PRACTICAL STATISTICS

(For BCom, BA, MCom, MA, MBA, ICWA, CA etc.) Solutions to the Statistics Text

R S N PILLAI
MA, MCom, LLB
Head of the Dept. of Commerce
Arignar Anna College, Arambaly
Kanyakumari

BAGAVATHI
MA, MCom
179, Chidambaranagar
Nagercoil
Kanyakumari

S. CHAND
PUBLISHING
empowering minds

S Chand And Company Limited
(ISO 9001 Certified Company)
RAM NAGAR, NEW DELHI - 110 055

S Chand And Company Limited

(ISO 9001 Certified Company)

Head Office: 7361, RAM NAGAR, QUTAB ROAD, NEW DELHI - 110 055
Phone: 23672080-81-82, 66672000 Fax: 91-11-23677446
www.**schandpublishing.com**; e-mail: **info@schandpublishing.com**

Branches:

Ahmedabad	:	Ph: 27541965, 27542369, ahmedabad@schandpublishing.com
Bengaluru	:	Ph: 22268048, 22354008, bangalore@schandpublishing.com
Bhopal	:	Ph: 4209587, bhopal@schandpublishing.com
Chandigarh	:	Ph: 2625356, 2625546, 4025418, chandigarh@schandpublishing.com
Chennai	:	Ph: 28410027, 28410058, chennai@schandpublishing.com
Coimbatore	:	Ph: 2323620, 4217136, coimbatore@schandpublishing.com (Marketing Office)
Cuttack	:	Ph: 2332580, 2332581, cuttack@schandpublishing.com
Dehradun	:	Ph: 2711101, 2710861, dehradun@schandpublishing.com
Guwahati	:	Ph: 2738811, 2735640, guwahati@schandpublishing.com
Hyderabad	:	Ph: 27550194, 27550195, hyderabad@schandpublishing.com
Jaipur	:	Ph: 2219175, 2219176, jaipur@schandpublishing.com
Jalandhar	:	Ph: 2401630, jalandhar@schandpublishing.com
Kochi	:	Ph: 2809208, 2808207, cochin@schandpublishing.com
Kolkata	:	Ph: 23353914, 23357458, kolkata@schandpublishing.com
Lucknow	:	Ph: 4065646, lucknow@schandpublishing.com
Mumbai	:	Ph: 22690881, 22610885, 22610886, mumbai@schandpublishing.com
Nagpur	:	Ph: 2720523, 2777666, nagpur@schandpublishing.com
Patna	:	Ph: 2300489, 2260011, patna@schandpublishing.com
Pune	:	Ph: 64017298, pune@schandpublishing.com
Raipur	:	Ph: 2443142, raipur@schandpublishing.com (Marketing Office)
Ranchi	:	Ph: 2361178, ranchi@schandpublishing.com
Sahibabad	:	Ph: 2771235, 2771238, delhibr-sahibabad@schandpublishing.com

First Edition 1987
Second Edition 2003; Reprint 2010, 2011, 2013, 2014
Reprint with Correction 2017
Reprint 2018 (Twice)

ISBN : 978-81-219-0044-7 **Code :** 1007A 182

PRINTED IN INDIA

By Vikas Publishing House Pvt. Ltd., Plot 20/4, Site-IV, Industrial Area Sahibabad, Ghaziabad-201010 and Published by S Chand And Company Limited, 7361, Ram Nagar, New Delhi-110 055.

PREFACE TO THE SECOND EDITION

Practical Statistics, carefully revised and thoroughly rechecked, steps into the second edition. All the errors in the first edition have been rectified. The problems selected have been rechecked. The latest questions asked the different examinations have been added. All the problems have been systematically graded. It contains 1001 problems and their solutions. Care has also been taken to make the book flawless.

The book in its present form will be useful to B.Com., B.A., M.Com., M.A. (Economics) MBA., ICWA., CA and other professional examinations. Further suggestions for the improvement of the book will be appreciated.

We are extremely thankful to Mr. R.K. Gupta, Managing Director and staff of M/s S. Chand and Company Ltd., New Delhi for bringing out the book in a nice manner.

Nagercoil

R.S.N. PILLAI
BAGAVATHI

PREFACE TO THE FIRST EDITION

Statistics occupies an important place in the study of all social sciences. Our statements need to be backed by statistical figures, lest they should be deemed mere speculations. Hence all branches of learning make extensive use of statistical methods.

The book **Practical Statistics** contains 1001 problems and their solutions. All the problems have been selected carefully from various university question papers and dealt with in such a manner that even an average student, without any remarkable aptitude for mathematics, can easily understand them. Only clear cut and direct techniques, successfully tested inside classrooms, have been employed in solving the problems. Every effort has been made to make the book self-teaching.

The book covers a comprehensive range of Statistics for undergraduate, postgraduate and professional examinations. The chapters have been systematically arranged. They begin with formulae and proceed to their application. Care has also been taken to present the subject in a graded and modulated manner.

We would immensely be thankful to those who would kindly point out the inadequacies and inaccuracies in the book and make suggestions for its further improvement.

Nagercoil

R.S.N. PILLAI
BAGAVATHI

CONTENTS

1

CLASSIFICATION AND TABULATION

CLASSIFICATION

Problem 1. Form a frequency distribution from the following data by inclusive method taking 4 as the magnitude of class intervals:

10	17	15	22	11	16	19	24	29	18
25	26	32	14	17	20	23	27	30	12
15	18	24	36	18	15	21	28	33	38
34	13	10	16	20	22	29	19	23	31

(*B.Com. Delhi*)

Solution :

Class interval	*Tally marks*	*Frequency*
10–13	~~||||~~	5
14–17	~~||||~~ |||	8
18–21	~~||||~~ |||	8
22–25	~~||||~~ ||	7
26–29	~~||||~~	5
30–33	||||	4
34–37	||	2
38–41	|	1
		40

Note : Lower limit of the first class is 10 as the minimum value of the variable is 10. The magnitude of the class intervals is given to be 4. To form a frequency distribution, first take the value 10, and put a tally mark against the class 10–13, for the second value 17, put a tally mark against the class 14–17, for the value 15, put a tally mark against the class 14–17, and for the value 22, put a tally mark against the class 22–25 and so on.

Problem 2. Marks obtained by 50 boys of a class are as under :

34	54	10	21	51	52	12	43	48	36
48	22	39	26	34	19	10	17	47	38
13	30	30	60	59	15	07	18	40	49
40	51	55	32	41	22	30	35	53	25
14	18	19	40	43	04	17	45	25	43

Construct a frequency table with a class interval 0–9, 10–19, 20–29 and so on.

(*B.Com. Calcutta*)

Solution: Under the inclusive method, the upper limit of each class is not repeated as the lower limit of the next class. That is, overlapping of class interval is avoided ; both lower and upper class limits are included in the class interval. Thus, a value of 49 will fall in 40–49 class.

Marks	*Tally Bars*	*Frequency*
0–9	||	2
10–19	𝍸 𝍸 ||	12
20–29	𝍸 |	6
30–39	𝍸 𝍸	10
40–49	𝍸 𝍸 ||	12
50-59	𝍸 ||	7
60–69	|	1
		N = 50

Problem 3. Following are the marks, out of 100, obtained by 50 students in Statistics:

70	45	33	64	50	25	65	75	30	20
55	65	60	58	52	56	45	42	35	40
47	51	39	61	33	59	49	41	15	55
42	63	82	65	45	63	54	52	48	46
57	53	55	42	45	39	64	55	26	18

Make a frequency distribution taking a class interval of 10 marks; take the first class interval as 0–10. (*B.Com. Banglore*)

Solution :

Frequency Distribution of marks

Marks	*Tally Bars*	*Frequency*
0-10	—	0
10-20	||	2
20-30	|||	3
30-40	𝍸 |	6
40-50	𝍸 𝍸 |||	13
50-60	𝍸 𝍸 ||||	14
60-70	𝍸 ||||	9
70–80	||	2
80–90	|	1
		N =50

Note: Under exclusive method, i.e. 0–10.....80–90, the upper limit of one class interval is the lower limit of the next class. Take the first mark, i.e. 70 which would be included in the class 70–80 and not in the class 60–70.

Problem 4. The following are the number of replacement parts used in a mill in 50 consecutive weeks for a certain groups of similar machines:

49	41	45	52	47	46	42	43	46	48
45	36	56	44	61	68	54	58	51	47
47	49	42	48	53	48	41	65	45	52
58	50	55	45	43	72	63	45	38	43
42	47	43	49	46	57	49	44	47	48

Construct a frequency distribution with a uniform class interval. (*M.A. Punjab*)

Solution: By using inclusive method and taking 5 as the width of class interval, the distribution is as follows :

Class Intervals	*Tally Bars*	*Frequency*
35–39	||	2
40–44	卌 卌 |	11
45–49	卌 卌 卌 卌 |	21
50–54	卌 |	6
55–59	卌	5
60–64	||	2
65–69	||	2
70–74	|	1
		N= 50

Problem 5. Form a frequency distribution by taking a suitable class interval for the following data giving the ages of 52 employees in a government agency :

67	34	36	48	49	31	61	34	43	45	38	32	28
61	29	47	36	50	46	30	46	32	30	33	45	49
48	41	53	36	37	47	47	30	46	50	28	35	35
38	46	43	34	36	62	69	50	28	44	43	60	39

(*B. A. Madurai*)

Solution: The lowest value is 28 and the highest value is 69. The difference between the two extreme values is 41 i.e. 69–28. When we take a class interval of 5 then the classes formed is $41 \div 5 = 8.2$. It means there will be nine classes including for the accommodation of fractional value.

Frequency Distribution of Ages

Class Intervals	*Tally Bars*	*Frequency*
25–30	||||	4
30–35	卌 卌	10
35–40	卌 卌	10
40–45	卌	5
45–50	卌 卌 |||	13
50–55	||||	4
55–60	—	—
60–65	||||	4
65–70	||	2
		N = 52

Problem 6. From the following observations prepare a classified frequency distribution :

110	108	126	132	149	136	125	112
138	155	125	138	136	130	120	148
140	125	119	111	154	147	165	137
145	132	150	137	142	135	125	126

(*B.Com. Andhra*)

Solution: The lowest value is 108 and the highest value 165. The difference between the two extreme is 57. If we take class interval of 10, there will be six classes, start from 100–110, 110–120 and so on.

Frequency Distribution

Class Intervals	*Tally Bars*	*Frequency*
100–110	|	1
110–120	||||	4
120–130	~~||||~~ ||	7
130–140	~~||||~~ ~~||||~~	10
140–150	~~||||~~ |	6
150–160	|||	3
160–170	|	1
		N=32

Problem 7. Prepare a bivariate frequency distribution for the following data for 20 students :

Marks in Law	10	11	10	11	11	14	12	12	13	10
Marks in Statistics	20	21	22	21	23	23	22	21	24	23
Marks in Law	13	12	11	12	10	14	14	12	13	10
Marks in Statistics	24	23	22	23	22	22	24	20	24	23

(*B.Com. Delhi*)

Solution :

Bivariate table will have 25 cells (5 × 5).

Marks in Law denoted by X (values 10 to 14 *i.e.*, 5 values)

Marks in Statistics denoted by Y (values 20 to 24 *i.e.*, 5 values.

Bivariate Frequency Table Shows Marks in Law and Statistics of 20 Students

Marks in Statistics (Y) \ Marks in Law (X)	10	11	12	13	14	Total
20	|(1)		|(1)			2
21		||(2)	|(1)			3
22	||(2)	|(1)	|(1)		|(1)	5
23	||(2)	|(1)	||(2)		|(1)	6
24				|||(3)	|(1)	4
Total	5	4	5	3	3	20

Note : The figures within brackets show the frequency corresponding to each cell.

Problem 8. The following figures give the ages in years of newly married husbands and wives. Represent the data by a frequency distribution.

Age of husband	24	26	27	25	28	24	27	28	25	26
Age of wife	17	18	19	17	20	18	18	19	18	19
Age of husband	25	26	27	25	27	26	25	26	26	26
Age of Wife	17	18	19	19	20	19	17	20	17	18

(*B.Com.* (*Hons.*)*Delhi*)

Solution :

X denote the age of husband

Y denote the age of wife

Bivariate Frequency Table of the Ages of Newly Married Couples.

<table>
<tr><th>Age of \ Age of
wife (Y) \ husband (X)</th><th>24</th><th>25</th><th>26</th><th>27</th><th>28</th><th>Total</th></tr>
<tr><td>17</td><td>|(1)</td><td>|||(3)</td><td>|(1)</td><td></td><td></td><td>5</td></tr>
<tr><td>18</td><td>|(1)</td><td>|(1)</td><td>|||(3)</td><td>|(1)</td><td></td><td>6</td></tr>
<tr><td>19</td><td></td><td>|(1)</td><td>||(2)</td><td>||(2)</td><td>|(1)</td><td>6</td></tr>
<tr><td>20</td><td></td><td></td><td>|(1)</td><td>|(1)</td><td>|(1)</td><td>3</td></tr>
<tr><td>Total :</td><td>2</td><td>5</td><td>7</td><td>4</td><td>2</td><td>20</td></tr>
</table>

Note : The figures within brackets show the frequency corresponding to each cell.

Problem 9. The data given below relate to the heights and weights of 20 persons. You are required to form a two way frequency table with class intervals 62″ to 64″, 64″ to 66″ and so on and 115 to 125 lbs, 125 to 135 lbs etc.

S. No.	*Weight*	*Height*	*S. No.*	*Weight*	*Height*
1.	170	70	11.	163	70
2.	135	65	12.	139	67
3.	136	65	13.	122	63
4.	137	64	14.	134	68
5.	148	69	15.	140	67
6.	124	63	16.	132	69
7.	117	65	17.	120	66
8.	128	70	18.	148	68
9.	143	71	19.	129	67
10.	129	62	20.	152	67

(*C. A.*)

Solution :

Two way frequency Table Shows the Height and Weight of 20 Persons

<table>
<tr><th>Weight \ Height
in lbs (Y) \ in lbs (X)</th><th>115–125</th><th>125–135</th><th>135–145</th><th>145–155</th><th>155–165</th><th>165–175</th><th>Total</th></tr>
<tr><td>62–64</td><td>||(2)</td><td>|(1)</td><td></td><td></td><td></td><td></td><td>3</td></tr>
<tr><td>64–66</td><td>|(1)</td><td></td><td>|||(3)</td><td></td><td></td><td></td><td>4</td></tr>
<tr><td>66–68</td><td>|(1)</td><td>|(1)</td><td>||(2)</td><td>|(1)</td><td></td><td></td><td>5</td></tr>
<tr><td>68–70</td><td></td><td>||(2)</td><td></td><td>||(2)</td><td></td><td></td><td>4</td></tr>
<tr><td>70–72</td><td></td><td>|(1)</td><td>|(1)</td><td></td><td>|(1)</td><td>|(1)</td><td>4</td></tr>
<tr><td>Total</td><td>4</td><td>5</td><td>6</td><td>3</td><td>1</td><td>1</td><td>20</td></tr>
</table>

Note: The figures within brackets show the frequency corresponding to each cell.

Problem 10. The ages of 20 husbands and wives are given below. Form a two way frequency table showing the relationship between the ages of husbands and wives with class intervals 20–25, 25–30 etc.

S. No.	Age of husband	Age of Wives	S. No.	Age of husband	Age of Wives
1.	28	23	11.	27	24
2.	37	30	12.	39	34
3.	42	40	13.	23	20
4.	25	26	14.	33	31
5.	29	25	15.	36	29
6.	47	41	16.	32	35
7.	37	35	17.	22	23
8.	35	25	18.	29	27
9.	23	21	19.	38	34
10.	41	38	20.	48	47

(C. A.)(B. Com. Madurai)

Solution :

Classification of Ages of Husbands and Wives

Age of wives \ *Age of* husbands	20–25	25–30	30–35	35–40	40–45	45–50	Total
20–25	|||(3)	||(2)					5
25–30		|||(3)		||(2)			5
30–35			|(1)	|||(3)			4
35–40			|(1)	|(1)	|(1)		3
40–45					|(1)	|(1)	2
45–50						|(1)	1
Total	3	5	2	6	2	2	20

Note : The figures within brackets show the frequency corresponding to each cell.

Problem 11. The following data represent the marks in Accountancy (X) and Statistics (Y) of 25 Students. Prepare a bivariate table from the following data :

X	35	28	30	18	40	45	27	36	52	38	40	38	35
Y	56	42	40	30	60	62	18	52	74	60	60	56	52
X	35	70	17	42	46	35	35	27	32	41	46	58	
Y	48	80	18	58	65	48	50	38	46	68	74	88	

(B. Com. Karnataka) (B.Com. Bangalore)

Solution :

Bivariate Frequency Distribution

Statistics (Y) \ *Accountancy* (X)	15–25	25–35	35–45	45–55	55–65	65–75	Total
15–25	|(1)	|(1)					2
25–35	|(1)						1
35–45		|||(3)					3
45–55		|(1)	||||(5)				6
55–65			|||| |(6)	|(1)			7
65–75			|(1)	|||(3)			4
75–85						|(1)	1
85–95					|(1)		1
Total	2	5	12	4	1	1	25

Problem 12. Convert the following distribution into more than cumulative frequency and less than cumulative frequency.

Weekly wages	*No. of workers*
0–20	41
20–40	51
40–60	64
60–80	38
80–100	7

(*B.Com. Delhi*)

Solution :

Weekly wages less than RS.	*No. of Workers*	*Weekly Wages more than RS.*	*No. of Workers*
20	41	0	201
40	92	20	160
60	156	40	109
80	194	60	45
100	201	80	7
		100	0

TABULATION

Problem 13. In a sample study about coffee habit in two towns, the following information was received :

Town A : Females were 40% : total coffee drinkers were 45% and males non-coffee drinkers were 20%.

Town B : Males were 55%; Males non-coffee drinkers were 30% and females coffee drinkers were 15%.

Present the above data in a tabular form. (*B.Com.*, (*Hons*) *Delhi*)

Solution :

Coffee Drinkers in Town A and B (*in percentage*)

	Town A			*Town B*		
	Male	*Female*	*Total*	*Male*	*Female*	*Total*
Coffee drinkers	40	5*	45	25*	15	40*
Non-coffee drinkers	20	35*	55	30	30*	60*
Total	60	40	100	55	45	100

*Figures are not given in the problems. These are given by minor calculations of additions and substractions.

Problem 14. Present in tabular form with suitable captions the information contained in the following:

In 2000 out of a total of 1.750 workers of a factory, 1,200 workers were members of a trade union. The number of women employed was 200 of which 175 did not belong to a trade union.

In 2001 the number of union workers increased to 1,510 of which 1,290 were men. On the other hand, the number of non-union workers fell down to 208 of which 180 were men.

In 2002 there were on the pay rolls of the factory, 1,800 employees who belonged to a trade union and 50 who did not. Of all the employees 2002 in 300 were women of whom only 8 did not belong to a trade union.

(*B.Com. Madras*)

Solution :

Comparative Study of the Members of Trade Union in a Factory in 2000, 2001 and 2002

Year	*Members of trade union*			*Non-members of trade union*			Total
	Male	Female	Total	Male	Female	Total	
2000	1175	25	1200	375	175	550	1750
2001	1290	220	1510	180	28	208	1718
2002	1508	292	1800	42	8	50	1850

Problem 15. Present the following information in a suitable tabular form, supplying the figures not directly given.

In 2001 out of 2,000 workers in a factory, 1550 were members of a trade union. The number of women workers employed was 250, out of which 200 did not belong to any trade union.

In 2002 the number of union workers was 1.725 of which 1,600 were men. The number of non-union workers was 380 among whom 155 were women. (*I.C.W.A.*)

Solution :

Comparative Study of the Membership of Trade Union in a Factory in 2001 and 2002

Year		2001			2002	
Trade Union	*Males*	*Females*	*Total*	*Males*	*Females*	*Total*
Members	1,500	50	1,550	1,600	125	1,725
Non-members	250	200	450	225	155	380
Total	1,750	250	2,000	1,825	280	2,105

Problem : 16. Present the following information in a suitable form.

In 2000, the number of workers in the trade union was 3,450 of which 3,200 were men. The number of non-trade union workers was 760 of which 330 were women.

In 2002, Out of a total of 4,000 workers in a factory, 3,300 were members of a trade union. The number of women workers employed was 500 out of which 400 did not belong to any union. (*B.Com. Madras*)

Solution :

Table Showing Membership of Trade Union by Sex.

Year		2001			2002	
Trade Union	*Males*	*Females*	*Total*	*Males*	*Females*	*Total*
Members	3,200	250	3,450	3,200	100	3,300
Non-members	430	330	760	300	400	700
Total	3,630	580	4,210	3,500	500	4,000

Problem 17. Draw a blank table to show the candidates sex-wise, appearing for Pre-University, First year, Second year and Third year Examinations of a University in the Faculties of Arts. Science and Commerce in a certain year.

(B.Com. Madras)

Solution:

Tables Showing the Distribution of Candidates Appearing in Various University Examinations

Faculty	*Boys*					*Girls*					*Total*					*Total*
	Pre University	Year				Pre University	Year				Pre University	Year				
		I	II	III	Total		I	II	III	Total		I	II	III	Total	
Art																
Science																
Commerce																
Total																

Problem 18. An investigation conducted by the Education Department in a Public Library revealed the following facts. You are required to tabulate the information as neatly and clearly as you can.

In 2000 the total number of readers was 46,000 and they borrowed some 16,000 volumes. In 2003 the number of books borrowed increased by 4,000 and the borrowers by 50%.

The classification was on the basis of three sections: Literature, Fiction and Illustrated News. There were 10,000 and 30,000 readers in the sections Literature and Fiction respectively in the year 2000. In the same year, 2,000 and 10,000 books were lent in the sections Illustrated News and Fiction respectively. Marked changes were seen in 2003. There were 7,000 and 42,000 readers in the Literature and Fiction Sections respectively. So also 4,000 and 13,000 books were lent in the sections Illustrated News and Fiction respectively.

(C.A. Nov.)

Solution : The given information can be tabulated as follows:

Table Showing the changes in the Readership and Type of Books (2000 and 2003)

Types of Books	2000		2003		*Changes in 2003 over 2000*	
	No. of Readers	*No. of Books Borrowed*	*No. of Readers*	*No. of Books Borrowed*	*No. of Readers*	*No. of Books Borrowed*
Literature	10,000	4,000	7,000	3,000	−3,000	−1,000
Fiction	30,000	10,000	42,000	13,000	+12,000	+3,000
Illustrated News	6,000	2,000	20,000	4,000	+14,000	+2,000
Total	46,000	16,000	69,000	20,000	23,000	4,000

Problem 19. Out of the total number of 1798 women, who were interviewed for employment in a textile factory, 512 were from textile areas, and the rest were from non-textile

areas. Amongst the married women who belonged to textile areas, 247 were experienced and 73 inexperienced. While in non-textile areas, the corresponding figures were 40 and 520. The total number of inexperienced women was 1341 of whom 111 resided in textile areas. Of the total number of women 918 were unmarried; and the number of experienced women in the textile and non-textile areas was 154 and 16 respectively. Tabulate.

Solution:

Table showing Employment Patten in a Textile Factory of Bombay

	Textile Areas			*Non-Textile Areas*			*Grand Total*		
	Married	Unmarried	Total	Married	Unmarried	Total	Married	Unmarried	Total
Experienced	247	154	401	40	16	56	287	170	457
In-experienced	73	38	111	520	710	1230	593	748	1341
Total	320	192	512	560	726	1286	880	918	1798

Problem 20. In a newspaper account describing the incidence of influenza among tubercular persons living in the same family the following passage appeared:

"Exactly $4/15^{th}$ of 60,000 inhabitants showed signs of tuberculosis and no less than 6,000 among them had an attack of influenza, but among them only 1,000 lived in infected houses. In contrast with this $1/5^{th}$ of the tubercular persons who did not have influenza were still exposed to infections. Altogether, 20,000 were attacked by influenza and 37,000 were exposed to the risk of infection but the number who having influenza but not tuberculosis lived in houses where no other case of influenza occurred was only 4,000."

Redraft the information in a concise and elegant tabular form. *(B.Com. Bombay)*

Solution :

Table Showing the Incidence of Influenza among Tubercular Persons Living in the Same Family

	Attacked by influenza			*Non attacked by Influenza*			*GrandTotal*
	Living in Infected house	Living in not infected house	Total	Living in Infected house	Living in not infected house	Total	
Attacked by tuberculosis	1,000	5,000	6,000	2,000	8,000	10,000	16,000
Not attacked by tuberculosis	10,000	4,000	14,000	24,000	6,000	30,000	44,000
Total	11,000	9,000	20,000	26,000	14,000	40,000	60,000

2
GRAPHIC AND DIAGRAMMATIC REPRESENTATION

GRAPH

Problem 1. The following are the share price quotations of a firm for five consecutive weeks. Present the data by an appropriate diagram.

Week	*High*	*Low*
1	102	100
2	103	101
3	107	103
4	106	105
5	105	104

(*B.com., Calicut M.B.A., Himachal Pradesh*)

Solution :

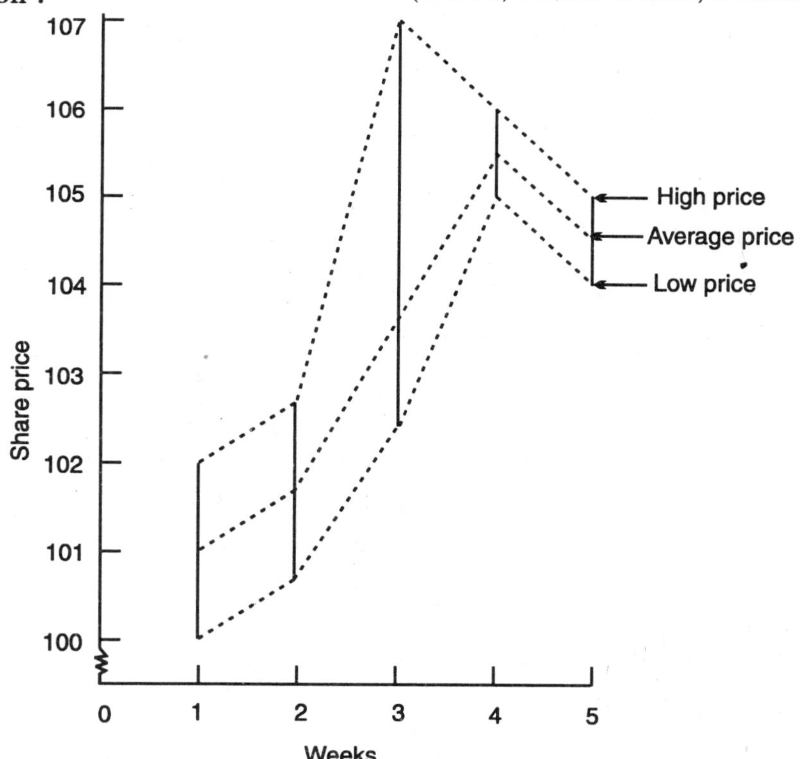

Problem. 2 . A firm reported that its net worth in the years 1999 to 2003 is as follows:

Year	1999	2000	2001	2002	2003
Net worth	100	112	120	133	147

Plot the above data in the form of a semi-logarithmic graph. Can you say anything about the approximate rate of growth of its networth ? (*B.A. Delhi*)

Solution :

Year	*Net Worth Y*	*Log Y*
1999	100	2.00
2000	112	2.05 (2.0492)
2001	120	2.08 (2.0792)
2002	133	2.12 (2.1239)
2003	147	2.17 (2.1673)

It reflects that the rate of growth is increasing for the whole period.

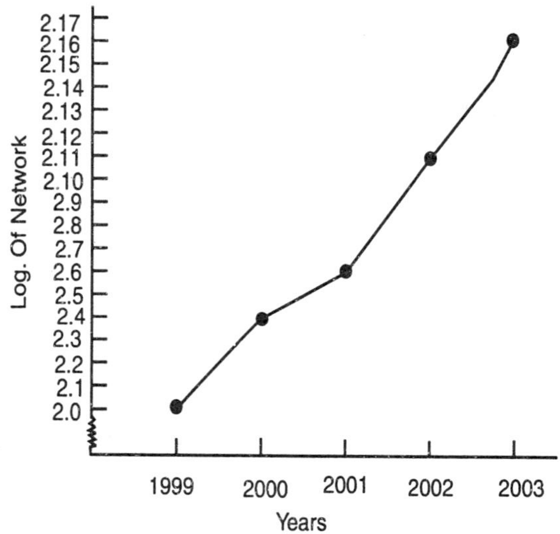

Problem 3. The following table gives the value of imports and exports of a country for the year 2003 in crores of rupees. Represent by means of a graph showing also the balance of trade :

Month	*Imports*	*Exports*
Jan.	22	28
Feb	24	28
Mar.	26	23
Apr.	28	21
May	31	20
June	29	22
July	32	21
Aug.	33	19
Sep.	32	20
Oct.	31	19
Nov.	25	18
Dec.	24	19

(*B.Com. Berhampur*)

Balance of Trade 2003

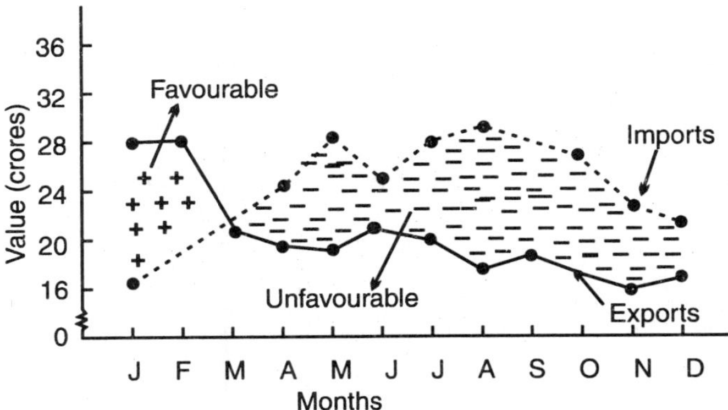

Problem 4. Draw a cumulative frequency curve for the following data :

Marks	:	0–10	10–20	20–30	30–40	40–50	50–60
Frequency	:	3	9	15	30	18	5

Also find out Quartiles and Median. (*B.A. Calicut*)

Solution : Cumulative frequency of the above problem:

Marks less than	10–3
Marks less than	20–12
Marks less than	30–27
Marks less than	40–57
Marks less than	50–75
Marks less than	60–80

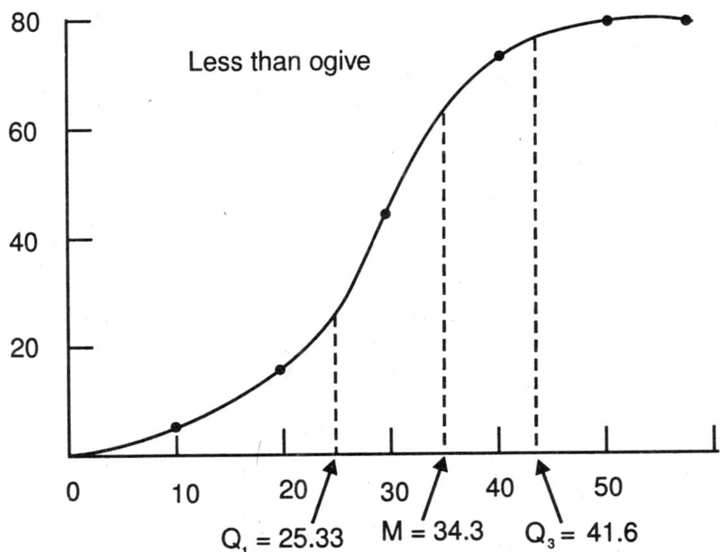

Problem 5. Convert the following distribution into 'more than' frequency distribution.

Weekly Wages less than (Rs.)	*No. of Workers*
20	41
40	92
60	156
80	194
100	201

For the data given above, draw 'less than' and 'more than' ogive and hence find the value of median (*B. Com. Delhi*)

Solution :

Weekly Wages	*No. of Workers (f)*	*Cumulative frequency*	
		Less than	*More than*
0–20	41	41	201
20–40	92–41 = 51	92	160
40–60	156–92 = 64	156	109
60–80	194–156 = 38	194	45
80–100	201–194 = 7	201	7

Ogive (less than and more than)

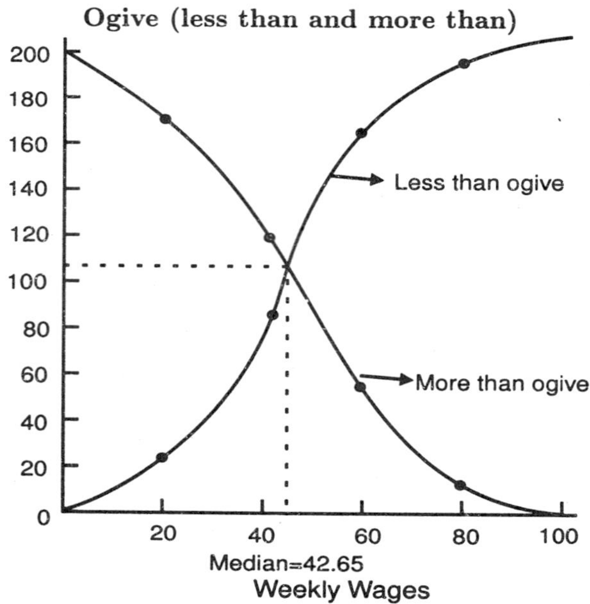

Problem 6. Draw histogram and frequency curve for the following data :
Profit range ;('000)

Rs.	0–15	15–30	30–45	45–60	60–75	75–90	90–105	105–120	120–135	135–150
No. of Companies	3	7	18	25	20	12	6	5	2	2

(*B.Com. Saurashtra*)

Solution : **Histogram and Frequency Curve**

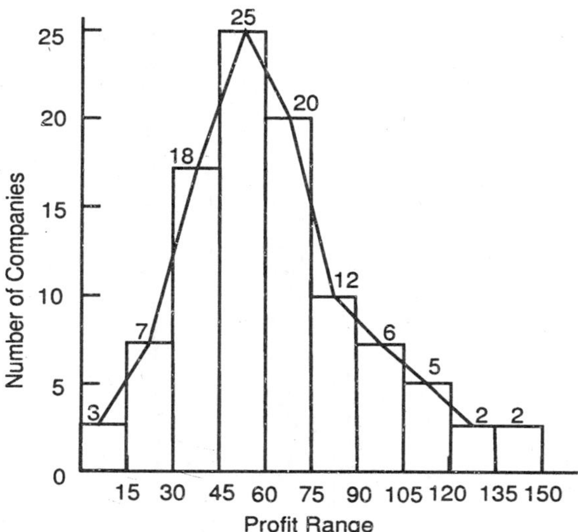

Problem 7. Draw an ogive from the following data and find graphically the number of observations lying between 360 and 440 :

Value	*No. of observations*
More than 200	400
More than 250	370
More than 300	315
More than 350	220
More than 400	115
More than 500	45
More than 600	15
More than 700	0

(*I.C.W.A.*)

Solution :

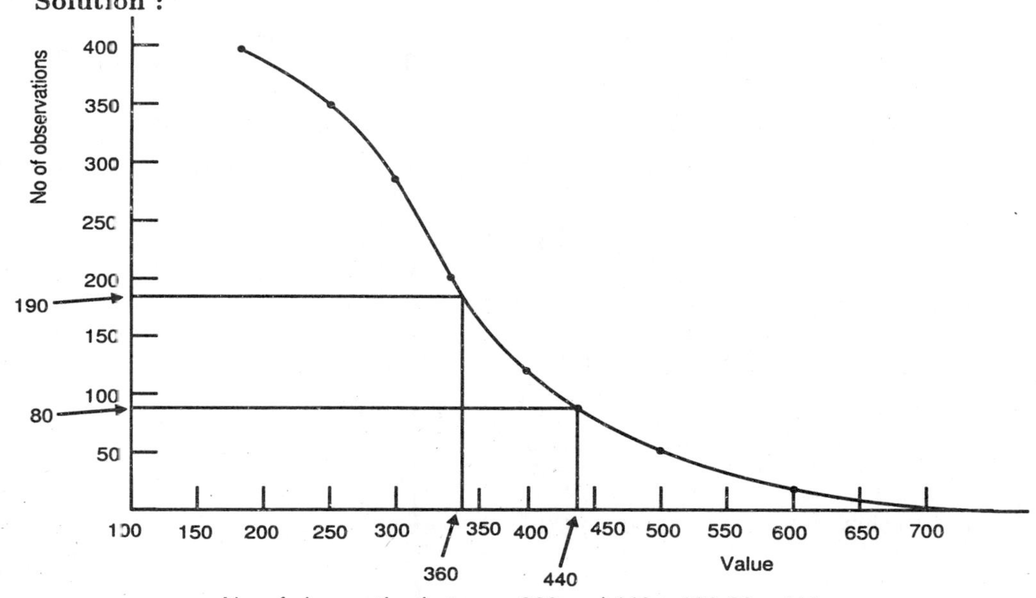

No. of observation between 360 and 440 = 190-80 = 110

Problem 8. The profits of a particular firm and that of the whole industry are given in the following table :

Year	1997	1998	1999	2000	2001	2002	2003
Firm ('00,000)	1.5	2.0	2.18	2.69	3.5	6.0	14.0
Industry (00,00,000)	3.2	4.0	5. 4	6. 8	8.0	11.0	19.0

	Firm		*Industry*	
Year	*Rs. '00,000*	*log*	*Rs. '00,00,000*	*log*
1997	1.50	4.1761	3.2	6.5051
1998	2.00	4.3010	4.0	6.6021
1999	2.18	4.3385	5.4	6.7324
2000	2.69	4.4298	6.8	6.8325
2001	3.50	4.5441	8.0	6.9031
2002	6.00	4.7782	11.0	7.0414
2003	14.00	4.1461	19.0	7.2788

Solution :

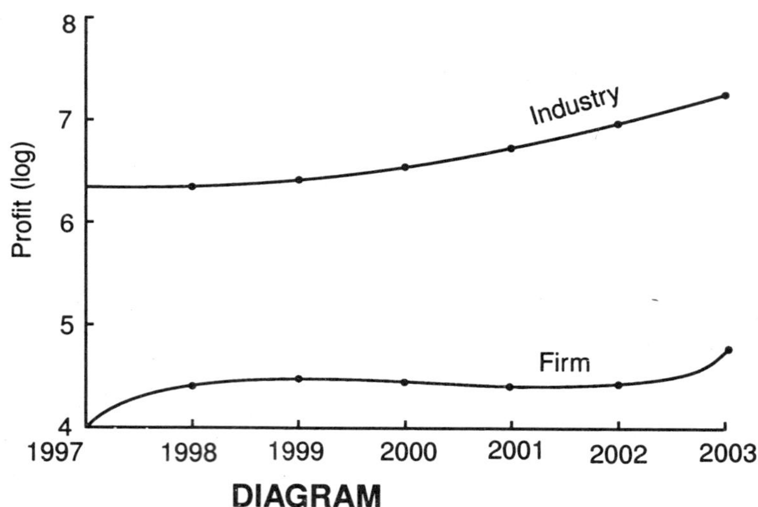

DIAGRAM

Problem 9. The sale proceeds, cost and the profit or loss per wooden chair of a firm are :

Particulars	2001	2002	2003
Sale proceeds	190	220	250
Cost per chair			
Material	100	110	130
Wages	40	75	90
Other costs	30	50	60
Total cost	170	235	280
Profit/loss	+20	−15	−30

Draw bars to show (a) absolute value and (b) relative values of the problem.

(*B.Com.*)

Solution :

Table Showing Absolute and Relative Values

Particulars	2001		2002		2003	
	Absolute values	*Relative values*	*Absolute values*	*Relative values*	*Absolute values*	*Relative values*
Sale proceeds per chair	190	100%	220	100%	250	100%
Material	100	52.63%	110	50	130	52
Wages	40	21.05%	75	34.41	90	36
Other costs	30	15.79%	50	22.73	60	24
Total cost	170	89.47%	235	106.82	280	112%
Profit (+) Loss (−)	+20	10.53%	−15	−6.82%	−30	−12%

Diagram show absolute Value

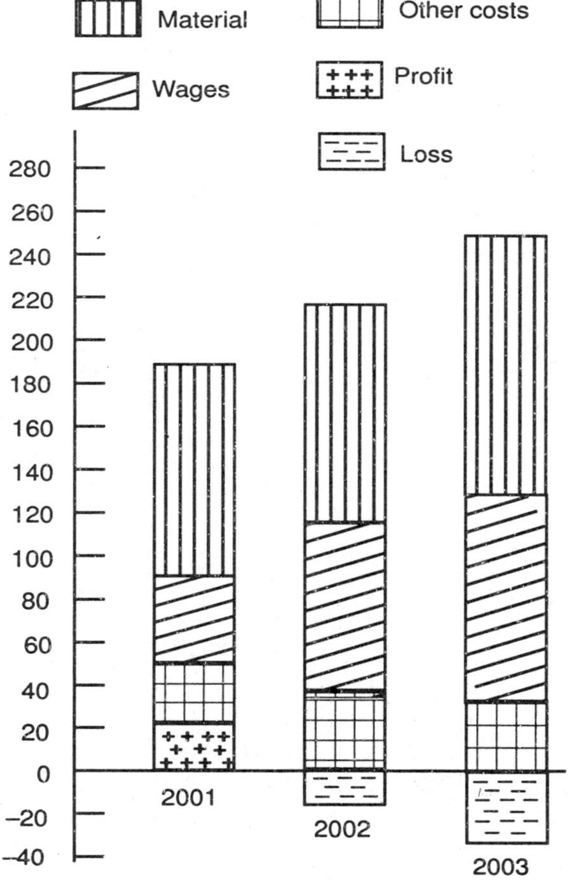

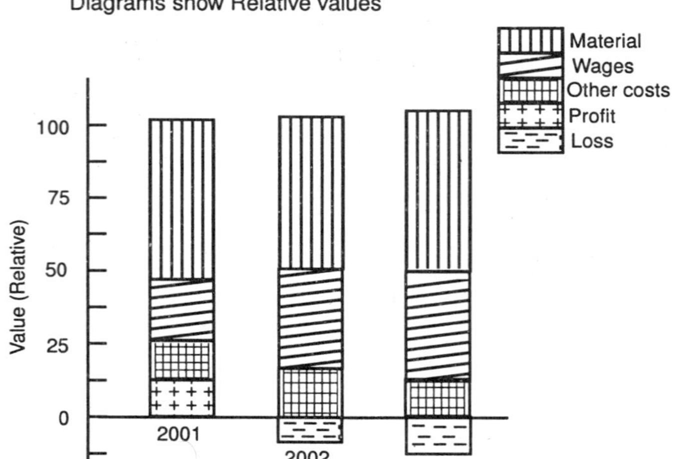

Problem 10. The data below give the yearly profits (in 000 of rupees) of the two companies A and B.

Year	*Profits in '000*	
	Company A	*Company B*
2000	120	90
2001	135	95
2002	140	108
2003	160	120

Represent the data by means of a suitable diagram. (*I.C.W.A. Inter*)

Solution : Yearly profits in '000 rupees

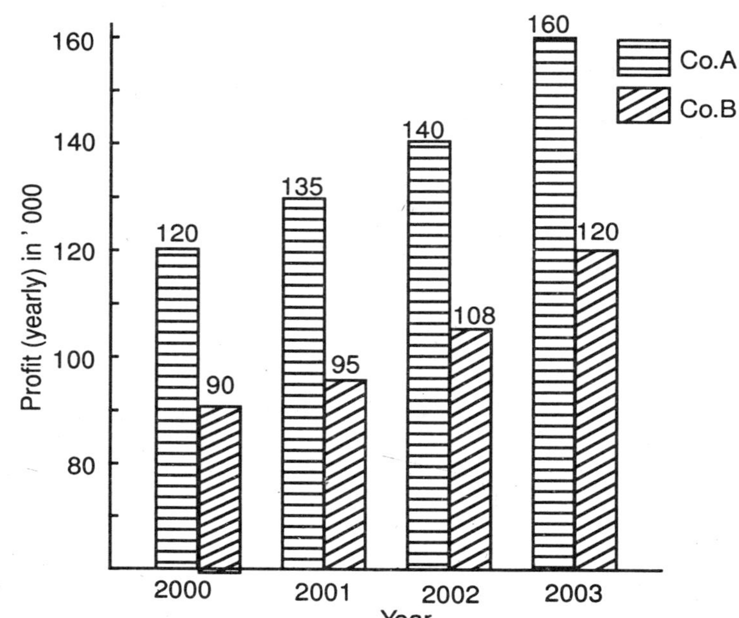

Problem 11. Draw a Multiple bar diagram for the following data :

Year	*Sales* ('000)	*Gross Profit* ('000)	*Net Profit* ('000)
2000	100	30	10
2001	120	40	15
2002	130	45	25
2003	150	50	25

(*B.Com. Delhi*)

Solution:

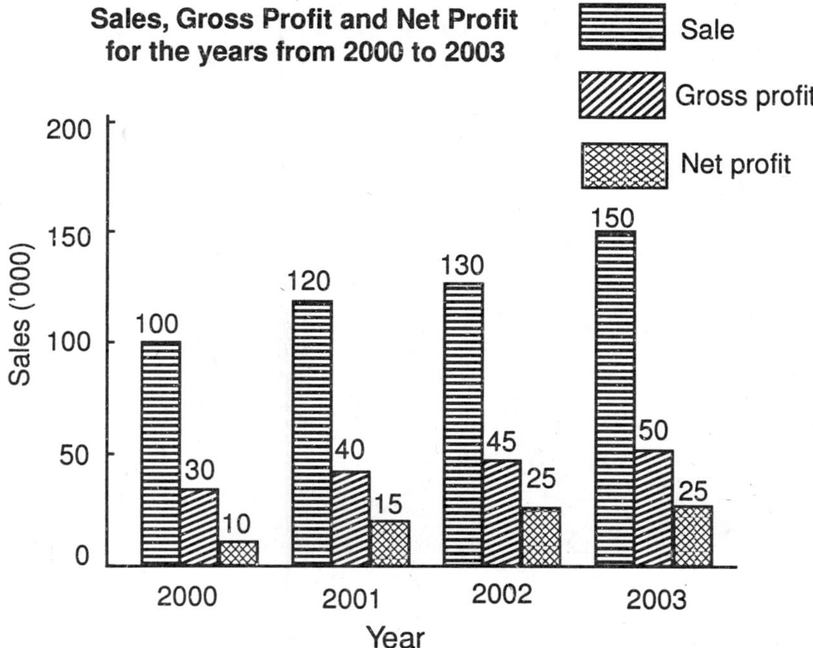

Problem 12. The following table gives the height of trees :

Height	*No. of trees*
Below 7 feet	26
,, 14 ,	57
,, 21 ,,	92
,, 28 ,,	134
,, 35 ,,	216
,, 42 ,,	287
,, 49 ,,	341
,, 56 ,,	360

Represent the data in the form of histogram. (*B.Sc. Himachal*)

Solution :

Histogram of the Height of Trees

To draw a histogram, we have to obtain simple frequencies :

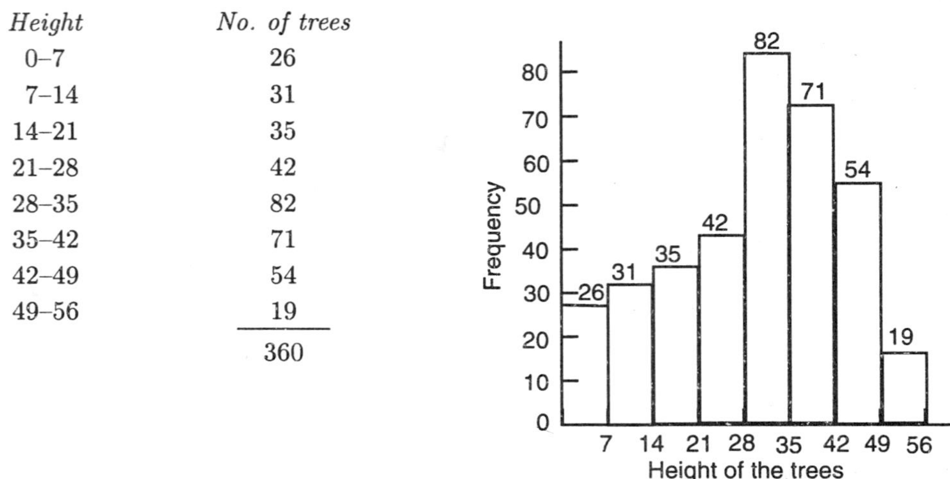

Height	*No. of trees*
0–7	26
7–14	31
14–21	35
21–28	42
28–35	82
35–42	71
42–49	54
49–56	19
	360

Problem 13. The following figures relate to the cost of construction of a house in Delhi :

Item	*Expenditure*
Cement	20%
Steel	18%
Bricks	10%
Timber	15%
Labour	25%
Miscellaneous	12%

Represent the data by a suitable diagram.

(*B.A.* (*Hons* :) *Kurukshetra*, *B.Sc. Madurai*)

Solution :

Item	*Expenditure*	*Degrees*
Cement	20%	$\frac{20}{100} \times 360 = 72$
Steel	18%	$\frac{18}{100} \times 360 = 64.8$
Bricks	10%	$\frac{10}{100} \times 360 = 36.0$
Timber	15%	$\frac{15}{100} \times 360 = 54.0$
Labour	25%	$\frac{25}{100} \times 360 = 90.0$
Misc.	12%	$\frac{12}{100} \times 360 = 43.2$
	100%	360

Pie diagram showing the cost of construction of a house in Delhi

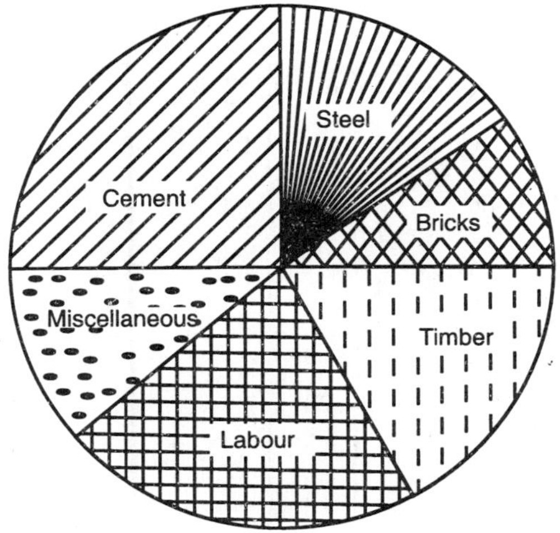

Problem 14. Find out the mode of the following data graphically and check the result through calculation :

Size	0–1	1–2	2–3	3–4	4–5	5–6	6–7	7–8	8–9	9–10	10–11
Frequency	3	7	9	15	25	20	14	12	8	6	2

(*B.Com. Delhi*)

Solution :

HISTOGRAM

Mode = 4.67
Size of items

$$\text{Check : Z} = L_1 + \frac{f_1 - f_0}{2f_1 - f_0 - f_2} \times i$$

$$= 4 + \frac{25 - 15}{2X25 - 15 - 20} \times I$$

$$= 4 + \frac{10}{15} = 4 + 0.67$$
$$= \mathbf{4.67}$$

Problem 15. Draw a histogram from the following data :

Mid Value	15	25	35	45	55	65	75
Frequency	10	24	40	32	20	14	4

(*B.Com. Kerala*)

Solution :

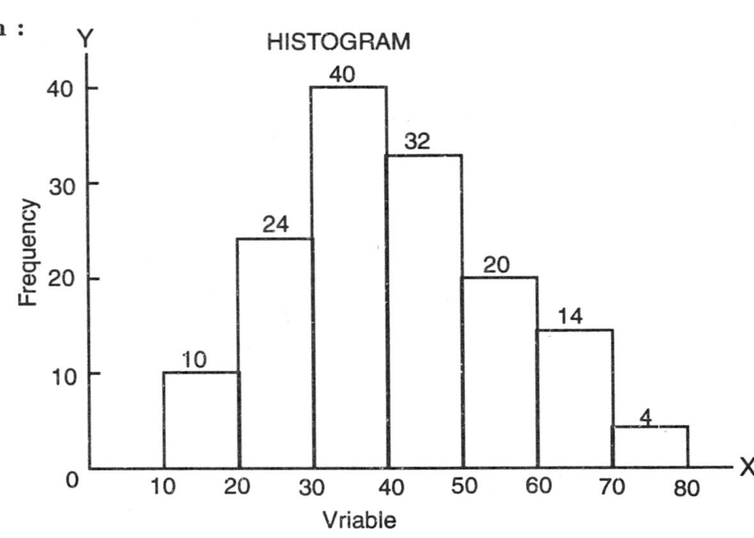

Note : we will have to find out the lower and upper value of each class and they are :

10–20	10	50–60	20
20–30	24	60–70	14
30–40	40	70–80	4
40–50	32	80–	

Problem 16 : Below is given the frequency distribution of weights of a group of 60 students of a class in a school :

Weight in kg.	*No. of students*
30–34	3
35–39	5
40–44	12
45–49	18
50–54	14
55–59	6
60–64	2

(*a*) Draw histogram for this distribution and find the modal value. Check this result by using the formula.

(*I.C.W.A. Inter*)

Solution :

We have to convert the distribution into continuous class intervals, as given below :

Weight in kg.	*f*
29.5–34.5	3
34.5–39.5	5
39.5–44.5	12
44.5–49.5	18
49.5–54.5	14
54.5–59.5	6
59.5–64.5	2

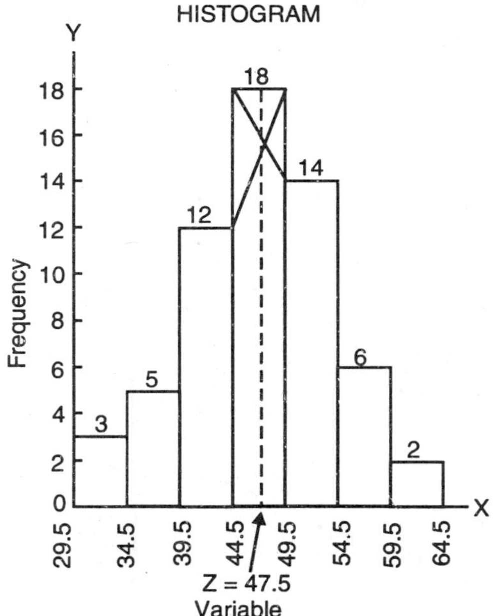

$$\text{Check : Z} = 44.5 + \frac{18 - 12}{36 - 12 - 14} \times 5$$

$$= 47.5$$

Problem 17. Draw a pie diagram to represent the following data of investment pattern in the Five Year Plan :

Agriculture and Community Development	14%
Irrigation and Power	16%
Small and Organised Industries and Minerals	29%
Transport and Communication	17%
Social services	16%
Inventories	8%

(*B.Com. Bombay*)

Solution :

Item	*% Investment*	*Degrees*
Agriculture and Community development	14	$\frac{14 \times 360}{100} = 50.4°$
Irrigation & Power	16	$\frac{16 \times 360}{100} = 57.6°$
Industries & Minerals	29	$\frac{29 \times 360}{100} = 104.4°$
Transport & Communication	17	$\frac{17 \times 360}{100} = 61.2°$
Social Services	16	$\frac{16 \times 360}{100} = 57.6°$
Inventories	8	$\frac{8 \times 360}{100} = 28.8°$
Total	100	360^0

Pie diagram showing the investment in the Five Year Plan

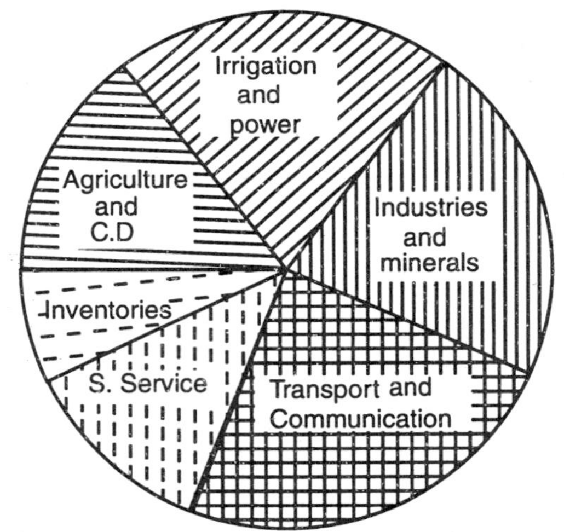

Problem 18. Draw a suitable diagram for the following :

Expenditure item	*Percentage of total expenditure*
Food	65
Clothing	10
Housing	12
Fuel and Lighting	5
Miscellaneous	8

(B.A. (Econ.) Madras)

Solution :

Item of Expenditure	*% of total expenditure*	*Degrees*
Food	65	$\frac{65}{100} \times 360 = 234$
Clothing	10	$\frac{10}{100} \times 360 = 36$
Housing	12	$\frac{12}{100} \times 360 = 43.2$
Fuel and Lighting	5	$\frac{5}{100} \times 360 = 18$
Miscellaneous	8	$\frac{8}{100} \times 360 = 28.8$
	100	360

Pie Diagram Showing expenditure

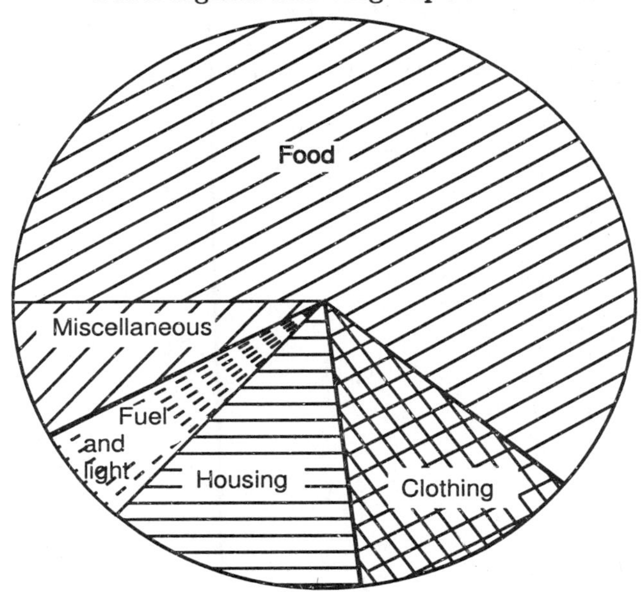

Problem 19. Draw a pie diagram to represent the following population in a town :

Males	*Females*	*Girls*	*Boys*	*Total*
2000	1800	4200	2000	10000

(*I.C.W.A Inter*)

Solution : **Calculation for a pie diagram**

Population	*Numbers*	*Degrees*
Males	2,000	$\frac{2,000}{10,000} \times 360 = 72°$
Females	1,800	$\frac{1,800}{10,000} \times 360 = 65°$
Girls	4,200	$\frac{4,200}{10,000} \times 360 = 151°$
Boys	2,000	$\frac{2,000}{10,000} \times 360 = 72°$
Total	10,000	360

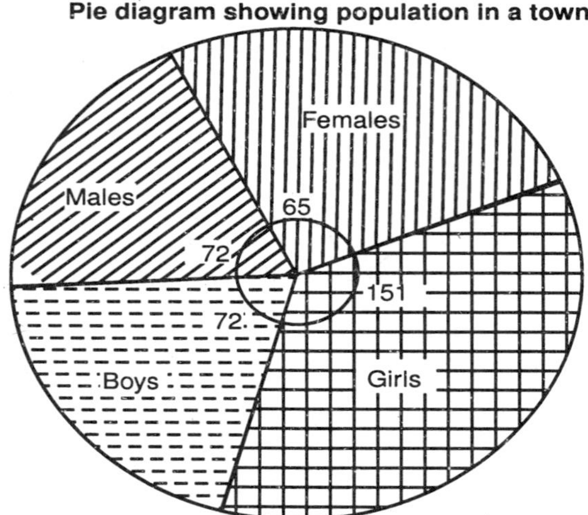

Problem 20. Draw a histogram from the following data and measure the modal value Verify it by actual calculation:

Size	*Frequency*
0–10	5
10–20	11
20–30	19
30–40	21
40–50	16
50–60	10
60–70	8
70–80	6
80–90	3
90–100	1

(*B.Com., Delhi*)

Solution :

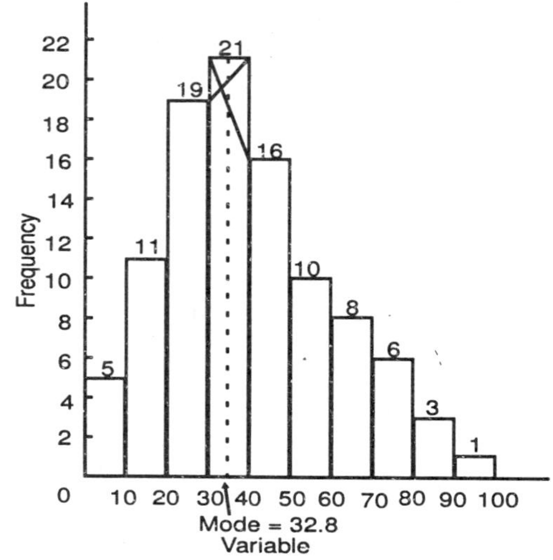

Verification

$$\text{Mode} = L_1 + \frac{f_1 - f_0}{2f_1 - f_0 - f_2} \times i$$

$$= 30 + \frac{21 - 19}{2 \times 21 - 19 - 16} \times 10 = 30 + \frac{2}{7} \times 10 = 30 + 2.8 = 32.8$$

Problem 21. Show the following with the help of pie diagram :

Accidents due to		*No. of Accidents*
(*a*) Fire		10
(*b*) Traffic		15
(*c*) Falls		20
(*d*) Cuts and bruises		15
(*e*) Mist		5
(*f*) Falling objects		35
	Total	100

Solution :

Central angles :

(*a*)	10/100×360	=	36°
(*b*)	15/100×360	=	54°
(*c*)	20/100×360	=	72°
(*d*)	15/100×360	=	54°
(*e*)	5/100×360	=	18°
(*f*)	35/100×360	=	126°
			360°

Pie Diagram Showing accidents

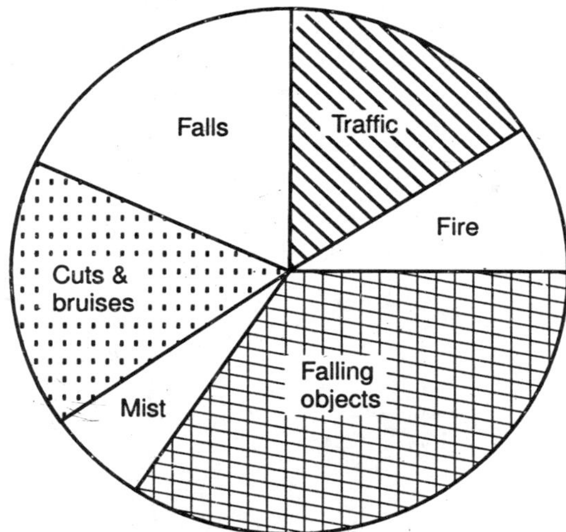

Problem 22. Construct a multiple bar diagram from the following data :

Year	*No. of Public Cos.* ('000)	*No. of Private Cos.* ('000)
2000	8	12
2001	13	20
2002	15	18
2003	12	21

(*B.Com. Madurai*)

Solution :

Multiple Bar Diagram

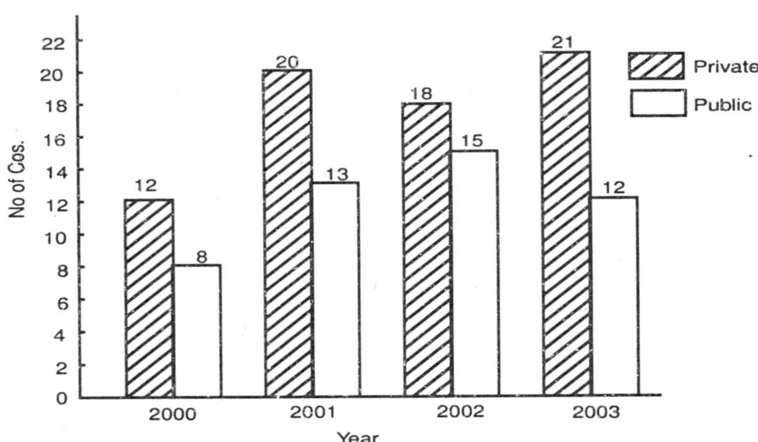

Problem 23. The following table gives the number of cars manufactured by a company, for different years :

Year	*No. of cars*
1999	4,000
2000	8,000
2001	10,000
2002	12,000
2003	14,000

Represent the data by pictogram.

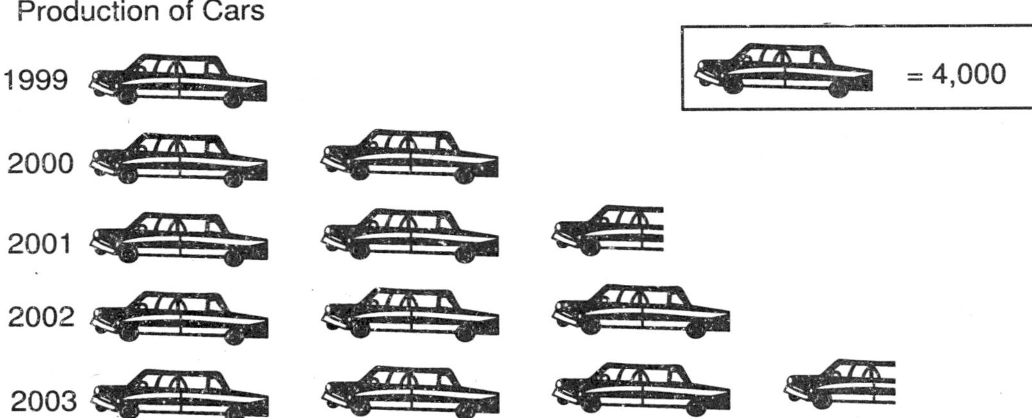

Problem 24. The following table gives the number of students studying in Colleges for different years of a particular state :

Year	*Students on roll on* 31st *March*
2000	1,00,000
2001	1,25,000
2002	1,12,500
2003	1,18,750

Represent the data by a pictogram :

Solution :

Students on role at colleges

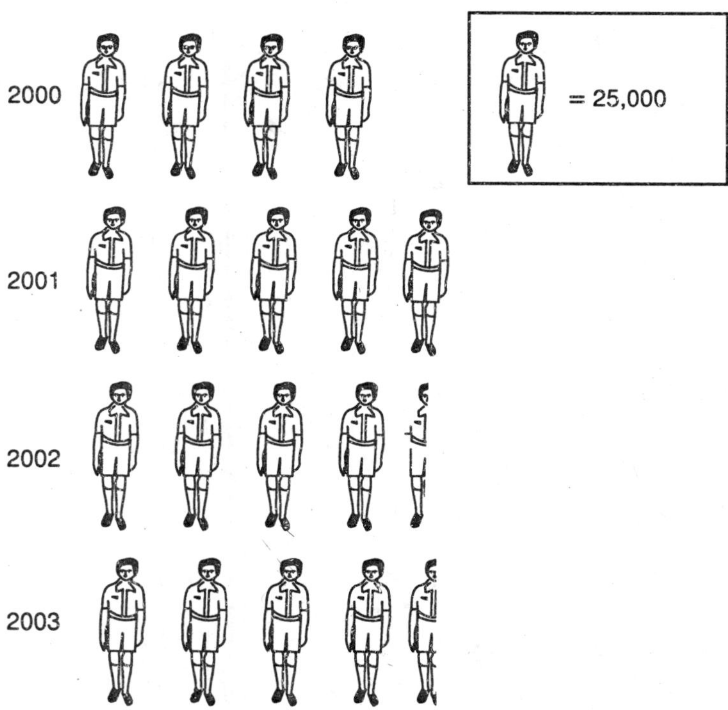

Problem 25. The following table gives the number of milk bottles produced by a Milk Society for four years :

Year	*No. of milk bottles*
2000	2,00,000
2001	2,50,000
2002	2,75,000
2003	3,00,000

Represent the data by a pictogram : **Solution :**

Number of milk bottles produced

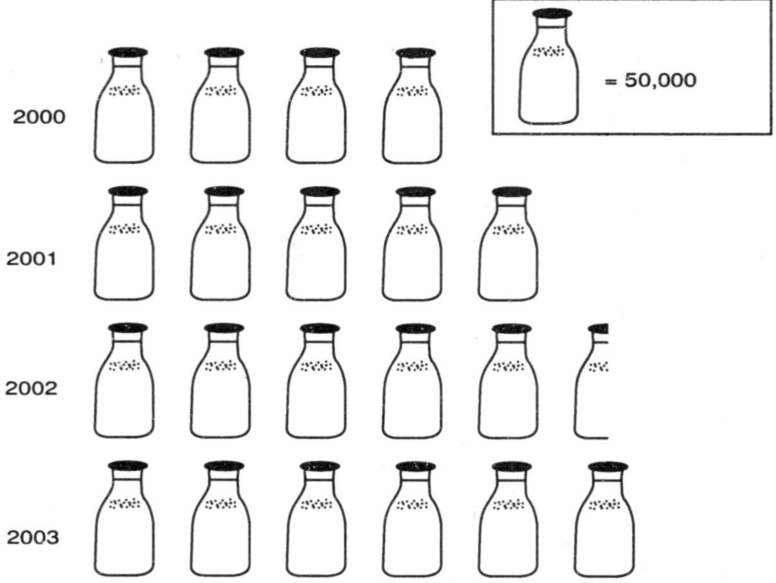

Problem 26. The following table gives the number of scooters manufactured by a Company, for different years :

Year	*No. of Scooters*
2000	30,000
2001	40,000
2002	65,000
2003	75,000

Represent the data by a pictogram.

Solution :

Number of scooters manufactured

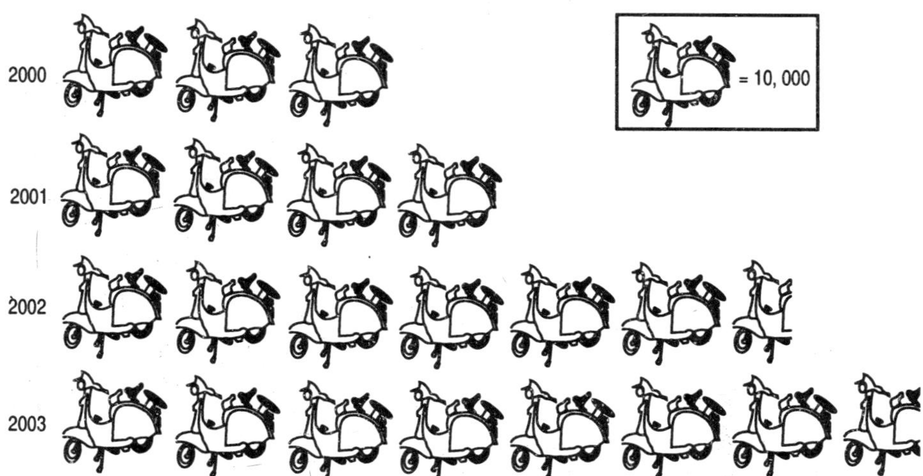

3

MEASURES OF CENTRAL TENDENCIES

Arithmetic Mean—Simple, Weighted and Combined , Median, Quartiles, Deciles and Percentiles, Mode, Geometric Mean, Harmonic Mean, Miscellaneous Problems.

FORMULAE

ARITHMETIC MEAN 1. *Individual Series* (A) *Direct Method* $\overline{X} = \frac{X_1 + X_2 + X_n}{N}$ or $\overline{X} = \frac{\Sigma X}{N}$ (B) Short Cut Method $\overline{X} = A \pm \frac{\Sigma d}{N}$ (C) Step Deviation Method $\overline{X} = A \pm \frac{\Sigma d'}{N} \times C$	$\overline{X}$ = Arithmetic Mean ΣX = The Sum of Variables N = Number of Observations A = Assumed Mean Σd = Sum of the deviations N = Number of items A = Assumed Mean $\Sigma d'$ = Sum of the deviations C = Common Factor
2. *Discrete Series* (A) *Direct Method* $\overline{X} = \frac{\Sigma fX}{N}$ (B) *Short Cut Method* $\overline{X} = A \pm \frac{\Sigma fd}{N}$ (C) *Step Deviation Method* $\overline{X} = A \pm \frac{\Sigma fd'}{N} \times C$	ΣfX = Sum of the products of the frequencies and the variable X N = Total number of items *i.e.* Σf A = Assumed Mean Σfd = Sum of total deviations N = Total Frequency A = Assumed Mean $\Sigma fd'$ = Sum of deviations N = Total frequency C = Common factor
3. *Continuous Series* (A) *Direct Method* $\overline{X} = \frac{\Sigma fm}{N}$	Σfm = Sum of the products of the frequencies and the mid points N = The total frequencies

(B) *Short Cut Method:* $\overline{X} = A \pm \frac{\Sigma fd}{N}$	A = Assumed Mean Σfd = Sum of total deviations N = Total frequency
(C) *Step Deviation Method:* $\overline{X} = A \pm \frac{\Sigma fd'}{N} \times C$	A = Assumed Mean $\Sigma fd'$ = The sum of deviations N = Number of items C = Common factor
Median (Med) 1. *Individual Series* Med: Size of $\left(\frac{N+1}{2}\right)$th item 2. *Discrete Series* Med = Size of $\left(\frac{N+1}{2}\right)$th item 3. *Continuous Series* Size of $\left(\frac{N}{2}\right)$ th item $Med = L_1 + \frac{\frac{N}{2} - C.f}{f} \times i$	$\frac{N}{2}$ = Median item L_1 = Lower limit of the median class f = frequency of the median class $C.f.$ = cumulative frequency of the class preceeding of median class (Total frequency of all lower classes) i = Class interval of median class
$Med = L_2 - \frac{\frac{N}{2} - C.f}{f} \times i$	L_2 = Upper limit of the median class $\frac{N}{2}$ = Median item i = Class interval
QUARTILES **Quartile One (Q_1)** *Individual Series and Discrete Series* Size of $\left(\frac{N+1}{4}\right)$th item *Continuous Series* Size of $\left(\frac{N}{4}\right)$th item	Q_1 = Lower Quartile N = Number of items L_1 = Lower limit of the Lower Quartile Class $\frac{N}{4}$ = Lower Quartile item

$Q_1 = L_1 + \dfrac{\frac{N}{4} - C.f}{f} \times i$	$C.f$ = Cumulative frequency of the class preceeding of Lower Quartile Class f = frequency of the Lower Quartile Class i = Class interval of Lower Quartile Class
Quartile Three(Q_3) *Individual Series and Discrete Series* *Size of* $3\left(\dfrac{N+1}{4}\right)$th item *Continuous Series* Size of $\left(\dfrac{3N}{4}\right)$th item $Q_3 = L_1 + \dfrac{\frac{3N}{4} - C.f}{f} \times i$	Q_3 = Upper Quartile N = Number of items L_1 = Lower limit of the upper Quartile class $\dfrac{3N}{4}$ = Upper Quartile item $C.f$ = Cumulative frequency of the class preceeding of upper Quartile class f = frequency of the upper Quartile class i = Class interval of upper Quartile class
Deciles *Individual Series* and *Discrete Series* D_5 = Size of $5\left(\dfrac{N+1}{10}\right)$ th item *Continuous Series* Size of $\left(\dfrac{5N}{10}\right)$th item $D_5 = L_1 + \dfrac{\frac{5N}{10} - C.f}{f} \times i$	D_5 = Decile 5 N = Number of items L_1 = Lower limit of the class $\dfrac{5N}{10} = D_5$ item $C.f$ = Cumulative frequency of the class preceeding of D_5 class f = frequency of D_5 class i = class interval of D_5 class
Percentiles: *Individual and Discrete Series* P_{70} = Size of $\dfrac{70(N+1)}{100}$ th item *Continuous Series* P_{70} = Size of $\dfrac{70N}{100}$th item	P_{70} = Percentile 70 N = Number of items L_1 = Lower limit of P_{70} class $\dfrac{70N}{100}$ = Percentile P_{70} item

$P_{70} = L_1 + \dfrac{\frac{70N}{100} - C.f}{f} \times i$	$C.f.$ = cumulative frequency of the class preceeding of P_{70} class f = frequency of P_{70} class i = class interval of P_{70} class
MODE (Z) (A) *Individual Series* Most Common Value (B) *Discrete Series* By inspection or grouping method (C) *Continuous Series* By grouping (Z) or $M_0 = L_1 + \dfrac{f_1 - f_0}{2f_1 - f_0 - f_2} \times i$ Alternative formula $Z = L_1 + \dfrac{\Delta_1}{\Delta_1 + \Delta_2} \times i$ Empirical Mode: $Z = 3$ Median $- 2$ Mean	Z = *Mode* L_1 = Lower limit of the modal class f_1 = Frequency of the modal class f_0 = Frequency of the class preceeding the modal class i = Class interval $\Delta_1 = f_1 - f_0$ $\Delta_2 = f_1 - f_2$
GEOMETRIC MEAN (G.M.) *Individual Series* G.M. = Anti log of $\dfrac{\log X_1 + \log X_2 + \ldots \log X_n}{N}$ or G.M. = Anti log $\left(\dfrac{\Sigma \log X}{N}\right)$ *Discrete Series* G.M. = Anti log $\left(\dfrac{\Sigma f \log X}{N}\right)$ *Continuous Series* G.M. = Anti log $\left(\dfrac{\Sigma f \log m}{N}\right)$	$\Sigma \log X$ = The sum of the values of log X N = Number of items $\Sigma f \log X$ = Total of the products N = The total frequency
HARMONIC MEAN (H.M.) *Individual Series* H.M. = $\dfrac{N}{\frac{1}{X_1} + \frac{1}{X_2} + \cdots \frac{1}{X_n}}$ H.M. = $\dfrac{N}{\Sigma \frac{1}{x}}$ *Discrete Series* H.M. = $\dfrac{N}{\Sigma f\left(\frac{1}{X}\right)}$ *Continuous Series* H.M. = $\dfrac{N}{\Sigma f\left(\frac{1}{m}\right)}$	$X_1, X_2 \ldots \quad X_n$ = Variables

Weighted Arithmetic Mean $\overline{X}\omega = \frac{\Sigma WX}{\Sigma W}$ **Weighted Geometric Mean** **G.M.** ω = Antilog $\left(\frac{\Sigma(logXW}{\Sigma W}\right)$ **Weighted Harmonic Mean** **H.M.** $\omega = \frac{\Sigma W}{(\frac{1}{a} \times W_1) + (\frac{1}{b} \times W_2)}$	
Combined Arithmetic Mean $\overline{X}_{12} = \frac{N_1 + \overline{X}_1 + N_2\overline{X}_2}{N_1 + N_2}$ $\overline{X}_{123} = \frac{N_1 + \overline{X_1} + N_2\overline{X}_2 + N_3\overline{X}_3}{N_1 + N_2 + N_3}$	$\overline{X}_{12}$, $\overline{X}_{123}$ = the combined means. $\overline{X}_1, \overline{X}_2, \overline{X}_3$ = Arithmetic Mean of first group, second group, and third group N_1, N_2, N_3 = Number of items in first, second and third groups.

(ARITHMETIC MEAN)

(1 to 45)

Problem 1. Calculate the arithmetic mean of the daily income of 10 families

Families	1	2	3	4	5	6	7	8	9	10
Income Rs.	18	20	35	55	38	54	100	85	37	53

(B. Com.)

Solution:

Calculation of Arithmetic Mean

Family	*Income (Rs.)*
1	18
2	20
3	35
4	55
5	38
6	54
7	100
8	85
9	37
10	53
N= 10	ΣX = 495

$$\overline{X} = \frac{\Sigma X}{N} \quad \Sigma X = 495; \quad N = 10$$

$$\overline{X} = \frac{495}{10} \quad = \text{Rs.}\mathbf{49.5}$$

Problem 2. The coins are tossed 1024 times. The theoretical frequencies of 10 heads, 9 heads ...... 0 heads are given below:

No. of heads	*Frequency*	*No. of heads*	*Frequency*
0	1	6	210
1	10	7	120
2	45	8	45
3	120	9	10
4	210	10	1
5	252		

(*Calcutta*)

Solution:

Computation of Mean

X	f	fX
0	1	0
1	10	10
2	45	90
3	120	360
4	210	840
5	252	1260
6	210	1260
7	120	840
8	45	360
9	10	90
10	1	10
	N= 1024	$\Sigma fX = 5,120$

$$\text{Mean:} \quad \overline{X} = \frac{\Sigma fX}{N} = \frac{5120}{1024} = \mathbf{5}$$

Problem 3. Six types of workers are employed in each of two workshops, but at different rates of wages as follows :

Type of workers	*Workshop A*		*Workshop B*	
	Rate of wages per workers (Rs.)	*No. of workers*	*Rate of wages per worker (Rs.)*	*No. of workers*
Mechanic	2.50	2	3.00	18
Fitter	3.50	14	3.00	50
Electrician	4.00	20	4.25	8
Carpenter	3.00	7	3.50	12
Smith	3.00	6	3.50	10
Clerk	2.00	1	5.00	2

In which of the two workshops is the average rate of wages per worker higher and by how much?

(*B Com., Madurai M.A. Economics, Lucknow*)

Solution:

Calculation of Average Wage

Type of Workers	*Workshop A*			*Workshop B*		
	X	f	fX	X	f	fX
Mechanic	2.50	2	5.00	3.00	18	54
Fitter	3.50	14	49.00	3.00	50	150
Electrician	4.00	20	80.00	4.25	8	34
Carpenter	3.00	7	21.00	3.50	12	42
Smith	3.00	6	18.00	3.50	10	35
Clerk	2.00	1	2.00	5.00	2	10
		N = 50	$\Sigma fX = 175$		N = 100	$\Sigma fX = 325$

$$\overline{X} = \Sigma fX/N = \frac{175}{50} = \textbf{Rs.3.50} \qquad X = \Sigma fX/N = \frac{325}{100} = \textbf{Rs.3.25}$$

Workshop A pays higher average rate of wages by Rs. 0.25.

Problem 4. Calculate mean from the following data:

Midpoints	1	2	3	4	5	6	7	8	9
Frequency	2	60	101	152	205	155	79	40	1

(*I.C.W.A.*)

Solution:

Computation of Arithmetic Mean

Midpoints (m)	*Frequency* (f)	$f\,m$
1	2	2
2	60	120
3	101	303
4	152	608
5	205	1025
6	155	930
7	79	553
8	40	320
9	1	9
	N = 795	$\Sigma fm = 3870$

$$\overline{X} = \frac{\Sigma fm}{N}.$$

$$\Sigma fm = 3870; N = 795$$

$$\overline{X} = \frac{3870}{795} = \mathbf{4.87}$$

Problem 5. The following data relate to size of shoes sold at a store during a given week. Find the average size by short cut method.

Size of shoes													
4.5	5	5.5	6	6.5	7	7.5	8	8.5	9	9.5	10	10.5	11
No. of pairs													
1	2	4	5	15	30	60	95	82	75	44	25	15	4

(*M. A. Calcutta*)

Solution:

Calculation of Mean

Size of shoes X	*No. of pairs*	$d = X - 8$	$f\,d$
4.5	1	−3.5	−3.5
5	2	−3	−6
5.5	4	−2.5	−10
6	5	−2	−10
6.5	15	−1.5	−22.5
7	30	−1	−30
7.5	60	−0.5	−30
8	95	0	0
8.5	82	+0.5	+41
9	75	+1	+75
9.5	44	+1.5	+66
10	25	+2	+50
10.5	15	+2.5	+37.5
11	4	+3	+12
	$N = 457$		$\Sigma fd = 169.5$

$$\overline{X} = A + \frac{\Sigma fd}{\text{N}}$$

$$A = 8; fd = +169.5; N = 457$$

$$\overline{X} = 8 + \frac{169.5}{457}$$

$$= 8 + 0.37$$

$$= \mathbf{8.37}$$

Problem 6. The pass result of 50 students who took up a test is given below:

Marks	: 4	5	6	7	8	9
No. of students	: 8	10	9	6	4	3

If the average marks of all the 50 students were 5.16, find out the average marks of the students who failed.

(*B. Com. Mysore*)

Solution:

Total Number of students = 50
Average Marks of 50 students = 5.16
Total Marks of 50 students = 5.16 × 50
= **258**

Total marks of 40 students

X	f	fX
4	8	32
5	10	50
6	9	54
7	6	42
8	4	32
9	3	27
	40	237

$\therefore$ Total marks of 40 students = 237

Average marks of the

Students failed $= \dfrac{258 - 237}{10} = \dfrac{21}{10} = \mathbf{2.1}$

$\therefore$ Average marks of the students failed =**2.1**

Problem 7. The numbers 3.2, 5.8, 7.9 and 4.5 have frequencies X, $(X + 2)$, $(X - 3)$ and $(X + 6)$ respectively. If the arithmetic mean is 4.876, find the value of X.

(M. Com. Calcutta, B. Com. Bombay, Agra)

Solution:

Calculation of The Value of X

Numbers X	f	fX
3.2	X	$3.2\ X$
5.8	$X + 2$	$5.8\ X + 11.6$
7.9	$X - 3$	$7.9\ X - 23.7$
4.5	$X + 6$	$4.5\ X + 27$
	$\Sigma f = 4\ X + 5$	$\Sigma f\, X = 21.4\ X + 14.9$

$$\overline{X} = \frac{\Sigma fx}{N}$$

$$4.876 = \frac{21.4\ X + 14.9}{4\ X + 5}$$

The above step will be multiplied with $4X + 5$,

thus, the simplified equation is:

$$\begin{aligned}
4.876(4X + 5) &= 21.4X + 14.9 \\
19.504\ X + 24.38 &= 21.4X + 14.9 \\
24.38 - 14.9 &= 21.4X - 19.504X \\
9.48 &= 1.896X \\
X &= \frac{9.48}{1.896} \\
&= \mathbf{5.}
\end{aligned}$$

Problem 8. Find the class intervals if the arithmetic mean of the following distribution is 33 and assumed mean 35 :

Step Deviation	−3	−2	−1	0	+1	+12
Frequency	5	10	25	30	20	10

(B. Com. Madurai, Bombay, Madrass)

Solution: **Computation of Class Intervals**

Step Deviation	*Frequency f*	*f d*
−3	5	−15
−2	10	−20
−1	25	−25
0	30	0
1	20	20
2	10	20
	N = 100	$\Sigma fd' = -20$

Mean:

$$\overline{X} = A \pm \frac{\Sigma fd'}{N} \times i$$

$$\overline{X} = 33, a = 35, N = 100, \Sigma fd' = -20$$

$$\text{Substituting the value, } 33 = 35 - \frac{20}{100} \times i$$

$$33 - 35 = -0.2\,i$$

$$0.2\,i = 2 \quad i = \frac{2}{0.2} = 10$$

Therefore the calss interval is 10 The value of assumed mean is happened to lie in the mid value of that with 0 as Step deviation. Therefore, the lower and upper limits of this class are:

$$35 + \frac{10}{2} = 40 \text{ and lower limit } 35 - \frac{10}{2} = 30.$$

In other words, the particular class is 30-40. Therefore, the entire classes: 0–10, 10–20, 20–30, 30–40, 40–50, 50–60

Problem 9. From the following data compute the mean marks of all the students of 50 schools in a city:

Marks obtained	*No. of Schools*	*Average No. of students in a school*
More than 35	7	200
30–35	10	250
25–30	15	300
20–15	9	200
15–20	5	150
Less than 15	4	100

(*B. Com, Rajasthan*)

Solution: First we have to rearrange the data given in the question and then calculate the mean.

Computation of Mean Marks

Marks (1)	*No. of Schools* (2)	*Average no. of students* (3)	*Total no of* students (2 × 3) *f*	*m.p.*	$(m - 27.5)/5 = d'$	fd'
10–15	4	100	400	12.5	−3	−1200
15–20	5	150	750	17.5	−2	−1500
20–25	9	200	1800	22.5	−1	−1800
25–30	15	300	4500	27.5	0	0
30–35	10	250	2500	32.5	1	2500
35–40	7	200	1400	37.5	2	2800
			$N = 11,350$			$\Sigma fd' = 800$

Mean:

$$\overline{X} = A + \frac{\Sigma fd'}{N} \times C$$
$$= 27.5 + \frac{800}{11,350} \times 5$$
$$= 27.5 + 0.35$$
$$= \mathbf{27.85} \text{ marks.}$$

Problem 10. Calculate the average marks of the students from the following data:

Marks	*No. of students*
Below 10	15
" 20	35
" 30	60
" 40	84
" 50	96
" 60	127
" 70	198
" 80	250

(*B. Com. Bangalore, Madurai, Bombay*)

Solution: Determine the simple frequencies from the cumulative frequencies given here and then calculate the mean.

Calculation of Arithmetic Mean

Marks	*No. of Students f*	*M.P. m*	$\left(\frac{m-35}{10}\right) d'$	fd'
0–10	15	5	−3	−45
10–20	20	15	−2	−40
20–30	25	25	−1	−25
30–40	24	35	0	0
40–50	12	45	1	+12
50–60	31	55	2	+62
60–70	71	65	3	+213
70–80	52	75	4	+208
	N = 250			$\Sigma fd' = +385$

$$\overline{X} = A + \frac{\Sigma fd'}{N} \times C$$
$$A = 35, \Sigma fd' = 385, N = 250, C = 10$$
$$\overline{X} = 35 + \frac{385}{250} \times 10$$
$$= 35 + 15 \cdot 4$$
$$= \mathbf{50.4}$$

Problem 11. Calculate the arithmetic mean from the following data:

Age (years)	18–21	22–25	26–35	36–45	46–55
No. of employees	8	32	54	36	20

(*B. Com. Madurai*)

Solution:

Computation of Mean

Age	*m.P*	*f*	$d = m - 30.5$	fd
18–21	19.5	8	−11	−88
22–25	23.5	32	−7	−224
26–35	30.5	54	0	0
36–45	40.5	36	10	360
46–55	50.5	20	20	400
		N = 150		$\Sigma fd = 448$

Note: It is not necessary to adjust the classes for the calculation of mean. But at the same time, adjustment of classes is necessary in case of Median and Mode.

$$\overline{X} = A \pm \frac{\Sigma fd}{N}$$

$$A = 30.5,\ \Sigma fd = 448,\ N = 150$$

$$= 30.5 + \frac{448}{150}$$

$$= 30.5 + 2.99$$

$$= \mathbf{33.49}$$

Problem 12. The following table gives the lifetime in hours of 400 radio tubes of a certain make. Find the mean lifetime of the radio tubes :

Lifetime (in hours)		*No. of tubes*	*Lifetime (in hours)*		*No. of tubes*
Less than	300	0	Less than	800	265
,,	400	20	,,	900	324
,,	500	60	,,	1000	374
,,	600	116	,,	1100	392
,,	700	194	,,	1200	400

(*B. Com. Madras*)

Solution:

Computation of Mean

Class Interval	*m*	*f*	$d' = \frac{m - 749.5}{100}$	fd'
300–399	349.5	20	−4	−80
400–499	499.5	40	−3	−120
500–599	549.5	56	−2	−112
600–699	649.5	78	−1	−78
700–799	749.5	71	0	0
800–899	849.5	59	+1	+59
900–999	949.5	50	+2	+100
1000–1099	1049.5	18	+3	+54
1100–1199	1149.5	8	+4	+32
		N = 400		$\Sigma fd' = -145$

Cumulative frequencies are given in the problem. Therefore, we have to find out the frequencies of the class-intervals. The number of tubes, which have lifetime, less than 300 is nil. Therefore, the lowest class limit is 300, and the class is 300–399. There are 20 tubes which have lifetime less than 400 hours *i.e.*, 300–399 class limits the number of tubes is 20. Then, 400–499 lifetime hours, there are 40 tubes *i.e.*, 60 – 20 = 40 and so on. The whole frequency table appears as above.

$$\begin{aligned} \overline{X} &= A \pm \frac{\Sigma fd'}{N} \times C \\ &= 749.5 - \frac{145}{400} \times 100 \\ &= 749.5 - 36.25 \\ &= \mathbf{713.25} \end{aligned}$$

Problem 13. Find mean for the following data:

Class interval	50–59	40–49	30–39	20–29	10–19	0–9
Frequency	1	3	8	10	15	3

(*B. Com. Karnatak*)

Solution: For finding out the mean, it is not necessary to write the class interval in ascending order and also not necessary to adjust the inclusive classes to exclusive classes.

Computation of Mean

Class	m	f	$d' = \frac{m - 34.4}{10}$	fd'
50–59	54.5	1	+2	+2
40–49	44.5	3	+1	+3
30-39	34.5	8	0	0
20–29	24.5	10	–1	–10
10–19	14.5	15	–2	–30
0–9	4.5	3	–3	–9
		N = 40		$\Sigma fd' = -44$

$$\begin{aligned} \overline{X} &= A \pm \frac{\Sigma fd'}{N} \times C \\ &= 34.5 - \frac{44}{40} \times 10 \\ &= 34.5 - 11 \\ &= \mathbf{23.5} \end{aligned}$$

Problem 14. Given the following frequency distribution, calculate the arithmetic mean:

Monthly wages (in Rs.)	*No. of workers*
12.5–17.5	2
17.5–22.5	22
22.5–27.5	10
27.5–32.5	14
32.5–37.5	3
37.5–42.5	4
42.5–47.5	6
47.5–52.5	1
52.5–57.5	1
	63

(*I.C.W.A., Inter*)

Solution:

Computation of Mean

Monthly Wages	m	f	$d' = \frac{m-35}{5}$	fd'
12.5–17.5	15	2	−4	−8
17.5–22.5	20	22	−3	−66
22.5–27.5	25	10	−2	−20
27.5–32.5	30	14	−1	−14
32.5–37.5	35	3	0	0
37.5–42.5	40	4	+1	+4
42.5–47.5	45	6	+2	+12
47.5–52.5	50	1	+3	+3
52.5–57.5	55	1	+4	+4
		N = 63		$\Sigma fd' = -85$

$$\overline{X} = A \pm \frac{\Sigma fd'}{N} \times C \quad = 35 + \frac{(-85)}{63} \times 5 \quad = 35 - \frac{425}{63} \quad = 35 - 6.75 \quad = \mathbf{28.25}$$

Problem 15. Following is the distribution of persons in U.K. according to difference income groups:

Income ('000£)	*No. of Persons*
0–1	13
1–2	90
2–3	81
3–5	117
5–10	66
10–25	27
25–50	6
50–100	2
100–1000	2

Calculate the average income per head.

(*B. Com. Rohtak*)

Solution:

Computation of Mean

Income £	*m.P(m)*	*No. of Persons (f)*	*f.m.*
0-1	0.5	13	6.5
1-2	1.5	90	135.0
2-3	2.5	81	202.5
3-5	4.0	117	468.0
5-10	7.5	66	495.0
10-25	17.5	27	472.5
25-50	37.5	6	225.0
50-100	75.0	2	150.0
100-1000	550.0	2	1100.0
		N = 404	$\Sigma fm = 3254.5$

Mean:

$$\overline{X} = \frac{\Sigma fm}{N} = \frac{3254.5}{404} = \mathbf{8.056}\ i.e.\ \pounds\,\mathbf{8,056}$$

Problem 16. Calculate the arithmetic mean for the following data:

Class Interval	5–10	10–15	15–20	20–25	25–30	30–35	35–40	40–45
Fre-Quency	6	5	15	10	5	4	3	2

(B.A. Bombay)

Solution:

Computation of Mean

$\overline{X}$	m	f	$d' = \frac{m - 27.5}{5}$	fd'
5–10	7.5	6	−4	−24
10–15	12.5	5	−3	−15
15–20	17.5	15	−2	−30
20–25	22.5	10	−1	−10
25–30	27.5	5	0	0
30–35	32.5	4	1	4
35–40	37.5	3	2	6
40–45	42.5	2	3	6
		N = 50		$\Sigma fd' = -63$

$$\overline{X} = A \pm \frac{\Sigma fd'}{N} \times C$$

$$A = 27.5;\ \Sigma fd' = -63;\ N = 50;\ C = 5$$

$$\overline{X} = 27.5 - \frac{63}{50} \times 5 = 27.5 - 6.3 = \mathbf{21.2}$$

Problem 17. The marks scored by 50 students in an examination paper are given below:

30	45	48	55	39	25	31	12	18	21
54	59	51	33	43	44	10	38	19	26
47	35	37	41	46	33	51	37	58	58
17	19	23	26	29	38	57	36	35	44
43	27	31	43	22	31	47	34	18	15

Prepare a frequency table taking a class interval of 10 and calculate the arithmetic mean.

(B.Com. Bombay)

Solution:

Computation of Mean

Marks	*Tally Marks*	*f*	*m*	$d' = \frac{m - 35}{10}$	*fd'*
10–20	𝍸 |||	8	15	–2	–16
20–30	𝍸 |||	8	25	–1	–8
30–40	𝍸 𝍸 𝍸	15	35	0	0
40–50	𝍸 𝍸		11	45	1	11
50–60	𝍸, |||	8	55	2	16
		N = 50			$\Sigma fd' = +3$

$$\overline{X} = A + \frac{fd'}{N} \times C$$

$$A = 35; \Sigma fd' = +3; N = 50; C = 10$$

$$\overline{X} = 35 + \frac{3}{50} \times 10 \quad = 35 + 0.6 \quad = \mathbf{35.6}.$$

Problem 18. Calculate the arithmetic mean from the following data:

Value	*Frequency*
0–4	328
5–9	350
10–19	720
20–29	664
30–39	598
40–49	524
50–59	378
60–69	244

(*B. Com., Kerala*)

Solution:

Combine the first and second classes so as to form equal class intervals throughout.

Compulation of Mean

Value	*f*	*m*	$\frac{(m - 34.5)}{10}$ d'	*fd'*
0–9	678	4.5	–3	–2034
10–19	720	14.5	–2	–1440
20–29	664	24.5	–1	–664
30–39	598	34.5	0	0
40–49	524	44.5	+1	+524
50–59	378	54.5	+2	+756
60–69	244	64.5	+3	+732
	N= 3806			$\Sigma fd' = -2126$

$$\overline{X} = A + \frac{\Sigma fd'}{N} \times C$$

$$\begin{aligned} A &= 34.5, \Sigma fd' = 2126, N = 3806, C = 10 \\ \overline{X} &= 34.5 + \left(\frac{-2126}{3806}\right) \times 10 \\ &= 34.5 - 5.59 \\ &= \mathbf{28.91}. \end{aligned}$$

Problem 19. The marks scored by 60 students in an examination in statistics are given below. Frame class intervals of ten and calculate the arithmetic mean.

6	10	58	56	0	25	32	35	35	9
78	17	60	50	35	38	31	10	48	5
68	48	35	30	31	21	23	23	50	72
19	25	35	40	46	42	45	25	60	41
35	36	38	35	33	46	28	31	35	42
46	38	39	45	48	50	28	29	31	55

(*B. Com., Mysore B.A. Madurai, M.S.*)

Solution:

Formation of Frequency Distribution and Calculation of Mean

Marks	*Tally Bars*	*f*	*m p*	$\left(\frac{m-35}{10}\right)$	*fd'*
			m	*d'*	
0–10	||||	4	5	–3	–12
10–20	||||	4	15	–2	–8
20–30	~~||||~~ ||||	9	25	–1	–9
30–40	~~||||~~ ~~||||~~ ~~||||~~ ~~||||~~	20	35	0	0
40–50	~~||||~~ ~~||||~~ ||	12	45	1	12
50–60	~~||||~~ |	6	55	2	12
60–70	|||	3	65	3	9
70–80	||	2	75	4	8
		N= 60			$\Sigma fd' = +12$

$$\begin{aligned} \overline{X} &= A + \frac{\Sigma fd'}{N} \times C \\ A &= 35, \Sigma fd' = +12, N = 60, C = 10 \\ \overline{X} &= 35 + \frac{12}{60} \times 10 \\ &= 35 + 2 = \mathbf{37} \end{aligned}$$

Problem 20. Calculate the arithmetic mean from the following data:

Temp. 'C'	*No. of days*
–40 to –30	10
–30 to –20	28
–20 to –10	30
–10 to 0	42
0 to 10	65
10 to 20	180
20 to 30	10

(*C. A., B.Com., Kerala, Bombay, Agra, Punjab*)

Solution:

Calculation of Arithmetic Mean

Temp 'C'	*No. of days* f	*M.P.* m	$\left(\frac{m-(+5)}{10}\right)$ d'	fd'
−40 to −30	10	−35	−4	−40
−30 to −20	28	−25	−3	−84
−20 to −10	30	−15	−2	−60
−10 to 0	42	−5	−1	−42
0 to 10	65	+5	0	0
10 to 20	180	+15	+1	+180
20 to 30	10	+25	+2	+20
	N = 365			$\Sigma fd' = -26$

$$\overline{X} = A + \frac{\Sigma fd'}{N} \times C$$

$$A = +5,\ \Sigma fd' = -26,\ N = 365,\ C = 10$$

$$\overline{X} = 5 + \left(\frac{-26}{365}\right) \times 10$$

$$= 5 - .71 = \mathbf{4.29°C}$$

Problem 21. Calculate the Mean of the following frequency distribution relating to the marks secured by students in Statistics :

Marks	*No. of Students*	*Marks*	*No. of Students*
0–5	1	40–45	20
5–10	6	45–50	25
10–15	8	50–55	12
15–20	7	55–60	7
20–25	11	60–65	6
25–30	10	65–70	5
30–35	10	70–75	4
35–40	17	75–80	1

(*B. Com., Delhi University*)

Solution: **Computation of Mean**

Marks	*Mid Point* (m)	*No. of Students* (f)	$d' = \frac{m - 37.5}{5}$	fd'
0–5	2.5	1	−7	−7
5–10	7.5	6	−6	−36
10–15	12.5	8	−5	−40
15–20	17.5	7	−4	−28
20–25	22.5	11	−3	−33
25–30	27.5	10	−2	−20
30–35	32.5	10	−1	−10
35–40	37.5	17	0	0
40–45	42.5	20	1	20
45–50	47.5	25	2	50

Cont..

50–55	52.5	12	3	36
55–60	57.5	7	4	28
60–65	62.5	6	5	30
65–70	67.5	5	6	30
70–75	72.5	4	7	28
75–80	77.5	1	8	8
		N = 150		$\Sigma fd' = 56$

$$\text{Mean : } \bar{X} = A + \frac{\Sigma fd'}{N} \times C$$

$$A = 37.5;\ \Sigma fd' = 56;\ N = 150;\ C = 5$$

$$= 37.5 + \frac{56}{150} \times 5 = 37.5 + 1.87$$

$$= \mathbf{39.37\ Marks.}$$

Problem 22. Find the missing frequency from the following data :

Marks	*Frequency*
0– 5	10
5–10	12
10–15	16
15–20	?
20–25	14
25–30	10
30–35	8

The mean is 16.82 (*B. Com. Gujarat*)

Solution: **Computation of Missing Frequency**

Marks	m	f	$d'\left(\frac{m-17.5}{5}\right)$	fd'
0–5	2.5	10	−3	−30
5–10	7.5	12	−2	−24
10–15	12.5	16	−1	−16
15–20	17.5	x	0	0
20–25	22.5	14	+1	14
25–30	27.5	10	+2	20
30–35	32.5	8	+3	24
		$N = 70 + x$		$\Sigma fd' = -12$

$$\bar{X} = A + \frac{\Sigma fd'}{N} C$$

$$16.82 = 17.5 + \frac{(-12)}{70 + x} 5$$

$$16.82 - 17.5 = \frac{-60}{70 + x}$$

$$-0.68(70 + x) = -60$$

$$-47.6 - 0.68x = -60$$

$$\text{(or)} 60 - 47.6 = 0.68x$$

$$12.4 = 0.68x$$

$$\text{Therefore} \quad x = \frac{12.4}{0.68}$$
$$= \mathbf{18.235}$$

Therefore, the missing frequency is 18.

Problem 23. The frequency distribution given below gives the cost of production of sugarcane in different holdings. Find the mean.

Cost Rs.	*Frequency*	*Cost Rs.*	*Frequency*
2–6	1	18–22	52
6–10	9	22–26	36
10–14	21	26–30	19
14–18	47	30–34	3

(*B. Com, Madras*)

Solution: **Computation of Mean**

Cost in (*Rs.*)	*M.P* (*m*)	*f*	$d' = \frac{m-20}{4}$	fd'
2–6	4	1	−4	−4
6–10	8	9	−3	−27
10–14	12	21	−2	−42
14–18	16	47	−1	−47
18–22	20	52	0	0
22–26	24	36	1	36
26–30	28	19	2	38
30–34	32	3	3	9
		N = 188		$\Sigma fd' = -37$

$$\text{Mean} = \overline{X} = A + \frac{\Sigma fd'}{N} \times C$$
$$A = 20;\ \Sigma fd' = -37;\ N = 188;\ C = 4$$
$$= 20 - \frac{37}{188} \times 4$$
$$= 20 - 0.79$$
$$= \mathbf{19.21}$$

Problem 24. The following are the monthly salaries in rupees of 20 employees of a firm:

130	62	145	118	125	75	151	142	110	98
65	116	100	103	71	85	80	122	132	95

The firm gives bonus of Rs. 10, 15, 20, 25 and 30 for individuals in the respective salary groups exceeding Rs. 60 but not exceeding Rs. 80, exceeding Rs. 80 but not exceeding Rs. 100 and so on upto Rs. 140 but not exceeding Rs. 160. Find the average bonus paid per employee.

(*B. Com. Gurunanak*)

Solution:

We have to convert the data into grouped frequency distribution with the help of tally sheet to decide the amount of bonus.

Computation of Mean

Salary	*Tally*	*Frequency (f)*	*Bonus (x)*	*fx*
61–80	~~||||~~	5	10	50
81–100	||||	4	15	60
101–120	||||	4	20	80
121–140	||||	4	25	100
141–161	|||	3	30	90
		$\Sigma f = 20$		$\Sigma f\overline{X} = 380$

$$\text{Average bonus paid per employee} = \frac{\Sigma fX}{\Sigma f} = \frac{380}{20} = \textbf{Rs. 19}$$

Problem 25. The table given below has been constructed from data obtained from a factory showing the distribution of the number of processed articles per day per person and the rate of payment:

No. of articles processed per person (x)	80–99	100–119	120–139	140–159	160–169
No. of persons processing (f)	12	63	87	56	3
Rate of payment per article (r)	3.1	3.2	3.3	3.4	3.5

Calculate the rate of payment per article.

(*I.C.W.A.*)

Solution: **Computation of Average Rate of Payment**

No. of articles processed per person X	*Mid-value (mv)*	*No. of persons processing (f)*	*Rate of payment per article (r)*	*fm*	*fmr*
80–99	89.5	12	3.1	1074.0	3329.40
100–119	109.5	63	3.2	6898.5	22075.20
120–139	129.5	87	3.3	11266.5	37179.45
140–159	149.5	56	3.4	8372.0	28464.80
160–169	164.5	3	3.5	493.5	1727.25
				Σfm = 28104.5	Σfmr = 92776.10

Average rate of payment person per article processed:

$$\frac{\Sigma fmr}{\Sigma fm} = \frac{92,776.10}{28,104.5} = \mathbf{3.3}$$

Problem 26. Below is given the frequency distribution of weights (lbs) of 100 children:

Class limits	*Frequency*
65–69	8
70–74	15
75–79	18
80–84	25
85–89	14
90–94	9
95–99	6
100–104	5
	100

Calculate mean of the distribution.

(*I.C.W.A.*)

Solution: **Computation of Mean**

	$m.p.$	f	$(m-82)/5 = d'$	fd'
65–69	67	8	−3	−24
70–74	72	15	−2	−30
75–79	77	18	−1	−18
80–84	82	25	0	0
85–89	87	14	1	14
90–94	92	9	2	18
95–99	97	6	3	18
100–104	102	5	4	20
		N = 100		$\Sigma fd' = -2$

$$\text{Mean : } \overline{\text{X}} = \text{A} + \frac{\Sigma fd'}{N} \times C$$

$$= 82 - \frac{2}{100} \times 5$$

$$= 82 - 0.1$$

$$= \mathbf{81.9}$$

Problem 27. Find the arithmetic mean from the following:

No. of days absent less than	5	10	15	20	25	30	35	40	45
No. of students	29	224	465	582	634	644	650	653	655

(*B. Com.*)

Solution:

To find out mean, the cumulative frequencies have to be converted into simple frequencies.

Computation of Mean

		Frequency			
	m.p.	*Cumulative*	*Single (f)*	*(m-22.5)/5* $= d'$	fd'
0–5	2.5	29	29	–4	–116
5–10	7.5	224	224 – 29 = 195	–3	–585
10–15	12.5	465	465 – 224 = 241	–2	–482
15–20	17.5	582	582 – 465 = 117	–1	–117
20–25	22.5	634	634 – 582 = 52	0	0
25–30	27.5	644	644 – 634 = 10	1	10
30–35	32.5	650	650 – 644 = 6	2	12
35–40	37.5	653	653 – 650 = 3	3	9
40–45	42.5	655	655 – 653 = 2	4	8
			N = 655		$\Sigma fd' = -1261$

$$\begin{aligned}\overline{X} &= A + \frac{\Sigma fd'}{N} \times C \\ &= 22.5 - \frac{1261}{655} \times 5 \\ &= 22.5 - 9.6 \\ &= \mathbf{12.9\ (13\ days)}\end{aligned}$$

Problem 28. A factory pays workers on piece rate basis and also a bonus to each worker on the basis of individual output in each quarter. The rate of bonus payble is as follows:

Output in units	*Bonus of rupees*
70–74	40
75–79	45
80–84	50
85–89	60
90–94	70
95–99	80
100–104	100

The individual output of a batch of 50 workers is given below:

94	83	78	76	88	86	93	80	91	82
89	97	92	84	82	80	85	83	98	103
87	88	88	81	95	86	99	81	87	90
84	97	80	75	93	101	82	82	89	72
85	83	75	72	83	98	77	87	71	80

By suitable classification you are required to find:

(1) Average bonus per worker for the quarter.

(2) Total quarterly bonus paid to the whole batch.

(3) Average output per worker.

Solution: Since the bonus figures are given for classes 70–74, 75–79 etc. the output data shall also be classified with the same class intervals.

Frequency Distribution by Output and Bonus

Output in-units	*Tally Bars*	*f*	*X*	*m*	$(m-87)/5 = d'$	fd'	fx
70–74	|||	3	40	72	−3	−9	120
75–79	~~||||~~	5	45	77	−2	−10	225
80–84	~~||||~~ ~~||||~~ ~~||||~~ |	16	50	82	−1	−16	800
85–89	~~||||~~ ~~||||~~ ||	12	60	87	0	0	720
90–94	~~||||~~ |	6	70	92	1	6	420
95–99	~~||||~~ |	6	80	97	2	12	480
100–104	||	2	100	102	3	6	200
		N = 50				$\Sigma fd' = -11$	$\Sigma fX = 2,965$

(*i*) Average bonus per worker for the quarter

$$\overline{X} = \frac{\Sigma fX}{N}$$

$$\Sigma fX = 2,965, \quad N = 50$$

$$= \frac{2965}{50}$$

$$\overline{X} = \mathbf{59.3}$$

(*ii*) Total quarterly bonus paid to the whole batch

$$= 59.3 \times 50$$

$$= \text{Rs.}\mathbf{2,965}$$

(*iii*) Average output per worker

$$\overline{X} = A + \frac{\Sigma fd'}{N} \times C$$

$$A = 87, \Sigma fd' = -11, N = 50, C = 5$$

$$= 87 - \frac{11}{50} \times 5$$

$$= 87 - \frac{55}{50}$$

$$= 87 - 1.1$$

$$\overline{X} = \mathbf{85.9} \text{ units or } \mathbf{86} \text{ units}$$

Problem 29. Following are the marks (out of 100) obtained by 50 students in Statistics :

70	55	51	42	57	45	60	47	63	53
33	65	39	82	55	64	50	25	65	75
30	20	58	52	36	45	42	35	40	61
53	59	49	41	15	52	46	42	45	39
55	65	45	63	54	48	64	35	26	18

(*i*) Make a frequency distribution taking a class-interval of 10 marks: (Take the first class-interval as 0–10).

(*ii*) Draw a histogram and a frequency polygon from the frequency distribution.

(*iii*) Find out the average marks of the students.

Solution:(*i*) **Computation of Frequency Distribution**

Marks	*Tally Marks*	*f*
10–20	||	2
20–30	|||	3
30–40	~~||||~~ ||	7
40–50	~~||||~~ ~~||||~~ |||	13
50–60	~~||||~~ ~~||||~~ |||	13
60–70	~~||||~~ ||||	9
70–80	||	2
80–90	|	1
		N = 50

(*ii*) **HISTOGRAM**

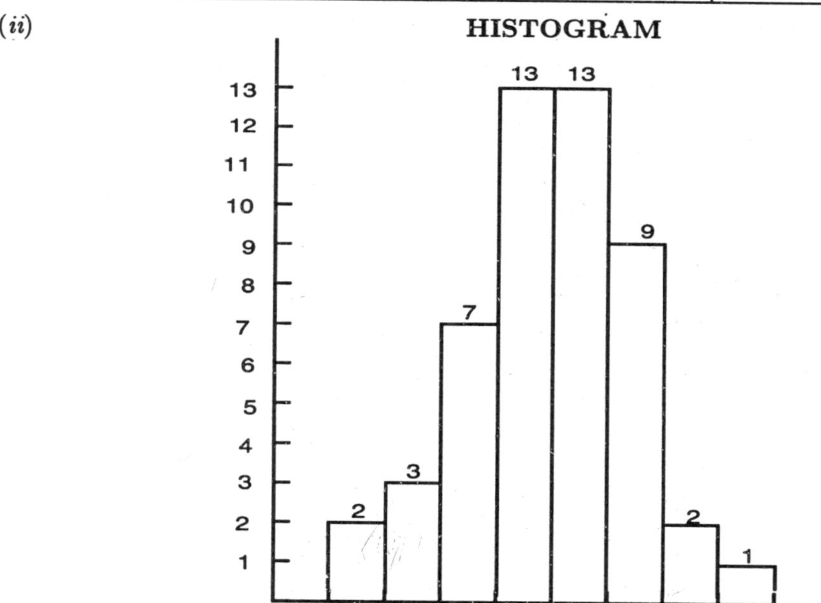

(*iii*) **Computation of Mean**

Marks	*m*	*f*	$d' = \frac{m-45}{10}$	fd'
10–20	15	2	−3	−6
20–30	25	3	−2	−6
30–40	35	7	−1	−7
40–50	45	13	0	0
50–60	55	13	1	13
60–70	65	9	2	18
70–80	75	2	3	6
80–90	85	1	4	4
		N = 50		$\Sigma fd' = +22$

$$\overline{X} = A + \frac{\Sigma fd'}{N} \times C$$

$$A = 45;\ \Sigma fd' = +22;\ N = 50;\ C = 10$$

$$\overline{X} = 45 + \frac{22}{50} \times 10$$

$$= 45 + 4.4$$

$$= \mathbf{49.4}$$

Problem 30. Calculate weighted mean and unweighted mean from the following data:

Article	*Price in Rs. per kg.*	*Quantity consumed*
Rice	Rs. 4.50	100 Kg.
Wheat	Rs. 3.00	50 Kg.
Sugar	Rs. 5.00	20 Kg.
Oil	Rs. 10.00	5 Kg.
Ghee	Rs. 35.00	2 Kg.

Solution:

Computation of Unweighted and Weighted Mean

Article	*Price* (*X*)	*Quantity* (*W*)	*WX*
Rice	4.50	100	450
Wheat	3.00	50	150
Sugar	5.00	20	100
Oil	10.00	5	50
Ghee	35.00	2	70
	$\Sigma X = 57.50$	$\Sigma W = 177$	$\Sigma WX = 820$

$$\overline{X} = \frac{\Sigma X}{N}$$

$$\overline{X} = \frac{57.50}{5}$$

$$= 11.50$$

Unweighted Mean = Rs. 11.50

Weighted Mean

$$\overline{X}_W = \frac{\Sigma WX}{\Sigma W}$$

$$= \frac{820}{177}$$

$$= \text{Rs. } \mathbf{4.63}$$

Problem 31. A man travelled by motor car for 3 days. He covered 960 kms. each day. He drove the first day 10 hours at 96 kms. per hour, the second day 12 hours at 80 kms. per hour and the third day 15 hours, at 64 kms. per hour. What was his average speed ?

(*B. Com. Jodhpur*)

Solution:

Calculation of Weighted Mean

Speed (*kms. per hour X*)	*Hour W*	*WX*
96	10	960
80	12	960
64	15	960
	$\Sigma W = 37$	$\Sigma WX = 2,880$

$$\text{AverageSpeed} = \frac{\Sigma WX}{\Sigma w} = \frac{2880}{37} = \mathbf{77.84 kms.p.h.}$$

Problem 32. Comment on the performance of the students of three Universities given below using simple and weighted averages :

University	*Bombay*		*Calcutta*		*Madras*	
Course of study	*% of pass*	*No. of students* ('00)	*% of pass*	*No. of students* ('00)	*% of pass*	*No. of students* ('00)
M.A.	71	3	82	2	81	2
M.Com.	83	4	76	3	76	3.5
B.A.	73	5	73	6	74	4.5
B.Com.	74	2	76	7	58	2
B.Sc.	65	3	65	3	70	7
M. Sc.	66	3	60	7	73	2

(*C.A.*)

Solution: **Computation of Simple and weighted Average**

University	*Bombay*			*Calcutta*			*Madras*		
Courses	*X*	*W*	*WX*	*X*	*W*	*WX*	*X*	*W*	*XW*
M.A.	71	3	213	82	2	164	81	2	162
M.Com.	83	4	332	76	3	228	76	3.5	266
B.A.	73	5	365	73	6	438	74	4.5	333
B Com.	74	2	148	76	7	532	58	2	116
B. Sc.	65	3	195	65	3	195	70	7	490
M. Sc.	66	3	198	60	7	420	73	2	146
	ΣX 432	ΣW 20	ΣWX 1451	ΣX 432	ΣW 28	ΣWX 1977	ΣX 432	ΣW 21	ΣWX 1513

ΣX is the same for all the three universities

$$\overline{X} = \frac{432}{6} = 72.$$

But the number of students (weight) is different. Therefore, we have to calculate the weighted mean.

$$\text{Bombay } \overline{X}_w = \frac{WX}{\Sigma W} = \frac{1451}{20} = 72.55$$

$$\text{Calcutta } \overline{X}_w = \frac{WX}{\Sigma W} = \frac{1977}{28} = 70.60$$

$$\text{Madras } \overline{X}_w = \frac{WX}{\Sigma W} = \frac{1513}{21} = 72.05$$

Bombay university is the best university because the weighted mean is greater than the other two universities.

Problem 33. An average monthly production of a certain factory for the first 9 months is 2, 584 units and for the remaining three months it is 2, 416 units, Calculate the average monthly production for the year.

(*B. Com. Delhi*)

Solution:

$$\overline{X}_{12} = \frac{N_1\overline{X}_2 + N_2\overline{X}_2}{N_1 + N_2}$$

$$N_1 = 9, \overline{X}_1 = 2,584, N_2 = 3, \overline{X}_2 = 2,416$$

$$\overline{X}_{12} = \frac{(9 \times 2,584) + (3 \times 2,416)}{9+3}$$

$$= \frac{23,256 + 7248}{12}$$

$$= \frac{30504}{12}$$

$$= \mathbf{2,542.}$$

Therefore the average monthly production for the year is 2.542 units.

Problem 34. There are two branches of a company, employing 280 and 320 persons respectively. If the arithmetic mean of the monthly salaries paid by the two companies are Rs. 750 and Rs. 937.5 respectively, find the arithmetic mean of the salaries of the employees of the companies as a whole.

(*B. Com.*)

Solution:

$$\overline{X}_{12} = \frac{N_1\overline{X}_1 + N_1\overline{X}_2}{N_1 + N_2}$$

$$= \frac{280 \times 750 + 320 \times 937.5}{280 + 320} = \frac{210000 + 300000}{600}$$

$$= \frac{510000}{600}$$

$$= \textbf{Rs. 850}$$

The average salaries of the employees of the companies as a whole = Rs. 850

Problem 35. The mean annual salaries paid to all employees of a company was Rs. 500. The mean annual salaries paid to male and female employees were Rs. 520 and Rs. 420 respectively. Determine the percentage of males and females employed by the company.

(*M.BA. Delhi*)

Solution:

Let N_1 = Percentage of males

N_2 = Percentage of females

Known values are: $\overline{X}_{12} = 500$; $\overline{X}_1 = 520$; $\overline{X}_2 = 420$

$$\overline{X}_{12} = \frac{N_1X_1 + N_2\overline{X}_2}{N_1 + N_2}$$

$$500 = \frac{N_1(520) + N_2(420)}{N_1 + N_2}$$

$$500 = \frac{N_1(520) + N_2(420)}{100}$$

$$500 \times 100 = 520\,N_1 + (100 - N_1)420 \qquad N_1 + N_2 = 100;\ N_2 = 100 - N_1$$

$$50000 = 520\,N_1 + 42000 - 420\,N_1$$

$$50000 - 42000 = 520\,N_1 - 420\,N_1$$

$$100\,N_1 = 8000$$

$$N_1 = \frac{8000}{100} = 80\%$$

$$\text{Thus } N_1 = 80\%$$
$$N_2 = 20\% (\text{since } N_1 + N_2 = 100\%)$$
$$N_2 = 100 - 80 = 20\%$$

Problem 36. The mean age of a combined group of men and women is 30 years. If the mean age of the group of men is 32 and that of the group of women is 27, find out the percentage of men and women in the group.

(*C.A.*)

Solution:

$$\overline{X}_{12} = \frac{N_1\overline{X}_1 + N_2\overline{X}_2}{N_1 + N_2}$$

We are given $\overline{X}_{12}$, $\overline{X_1}$, $\overline{X_2}$ and have no N_1 and N_2

Let the percentage of men be N_1

$\therefore$ Percentage of women will be $(100-N_1)$

So that $N_1+N_2 = 100$

$$\overline{X}_{12} = 30; \overline{X}_1 = 32; \overline{X}_2 = 27$$
$$30 = \frac{N_1 \times 32 + (100 - N_1)27}{100}$$
$$3000 = 32\,N_1 + 2700 - 27\,N_1$$
$$= 3000 - 2700 = 32\,N_1 - 27\,N_1$$
$$5\,N_1 = 300$$
$$\therefore \quad N_1 = 60\%$$
$$N_2 = 100 - 60$$
$$= \mathbf{40\ \%}$$

Problem 37. The mean weight of 150 students in a class is 60 kg. The mean weight of boys in the class is 70 kg. and that of the girls is 55 kg. Find the number of girls in the class.

(*B. Com. Madurai*)

Solution:

$$N_1 = \text{No. of boys}; N_2 = \text{No. of girls}$$
$$N_1 + N_2 = 150; \overline{X_1} = 70; \overline{X_2} = 55; \overline{X_{12}} = 60$$
$$N_{12} = \frac{N_1\overline{X_1} + N_2\overline{X_2}}{N_1 + N_2}$$
$$60 = \frac{70\,N_1 + 55(150 - N_1)}{150}$$
$$9000 = 70\,N_1 + 8250 - 55\,N_1$$
$$9000 - 8250 = 70\,N_1 - 55\,N_1$$
$$750 = 15\,N_1$$
$$N_1 = \frac{750}{15} = 50$$
$$\text{No. of boys} = 50$$
$$\text{No. of girls} = 150 - 50 = 100$$

Problem 38. The mean wage of 100 labourers working in a factory, running two shifts of 60 and 40 workers respectively, is Rs. 38. The mean wage of 60 labourers working in the morning shift is Rs. 40. Find the mean wage of 40 labourers working in the evening shift.

(*B. Com (Hons.) Delhi*)

Solution: $N_1+N_2 = 100$

Morning shift workers $N_1 = 60$

Mean wage of 60 labourers $\overline{X_1} = 40$

Mean wage of 100 labourers, $\overline{X}_{12} = 38$

Evening shift workers $N_2 = 40$

$$\overline{X}_{12} = \frac{\overline{X_1}N_1 + \overline{X_2}N_2}{N_1 + N_2}$$

$$38 = \frac{40 \times 60 + \overline{X_2} \times 40}{60 + 40}$$

$$38 = \frac{40 \times 60 + \overline{X_2} \times 40}{100}$$

$$3800 = 2400 + 40\,\overline{X_2}$$

$$\text{or } 40\,\overline{X_2} = 1400$$

$$\overline{X_2} = \frac{1400}{40} = 35$$

Mean wage of 40 labourers = **Rs. 35**

Problem 39. For a certain frequency table which is partly reproduced here, the mean was found to be 1.46.

No. of accidents	*Number of days*
0	46
1	?
2	?
3	25
4	10
5	5
	200

Calculate the missing frequencies. (*B. Com. Calcutta*)

Solution:

Computation of missing figures

No. of accidents (X)	*Frequencies* (f)	fX
0	46	0
1	f_1	f_1
2	f_2	$2f_2$
3	25	75
4	10	40
5	5	25
Total	$86 + f_1 + f_2$ (or) $\Sigma f = 200$	$\Sigma fX = 140 + f_1 + 2f_2$

We know

$$200 = 86 + f_1 + f_2$$

$$200 - 86 = f_1 + f_2 \qquad \text{........}\otimes$$

$$114 = f_1 + f_2$$

$$\overline{X} = \frac{\Sigma fx}{\Sigma f} = 1.46 = \frac{140 + f_1 + 2f_2}{200}$$

$$140 + f_1 + 2f_2 = 1.46 \times 200$$
$$140 + f_1 + 2f_2 = 292$$
$$f_1 + 2f_2 = 292 - 140$$
$$f_1 + 2f_2 = 152 \qquad \ldots\ldots\ldots @$$

Subtract ⊗ from @

$$\begin{array}{r} f_1 + 2f_2 = 152 \\ \underline{f_1 + f_2 = 114} \\ f_2 = 38 \end{array}$$

Substituting in ⊗ we get $f_1 = 114 - f_2 = 114 - 38 = 76$ $f_1 = 76$ and $f_2 = 38$.

Problem 40. The mean age of a group as 100 persons was found to be 32.02. Later it was discovered that age 57 was misread as 27. Find the correct mean. (*M. A. Punjab*)

Solution:

$$\overline{X} = \frac{\Sigma X}{N}$$

Putting the values in the formula we get wrong

$$\overline{X} = 32.02 \times 100 = 3202$$

Correct ΣX = Incorrect Σ X−wrong item + correct item

Correct $\Sigma X = 3202 - 27 + 57$

Correct $\Sigma X = 3232$

Correct Mean $= \dfrac{3232}{100}$

$= \mathbf{32.32}$

Problem 41. In a class of 50 students, 10 have failed and their average marks is 2.5. The total marks secured by the entire classes were 281. Find the average marks of those who passed.

(*B. Com. Bangalore*)

Solution:

Number of failures = 10
Average marks of those who failed = 2.5
Total number of students = 50
Total marks secured by all students = 281
Marks secured by 10 students who failed = 10 × 2.5 = 25
Out of 50 ten have failed
Total marks of those who passed = 281 − 25
= 256
Average marks of those who passed $= \dfrac{256}{40}$
= **6.4**

Problem 42. The value of mode and median for a moderately skewed distribution are 64.2 and 68.6 respectively. Find the value of the mean.

(*B. Com. Osmania*)

Solution: Using the empirical formula

$$\text{Mean} = \text{Mode} + \frac{3}{2}(\text{Median} - \text{Mode})$$

$$\text{Mean} = 64.2 + \frac{3}{2}(68.6 - 64.2)$$

$$= \mathbf{70.8}.$$

Problem 43. The average weight of a group of 25 boys was calculated to be 78.4 lbs. It was later discovered that one weight was misread as 69 lbs, instead of 96 lbs. Calculate the correct mean.

(*B. Com. Poona*)

Solution: Mean (given) = 78.4 lbs

Therefore the wrong total weight = 78.4 × 25 = 1,960

Correct total weight = wrong total − wrong value + correct value = 1960 − 69 + 96 = 1987

$$\text{Correct Mean} = \frac{1987}{25}$$

$$= \mathbf{79.48\ lbs.}$$

(Alternatively):

$$\text{Correct Mean} = \text{Uncorrected Mean} - \frac{(\text{Misread item}) - (\text{Correct item})}{\text{No.of items}}$$

$$= 78.4 - \frac{69 - 96}{25}$$

$$= 78.4 + 1.08 = \mathbf{79.48\ lbs.}$$

Problem 44. Mean of 100 items is found to be 30. If at the time of calculation two items are wrongly taken as 32 and 12 instead of 23 and 11, find the correct mean.

(*B. Com. Shivaji*)

Solution:

$$\text{Wrong } \Sigma X = \overline{X} \times N$$

$$= 30 \times 100$$

$$= 3,000$$

$$\text{Correct } \Sigma X = \text{Wrong } \Sigma X - \text{Misread items} + \text{Correct items}$$

$$= 3000 - (32 + 12) + (23 + 11)$$

$$= 3000 - 44 + 34$$

$$= \mathbf{2990}$$

$$\text{Correct mean} = \frac{\text{Corrected } \Sigma X}{N}$$

$$= \frac{2990}{100}$$

$$= \mathbf{29.9}$$

Problem 45. The mean marks of 100 students were found to be 40. Later on it was discovered that a score of 53 was misread as 83. Find the corrected mean corresponding to the corrected score.

(*B. Com. Bombay*)

Solution:

$$\begin{aligned}
\text{Wrong } \Sigma X &= \overline{X} \times N \\
&= 40 \times 100 \\
&= 4000 \\
\text{Correct } \Sigma X &= \text{Wrong } \Sigma X - \text{Wrong item} + \text{Correct item} \\
&= 4000 - 83 + 53 \\
&= 3970 \\
\text{Correct mean} &= \frac{\text{Corrected } \Sigma X}{N} \\
&= \frac{3970}{100} \\
&= \mathbf{39.7}
\end{aligned}$$

MEDIAN, QUALITILES etc.

Problem 46. Find out the median of the following items:

10, 8, 5, 13, 4, 9, 7

Solution:

The items are arranged in ascending order of magnitude.

4
5
7
8
9
10
13

$$\begin{aligned}
\text{Median} &= \text{Size of } \frac{N+1}{2}\text{th item} \\
&= \text{Size of } \frac{7+1}{2}\text{th item} \\
&= \text{Size of } \frac{8}{2}\text{th item} \\
&= \text{Size of 4th item} \\
&= \mathbf{8}
\end{aligned}$$

Problem 47. **The following table gives the monthly incomes of 12 families in a town:**

S.No.	1	2	3	4	5	6	7	8	9	10	11	12
Monthly incomes	280	180	96	98	104	75	80	94	100	75	600	200

Calculate the median of the above incomes.

(M. A.)(Econ.) Lucknow)

Solution:

To Calculate the median, first we have to arrange the data either in ascending or decending order. In this problem the incomes have been arranged in ascending order.

Computation of Median

S. No.	*Incomes*
1.	75
2.	75
3.	80
4.	94
5.	96
6.	98
7.	100
8.	104
9.	180
10.	200
11.	280
12.	600

$$\text{Median} = \text{Size of } \frac{(N+1)}{2}\text{th item}$$
$$= \text{Size of } \frac{12+1}{2}\text{th item}$$
$$= 6.5\text{th item}$$
$$\text{Size of 6.5th item} = \frac{\text{6th item} + \text{7th item}}{2}$$
$$= \frac{98+100}{2} = 99$$

Therefore median income is Rs. **99**

Problem 48. You are given below a certain statistical distribution:

Value	*Frequency*
Less than 100	40
100–200	89
200–300	148
300–400	64
400 and above	39
Total:	380

Calculate the most suitable average giving reasons for your choice.

(*C.A. Inter*)

Solution:

Median and mode are suitable averages. However, we calculate median for the above problem.

Value	*f*	*cf*
Less than 100	40	40
100–200	89	129
200–300	148	277
300–400	64	341
400 and above	39	380

$$\text{Median} = \text{Size } \frac{N}{2}\text{th item} = \text{Size of} \frac{380}{2} \text{ th item} = 190 \text{ th item}$$

The median lies in the group 200–300 (190th item)

$$\text{Median} = L_1 + \frac{\frac{N}{2} - cf}{f} \times i$$

$$L_1 = 200; \frac{N}{2} = 190; c.f. = 129, f = 148; i = 100.$$

$$= 200 + \frac{190 - 129}{148} \times 100$$

$$= 200 + 41.22$$

$$= \mathbf{241.22}.$$

Problem 49. Find the median:

Wages Rs.	*No. of labours*
60–70	5
50–60	10
40–50	20
30–40	5
20–30	3

(*B. Com. Madras*)

Solution:

Computation of Median

x	f	$c.f.$
20–30	3	3
30–40	5	8
40–50	20	28
50–60	10	38
60–70	5	43

$$\text{Median} = \text{Size of} \left(\frac{N}{2}\right) \text{th item}$$

$$= \text{Size of } \frac{43}{2} \text{th item}$$

$$= 21.5\text{th item which lies in the calss } 40\text{–}50$$

$$\text{Median} = L_1 + \frac{\frac{N}{2} - cf}{f} \times i$$

$$L_1 = 40; \frac{N}{2} = 21.5; c.f = 8; f = 20; i = 10$$

$$= 40 + \frac{21.5 - 8}{20} \times 10$$

$$= 40 + \frac{135}{20} = 40 + 6.75$$

$$= \mathbf{46.75}$$

Problem 50. Find the median and the quartiles of the following series:

Size	*Frequency*	*Size*	*Frequency*
4	40	12	50
5	48	13	52
6	52	14	41
7	56	15	57
8	60	16	63
9	63	17	52
10	57	18	48
11	55	19	40

(*B.Com*)

Solution:

Calculation of Median and Quartiles

Size	*Frequency*	*c.f*
4	40	40
5	48	88
6	52	140
7	56	196
8	60	256
9	63	319
10	57	376
11	55	431
12	50	481
13	52	533
14	41	574
15	57	631
16	63	694
17	52	746
18	48	794
19	40	834

Median $=$ Size of $\frac{N+1}{2}$th item $=$ Size of $\frac{835}{2}$th item

$=$ 417.5th item which lies in 11 th size

Median $=$ **11**

Q_1 $=$ Size of $\left(\frac{N+1}{4}\right)$ th item

$=$ Size of $\frac{835}{4}$th item

$=$ 208.75th item which lies in the size 8.

Q_1 $=$ **8**.

Q_3 $=$ size of $\frac{3(N+1)}{4}$th item

$=$ size of $3 \times \frac{835}{4}$th item

$=$ 626.25th item which lies in the size 15.

Q_3 $=$ **15**

Problem 51. What are the various measures of central tendency ? Choose an appropriate measure for the following distribution :

Monthly income (in Rs.) in locality X	*No. of families*
Below 100	50
100–200	500
200–300	555
300–400	100
400–500	3
500 and above	2

(*B.A. Delhi*)

Solution:

Computation of Median

Monthly income in (Rs.)	*No. of families (f)*	*f*
Below 100	50	50
100–200	500	550
200–300	555	1105
300–400	100	1205
400–500	3	1208
500 and above	2	1210

$$\text{Median} = \text{Size of } \frac{N}{2}\text{th item}$$

$$= \text{Size of } \frac{1210}{2}\text{th item}$$

$$= 605\text{th item which lies in the class 200–300}$$

$$\text{Median} = L_1 + \frac{\frac{N}{2} - c.f}{f} \times i$$

$$L_1 = 200;\ \frac{N}{2} = 605;\ c.f. = 550;\ i = 100;\ f = 555$$

$$= 200 + \frac{605 - 550}{555} \times 100 \quad = 200 + 9.91 \quad = \mathbf{209.91}.$$

Problem 52. The following table gives the marks obtained by a batch of 25 students in a certain class test in Accountancy and Statistics.

R. No.	*Marks in Statistics*	*Marks in Accountancy*	*R. No.*	*Marks in Statistics*	*Marks in Accountancy*
1	29	36	14	47	44
2	65	30	15	60	15
3	33	38	16	30	20
4	45	39	17	32	32
5	51	64	18	52	25
6	72	50	19	54	55
7	48	46	20	56	35
8	33	15	21	58	40
9	42	42	22	49	62
10	25	10	23	38	58
11	28	72	24	40	28
12	35	33	25	46	53
13	46	80			

In which subject is the level of knowledge of students, as revealed by these figures higher ? Give reasons.

(*B. Com. Gorakhpur*)

Solution:

To solve this problem, computation of median marks is necessary, in both subjects.

Computation of Median Marks

S. No.	*Marks*		*S. No.*	*Marks*	
	Statistics	*Accountancy*		*Statistics*	*Accountancy*
1	25	10	14	46	42
2	28	15	15	47	44
3	29	20	16	48	46
4	30	25	17	49	50
5	32	28	18	51	53
6	33	30	19	52	55
7	33	32	20	54	58
8	35	33	21	56	62
9	38	35	22	58	64
10	40	36	23	60	72
11	42	38	24	65	80
12	45	39	25	72	85
13	46	40			

Size of 13 th item = 46 marks (Statistics)

= 40 marks (Accountancy)

Therefore, it is clear that the level of knowledge of the student is higher in Statistics as compared with Accountancy.

Problem 53. Calculate the values of the median and the two quartiles for the following :

Limits of percentage recovery of sugar	*Factories in India* (2002–03)
80.–8.2	2
8.2–	5
8.4–	4
8.6–	11
8.8–	11
9.0–	11
9.2–	13
9.4–	10
9.6–	7
9.8–	6
10.0–	3
10.2–	1
10.4–10.6	1

(*M.A. Punjab*)

Solution: **Computation of Median and Quartiles**

Limits of % recovery of sugar	*f*	*c.f*
8.0–8.2	2	2
8.2–8.4	5	7
8.4–8.6	4	11
8.6–8.8	11	22
8.8–9.0	11	33
9.0–9.2	11	44
9.2–9.4	13	57
9.4–9.6	10	67
9.6–9.8	7	74
9.8–10.0	6	80
10.0–10.2	3	83
10.2–10.4	1	84
10.4–10.6	1	85

$$\text{Median} = \text{Size of } \frac{N}{2}\text{th item}$$
$$= \text{Size of } \frac{85}{2}\text{th item}$$
$$= 42.5\text{th item which lies in the class } 9.0\text{–}9.2$$
$$\text{Median} = L_1 + \frac{\frac{N}{2} - c.f}{f} \times i$$
$$L_1 = 9;\ \frac{N}{2} = 42.5;$$
$$c.f. = 33;\ f = 11;\ i = 0.2$$
$$= 9 + \frac{42.5 - 33}{11} \times 0.2 = 9 + 0.17$$
$$= \mathbf{9.17}$$
$$Q_1 = \text{Size of } \frac{N}{4}\text{th item}$$
$$= \text{Size of } \frac{85}{4}\text{th item}$$
$$= 21.25\text{th item which lies in the class } 8.6\text{–}8.8$$
$$Q_1 = L_1 + \frac{\frac{N}{4} - c.f}{f} \times i$$
$$L_1 = 8.6;\ \frac{N}{4} = 21.25;$$
$$c.f. = 11;\ f = 11;\ i = 0.2$$
$$= 8.6 + \frac{21.25 - 11}{11} \times 0.2 = 8.6 + 0.19$$
$$= \mathbf{8.79}$$
$$Q_3 = \text{size of } \frac{3N}{4}\text{th item}$$
$$= \text{size of } 3 \times \frac{85}{4}\text{th item}$$
$$= 63.75\text{th item which lies in the class } 9.4\text{–}9.6$$

$$Q_3 = L_1 + \frac{\frac{3N}{4} - c.f}{f} \times i$$

$$L_1 = 9.4\,;\ \frac{3N}{4} = 63.75\,;\ c.f = 57$$

$$f = 10 \cdot\ i = 0.2$$

$$= 9.4 + \frac{63.75 - 57}{10} \times 0.2 = 9.4 + 0.14$$

$$= \mathbf{9.54}$$

Problem 54. The following table gives the distribution of males in an Indian town. Find the median age.

Age group	*Males*	*Age group*	*Males*
0–9	2756	50–59	610
10–19	2124	60–69	245
20–29	1677	70–79	67
30–39	1481	80–89	6
40–49	1021	90–99	3

(*B. Com. Madras, Madurai, Agra*)

Solution:

Computation of Median age

Age group	*f*	*c.f*
0–9	2756	2756
10–19	2124	4880
20–29	1677	6557
30–39	1481	8038
40–49	1021	9059
50–59	610	9669
60–69	245	9914
70–79	67	9981
80–89	6	9987
90–99	3	9990
	N = 9990	

$$\text{Me} = \text{Size of } \frac{N}{2}\text{th item}$$

$$= \text{Size of } \frac{9990}{2} = 4995\text{th item}$$

which lies in the class 20–29 and its real limit is 19.5–29.5

$$\text{Median} = L_1 + \frac{\frac{N}{2} - e.f}{f} \times i$$

$$L_1 = 19.5,\ \frac{N}{2} = 4995,\ cf = 4880$$

$$f = 1677, i = 10$$

$$\text{Median} = 19.5 + \frac{4995 - 4880}{1677} \times 10$$

$$= 19.5 + 0.686$$

$$= \mathbf{20.186(20.2)}\text{years.}$$

Problem 55. The following table gives you the distribution of marks secured by some students in an examination:

Marks	*No. of students*
0–20	42
21–30	38
31–40	120
41–50	84
51–60	48
61–70	36
71–80	31

Find: (*a*) Median marks.

(*b*) The percentage of failures if the minimum for a pass is 35 marks.

(*C.A. B. Com., Punjab, Kerala, Jammu*)

Solution: **Computation of Median Marks**

Marks	*No. of students f*	*c.f.*
0–20	42	42
21–30	38	80
31–40	120	200
41–50	84	284
51–60	48	332
61–70	36	368
71–80	31	399
	N = 399	

(*a*) $$\text{Median} = \text{Size of } \left(\frac{N}{2}\right) \text{th item}$$

$$= \text{Size of } \left(\frac{399}{2}\right) \text{th item} = 199.5\text{th item}$$

which lies in the class 31–40 and its real limit is 30.5–40.5.

$$\text{Median} = L_1 + \frac{\frac{N}{2} - c.f}{f} \times i$$

$$L_1 = 30.5, \frac{N}{2} = 199.5, \; c.f = 80, \; f = 120,$$

$$i = 10.$$

$$\text{Median} = 30.5 + \frac{199.5 - 80}{120} \times 10$$

$$= 30.5 + 9.96$$

$$= \mathbf{40.46}$$

(*b*) Percentage of failures if the minimum for a pass is 35 marks.

$$= \frac{\left(42 + 38 + \frac{120}{2}\right)}{399} \times 100$$

$$= \frac{140}{399} \times 100$$

$$= \mathbf{35.09\%}$$

Problem 56. Find the median and quartiles from the following data:

Monthly income	*No. of persons.*
Below 50	35
50–60	24
60–70	21
70–80	18
80–90	6
90 and above	3

(*B. Com. Banaras, Agra, Bombay, Bangalore*)

Solution:

Computation of Median and Quartiles

Income	f	*c.f.*
Below 50	35	35
50–60	24	59
60–70	21	80
70–80	18	98
80–90	6	104
90 and above	3	107
	N = 107	

Median:

$$\text{Median} = \text{size of } \frac{N}{2}\text{th item}$$
$$= \text{size of } \frac{107}{2} = 53.5\text{th item}$$

which lies in the class 50–60.

$$\textbf{Me} = L_1 + \frac{\frac{N}{2} - c.f}{f} \times i$$
$$L_1 = 50, \frac{N}{2} = \frac{107}{2} = 53.5, c.f. = 35$$
$$f = 24,\ i = 10$$
$$\textbf{Me} = 50 + \frac{53.5 - 35}{24} \times 10 = 50 + 7.7$$
$$= \textbf{Rs.57.7}$$
$$Q_1 = \text{size of } \frac{N}{4}\text{th item}$$
$$= \text{size of } \frac{107}{4} = 26.75\text{th item}$$

Which lies in the class 40–50.

$$Q_1 = L_1 + \frac{\frac{N}{4} - c.f}{f} \times i$$
$$L_1 = 40, \frac{N}{4} = 26.75,\ c.f = 0,\ f = 35$$
$$i = 10$$
$$Q_1 = 40 + \frac{26.75 - 0}{35} \times 10 = 40 + 7.64$$
$$= \mathbf{47.64}$$

$$Q_3 = \text{size of } \frac{3N}{4}\text{th item}$$

$$= \text{size of } \left(\frac{3 \times 107}{4}\right) \text{th item} = 80.25\text{th item}$$

which lies in the class 70–80.

$$Q_3 = L_1 + \frac{\frac{3N}{4} - c.f}{f} \times i$$

$$L_1 = 70,\ \frac{3N}{4} = 80.25,\ c.f = 80,$$

$$f = 18,\ i = 10$$

$$Q_3 = 70 + \frac{80.25 - 80}{18} \times 10 = 70 + .14$$

$$= \mathbf{70.14}$$

Problem 57. Calculate the value of median and the two quartiles for the data given below:

Income Under ('000)	1	1–2	2–3	3–5	5–10	10–25	25–50	50–100	100–1000
No. of Persons	13	90	81	117	66	27	6	2	2

(B. Com. Punjab, M. Com. Calcutta, Agra, Punjab)

Solution:

Calculation of Median and Quartile

Income	*No. of persons*	*Cumulative frequency*
Under 1	13	13
1–2	90	103
2–3	81	184
3–5	117	301
5–10	66	367
10–25	27	394
25–50	6	400
50–100	2	402
100–1000	2	404

$$\text{Median} = \text{size of } \frac{N}{2}\text{th item}$$

$$= \text{size of } \frac{404}{2}\text{th item}$$

$$= 202\text{th item which lies in the class 3–5}$$

$$\text{Median} = L_1 + \frac{\frac{N}{2} - c.f}{f} \times i$$

$$= 3 + \frac{202 - 184}{117} \times 2 = 3 + 0.3$$

$$= \mathbf{3.3}$$

$$Q_1 = \text{size of } \frac{N}{4}\text{th item}$$

$$= \text{size of } \frac{404}{4}\text{th item}$$

$$= \text{101th item which lies in the class 1–2.}$$

$$Q_1 = L_1 + \frac{\frac{N}{4} - c.f}{f} \times i$$

$$= 1 + \frac{101 - 13}{90} \times 1 = 1 + 0.98 \qquad = \mathbf{1.98}$$

$$Q_3 = \text{size of } \frac{3N}{4}\text{th item}$$

$$= \text{size of } \frac{3 \times 404}{4}\text{th item}$$

$$= \text{303th item which lies in the class 5–10}$$

$$Q_3 = L_1 + \frac{\frac{3N}{4} - c.f}{f} \times i$$

$$= 5 + \frac{303 - 301}{66} \times 5 = 5 + 0.15$$

$$= \mathbf{5.15}$$

Problem 58. From the following table, find out first quartile, third quartile and first decile.

Size of item

	0–10	10–20	20–30	30–40	40–50	50–60	60–70	70–80
f	2	18	30	45	35	20	6	3

(*B. Com. Nagpur, Agra, Bombay, Madras*)

Solution:

Calculation of quartiles and decile

Size of Item	*Frequency*	*Cumulative Frequency*
0–10	2	2
10–20	18	20
20–30	30	50
30–40	45	95
40–50	35	130
50–60	20	150
60–70	6	156
70–80	3	159

$$Q_1 = \text{size of } \frac{N}{4}\text{th item} = \frac{159}{4}\text{th item}$$

$$= \text{39.75 which lies in the class } 20 - 30$$

$$Q_1 = L_1 + \frac{\frac{N}{4} - c.f}{f} \times i$$

$$= 20 + \frac{39.75 - 20}{30} \times 10 = 20 + 6.58$$

$$= \mathbf{26.58}$$

$$Q_3 = \text{size of } \frac{3N}{4}\text{th item} = \frac{3 \times 159}{4}\text{th item}$$

$$= \text{119.25 which lies in the class } 40 - 50$$

$$Q_3 = L_1 + \frac{\frac{3N}{4} - c.f}{f} \times i$$

$$= 40 + \frac{119.25 - 95}{35} \times 10 = 40 + 6.93$$

$$= \mathbf{46.93}$$

$$D_1 = \text{size of } \frac{N}{10}\text{th item} = \frac{159}{10}\text{th item}$$

15.9th item which lies in the class 10 – 20

$$D_1 = L_1 + \frac{\frac{N}{10} - c.f}{f} \times i$$

$$= 10 + \frac{15.9 - 2}{18} \times 10$$

$$= 10 + 7.72$$

$$= \mathbf{17.72}$$

Problem 59. Following is the distribution of marks obtained by 50 students in mercantile law:

Marks more than	0	10	20	30	40	50
No. of students	50	46	40	20	10	3

Calculate the median marks. If 60% of the students pass the test, find the minimum marks obtained by a pass candidate.

(B. Com. (Hons) Delhi, Punjab, Jabalpur Jammu, Kerala)

Solution:

Calculation of Median Marks

	Frequency			
Marks More than	*Cumulative*	*Single*	*Class of Intervals*	*c.f*
0	50 = N	50 – 46 = 4	0–10	4
10	46	46 – 40 = 6	10–20	10
20	40	40 – 20 = 20	20–30	30
30	20	20 – 10 = 10	30–40	40
40	10	10 – 3 = 7	40–50	47
50	3	3	50–60	50

$$\text{Median} = \text{size of } \frac{N}{2}\text{th item}$$

$$= \text{size of } \frac{50}{2}\text{th item}$$

= 25th item which lies in the class 20 – 30

$$\text{Me} = L_1 + \frac{\frac{N}{2} - c.f}{f} \times i$$

$$= 20 + \frac{25 - 10}{20} \times 10 = 20 + 7.5$$

$$= \textbf{27.5 marks}$$

60 % of the students passed the test and 40% of the students failed the test. Therefore the minimum marks for a pass D_4

$$D_4 = \frac{4N}{10}\text{th item}$$

$$= \frac{4 \times 50}{10}\text{th item} = 20\text{th item}$$

$$D_4 = L_1 + \frac{\frac{4N}{10} - c.f}{f} \times i$$

$$= 20 + \frac{20 - 10}{20} \times 10 = 20 + 5$$

$$= 25 \textbf{ marks}$$

Problem 60. Determine the quartiles and the median from the following table:

Income	*No. of persons*
Below Rs. 30	69
Rs. 30 and below Rs. 40	167
Rs. 40 and below Rs. 50	207
Rs. 50 and below Rs. 60	65
Rs. 60 and below Rs. 70	58
Rs. 70 and below Rs. 80	27
Rs. 80 and over	10
Total:	603

(*B. Com. Andhra, Bombay*)

Solution: **Computation of Median and Quartiles**

Income Rs.	*f*	*c. f.*
20–30	69	69
30–40	167	236
40–50	207	443
50–60	65	508
60–70	58	566
70–80	27	593
80–90	10	603

$$\text{Median} = \text{size of } \left(\frac{N}{2}\right) \text{th item}$$

$$= \text{size of } \frac{603}{2} \text{th item}$$

$$= 301.5\text{th item which lies in the class } 40 - 50$$

$$\text{Median} = L_1 + \frac{\frac{N}{2} - c.f}{f} \times i$$

$$L_1 = 40; \frac{N}{2} = 301.5$$

$$c.f = 236; f = 207; i = 10$$

$$= 40 + \frac{301.5 - 236}{207} \times 10 = 40 + 3.16 = \mathbf{43.16}$$

$$Q_1 = \text{size of } \frac{N}{4} \text{th item}$$

$$= \text{size of } \frac{603}{4} \text{th item}$$

$$= 150.75\text{th item which lies in the class } 30 - 40$$

$$Q_1 = L_1 + \frac{\frac{N}{4} - c.f}{f} \times i$$

$$L_1 = 30; \frac{N}{4} = 150.75, cf = 69, f = 167, i = 10$$

$$= 30 + \frac{150.75 - 69}{167} \times 10$$
$$= 30 + 4.89$$
$$= \mathbf{34.89}$$

$$Q_3 = \text{size of } \frac{3N}{4}\text{th item}$$
$$= \text{size of } \frac{3 \times 603}{4}\text{th item}$$
$$= \text{452.25th item which lies in the class 50–60}$$
$$Q_3 = L_1 + \frac{\frac{3N}{4} - c.f}{f} \times i$$
$$L_1 = 50; \frac{3N}{4} = 452.25$$
$$c.f = 443;\ f = 65;\ i = 10$$
$$= 50 + \frac{452.25 - 443}{65} \times 10$$
$$= 50 + 1.42$$
$$= \mathbf{51.42}$$

Problem 61. The following series relates to the marks secured by students in an examination:

Marks	*No. of students*	*Marks*	*No. of students*
0–10	11	50–60	33
10–20	18	60–70	22
20–30	25	70–80	15
30–40	28	80–90	12
40–50	30	90–100	10

Find the median, quartiles, and 1st and the 9th deciles.

(*B. Com., Kerala, Agra, Delhi, Madras*)

Solution: **Computation of Median, Quartiles and Deciles**

Marks	*No. of students*	*c.f*
0–10	11	11
10–20	18	29
20–30	25	54
30–40	28	82
40–50	30	112
50–60	33	145
60–70	22	167
70–80	15	182
80–90	12	194
90–100	10	204

$$\text{Median} = \text{size of } \left(\frac{N}{2}\right)\text{th item}$$
$$= \text{size of } \left(\frac{204}{2}\right)\text{th item}$$
$$= \text{102th item which lies in the class 40–50}$$

$$\text{Median} = L_1 + \frac{\frac{N}{2} - c.f}{f} \times i$$

$$L_1 = 40;\ \frac{N}{2} = 102;$$

$$c.f = 82;\ f = 30;\ i = 10$$

$$= 40 + \frac{102 - 82}{30} \times 10$$

$$= 40 + 6.66$$

$$= \mathbf{46.66}$$

$$Q_1 = \text{size of } \left(\frac{N}{4}\right) \text{th item}$$

$$= \text{size of } \left(\frac{204}{4}\right) \text{th item}$$

= 51th item which lies in the class 20–30

$$Q_1 = L_1 + \frac{\frac{N}{4} - c.f}{f} \times i$$

$$L_1 = 20;\ \frac{N}{4} = 51$$

$$c.f = 29;\ f = 25;\ i = 10$$

$$= 20 + \frac{51 - 29}{25} \times 10 = 20 + 8.8$$

$$= \mathbf{28.8}$$

$$Q_3 = \text{size of } \frac{3N}{4} \text{th item}$$

$$= \text{size of } \frac{3 \times 204}{4} \text{th item}$$

= 151th item which lies in the class 60–70

$$Q_3 = L_1 + \frac{\frac{3N}{4} - c.f}{f} \times i$$

$$L_1 = 60;\ \frac{3N}{4} = 151$$

$$c.f = 145;\ f = 22;\ i = 10$$

$$= 60 + \frac{151 - 145}{22} \times 10 = 60 \times 2.73$$

$$= 62.73$$

$$D_1 = \text{size of } \frac{N}{10} \text{th item}$$

$$= \text{size of } \frac{204}{10} \text{th item}$$

= 20.4th item which lies in the class 10–20

$$D_1 = L_1 + \frac{\frac{N}{10} - c.f}{f} \times i$$

$$L_1 = 10;\ \frac{N}{10} = 20.4;$$

$$c.f = 11;\ f = 18;\ i = 10$$

$$= 10 + \frac{20.4 - 11}{18} \times 10 = 10 + 5.22 \qquad = \mathbf{15.22}$$

$$D_9 = \text{size of } \frac{9N}{10}\text{th item}$$
$$= \text{size of } 9 \times \frac{204}{10}\text{th item}$$
$$= 183.6\text{th item which lies in the class 80–90}$$
$$D_9 = L_1 + \frac{\frac{9N}{10} - c.f}{f} \times i$$
$$L_1 = 80;\ \frac{9N}{10} = 1836;$$
$$c.f = 182;\ f = 12;\ i = 10$$
$$= 80 + \frac{183.6 - 182}{12} \times 10 = 80 + 1.33$$
$$= \mathbf{81.33}$$

Problem 62. The following table shows the age distribution of heads of families in a certain country. Find the median, third quartile and the second decile of the distribution. Check your results by the graphical method.

Age of head of family (years)	*Numbers (million)*
Under 25	2.3
25–29	4.1
30–34	5.3
35–44	10.6
45–54	9.7
55–64	6.8
65–74	4.4
above 74	1.8

(*I.C.W.A.*)

Solution:

Computation of Median, Quartiles and Deciles

Age (years)	*No. (Million)* f	$c.f$
Under 25	2.3	2.3
25–30	4.1	6.4
30–35	5.3	11.7
35–45	10.6	22.3
45–55	9.7	32
55–65	6.8	38.8
65–75	4.4	43.2
Above 75	1.8	45

$$\text{Median} = \text{size of } \frac{N}{2}\text{th item} = \text{size of } \frac{45}{2}\text{th item}$$
$$= 22.5\text{th item which lies in the class 45–55}$$
$$\text{Median} = L_1 + \frac{\frac{N}{2} - c.f}{f} \times i$$
$$L_1 = 45,\ \frac{N}{2} = 22.5$$
$$c.f = 22.3,\ f = 9.7,\ i = 10$$

$$= 45 + \frac{22.5 - 22.3}{9.7} \times 10 \quad = \mathbf{45.21}$$

$$Q_3 = \text{size of } \frac{3N}{4}\text{th item} \quad = \text{size of } \frac{3 \times 45}{4}$$

$$= 33.75\text{th item which lies in the class 55–65}$$

$$Q_3 = L_1 + \frac{\frac{3N}{4} - c.f}{f} \times i$$

$$L_1 = 55, \frac{3N}{4} = 33.75$$

$$c.f. = 32, f = 6.8, i = 10$$

$$= 55 + \frac{33.75 - 32}{6.8} \times 10 = 55 + 2.57 \quad = \mathbf{57.57}$$

$$D_2 = \text{size of } \frac{2N}{10}\text{th item} \quad = \text{size of } \frac{2 \times 45}{10}\text{th item}$$

$$= 9\text{th item which lies in the class 30–35}$$

$$D_2 = L_1 + \frac{\frac{2N}{10} - c.f}{f} \times i$$

$$L_1 = 30, \frac{2N}{10} = 9$$

$$c.f. = 6.4, f = 5.3, i = 5$$

$$= 30 + \frac{9 - 6.4}{5.3} \times 5 = 30 + 2.45 \quad = \mathbf{32.45}$$

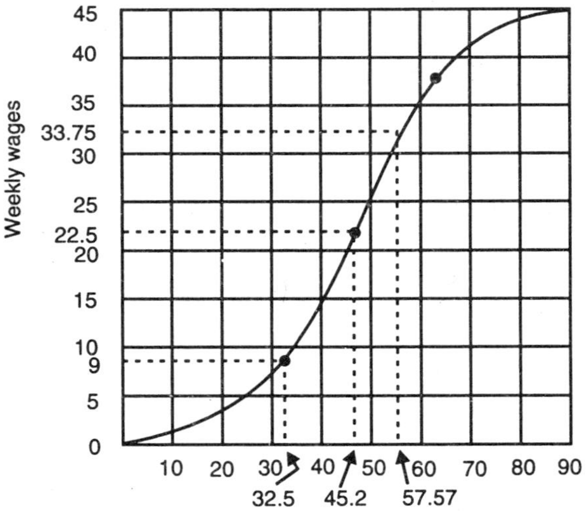

Problem 63. From the following data, calculate the median and the first and third quartile wages:

Weekly wages (Rs.)	*No. of workers*	*Weekly wages (Rs.)*	*No. of workers*
30–32	2	40–42	62
32–34	9	42–44	39
34–36	25	44–46	20
36–38	30	46–48	11
38–40	49	48–50	3

(*B Com. Himachal*)

Solution: **Computation of Median and Quartiles**

Weekly wages Rs.	*No. of workers f*	*c.f.*
30–32	2	2
32–34	9	11
34–36	25	36
36–38	30	66
38–40	49	115
40–42	62	177
42–44	39	216
44–46	20	236
46–48	11	247
48–50	3	250
	N = 250	

Median $=$ size of $\frac{N}{2}$th item

$=$ size of $\frac{250}{2}$th item

$=$ 125th item which lies in the class 40–42

Median $= L_1 + \frac{\frac{N}{2} - c.f}{f} \times i$

$L_1 = 40,\ \frac{N}{2} = 125$

$c.f = 115,\ f = 62, i = 2$

$= 40 + \frac{125 - 115}{62} \times 2 = 40 + 0.32 \quad = \mathbf{40.32}$

Lower quartile (Q_1) $=$ size of $\frac{N}{4}$th item

$=$ size of $\frac{250}{4}$th item

$=$ 62.5th item which lies in the class 36–38.

$Q_1 = L_1 + \frac{\frac{N}{4} - c.f}{f} \times i$

$L_1 = 36,\ \frac{N}{4} = 62.5$

$c.f. = 36,\ f = 30,\ i = 2$

$= 36 + \frac{62.5 - 36}{30} \times 2 = 36 + 1.77 \quad = \mathbf{37.77}$

Upper quartile Q_3 $=$ size of $\frac{3N}{4}$th item

$=$ size of $\frac{3 \times 250}{4}$th item

$=$ 187.5th item which lies in the class 42–44

$Q_3 = L_1 + \frac{\frac{3N}{4} - c.f}{f} \times i$

$L_1 = 42,\ \frac{3N}{4} = 187.5,\ cf = 177,\ f = 39,\ i = 2$

$= 42 + \frac{187.5 - 177}{39} \times 2 = 42 + 0.54 \quad = \mathbf{42.54}$

Problem 64. Given the following information, determine the quartiles sixth and ninth deciles:

Age	*No. of persons*	*Age*	*No. of persons*
20–24	50	40–45	150
25–30	70	45–50	120
30–35	100	50–55	70
35–40	180	55–60	60

(*B. com. Madurai.*)

Solution:

Computation of Quartiles and Deciles

Age	*No. of persons f*	*c.f*
20–24	50	50
25–30	70	120
30–35	100	220
35–40	180	400
40–45	150	550
45–50	120	670
50–55	70	740
55–60	60	800

$$Q_1 = \text{size of } \frac{N}{4}\text{th item} = \text{size of } \frac{800}{4}\text{th item}$$

$$= \text{200th item which lies in the class 30–35}$$

$$Q_1 = L_1 + \frac{\frac{N}{4} - c.f}{f} \times i$$

$$L_1 = 30;\ \frac{N}{4} = 200$$

$$c.f. = 120;\ f = 100;\ i = 5$$

$$= 30 + \frac{200 - 120}{100} \times 5 = 30 + 4 \quad = \mathbf{34}$$

$$Q_3 = \text{size of } \frac{3N}{4}\text{th item} = \frac{3 \times 800}{4}\text{th item}$$

$$= \text{size of 600 th item which lies in the class 45–50}$$

$$Q_3 = L_1 + \frac{\frac{3N}{4} - c.f}{f} \times i$$

$$L_1 = 45;\ \frac{3N}{4} = 600$$

$$c.f = 550;\ f = 120,\ i = 5$$

$$= 45 + \frac{600 - 550}{120} \times 5 = 45 + 2.08$$

$$= \mathbf{47.08}$$

$$D_6 = \text{size of } \frac{6N}{10}\text{th item}$$

$$= \text{size of } \frac{6 \times 800}{10}\text{th item}$$

$$= \text{480th item which lies in the class 40–45}$$

$$D_6 = L_1 + \frac{\frac{6N}{10} - c.f}{f} \times i$$

$$L_1 = 40;\ \frac{6N}{10} = 480; \qquad c.f = 400;\ f = 150;\ i = 5$$

$$= 40 + \frac{480 - 400}{150} \times 5 = 40 + 2.67 \qquad = \mathbf{42.67}$$

$$D_9 = \text{size of } \frac{9N}{10}\text{th item}$$

$$= \text{size of } \frac{9 \times 800}{10}\text{th item}$$

$$= 720\text{th item which lies in the class } 50–55$$

$$D_9 = L_1 + \frac{\frac{9N}{10} - c.f}{f} \times i$$

$$L_1 = 50;\ \frac{9N}{10} = 720; \qquad c.f = 670;\ f = 70;\ i = 5$$

$$= 50 + \frac{720 - 670}{70} \times 5 = 50 + 3.57 \qquad = \mathbf{53.57}$$

Problem 65. Calculate the median age of married females and also two quartiles for the following data :

Age in years	*No. of Married females*	*Age in years*	*No. of married females*
0–5	3	40–45	963
5–10	31	45–50	762
10–15	410	50–55	531
15–20	1809	55–60	317
20–25	2446	60–65	156
25–30	2233	65–70	59
30–35	1723	70–75	37
35–40	1292		

(*B. Com. Andhra, kerala*)

Solution: **Computation of Median and Quartiles**

Age in years X	*No. of married females f*	*c.f*
0–5	3	3
5–10	31	34
10–15	410	444
15–20	1809	2253
20–25	2446	4699
25–30	2233	6932
30–35	1723	8655
35–40	1292	9947
40–45	963	10910
45–50	762	11672
50–55	531	12203
55–60	317	12520
60–65	156	12676
65–70	59	12735
70–75	37	12772

$$\text{Median} = \text{size of } \frac{N}{2}\text{th item}$$

$$= \text{size of } \frac{12772}{2}\text{th item}$$

$$= \text{6386th item which lies in the class 25–30}$$

$$\text{Median} = L_1 + \frac{\frac{N}{2} - c.f}{f} \times i$$

$$L_1 = 25;\ \frac{N}{2} = 6386$$

$$c.f = 4699;\ f = 2233;\ i = 5$$

$$= 25 + \frac{6386 - 4699}{2233} \times 5$$

$$= 25 + \frac{1687}{2233} \times 5$$

$$= 25 + 3.78$$

$$= \mathbf{28.78}$$

$$Q_1 = \text{size of } \frac{N}{4}\text{th item}$$

$$= \text{size of } \frac{12772}{4}\text{th item}$$

$$= \text{3193rd item which lies in the class 20–25}$$

$$Q_1 = L_1 + \frac{\frac{N}{4} - c.f}{f} \times i$$

$$L_1 = 20;\ \frac{N}{4} = 3193$$

$$c.f = 2253;\ f = 2446;\ i = 5$$

$$= 20 + \frac{3193 - 2253}{2446} \times 5$$

$$= 20 + \frac{940 \times 5}{2446} \quad = 20 + 1.92 \quad = \mathbf{21.92}$$

$$Q_3 = \text{size of } \left(\frac{3N}{4}\right) \text{th item}$$

$$= \text{size of } \frac{3 \times 12772}{4}\text{th item}$$

$$= \text{9579th item which lies in the class 35–40}$$

$$Q_3 = L_1 + \frac{\frac{3N}{4} - c.f}{f} \times i$$

$$L_1 = 35;\ \frac{3N}{4} = 9579$$

$$c.f = 8655 :\ f = 1292;\ i = 5$$

$$= 35 + \frac{9579 - 8655}{1292} \times 5$$

$$= 35 + \frac{4620}{1292} \quad = 35 + 3.58 \quad = \mathbf{38.58}$$

Problem 66. Calculate the Median and Quartiles and interpret :

Monthly Income	*No. of teachers*
250–275	15
275–300	51
300–325	240
325–350	681
350–375	978
375–400	744
400–425	264
425–450	27

(*B. Com. Madras*)

Solution:

Computation of Median and Quartiles

Monthly Income *Rs.*	*No. of Teachers* *f*	*c.f*
250–275	15	15
275–300	51	66
300–325	240	306
325–350	681	987
350–375	978	1965
375–400	744	2709
400–425	264	2973
425–450	27	3000

$$\text{Median} = \text{size of } \frac{N}{2}\text{th item}$$

$$= \text{size of } \frac{3000}{2}\text{th item}$$

$= 1500$th item which lies in the class 350–375

$$\text{Median} = L_1 + \frac{\frac{N}{2} - c.f}{f} \times i$$

$$L_1 = 350; \frac{N}{2} = 1500$$

$$c.f = 987,\ f = 978;\ i = 25$$

$$= 350 + \frac{1500 - 987}{978} \times 25 = 350 + 13.11$$

$$= \mathbf{363.11}$$

$$Q_1 = \text{size of } \frac{N}{4}\text{th item}$$

$$= \text{size of } \frac{3000}{4}\text{th item}$$

$= 750$th item which lies in the class 325–350

$$Q_1 = L_1 + \frac{\frac{N}{4} - c.f}{f} \times i$$

$$L_1 = 325; \frac{N}{4} = 750$$

$$c.f = 306;\ f = 681;\ i = 25$$

$$Q_1 = 325 + \frac{750 - 306}{681} \times 25 = 325 + 16.3$$
$$= \mathbf{341.3}$$
$$Q_3 = \text{size of } \frac{3N}{4}\text{th item}$$
$$= \text{size of } 3 \times \frac{3000}{4}\text{th item}$$
$$= \text{2250th item which lies in the class 375–400}$$
$$Q_3 = L_1 + \frac{\frac{3N}{4} - c.f}{f} \times i$$
$$L_1 = 375; \frac{3N}{4} = 2250$$
$$c.f = 1965; f = 744; i = 25$$
$$= 375 + \frac{2250 - 1965}{744} \times 25 = 375 + 9.58$$
$$= \mathbf{384.58}$$

Problem 67. In a small branch of a bank in a rural area the following is the average deposit balance of current accounts (x) during a month. Calculate median, seventh decile and 85th percentile.

Deposit balance less than	*No. of deposits*
1000	500
900	498
800	480
600	475
550	440
500	374
400	300
250	125
100	25

(*B. Com. Bombay*)

Solution: **Computation of Median, Deciles and Percentiles**

x	f	$c.f$
0–100	25	25
100–250	125 − 25 = 100	125
250–400	300 − 125 = 175	300
400–500	374 − 300 = 74	374
500–550	440 − 374 = 66	440
550–600	475 − 440 = 35	475
600–800	480 − 475 = 5	480
800–900	498 − 480 = 18	498
900–1000	500 − 498 = 2	500

$$\text{Median} = \text{size of } \frac{N}{2}\text{th item}$$
$$= \text{size of } \frac{500}{2}\text{th item}$$
$$= \text{250 th item which lies in the class 250–400}$$

$$\text{Median} = L_1 + \frac{\frac{N}{2} - c.f}{f} \times i$$

$$L_1 = 250; \frac{N}{2} = 250$$

$$c.f = 125;\ f = 175;\ i = 150$$

$$= 250 + \frac{250 - 125}{175} \times 150 = 250 + 107.14$$

$$= 357.14$$

$$D_7 = \text{size of } \frac{7N}{10}\text{th item}$$

$$= \text{size of } \frac{7 \times 500}{10}\text{th item}$$

= 350th item which lies in the class 400–500

$$D_7 = L_1 + \frac{\frac{7N}{10} - c.f}{f} \times i$$

$$L_1 = 400; \frac{7N}{10} = 350$$

$$c.f = 300;\ f = 74;\ i = 100$$

$$= 400 + \frac{350 - 300}{74} \times 100 = 400 + 67.57$$

$$= \mathbf{467.57}$$

$$P_{85} = \text{size of } 85 \times \frac{N}{100}\text{th item}$$

$$= \text{size of } 85 \times \frac{500}{100}\text{th item}$$

= 425th item which lies in the class 500–550

$$P_{85} = L_1 + \frac{\frac{85N}{100} - c.f}{f} \times i$$

$$L_1 = 500; \frac{85N}{100} = 425$$

$$c.f = 374 :\ f = 66;\ i = 50$$

$$= 500 + \frac{425 - 374}{66} \times 50 = 500 + 38.64$$

$$= \mathbf{538.64}$$

Problem 68. From the following table, find out quartiles and first decile.

Size of item	0–10	10–20	20–30	30–40	40–50	50–60	60–70	70–80
Frequency	2	18	30	45	35	20	6	3

(*B. Com. Nagpur*)

Solution:

Computation of Quartiles and Deciles

X	f	$c.f$
0–10	2	2
10–20	18	20
20–30	30	50
30–40	45	95
40–50	35	130
50–60	20	150
60–70	6	156
70–80	3	159

$$Q_1 = \text{size of } \left(\frac{N}{4}\right) \text{th item}$$

$$= \text{size of } \frac{159}{4}\text{th item}$$

$$= 39.75\text{th item which lies in the class 20–30}$$

$$Q_1 = L_1 + \frac{\frac{N}{4} - c.f}{f} \times i$$

$$L_1 = 20;\ \frac{N}{4} = 39.75;\ c.f. = 20;\ f = 30;\ i = 10$$

$$= 20 + \frac{39.75 - 20}{30} \times 10 = 20 + 6.58$$

$$= \mathbf{26.58}$$

$$Q_3 = \text{size of } \frac{3N}{4}\text{th item}$$

$$= \text{size of } \frac{3 \times 159}{4}\text{th item}$$

$$= 119.25\text{th item which lies in the class 40–50}$$

$$Q_3 = L_1 + \frac{\frac{3N}{4} - c.f}{f} \times i$$

$$L_1 = 40;\ \frac{3N}{4} = 119.25$$

$$c.f = 95;\ f = 35;\ i = 10$$

$$= 40 + \frac{119.25 - 95}{35} \times 10 = 40 + 6.93$$

$$= \mathbf{46.93}$$

$$D_1 = \text{size of } \frac{N}{10}\text{th item}$$

$$= \text{size of } \frac{159}{10}\text{th item}$$

$$= 15.9\text{th item which lies in the class 10–20}$$

$$D_1 = L_1 + \frac{\frac{N}{10} - c.f}{f} \times i$$

$$L_1 = 10;\ \frac{N}{10} = 15.9$$

$$c.f = 2;\ f = 18;\ i = 10$$

$$= 10 + \frac{15.9 - 2}{18} \times 10 = 10 + 7.72$$

$$= \mathbf{17.72}$$

Problem 69. The following table gives the distribution of male population according to age groups. Find out the median, first quartile and third quartile.

Age group	*Males*	*Age group*	*Males*
0–10	150	40–50	75
10–20	350	50–60	50
20–30	400	60–70	25
30–40	200		
		Total	1, 250

(*B. Com. Jodhpur*)

Solution:

Computation of Median and Quartiles

Age group	*f*	*c.f*
0–10	150	150
10–20	350	500
20–30	400	900
30–40	200	1100
40–50	75	1175
50–60	50	1225
60–70	25	1250

$$\text{Median} = \text{size of } \left(\frac{N}{2}\right) \text{th item}$$

$$= \text{size of } \frac{1250}{2} \text{th item 625th item}$$

$\therefore$ Median lies in the class 20–30

$$M = L + \frac{\frac{N}{2} - c.f}{f} \times 10$$

$$= 20 + \frac{625 - 500}{400} \times 10$$

$$= 20 + \frac{1250}{400} = 20 + 3.125 \quad = \mathbf{23.125}$$

$$Q_1 = \text{size of } \left(\frac{N}{4}\right) \text{th item}$$

$$= \text{size of } \frac{1250}{4} \text{th item which is 312.5th item}$$

$\therefore$ first quartile lies in the class 10–20

$$Q_1 = L + \frac{\frac{N}{4} - c.f}{f} \times i$$

$$L = 10; \frac{N}{4} = 312.5$$

$$c.f = 150;\ f = 350;\ i = 10$$

$$Q_1 = 10 + \frac{312.5 - 150}{350} \times 10 = 10 + 4.643 \quad = \mathbf{14.643}$$

$$Q_3 = \text{size of } \frac{3N}{4}\text{th item}$$

$$= \text{size of } \frac{3 \times 1250}{4}\text{th item, which is } 937.5$$

$\therefore$ Third quartile lies in the class 30–40

$$Q_3 = L + \frac{\frac{3N}{4} - c.f}{f} \times i$$

$$L = 30;\ \frac{3N}{4} = 937.5$$

$$c.f = 900;\ f = 200;\ i = 10$$

$$= 30 + \frac{937.5 - 900}{200} \times 10 = 30 + 1.875 \quad = \mathbf{31.875}$$

Problem 70. The median and mode of the following wage distribution are known to be Rs. 33.5 and Rs. 34 respectively. Three frequency values from the table are however missing. Find these missing values.

Wages Rs. :	0–10	10–20	20–30	30–40	40–50	50–60	60–70
Frequencies :	4	16	?	?	?	6	4

Total: 230 Find also Q_1 and Q_3

(*Rajasthan*)

Solution:

Calculation of Missing Values

Wages	*f*	*c.f*
0–10	4	4
10–20	16	20
20–30	a	$20 + a$
30–40	b	$20 + a + b$
40–50	c	220*
50–60	6	226
60–70	4	230
	N = 230	

Known values $= 4 + 16 + 6 + 4 = 30$

$\therefore$ $a + b + c = 230 - 30 = 200$ (*or*) $c = 200 - a -$

$200 - a - b($

$20 + a + b$

220 (at $c.f.$)

$$\text{Median} = 33.5 = 30 + \frac{230/2 - (20 + a)}{b} \times 10$$

$$33.5 = 30 + \frac{115 - (20 + a)}{b} \times 10$$

$$33.5 = 30 + \frac{95 - a}{b} \times 10$$

$$3.5 = \frac{950 - 10a}{b}$$

$$3.5b = 950 - 10a$$

$$3.5b + 10a = 950 \quad \ldots(1)$$

$$\text{Mode} = 34 = 30 + \frac{b - a}{2b - a - (200 - a - b)} \times 10$$

$$.34 = 30 + \frac{10b - 10a}{3b - 200}$$

$$4 = \frac{10b - 10a}{3b - 200}$$

(*or*) $12b - 800 = 10b - 10a$

$$2b + 10a = 800 \quad \ldots(2)$$

subtract (2) from (1)

$$\therefore \quad \begin{array}{r} 3.5b + 10a = 950 \\ \underline{2b + 10a = 800} \\ 1.5b = 150 \end{array}$$

or $b = \frac{150}{1.5} = \mathbf{100}$

Substituting equation (1)

$$3.5(100) + 10a = 950$$

$$350 + 10a = 950$$

$$10a = 950 - 350$$

$$10a = 600$$

$$a = \frac{600}{10} = \mathbf{60}$$

$c = 200 - a - b = 200 - 100 - 60 = 40$

Therefore the missing figures are:

60, 100 and 40

$$Q_1 = 20 + \frac{57.5 - 20}{60} \times 10 = 20 + 6.25 = \mathbf{26.25}$$

$$Q_3 = 30 + \frac{172.5 - 80}{100} \times 10 = 30 + 9.25 = \mathbf{39.25}$$

Problem 71. Find the median, lower quartile, 7th decile and 85th percentile of the frequency distribution given below:

Marks in Statistics:							
Below 10	10–20	20–30	30–40	40–50	50–60	60–70	above 70
No. of students:							
8	12	20	32	30	28	12	4

(*B. Com. Allahabad, Agra, Delhi*)

Solution:

Computation of Median, Quartile Decile and Percentile

Marks in Statistics	*No. of Students*	*c.f.*
0–10	8	8
10–20	12	20
20–30	20	40
30–40	32	72
40–50	30	102
50–60	28	130
60–70	12	142
70 and above	4	146

$$\text{Median} = \text{size of } \frac{N}{2}\text{th item} = \text{size of } \frac{146}{2}\text{th item}$$

$$= \text{73rd item which lies in the class 40–50}$$

$$\text{Median} = L_1 + \frac{\frac{N}{2} - c.f}{f} \times i$$

$$L_1 = 40;\ \frac{N}{2} = 73;\ c.f = 72 : f = 30;\ i = 10$$

$$= 40 + \frac{73 - 72}{30} \times 10 = 40 + 0.33$$

$$= \mathbf{40.33}$$

$$\text{First quartile} = \text{size of } \frac{N}{4}\text{th item}$$

$$= \text{size of } \frac{146}{4}\text{th item}$$

$$= \text{36.5th item which lies in the class 20–30}$$

$$Q_1 = L_1 + \frac{\frac{N}{4} - c.f}{f} \times i$$

$$L_1 = 20;\ \frac{N}{4} = 36.5;\ c.f = 20;\ f = 20;\ i = 10$$

$$= 20 + \frac{36.5 - 20}{20} \times 10$$

$$= 20 + 8.25$$

$$= \mathbf{28.25}$$

$$D_7 = \text{size of } \frac{7 \times N}{10}\text{th item}$$

$$= \text{size of } \frac{7 \times 146}{10}\text{th item}$$

$$= \text{102.2th item which lies in the class 50–60}$$

$$D_7 = L_1 + \frac{\frac{7 \times N}{10} - c.f}{f} \times i$$

$$L_1 = 50;\ \frac{7N}{10} = 102.2;\ c.f = 102;\ f = 28;\ i = 10$$

$$= 50 + \frac{102.2 - 102}{28} \times 10 = 50 + 0.07$$

$$= \mathbf{50.07}$$

$$P_{85} = L_1 + \frac{\frac{85\,N}{100} - c.f}{f} \times i$$

$$P_{85} = \text{size of } \frac{85N}{100}\text{th item}$$

$$= \text{size of } \frac{85 \times 146}{100}\text{th item}$$

$= 124.1$th item which lies in the class 50–60

$$P_{85} = L_1 + \frac{\frac{85N}{100} - c.f}{f} \times i$$

$$L_1 = 50;\ \frac{85N}{100} = 124.1;\ c.f = 102;\ f = 28;\ i = 10$$

$$= 50 + \frac{124.1 - 102}{28} \times 10$$

$$= 50 + 7.89$$

$$= \mathbf{57.89}$$

Problem 72. An incomplete distribution is given as follows :

Class	10–20	20–30	30–40	40–50	50–60	60–70	70–80	Total
Frequency:	12	30	?	65	?	25	18	229

You are given the median value as 46. Using the median formula, fill up the missing frequencies. (*C.A*)

Solution: Let us assume that the missing frequencies under the class intervals, 30–40 and 50–60 be x and y respectively.

Total frequency = 229.

Given frequencies = 150.

Therefore, the sum of missing frequencies $(x + y) = 229 - 150 = 79$

$$\text{That is } x + y = 79$$

$$\text{The Median} = 46.$$

$$\text{Median} = L_1 + \frac{\frac{N}{2} - c.f}{f} \times i$$

$$46 = 40 + \frac{\frac{229}{2} - (12 + 30 + x)}{65} \times 10$$

$$46 - 40 = \frac{114.5 - 42 - x}{65} \times 10$$

$$6 = \frac{114.5 - 42 - x}{65} \times 10$$

$$6 \times 65 = 114.5 - 42 - x \quad \times 10$$

$$390 = 1145 - 420 - 10\,x$$

$$390 - 1145 + 420 = -10\,x$$

$$-335 = -10\,x$$

$x = 33.5$(Frequency cannot be in fraction therefore 33.5=34)

$$\therefore\ x = 34$$

$$\therefore\ y = 79 - 34 = 45$$

Therefore the missing frequencies are 34 and 45 under the class intervals 30–40 and 50–60.

Problem 73. In as moderately a symmetrical distribution the value of mode and mean are 32.1 and 35.4 respectively. Find median value.

(B. Com. Andhra)

Solution:

Using the empirical formula:

$$\begin{aligned} \text{Median} &= \frac{1}{3}(2\text{ Mean} + \text{Mode}) \\ &= \frac{1}{3}(2 \times 35.4 + 32.1) \\ &= \mathbf{34.3} \end{aligned}$$

Problem 74. In the frequency distribution of 100 families given below, the number of families corresponding to expenditure groups 20–40 and 60–80 are missing from the table. However, the median is known to be 50. Find the missing frequencies.

Expenditure	0–20	20–40	40–60	60–80	80–100
No. of families	14	?	27	?	15

(B. Com. (Hons) Delhi)

Solution:

Median = 50, which is in the class 40–60

Let us assume the frequency of 20–40 be f_1 and 60–80 be f_2.

$$\begin{aligned} \text{Median} &= \text{L} + \frac{\frac{100}{2} - c.f}{27} \times 20 \\ 50 &= 40 + \frac{50 - (14 + f_1)}{27} \times 20 \\ 50 &= 40 + \frac{36 - f_1}{27} \times 20 \\ 50 - 40 &= \frac{36 - f_1}{27} \times 20 \\ 10 &= \frac{36 - f_1}{27} \times 20 \\ 10 \times 27 &= (36 - f_1)20 \\ 270 &= 720 - 20f_1 \\ \text{(or)} \quad 20f_1 &= 720 - 270 \\ 20f_1 &= 450 \\ f_1 &= \frac{450}{20} \\ &= 22.5 \\ &= 23 \text{ Because the value of frequency can not be a fractional one.} \\ \Sigma f &= 56 + f_1 + f_2 \\ &= 100 \\ f_1 + f_2 &= 100 - 56 \\ &= 44 \\ f_2 &= 44 - 23 \\ &= \mathbf{21} \end{aligned}$$

Therefore the missing frequencies are 23 and 21 respectively.

Problem 75. Find the median of the following data:

Class interval	*Frequency*	*Class interval*	*Frequency*
7.5–10.5	12	22.5–25.5	14
10.5–13.5	10	25.5–28.5	3
13.5–16.5	15	28.5–31.5	0
16.5–19.5	19	31.5–34.5	4
19.5–22.5	12	34.5–37.5	1

(*B. Com. Madurai*)

Solution:

Computation of Median

Class interval	*f*	*cf*
7.5–10.5	12	12
10.5–13.5	10	22
13.5–16.5	15	37
16.5–19.5	19	56
19.5–22.5	12	68
22.5–25.5	14	82
25.5–28.5	3	85
28.5–31.5	0	85
31.5–34.5	4	89
34.5–37.5	1	90

$$\text{Median} = \text{size of } \frac{N}{2}\text{th item}$$

$$= \text{size of } \frac{90}{2}\text{th item}$$

= 45th item which lies in the class 16.5–19.5

$$\text{Median} = L_1 + \frac{\frac{N}{2} - c.f}{f} \times i$$

$$L_1 = 16.5; \frac{N}{2} = 45; c.f = 37; f = 19; i = 3$$

$$= 16.5 + \frac{45 - 37}{19} \times 3$$

$$= 16.5 + 1.26$$

$$= \mathbf{17.76}$$

Problem 76. The following table gives the marks obtained by 65 students in statistics in a certain examination. Calculate the median.

Marks	*No. of students*
More than 70 %	7
,, 60 %	18
,, 50 %	40
,, 40 %	45
,, 20 %	63
,, 10 %	65

(*B.A., Madurai*)

Solution: **Computation of Median**

Marks	*No. of Students f*	*c.f*
10–20	65 – 63 = 2	2
20–40	63 – 45 = 18	20
40–50	45 – 40 = 5	25
50–60	40 – 18 = 22	47
60–70	18 – 7 = 11	58
70–80	7	65

$$\text{Median} = \text{size of } \left(\frac{N}{2}\right)\text{th item}$$

$$= \text{size of } \frac{65}{2}\text{th item}$$

$= 32.5$th item which lies in the class 50–60.

$$\text{Median} = L_1 + \frac{\frac{N}{2} - c.f}{f} \times i$$

$$L_1 = 50;\ \frac{N}{2} = 32.5;\ c.f = 25;\ f = 22;\ i = 10$$

$$= 50 + \frac{32.5 - 25}{22} \times 10 = 50 + 3.41$$

$$= \mathbf{53.41}.$$

Problem 77. Calculate mean and median from the following data:

Size of items	14	16	18	20	22	24	26
Frequency	2	4	5	3	2	1	4

(*B. A. Madurai*)

Solution:

Computation of Mean and Median

Size of Items X	$d' = \frac{X-20}{2}$	*Frequency f*	fd'	*c.f.*
14	−3	2	−6	2
16	−2	4	−8	6
18	−1	5	−5	11
20	0	3	0	14
22	1	2	2	16
24	2	1	2	17
26	3	4	12	21
		N = 21	$\Sigma fd' = -3$	

$$\text{Mean} = \overline{X} = A + \frac{\Sigma fd'}{N} \times C$$

$$\Sigma fd' = -3;$$

$$N = 21;$$

$$C = 2$$

$$\overline{X} = 20 - \frac{3}{21} \times 2$$

$$= 20 - 0.29$$

$$= \mathbf{19.71}$$

$$\text{Median} = \text{size of } \frac{N+1}{2}\text{th item}$$

$$= \text{size of } \frac{21+1}{2}\text{th item}$$

= Size of 11th item which lies in the size 18.

Hence the median size of item = **18**

Problem 78. Determine the quartiles and the median from the following table:

Income	*No. of persons*
Below Rs. 30	69
Rs. 30 and below Rs. 40	167
Rs. 40 and below Rs. 50	207
Rs. 50 and below Rs. 60	65
Rs. 60 and below Rs. 70	58
Rs. 70 and below Rs. 80	27
Rs. 80 and over	10
	603

(*B. Com. Bombay, Andhra*)

Solution:

Computation of Median and Quartiles

Income	*f*	*c.f.*
Below Rs. 30	69	69
Rs. 30 and below Rs. 40	167	236
Rs. 40 and below Rs. 50	207	443
Rs. 50 and below Rs. 60	65	508
Rs. 60 and below Rs. 70	58	566
Rs. 70 and below Rs. 80	27	593
Rs. 80 and over	10	603

$$\text{Median} = \text{size of } \frac{N}{2}\text{th item} = \text{size of } \frac{603}{2}\text{th item}$$

= 301.5th item which lies in the class Rs. 40 and below Rs. 50

$$\text{Median} = L_1 + \frac{\frac{N}{2} - c.f}{f} \times i.$$

$$L_1 = 40; \frac{N}{2} = 301.5; c.f = 236$$

$$f = 207; i = 10$$

$$= 40 + \frac{301.5 - 236}{207} \times 10$$

$$= 40 + 3.16 = \mathbf{43.16}$$

$$Q_1 = \text{size of } \frac{N}{4}\text{th item} = \text{size of } \frac{603}{4}\text{th item}$$

= 150.75th item which lies in the class Rs. 30 and below Rs. 40

$$Q_1 = L_1 + \frac{\frac{N}{4} - c.f}{f} \times i$$

$$
\begin{aligned}
L_1 &= 30; \\
\frac{N}{4} &= 150.75; \\
c.f &= 69;\ f = 167;\ i = 10 \\
&= 30 + \frac{150.75 - 69}{167} \times 10 \\
&= 30 + 4.895 \quad = \mathbf{34.895} \\
Q_3 &= \text{size of } \frac{3N}{4}\text{th item} \\
&= \text{size of } \frac{3 \times 603}{4}\text{th item} \\
&= 452.25\text{th item which lies in the class Rs. 30} \\
&\quad \text{and below Rs. 60} \\
Q_3 &= L_1 + \frac{\frac{3N}{4} - c.f}{f} \times i \qquad L_1 = 50;\ \frac{3N}{4} = 452.25 \\
c.f &= 443;\ f = 65;\ i = 10 \\
&= 50 + \frac{452.25 - 443}{65} \times 10 = 50 + 1.423 \\
&= \mathbf{51.423}
\end{aligned}
$$

Problem 79. From the distribution of income in a Factory given below obtain the median income of a worker graphically;

Income in Rs.						
Less than :	50	50–99	100–149	150–199	200–249	250–299
No. of workers:	19	46	75	32	23	5

Use the graph to find the number of workers whose income lies between Rs. 130 and Rs. 180.

(*B. A. Kerala*)

Solution:

Calculation of Median

Income	*f*	*Income less than (−)*	*c.f*	*Income more than (+)*	*c.f*
50	19	49.5	19	0	200
50–99	46	99.5	65	49.5	181
100–149	75	149.5	140	99.5	135
150–199	32	199.5	172	149.5	60
200–249	23	249.5	195	199.5	28
250–299	5	299.5	200	249.5	5

The median corresponding to the cumulative frequency can be read as 123 $(99.5 + \frac{100 - 65}{75} \times 50 = 122.8)$. The number of workers who get income less than Rs. 130 is 115 and the number of workers who get income less than Rs. 180 is 165.

Thus the number of workers whose income, between Rs. 130 and Rs. 180 is 165 − 115 = 50.

Problem 80. Following figures show length of life of 3700 motor buses which were operated until scrapped by a large transport company. Construct a frequency polygon and

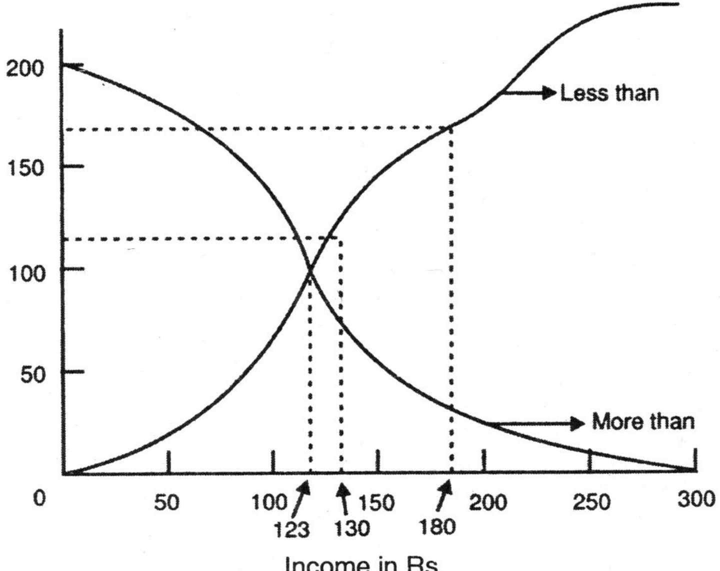

Problem 80. Following figures show length of life of 3700 motor buses which were operated until scrapped by a large transport company. Construct a frequency polygon and orgives for the distribution, determining the quartiles graphically.

Life in years :	1	2	3	4	5	6	7	8	9	Total
No.of buses :	21	270	640	922	814	520	456	31	26	3700

[*B. Com.* (*Hons.*) *Delhi*]

Solution :

Computation of Quartiles

Life in Years	*No. of Buses*	*c.f*
1	21	21
2	270	291
3	640	931
4	922	1853
5	814	2667
6	520	3187
7	456	3643
8	31	3674
9	26	3700

Median = 3.9
Quartile One = 2.9
Quartile Three = 5.2

FREQUENCY POLYGON

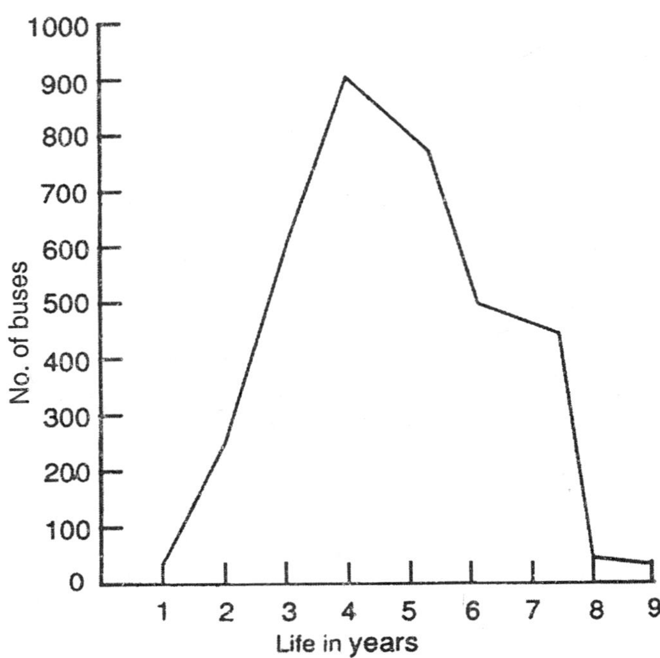

OGIVE

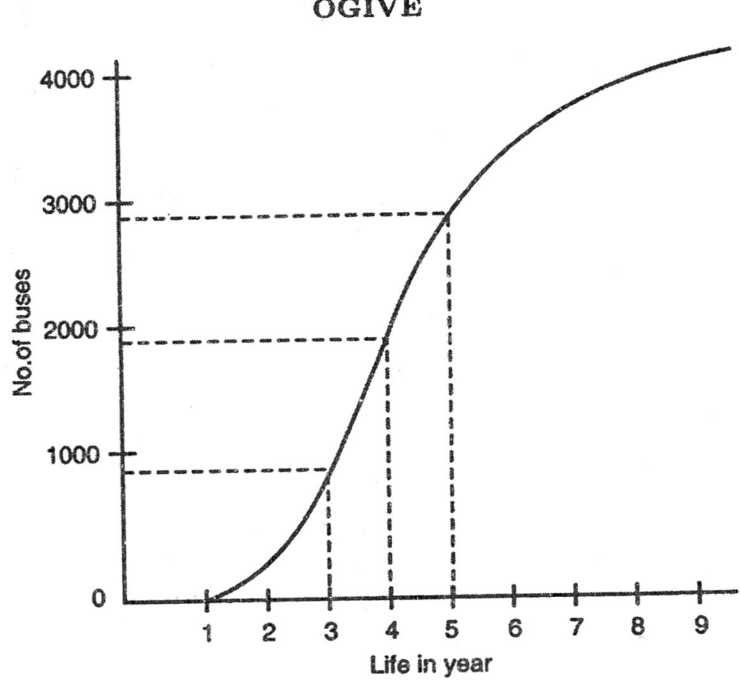

Problem 81. The following table gives the distribution of monthly income of 600 families in a certain city.

Monthly income (Rs.)	*No. of families*
Below 75	60
75–150	170
150–225	200
225–300	60
300–375	50
375–450	40
450 and over	20

Draw a 'less than' and 'a more than' ogive curve for the above data on the same graph.

Read the median income and obtain the limits of income of central 50% of the observed frequencies. [*B.Com. (Hons.) Delhi*]

Solution :

The less than and more than cumulative frequency form is given below :

Monthly Income	*f*	*Monthly income less than*	*f*	*Monthly income more than*	*f*
Below 75	60	60	60	0	600
75–150	170	150	230	75	540
150–225	200	225	430	150	370
225–300	60	300	490	225	170
300–375	50	375	540	300	110
375–450	40	450	580	375	60
above 450	20	525	600	450	20

Now see the graph.

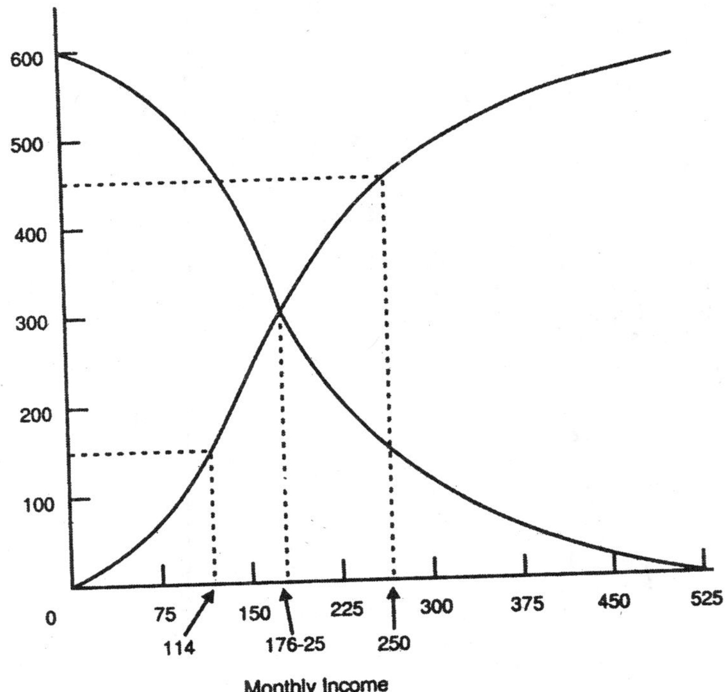

MODE

Problem 82. Calculate the mode from the following :

Size	10	11	12	13	14	15	16	17	18
Frequency	10	12	15	19	20	8	4	3	2

(*B.Com. Madurai*)

Solution:

Grouping table

Frequency

Size	1	2	3	4	5	6
10	10	22		37		
11	12		27		46	
12	15	34				54
13	19		39	47		
14	20	28			32	
15	8		12			15
16	4	7		9		
17	3		5			
18	2					

Size of Item Containing Maximum Frequency

Col. No.	11	12	13	14	15
1				I	
2		I	I		
3			I	I	
4			I	I	I
5	I	I	I		
6		I	I	I	
	1	3	5	4	1

The mode is 13, as this size of item repeats five times. But through inspection, we say the mode is 14, because the size 14 occurs 20 times. But this wrong decision is revealed by analysis table.

Problem 83. Find the mode

Size	*Frequency*
0–10	5
10–20	7
20–30	12
30–40	18
40–50	16
50–60	10
60–70	5

(*B.Com. Madras*)

Solution:

Grouping Table

Size	*Frequency*					
	1	2	3	4	5	6
0–10	5	12		24		
10–20	7		19		37	
20–30	12	30				
30–40	18		34	44		46
40–50	16	26			31	
50–60	10		15			
60–70	5					

Analysis Table

Col. No.	10–20	20–30	30–40	40–50	50–60
1			I		
2		I	I		
3			I	I	
4			I	I	I
5	I	I	I		
6		I	I	I	
Total	1	3	6	3	1

From the analysis table we find that mode lies in the class 30–40

$$Z = L_1 + \frac{f_1 - f_0}{2f_1 - f_0 - f_2} \times i$$

$$L_1 = 30;\ f_1 = 18;\ f_0 = 12;\ f_2 = 16;\ i = 10$$

$$= 30 + \frac{18 - 12}{2 \times 18 - 12 - 16} \times 10 = 30 + 7.5$$

$$= \mathbf{37.5}$$

Problem 84. Find out the mode of the following series :

Wages (Rs.)	*No. of persons*	*Wages (Rs.)*	*No. of persons*
Below 25	10	75–100	25
25–50	30	100–125	20
50–75	40	Above 125	15

(*B. Com. Andhra*)

Solution:

Computation of Mode

Wages in Rs.	*Frequency*							
	1	2	3	4	5	6	Analysis	Total
Below 25	10	40		80			|	1
25–50	30		70		95		|||	3
50–75	40	65				85	~~||||~~ |	6
75–100	25		45	60			|||	3
100–125	20	35					|	1
Above 125	15							0

From the above table we can find that the mode lies in the class 50–75

$$Z = L_1 + \frac{f_1 - f_0}{2f_1 - f_0 - f_2} \times i$$

$$L_1 = 50;\ f_1 = 40;\ f_0 = 30;\ f_2 = 25;\ i = 25$$

$$= 50 + \frac{40 - 30}{2 \times 40 - 30 - 25} \times 25 \quad = 50 + 10$$

$$= \text{Rs. } \mathbf{60}$$

Problem 85. Compute the mode of the following distribution:

	Size of item = x				*Frequency = f*				
x:	0–5	5–10	10–15	15–20	20–25	25–30	30–35	35–40	40–45
f:	20	24	32	28	20	16	37	10	8

Solution: (*B. Com. Delhi*)

Grouping Table

x	*Frequency*					
	1	2	3	4	5	6
0–5	20	44		76		
5–10	24		56		84	
10–15	32	60				80
15–20	28		48	64		
20–25	20	36			73	
25–30	16		53			63
30–35	37	47		55		
35–40	10		18			
40–45	8					

Analysis Table

Column	*Grouping*	*Containing*	*Maximum*	*Frequency*	
1			10–15		
2			10–15	15–20	
3		5–10	10–15		
4	0–5	5–10	10–15		
5		5–10	10–15	15–20	
6			10–15	15–20	20–25
Total .	1	3	6	3	1

From the analysis table we find that mode lies in the class 10–15.

$$\text{Mode: Z} = \text{L}_1 + \frac{f_1 - f_0}{2f_1 - f_0 - f_2} \times i$$

$$\text{L}_1 = 10 \quad ; f_1 = 32;\ f_0 = 24;\ f_2 = 28;\ i = 5$$

$$= 10 + \frac{32 - 24}{2 \times 32 - 24 - 28} \times 5$$

$$= 10 + 3.33$$

$$= \mathbf{13.33}$$

Problem 86. From the data given below, find the mode:

Ages	*No. of Persons*
20–25	50
25–30	70
30–35	80
35–40	180
40–45	150
45–50	120
50–55	70
55–60	50

(*B. Com. Delhi*)

Solution:

Grouping Table

Age	*Frequencies* 1	2	3	4	5	6
20–25	50					
		120				
25–30	70			200		
			150			
30–35	80				330	
		260				
35–40	180					
			330			410
40–45	150			450		
		270				
45–50	120				340	
			190			
50–55	70					
		120				240
55–60	50					

Analysis Table

Column	30–35	35–40	40–45	45–50	50–55
1		I			
2			I	I	
3		I	I		
4		I	I	I	
5			I	I	I
6	I	I	I		
Total	1	4	5	3	1

When frequencies of the proceeding class is greater than the modal class frequency, the following formula is used

$$Z = L_1 + \frac{f_2}{f_0 + f_2} \times i$$

$$L_1 = 40;\ f_2 = 120;\ f_0 = 180;\ i = 5$$

$$= 40 + \frac{120}{180 + 120} \times 5 = 40 + 2 \quad = \mathbf{42}$$

Problem 87. Find out the mode from the following data showing frequency with which profits are made:

Profits in thousands

of rupees :	3–4	4–5	5–6	6–7	7–8	8–9	9–10
Frequency :	83	27	25	50	75	38	18

(*M. A. Eco. Delhi*)

Solution:

Grouping Table

Marks	*Frequency*					
	1	2	3	4	5	6
3–4	83	110				
4–5	27		52	135		
5–6	25	75			102	
6–7	50		125			150
7–8	75	113		163		
8–9	38		56		131	
9–10	18					

Analysis Table

Column	5–6	6–7	7–8	8–9	9–10
1			I		
2			I	I	
3		I	I		
4		I	I	I	
5			I	I	I
6	I	I	I		
Total	1	3	6	3	1

From the analysis table we find that mode lies in the class 7–8.

Mode:

$$Z = L_1 + \frac{f_1 - f_0}{2f_1 - f_0 - f_2} \times i$$

$$L_1 = 7;\ f_1 = 75;\ f_0 = 50;\ f_2 = 38;\ i = 1$$

$$= 7 + \frac{75 - 50}{2 \times 75 - 50 - 38} \times 1 = 7 + 0.40$$

$$= \mathbf{7.40}$$

Problem 88. Calculate mode for the following data:

Class	:	10–20	20–30	30–40	40–50	50–60	60–70	70–80
f	:	24	42	56	66	108	130	154

(*B. Com. Kanpur*)

Solution:

By inspection method, the mode lies in 70–80 class:

$$Z = L + \frac{f_1 - f_0}{2f_1 - f_0 - f_2} \times i$$

$$L = 70;\ f_1 = 154;\ f_0 = 130;$$

$$f_2 = 0; i = 10$$

$$Z = 70 + \frac{154 - 130}{2 \times 154 - 130 - 0} \times 10$$

$$= 70 + \frac{240}{178}$$

$$= 70 + 1.348$$

$$= \mathbf{71.348}$$

Problem 89. Find the mode of the following data:

% marks	No. of students	% marks	No. of students
Below 15	10	Below 55	195
,, 25	25	,, 65	255
,, 35	55	,, 75	300
,, 45	110	,, 85	325

(*B. Com. Madras*)

Solution:

The Cumulative frequencies have to be converted into simple frequencies to solve the problem.

Grouping Table

Marks	*Frequency*					
	1	2	3	4	5	6
Below 15	10					
		25				
15–25	15			55		
			45			
25–35	30					
		85			100	
35–45	55					170
			140			
45–55	85			200		
		145				
55–65	60					
			105		190	
65–75	45					130
		70				
75–85	25					

Analysis Table

Column	25–35	35–45	45–55	55–65	65–75
1			I		
2			I	I	
3		I	I		
4		I	I	I	
5			I	I	I
6	I	I	I		
Total	1	3	6	3	1

From the analysis Table, we find that the mode is 45–55. Its frequency occur the maximum times. Mode is estimated by the formula:

Mode:

$$Z = L_1 + \frac{f_1 - f_0}{2f_1 - f_0 - f_2} \times i$$

$$L_1 = 45;\ f_1 = 85;\ f_0 = 55;\ f_2 = 60;\ i = 10$$

$$= 45 + \frac{85 - 55}{2 \times 85 - 55 - 60} \times 10 = 45 + 5.45$$

$$= \mathbf{50.45}$$

Problem 90. Obtain the mode of the following data:

Monthly rent	*No. of families*	*Monthly rent*	*No. of families*
20–40	6	120–140	15
40–60	9	140–160	10
60–80	11	160–180	8
80–100	14	180–200	7
100–120	20		

(*B. Com. Poona*)

Solution:

Grouping Table

Class Interval	1	2	3	4	5	6
20–40	6					
		15				
40–60	9			26		
			20			
60–80	11				34	
		25				
80–100	14					45
			34			
100–120	20			49		
		35				
120–140	15				45	
			25			
140–160	10					33
		18				
160–180	8			25		
			15			
180–200	7					

Analysis Table

Column No.	60–80	80–100	100–120	120–140	140–160
1			I		
2			I	I	
3		I	I		
4		I	I	I	
5			I	I	I
6	I	I	I		
Total	1	3	6	3	1

$$\begin{aligned}
M_0 &= L_1 + \frac{f_1 - f_0}{2f_1 - f_0 - f_2} \times i \\
L_1 &= 100,\ f_1 = 20,\ f_0 = 14,\ f_2 = 15,\ i = 20 \\
&= 100 + \frac{20 - 14}{2 \times 20 - 14 - 15} \times 20 \\
&= 100 + \frac{120}{11} \\
&= 100 = 10.91 \\
&= \mathbf{110.91} \\
\text{Mode} &= \mathbf{110.91}
\end{aligned}$$

Alternatively:

$$\begin{aligned}
Z &= L_2 - \frac{f_1 - f_2}{2f_1 - f_0 - f_2} \times i \\
&= 120 - \frac{20 - 15}{2 \times 20 - 14 - 15} \times 20 \\
&= 120 - 9.09 \\
&= \mathbf{110.91}.
\end{aligned}$$

$$= 120 - 9.09$$
$$= \mathbf{110.91}.$$

Problem 91. Calculate mode for the distribution of monthly rent paid by 500 families in a locality:

Monthly Rent (Rs.)	*No. of families*	*Monthly Rent (Rs)*	*No. of families*
0–50	5	250–300	87
50–100	14	300–350	60
100–150	40	350–400	38
150–200	91	400 and above	15
200–250	150		

(*B. Com. Bombay*)

Solution:

From the distribution, it is evident that the class, 200–250, is the mode and its frequency is maximum.

$$L_1 = 200,\ f_1 = 150,\ f_0 = 91,\ f_2 = 87,\ i = 50$$

$$\text{Mode} = L_1 + \frac{f_1 - f_0}{2f_1 - f_0 - f_2} \times i$$

$$= 200 + \frac{150 - 91}{2 \times 150 - 91 - 87} \times 50$$

$$= 200 + \frac{2950}{122}$$

$$= 200 + 24.18$$

$$\text{Mode} = \mathbf{224.18}$$

Alternatively:

$$Z = L_2 - \frac{f_1 - f_0}{2f_1 - f_0 - f_2} \times i$$

$$= 250 - \frac{150 - 87}{2 \times 150 - 91 - 87} \times 50$$

$$= 250 - \frac{63 \times 50}{122}$$

$$= 250 - 25.82$$

$$= \mathbf{224.18}$$

Problem 92. Calculate the value of mode by the usual formula.

Class Interval	*Frequency*	*Class Interval*	*Frequency*
10–20	4	60–70	22
20–30	6	70–80	24
30–40	5	80–90	6
40–50	10	90–100	2
50–60	20	100–110	1

(*C. A. Inter*)

Solution:

Grouping Table

Class Interval	*Frequency*						*Analysis col.*
	I	II	III	IV	V	VI	
10–20	4						–
		10					
20–30	6			15			–
			11				
30–40	5				21		–
		15					
40–50	10					35	I
			30				
50–60	20			52			III
		42					
60–70	22				66		IIIII
			46				
70–80	24					52	IIII
		30					
80–90	6			32			I
			8				–
90–100	2				9		
		3					
100–110	1						

The last column shows the maximum frequency. Thus, it is evident that the mode is 60–70

$$Z = L_1 + \frac{f_1 - f_0}{2f_1 - f_0 - f_2} \times i$$

$$= 60 + \frac{22 - 20}{2 \times 22 - 20 - 24} \times 10$$

$$2f_1 - f_0 - f_2 = 0$$

which is meaningless, therefore, the following formulae is used.

$$\text{Z} = \text{L}_1 + \frac{f_2}{f_1 + f_2} \times i$$

$$= 60 + \frac{24}{22 + 24} \times 10$$

$$= 60 + 5.21$$

$$= \mathbf{65.21}$$

Problem 93. Calculate Mean and Mode of the following distribution:

Size of the item below:	15	20	25	30	35	40	45	50
No. of items	4	12	30	60	80	90	95	97

(*B. Com. Bangalore, Mysore, Punjab, Delhi*)

Solution:

Computation of Mean and Mode

Size of Item	*M.P.*	f	$(m - 27.5)/5 = d'$	fd'
10–15	12.5	4	−3	−12
15–20	17.5	8	−2	−16
20–25	22.5	18	−1	−18
25–30	27.5	30	0	0
30–35	32.5	20	1	20
35–40	37.5	10	2	20
40–45	42.5	5	3	15
45–50	47.5	2	4	8
		N = 97		$\Sigma fd' = 17$

$$\text{Mean} \quad \overline{X} = A + \frac{\Sigma fd'}{N} \times C$$

$$A = 27.5,\ \Sigma fd' = 17,\ \text{N} = 97,\ C = 5$$

$$= 27.5 + \frac{17}{97} \times 5$$

$$= 27.5 + 0.88$$

$$= \mathbf{28.38}$$

By inspection method mode lies in the class 25–30

Mode:

$$\text{Z} = \text{L}_1 + \frac{f_1 - f_0}{2f_1 - f_0 - f_2} \times i$$

$$\text{L}_1 = 25,\ f_1 = 30,\ f_0 = 18,\ f_2 = 20,\ i = 5$$

$$= 25 + \frac{30 - 18}{2 \times 30 - 18 - 20} \times 5$$

$$= 25 + \frac{60}{22}$$

$$= 25 + 2.73$$

$$= \mathbf{27.73}$$

Problem 94. Below is given the distribution of heights of a group of 60 students.

Height (in cms)	*No. of students*
145.0–149.9	2
150.00–154.9	5
155.0–159.9	9
160.0–164.9	15
165.0–169.9	16
170.0–174.9	7
175.0–179.9	5
180.0–184.9	1

Draw a histogram of the distribution and find the model height therefrom. Check the result by using the formula.

(*ICAW, Inter*)

$$\text{Z} = \text{L}_1 + \frac{f_1 - f_0}{2f_1 - f_0 - f_2} \times i$$

Solution:

Computation of Mode

Height (in crores)	*No. of students*
144.95–149.95	2
149.95–154.95	5
154.95–159.95	9
159.95–164.95	15
164.95–169.95	16
169.95–174.95	7
174.95–179.95	5
179.95–184.95	1

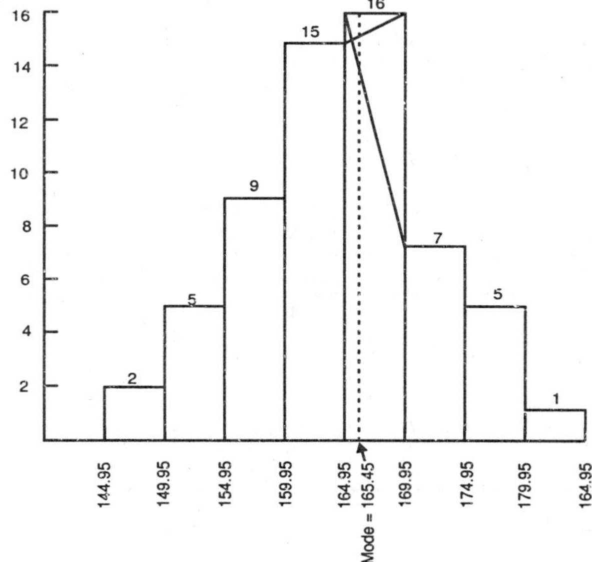

$$= \quad 164.95 + \frac{16-15}{2 \times 16 - 15 - 7} \times 5 \quad = 164.95 + 0.50 \quad = \mathbf{165.45}$$

Problem 95. Given below is the distribution of profits ('000) in rupees earned by 94 Book Depots in a certain territory.

Profit	*No. of Book Depots*
Below 20	5
,, 30	14
,, 40	27
,, 50	48
,, 60	68
,, 70	83
,, 80	91
,, 90	94

Find the modal value.

(B. Com. Bombay)

Solution:

Computation of Mode

Profit	1	2	3	4	5	6
10–20	5					
		14				
20–30	14 – 5 = 9			27		
			22			
30–40	27 – 14 = 13				43	
		34				
40–50	48 – 27 = 21					54
			41			
50–60	68 – 48 = 20			56		
		35				
60–70	83 – 68 = 15				43	
			23			
70–80	91 – 83 = 8					26
		11				
80–90	94 – 91 = 3					

Analysis Table

Column	*Grouping Containing Maximum Frequency*					
1			40–50			
2				50–60	60–70	
3			40–50	50–60		
4			40–50	50–60	60–70	
5	20–30	30–40	40–50	50–60	60–70	70–80
6		30–40	40–50	50–60		
Total	1	2	5	5	3	

The mode is ill-defined. Therefore, the value of mode is to be estimated by adopting the following formula.

Mean−Mode = 3 (Mean−Median)

Now the value of median and mean has to be computed.

Computation of Mean and Median

Mid Point	*Frequency*	$(m-55)/10 = d'$	fd'	$c.f.$
15	5	−4	−20	5
25	9	−3	−27	14
35	13	−2	−26	27
45	21	−1	−21	48
55	20	0	0	68
65	15	1	15	83
75	8	2	16	91
85	3	3	9	94
	N = 94		$\Sigma fd' = -54$	

$$\text{Mean:} \quad \overline{X} = A + \frac{\Sigma fd'}{N} \times C$$

$$A = 55,\ \Sigma fd' = -54,\ N = 94,\ C = 10$$

$$= 55 - \frac{54}{94} \times 10$$

$$= 55 - 5.74$$

$$= \mathbf{49.26}.$$

$$\text{Median: } L_1 + \frac{\frac{N}{2} - c.f.}{f} \times i$$

$$L_1 = 40,\ \frac{N}{2} = 47$$

$$f_1 = 21,\ c.f. = 27,\ i = 10$$

$$= 40 + \frac{47 - 27}{21} \times 10$$

$$= 40 + 9.52$$

$$= \mathbf{49.52}$$

By substituting the values of mean and median in the above formula, we get:

$$49.26 - M_0 = 3(49.26 - 49.52)$$

$$49.26 - M_0 = 147.78 - 148.56$$

$$M_0 = 49.26 + 0.78$$

$$\text{Mode} = \mathbf{50.04}$$

Problem 96. Compute mode from the following data relating to dividend paid by joint stock companies in the year 2002.

Dividend (in the share value)	*No. of Cos.*	*Dividend in the share value)*	*No. of Cos.*
0–1.0	10	10.0–12.5	104
1.0–2.5	15	12.5–14.0	250
2.5–3.5	20	14.0–15.0	164
3.5–4.0	23	15.0–17.5	278
4.0–5.0	30	17.5–19.0	100
5.0–7.5	172	19.0–20.0	72
7.5–9.0	60	20.0–22.5	331
9.0–10.0	39	22.5–25.0	150

(*B. Com Delhi*)

Solution:

Before finding out the value of mode, the class intervals are to be arranged as under:

Computation of Mode

Dividend	*No of Companies*
0–2.5	25
2.5–5.0	73
5.0–7.5	172
7.5–10.0	99
10.0–12.5	104
12.5–15.0	414
15.0–17.5	278
17.5–20.0	172
20.0–22.5	331
22.50–25.0	150

By inspection group mode lies in the class 12.5–15.0

Mode: $Z = L_1 + \dfrac{f_1 - f_0}{2f_1 - f_0 - f_2} \times i$

$L_1 = 12.5;\ f_1 = 414;\ f_0 = 104,\ f_2 = 278;\ i = 2.5$

$$= 12.5 + \frac{414 - 104}{2 \times 414 - 104 - 278} \times 2.5$$

$$= 12.5 + \frac{310 \times 2.5}{446} = 12.5 + 1.74$$

$$= \mathbf{14.24}$$

Problem 97. Find out the mode from the following data showing frequency with which profits are made:

Profits in Rs. ('000)	3–4	4–5	5–6	6–7	7–8	8–9	9–10
Frequency	83	27	25	50	75	38	18

(*M.A. Delhi*)

Solution:

Grouping Table

Profits	*frequencies* 1	2	3	4	5	6	*No. of times group occurs in the maximum*
3–4	83	110		135			1
4–5	27		52		102		1
5–6	25	75				150	3
6–7	50		125	173			5
7–8	75	113			131		3
8–9	38		56				1
9–10	18						

Therefore mode lies in the class interval 7–8.

By interpolation mode $= L + \dfrac{f_1 - f_0}{2f_1 - f_2 - f_0} \times i$

$L = 7;\ f_1 = 75;\ f_0 = 50;\ f_2 = 38;\ i = 1.$

$$\begin{aligned}\text{Mode} &= 7 + \frac{75-50}{7\times 75 - 38 - 50}\times 1\\ &= 7+\frac{25}{62} = 7 + .40\\ &= \mathbf{7.40}\end{aligned}$$

Problem 98. Estimate the mode for the following table consisting of frequency distribution:

Class interval	*Frequency*	*Class interval*	*Frequency*
0–10	5	50-60	28
10–20	20	60-70	22
20–30	24	70-80	48
30–40	48	80-90	23
40–50	32		

(*B. A. Madurai*)

Solution:

Grouping Table

Class Interval	*Frequency* 1	2	3	4	5	6
0–10	5					
		25				
10–20	20			49		
			44			
20–30	24					
		72			92	
30–40	48					104
			80			
40–50	32					
		60		108		
50–60	28				82	
			50			98
60–70	22					
		70				
70–80	48			93		
			71			
80–90	23					

Analysis Table
Size of Item Containing Maximum Frequency

Column	10–20	20–30	30–40	40–50	50–60	60–70	70–80
1			I				I
2		I	I				
3			I	I			
4			I	I	I		
5	I	I	I				
6		I	I	I			
Total	1	3	6	3	1		1

From the above analysis table, we find that the mode is 30–40, as its frequencies occur the maximum times. Mode is estimated by the formula:

$$Z = L_1 + \frac{f_1 - f_0}{2f_1 - f_0 - f_2} \times i$$

$$L_1 = 30;\ f_1 = 48;\ f_0 = 24;\ f_2 = 32;\ i = 10$$

$$= 30 + \frac{48 - 24}{2 \times 48 - 24 - 32} \times 10$$

$$= 30 + 6$$

$$= \mathbf{36}$$

Problem 99. Classify the following scores in class intervals 0–9, 10–19, etc. and represent the data by a histogram Compute the modal value of the frequency table. Also making a suitable choice of scale and origin, calculate the variance of the distribution in a systematic manner.

24	12	37	49	30	6	28	10	13	18
12	19	2	33	4	25	42	22	16	29
0	21	23	31	21	34	20	27	23	35

(*B. Sc. Delhi*)

Solution:

Computation of Variance

Class interval	*Tally Bar*	f	*m.p.*	$d' = \frac{m-25}{10}$	fd'	fd'^2
0–9	||||	4	5	−2	−8	16
10–19	~~||||~~ ||	7	15	−1	−7	7
20–29	~~||||~~ ~~||||~~ |	11	25	0	0	0
30–39	~~||||~~ |	6	35	1	6	6
40–49	||	2	45	2	4	8
		N = 30			$\Sigma fd = -5$	$\Sigma fd'^2 = 37$

N.B. Since classes are not continuous, the given distribution is to be converted into a continuous frequency distribution, as shown in the histogram.

Mode lies in the class 19.5–29.5

$$Z = L_1 + \frac{f_1 - f_0}{2f_1 - f_0 - f_2} \times i$$

$$L_1 = 19.5;\ f_1 = 11;\ f_0 = 7;\ f_2 = 6;\ i = 10$$

$$= 19.5 + \frac{11 - 7}{2 \times 11 - 7 - 6} \times 10$$

$$= \mathbf{23.94}$$

The variance

$$= \sigma^2 = \frac{\Sigma fd'^2}{N} - \left(\frac{\Sigma fd'}{N}\right)^2 \times i^2$$

$$= \left[\frac{37}{30} - \left(\frac{-.5}{30}\right)^2\right] 10^2$$

$$= [1.233 - 0.028] \times 100 = \mathbf{120.5}$$

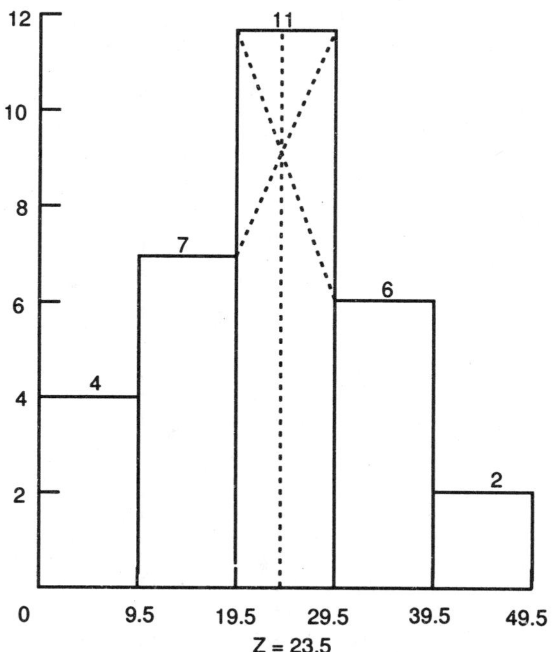

Problem 100. Calculate modal value from the following data:

Income Rs.	*No. of persons*
Less than 100	8
,, 200	22
,, 300	35
,, 400	50
,, 500	57
,, 600	60

(*B.A. Eco. Hons*) *Kurukshetra*)

Solution:

Grouping Table

Income Rs	*Frequency*					
	1	2	3	4	5	6
0–100	8	22				
100–200	14		27	35		
200–300	13	28			42	
300–400	15		22			35
400–500	7	10		35		
500–600	3					

Analysis Table

Column	0–100	100–200	200–300	300–400	400–500	500–600
1				I		
2			I	I		
3		I	I			
4	I	I	I	I	I	I
5		I	I	I		
6			I	I	I	
Total	1	3	5	5	2	.1

The mode is ill defined. Therefore the value of mode is to be estimated by adopting the following formula.

Mode = 3 Median−2 Mean

Now we have to compute the value of Mean and Median.

Computation of Mean and Median

Income	*M.P. (m)*	*f*	$d' = \frac{m-250}{100}$	fd'	*c.f.*
0–100	50	8	−2	−16	8
100–200	150	14	−1	−14	22
200–300	250	13	0	0	35
300–400	350	15	1	15	50
400–500	450	7	2	14	57
500–600	550	3	3	9	60
		N = 60		$\Sigma fd' = 8$	

Mean: $\overline{X} = A + \frac{\Sigma fd'}{N} \times C$

$A = 250, \Sigma fd' = 8, N = 60, C = 100$

$\overline{X} = 250 + \frac{8}{60} \times 100 = 250 + 13.33 = \mathbf{263.33}$

Median $= \text{size of } \frac{N}{2}\text{th item} = \text{size of } \frac{60}{2}\text{th item}$

= 30thitem which lies in the class 200–300

Median $= L_1 + \frac{\frac{N}{2} - c.f}{f} \times i$

$L_1 = 200; \frac{N}{2} = 30; c.f = 22; f = 13; i = 100$

Median $= 200 + \frac{30-22}{13} \times 100 = 200 + 61.54 = \mathbf{261.54}$

By substituting the value of mean and median in the formula:

Mode = 3 Median − 2 Mean

$= (3 \times 261.54) - (2 \times 263.33)$

$= 704.62 - 526.66 = \mathbf{257.96}$

Problem 101. Calculate mode from the following data:

Marks	*No. of students*	*Marks*	*No. of Students*
Below 10	4	Below 60	86
,, 20	6	,, 70	96
,, 30	24	,, 80	99
,, 40	46	,, 90	100
,, 50	67		

(*B. Com. Delhi*)
(*Madurai, Agra, Madras, Bombay*)

Solution:

Grouping Table

Marks	*Frequencies* 1	2	3	4	5	6
0–10	4	6				
10–20	6 – 4 = 2		20	24	42	
20–30	24 – 6 = 18	40				61
30–40	46 – 24 = 22		43			
40–50	67 – 46 = 21	40		62	50	
50–60	86 – 67 = 19		29			32
60–70	96 – 86 = 10	13				
70–80	99 – 96 = 3		4	14		
80–90	100 – 99 = 1					

Marks	*Size of items Containing Maximum Frequency* 20–30	30–40	40–50	50–60	60–70
1		I			
2	I	I	I	I	
3		I	I		
4		I	I	I	
5			I	I	I
6	I	I	I		
No. of times Each class occurs	2	5	5	3	1

The mode is ill defined. Therefore the value of mode is to be estimated by adopting the following formula.

Méar–Mode = 3 (Mean = Median

or

Mode = 3 Media – 2 Mean

Now we have to compute the value of Mean and Median

$$\text{Mean} : \overline{X} = A \pm \frac{\Sigma fd'}{N} \times C$$

$$A = 45,\ \Sigma fd' = -28,\ \text{N} = 100, C = 10$$

$$= 45 - \frac{28}{100} \times 10 = 45 - 2.8 \quad = \mathbf{42.2}$$

$$\text{Median} = \text{L}_1 + \frac{\frac{\text{N}}{2} - c.f}{f} \times i$$

$$\text{L}_1 = 40, \frac{\text{N}}{2} = \frac{100}{2} = 50$$

$$c.f = 46,\ f = 21,\ i = 10$$

$$= 40 + \frac{50 - 46}{21} \times 10 = 40 + 1.9 \quad = \mathbf{41.9}$$

Computation of Mean and Median

Marks	*M.P.*	*f*	$(m-45)/10 = d'$	fd'	$c.f$
0–10	5	4	−4	−16	4
10–20	15	2	−3	− 6	6
20–30	25	18	−2	−36	24
30–40	35	22	−1	−22	46
40–50	45	21	0	0	67
50–60	55	19	1	19	86
60–70	65	10	2	20	96
70–80	75	3	3	9	99
80–90	85	1	4	4	100
		N = 100		$\Sigma fd' = -28$	

By substituting the value of mean and median in the formula Mode = 3 Median −2 Mean we get. Mode = 3 × 41.9 − 2 × 42.2 = 125.7 − 84.4 = **41.3**

Problem 102. Find the mode in the following distribution:

Class Intervals	0–10	10–20	20–30	30–40	40–50
Frequency	4	18	30	42	24

(*B. Com. Banaras*)

Solution:

Analysis Table

	Size of Item Containing Maximum Frequency				
Col. No.	0–10	10–20	20–30	30–40	40–50
1				I	
2			I	I	
3				I	I
4	I	I	I		
5		I	I	I	
6			I	I	I
Total	1	2	4	5	2

Modal class is 30–40

Mode:

$$Z = L_1 + \frac{f_1 - f_0}{2f_1 - f_0 - f_2} \times i$$

$$L_1 = 30,$$
$$f_1 = 42,$$
$$f_0 = 30,$$
$$f_2 = 24,$$
$$i = 10$$

$$= 30 + \frac{42 - 30}{2 \times 42 - 30 - 24} \times 10$$

$$= 30 + \frac{12}{3} = 30 + 4$$

Grouping Table

Class Interval	*Frequency*					
	1	2	3	4	5	6
0–10	4					
		22				
10–20	18			52		
			48			
20–30	30				90	
		72				96
30–40	42					
			66			
40–50	24					

Problem 103. Find out the median and the mode for the following table:

No. of days absent	*No. of students*
Less than 5	29
Less than 10	224
Less than 15	465
Less than 20	582
Less than 25	634
Less than 30	644
Less than 35	650
Less than 40	653
Less than 45	655

(*B. Com. Lucknow, Madras, Madurai, Punjab, Bombay*)

Solution:

Computation of Mode

No. of days absent	*No. of students*						*No. of times group occurs in the maximum*	*c.f.*
	1	2	3	4	5	6		
0–5	29						1	29
		224						
5–10	195						3	224
			436					
10–15	241						6	465
		358		465				
15–20	117						3	582
			169		553			
20–25	52						1	634
		62		179		410		
25–30	10							644
			16		68			
30–35	6							650
		9				19		
35–40	3							653
			5					
40–45	2							655

$$\text{Median} = \text{size of } \left(\frac{N}{2}\right) \text{th item}$$

$$= \text{size of } \left(\frac{655}{2}\right) \text{th item} = 327.5$$

which lies in the group 10–15 days.

By interpolation, median $= L_1 + \dfrac{\frac{N}{2} - c.f. \times i}{f}$

$$= 10 + \frac{327.5 - 224}{241} \times 5 = 10 + 2.15 \quad = \mathbf{12.15 \text{ days.}}$$

Modal class = 10 – 15

By interpolation, mode $= L_1 + \dfrac{f_1 - f_0}{2f_1 - f_0 - f_2} \times i$

$$= 10 + \frac{241 - 195}{2 \times 241 - 195 - 117} \times 5$$

$$= 10 + 1.35 \quad = \mathbf{11.35 \text{ days.}}$$

Problem 104. The monthly profits in rupees of 100 shops are distributed as follows:

Profits per shop	*No. of shops*
0–100	12
100–200	18
200–300	27
300–400	20
400–500	17
500–600	6

Draw a histogram of the data and find the modal value. Check this value by direct calculation.

(*B. Com. Delhi*)

Solution:

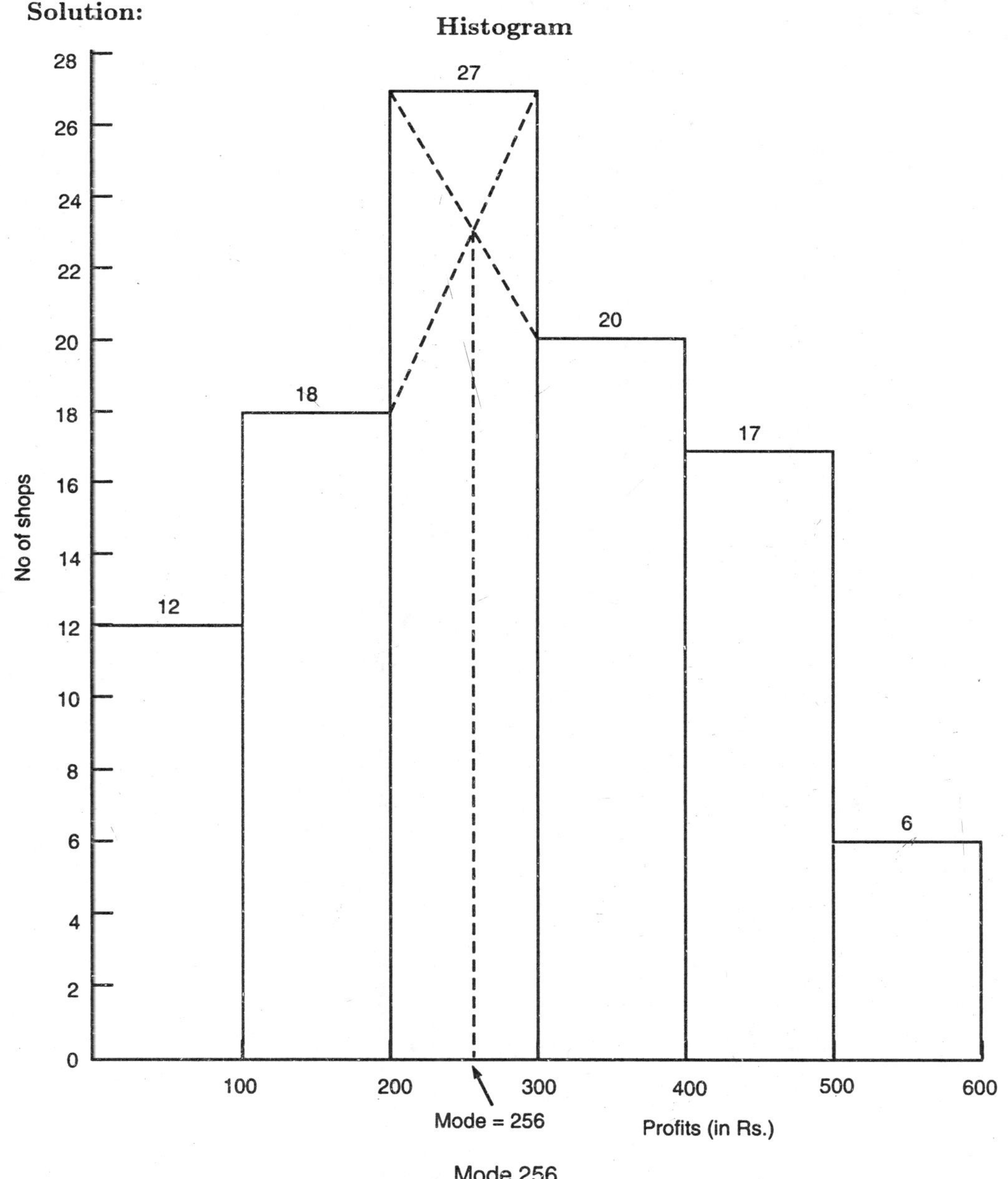

Mode 256

Mode lies in the class 200–300

$$Z = L_1 + \frac{f_1 - f_0}{2f_1 - f_0 - f_2} \times i$$

$$= 200 + \frac{27 - 18}{2 \times 27 - 18 - 20} \times 100 = 200 + 56.25$$

$$= \mathbf{256.25}$$

Problem 105. If the mean and median of a moderately asymmetrical series are 26.8 and 27.9 respectively, what would be its most probable mode? (*B. Com. Mysore*)

Solution:

$$\begin{aligned} \text{Mode} &= 3 \text{ Median} - 2 \text{ Mean} \\ &= 3 \times 27.9 - 2 \times 26.8 \\ &= \mathbf{30.1}. \end{aligned}$$

Problem 106. If in a moderately asymmetrical frequency distribution, the values of median and arithmetic mean are 72 and 78 respectively, estimate the value of the mode. (*B. Com. Andhra*)

Solution:

The value of the mode is estimated by applying the following formula:

$$\begin{aligned} Mean - Mode &= 3(Mean - Median) \\ 78 - Mode &= 3(78 - 72) \\ 78 - Mode &= 3\ (6) \\ 78 - Mode &= 18 \\ -Mode &= 18 - 78 \\ -Mode &= -60 \\ 60 &= Mode \end{aligned}$$

Therefore the mode is 60.

Geometric Mean

Problem 107. Calculate geometric mean of the following;

50 72 54 82 93

Solution:

X	*log of X*
50	1.6990
72	1.8573
54	1.7324
82	1.9138
93	1.9685
	$\Sigma \log X = 9.1710$

$$\text{Geometric mean} = \sqrt[n]{50 \times 72 \times 54 \times 82 \times 93}$$

$$(or) \quad \text{Geometric mean} = \text{Antilog } \frac{\Sigma log X}{N}$$

$$\begin{aligned} &= \text{Antilog } \frac{9.1710}{5} \\ &= \text{Antilog } 1.8342 \\ &= \mathbf{68.26} \end{aligned}$$

Problem 108. The monthly incomes of twenty families are given below in rupees:

2,000 35 400 15 1,500 300 6 90 250 20 12 450
10 150 8 25 30 1,200 60 40

Calculate the Geometric mean. Calculate Arithmetic mean and median also.

(*B. Com. Allahabad*)

Solution:

Computation of Geometric Mean, Arithmetic Mean and Median

S.No.	*X*	*log X*
1	6	0.7782
2	8	0.9031
3	10	1.000
4	12	1.0792
5	15	1.1761
6	20	1.3010
7	25	1.3979
8	30	1.4771
9	35	1.5441
10	40	1.6021
11	60	1.7782
12	90	1.9542
13	150	2.1761
14	250	2.3979
15	300	2.4771
16	400	2.6021
17	450	2.6532
18	1200	3.0792
19	1500	3.1761
20	2000	3.3010
	$\Sigma X = 6601$	$\Sigma \log X = 37.8539$

$$\text{Mean} = \frac{\Sigma X}{N} = \frac{6601}{20} = \mathbf{330}$$

Geometric Mean

$$= \text{Antilog } \frac{\Sigma \log X}{\text{N}}$$

$$= \text{Antilog of } \frac{37.8539}{20}$$

$$= \text{Antilog of } 1.8927 \quad = \mathbf{78.11}$$

$$\text{Median} = \text{size of } \frac{(N+1)}{2}\text{th item}$$

$$= \text{size of } \frac{21}{2}\text{th item}$$

$$= \frac{10\text{th item} + 11\text{th item}}{2}$$

$$= \frac{40+60}{2} \quad = \mathbf{50}$$

Problem 109. From the monthly incomes of ten families given below, calculate the geometric mean.

S. No.	1	2	3	4	5	6	7	8	9	10
Income (Rs.)	145	367	268	73	185	619	280	115	870	315

(*B. Com. Rajasthan*)

Solution:

X	log X
145	2.1614
367	2.5647
268	2.4281
73	1.8633
185	2.2672
619	2.7919
280	2.4472
115	2.0607
870	2.9395
315	2.4983
	$\Sigma log X = 24.0223$

$$\text{Geometric mean} = \text{Antilog } \frac{\Sigma \log X}{N}$$
$$= \text{Antilog } \frac{24.0223}{10}$$
$$= \text{Antilog of } 2.40223$$
$$= \textbf{Rs. 252.40}$$

Problem 110. The monthly income of families in rupees in a certain locality are given below:

Family :	A	B	C	D	E	F	G	H	I	J
Income :	85	70	10	75	500	8	42	250	40	36

Calculate the Geometric Mean.

(*B. Com., Agra*)

Solution:

Computation of G. M. and H. M.

Family	*Income*	*LogX*
A	85	1.9294
B	70	1.8451
C	10	1.0000
D	75	1.8751
E	500	2.6990
F	8	0.9031
G	42	1.6232
H	250	2.3979
I	40	1.6021
J	36	1.5563
N = 10		$\Sigma \log X = 17.4312$

$$\text{Geometric Mean} = \text{Antilog of } \frac{\Sigma \log X}{\text{N}}$$
$$= \text{Antilog of } \frac{17.4312}{10}$$
$$= \text{Antilog of } 1.74312$$
$$= \textbf{Rs. 55.35}$$

Problem 111. Calculate the average income per head from the data given below. Use geometric mean.

Class of people	*No. of families*	*Annual income per head*
Landlords	2	5,000
Cultivators	100	400
Landless labourers	50	200
Money lenders	4	3750
School teachers	6	3000
Shop-keepers	8	750
Carpenters	6	600
Weavers	10	300

(*B. Com., Andhra*)

Solution:

Computation of Geometric Mean

Class of people	*No. of families (f)*	*Income X*	*log X*	*f log X*
Landlords	2	5000	3.6990	7.398
Cultivators	100	400	2.6021	260.210
Landless labours	50	200	2.3010	115.050
Money lenders	4	3750	3.5740	14.296
School teachers	6	3000	3.4771	20.863
Shop keepers	8	750	2.8751	23.001
Carpenters	6	600	2.7782	16.669
Weavers	10	300	2.4771	24.771
				$\Sigma f log X = 482.258$

$$\text{Geometric Mean} = \text{Antilog}\ \frac{\Sigma f \log X}{\text{N}}$$

$$= \text{Antilog}\ \frac{482.258}{186}$$

$$= \text{Antilog}\ 2.5928$$

$$= \textbf{Rs. 391.5}$$

Problem 112. In the construction of the cost of living index number of a certain place, the following group index numbers were found. Calculate the cost of living index number by using (*a*) weighted arithmetic mean and (*b*) weighted geometric mean:

Group	*Index No.*	*Weight*
Food	352	48
Fuel	220	10
Clothing	230	8
House rent	160	12
Miscellaneous	190	15

(*B. Com., Andhra*)

Solution:

Computation of Arithmetic and Geometric Mean

Group	*I No.* (X)	*Weight* (w)	*Weighted index No.*	*Log X*	*w log X*
Food	352	48	16896	2.5465	122.2320
Fuel	220	10	2200	2.3424	23.4240
Clothing	230	8	1840	2.3617	18.8936
House rent	160	12	1920	2.2041	26.4492
Misc.	190	15	2850	2.2788	34.1820
		$\Sigma w = 93$	$\Sigma wX = 25706$		$\Sigma w log X$ = 225.1808

$$\text{Weighted mean} = \frac{\Sigma wX}{\Sigma w} = \frac{25706}{93} = 276.41$$

$$\text{Weighted geometric mean} = \text{Antilog } \frac{\Sigma w \log X}{w} = \text{Antilog } \frac{225.1809}{93} = \text{Antilog of } 2.4213 = \mathbf{263.8}$$

Problem 113. Find out the geometric mean.

Yeild in Tons	*No. of farms*
7.5 to 10.5	5
10.5 to 13.5	9
13.5 to 16.5	19
16.5 to 19.5	23
19.5 to 22.5	7
22.5 to 25.5	4
25.5 to 28.5	1

(*B. Com. Osmania*)

Solution:

Yield in tons	m	f	*log m*	*f log X*
7.5 to 10.5	9	5	0.9542	4.7710
10.5 to 13.5	12	9	1.0792	9.7128
13.5 to 16.5	15	19	1.1761	22.3459
16.5 to 19.5	18	23	1.2553	28.8719
19.5 to 22.5	21	7	1.3222	9.2554
22.5 to 25.5	24	4	1.3802	5.5208
25.5 to 28.5	27	1	1.4314	1.4314
		N = 68		Σ log X = 81.9092

$$\text{Geometric mean} = \text{Antilog } \frac{\Sigma \log X}{N}$$
$$= \text{Antilog } \frac{81.9092}{68}$$
$$= \text{Antilog of } 1.2045$$
$$= \mathbf{16.02}$$

Problem 114. Compute the geometric mean from the following data:

Marks	0–10	10–20	20–30	30–40	40–50
No. of students	5	7	15	25	8

(*B. Com., Andhra*)

Solution:

Marks	m	f	*log m*	*f log m*
0–10	5	5	0.6990	3.4950
10–20	15	7	1.1761	8.2327
20–30	25	15	1.3979	20.9685
30–40	35	25	1.5441	38.6025
40–50	45	8	1.6532	13.2256
		$N = 60$		$= \Sigma f \log m$ $= 84.5243$

$$\text{Geometric mean} = \text{Antilog } \frac{\Sigma f \log m}{\text{N}}$$
$$= \text{Antilog } \frac{84.5243}{60}$$
$$= \text{Antilog of } 1.4087$$
$$= \mathbf{25.63}$$

Problem 115. The following table gives the weight of 31 persons in a sample survey. Calculate geometric mean.

Weight (Ibs) :	130	135	140	145	146	148	149	150	157
No. of persons:	3	4	6	6	3	5	2	1	1

Solution:

Computation of Geometric Mean

Size of item	*frequency*	*log X*	*f log X*
130	3	2.1139	6.3417
135	4	2.1303	8.5212
140	6	2.1461	12.8766
145	6	2.1614	12.9684
146	3	2.1644	6.4932
148	5	2.1703	10.8515
149	2	2.1732	4.3464
150	1	2.1761	2.1761
157	1	2.1959	2.1259
	N = 31		$\Sigma f \log X = 66.7010$

$$\text{Geometric mean} = \text{Antilog } \frac{\Sigma f \log X}{N}$$
$$= \text{Antilog } \frac{66.7010}{31}$$
$$= \text{Antilog of } 2.1516$$
$$= \mathbf{141.8}$$

Problem 116. Find out the geometric mean of the following:

Marks	*No. of students*
10–25	6
25–40	22
40–55	44
55–70	26
70–85	3
85–100	1

(*B.Com Madurai*)

Solution:

Computation of Geometric Mean

Marks	*m*	*f*	*log m*	*f log m*
10–25	17.5	6	1.2430	7.4580
25–40	32.5	22	1.5119	33.2618
40–55	47.5	44	1.6767	73.7748
55–70	62.5	26	1.7959	46.6934
70–85	77.5	3	1.8893	5.6679
85–100	92.5	1	1.9661	1.9661
		$N = 102$		$\Sigma f \log m = 168.8220$

$$\text{Geometric mean} = \text{Antilog } \frac{\Sigma f \log m}{\text{N}}$$
$$= \text{Antilog } \frac{168.8220}{102}$$
$$= \text{Antilog } 1.6551$$
$$= \mathbf{45.2 \text{ marks}}$$

HARMONIC MEAN

Problem 117. The monthly incomes of 10 families in rupees in a certain village are given below:

Family :	1	2	3	4	5	6	7	8	9	10
Income :	85	70	10	75	500	8	42	250	40	36

Calculate the harmonic mean.

(*B. Com. Agra*)

Solution:

Computation of Harmonic Mean

Family	*Income*	*Reciprocal* (1/X)
1	85	0.01176
2	70	0.01426
3	10	0.10000
4	75	0.01333
5	500	0.00200
6	8	0.12500
7	42	0.02381
8	250	0.00400
9	40	0.02500
10	36	0.02778
		$\Sigma 1/X = 0.34694$

$$\text{Harmonic mean} = \frac{N}{\frac{1}{X_1} + \frac{1}{X_2} + \frac{1}{X_3} + \dots \frac{1}{X_n}}$$

$$= \frac{N}{\Sigma 1/X}$$

$$= \frac{10}{0.34694}$$

$$= \textbf{Rs 28.82}$$

Problem 118. The monthly income of 8 families in rupees in a certain locality are given below. Calculate the mean, the geometric mean and harmonic mean and confirm that the relationship $\overline{X} > G.M. > H.M$ holds true:

Family	: A	B	C	D	E	F	G	H
Income Rs.	: 70	10	500	75	8	250	8	42

(*B. Com., Saugar*)

Solution:

Computation of $\overline{X}$ GM and HM

X	*log of X*	*Reciprocals* (1/X)
70	1.8451	0.01429
10	1.0000	0.10000
500	2.6990	0.00200
75	1.8751	0.01333
8	0.9031	0.12500
250	2.3979	0.00400
8	0.9031	0.12500
42	1.6232	0.02381
$\Sigma X = 963$	$\Sigma log X = 13.2465$	$\Sigma \frac{1}{X} = 0.40743$

$$\overline{X} = \frac{\Sigma X}{8} = \frac{963}{8}$$

$$= \textbf{Rs.120.375}$$

$$\text{G.M.} = \text{Anti log } \frac{\Sigma log X}{N} = \frac{13.2465}{8}$$

$$= 1.6558$$

$$= \textbf{Rs.45.27}$$

$$\text{H.M.} = \frac{N}{\Sigma \frac{1}{X}} = \frac{8}{0.40743}$$

$$= \textbf{Rs. 19.635}$$

Rs. 120.375 > Rs. 45.27 > Rs. 19.635

Problem 119. Calculate the Arithmetic mean, Geometric mean and Harmonic mean from the following frequency distribution.

Variable	: 3	4	5	6	7	8	9	10	11
Frequency	: 2	5	9	14	15	8	6	3	1

(*B. Com., Andhra*)

Solution: **Computation of Mean, G. M. and H. M.**

Variable X	*Frequency* f	fX	*log X*	*f log X*	*Reciprocals* $\frac{1}{X}$	$f\frac{1}{X}$
3	2	6	0.4771	0.9542	0.3333	0.6666
4	5	20	0.6021	3.0105	0.2500	1.2500
5	9	45	0.6990	6.2910	0.2000	1.8000
6	14	84	0.7782	10.8948	0.1667	2.3338
7	15	105	0.8451	12.6765	0.1429	2.1435
8	8	64	0.9031	7.2248	0.1250	1.0000
9	6	54	0.9542	5.7252	0.1111	0.6666
10	3	30	1.0000	3.0000	.1000	0.3000
11	1	11	1.0414	1.0414	0.0909	0.0909
	$N = 63$	$\Sigma fX = 419$		$\Sigma f log X = 50.8184$		$\Sigma f\frac{1}{X} = 10.2514$

$$\text{Mean:}\overline{X} = \frac{\Sigma fX}{N} = \frac{419}{63}$$

$$= \textbf{6.65}$$

$$\text{Geometric Mean: Antilog } \frac{\Sigma f \, log \, X}{N}$$

$$= \text{Antilog } \frac{50.8184}{63} = \text{Antilog } 0.8066$$

$$= \textbf{6.41}$$

$$\text{Harmonic Mean} = \frac{N}{\Sigma f\frac{1}{X}}$$

$$= \frac{63}{10.2514}$$

$$= \textbf{6.1455}$$

Problem 120. Calculate the Geometric and the harmonic mean of the following series:

3,543.03; 8,935.23; 9,345.07; 10,532.45; 0.3231
0.8934; 0.0041; 0.0005; 0.0043; and 0.00004

(*B. Com., Andhra*)

Solution :

Computation of Geometric Mean and Harmonic Mean

Size of item	*Log X*	*Reciprocals* $1/X$
3,543.03	3.5494	.000282
8,935.23	3.9511	.000112
9,345.07	3.9705	.000107
10,532.45	4.0224	.000095
0.3231	$\bar{1}.5093$	3.095
0.8934	$\bar{1}.9511$	1.119
0.0041	$\bar{3}.6128$	243.9
0.0005	$\bar{4}.6990$	2000.0
0.0043	$\bar{3}.6335$	232.6
0.00004	$\bar{5}.6021$	25000.0
	$\Sigma log X = 2.5012$	$\Sigma\frac{1}{X} = 27480.714596$

Geometric Mean:

$$\begin{aligned} \text{G.M.} &= \text{Antilog}\ \frac{\Sigma log X}{N} \\ &= \text{Antilog}\ \frac{2.5012}{10} \\ &= \text{Antilog}\ 0.25012 \\ &= \mathbf{1.778} \end{aligned}$$

Harmonic Mean:

$$\begin{aligned} \text{H.M.} &= \frac{N}{\Sigma\frac{1}{X}} \\ &= \frac{10}{27480.714596} \\ &= \mathbf{0.00036} \end{aligned}$$

Problem 121. Calculate harmonic mean from the following data:

Size of item	: 6	7	8	9	10	11
Frequency	: 4	6	9	5	2	8

Solution:

Size of item	f	*Reciprocal* $(1/X)$	$f1/X$
6	4	.1667	.6668
7	6	.1429	.8574
8	9	.1250	1.1250.
9	5	.1111	.5555
10	2	.1000	.2000
11	8	.0909	.7272
	$\Sigma f = 34$		$\Sigma f1/X = 4.1319$

$$\begin{aligned} \text{Harmonic mean} &= \frac{N}{\Sigma f1/X} \\ &= \frac{34}{4.1319} \\ &= \mathbf{8.23} \end{aligned}$$

Problem 122. In a certain factory, a unit of work is completed by A in 4 minutes, by B in 5 minutes, by C in 6 minutes, by D in 10 minutes and by E in 12 minutes. What is their average rate of working ? What is the average number of units of work completed per minute ? At this rate how many units will they complete in a six-hour day.

(*B. Com. Hons. Delhi*)

Solution:

$$\text{Harmonic Mean} = \frac{5}{1/4 + 1/5 + 1/6 + 1/10 + 1/12}$$

$$= \frac{5}{\frac{15+12+10+6+5}{60}}$$

$$= \frac{5 \times 60}{48} = \frac{25}{4} \text{ minutes per unit.}$$

Hence the average number of units of work completed per minute is 25/4.

Now, 25/4 minutes are required for one unit. At this rate the number of units that will be completed in a six hour day are:

$$360 \times \frac{4}{25} = 57.6 = \mathbf{58}.$$

Problem 123. Calculate the geometric mean and the harmonic mean of the following series:

2000 35 400 15 40 1500 300 6 90 250 20

(B. Com., Mysore)

Solution:

Computation of G.M. and H.M.

X	$log\,of\,X$	*Reciprocals* $(\frac{1}{X})$
2000	3.3010	0.0005
35	1.5441	0.0285
400	2.6021	0.0025
15	1.1761	0.0667
40	1.6021	0.0250
1500	3.1761	0.0007
300	2.4771	0.0033
6	0.7782	0.1667
90	1.9542	0.0111
250	2.3979	0.0040
20	1.3010	0.0500
	$\Sigma log X = 22.3099$	$\Sigma\frac{1}{X} = 0.3590$

$$\text{G.M.} = \text{Antilog}\ \frac{\Sigma log X}{N}$$

$$= \text{Antilog}\ \frac{22.3099}{11} = \text{Antilog of } 2.0282 = \mathbf{Rs106.70}$$

$$\text{H.M.} = \frac{N}{\Sigma\frac{1}{x}} = \frac{11}{0.3590} = \mathbf{Rs\ 30.64}$$

Problem 124. Calculate the geometric and the harmonic means of the following series of monthly expenditure of a batch of students:

Rs. 142, 110, 95, 175, 162, 180, 75, 133

(*B. Com. Madurai*)

Solution:

Computation of Geometric Mean and Harmonic Mean

X	*Log of X*	*Reciprocals of X*
142	2.1523	0.0070
110	2.0414	0.0091
95	1.9777	0.0105
175	2.2430	0.0057
162	2.2095	0.0062
180	2.2553	0.0056
75	1.8751	0.0133
133	2.1239	0.0075
$N = 8$	$\Sigma Log X = 16.8782$	$\Sigma \frac{1}{X} = 0.0649$

$$\text{Geometric Mean} = \text{Antilog } \frac{\Sigma log X}{\text{N}}$$

$$= \text{Antilog } \frac{16.8782}{8}$$

$$= \text{Antilog } 2.1098 \quad = \textbf{Rs. 128.70}$$

$$\text{Harmonic Mean} = \frac{\text{N}}{\Sigma \frac{1}{\text{X}}} = \frac{8}{0.0649} \quad = \textbf{Rs. 123.50}$$

Problem 125. Find the H.M. from the data given below:

Class boundaries :	15–25	25–35	35–45	45–55	55-65	65–75
Frequency :	4	11	19	14	0	2

(*B. Com.*,)

Solution:

Computation of Harmonic Mean

Class Boundaries	*M.P.* m	f	$\frac{1}{m}$	$f \times \frac{1}{m}$
15–25	20	4	0.05	0.2000
25–35	30	11	0.0333	0.3663
35–45	40	19	0.025	0.4750
45–55	50	14	0.02	0.2800
55–65	60	0	0.0166	0.0000
65–75	70	2	0.0148	0.0286
		N = 50		$\Sigma f \times \frac{1}{m} = 1.3499$

$$\text{Harmonic Mean} = \frac{n}{\Sigma \left(f \times \frac{1}{m}\right)}$$

$$\text{N} = 50, \Sigma f \times \frac{1}{m} = 1.3499$$

$$\text{Harmonic Mean} = \frac{50}{1.3499}$$

$$= 37.0398$$
$$= \mathbf{37.04}$$

Problem 126. Find the geometric mean, mean and harmonic mean for the following distribution:

Marks	0–10	10–20	20–30	30–40	40–50
No. of students	5	7	15	25	8

(*B. Com. Madurai, Kerala*)

Solution:

Computation of Geometric Mean, Mean and Harmonic Mean

Marks	m	f	$d' = \frac{m-25}{5}$	fd'	$\log m$	$f \log m$	$1/X$	$f1/X$
0–10	5	5	−4	−20	0.6990	3.4950	0.2000	1.000
10–20	15	7	−2	−14	1.1761	8.2327	0.6667	4.6669
20–30	25	15	0	0	1.3939	20.9685	0.0400	0.6000
30–40	35	25	+2	+50	1.5441	38.6025	0.2857	7.1425
40–50	45	8	+4	+32	1.6532	13.2256	0.0222	0.1776
		$N = 60$		$\Sigma fd' =$ +48		$\Sigma f \log m =$ 84.5243		$\Sigma f\, 1/X =$ 13.5870

$$\text{Mean or } \overline{X} = A \pm \frac{\Sigma fd}{N} \times C$$
$$= 25 + \frac{48}{60} \times 5 = 25 + 4 = \mathbf{29}$$

$$\text{Geometric Mean} = \text{Antilog } \frac{\Sigma f \log X}{N} = \frac{84.5243}{60} = \text{Antilog of } 1.4087 = \mathbf{25.63}$$

$$\text{Harmonic Mean} = \frac{N}{\Sigma f 1/X} = \frac{60}{13.5870} = \mathbf{4.42}$$

Problem 127. Peter travelled by car for 4 days. He drove 10 hours each day. He drove: first day at the rate of 45 km. per hour, second day at the rate of 40 km. per hour, third day at the rate of 38 km. per hour, and fourth day at the rate of 37 km. per hour. What was his average speed?

(*B. Com., Delhi*)

Solution:

$$\text{H.M.} = \frac{N}{\Sigma\left(\frac{1}{X}\right)}$$
$$= \frac{4}{\frac{1}{45} + \frac{1}{40} + \frac{1}{38} + \frac{1}{37}}$$
$$= \frac{4}{0.022 + 0.025 + 0.026 + 0.027}$$
$$= \frac{4}{0.1}$$
$$= \mathbf{40\,km.}$$

Problem 128. An auto ride in Delhi costs Rs. one for the first kilometre and sixty paise for each additional kilometre. The cost for each kilometre is incurred at the beginning of the kilometre, so that the rider pays for a whole kilometre. What is the average cost for $2\frac{3}{4}$ kilometre.

(*B. Com. Delhi*)

Solution:

The average cost for $2\frac{3}{4}$ k.m.

$$= \frac{\text{Rs } 1 + 0.60 + 0.60}{2\frac{3}{4}}$$

$$= \frac{2.20 \times 4}{11}$$

$$= \mathbf{0.80 \text{ paise}}$$

Problem 129. Mr. Dushmants of Bhubaneswar started for a village at a distance of six miles. He travelled in his car at a speed of 40 miles per hour. After travelling for 4 miles the car stopped running. He then travelled in a rickshaw at a speed of 10 miles per hour. After travelling a distance of $1\frac{1}{2}$ miles, he left the rickshaw and covered the remaining distance on foot at a speed of 4 miles per hour. Find the average speed per hour of Mr. Dushmanta and verify the calculations.

(*B. Com., Utkal*)

Solution:

$$\text{H.M.} = \frac{\Sigma W}{(\frac{1}{a} \times W_1) + (\frac{1}{b} \times W_2) + (\frac{1}{c} \times W_3)}$$

$$\text{H.M.} = \frac{4 + 1.5 + 0.5}{(\frac{1}{40} \times 4) + (\frac{1}{10} \times 1.5) + (\frac{1}{4} \times 0.5)}$$

$$= \frac{6}{\frac{1}{10} + \frac{3}{20} + \frac{1}{8}}$$

$$= \frac{6}{0.375}$$

$$= \mathbf{16 \text{ m.p.h.}}$$

Verification

4 miles in car at the speed of 40 m.p.h. Thus time taken 6 minutes.

1.5 miles in Rickshaw at 10 m.p.h. Thus time taken 9 minutes.

0.5 miles on foot at 4 m.p.h. Thus time taken 7.5 minutes.

Therefore total distance covered = 6 miles

Total time taken = 22.5 minutes

Therefore, his speed $= \frac{6}{22.5} \times 60 = \mathbf{16 \text{ m.p.h.}}$

Problem 130. A man travelled by car for 3 days. He covered 480 miles each day. On the first day he drove for 10 hours at 48 miles an hour, on the second day he drove for 12 hours at 40 miles an hour and on last day he drove for 15 hours at 32 miles per hour. What was his average speed?

(*B. Com., Bangalore*)

Solution:

$$\text{Harmonic Mean} = \frac{N}{\frac{1}{X^1} + \frac{1}{X^2} + \frac{1}{X^3}}$$

$$= \frac{3}{\frac{1}{48} + \frac{1}{40} + \frac{1}{32}}$$

$$= \frac{3}{\frac{37}{480}}$$

$$= \frac{3 \times 480}{37} = \mathbf{38.92 \text{ m.p.h.}}$$

Problem 131. An invester buys Rs. 1200 worth of shares in a company each month. During the first 5 months he bought the shares at a price of Rs. 10, Rs. 12, Rs. 15, Rs. 20 and Rs, 24 per share. After 5 months what is the average price paid for the shares by him?

(B. Com., (H) Delhi)

Solution:

Harmonic mean is suitable to solve the problem.

$$\text{Harmonic Mean} = \frac{N}{\frac{1}{X^1} + \frac{1}{X^2} + \frac{1}{X^3} \cdots \frac{1}{X^n}}$$

$$= \frac{5}{\frac{1}{10} + \frac{1}{12} + \frac{1}{15} + \frac{1}{20} + \frac{1}{24}}$$

$$= \frac{5}{\frac{41}{120}} = \frac{5 \times 120}{41}$$

$$= \textbf{Rs.14.63}$$

Problem 132. A motor car covered a distance of 50 miles four times. The first time at 50 m.p.h., the second at 20 m.p.h. the third at 40 m.p.h. and the fourth at 25 m.p.h. Calculate the average speed and explain the choice of average.

(C.A.)

Solution:

$$\text{Harmonic Mean} = \frac{N}{\frac{1}{X^2} + \frac{1}{X^2} + \frac{1}{X^3} + \frac{1}{X^4}}$$

$$= \frac{4}{\frac{1}{50} + \frac{1}{20} + \frac{1}{40} + \frac{1}{25}}$$

$$= \frac{4}{\frac{27}{300}}$$

$$= \frac{4 \times 200}{27}$$

$$= \textbf{29.63 m.p.h.}$$

Therefore the average speed is 29.63 m.p.h.

Problem 133. A vehicle, when climbing up a gradient, consumes petrol at the rate of one litre per 8 kms. While climbing down, it gives 12 kms per litre. Find its average rate of consumption for a to and fro travel between two places situated at the two ends of a 25 kilometres long gradiant.

(B. Com., Bombay)

Solution:

$$\text{Harmonic Mean} = \frac{N}{\Sigma\left(\frac{1}{X}\right)}$$

$$= \frac{2}{\frac{1}{8} + \frac{1}{12}}$$

$$= 2 \times \frac{24}{5}$$

$$= \textbf{9.6 km. per litre.}$$

Problem 134. A cyclist covers his three miles at an average speed of 8 m.p.h. Another two miles at 3 m.p.h. and the last 2 miles at 2 m.p.h. Find the average speed for the entire journey.

(*B. Com., Agra*)

Solution:

$$\begin{aligned}
\text{H.M.} &= \frac{\Sigma w}{\Sigma\left(w\frac{1}{X}\right)} \\
&= \frac{3+2+2}{\left(\frac{1}{8}\times 3\right)+\left(\frac{1}{3}\times 2\right)+\left(\frac{1}{2}\times 2\right)} \\
&= \frac{7}{\frac{3}{8}+\frac{2}{3}+\frac{2}{2}} \\
&= \frac{7\times 24}{49} \\
&= \frac{24}{7} \\
&= \mathbf{3.43\ m.p.h.}
\end{aligned}$$

Problem 135. A taxi cab drives from a plain town to a hill station, 60 miles distance, at a mileage rate of 10 miles per gallon of petrol and on the return trip at 15 miles per gallon. Find the harmonic mean, rate of mileage per gallon.

(*M. Com., Delhi*)

Solution:

$$\begin{aligned}
\text{H.M.} &= \frac{N}{\Sigma\left(\frac{1}{X}\right)} \\
&= \frac{2}{\frac{1}{10}+\frac{1}{15}} \\
&= \frac{2}{\frac{3+2}{30}} \\
&= 2\times\frac{30}{5} \\
&= \mathbf{12\ Miles\ per\ gallon.}
\end{aligned}$$

Problem 136. You take a trip which entails travelling 900 miles by train at an average speed of 60 m.p.h., 300 miles by boat at an average of 25 m.p.h., 400 miles by plane at 350 m.p.h. and finally 15 miles by taxi at 25 m.p.h. What is your average speed for the entire distance?

(*M. Com., Agra*)

Solution:

Weighted harmonic mean is suitable

$$\begin{aligned}
\text{H.M.} &= \frac{\Sigma w}{\Sigma\left(w\frac{1}{X}\right)} \\
&= \frac{900+300+400+15}{\left(\frac{1}{60}\times 900\right)+\left(\frac{1}{25}\times 300\right)+\left(\frac{1}{350}\times 400\right)\times\frac{1}{25}\times 15} \\
&= \frac{1615}{15+12+1.14+0.6} \\
&= \frac{1615}{28.74} \\
&= \mathbf{56.19\ k.p.h.}
\end{aligned}$$

Miscellaneous

Problem 137. The number of telephone calls received in 245 successive one minute intervals at an exchange are shown in the following frequency distribution:

No. of calls	: 0	1	2	3	4	5	6	7
Frequency	: 14	21	25	43	51	40	39	12

(*I.C.W.A.*)

Evaluate the mean, median and mode.

Solution:

Computation of Mean, Median and Mode

No. of calls. X	*f*	*fX*	*c.f.*
0	14	0	14
1	21	21	35
2	25	50	60
3	43	129	103
4	51	204	154
5	40	200	194
6	39	234	233
7	12	84	245
	N = 245	$\Sigma fX = 922$	

$$\text{Mean} : \overline{X} = \frac{\Sigma fX}{N} \qquad \Sigma fX = 922;\ N = 245$$

$$= \frac{922}{245}$$

$$= \mathbf{3.76}$$

$$\text{Median} = \text{size of } \frac{N+1}{2}\text{th item}$$

$$= \text{size of } \frac{246}{2}\text{th item}$$

= 123rd item which lies in 4th call. So

Median = **4.**

Mode :

By inspection method mode lies as it is having the highest frequency.

Mode = **4.**

Problem 138. Find the mean, median and model ages of married women at the first child birth.

Age at the birth of First child	13	14	15	16	17	18	19	20	21	22	23	24	25
No. of married women	37	162	343	390	256	433	161	355	65	85	49	46	40

(*I.C.W.A.*)

Solution:

Computation of Mean, Median and Mode

Age at the birth of first child	*No. of married women*	$d = X - 19$	fd	cf
13	37	−6	−222	37
14	162	−5	−810	199
15	343	−4	−1372	542
16	390	−3	−1170	932
17	256	−2	−512	1183
18	433	−1	−433	1621
19	161	0	0	1782
20	355	1	355	2137
21	65	2	130	2202
22	85	3	255	2287
23	49	4	196	2336
24	46	5	230	2382
25	40	6	240	2422
	N = 2422		$\Sigma fd = -3113$	

$$\overline{X} = A - \frac{\Sigma fd}{N}$$

$$A = 19, \Sigma fd = -3113, N = 2422$$

$$\overline{X} = 19 - \frac{3113}{2422}$$

$$= 19 - 1.285 \quad = \mathbf{17.715}$$

$$\text{Median} = \text{size of } \left(\frac{N+1}{2}\right) \text{th item}$$

$$= \text{size of } \left(\frac{2422+1}{2}\right) \text{th item}$$

$$= \text{size of 1211.5th item}$$

$$= \mathbf{18}$$

By inspection the mode is **18**

Problem 139. Find the mean and median of the following distribution.

Size of farm (acres)	up to 50	50–100	100–150	150–200	200–250	Over 250
Number of occupiers	57	256	132	25	10	12

(*B.Com., Madras*)

Solution:

Computation of Mean and Median

Size of farm	m	f	$d' = \frac{m - 125}{50}$	fd'	*c.f.*
0–50	25	57	−2	−114	57
50–100	75	256	−1	−256	313
100–150	125	132	0	0	445
150–200	175	25	1	25	470
200–250	225	10	2	20	480
250–300	275	12	3	36	492
		N = 492		$\Sigma fd' = -289$	

$$\text{Mean} = A + \frac{\Sigma fd'}{N} \times C$$

$$A = 125; \Sigma fd' = -289; N = 492; C = 50$$

$$= 125 - \frac{289}{492} \times 50 = 125 - 29.37$$

$$= \mathbf{95.63}$$

$$\text{Median} = \text{Size of } \frac{N}{2}\text{th item}$$

$$= \text{Size of } \frac{492}{2}\text{th item}$$

$$= \text{246th item which lies in the class 50–100}$$

$$\text{Median} = L_1 + \frac{\frac{N}{2} - c.f.}{f} \times i$$

$$L_1 = 50; \frac{N}{2} = 246; c.f. = 57; f = 256; i = 50$$

$$= 50 + \frac{246 - 57}{256} \times 50 = 50 + 36.91$$

$$= \mathbf{86.91}$$

Problem 140. Find the median and mode from the data given below:

Size	*Frequency*	*Size*	*Frequency*
Below 10	5	Below 50	190
,, 20	20	,, 60	250
,, 30	50	,, 70	295
,, 40	105	,, 80	320

(*B. Com., Madurai*)

Solution:

Computation of Median and Mode

Size	*Frequency*	*c.f.*
0–10	5	5
10–20	20-5 = 15	20
20–30	50-20 = 30	50
30–40	105-50 = 55	105
40–50	190-105 = 85	190
50–60	250-190 = 60	250
60–70	295-250 = 45	295
70–80	320-295 = 25	320
	N = 320	

$$\text{Median} = \text{size of } \frac{N}{2}\text{th item}$$
$$= \text{size of } \frac{320}{2}\text{th item}$$
$$= \text{160th item which lies in the class 40–50}$$
$$\text{Median} = L_1 + \frac{\frac{N}{2} - c.f.}{f} \times i$$
$$L_1 = 40; \frac{N}{2} = 160;$$
$$c.f. = 105;\ f = 85;\ i = 10$$
$$= 40 + \frac{160 - 105}{85} \times 10 = 40 + 6.47$$
$$= \mathbf{46.47}$$

Mode : By inspection method mode lies in the class 40–50

$$Z = L_1 + \frac{f_1 - f_0}{2f_1 - f_0 - f_2} \times i$$
$$L_1 = 40;\ f_1 = 85;\ f_0 = 55;\ f_2 = 60;\ i = 10$$
$$= 40 + \frac{85 - 55}{2 \times 85 - 55 - 60} \times 10 = 40 + 5.45$$
$$= \mathbf{45.45}$$

Problem 141. Calculate the Median and the Mode.

No. of day absent	*No. of students*	*No. of days absent*	*No. of students*
Less than 5	29	Less than 30	644
,, 10	224	,, 35	650
,, 15	465	,, 40	653
,, 20	582	,, 45	655
,, 25	634		

(*B. Com., Madras, Madurai, Punjab*)

Solution:

Computation of Median and Mode

No. of days absent	*No. of students f*	*c.f.*
0–5	29	29
5–10	224 – 29 = 195	224
10–15	465 – 224 = 241	465
15–20	582 – 465 = 117	582
20–25	634 – 582 = 52	634
25–30	644 – 634 = 10	644
30–35	650 – 644 = 6	650
35–40	653 – 650 = 3	653
40–45	655 – 653 = 2	655

$$\text{Median} = \text{size of } \frac{N}{2}\text{th item} = \text{size of } \frac{655}{2}\text{th item}$$

$$= 327.5\text{th item which lies in the class 10–15}$$

$$\text{Median} = L_1 + \frac{\frac{N}{2} - c.f.}{f} \times i$$

$$L_1 = 10; \frac{N}{2} = 327.5;$$

$$c.f = 224;\ f = 241;\ i = 5$$

$$= 10 + \frac{327.5 - 224}{241} \times 5 = 10 + 2.15 \quad = \mathbf{12.15}$$

Mode : By inspection method mode lies in the class 10–15

$$Z = L_1 + \frac{f_1 - f_0}{2f_1 - f_0 - f_2} \times i$$

$$L_1 = 10;\ f_1 = 241;\ f_0 = 195;\ f_2 = 117;\ i = 5$$

$$= 10 + \frac{241 - 195}{2 \times 241 - 195 - 117} \times 5 = 10 + 1.35 \quad = \mathbf{11.35}$$

Problem 142. Calculate the geometric and the harmonic means of the following series of monthly expenditure of a batch of students :

Rs. 125	130	75	10	45	0.50	0.40	500	150	5

(*B. Com. Andhra*)

Solution:

Computation of Geometric Mean and Harmonic Mean

X	*Log of X*	*Reciprocals*
125	2.0969	0.0080
130	2.1139	0.0077
75	1.8751	0.0133
10	1.0000	0.1000
45	1.6532	0.0222
0.50	$\bar{1}.6990$	2.0000
0.40	$\bar{1}.6021$	2.5000
500	2.6990	0.0020
150	2.1761	0.0067
5	0.6990	0.2000
	$\Sigma log_X = 13.6143$	$\Sigma \frac{1}{X} = 4.8599$

$$\text{Geometric mean} = \text{Antilog } \frac{\Sigma \log x}{N} = \frac{13.6143}{10}$$
$$= \text{Antilog of } 1.36143 = \mathbf{22.98}$$
$$\text{Harmonic Mean} = \frac{N}{\Sigma 1/X} = \frac{10}{4.8599}$$
$$= \mathbf{2.06}$$

Problem 143. If the mode and the mean of a moderately asymetrical series are 16″ and 15.6″ respectively. What would be its most probable median ?

(*B. Com. Agra*)

Solution:

$$\begin{aligned}
\text{Mean} - \text{Mode} &= 3(\text{Mean} - \text{Median}) \\
15.6 - 16 &= 3(15.6 - \text{Median}) \\
-0.4 &= 46.8 - 3\text{ Median.} \\
3\text{ Median} &= 46.8 + 0.4 \\
3\text{ Median} &= 47.2 \\
\text{Median} &= \frac{47.2}{3} \\
&= \text{Median } 15.73''
\end{aligned}$$

Problem 144. Calculate the mean, median and mode of the following distribution.

Mid	: 59	61	63	65	67	69	71	73
Frequency	: 1	2	9	48	131	102	40	17

(*B.A. Kerala*)

Solution:

m	f	$d' = \frac{m-65}{2}$	fd'	$c.f.$
59	1	−3	−3	1
61	2	−2	−4	3
63	9	−1	−9	12
65	48	0	0	60
67	131	1	131	191
69	102	2	204	293
71	40	3	120	333
73	17	4	68	350
	N = 350		$\Sigma fd' = 507$	

$$\overline{X} = A + \frac{\Sigma fd'}{N} \times c$$
$$A = 65;\ \Sigma fd' = 507;\ C = 2;\ N = 350$$
$$= 65 + \frac{507}{350} \times 2$$
$$= 65 + 2.9 = \mathbf{67.9}$$
$$\text{Median} = \frac{N}{2}\text{th item } i.e., 175\text{ th item } = 67$$

The class is 66–68

$$\therefore \quad \text{Median} = L_1 + \frac{\frac{N}{2} - cf}{f} \times i$$

$$L_1 = 66; \frac{N}{2} = 175; c.f = 64; f = 131; i = 2$$

$$\text{Median} = 66 + \frac{175 - 60}{131} \times 2$$

$$= 66 + 1.76 = \mathbf{67.76}$$

Mode lies in the class 66–68

$$\therefore \quad Z = L + \frac{f_1 - f_0}{3f_1 - f_0 - f_2} \times i$$

$$L = 66; f = 131; f_0 = 48; f_2 = 102; i = 2$$

$$= 66 + \frac{131 - 40}{262 - 48 - 102} \times 2$$

$$= 66 + 1.48$$

$$= \mathbf{67.48}$$

Problem 145. Calculate median and mode from the following data :

Class :	0–7	7–14	14–21	21–28	28–35	35–42
Frequency :	7	11	24	19	12	9

(*B. Com., Baroda*)

Solution:

Computation of Median and Mode

x	m	f	cf
0–7	3.5	7	7
7–14	10.5	11	18
14–21	17.5	24	42
21–28	24.5	19	61
28–35	31.6	12	73
35–42	38.5	9	82
		N = 82	

$$\text{Median} = \text{size of } \frac{N}{2}\text{th item}$$

$$= \text{size of } \frac{82}{2}\text{th item}$$

$$= \text{41th item which lies in the class 14–21}$$

$$\text{Median} = L_1 + \frac{\frac{N}{2} - c.f.}{f} \times C$$

$$L_1 = 14, \frac{N}{2} = 41, c.f. = 18, f = 24, C = 7$$

$$= 14 + \frac{41 - 18}{24} \times 7$$

$$= 14 + \frac{161}{24} = 14 + 6.71$$

$$= \mathbf{20.71}.$$

Grouping Table

x	1	2	3	4	5	6
0–7	7					
		18				
7–14	11					
			3.5			
14–21	24					55
		43		42		
21–28	19					
			31		54	
28–35	12					
		21		40		
35–42	9					

Analysis Table

Col No.	0–7	7–14	14–21	21–28	28–35
1			1		
2			1	1	
3		1	1		
4	1	1	1		
5		1	1	1	
6			1	1	1
	1	3	6	3	1

Therefore mode lies in the class 14–21

$$
\begin{aligned}
\text{M}_0 &= L_1 + \frac{f_1 - f_0}{2f_1 - f_0 - f_2} \times i \\
\text{L}_1 &= 14, f_1 = 24, f_0 = 11, f_2 = 19, i = 7 \\
&= 14 + \frac{24 - 11}{2 \times 24 - 11 - 19} \times 7 \\
&= 14 + \frac{91}{18} = 14 + 5.06 \\
\text{Mode} &= \mathbf{19.06}.
\end{aligned}
$$

Problem 146. Find arithmetic mean, median and mode from the following :

Marks below	:	10	20	30	40	50	60	70	80
No. of students	:	15	35	60	84	96	127	198	250

(*B.Com. Bombay*)

Solution:

Computation of Mean, Median and Mode

Marks	*m.p.*	*f*	$fd' = \frac{m-35}{10}$	*fd'*	*c.f.*
0–5	5	15	−3	−45	.5
10–20	15	35 − 15 = 20	−2	−40	35
20–30	25	60 − 35 = 25	−1	−25	60
30–40	35	84 − 60 = 24	0	0	84
40–50	45	96 − 84 = 12	1	12	96
50–60	55	127 − 96 = 31	2	62	127
60–70	65	198 − 127 = 71	3	213	198
70–80	75	250 − 198 = 52	4	208	250
			N = 250		$\Sigma fd' = 385$

Mean :

$$\overline{X} = A + \frac{\Sigma fd'}{N} \times C$$

$$A = 35, \Sigma fd' = 385, N = 250, C = 10$$

$$= 35 + \frac{385}{250} \times 10$$

$$= 35 + 15.4$$

$$= \mathbf{50.4}$$

Median :

$$\text{Median} = \text{size of } \frac{N}{2}\text{th item}$$

$$= \text{size of } \frac{250}{2}\text{th item}$$

$$= \text{125th item which lies in the class 50–60}$$

$$\text{Median} = L_1 + \frac{\frac{N}{2} - c.f.}{f} \times i$$

$$L_1 = 50, \frac{N}{2} = 125, c.f. = 96,$$

$$f = 31, C = 10$$

$$= 50 + \frac{125 - 96}{31} \times 10$$

$$= 50 + \frac{290}{31} = 50 + 9.35$$

$$= \mathbf{59.35}$$

Mode :

By inspection method mode lies in the class 60–70,

$$Z = L_1 + \frac{f_1 - f_0}{2f_1 - f_0 - f_2} \times i$$

$$L_1 = 60, f_1 = 71, f_0 = 31, f_2 = 52, C = 10$$

$$= 60 + \frac{71 - 31}{2 \times 71 - 31 - 52} \times 10$$

$$= 60 + \frac{400}{59} = 60 + 6.78$$

$$= \mathbf{66.78}$$

Problem 147. Form an ordinary frequency table from the following cumulative distribution of marks obtained by 22 students and calculate mean, median and mode.

Marks	*No. of students*
Below 10	3
,, 20	8
,, 30	17
,, 40	20
,, 50	22

(*ICWA Inter*)

Solution:

Computation of Mean, Median and Mode

Marks	*m.p.*	*f*	$(m-24.5)/10 = d'$	fd'	*c.f.*
Below 9.5	4.5	3	−2	−6	3
9.5−19.5	14.5	5	−1	−5	8
19.5−29.5	24.5	9	0	0	17
29.5−39.5	34.5	3	1	3	20
39.5−49.5	44.5	2	2	4	22
		N = 22		$\Sigma fd' = -4$	

Mean :

$$\begin{aligned}\overline{X} &= A + \frac{\Sigma fd'}{N} \times C \\ A &= 24.5,\ \Sigma fd' = -4,\ N = 22,\ C = 10 \\ &= 24.5 - \frac{4}{22} \times 10 \\ &= 24.5 - 1.82 \\ &= \mathbf{22.68}\end{aligned}$$

Median :

$$\begin{aligned}&= L_1 + \frac{\frac{N}{2} - c.f.}{f} \times i \\ L_1 &= 19.5, \frac{N}{2} = \frac{22}{2} = 11, \\ c.f. &= 8,\ f = 9, i = 10 \\ &= 19.5 + \frac{11-8}{9} \times 10 \\ &= 19.5 + 3.33 \\ &= \mathbf{22.83}.\end{aligned}$$

By inspection method mode lies in the class 19.5–29.5

Mode :

$$\begin{aligned}Z &= L_1 + \frac{f_1 - f_0}{2f_1 - f_0 - f_2} \times i \\ L_1 &= 19.5, f_1 = 9, f_0 = 5, f_2 = 3, i = 10 \\ &= 19.5 + \frac{9-5}{2 \times 9 - 5 - 3} \times 10 \\ &= 19.5 + 4 \\ &= \mathbf{23.5}\end{aligned}$$

Problem 148. Calculate the mean, the median and the mode for the following frequency table.

Monthly Income :	300–325	325–350	350–375	375–400	
No. of clerks :	5	17	80	227	
		400–425	425–450	450–475	475–500
		326	248	88	9

(*B. Com., Nagpur*)

Solution:

Computation of Mean, Median and Mode

Monthly Income (Rs)	*M.P* m	f	$d' = \frac{m - 412.5}{25}$	fd'	*c.f.*
300–325	312.5	5	−4	−20	5
325–350	337.5	17	−3	−51	22
350–375	362.5	80	−2	−160	102
375–400	387.5	227	−1	−227	329
400–425	412.5	326	0	0	655
425–450	437.5	248	1	248	903
450–475	462.5	88	2	176	991
475–500	487.5	9	3	27	1000
		N = 1000		$\Sigma fd' = -7$	

Mean :

$$\overline{X} = A \pm \frac{\Sigma fd'}{N} \times C$$

$$A = 412.5;\ \Sigma fd' = -7;\ N = 1000$$

$$C = 25$$

$$= 412.5 - \frac{7}{1000} \times 25 = 412.5 - 0.175$$

$$= \mathbf{412.325}.$$

$$\text{Median} = \text{size of } \frac{N}{2}\text{th item}$$

$$= \frac{1000}{2}\text{th item}$$

= 500th item which lies in the class400–425

$$\text{Median} = L_1 + \frac{\frac{N}{2} - c.f.}{f} \times i$$

$$L_1 = 400;\ \frac{N}{2} = 500;\ c.f. = 329;$$

$$f = 326;\ i = 25$$

$$= 400 + \frac{500 - 329}{326} \times 25 = 400 + 13.11$$

$$= \mathbf{413.11}.$$

Mode :

By inspection method mode lies in the class 400–425

$$Z = L_1 + \frac{f_1 - f_0}{2f_1 - f_0 - f_2} \times i$$

$$L_1 = 400;\ f_1 = 326;\ f_0 = 227;$$
$$f_2 = 248;\ i = 25$$
$$= 400 + \frac{326 - 227}{2 \times 326 - 227 - 248} \times 25$$
$$= 400 + 13.98$$
$$= \mathbf{413.98.}$$

Problem 149. Compute the arithmetic mean, median and mode from the following data.

Age at last birth day	*Number*
15–19	4
20–24	20
25–29	38
30–34	24
35–39	10
40–44	9

(*M.A, Kerala*)

Solution:

Computation of Mean, Median and Mode

Age	*M.P.*	*f*	$d' = \frac{m - 27}{5}$	fd'	*c.f.*
14.5–19.5	17	4	−2	−8	4
19.5–24.5	22	20	−1	−20	24
24.5–29.5	27	38	0	0	62
29.5–34.5	32	24	1	24	86
34.5–39.5	37	10	2	20	96
39.5–44.5	42	9	3	27	105
		N = 105		$\Sigma fd'$=43	

Mean:

$$\overline{X} = A + \frac{\Sigma fd'}{N} \times C$$
$$A = 27;\ \Sigma fd' = 43;\ N = 105;\ C = 5$$
$$= 27 + \frac{43}{105} \times 5 = 27 + 2.05 = \mathbf{29.05.}$$

$$\text{Median} = \text{size of } \frac{N}{2}\text{th item} = \frac{105}{2} = 52.5\text{th item}$$

$$\therefore \quad \text{Median} = L_1 + \frac{\frac{N}{2} - c.f.}{f} \times i$$
$$= 24.5 + \frac{52.5 - 24}{38} \times 5 = 24.5 + 3.75 = \mathbf{28.25.}$$

Mode lies in the class 24.5–29.5

$$Z = L_1 + \frac{f_1 - f_0}{2f_1 - f_0 - f_2} \times i$$
$$L_1 = 24.5;\ f_1 = 38;\ f_0 = 20;\ f_2 = 24;\ i = 5$$
$$= 24.5 + \frac{38 - 20}{76 - 20 - 24} \times 5$$
$$= 24.5 + 2.81 = \mathbf{27.31}$$

Problem 150. Calculate the mean, median and the mode for the following data.

Profits per shop (Rs. in lakhs)	*No. of shops*
0–10	12
10–20	18
20–30	27
30–40	20
40–50	17
50–60	6

(*B.A. Bombay*)

Solution:

Computation of Mean Median and Mode

Profits (*in Rs.*)	m	*No. of shops f*	$d' = \frac{m-25}{10}$	fd'	*c.f*
0–10	5	12	−2	−24	12
10–20	15	18	−1	−18	30
20–30	25	27	0	0	57
30–40	35	20	1	20	77
40–50	45	17	2	34	94
50–60	55	6	3	18	100
		N = 100		$\Sigma fd' = 30$	

Mean :

$$\overline{X} = A + \frac{\Sigma fd'}{N} \times C$$

$$A = 25; \Sigma fd^2 = 30; N = 100; C = 10$$

$$= 25 + \frac{30}{100} \times 10 = 25 + 3 \quad = \mathbf{28}$$

$$\text{Median} = \text{size of } \frac{N}{2}\text{th item}$$

$$= \text{size of } \frac{100}{2}\text{th item}$$

$$= \text{50th item which lies in the class 20–30}$$

$$\text{Median} = L_1 + \frac{\frac{N}{2} - c.f.}{N} \times i$$

$$L_1 = 20; \frac{N}{2} = 50; c.f = 30; f = 27; i = 10$$

$$= 20 + \frac{50 - 30}{27} \times 10 = 20 + 7.41$$

$$= \mathbf{27.41}$$

Made : By inspection method mode lies in the class 20–30

$$Z = L_1 + \frac{f_1 - f_0}{2f_1 - f_0 - f_2} \times i$$

$$L_1 = 20; f_1 = 27; f_0 = 18; f_2 = 20; i = 10$$

$$= 20 + \frac{27 - 18}{2 \times 27 - 18 - 20} \times 10 = 20 + 5.63$$

$$= \mathbf{25.63}$$

Problem 151. Calculate the mean, the median and the mode from the following data :

Age	*No. of people*
55–60	7
50–55	13
45–50	15
40–45	20
35–40	30
30–35	33
25–30	28
20–25	14

(*B.Com. Madurai*)

Solution: **Computation of Mean, Median and Mode**

Age	m	f	$d' = \frac{m - 37.5}{5}$	fd'	*c.f.*
20–25	22.5	14	−3	−42	14
25–30	27.5	28	−2	−56	42
30–35	32.5	33	−1	−33	75
35–40	37.5	30	0	0	105
40–45	42.5	20	1	20	125
45–50	47.5	15	2	30	145
50–55	52.5	13	3	39	153
55–60	57.5	7	4	28	260
		N = 160		$\Sigma fd' = -14$	

Mean :

$$\overline{X} = A + \frac{\Sigma fd'}{N} \times C$$

$$A = 37.5; \Sigma fd' = -14; N = 160; C = 5$$

$$= 37.5 - \frac{14}{160} \times 5 = 37.5 - 0.44 \quad = \mathbf{37.06}$$

$$\text{Median} = \text{size of } \frac{N}{2}\text{th item}$$

$$= \text{size of } \frac{160}{2}\text{th item}$$

$$= \text{80th item which lies in the class } 35 - 40$$

$$\text{Median} = L_1 + \frac{\frac{N}{2} - c.f.}{f} \times i$$

$$L_1 = 35; \frac{N}{2} = 80;$$

$$c.f = 75; f = 30; i = 5$$

$$= 35 + \frac{80 - 75}{30} \times 5 = 35 + 0.83 \quad = \mathbf{35.83}$$

Mode : By inspection method mode lies in the class 30–35

$$Z = L_1 + \frac{f_1 - f_0}{2f_1 - f_0 - f_2} \times i$$

$$L_1 = 30; f_1 = 33; f_0 = 28; f_2 = 30; i = 5$$

$$= 30 + \frac{33 - 28}{2 \times 33 - 28 - 30} \times 5 = 30 + 3.13$$

$$= \mathbf{33.13}$$

Problem 152. Calculate the mean and mode for the data given below :

Weekly earnings (in Rs.)	*No. of persons*	*Weekly earnings (in Rs.)*	*No. of persons*
50–53	3	65–68	28
53–56	8	68–71	16
56–59	14	71–74	10
59–62	30	74–77	5
62–65	36		

(*B.Com., Nagpur*)

Solution:

Computation of Mean, Median and Mode

Weekly earnings in Rs.	*fm*	*f*	$d' = \frac{m - 63.5}{3}$	*fd'*	*c.f*
50–53	51.5	3	–4	–12	3
53–56	54.5	8	–3	–24	11
56–59	57.5	14	–2	–28	25
59–62	60.5	30	–1	–30	55
62–65	63.5	36	0	0	91
65–68	66.5	28	1	28	119
68–71	69.5	16	2	32	135
71–74	72.5	10	3	30	145
74–77	75.5	5	4	20	150
		N = 150		$\Sigma fd' = 16$	

Mean :

$$\overline{X} = A + \frac{\Sigma fd'}{N} \times C$$

$$A = 63.5;\ \Sigma fd' = 16;\ N = 150;\ C = 3$$

$$= 63.5 + \frac{16}{150} \times 3 = 63.5 + 0.32 \quad = \mathbf{63.82}$$

$$\text{Median} = \text{size of } \frac{N}{2}\text{th item}$$

$$= \text{size of } \frac{150}{2}\text{th item}$$

= 75th item which lies in the class 62–65

$$\text{Median} = L_1 + \frac{\frac{N}{2} - c.f.}{f} \times i$$

$$L_1 = 62, \frac{N}{2} = 75;$$

$$c.f = 55;\ f = 36;\ i = 3$$

$$= 62 + \frac{75 - 55}{36} \times 3 = 62 + 1.67 \quad = \mathbf{63.67}$$

By inspection method mode lies in the class 62–65

$$\text{Mode}: Z = L_1 + \frac{f_1 - f_0}{2f_2 - f_0 - f_2} \times i$$

$$L_1 = 62;\ f_1 = 36;\ f_0 = 30;\ f_2 = 28;\ i = 3$$

$$= 62 + \frac{36 - 30}{2 \times 36 - 30 - 28} \times 3 = 62 + 1.29 \quad = \mathbf{63.29}$$

Problem 153. Define mean, median and mode in a statistical data. For the following distribution of income groups, find mean, median and mode :

Income (in Rs.)	*No. of persons*	*Income (in Rs.)*	*No. of persons*
0–200	80	600–800	80
200–400	165	800–1,000	32
400–600	230	1,000–1,200	13

(*B.Com., Bombay*)

Solution:

Computation of Mean Median and Mode

Income in Rs.	m	f	$d' = \frac{m-500}{200}$	fd'	*c.f.*
0–200	100	80	–2	–160	80
200–400	300	165	–1	–165	245
400–600	500	230	0	0	475
600–800	700	80	1	80	555
800–1,000	900	32	2	64	587
1,000–1,200	1,100	13	3	39	600
		N = 600		$\Sigma fd' = -142$	

Mean :

$$\overline{X} = A + \frac{\Sigma fd'}{N} \times C$$

$$A = 500; \Sigma fd' = -142; N = 600; C = 200$$

$$= 500 - \frac{142}{600} \times 200 = 500 - 47.33$$

$$= \mathbf{452.67}$$

Median

$$= \text{size of } \frac{N}{2}\text{th item}$$

$$= \text{size of } \frac{600}{2}\text{th item}$$

= 300th item which lies in the class 400–600

Median

$$= L_1 + \frac{\frac{N}{2} - c.f.}{f} \times i$$

$$L_1 = 400;\ \frac{N}{2} = 300;$$

$$c.f = 245;\ f = 230;\ i = 200$$

$$= 400 + \frac{300 - 245}{230} \times 200 = 400 + 47.83$$

$$= \mathbf{447.83}$$

Mode : By inspection method mode lies in the class 400–600

$$Z = L_1 + \frac{f_1 - f_0}{2f_1 - f_0 - f_2} \times i$$

$$L_1 = 400;\ f_1 = 230;\ f_0 = 165;\ f_2 = 80;\ i = 200$$

$$= 400 + \frac{230 - 165}{2 \times 230 - 165 - 80} \times 200 = 400 + 60.47$$

$$= \mathbf{460.47}$$

Problem 154. The following is the frequency distribution of the marks obtained by 250 students in an examination. Compute the mean, the median and the mode :

Marks obtained	*No. of students*	*Marks obtained*	*No. of students*
0–10	15	40–50	12
10–20	20	50–60	31
20–30	25	60–70	71
30–40	24	70–80	52

(*B. Com., Nagpur*)

Solution:

Computation of Mean, Median and the Mode

Marks	*m*	*f*	$d' = \frac{m - 35}{10}$	fd'	*c.f.*
0–10	5	15	−3	−45	15
10–20	15	20	−2	−40	35
20–30	25	25	−1	−25	60
30–40	35	24	0	0	84
40–50	45	12	1	12	96
50–60	55	31	2	62	127
60–70	65	71	3	213	198
70–80	75	52	4	208	250
		N = 250		$\Sigma fd' = 385$	

$$\text{Mean} : \bar{X} = A + \frac{\Sigma fd'}{N} \times C$$

$$A = 35;\ \Sigma fd' = 385;\ N = 250;\ i = 10$$

$$= 35 + \frac{385}{250} \times 10 = 35 + 15.4 = \mathbf{50.4}$$

$$\text{Median} = \text{size of } \frac{N}{2}\text{th item}$$

$$= \text{size of } \frac{250}{2}\text{th item}$$

= 125th item which lies in the class 50–60

$$\text{Median} = L_1 + \frac{\frac{N}{2} - c.f.}{f} \times i$$

$$L_1 = 50;\ \frac{N}{2} = 125$$

$$c.f = 96;\ f = 31;\ i = 10$$

$$= 50 + \frac{125 - 96}{31} \times 10 = 50 + 9.35 = \mathbf{59.35}$$

Mode : By inspection method mode lies in the class 60–70

$$Z = L_1 + \frac{f_1 - f_0}{2f_1 - f_0 - f_2} \times i$$

$$L_1 = 60;\ f_1 = 71;\ f_0 = 52;\ i = 10$$

$$= 60 + \frac{71 - 31}{2 \times 71 - 31 - 52} \times 10 = 60 + 6.78 \quad = \mathbf{66.78}$$

Problem 155. The age in completed years of 50 persons is given below :

32	61	52	56	22	49	97	35	20	30
95	67	42	20	31	64	20	10	62	60
27	53	31	9	54	25	43	47	35	21
43	75	45	22	36	13	46	23	51	11
15	39	50	42	77	73	81	40	40	55

Prepare frequency table taking 10–19, 20–29,. . . as class intervals and calculate mean and modal age.

(*B.Com., Bombay*)

Solution:

Computation of Mean and Mode

Age	*Tally sheet*	*f*	*m*	$d' = \frac{m - 44.5}{10}$	*fd'*
0–9	|	1	4.5	−4	−4
10–19	||||	4	14.5	−3	−12
20–29	卌 |||	8	24.5	−2	−16
30–39	卌 ||||	9	34.5	−1	−9
40–49	卌 卌	10	44.5	0	0
50–59	卌 ||	7	54.5	1	7
60–69	卌	5	64.5	2	10
70–79	|||	3	74.5	3	9
80–89	|	1	84.5	4	4
90–99	||	2	94.5	5	10
		N = 50			$\Sigma fd' = -1$

$$\bar{X} = A + \frac{\Sigma fd'}{N} \times C$$

$$A = 44.5; \Sigma fd' = -1; N = 50; i = 10$$

$$= 44.5 - \frac{1}{50} \times 10 = 44.5 - 0.2 = \mathbf{44.3}$$

$$Z = L_1 + \frac{f_1 - f_0}{2f_1 - f_0 - f_2} \times i$$

$$L = 39.5; f_1 = 10; f_0 = 9; f_2 = 7; i = 10$$

$$= 39.5; + \frac{10 - 9}{20 - 9 - 7} \times 10 = 39.5 + 2.5 \quad = \mathbf{42\ years}$$

Problem 156. The following table gives the marks obtained by students in a class test:

Marks	*Students*	*Marks*	*Students*
32–36	10	48–52	51
36–40	37	52–56	35
40–44	65	56–60	18
44–48	80	60–64	4

Find the mean, median and modal marks.

(*M. Com., Kurukshetra*)

Solution:

Computation of Mean, Median and Mode

Marks	*m*	*f*	$d' = \frac{m - 46}{4}$	*fd'*	*c.f.*
32–36	34	10	−3	−30	10
36–40	38	37	−2	−74	47
40–44	42	65	−1	−65	112
44–48	46	80	0	0	192
48–52	50	51	1	51	243
52–56	54	35	2	70	278
56–60	58	18	3	54	296
60–64	62	4	4	16	300
		N = 300		$\Sigma fd' = +22$	

$$\overline{X} = A + \frac{\Sigma fd'}{N} \times C$$

$$A = 46;\ \Sigma fd' = +22;\ N = 300;\ C = 4$$

$$\overline{X} = 46 + \frac{22}{300} + 4$$

$$= 46 + 0.29$$

$$= \mathbf{46.29}$$

$$\text{Median} = \text{size of } \left(\frac{N}{2}\right) \text{th item}$$

$$= \text{size of } \left(\frac{300}{2}\right) \text{th item} = 150\text{th item}$$

∴ Median lies in the class 44–48

$$\text{Median} = L + \frac{\frac{N}{2} - c.f.}{f} \times i$$

$$L = 44;\ \frac{N}{2} = 150$$

$$c.f = 112;\ f = 80;\ i = 4$$

$$\text{Median} = 44 + \frac{150 - 112}{80} \times 4$$

$$= 44 + \frac{152}{80}$$

$$= 44 + 1.9$$

$$= \mathbf{45.9}$$

By inspection mode, lies in the class 44–48

$$\text{Mode} = L_1 + \frac{f_1 - f_0}{2f_1 - f_0 - f_2} \times i$$

$$L_1 = 44;\ f_1 = 80;\ f_0 = 65;\ f_2 = 51;\ i = 4$$

$$Z = 44 + \frac{80 - 65}{2 \times 80 - 65 - 51} \times 4$$

$$= 44 + 1.36$$

$$= \mathbf{45.36}$$

Problem 157. Compute the mean, median and the mode wages from the following :

Wages in Rs.	*No. of workers*
30–35	12
35–40	18
40–45	22
45–50	27
50–55	17
55–60	23
60–65	29
65–70	8

(*B.A. Bombay*)

Solution:

Computation of Mean, Median and Mode

Wages (Rs.)	m	f	$d' = \frac{m - 47.5}{5}$	fd'	*c.f.*
30–35	32.5	12	–3	–36	12
35–40	37.5	18	–2	–36	30
40–45	42.5	22	–1	–22	52
45–50	47.5	27	0	0	79
50–55	52.5	17	1	17	96
55–60	57.5	23	2	46	119
60–65	62.5	29	3	87	148
65–70	67.5	8	4	32	156
		N = 156		$\Sigma fd' = 88$	

$$\text{Mean: } \overline{X} = A + \frac{\Sigma fd'}{N} \times C$$

$$A = 47.5; \Sigma fd' = 88; N = 156; C = 5$$

$$= 47.5 + \frac{88}{156} \times 5 = 47.5 + 2.82 \quad = \mathbf{50.32}$$

$$\text{Median} = \text{size of } \frac{N}{2}\text{th item}$$

$$= \text{size of } \frac{156}{2}\text{th item}$$

= 78th item which lies in the class 45–50

$$\text{Median} = L_1 + \frac{\frac{N}{2} - c.f.}{f} \times i$$

$$L_1 = 45; \frac{N}{2} = 78; c.f. = 52;$$

$$f = 27; i = 5$$

$$= 45 + \frac{78 - 52}{27} \times 5 = 45 + 4.81 \quad = \mathbf{49.81}$$

Mode : By inspection method mode lies in the class 45–50

$$Z = L_1 + \frac{f_1 - f_0}{2f_1 - f_0 - f_2} \times i$$

$$L_1 = 45;\ f_1 = 27;\ f_0 = 22;$$

$$f_2 = 17;\ i = 5$$

$$= 45 + \frac{27 - 22}{2 \times 27 - 22 - 17} \times 5 = 45 + 1.67 \quad = \mathbf{46.67}$$

Problem 158. Calculate mean, median and mode from the following data :

Class interval	*Frequency*	*Class interval*	*frequency*
10–20	4	10–60	124
10–30	16	10–70	137
10–40	56	10–80	146
10–50	97	10–90	150

(*B. Com. Kurukhetra, Madurai*)

Solution:

Computation of Mean, Median and Mode

Class	m	f	$d' = \frac{m-45}{10}$	fd'	*c.f.*
10–20	15	4	–3	–12	4
20–30	25	(16 – 4) = 12	–2	–24	16
30–40	35	(56 – 16) = 40	–1	–40	56
40–50	45	(97 – 56) = 41	0	0	97
50–60	55	(124 – 97) = 27	1	27	124
60–70	65	(137 – 124) = 13	2	26	137
70–80	75	(146 – 137) = 9	3	27	146
80–90	85	(150 – 146) = 4	4	16	150
		N = 150		$\Sigma fd'$ = 20	

First we have to find out simple frequencies to solve the problem. The process is shown above.

$$\overline{X} = A + \frac{\Sigma fd'}{N} \times C$$

$$A = 45;\ \Sigma fd' = +20;\ N = 150;\ C = 10$$

$$\overline{X} = 45 + \frac{20}{150} \times 10$$

$$= 45 + 1.33$$

$$= \mathbf{46.33}$$

$$\text{Median} = \text{size of } \left(\frac{N}{2}\right) \text{th item}$$

$$= \text{size of } \left(\frac{150}{2}\right) \text{th item}$$

$$= \text{size of 75th item}$$

$\therefore$ Median lies in the class 40–50

$$\text{Median} = L + \frac{\frac{N}{2} - c.f.}{f} \times i$$

$$L = 40; \frac{N}{2} = 75; c.f. = 56;$$

$$f = 41; i = 10$$

$$\text{Median} = 40 + \frac{75 - 56}{41} \times 10$$

$$= 40 + \frac{190}{41}$$

$$= 40 + 4.634$$

$$= \mathbf{44.634}$$

By inspection method, mode lies in the class 40–50

$$z = L + \frac{f_1 - f_0}{2f_1 - f_0 - f_2} \times i$$

$$L = 40; f_1 = 41; f_0 = 40;$$

$$f_2 = 27; i = 10$$

$$z = 40 + \frac{41 - 40}{2 \times 41 - 40 - 27} \times 10$$

$$= 40 + 0.67$$

$$= \mathbf{40.67}$$

Problem 159. Find the mean, median and mode from the following frequency distribution :

Output in units	*No. of workers*
300–309	9
310–319	20
320–329	24
330–339	38
340–349	48
350–359	27
360–369	17
370–379	6

(*B. Com. Calcutta, Bombay*)

Solution:

Computation of Mean, Median and Mode

Output in units	*Class adjustment*	*m.p.*	*f*	$d' = \frac{m - 334.5}{10}$	fd'	*c.f*
300–309	299.5–309.5	304.5	9	–3	–27	9
310–319	309.5–319.5	314.5	20	–2	–40	29
320–329	319.5–329.5	324.5	24	–1	–24	53
330–339	329.5–339.5	334.5	38	0	0	91
340–349	339.5–349.5	344.5	48	1	48	139
350–359	349.5–359.5	355.5	27	2	54	166
360–369	359.5–369.5	365.5	17	3	51	183
370–379	369.5–379.5	375.5	6	4	24	189
			N = 189		$\Sigma fd' = 86$	

$$\text{Mean}: \overline{X} = A + \frac{\Sigma fd'}{N} \times C$$

$$A = 334.5, \Sigma fd' = 86, N = 189, C = 10$$

$$= 334.5 + \frac{86}{189} \times 10$$

$$= 334.5 + 4.55$$

$$= \mathbf{339.05}$$

Median :

$$\text{Median} = \text{size of } \frac{N}{2}\text{th item}$$

$$= \text{size of } \frac{189}{2}\text{th item}$$

$$= 94.5\text{th item which lies in the class } 339.5\text{–}349.5$$

$$\text{Median} = L_1 + \frac{\frac{N}{2} - c.f.}{N} \times i$$

$$= 339.5 + \frac{94.5 - 91}{48} \times 10$$

$$= 339.5 + \frac{35}{48} = 339.5 + 0.73$$

$$= \mathbf{340.23}$$

Mode :

By inspection method mode lies in the class 339.5–349.5

$$Z = L_1 + \frac{f_1 - f_0}{2f_1 - f_0 - f_2} \times i$$

$$L_1 = 339.5,\ f_1 = 48,\ f_0 = 38,\ f_2 = 27,\ i = 10$$

$$= 339.5 + \frac{48 - 38}{2 \times 48 - 38 - 27} \times 10$$

$$= 339.5 + \frac{100}{31} = 339.5 + 3.23$$

$$= \mathbf{342.73}$$

Problem 160. In an examination of 675 candidates, the examiner supplied the following information:

Marks obtained	*No. of candidates*
Less than 10 %	7
,, 20 %	39
,, 30 %	95
,, 40 %	201
,, 50 %	381
,, 60 %	545
,, 70 %	631
,, 80 %	675

Calculate the mean, median and mode of the percentage marks obtained.

(*B.A. Ecos.* (*Hons*), *Delhi*)

Solution:

Computation of Mean, Median and Mode

Marks	*m.p.*	*f*	$(m-35)/10d'$	fd'	*c.f.*
0–10	5	7	–3	–21	7
10–20	15	32	–2	–64	39
20–30	25	56	–1	–56	95
30–40	35	106	0	0	201
40–50	45	180	1	180	381
50–60	55	164	2	328	545
60–70	65	86	3	258	631
70–80	75	44	4	176	675
		N = 675		$\Sigma fd' = 801$	

$$\text{Mean: } \overline{X} = A + \frac{\Sigma fd'}{N} \times C$$

$$= 35 + \frac{801}{675} \times 10 = 35 + 11.87 \qquad = \mathbf{46.87}$$

$$\text{Median} = L_1 + \frac{\frac{N}{2} - c.f.}{f} \times i$$

$$= 40 + \frac{337.5 - 201}{180} \times 10 = 40 + 7.58 \qquad = \mathbf{47.58}$$

By inspection method mode lies in the class 40–50

$$\text{Mode, } Z = L_1 + \frac{f_1 - f_0}{2f_1 - f_0 - f_2} \times i$$

$$= 40 + \frac{180 - 106}{2 \times 180 - 106 - 164} \times 10$$

$$= 40 + 8.22 \qquad = \mathbf{48.22}$$

Problem 161. Calculate the arithmetic mean, median and mode from the following distribution :

Height (inches)	*No. of men*	*Height (inches)*	*No. of men*
60–63	8	69–72	66
63–66	28	72–75	16
66–69	118	75–78	4

(*B. Com. Andhra*)

Solution:

Computation of Mean, Median and Mode

Height	*m.p.*	*No. of men*	$(m-67.5)/3 = d'$	fd'	*c.f.*
60–63	61.5	8	–2	–16	8
63–66	64.5	28	–1	–28	36
66–69	67.5	118	0	0	154
69–72	70.5	66	1	66	220
72–75	73.5	16	2	32	236
75–78	76.5	4	3	12	240
		N = 240		$\Sigma fd' = 66$	

$$\text{Mean} : \overline{X} = A + \frac{\Sigma fd'}{N} \times C$$
$$= 67.5 + \frac{66}{240} \times 3$$
$$= 67.5 + 0.83$$
$$= \mathbf{68.33}$$

$$\text{Median} = L_1 + \frac{\frac{N}{2} - c.f.}{f} \times i$$
$$= 66 + \frac{120 - 36}{118} \times 3$$
$$= 66 + \frac{84 \times 3}{118}$$
$$= 66 + 2.14$$
$$= \mathbf{68.14}$$

By inspection method mode lies in the class 66–69.

$$\text{Mode} : Z = L_1 + \frac{f_1 - f_0}{2f_1 - f_0 - f_2} \times i$$
$$= 66 + \frac{118 - 28}{2 \times 118 - 28 - 66} \times 3$$
$$= 66 + \frac{270}{142}$$
$$= 66 + 1.9$$
$$= \mathbf{67.9}$$

Problem 162. Calculate the mean, median and mode for the data given below :

Weekly earnings (in Rs.)	*No. of workers*	*Weekly earnings (in Rs.)*	*No. of workers*
50–53	3	65–68	28
53–56	8	68–71	16
56–59	14	71–74	10
59–62	30	74–77	5
62–65	36		

(*B.Com. Nagpur*)

Solution:

Computation of Mean, Median and Mode

Weekly earnings	f	m	$d' = \frac{m - 63.5}{3}$	fd'	*c.f.*
50–53	3	51.5	−4	−12	3
53–56	8	54.5	−3	−24	11
56–59	14	57.5	−2	−28	25
59–62	30	60.5	−1	−30	55
62–65	36	63.5	0	0	91
65–68	28	66.5	+1	+28	119
68–71	16	69.5	+2	+32	135
71–74	10	72.5	+3	+30	145
74–77	5	75.5	+4	+20	150
	N = 150			$\Sigma fd' = +16$	

$$\overline{X} = A \pm \frac{\Sigma fd'}{N} \times C = 63.5 + \frac{16}{150} \times 3$$
$$= 63.5 + 0.32 = \mathbf{63.82}$$

$$\text{Median} = \frac{N}{2} = \frac{150}{2} = 75\text{th item}$$

$$\text{Median} = L_1 + \frac{\frac{N}{2} - c.f.}{f} \times i$$
$$= 62 + \frac{75 - 55}{36} \times 3 = 62 + 1.67 = \mathbf{63.67}$$

Mode lies in the class, 62–65

$$Z = L_1 + \frac{f_1 - f_0}{2f_1 - f_0 - f_2} \times i$$
$$= 62 + \frac{36 - 30}{2 \times 36 - 30 - 28} \times 3$$
$$= 62 + 1.29$$
$$= \mathbf{63.29}$$

Problem 163. A time and motion study of a certain operation shows the following distribution for 100 workers. Calculate mean, median and mode of the distribution :

Time (minutes)	10–15	15–20	20–25	25–30	30–35	35–40	40–45
No. of workers	8	14	18	25	15	14	6

(*B. Com. Bombay*)

Solution:

Time	*m.p.*	*f*	$(m - 27.5)/5 = d'$	fd'	*c.f*
10–15	12.5	8	−3	−24	8
15–20	17.5	14	−2	−28	22
20–25	22.5	18	−1	−18	40
25–30	27.5	25	0	0	65
30–35	32.5	15	1	15	80
35–40	37.5	14	2	28	94
40–45	42.5	6	3	18	100
		N = 100		$\Sigma fd' = -9$	

Mean: $$\overline{X} = A + \frac{\Sigma fd'}{N} \times C$$
$$= 27.5 - \frac{9}{100} \times 5 = 27.5 - 0.45$$
$$= \mathbf{27.05}$$

Median: $$Me = L_1 + \frac{\frac{N}{2} - c.f.}{f} \times i$$

$$= 25 + \frac{50 - 40}{25} \times 5 = 25 + 2$$

$$= \mathbf{27}$$

Mode : $$Z = L_1 + \frac{f_1 - f_0}{2f_1 - f_0 - f_2} \times i$$

$$= 25 + \frac{25 - 18}{50 - 18 - 15} \times 5 = 25 + 2.06$$

$$= \mathbf{27.06}$$

Problem 164. Find the mean, median and mode for the following data.

Weight of students (lbs)	*No. of students*
90–100	10
100–110	37
110–120	65
120–130	80
130–140	51
140–150	35
150–160	18
160–170	4

(*B. Com. Madurai*)

Solution:

Computation of Mean, Median and Mode

	m.p.	*f*	$(m - 125)/10 = d'$	fd'	*c.f*
90–100	95	10	−3	−30	10
100–110	105	37	−2	−74	47
110–120	115	65	−1	−65	112
120–130	125	80	0	0	192
130–140	135	51	1	51	243
140–150	145	35	2	70	278
150–160	155	18	3	54	296
160–170	165	4	4	16	300
		N = 300		$\Sigma fd' = 22$	

Mean : $$\overline{X} = A + \frac{\Sigma fd'}{N} \times C$$

$$= 125 + \frac{22}{300} \times 10$$

$$= 125 + 0.73$$

$$= \mathbf{125.73}$$

Median : $$Me = L_1 + \frac{\frac{N}{2} - c.f.}{f} \times i$$

$$= 120 + \frac{\frac{300}{2} - 112}{80} \times 10$$

$$= 120 + \frac{150 - 112}{80} \times 10 = 120 + 4.75$$

$$= \mathbf{124.75}$$

Mode : $$Z = L_1 + \frac{f_1 - f_0}{2f_1 - f_0 - f_2} \times i$$

$$= 120 + \frac{80 - 65}{2 \times 80 - 65 - 51} \times 10$$

$$= 120 + \frac{150}{44} = 120 + 3.41$$

$$= \mathbf{123.41}$$

Problem 165. For the following frequency table calculate mean, median and mode.

Weekly packet expenditure	*No. of persons*
20–40	6
40–60	9
60–80	11
80–100	14
100–120	20
120–140	15
140–160	10
160–180	8
180–200	7

(*B. Com., Madras*)

Solution:

Weekly packet expend.	*m.p.*	*f*	$(m - 110)/20 = d'$	fd'	*c.f*
20–40	30	6	−4	−24	6
40–60	50	9	−3	−27	15
60–80	70	11	−2	−22	26
80–100	90	14	−1	−14	40
100–120	110	20	0	0	60
120–140	130	15	1	15	75
140–160	150	10	2	20	85
160–180	170	8	3	24	93
180–200	190	7	4	28	100
		N = 100		$\Sigma fd' = 0$	

Mean : $$\overline{X} = A + \frac{\Sigma fd'}{N} \times C$$

$$= 110 + \frac{0}{100} \times 20$$

$$= \mathbf{110}$$

Median : $$Me = L_1 + \frac{\frac{N}{2} - c.f.}{f} \times i$$

$$= 100 + \frac{\frac{100}{2} - 40}{20} \times 20$$

$$= 100 + \frac{50 - 40}{20} \times 20 = 100 + \frac{200}{20}$$

$$= \mathbf{110}$$

Mode : $$Z = L_1 + \frac{f_1 - f_0}{2f_1 - f_0 - f_2} \times i$$

$$= 100 + \frac{20 - 14}{2 \times 20 - 14 - 15} \times 20$$

$$= 100 + \frac{120}{11}$$

$$= 100 + 10.91$$

$$= \mathbf{110.91}$$

Problem 166. The I. Q. test of 510 students, of a college is as follows :

I.Q.							
20–29	30–39	40–49	50–59	60–69	70—79	80–89	90–99
No. of students							
41	52	61	190	67	45	40	14

Find mean, median and mode.

(*B.Com. Jabalpur*)

Solution:

I.Q. Test	*m.p.*	*f*	$(m - 54.5)/10 = d'$	fd'	*c.f*
19.5–29.5	24.5	41	−3	−123	41
29.5–39.5	34.5	52	−2	−104	93
39.5–49.5	44.5	61	−1	−61	154
49.5–59.5	54.5	190	0	0	344
59.5–69.5	64.5	67	1	67	411
69.5–79.5	74.5	45	2	90	456
79.5–89.5	84.5	40	3	120	496
89.5–99.5	94.5	14	4	56	510
		N = 510		$\Sigma fd' = 45$	

Mean: $$\overline{X} = A + \frac{\Sigma fd}{N} \times C$$

$$= 54.5 + \frac{45}{510} \times 10$$
$$= 54.5 + 0.88 \quad = \mathbf{55.38}$$

Median: $$Me = L_1 + \frac{\frac{N}{2} - c.f.}{f} \times i$$
$$= 49.5 + \frac{\frac{510}{2} - 154}{190} \times 10$$
$$= 49.5 + \frac{255 - 154}{190} \times 10$$
$$= 49.5 + \frac{101}{19} = 49.5 + 5.32 \quad = \mathbf{54.82}$$

Mode: $$Z = L_1 + \frac{f_1 - f_0}{2f_1 - f_0 - f_2} \times i$$
$$= 49.5 + \frac{190 - 61}{2 \times 190 - 61 - 67} \times 10$$
$$= 49.5 + \frac{1290}{252}$$
$$= 49.5 + 5.12 \quad = \mathbf{54.62}$$

Problem 167. The table below gives the distribution of the sample of 50 people according to weight. Calculate the mean and mode.

Weight (in kilograms)	*Frequency*
45–50	2
50–55	3
55–60	5
60–65	7
65–70	9
70–75	11
75–80	7
80–85	2
85–90	3
90–95	1

(*B.A. Bombay*)

Solution:

Computation of Mean and Mode

X	m	f	$d' = \frac{m - 62.5}{5}$	fd'
45–50	47.5	2	−3	−6
50–55	52.5	3	−2	−6
55–60	57.5	5	−1	−5
60–65	62.5	7	0	0
65–70	67.5	9	1	9
70–75	72.5	11	2	22
75–80	77.5	7	3	21
80–85	82.5	2	4	8
85–90	87.5	3	5	15
90–95	92.5	1	6	6
		N = 50		$\Sigma fd' = +64$

$$\overline{X} = A \pm \frac{\Sigma fd'}{N} \times C$$

$$A = 62.5;\ \Sigma\, fd' = +64;\ N = 50;\ C = 5$$

$$\overline{X} = 62.5 + \frac{64}{50} \times 5$$

$$= 62.5 + 6.4 = \mathbf{68.9}$$

Mode lies in the class 70–75

$$= L_1 + \frac{f_1 - f_0}{2f_1 - f_0 - f_2} \times i$$

$$L_1 = 70;\ f_1 = 11;\ f_0 = 9;\ f_2 = 7;\ i = 5$$

$$Z = 70 + \frac{11 - 9}{2 \times 11 - 9 - 7} \times 5$$

$$= 70 + 1.67 \quad = \mathbf{71.67}$$

Problem 168. The frequency distribution of weight in grams of mangoes of a given variety is given below. Calculate the arithmetic mean, median and mode.

Weight (gms.)	*No. of mangoes*	*Weight (gms.)*	*No. of mangoes*
410–419	14	450–459	45
420–429	20	460–469	11
420–439	42	470–479	7
440–449	54		

(B.A. (Hons) Delhi)

Solution:

Computation of Mean, Median and Mode

Weight	*Weight*	f	*m.p.*	$d' = \frac{m - 444.5}{10}$	fd''	cf
410–419	409.5–419.5	14	414.5	−3	−42	14
420–429	419.5–429.5	20	424.5	−2	−40	34
430–439	429.5–439.5	42	434.5	−1	−42	76
440–449	439.5–449.5	54	444.5	0	0	130
450–459	449.5–459.5	45	454.5	1	45	175
460–469	459.5–469.5	18	464.5	2	36	193
470–479	469.5–479.5	7	474.5	3	21	200
		N = 200			$\Sigma\, fd' = -22$	

Mean $\overline{X} = A + \frac{\Sigma\, fd'}{N} \times C$

$$A = 444.5,\ N = 200, C = 10,\ \Sigma\, fd' = -22$$

$$\overline{X} = 444.5 - \frac{22}{200} \times 10$$

$$= 444.5 - \frac{220}{200}$$

$$= 444.5 - 1.1$$

$$\overline{X} = \mathbf{443.4}$$

Median.

$$\text{Median} = \text{size of } \frac{N}{2}\text{th item} = \frac{200}{2} = 100\text{th item}$$

Which lies in the class 439.5–449.5

$$\text{Me} = \text{L} + \frac{N/2 - Cf}{f} \times \text{C}$$

$$\text{N}/2 = \frac{200}{2} = 100, \text{L} = 439.5, cf = 76$$

$$f = 54, \text{C} = 10$$

$$\text{Me} = 439.5 + \frac{100 - 76}{54} \times 10$$

$$= 439.5 + \frac{240}{54}$$

$$= 439.5 + 4.44$$

$$\text{Median} = \mathbf{443.94}$$

$$\text{Mode:} \quad = \text{L}_1 + \frac{f_1 - f_0}{2f_1 - f_0 - f_2} \times \text{C}$$

By inspection mode lies in the class 439.5–449.5 L= 439.5, $f_1 = 54$, $f_0 = 42$, $f_2 = 45$ C=10

$$\text{M} = 439.5 + \frac{54 - 42}{2 \times 54 - 42 - 45} \times 10$$

$$= 439.5 + \frac{120}{21}$$

$$= 439.5 + 5.71$$

$$\text{Mode} = \mathbf{445.21}$$

Problem 169. The following are the marks obtained by 40 students in statistics. Tabulate the above data in the form of a continuous series with class interval 10, one of the groups being 20–29. Calculate mean, median, mode and fourth decile of tabulated data :

35	10	55	22	5	48	30	20	30	23
50	32	7	18	15	55	37	29	25	42
33	45	37	26	29	32	38	24	30	10
8	7	15	45	48	50	27	29	30	15

(*B. Com. Bombay*)

Solution:

Computation of Mean, Median, Mode and Fourth Deciles

Class	*Tally marks*	*f*	*m*	$d' = \frac{m - 24.5}{10}$	*fd'*	*c.f.*
0–9	||||	4	4.5	−2	−8	4
10–19	~~||||~~ |	6	14.5	−1	−6	10
20–29	~~||||~~ ~~||||~~	10	24.5	0	0	20
30–39	~~||||~~ ~~||||~~ |	11	34.5	1	11	31
40–49	~~||||~~	5	44.5	2	10	36
50–59	||||	4	54.5	3	12	40
		N = 40			$\Sigma fd' = 19$	

$$\text{Mean :} \quad \overline{\text{X}} = \text{A} + \frac{\Sigma fd'}{\text{N}} \times \text{C}$$

$$A = 24.5; \Sigma fd' = 19; N = 40; C = 10$$
$$= 24.5 + \frac{19}{40} \times 10 = 24.5 + 4.75$$
$$= \mathbf{29.25}$$

$$\text{Median} = \text{size of } \frac{N}{2}\text{th item}$$
$$= \text{size of } \frac{40}{2}\text{th item}$$
$$= \text{20th item which lies in the class} 19.5 - 29.5$$
$$\text{Median} = L_1 + \frac{\frac{N}{2} - c.f.}{f} \times i$$
$$L_1 = 19.5; \frac{N}{2} = 20;$$
$$c.f = 10; f = 10; i = 10$$
$$= 19.5 + \frac{20 - 10}{10} \times 10 = 19.5 + 10 \qquad = \mathbf{29.5}$$

By inspection method mode lies in the class 29.5–39.5

$$\text{Mode : } Z = L_1 + \frac{f_1 - f_0}{2f_1 - f_0 - f_2} \times i$$
$$L_1 = 29.5; f_1 = 11; f_0 = 10; f_2 = 5; i = 10$$
$$= 29.5 + \frac{11 - 10}{2 \times 11 - 10 - 5} \times 10 = 29.5 + 1.43$$
$$= \mathbf{30.93}$$
$$D_4 = \text{size of } \frac{4N}{10}\text{th item}$$
$$= \text{size of } \frac{4 \times 40}{10}\text{th item}$$
$$= \text{16th item which lies in the class 19.5–29.5}$$
$$D_4 = L_1 + \frac{\frac{4N}{10} - c.f.}{f} \times i$$
$$L_1 = 19.5; \frac{4N}{10} = 16;$$
$$c.f = 10; f = 10; i = 10$$
$$= 19.5 + \frac{16 - 10}{10} \times 10 = 19.5 + 6$$
$$= \mathbf{25.5}$$

Problem 170. From the following table, find the median and the mode.

Income (Rs.) :	100–200	100–300	100–400	100–500	100–600
No. of Persons :	15	33	63	83	100

(*B. Com. Agra*)

Solution: **Computation of Median and Mode**

Income	*No. of Persons (f)*	*c.f*
100–200	15	15
200–300	33 – 15 = 18	33
300–400	63 – 33 = 30	63
400–500	83 – 63 = 20	83
500–600	100 – 83 = 17	100

$$\text{Median} = \text{size of } \frac{N}{2}\text{th item}$$

$$= \text{50th item which lies in the class 300–400}$$

$$\text{Median} = L_1 + \frac{\frac{N}{2} - c.f.}{f} \times i$$

$$L_1 = 300;\ \frac{N}{2} = 50$$

$$c.f = 33;\ f = 30;\ i = 100$$

$$\text{Median} = 300 + \frac{50 - 33}{30} \times 100 = 300 + 56.67 \qquad = \mathbf{356.67}$$

By inspection method mode lies in the class 300–400

$$\text{Mode}: \quad Z = L_1 + \frac{f_1 - f_0}{2f_1 - f_0 - f_2} \times i$$

$$L_1 = 300;\ f_1 = 30;\ f_0 = 18;\ f_2 = 20,\ i = 100$$

$$Z = 300 + \frac{30 - 18}{2 \times 30 - 18 - 20} \times 100$$

$$= 300 + 54.55 \qquad = \mathbf{354.55}$$

Problem 171. Incomes of employees in an industrial concern are given below. The total income of the 10 employees in the class over Rs. 250 is Rs. 3,000. Compute the mean income. Every employee belonging to the top 25% of the earners is required to pay 1% of his income to workers' relief fund. Estimate the contribution to this fund :

Income Rs.	*Frequency*
0–50	90
50–100	150
100–150	100
150–200	80
200–250	70
above 250	10

(*ICWA*)

Solution:

Income	*Mid Point X*	*Frequency*	*fx*	*c.f.*
0–50	25	90	2,250	90
50–100	75	150	11,250	240
100–150	125	100	12,500	340
150–200	175	80	14,000	420
200–250	225	70	15,750	490
250–over	300	10	3000	500
		N = 500	$\Sigma fx = 58750$	

$$\text{Mean income} \qquad \overline{X} = \frac{\Sigma fx}{N} = \frac{58750}{500} = 117.50$$

$$Q_3 = \text{size of } \frac{3N}{4}\text{th item}$$

$$= \text{size of } \frac{3 \times 500}{4} = 375\text{th item}$$

Which lies in the class 150–200

$$Q_3 = L_1 + \frac{\frac{3N}{4} - c.f.}{f} \times i$$

$$= 150 + \frac{375 - 340}{80} \times 50 = \mathbf{171.88}$$

Top 25% employees earn Rs. 171.88 and over. So their total income will be Rs. 27,120 *i.e.*

	x	f	fx
172–200	186	45	8,370
200–250	225	70	15,750
250–over	300	10	3,000
		125	Rs. 27,120

Contribution to Relief fund = 1% of 27, 120

= **Rs. 271.20**

Problem 172. From the following distribution of weekly earnings, calculate (*i*) the most usual wage and (*ii*) the percentage earning more than Rs. 31.50.

Weekly earnings	*No. of persons*
25–26	25
26–27	70
27–28	210
28–29	275
29–30	430
30–31	550
31–32	340
32–33	130
33–34	90
34–35	55
35–36	25
	Total : 2, 200

(ICWA)

Solution:

Weekly earnings	*No. of persons*	*Cumulative frequency*
25–26	25	25
26–27	70	95
27–28	210	305
28–29	275	580

Cont....

29–30	430	1010
30–31	550	1560
31–32	340	1900
32–33	130	2030
33–34	90	2120
34–35	55	2175
35–36	25	2200

$$\text{Median} = \text{size of } \frac{N}{2}\text{th item}$$

$$= \frac{2200}{2} = 1100\text{th item}$$

which lies in the class 30–31

$$\text{Median} = L_1 + \frac{\frac{N}{2} - c.f.}{f} \times i$$

$$= 30 + \frac{1100 - 1010}{550} \times 1$$

The most usual wage = 30.16

Persons earning 31.50 = $1560 + \frac{1}{2}$ of 340 = 1730

Percentage earning more than 31.50 = $\frac{2200 - 1730}{2200} \times 100$

= **21.36%**

Problem 173. The arithmetic mean calculated from the following frequency distribution is known to be 67.45 inches. Find the value of f_1

Height (inches)	*Frequency*
60–62	15
63–65	54
66–68	f_1
69–71	81
72–74	24

(*ICWA*)

Solution:

$$\overline{X} = \frac{\Sigma f x}{N}$$

$$\overline{X} = 67.45; \text{ (given)}$$

$$67.45 = \frac{61 \times 15 + 64 \times 54 + 67f_1 + 70 \times 81 + 73 \times 24}{15 + 54 + f_1 + 81 + 24}$$

$$67.45 = \frac{915 + 3456 + 67f_1 + 5670 + 1752}{174 + f_1}$$

$$67.45 = \frac{11793 + 67f_1}{174 + f_1}$$

$$11736.3 + 67.45f_1 = 11793 + 67f_1$$

$$67.45f_1 - 67f_1 = 11793 - 11736.3$$

$$0.45f_1 = 56.7$$

$$f_1 = \frac{56.7}{0.45}$$

$$f_1 = \mathbf{126}$$

4

MEASURES OF DISPERSON

Range, Quartile Deviation, Mean Deviation, Standard Deviation, Coefficient of Variation, Lorenz Curve

FORMULAE

Range (R) Individual Series, Discrete and Continuous Series R = L − S	R = Range L = Largest value S = Smallest value
Coefficient of Range (C.R.) Individual Discrete and Continuous Series $\text{C.R.} = \frac{L-S}{L+S}$	
Quartile Deviation (Q.D.) Individual, Discrete and Continuous Series $\text{Q.D.} = \frac{Q_3 - Q_1}{2}$	Q.D. = Quartile Deviation Q_1 = Lower quartile Q_3 = Upper Quartile
Coefficient of Quartile Deviation (Coeff. Of Q.D.) Individual, Discrete and Continuous Series $\text{Coeff. of Q.D} = \frac{Q_3 - Q_1}{Q_3 + Q_1}$	
Mean Deviation Individual Series $\text{M.D.} = \left.\begin{array}{l}\frac{\sum(X-\overline{X})}{N}\\ \frac{\Sigma(X-\text{Med})}{N}\\ \frac{\Sigma(X-Z)}{N}\end{array}\right] \frac{\sum\lvert D\rvert}{N}$ Discrete and Continuous Series $\text{M.D.} = \frac{\Sigma f\lvert D\rvert}{N}$ When Mean or Median is in fraction M.D.	M.D = Mean Deviation $\sum\lvert D\rvert$ = Total of Deviations from Mean, Median or Mode ignoring signs N = Numbers of items $\Sigma f\,[D]$ =Sum of the products of frequency and respective deviation from $\overline{X}$ or Med. or Z $\sum fm_a$ and $\sum fm_b$= Totals of products of mid points and frequencies corresponding to mid

$= \dfrac{\Sigma m f_a - \Sigma f m_b - (\Sigma f_a - \Sigma f_b) \times \overline{X}}{N}$	points above and below the average value (or median value) respectively.
M.D. $= \dfrac{\Sigma m f_a - \Sigma f m_b - (\Sigma f_a - \Sigma f_b)}{N} \times \text{Med}$	$\sum fm_a$ and $\sum fm_b$ = The totals of frequencies corresponding to mid points above and below the mean value or Median value. N = Total number of items
Coefficient of Mean Deviation Individual, Discrete and Continuous Series Coeff. M.D. $= \dfrac{\text{Mean Deviation}}{\overline{X}\text{or Med. or} Z}$	
Standard Deviation (σ)Individual Series $\sigma = \sqrt{\dfrac{\Sigma(X-\overline{X})}{N}} = \sqrt{\dfrac{\Sigma X^2}{N}}$	ΣX^2 = Total square deviations from Mean. N = Number of items
Assumed Mean $\sigma = \sqrt{\frac{\Sigma d^2}{N} - \left(\frac{\Sigma d}{N}\right)^2}$	$d = x-$ Assumed Mean
Step Deviation Method $\sigma = \sqrt{\frac{\sum d^2}{N} - \left(\frac{\overline{X} d}{N}\right)^2} \times C$	
Discrete and Continuous Series Actual Mean Method $\sigma = \dfrac{\sum f\,(X-X)^2}{N}$ $= \sqrt{\frac{\Sigma f d^2}{N}}$ Assumed Mean Method $\sigma = \sqrt{\dfrac{\Sigma f d^2}{N} - \left(\dfrac{\Sigma f d}{N}\right)^2}$ Step deviation Method $\sigma = \sqrt{\dfrac{\Sigma f d' 2}{N} - \left(\dfrac{\Sigma f d'}{N}\right)^2} \times C$	$d = X - \overline{X}$
Coefficient of variation (C.V.) C.V. $= \dfrac{\sigma}{\overline{X}} \times 100$	C.V. = Coefficient of Variation σ = Standard Deviation $\overline{X}$ = Mean
Combined Standard Deviation (σ_{12}) $\sigma_{12} = \sqrt{\dfrac{N_1\sigma_1^2 + N_2\sigma^2 + Nd^2 + N_2 d_2}{N_1 + N_2}}$	$d_1 = \overline{X}_1 - \overline{X}_{12}$ $d_2 = \overline{X}_2 - \overline{X}_{12}$

RANGE AND QUARTILE DEVIATION

Problem 1. Find the range of weight of 10 students from the following :

41 11 14 65 73 64 53 35 71 55

Solution : (*B. Com.*)

Range $= L-S$

L= largest value $= 73$, S = smallest value = 11

$= 73-11$

Range $= 62$

Coefficient of Range $= \dfrac{L-S}{L+S} = \dfrac{73-11}{73+11}$

$= 0.738$

Problem 2. The following are the marks of 100 students of B. Com. Find the range of variation of marks and also compute coefficient of range.

Marks	*No. of students*
0–10	13
10–20	6
20–30	9
30–40	11
40–50	10
50–60	18
60–70	23
70–80	10

(*B. Com*)

Solution :

Range $= L-S$

$= L = 80$; $S = 0$

Range $= 80-0 = 80$

Coefficient of range $= \dfrac{L-S}{L+S}$

$= \dfrac{80-0}{80+0} = \dfrac{80}{80}$

$= 1$

Problem 3. Calculate the quartile deviation and its coefficient from the following data :

Months	*Monthly earnings*	*Months*	*Monthly earnings*
1	39	7	42
2	40	8	43
3	40	9	43
4	41	10	44
5	41	11	44
6	42	12	45

(*B. Com. Meerut*)

Solution :

Computation of Quartiles

Months	*Monthly Earnings*
1	39
2	40
3	40
4	41
5	41
6	42
7	42
8	43
9	43
10	44
11	44
12	45

$$Q_1 = \text{size of } \frac{N+1}{4}\text{th item}$$
$$= \text{size of } \frac{12+1}{4}\text{th item}$$
$$= 3.25\text{th item}$$
$$= 40 + 0.25\,(41 - 40)$$
$$= \mathbf{40.25}$$
$$Q_3 = \text{size of } 3\left(\frac{N+1}{4}\right)\text{th item}$$
$$= \text{size of } 3\left(\frac{12+1}{4}\right)\text{th item}$$
$$= \text{size of } 9.75\text{th item}$$
$$= 43 + 0.75\,(44\text{–}43)$$
$$= \mathbf{43.75}$$
$$\text{Q.D} = \frac{Q_3 - Q_1}{2} = \frac{43.75 - 40.25}{2} = \frac{3.50}{2}$$
$$= \mathbf{1.75}$$
$$\text{Coefficient of Q.D.} = \frac{Q_3 - Q_1}{Q_3 + Q_1}$$
$$= \frac{43.75 - 40.25}{43.75 + 40.25} = \frac{3.5}{84}$$
$$= \mathbf{0.042}$$

Problem 4. Calculate the semi-interquartile range and quartile coefficient from the following :

Age in years	20	30	40	50	60	70	80
No. of members	3	61	132	153	140	51	3

(*B. Com., Nagpur*)

Solution :

Computation of Quartile coefficient

Age in years	*No. of members*	*c.f*
20	3	3
30	61	64
40	132	196
50	153	349
60	140	489
70	51	540
80	3	543

$$\begin{aligned}
Q_1 &= \text{value of } \left(\frac{N+1}{4}\right) \text{th item} \\
&= \text{value of } \frac{543+1}{4} \text{th item} \\
&= 136\text{th item} \\
&= 40 \text{ years.} \\
Q_3 &= \text{value of } 3\left(\frac{N+1}{4}\right) \text{th item} \\
&= \text{value of } 3\left(\frac{543+1}{4}\right) \text{th item} \\
&= 408\text{th item} \\
&= 60 \text{ years.} \\
\text{Quartile Deviation} &= \frac{Q_3 - Q_1}{2} \\
Q_3 &= 60, Q_1 = 40 \\
&= \frac{60-40}{2} = \frac{20}{2} \\
&= \textbf{10 years} \\
\text{Coefficient of Q.D.} &= \frac{Q_3 - Q_1}{Q_3 + Q_1} \\
&= \frac{60-40}{60+40} = \frac{20}{100} \\
&= \textbf{0.2}
\end{aligned}$$

Problem 5. Compute quartile deviation from the following data :

Height in inches	*No. of students*
58	15
59	20
60	32
61	35

Height in inches	*No. of students*
62	33
63	22
64	20
65	10
66	8

(*B. Com., Agra*)

Solution :

Computation of Quartile Deviation

Height in inches	*f*	*c.f*
58	15	15
59	20	35
60	32	67
61	35	102
62	33	135
63	22	157
64	20	177
65	10	187
66	8	195

$$Q1 = \text{size of } \left(\frac{N+1}{4}\right) \text{th item}$$

$$= \text{size of } \left(\frac{195+1}{4}\right) \text{th item}$$

$$= 49\text{th item} = 60$$

$$Q_1 = \mathbf{60}$$

$$Q_3 = \text{size of } 3\left(\frac{N+1}{4}\right) \text{th item}$$

$$= \text{size of } 3\left(\frac{195+1}{4}\right) \text{th item}$$

$$= 147\text{th} = 63$$

$$Q_3 = \mathbf{63}$$

$$\text{Q.D.} = \frac{Q_3 - Q_1}{2} = \frac{63-60}{2}$$

$$= \mathbf{1.5}$$

Problem 6. From the following data compute Quartile Deviation :

Size	:	4–7	8–10	11–13	14–16	17–19
Frequency	:	14	24	38	20	4

(*B. Com., Osmania*)

Solution :

Computation of Quartile Deviation

Size	*f*	*c.f*
4–7	14	14
8–10	24	38
11–13	38	76
14–16	20	96
17–19	4	100

We need the values of Q_1 and Q_3 which are as follows :

$$Q_1 = \text{size of } \left(\frac{N}{4}\right) \text{th item}$$

$$= \text{size of } \left(\frac{100}{4}\right) \text{th item} = 25\text{th item}$$

$\therefore$ Q_1 lies in the class 8 to 10

But the real values are 7.5 to 10.5

$$Q_1 = L_1 + \frac{\frac{N}{4} - c.f}{f} \times i$$

$$L_1 = 7.5\ ;\ \frac{N}{4} = 25\ ;\ c.f = 14\ ;\ f = 24\ ;\ i = 2$$

$$= 7.5 + \frac{25 - 14}{24} \times 2$$

$$= 7.5 + 0.92 = \mathbf{8.42}$$

$$Q_3 = \text{size of } \frac{3N}{4} \text{th item}$$

$$= \text{size of } \frac{3 \times 100}{4} \text{th item} = 75\text{th item}$$

$\therefore$ Q_3 lies in the class 11–13 (10.5 – 13.5)

$$Q_3 = L_1 + \frac{\frac{3N}{4} - c.f}{f} \times i$$

$$L_1 = 10.5;\ \frac{3N}{4} = 75$$

$$c.f = 38; f = 38; i = 2$$

$$Q_3 = 10.5 + \frac{75 - 38}{38} \times 2$$

$$= 10.5 + 1.95 = \mathbf{12.45}$$

$$Q.D. = \frac{Q_3 - Q_1}{2} = \frac{12.45 - 8.42}{2} = \mathbf{2.015}$$

Problem 7. Calculate Inter Quartile Range for the data given below :

Class	:	0–10	10–20	20–30	30–40	40–50
Frequency	:	4	15	28	16	7

(*B.A. Madurai*)

Solution :

Computation of Quartile Deviation

Class	*f*	*c.f*
0–10	4	4
10–20	15	19
20–30	28	47
30–40	16	63
40–50	7	70

We need the values of Q_1 and Q_3

$$Q_1 = \text{size of } \left(\frac{70}{4}\right) \text{th item} = 17.5 \text{ th item}$$

Which lies in the class = 10–20

$$Q_1 = L_1 + \frac{\frac{N}{4} - c.f}{f} \times i$$

$$L_1 = 10 \; ; \; \frac{N}{4} = 17.5 \; ; \; f = 15 \; ; \; cf = 4 \; ; \; i = 10$$

$$= 10 + \frac{17.5 - 4}{15} \times 10 = \mathbf{19}$$

$$Q_3 = \text{size of } \left(\frac{3N}{4}\right) \text{th item} = 52.5 \text{ th item}$$

Which lies in the class 30–40

$$Q_3 = L_1 + \frac{\frac{3N}{4} - c.f}{f} \times i$$

$$L_1 = 30 \; ; \; \frac{3N}{4} = 52.5 \; ; \; c.f = 47 \; ; \; f = 16 \; ; \; i = 10$$

$$= 30 + \frac{52.5 - 47}{16} \times 10$$

$$= 30 + 3.44 = 33{\cdot}44$$

$$\text{Q.D.} = \frac{Q_3 - Q_1}{2} = \frac{33.44 - 19}{2}$$

$$= \mathbf{7.22}$$

Problem 8. The following table gives the heights of students in a class. Find out the quartile deviation :

Height (in inches)	*No. of students*
50–53	2
53–56	7
56–59	24
59–62	27
62–65	13
65–68	3

(*B. Com. Madurai*)

Solution :

Computation of Quartile Deviation

Height (in inches)	*No. of students (f)*	*c.f*
50–53	2	2
53–56	7	9
56–59	24	33
59–62	27	60
62–65	13	73
65–68	3	76

$$\text{Lower Quartile}\,(Q_1) = \text{size of } \frac{N}{4}\text{th item}$$

$$= \text{size of } \frac{76}{4}\text{th item}$$

$$= \text{19th item which lies in the class 56–59}$$

$$Q_1 = L_1 + \frac{\frac{N}{4} - c.f}{f} \times i$$

$$L_1 = 56 \; ; \; \frac{N}{4} = 19 \; ; \; c.f. = 9 \; ;$$

$$f = 24 \; ; \; i = 3$$

$$= 56 + \frac{19 - 9}{24} \times 3 = 56 + 1.25$$

$$= \mathbf{57.25}$$

$$\text{Upper Quartile}\,(Q_3) = \text{size of } \frac{3N}{4}\text{th item}$$

$$= \text{size of } 3 \times \frac{76}{4}\text{th item}$$

$$= \text{57th item which lies in the class 59–62}$$

$$Q_3 = L_1 + \frac{\frac{3N}{4} - c.f}{f} \times i$$

$$L_1 = 59 \; ; \; \frac{3N}{4} = 57$$

$$c.f = 33 \; ; \; f = 27 \; ; \; i = 3$$

$$= 59 + \frac{57 - 33}{27} \times 3 = 59 + 2.67$$

$$= \mathbf{61.67}$$

$$\text{Quartile Deviation} = \frac{Q_3 - Q_1}{2} = \frac{61.67 - 57.25}{2} = \frac{4.42}{2}$$

$$= \mathbf{2.21}$$

Problem 9. Calculate Quartile Deviation for the data given below :

weekly wage Rs.	*No. of Wage Earners*
35–36	14
36–37	20

weekly wage Rs.	*No. of Wage Earners*
37–38	42
38–39	54
40–41	45
41–42	21
42–43	8

(*B. Com., Annamalai*)

Solution :

Computation of Quartile Deviation

Weekly Wages (Rs.)	*No of wage Earners* (*f*)	*cf*
35–36	14	14
36–37	20	34
37–38	42	76
38–39	54	130
40–41	45	175
41–42	21	196
42–43	8	204

$$Q1 = \text{size of } \frac{N}{4}\text{th item}$$

$$= \text{size of } \frac{204}{4}\text{th item}$$

= 51th itemwhich lies in the class 37–38

$$Q_1 = L_1 + \frac{\frac{N}{4} - c.f}{f} \times i$$

$$L_1 = 37\ ;\ \frac{N}{4} = 51\ ;$$

$$c.f = 34\ ;\ f = 42\ ;\ i = 1$$

$$= 37 + \frac{51 - 34}{42} \times 1 = 37 + 0.40$$

= **37.40**

$$Q_3 = \text{size of} \frac{3N}{4}\text{th item}$$

$$= \text{size of} \frac{3 \times 204}{4}\text{th item}$$

= 153th item which lies in the class 40–41

$$Q_3 = L_1 + \frac{\frac{3N}{4} - c.f}{f} \times i$$

$$L_1 = 40\ ;\ \frac{3N}{4} = 153\ ;$$

$$c.f = 130\ ;\ f = 45\ ;\ i = 1$$

$$= 40 + \frac{153 - 130}{45} \times 1 = 40 + 0.51$$

$$= \mathbf{40.51}$$

$$Q.\,D = \frac{Q_3 - Q_1}{2}, \; Q_3 = 40.51 \; ; \; Q_1 = 37.40$$

$$= \frac{40.51 - 37.40}{2} = \frac{3.11}{2}$$

$$= \mathbf{1.56}$$

Problem 10. Compute quartile deviation from the following data :

Size	*Frequency*
4–8	6
8–12	10
12–16	18
16–20	30
20–24	15
24–28	12
28–32	10
32–36	6
36–40	2

(*CA*)

Solution :

Computation of Quartile Deviation

Size	*f*	*c.f*
4–8	6	6
8–12	10	16
12–16	18	34
16–20	30	64
20–24	15	79
24–28	12	91
28–32	10	101
32–36	6	107
36–40	2	109

$$Q_1 = \text{size of } \left(\frac{N}{4}\right) \text{th item}$$

$$= \text{size of } \frac{109}{4} \text{ th item}$$

$$= 27.25\text{th item which lies in the class } 12\text{–}16$$

$$Q_1 = L_1 + \frac{\frac{N}{4} - c.f}{f} \times i$$

$$L_1 = 12 \; ; \; \frac{N}{4} = 27.25, ; \quad c.f = 16 \; ; \; f = 18 \; ; \; i = 4$$

$$= 12 + \frac{27.25 - 16}{18} \times 4 = 12 + 2.5$$

$$= \mathbf{14.5}$$

$$Q_3 = \text{size of } \frac{3N}{4}\text{th item}$$

$$= \text{size of } \frac{3 \times 109}{4}\text{th item}$$

$= 81.75$th item which lies in the class 24–28

$$Q_3 = L_1 + \frac{\frac{3N}{4} - c.f}{f} \times i$$

$$L_1 = 24 \; ; \frac{3N}{4} = 81.75;$$

$$c.f = 79 \; ; \; f = 12 \; ; \; i = 4$$

$$= 24 + \frac{81.75 - 79}{12} \times 4 = 24 + 0.92$$

$$= \mathbf{24.92}$$

$$\text{Q.D.} = \frac{Q_3 - Q_1}{2} = \frac{24.92 - 14.5}{2} = \frac{10.42}{2}$$

$$= \mathbf{5.21}$$

Problem 11. From the following data, calculate the percentage of workers getting wages:

(*a*) more than Rs. 44,
(*b*) between Rs. 22 and Rs. 58,
(*c*) the quartile deviation

wages	0–10	10–20	20–30	30–40	40–50	50–60	60–70	70–80
No. of workers	20	45	85	160	70	55	35	30

(*C.A*)

Solution : (*a*) Number of persons getting wages more than Rs. 44 is :

$$\left[\frac{50 - 44}{10} \times 70\right] + 55 + 35 + 30$$

$$= 42 + 55 + 35 + 30 = 162$$

The percentage of workers getting wages over Rs. 44 is :

$$\frac{162}{500} \times 100 = \mathbf{32.4\%}$$

(*b*) Number of workers getting wages between Rs. 22 and 58 is :

$$\left[\frac{30 - 22}{10} \times 85\right] + 160 + 70 \left[\frac{58 - 50}{10} \times 55\right]$$

$$= 68 + 160 + 70 + 44 = 342$$

The percentage of workers getting wges between Rs. 22 and Rs. 58 is :

$$\frac{342}{500} \times 100 = \mathbf{68.4\%}$$

$$Q_1 = \text{size of } \frac{N}{4}\text{th item} = \text{size of } \frac{500}{4}\text{th item}$$

$$= \text{125th item which lies in the class 20–30}$$

Computation of Q_1 and Q_3

Wages in (Rs.)	*No. of workes (f)*	*c.f*
0–10	20	20
10–20	45	65
20–30	85	150
30–40	160	310
40–50	70	380
50–60	55	435
60–70	35	470
70–80	30	500

$$Q_1 = L_1 + \frac{\frac{N}{4} - c.f}{f} \times i$$

$$L_1 = 20 ; \frac{N}{4} = 125 ;$$

$$c.f = 65 ; f = 85 ; i = 10$$

$$= 20 + \frac{125 - 65}{85} \times 10 = 20 + 7.06$$

$$= \mathbf{27.06}$$

$$Q_3 = \text{size of } \frac{3N}{4}\text{th item}$$

$$= \text{size of } \frac{3 \times 500}{4}\text{th item}$$

$$= \text{375th item which lies in the class 40–50}$$

$$Q_3 = L_1 + \frac{\frac{3N}{4} - c.f}{f} \times i$$

$$L_1 = 40 ; \frac{3N}{4} = 375 ;$$

$$c.f = 310 ; f = 70 ; i = 10$$

$$= 40 + \frac{375 - 310}{70} \times 10 = 40 + 9.29$$

$$= \mathbf{49.29}$$

(c) $$Q.D. = \frac{Q_3 - Q_1}{2}$$

$$= \frac{49.29 - 27.06}{2} = \frac{22.23}{2}$$

$$= \mathbf{11.115}$$

Problem 12. Evaluate an appropriate measure of dispersion for the following data.

Income (in Rs.)	*Number of persons*
Less than 50	54
50–70	100
70–90	140
90–110	300
110–130	230
130–150	125
Above 150	51

(*B. Com., Calicut*)

Solution : The classes are open end intervals. Therefore, we may measure of dispersion and adopt only quartile deviation.

Income (in Rs.)	*Number of persons (f)*	*Less than c. f*
Less than 50	54	54
50–70	100	154
70–90	140	294
90–110	300	594
110–130	230	824
130–150	125	949
Above 150	51	1000

$$Q_1 = \text{size of } \frac{N}{2}\text{th item}$$

$$= \text{size of } \frac{1000}{4}\text{th item}$$

$$= \text{250th item which lies in the class 70–90}$$

$$Q_1 = L_1 + \frac{\frac{N}{4} - c.f}{f} \times i$$

$$L_1 = 70, \ \frac{N}{4} = 250,$$

$$c.f = 154, \ f = 140 \ ; \ i = 20$$

$$= 70 + \frac{250 - 154}{140} \times 20 = 70 + 13.714$$

$$= \mathbf{83.714}$$

$$Q_3 = \text{size of } \frac{3N}{4}\text{th item}$$

$$= \text{size of } \frac{3 \times 1000}{4}\text{th item}$$

$$= \text{750th item which lies in the class 110–130}$$

$$Q_3 = L_1 + \frac{\frac{3N}{4} - c.f}{f} \times i$$

$$L_1 = 110, \ \frac{3N}{4} = 750,$$

$$c.f = 594,\ f = 230\ ;\ i = 20$$

$$= 110 + \frac{750 - 594}{230} \times 20 = 110 + 13.365$$

$$= \mathbf{123.565}$$

$$\text{Q.D.} = \frac{Q_3 - Q_1}{2}$$

$$Q_3 = 123.565,\ Q_1 = 83.714$$

$$= \frac{123.565 - 83.714}{2} = \frac{39.851}{2}$$

$$= \mathbf{19.925}$$

Problem 13. Calculate the range and semi-inter quartile range for wages :

Wages (Rs.)	30–32	32–34	34–36	36–38	38–40	40–42	42–44
Labourers	12	18	16	14	12	8	6

Also calculate the quartile coefficient of dispersion.

(*B. Com.*)

Solution :

$$\text{A. Range} = \text{L–S}$$

$$= 44\text{–}30 = 14 \text{ Rs.}$$

B. Calculation of Quartiles

X	*f*	*c.f*
30–32	12	12
32–34	18	30
34–36	16	46
36–38	14	60
38–40	12	72
40–42	8	80
42–44	6	86

$$Q_1 = \text{size of } \frac{N}{4}\text{th item}$$

$$= \text{size of } \frac{86}{4}\text{th item} = 21.5$$

Which lies in the group 32–34

$$Q_1 = L_1 + \frac{\frac{N}{4} - c.f}{f} \times i$$

$$L_1 = 32,\ \frac{N}{4} = 21.5,\ c.f = 12,\ f = 18,\ i = 2$$

$$= 32 + \frac{21.5 - 12}{18} \times 2 = 32 + \frac{19}{18}$$

$$= 32 + 1.06$$

$$= \mathbf{33.06}$$

$$Q_3 = \text{size of } \frac{3N}{4}\text{th item}$$

$$= \text{size of } \frac{3 \times 86}{4} = 64.5\text{th item which lies}$$

in the class 38–40

$$Q_3 = L_1 + \frac{\frac{3N}{4} - c.f}{f} \times i$$

$$L_1 = 38, \quad \frac{3N}{4} = 64.5, \quad c.f = 12, \quad i = 2.$$

$$= 38 + \frac{64.5 - 60}{12} \times 2$$

$$= 38 + 0.75$$

$$= \mathbf{38.75}$$

$$\text{Q.D.} = \frac{Q_3 - Q_1}{2}$$

$$= \frac{38.75 - 33.06}{2}$$

$$= \frac{5.69}{2}$$

$$= \mathbf{2.85}$$

$$\text{Coefficient of Q.D.} = \frac{Q_3 - Q_1}{Q_3 + Q_1}$$

$$= \frac{38.75 - 33.06}{38.75 + 33.06}$$

$$= \frac{5.69}{71.81}$$

$$= \mathbf{0.08}$$

MEAN DEVIATION

Problem 14. Calculate the mean deviation from (1) arithmetic mean (2) mode, (3) median in respect of the marks obtained by nine students given below and show that the mean deviation from median is minimum. Marks, (out of 25) 7, 4, 10, 9, 15, 12, 7, 9, 7. If the marks are doubled (converted out of 50) will the variation in marks increase ? Give reasons.

(B. Com., Bombay)

Solution :

(1) $$\overline{X} = \frac{\Sigma X}{N}$$

$$= \frac{80}{9} = \mathbf{8.9}$$

(2) Mode = 7 (as 7 repeats for 3 times)

(3) $$\text{Median} = \text{size of } \left(\frac{N+1}{2}\right) \text{th item}$$

$$= 5\text{th item}$$

$$(4, 7, 7, 7, 9, 9, 10, 12, 15)$$

$$\text{Median} = \mathbf{9}$$

Computations of Mean Deviation

Marks	$\mid D \mid (Mean)$	$\mid D \mid (Medium)$	$\mid D \mid (Mode)$
7	1.9 .	2	0
4	4.9	5	3
10	1.1	1	3
9	0.1	0	2
15	6.1	6	8
12	3.1	3	5
7	1.9	2	0
9	0.1	0	2
7	1.9	2	0
	$\Sigma \mid D \mid = 21.1$	$\Sigma \mid D \mid = 21$	$\Sigma \mid D \mid = 23$

$$\text{MD (from)}\overline{X} = \frac{\Sigma \mid \text{D} \mid}{\text{N}} = \frac{21.1}{9} = 2.34$$

$$\text{MD (from med.)} = \frac{\Sigma \mid \text{D} \mid}{\text{N}} = \frac{21}{9} = 2.33$$

$$\text{M D (from Z)} = \frac{\Sigma \mid \text{D} \mid}{\text{N}} = \frac{23}{9} = 2.56$$

When the marks are doubled, the variations would also be doubled. Because the value of mean, median, mode, mean deviation and standard deviation would also be increased.

Problem 15. Calculate mean deviation (take deviation from (mean) from the following data :

X	2	4	6	8	10
f	1	4	6	4	1

(*B. Com., Banaras*)

Solution :

Computation of Mean and Mean Deviation

X	*f*	*fX*	*Deviation from Mean* $= \mid D \mid$	$f \mid D \mid$
2	1	2	4	4
4	4	16	2	8
6	6	36	0	0
8	4	32	2	8
10	1	10	4	4
	N=16	$\Sigma fX = 96$		$\Sigma f \mid \text{D} \mid = 24$

$$\text{Mean : } \overline{X} = \frac{\Sigma fX}{\text{N}} \quad \Sigma fX = 96 \text{ ; N} = 16$$

$$= \frac{96}{16}$$

$$= \mathbf{6}$$

$$\text{M.D.} = \frac{\Sigma f\,|D|}{N} \quad \Sigma f\,|D| = 24\ ;\ N = 16$$

$$= \frac{24}{16}$$

$$= \mathbf{1.5}$$

Problem 16. Find the mean deviation and the mean coefficient of dispersion from median of the following series :

Size	:	5	6	7	8	9	10
Frequency	:	8	12	18	8	3	1

(*B. Com., Mysore*)

Solution :

Calculation of Median and M.D.

Size X	f	$c.f$	$\|D\|(X-7)$	$f\,\|D\|$
5	8	8	2	16
6	12	20	1	12
7	18	38	0	0
8	8	46	1	8
9	3	49	2	6
10	1	50	3	3
	N = 50			$\Sigma f\,\|D\| = 45$

$$\text{Median} = \text{size of } \frac{N+1}{2} \text{th item}$$

$$= \text{size of } \frac{50+1}{2} \text{th item}$$

$$= 25.5\text{th item i.e. 7th item}$$

$$\text{M.D} = \frac{\Sigma f\,|D|}{N} = \frac{45}{50}$$

$$= \mathbf{0.9}$$

$$\text{Coefficient of M.D.} = \frac{\text{M.D}}{\text{Median}} = \frac{0.9}{7} = \mathbf{0.129}$$

Problem 17. Calculate mean deviation of the following series :

X	10	11	12	13	14
F	3	12	18	12	3

(*C.A*)

Solution :

Calculation of Median and M.D

X	f	$c.f$	$\|D\| = X - 12$	$f\,\|D\|$
10	3	3	2	6
11	12	15	1	12
12	18	33	0	0

X	f	$c.f$	$\mid D \mid = X - 12$	$f \mid D \mid$
13	12	45	1	12
14	3	48	2	6
	N=48			$\Sigma f \mid D \mid = 36$

$$\text{Median} = \text{value of } \frac{N+1}{2}\text{th item}$$

$$= \text{value of } \frac{48+1}{2}\text{th item}$$

$$= \text{value of 24.5th item} = \mathbf{12}$$

$$\text{M. D. from Median} = \frac{\Sigma f\,|D|}{N} = \frac{36}{48} = \mathbf{0.75}$$

Problem : 18 Calculate mean deviation (take deviation from mean) from the following data :

X	10	12	14	16	18
f	5	9	10	9	7

(B. Com. Banaras)

Solution :

Calculation of Mean Deviation

X	f	fX	*Deviation of X from* $\overline{X}$: $\|D\|$	$f\,\|D\|$
10	5	50	4.2	85.6
12	9	108	2.2	19.8
14	10	140	0.2	2.0
16	9	144	1.8	16.2
18	7	126	3.8	26.6
	$N = 40$	$\Sigma fX = 568$		$\Sigma f\,\|D\| = 85.6$

$$\overline{X} = \frac{\Sigma fX}{N} = \frac{568}{40} = 14.2$$

$$\text{Mean Deviation} = \frac{\Sigma f\,|D|}{N}$$

$$\Sigma f\,|D| = 85.6;\ N = 40$$

$$= \frac{85.6}{40}$$

$$= \mathbf{2.14}$$

Problem 19. Calculate mean deviation from median of mark obtained by the following students :

8,	20,	15,	17,	2,	10,	30,	38,	28,
39,	4,	8,	6,	12,	18,	18,	29,	37,
23,	18,	16,	15,	24,	14,	28,	27,	35,
49,	9,	13,	6,	18,	22,	25,	30.	

(B. Com, Rajasthan)

Solution :

Computation of Mean Deviation

Marks X	*f*	*c.f*	$\|D\| = X - 18$	$f\ \|D\|$
2	1	1	16	16
4	1	2	14	14
6	2	4	12	24
8	2	6	10	20
9	1	7	9	9
10	1	8	8	8
12	1	9	6	6
13	1	10	5	5
14	1	11	4	4
15	2	13	3	6
16	1	14	2	2
17	1	15	1	1
18	3	18	0	0
20	1	19	2	2
22	1	20	4	4
23	1	21	5	5
24	1	22	6	6

Marks X	*f*	*c.f*	$\|D\| = X - 18$	$f\ \|D\|$
25	1	23	7	7
26	1	24	8	8
27	1	25	9	9
28	2	27	10	20
29	1	28	11	11
30	2	30	12	24
35	1	31	17	17
37	1	32	19	19
38	1	33	20	20
39	1	34	21	21
49	1	35	31	31
				$\Sigma f\ \|D\| = 319$

$$\text{Median} = \text{size of } \left(\frac{\text{N}+1}{2}\right) \text{th item}$$

$$= \text{size of } \left(\frac{35+1}{2}\right) \text{th item}$$

$$= \text{size of 18th item.}$$

$$\therefore \quad \text{Median} = 18 \text{ marks.}$$

$$\text{M.D} = \frac{\Sigma f\,|D|}{N} \quad \Sigma f\,|D| = 319\ ;\ N = 35$$

$$= \frac{319}{35}$$

$$= \mathbf{9.114}$$

Problem 20. Calculate mean deviation for the following frequency distribution:

No. of colds experienced in 12 months	:	0	1	2	3	4	5	6	7	8	9
No. of persons	:	25	46	91	162	110	95	82	26	13	2

(*I.C.W.A*)

Solution :

Computation of Mean Deviation

X	f	*c.f.*	*Deviation from Med* : 4 $\|D\|$	$f\ \|D\|$
0	25	25	−4	100
1	46	71	−3	138
2	91	162	−2	182
3	162	324	−1	162
4	110	434	0	0
5	95	529	1	95
6	82	611	2	164
7	26	637	3	78
8	13	650	4	52
9	2	652	5	10
	$N = 652$			$\Sigma f\,\|D\| = 981$

$$\text{Median} = \frac{652}{2} = 326 = 4\text{th month}$$

$$\text{M.D.} = \frac{\Sigma f\,|\text{D}|}{\text{N}} = \frac{981}{652}$$

$$= \mathbf{1.5}$$

Problem 21. With median as the base calculate the mean deviation and compare the variability of the two series A and B :

Series A	*Series B*
3484	487
4572	508
4124	620
3682	382
5624	408
4388	266
3680	186
4308	218

(*C.A.*)

Solution :

We have to rearrange the data in an ascending order to find out median.

$$\text{Median} = \text{size of } \frac{N+1}{2}\text{th item} = \frac{8+1}{2}\text{th item}$$

$$= 4.5\text{th item i.e. the average of the 4th and 5th item.}$$

$$\text{Series A} = \frac{4124+4308}{2} = 4216$$

$$\text{Series B} = \frac{382+408}{2} = 395$$

Computation of Mean deviation

Series A		*Series B*	
X_1	$\|D\| = X - 4216$	X_2	$\|D\| = X - 395$
3484	732	186	209
3680	536	218	177
3682	534	266	129
4124	92	382	13
4308	92	408	13
4388	172	487	92
4572	356	508	113
5624	1408	620	225
	$\Sigma\|D\| = 3922$		$\Sigma\|D\| = 971$

$$\text{M.D. (Series) A} = \frac{\Sigma|D_1|}{N} = \frac{3922}{8}$$

$$= \mathbf{490.25}$$

$$\text{M.D. (Series) B} = \frac{\Sigma|D_2|}{N} = \frac{971}{8}$$

$$= \mathbf{121.38}$$

$$\text{The Coefficient of mean Deviation} = \frac{M.D}{Median} \times 100$$

$$\text{Series A} = \frac{490.25}{4216} \times 100$$

$$= \mathbf{11.63\%}$$

$$\text{Sereis B} = = \frac{121.38}{395} \times 100$$

$$= \mathbf{30.73\%}$$

The coefficient of M.D. for series B (30.73%) is greater than the coefficient of M.D. for series A (11.63%). Therefore series B has greater variability.

Problem 22. Calculate mean deviation from mean and median for the following data :

100 150 200 250 360 490 500 600 671

Also calculate coefficient of mean deviation. *(B. Com.)*

Solution :

Computation of Mean Deviation

X	$\lvert D\rvert = X - \overline{X}$ $= X - 369$	$\lvert D\rvert = X - Median$ $= X - 360$
100	269	260
150	219	210
200	169	160
250	119	110
360	9	0
490	121	130
500	131	140
600	231	240
671	302	311
$\Sigma X = 3321$	$\Sigma \lvert D\rvert = 1570$	$\Sigma \lvert D\rvert = 1561$

Mean =

$$\overline{X} = \frac{\Sigma X}{N} = \frac{3321}{9} = \mathbf{369}$$

M.D. from mean =

$$\frac{\Sigma|D|}{9} = \frac{1570}{9} = \mathbf{174.44}$$

Coefficient of M.D.

$$= \frac{M.D.}{\overline{X}} = \frac{174.44}{369} = \mathbf{0.47}$$

Median

$$= \text{value of } \frac{(N+1)}{2} \text{ th item}$$

$$= \text{value of } \frac{(9+1)}{2} \text{ th item}$$

$$= \text{value of 5th item}$$

$$= \mathbf{360}$$

M.D. from Median

$$= \frac{\Sigma|D|}{N} = \frac{1561}{9} = \mathbf{173.44}$$

Coefficient of M. D.

$$= \frac{M.D.}{Median} = \frac{173.44}{360} = \mathbf{0.48}$$

Problem 23. Find out the coefficient of mean deviation in the following series :

Age in year :	0–10	10–20	20–30	30–40	40–50	50–60	60–70	70–80
No. of men	20	25	32	40	42	35	10	8

Calculation to be made correct to one decimel place only. (*B. Com. Andhra*)

Solution :

Computation of Mean Deviation

X	m	f	$d' = \frac{m-35}{10}$	fd'	$\|D\|$	$f\ \|D\|$
0–10	5	20	−3	-60	31.5	530
10–20	15	25	−2	−50	21.5	537.5
20–30	25	32	−1	−32	11.5	368
30–40	35	40	0	0	1.5	60
40–50	45	42	1	42	8.5	357
50–60	55	35	2	70	18.5	674.5
60–70	65	10	3	30	28.5	285
70–80	75	8	4	32	38.5	308
		$N = 212$		$\Sigma fd' = 32$		$\Sigma f\ \|D\| = 3093$

Mean : $\overline{X} = A + \frac{\Sigma fd'}{N} \times i$

$$= 35 + \frac{32}{212} \times 10 = 35 + 1.5$$

$$= \mathbf{36.5} \text{ years.}$$

Mean Deviation from Mean :

$$= \frac{\Sigma f\,|D|}{N}$$

$$= \frac{3093}{212}$$

$$= \mathbf{14.59}$$

Coefficient of M.D. :

$$= \frac{\text{M.D.}}{\overline{X}}$$

$$= 14.59 \div 36.5$$

$$= \mathbf{0.399 \text{ or } 0.4}$$

Problem 24. Calculate mean deviation from median from the following data :

Marks less than	*No. of Students*	*Marks less than*	*No. of Students*
80	100	40	32
70	90	30	20
60	80	20	13
50	60	10	5

(*B. Com. (Hons.) Delhi*)

Solution:

Computation of Mean Deviation

Class interval	*Mid point* (m)	*Frequency* f	*c.f.*	$\lvert D\rvert =$ $m - 46.43$	$f\,\lvert D\rvert$
0–10	5	5	5	41.43	207.15
10–20	15	13– 5= 8	13	31.43	251.44
20–30	25	20–13= 7	20	21.43	150.01
30–40	45	32–20=12	32	11.43	137.16
40–50	45	60–32=28	60	1.43	40.04
50–60	55	80–60=20	80	8.57	171.14
60–70	65	90–80=10	90	18.57	185.70
70–80	75	100–90=10	100	28.57	285.70
		N=100			$\Sigma f\,\lvert D\rvert$ = 1428.34

$$\text{Median} = \text{size of } \frac{N}{2}\text{th item}$$

$$= \text{size of } \frac{100}{2}\text{th item}$$

$$= \text{size of 50th item which lies in the class 40–50}$$

$$\text{Median} = L_1 + \frac{\frac{N}{2} - c.f}{f} \times i$$

$$L_1 = 40;\ \frac{N}{2} = 50;\ c.f. = 32;\ f = 28;\ i = 10$$

$$= 40 + \frac{50 - 32}{28} \times 10 = 40 + 6.43$$

$$= \mathbf{46.43.}$$

$$\text{M.D.} = \frac{\Sigma f\,\lvert D\rvert}{N}$$

$$= \frac{1428.34}{100} = 14.2834$$

$$= \mathbf{14.28}$$

Problem 25 : Calculate Mean deviation from median from the following data :

Class interval	f
20–25	6
25–30	12
30–40	17
40–45	30
45–50	10
20–25	6
50–55	10

Class interval	*f*
55–60	8
60–70	5
70–80	2

Also calculate co-efficient of mean deviation. (*B. Com. Delhi*)

Solution :

Computation of Mean Deviation from Median

Class interval	*Mid point* (m)	f	$c.f.$	$\lvert D \rvert = m - 42.5$	$f\lvert D\rvert$
20–25	22.5	6	6	20	120
25–30	27.5	12	18	15	180
30–40	35	17	35	7.5	127.5
40–45	42.5	30	65	0	0
45–50	47.5	10	75	5	50
50–55	52.5	10	85	10	100
55–60	57.5	8	93	15.0	120
60–70	65	5	98	22.5	112.5
70–80	75	2	100	32.5	65
		N=100			$\Sigma f\lvert D\rvert = 875.0$

$$\text{Median} = \text{size of } \frac{N}{2}\text{th item}$$

$$= \text{size of } \frac{100}{2}\text{th item}$$

$$= \text{50th item which lies in the class 40–45}$$

$$\text{Median} = L_1 + \frac{\frac{N}{2} - c.f}{f} \times i$$

$$L_1 = 40\ ;\ \frac{N}{2} = 50\ ;\ c.f. = 35\ ;\ f = 30\ ;\ i = 5$$

$$= 40 + \frac{50 - 35}{30} \times 5$$

$$= 40 + \frac{75}{30} = 40 + 2.5$$

$$= \mathbf{42.5}$$

$$\text{M.D.} = \frac{\Sigma f\lvert D\rvert}{N} = \frac{875}{100}$$

$$= \mathbf{8.75}$$

$$\text{The Coefficient of M.D.} = \frac{\text{M.D.}}{\text{Median}} = \frac{8.75}{42.5}$$

$$= \mathbf{0.206}$$

Problem 26. Calculate mean deviation (from. Mean) from the following data :

size of item	*Frequency*
3–4	3
4–5	7
5–6	22
6–7	60
7–8	85
8–9	32
9–10	8

(*B. Com. Meerut*)

Solution :

Computation of Mean Deviation from Mean

size of item	*M.P.* m	f	$d = m - 6.5$	fd	fm	
3–4	3.5	3	−3	−9	10.5	$\Sigma fm_b = 553$
4–5	4.5	7	−2	−14	31.5	$\Sigma fb = 92$
5–6	5.5	22	−1	−22	121.0	
6–7	6.5	60	0	0	390.0	
7–8	7.5	85	1	85	637.5	$\Sigma fm_a = 985.5$
8–9	8.5	32	2	64	272.0	$\Sigma fa = 125$
9–10	9.5	8	3	24	76.0	
		$N = 217$		$\Sigma fd = 128$		

$$\text{Mean} : \overline{X} = A + \frac{\Sigma fd}{N} \qquad A = 6.5\,;\ \Sigma fd = 128\ ;\ \text{N} = 217$$

$$= 6.5 + \frac{128}{217} = 6.5 + 0.59$$

$$= \mathbf{7.09}$$

Since the mean is in fraction we can use an alternative formula for an easy calculation.

$$\text{M.D.} = \frac{\Sigma mf_a - \Sigma fm_b - (\Sigma fa - fb) \times \overline{X}}{N}$$

$$\Sigma mf_a = 985.5\,;\ \Sigma fm_b = 553\,;\ \Sigma fa = 125\,;\ \Sigma fb = 92\,;$$

$$N = 217\,;\ \overline{X} = 7.09$$

$$\text{M.D.} = \frac{985.5 - 553 - [(125 - 92) \times 7.09]}{217}$$

$$= \frac{985.5 - 553 - 233.97}{217} = \frac{198.53}{217}$$

$$= \mathbf{0.915}$$

Problem 27 : Calculate any measure of dispersion for the following distribution of the number of particles emitted by a radio active substance :

No. of particles emitted	:	0–2	3–5	6–8	9–11	12–14
Frequency	:	643	1465	451	86	2

(*B. Com.*)

Solution :

Calculation of Mean Deviation

No. of Particles emitted	*M.P.*	*f*	$d' = \frac{m-4}{3}$	fd'	$\|D\| = m\text{-}3.98$	$f\ \|D\|$
0– 2	1	643	−1	−643	2.98	1961.14
3– 5	4	1465	0	0	.02	29.30
6– 8	7	451	1	451	3.02	1362.02
9–11	10	86	2	172	6.02	517.72
12–14	13	2	3	6	9.02	18.04
		N =2647		$\Sigma fd'$ = −14		$\Sigma f\ \|D\|$ = 3843.22

$$\text{Mean : } \bar{X} = A + \frac{\Sigma fd'}{N} \times C$$

$$A = 4;\ \Sigma fd' = -14;\ N = 2647;\ C = 3$$

$$= 4 - \frac{14}{2647} \times 3 = 4 - 0.016 \text{ or } 4 - 0.02$$

$$= \mathbf{3.98}$$

Mean Deviation :

$$\text{M.D.} = \frac{\Sigma f\ |D|}{N} \quad \Sigma f\ |D| = 3843.22\ N = 2647$$

$$= \frac{3843.22}{2647}$$

$$= \mathbf{1.45.}$$

Problem 28. Calculate the mean deviation from the following data. What light does it throw on the social condition of the community? Diffrence in age between husband and wife.

Difference in years	:	0–5	5–10	10–15	15–20	20–25	25–30	30–35	35–40
Frequency	:	449	705	507	281	109	52	16	4

(*B. Com. Bombay*)

Solution :

Computation of Mean Deviation from Median

Difference inyears	m	f	$c.f$	fm	
0 – 5	2.5	449	449	1122.5	$\Sigma fm_b = 6410$
5 – 10	7.5	705	1154	5287.5	$\Sigma fb = 1154$
10 – 15	12.5	507	1661	6337.5	
15 – 20	17.5	281	1942	4917.5	
20 – 25	22.5	109	2051	2452.5	$\Sigma fm_a = 15827.5$
25 – 30	27.5	52	2103	1430	$\Sigma fa = 969$
30 – 35	32.5	16	2119	520	
35 – 50	42.5	4	2123	170	
		$N = 2123$			

$$\text{Median} = \text{size of} \frac{N}{2} \text{ th item}$$

$$= \text{size of} \frac{2123}{2} \text{ th item}$$

$$= 1061.5 \text{ th item which lies in the class 5–10}$$

$$\text{Median} = L_1 + \frac{\frac{N}{2} - c.f}{f} \times i$$

$$L_1 = 5\ ;\ \frac{N}{2} = 1061.5;\ c.f. = 449;\ f = 705;\ i = 5$$

$$= 5 + \frac{1061.5 - 449}{705} \times 5 = 5 + 4.34$$

$$= \mathbf{9.34}.$$

Since the value of median is in fraction, the following formula is used.

$$\text{M.D.} = \frac{\Sigma mf_a - \Sigma fm_b - (\Sigma fa - \Sigma fb) \times \text{Median}}{N}$$

$$\Sigma mf_a = 15827.5;\ \Sigma fm_b = 6410;\ \Sigma fa = 969;\ \Sigma fb = 1154;$$

$$N = 2123.$$

$$= \frac{15827.5 - 6410 - \{(969 - 1154) \times 9.34\}}{2123}$$

$$= \frac{9417.5 - \{(-185) \times 9.34\}}{2123}$$

$$= \frac{9417.5 - (-1727.9)}{2123}$$

$$= \frac{11,145.4}{2123} = \mathbf{5.25}$$

STANDARD DEVIATION

Problem 29. The table below gives the marks obtained by 10 B. Com students in statistics examination. Calculate standard deviation.

R. No.	1	2	3	4	5	6	7	8	9	10
Marks	43	48	65	57	31	60	37	48	78	59

(*B. Com. Madras*)

Solution :

Computation of Standard Deviation
(Deviations from assumed mean)

R. No.	*Marks* (*X*)	$d : X - A$ ($A = 50$)	d^2
[-9pt] 1	43	−7	49
2	48	−2	4
3	65	+15	225
4	57	+7	49
5	31	−19	361
6	60	+10	100
7	37	−13	169
8	48	−2	4
9	78	+28	784
10	59	+9	81
$N = 10$		$\Sigma d = 26$	$\Sigma d^2 = 1826$

$$\sigma = \sqrt{\frac{\Sigma d^2}{N} - \left(\frac{\Sigma d}{N}\right)^2} = \sqrt{\frac{1826}{10} - \left(\frac{26}{10}\right)^2}$$

$$= \sqrt{182.6 - (2.6)^2} = \sqrt{182.6 - 6.76}$$

$$= \sqrt{175.84}$$

$$= \mathbf{13.26}$$

Problem 30. 10 students of the B. Com class of a college obtained the following marks in statistics out of 100. Calculate the standard deviation.

S. No.	1	2	3	4	5	6	7	8	9	10
Marks	5	10	20	25	40	42	45	48	70	80

(*B. Com. Osmania*)

Solution :

Calculation of Standard Deviation

S.No.	*Marks*	$d = (X - 40)$	d^2
1	5	−35	1225
2	10	−30	900
3	20	−20	400
4	25	−15	225

S.No.	*Marks*	$d = (X - 40)$	d^2
5	40	0	0
6	42	2	4
7	45	5	25
8	48	8	64
9	70	30	900
10	80	40	1600
$N = 10$		$\Sigma d = -15$	$\Sigma d^2 = 5343$

$$\sigma = \sqrt{\frac{\Sigma d^2}{N} - \left(\frac{\Sigma d}{N}\right)^2}$$

$$\Sigma d^2 = 5343, \quad N = 10, \quad \Sigma d = -15$$

$$= \sqrt{\frac{5343}{10} - \left(-\frac{15}{10}\right)^2}$$

$$= \sqrt{534.3 - 2.25} = \sqrt{532.05}$$

$$= \mathbf{23.07}$$

Problem 31. Calculate standard deviation from the following :

Marks	*No. of students*	*Marks*	*No. of students*
10	8	40	10
20	12	50	7
30	20	60	3

(*B. Com.*)

Solution :

Computation of Standard Deviation

Marks	f	$d' = \frac{X-30}{10}$	fd'	fd'^2
10	8	−2	−16	32
20	12	−1	−12	12
30	20	0	0	0
40	10	1	10	10
50	7	2	14	28
60	3	3	9	27
	$N = 60$		$\Sigma fd' = 5$	$\Sigma fd'^2 = 109$

$$\sigma = \sqrt{\frac{\Sigma fd'^2}{N} - \left(\frac{\Sigma fd'}{N}\right)^2}$$

$$\Sigma fd'^2 = 109, \quad \Sigma fd' = 5, \quad N = 60, \quad C = 10$$

$$= \sqrt{\frac{109}{60} - \left(\frac{5}{60}\right)^2} \times C$$

$$= \sqrt{8.817 - 0.0069} \times 10$$
$$= \sqrt{1.81} \times 10 = 1.35 \times 10$$
$$= \mathbf{13.5}$$

Problem 32. Calculate standard deviation from the following data regarding the marks obtained by students in an Accountancy practical test :

Marks	1	2	3	4	5	6	7	8	9
No. of students	32	41	57	98	123	83	46	17	3

What will be the value of standard deviation if the marks obtained by each of the students are increased by one ? (*B. Com. Shivaji*)

Solution :

Computation of Standard Deviation

Marks (X)	*No. of students* (f)	$d = X - 5$	fd	fd^2
1	32	−4	−128	512
2	41	−3	−123	369
3	57	−2	−114	228
4	98	−1	−98	98
5	123	0	0	0
6	83	1	83	83
7	46	2	92	184
8	17	3	51	153
9	3	4	12	48
	$N = 500$		$\Sigma fd = -225$	$\Sigma fd^2 = 1675$

Standard Deviation :

$$\sigma = \sqrt{\frac{\Sigma fd^2}{N} - \left(\frac{\Sigma fd}{N}\right)^2}$$

$$\Sigma fd^2 = 1675, \quad N = 500, \quad \Sigma fd = -225$$

$$= \sqrt{\frac{1675}{500} - \left(-\frac{225}{500}\right)^2}$$

$$= \sqrt{3.35 - 0.203} = \sqrt{3.147}$$

$$= \mathbf{1.774}$$

If the marks obtained by each of the students are increased by one, the result obtained above would not be affected i.e. same value.

Problem 33. Compute the standard deviation of household size from the following frequence distribution of 500 household covered in a sample survey :

Household size	:	1	2	3	4	5	6	7	8	9
No. of household	:	92	49	52	82	102	60	35	24	4

(*B.A (Ecos.) (Hons) Calcutta*)

Solution :

Computation of Standard Deviation

Household size X	*No. of house-hold (f)*	$d = X - 5$	*fd*	*fd*²
1	92	−4	−368	1472
2	49	−3	−147	441
3	52	−2	−104	208
4	82	−1	−82	82
5	102	0	0	0
6	60	1	60	60
7	35	2	70	140
8	24	3	72	216
9	4	4	16	64
	$N = 500$		$\Sigma fd = -483$	$\Sigma fd^2 = 2683$

Standard Deviation: $\sigma = \sqrt{\frac{\Sigma fd^2}{N} - \left(\frac{\Sigma fd}{N}\right)^2}$

$\Sigma fd^2 = 2683, \quad N = 500, \quad \Sigma fd = -483$

$$= \sqrt{\frac{2683}{500} - \left(\frac{-483}{500}\right)^2}$$

$$= \sqrt{5.366 - (-0.966)^2}$$

$$= \sqrt{5.366 - 0.933} = \sqrt{4.433}$$

$$= \mathbf{2.106}$$

Problem 34. Calculate standard deviation from the following data :

X	1	3	5	7	9	11
F	4	6	5	5	8	2

(*B.A. madurai*)

Solution :

Computation of Standard Deviation

X	*f*	$d = X - 5$	*fd*	*fd*²
1	4	−4	−16	64
3	6	−2	−12	24
5	5	0	0	0
7	5	2	10	20
9	8	4	32	128
11	2	6	12	72
	$N = 30$		$\Sigma fd = 26$	$\Sigma fd^2 = 308$

$$\sigma = \sqrt{\frac{\Sigma fd^2}{N} - \left(\frac{\Sigma fd}{N}\right)^2}$$

$$\Sigma fd^2 = 308; \quad N = 30; \quad \Sigma fd = 26$$

$$\sigma = \sqrt{\frac{308}{30} - \left(\frac{26}{30}\right)^2}$$

$$= \sqrt{10.27 - 0.75} = \sqrt{9.52}$$

$$= \mathbf{3.09}$$

Problem 35: Calculate the S.D. of the following:

size of the item	: 6	7	8	9	10	11	12
Frequency	: 3	6	9	13	8	5	4

(*B. Com., Madras*)

Solution :

Computation of Standard Deviation

size of item X	f	$d = X - 9$	fd	fd^2
6	3	−3	− 9	27
7	6	−2	−12	24
8	9	−1	−9	9
9	13	0	0	0
10	8	1	8	8
11	5	2	10	20
12	4	3	12	36
	$N = 48$		$\Sigma fd = 0$	$\Sigma fd^2 = 124$

Standard Deviation :

$$\sigma = \sqrt{\frac{\Sigma fd^2}{N} - \left(\frac{\Sigma fd}{N}\right)^2}$$

$$\Sigma fd^2 = 124; \quad N = 48; \quad \Sigma fd = 0$$

$$= \sqrt{\frac{124}{48} - \left(\frac{0}{48}\right)^2} = \sqrt{2.58 - 0} = \mathbf{1.6.}$$

Problem 36 : Calculate the standard deviation for the data :

X	: 50	60	70	80	90	100	110	120
F	: 14	40	54	46	26	12	6	2

(*B. Com. Madurai*)

Solution :

Computation of Standard Deviation

X	f	$d' = \frac{X-80}{10}$	fd'	fd'^2
50	14	−3	−42	126
60	40	−2	−80	160
70	54	−1	−54	54
80	46	0	0	0
90	26	1	26	26
100	12	2	24	48
110	6	3	18	54
120	2	4	8	32
	$N = 200$		$\Sigma fd' = -100$	$\Sigma fd^2 = 500$

Standard Deviation : $\sigma = \sqrt{\frac{\Sigma fd'^2}{N} - \left(\frac{\Sigma fd'}{N}\right)^2} \times C$

$\Sigma fd'^2 = 500; \quad N = 200, \quad \Sigma fd' = -100; \quad C = 10$

$$\sigma = \sqrt{\frac{500}{200} - \left(\frac{-100}{200}\right)^2} \times 10$$

$$= \sqrt{2.5 - (-0.05)^2} \times 10$$

$$= \sqrt{2.5 - 0.25} \times 10$$

$$= \sqrt{2.25} \times 10 = 1.5 \times 10$$

$$= \mathbf{15.}$$

Problem 37 : Calculate standard deviation from the following data :

Mid points	*Frequency*	*Mid point*	*Frequency*
1	2	6	155
2	60	7	79
3	101	8	40
4	152	9	1
5	205		

(*ICWA*

Solution :

Computation of Standard Deviation

Mid points	f	$d = (m - 5)$	fd	fd^2
1	2	−4	−8	32
2	60	−3	−180	540
3	101	−2	−202	404
4	152	−1	−152	152

Mid points	*f*	$d = (m-5)$	*fd*	fd^2
5	205	0	0	0
6	155	1	155	155
7	79	2	158	316
8	40	3	120	360
9	1	4	4	16
	$N = 795$		$\Sigma fd = -105$	$\Sigma fd^2 = 1975$

Standard Deviation : $\sigma = \sqrt{\frac{\Sigma fd^2}{N} - \left(\frac{\Sigma fd}{N}\right)^2}$

$$\Sigma fd^2 = 1975; \quad N = 795, \quad \Sigma fd = -105$$

$$= \sqrt{\frac{1975}{795} - \left(\frac{-105}{795}\right)^2}$$

$$= \sqrt{2.484 - (0.132)^2}$$

$$= \sqrt{2.484 - 0.017} = \sqrt{2.467}$$

$$= \mathbf{1.57}$$

Problem 38. Daily sales (recorded in rupees) of a retail shop are given below :

Daily sales in Rs. (X-Mid pt. of interval)	102	106	110	114	118	122	126
No. of days (*Frequecy-f*)	3	9	25	35	17	10	1

Calculate the mean and the standard deviation of the above data and explain what they indicate about the distribution of daily sales ?

(*M.A. Eco. Madurai,*)

Solution :

Computation of Mean and Standard Deviation

No. of days (X)	*f*	$d' = \frac{X-114}{4}$	fd'	fd^2
102	3	−3	−9	27
106	9	−2	−18	36
110	25	−1	−25	25
114	35	0	0	0
118	17	1	17	17
122	10	2	20	40
126	1	3	3	9
	$N = 100$		$\Sigma fd' = -12$	$\Sigma fd'^2 = 154$

$$\text{Mean} : \overline{X} = A + \frac{\Sigma fd}{N} \times C$$

$$A = 114; \quad \Sigma fd = -12; \quad N = 100; \quad C = 4$$

$$= 114 - \frac{12}{100} \times 4 = 114 - 0.48$$

$$= \mathbf{113.52}$$

Standard Deviation : $\sigma = \sqrt{\frac{\Sigma fd^2}{N} - \left(\frac{\Sigma fd}{N}\right)^2} \times C$

$\Sigma fd^2 = 154; \quad N = 100; \Sigma fd = -12; \quad C = 4$

$$= \sqrt{\frac{154}{100} - \left(-\frac{12}{100}\right)^2} \times 4$$

$$= \sqrt{1.54 - (-0.12)^2} \times 4$$

$$= \sqrt{1.54 - 0.0144} \times 4$$

$$= \sqrt{1.5256} \times 4 = 1.235 \times 4$$

$$= \mathbf{4.94}$$

Problem 39. The following table gives the number of finished articles turned out pe day by different number of workers in a factory. Find the mean value and the standar deviation of the output of finished articles :

No. of articles	*No. of workers*	*No. of articles*	*No. of workers*
18	3	23	17
19	7	24	13
20	11	25	8
21	14	26	5
22	18	27	4

(*B. Com., Madurai,*

Solution

Computation of Mean and Standard Deviation

No. of articles X	*f*	$d = X - 22$	*fd*	fd^2
18	3	−4	−12	48
19	7	−3	−21	63
20	11	−2	−22	44
21	14	−1	−14	14
22	18	0	0	0
23	17	1	17	17
24	13	2	26	52
25	8	3	24	72
26	5	4	20	80
27	4	5	20	100
	$N = 100$		$\Sigma fd = 38$	$\Sigma fd^2 = 490$

Mean : $\overline{X} = A + \frac{\Sigma fd}{N}$

$$A = 22; \quad \Sigma fd = 38; \quad N = 100$$
$$= 22 + \frac{38}{100} = 22 + 0.38$$
$$= \mathbf{22.38}$$

Standard deviation :

$$\sigma = \sqrt{\frac{\Sigma fd^2}{N} - \left(\frac{\Sigma fd}{N}\right)^2}$$
$$\Sigma fd^2 = 490; \quad N = 100; \quad \Sigma fd = 38$$
$$= \sqrt{\frac{490}{100} - \left(\frac{38}{100}\right)^2}$$
$$= \sqrt{4.90 - (0.38)^2}$$
$$= \sqrt{4.90 - 0.1444} = \sqrt{4.7556}$$
$$= \mathbf{2.18}$$

Problem 40. Calculate standard deviation for the following data :

Mid point	1	2	3	4	5	6	7	8	9
Frequency	6	45	103	147	205	160	80	40	4

(*B.A. Madurai*)

Solution :

Computation of Standard Deviation

Mid point	*Frequency*	$d = X - 5$	fd	fd^2
1	6	−4	−24	96
2	45	−3	−135	405
3	103	−2	−206	412
4	147	−1	−147	147
5	205	0	0	0
6	160	1	160	160
7	80	2	160	320
8	40	3	120	360
9	4	4	60	64
	$N = 790$		$\Sigma fd = -56$	$\Sigma fd^2 = 1964$

$$\text{Standard Deviation} = \sqrt{\frac{\Sigma fd^2}{N} - \left(\frac{\Sigma fd}{N}\right)^2}$$
$$\Sigma fd^2 = 1964; \quad N = 790; \quad \Sigma fd = -56$$
$$= \sqrt{\frac{1964}{790} - \left(\frac{-56}{790}\right)^2}$$
$$= \sqrt{2.486 - 0.005}$$
$$= \sqrt{2.481}$$
$$= \mathbf{1.575}$$

Problem 41. Compute the standard deviation of the following data :

Wages per day (Rs.)	*No. of workers*
1–3	15
3–5	18
5–7	27
7–9	10
9–11	6

(*B. Com. Andhra*)

Solution :

X	m	f	$d' = \frac{m-6}{2}$	fd'	fd'^2
1–3	2	15	−2	−30	60
3–5	4	18	−1	−18	18
5–7	6	27	0	0	0
7–9	8	10	1	10	10
9–11	10	6	2	12	24
		N=76		$\Sigma fd' = -26$	$\Sigma fd'^2 = 112$

$$\sigma = \sqrt{\frac{\Sigma fd'^2}{N} - \left(\frac{\Sigma fd'}{N}\right)^2} \times C$$

$$\Sigma fd'^2 = 112; \quad \Sigma fd' = -26; \quad N = 76; \quad C = 2$$

$$= \sqrt{\frac{112}{76} - \left(-\frac{26}{76}\right)^2} \times 2$$

$$= \sqrt{1.474 - (0.34)^2} \times 2$$

$$= \sqrt{1.474 - 0.1156} \times 2$$

$$= \sqrt{1.3584.} \quad \times 2$$

$$= 1.166 \times 2$$

$$= \mathbf{2.33}$$

Problem 42. Find out the arithmetic mean and standard deviation from following data :

Variable	*Frequency*	*Variable*	*Frequency*
5–10	2	20–25	54
10–15	9	25–30	11
15–20	29	30–35	6

(*B. Com. Madurai*)

Solution :

Computation of Mean and Standard Deviation

Variable	$m.p(m)$	f	$d' = \frac{m-17.5}{5}$	fd^1	$fd^{\prime 2}$
5–10	7.5	2	−2	−4	8
10–15	12.5	9	−1	−9	9
15–20	17.5	29	0	0	0
20–25	22.5	54	1	54	54
25–30	27.5	11	2	22	44
30–35	32.5	6	3	18	54
		$N = 111$		$\Sigma fd^1 = 81$	$\Sigma fd'^2 = 169$

$$\text{Mean : } \overline{X} = A + \frac{\Sigma fd'}{N} \times C$$

$$A = 17.5; \quad \Sigma fd' = 81; \quad N = 111; \quad C = 5$$

$$= 17.5 + \frac{81}{111} \times 5 = 17.5 + 3.65$$

$$= \mathbf{21.15}$$

Standard Deviation :

$$\sigma = \sqrt{\frac{\Sigma fd'^2}{N} - \left(\frac{\Sigma fd'}{N}\right)^2} \times C$$

$$\Sigma fd'^2 = 169; \quad \Sigma fd' = 81; \quad N = 111; \quad C = 5$$

$$= \sqrt{\frac{169}{111} - \left(\frac{81}{111}\right)^2} \times 5$$

$$= \sqrt{1.52 - (0.73)^2} \times 5$$

$$= \sqrt{1.52 - .533} \times 5$$

$$= \sqrt{0.987} \times 5$$

$$= 0.99 \times 5$$

$$= \mathbf{4.95}$$

Problem 43. Compute the S.D. for the following frequency distribution of wage earners in a factory :

Wages per hour (in Rs.)	: 9	12	15	18	21	24	27	30
No. of Wage Earners	: 20	60	150	250	200	120	50	40

(*B. Com., Madurai*)

Solution :

Computation of Standard Deviation

Wages per hour (in Rs.) (X)	No. of wage earners f	$d = \frac{X-18}{3}$	fd	fd^2
9	20	−3	−60	180
12	60	−2	−120	240
15	150	−1	−150	150
18	250	0	0	0
21	200	1	200	200
24	120	2	240	480
27	50	3	150	450
30	40	4	160	640
	$N = 890$		$\Sigma fd =$ 420	$\Sigma fd^2 =$ 2340

Standard Deviation :

$$\sigma = \sqrt{\frac{\Sigma fd^2}{N} - \left(\frac{\Sigma fd}{N}\right)^2} \times C$$

$$\Sigma fd^2 = 2340; \quad \Sigma fd = 420; \quad \text{N} = 890; \quad C = 3$$

$$\sigma = \sqrt{\frac{2340}{890} - \left(\frac{420}{890}\right)^2} \times 3$$

$$= \sqrt{2.629 - (0.472)^2 \times 3}$$

$$= \sqrt{2.406} \times 3$$

$$= \sqrt{1.551 \times 3}$$

$$= \mathbf{4.653}$$

Problem 44. The daily temperature recorded in a city in Russia in an year is given below :

Temperature °C	*No. of days*
−40 to −30	10
−30 to −20	28
−20 to −10	30
−10 to −00	42
0 to 10	65
10 to 20	180
20 to 30	10
	365

Calculate the mean and standard deviation. (*C.A.*)

Solution :

Computation of mean and Standard Deviation

Temperature C°	*Mid value* (m)	*No. of days f*	$d' = \frac{m-0}{5}$	fd'	fd'^2
−40 to −30	−35	10	−7	−70	490
−30 to −20	−25	28	−5	−140	700
−20 to −10	−15	30	−3	−90	270
−10 to 0	−5	42	−1	−42	42
0 to 10	+5	65	+1	+65	65
10 to 20	+15	180	+3	+540	1620
20 to 30	+25	10	+5	+50	250
		$N : 365$		$\Sigma fd' =$ 313	$\Sigma fd'^2 =$ 3437

$$\text{Mean : } \overline{X} = A + \frac{\Sigma fd'}{N} \times C = 0 + \frac{313 \times 5}{365}$$

$$= \mathbf{4.3°C}$$

$$\sigma = \sqrt{\frac{\Sigma fd'^2}{N} - \left(\frac{\Sigma fd'}{N}\right)^2} \times C$$

$$\sigma = \sqrt{\frac{3437}{365} - \left(\frac{313}{365}\right)^2} \times 5$$

$$= \sqrt{9.4164 - 0.736} \times 5$$

$$= \sqrt{8.6804} \times 5$$

$$= 2.946 \times 5$$

$$= \mathbf{14.73°C}$$

Problem 45. Compute the standard deviation and mean deviation from the following data :

Class (X)	:	0–10	10–20	20–30	30–40	40–50	50–60	60–70
Frequency (f)	:	8	12	17	14	9	7	4

(*B. Sc. Madras*)

Solution :

Computation of Mean Deviation and Standard Deviation

Class (X)	*M.V.* (m)	$d' = \frac{m-35}{10}$	f	fd'	fd'^2	$\lvert D\rvert$ $(X - \overline{X})$ $(\overline{X}) =$ 30.775	$f\lvert D\rvert$
0–10	5	−3	8	−24	72	25.775	206.200
10–20	15	−2	12	−24	48	15.775	189.300

Class (X)	*M.V.* (m)	$d' = \frac{m-35}{10}$	f	fd'	fd'^2	$\lvert D \rvert$ $(X - \overline{X})$ $(\overline{X}) =$ 30.775	$f\lvert D \rvert$
20–30	25	−1	17	−17	17	5.775	98.175
30–40	35	0	14	0	0	4.225	59.150
40–50	45	1	9	9	9	14.225	128.025
50–60	55	2	7	14	28	24.225	169.575
60–70	65	3	4	12	36	34.225	136.900
			$N : 71$	$\Sigma fd' =$ −30	$\Sigma fd'^2$ = 210		$\Sigma f\lvert D \rvert$ = 987.325

$$\text{Mean : } \overline{X} = A - \frac{\Sigma fd'}{N} \times C$$

$$A : 35; \quad \Sigma fd' = -30; \quad N = 71; \quad C = 10$$

$$= 35 - \frac{30}{71} \times 10$$

$$= 35 - 4.225$$

$$= \mathbf{30.775}$$

$$\text{M.D. : } \frac{\Sigma f\lvert D \rvert}{N} = \frac{987.325}{71}$$

$$= \mathbf{13.906}$$

Standard Deviation :

$$= \sqrt{\frac{\Sigma fd'^2}{N} - \left(\frac{\Sigma fd'}{N}\right)^2} \times C$$

$$= \sqrt{\frac{210}{71} - \left(\frac{-30}{71}\right)^2} \times 10$$

$$= \sqrt{2.957 - (-0.4225)^2} \times 10$$

$$= \sqrt{2.957 - 0.1785} \times 10$$

$$= 1.667 \times 10$$

$$= \mathbf{16.67}$$

Problem 46. Calculate the arithmetic Mean and standard deviation for the following data :

Class interval :	5–10	10–15	15–20	20–25	25–30	30–35	35–40	40–45
Frequency :	6	5	15	10	5	4	3	2

(*B.A. Bombay*)

Solution :

Computation of Mean and Standard Deviation

X	m	f	$d' = \frac{m - 27.5}{5}$	fd'	fd'^2
5–10	7.5	6	−4	−24	96
10–15	12.5	5	−3	−15	45
15–20	17.5	15	−2	−30	60
20–25	22.5	10	−1	−10	10
25–30	27.5	5	0	0	0
30–35	32.5	4	1	4	4
35–40	37.5	3	2	6	12
40–45	42.5	2	3	6	18
		$N = 50$		$\Sigma fd' = -63$	$\Sigma fd'^2 = 245$

$$\overline{X} = A + \frac{\Sigma fd'}{N} \times C$$

$$A = 27.5; \quad \Sigma fd' = -63; \quad N = 50; \quad C = 5$$

$$= 27.5 - \frac{63}{50} \times 5$$

$$= 27.5 - 6.3$$

$$= \mathbf{21.2}$$

$$\sigma = \sqrt{\frac{\Sigma fd'^2}{N} - \left(\frac{\Sigma fd'}{N}\right)^2} \times C$$

$$\sigma = \sqrt{\frac{245}{50} - \left(\frac{-63}{50}\right)^2} \times 5$$

$$= \sqrt{4.9 - (1.26)^2} \times 5$$

$$= \sqrt{4.9 - 1.5876} \times 5$$

$$= \sqrt{3.3124} \times 5$$

$$= 1.82 \times 5$$

$$= \mathbf{9.1}$$

Problem 47. A charitable organization decided to give old age pensions to people over sixty years of age. The scale of pensions were fixed as follows :

Age group	60–65	Rs. 20 per month
"	65–70	Rs. 25 per month
"	70–75	Rs. 30 per month
"	75–80	Rs. 35 per month
"	80–85	Rs. 40 per month

The ages of 25 persons who secured the pensions right are as given below :

74	62	84	72	61	83	72	81	64	71	63	61	60
67	74	64	79	73	75	76	69	68	78	66	67	

Calculate the monthly average pensions payable per person and the standard deviation.

(B. Com. (Hons) Delhi)

Solution : We must prepare a frequency distribution of 25 persons, in the age groups 60–65, 65–70 etc. Then we calculate the mean of pension payable and standard deviation.

Computation of Mean and Standard Deviation

Age group	*Tally marks*	f	*Monthly pension in Rs.*	$d' = \frac{X-30}{5}$	fd'	fd'^2
60–65	$\cancel{||||}$ ||	7	20	−2	−14	28
65–70	$\cancel{||||}$	5	25	−1	−5	5
70–75	$\cancel{||||}$ |	6	30	0	0	0
75–80	||||	4	35	1	4	4
80–85	|||	3	40	2	6	12
		$N = 25$			$\Sigma fd' = -9$	$\Sigma fd'^2 = 49$

$$\text{Mean : } \quad \overline{X} = A \pm \frac{\Sigma fd'}{N} \times C$$

$$A = 30, \quad \Sigma fd' = -9 \quad N = 25, \quad C = 5$$

$$= 30 - \frac{9}{25} \times 5 = 30 - 1.8$$

$$= 28.2$$

$$\sigma = \sqrt{\frac{\Sigma fd'^2}{N} - \left(\frac{\Sigma fd'}{N}\right)^2} \times C$$

$$\Sigma fd'^2 = 49, \quad N = 25, \quad \Sigma fd' = -9, \quad C = 15$$

$$= \sqrt{\frac{49}{25} - \left(\frac{-9}{25}\right)^2} \times 5$$

$$= \sqrt{1.96 - 0.13} \times 5$$

$$= \sqrt{1.83} \times 5$$

$$= 1.35 \times 5$$

$$= \mathbf{6.75}$$

Problem 48. Calculate the mean and standard deviation from the following data :

X below	:	20–25	25–30	30–35	35–40	40–45	45-50	50–55	above 55
f 20	:	26	44	60	101	109	84	66	10

(B. Com. Delhi)

Solution :

Mean and standard deviation cannot be found out in the open end class and therefore an assumption is to be made to decide the width of the class. In this problem the class width is 5 in all the cases and therefore the classes are 15–20 and 55–60.

Computation of Mean and Standard Deviation

Age group	*Mid point*	$d' = \frac{m - 37.5}{5}$	f	fd'	fd'^2
15–20	17.5	−4	20	−80	320
20–25	22.5	−3	26	−78	234
25–30	27.5	−2	44	−88	176
30–35	32.5	−1	60	−60	60
35–40	37.5	0	101	0	0
40–45	42.5	1	109	109	109
45–50	47.5	2	84	168	336
50–55	52.5	3	66	198	594
55–60	57.5	4	10	40	160
			$\Sigma f = 520$	$\Sigma fd' = 209$	$\Sigma fd'^2 = 1989$

Mean : $\overline{X} = A + \frac{\Sigma fd'}{N} \times C$

$$A = 37.5, \quad \Sigma fd' = 209, \quad N = 520, \quad C = 5$$

$$= 37.5 + \frac{209}{520} \times 5 = 37.5 + 2$$

$$= \mathbf{39.5}$$

$$\sigma = \sqrt{\frac{\Sigma fd'^2}{N} - \left(\frac{\Sigma fd'}{N}\right)^2} \times C$$

$$\Sigma fd'^2 = 1989, \quad \Sigma fd' = 209; \quad N = 520, \quad C = 5$$

$$= \sqrt{\frac{1989}{520} - \left(\frac{209}{520}\right)^2} \times 5$$

$$= \sqrt{3.83 - 0.16} \times 5$$

$$= \sqrt{3.67} \times 5$$

$$= 1.916 \times 5$$

$$= \mathbf{9.58}$$

Problem 49. Calculate the proportion of farms in which costs of production are within the range A.M. ± S.D. in the following distribution :

Cost of production (Rs. Per liter)	No. of dairy farms
4–6	13
6–8	111
8–10	182
10–12	105
12–14	19
14–16	7
	437

(*ICWA*)

Solution :

Computation of Mean and Standard Deviation

Cost of production (Rs. per litre)	*Mid point m*	*No. of dairy farms f f*	$d' = \frac{m-9}{2}$	fd'	$fd'2$
4–6	5	13	−2	− 26	52
6–8	7	111	−1	−111	111
8–10	9	182	0	0	0
10–12	11	105	1	105	105
12–14	13	19	2	38	76
14–16	15	7	3	21	63
		$N = 437$		$\Sigma fd' = -27$	$\Sigma fd'^2 = 407$

$$\text{Mean} : \overline{X} = A + \frac{\Sigma fd'}{N} \times C$$

$$A = 9, \quad \Sigma fd' = -27, \quad N = 437, \quad C = 2$$

$$= 9\frac{-27}{437} \times 2 = 9 + 0.12$$

$$= \mathbf{9.12}$$

$$\sigma = \sqrt{\frac{\Sigma fd'^2}{N} - \left(\frac{\Sigma fd'}{N}\right)^2} \times C$$

$$\Sigma fd'^2 = 407, \quad N = 437, \quad \Sigma fd' = -27, \quad C = 2$$

$$= \sqrt{\frac{407}{437} - \left(\frac{-27}{437}\right)^2} \times 5$$

$$= \sqrt{0.931 - 0.004} \times 2$$

$$= \sqrt{0.927} \times 2$$

$$= 0.963 \times 2$$

$$= \mathbf{1.926}$$

Problem 50. Given below is the frequency distribution of marks obtained by 90 students. Compare the arithmetic mean and standard deviation.

Marks	*No. of students*	*Marks*	*No. Students*
20–29	5	60–69	18
30–39	12	70–79	10
40–49	15	80–89	6
50–59	20	90–99	4

(*ICWA*)

Solution :

Computation of Mean and Standard Deviation

Marks	*Mid Point* (m)	*No. of Students* (f)	$d' = \frac{m-54.5}{10}$	fd'	fd'^2
20–29	24.5	5	−3	−15	45
30–39	34.5	12	−2	−24	48
40–49	44.5	15	−1	−15	15
50–59	54.5	20	0	0	0
60–69	64.5	18	1	18	18
70–79	74.5	10	2	20	40
80–89	84.5	6	3	18	54
90–99	94.5	4	4	16	64
		$N = 90$		$\Sigma fd' = 18$	$\Sigma fd'^2 = 284$

$$\text{Mean : } \overline{X} = A + \frac{\Sigma fd'}{N} \times C$$

$$A = 54.5, \quad \Sigma fd' = 18, \quad N = 90, \quad C = 10$$

$$= 54.5 + \frac{18}{90} \times 10 \qquad = 54.5 + 2$$

$$= \mathbf{56.5}$$

$$\sigma = \sqrt{\frac{\Sigma fd'^2}{N} - \left(\frac{\Sigma fd'}{N}\right)^2} \times C$$

$$\Sigma fd'^2 = 284, \quad \Sigma fd' = 18; \quad N = 90; \quad C = 10$$

$$= \sqrt{\frac{284}{90} - \left(\frac{18}{90}\right)^2} \times 10$$

$$= \sqrt{3.156 - 0.04} \times 10 \qquad = \sqrt{3.116} \times 10$$

$$= 1.765 \times 10 \qquad = \mathbf{17.65}$$

Problem 51. Calculate standard deviation of the following series:

Weekly wages (Rs)	*No. of workers*	*Weekly wages (Rs)*	*No. of workers*
100–105	200	130–135	410
105–110	210	135–140	320
110–115	230	140–145	280
115–120	320	145–150	210
120–125	350	150–155	160
125–130	520	155–160	90

(*B. Com. Delhi*)

Solution :

Computation of Standard Deviation

Weekly wages of workers in Rs.	*Mid point m*	*No. of workers f*	$d' = \frac{m-132.5}{5}$	fd'	fd'^2
100–105	102.5	200	−6	−1200	7200
105–110	107.5	210	−5	−1050	5250
110–115	112.5	230	−4	−920	3680
115–120	117.5	320	−3	−960	2880
120–125	122.5	350	−2	−700	1400
125–130	127.5	520	−1	−520	520
130–135	132.5	410	0	0	0
135–140	137.5	320	1	320	320
140–145	142.5	280	2	560	1120
145–150	147.5	210	3	630	1890
150–155	152.5	160	4	640	2560
155–160	157.5	90	5	450	2250
		$N = 3300$		$\Sigma fd' = -2750$	$\Sigma fd'^2 = 29070$

$$\sigma = \sqrt{\frac{\Sigma fd'^2}{N} - \left(\frac{\Sigma fd'}{N}\right)^2} \times C$$

$$\Sigma fd'^2 = 29070, \quad N = 3300, \quad \Sigma fd' = -2750, \quad C = 5$$

$$= \sqrt{\frac{29070}{3300} - \left(\frac{-2750}{3300}\right)^2} \times 5$$

$$= \sqrt{8.809 - (0.833)^2} \times 5 \qquad = \sqrt{8.809 - 0.694} \times 5$$

$$= \sqrt{8.115} \times 5 = 2.849 \times 5 \qquad = \mathbf{14.245}$$

Problem 52. Calculate the standard deviation of the distribution :

Age	:	20–25	25–30	30–35	35–40	40–45	45–50
No. of persons	:	170	100	80	45	40	45

(*ICWA*)

Solution :

Computation of Standard Deviation

Age	*Mid Point (m)*	*No. of persons f*	$d' = \frac{m - 27.5}{5}$	fd'	$fd'2$
20–25	22.5	170	−1	−170	170
25–30	27.5	100	0	0	0
30–35	32.5	80	1	80	80

Age	*Mid Point (m)*	*No. of persons f*	$d' = \frac{m - 27.5}{5}$	*fd'*	*fd'2*
35–40	37.5	45	2	90	180
40–45	42.5	40	3	120	360
45–50	47.5	45	4	180	720
		$N = 480$		$\Sigma fd' = 300$	$\Sigma fd'^2 = 1510$

Standard Deviation :

$$\sigma = \sqrt{\frac{\Sigma fd'^2}{N} - \left(\frac{\Sigma fd'}{N}\right)^2} \times C$$

$$\Sigma fd'^2 = 1510, \quad N = 480, \quad \Sigma fd' = 300, \quad C = 5$$

$$= \sqrt{\frac{1510}{480} - \left(\frac{300}{480}\right)^2} \times 5$$

$$= \sqrt{3.146 - (0.625)^2} \times 5$$

$$= \sqrt{3.146 - 0.391} \times 5$$

$$= \sqrt{2.755} \times 5$$

$$= 1.660 \times 5$$

$$= \mathbf{8.30}$$

Problem 53. Calculate the arithmetic mean and standard deviation from the following data :

Value	*Frequency*
More than 800	14
,, 700	44
,, 600	96
,, 500	175
,, 400	381
,, 300	527
,, 200	615
,, 100	660

(*CA Inter*)

Solution :

Computation of Mean and Standard Deviation

Class Interval	*M.P (m)*	*Frequency*	$d' = \frac{m - 450}{100}$	*fd'*	*fd'2*
100–200	150	660–615=45	−3	−135	405
200–300	250	615–527=88	−2	−176	352
300–400	350	527–381=146	−1	−146	146
400–500	450	381–175=206	0	0	0

Class Interval	*M.P (m)*	*Frequency*	$d' = \frac{m-450}{100}$	*fd'*	*fd'*^{2}
500–600	550	175–96=79	1	79	79
600–700	650	96–44=52	2	104	208
700–800	750	44–14=30	3	90	270
800–900	850	14	4	56	224
		$N = 660$		$\Sigma fd' = -128$	$\Sigma fd'^2 = 1684$

$$\text{Mean :} \quad \overline{X} = A + \frac{\Sigma fd'}{N} \times C$$

$$A = 450, \quad \Sigma fd' = -128, \quad N = 660, \quad C = 100$$

$$= 450 - \frac{128}{660} \times 100 = 450 - 19.39$$

$$= \mathbf{430.61}$$

Standard Deviation :

$$\sigma = \sqrt{\frac{\Sigma fd'^2}{N} - \left(\frac{\Sigma fd'}{N}\right)^2} \times C$$

$$\Sigma fd'^2 = 1684, \quad \Sigma fd' = -128; \quad N = 660, \quad C = 100$$

$$= \sqrt{\frac{1684}{660} - \left(\frac{-128}{660}\right)^2} \times 100$$

$$= \sqrt{2.552 - (0.194)^2} \times 100$$

$$= \sqrt{2.552 - 0.038}$$

$$= \sqrt{2.154 \times 100}$$

$$= 1.586 \times 100$$

$$= \mathbf{158.6}$$

Problem 54. Find any one of the measures of dispersion from the following data :

Profits (in Rs.)	*No. of Firms*
5000 to 6000	10
4000 to 5000	15
3000 to 4000	30
2000 to 3000	10
1000 to 2000	5
0 to 1000	4
−1000 to 0	6
−2000 to −1000	8
−3000 to −2000	10

(*B. Com., Madras*)

Solution :

Computation of Standard Deviation

Profits (in Rs.)	*M.P (m)*	*f*	$d' = \frac{m-1500}{1000}$	*fd'*	*fd'2*
5000 to 6000	5500	10	4	40	160
4000–5000	4500	15	3	45	135
3000–4000	3500	10	2	60	120
2000–3000	2500	10	1	10	10
1000–2000	1500	5	0	0	0
0–1000	500	4	–1	–4	4
–1000–0	500	6	–2	–12	24
–2000 to –1000	1500	8	–3	–24	72
–3000 to –2000	2500	10	–4	–40	160
		$N = 98$		$\Sigma fd' = 75$	$\Sigma fd'^2 = 685$

Standard Deviation :

$$\sigma = \sqrt{\frac{\Sigma fd'^2}{N} - \left(\frac{\Sigma fd'}{N}\right)^2} \times C$$

$$\Sigma fd'^2 = 685; \quad \Sigma fd' = 75; \quad N = 98; \quad C = 1000$$

$$= \sqrt{\frac{685}{98} - \left(\frac{75}{98}\right)^2} \times 1000$$

$$= \sqrt{6.989 - (0.765)^2} \times 1000$$

$$= \sqrt{6.989 - 0.586} \times 1000$$

$$= \sqrt{6.403 \times 1000}$$

$$= 2.530 \times 1000$$

$$= \mathbf{2530}$$

Problem 55. Compute the S.D. and M.D. from the mean for the distribution given below :

Class (X)	: 0–10	10–20	20–30	30–40	40–50	50–60	60–70
Frequency (y)	: 8	12	17	14	9	7	4

(*B.Sc. Madurai*)

Solution :

Computation of Mean, M.D. and Standard Deviation

Class X	M.P. m	f	$d' = \dfrac{m-35}{10}$	fd'	fd'^{2}	$\lvert D\rvert = m - 30.78$	$f\lvert D\rvert$
0–10	5	8	–3	–24	72	25.78	206.24
10–20	15	12	–2	–24	48	15.78	189.36
20–30	25	17	–1	–17	17	5.78	98.26
30–40	35	14	0	0	0	4.22	59.08
40–50	45	9	1	9	9	14.22	127.98
50–60	55	7	2	14	28	24.22	169.54
60–70	65	4	3	12	36	34.22	136.88
		$N = 71$		$\Sigma fd' = -30$	$\Sigma fd'^2 = 210$		$\Sigma f\lvert D\rvert = 987.34$

$$\text{Mean} = \overline{X} = A + \frac{\Sigma fd'}{N} \times C \quad A = 35; \quad \Sigma fd' = -30 \quad N = 71 \quad C = 10$$

$$= 35 - \frac{30}{71} \times 10 = 35 - 4.225 = 30.775$$

$$= \mathbf{30.78}$$

$$\text{M.D.} = \frac{\Sigma f|D|}{N} \quad \Sigma f|D| = 987.34; \quad N = 71$$

$$= \frac{987.34}{71}$$

$$= \mathbf{13.91}$$

Standard Deviation :

$$\sigma = \sqrt{\frac{\Sigma fd'^2}{N} - \left(\frac{\Sigma fd'}{N}\right)^2} \times C$$

$$\Sigma fd'^2 = 210; \quad N = 71; \quad \Sigma fd' = -30; \quad C = 10$$

$$= \sqrt{\frac{210}{71} - \left(-\frac{30}{71}\right)^2} \times 10$$

$$= \sqrt{2.958 - 0.423} \times 10$$

$$= \sqrt{2.958 - 0.179} \times 10$$

$$= \sqrt{2.779 \times 10}$$

$$= 1.667 \times 10$$

$$= \mathbf{16.67}$$

Problem 56. Calculate the S.D for following distribution giving 300 telephone calls according to their duration in seconds :

Duration (in seconds)	0–30	30–60	60–90	90–120	120–150	150–180	180–210
No. of calls	9	17	43	82	81	44	24

(*B. Com., Bombay*)

Solution :

Computation of Standard Deviation

Deviation in seconds	*M.P.* (*m*)	*f*	$d' = \frac{m - 105}{30}$	fd'	fd'^2
0–30	15	9	−3	−27	81
30–60	45	17	−2	−34	68
60–90	75	43	−1	−43	43
90–120	105	82	0	0	0
120–150	135	81	1	81	81
150–180	165	44	2	88	176
180–210	195	24	3	72	216
		$N = 300$		$\Sigma fd' = 137$	$\Sigma fd'^2 = 665$

Standard Deviation :

$$\sigma = \sqrt{\frac{\Sigma fd'^2}{N} - \left(\frac{\Sigma fd'}{N}\right)^2} \times C$$

$$\Sigma f d'^2 = 665; \quad \Sigma f d' = 137; \quad N = 300; \quad C = 30$$

$$= \sqrt{\frac{665}{300} - \left(\frac{137}{300}\right)^2} \times 30 \qquad = \sqrt{2.217 - (-0.457)^2} \times 30$$

$$= \sqrt{2.217 - 0.209} \times 30 \qquad = \sqrt{2.008} \times 30$$

$$= 1.417 \times 30 \qquad = \mathbf{42.51}$$

Problem 57 : calculate the standard deviation from the following data, using the short cut method and show symbolically the formula on which your calculations are based.

Age (years)	*Frequency*	*Age (years)*	*Frequency*
10–19	3	50–59	53
20–29	61	60–69	19
30–39	223	70–79	4
40–49	137		

(*ICWA*)

Solution :

Computation of Standard Deviation

Age (years)	*m.p (m)*	*f*	$d' = \frac{m - 44.5}{10}$	*fd'*	*fd'*^{2}
10–19	14.5	3	−3	9	27
20–29	24.5	61	−2	122	244
30–39	34.5	223	−1	223	223
40–49	44.5	137	0	0	0
50–59	54.5	53	1	53	53
60–69	64.5	19	2	38	76
70–79	74.5	4	3	12	36
		$N = 500$		$\Sigma fd' = -251$	$\Sigma fd'^2 = 659$

Standard Deviation :

$$\sigma = \sqrt{\frac{\Sigma f d'^2}{N} - \left(\frac{\Sigma f d'}{N}\right)^2} \times C$$

$$\Sigma f d'^2 = 659; \quad N = 500; \quad \Sigma f d' = -251; \quad C = 10$$

$$= \sqrt{\frac{659}{500} - \left(\frac{-251}{500}\right)^2} \times 10$$

$$= \sqrt{1.318 - (-0.502)^2} \times 10$$

$$= \sqrt{1.318 - 0.252} \times 10$$

$$= \sqrt{1.066} \times 10$$

$$= 1.032 \times 10$$

$$= \mathbf{10.32}$$

Problem 58. Find the arithmetic average and standard deviation from the following data :

Age under	*No. of persons dying*	*Age under*	*No. of persons dying*
10	15	50	100
20	30	60	110
30	53	70	115
40	75	80	125

(*B. Com. Kerala*)

Solution :

Computation of Mean and Standard Deviation

Age	*M.P.* (m)	f	$d' = \frac{(m-35)}{10}$	fd'	fd'^2
0–10	5	15	−3	−45	135
10–20	15	15	−2	−30	60
20–30	25	23	−1	−23	23
30–40	35	22	0	0	0
40–50	45	25	1	25	25
50–60	55	10	2	20	40
60–70	65	5	3	15	45
70–80	75	10	4	40	160
		$N = 125$		$\Sigma fd' = 2$	$\Sigma fd'^2 = 488$

$$\text{Mean} : \overline{X} = A \pm \frac{\Sigma fd'}{N} \times C$$

$$\Sigma fd' = 2 : \quad N = 125; \quad C = 10$$

$$= 35 + \frac{2}{125} \times 10 = 35 + 0.16$$

$$= \mathbf{35.16}$$

Standard Deviation :

$$\sigma = \sqrt{\frac{\Sigma fd'^2}{N} - \left(\frac{\Sigma fd'}{N}\right)^2} \times C$$

$$\Sigma fd'^2 = 488; \quad \Sigma fd' = 2; \quad N = 125; \quad C = 10$$

$$= \sqrt{\frac{488}{125} - \left(\frac{2}{125}\right)^2} \times 10$$

$$= \sqrt{3.904 - (0.016)^2 \times 10}$$

$$= \sqrt{3.904 - 0.0003 \times 10}$$

$$= \sqrt{3.9037 \times 10}$$

$$= 1.976 \times 10$$

$$= \mathbf{19.76}$$

Problem 59. From the following observations prepare a frequency distribution table in ascending order starting with 5–10 (exclusive method)and find out the mean and the standard deviation.

Scores :

19	18	15	35	32	30	8	12	
17	8	18	19	18	30	36	42	
35	37	30	39	25	24	26	28	8
17	19	21	24	10	16	15	18	17
12	21	29	30	31	19	26	24	24
29	27	25	28	22	22	21	28	35

(*B. Com. Mysore*)

Solution :

Computation of Mean and Standard Deviation

Scores	*Tally Marks*	f	*M.P.* (m)	$d' = \frac{m - 22.5}{5}$	fd'	fd'^2
5–10	|||	3	7.5	−3	−9	27
10–15	|||	3	12.5	−2	−6	12
15–20	~~||||~~ ~~||||~~ ||||	14	17.5	−1	−14	14
20–25	~~||||~~ ||||	9	22.5	0	0	0
25–30	~~||||~~ ~~||||~~	10	27.5	1	10	10
30–35	~~||||~~ |	6	32.5	2	12	24
35–40	~~||||~~ |	6	37.5	3	18	54
40–45	|	1	42.5	4	4	16
		$N = 52$			$\Sigma fd' = 15$	$\Sigma fd'^2 = 157$

Mean :

$$\overline{X} = A + \frac{\Sigma fd'}{N} \times C$$

$$A = 22.5; \quad \Sigma fd' = 15; \quad N = 52; \quad C = 5$$

$$= 22.5 + \frac{15}{52} \times 5 = 22.5 + 1.44$$

$$= \mathbf{23.94}$$

Standard Deviation :

$$\sigma = \sqrt{\frac{\Sigma fd'^2}{N} - \left(\frac{\Sigma fd'}{N}\right)^2} \times C$$

$$\Sigma fd'^2 = 157; \quad N = 52; \quad \Sigma fd' = 15; \quad N = 52; C = 5$$

$$= \sqrt{\frac{157}{52} - \left(\frac{15}{52}\right)^2} \times 5$$

$$= \sqrt{3.019 - (0.288)^2} \times 5$$

$$= \sqrt{3.019 - 0.083} \times 5$$

$$= \sqrt{2.936} \times 5$$

$$= 1.713 \times 5$$

$$= \mathbf{8.57}$$

Problem 60. Calculate the standard deviation for the following distribution giving 600 telephone calls according to their duration in seconds :

Duration in seconds	0–30	30–60	60–90	90–120	12–150	150–180	180–210
No. of calls	20	35	88	165	154	75	63

(*B. Com. Bombay, Calcutta, Kerla, Agra, Madras*)

Solution :

Computation of Standard Deviation

Class Interval	*M.P.*	f	$d' = \frac{m-105}{30}$	fd'	fd'^2
0–30	15	20	−3	−60	180
30–60	45	35	−2	−70	140
60–90	75	88	−1	−88	88
90–120	105	165	0	0	0
120–150	135	154	1	154	154
150–181	165	75	2	150	300
180–210	195	63	3	189	567
		$N = 600$		$\Sigma fd' = 275$	$\Sigma fd'^2 = 1429$

$$\text{Standard Deviation} : \sigma = \sqrt{\frac{\Sigma fd'^2}{N} - \left(\frac{\Sigma fd'}{N}\right)^2} \times C$$

$$\Sigma fd'2 = 1429; \quad \Sigma fd' = 275; \quad N = 600; \quad C = 30$$

$$= \sqrt{\frac{1429}{600} - \left(\frac{275}{600}\right)^2} \times 30$$

$$= \sqrt{2.4483 - (0.4583)^2} \times 30$$

$$= \sqrt{2.4483 - 0.210} \times 30$$

$$= \sqrt{2.2383} \times 30$$

$$= 1.496 \times 30$$

$$= \mathbf{44.88}$$

Problem 61. Calculate the mean and standard deviation from the following :

Age	below 20	20–25	25–30	30–35	35–40	40–45	45–50	50–55	55 and above
f :	20	26	44	60	101	109	84	66	10

(*B. Com., Delhi*)

Solution :

Computation of Mean and Standard Deviation

Age	*M.P.(m)*	*f*	$d' = \frac{m - 37.5}{5}$	*fd'*	*fd'2*
15–20	17.5	20	−4	− 80	320
20–25	22.5	26	−3	− 78	234
25–30	27.5	44	−2	− 88	176
30–35	32.5	60	−1	− 60	60
35–40	37.5	101	0	0	0
40–45	42.5	109	1	109	109
45–50	47.5	84	2	168	336
50–55	52.5	66	3	198	594
55–60	57.5	10	4	40	160
		$N = 520$		$\Sigma fd' = 209$	$\Sigma fd'^2 = 1989$

$$\text{Mean : } \overline{X} = A + \frac{\Sigma fd'}{N} \times C$$

$$A = 37.5; \quad \Sigma fd' = 209; \quad N = 520; \quad C = 5$$

$$= 37.5 + \frac{209}{520} \times 5 = 37.5 + 2.01$$

$$= \mathbf{39.51}$$

$$\text{Standard Deviation : } \quad \sigma = \sqrt{\frac{\Sigma fd'^2}{N} - \left(\frac{\Sigma fd'}{N}\right)^2} \times C$$

$$\Sigma fd'2 = 1989; \quad \Sigma fd' = 209; \quad N = 520; \quad C = 5$$

$$= \sqrt{\frac{1989}{520} - \left(\frac{209}{520}\right)^2} \times 5$$

$$= \sqrt{3.825 - (0.402)^2} \times 5$$

$$= \sqrt{3.825 - 0.162} \times 5 \quad = \sqrt{3.663} \times 5$$

$$= 1.914 \times 5 \quad = \mathbf{9.57}$$

Problem 62. Calculate the standard deviation and semiquartile range of the following table:

Age in years	: 20–30	30–40	40–50	50–60	60–70	70–80	80–90
No. of persons	: 3	61	132	153	140	51	2

(*M.A. Ecos. Calcutta*)

Solution :

Age	*M.P.(m)*	*No. of persons f*	*c.f.*	$d' = \frac{m-55}{10}$	*fd'*	*fd'2*
20–30	25	3	3	–3	– 9	27
30–40	35	61	64	–2	–122	244
40–50	45	132	196	–1	–132	132
50–60	55	153	349	0	0	0
60–70	65	140	489	1	140	140
70–80	75	51	540	2	102	204
80–90	85	2	542	3	6	18
		$N = 542$			$\Sigma fd' = -15$	$\Sigma fd'^2 = 765$

$$Q_1 = \text{size of} \frac{N}{4} \text{th item} = \text{size of} \frac{542}{4} \text{th item}$$

$$= 135.5\text{th item Which lies in the group 40–50}$$

$$Q_1 = L_1 + \frac{\frac{N}{4} - c.f}{f} \times i$$

$$L_1 = 40; \quad \frac{N}{4} = 135.5; \quad c.f = 64; \quad f = 132; \quad i = 10$$

$$= 40 + \frac{135.5 - 64}{132} \times 10 = 40 + 5.42 \qquad = \mathbf{45.42}$$

$$Q_3 = \text{size of} \frac{3N}{4} \text{th item} = \text{size of} \frac{3 \times 542}{4} \text{th item}$$

$$= 406.5\text{th item which lies in the class 60–70}$$

$$Q_3 = \text{L}_1 + \frac{\frac{3N}{4} - c.f}{f} \times i$$

$$L_1 = 60; \quad \frac{3N}{4} = 406.5; \quad c.f = 349; \quad f = 140; \quad i = 10$$

$$= 60 + \frac{406.5 - 349}{140} \times 10 = 60 + 4.11 \qquad = \mathbf{64.11}$$

$$\text{Semi Quartile Range} = \frac{Q_3 - Q_1}{2}$$

$$= \frac{64.11 - 45.42}{2} = \frac{18.69}{2} \qquad = \mathbf{9.35}$$

$$\text{Standard Deviation :} \quad \sigma = \sqrt{\frac{\Sigma fd'^2}{N} - \left(\frac{\Sigma fd'}{N}\right)^2} \times C$$

$$\Sigma fd'^2 = 765; \quad \Sigma fd' = -15; \quad N = 542; \quad C = 10$$

$$= \sqrt{\frac{765}{542} - \left(\frac{-15}{542}\right)^2} \times 10$$

$$= \sqrt{1.411 - (0.028)^2} \times 10$$

$$= \sqrt{1.411 - 0.0007} \times 10 \qquad = \sqrt{1.4103} \times 10$$

$$= 1.187 \times 10 \qquad = \mathbf{11.87}.$$

Problem 63. The following table gives the distribution of monthly income of 600 middle class families in a city :

Monthly Income (Rs.)	*No. of families*
0–75	69
75–150	167
150–225	207
225–300	65
300–375	58
375–450	24
450–525	10

Calculate the standard Deviation and Quartile Deviation.

(*B. Com. Madurai, Bhopal, Delhi.*)

Solution :

Computation of Standard Deviation and Quartile Deviation

Monthly income (Rs.)	*M.P. (m)*	f	$d' = \frac{m - 262.5}{75}$	fd'	$fd'2$	*c.f.*
0–75	37.5	69	−3	−207	621	69
75–150	112.5	167	−2	−334	668	236
150–225	187.5	207	−1	−207	207	443
225–300	262.5	65	0	0	0	508
300–375	337.5	58	1	58	58	566
375–450	412.5	24	2	48	96	590
450–525	487.5	10	3	30	90	600
		$N = 600$		$\Sigma fd' = -162$	$\Sigma fd'^2 = 1740$	

$Q_1 =$ size of $\frac{N}{4}$th item = size of $\frac{600}{4}$ th item = 150 th Which lies in the group 75–150

$$Q_1 = L_1 + \frac{\frac{N}{4} - c.f}{f} \times i \quad L_1 = 75; \quad \frac{N}{4} = 150; \quad c.f = 69$$

$$f = 167; \quad i = 75$$

$$= 75 + \frac{150 - 69}{167} \times 75 = 75 + 36.38$$

$$= \mathbf{111.38}$$

$$Q_3 = \text{size of } \frac{3N}{4}\text{th item}$$

$$= \text{size of } 3 \times \frac{600}{4}\text{th item}$$

$$= \text{size of 450th item which lies in the class } 225 - 300$$

$$Q_3 = L_1 + \frac{\frac{3N}{4} - c.f}{f} \times i \qquad L_1 = 225; \frac{3N}{4} = 450$$

$$c.f. = 443; \quad f = 65; \quad i = 75.$$

$$= 225 + \frac{450 - 443}{65} \times 75 = 225 + 8.07$$

$$= \mathbf{233.07}$$

$$Q.D. = \frac{Q_3 - Q_1}{2}$$

$$= \frac{233.07 - 111.38}{2}$$

$$= \mathbf{60.85}$$

Standard Deviation :

$$\sigma = \sqrt{\frac{\Sigma fd'^2}{N} - \left(\frac{\Sigma fd'}{N}\right)^2} \times C$$

$$\Sigma fd'^2 = 1740; \quad \Sigma fd' = -612; \quad N = 600; \quad C = 75$$

$$= \sqrt{\frac{1740}{600} - \left(\frac{-612}{600}\right)^2} \times 75$$

$$= \sqrt{2.9 - 1.0404} \times 75$$

$$= \sqrt{1.8596} \times 75$$

$$= 1.364 \times 75$$

$$= \mathbf{102.28}.$$

Problem 64. Calculate the arithmetic mean and standard deviation from the following series :

Class-interval	: 5–15	15–25	25–35	35–45	45–55
Frequency	: 8	12	15	9	6

(*B. Com., Delhi*)

Solution :

Computation of Mean and Standard Deviation

Class Interval	*m.P.* m	f	$d' = \frac{m - 30}{10}$	fd'	fd'^2
5–15	10	8	−2	−16	32
15–25	20	12	−1	−12	12
25–35	30	15	0	0	0
35–45	40	9	1	9	9
45–55	50	6	2	12	24
		$N = 50$		$\Sigma fd' = -7$	$\Sigma fd'^2 = 77$

$$\text{Mean : } \overline{X} = A + \frac{\Sigma fd'}{N} \times C$$

$$A = 30; \quad \Sigma fd' = -7; \quad N = 50; \quad C = 10$$

$$= 30 - \frac{7}{50} \times 10 = 30 - 1.4$$

$$= \mathbf{28.6}$$

Standard Deviation :

$$\sigma = \sqrt{\frac{\Sigma f d'^2}{N} - \left(\frac{\Sigma f d'}{N}\right)^2} \times C$$

$$\Sigma f d'^2 = 77; \quad \Sigma f d' = -7; \quad N = 50; \quad C = 10$$

$$\sigma = \sqrt{\frac{77}{50} - \left(\frac{-7}{50}\right)^2} \times 10$$

$$= \sqrt{1.54 - (0.14)^2} \times 10 \qquad = \sqrt{1.54 - 0.0196} \times 10$$

$$= \sqrt{1.5204} \times 10 \qquad = 1.233 \times 10$$

$$= \mathbf{12.33}$$

Problem 65. The weekly earnings of workers in a factory are given below :

Compute the standard deviation and coefficienct of quartile deviation of the weekly earnings :

Weekly earnings (Rs.)	:	5–9	10–14	15–19	20–24	25–29	30–34
No. of Workers	:	62	273	314	75	22	5

(*B.A., Madras*)

Solution :

Earnings	m	f	$d' = \frac{m-17}{5}$	fd'	fd'^2	$c.f.$
5–9	7	62	−2	−124	248	62
10–14	12	272	−1	−272	272	334
15–19	17	314	0	0	0	648
20–24	22	75	1	75	75	723
25–29	27	22	2	44	88	745
30–34	32	5	3	15	45	750
				$\Sigma fd' = -262$	$\Sigma fd'^2 = 728$	

$$\sigma = \sqrt{\frac{\Sigma f d'^2}{N} - \left(\frac{\Sigma f d'}{N}\right)^2} \times C$$

$$\Sigma f d'^2 = 728; \quad \Sigma f d' = -262; \quad N = 750; \quad C : 5$$

$$\sigma = \sqrt{\frac{728}{750} - \left(\frac{-262}{750}\right)^2} \times 5 = \sqrt{0.97 - 0.12} \times 5$$

$$= \sqrt{0.85} \times 5 = 0.92 \times 5 = \mathbf{4.6}$$

$$Q_1 = \frac{N}{4}\text{th item} = 187.5\text{th item which is 10–14 class}$$

$$Q_1 = L_1 + \frac{\frac{N}{4} - c.f}{f} \times i = 9.5 + \frac{187.5 - 62}{272} \times 4 = \mathbf{11.35}$$

$$Q_3 = \frac{3N}{4}\text{th item which is 15–19 class.}$$

$$Q_3 = L_1 + \frac{\frac{3N}{4} - c.f}{f} \times i = 14.5 + \frac{562.5 - 334}{314} \times 4 = \mathbf{17.41}$$

$$\text{co-eff of } Q.D. = \frac{Q_3 - Q_1}{Q_3 + Q_1} = \frac{17.41 - 11.35}{17.41 + 11.35} = \frac{6.06}{28.76} = \mathbf{0.21}$$

Problem 66. Calculate the mean and the S.D. of the quantity of grain produced for the following data :

No. of kilograms of grain produced		*No. of plots*
200–299		5
300–399		9
400–499		15
500–599		17
600–699		22
700–799		17
800–899		7
900–999		6
1,000–1,099		2
	Total	100

(*B. Com., Guahati*)

Solution :

Computation of Mean and Standard Deviation

No. of kgs. Of grains produced	m	f	$d' = \frac{m - 649.5}{100}$	fd'	fd'^2
199.5–299.5	249.5	5	−4	−20	80
299.5–399.5	349.5	9	−3	−27	81
399.5–499.5	449.5	15	−2	−30	60
499.5–599.5	549.5	17	−1	−17	17
599.5–699.5	649.5	22	0	0	0
699.5–799.5	749.5	17	1	17	17
799.5–899.5	849.5	7	2	14	28
899.5–999.5	949.5	6	3	18	54
999.5–1099.5	1049.5	2	4	8	32
		$N = 100$		$\Sigma fd' = -37$	$\Sigma fd'^2 = 369$

$$\text{Mean : } \overline{X} = A + \frac{\Sigma fd'}{N} \times C$$

$$A = 649.5; \quad \Sigma fd' = -37; \quad N = 100; \quad C = 100$$

$$= 649.5 - \frac{37}{100} \times 100 = 649.5 - 37$$

$$= \mathbf{612.5}$$

Standard Deviation :

$$\sigma = \sqrt{\frac{\Sigma fd'^2}{N} - \left(\frac{\Sigma fd'}{N}\right)^2} \times C$$

$$\Sigma fd'^2 = 369; \quad \Sigma fd' = -37; \quad N = 100; \quad C = 100$$

$$= \sqrt{\frac{369}{100} - \left(\frac{-37}{100}\right)^2} \times 100$$

$$= \sqrt{3.69 - (-0.37)^2} \times 100$$

$$= \sqrt{3.69 - 0.1369} \times 100$$

$$= \sqrt{3.5531} \times 100$$

$$= 1.8849 \times 100$$

$$= \mathbf{188.49}$$

Problem 67. Find the standard deviation from the following data :

Wages (Rs.)	No. of workers
Upto Rs. 10	12
Upto Rs. 20	30
Upto Rs. 30	65

Wages (Rs.)	No. of workers
Upto Rs. 40	107
Upto Rs. 50	157
Upto Rs. 60	202
Upto Rs. 70	222
Upto Rs. 80	230

(*B. Com. Punjab, Madurai, Bombay, Delhi*)

Solution : **Calculation of Standard Deviation**

Wages	m	f	$d' = \frac{m-35}{10}$	fd'	fd'^2
0–10	5	12	−3	−36	108
10–20	15	18	−2	−36	72
20–30	25	35	−1	−35	35
30–40	35	42	0	0	0
40–50	45	50	1	50	50
50–60	55	45	2	90	180
60–70	65	20	3	60	180
70–80	75	8	4	32	128
		$N = 230$		$\Sigma fd' = +125$	$\Sigma fd'^2 = 753$

Standard Deviation : $\sigma = \sqrt{\frac{\Sigma fd'^2}{N} - \left(\frac{\Sigma fd'}{N}\right)^2} \times C$

$$\Sigma fd'^2 = 753; \quad \Sigma fd' = 125; \quad N = 230; \quad C = 10$$

$$\sigma = \sqrt{\frac{753}{230} - \left(\frac{125}{230}\right)^2} \times 10$$

$$= \sqrt{3.274 - 0.295} \times 10$$

$$= \sqrt{2.979} \times 10$$

$$= 1.726 \times 10$$

$$= \mathbf{17.26}$$

Problem 68. The following table gives the distribution of income of 100 families in a village:

Annual Income (in Rs.)	*Number of families*
0-1,000	18
1,000–2,000	26
2,000–3,000	30
3,000–4,000	12
4,000–5,000	10
5,000–6,000	4

Find the mean and standard deviation of the distribution: (*B.A. Gauhati*)

Solution:

Computation of Mean and Standard Deviation

Annual Income in Rs.	m	f	$d' = \frac{m - 2500}{1000}$	fd'	fd'^2
0–1000	500	18	−2	−36	72
1000–2000	1500	26	−1	−26	26
2000–3000	2500	30	0	0	0
3000–4000	3500	12	1	12	12
4000–5000	4500	10	2	20	40
5000–6000	5500	4	3	12	36
		$N = 100$		$\Sigma fd' = -18$	$\Sigma fd'^2 = 186$

$$\text{Mean: } \overline{X} = A + \frac{\Sigma fd'}{N} \times C$$

$$A = 2500; \quad \Sigma fd' = -18; \quad N = 100; \quad C = 1000$$

$$= 2500 - \frac{18}{100} \times 1000 = 2500 - 180$$

$$= \mathbf{2320.}$$

Standard Deviation:

$$\sigma = \sqrt{\frac{\Sigma fd'}{N} - \left(\frac{\Sigma fd'}{N}\right)^2} \times C$$

$$\Sigma fd'^2 = 186; \quad N = 100; \quad \Sigma fd' = -18; \quad C = 1000$$

$$= \sqrt{\frac{186}{100} - \left(-\frac{18}{100}\right)^2} \times 1000$$

$$= \sqrt{1.86 - 0.032} \times 1000$$
$$= \sqrt{1.828} \times 1000$$
$$= 1.352 \times 1000$$
$$= \mathbf{1352}.$$

Problem 69. Find the standard Deviation for the following distribution :

X:	4.5	14.5	24.5	34.5	44.5	54.5	64.5
Y:	1	5	12	22	17	9	4

Solution :

Computation of Standard Deviation

X	f	$d' = \frac{X - 34.5}{10}$	fd'	fd'^2
4.5	1	−3	− 3	9
14.5	5	−2	−10	20
24.5	12	−1	−12	12
34.5	22	0	0	0
44.5	17	1	17	17
54.5	9	2	18	36
64.5	4	3	12	36
	$N = 70$		$\Sigma fd' = 22$	$\Sigma fd'^2 = 130$

Standard Deviation :

$$\sigma = \sqrt{\frac{\Sigma fd'^2}{N} - \left(\frac{\Sigma fd'}{N}\right)^2} \times C$$

$$\Sigma fd'^2 = 130; \quad \Sigma fd' = 22; \quad N = 70; \quad C = 10$$

$$= \sqrt{\frac{130}{70} - \left(\frac{22}{10}\right)^2} \times 10$$
$$= \sqrt{1.857 - (0.314)^2} \times 10$$
$$= \sqrt{1.758} \times 10$$
$$= 1.326 \times 10$$
$$= \mathbf{13.26}$$

Problem 70. Find the standard devition and mean of breaking strength of 80 test pieces of certin alloy from the following table :

Breking strength	*Number of pieces*
44–46	3
46–48	24
48–50	27
50–52	21
52–54	5

the unit being given to the nearest thousand pounds per square inch.

(*B.A. Calicut*)

Solution :

Computation of Mean and Standard Deviation

Breaking strength	m	f	$d' = \frac{m-49}{2}$	fd'	fd'^2
44–46	45	3	−2	− 6	12
46–48	47	24	−1	−24	24
48–50	49	27	0	0	0
50–52	51	21	1	21	21
52–54	53	5	2	10	20
		$N = 80$		$\Sigma fd' = 1$	$\Sigma fd'^2 = 77$

Mean :

$$\overline{X} = A + \frac{\Sigma fd'}{N} \times C$$

$$A = 49; \quad \Sigma fd' = 1 \quad N = 80; \quad C = 2$$

$$= 49 + \frac{1}{80} \times 2 = 49 + 0.025$$

$$= \mathbf{49.025}$$

Standard Deviation :

$$\sigma = \sqrt{\frac{\Sigma fd'^2}{N} - \left(\frac{\Sigma fd'}{N}\right)^2} \times C$$

$$\Sigma fd'^2 = 77; \quad \Sigma fd' = 1; \quad N = 80; \quad C = 2$$

$$= \sqrt{\frac{77}{80} - \left(\frac{1}{80}\right)^2} \times 2$$

$$= \sqrt{.9625 - (0.0125)^2} \times 2$$

$$= \sqrt{0.9625 - 0.0002} \times 2$$

$$= \sqrt{0.9623} \times 2$$

$$= 0.98 \times 2$$

$$= \mathbf{1.96}$$

Problem 71. Find out the S.D. of the following series.

size of the holdings (Hectares)	*No. of farmers*
2.5–3.5	1,000
3.5–4.5	2,300
4.5–5.5	3,600
5.5–6.5	2,400
6.5–7.5	1,700
7.5–8.5	3,000
8.5–9.5	500

What conclusion do you draw from your results ?

(*B. Com. Delhi*)

Solution :

Computation of Standard Deviation

size of Holdings (Hrs.)	m	f	$d = m - 6$	fd	fd^2
2.5–3.5	3	1,000	–3	–3,000	9,000
3.5–4.5	4	2,300	-2	–4,600	9,200
4.5–5.5	5	3,600	–1	–3,600	3,600
5.5–6.5	6	2,400	0	0	0
6.5–7.5	7	1,700	1	1,700	1,700
7.5–8.5	8	3,000	2	6,000	12,000
8.5–9.5	9	500	3	1,500	4,500
		$N = 14500$		$\Sigma fd = -2000$	$\Sigma fd^2 = 40,000$

Standard Deviation :

$$\sigma = \sqrt{\frac{\Sigma fd'^2}{N} - \left(\frac{\Sigma fd'}{N}\right)^2} \times C$$

$$\Sigma fd^2 = 40,000; \quad \Sigma fd = -2000; \quad N = 14,500; \quad \Sigma fd = -2000$$

$$= \sqrt{\frac{40,000}{14,500} - \left(\frac{-2000}{14500}\right)^2}$$

$$= \sqrt{2.7586 - (-0.1379)^2}$$

$$= \sqrt{2.7586 - 0.019}$$

$$= \sqrt{2.7396}$$

$$= \mathbf{1.655}$$

Problem 72. The following table gives the rent of 200 houses surveyed in the city.

Rent (in Rs.)	*No. of houses*	*Rent* (*in Rs.*)	*No. of Houses*
75 and under 125	12	275 and under 325	37
125 and under 175	26	325 and under 375	13
175 and under 225	45	375 and under 425	5
225 and under 275	60	425 and under 475	2

Calculate the mean and standard deviation of the distribution.

(*M.A., Gauhati*)

Solution :

Computation of Mean and Standard Deviation

Rent in Rs.	m	f	$d' = \frac{m-250}{50}$	fd'	fd'^2
75 and under 125	100	12	-3	-36	108
125–175	150	26	-2	-52	104
175–225	200	45	-1	-45	45
225–275	250	60	0	0	0
275–325	300	37	1	37	37
325–375	350	13	2	26	52
375–425	400	5	3	15	45
425–475	450	2	4	8	32
		$N = 200$		$\Sigma fd' = -47$	$\Sigma fd'^2 = 423$

Mean :

$$\overline{X} = A \pm \frac{\Sigma fd'}{N} \times C$$

$$A = 250; \quad \Sigma fd' = -47; \quad N = 200; \quad C = 50$$

$$= 250 - \frac{47}{200} \times 50 = 250 - 11.75$$

$$= \mathbf{238.25}$$

Standard Deviation :

$$\sigma = \sqrt{\frac{\Sigma fd'^2}{N} - \left(\frac{\Sigma fd'}{N}\right)^2} \times C$$

$$\Sigma fd'^2 = 423; \quad \Sigma fd' = -47; \quad N = 200; \quad C = 50$$

$$= \sqrt{\frac{423}{200} - \left(\frac{-47}{200}\right)^2} \times 50$$

$$= \sqrt{2.115 - (-0.235)^2} \times 50$$

$$= \sqrt{2.115 - 0.055} \times 50$$
$$= \sqrt{2.06} \times 50$$
$$= 1.435 \times 50$$
$$= \mathbf{71.75}$$

Problem 73. You are provided with the following raw sums in a statistical investigation of two variables, x and y

$\Sigma X = 235; \quad \Sigma Y = 250; \quad \Sigma X^2 = 6750; \quad \Sigma Y^2 = 6840$

Ten pairs of values are included in the survey, compute the standard deviation of the x and y variables.

(*B. Com. Madras*)

Solution :

$$\sigma_x = \sqrt{\frac{\Sigma X^2}{N} - (\overline{X}^2)}$$
$$\Sigma X = 235 \text{ (given in the problem)}$$
$$\therefore \quad \overline{X} = 235 \div 10 = 23.5$$
$$\sigma X = \sqrt{\frac{6750}{10} - (23.5)^2}$$
$$= \sqrt{675 - 552.25}$$
$$= \sqrt{122.75}$$
$$= \mathbf{11.08}$$
$$\sigma_y = \sqrt{\frac{\Sigma Y^2}{N} - (\overline{Y})^2}$$
$$\overline{Y} = 250 \div 10 = 25$$
$$\sigma Y = \sqrt{\frac{6840}{10} - (25)^2}$$
$$= \sqrt{684 - 625}$$
$$= \sqrt{59}$$
$$= \mathbf{7.68}$$

Problem 74. The mean and standard deviation of 100 items are found to be 40 and 10. At the time of calculations two items are wrongly taken as 30 and 72 instead of 3 and 27. Find the correct mean and correct standard deviations.

(*B. Com. Bombay*)

Solution :

To find the correct sum of 100 observations we have to subtract the wrong values and add the correct values.

$$\Sigma X = N\overline{X}$$
$$= 100 \times 40 = 4000 \text{(incorrect total)}$$
$$\text{Correct Total} = 4000 - 72 - 30 + 3 + 27$$
$$= 3928$$

$\therefore$ The Correct mean

$$
\begin{aligned}
&= \frac{3928}{100} = 39.28 \\
\sigma &= \sqrt{\frac{\Sigma X^2}{N} - (\overline{X})^2} \\
\sigma^2 &= \frac{\Sigma X^2}{N} - (X)^{(2)} \ldots \text{ Multiply by N.} \\
N\sigma^2 &= \Sigma X^2 - N(\overline{X})^2 \\
\therefore\ \Sigma X^2 &= N(\overline{X})^2 + N\sigma^2 \\
\Sigma X^2 &= N\left(\overline{X}^2 + \sigma^2\right)
\end{aligned}
$$

Before correction

$$
\begin{aligned}
(\Sigma X^2) &= 100(40^2 + 10^2) \\
&= 100(1600 + 100) \\
&= 1,70,000
\end{aligned}
$$

ΣX^2 after correction $= 1,70,000 - 72^2 - 30^2 + 3^2 + 27^2$

$$
\begin{aligned}
&= 1,70,000 - 5184 - 900 + 9 + 729 \\
&= 1,64,654 \\
\sigma^2 &= \frac{1,64,654}{100} - (39.28)^2
\end{aligned}
$$

$$
\begin{aligned}
&= 1646.54 - 1542.92 \\
&= 103.62 \\
\sigma &= \sqrt{103.62} \\
&= \mathbf{10.18}
\end{aligned}
$$

Problem 75. Find the actual class groups from the data given below :

d'	-3	-2	-1	0	1	2	3
f	10	15	25	25	10	10	5

You are given that the mean of the distribution is 31 and standard deviation is 15.9. *(B. Com. Calcutta)*

Solution :

To find the class groups, we need two values–class interval and the assumed mean. These are calculated as follows :

d'	f	fd'	fd'^2
−3	10	−30	90
−2	15	−30	60
−1	25	−25	25
0	25	0	0
1	10	10	10
2	10	20	40
3	5	15	45
	$N = 100$	$\Sigma fd = -40$	$\Sigma fd^2 = 270$

$$\sigma = \sqrt{\frac{\Sigma fd'^2}{N} - \left(\frac{\Sigma fd'}{N}\right)^2} \times C$$

$$= \sqrt{\frac{270}{100} - \left(\frac{-40}{100}\right)^2} \times C$$

$$= \sqrt{2.7 - 0.16} \times C$$

$$\sigma(15.9) = 1.59 \times C$$

$$\therefore C = \frac{15.9}{1.59}$$

$$= \mathbf{10}.$$

$$\overline{X} = A + \frac{\Sigma fd'}{N} \times C$$

$$31 = A - \frac{40}{100} \times 10$$

$$31 = A - 4$$

$$A = 31 + 4$$

$$= \mathbf{35}$$

The variable under study is a continuous one, the class for which $d' = 0$ the mid-value is 35 and the class is 30–40. Take the next class, the $d' = 1$ which means the mid-value is 45 and the deviation of 10 is divided by 10 is 1 (d'). Thus the whole distribution :

Class :	0–10	10–20	20–30	30–40	40–50	50–60	60–70
f:	10	15	25	25	10	10	5

Problem 76. The mean of 5 observations is 4.4 and the variance is 8.24. If three of the five observations are 1, 2 and 6, find the other two.

(*M.A. Econ. Delhi*)

Solution :

Let the two missing items by x and y

$$\Sigma X = \overline{X} \times N$$

$$= 4.4 \times 5 = 22$$

$$
\begin{aligned}
1+2+6+x+y &= 22 \\
x+y &= 22-9=13 \\
i.e. x+y &= 13 \\
\sigma^2 &= \frac{\Sigma X^2}{N} - (\overline{X})^2 \\
8.24 &= \frac{\Sigma X^2}{5} - (4.4)^2 \\
8.24 \times 5 &= \Sigma X^2 - (4.4^2 \times 5) \\
41.2 &= \Sigma X^2 - 96.8 \\
-\Sigma X^2 &= -96.8 - 41.2 \\
X^2 &= 138 \\
\Sigma X^2 &= 1^2 + 2^2 + 6^2 + x^2 + y^2 \\
\Sigma X^2 &= 41 + x^2 + y^2 \\
x^2 + y^2 &= 138 - 41 = 97 \\
(x+y)^2 &= x^2 + 2xy + y^2 \\
(13)^2 &= 97 + 2xy \\
2xy &= 169 - 97 \\
xy &= 36 \\
(x-y)^2 &= x^2 + y^2 - 2xy \\
&= 97 - 2(36) \\
x - y &= \sqrt{25} = 5 \\
x + y &= 13 \\
2x &= 18 \quad \therefore\ x = 9 \\
9 + y &= 13 \quad \therefore\ y = 4
\end{aligned}
$$

Therefore the two missing items are 9 and 4

Problem 77. the mean of 200 items is 48 and their standard deviation is 3, find the sum of squares of all items.

(B. Com. (Hons.) Delhi)

Solution :

$$
\begin{aligned}
N &= 200, \overline{X} = 48 \ \ \sigma = 3 \\
\overline{X} &= \frac{\Sigma X}{N} or \\
\Sigma X &= 200 \times 48 \\
&= \mathbf{9,600} \\
\sigma &= \sqrt{\frac{\Sigma X^2}{N} - \left(\frac{\Sigma X}{N}\right)^2}
\end{aligned}
$$

$$3 = \sqrt{\frac{\Sigma X^2}{200} - \left(\frac{9600}{200}\right)^2}$$

$$3^2 = \frac{\Sigma X^2}{200} - \left(\frac{9600}{200}\right)^2$$

$$9 = \frac{\Sigma X^2}{200} - 2304$$

$$9 \times 200 = \Sigma X^2 - 2304 \times 200$$

$$1800 = \Sigma X^2 - 4,60,800$$

$$\Sigma X^2 = 1800 + 4,60,800$$

$$\Sigma X^2 = \mathbf{4,62,600}$$

Problem 78. The mean and the standard deviation of a sample of size 10 were found to be 9.5 and 2.5 respectively. Later on, an additional observation became available. This 15.0 was included in the orginal sample. Find the mean and the standard deviation of the 11 observations.

(*ICWA*)

Solution :

$$N = 10; \quad \overline{X} = 9.5, \quad \sigma = 2.5 \text{(all value given)}$$

$$\Sigma X \text{(excluding 15)} = N\overline{X} = 10 \times 9.5 = 95$$

$$\Sigma X \text{(including 15)} = 95 + 15 = 110$$

$$\text{New Mean} = \frac{110}{11}$$

$$= \mathbf{10}$$

$$\Sigma X^2 \text{(excluding 15)} = N(\sigma^2 + \overline{X}^2)$$

$$= 10(2.5^2 + 9.5^2)$$

$$= 10(6.25 + 90.25)$$

$$= 965$$

$$\Sigma X^2 \text{(including 15)} = 965 + 15^2$$

$$= 1190$$

$$\text{New } \sigma = \sqrt{\frac{\text{New}\Sigma X^2}{N} - (\text{New Mean})^2}$$

$$= \sqrt{\frac{1190}{11} - (10)^2}$$

$$= \sqrt{108.18 - 100}$$

$$= \sqrt{8.18}$$

$$= \mathbf{2.86}$$

Problem 79. The mean and standard deviation of 20 items is found to be 10 and 2 respectively. At the time of checking it was found that one item 8 was incorrect. Calculate the mean and standard deviation if :

(*a*) the wrong item is omitted, and

(*b*) it is replaced by 12.

(*ICWA*)

Solution :

(*a*) When the wrong item is omitted, $N_1 = 20 - 1 = 19$

$$\begin{aligned}
\text{uncorrected } \Sigma X &= (10 \times 20) = 200 \\
\text{corrected } \Sigma X &= 200 - 8 = 192 \\
\text{uncorrected } \Sigma X^2 &= N(\sigma^2 + X^2) \\
&= 20(4 + 100) \\
&= 2080 \\
\text{corrected } \Sigma X^2 &= 2080 - (8)^2 \\
&= 2016 \\
\text{corrected } \overline{X} &= \frac{\text{corrected } \Sigma X}{\text{corrected} \quad N_1} \\
&= \frac{192}{19} \\
&= \mathbf{10.105} \\
\text{corrected } \sigma &= \sqrt{\frac{\text{corrected } \Sigma X^2}{N_1} - \left(\text{corrected } \overline{X}\right)^2} \\
&= \sqrt{\frac{2016}{19} - (10.105)^2} \\
&= \sqrt{106.1 - 102.1} \\
&= \sqrt{4} \\
&= \mathbf{2}
\end{aligned}$$

(*b*)

$$\begin{aligned}
\text{corrected } \Sigma X &= 200 - 8 + 12 = 204 \\
\therefore \quad \text{corrected } \overline{X} &= \frac{204}{20} = 10.2 \\
\text{corrected } \Sigma X^2 &= 2080 - (8)^2 + (12)^2 \\
&= 2080 - 64 + 144 \\
&= 2160 \\
\text{corrected } \sigma &= \sqrt{\frac{2160}{20} - (10.2)^2} \\
&= \sqrt{108 - 104.04} \\
&= \sqrt{3.96} \\
&= \mathbf{1.99}
\end{aligned}$$

Problem 80. The arithmetic mean and standard deviation of series of 20 items were calculated by a student as 20 cm and 5 cm, respectively. But while calculating them an item 13 was misread as 30. Find the correct arithmetic mean and standard deviation.

(*B. Com.(Hons.) Delhi*)

Solution :

$$\begin{aligned}
N &= 20; \quad \overline{X} = 20\text{cms.} \quad \sigma = 5\text{cms.} \\
\overline{X} &= \frac{\Sigma X}{N} \\
\text{wrong } \Sigma X &= N\overline{X} = 20 \times 20 = 400 \\
\text{correct } \Sigma X &= \text{wrong } \Sigma X - \text{wrong item} + \text{correct item} \\
&= 400 - 30 + 13 \\
&= 383
\end{aligned}$$

$$\therefore \quad \text{corrected } \overline{X} = \frac{383}{20} = \mathbf{19.15}$$

$$\text{wrong } \Sigma X^2 = N(\sigma^2 + \overline{X}^2) = 20(5^2 + 20^2) = 8500$$

$$\text{corrected } \Sigma X^2 = 8500 - (30)^2 + (13)^2 = 7769$$

$$\text{corrected } \sigma = \sqrt{\frac{\text{corrected } \Sigma X^2}{N} - (\text{corrected } \overline{X})^2}$$

$$= \sqrt{\frac{7769}{20} - (19.15)^2}$$

$$= \sqrt{388.45 - 366.72}$$

$$= \sqrt{21.73}$$

$$= \mathbf{4.66}$$

Problem 81. The means of two samples of sizes 50 and 100 respectively are 54.1 and 50.3 and the standard deviations are 8 and 7. Obtain the standard deviation of the sample of size 150 obtained by combining the two samples.

(*ICWA*)

Solution :

$$N_1 = 50 \qquad \overline{X}_1 = 54.1 \qquad \sigma_1 = 8$$

$$N_2 = 100 \qquad \overline{X}_2 = 50.3 \qquad \sigma_2 = 7$$

$$\text{Combined Mean } \overline{X}_{12} = \frac{N_1\overline{X}_1 + N_2\overline{X}_2}{N_1 + N_2}$$

$$= \frac{50 \times 54.1 + 100 \times 50.3}{50 + 100}$$

$$= \frac{2705 + 5030}{150}$$

$$= \frac{7735}{150}$$

$$= \mathbf{51.57}$$

$$\text{Combined } \sigma_{12} = \sqrt{\frac{N_1\sigma_1^2 + N_2\sigma_2^2 + N_1d_1^2 + N_2d_2^2}{N_1 + N_2}}$$

$$d_1 = (\overline{X}_1 - \overline{X}_{12}); \quad d_2 = (\overline{X}_2 - \overline{X}_{12})$$

$$\text{Thus } \sigma_{12} = \sqrt{\frac{50 + 8^2 + 100 \times 7^2 + 50(54.1 - 51.57)^2 + 100(50.3 - 51.57)^2}{150}}$$

$$= \sqrt{\frac{50 \times 64 + 100 \times 49 + 50(2.53)^2 + 100(-1.27)^2}{50 + 100}}$$

$$= \sqrt{\frac{3200 + 4900 + 320.045 + 161.29}{150}}$$

$$= \sqrt{\frac{8581.335}{150}}$$

$$= \mathbf{7.5636}$$

Problem 82. A sample of size 15 has mean 3.5 and S.D 3.0. Another sample of size 22 has mean 4.7 and S.D. 4.0. If the two samples are pooled together, find the mean and the SD. of the combined sample.

(*I.C.W.A. Intermediate*)

Solution :

Combined Mean $\overline{X}_{12} = \frac{N_1\overline{X}_1+N_2\overline{X}_2}{N_1+N_2}$

$$N_1 = 15 \qquad \overline{X}_1 = 3.5 \qquad \sigma_1 = 3$$

$$N_2 = 22 \qquad \overline{X}_2 = 4.7 \qquad \sigma_2 = 4$$

$$\overline{X}_{12} = \frac{15 \times 3.5 + 22 \times 4.7}{15+22}$$

$$= \frac{52.5 + 103.4}{37}$$

$$= \mathbf{4.2135}$$

Combined Standard Deviation (σ_{12})

$$\sigma_{12}^2 = \frac{N_1\sigma_1^2 + \sigma_2^2 N_2^2 + N_1(\overline{X}_1 - \overline{X}_{12}) + N_2(X_2 - X_{12})}{N_1 + N_2}$$

$$= \frac{15 \times (3)^2 + 22 \times (4)^2 + 15(3.5 - 4.2135)^2 + 22(4.7 - 4.2135)^2}{15+22}$$

$$= \frac{135 + 352 + 7.636 + 5.207}{37}$$

$$= \frac{499.943}{37} = 13.512$$

$$\therefore \quad \sigma_{12} = \sqrt{13.512}$$

$$= \mathbf{3.676}$$

Problem 83. The mean and standard deviation calculated from 20 observations are 15 and 10 respectively. If an additional observation 36, left out through oversight, be included in the calculations, find the corrected mean and standard deviation.

(*ICWA*)

Solution :

$$\overline{X} = \frac{\Sigma X}{N} \quad \therefore \quad \Sigma X = \overline{X} \times N$$

$$\therefore \Sigma X = 20 \times 15 = 300 \text{(which is incorrect)}$$

$$\text{But correct } \Sigma X = 300 + 36 = 336$$

$$\text{Then } N = 20 + 1 = 21$$

$$\therefore \quad \text{Corrected Mean} = \frac{336}{21}$$

$$= \mathbf{16.}$$

$$\sigma^2 = \frac{\Sigma X^2}{N} - (X)^2$$

$$(10)^2 = \frac{\Sigma X^2}{20} - (15)^2$$

$$2000 = \Sigma X^2 - 4500$$

$$6500 = \Sigma X^2 \text{(which is incorrect)}$$

$$\text{Correct } \Sigma X^2 = 6500 + (36)^2$$

$$= \mathbf{7796}$$

$$\text{Correct } \sigma = \sqrt{\frac{\text{Correct } (\Sigma X)^2}{N} - (\text{Correct } \overline{X})^2}$$

$$= \sqrt{\frac{7796}{21} - (16)^2}$$

$$= \sqrt{371.24 - 256}$$

$$= \sqrt{115.24}$$

$$= \mathbf{10.73}$$

Problem 84. Mean and standard deviations of two distribution of 100 and 150 items are 50, 5 and 40, 6 respectively. Find the mean and standard deviation of all the 150 items taken together.

(*ICWA*)

Solution :

$N_1 = 100$	$\overline{X}_1 = 50$	$\sigma_1 = 5$
$N_2 = 150$	$\overline{X}_2 = 40$	$\sigma_2 = 6$

$$\text{Combined } \overline{X}_{12} = \frac{N_1\overline{X}_1 + N_2\overline{X}_2}{N_1 + N_2}$$

$$(\overline{X}_{12}) = \frac{(100 \times 50) + (150 \times 40)}{100 + 150}$$

$$= \frac{5000 + 6000}{250}$$

$$= \mathbf{44.}$$

$$\text{Combined } \sigma = \sqrt{\frac{N_1\sigma_1^2 + N_2\sigma_2^2 + N_1d_1^2 + N_2d_2^2}{N_1 + N_2}}$$

$$d_1 = (\overline{X}_1 = \overline{X}_{12})d_2 = (\overline{X}_2 - \overline{X}_{12})$$

$$\sigma_{12} = \sqrt{\frac{100 \times (5)^2 + 150(6)^2 + 100(+6)^2 + 150(-4)^2}{100 + 150}}$$

$$= \sqrt{\frac{2500 + 5400 + 3600 + 2400}{250}}$$

$$= \sqrt{\frac{13900}{250}} = \sqrt{55.6}$$

$$= \mathbf{7.46.}$$

Problem 85. The first two sub groups has 100 items with mean 15 and standard deviation 3. If the whole group has 250 items with mean 15.6 and standard deviation $\sqrt{13.44}$, find the standard deviation of the second sub-group.

(*M.A. Ecos. Delhi*)

Solution :

$$N_1 = 100 \qquad \overline{X}_1 = 15 \qquad \sigma_1 = 3$$
$$N_2 = (250 - 100) \quad \overline{X}_2 = 15.6 \quad \sigma_{12} = \sqrt{13.44}$$
$$\overline{X}_{12} = \frac{N_1\overline{X}_1 + N_2\overline{X}_2}{N_1 + N_2}$$
$$15.6 = \frac{100 \times 15 + 150\overline{X}_2}{250}$$
$$3900 = 1500 + 150\overline{X}_2$$
$$-150\overline{X}_2 = -3900 + 1500$$
$$-150\overline{X}_2 = -2400$$
$$-\overline{X}_2 = -2400 \div 150$$
$$\overline{X}_2 = 16$$
$$d_1 = 15.6 - 15 = 0.6$$
$$d_2 = 15.6 - 16 = -0.4$$
$$\sigma_{12}^2 = \frac{N_1\sigma_1^2 + N_2\sigma_2^2 + N_1d_1^2 + N_2d_2^2}{N_1 + N_2}$$
$$13.44 = \frac{100(3)^2 + 150\sigma_2^2 + 100(0.6)^2 + 150(-0.4)^2}{250}$$
$$3360 = 900 + 150\sigma_2^2 + 36 + 24$$
$$3360 - 960 = 150\sigma_2^2$$
$$2400 = 150\sigma_2^2$$
$$\therefore \sigma_2^2 = \frac{2400}{150} = 16$$
$$\therefore \sigma_2 = \sqrt{16} = 4.$$

The standard deviation of the second sub-group

= **4.**

Problem 86. In a certain distribution of N=25 measurement it was found that mean=56 and standard deviation=2. After these results were computed it was discovered that a mistake had been made in one of the measurement which was recorded as 64. Find the mean and standard deviation if the incorrect value 64 is omitted.

(M.Com. Calcutta)

Solution :

$$\overline{X} = 56; \quad N = 25; \quad \sigma : 2(\text{given})$$
$$\overline{X} = \frac{\Sigma X}{N}$$
$$\therefore \Sigma X = \overline{X}N = 56 \times 25 = 1400(\text{uncorrected})$$
$$\text{Correct } \Sigma X = \text{uncorrected } \Sigma X - \text{wrong item}$$
$$= 1400 - 64 = 1336$$
$$\text{Corrected } \overline{X} = \frac{1336}{24} = \mathbf{55.667}.$$

$$\begin{aligned}
\Sigma X^2 &= N(\sigma^2 + \overline{X}^2) \\
&= 25(2^2 + 56^2) \\
&= 78,500(\text{uncorrected } \Sigma X^2) \\
\text{Corrected } \Sigma X^2 &= \text{uncorrected } \Sigma X^2 - \text{wrong item(square)} \\
&= 78,500 - (64)^2 \\
&= 74,404 \\
\text{Corrected } \sigma &= \sqrt{\frac{\text{Corrected } \Sigma X^2}{N} - (\text{Corrected } \overline{X})^2} \\
&= \sqrt{\frac{74,404}{24} - (55.667)^2} \\
&= \sqrt{3100.17 - 3098.81} \\
&= \sqrt{1.36} \\
&= \mathbf{1.17.}
\end{aligned}$$

Problem 87. A sample of 35 values has mean 80 and standard deviation 4. A second sample of 65 values from the same population has mean 70 and standard deviation 3. Find the mean and the standard deviation of the combined sample of 100 values.

(B. Com Punjab)

Solution :

$$\begin{aligned}
N_1 &= 35; \quad \overline{X}_1 = 80; \quad \sigma_1 = 4 \\
N_2 &= 65; \quad \overline{X}_2 = 70; \quad \sigma_2 = 3 \\
\overline{X}_{12} &= \frac{N_1\overline{X}_1 + N_2\overline{X}_2}{N_1 + N_2} \\
&= \frac{35 \times 80 + 65 \times 70}{35 + 65} \\
&= \frac{2800 + 4550}{100} \\
&= \frac{7350}{100} = \mathbf{73.5.} \\
\sigma_{12} &= \sqrt{\frac{N_1\sigma_1^2 + N_2\sigma_2^2 + N_1d_1^2 + N_2d_2^2}{N_1 + N_2}} \\
d_1 &= (\overline{X}_1 - \overline{X}_{12}) = 80 - 73.5 = 6.5 \\
d_2 &= (\overline{X}_2 - \overline{X}_{12}) = 70 - 73.5 = -3.5 \\
\sigma_{12} &= \sqrt{\frac{35 \times (4)^2 + 65 \times (3)^2 + 35 \times (6.5)^2 + 65 \times (-3.5)^2}{100}} \\
&= \sqrt{\frac{560 + 585 + 1478.75 + 796.25}{100}} \\
&= \sqrt{34.2} \\
&= \mathbf{5.8.}
\end{aligned}$$

Problem 88. The analysis of the results of a budget survey of 150 families gave an average monthly expenditure of Rs. 120 on food items with a standard deviation of Rs 15. After the analysis was completed it was noted that the figure recorded for one household was wrongly taken as Rs. 15 instead of Rs. 105. Determine the correct value of the average expenditure and its standard deviation. *(B.A. Kerala)*

Solution :

$$N = 150; \quad \overline{X} = 120; \quad \sigma = 15(\text{given})$$

$\therefore \quad \Sigma X(\text{Before correction}) = 120 \times 150 = 18,000$

$$\begin{aligned}
\text{Correct } \Sigma X &= \text{wrong } \Sigma X - \text{wrong item } + \text{correct item} \\
&= 18000 - 15 + 105 \\
&= 18090 \\
\therefore \quad \text{Corrected } \overline{X} &= \frac{18090}{150} = (\mathbf{120.6}) \\
\Sigma X^2(\text{Before Corrections}) &= N(\sigma^2 + \overline{X}^2) \\
&= 150(15^2 + 120^2) \\
&= 21,93,750 \\
\text{Correct } \Sigma X^2 &= \text{wrong } \Sigma X^2 - \text{square of wrong item} \\
&\quad + \text{square of correct item} \\
&= 21,93,750 - 225 + 11,025 \\
&= 22,04,550 \\
\text{Corrected } \sigma &= \sqrt{\frac{\text{Corrected } \Sigma X^2}{N} - (\text{Corrected } \overline{X}^2)} \\
&= \sqrt{\frac{2204550}{150} - (120.6)^2} \\
&= \sqrt{14,697 - 14,544.36} \\
&= \sqrt{152.64} \\
&= \mathbf{12.35}.
\end{aligned}$$

Problem 89. A student obtained the mean and standard deviation of 100 observations as 40 and 5.1 respectively. It was later discovered that he had wrongly copied down an observation as 50 instead of 40. Calculate the correct mean and standard deviation. *(B.Sc. Delhi)*

Solution :

$$\begin{aligned}
N &= 100; \quad \overline{X} = 40; \quad \sigma = 5.1 \\
\overline{X} &= \frac{\Sigma X}{N} \\
40 &= \frac{\Sigma X}{100} \\
\therefore \quad \Sigma X &= 40 \times 100 = 4,000(\text{uncorrected}) \\
\text{Correct } \Sigma X &= \text{uncorrected } \Sigma X - \text{wrong item} + \text{correct item} \\
&= 4000 - 50 + 40 \\
&= 3990 \\
\therefore \quad \text{Corrected} \overline{X} &= \frac{3990}{100} = \mathbf{39.9}
\end{aligned}$$

$$\begin{aligned}
\text{uncorrected}\Sigma X^2 &= N(\sigma^2 + \overline{X}^2) \\
&= 100(5.1)^2 + (40)^2 \\
&= 1,62,601 \\
\text{Correct}\Sigma X^2 &= 1,62,601 - 50^2 + 40^2 \\
&= 1,61,701 \\
\text{Corrected}\sigma &= \sqrt{\frac{\text{Corrected}\Sigma X^2}{N} - (\text{Corrected}\overline{X})^2} \\
&= \sqrt{\frac{161701}{100} - (39.9)^2} \\
&= \sqrt{1617.01 - 1592.01} \\
&= \sqrt{25} \\
&= \mathbf{5.}
\end{aligned}$$

Problem 90. The mean and standard deviation of a set of 100 observations were worked out as 40 and 5 respectively by a computer who by mistake took the value 50 in place of 40 for one observation. Re-calculate the correct mean and variance. (*B. Com., Bangalore*)

Solution :

Correct Mean:

We are given

$$\begin{aligned}
= \overline{X} &= 40; \quad \sigma = 5; \quad N = 100 \\
\overline{X} &= \frac{\Sigma X}{N} = 40 = \frac{\Sigma X}{100} \\
\Sigma X &= 4,000 \\
\text{But Correct } \Sigma X &= \Sigma X - \text{Wrong item} + \text{Correct item} \\
&= 4000 - 50 + 40 = 3990 \\
\therefore \text{Correct Mean} = \frac{\text{Correct } \Sigma X}{N} &= \frac{3990}{100} \\
&= \mathbf{39.90}
\end{aligned}$$

Correct Standard deviation:

$$\sigma = \sqrt{\frac{\Sigma X^2}{N} - (X)^2} = 5 = \sqrt{\frac{\Sigma X^2}{100} - (40)^2}$$

$$\begin{aligned}
(5)^2 &= \frac{\Sigma X^2}{100} - (40)^2 = 25 = \frac{\Sigma X^2}{100} - 1600 \\
25 \times 100 &= \Sigma X^2 - 1600 \times 100 = 2500 = \Sigma X^2 - 1,60,000 \\
\Sigma X^2 &= 2500 + 1,60,000 = 1,62,500 \\
\text{But Correct } \Sigma X^2 &= \text{Incorrect } \Sigma X^2 - \text{Wrong items square} \\
&\qquad + \text{Correct item square.} \\
\therefore \text{ Correct } \Sigma X^2 &= 1,62,500 - (50)^2 + (40)^2 \\
&= 1,62,500 - 2500 + 1600 \\
&= 1,61,600 \\
\text{Again Correct } \sigma &= \sqrt{\frac{\text{Correct } \Sigma X^2}{N} - (\text{Correct } \overline{X})^2}
\end{aligned}$$

$$= \sqrt{\frac{1,61,600}{100} - (39.90)^2}$$
$$= \sqrt{1616 - 1592.01}$$
$$\sigma = \sqrt{23.99}$$
$$= 4.89$$
$$\text{Variance} = \sigma^2 = \mathbf{23.99}.$$

Problem 91. Coefficient of variation of two series are 58% and 69%. Their standard deviations are 21.2 and 15.6. What are their arithmetic means?

(*B. Com., Delhi*)

Solution:

Coefficient of Variation

$$= \frac{\sigma \times 100}{\overline{X}}$$
$$\text{Therefore } \overline{X} = \frac{\sigma}{C.V} \times 100$$

Mean of the first series

$$= \frac{21.2}{58} \times 100$$
$$= \mathbf{36.6}$$

Mean of the second series

$$= \frac{15.6}{69} \times 100$$
$$= \mathbf{22.6}$$

Problem 92. The number of members, mean and S.D. of two distributions are :

Number of members	280	350
Mean	45	54
Standard Deviation	6	4

Find the mean and S.D. of the distribution formed by the two distribution taken together.

(*B.A. Econ. Hon. Delhi,*)

Solution:

Combined Mean :

$$\overline{X}_{12} = \frac{N_1\overline{X}_1 + N_2\overline{X}_2}{N_1 + N_2}$$
$$N_1 = 280; \quad \overline{X}_1 = 45; \quad N_2 = 350; \quad \overline{X}_2 = 54$$
$$= \frac{280 \times 45 + 350 \times 54}{280 + 350}$$
$$= \frac{12,600 + 18900}{630} = \frac{31500}{630}$$
$$= \mathbf{50}.$$

Combined Standard Deviation:

$$\sigma_{12} = \sqrt{\frac{N_1(\sigma_1^2 + d_1^2) + N_2(\sigma_2^2 + d_2^2)}{N_1 + N_2}}$$

$$d_1 = 45 - 50 = -5$$

$$d_2 = 54 - 50 = 4$$

$$N_1 = 280; \quad \sigma_1 = 6; \quad \text{d}_1^2 = (5)^2; \quad N_2 = 350; \quad \sigma_2^2 = (4)^2, \text{d}_2^2 = (4)^2$$

$$= \sqrt{\frac{280(6^2 + 5^2) + 350(4^2 + 4^2)}{280 + 350}}$$

$$= \sqrt{\frac{280(36 + 25) + 350(16 + 16)}{630}}$$

$$= \sqrt{\frac{280 \times 61 + 350 \times 32}{630}} = \sqrt{\frac{17,080 + 11,200}{630}}$$

$$= \sqrt{\frac{28280}{630}} = \sqrt{44.88}$$

$$= \mathbf{6.7}.$$

Problem 93. The numbers examined, the mean weight and the S.D. in each group of examination by two medical examiners are given below. Find the mean weight and S.D. deviation of both the groups taken together.

Medical Examiner	*Number Examined*	*Mean Weight Ibs.*	*Standard Deviation 1bs.*
A	50	113	6.5
B	60	120	8.2

(*B. Com. Madras*)

Solution:

$$\text{Combined Mean}(X_{12}) = \frac{N_1\overline{X}_1 + N_2\overline{X}_2}{N_1 + N_2}$$

$$N_1 = 50; \quad \overline{X}_1 = 113; \quad N_2 = 60; \overline{X}_2 = 120$$

$$\overline{X}_{12} = \frac{50 \times 113 + 60 \times 120}{50 + 60}$$

$$= \frac{5650 + 7200}{110}$$

$$= \frac{12850}{110}$$

$$= \mathbf{116.82}.$$

Combined σ

$$(\sigma_{12})\sqrt{\frac{N_1\sigma_1^2 + N_2\sigma_2^2 + N_1 d_1^2 + N_2 d_2^2}{N_1 + N_2}}$$

$$d_1 = \overline{X}_1 - \overline{X}_{12} = 113 - 116.82 = -3.82$$

$$d_2 = \overline{X}_2 - \overline{X}_{12} = 120 - 116.82 = 3.18$$

$$\sigma_{12} = \sqrt{\frac{50 \times (6.5)^2 + 60 \times (8.2)^2 + 50(-3.82)^2 + 60(3.18)^2}{50 + 60}}$$

$$= \sqrt{\frac{2112.5 + 4034.4 + 729.6 + 606.7}{110}}$$

$$= \sqrt{\frac{7483.2}{110}} = \sqrt{68.029}$$

$$= \mathbf{8.25}.$$

COEFFICIENT OF VARIATION

Problem 94. Calculate Range, standard deviation, coefficient of variation in respect of the marks obtained by ten students given below :

50 55 57 49 54 61 64 59 59 56

How would your results be affected if it is decided to increase the marks of each of the above students by 5 marks.

(B. Com., Bombay)

Solution :

Range = $L - S = 64 - 49 = 15$

Calculation of Standard Deviation

Marks	$d = X - 55$	d^2
50	−5	25
55	0	0
57	+2	4
49	−6	36
54	−1	1
61	+6	36
64	+9	81
59	+4	16
59	+4	16
56	+1	1
	$\Sigma d = +14$	$\Sigma d^2 = 216$

$$\sigma = \sqrt{\frac{\Sigma d^2}{N} - \left(\frac{\Sigma d}{N}\right)^2} = \sqrt{\frac{216}{10} - \left(\frac{14}{10}\right)^2}$$

$$= \sqrt{21.6 - 1.96} = \sqrt{19.64} = 4.43$$

$$\overline{X} = A + \frac{\Sigma d}{N} = 55 + \frac{14}{10} = \mathbf{56.4}$$

$$C.V. = \frac{\sigma}{\overline{X}} \times 100 = \frac{4.43 \times 100}{56.4} = \mathbf{7.85\%}$$

The standard diviation will not be affected even if all the items are increased by 5 marks.

Problem 95. Calculate the standard deviation and the coefficient of variation from the following table :

Age :	20–30	30–40	40–50	50–60	60–70	70–80	80–90
No. of members :	3	61	132	153	140	51	2

(*B. Com. Andhra, Madurai, Jammu*)

Solution :

Calculation of Standard Deviation

X	m	f	$d' = \frac{m-55}{10}$	fd'	fd^2
20–30	25	3	–3	–9	27
30–40	35	61	–2	–122	244
40-50	45	132	–1	–132	132
50–60	55	153	0	0	0
60–70	65	140	1	140	140
70–80	75	51	2	102	204
80–90	85	2	3	6	18
		$N = 542$		$\Sigma fd' = -15$	$\Sigma fd'^2 = 765$

$$\overline{X} = A \pm \frac{\Sigma fd'}{N} \times C$$

$$A = 55; \quad \Sigma fd' = -15; \quad N = 542; \quad C = 10$$

$$\overline{X} = 55 - \frac{15}{542} \times 10 = 55 - 0.28 = 54.72$$

$$\sigma = \sqrt{\frac{\Sigma fd'^2}{N} - \left(\frac{\Sigma fd'}{N}\right)^2} \times C$$

$$\Sigma fd'^2 = 765; \quad \Sigma fd' = -15; \quad N = 542; \quad C = 10$$

$$\sigma = \sqrt{\frac{765}{542} - \left(\frac{-150}{542}\right)^2} \times 10$$

$$= \sqrt{1.41 - 0.08} \times 10$$

$$= \sqrt{1.33} \times 10$$

$$= 1.15 \times 10$$

$$= \mathbf{11.5}$$

$$C.V. = \frac{\sigma}{\overline{X}} \times 100 = \frac{11.5}{54.72} \times 100$$

$$= \mathbf{21.02\%}$$

Problem 96 : The table below gives the distribution by size (No. of workes employed) of 40 different companies :

No. of workers	*No. of companies*	*No. of workers*	*No. of companies*
1–50	13	201–250	4
51–100	9	251–300	5
101–150	0	301–350	2
151–200	7		

Calculate :

(*a*) The total number of persons employed in theses 40 companies.

(*b*) The standard deviation.

(*c*) Coefficient of variation.

(*B. Com. Osmania*)

Solution :

Computation of Mean, Standard Deviation and C.V.

No. of workers	m	f	$d' = \frac{m - 175.5}{250}$	fd'	fd'^2
1–50.5	25.5	13	−3	−39	117
50.5–100.5	75.5	9	−2	−18	36
100.5–150.5	125.5	0	−1	0	0
150.5–200.5	175.5	7	0	0	0
200.5–250.5	225.5	4	1	4	4
250.5–300.5	275.5	5	2	10	20
300.5–350.5	325.5	2	3	6	18
		$N = 40$		$\Sigma fd' = -37$	$\Sigma fd^{12} = 195$

(*a*) Mean :

$$\overline{X} = A + \frac{\Sigma fd'}{N} \times C$$

$$A = 175.5; \quad \Sigma fd' = -37; \quad N = 40; \quad C = 50$$

$$= 175.5 - \frac{37}{40} \times 50 = 175.5 - 46.25$$

$$= 129.25.$$

Total number of workers $= 129.25 \times 40$

$= \mathbf{5,170}.$

(*b*) Standard deviation :

$$\sigma = \sqrt{\frac{\Sigma fd'^2}{N} - \left(\frac{\Sigma fd'}{N}\right)^2} \times C$$

$$\Sigma fd'^2 = 195; \quad \Sigma fd' = -37; \quad N = 40; \quad C = 50$$

$$= \sqrt{\frac{195}{40} - \left(-\frac{37}{40}\right)^2} \times C$$

$$= \sqrt{4.875 - (0.0925)} \times 50$$

$$= \sqrt{4.875 - 0.856} \times 50$$

$$= \sqrt{4.019} \times 50$$

$$= 2.005 \times 50$$

$$= \mathbf{100.25}$$

(*c*) Coefficient of variation :

$$C.V. = \frac{\sigma}{\overline{X}} \times 100 \quad \sigma = 100.25; \quad \overline{X} = 129.25$$

$$= \frac{100.25}{129.25} \times 100$$

$$= \mathbf{77.56\%}$$

Problem 97. In a small town, a survey was conducted in respect of profits made by retail shops. The following results werer obtained.

Profits ('000 Rs.)	*No. of shops*	*Profits* ('000 Rs.)	*No. of shops*
−4 to −3	4	1 to 2	56
−3 to −2	10	2 to 3	40
−2 to −1	22	3 to 4	24
−1 to 0	28	4 to 5	18
0 to 1	38	5 to 6	10

Calculate (*a*) the average profit made by a retail shop,

(*b*) total profit by all shops and

(*c*) the coefficient of variation of earnings.

(C.A)

Solution :

Computation of Coefficient of Variation

Profits of loss in ('000 Rs.)	m	f	fm	fm^2
−4 to −3	−3.5	4	−14	49
−3 to −2	−2.5	10	−25	62.5
−2 to −1	−1.5	22	−33	49.5
−1 to −0	−0.5	28	−14	7.0
0–1	0.5	38	19	9.5

Profits of loss in ('000 Rs.)	m	f	fm	fm^2
1–2	1.5	56	84	126.0
2–3	2.5	40	100	250.0
3–4	3.5	24	84	294.0
4–5	4.5	18	81	364.5
5–6	5.5	10	55	302.5
		$\Sigma f = 250$	$\Sigma fm = 337$	$\Sigma fm^2 = 1514.5$

$$\text{Mean: } \quad \overline{X} = \frac{\Sigma fm}{\Sigma f} = \frac{337}{250} = \mathbf{1.35}$$

$$\text{Total profit} = 1.35 \times 250 = \mathbf{337.50}$$

$$\sigma = \sqrt{\frac{\Sigma fm^2}{\Sigma f} - \left(\frac{\Sigma fm}{\Sigma f}\right)^2} = \sqrt{\frac{1514.5}{250} - \left(\frac{337}{250}\right)^2} = \sqrt{6.06 - 1.82} = \sqrt{4.24} = \mathbf{2.059}$$

$$C.V. = \frac{2.059}{1.35} \times 100 = \mathbf{152.52\%}$$

Problem 98. Calculate the S.D. and C.V. for the following :

X	: 10–30	30–50	50–70	70–90	90–110	110–130	130–150
f	: 14	59	101	61	28	17	4

Solution :

Computation of Standard Deviation and C.V

X	$M.P.$ (m)	f	$d' = \frac{m-80}{20}$	fd'	fd'^2
10–30	20	14	−3	−42	126
30–50	40	59	−2	−118	236
50–70	60	101	−1	−101	101
70–90	80	61	0	0	0

X	$M.P.$ (m)	f	$d' = \frac{m-80}{20}$	fd'	fd'^2
90–110	100	28	1	28	28
110–130	120	17	2	34	68
130–150	140	4	3	12	36
		$N = 284$		$\Sigma fd' = -187$	$\Sigma fd^2 = 595$

$$\text{Mean} : \overline{X} = A + \frac{\Sigma fd'}{N} \times C$$

$$A = 80; \quad \Sigma fd' = -187; \quad N = 284; \quad C = 20$$

$$= 80 \frac{-187}{284} \times 20 = 80 - 13.17$$

$$= 66.83.$$

Standard Deviation :

$$\sigma = \sqrt{\frac{\Sigma fd'^2}{N} - \left(\frac{\Sigma fd'}{N}\right)^2} \times C$$

$$\Sigma fd'^2 = 595; \quad \Sigma fd' = -187; \quad N = 284; \quad C = 20$$

$$= \sqrt{\frac{595}{284} - \left(\frac{-187}{284}\right)^2} \times 20 = \sqrt{2.095 - (0.658)^2} \times 20$$

$$= \sqrt{2.095 - 0.433} \times 20 = \sqrt{1.662} \times 20$$

$$= 1.289 \times 20$$

$$= \mathbf{25.78}$$

Coefficient of variation :

$$C.V. = \frac{\sigma}{\overline{X}} \times 100 \quad \sigma = 25.78; \quad \overline{X} = 66.83$$

$$= \frac{25.78}{66.83} \times 100$$

$$= \mathbf{38.58}$$

Problem 99. From the following figures find the S.D. and the coefficient of variation :

Marks :	0–10	10–20	20–30	30–40	40–50	50–60	60–70	70–80
No. of person:	5	10	20	40	30	20	10	4

(*B. Com. Agra, Madurai*)

Solution:

Computation of Standard Deviation and Coefficient of Variation

Marks	*M.P.* m	f	$d' = \frac{m-35}{10}$	fd'	fd'^2
0–10	5	5	−3	−15	45
10–20	15	10	−2	−20	40
20–30	25	20	−1	−20	20
30–40	35	40	0	0	0
40–50	45	30	1	30	30
50–60	55	20	2	40	80
60–70	65	10	3	30	90
70–80	75	4	4	16	64
		$N = 139$		$\Sigma fd' = 61$	$\Sigma fd'^2 = 369$

Mean :

$$\overline{X} = A + \frac{\Sigma fd'}{N} \times C \quad A = 35; \quad \Sigma fd' = 61; \quad N = 139; \quad C = 10$$

$$= 35 + \frac{61}{139} \times 10 = 35 + 4.39$$

$$= \mathbf{39.39}.$$

Standard Deviation :

$$\sigma = \sqrt{\frac{\Sigma fd'^2}{N} - \left(\frac{\Sigma fd'}{N}\right)^2} \times C$$

$$\Sigma fd'^2 = 369; \quad \Sigma fd' = 61; \quad N = 139; \quad C = 10$$

$$= \sqrt{\frac{369}{139} - \left(\frac{61}{139}\right)^2} \times 10$$

$$= \sqrt{2.655 - (0.439)^2} \times 10$$

$$= \sqrt{2.655 - 0.193} \times 10$$

$$= \sqrt{2.462} \times 10 \qquad = 1.569 \times 10$$

$$= \mathbf{15.69}$$

$$C.V. = \frac{\sigma}{\overline{X}} \times 100 \quad \sigma = 15.69; \quad \overline{X} = 39.39$$

$$= \frac{15.69}{39.39} \times 100$$

$$= \mathbf{39.83\%}$$

Problem 100. Compute an absolute measure of variance and a relative measure of dispersion from the following data :

Income	*No. of families*
300–399	30
400–499	46
500–599	58
600–699	76
700–799	60
800–899	50
900–999	20

(*B.A. Hons, Ecos., Delhi*)

Solution :

Computation of Variance and Coefficient of Dispersion

Income	*Mid Point* m	*No. of families* f	$d' = \frac{m-649.5}{100}$	fd'	fd'^2
300–399	349.5	30	−3	−90	270
400–499	449.5	46	−2	-92	184
500–599	549.5	58	−1	−58	58
600–699	649.5	76	0	0	0
700–799	749.5	60	1	60	60
800–899	849.5	50	2	100	200
900–999	949.5	20	3	60	180
		$N = 340$		$\Sigma fd^2 = -20$	$\Sigma fd'^2 = 952$

$$\text{Variance} = \sigma^2$$

$$\sigma = \sqrt{\frac{\Sigma fd'^2}{N} - \left(\frac{\Sigma fd'}{N}\right)} \times C$$

Variance

or $\sigma^2 = \frac{\Sigma fd'}{N} - \left(\frac{\Sigma fd'}{N}\right)^2 \times C^2$

$\Sigma fd'^2 = 952$; $N = 340$; $\Sigma fd' = -20$; $C^2 = 100^2$

$$= \frac{952}{340} - \left(\frac{-20}{340}\right)^2 \times 100^2$$

$$= 2.8 - 0.0035 \times 10,000$$

$$= 2.7965 \times 10,000 \quad = \mathbf{27,965.}$$

$$\overline{X} = A \pm \frac{\Sigma fd'}{N} \times C = 649.5 - \frac{20}{340} \times 100$$

$$= 649.5 - 5.9 \quad = \mathbf{643.6.}$$

Coefficient of variation :

$$C.V. = \frac{\sigma}{\overline{X}} \times 100 \quad \sigma = \sqrt{27965} = 167.23 \quad \overline{X} = 643.6$$

$$= \frac{167.23}{643.6} \times 100 \quad = \mathbf{25.98\%}.$$

Problem 101. The following data were collected randomly from a population of a particular university :

Monthly Expenditure	*No. of students*
72.0–73.9	7
74.0–75.9	31
76.0–77.9	42
78.0–79.9	54
80.0–81.9	33
82.0–83.9	24
84.0–85.9	22
86.0–87.9	8
88.0–89.9	4

Find mean, standard deviation and coefficient of variation from this data.

(*M.A. Ecos., Rajasthan*)

Solution:

Computation of Mean and Standard Deviation

Monthly Expenditure Rs.	*M.P.* m	f	$d' = \frac{m - 80.95}{2}$	fd'	fd'^2
72–73.9	72.95	7	−4	−28	112
74–75.9	74.95	31	−3	−93	279
76–77.9	76.95	42	−2	−84	168
78–79.9	78.95	54	−1	−54	54
80–81.9	80.95	33	0	0	0
82–83.9	82.95	24	1	24	24
84–85.9	84.95	22	2	44	88
86–87.9	86.95	8	3	24	72
88–89.9	88.95	4	4	16	64
		$N = 225$		$\Sigma fd' = -151$	$\Sigma fd'^2 = 861$

Mean : $\overline{X} = A + \frac{\Sigma fd'}{N} \times C$

$A = 80.95; \quad \Sigma fd' = -151; \quad N = 225; C = 2.$

$$= 80.95 - \frac{151}{225} \times 2 = 80.95 - 1.34$$

$$= \mathbf{79.61}.$$

Standard Deviation :

$$\sigma = \sqrt{\frac{\Sigma fd'^2}{N} - \left(\frac{\Sigma fd'}{N}\right)^2} \times C$$

$$\Sigma fd'^2 = 861; \quad \Sigma fd' = -151; \quad N = 225; \quad C = 2$$

$$= \sqrt{\frac{861}{225} - \left(\frac{-151}{225}\right)^2} \times 2 = \sqrt{3.826 - 0.449} \times 2$$

$$= \sqrt{3.377} \times 2$$

$$= 1.838 \times 2$$

$$= \mathbf{3.675}$$

Coefficient of variation : $\sigma = 3.675; \overline{X} = 79.61$

$$C.V. = \frac{\sigma}{\overline{X}} \times 100$$

$$= \frac{3.675}{79.61} \times 100$$

$$= \mathbf{4.62\%}.$$

Problem 102. The following are the marks obtained by 40 students of a class :

Marks	*Students*	*Marks*	*Students*
80–84	1	50–54	6
75–79	1	45–49	6
70–74	1	40–44	6
65–69	4	35–39	3
60–64	4	30–34	0
55–59	7	25–29	1

(*B. Com., Agra*)

Solution :

Calculation coefficient of variation.

Marks	*M.P.* m	f	$d = \frac{m - 52}{5}$	fd'	fd'^2
80–84	82	1	6	6	36
75–79	77	1	5	5	25
70–74	72	1	4	4	16
65–69	67	4	3	12	36
60–64	62	4	2	8	16
55–59	57	7	1	7	7

Marks	*M.P.* m	f	$d = \frac{m-52}{5}$	fd'	fd'^2
50–54	52	6	0	0	0
45–49	47	6	−1	−6	6
40–44	42	6	−2	−12	24
35–39	37	3	−3	−9	27
30–34	32	0	−4	0	0
25–29	27	1	−5	−5	25
		$N = 40$		$\Sigma fd' = 10$	$\Sigma fd'^2 = 218$

Mean : $\overline{X} = A + \frac{\Sigma fd'}{N} \times C \quad A = 52; \quad \Sigma fd' = 10; \quad N = 40; \quad C = 5$

$$= 52 + \frac{10}{40} \times 5 = 52 + 1.25$$

$$= \mathbf{53.25}.$$

Standard Deviation :

$$\sigma = \sqrt{\frac{\Sigma fd'^2}{N} - \left(\frac{\Sigma fd'}{N}\right)^2} \times C$$

$$\Sigma fd'^2 = 218; \quad \Sigma fd' = 10; \quad N = 40; \quad C = 5$$

$$= \sqrt{\frac{218}{40} - \left(\frac{10}{40}\right)^2} \times 5$$

$$= \sqrt{5.45 - 0.0625} \times 5 = \sqrt{5.3875} \times 5$$

$$= 2.321 \times 5$$

$$= \mathbf{11.61}.$$

$$C.V. = \frac{\sigma}{\overline{X}} \times 100 \quad \sigma = 11.61; \quad \overline{X} = 53.25$$

$$= \frac{11.61}{53.25} \times 100$$

$$= \mathbf{21.80\%}$$

Problem 103. From the prices of shares X and Y given below, state which share is more stable in value :

X :	55	54	52	53	56	58	52	50	51	49
Y :	108	107	105	105	106	107	104	103	104	101

(*B. Com. Srivenkateswara*)

Solution :

Computation of Coefficient of Variation

X shares			*Y Series*		
Prices of X shares X	*Deviation from mean (53) dx*	*Square of Deviations dx^2*	*Prices of Y share Y*	*Deviations from X (105) dy*	*Square of deviations dy^2*
55	+2	4	108	+3	9
54	+1	1	107	+2	4
52	–1	1	105	0	0
53	0	0	105	0	0
56	+3	9	106	1	1
58	+5	25	107	2	4
52	–1	1	104	–1	1
50	–3	9	103	–2	4
51	–2	4	104	–1	1
49	–4	16	101	–4	16
$\Sigma X = 530$		$\Sigma dx^2 = 70$	$\Sigma Y = 1050$		$\Sigma y^2 = 40$

X Series

$$\bar{X} = \frac{\Sigma X}{N} = \frac{530}{10}$$

$$= 53$$

$$\sigma = \sqrt{\frac{\Sigma dx^2}{N}} = \sqrt{\frac{70}{10}}$$

$$= \sqrt{7}$$

$$= 2.65$$

$$C.V. = \frac{\sigma}{\bar{X}} \times 100$$

$$= \frac{2.65}{53} \times 100$$

$$= 5\%$$

Y Series

$$\bar{X} = \frac{\Sigma Y}{N} = \frac{1050}{10}$$

$$= 105$$

$$\sigma = \sqrt{\frac{\Sigma dy^2}{N}} = \sqrt{\frac{40}{10}}$$

$$= \sqrt{4}$$

$$= 2$$

$$C.V. = \frac{\sigma}{\bar{X}} \times 100$$

$$= \frac{2}{105} \times 100$$

$$= 1.9\%$$

Y shares are more stable value than *X* shares because the coefficient of variation of *y* shares in lower than the coefficient of variation of *X* shares.

Problem 104. The following is the record of number of bricks laid each day for 10 days by two bricks-layers A and B. Calculate the co-efficient of variation in each case and discuss the relative consistency.

A	:	700	675	725	625	650	700	650	700	600	650
B	:	550	600	575	550	650	600	550	525	625	600

(*B. Com. Bangalore*)

Solution :

Computation of S.D. and C.V.

A			B		
X	$dx = x - 700$	dx^2	y	$dy = y - 600$	dy^2
700	0	0	550	−50	2500
675	−25	625	600	0	0
625	+25	625	575	−25	625
625	−75	5625	550	−50	2500
650	−50	2500	650	+50	2500
700	0	0	600	0	0
650	−50	2500	550	−50	2500
700	0	0	525	−75	5625
600	−100	10,000	625	+25	625
650	−50	2,500	600	0	0
	$\Sigma dx = -325$	$\Sigma dx^2 = 24375$		$\Sigma dy = -175$	$\Sigma dy^2 = 16875$

Mean :

$$\overline{X} = A + \frac{\Sigma dx}{N}$$

$$A = 700; \Sigma dx = -325; \quad N = 10$$

$$= 700 - \frac{325}{10} = 700 - 32.5$$

$$= \mathbf{667.5}$$

Mean

$$A = 600; \Sigma dy = -175; \quad N = 10$$

$$\overline{X} = 600 - \frac{175}{10} = 600 - 17.5$$

$$= \mathbf{582.5}$$

Standard Deviation :

$$\sigma = \sqrt{\frac{\Sigma d^2}{N} - \left(\frac{\Sigma dx}{N}\right)^2}$$

$$\Sigma dx^2 = 24375; \quad N = 10 \quad \Sigma dx = -325$$

Standard Deviation :

$$\Sigma dy^2 = 16875; \quad N = 10; \quad \Sigma dy = -175$$

$$\sigma = \sqrt{\frac{16875}{10} - \left(\frac{-175}{10}\right)^2}$$

$$= \sqrt{\frac{24375}{10} - \left(\frac{-325}{10}\right)^2}$$

$$= \sqrt{2437.5 - (-32.5)^2}$$

$$= \sqrt{2437.5 - 1056.25}$$

$$= \sqrt{1381.25}$$

$$= \mathbf{37.17.}$$

$$= \sqrt{1687.5 - (-17.5)^2}$$

$$= \sqrt{1687.5 - 306.25}$$

$$= \sqrt{1381.25}$$

$$= \mathbf{37.17.}$$

Coefficient of variartion :

$$C.V. = \frac{\sigma}{\overline{X}} \times 100$$

$$\sigma = 37.17; \overline{X} = 667.5$$

$$= \frac{37.17}{667.5} \times 100$$

$$= \mathbf{5.57\%}$$

Coefficient of variartion :

$$C.V. = \frac{\sigma}{\overline{X}} \times 10$$

$$\sigma = 37.17; \overline{X} = 582.5$$

$$= \frac{37.17}{582.5} \times 100$$

$$= \mathbf{6.38\%}$$

Bricks–layer A is more consistent in his performance.

Problem 105. The index number of prices of cotton and coal shares in 2002 were as under :

Months	*Index number of prices of cotton shares*	*Index number of prices of coal shares*
January	188	131
February	178	130
March	173	130
April	164	129
May	172	129
June	183	120
July	184	127
August	185	127
September	211	130
October	217	137
November	232	140
December	240	142

Which of the two shares do you consider more variable in prices ?

(*B. Com. Allahabad, M.A., Agra*)

Solution :

Computation of Coefficient of Variation

Month	*X Series*			*Y Series*		
	Index No. (cotton) X	*Deviation from A (184) (dx)*	*Square of Deviations $(dx)^2$*	*Index No. (coal) Y*	*Deviation from A (130) dy*	*Square of Deviation $(dy)^2$*
January	188	+4	16	131	+1	1
February	178	−6	36	130	0	0
March	173	−11	121	130	0	0
April	164	−20	400	129	−1	1
May	172	−12	144	129	−1	1
June	183	−1	1	120	−10	100
July	184	0	0	127	−3	9
August	185	1	1	127	−3	9
September	211	27	729	130	0	0
October	217	33	1089	137	+7	49
November	232	48	2304	140	+10	100
December	240	56	3136	142	+12	144
		$\Sigma dx = 119$	$\Sigma d^2x =$ 7,977		$\Sigma dy = 12$	$\Sigma d^2y = 414$

Cotton Shares

Mean :

$$\overline{X} = A + \frac{\Sigma fd'}{N}$$

$$A = 184; \Sigma dx = 119; \quad N = 12$$

$$= 184 + \frac{119}{12} = 184 + 9.9$$

$$= \mathbf{193.9}$$

$$\sigma = \sqrt{\frac{\Sigma d^2x}{N} - \left(\frac{\Sigma dx}{N}\right)^2}$$

$$\Sigma d^2x = 7,977, \quad N = 12, \quad \Sigma dx = 119.$$

$$= \sqrt{\frac{7,977}{12} - \left(\frac{119}{12}\right)^2}$$

$$= \sqrt{664.75 - (9.9)^2}$$

$$= \sqrt{664.75 - 98.01}$$

$$= \sqrt{566.74}$$

Coal Shares

$$\overline{X} = A + \frac{\Sigma dy}{N}$$

$$A = 130; \Sigma dy = 12; \quad N = 12$$

$$= 130 + \frac{12}{12} = 130 + 1$$

$$= \mathbf{131}.$$

$$\sigma = \sqrt{\frac{\Sigma d^2y}{N} - \left(\frac{\Sigma dy}{N}\right)^2}$$

$$\Sigma d^2y = 414, \quad N = 12, \quad \Sigma dy = 12$$

$$= \sqrt{\frac{414}{12} - \left(\frac{12}{12}\right)^2}$$

$$= \sqrt{34.5 - (1)^2}$$

$$= \sqrt{34.5 - 1}$$

$$= \sqrt{33.5}$$

$$= \mathbf{23.81}. \qquad\qquad = \mathbf{5.79}.$$

$$C.V. = \frac{\sigma}{\overline{X}} \times 100 \qquad\qquad C.V. = \frac{\sigma}{\overline{X}} \times 100$$

$$= \frac{23.81}{193.9} \times 100 \qquad\qquad = \frac{5.79}{131} \times 100$$

$$= \mathbf{12.28\%} \qquad\qquad = \mathbf{4.42\%}$$

Hence cotton shares are more variable in price than the coal shares.

Problem 106. Goal scored by two team A and B in a football season were as follows :

Number of goals scored in match	*No. of matches* Team A	Team B
0	27	17
1	9	9
2	8	6
3	5	5
4	4	3

By calculating the coefficient of variation in each case, find which team may be considered nore consistent.

(*B. Com. Calicut*)

Solution :

Computation of Coeffcient of Variation

No. of goals scored	*Deviation from* $A = 2(d)$	d^2	*Team A*			*Team B*		
			No. of matches f	fd	fd^2	*No. of matches* f	fd	fd^2
0	−2	4	27	−54	108	17	−34	68
1	−1	1	9	−9	9	9	−9	9
2	0	0	8	0	0	6	0	0
3	1	1	5	5	5	5	5	5
4	2	4	4	8	16	3	6	12
			$N = 53$	$\Sigma fd = -50$	$\Sigma fd^2 = 138$	$N = 40$	$\Sigma fd = -32$	$\Sigma fd^2 = 94$

Mean :

$$\overline{X} = A \pm \frac{\Sigma fd}{N} \qquad\qquad \overline{X} = 2 - \frac{32}{40} = 2 - 0.8$$

$$= 2 - \frac{50}{53} = 2 - 0.94 \qquad\qquad = \mathbf{1.2}.$$

$$= \mathbf{1.06}. \qquad\qquad \sigma = \sqrt{\frac{94}{40} - \left(\frac{-32}{40}\right)^2}$$

$$\sigma = \sqrt{\frac{\Sigma fd^2}{N} - \left(\frac{\Sigma fd}{N}\right)^2} \qquad\qquad = \sqrt{2.35 - (-0.8)^2}$$

$$= \sqrt{\frac{138}{53} - \left(\frac{-50}{53}\right)^2}$$
$$= \sqrt{2.6 - (-0.94)^2}$$
$$= \sqrt{2.6 - 0.8836}$$
$$= \sqrt{1.7164}$$
$$= \mathbf{1.31}.$$
$$C.V. = \frac{\sigma}{\overline{X}} \times 100$$
$$= \frac{1.31}{1.06} \times 100$$
$$= \mathbf{123.6\%}$$

$$= \sqrt{2.35 - 0.64}$$
$$= \sqrt{1.71}$$
$$= \mathbf{1.308}.$$
$$C.V. = \frac{1.308}{1.2} \times 100$$
$$= \mathbf{109\%}$$

Therefore *B* Team is more consistent in its performance.

Problem 107. Two cricketers scored the following runs in the several innings. Find who is a better run-getter and who more consistent player.

A:	42	17	83	59	72	76	64	45	40	32
B:	28	70	31	0	59	108	82	14	3	95

(*B. Com., Madras*)

Solution :

Computation of Mean and Coefficient of Variation

Cricketer A			*Cricketer B*		
X	$(X - \overline{X})(53)$	$(X - \overline{X})^2$	X	$(X - \overline{X})(49)$	$(X - \overline{X})^2$
42	−11	121	28	−21	441
17	−36	1296	70	+21	441
83	+30	900	31	−18	324
59	+6	36	0	−49	2401
72	+19	361	59	+10	100
76	+23	529	108	+59	3481
64	+11	121	82	+33	1089
45	−8	84	14	−35	1225
40	−13	169	3	−46	2116
32	−21	441	95	+46	2116
$\Sigma X = 530$	$\Sigma(X - \overline{X}) = 0$	$(X - \overline{X})^2 = 4058$	$\Sigma X = 490$	$\Sigma(X - \overline{X}) = 0$	$\Sigma(X - \overline{X})^2 = 13734$

$$\overline{X} = \frac{\Sigma X}{N}$$
$$= \frac{530}{10} = 53$$

$$\overline{X} = \frac{\Sigma X}{N}$$
$$= \frac{490}{10} = 49$$

$$\sigma = \sqrt{\frac{\Sigma X^2}{N}} \qquad \sigma = \sqrt{\frac{\Sigma X^2}{N}}\sqrt{\frac{13734}{10}}$$

$$= \sqrt{\frac{4058}{10}} \qquad = \sqrt{\frac{13734}{10}}$$

$$= \sqrt{405.8} \qquad = \sqrt{1373.4}$$

$$= 20.14 \qquad = 37.06$$

$$C.V. = \frac{\sigma}{\overline{X}} \times 100 \qquad C.V. = \frac{\sigma}{\overline{X}} \times 100$$

$$= \frac{20.14}{53} \times 100 \qquad = \frac{37.06}{49} \times 100$$

$$= \mathbf{38\%} \qquad = \mathbf{75.6\%}$$

A is better run getter as average is higher than *B*.
A is also more consistent player as the C.V. is lesser than *B*.

Problem 108. The following are the runs scored by two batsmen *A* and *B* in ten innings.

A :	101	27	0	36	82	45	7	13	65	14
B :	97	12	40	96	13	8	85	8	56	15

Who is the more consistent batsman?

(*B.Com., Bombay*)

Solution :

Computation of Coefficient of Variation

Batsman A			*Batsman B*		
Runs scored $\overline{X}$	$dx = X - 39$	dx^2	*Runs scored Y*	$dy = Y - 43$	dy^2
101	+62	3844	97	+54	2916
27	−12	144	12	−31	961
0	−39	1521	40	−3	9
36	−3	9	96	+53	2809
82	+43	1849	13	−30	900
45	+6	36	8	−35	1225
7	−32	1024	85	+42	1764
13	−26	676	8	−35	1225
65	+26	676	56	+13	169
14	−25	625	15	−28	784
		$\Sigma dx^2 = 10404$			$\Sigma dy^2 = 12762$

Batsman A

Mean: $\overline{X} = \frac{\Sigma X}{N} = \frac{390}{10}$

$= \mathbf{39}$

Standard Deviation :

$\sigma = \sqrt{\frac{\Sigma dX^2}{N}} = \sqrt{\frac{10404}{10}}$

$= \sqrt{1040.4}$

$= \mathbf{32.26}.$

$C.V. = \frac{\sigma}{\overline{X}} \times 100$

$\sigma = 32.26; \overline{X} = 39$

$= \frac{32.26}{39} \times 100$

$= \mathbf{82.72\%}$

Batsman B

Mean: $\overline{X} = \frac{430}{10}$

$= \mathbf{43}$

Standard Deviation :

$\sigma = \sqrt{\frac{\Sigma dy^2}{N}} = \sqrt{\frac{12762}{10}}$

$= \sqrt{1276.2}$

$= \mathbf{35.72}.$

$C.V. = \frac{\sigma}{\overline{X}} \times 100$

$\sigma = 35.72; \overline{X} = 43$

$= \frac{35.72}{43} \times 100$

$= \mathbf{83.07\%}$

Batsman A is more consistent as the coefficient of variation is less.

Problem 109. Find out which of the following is more consitent in scoring. Would you also accept him as a better batsman? Why ?

Batsman A :	5	7	16	27	39	53	56	61	80	101	105
Batsman B :	0	4	16	21	41	43	57	78	83	90	95

(*B. Com., Poona*)

Solution :

To find out more consistent batsman we compare the coefficient of variation. To know better batsman, we compare the arithmatic mean.

Computation of Coefficient of Variation

Batsman A			*Batsman B*		
X	$(X - \overline{X}) = (50)$	$(X - \overline{X})^2$	X	$(X - \overline{X}) = (48)$	$(X - \overline{X})^2$
5	−45	2025	0	−48	2304
7	−43	1849	4	−44	1936
16	−34	1156	16	−32	1024
27	−23	529	21	−27	729
39	−11	121	41	−7	49
53	+3	9	43	−5	25
56	+6	36	57	+9	81

Batsman A			Batsman B		
X	$(X-\overline{X}) = (50)$	$(X-\overline{X})^2$	X	$(X-\overline{X}) = (48)$	$(X-\overline{X})^2$
61	+11	121	78	+30	900
80	+30	900	83	+35	1225
101	+51	2601	90	+42	1764
105	+55	3025	95	+47	2209
$\Sigma X = 550$	$\Sigma(X-\overline{X}) = 0$	$(X-\overline{X})^2 = 12372$	$\Sigma X = 528$	$\Sigma(X-\overline{X}) = 0$	$\Sigma(X-\overline{X})^2 = 12246$

$$\overline{X} = \frac{\Sigma X}{N} = \frac{550}{11} = 50$$

$$\sigma = \sqrt{\frac{\Sigma X^2}{N}} \text{ or } \sqrt{\frac{\Sigma(X-\overline{X})^2}{N}}$$

$$= \sqrt{\frac{12372}{11}} = \sqrt{1124.73}$$

$$= \mathbf{33.54.}$$

$$\text{C.V.} = \frac{\sigma}{\overline{X}} \times 100$$

$$= \frac{33.54}{50} \times 100$$

$$= \mathbf{67.08}$$

$$\overline{X} = \frac{\Sigma X}{N} = \frac{528}{11} = 48$$

$$\sigma = \sqrt{\frac{\Sigma X^2}{N}} \text{ or } \sqrt{\frac{\Sigma(X-X)^2}{N}}$$

$$= \sqrt{\frac{12246}{11}} = \sqrt{1113.27}$$

$$= \mathbf{33.37.}$$

$$\text{C.V.} = \frac{\sigma}{\overline{X}} \times 100$$

$$= \frac{33.37}{48} \times 100$$

$$= \mathbf{69.52}$$

Batsman *A* is more consistent as the coefficient of variation is less. *A* is better batsman as the average is higher.

Problem 110. Prices of a particular commodity in five years in two cities are given below :

Price in city A :	20	22	19	23	16
Price in city B :	10	20	18	12	15

Find from the above data the city which had more stable prices.

(*B. Com., Andhra*)

Solution :

Computation of coefficient of Variation

Prices in city A X	*Deviation from* $\overline{X} = 20$	$d^2_{(X)}$	*Prices in city B* Y	*Deviations from* $\overline{Y} = 15$	$d^2(y)$
20	0	0	10	−5	25
22	2	4	20	5	25

Prices in city A X	*Deviation from* $\overline{X} = 20$	$d^2_{(X)}$	*Prices in city B* Y	*Deviations from* $\overline{Y} = 15$	$d^2(y)$
19	−1	1	18	3	9
23	+3	9	12	−3	9
16	−4	16	15	0	0
$\Sigma X = 100$	$\Sigma d = 0$	$\Sigma d^2_{(X)} = 30$	$\Sigma Y = 75$	$\Sigma d = 0$	$\Sigma d^2_{(y)} = 68$

City A City B

$$\overline{X} = \frac{\Sigma X}{N} = \frac{100}{5} = 20 \qquad \overline{Y} = \frac{\Sigma Y}{N} = \frac{75}{5} = \mathbf{15}$$

$$\sigma = \sqrt{\frac{\Sigma d^2(x)}{N}} \qquad \sigma = \sqrt{\frac{\Sigma d^2(y)}{N}}$$

$$= \sqrt{\frac{30}{5}} = \sqrt{6} = \mathbf{2.45.} \qquad = \sqrt{\frac{68}{5}} = \sqrt{13.6} = \mathbf{3.69.}$$

$$C.V. = \frac{\sigma}{\overline{X}} \times 100 \qquad C.V. = \frac{\sigma}{\overline{Y}} \times 100$$

$$= \frac{2.45}{20} \times 100 \qquad = \frac{3.69}{15} \times 100$$

$$= \mathbf{12.25\%} \qquad = \mathbf{24.6\%}$$

Since the *C: V.* is less in city *A*, we can conclude that the prices are more sable in city *A* than city *B*.

Problem 111. The following data refer to the dividend (%) paid by two companies A and B over the last seven years.

A :	4	8	4	15	10	11	9
B :	12	8	3	15	6	4	10

Calculate the co-efficient variation and comment. (*I.C.W.A. Final*)

Solution :

Computation of Mean, Standard Deviation and Coefficient of Variation

$A(x)$	$dx = x - 10$	dx^2	$B(y)$	$dy = y - 10$	dy^2
4	−6	36	12	2	4
8	−2	4	8	−2	4
4	−6	36	3	−7	49
15	5	25	15	5	25
10	0	0	6	−4	16
11	1	1	4	−6	36

$A(x)$	$dx = x - 10$	dx^2	$B(y)$	$dy = y - 10$	dy^2
9	−1	1	10	0	0
	$\Sigma dx = -9$	$\Sigma dx^2 = 103$		$\Sigma dy = -12$	$\Sigma dy = 134$

$$\text{Mean} : \overline{X} = A \pm \frac{\Sigma dx}{N}$$

$$A = 10; \Sigma dx = -9; N = 7$$

$$= 10 - \frac{9}{7} = 10 - 1.29$$

$$= \mathbf{8.71}.$$

$$A = 10; \Sigma dy = -12; \quad N = 7$$

$$\overline{X} = 10 - \frac{12}{7} = 10 - 1.71$$

$$= \mathbf{8.29}$$

Standard Deviation

$$\sigma = \sqrt{\frac{\Sigma dx^2}{N} - \left(\frac{\Sigma dx}{N}\right)^2}$$

$$\Sigma dx^2 = 103; \quad N = 7; \quad \Sigma dx = -9;$$

$$= \sqrt{\frac{103}{7} - \left(\frac{-9}{7}\right)^2}$$

$$= \sqrt{14.71 - (-1.29)^2}$$

$$= \sqrt{14.71 - 1.66}$$

$$= \sqrt{13.05}$$

$$= \mathbf{3.61}.$$

Standard Deviation

$$\Sigma dy^2 = 134; \quad N = 7; \quad \Sigma dy = -12$$

$$\sigma = \sqrt{\frac{134}{7} - \left(\frac{-12}{7}\right)^2}$$

$$= \sqrt{19.14 - (-1.71)^2}$$

$$= \sqrt{19.14 - 2.92}$$

$$= \sqrt{16.22}$$

$$= \mathbf{4.03}$$

Coefficient of Variation

$$C.V. = \frac{\sigma}{\overline{X}} \times 100$$

$$\sigma = 3.61; \quad \overline{X} = 8.71$$

$$= \frac{3.61}{8.71} \times 100$$

$$= \mathbf{41.45\%}.$$

Coefficient of Variation

$$\sigma = 4.03; \overline{X} = 8.29$$

$$C.V. = \frac{4.03}{8.29} \times 100$$

$$= \mathbf{48.61\%}$$

Company A is better. Because dividend percentage is more and has less variability.

Problem 112. From data given below state which series is more consistent.

Variable	*Series A*	*Series B*
10–20	10	18
20–30	18	22
30–40	32	40
40–50	40	32

Variable	*Series A*	*Series B*
50–60	22	18
60–70	18	10

(*B. Com. Bangalore*)

Solution :

Computation of Coefficient of Variation

Variable	m	$d' = \frac{m-35}{10}$	*Series A*			*Series B*		
			f	fd'	fd'^2	f	fd'	fd'^2
10–20	15	−2	10	−20	40	18	−36	72
20–30	25	−1	18	−18	18	22	−22	22
30–40	35	0	32	0	0	40	0	0
40–50	45	1	40	40	40	32	32	32
50–60	55	2	22	44	88	18	36	72
60–70	65	3	18	54	162	10	30	90
			$N = 140$	$\Sigma fd' = 100$	$\Sigma fd'^2 = 348$	$N = 140$	$\Sigma fd' = 40$	$\Sigma fd'^2 = 288$

Series A

Mean :

$$\overline{X} = A + \frac{\Sigma fd'}{N} \times C$$

$$A = 35; \Sigma fd' = 100; \quad N = 140; C = 10$$

$$= 35 + \frac{100}{140} \times 10 = 35 + 7.14$$

$$= \mathbf{42.14}.$$

Standard Deviation

$$\sigma = \sqrt{\frac{\Sigma fd'^2}{N} - \left(\frac{\Sigma fd'}{N}\right)^2} \times C$$

$$\Sigma fd'^2 = 348; \Sigma fd' = 100; \quad N = 140; C = 10$$

$$= \sqrt{\frac{348}{140} - \left(\frac{100}{140}\right)^2} \times 10$$

$$= \sqrt{2.486 - (0.714)^2} \times 10$$

$$= \sqrt{2.486 - 0.510} \times 10$$

$$= \sqrt{1.976} \times 10$$

$$= 1.405 \times 10$$

Series B

$$A = 35; \Sigma fd' = 40; \quad N = 140; C = 10$$

$$\overline{X} = 35 + \frac{40}{140} \times 10 = 35 + 2.86$$

$$= \mathbf{37.86}$$

Standard Deviation

$$\Sigma fd'^2 = 288; N = 140; \Sigma fd' = 40; C = 10$$

$$\sigma = \sqrt{\frac{288}{140} - \left(\frac{40}{140}\right)^2} \times 10$$

$$= \sqrt{2.057 - (0.286)^2} \times 10$$

$$= \sqrt{2.057 - 0.082} \times 10$$

$$= \sqrt{1.975} \times 10$$

$$= 1.405 \times 10$$

$$= \mathbf{14.05}.$$

$= \mathbf{14.05}$.

Coefficient of Variation

$$C.V. = \frac{\sigma}{\overline{X}} \times 100 \quad \sigma = 14.05$$

$$\overline{X} = 42.14$$

$$= \frac{14.05}{42.14} \times 100$$

$$= \mathbf{33.34\%}$$

Coefficient of Variation

$$\sigma = 14.05; \overline{X} = 37.86$$

$$C.V. = \frac{14.05}{37.86} \times 100$$

$$= \mathbf{37.11\%}$$

Series **A** is more consistent.

Problem 113. You are given the daily wages paid to workers in two factories X and Y.

Daily wages : (Rs)	2–3	3–4	4–5	5–6	6–7	7–8	8–9
Factory X :	15	30	44	60	30	14	7
Factory Y :	25	40	60	35	20	15	5

Using arithmetic mean and standard deviation, answer the following points :

(*a*) Which factory pays higher average wages? By how much?

(*b*) In which factory are wages more variable?

(*c*) Which factory has to pay more wages in a month assuming that both work for 20 days in a month?

(*C.A.*)

Solution :

Computation of Coefficient of Variation

			Factory X			*Factory Y*		
Daily wages	*M.P.* m	$d = m - 5.5$	f	fd	fd^2	f	fd	fd^2
2–3	2.5	−3	15	−45	135	25	−75	225
3–4	3.5	−2	30	−60	120	40	−80	160
4–5	4.5	−1	44	−44	44	60	−60	60
5–6	5.5	0	60	0	0	35	0	0
6–7	6.5	1	30	30	30	20	20	20
7–8	7.5	2	14	28	56	15	30	60
8–9	8.5	3	7	21	63	5	15	45
			$N = 200$	$\Sigma fd = -70$	$\Sigma fd^2 = 448$	$N = 200$	$\Sigma fd = -150$	$\Sigma fd^2 = 570$

Factory X

Mean :

$$\overline{X} = A + \frac{\Sigma fd}{N}$$

$$A = 5.5; \Sigma fd = -70; \quad N = 200$$

$$= 5.5 - \frac{70}{200} = 5.5 - 0.35$$

$$= \mathbf{5.15}.$$

Standard Deviation :

$$\sigma = \sqrt{\frac{\Sigma fd^2}{N} - \left(\frac{\Sigma fd}{N}\right)^2}$$

$$\Sigma fd^2 = 448; N = 200 \quad \Sigma fd = -70;$$

$$= \sqrt{\frac{448}{200} - \left(\frac{-70}{200}\right)^2}$$

$$= \sqrt{2.24 - (-0.35)^2}$$

$$= \sqrt{2.24 - 0.12}$$

$$= \sqrt{2.12}$$

$$= \mathbf{1.46}.$$

$$C.V. = \frac{\sigma}{\overline{X}} \times 100$$

$$\sigma = 1.46; \overline{X} = 5.15$$

$$= \frac{1.46}{5.15} \times 100$$

$$= \mathbf{28.35\%}$$

Factory Y

Mean :

$$A = 5.5; \Sigma fd = -150; \quad N = 200$$

$$\overline{X} = 5.5 - \frac{150}{200} = 5.5 - 0.75$$

$$= \mathbf{4.75}$$

Standard Deviation :

$$\Sigma fd^2 = 570; \quad N = 200; \quad \Sigma fd = -150$$

$$\sigma = \sqrt{\frac{570}{200} - \left(\frac{-150}{200}\right)^2}$$

$$= \sqrt{2.85 - (-0.75)^2}$$

$$= \sqrt{2.85 - 0.56}$$

$$= \sqrt{2.29}$$

$$= \mathbf{1.51}.$$

$$\sigma = 1.51; \overline{X} = 4.75$$

$$C.V. = \frac{1.51}{4.75} \times 100$$

$$= \mathbf{31.79\%}.$$

(*a*) The average wage of Factory *X* is Rs. 5.15 which is more than the average wage of Factory *Y* (Rs. 4.75). Therefore, the factory *X* pays higher average wage.

Factory *X* pays Rs. 0.40 (Rs. 5.15–4.75) more than Factory *Y* per worker on the basis of average.

(*b*) There is a greater variability of wages in Factory *Y* than the factory *X* as the co-efficient of variation is more. This is because the C.V. of Factory *Y* is 31.79 % which is more than the C.V. of Factory *X* (28.35%).

(*c*) Factory *X* pays out more wages in a month on the basis of total monthly wages, which is :

Total Monthly wages = Mean wage × No. of workers × working days

Factory X = Rs. 5.15×200 × 20 = 20,600

Factory Y = Rs. 4.75×200 × 20 = 19,000

Problem 114. The data given below relate to the heights and weights of 20 persons. You are required to form a two way frequency table with class intervals 62" to 64", 64" to 66" and so on, and, 115 to 125 Ibs., 125 to 135 Ibs and so on.

S. No.	*Weight*	*Height*	*S.No.*	*Weight*	*Height*	*S.No.*	*Weight*	*Height*
1	170	70	8	128	70	15	140	67
2	135	65	9	143	71	16	132	69
3	136	65	10	129	62	17	120	66
4	137	64	11	163	70	18	148	68
5	148	69	12	139	67	19	129	67
6	124	63	13	122	63	20	152	67
7	117	65	14	134	68			

Using the standard deviation and its coefficient, state whether there is greater variation in heights or weights.

(*C.A.*)

Solution :

Two way frequency table

	115–125	125–135	135–145	145–155	155–165	165–175	Total
62–64	II(2)	I(1)					3
64–66	I(1)		III(3)				4
66–68	I(1)	I(1)	II (2)	I(1)			5
68–70		II (2)		II (2)			4
70–72		I(1)	I(1)		I(1)	I(1)	4
Total	4	5	6	3	1	1	20

Mean : $\overline{X} = A + \dfrac{\Sigma fd'}{N} \times C$

$A = 67$; $\Sigma fd' = 2$; $N = 20$; $C = 10$

$= 67 + \dfrac{2}{20} \times 2 = 67 + 0.2$

$=$ **67.2inches.**

$A = 140; \Sigma fd' = -5; \quad N = 20; \quad C = 10$

$\overline{X} = 140 - \dfrac{5}{20} \times 10 = 140 - 2.5$

$=$ **137.5Ibs.**

Standard Deviation

$$\sigma = \sqrt{\frac{\Sigma fd'^2}{N} - \left(\frac{\Sigma fd'}{N}\right)^2} \times C$$

$\Sigma fd'^2 = 36; \Sigma fd' = 2; \quad N = 20; \quad C = 2$

$$= \sqrt{\frac{36}{20} - \left(\frac{2}{20}\right)^2} \times 2$$

$$= \sqrt{1.8 - (0.1)^2} \times 2$$

$\Sigma fd'^2 = 37; \quad \Sigma fd' = -5; \quad N = 20; \quad C = 10$

$$= \sqrt{\frac{37}{20} - \left(\frac{-5}{20}\right)^2} \times 10$$

$$= \sqrt{1.85 - (0.25)^2} \times 10$$

$$= \sqrt{1.85 - 0.0625} \times 10$$

$$= \sqrt{1.8 - 0.01} \times 2$$
$$= \sqrt{1.79 \times 2}$$
$$= 1.34 \times 2$$
$$= \mathbf{2.68.}$$
$$C.V. = \frac{\sigma}{\overline{X}} \times 100$$
$$\sigma = 2.68; \overline{X} = 67.2$$
$$= \frac{2.68}{67.2} \times 100$$
$$= \mathbf{3.99\%.}$$

$$= \sqrt{1.7875} \times 10$$
$$= 1.337 \times 10$$
$$= \mathbf{13.37.}$$
$$\sigma = 13.37; \overline{X} = 137.5$$
$$C.V. = \frac{13.37}{137.5} \times 100$$
$$= \mathbf{9.72\%.}$$

There is greater variation in weight. Since the coefficient of variation of weight (9.72%) is greater than the coefficient of variation of height (3.99%).

Computation of Mean and Standard Deviation

Height	*M.P.* m	f	$d' = \frac{m-67}{2}$	fd'	fd'^2	*Weight*	*M.P.* m	f	$d' = \frac{m-140}{10}$	fd'	fd'^2
62–64	63	3	–2	–6	12	115–125	120	4	–2	–8	16
64–66	65	4	–1	–4	4	125–135	130	5	–1	–5	5
66–68	67	5	0	0	0	135–145	140	6	0	0	0
68–70	69	4	1	4	4	155–165	150	3	1	3	3
70–72	71	4	2	8	16	155–165	160	1	2	2	4
						165–175	170	1	3	3	9
		$N = 20$		$\Sigma fd' = +2$	$\Sigma fd'^2 = 36$			$N = 20$		$\Sigma fd' = -5$	$\Sigma fd'^2 = 37$

Problem 115. Lives of two models of refrigerators turned in for new models in a recent survey are :

Life (No. of years)	*No. of refrigerators* Model A	Model B
0–2	5	2
2–4	16	7
4–6	13	12
6–8	7	19
8–10	5	9
10–12	4	1

What is the average life of each model of these refrigerators ? Which model has more uniformity?

(*MBA Delhi*)

Solution :

Computation of Mean and Standard Deviation

		Model A				Model B			
Life (NO. of years)	M.P. m	f	$\frac{(m-5)}{2} = a'$	fd'	fd'^2	f	$d' = \frac{m-5}{2}$	fd'	fd'^2
0–2	1	5	−2	−10	20	2	−2	−4	8
2–4	3	16	−1	−16	16	7	−1	−7	7
4–6	5	13	0	0	0	12	0	0	0
6–8	7	7	1	7	7	19	1	19	19
8–10	9	5	2	10	20	9	2	18	36
10–12	11	4	3	12	36	1	3	3	9
		$N = 50$		$\Sigma fd' = 3$	$\Sigma fd'^2 = 99$	$N = 50$		$\Sigma fd' = 29$	$\Sigma fd'^2 = 79$

$$\overline{X} = A + \frac{\Sigma fd'}{N} \times C$$

$$A = 5; \quad \Sigma fd' = 3; \ N = 50; \quad C = 2$$

$$= 5 + \frac{3}{50} \times 2 = 5 + 0.12$$

$$= \mathbf{5.12}$$

$$A = 5; fd' = 29; \quad N = 50; C = 2$$

$$\overline{X} = 5 + \frac{29}{50} \times 2 = 5 + 1.16$$

$$= \mathbf{6.16}.$$

$$\sigma = \sqrt{\frac{\Sigma fd'^2}{N} - \left(\frac{\Sigma fd'}{N}\right)^2} \times C$$

$$\Sigma fd'^2 = 99; \Sigma fd' = 3; \quad N = 50; C = 2$$

$$= \sqrt{\frac{99}{50} - \left(\frac{3}{50}\right)^2} \times 2$$

$$= \sqrt{1.98 - 0.0036} \times 2$$

$$= \sqrt{1.9764} \times 2$$

$$= 1.406 \times 2$$

$$= \mathbf{2.812}.$$

$$\Sigma fd'^2 = 79; \ \Sigma fd' = 29; \ N = 50; \ C = 2$$

$$\sigma = \sqrt{\frac{79}{50} - \left(\frac{29}{50}\right)^2} \times 2$$

$$= \sqrt{1.58 - 0.3364} \times 2$$

$$= \sqrt{1.2436} \times 2$$

$$= 1.115 \times 2$$

$$= \mathbf{2.23}.$$

$$C.V. = \frac{\sigma}{\overline{X}} \times 100$$

$$\sigma = 2.812; \overline{X} = 5.12$$

$$C.V. = \frac{2.812}{5.12} \times 100$$

$$= \mathbf{54.92\%}$$

$$C.V. = \frac{2.23}{6.16} \times 100$$

$$= \mathbf{36.2\%}$$

Coefficient of variation is less for model B. Therefore B modal has greater uniformity.

Problem 116. The following table gives the frequency distribution of marks obtained by studens of two classes. Find the arithmetic mean, the standard deviation and coefficients of variations of the marks of two classes :

Marks :	5–10	10–15	15–20	20–25	25–30	30–35	35–40	40–45
Class A :	1	10	20	8	6	3	1	0
Class B :	5	6	15	10	5	4	2	2

(*B. Com. Punjab*)

Solution :

		Class A				Class B		
Mark	*M.P.(m)*	f	$d' = \frac{m-22.5}{5}$	fd'	fd'^2	f	fd'	fd'^2
5–10	7.5	1	−3	−3	9	5	−15	45
10–15	12.5	10	−2	−20	40	6	−12	24
15–20	17.5	20	−1	−20	20	15	−15	15
20–25	22.5	8	0	0	0	10	0	0
25–30	27.5	6	1	6	6	5	5	5
30–35	32.5	3	2	6	12	4	8	16
35–40	37.5	1	3	3	9	2	6	18
40–45	42.5	0	4	0	0	2	8	32
		$N = 49$		$\Sigma fd' = -28$	$\Sigma fd'^2 = 96$	$N = 49$	$\Sigma fd' = -15$	$\Sigma fd'^2 = 155$

Mean :

$$\overline{X} = A + \frac{\Sigma fd'}{N} \times C$$

$$A = 22.5;\ \Sigma fd' = -28;\ N = 49;\ C = 5$$

$$= 22.5 - \frac{28}{49} \times 5 = 22.5 - 2.86$$

$$= \mathbf{19.64.}$$

$$\sigma = \sqrt{\frac{\Sigma fd'^2}{N} - \left(\frac{\Sigma fd'}{N}\right)^2} \times 5$$

$$\Sigma fd'^2 = 96;\quad N = 49;$$

$$\Sigma fd' = -28; C = 5$$

$$\sigma = \sqrt{\frac{96}{49} - \left(\frac{-28}{49}\right)^2} \times 5$$

$$= \sqrt{1.96 - 0.32} \times 5$$

$$= \sqrt{1.64} \times 5 = 1.28 \times 5$$

$$A = 22.5; \Sigma fd' = -15$$

$$N = 49;\ C = 5$$

$$= 22.5 - \frac{15}{49} \times 5 = 22.5 - 1.53$$

$$= \mathbf{20.97.}$$

$$\Sigma fd'^2 = 155;\quad N = 49;$$

$$\Sigma fd' = -15;\quad C = 5$$

$$\sigma = \sqrt{\frac{155}{49} - \left(\frac{-15}{49}\right)^2} \times 5$$

$$= \sqrt{3.16 - 0.09} \times 5$$

$$= \sqrt{3.07} \times 5$$

$$= 1.75 \times 5$$

$= \mathbf{6.40}.$ $\qquad\qquad = \mathbf{8.75}$

$$C.V. = \frac{\sigma}{\overline{X}} \times 100 = \frac{6.40}{19.64} \times 100 \qquad C.V. = \frac{8.75}{20.97} \times 100$$

$= \mathbf{32.59\%}.$ $\qquad\qquad = \mathbf{41.73\%}.$

Problem 117. *A* factory produces two types of electric lamps *A* and *B*. In an experiement relating to their life, the following results were obtained.

Length of life (in hours)	*No. of lamps A*	*No. of lamps B*
500–700	5	4
700–900	11	30
900–1,100	26	12
1,100–1,300	10	8
1,300–1,500	8	6
	60	60

Compare the variability of the life of the two varieties using coefficient of variation.

(*C.A. Inter*)

Solution :

Computation of Coefficient of Variation

			A			*B*		
Length of life in hours	m	$d' = \frac{m-1000}{200}$	f	fd'	fd'^2	f	fd'	fd'^2
500–700	600	−2	5	−10	20	4	−8	16
700–900	800	−1	11	−11	11	30	−30	30
900–1100	1000	0	26	0	0	12	0	0
1100–1300	1200	1	10	10	10	8	8	8
1300–1500	1400	2	8	16	32	6	12	24
			$N = 60$	$\Sigma fd' = 5$	$\Sigma fd'^2 = 73$	$N = 60$	$\Sigma fd' = -18$	$\Sigma fd'^2 = 78$

A

Mean : $\overline{X} = A + \frac{\Sigma fd'}{N} \times C$

$A = 1000; \quad \Sigma fd' = 5; \quad N = 60;$

$C = 200$

$= 1000 + \frac{5}{60} \times 200 = 100 + 16.67$

$= \mathbf{1016.67}.$

B

Mean:

$A = 1000; \Sigma fd' = -18;$

$N = 60; \quad C = 200$

$\overline{X} = 1000 - \frac{18}{60} \times 200$

$= 1000 - 60$

$= \mathbf{940}$

Standard Deviation

$$\sigma = \sqrt{\frac{\Sigma fd'^2}{N} - \left(\frac{\Sigma fd'}{N}\right)^2} \times C$$

$$\Sigma fd'^2 = 73; \quad N = 60; \quad \Sigma fd' = 5; \quad C = 200$$

$$= \sqrt{\frac{73}{60} - \left(\frac{5}{60}\right)^2} \times 200$$

$$= \sqrt{1.217 - (-0.083)^2} \times 200$$

$$= \sqrt{1.217 \times 0.007} \times 200$$

$$= \sqrt{1.210} \times 200 = 1.1 \times 200$$

$$= \textbf{220 hours.}$$

Standard Deviation

$$\Sigma fd'^2 = 78; \quad N = 60$$

$$\Sigma fd' = -18; C = 200$$

$$= \sqrt{\frac{78}{60} - \left(\frac{-18}{60}\right)^2} \times 200$$

$$= \sqrt{1.3 - (0.3)^2} \times 200$$

$$= \sqrt{1.3 - 0.09} \times 200$$

$$= \sqrt{1.21} \times 200$$

$$= 1.1 \times 200$$

$$= \textbf{220 hours}$$

Coefficient of Variation

$$C.V. = \frac{\sigma}{\overline{X}} \times 100$$

$$\sigma = 220; \overline{X} = 1016.67$$

$$= \frac{220}{1016.67} \times 100$$

$$= \textbf{21.64\%}$$

Coefficient of Variation

$$\sigma = 220; \overline{X} = 940$$

$$C.V. = \frac{220}{940} \times 100$$

$$= \textbf{23.40\%}$$

Electric lamp A is more uniform.

Problem 118. The following table gives the distribution of wages in the two branches of a factory :

Monthly wages (Rs.)	*Number of workers*	
	Branch A	*Branch B*
100–150	167	63
150–200	207	93
200–250	253	157
250–300	205	105
300–350	168	82
Total	1000	500

Find the mean and standard deviation for the two branches for the wages seperatrely.

(*a*) Which branch pays higher average wages?

(*b*) Which branch has greater variability in wages in relation to the average wages ?

(*c*) What is the average monthly wage of the factory as a whole?

(*d*) What is the variance of wages of all the workers in the two branches *A* and *B* taken together?

(*B. Com., Mysore*)

Solution :

Computation of Coefficient of Variation

Monthly Wages in Rs.			*Branch A*			*Branch B*		
	m	$d' = \frac{m-225}{50}$	f	fd'	fd'^2	f	fd'	fd'^2
100–150	125	−2	167	−334	668	63	−126	252
150–200	175	−1	207	−207	207	93	−93	93
200–250	225	0	253	0	0	157	0	0
250–300	275	1	205	205	205	105	105	105
300–350	325	2	168	336	672	82	164	328
			N= 1000	$\Sigma fd' = 0$	$\Sigma fd'^2 = 1752$	$N = 500$	$\Sigma fd' = 50$	$\Sigma fd'^2 = 778$

Branch A

(A) Mean :

$$\overline{X} = A + \frac{\Sigma fd'}{N} \times C$$

$$A = 225; \Sigma fd' = 0; \quad N = 1000;$$

$$C = 50$$

$$= 225 + \frac{0}{1000} \times 50$$

$$= \mathbf{225}$$

Branch B

Mean :

$$A = 225; \Sigma fd' = 50$$

$$N = 500; \quad C = 50$$

$$\overline{X} = 225 + \frac{50}{500} \times 50$$

$$= \mathbf{230}$$

Branch B pays higher average wages.

(B) Standard Deviation

$$\sigma = \sqrt{\frac{\Sigma fd'^2}{N} - \left(\frac{\Sigma fd'}{N}\right)^2} \times C$$

$$\Sigma fd'^2 = 1752; \quad N = 1000; \quad \Sigma fd' = 0;$$

$$C = 50$$

$$= \sqrt{\frac{1752}{1000} - (0)^2} \times 50$$

$$= \sqrt{1.752} \times 50 = 1.324 \times 50$$

$$= \mathbf{66.2}$$

Standard Deviation

$$\Sigma fd'^2 = 778; N = 500; \quad \Sigma fd' = 50$$

$$C = 50$$

$$\sigma = \sqrt{\frac{778}{500} - \left(\frac{50}{500}\right)^2} \times 50$$

$$= \sqrt{1.556 - (0.1)^2} \times 50$$

$$= \sqrt{1.556 - 0.01} \times 50$$

$$= \sqrt{1.546} \times 50 = 1.243 \times 50$$

$$= \mathbf{62.15}$$

Coefficient of Variation

Coefficient of Variation

$$C.V. = \frac{\sigma}{\overline{X}} \times 100 \quad \sigma = 66.2; \overline{X} = 225 \qquad \sigma = 62.15; \overline{X} = 230$$

$$\sigma = \frac{66.2}{225} \times 100 \qquad C.V. = \frac{62.15}{230} \times 100$$

$$= \mathbf{29.42\%} \qquad = \mathbf{27.02\%}$$

(C.) Average Monthly wages for the whole factory :

Combined Mean :

$$\overline{X}_{12} = \frac{N_1X_1 + N_2X_2}{N_1 + N_2} \qquad N_1 = 1000; \overline{X_1} = 225$$

$$N_2 = 500; \overline{X}_2 = 230$$

$$= \frac{1000 \times 225 + 500 \times 230}{1000 + 500} = \frac{225,000 + 1,15,000}{1500}$$

$$= \frac{3,40,000}{1500}$$

$$= \textbf{Rs.226.67}$$

(D) Variance.

Combined Varience

$$\sigma_{12}^2 = \frac{N_1(\sigma_1^2 + d_1^2) + N_2(\sigma_2^2 + d_2^2)}{N_1 + N_2}$$

$$\sigma_{12}^2 = \frac{1000(66.2^2 + 1.67^2) + 500(62.15^2 + 3.33^2)}{1000 + 500}$$

$$= \frac{1000 \times 4385.23 + 500 \times 3873.71}{1000 + 500}$$

$$= \frac{63,22,085}{1500}$$

$$= \textbf{Rs.4215.}$$

Problem 119. The mean and standard deviation of 200 items are found to be 60 and 20 respectively. If at the time of calculation, two items were wrongly taken as 3 and 67 instead of 13 and 17, find the correct mean and standard deviation. What is the correct coefficient of variation ?

(*B. Com., Delhi*)

Solution :

Correct Mean:

$$\text{We are given } \overline{X} = 60; \sigma = 20; \text{N} = 200$$

$$\overline{X} = \frac{\Sigma X}{N} = 60 = \frac{\Sigma X}{100}$$

$$\text{or} \quad \Sigma X = 12,000$$

$$\text{But Correct } \Sigma X = \Sigma X - \text{Wrong items} + \text{Correct items}$$

$$= 12000 - 3 - 67 + 13 + 17 = 11,960$$

$$\text{Correct Mean } \overline{X} = \frac{\text{Correct } \Sigma X}{N} = \frac{11,960}{200}$$

$$= \mathbf{59.8}$$

Correct Standard Deviation:

$$\sigma = \sqrt{\frac{\Sigma X^2}{N} - (\overline{X})^2}$$

$$20 = \sqrt{\frac{\Sigma X^2}{200} - (60)^2}$$

$$(20)^2 = \frac{\Sigma X^2}{200} - (60)^2$$

$$400 = \frac{\Sigma X^2}{200} - 3600$$

$$400 \times 200 = \Sigma X^2 - 3600 \times 200$$

$$80,000 = \Sigma X^2 - 7,20,000$$

$$80,000 + 7,20,000 = \Sigma X^2$$

$$\Sigma X^2 = 80,000 + 7,20,000$$

$$\Sigma X^2 = 8,00,000$$

But Correct ΣX^2 = Incorrect ΣX^2 – Wrong items square + Correct item square.

$$\therefore \text{ Correct } \Sigma X^2 = 8,00,000 - (3)^2 + (67)^2 + (13)^2 + (17)^2$$

$$= 8,00,000 - 9 - 4489 + 169 + 289$$

$$= 7,95,960$$

$$\text{Again Correct } \sigma = \sqrt{\frac{\text{Correct } \Sigma X^2}{N} - (\text{Correct } \overline{X})^2}$$

$$= \sqrt{\frac{7,95,960}{200} - (59.8)^2}$$

$$= \sqrt{3979.8 - 3576.04}$$

$$= \sqrt{403.76}$$

$$= \mathbf{20.09}$$

Coefficient of Variation

$$= \frac{\sigma}{\overline{X}} \times 100$$

$$= \frac{20.09}{59.8} \times 100$$

$$= \mathbf{33.59}.$$

Problem 120. In two factories A and B engaged in the same industry in the area, the averge weekly wages (in Rs.) and the standard deviations are as follows :

Factory	*Average*	*Standard Deviation*	*No. of employees*
A	34.5	5	476
B	28.5	4.5	524

(*a*) Which factory A or B pays out a larger amount as weekly wages?

(*b*) Which factory A or B has greater variability in industrial wages?

(*B. Com.* (*Hons*) *Delhi*)

Solution :

$$N_1 = 476\,\overline{X}_1 = 34.5, \quad \sigma_1 = 5.0$$
$$N_2 = 524\,\overline{X}_2 = 28.5, \quad \sigma_2 = 4.5$$

(*a*) Total wages = Average wages of workers × No. of workers.
Total wages paid by factory *A*.

$$= \mathrm{N}_1\overline{X}_1 = 476 \times 34.5$$
$$= \mathbf{16,422}$$

∴ Total wages paid by factory *B*.

$$= \mathrm{N}_2\overline{X}_1 = 524 \times 28.5$$
$$= \mathbf{14,934}$$

Therefore factory *A* pays out larger amont as weekly wages

(*b*)

$$C.V.(A) = \frac{\sigma_1 \times 100}{\overline{X}_1}$$
$$= \frac{5 \times 100}{34.5}$$
$$= \mathbf{14.49\%}$$
$$C.V.(B) = \frac{\sigma_2 \times 100}{\overline{X}_2} = \frac{4.5}{28.5} \times 100$$
$$= \mathbf{15.79\%}$$

Factory *B* has greater variability in industrial wages.

Problem 121. Comment on the statement "after settlement the average weekly wage in a factory had increased from Rs. 8 to Rs. 12 and standard deviation has increased from 2 to 2.5. After the settlement, the wage has become higher and more uniform".

(*B.A. Ecos.* (*Hons*) *Delhi*)

Solution : According to the statement it is understood that the average weekly wages have increased from Rs. 8 to Rs. 12 i.e. the total wages received per week by all the workers have increased. Therefore, after the settlement the weekly average wage increased. In order to measure uniformity of the wages, the coefficient of variation of the wages of the workers before and after the settlement has to be calculated, which is:

	Before settlement	*After settlement*
Coefficient of variation:	$\frac{2}{8} \times 100 = 25\%$	$\frac{2.5}{12} \times 100 = \mathbf{20.83\%}$

Thus after the settlement (20.83) there is less variation i.e. more uniform.

Therefore, the statement is correct.

Problem 122. Coefficient of variation of two series are 60% and 80%. Their standard deviations are 20 and 16. What are their arithmetic mean?

(B. Com. (Hons) Delhi)

Solution : Let $\overline{X}_1$ and $\overline{X}_2$ be the means of First and Second Series. Let corresponding standard deviations be σ_1 and σ_2 Thus :

First Series = Coefficient of Variation = $60 = \frac{\sigma_1}{\overline{X}_1} \times 100$

$$\begin{aligned} 60 &= \frac{20}{\overline{X}_1} \times 100 \\ 60\overline{X}_1 &= 20 \times 100 \\ 60\overline{X}_1 &= 2000 \\ \overline{X}_1 &= \frac{2000}{60} \\ &= \mathbf{33.3} \end{aligned}$$

Second Series

$$\begin{aligned} C.V. &= \frac{\sigma_2}{\overline{X}_2} \times 100 \\ 80 &= \frac{16}{\overline{X}_2} \times 100 \\ 80\overline{X}_2 &= 1600 \\ \overline{X}_2 &= \frac{1600}{80} \\ &= \mathbf{20} \end{aligned}$$

Problem 123. In an industrial establishment, the coefficients of variation of wages of male and female workers were 55% and 70% respectively. The standard deviation were Rs. 22.00 and Rs. 15.40 respectively. Calculate the combined average wages of all the workers if 80% of the workers were males. *(CA)*

Solution :

$$\begin{aligned} C.V.(\text{ Males}) &= 55\%; C.V.(\text{ Female}) = 70\% \\ \sigma_1(\text{ Males}) &= 22 \qquad \sigma_2 = (\text{ Females}) = 15.4 \end{aligned}$$

Let $\overline{X}_1$ and $\overline{X}_2$ be average wage of males and female.

$$\begin{aligned} C.V.(\text{Males}) &= \frac{\sigma_1}{X_2} \times 100 \\ 55 &= \frac{22 \times 100}{X_1} \end{aligned}$$

$$55\overline{X}_1 = 2200$$
$$\overline{X}_1 = \frac{2200}{55}$$
$$= \textbf{Rs.40}$$
$$C.V.(\text{Females}) = \frac{\sigma_2}{\overline{X}_2} \times 100$$
$$70 = \frac{15.4 \times 100}{\overline{X}_2}$$
$$70\overline{X}_2 = 1540$$
$$\overline{X}_2 = \textbf{Rs.22}$$

N_1 and N_2 be the number of male and female workers. Thus

$$N_1 = 80(given)$$
$$\therefore N_2 = 100 - 80 = 20$$
$$\overline{X}_{12} = \frac{N_1\overline{X}_1 + N_2\overline{X}_2}{N_1 + N_2}$$
$$= \frac{80 \times 40 + 20 \times 22}{80 + 20}$$
$$= \frac{3200 + 440}{100}$$
$$= \frac{3640}{100}$$
$$= \textbf{Rs.36.40}$$

Problem 124. From the data relating to two factories A and B find the following :

(*a*) Average of both the factories put together,

(*b*) Standard deviation of both put together,

(*c*) State also in which factory wages are more variable.

	Factory A	*Factory B*
No. of workers	100	150
Mean wages	45	55
Standard deviation	7	12

(*B. Com. Madurai*)

Solution :

(*a*) Combined Mean

$$\overline{X}_{12} = \frac{N_1\overline{X}_1 + N_2\overline{X}_2}{N_1 + N_2}$$
$$N_1 = 100; \overline{X}_1 = 45; N_2 = 150; \overline{X}_2 = 55$$
$$\overline{X}_{12} = \frac{(100 \times 45) + (150 \times 55)}{100 + 150}$$
$$= \frac{4500 + 8250}{100 + 150} = \frac{12750}{250}$$
$$= \textbf{Rs.51}$$

(*b*) Combined Standard Deviation

$$\sigma_{12} = \sqrt{\frac{N_1\sigma_1^2 + N_2\sigma_2^2 + N_1d_1^2 + N_2d_2^2}{N_1 + N_2}}$$

$$N_1 = 100; \quad \sigma_1 = 7; \quad N_2 = 150; \quad \sigma_2 = 12 \quad d_1 = (\overline{X}_1 - \overline{X}_{12})$$

$$d_1 = 45 - 51 = -6; \quad d_2 = (\overline{X}_2 - \overline{X}_{12}) = (55 - 51) = +4$$

$$\sigma_{12} = \sqrt{\frac{100 \times (7)^2 + 150 \times (12)^2 + 100 \times (-6)^2 + 150 \times (+4)^2}{100 + 150}}$$

$$= \sqrt{\frac{4900 + 21600 + 3600 + 2400}{250}} = \sqrt{\frac{32500}{250}}$$

$$= \sqrt{130}$$

$$= \mathbf{11.4}$$

(*c*) Factory in which wages are more variable.

Factory A

$$C.V. = \frac{\sigma}{\overline{X}} \times 100$$

$$= \frac{7}{45} \times 100$$

$$= \mathbf{15.56\%}$$

Factory B

$$C.V. = \frac{12}{55} \times 100$$

$$= \mathbf{21.82\%}$$

Coefficient of variation of factory *B* (21.82%) is greater than *A* (15.56%). The wages are more variable in factory *B* than factory *A*.

Problem 125. Particulars regarding income of two villages are given below :

	Village	
	A	*B*
No. of people	600	600
Average income	175	186
Variance of income	100	81

(*a*) In which village is the variation in income greater ?
(*b*) What is the total income of both the villages put together ?
(*c*) What is the average income of the people of both the villages put together ?
(*d*) What is the combined standard deviation ?

(*C.A*

Solution :

(*a*) Variation of distribution of income of villages A

$$C.V. = \frac{\sigma}{\overline{X}} \times 100 \quad \sigma^2 = 100; \overline{X} = 175$$

$$= \frac{\sqrt{100}}{175} \times 100 = \frac{10 \times 100}{175}$$

$$= \mathbf{5.71\%}$$

Similarly for village P

$$C.V. = \frac{\sigma \times 100}{\overline{X}} \quad \sigma^2 = 81; \overline{X} = 186$$

$$= \frac{\sqrt{81} \times 100}{186}$$

$$= \mathbf{4.8}$$

$\therefore$ Village A has greater variation than village B.

(b) Total Income.

No of People (A) $\times \overline{X}$ income (A) + No. of people (B) $\times \overline{X}$ income (B)

$175 \times 600 + 186 \times 500 =$ Rs. **1,98,000**

(c) Combined average income

$$\overline{X}_{12} = \frac{N_1\overline{X}_1 + N_2\overline{X}_2}{N_1 + N_2} = \frac{175 \times 600 + 186 \times 500}{600 + 500}$$

$$= \mathbf{180}$$

(d) Combined Standard Deviation

$$= \sqrt{\frac{N_1(\sigma_1^2 + d_1^2) + N_2(\sigma_2^2 + d_2^2)}{N_1 + N_2}}$$

$$= \sqrt{\frac{600\left[100 + (175 - 180)^2\right] + 500\left[81 + (186 - 180)^2\right]}{600 + 500}}$$

$$= \sqrt{\frac{600\,(100 + 25) + 500\,(81 + 36)}{1100}} = \sqrt{\frac{600 \times 125 + 500 \times 117}{1100}}$$

$$= \sqrt{\frac{1,33,500}{1100}} = \sqrt{\frac{1335}{11}} = \sqrt{121.364} = \mathbf{Rs.11.02}$$

Problem 126. An analysis of the monthly wages gives the following results :

	Factory X	*Factory Y*
No. of workers	100	150
Average monthly wages	Rs. 300	250
Variance of the distribution of wages	49	64

(i) Which factory, X or Y, has a larger wage bill ?

(ii) In which, X or Y, is there greater variability in individual wages?

(iii) Calculate (1) the average monthly wage and (2) the variance of the distribution of the wage of all the workers in the factory X and Y taken together ?

(*B. Com. Bombay, Madurai*)

Solution :

(i) Factory X. Total wage bill $= N_1\overline{X}_1$

$= 100 \times 300$

$=$ **Rs.30.00**

$$\text{Factory Y Total wage bill} = N_2\overline{X}_2$$
$$= 150 \times 250$$
$$= \textbf{Rs.37.500}$$

The factory Y has larger wage bill.

(*ii*) Variability

$$\text{Factory}X \quad C.V. = \frac{\sigma_1}{\overline{X}_1} \times 100$$
$$= \frac{\sqrt{49}}{300} \times 100$$
$$= \frac{7}{300} \times 100$$
$$= \mathbf{2.33\%}$$
$$\text{Factory Y} = \frac{\sqrt{64}}{250} \times 100$$
$$= \frac{8}{250} \times 100$$
$$= \mathbf{3.2\%}$$

Since the coefficient of variation is greater in the case of Factory Y, there is greater variability in individual wages in respect of Factory Y.

(*iii*) Average monthly wages of X and Y taken together :

$$\overline{X}_{12} = \frac{N_1\overline{X}_1 + N_2\overline{X}_2}{N_1 + N_2}$$
$$N_1 = 100; \quad \overline{X}_1 = 300 N_2 = 150; \quad \overline{X}_2 = 250$$
$$= \frac{100 \times 300 + 150 \times 250}{100 + 150} = \frac{30,000 + 37,500}{250}$$
$$= \textbf{Rs.270}$$

Combined Standard Deviation :

$$\sigma_{12} = \sqrt{\frac{N_1\sigma_1^2 + N_2\sigma_2^2 + N^1 d_1^2 + N_2 d_2^2}{N_1 + N_2}}$$
$$\text{Variance or } \sigma_{12}^2 = \frac{N_1\sigma_1^2 + N_2\sigma_2^2 + N^1 d_1^2 + N_2 d_2^2}{N_1 + N_2}$$
$$d = \overline{X}_1 - \overline{X}_{12} = 300 - 270 = 30$$
$$d = \overline{X}_1 - \overline{X}_{12} = 250 - 270 = -20$$
$$= \frac{100 \times 49 + 150 \times 64 + 100\,(30)^2 + 150\,(-20)^2}{100 + 150}$$
$$= \frac{4900 + 9600 + 90000 + 60000}{250}$$
$$= \frac{164500}{250}$$
$$= \mathbf{658}$$

Problem 127. An analysis of monthly wages paid to workers in two firms A and B, belonging to the same industry, gives the following results :

	Firm A	*Firm B*
No. of wage earners	300	200
Average monthly wages (in Rs.)	52.5	47.5
Standard deviation of the distribution of wages	10	11

(*i*) In which firm A or B is there greater variability in individual wages ?

(*ii*) Find the average monthly wages and the standard deviation of the wages of all the workers in the two firms taken together.

(*B. Com. Shivaji*)

Solution :

Coffiecient of variantion

Firm A

$$C.V. = \frac{\sigma}{\overline{X}} \times 100$$

$$\sigma = 10; \quad \overline{X} = 52.5$$

$$= \frac{10}{52.5} \times 100$$

$$= \mathbf{19.05\%.}$$

Firm B

$$\sigma = 11; \quad \overline{X} = 47.5$$

$$C.V. = \frac{11}{47.5} \times 100$$

$$= \mathbf{23.16\%.}$$

(*ii*) Combined Mean :

$$\overline{X}_{12} = \frac{N_1\overline{X}_1 + N_2\overline{X}_2}{N_1 + N_2}$$

$$N_1 = 300; \overline{X}_1 = 52.5; N_2 = 200; \overline{X}_2 = 47.5$$

$$= \frac{300 \times 52.5 + 200 \times 47.5}{300 + 200} = \frac{15750 + 9500}{500}$$

$$= \frac{25250}{500}$$

$$= \mathbf{50.5.}$$

Combined Standard Deviation :

$$\sigma^{12} = \sqrt{\frac{N_1(\sigma_1^2 + d_1^2) + N_2(\sigma_2^2 + d_2^2)}{N_1 + N_2}}$$

$$N_1 = 300; \quad \sigma_1^2 = 10^2; \quad d_1^2 = (50.5 - 52.5)^2$$

$$N_2 = 200; \sigma_2^2 = 11^2; \mathrm{d}_2^2 = (50.5 - 47.5)^2$$

$$= \sqrt{\frac{300\,[10^2 + (50.5 - 52.5)^2] + 200\,[11^2 + (50.5 - 47.5)^2]}{300 + 200}}$$

$$= \sqrt{\frac{300(100 + (-0.2)^2 + 200(121 + (3)^2}{500}}$$

$$= \sqrt{\frac{300 \times 104 + 200 \times 130}{500}} = \sqrt{\frac{31200 + 26000}{500}}$$

$$= \sqrt{\frac{57200}{500}} = \sqrt{114.4}$$

$$= \mathbf{10.695}$$

Problem 128. For a set of 100 observations, the sum of the deviations from 4 c.m is – 11 c.m. and the sum of the squares of these deviations is 257 c.m. Find the coefficient of variation. *(ICWA)*

Solution :

To find out coefficient of variation, mean and standard deviation are needed. They are calculated as follows :

$$\overline{X} = A \pm \frac{\Sigma d}{N}$$

$$= 4 - \frac{11}{100}$$

$$= 4 - 0.11$$

$$\overline{X} = \mathbf{3.89}$$

$$\sigma = \sqrt{\frac{\Sigma f d^2}{N} - \left(\frac{\Sigma f d'^2}{N}\right)^2}$$

$$= \sqrt{\frac{257}{100} - \left(\frac{11}{100}\right)^2}$$

$$= \sqrt{2.57 - 0.012}$$

$$= \sqrt{2.558}$$

$$\sigma = \mathbf{1.6}$$

$$\text{Coefficient of Variation} = \frac{\sigma}{\overline{X}} \times 100$$

$$= \frac{1.6}{3.89} \times 100$$

$$= \mathbf{41.13\%}.$$

LORENZ CURVE

Problem 129. The frequency distribution of marks obtained in mathematics and Englsh are as follows :

Mid value of marks :	5	15	25	35	45	55	65	75	85	95
No. of students (M)	10	12	13	14	22	27	20	12	11	9
No. of students (E)	1	2	26	50	59	40	10	8	3	1

Analyse the data by drawing the Lorenz curves. *(B. A. Kerala)*

Solution :

Marks			*Mathematics*			*English*		
M.V.	*Cumulative*	*Cumulative%*	*No. of students*	*c.f. of students*	*c.f. %*	*No. of students*	*c.f. of students*	*c.f.%*
5	5	1	10	10	6.6	1	1	0.5
15	20	4	12	22	14.52	2	3	1.5
25	45	9	13	35	23.10	26	29	14.5

Marks			Mathematics			English		
M.V.	*Cumulative*	*Cumulative%*	*No. of students*	*c.f. of students*	*c.f. %*	*No. of students*	*c.f. of students*	*c.f.%*
35	80	16	14	49	32.34	50	79	39.3
45	125	25	22	71	46.86	59	138	69.0
55	180	36	27	98	64.68	40	178	89.0
65	245	49	20	118	77.88	10	188	94.0
75	320	64	12	130	85.80	8	196	98.0
85	405	81	11	141	93.06	3	199	99.5
95	500	100	9	150	100.00	1	200	100

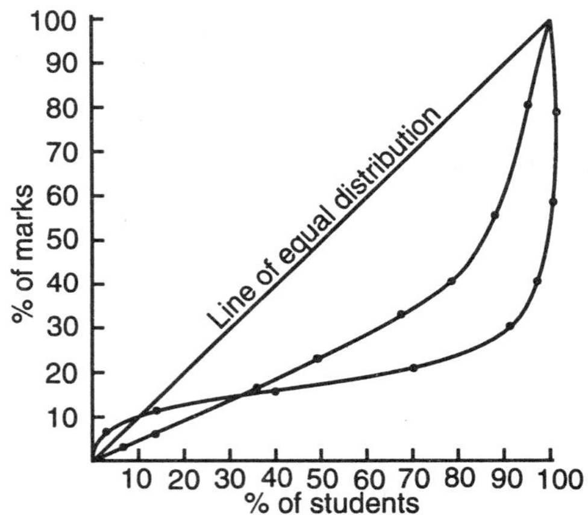

Problem 130. Draw Lorenz curve for the following data and compare the variability of the two distributions.

Income per head Rs.	*No. of persons*	
	Company A	*Company B*
100	13	5
200	8	6
400	2	5
500	1	3
800	1	1

(*B. Com.*)

Solution :

Company A

Income per head	*No. of persons*	*Total income*	*c.f.*	*%of c.f.*	*c.f. of income*	*% of cf. of income*
100	13	1300	13	52	1300	26
200	8	1600	21	84	2900	58
400	2	800	23	92	3700	74
500	1	500	24	96	4200	84
800	1	800	25	100	5000	100

Company B

Income per head	*No. of persons*	*Total income*	*c.f.*	*%of c.f.*	*c.f. of income*	*%of c.f. of income*
100	5	500	5	25	500	8
200	6	1200	11	55	1700	28
400	5	2000	16	80	3700	62
500	3	1500	19	95	5200	87
800	1	800	20	100	6000	100

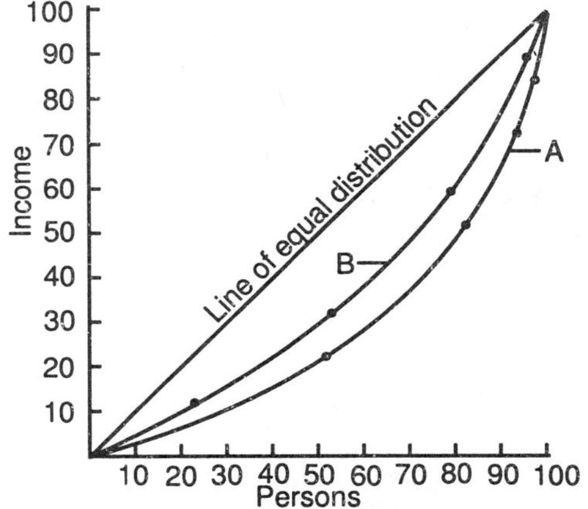

Problem 131. From the following table giving data regarding income of workers in two factories, draw a graph (Lorenz curve) to show which factory has greater inequalities of income.

Income Rs.	*Factory A*	*Factory B*
Below 500	6000	5000
500–1000	4250	4500
1000–2000	3600	4800
2000–3000	1500	2200
3000–4000	650	1500

(B. Com. Meerut, Karnataka)

Solution :

Factory A

Income	*m.p.*	*f.*	*Total income*	*Cumulative income*	*% of Cu. Income*	*c.f.*	*% of c.f.*
0–500	250	6000	15,00,000	15,00,000	9.3	6000	37.5
500–1000	750	4250	31,87,500	46,87,500	29.1	10,250	64.0
1000–2000	1500	3600	54,00,000	100,87,500	62.6	13,850	86.5
2000–3000	2500	1500	37,50,000	138,37,500	85.9	15,350	96.0
3000–4000	3500	650	22,75,000	161,12,500	100	16,000	100

Factory B

Income	*m.p.*	*f.*	*Total income*	*Cumulative income*	*%. Cu. Income*	*c.f.*	*% of c.f.*
0–500	250	5000	12,50,000	12,50,000	5.5	5000	27.7
500–1000	750	4500	33,75,000	46,25,000	20.5	9500	52.7
1000–2000	1500	4800	72,00,000	1,18,25,000	52.0	14300	79.5
2000–3000	2500	2200	55,00,000	1,73,25,000	76.5	16500	91.6
3000–4000	3500	1500	52,50,000	2,25,75,000	100.0	18000	100.0

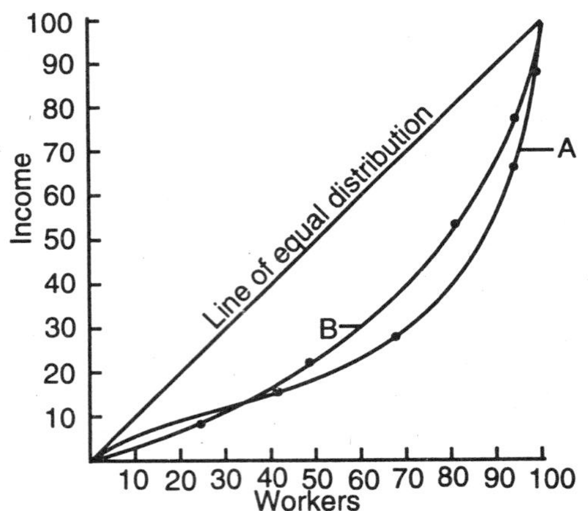

5

MEASURES OF SKEWNESS, MOMENTS, KURTOSIS

FORMULAE

Absolute Skewness (Karl Pearson) $SK_p = \overline{X}; Z$ Bowley $= SK_B = Q_3 + Q_1 - 2\,\text{Med}$	$\overline{X}$ = Mean Z = Mode Q_3 = Upper Quartile Q_1 = Lower Quartile Med = Median
Coefficient of Skewness 1. Karl Pearson' Coefficient of Skewness (*a*) $Sk_p \doteq \dfrac{\text{Mean} - \text{Mode}}{\text{Standard Deviation}}$ If Mode is ill defined (*b*) $Sk_P = \dfrac{3(\overline{X} - Med)}{\sigma}$	SK_P = Karl Pearson's Coefficient of Skewness $\overline{X}$ = Mean Med = Median σ = Standard Deviation
2. Bowley's Coefficient of Skewness $Sk_B = \dfrac{Q_3 + Q_1 - 2Med)}{Q_3 + Q_1}$	Sk_B=Bowley's Coefficient of Skewness
3. Kelly's Coefficient of Skewness $Sk_K = \dfrac{P_{10} + P_{90} - 2\text{Med}}{P_{90} + P_{10}}$ $Sk_K = \dfrac{D_1 + D_9 - 2\text{Med}}{D_9 + D_1}$	Sk_k= Kelly's Coefficient of Skewness $P_{10} + P_{10}$ = Percentiles D_1 and D_9= Deciles

Moments	μ_1	μ_2	μ_3	μ_4
Moment about Mean Individual Series	$\dfrac{\Sigma(X - \overline{X})}{N}$ or $\dfrac{\Sigma d}{N} = 0$	$\dfrac{\Sigma d^2}{N} = \sigma^2$	$\dfrac{\Sigma d^3}{N}$	$\dfrac{\Sigma d^4}{N}$
Frequency Distribution	$\dfrac{\Sigma f(X - \overline{X})}{N}$ or $\dfrac{\Sigma fd}{N} = 0$	$\dfrac{\Sigma fd^2}{N} = \sigma^2$	$\dfrac{\Sigma fd^3}{N}$	$\dfrac{\Sigma fd^4}{N}$

	μ_1'	μ_2'	μ_3'	μ_4'
Moments about arbitrary origin. Individual Series	$\frac{\Sigma(X-A)}{N}$ or $\frac{\Sigma d}{N}$	$\frac{\Sigma d^2}{N}$	$\frac{\Sigma d^3}{N}$	$\frac{\Sigma d^4}{N}$
Frequency Distribution	$\frac{\Sigma f(X-A)}{N} = \frac{\Sigma fd}{N}$ $\frac{\Sigma fd'}{N}\times C$	$\frac{\Sigma fd^2}{N}$ $\frac{\Sigma fd'^2}{N}\times C$	$\frac{\Sigma fd^3}{N}$ $\frac{\Sigma fd'^3}{N}\times C$	$\frac{\Sigma fd^4}{N}$ $\frac{\Sigma fd'^4}{N}\times C$

Converting Moments about $\overline{X}$	$\mu_1 = \mu_1' - \mu_1' = 0$ $\mu_2 = \mu_2' - (\mu_1')^2$ $\mu_3 = \mu_3' - 3\mu_1'\mu_2' + 2(\mu_1')^3$ $\mu_4 = \mu_4' - 4\mu_1'\mu_3' + 6\mu_2'(\mu_1')^2 - 3(\mu_1')4$
Kurtosis $\beta_1 = \frac{\mu_{32}}{\mu_{23}}$ $\beta_2 = \frac{\mu_4}{\mu_{22}}$	

Problem 1. Calculate skewness from the following distribution :

X	1	2	3	4	5	6	7
F	5	7	3	1	4	6	9

(*B.Com.Kerala*)

Solution :

Computation of Coefficient of Skewness

X	f	$d = x - 4$	fd	fd^2
1	5	−3	−15	225
2	7	−2	−14	196
3	3	−1	−3	9
4	1	0	0	0
5	4	1	4	16
6	6	2	12	144
7	9	3	27	729
	N = 35		$\Sigma fd = -11$	$\Sigma fd^2 = 1319$

$$\overline{X} = A + \frac{\Sigma fd}{N}$$

$$\overline{X} = 4 - \frac{11}{35} = 4 - 0.31 = 3.69$$

$$\sigma = \sqrt{\frac{\Sigma fd^2}{N} - \left(\frac{\Sigma fd}{N}\right)^2}$$

$$\sigma = \sqrt{\frac{1319}{35} - \left(-\frac{11}{35}\right)^2}$$
$$= \sqrt{37.69 - 0.096}$$
$$= 6.13$$
$$Z = 7$$
$$Sk = \frac{\text{Mean} - \text{Mode}}{\sigma}$$
$$= \frac{3.69 - 7}{6.13}$$
$$= \mathbf{-0.54}$$

Problem 2 . Calculate any measure of skewness for the following :

No. of headless Matches in a Box	:	0	1	2	3	4	5	6	7
No. of Boxes	:	12	17	29	19	8	4	1	0

(*B.Com. Madras*)

Solution :

Computation of Coefficient of Skewness

No. of headless matches in a box	*No. of Boxes (f)*	*fx*	*fx*^{2}
0	12	0	0
1	17	17	17
2	29	58	116
3	19	57	171
4	8	32	128
5	4	20	100
6	1	6	36
7	0	0	0
	$N = 90$	$\Sigma fx = 190$	$\Sigma fx^2 = 568$

$$\overline{X} = \frac{\Sigma fx}{N}$$
$$\Sigma fx = 190;\ N = 90$$
$$= \frac{190}{90}$$
$$= \mathbf{2.11}$$

By inspection method mode lies in 2.

Standard Deviation :

$$\sigma = \sqrt{\frac{\Sigma fx^2}{N} - \left(\frac{\Sigma fx}{N}\right)^2}$$
$$\Sigma fx^2 = 568;\ N = 90;\ \Sigma fx = 190$$
$$= \sqrt{\frac{568}{90} - \left(\frac{190}{90}\right)^2}$$

$$= \sqrt{6.31 - (2.11)^2}$$
$$= \sqrt{6.31 - 4.46}$$
$$= \sqrt{1.85}$$
$$= \mathbf{1.36}$$

Coefficient of Skewness :

$\frac{\text{Mean–Mode}}{\sigma}$ Mean = 2.11; Mode=2; $\sigma = 1.36$

$$= \frac{2.11 - 2}{1.36} = \frac{0.11}{1.36}$$
$$= \mathbf{0.08}$$

Problem 3. From the following table calculate the standard deviation and Coefficient of Skewness :

Weekly Wages of Rs.	:	15	20	25	30	35	40	45
No. of Earners	:	3	25	19	16	4	5	6

(*M.A. Eco. B.Com. Madras*)

Solution :

Computation of Standard Deviation and Coefficient of Skewness

Weekly Wages in (Rs.)	$d = \frac{x-30}{5}$	*Wage earners f*	*fd*	*fd*^{2}	*c.f.*
15	−3	3	−9	27	3
20	−2	25	−50	100	28
25	−1	19	−19	19	47
30	0	16	0	0	63
35	1	4	4	4	67
40	2	5	10	20	72
45	3	6	18	54	78
		N=78	$\Sigma fd = -46$	$\Sigma fd^2 = 224$	

Mean :

$$\overline{X} = A \pm \frac{\Sigma fd}{N} \times C A = 30; \Sigma fd = -46; N = 78; C = 5$$
$$= 30 \frac{-46}{78} \times 5$$
$$= 30 - 2.95$$
$$= \mathbf{27.05}.$$

Standard Deviation :

$$\sigma = \sqrt{\frac{\Sigma fd^2}{N} - \left(\frac{\Sigma fd}{N}\right)^2} \times C$$
$$\Sigma fd^2 = 224; N = 78; \Sigma fd = -46; C = 5$$
$$= \sqrt{\frac{224}{78} - \left(\frac{-46}{78}\right)^2} \times 5$$

$$= \sqrt{2.87 - (-0.6)^2} \times 5$$
$$= \sqrt{2.87 - 0.36} \times 5$$
$$= \sqrt{2.51} \times 5$$
$$= 1.6 \times 5$$
$$= \mathbf{8.}$$

By inspection method mode is 20.

Coefficient of Skewness :

$$= \frac{\overline{X} - \text{Mode}}{\sigma} \qquad \overline{X} = 27.05;\ \text{Mode} = 20;\ \sigma = 8$$
$$= \frac{27.05 - 20}{8} = \frac{7.05}{8}$$
$$= \mathbf{0.88.}$$

Problem 4 . Calculate the coefficient of skewness for the following :

Height inches	:	58	59	60	61	62	63	64	65
No. of persons	:	10	18	30	42	35	28	16	8

(*B.Com. Madurai*)

Solution :

Computation of Coefficient of Skewness

Height in inches	$d = X - 61$	f	fd	fd^2
58	−3	10	−30	90
59	−2	18	−36	72
60	−1	30	−30	30
61	0	42	0	0
62	1	35	35	35
63	2	28	56	112
64	3	16	48	144
65	4	8	32	128
		$N = 187$	$\Sigma fd = 75$	$\Sigma fd^2 = 611$

Mean :

$$\overline{X} = A + \frac{\Sigma fd}{N} \qquad A = 61;\ \Sigma fd = 75;\ N = 187$$
$$= 61 + \frac{75}{187} = 61 + 0.40$$
$$= \mathbf{61.40}$$

Since the highest frequency is 42 mode is 61.

Standard Deviation :

$$\sigma = \sqrt{\frac{\Sigma fd^2}{N} - \left(\frac{\Sigma fd}{N}\right)^2}$$
$$\Sigma fd^2 = 611;\ N = 187;\ \Sigma fd = 75$$

$$\sigma = \sqrt{\frac{611}{187} - \left(\frac{75}{187}\right)^2}$$
$$= \sqrt{3.267 - (0.40)^2}$$
$$= \sqrt{3.267 - 0.16}$$
$$= \sqrt{3.107}$$
$$= \mathbf{1.76.}$$

$$\text{Coefficient of Skewness} = \frac{\text{Mean} - \text{Mode}}{\text{S.D.}}$$

$$\overline{X} = 61.40;$$
$$\sigma = 1.76$$
$$\text{Sk.} = \frac{61.40 - 61}{1.76} = \frac{0.40}{1.76}$$
$$= \mathbf{0.23}$$

Problem 5. Find the coefficient of skewness from the given data :

Size	:	3	4	5	6	7	8	9	10
Frequency	:	7	10	14	35	102	136	43	8

(*B.Com. Andhra*)

Solution :

Computation of Coefficient of Skewness

Size (X)	$d = X - 6$	f	fd	fd^2
3	−3	7	−21	63
4	−2	10	−20	40
5	−1	14	−14	14
6	0	35	0	0
7	1	102	102	102
8	2	136	272	544
9	3	43	129	387
10	4	8	32	128
		$N = 355$	$\Sigma fd = 480$	$\Sigma fd^2 = 1{,}278$

$$\text{Mean} = A + \frac{\Sigma fd}{N}$$
$$A = 6;\ \Sigma fd = 480;\ N = 355$$
$$\overline{X} = 6 + \frac{480}{355} = 6 + 1.35$$
$$= \mathbf{7.35}$$

Since highest frequency is 136 Mode is 8

Standard Deviation :

$$\sigma = \sqrt{\frac{\Sigma fd^2}{N} - \left(\frac{\Sigma fd}{N}\right)^2}$$

$$\Sigma fd^2 = 1278;\ N = 355;\ \Sigma fd = 480$$

$$\sigma = \sqrt{\frac{1278}{355} - \left(\frac{480}{355}\right)^2}$$

$$= \sqrt{3.6 - (1.35)^2}$$

$$= \sqrt{3.6 - 1.8} = \sqrt{1.8}$$

$$= \mathbf{1.34}$$

Coefficient of Skewness : $\dfrac{\text{Mean} - \text{Mode}}{S.D.}$

$$\overline{X} = 7.35$$

$$\text{Mode} = 8$$

$$\text{S.D.} = 1.34$$

$$\text{Sk. or j} = \frac{7.35 - 8}{1.34} = \frac{-0.65}{1.34}$$

$$= \mathbf{-0.5.}$$

Problem 6. Calculate Karl Pearson's Coefficient of skewness for the following data :

25 15 23 40 27 25 23 25 20

(*B.Com. Sri Venkateswara*)

Solution :

Calculation of Coefficient of Skewness

Size (*X*)	$d = X - 25$	d^2
25	0	0
15	−10	100
23	− 2	4
40	+15	225
27	+2	4
25	0	0
23	−2	4
25	0	0
20	−5	25
	$\Sigma d = -2$	$\Sigma d^2 = 362$

$$\text{Mean} : \overline{X} = A + \frac{\Sigma fd}{N}$$

$$A = 25;\ \Sigma d = -2;\ N = 9$$

$$\overline{X} = 25 - \frac{2}{9} = 25 - 0.22$$

$$= \mathbf{24.78}$$

$$\text{S.D.} = \sqrt{\frac{\Sigma d^2}{N} - \left(\frac{\Sigma d}{N}\right)^2}$$

$$\Sigma d^2 = 362;\ \Sigma d = -2;\ N = 9$$

$$= \sqrt{\frac{362}{9} - \left(\frac{-2}{9}\right)^2}$$

$$= \sqrt{40.22 - 0.05}$$

$$= \sqrt{40.17} = 6.3$$

$$\text{Mode} = 25$$

Karl Pearson's Coefficient of Skewness :

$$= \frac{\text{Mean} - \text{Mode}}{S.D.}$$

$$\bar{X} = 24.78;\ \text{Mode} = 25;\ \text{S.D.} = 6.3$$

$$j = \frac{24.78 - 25}{6.3}$$

$$= \frac{-0.22}{6.3}$$

$$= \mathbf{-0.03}.$$

Problem 7. Calculate the Pearson's measure of skewness on the basis of Mean, Mode and Standard Deviation.

X	:	14.5	15.5	16.5	17.5	18.5	19.5	20.5	21.5
F	:	35	40	48	100	125	87	43	22

(*C.A. Inter*)

Solution :

Computation of Skewness

X	$D = X - 17.5$	f	fd	fd^2
14.5	−3	35	−105	315
15.5	−2	40	−80	160
16.5	−1	48	−48	48
17.5	0	110	0	0
18.5	1	125	125	125
19.5	2	87	174	348
20.5	3	43	129	387
21.5	4	22	88	352
		$N = 500$	$\Sigma fd = 283$	$\Sigma fd^2 = 1735$

$$\text{Mean} : \bar{X} = A + \frac{\Sigma fd}{N} \quad A = 17.5;\ \Sigma fd = 283;\ N = 500$$

$$= 17.5 + \frac{283}{500} = 17.5 + 0.57$$

$$= \mathbf{18.07}$$

Since the highest frequency is 125 Mode is 18.5 Standard Deviation :

$$\sigma = \sqrt{\frac{\Sigma fd^2}{N} - \left(\frac{\Sigma fd}{N}\right)^2}$$

$$\Sigma fd^2 = 1735;\ N = 500;\ \Sigma fd = 283$$

$$\sigma = \sqrt{\frac{1735}{500} - \left(\frac{283}{500}\right)^2}$$

$$= \sqrt{3.47 - (0.566)^2}$$

$$= \sqrt{3.47 - 0.32} = \sqrt{3.15}$$

$$= \mathbf{1.77.}$$

Karl Pearson's Coefficient of Skewness $= \dfrac{\text{Mean} - \text{Mode}}{\sigma}$

$$\overline{X} = 18.07;\ \text{Mode} = 18.5;\ \sigma = 1.77$$

$$Sk- = \frac{18.07 - 18.5}{1.77}$$

$$= \frac{-0.43}{1.77}$$

$$= \mathbf{-0.24.}$$

Problem 8. Calculate the Karl Pearson's coefficient of skewness from the following data :

Marks above = X; *No. of Students = f*

X	: 0	10	20	30	40	50	60	70	80
f	: 150	140	100	80	80	70	30	14	0

(*B.Com., Hons. Delhi.*)

Solution :

Calculation of Skewness

Marks X	m	$d = \frac{m-45}{10}$	f	fd'	fd'^2	$c.f.$
0–10	5	−4	10	−40	160	10
10–20	15	−3	40	−120	360	50
20–30	25	−2	20	−40	80	70
30–40	35	−1	0	0	0	70
40–50	45	0	10	0	0	80
50–60	55	1	40	40	40	120
60–70	65	2	16	32	64	136
70–80	75	3	14	42	126	150
			$N = 150$	$\Sigma fd' = 86$	$\Sigma fd'^2 = 830$	

Mean :

$$\overline{X} = A + \frac{\Sigma fd'}{N} \times C \qquad A = 45;\ \Sigma fd' = -86;$$

$$N = 150;\ C = 10$$

$$= 45 - \frac{86}{150} \times 10 = 45 - 5.73$$

$$= \mathbf{39.27}$$

Mode is ill defined, therefore we must use median to calculate the coefficient of Skewness.

Median $= \frac{N}{2} = \frac{150}{2} = 75$th item which lies in the class 40–50

$$\text{Median} = L_1 + \frac{\frac{N}{2} - c.f.}{f} \times i \quad L_1 = 40;\ \frac{N}{2} = 75;$$

$$\text{c.f.} = 70;\ f = 10;\ i = 10$$

$$= 40 + \frac{75 - 70}{10} \times 10 = 40 + 5$$

$$= \mathbf{45.}$$

Standard Deviation : $\sigma - \sqrt{\frac{\Sigma fd'^2}{N} - \left(\frac{\Sigma fd'}{N}\right)^2} \times \text{C}$

$$\Sigma fd'^2 = 830;\ N = 150;\ \Sigma fd' = -86;\ C = 10$$

$$\sigma = \sqrt{\frac{830}{150} - \left(\frac{-86}{150}\right)^2} \times 10$$

$$= \sqrt{5.533 - (-0.573)^2} \times 10$$

$$= \sqrt{5.533 - 0.328} \times 10 = \sqrt{5.205} \times 10 = 2.281 \times 10$$

$$= \mathbf{22.81}$$

$$\text{Coefficient of Skewness} = \frac{3\,(\text{Mean} - \text{Median})}{\text{S.D.}}$$

$$\text{Mean} = 39.27;\ \text{Median} = 45;\ S.D. = 22.81$$

$$j = \frac{3(39.27 - 45)}{22.81} = \frac{3\,(-5.73)}{22.81}$$

$$= \frac{-17.19}{22.81}$$

$$= \mathbf{-0.75.}$$

Problem 9. Calculate the coefficient of skewness for the following distribution :

Central value	:	1	2	3	4	5	6	7	8	9	10
Frequency	:	2	9	11	14	20	24	20	16	5	2

(*B.Com. Madras*)

Solution :

Computation of Skewness

Central value (X)	$d = X - 5$	f	fd	fd^2
1	−4	2	−8	32
2	−3	9	−27	81
3	−2	11	−22	44
4	−1	14	−14	14
5	0	20	0	0
6	1	24	24	24
7	2	20	40	80
8	3	16	48	144
9	4	5	20	80
10	5	2	10	50
		$N = 123$	$\Sigma fd = 71$	$\Sigma fd^2 = 549$

$$\text{Mean} : \overline{X} = A + \frac{\Sigma fd}{N} \quad A = 5;\ \Sigma fd = 71;\ N = 123;$$

$$= 5 + \frac{71}{123} = 5 + 0.58$$

$$= \mathbf{5.58}.$$

Since the highest frequency is 24 Mode is 6.

Standard Deviation :

$$\sigma = \sqrt{\frac{\Sigma fd^2}{N} - \left(\frac{\Sigma fd}{N}\right)^2}$$

$$\Sigma fd^2 = 549;\ N = 123;\ \Sigma fd = 71$$

$$\sigma = \sqrt{\frac{549}{123} - \left(\frac{71}{123}\right)^2} = \sqrt{4.463 - (0.58)^2}$$

$$= \sqrt{4.463 - 0.336} = \sqrt{4.127}$$

$$= \mathbf{2.03}.$$

Karl Pearson's Coefficient of Skewness :

$$\text{Sk.} = \frac{\text{Mean} - \text{Mode}}{\sigma} \quad \overline{X} = 5.58;\ \text{Mode} = 6;\ \sigma = 2.03$$

$$= \frac{5.58 - 6}{2.03} = \frac{-0.42}{2.03}$$

$$= \mathbf{-0.207}.$$

Problem 10. Calculate the coefficient of skewness for the following distribution of daily wages in a factory :

Wages	5	6	7	8	9	10	11	12
Workers	25	45	65	100	30	75	40	50

(*B.Com. Bombay, Sambalpur*)

Solution :

Computation of Coefficient of Skewness

Wages X	*Workers* f	$d = X - 9$	fd	fd^2
5	25	−4	−100	400
6	45	−3	−135	405
7	65	−2	−130	260
8	100	−1	−100	100
9	30	0	0	0
10	75	1	75	75
11	40	2	80	160
12	50	3	150	450
	$N = 430$		$\Sigma fd = -60$	$\Sigma fd^2 = 1850$

Mean: $\overline{X} = A + \frac{\Sigma fdx}{N}$

$X = 9 - \frac{60}{430} = 9 - 0.14 = 8.86$

By inspection the maximum frequency is 100, hence Mode = **8**

$$\text{Standard Deviation} = \sigma = \sqrt{\frac{\Sigma fd^2}{N} - \left(\frac{\Sigma fd}{N}\right)^2}$$

$$= \sqrt{\frac{1850}{430} - \left(\frac{-60}{430}\right)^2}$$

$$= \sqrt{4.302 - 0.0196}$$

$$= \sqrt{4.2824} \quad = \mathbf{2.07}$$

Karl Pearson's Coefficient of Skewness:

$$\text{Sk.} = \frac{\overline{X} - Mode}{\sigma}$$

$$\text{Sk.} = \frac{8.86 - 8}{2.07}$$

$$= \mathbf{+0.42}$$

Problem 11. Calculate Pearson's Coefficient of Skewness from the table given below :

Life Time (Hours)	*No. of Tubes*
300–400	14
400–500	46
500–600	58
600–700	76
700–800	68
800–900	62
900–1,000	48
1,000–1,100	22
1,100–1,200	6

(*B.Com., Bombay*)

Solution :

Computation of Coefficient of Skewness

Life time (Hours)	m	$d' = \frac{m-750}{100}$	f	fd'	fd'^2
300–400	350	−4	14	−56	224
400–500	450	−3	46	−138	414
500–600	550	−2	58	−116	232
600–700	650	−1	76	76	76
700–800	750	0	68	0	0
800–900	850	1	62	62	62
900–1000	950	2	48	96	192
1000–1100	1050	3	22	66	198
1100–1200	1150	4	6	24	96
			$N = 400$	$\Sigma fd' = -138$	$\Sigma fd'^2 = 1494$

$$\text{Mean} : \overline{X} = A \pm \frac{\Sigma fd'}{N} \times C \quad A = 750;\ N = 400;\ \Sigma fd' = -138;$$

$C = 100$

$$= 750 - \frac{138}{400} \times 100 = 750 - 34.5$$

$$= \mathbf{715.5}$$

By inspection method mode lies in the class 600–700.

Mode :

$$Z = L_1 + \frac{f_1 - f_0}{2f_1 - f_0 - f_2} \times i$$

$$L_1 = 600;\ f_1 = 76;\ f_0 = 58;\ f_2 = 68;\ i = 100$$

$$= 600 + \frac{76 - 58}{2 \times 76 - 58 - 68} \times 100 = 600 + 69.23$$

$$= \mathbf{669.23}$$

Standard Deviation :

$$\sigma = \sqrt{\frac{\Sigma fd^2}{N} - \left(\frac{\Sigma fd'}{N}\right)^2} \times C$$

$$\Sigma fd'^2 = 1494;\ N = 400;\ \Sigma fd' = -138;\ C = 100$$

$$= \sqrt{\frac{1494}{400} - \left(\frac{-138}{400}\right)^2} \times 100$$

$$= \sqrt{3.735 - (-0.345)^2} \times 100$$

$$= \sqrt{3.735 - 0.119} \times 100$$

$$= \sqrt{3.616} \times 100$$

$$= 1.9015 \times 100$$

$$= \mathbf{190.15}.$$

Karl Pearson's Coefficient of Skewness :

$$= \frac{\overline{X} - \text{Mode}}{\sigma} \quad \overline{X} = 715.5;\ Z = 669.23;\ \sigma = 190.15$$

$$= \frac{715.5 - 669.23}{190.15} = \frac{46.27}{190.15}$$

$$= \mathbf{0.243}$$

Problem 12. From the following table, compute the quartile deviation as well as the coefficient of skewness :

Size :	4–8	8–12	12–16	16-20	20-24	24-28	28-32	32-36	36-40
Frequency :	6	10	18	30	15	12	10	6	2

(*C.A.*)

Solution :

Computation of Quartile Deviation and Coefficient of Skewness

Size	*f*	*c.f.*
4–8	6	6
8–12	10	16
12–16	18	34
16–20	30	64
20–24	15	79
24–28	12	91
28–32	10	101
32–36	6	107
36–40	2	109

Median = Size of $\frac{N}{2}$th item = Size of $\frac{109}{2}$th item

= 54.5th item which lies in the class 16–20

$$\text{Median} = L_1 + \frac{\frac{N}{2} - c.f.}{f} \times i$$

$$L_1 = 16;\ \frac{N}{2} = 54.5;\ c.f. = 34;\ f = 30;\ i = 4$$

$$= 16 + \frac{54.5 - 34}{30} \times 4 = 16 + 2.73$$

$$= \mathbf{18.73}$$

Q_1 = Size of $\frac{N}{4}$th item = Size of $\frac{109}{4}$th item

= 27.25th item which lies in the class 12–16

$$Q_1 = L_1 + \frac{\frac{N}{4} - c.f}{f} \times i$$

$$L_1 = 12;\ \frac{N}{4} = 27.25;\ c.f. = 16;\ f = 18;\ i = 4$$

$$= 12 + \frac{27.25 - 16}{18} \times 4 = 12 + 2.5$$

$$= \mathbf{14.5}$$

Q_3 = Size of $\frac{3N}{4}$th item = Size of 3 × $\frac{109}{4}$th item

= 81.75th item which lies in the cless 24–28.

$$Q_3 = L_1 + \frac{\frac{3N}{4} - c.f.}{f} \times i$$

$$L_1 = 24;\ \frac{3N}{4} = 81.75;\ c.f. = 79;\ f = 12;\ i = 4$$

$$= 24 + \frac{81.75 - 79}{12} \times 4 = 24 + 0.92$$

$$= \mathbf{24.92}$$

$$Q.D. = \frac{Q_3 - Q_1}{2} = \frac{24.92 - 14.5}{2} = \frac{10.42}{2}$$

$$= \mathbf{5.21}$$

Coefficient of Skewness :

$$= \frac{Q_3 + Q_1 - 2\text{Median}}{Q_3 - Q_1}$$

$$Q_3 = 24.92;\ Q_1 = 14.5;\ \text{Median} = 18.73$$

$$= \frac{24.92 + 14.5 - 2 \times 18.73}{24.92 - 14.5} = \frac{39.42 - 37.46}{10.42}$$

$$= \frac{1.96}{10.42}$$

$$= \mathbf{0.188}.$$

Problem 13. Calculate one measure of central tendency, dispersion and skewness for the following data :

Difference in *years*	:	0–5	5–10	10–15	15–20	20–25	25–30	30–35
Frequency	:	449	705	507	281	109	53	11

(*B. Com., Madras*)

Solution :

Computation of Skewness

Difference in years	m	$d' = \frac{m - 17.5}{5}$	f	fd'	fd'^2
0–5	2.5	−3	449	−1347	4041
5–10	7.5	−2	705	−1410	2820
10–15	12.5	−1	507	−507	507
15–20	17.5	0	281	0	0
20–25	22.5	1	109	109	109
25–30	27.5	2	53	106	212
30–35	32.5	3	11	33	99
			$N = 2115$	$\Sigma fd' = -3016$	$\Sigma fd'^2 = 7788$

Mean :

$$\overline{X} = A \pm \frac{\Sigma fd'}{N} \times C$$

$$A = 17.5;\ \Sigma fd' = -3016;\ N = 2115;\ C = 5$$

$$= 17.5 - \frac{3016}{2115} \times 5 = 17.5 - 7.13$$

$$= \mathbf{10.37}$$

By inspection method mode lies in the class 5–10

Mode :

$$
\begin{aligned}
Z &= L_1 + \frac{f_1 - f_0}{2f_1 - f_0 - f_2} \times i \\
L_1 &= 5;\ f_1 = 705;\ f_0 = 449;\ f_2 = 507;\ i = 5 \\
L_1 &= 5 + \frac{705 - 449}{2 \times 705 - 449 - 507} \times 5 = 5 + 2.82 \\
&= \mathbf{7.82}.
\end{aligned}
$$

Standard Deviation :

$$
\begin{aligned}
\sigma &= \sqrt{\frac{\Sigma f d'^2}{N} - \left(\frac{\Sigma f d'}{N}\right)^2} \times C \\
\Sigma f d'^2 &= 7788;\ N = 2115;\ \Sigma f d' = 3016;\ C = 5 \\
&= \sqrt{\frac{7788}{2115} - \left(\frac{-3016}{2115}\right)^2} \times 5 \\
&= \sqrt{3.682 - (-1.426)^2} \times 5 \\
&= \sqrt{3.682 - 2.033} \times 5 = \sqrt{1.649} \times 5 \\
&= 1.284 \times 5 = \mathbf{6.42}.
\end{aligned}
$$

Coefficient of Skewness

$$
\begin{aligned}
&= \frac{\text{Mean} - \text{Mode}}{\text{S.D.}} \\
\overline{X} &= 10.37;\ \text{Mode} = 7.82;\ \sigma = 6.42 \\
&= \frac{10.37 - 7.82}{6.42} = \frac{2.55}{6.42} \\
&= \mathbf{0.397}.
\end{aligned}
$$

Problem 14. From the following data given below calculate Karl Pearson's coefficient of skewness and explain its significance.

Wages Rs.	*No. of Persons*	*Wages Rs.*	*No. of persons*
70–80	12	110–120	50
80–90	18	120–130	45
90–100	35	130–140	20
100–110	42	140–150	8

(*M.A. Ecos. Punjab*)

Solution :

Computation of Coefficient of Skewness

Wages	m	f	$d' = \frac{m-105}{10}$	fd'	fd'^2
70–80	75	12	−3	−36	108
80–90	85	18	−2	−36	72
90–100	95	35	−1	−35	35
100–110	105	42	0	0	0
110–120	115	50	1	50	50
120–130	125	45	2	90	180
130–140	135	20	3	60	180
140–150	145	8	4	32	128
		$N = 230$		$\Sigma fd' = 125$	$\Sigma fd'^2 = 753$

$$\overline{X} = A \pm \frac{\Sigma fd'}{N} \times C$$

$$A = 105;\ \Sigma fd' = 125;\ N = 230;\ C = 10$$

$$\overline{X} = 105 + \frac{125}{230} \times 10$$

$$= 105 + 5.43$$

$$= \mathbf{110.43}$$

Highest frequency is 50.
Therefore, $Z = 110 - 120$

$$\text{Mode} = L_1 + \frac{f_1 - f_0}{2f_1 - f_0 - f_2} \times i$$

$$L_1 = 110;\ f_1 = 50;\ f_0 = 42;\ f_2 = 45;\ C = 10$$

$$Z = 110 + \frac{50 - 42}{2 \times 50 - 42 - 45} \times 10$$

$$= 110 + 6.15 \quad = \mathbf{116.15}.$$

$$\sigma = \sqrt{\frac{\Sigma fd'^2}{N} - \left(\frac{\Sigma fd'}{N}\right)^2} \times C$$

$$\Sigma fd'2 = 753; \Sigma fd' = 125;\ N = 230;\ C = 10$$

$$\sigma = \sqrt{\frac{753}{230} - \left(\frac{125}{230}\right)^2} \times 10$$

$$= \sqrt{3.27 - 0.29} \times 10$$

$$= \sqrt{2.98 \times 10} = 1.73 \times 10$$

$$= \mathbf{17.3}$$

$$\text{Sk.} = \frac{\overline{X} - Z}{\sigma}$$

$$\overline{X} = 110.43;\ Z = 116.15;\ \sigma = 17.3$$

$$\text{Sk.} = \frac{110.43 - 116.15}{17.3} = \frac{-5.72}{17.3}$$
$$= \mathbf{-0.33}.$$

Problem 15. The following series gives the height of trees in a garden. From these data, calculate the Karl Pearson's coefficient of skewness and also find coefficient of variation.

Height	*(ft.)*	*No. of trees*	*Height*	*(ft.)*	*No. of tress*
Below	7	26	Below	35	216
"	14	57	"	42	287
"	21	92	"	49	341
"	28	134	"	56	360

(*B.Com., Lucknow*)

Solution :

Computation of Coefficient of Skewness

Height	m	f	$d' = \frac{m-31.5}{7}$	fd'	fd'^2
0–7	3.5	26	−4	−104	416
7–14	10.5	31	−3	−93	279
14–21	17.5	35	−2	−70	140
21–28	24.5	42	−1	−42	42
28–35	31.5	82	0	0	0
35–42	38.5	71	1	71	71
42–49	45.5	54	2	108	216
49–56	52.5	19	3	57	171
		$N = 360$		$\Sigma fd' = -73$	$\Sigma fd'^2 = 1335$

$$\overline{X} = A \pm \frac{\Sigma fd'}{N} \times C$$
$$A = 31.5;\ \Sigma fd' = -73;\ N = 360;\ C = 7$$
$$\overline{X} = 31.5 - \frac{73}{360} \times 7$$
$$= 31.5 - 1.42 \quad = \mathbf{30.08}$$

Since the highest frequency is 82, Z lies in 28–35

$$Z = L_1 + \frac{f_1 - f_0}{2f_1 - f_0 - f_2} \times i$$
$$L_1 = 28;\ f_1 = 82;\ f_0 = 42;\ f_2 = 71;\ i = 7$$
$$Z = 28 + \frac{82 - 42}{2 \times 82 - 42 - 71} \times 7$$
$$= 28 + 5.49$$
$$= \mathbf{33.49}$$
$$\sigma = \sqrt{\frac{\Sigma fd'^2}{N} - \left(\frac{\Sigma fd'}{N}\right)^2} \times C$$
$$\Sigma fd'^2 = 1335;\ \Sigma fd' = -73;\ N = 360;\ C = 7$$

$$\sigma = \sqrt{\frac{1335}{360} - \left(\frac{-73}{360}\right)^2} \times 7$$
$$= \sqrt{3.71 - 0.041} \times 7$$
$$= \sqrt{3.669} \times 7$$
$$= 1.915 \times 7$$
$$= \mathbf{13.405.}$$
$$\text{Sk.} = \frac{\overline{X} - Z}{\sigma}$$
$$\overline{X} = 30.08\ Z = 33.49;\ \sigma = 13.405$$
$$\text{Sk.} = \frac{30.08 - 33.49}{13.405}$$
$$= \frac{-3.41}{13.405}$$
$$= \mathbf{-0.254}$$
$$\text{C.V.} = \frac{\sigma}{\overline{X}} \times 100$$
$$\sigma = 13.405;\ \overline{X} = 30.08$$
$$\text{C.V.} = \frac{13.405}{30.08} \times 100$$
$$= \mathbf{44.56\%}.$$

Problem 16. Calculate the coefficient of skewness based, on mean median and standard deviation from the following data :

Variable	*Frequency*	*Variable*	*Frequency*
100–110	4	140–150	64
110–120	16	150–160	40
120–130	36	160–170	32
130–140	52	170–180	11

(*C.A.*)

Solution :

Computation of Mean, Median and S.D.

Variable	m	f	$d' = \frac{m - 135}{10}$	fd'	fd'^2	cf
100–110	105	4	−3	−12	36	4
110–120	115	16	−2	−32	64	20
120–130	125	36	−1	−36	36	56
130–140	135	52	0	0	0	108
140–150	145	64	1	64	64	172
150–160	155	40	2	80	160	212
160–170	165	32	3	96	288	244
170–180	175	11	4	44	176	255
		$N = 255$		$\Sigma fd' = 204$	$\Sigma fd'^2 = 824$	

$$\overline{X} = A + \frac{\Sigma fd'}{N} \times C$$

$$A = 135;\ \Sigma fd' = 204;\ C = 10$$

$$\overline{X} = 135 + \frac{204}{255} \times 10$$

$$= 135 + 8$$

$$= \mathbf{143}.$$

$$\text{Median} = \text{Size of } \left(\frac{N}{2}\right) \text{th item}$$

$$= \text{Size of } \left(\frac{255}{2}\right) \text{th item}$$

$$= \text{Size of 127.5th item}$$

Therefore median lies in the class 140–150

$$\text{Median} = L_1 + \frac{\frac{N}{2} - cf}{f} \times i$$

$$L_1 = 140;\ \frac{N}{2} = 127 \cdot 5;\ c.f. = 108;\ f = 64;\ i = 10$$

$$\text{Median} = 140 + \frac{127 \cdot 5 - 108}{64} \times 10$$

$$= 140 + 3.05$$

$$= \mathbf{143.05}.$$

$$\sigma = \sqrt{\frac{\Sigma fd'^2}{N} - \left(\frac{\Sigma fd'}{N}\right)^2} \times C$$

$$\Sigma fd'^2 = 824;\ \Sigma fd' = 204;\ N = 255;\ C = 10$$

$$\sigma = \sqrt{\frac{824}{255} - \left(\frac{204}{255}\right)^2} \times 10$$

$$= \sqrt{3 \cdot 23 - 0 \cdot 65} \times 10$$

$$= \sqrt{2 \cdot 59} \times 10$$

$$= 1.609 \times 10 \quad = \mathbf{16.09}$$

$$\text{Sk.} = \frac{3\left(\overline{X} - Med.\right)}{\sigma}$$

$$\overline{X} = 143;\ Med = 143 \cdot 05;\ \sigma = 16 \cdot 09$$

$$\text{Sk.} = \frac{3\,(143 - 143 \cdot 05)}{16 \cdot 09}$$

$$= \frac{3 \times 0 \cdot 05}{16 \cdot 09}$$

$$= \frac{-0 \cdot 15}{16 \cdot 9}$$

$$= \mathbf{-0.0093}.$$

Problem 17. For the frequency distribution given below, calculate the coefficient of skewness based on the quartiles:

Class limits	*Frequency*	*Class limits*	*Frequency*
10–19	5	40–59	25
20–29	9	50–69	15
30–39	10	60–79	8
40–49	20	70–89	4

(*I.C.W.A. Inter*)

Solution:

Calculation of Coefficient of Skewness

Class Interval	*f*	*c.f.*
9.5–19.5	5	5
19.5–29.5	9	14
29.5–39.5	14	28
39.5–49.5	20	48
49.5–59.5	25	73
59.5–69.5	15	88
69.5–79.5	8	96
79.5–89.5	4	100

$$\text{Median} = \text{Size of } \frac{N}{2}\text{th item} = \text{Size of } \frac{100}{2}\text{th item}$$

$$= \text{50th item which lies in the class 49.5–59.5}$$

$$\text{Median} = L_1 + \frac{\frac{N}{2} - c.f.}{f} \times i$$

$$L_1 = 49 \cdot 5;\ \frac{N}{2} = 50;\ c.f. = 48;\ f = 25;\ i = 10$$

$$\text{Median} = 49 \cdot 5 + \frac{50 - 48}{25} \times 10 = 49 \cdot 5 + 0 \cdot 8$$

$$= \mathbf{50.3}.$$

$$Q_1 = \text{Size of } \frac{N}{4}\text{th item} = \text{Size of } \frac{100}{4}\text{th item}$$

$$= \text{25th item which lies in the class 29.5 –39.5}$$

$$Q_1 = L_1 + \frac{\frac{N}{4} - c.f.}{f} \times i$$

$$L_1 = 29 \cdot 5;\ \frac{N}{4} = 25;\ c.f. = 14;\ f = 14;\ i = 10$$

$$Q_1 = 29 \cdot 5 + \frac{25 - 14}{14} \times 10 = 29 \cdot 5 + 7 \cdot 86$$

$$= \mathbf{37.36}.$$

$$Q_3 = \text{Size of } \frac{3N}{4}\text{th item} = \text{size of } 3 \times \frac{100th}{4}\text{item}$$

$$= \text{75th item which lies in the class 59.5–69.6}$$

$$Q_3 = L_1 + \frac{\frac{3N}{4} - c.f.}{f} \times i$$

$$L_1 = 59 \cdot 5; \frac{3N}{4} = 75; c.f. = 73; f = 15; i = 10$$

$$Q_1 = 59 \cdot 5 + \frac{75 - 73}{15} \times 10 = 59 \cdot 5 + 1 \cdot 33$$

$$= \mathbf{60.83}$$

$$\text{Bowley's Coefficient of Skewness} = \frac{Q_3 + Q_1 - 2\text{Median}}{Q_3 - Q_1}$$

$$Q_3 = 60.83; Q_1 = 37.36; \text{Median} = 50.3$$

$$Sk. = \frac{60.83 + 37.36 - 2 \times 50.3}{60.83 - 37.36} = \frac{-2.41}{23.47}$$

$$= \mathbf{-0.103}.$$

Problem 18. From the following data compute quartile deviation and the Coefficient of Skewness.

Size	: 5–7	8–10	11–13	14–16	17–19
Frequency	: 14	24	38	20	4

(*B.Com., Osmania*)

Solution :

Computation of Quartile Deviation and Coefficient of Skewness.

Size	*f*	*c.f.*
4.5–7.5	14	14
7.5–10.5	24	38
10.5–13.5	38	76
13.5–16.5	20	96
16.5–19.5	4	100

$$Q_1 = \text{Size of } \frac{N}{4}\text{th item} = \text{Size of } \frac{100}{4}\text{th item}$$

$$= \text{25th item which lies in the class 7.5–10.5}$$

$$Q_1 = L_1 + \frac{\frac{N}{4} - c.f.}{f} \times C$$

$$L_1 = 7.5; \frac{N}{4} = 25; c.f. = 14; f = 24; i = 3$$

$$= 7.5 + \frac{25 - 14}{24} \times 3 = 7.5 + 1.38$$

$$= \mathbf{8.88}$$

$$Q_3 = \text{Size of } \frac{3N}{4}\text{th item} = \text{Size of } 3 \times \frac{100}{4}\text{th item}$$

$$= \text{75th item which lies in the class 10.5–13.5}$$

$$Q_3 = L_1 + \frac{\frac{3N}{4} - c.f.}{f} \times C$$

$$L_1 = 10.5; \frac{3N}{4} = 75; c.f. = 38; f = 38; i = 3$$

$$= 10.5 + \frac{75-38}{38} \times 3 = 10.5 + 2.92$$
$$= \mathbf{13.42.}$$
$$Q.D. = \frac{Q_3 - Q_1}{2} = \frac{13.42 - 8.88}{2}$$
$$= \mathbf{2.27.}$$
$$\text{Median} = \text{Size of } \frac{N}{2} \text{ th item} = \text{Size of } \frac{100}{2}\text{th item}$$
$$= \text{50th item which lies in the class 10.5–13.5}$$
$$\text{Median} = L_1 + \frac{\frac{N}{2} - c.f.}{f} \times i$$
$$L_1 = 10.5; \frac{N}{2} = 50; c.f. = 38; f = 38; i = 3$$
$$= 10.5 + \frac{50-38}{38} \times 3 = 10.5 + 0.947$$
$$= \mathbf{11.447.}$$
$$\text{Coefficient of Skewness} = \frac{Q_3 + Q_1 - 2\text{Median}}{Q_3 - Q_1}$$
$$Q_3 = 13.42; Q_1 = 8.88; \text{Median} = 11.447$$
$$= \frac{13.42 + 8.88 - 2 \times 11.447}{13.42 - 8.88} = \frac{22.30 - 22.89}{4.54}$$
$$= \frac{-0.59}{4.54} = \mathbf{-0.13.}$$

Problem 19. Calculate any measure of skewness for the following distributions :

Class Interval :	35–40	40–45	45–50	50–55	55–60
Frequency :	2	14	24	30	15

(*B.Com., Madras*)

Solution :

Computation of Coefficient of Skewness

Class Interval	m	$d' = \frac{m - 47.5}{5}$	f	fd'	fd'^2
35–40	37.5	−2	2	−4	8
40–45	42.5	−1	14	−14	14
45–50	47.5	0	24	0	0
50–55	52.5	1	30	30	30
55–60	57.5	2	15	30	60
			$N = 85$	$\Sigma fd' = 42$	$\Sigma fd'2 = 112$

$$\text{Mean}\overline{X} = A + \frac{\Sigma fd'}{N} \times C \quad A = 47.5; \Sigma fd' = 42; N = 85; C = 5$$
$$= 47.5 + \frac{42}{85} \times 5 = 47.5 + 2.47$$
$$= \mathbf{49.97}$$

By inspection method mode lies in the class 50–55

$$\text{Mode} : Z = L_1 + \frac{f_1 - f_0}{2f_1 - f_0 - f_2} \times i$$

$$L_1 = 50;\ f_1 = 30;\ f_0 = 24;\ f_2 = 15;\ i = 5$$

$$= 50 + \frac{30 - 24}{2 \times 30 - 24 - 15} \times 5 = 50 + 1.43 = \mathbf{51.43}.$$

Standard Deviation :

$$\sigma = \sqrt{\frac{\Sigma f d'^2}{N} - \left(\frac{\Sigma f d'}{N}\right)^2} \times C$$

$$\Sigma f d'^2 = 112;\ N = 85;\ \Sigma f d' = 42;\ C = 5$$

$$= \sqrt{\frac{112}{85} - \left(\frac{42}{85}\right)^2} \times 5 = \sqrt{1.318 - (-0.494)^2} \times 5$$

$$= \sqrt{1.318 - 0.244} \times 5 = \sqrt{1.074} \times 5$$

$$= 1.036 \times 5 = \mathbf{5.18}.$$

Coefficient of Skewness : $\dfrac{\overline{X} - \text{Mode}}{\sigma}$

$$\overline{X} = 49.97;\ Mode = 51.43;\ \sigma = 5.175$$

$$= \frac{49.97 - 51.43}{5.18}$$

$$= \frac{-1.46}{5.18}$$

$$= \mathbf{-0.282}.$$

Problem 20. Calculate the quartile coefficient of skewness of the following frequency distribution:

Weight	*No. of persons*	*Weight*	*No. of persons*
Under 100	1	150–159	65
100–109	14	160–169	31
110–119	66	170–179	12
120–129	122	180–189	5
130–139	145	190–199	2
140–149	121	Over 200	2

(*B.A., Eco., Hons.*)

Solution :

Computation of Quartile Coefficient of Skewness

X	f	$c.f.$
Under 100	1	1
100.5–109.5	14	15
109.5–119.5	66	81
119.5–129.5	122	203
129.5–139.5	145	348
139.5–149.5	121	469
149.5–159.5	65	534
159.5–169.5	31	565
169.5–179.5	12	577
179.5–189.5	5	582
189.5–200.5	2	584
Over 200.5	2	586

$$\text{Median} = \text{Size of } \frac{N}{2}\text{th item} = \text{Size of } \frac{586}{2}\text{th item}$$
$$= 293 \text{ item which lies in the class } 129.5\text{–}139.5$$
$$\text{Median} = L_1 + \frac{\frac{N}{2} - c.f.}{f} \times i$$
$$L_1 = 129.5;\ \frac{N}{2} = 293;\ c.f. = 203;\ f = 145;\ i = 10$$
$$\text{Medain} = 129.5 + \frac{293 - 203}{145} \times 10$$
$$= 129.5 + 6.2 = \mathbf{135.7}.$$
$$Q_1 = \text{Size } \frac{N}{4}\text{th item} = \text{Size of } \frac{586}{4}\text{th item}$$
$$= 146.5^{\text{th}} \text{ item which lies in the class } 119.5 - 129.$$
$$Q_1 = L_1 + \frac{\frac{N}{3} - c.f.}{f} \times i$$
$$L_1 = 119.5;\ \frac{N}{4} = 146.5;\ c.f. = 81;\ i = 10;\ f = 122$$
$$Q_1 = 119.5 + \frac{146.5 - 81}{122} \times 10 = 119.5 + 5.37$$
$$= \mathbf{124.87}.$$
$$Q_3 = \text{Size of } \frac{3N}{4}\text{th item} = \text{Size of } 3 \times \frac{586}{4} \text{ th item}$$
$$= 439.5\text{th item which lies in the class } 139.5\text{–}149.5$$
$$Q_3 = L_1 + \frac{\frac{3N}{4} - c.f.}{f} \times i$$
$$L_1 = 139.5;\ \frac{3N}{4} = 439.5;\ c.f. = 348;\ f = 121;\ i = 10$$
$$= 139.5 + \frac{439.5 - 348}{121} \times 10 = 139.5 + 7.6$$
$$= \mathbf{147.1}.$$

$$\text{Bowley's Coefficient of Skewness} = \frac{Q_3 + Q_1 - 2\text{Median}}{Q_3 - Q_1}$$

$$Q_3 = 147.1;\ Q_1 = 124.87;\ \text{Median} = 135.7$$

$$Sk. = \frac{147.1 + 124.87 - 2 \times 135.7}{147.1 - 124.87} = \frac{0.57}{22.23}$$

$$= \mathbf{0.026.}$$

Problem 21. Calculate Karl Pearson's co-efficient of skewness from the following data :

Marks		*No. of Students*	*Marks*		*No. of Students*
Above	0	100	Above	50	50
"	10	98	"	60	35
"	20	95	"	70	23
"	30	90	"	80	13
"	40	80	"	90	5

(*B.Com. Madurai*)

Solution :

Computation of Pearson's Coefficient of Skewness

Marks	m	$d' = \frac{m-45}{10}$	f	fd'	fd'^2
0–10	5	−4	100–98 = 2	−8	32
10–20	15	−3	98–95 = 3	−9	27
20–30	25	−2	95–90 = 5	−10	20
30–40	35	−1	90–80 =10	−10	10
40–50	45	0	80–50 =30	0	0
50–60	55	1	50–35 =15	15	15
60–70	65	2	35–23 =12	24	48
70–80	75	3	23–13 =10	30	90
80–90	85	4	13–5 = 8	32	128
90–100	95	5	5	25	125
			$N = 100$	$\Sigma fd' = 89$	$\Sigma fd'^2 = 495$

$$\text{Mean:}\overline{X} = A + \frac{\Sigma fd'}{N} \times C \quad A = 45;\ \Sigma fd' = 89;\ N = 100;\ C = 10$$

$$= 45 + \frac{89}{100} \times 10 = 45 + 8.9$$

$$= \mathbf{53.9}.$$

By inspection method mode lies in the class 40–50

$$\text{Mode:} \quad Z; = L_1 + \frac{f_1 - f_0}{2f_1 - f_0 - f_2} \times i$$

$$L_1 = 40;\ f_1 = 30\ f_0 = 10;\ f_2 = 15;\ i = 10$$

$$Z = 40 + \frac{30 - 10}{2 \times 30 - 10 - 15} \times 10 = 40 + 5.71$$

$$= \mathbf{45.71}.$$

Standard Deviation:

$$\sigma = \sqrt{\frac{\Sigma f d'^2}{N} - \left(\frac{\Sigma f d'}{N}\right)^2} \times C$$

$$\Sigma f d'^2 = 495;\ N = 100;\ \Sigma f d' = 89;\ C = 10$$

$$\sigma = \sqrt{\frac{495}{100} - \left(\frac{89}{100}\right)^2} \times 10$$

$$= \sqrt{4.95 - (0.89)^2} \times 10$$

$$= \sqrt{4.95 - 0.79} \times 10$$

$$= \sqrt{4.16} \times 10 = 2.04 \times 10$$

$$= \mathbf{20.4}$$

$$\text{Pearson's Coefficient of Skewness} = \frac{\text{Mean} - \text{Mode}}{\sigma}$$

$$\overline{X} = 53.9;\ Mode =;\ 45.71;\ \sigma = 20.4$$

$$Sk = \frac{53.9 - 45.71}{20.4} = \mathbf{0.40}$$

Problem 22. Find the standard deviation and a coefficient of skewness for the following distribution.

Variable :	0–5	5–10	10–15	15–20	20–25	25–30	30–35	35–40
Frequency :	2	5	7	13	21	16	8	3

(*B.Com., Madras : Poona ; Delhi*)

Solution :

Computation of Mean and Standard Deviation

Variable X	m	$d' = \frac{m - 22.5}{5}$	$f.$	fd'	fd'^2
0–5	2.5	−4	2	−8	32
5–10	7.5	−3	5	−15	45
10–15	12.5	−2	7	−14	28
15–20	17.5	−1	13	−13	13
20–25	22.5	0	21	0	0
25–30	27.5	1	16	16	16
30–35	32.5	2	8	16	32
35–40	37.5	3	3	9	27
			N=75	$\Sigma f d' = -9$	$\Sigma f d'^2 = 193$

$$\text{Mean} : \overline{X} = A \pm \frac{\Sigma fd'}{N} \times C \quad A = 22.5; \Sigma fd' = -9; N = 75; i = 5$$

$$= 22.5 - \frac{9}{75} \times 5 = 22.5 - 0.6$$

$$= \mathbf{21.9.}$$

By inspection method mode lies in the group 20–25

$$\text{Mode} : \quad Z; = L_1 + \frac{f_1 - f_0}{2f_1 - f_0 - f_2} \times i$$

$$L_1 = 20; f_1 = 21; f_0 = 13; f_2 = 16; i = 5$$

$$Z = 20 + \frac{21 - 13}{2 \times 21 - 13 - 16} \times 5 = 20 + 3.08$$

$$= \mathbf{23.08}$$

$$\text{Standard Deviation} : \sigma = \sqrt{\frac{\Sigma fd'^2}{N} - \left(\frac{\Sigma fd'}{N}\right)^2} \times C$$

$$\Sigma fd'^2 = 193; N = 75; \Sigma fd' = -9; C = 5$$

$$= \sqrt{\frac{193}{75} - \left(\frac{-9}{75}\right)^2} \times 5 = \sqrt{2.573 - (-0.12)^2} \times 5$$

$$= \sqrt{2.573 - 0.014} \times 5 = \sqrt{2.559} \times 5 = 1.599 \times 5$$

$$= \mathbf{7.99.}$$

Karl Pearson's Coefficient of Skewness :

$$j = \frac{\text{Mean} - \text{Mode}}{S.D.} \quad \text{Mean} = 21.9; \text{Mode} = 23.08; S.D. = 7.99$$

$$= \frac{21.9 - 23.08}{7.99} = \frac{-1.18}{7.99}$$

$$= \mathbf{-0.148.}$$

Problem 23. Assume that a firm has selected a random sample of 100 from its production line and has obtained the data shown in the table below:

Class interval	*Frequency*	*Class interval*	*Frequency*
130–134	3	150–154	19
135–139	12	155–159	12
140–144	21	160–164	5
145–149	28	Total	**100**

Compute the following:

(*a*) the arithmetic mean,

(*b*) the standard deviation,

(*c*) Karl Pearson's coefficient of skewness.

(*B.Com. Punjab*)

Solution:

Computation of Mean, Standard Deviation and Coefficient of Skewness

Class Interval	m	$d' = \frac{m-147}{5}$	f	fd'	fd'^2
129.5–135.5	132	−3	3	−9	27
134.5–139.5	137	−2	12	−24	48
139.5–144.5	142	−1	21	−21	21
144.5–149.5	147	0	28	0	0
149.5–154.5	152	1	19	19	19
154.5–159.5	157	2	12	24	48
159.5–164.5	162	3	5	15	45
			$N = 100$	$\Sigma fd' = 4$	$\Sigma fd'2 = 208$

Mean :

$$\overline{X} = A + \frac{\Sigma fd'}{N} \times C \quad A = 147;\ \Sigma fd' = 4;\ N = 100;\ C = 5$$

$$= 147 + \frac{4}{100} \times 5 = 147 + 0.2$$

$$= \mathbf{147.2.}$$

By inspection method mode lies in the class 144.5–149.5

Mode :

$$Z = L_1 + \frac{f_1 - f_0}{2f_1 - f_0 - f_2} \times i$$

$$L_1 = 144.5;\ f_1 = 28;\ f_0 = 21;\ f_2 = 19;\ i = 5$$

$$= 144.5 + \frac{28 - 21}{2 \times 28 - 21 - 19} \times 5 = 144.5 + 2.19$$

$$= \mathbf{146.69.}$$

Standard Deviation :

$$\sigma = \sqrt{\frac{\Sigma fd'^2}{N} - \left(\frac{\Sigma fd'}{N}\right)^2} \times C$$

$$\Sigma fd'^2 = 208;\ N = 100;\ \Sigma fd' = 4;\ C = 5$$

$$\sigma = \sqrt{\frac{208}{100} - \left(\frac{4}{100}\right)^2} \times 5 = \sqrt{2.08 - (0.04)^2} \times 5$$

$$= \sqrt{2.08 - 0.0016} \times 5$$

$$= \sqrt{2.0784} \times 5 = 1.442 \times 5$$

$$= \mathbf{7.21}$$

Karl Pearson's Coefficient of Skewness :

$$Sk = \frac{\text{Mean} - \text{Mode}}{\sigma} \quad \overline{X} = 147.2;\ \text{Mode} = 146.69;\ \sigma = 7.21$$

$$= \frac{147.2 - 146.69}{7.21} = \frac{-0.51}{7.21}$$

$$= \mathbf{-0.071.}$$

Problem 24. The following data represent the percentage of ash contents in a particular variety of coal as determined by test on 280 wagon loads.

Percentage of ash contents	*Frequency*	*Percentage of ash contents*	*Frequency*
6.0–6.9	1	11.0–11.9	45
7.0–7.9	7	12.0–12.9	28
8.0–8.9	28	13.0–13.9	7
9.0–9.9	78	14.0–14.9	2
10.0–10.9	84		

Calculate the quartile coefficient of skewness for the distribution. (*B.Com., Bombay*)

Solution:

% of ash content	*f*	*c.f.*
5.95–6.95	1	1
6.95–7.95	7	8
7.95–8.95	28	36
8.95–9.95	78	114
9.95–10.95	84	198
10.95–11.95	45	243
11.95–12.95	28	271
12.95–13.95	7	278
13.95–14.95	2	280

$$\text{Median} = \text{Size of } \frac{N}{2} \text{ th item} = \text{Size of } \frac{280}{2} \text{th item}$$

$$= 140th \text{ item which lies in the class } 9.95\text{–}10.95$$

$$\text{Median} = L_1 + \frac{\frac{N}{2} - c.f.}{f} \times i$$

$$L_1 = 9.95;\ \frac{N}{2} = 140;\ c.f. = 114;\ f = 84;\ i = 1$$

$$\text{Median} = 9.95 + \frac{140 - 114}{84} \times 1$$

$$= 9.95 + 0.31$$

$$= \mathbf{10.26}$$

$$Q_1 = \text{Size of } \frac{N}{4} \text{ th item} = \frac{280}{4} \text{ th item}$$

$$= 70\text{th item which lies in the class } 8.95\text{–}9.95$$

$$Q_1 = L_1 + \frac{\frac{N}{4} - c.f.}{f} \times i$$

$$L_1 = 8.95;\ \frac{N}{4} = 70;\ c.f. = 36;\ f = 78;\ i = 1$$

$$= 8.95 + \frac{70 - 36}{78} = 8.95 + 0.44$$

$$= \mathbf{9.39}.$$

$$Q_3 = \text{Size of } \frac{3N}{4}\text{th item} = 3 \times \frac{380}{4}\text{th item}$$
$$= \text{210th item which lies in the class 10.95–11.95}$$
$$Q_3 = L_1 + \frac{\frac{3N}{4} - c.f.}{f} \times i$$
$$L_1 = 10.95;\ \frac{3N}{4} = 210;\ c.f. = 198;\ f = 45;\ i = 1$$
$$= 10.95 + \frac{210 - 198}{45} = 10.95 + 0.27 = \mathbf{11.22}.$$

$$\text{Bowley's coefficient of Skewness} = \frac{Q_3 + Q_1 - 2\text{Median}}{Q_3 - Q_1}$$
$$Q_3 = 11.22;\ Q_1 = 9.39;\ \text{Median} = 10.26$$
$$Sk. = \frac{11.22 + 9.39 - 2 \times 10.26}{11.22 - 9.39} = \frac{0.09}{1.83}$$
$$= \mathbf{0.05}.$$

Problem 25 : Find out the coefficient of skewness from the following data and show hich section is more skewed :

Income	55–58	58–61	61–64	64–67	67–70
Section A :	12	17	23	18	11
Section B :	20	22	25	13	7

(*B.Com. Kerala*)

Solution :

Computation of Coefficient of Skewness

Income	*Section A*		*Section B*	
	f	*c.f.*	*f*	*c.f.*
55–58	12	12	20	20
58–61	17	29	22	42
61–64	23	52	25	67
64–67	18	70	13	80
67–70	11	81	7	87

Section A

$$\text{Median} = \text{Size of } \frac{N}{2} \text{ th item}$$
$$= \text{Size of } \frac{81}{2} \text{ th item}$$
$$= \text{40.5th item which lies in the class 61-64}$$
$$\text{Median} = L_1 + \frac{\frac{N}{2} - c.f.}{f} \times i$$
$$L_1 = 61;\ \frac{N}{2} = 40.5;$$
$$c.f. = 29;\ f = 23;\ C = 3$$
$$\text{Median} = 61 + \frac{40.5 - 29}{23} \times 3$$
$$= 61 + 1.5$$
$$= \mathbf{62.5}$$

Section B

$$\text{Median} = \text{Size of } \frac{N}{2} \text{ th item}$$
$$= \text{Size of } \frac{87}{2} \text{ th item}$$
$$= \text{43.5th item which lies in the class 61–64}$$
$$\text{Median} = L_1 + \frac{\frac{N}{2} - c.f.}{f} \times i$$
$$L_1 = 61;\ \frac{N}{2} = 43.5;$$
$$c.f. = 42;\ f = 25;\ i = 3$$
$$\text{Median} = 61 + \frac{43.5 - 42}{25} \times 3$$
$$= \mathbf{61.18}.$$

Q_1 = Size of $\frac{N}{4}$ th item

= Size of $\frac{81}{4}$ th item

= 20.25^{th} item which lies in the class 58–61

$$Q_1 = L_1 + \frac{\frac{N}{4} - c.f.}{f} \times i$$

$L_1 = 58$; $\frac{N}{4} = 20.25$;

$c.f. = 12$; $f = 17$; $i = 3$

$$Q_1 = 58 + \frac{20.25 - 12}{17} \times 3$$

$= 58 + 1.46$

$= \mathbf{59.46}$.

Q_3 = Size of $\frac{3N}{4}$th item

= Size of $\frac{3 \times 81}{4}$ th item

= 60.75th item which lies in the class 64–67

$$Q_3 = L_1 + \frac{\frac{3N}{4} - c.f.}{f} \times i$$

$L_1 = 64$; $\frac{3N}{4} = 60.75$;

$c.f. = 52$; $f = 18$; $i = 3$

$$Q_3 = 64 + \frac{60.75 - 52}{18} \times 3$$

$= 64 + 1.46 = \mathbf{65.46}$

Bowley's Coefficient of Skewness :

$$Sk. = \frac{Q_3 + Q_1 - 2\,\text{Median}}{Q_3 - Q_1}$$

$Q_3 = 65.46$; $Q_1 = 59.46$;

Median=62.5

$$Sk. = \frac{65.46 + 59.46 - 2 \times 62.5}{65.46 - 59.46}$$

$$= \frac{-0.08}{6} = \mathbf{-0.013}.$$

Q_1 = Size of $\frac{87}{4}$ th item

= 21.75th item which lies in the class 58–61

$$Q_1 = 58 + \frac{21.75 - 20}{22} \times 3$$

$= \mathbf{58+0.24}$

$$Q_3 = \frac{3 \times 87}{4}\text{th item}$$

= 65.25th item which lies in the class 61–64

$L_1 = 61$; $\frac{3N}{4} = 65.25$;

$c.f. = 42$; $f = 25$; $i = 3$

$$Q_3 = 61 + \frac{65.25 - 42}{25} \times 3$$

$= 61 + 2.79$

$= \mathbf{63.79}$

Bowley's Coefficient of Skewness:

$Q_3 = 63.79\, Q_1 = 58.24$;

Median = 61.18

$$Sk. = \frac{63.79 + 58.24 - 2 \times 61.18}{63.79 - 58.24}$$

$$= \frac{-0.33}{5.55} = \mathbf{-0.06}$$

Problem 26. Find the appropriate measure of skewness from the following data :

Age (years)	*No. of men*	*Age (years)*	*No. of men*
Below 20	13	35–40	112
20–25	29	40–45	94
25–30	46	45–50	45
30–35	60	Above 50	21

(ICWA Inter)

Solution :

Computation of Skewness

Age (years)	*f*	*c.f.*
Below 20	13	13
20–25	29	42
25–30	46	88
30–35	60	148
35–40	112	260
40–45	94	354
45–50	45	399
50 and above	21	420

$$\text{Median} = \text{Size of } \frac{N}{2}\text{th item} = \text{Size of } \frac{420}{2}\text{th item}$$

$$= \text{210th item which lies in the class 35–40}$$

$$\text{Median} = L_1 + \frac{\frac{N}{2} - c.f.}{f} \times i$$

$$L_1 = 35;\ \frac{N}{2} = 210;\ c.f. = 148;\ f = 112;\ i = 5$$

$$\text{Median} = 35 + \frac{210 - 148}{112} \times 5 = 35 + 2.77$$

$$= \mathbf{37.77}.$$

$$Q_1 = \text{Size of } \frac{N}{4}\text{th item} = \text{Size of } \frac{420}{4}\text{th item}$$

$$= \text{105th item which lies in the class 30–35}$$

$$Q_1 = L_1 + \frac{\frac{N}{2} - c.f.}{f} \times i;$$

$$L_1 = 30;\ \frac{N}{4} = 105;\ c.f. = 88;\ f = 60;\ i = 5$$

$$= 30 + \frac{105 - 88}{60} \times 5 = 30 + 1.42$$

$$= \mathbf{31.42}.$$

$$Q_3 = \text{Size of } \frac{3N}{4} \text{ th item} = \text{Size of } \frac{3 \times 420}{4}\text{th item}$$

$$= \text{315th item which lies in the class 40–45.}$$

$$Q_3 = L_1 + \frac{\frac{3N}{4} - c.f.}{f} \times i;\ L_1 = 40;\ \frac{3N}{4} = 315;$$

$$c.f. = 260;\ f = 94;\ i = 5$$

$$= 40 + \frac{315 - 260}{94} \times 5 = 40 + 2.93$$

$$= \mathbf{42.93}.$$

$$\text{Bowley's coefficient of skewness} = \frac{Q_3 + Q_1 - 2\text{Median}}{Q_3 - Q_1}$$

$$Q_3 = 42.93;\ Q_1 = 31.42;\ \text{Median} = 37.77$$

$$Sk. = \frac{42.93 + 31.42 - 2 \times 37.77}{42.93 - 31.42}$$

$$= \frac{-1.19}{11.51} = \mathbf{-0.103}$$

Problem 27. Examine for skewness the following frequency distribution of blood donors :

Age (in years)	10–19	20–29	30–39	40–49	50–59	60–69	70–79	80–89
Frequency	3620	7045	9030	5029	2710	1200	175	11

(*B.Com., Madras*)

Solution :

Computation of Coefficient of Skewness

Age in years	*f*	*c.f.*
9.5–19.5	3620	3,620
19.5–29.5	7045	10,665
29.5–39.5	9030	19,695
39.5–49.5	5029	24,724
49.5–59.5	2710	27,434
59.5–69.5	1200	28,634
69.5–79.5	175	28, 809
79.5–89.5	11	28,820

$$\text{Median} = \text{Size of } \frac{N}{2}\text{th item} = \text{Size of } \frac{28820}{2}\text{th item}$$

$$= 14,410\text{th item which lies in the class 29.5–39.5}$$

$$\text{Median} = L_1 - \frac{\frac{N}{2} - c.f.}{f} \times i$$

$$L_1 = 29.5;\ \frac{N}{2} = 14,410;\ c.f. = 10,665;\ f = 9030;\ i = 10$$

$$\text{Median} = 29.5 + \frac{14,410 - 10,655}{9030} \times 10 = 29.5 + 4.15$$

$$= \mathbf{33.65}$$

$$Q_1 = \text{Size of } \frac{N}{4}\text{th item} = \text{Size of } \frac{28820}{4}\text{th item}$$

$$= 7205\text{th item which lies in the class 19.5–29.5}$$

$$Q_1 = L_1 - \frac{\frac{N}{4} - c.f.}{f} \times i$$

$$L_1 = 19.5;\ \frac{N}{4} = 7205;\ c.f. = 3620;\ f = 7045;\ i = 10$$

$$Q_1 = 19.5 + \frac{7205 - 3620}{7045} \times 10 = 19.5 + 5.09$$

$$= \mathbf{24.59}$$

$$Q_3 = \text{Size of } \frac{3N}{4}\text{th the item} = \text{Size of } \frac{3 \times 28820}{4}\text{th item}$$

$$= 21,615\text{th item which lies in the class 39.5–49.5}$$

$$Q_3 = L_1 - \frac{\frac{3N}{4} - c.f.}{f} \times i$$

$$L_1 = 39.5;\ \frac{3N}{4} = 21,615;\ c.f. = 19,695;\ f = 5029;\ i = 10$$

$$Q_3 = 30.5 + \frac{21615 - 19695}{5029} \times 10 = 39.5 + 3.82$$

$$= \mathbf{43.32}.$$

Bowley's Coefficient of Skewness

$$= \frac{Q_3 + Q_1 - 2\text{Median}}{Q_3 - Q_1}$$

$$Q_3 = 43.32;\ Q_1 = 24.59;\ \text{Median} = \mathbf{33.65}$$

$$Sk. = \frac{43.32 + 24.59 - 2 \times 33.65}{43.32 - 24.59} = \frac{0.61}{18.73} = \mathbf{0.033}.$$

Problem 28. Calculate Karl Pearson's coefficient of skewness from the data given below :

Income (Rs.) :	400-500	500-600	600-700	700-800	800-900
No. of Employees :	8	16	20	17	3

(*B.Com., Banaras*)

Solution :

Computation of Coefficient of Skewness

Income (Rs.)	m	f	$d' = \frac{m - 650}{100}$	fd'	fd'^2
400–500	450	8	–2	–16	32
500–600	550	16	–1	–16	16
600–700	650	20	0	0	0
700–800	750	17	1	17	17
800–900	850	3	2	6	12
		N = 64		$\Sigma fd' = -9$	$\Sigma fd'^2 = 77$

$$\text{Mean : } \overline{X} = A \pm \frac{\Sigma fd'}{N} \times C$$

$$A = 650;\ \Sigma fd' = -9;\ N = 64;\ C = 100$$

$$= 650 - \frac{9}{64} \times 100 = 650 - 14.06$$

$$= \mathbf{635.94}.$$

By inspection mode lies in the class 600–700

$$\text{Mode} : Z = L_1 + \frac{f_1 - f_0}{2f_1 - f_0 - f_2} \times i$$

$$L_1 = 600;\ f_1 = 20;\ f_0 = 16;\ f_2 = 17;\ i = 100$$

$$Z = 600 + \frac{20 - 16}{2 \times 20 - 16 - 17} \times 100 = 600 + 57.14$$

$$= \mathbf{657.14}.$$

Standard Deviation :

$$\sigma = \sqrt{\frac{\Sigma fd'^2}{N} - \left(\frac{\Sigma fd'}{N}\right)^2} \times C$$

$$\Sigma fd'^2 = 77;\ N = 64;\ \Sigma fd' = -9;\ C = 100$$

$$\sigma = \sqrt{\frac{77}{64} - \left(\frac{-9}{64}\right)^2} \times 100$$

$$= \sqrt{1.2031 - 0.0198} \times 100$$

$$= \sqrt{1.1813} \times 100$$

$$= 1.087 \times 100$$

$$= \mathbf{108.7}.$$

Coefficient of skewness $= \dfrac{\overline{X} - \text{Mode}}{\sigma}$

$$\overline{X} = 635.94;\ Z = 657.14;\ \sigma = 108.7$$

$$\sigma = \frac{635.94 - 657.14}{108.7} = \frac{-21.20}{108.7}$$

$$= \mathbf{-0.195}.$$

Problem 29. Calculate the coefficient of skewness based on the quartiles from the following :

More than

0	10	20	30	40	50	60	70	80	90	100	110
5474,	5426,	5259	5023,	4475	3712	2718,	1406	764,	370,	160,	39

(*C.A.*)

Solution. Here the distribution is in more than cumulative frequency and we may first convert this into less than cumulative frequency form as follows.

Computation of Coefficient of Skewness

Class Interval	*More than c.f.*	*f*	*Less than c.f.*
0–10	5474	48	48
10–20	5426	167	215
20–30	5259	236	451
30–40	5023	548	999
40–50	4475	763	1762
50–60	3712	994	2756
60–70	2718	1312	4068
70–80	1406	642	4710
80–90	764	394	5104
90-100	370	210	5314
100–110	160	121	5435
Over 110	39	39	5474

$$Q_1 = \frac{N}{4} = \frac{5474}{4}$$

$$= 1368.5 \text{ which lies in the class 40–50}$$

$$Q_1 = L_1 + \frac{\frac{N}{4} - c.f.}{f} \times i$$

$$L_1 = 40; \frac{N}{4} = 1368.5; c.f. = 999; f = 763; i = 10$$

$$Q_1 = 40 + \frac{1368.5 - 999}{763} \times 10$$

$$= 40 + 4.84$$

$$= 44.84$$

$$\text{Median} = \frac{N}{2} = \frac{5474}{2} = 2737$$

Which lies in the class 50–60

$$\text{Median} = L_1 + \frac{\frac{N}{2} - c.f.}{f} \times i; L_1 = 50; \frac{N}{2} = 2737;$$

$$c.f. = 1762; f = 763; i = 10$$

$$= 50 + \frac{2737 - 1762}{994} \times 10 = 50 + 9.80$$

$$= 59.80$$

$$Q_3 = \frac{3N}{4} = \frac{3 \times 5474}{4}$$

$$= 4105.5 \text{ which lies in the class 70–80}$$

$$Q_3 = L_1 + \frac{\frac{3N}{4} - c.f.}{f} \times i; L_1 = 70; \frac{3N}{4} = 4105.5;$$

$$c.f. = 4068; f = 642; i = 13$$

$$= 70 + \frac{4105.56 - 4068}{642} \times 10 = 70.58$$

Bowley's Coefficient of Skewness :

$$Sk = \frac{Q_3 + Q_1 - 2\text{Median}}{Q_3 - Q_1}$$

$$= \frac{70.58 + 44.85 - 2 \times 59.80}{70.58 - 44.85} = -\frac{4.17}{25.73}$$

$$= \mathbf{-0.16.}$$

Problem 30. Calculate the measure of skewness based on quartiles and median from the following data :

Variable	10–20	20–30	30–40	40–50	50–60	60–70	70–80
Frequency	358	2417	976	129	62	18	10

(*C.A.*)

Solution :

Variable	*f*	*c.f.*
10–20	358	358
20–30	2417	2775
30–40	976	3751
40–50	129	3880
50–60	62	3942
60–70	18	3960
70–80	10	3970

$$\text{Median} = \text{Size of } \frac{N}{2}\text{th item}$$

$$= \text{Size of } \frac{3970}{2}\text{th item}$$

$$= \text{1985th item which lies in the class 20–30}$$

$$\text{Median} = L_1 + \frac{\frac{N}{2} - c.f.}{f} \times i$$

$$L_1 = 20;\ \frac{N}{2} = 1985;\ c.f. = 358;\ f = 2417;\ i = 10$$

$$\text{Median} = 20 + \frac{1985 - 358}{2417} \times 10 = 20 + 6.73$$

$$= \mathbf{26.73}.$$

$$Q_1 = \text{Size of } \frac{N}{4} \text{ th item} = \text{Size of } \frac{3970}{4} \text{ th item}$$

$$= \text{992.5 th item which lies in the class 20–30}$$

$$Q_1 = L_1 + \frac{\frac{N}{4} - c.f.}{f} \times i$$

$$L_1 = 20;\ \frac{N}{4} = 992.5;\ c.f. = 358;\ f = 2417;\ i = 10$$

$$= 20 + \frac{992.5 - 358}{2417} \times 10 = 20 + 2.63$$

$$= \mathbf{22.63}.$$

$$Q_3 = \text{Size of } \frac{3N}{4} \text{ th item} = \text{Size of } \frac{3 \times 3970}{4} \text{ th item}$$

$$= \text{2977.5 th item which lies in the class 30–40}$$

$$Q_3 = L_1 + \frac{\frac{3N}{4} - c.f.}{f} \times i$$

$$L_1 = 30;\ \frac{3N}{4} = 2977.5;\ c.f. = 2775;\ f = 976;\ i = 10$$

$$= 30 + \frac{2977.5 - 2775}{976} \times 10$$

$$= 30 + 2.07$$

$$= \mathbf{32.07}.$$

Bowley's coefficient of Skewness

$$= \frac{Q_3 + Q_1 - 2\text{Median}}{Q_3 - Q_1}$$

$$Q_3 = 32.07;\ Q_1 = 22.63;\ \text{Median} = 26.73$$

$$Sk = \frac{32.07 + 22.63 - 2 \times 26.73}{32.07 - 22.63}$$

$$= \frac{+1.24}{9.44}$$

$$= \mathbf{0.13}.$$

Problem 31. Calculate the appropriate measure of skewness from the following income distribution :

Monthly income (Rs.)	*Frequency*
up to 100	9
101–150	51
151–200	120
201–300	240
301–500	136
501–750	33
751–1000	9
Above 1000	2
	600

(*ICWA*)

Solution :

Computation of coefficient of Skewness

Monthly Income (Rs.)	*f*	*c.f.*
upto 100	9	9
101–150	51	60
151–200	120	180
201–300	240	420
301–500	136	556
501–750	33	589
751–1000	9	598
Above 1000	2	600

$$\text{Median} = \text{Size of } \frac{600}{2} \text{ th item}$$

$$= 300 \text{ th item which lies in the class } 201\text{–}300$$

The real limit is 200.5–300.5

$$\text{Median} = L_1 + \frac{\frac{N}{2} - c.f.}{f} \times i$$

$$L_1 = 200.5;\ \frac{N}{4} = 300;\ ,c.f. = 180;\ f = 240;\ i = 100$$

$$\begin{aligned}
\text{Median} &= 200.5 + \frac{300 - 180}{240} \times 100 = 200.5 + 50 \\
&= \mathbf{250.5}. \\
Q_1 &= \text{Size of } \frac{N}{4} \text{ th item} = \text{Size of } \frac{600}{4} \text{ th item} \\
&= 150 \text{ th item which lies in the class } 151\text{–}200 \\
Q_1 &= L_1 + \frac{\frac{N}{4} - c.f.}{f} \times i \\
L_1 &= 150.5; \frac{N}{4} = 150; c.f. = 60; f = 120; i = 100 \\
&= 150.5 + \frac{150 - 60}{120} \times 50 = 150.5 + 37.50 \\
&= \mathbf{188}. \\
Q_3 &= \text{Size of } \frac{3N}{4} \text{ th item} = \text{Size of } \frac{3 \times 600}{4} \text{ th item} \\
&= 450 \text{ th item which lies in the class } 301\text{–}500.
\end{aligned}$$

The real limit is 300.5–500.5

$$\begin{aligned}
Q_3 &= L_1 + \frac{\frac{3N}{4} - c.f.}{f} \times i \\
L_1 &= 300.5; \frac{3N}{4} = 450; c.f. = 420; f = 136; i = 200 \\
&= 300.5 + \frac{450 - 420}{136} \times 200 = 300.5 + 44.12 \\
&= \mathbf{344.62}.
\end{aligned}$$

Coefficient of Skewness

$$\begin{aligned}
&= \frac{Q_3 + Q_1 - 2 \text{ Median}}{Q_3 - Q_1} \\
Q_3 &= 344.62 \\
Q_1 &= 188; \text{ Median} = 250.5 \\
Sk &= \frac{344.62 + 188 - 2 \times 250.5}{344.62 - 188} = \frac{532.62 - 501}{156.62} \\
&= \frac{31.62}{156.62} \\
&= \mathbf{0.2}.
\end{aligned}$$

Problem 32. From the information given below, calculate Karl Pearson's coefficient of skewness and also quartile coefficient of skewness.

Measure	*Firm A*	*Firm B*
Mean	150	140
Median	142	155
Standard deviation	30	55
Third quartile	195	260
First quartile	62	80

(*B.Com., Osmania*)

Solution :

Karl Pearson's coefficient of Skewness :

$$Sk = \frac{3(\overline{X} - \text{ Median})}{\sigma}$$

Place A

$\overline{X} = 150$; Median $= 142$; $\sigma = 30$

$$Sk = \frac{3(150 - 142)}{30} = \frac{24}{30} = \mathbf{0.8}$$

Place B

$\overline{X} = 140$; median $= 155$; $\sigma = 55$

$$Sk = \frac{3(140 - 155)}{55} = -\frac{45}{55} = \mathbf{0.82}$$

Quartile coefficient of Skewness :

$$Sk = \frac{Q_3 + Q_1 - 2\text{Median}}{Q_3 - Q_1}$$

$Q_3 = 195$; $Q_1 = 62$;
Median $= 142$

$$Sk = \frac{195 + 62 - 2 \times 142}{195 - 62} = \frac{-27}{133} = \mathbf{-0.2}$$

$Q_3 = 260$; $Q_1 = 80$
Median $= 155$

$$Sk = \frac{260 + 80 - 2 \times 155}{260 - 80} = \frac{30}{180} = \mathbf{0.17}$$

Problem 33. From the information given below calculate Karl Pearson's coefficient of skewness and also quartile coefficient of skewness.

Measure	*Place A*	*Place B*
Mean	256.5	240.8
Median	201.0	201.6
S.D.	215.4	181.1
Third quartile	260.0	242.0
First quartile	157.0	164.2

(*B.Com. Mysore*)

Solution : *Place A:*

The value of mode is not given therefore it is to be found out by using the following formula.

$$\begin{aligned} \text{Mode} &= 3 \text{ Median} - 2 \text{ Mean} \\ \text{Median} &= 201; \text{ Mean } = 256.5 \\ \text{Mode} &= 3(201) - 2(256.5) \\ &= 603 - 513 \\ &= \mathbf{90}. \\ \text{Sk} &= \frac{\overline{X} - \text{Mode}}{\sigma} \\ \overline{X} &= 256.5; \text{Mode} = 90; \sigma = 215.4 \end{aligned}$$

$$\text{Sk} = \frac{256.5 - 90}{215.4}$$
$$= \frac{166.5}{215.4}$$
$$= \mathbf{0.773}.$$

Place B :

$$\text{Mode} = 3 \text{ Median} - 2 \text{ Mean}$$
$$\text{Median} = 201.6; \text{ Mean} = 240.8$$
$$\text{Mode} = 3(201.6) - 2(240.8)$$
$$= 604.8 - 481.6$$
$$= \mathbf{123.2}$$
$$\text{Sk} = \frac{\overline{X} - \text{ mode}}{\sigma}$$
$$\overline{X} = 240.8; \text{ mode} = 123.2; \sigma = 181.1$$
$$\text{Sk.} = \frac{240.8 - 123.2}{181.1}$$
$$= \frac{117.6}{181.1}$$
$$= 0.649$$
$$= \mathbf{0.65}.$$

Quartile Coefficient of Skewness

Place A

$$\text{Sk.} = \frac{Q_3 + Q_1 - 2 \text{ Med}}{Q_3 - Q_1}$$
$$Q_3 = 260; \; Q_1 = 157; \; \text{Med} = 201$$
$$\text{Sk} = \frac{260 + 157 - 2\,(201)}{260 - 157}$$
$$= \frac{417 - 402}{103}$$
$$= \frac{15}{103}$$
$$= \mathbf{0.146}.$$

Place B

$$\text{Sk.} = \frac{Q_3 + Q_1 - 2\text{Med}}{Q_3 - Q_1}$$
$$Q_3 = 242; \; Q_1 = 164.2; \; \text{Med} = 210.6$$
$$\text{Sk} = \frac{242 + 164.2 - 2\,(201.6)}{242 - 164.2}$$
$$= \frac{406.2 - 403.2}{77.8}$$
$$= \frac{3}{77.8}$$
$$= 0.385$$
$$= \mathbf{0.039}.$$

Problem 34. Calculate coefficient of skewness from the following data by the Karl Pearson's method.

Wages in Rs. More than	*No. of workers*	*Wages in Rs. more than*	*No. of workers*
0	100	40	25
10	90	50	15
20	75	60	5
30	50	70	0

(*B.Com. Madras, Delhi*)

Solution :

First convert the cumulative frequency into simple frequency then calculate coefficient of skewness :

Wages Rs.	*f*	*m.p.*	$d' = \frac{m-35}{10}$	*fd'*	*fd'2*	*c.f.*
0–10	10	5	–3	–30	90	10
10–20	15	15	–2	–30	60	25
20–30	25	25	–1	–25	25	50
30–40	25	35	0	0	0	75
40–50	10	45	1	10	10	85
50–60	10	55	2	20	40	95
60–70	5	65	3	15	45	100
	$N = 100$			$\Sigma fd' = -40$	$\Sigma fd'^2 = 270$	

Coefficient of skewness = 3 ($\overline{X}$– Median)

$$\text{Mean} = A \pm \frac{fd'}{N} \times C = 35 - \frac{40}{100} \times 10 = 35 - 4 = \mathbf{31}$$

Standard deviation

$$= \sqrt{\frac{270}{100} - \frac{(-4)^2}{100}} \times 10$$
$$= \sqrt{2.7 - 0.16} \times 10$$
$$= \sqrt{2.54} \times 10$$
$$= 1.594 \times 10 = \mathbf{15.94}$$

Median = 50 th item, which lies in the class 20–30

$$= 20 + \frac{50-25}{25} \times 10 = \mathbf{30}$$

$$\text{Coefficient of skewness} = \frac{3(31-30)}{15.94} = \frac{3}{15.94} = \mathbf{+0.188}$$

Problem 35. Consider the following distribution :

	Distribution A	*Distribution B*
Mean	100	90
Median	90	80
Standard deviation	10	10

(*a*) Distribution has the same degree of variation as distribution *B*.

(*b*) Both distributions have the same degree of skewness.

True or false. (*B.Com. Delhi*)

Solution :

$$(a)\ \text{C.V. (for distribution } A) = \frac{\sigma A}{\overline{X}A} \times 100$$

$$\sigma = 10;\ \overline{X} + 100$$

$$\text{C.V.} = \frac{10}{100} \times 100$$
$$= \mathbf{10\%}.$$

$$\text{C.V. (For distribution } B) = \frac{10}{90} \times 100$$
$$= \mathbf{11.1\%}.$$

(*a*) False. The coefficients of variations of distribution *A* and *B* are different. Degree of variation is different.

(*b*) Coefficient of Distribution *A* :

$$\text{Sk.} = \frac{3\text{ Mean} - \text{ Median}}{\sigma}$$

$$\overline{X} = 100; \text{ Median} = 90; \sigma = 10$$

$$\text{Sk.} = \frac{3(100-90)}{10} = \frac{30}{10}$$

$$= \mathbf{3}.$$

Coefficient of Distribution *B*:

$$\overline{X} = 90; \text{ median} = 80; \sigma = 10$$

$$\text{Sk.} = \frac{3(90-90)}{10} = \frac{30}{10} = \mathbf{3}.$$

(*b*) True. Distribution *A* and *B* have the same degree of Skewness.

Problem 36. The following table gives the distribution of population in towns *A* and *B* in age groups. Compare the variation and skewness of their frequencies.

	Population in '000	
Age group	*A*	*B*
0–10	18	10
10–20	16	12
20–30	15	24
30–40	12	32
40–50	10	29
50–60	5	11
60–70	2	3
Above 70	1	1

(*B.Com.*)

Solution :

Computation of Variation and Skewness

A							*B*				
Age group	*m*	*f*	$d' = \frac{m-25}{10}$	fd'	fd'^2	c.f.	*f*	fd'	fd'^2	c.f.
0–10	5	18	–2	–36	72	18	10	–20	40	10
10–20	15	16	–1	–16	16	34	12	–12	12	22
20–30	25	15	0	0	0	49	24	0	0	46
30–40	35	12	1	12	12	61	32	32	32	78
40–50	45	10	2	20	40	71	29	58	116	107
50–60	55	5	3	15	45	76	11	33	99	118
60–70	65	2	4	8	32	78	3	12	48	121
70–80	75	1	5	5	25	79	1	5	25	122
		$N = 79$		$\Sigma fd' = +8$	$\Sigma fd'^2 = 242$		$N = 122$	$\Sigma fd' = 108$	$\Sigma fd'^2 = 372$	

Place A

Mean : $\overline{X} = A + \frac{\Sigma fd'}{N} \times C$

$A = 25;\ \Sigma fd' = 8;\ N = 79;\ C = 10$

$\overline{X} = 25 + \frac{8}{79} \times 10 = 25 + 1.01$

$= \mathbf{26.01}$

Standard Deviation

$\sigma = \sqrt{\frac{\Sigma fd'^2}{N} - \left(\frac{\Sigma fd'}{N}\right)^2} \times C$

$\Sigma fd'^2 = 242;\ N = 79;\ \Sigma fd' = 8;$

$C = 10$

$\sigma = \sqrt{\frac{242}{79} - \left(-\frac{8}{79}\right)^2} \times 10$

$= \sqrt{3.063 - (0.101)^2} \times 10$

$= \sqrt{3.063 - 0.01} \times 10$

$= \sqrt{3.053} \times 10 = 1.747 \times 10$

$= \mathbf{17.5\ Years}$

C.V. $= \frac{\sigma}{\overline{X}} \times 100$

$= \frac{17.5}{26.01} \times 100 = \mathbf{67.3\%}$

Median = Size of $\frac{N}{2}$ th item

= Size of $\frac{79}{2}$th item

= 39.5th item which lies in the class 20–30

Median $= L_1 + \frac{\frac{N}{2} - c.f.}{f} \times i$

$L_1 = 20;\ \frac{N}{2} = 39.5;\ c.f. = 34;$

$f = 15;\ i = 10$

Median $= 20 + \frac{39.5 - 34}{15} \times 10$

$= 20 + 3.67 = $ **23.67 Yrs.**

Coefficient of Skewness

$Sk = \frac{3(\text{Mean} - \text{Median})}{\sigma}$

$\sigma = \mathbf{17.5}$

$\overline{X} = 26.01;$ Median $= 23.67$

$Sk = \frac{3(26.01 - 23.67)}{17.5}$

$= \frac{7.02}{17.5}$

$= \mathbf{0.40.}$

Place B

$A = 25;\ \Sigma fd' = 108;\ N = 122;$

$C = 10$

$\overline{X} = 25 + \frac{108}{122} \times 10 = 25 + 8.85$

$= \mathbf{33.85}$

Standard Deviation

$\Sigma fd'^2 = 372;\ N = 122;\ \Sigma fd' = 108;$

$C = 10$

$\sigma = \sqrt{\frac{372}{122} - \left(\frac{108}{122}\right)^2} \times 10$

$= \sqrt{3.049 - (0.885)^2} \times 10$

$= \sqrt{3.049 - 0.784} \times 10$

$= \sqrt{2.265} \times 10 = 1.505 \times 10$

$= \mathbf{15.05}$ Yrs

$\sigma = 15.05;\ \overline{X} = 33.85$

C.V. $= \frac{15.05}{33.85} \times 100 = \mathbf{44.5\%}$

Median $= \frac{122}{2} = 61$th item

Which lies in the class 30–40

Median :

$L_1 = 30;\ \frac{N}{2} = 61;\ c.f. = 46;$

$f = 32;\ i = 10$

Median $= 30 + \frac{61 - 46}{32} \times 10$

$= 30 + 4.69 = $ **34.69 Yrs.**

Coefficient of Skewness

Mean = 33.85; Median = 34.69; $\sigma = 15.05$

$Sk = \frac{3(33.85 - 34.69)}{15.05}$

$= \frac{-2.52}{15.05}$

$= \mathbf{-0.17.}$

Problem 37. The following facts were gathered before and after an industrial dispute.

	Before dispute	*After dispute*
No. of workers	516	508
Mean wages	Rs. 49.50	Rs. 51.75
Median wages	Rs. 52.70	Rs. 50.00
Variance of wages	100	121

Compare the position before and after the dispute in respect of (*a*) total wages, (*b*) median wages, (*c*) modal wages, (*d*) standard deviation, (*e*) coefficient of variation and (*f*) skewness. (*C.A.*)

Solution:

	Before dispute		*After dispute*
(*a*)	Total wages ($\overline{X} \times N$) Rs. 49.50 × 516 =**25542**	(*a*)	Rs. 51.75 × 508 = **26289.**
(*b*)	Median wages (given) **Rs. 52.70**	(*b*)	**Rs. 50.00.**
(*c*)	Modal wages Mode = 3 Med − 2 Mean = 3 × 52.70 − 2 × 49.50 = 158.10 − 99 = **59.10.**	(*c*)	$Z = 3 \times 50 - 2 \times 51.75$ = 150 − 103.50 = 46.50
(*d*)	Standard deviation $\sigma = \sqrt{100} = \mathbf{10}.$	(*d*)	$\sigma = \sqrt{121} = \mathbf{11}.$
(*e*)	Coefficient of variation $\text{C.V.} = \frac{\sigma}{\overline{X}} \times 100$ $= \frac{10}{49.50} \times 100$ = **20.2%**	(*e*)	$\text{C.V.} = \frac{11}{51.75} \times 100$ = **21.26%.**
(*f*)	Skewness $\text{Sk.} = \frac{3(\text{ mean} - \text{Med})}{\sigma}$ $\frac{3(49.5 - 52.72)}{10}$ = **−0.96.**	(*f*)	$\text{Sk.} = \frac{3(51.75) -- 50}{11}$ = **+0.48.**

(*a*) Total wage bill has gone up to Rs. 26,289. There is an additional amount of Rs. 747 which has to be paid by the firm. The workers gain and it is a loss to the firm. But the production can be increased by bringing the industrial peace.

(*b*) The median wage has come down from Rs. 52.70 to 50.00. The number of employees also reduced to 508 (after dispute). This shows that there might be more changes in the extremes.

(*c*) After the dispute most of the workers get Rs. 46.50 as against Rs. 59.10 (before dispute). It means after the dispute concentration of wages around smaller value.

(*d*) After the dispute the variability in individual wages has increased.

(*e*) On the basis of the coefficient of variation, we can conclude that after the settlement the variability has increased. It means that the wages are not distributed in a uniform manner. Thus the variability is increased and is a loss to the workers.

(*f*) Before the dispute the distribution was negatively skewed. After the dispute the negative skewness has become positive skewness. It means the number of workers getting higher wages has decreased. The number of workers getting low wages has increased.

Problem 38. The following facts were gathered from a firm before and after an industrial dispute :

	Before dispute	*After dispute*
Mean wages	185	190
Median wages	182	180
Modal wages	176	160
Quartiles	175,192	175,195
S.D.	13	19
Persons employed	600	550

Compare the position of the firm before and after the dispute by making use to the above as fully as possible. *(C.A. M.B.A. Himachal)*

Solution :

	Before dispute	*After dispute*
1.	Total wage $= 185 \times 600$ $= 1,11,000$	Total wage $= 190 \times 550$ $= 1,04,500$
2.	Median=182 Mode = 176	Median = 180 Mode = 160
4.	C.V. $= \frac{13 \times 100}{185} = 7.03\%$	C.V. $= \frac{19}{190} \times 100 = 10\%$
5.	S.K. $(k) = \frac{3\ (185 - 182)}{13}$ $= \mathbf{0.69}$	S.K.$(k) = \frac{3(190 - 180)}{19}$ $= \mathbf{1.58}$
6.	S.K. $(B) = \frac{192 + 175 - 2 \times 182}{192 - 175}$ $= \frac{3}{17} = +\ \ 0.18.$	S.K. $(B) = \frac{195 + 175 - 2 \times 180}{195 - 175}$ $= \frac{10}{20} = +.5$

1. Number of workers has come down from 600 to 550. But mean wage has increased from Rs. 185 to Rs. 190. It implies that labourers at the low level have been retrenched.

2. The median wages has come down from Rs. 182 to 180. However the median is not affected by extreme values.

3. The modal wage has come down from 176 to Rs. 160. It means that the effect of the settlement on the low wage level is concentrated.

4. Quartile three gone up from 192 to 195. It means that more wages are earned by half of the employees, after the dispute.

5. C.V. has gone upto 10% (after settlement) from 7.03%. It means variability has increased after the settlement.

6. Since the Sk is 1.58 (after settlement) whereas the Sk. was 0.69 (before dispute), the distribution is more skewed after the dispute. The number of persons getting high wages has increased.

7. Bowley's measure also indicates that the distribution is more skewed after the dispute.

Problem 39. You are given the following information before and after the settlement of an industrial dispute:

	Before the dispute	*After the dispute*
No. of workers	1000	950
Average wage	308	325
Standard deviation	25	20
Median wage	320	300

Comment on the gains and losses from the point of view of workers and that of management.

(*M.B.A. Delhi*)

Solution .

	Before Settlement		*After Settlement*
(*a*)	Total wage = 308 × 1000 = 3, 08,000	(*a*)	Rs. 325 × 950 = Rs. 3,08,750
(*b*)	Workers 1000	(*b*)	950
(*c*)	Mode = 3 Median - 2 Mean = 3 × 320 − 2 × 308 = 960 − 616 = Rs. 344	(*c*)	Mode = 3 Median-2 Mean = 3 × 300 − 2 × 325 = 900 − 650 = Rs. 250
(*d*)	$\text{C.V.} = \frac{\sigma}{\overline{\overline{X}}} \times 100$ $= \frac{25}{308} \times 100$ = 8.12%	(*d*)	$C.V. = \frac{\sigma}{\overline{\overline{X}}} \times 100$ $= \frac{20}{325} \times 100$ = 6.15%
(*e*)	$Sk = \frac{3\,(\text{Mean} - \text{Median})}{\sigma}$ $= \frac{3(308 - 320)}{25}$ = −1.44	(*e*)	$Sk = \frac{3(\text{Mean} - \text{Median})}{\sigma}$ $= \frac{3(325 - 300)}{-20}$ = + 3.75

(*a*) The total wages paid by the management after the settlement, has increased from Rs. 3,08,000 to Rs. 3,08,750. At the same time, the number of workers has gone down from 1000 to 950. Thus there is an advantage to the workers and disadvantage to the management as the wage bill has increased, irrespective of the decreased number of employees.

(*b*) The number of employees has come down after the settlement from 1000 to 950. It may affect the efficiency of work adversely.

(*c*) The value of modal wage has come down from Rs. 344 to 250. It mean s, following the settlement, there is concentration of wages at the low level.

(*d*) The distribution of wages after the settlement is more uniform. Workers get more satisfaction as there is less disparity in wages. The C.V. is 8.12% (Before dispute) and now the C.V. is 6.15%. Thus, after the settlement, greater satisfaction to the workers is expected.

(*e*) The negative skewed distribution has become highly positively skewed distribution after the settlement. It implies that number of employees getting higher wages have decreased.

Problem 40. The following information was obtained from the records of a factory relating to wages :

Arithemetic mean = Rs. 56.8, Median = Rs. 59.5.

Standard Deviation = Rs. 12.4.

Give as much information as you can about the distribution of wages. *(B.Com., Punjab)*

Solution.

$$\text{Coefficient of Skewness} = \frac{3(\text{ Mean} - \text{ Median})}{\sigma}$$

$$\overline{X} = 56.8; \text{ Median} = 59.5; \sigma = 12.4$$

$$= \frac{3(56.8 - 59.5)}{12.4} = \frac{3 \times -2.7}{12.4}$$

$$= -0.65$$

Mode can be estimated by using the formula

$$\text{Mode} = 3 \text{ Median} - 2 \text{ Mean}$$

$$= 3 \times 59.5 - 2 \times 56.8$$

$$= 178.5 - 113.6$$

$$= \mathbf{64.9}.$$

Problem 41. In a distribution Mean = 65, Median =70, Coefficient of skewness = −0.6. Find (*i*) mode, (*ii*) Coefficient of variation. *(C.A.)*

Solution :

$$\text{Mode} = 3 \text{ Median} - 2 \text{ Mean}$$

$$= 3 \times 70 - 2 \times 65$$

$$= 210 - 130$$

$$= \mathbf{80}.$$

$$\text{Coefficient of Skewness} = \frac{(\text{ Mean} - \text{ Median})}{\sigma}$$

$$\overline{X} = 65; \text{ Mode} = 80; Sk = -0.6$$

$$-0.6 = \frac{65 - 80}{\sigma}$$

$$\sigma = \frac{15}{0.6}$$

$$= \mathbf{25}.$$

Coefficient of Variation :

$$C.V. = \frac{\sigma}{\overline{X}} \times 100$$

$$= \frac{25}{65} \times 100$$

$$= \mathbf{38.46\%}.$$

Problem 42. For a distribution Bowley's coefficient of skewness is -0.36, $Q_1 = 8.6$ and median $= 12.3$ What is its quartile coefficient of dispersion ? *(B.Com., Punjab)*

Solution :

Bowley's Coefficient of Skewness $= \dfrac{Q_3 + Q_1 - 2 \text{ median}}{Q_3 - Q_1}$

$Sk = -0.36$; $Q_1 = 8.6$; Median $= 12.3$

$$\begin{aligned}
-0.36 &= \frac{Q_3 + 8.6 - 2 \times 12.3}{Q_3 - 8.6} \\
-0.36\,Q_3 + 3.096 &= Q_3 + 8.6 - 2 \times 12.3 \\
-1.36\,Q_3 &= 8.6 - 24.6 - 3.096 \\
-1.36\,Q_3 &= 8.6 - 27.696 \\
-1.36\,Q_3 &= -19.096 \\
\therefore \quad Q_3 &= \frac{19.096}{1.36} \\
&= \mathbf{14.04}
\end{aligned}$$

Coefficient of Quartile deviation

$$\begin{aligned}
&= \frac{Q_3 - Q_1}{Q_3 + Q_1} \\
&= \frac{14.04 - 8.6}{14.04 + 8.6} \\
&= \frac{5.44}{22.64} \\
&= \mathbf{0.24}
\end{aligned}$$

Problem 43. Compute quartile Deviation and the coefficient of skewness from the following values :

$M = 18.8''$ $Q_1 = 14.6''$ $Q_3 = 25.2''$

(B.Com., Delhi)

Solution.

$$\begin{aligned}
\text{Quartile Deviation} &= \frac{Q_3 - Q_1}{2} \\
Q_3 &= 25.2;\ Q_1 = 14.6 \\
&= \frac{25.2 - 14.6}{2} \\
&= \frac{10.6}{2} \\
&= \mathbf{5.3.}
\end{aligned}$$

$$\begin{aligned}
\text{Coefficient of Skewness} &= \frac{Q_3 + Q_1 - 2 \text{ Median}}{Q_3 - Q_1} \\
Q_3 &= 25.2;\ Q_1 = 14.5;\ \text{Median} = 18.8 \\
&= \frac{25.2 + 14.6 - 2 \times 18.8}{25.2 - 14.6} \\
&= \frac{39.8 - 37.6}{10.6} \\
&= \frac{2.2}{10.6} \\
&= \mathbf{0.207.}
\end{aligned}$$

Problem 44. The Median, Mode and coefficient of skewness for a certain distribution are respectively 17.4, 15.3 and 0.35. Calculate the coefficient of variation.

(*I.C.W.A., Final*)

Solution :

Median = 17.4; Mode = 15.3; $Sk = 0.35$

In a moderately assymmetrical distribution

$$\text{Mode} = 3 \text{ Median} - 2 \text{ Mean}$$

$$\text{Mean} = \frac{(3 \text{ Median} - \text{ Mode})}{2}$$

$$\overline{X} = \frac{(3 \times 17.4 - 15.3)}{2} = \frac{36.9}{2}$$

$$= \mathbf{18.45}$$

$$\text{Karl Pearson's Coefficient of Skewness} = \frac{\overline{X} - \text{ Mode}}{\sigma}$$

$$0.35 = \frac{18.45 - 15.3}{\sigma}$$

$$\sigma = \frac{18.45 - 15.3}{0.35} = \frac{3.15}{0.35}$$

$$= \mathbf{9}.$$

Coefficient of Variation:

$$C.V. = \frac{\sigma}{\overline{X}} \times 100 = \frac{9}{18.45} \times 100$$

$$= \mathbf{48.78\%}.$$

Problem 45. From the marks secured by 120 students in section A and 120 students in section B of a class, the following measures are obtained :

Section $A\ \overline{X} = 46.83$, $S.D. = 14.8$

Section $B\ \overline{X} = 47.83$, $S.D. = 14.8$

Section (A) $Z = 51.67$

Section (B) $Z = 47.07$

Determine which distribution of marks is more skewed. (*B.Com., Mysore*)

Solution :

We have to compute the coefficient of Skewness for both the sections, A and B.

Section A :

$$Sk = \frac{\text{Mean} - \text{ Mode}}{S.D.}$$

$$\overline{X} = 46.83;\ Z = 51.67\ \sigma = 14.8$$

$$= \frac{46.83 - 51.67}{14.8}$$

$$= \frac{-4.84}{14.8}$$

$$= \mathbf{-0.327}.$$

Section B :

$$\text{Mean} = 47.83;\ \text{Mode} = 47.07;\ S.D. = 14.8$$

$$Sk = \frac{47.83 - 47.07}{14.8} = \frac{0.76}{14.8} = \mathbf{0.0514}.$$

Problem 46. You are given Mean = 50, $C.V. = 40\%$ Sk = -0.4
You are required to find standard deviation, mode and median.

(C.A.)

Solution :

$$\overline{X} = 50;\ C.V.\ 40\%$$

$$C.V. = \frac{\sigma}{\overline{X}} \times 100 = 40\% = \frac{\sigma}{50} \times 100$$

$$\text{or} \quad 40 = 2\sigma \quad \text{or} \quad 2\sigma 40$$

$$\sigma = \mathbf{20}.$$

$$\text{Coefficient of Skewness} = \frac{\text{Mean} - \text{Mode}}{\sigma}$$

$$-0.4 = \frac{50 - \text{Mode}}{20}$$

$$20 \times -0.4 = 50 - \text{Mode} = -8 = 50 - \text{Mode}$$

$$\text{Mode} = 50 + 8 = \mathbf{58}.$$

$$\text{Mean} - \text{Mode} = 3(\text{Mean} - \text{Median})$$

$$50 - 58 = 3(50 - \text{Median})$$

$$-8 = 150 - 3\ \text{Median}$$

$$3\ \text{Median} = 150 + 8$$

$$\text{Median} = \frac{158}{3} = \mathbf{52.67}.$$

Problem 47. From a moderately skewed distribution of retail prices for men's shoes, it is found that the mean price is Rs. 20 and the median price is Rs. 17. If the coefficient of variation is 20%, find the pearsonian coefficient of skewness of the distribution.

(B.Com. Bombay)

Solution :

$$Sk. = \frac{(3\ \text{Mean} - \text{Median})}{S.D.}$$

Mean = 20; Median = 17 . To find the Coefficient of Skewness we need Standard Deviation.

$$C.V. = \frac{\sigma}{\text{Mean}} \times 100$$

$$20 = \frac{\sigma}{20} \times 100$$

$$5\sigma = 20$$

$$\sigma = \frac{20}{5}$$

$$= 4$$

$$Sk. = \frac{3(20-17)}{4}$$

$$= \frac{9}{4}$$

$$= \mathbf{2.25}.$$

Problem 48. For a moderately skewed distribution, arithmetic mean = 160, mode = 157 and standard deviation = 50. Find (*a*), Coefficient of variation, (*b*) Pearsonian coefficient of skewness, and, (*c*) Median. (*B.Com., Bombay*)

Solution :

(*a*)
$$C.V. = \frac{\sigma}{\overline{X}} \times 100 \qquad \sigma = 50; \overline{X} = 160$$

$$= \frac{50}{160} \times 100$$

$$= \mathbf{31.25\%}.$$

(*b*) Pearsonian coefficient of skewness :

$$Sk. = \frac{\overline{X} - \text{Mode}}{\sigma} \qquad \overline{X} = 160; \ \text{Mode} = 157; \sigma = 50$$

$$= \frac{160-157}{50} = \frac{3}{50}$$

$$= \mathbf{+0.06}.$$

(*c*)
$$\text{Median} = \frac{1}{3}(2 \text{ Mean} + \text{ Mode})$$

$$= \frac{1}{3}(2 \times 160 + 157)$$

$$= \frac{1}{3}(320 + 157)$$

$$= \frac{1}{3} \times 477$$

$$= \mathbf{159}.$$

Problem 49. For a group of 10 items $\Sigma X = 452$, $\Sigma \overline{X}^2 = 24,270$ and Mode = 43.7. Find the Pearsonian coefficient of skewness.

(*B.Com. Bombay*)

Solution :

$$\text{Mean} : \overline{X} = \frac{\Sigma X}{N} \Sigma X = 452; N = 10$$

$$= \frac{452}{10}$$

$$= \mathbf{45.2}$$

$$\text{Standard Deviation} = \sqrt{\frac{\Sigma X^2}{N} - \left(\frac{\Sigma X}{N}\right)^2}$$

$$\Sigma X^2 = 24,270; N = 10; \Sigma X = 452$$

$$\sigma = \sqrt{\frac{24,270}{10} - \left(\frac{452}{10}\right)^2}$$

$$= \sqrt{2427 - (45.2)^2}$$

$$= \sqrt{2427 - 2043.04}$$
$$= \sqrt{383.96}$$
$$= \mathbf{19.59}.$$

Karl Pearson's Coefficient of Skewness :

$$Sk. = \frac{\overline{X} - \text{Mode}}{\sigma}$$
$$\overline{X} = 45.2;\ \text{Mode} = 43.7;\ \sigma = 19.59$$
$$= \frac{45.2 - 43.7}{19.59} = \frac{1.5}{19.59}$$
$$= \mathbf{0.077}.$$

Problem 50. The Karl Pearson's coefficient of skewness of a distribution is 0.32. Its standard deviation is 6.5 and the mean is 29.6. Find the mode. (*B.Com. Mysore*)

Solution :

$$Sk. = \frac{\overline{X} - Z}{\sigma}$$
$$0.32 = \frac{29.6 - Z}{6.5}$$
$$2.08 = 29.6 - Z$$
$$Z = 29.6 - 2.08$$
$$= \mathbf{27.52}.$$

Problem 51. You are given : Mean = 15; Coefficient of variance = 30%; Skewness = −0.667. Find standard deviation, mode and median. (*CA*)

Solution :

$$C.V. = \frac{\sigma}{\overline{X}} \times 100$$
$$30 = \frac{\sigma}{15} \times 100$$
$$450 = 100\sigma$$
$$\sigma = \frac{450}{100}$$
$$= \mathbf{4.5}$$

$$\text{Pearson's coefficient of skewness} = \frac{\overline{X} - Z}{\sigma}$$

$$\text{S.k.} = -0.667;\ \overline{X} = 15;\ \sigma = 4.5$$
$$-0.667 = \frac{15 - Z}{4.5}$$
$$-3 = 15 - Z$$
$$Z = 15 + 3 = \mathbf{18}$$
$$\text{Median} = \frac{1}{3}(2\ \text{Mean} + \text{Mode})$$
$$= \frac{1}{3}(2 \times 15 + 18)$$
$$= \frac{1}{3} \times 48$$
$$= \mathbf{16}$$

Problem 52. Find coefficient of skewness from the following information.

Difference of the two quartiles = 8

Sum of the two quarliles = 22

Median = 10.5

(*B.Com. Rajasthan*)

Solution.

Bowley's Coefficient of Skewness :

$$Sk = \frac{Q_3 + Q_1 - 2 \text{ Median}}{Q_3 - Q_1}$$

$$Q_3 + Q_1 = 22$$

$$Q_3 - Q_1 = 8$$

$$\text{Median} = 10.5$$

$$\frac{22 - 2 \times 10.5}{8}$$

$$= \frac{1}{8}$$

$$= \mathbf{0.125}.$$

Problem 53. The measure of skewness for a certain distribution is −0.8. If the lower and the upper quartiles are 44.1 and 56.6 respectively, find the median.

(*ICWA*)

Solution :

$$\text{Bowley's Coefficient of Skewness} = \frac{Q_3 + Q_1 - 2 \text{ Median}}{Q_3 - Q_1}$$

$$Sk = -0.8; Q_3 = 56.6; Q_1 = 44.1$$

$$-0.8 = \frac{56.6 + 44.1 - 2 \text{ Median}}{56.6 - 44.1}$$

$$-0.8 = \frac{100.7 - 2 \text{ Median}}{12.5}$$

$$-0.8 \times 12.5 = 100.7 - 2\text{Median}$$

$$2 \text{ Median} = 100.7 + 10 = 110.7$$

$$\text{Median} = \frac{110.7}{2}$$

$$= \mathbf{55.35}.$$

Problem 54. In a frequency distribution the coefficient of skewness based on quartiles is 0.6. If the sum of the upper and lower quartiles is 100 and median is 38, find the value of upper quartile.

(*B.Com. Delhi*)

Solution :

$$\text{Bowley's Coefficient of Skewness} = \frac{Q_3 + Q_1 - 2 \text{ Median}}{Q_3 - Q_1}$$

$$Sk = 0.6; Q_3 + Q_1 = 100; \text{ Median} = 38$$

$$0.6 = \frac{100 - 2 \times 38}{Q_3 - Q_1}$$

$$Q_2 - Q_1 = \frac{100 - 76}{0.6} = \frac{24}{0.6}$$

$$= \mathbf{40}.$$

$$\begin{aligned} Q_3 + Q_1 &= 100 \\ Q_3 - Q_1 &= 40 \\ \therefore \quad 2Q_3 &= 100 + 40 = 140 \\ Q_3 &= \frac{140}{2} \\ &= \mathbf{70}. \end{aligned}$$

$$\text{Further,} \quad Q_1 = 100 - 70 = 30$$

Problem 55. From the data given below calculate the coefficient of variation.

Pearson's measure of skewness = 0.42
Arithmetic mean = 86
Median = 80

(*C.A.*)

Solution :

Karl Pearson's Coefficient of Skewness :

$$\begin{aligned} Sk &= \frac{3(\text{ Mean } - \text{ Median})}{\sigma} \\ Sk &= 0.42, \overline{X} = 86; \text{ Median} = 80 \\ 0.42 &= \frac{3(86 - 80)}{\sigma} \\ 0.42 &= \frac{18}{\sigma} \\ 0.42\sigma &= 18 \\ \sigma &= \frac{18}{0.42} = \mathbf{42.86} \end{aligned}$$

Coefficient of Variation

$$\begin{aligned} &= \frac{\sigma}{\overline{X}} \times 100 \\ \sigma &= 42.86; \overline{X} = 86 \\ C.V. &= \frac{42.86}{86} \times 100 \\ &= \mathbf{49.84}. \end{aligned}$$

Problem 56. The Median mode and coefficient of skewness for a certain distribution are 17.4, 15.3 and 0.35 respectively. Calculate the coefficient of variation.

(*ICWA*)

Solution :

In a mode rately asymmetrical distribution

$$\begin{aligned} \text{Mode} &= 3 \text{ Median} - 2 \text{ Mean} \\ \therefore \quad \text{Mean} &= \frac{1}{2}(3 \text{ Median} - \text{ Mode}) \\ &= \frac{1}{2}(3 \times 17.4 - 15.3) \\ &= \frac{1}{2}(52.2 - 15.3) \end{aligned}$$

$$= \frac{1}{2} \times 36.9$$
$$= \mathbf{18.45.}$$

Karl Pearson's Coefficient of Skewness $= \dfrac{\overline{X} - \text{Mode}}{\sigma}$

$$Sk = 0.35;\ \overline{X} = 18.45;\ \text{Mode} + 15.3$$
$$0.35 = \frac{18.45 - 15.3}{\sigma}$$
$$0.35\sigma = 3.15$$
$$\sigma = \frac{3.15}{0.35}$$
$$= \mathbf{9.}$$

Coefficient of Variation $= \dfrac{\sigma}{\overline{X}} \times 100$

$$\sigma = 9;\ \overline{X} = 18.45$$
$$C.V. = \frac{9}{18.45} \times 100$$
$$= \mathbf{48.78\%.}$$

Problem 57. In a moderately skewed frequency distribution, the mean is Rs. 15 and the median is Rs. 14. If the coefficient of variation is 30% find the Pearsonian coefficient of skewness.

(*B.Com.*)

Solution :

In order to find the coefficient of skewness we have to find out the value of σ and mode.

$$\text{C.V.} = \frac{\sigma}{\overline{X}} \times 100 \qquad \text{C.V.} = 30;\ \overline{X} = 15$$
$$30 = \frac{\sigma}{15} \times 100 \qquad \therefore 100\sigma = 30 \times 15$$
$$\sigma = \frac{450}{100} = \mathbf{4.5}$$
$$\text{Mode} = 3\ \text{Median} - 2\ \text{Mean}$$
$$\text{Median} = 14;\ \overline{X} = 15$$
$$Z = 3 \times 14 - 2 \times 15 = 42 - 30$$
$$= \mathbf{12.}$$

Coefficient of Skewness

$$= \frac{\overline{X} - \text{Mode}}{\sigma}$$
$$\overline{X} = 15;\ \text{Mode} = 12;\ \sigma = 4.5$$
$$Sk = \frac{15 - 12}{4.5} = \frac{3}{4.5}$$
$$= \mathbf{0.67.}$$

Problem 58. The sum of 20 observations is 300 and its sum of square is 5000 and median is 15. Then find its coefficient of skewness and coefficient of variation.

(B.A. Gujarat)

Solution :

$$\overline{X} = \frac{\Sigma X}{N} \quad \Sigma X = 300; N = 20$$

$$= \frac{300}{20} = 15$$

$$\text{Mode} = 3 \text{ Median} - 2 \text{ Mean}; \quad \text{Median} = 15; \overline{X} = 15$$

$$= 3 \times 15 - 2 \times 15$$

$$= 45 - 30 = \mathbf{15}.$$

$$\text{Standard Deviation} = \sqrt{\frac{\Sigma X^2}{N} - \left(\frac{\Sigma X}{N}\right)^2}$$

$$\Sigma X^2 = 5000; N = 20; \Sigma X = 300$$

$$\sigma = \sqrt{\frac{5000}{20} - \left(\frac{300}{20}\right)^2}$$

$$= \sqrt{250 - (15)^2}$$

$$= \sqrt{250 - 225}$$

$$= \sqrt{25}$$

$$= \mathbf{5}.$$

$$\text{Coefficient of Skewness} = \frac{\overline{X} - \text{Mode}}{\sigma}$$

$$\overline{X} = 15; \text{ Mode} = 15; \sigma = 5$$

$$Sk. = \frac{15 - 15}{5}$$

$$= \mathbf{0}.$$

$$\text{Coefficient of Variation} = \frac{\sigma}{\overline{X}} \times 100$$

$$\sigma = 5; \overline{X} = 15$$

$$C.V. = \frac{5}{15} \times 100$$

$$= \mathbf{33.33\%}.$$

Problem 59. From the marks secured by 120 students in Section A, 120 students in section B of a class, the following measures are obtained :

Section A :	$\overline{X} = 46.83$,	S.D. $= 14.8$	$Z = 51.67$
Section B :	$\overline{X} = 47.83$,	S.D. $= 14.8$	$Z = 47.07$

Determine which distribution of marks is more skewed.

(B.Com. Mysore)

Solution :

Section A :

$$Sk. = \frac{\text{Mean} - \text{Mode}}{\sigma}$$

$$\overline{X} = 46.83; \text{ Mode} = 51.67; \sigma = 14.8$$

$$Sk. = \frac{46.83 - 51.67}{14.8} = \frac{-4.84}{14.8} = \mathbf{-0.327}.$$

Section B :

$$\overline{X} = 47.83; \text{ Mode} = 47.07; \sigma = 14.8$$

$$Sk. = \frac{14.83 - 47.07}{14.8} = \frac{0.76}{14.8} = \mathbf{0.0514}.$$

The distribution of marks of section A is more skewed.

MOMENTS

Problem 60 : The first four moments of a distribution about the value 5 are 2, 20, 40 and 50. Obtain, as far as possible, the various characteristics of the distribution on the basis of the information given. Comment upon the nature of the distribution. (*M.Com. Delhi*)

Solution :

$$A = 5; \mu_1' = 2; \mu_2' = 20; \mu_3' = 40; \mu_4' = 50$$

1. $$\text{mean} = A + \mu_1'$$
$$5 + 2 = 7.$$

2. $$\text{Variance} = \mu_2' - (\mu_1')^2 = 20 - (2)^2 = \mathbf{16}.$$

3. $$\mu_3 = \mu_3' - 3\mu_1'\mu_2' + 2\mu_1'^3 = 40 - 3 \times 2 \times 20 + 2 \times (2)^3 = 40 - 120 + 16 = \mathbf{-64}.$$

4. $$\mu_4 = \mu_4' - 4\mu_1'\mu_3' + 6\mu_1'^2\mu_2' - 3\,\mu_1'^4 = 50 - 4 \times 2 \times 40 + 6 \times (2)^2 X 20 - 3X(2)^4 = 50 - 320 + 480 - 48 = \mathbf{162}.$$

$$\beta_1 = \frac{\mu_3^2}{\mu_2^3} = \frac{(-64)^2}{(16)^3} = \frac{4096}{4096} = \mathbf{1}.$$

$$\beta_2 = \frac{\mu_4}{\mu_2^2} = \frac{162}{(16)^2} = \frac{162}{256} = \mathbf{0.63}.$$

Since β_2 is less than 3, the curve is platykurtic.

Problem 61. Find the first four moments for the following distribution :

Size	:	0–5	5–10	10–15	15–20	20–25
Frequency	:	1	2	6	7	4

(*B.Com.*)

Solution :

Size	m	f	$d' = \frac{m - 12.5}{5}$	fd'	fd'^2	fd'^3	fd'^4
0–5	2.5	1	−2	−2	4	−8	16
5–10	7.5	2	−1	−2	2	−2	2
10–15	12.5	6	0	0	0	0	0
15–20	17.5	7	1	7	7	7	7
20–25	22.5	4	2	8	16	32	64
		N= 20		$\Sigma fd' = 11$	$\Sigma fd'^2$=29	$\Sigma fd'^3$ =29	$\Sigma fd'^4$=89

$$\mu_1' = \frac{\Sigma fd'}{N} \times C = \frac{11}{20} \times 5 = 2.75$$

$$\mu_2' = \frac{\Sigma fd'^2}{N} \times C^2 = \frac{29}{20} \times (5)^2 = 36.25$$

$$\mu_3' = \frac{\Sigma fd'^3}{N} \times C^3 = \frac{29}{20} \times (5)^3 = 181.25$$

$$\mu_4' = \frac{\Sigma fd'^4}{N} \times C^4 = \frac{89}{20} \times (5)^4 = 2781.25$$

$$\mu^1 = 0$$

$$\begin{aligned} \mu_2 &= \mu_2' - (\mu_1')^2 = 36.25 - (2.75)^2 \\ &= 36.25 - 7.5625 \\ &= -28.6875 \end{aligned}$$

$$\begin{aligned} \mu_3 &= \mu_3' - 3\mu_1'\mu_2' + 2\mu'3 \\ &= 181.25 - 3(2.75)(36.25) + 2(2.75)^3 \\ &= 181.25 - 299.0625 + 41.5938 \\ &= 222.8438 - 299.0625 \\ &= \mathbf{-76.2187.} \end{aligned}$$

$$\begin{aligned} \mu_4 &= \mu'_4 - 4\mu'_1\mu'_3 + 6\mu'^2\mu'_2 - 3_{\mu_1}{}'^4 \\ &= 2781.25 - 4(2.75)(181.25) + 6(2.75)^2(36.25) - 3(2.75)^4 \\ &= 2781.25 - 1993.75 + 1644.8438 - 171.5742 \\ &= 4426.0938 - 2165.3242 \\ &= \mathbf{2260.7696.} \end{aligned}$$

Problem 62. The first two moments of a distribution about the value 5 of the variable are 2 and 20. Find the mean and the variance.

(*ICWA*)

Solution:

$$\begin{aligned} A &= 5, \mu_1' = 2 \quad \mu_2' = 20 \\ \text{Mean} &= A + \mu_1' \\ &= 5 + 2 \\ &= \mathbf{7.} \end{aligned}$$

$$\begin{aligned}\text{Variance}(\sigma^2) &= \mu_2' - \mu_1'^2 \\ &= 20 - (2)^2 \\ &= 20 - 4 \\ &= \mathbf{16}.\end{aligned}$$

Problem 63. Calculate first four moments from the following data and find out β_1 and β_2.

X	0	1	2	3	4	5	6	7	8
F	5	10	15	20	25	20	15	10	5

(*B.Com.*)

Solution:

Computation of Moments

X	f	fx	$d = (X-4)$	fd	fd^2	fd^3	fd^4
0	5	0	−4	−20	80	−320	1280
1	10	10	−3	−30	90	−270	810
2	15	30	−2	−30	60	−120	240
3	20	60	−1	−20	20	−20	20
4	25	100	0	0	0	0	0
5	20	100	1	20	20	20	20
6	15	90	2	30	60	120	240
7	10	70	3	30	90	270	810
8	5	40	4	20	80	320	1280
	N=125	$\Sigma fx = 500$	$\Sigma d = 0$	$\Sigma fd = 0$	$\Sigma fd^2 = 500$	$\Sigma fd^3 = 0$	$\Sigma fd^4 = 4700$

$$\begin{aligned}\overline{X} &= \frac{\Sigma fx}{N} = \frac{500}{125} = 4 \\ \mu_1 &= \frac{\Sigma fd}{N} = \frac{0}{125} = 0 \\ \mu_2 &= \frac{\Sigma fd^2}{N} = \frac{500}{125} = 4 \\ \mu_3 &= \frac{\Sigma fd^3}{N} = \frac{0}{125} = 0 \\ \mu_4 &= \frac{\Sigma fd^4}{N} = \frac{4700}{125} = 37.6 \\ \beta_2 &= \frac{\mu^4}{\mu_{2^2}} = \frac{37.6}{4^2} = \frac{37.6}{16} = \mathbf{2.35}.\end{aligned}$$

The value of $\beta_2 < 3$, therefore the curve is platykurtic.

$$\beta_1 = \frac{\mu_3^2}{\mu_2^3} = \frac{0^2}{4^3} = 0$$

Problem 64. Calculate the first four moments about the mean and also the value of β_1 and β_2 from the data :

Marks	:	0–10	10–20	20–30	30–40	40–50	50–60	60–70
No. of Students	:	8	12	20	30	15	10	5

(*M.Com. Jodhpur*)

Solution:

Computation of Moments β_1 and β_2

Marks	m	f	$d' = \frac{m-35}{10}$	fd'	fd'^2	fd'^3	fd'^4
0–10	5	8	−3	−24	72	−216	648
10–20	15	12	−2	−24	48	−96	192
20–30	25	20	−1	−20	20	−20	20
30–40	35	30	0	0	0	0	0
40–50	45	15	1	15	15	15	15
50–60	55	10	2	20	40	80	160
60–70	65	5	3	15	45	135	405
		$N = 10$		$\Sigma fd' = -18$	$\Sigma fd'^2 = 240$	$\Sigma fd'^3 = -102$	$\Sigma fd'^4 = 1440$

$$\mu_1' = \frac{\Sigma fd'}{N} \times C = \frac{-18}{100} \times 10 = \mathbf{1.8}$$

$$\mu_2' = \frac{\Sigma fd'^2}{N} \times C^2 = \frac{240}{100} \times 10^2 = \mathbf{240}$$

$$\mu_3' = \frac{\Sigma fd^3}{N} \times C^3 = \frac{-102}{100} \times 10^3 = \mathbf{-1020}$$

$$\mu_4' = \frac{\Sigma fd'^4}{N} \times C^4 = \frac{1440}{100} \times 10^4 = \mathbf{1,44,000}$$

Now we have to convert moments about arbitrary origin to moments about mean.

$$\mu_2 = \mu_2' - (\mu_1')^2 = 240 - (1.8)^2 = 240 - 3.24 = \mathbf{236.76}$$

$$\begin{aligned} \mu_3 &= \mu_3' - 3\mu_1'\mu_2' + 2\mu_1'^3 \\ &= -1020 - 3 \times -1.8 \times 240 + 2 \times (-1.8)^3 \\ &= -1020 + 1296 - 11.664 = 1296 - 1031.664 \\ &= \mathbf{264.336} \end{aligned}$$

$$\begin{aligned} \mu_4 &= \mu_4' - 4\mu_1'\mu_3' + 6(\mu_1')^2\mu_2' - 3(\mu_1')^4 \\ &= 144000 - 4 \times -1.8 \times -1020 + 6(-1.8)^2 \times 240 - 3(-1.8)^4 \\ &= 144000 - 7344 + 4665.6 - 31.49 \\ &= 141290.11 \end{aligned}$$

$$\beta_1 = \frac{\mu_3^2}{\mu_2^3} = \frac{(264.336)^2}{(236.76)^3} = \mathbf{0.005}$$

$$\beta_2 = \frac{\mu_4}{\mu_2^2} = \frac{141290.11}{(236.76)^2} = 2.52$$

Here $\beta_2 = 2.52$ which is less than 3, hence the curve is a platykurtic.

KURTOSIS

Problem 65. The four moments of a frequency distribution about an arbitrary origin are :

$$\mu'_1 = -2;\ \mu'_2 = 14;\ \mu'_3 = -20;\ \mu'_4 = 50$$

Find the value of β_1 and β_2.

(*B.Sc., Madras*)

Solution:

$$\begin{aligned}
\mu_2 &= \mu'_2; - (\mu'_1)^2 \\
&= 14 - (-2)^2 = 10 \\
\mu_3 &= \mu'_3 - 3\mu'_1 \mu'_2 + 2(\mu'_1)^3 \\
&= -20 - 3(-2)(14) + 2(-2)^3 \\
&= -20 + 84 - 16 = 84 - 36 = \mathbf{48} \\
\mu_4 &= \mu'_4 - 4\mu'_1 \mu'_3 + 6(\mu'_1)^2 \mu'_2 - 3(\mu'_1)^4 \\
&= 50 - 4(-2)(-20) + 6(-2)^2(14) - 3(-2)^4 \\
&= 50 - 160 + 336 - 48 \\
&= 386 - 208 = \mathbf{178} \\
\beta_2 &= \frac{\mu_3^2}{\mu_2^3} = \frac{(48)^2}{(10)^3} = \frac{2304}{1000} = 2.304 \\
\beta_2 &= \frac{\mu_4}{\mu_2^2} = \frac{178}{(10)^2} = \frac{178}{100} = \mathbf{1.78}
\end{aligned}$$

Problem 66. The first four central moments of a distribution are 0, 2.5, 0.7 and 18.75. Test the skewness and kurtosis of the distribution. (*M.Com., Delhi*)

Solution:

$$\begin{aligned}
\beta_1 &= \frac{\mu_3^2}{\mu_2^3} \\
&= \frac{(0.7)^2}{(2.5)^3} \\
&= \frac{0.49}{15.625} = \mathbf{+0.031}
\end{aligned}$$

$\therefore$ The distribution is skewed.

$$\begin{aligned}
\beta_2 &= \frac{\mu_4}{\mu_2^2} \\
&= \frac{18.75}{(2.5)^2} \\
&= +3
\end{aligned}$$

$\therefore$ The distribution is symmetrical.

Problem 67. The following data are given to an economist for the purpose of economic analysis. The data refer to the length of the life of a sample of Good Year Tyres. Is the distribution platykurtic ?

$$N = 100; \Sigma f dx = 50; \Sigma f dx^2 = 1967.2;$$
$$\Sigma f dx^3 = 2925.8; \Sigma f dx^4 = 86650.2$$

(*M.Com. Delhi*)

Solution:

$$\begin{aligned}
\mu'_1 &= \frac{\Sigma f dx}{N} = \frac{50}{100} = 0.5 \\
\mu'_2 &= \frac{\Sigma f dx^2}{N} = \frac{1967.2}{100} = 19.672 \\
\mu'_3 &= \frac{\Sigma f dx^3}{N} = \frac{2925.8}{100} = 29.258
\end{aligned}$$

$$\mu'_4 = \frac{\Sigma f dx^4}{N} = \frac{86650.2}{100} = 866.502$$

$$\mu_1 = 0$$

$$\mu_2 = \mu'_2; - (\mu'_1)^2 = 19.672 - (0.5)^2$$

$$= 19.672 - 0.25$$

$$= 19.422$$

$$\mu_3 = \mu'_3 - 3\mu'_1\mu'_2 + 2\mu'^3_1$$

$$= 29.258 - 3(0.5)(19.672) + 2(0.5)^3$$

$$= 29.258 - 29.508 + 0.25 = 0$$

$$\mu_4 = \mu'_4 - 4\mu'_1\,\mu'_3 + 6\,\mu'^2_1\,\mu'_2 - 3\,\mu_1'^4$$

$$= 866.502 - 4(0.5)(29.258) + 6(0.5)^2(19.672) - 3(0.5)^4$$

$$= 866.502 - 58.516 + 29.508 - 0.1875$$

$$= 837.3065$$

$$\beta_2 = \frac{\mu_4}{\mu_2^2}$$

$$= \frac{837.3065}{(19.422)^2}$$

$$= \frac{837.3065}{377.214}$$

$$= \mathbf{2.219}$$

6

CORRELATION

KARL PEARSON'S COEFFICIENT OF CORRELATION, RANK CORRELATION, CONCURRENT DEVIATION

FORMULAE

Karl Pearson' Coefficient of Correlation 1. When deviations are taken from actual mean $r = \frac{\Sigma xy}{N\sigma_x\sigma_y}$ or $= \frac{\Sigma xy}{\sqrt{\Sigma x^2 \times \Sigma y^2}}$	r = Karl Pearson's Coefficient of Correlation $x = (X - \overline{X})$ $y = (Y - \overline{Y})$ N = Number of Pairs of observations σ_x = Standard deviation of X series. σ_y = Standard deviation of Y series.
2. When deviations are taken from assumed mean $r = \frac{\Sigma dxdy - \frac{(\Sigma dx)(\Sigma dy)}{N}}{\sqrt{\Sigma dx^2 - \frac{(\Sigma dx)^2}{N}}\sqrt{\Sigma dy^2 - \frac{(\Sigma dy)^2}{N}}}$	$dx = (X - A)$ $dy = (Y - A)$
3. Bivariate frequency Distribution $r = \frac{\Sigma fdxdy - \frac{(\Sigma fdx)(\Sigma fdy)}{N}}{\sqrt{\Sigma fdx^2 - \frac{(\Sigma fdx)^2}{N}}\sqrt{\Sigma fdy^2 - \frac{(\Sigma fdy)^2}{N}}}$	
4. When we take actual value of X and Y $r = \frac{N\Sigma XY - \Sigma X\Sigma Y}{\sqrt{N\Sigma X^2 - (\Sigma X)^2}\sqrt{N\Sigma Y^2 - (\Sigma Y)^2}}$	
5. Spearman's Rank Correlation Coefficient $r = 1 - \frac{6\Sigma D^2}{N(N^2-1)}$ or $1 - \frac{6\Sigma D^2}{(N^3 - N)}$	r = Spearman's Rank Correlation D = Difference of Rank N = Number of pairs of observations
6. When Ranks are repeated	m = The number of times, the values are repeated or

$r = 1 - \dfrac{6\left[\Sigma D^2 + \frac{1}{12}(m^3 - m) + \frac{1}{12}(m^3 - m)\ldots\right]}{N^3 - N}$	the ranks are common
7. Concurrent Deviation $r_c = \pm\sqrt{\pm\dfrac{2C - N}{N}}$	r_c = Coefficient of correlation by the concurrent deviation method C = Number of concurrent deviations or the number of positive signs N = Number of pairs of deviation compared *i.e.*$(N - 1)$
8. Probable Error $\text{P.E}_r. = 0.6745\ \dfrac{1 - r^2}{\sqrt{N}}$ $\text{S.E}_r. = \dfrac{1 - r^2}{\sqrt{N}}$	P.E$_r$. = Probable Error r = Correlation N = Number of pairs of observation S.E$_r$. = Standard Error
9. Coefficient of Determination $= r^2$ 10. Coefficient of non-Determination $= 1 - r^2$	

CORRELATION

Problem 1. Calculate the coefficient of correlation between x and y from the following data :

X	1	2	3	4	5	6	7
Y	2	4	5	3	8	6	7

(*B.A. Punjab*)

Solution: **Computation of Coefficient of Correlation**

X	$x = (X - \overline{X})$ $\overline{X} = 4$	X^2	Y	$y = Y - \overline{Y}$ $\overline{Y} = 5$	y^2	xy
1	−3	9	2	−3	9	9
2	−2	4	4	−1	1	2
3	−1	1	5	0	0	0
4	0	0	3	−2	4	0
5	1	1	8	3	9	3
6	2	4	6	1	1	2
7	3	9	7	2	4	6
$\Sigma X = 28$		$\Sigma x^2 = 28$	$\Sigma y = 35$		$\Sigma y^2 = 28$	$\Sigma xy = 22$

Mean : $\overline{X} = \dfrac{\Sigma x}{N} = \dfrac{28}{7} = \mathbf{4}.$

Mean : $\overline{Y} = \dfrac{\Sigma y}{N} = \dfrac{35}{7} = \mathbf{5}.$

$$\text{Mean :} \qquad \overline{Y} = \frac{\Sigma y}{N} = \frac{35}{7} = \mathbf{5}.$$

Coefficient of correlation :

$$r = \frac{\Sigma xy}{\sqrt{\Sigma x^2 \times \Sigma y^2}} \qquad \Sigma xy = 22;$$

$$\Sigma x^2 = 28;\ \Sigma y^2 = 28$$

$$= \frac{22}{\sqrt{28 \times 28}} = \frac{22}{28} \quad +0.79$$

Problem 2. Calculate Karl Pearson's coefficient of correlation from the data given below :

X	2	4	6	8	10
Y	12	14	16	18	20

Solution :

Computation of Coefficient of Correlation

X	$dx = \frac{X-6}{2}$	dx^2	Y	$dy = \frac{Y-16}{2}$	dy^2	$dxdy$
2	−2	4	12	−2	4	4
4	−1	1	14	−1	1	1
6	0	0	16	0	0	0
8	1	1	18	1	1	1
10	2	4	20	2	4	4
	$\Sigma dx = 0$	Σdx^2 =10		$\Sigma dy = 0$	Σdy^2 =10	$\Sigma dxdy$ =10

$$\Sigma dxdy = 10$$

$$\Sigma dx^2 = 10$$

$$\Sigma dy^2 = 10$$

$$r = \frac{\Sigma dxdy}{\sqrt{\Sigma dx^2 \times \Sigma dy^2}}$$

$$= \frac{10}{\sqrt{10 \times 10}}$$

$$= \frac{10}{10}$$

$$= +1.$$

Since $r = +1$, there is perfect positive correlation between X and Y.

Problem 3. The following data give the marks obtained by 10 students in Accountancy and Statistics :

R. No.	*Accountancy*	*Statistics*
1	45	35
2	70	90
3	65	70
4	30	40
5	90	95
6	40	40
7	50	60
8	75	80
9	85	80
10	60	50

Find the coefficient of correlation and interpret it.

(*B.Com. Delhi*)

Solution :

(Deviations are taken from actual mean)

Computation of Coefficient of Correlation

X	$dx = (X - \overline{X})$ $\overline{X} = 61$	dx^2	Y	$dy = (Y - \overline{Y})$ $\overline{Y} = 64$	dy^2	$dxdy$
45	−16	256	35	−29	841	464
70	+9	81	90	26	676	234
65	4	16	70	6	36	24
30	−31	961	40	−24	576	744
90	29	841	95	31	961	899
40	−21	441	40	−24	576	504
50	−11	121	60	−4	16	44
75	14	196	80	16	256	224
85	24	576	80	16	256	384
60	−1	1	50	−14	196	14
$\Sigma X = 610$	$\Sigma dx = 0$	$\Sigma dx^2 = 3490$	$\Sigma y = 640$	$\Sigma dy = 0$	$\Sigma dy^2 = 4390$	$\Sigma dxdy = 3535$

Mean : $\overline{X} = \frac{\Sigma X}{N} = \frac{610}{10} = \mathbf{61}$ $\qquad \overline{Y} = \frac{\Sigma Y}{N} = \frac{640}{10} = \mathbf{64}$

Coefficient of Correlation :

$$r = \frac{\Sigma dxdy}{\sqrt{\Sigma dx^2 \times \Sigma dy^2}}$$

$$\Sigma dxdy = 3535 \quad ; \quad \Sigma dx^2 = 3490 \quad ; \quad \Sigma dy^2 = 4390$$

$$r = \frac{3535}{\sqrt{3490 \times 4390}} = \frac{3535}{3914.22} = \mathbf{+0.903}$$

Alternatively :

$$= \text{Antilog}\left[3535 - \frac{1}{2}(\log 3490 + \log 4390)\right]$$

$$= \text{Antilog}\left[3.5484 - \frac{1}{2}(3.5428 + 3.6425)\right]$$

$$= \text{Antilog}\left[3.5484 - \frac{1}{2}(7.1853)\right]$$

$$= \text{Antilog}\ (3.5484 - 3.5927)$$

$$= \text{Antilog}\ \bar{1}.9557$$

$$= 0.9031$$

$$r = \mathbf{+0.903.}$$

Problem 4. (Taking assumed mean).

The above problem (No. 3) is solved by taking deviations from assumed mean. We get similar answer as above.

Solution :

Computation of Coefficient of Correlation

X	$dx = \dfrac{X-65}{5}$	dx^2	Y	$dy = \dfrac{Y-60}{5}$	dy^2	$dxdy$
45	−4	16	35	−5	25	20
70	+1	1	90	+6	36	6
65	0	0	70	+2	4	0
30	−7	49	40	−4	16	28
90	+5	25	95	+7	49	35
40	−5	25	40	−4	16	20
50	−3	9	60	0	0	0
75	+2	4	80	+4	16	8
85	+4	16	80	+4	16	16
60	−1	1	50	−2	4	2
	$\Sigma dx = -8$	$\Sigma dx^2 = 146$		$\Sigma dy = 8$	$\Sigma dy^2 = 182$	$\Sigma dxdy = 135$

$$r = \frac{\Sigma dxdy - \dfrac{\Sigma dx \times \Sigma dy}{N}}{\sqrt{\Sigma dx^2 - \dfrac{(\Sigma dx)^2}{N}}\sqrt{\Sigma dy^2 - \dfrac{(\Sigma dy)^2}{N}}}$$

$\Sigma dxdy = 135; \Sigma dx = -8; \Sigma dy = 8; \Sigma dx^2 = 146 : \Sigma dy^2 = 182; N = 10$

$$= \frac{(135 \times 10) - (-8 \times 8)}{\sqrt{(146 \times 10) - (-8)^2}\sqrt{182 \times 10 - (8)^2}}$$

$$= \frac{1350 + 64}{\sqrt{(1460 - 64)(1820 - 64)}}$$

$$= \frac{1414}{\sqrt{1396 \times 1756}} = \frac{1414}{1565.69}$$

$$= 0.9031$$

$$r = \mathbf{+0.903.}$$

Problem 5. Calculate Karl Pearson's coefficient correlation from the data given below:

X	2	4	6	8	10
Y	20	18	16	14	12

Solution :

Computation of Coefficient of Correlation

X	$dx = \frac{X-6}{2}$	dx^2	Y	$dy = \frac{Y-16}{2}$	dy^2	$dxdy$
2	−2	4	20	2	4	−4
4	−1	1	18	1	1	−1
6	0	0	16	0	0	0
8	1	1	14	−1	1	−1
10	2	4	12	−2	4	−4
	$\Sigma dx = 0$	$\Sigma dx^2 = 10$		$\Sigma dy = 0$	$\Sigma dy^2 = 10$	$\Sigma dxdy = -10$

$$r = \frac{\Sigma dxdy}{\sqrt{\Sigma dx^2 \times \Sigma dy^2}} \qquad \begin{aligned} \Sigma dxdy &= -10 \\ \Sigma dx^2 &= 10 \\ \Sigma dy^2 &= 10 \end{aligned}$$

$$= \frac{-10}{\sqrt{10 \times 10}}$$

$$= \frac{-10}{10}$$

$$= \mathbf{-1}$$

Since $r = -1$, there is perfect negative correlation between X and Y.

Problem 6. From the following table calculate the coefficient of correlation by Karl Pearson's method.

X	6	2	10	4	8
Y	9	11	?	8	7

Arithmetic mean of X and Y are 6 and 8 respectively. (*B.Com. Delhi*)

Solution :

First we have to find out the missing figure in Y series.

$$\textbf{Mean (Y series)} = \frac{9 + 11 + A + 8 + 7}{5} = \frac{35 + A}{5} = 8$$

$$\begin{aligned} 35 + A &= 8 \times 5 \\ A &= 40 - 35 \\ A &= 5 \end{aligned}$$

Computation of Coefficient of Correlation

X	$x = (X - \overline{X})$	x^2	Y	$y = Y\text{-}\overline{Y}$	y^2	xy
6	0	0	9	1	1	0
2	−4	16	11	3	9	−12
10	4	16	5	−3	9	−12
4	−2	4	8	0	0	0
8	2	4	7	−1	1	−2
$\Sigma x = 30$		$\Sigma x^2 = 40$	$\Sigma y = 40$		$\Sigma y^2 = 20$	$\Sigma xy = -26$

Coefficient of Correlation :

$$r = \frac{\Sigma xy}{\sqrt{\Sigma x^2 \times \Sigma y^2}} \qquad \Sigma xy = -26\,;\ \Sigma x^2 = 40\,;\ \Sigma y^2 = 20$$

$$= \frac{-26}{\sqrt{40 \times 20}}$$

$$= \frac{-26}{28.28}$$

$$r = \mathbf{-0.92.}$$

Problem 7. Calculate the coefficient of correlation from the following data shown :

X	12	9	8	10	11	13	7
Y	14	8	6	9	11	12	3

(*B.Com. Baroda*)

Solution : In both the series items are in small number, hence r can be calculated under product method.

Computation of Coefficient of Correlation

X	Y	X^2	Y^2	XY
12	14	144	196	168
9	8	81	64	72
8	6	64	36	48
10	9	100	81	90
11	11	121	121	121
13	12	169	144	156
7	3	49	9	21
$\Sigma X = 70$	$\Sigma Y = 63$	$\Sigma X^2 = 728$	$\Sigma Y^2 = 651$	$\Sigma XY = 676$

$$r = \frac{(\Sigma XY_X N)(\Sigma X \times \Sigma Y)}{\sqrt{\Sigma X^2 \times N - (\Sigma X)^2}\sqrt{\Sigma Y \times N - (\Sigma Y^2)}}$$

$$\Sigma XY = 676; \Sigma X = 70; \Sigma Y = 63; \Sigma X^2 = 728; \Sigma Y^2 = 651; N = 7.$$

$$r = \frac{(676 \times 7) - (70 \times 63)}{\sqrt{728 \times 7 - (70)^2}\sqrt{651 \times 7 - (63)^2}}$$

$$= \frac{4732 - 4410}{\sqrt{5096 - 4900}\sqrt{4557 - 3969}}$$

$$= \frac{322}{\sqrt{196 \times 588}}$$

$$= \frac{322}{339.48}$$

$$= +\,0.9485$$

$$r = \mathbf{+\,0.95}$$

Problem 8. Calculate the coefficient of correlation between X and Y for the values given below :

X	2	5	7	9	19	16
Y	25	27	26	29	34	39

(*B.A. Madurai*)

Solution :

Computation of Coefficient of Correlation

X			Y			
X	$dx = X - 9$	dx^2	Y	$dy = Y - 29$	dy^2	$dxdy$
2	−7	49	25	−4	16	28
5	−4	16	27	−2	4	8
7	−2	4	26	−3	9	6
9	0	0	29	0	0	0
19	10	100	34	5	25	50
16	7	49	39	10	100	70
	$\Sigma dx = 4$	$\Sigma dx^2 = 218$		$\Sigma dy = 6$	$\Sigma dy^2 = 154$	$\Sigma dxdy = 162$

Coefficient of correlation :

$$r = \frac{\Sigma dxdy \times N - \Sigma dx \times \Sigma dy}{\sqrt{\Sigma dx^2 \times N - (\Sigma dx)^2 \times \Sigma dy^2 \times N - (\Sigma dy)^2}}$$

$$\Sigma dxdy = 162; N = 6; \Sigma dx = 4; \Sigma dy = 6; \Sigma dx^2 = 218; \Sigma dy^2 = 154$$

$$\begin{aligned} r &= \frac{162 \times 6 - (4 \times 6)}{\sqrt{218 \times 6 - (4)^2 \times 154 \times 6 - (6)^2}} \\ &= \frac{972 - 24}{\sqrt{1308 - 16 \times 924 - 36}} \\ &= \frac{948}{\sqrt{1292 \times 888}} \\ &= \frac{948}{1071.12} \\ &= \mathbf{+0.885}. \end{aligned}$$

Problem 9. Calculate the coefficient of correlation for the following:

X :	128	140	125	121	122	146
Y :	87	96	101	93	99	140

(*B.Com. Madurai*)

Solution :

Computation of Coefficient of Correlation

X	$dx = X - 128$	dx^2	Y	$dy = Y - 99$	dy^2	$dxdy$
128	0	0	87	−12	144	0
140	+12	144	96	−3	9	−36
125	−3	9	101	+2	4	6
121	−7	49	93	−6	36	+42
122	−6	36	99	0	0	0
146	+18	324	140	+41	1681	738
	$\Sigma dx = 14$	$\Sigma dx^2 = 562$		$\Sigma dy = 22$	$\Sigma dy^2 = 1874$	$\Sigma dxdy = 738$

Coefficient of Correlation :

$$r = \frac{\Sigma dxdy \times N - (\Sigma dx)(\Sigma dy)}{\sqrt{\Sigma dx^2 \times N - (\Sigma dx)^2}\sqrt{\Sigma dy^2 \times N - (\Sigma dy)^2}}$$

$\Sigma dxdy = 738$; $N = 6$; $\Sigma dx = 14$; $\Sigma dy = 22$; $\Sigma dx^2 = 562$; $\Sigma dy^2 = 1874$

$$r = \frac{738 \times 6 - (14)(22)}{\sqrt{526 \times 6 - (14)^2}\sqrt{1874 \times 6 - (22)^2}}$$

$$= \frac{4428 - 308}{\sqrt{3156 - 196}\sqrt{11,244 - 484}}$$

$$= \frac{4120}{\sqrt{2960 \times 10760}}$$

$$= \frac{4120}{5643.54}$$

$$= \mathbf{+0.73}.$$

Problem 10. Calculate the coefficient of correlation from the following data and comment on the result :

Experience (X)	:	16	12	18	4	3	10	5	12
Performance (Y)	:	23	22	24	17	19	20	18	21

(B.Com. Andhra)

Solution :

Computation of Coefficient of Correlation

Experience			*Performance*			
X	$dx = X - 10$	dx^2	Y	$dy = Y - 20$	dy^2	$dxdy$
16	+6	36	23	+3	9	18
12	+2	4	22	+2	4	4
18	+8	64	24	+4	16	32
4	−6	36	17	−3	9	18
3	−7	49	19	−1	1	7
10	0	0	20	0	0	0
5	−5	25	18	−2	4	10
12	+2	4	21	+1	1	2
	$\Sigma dx = 0$	$\Sigma dx^2 = 218$		$\Sigma dy = 4$	$\Sigma dy^2 = 44$	$\Sigma dxdy = 91$

Coefficient of Correlation :

$$r = \frac{\Sigma dxdy \times N - (\Sigma dx)(\Sigma dy)}{\sqrt{\Sigma dx^2 \times N - (\Sigma dx)^2}\sqrt{\Sigma dy^2 \times N - (\Sigma dy)^2}}$$

$\Sigma dxdy = 91; N = 8; \Sigma dx = 0; \Sigma dy = 4;$

$\Sigma dx^2 = 218; \Sigma dy^2 = 44$

$$r = \frac{91 \times 8 - (0)(4)}{\sqrt{218 \times 8 - (0)^2}\sqrt{44 \times 8 - (4)^2}}$$

$$= \frac{728}{\sqrt{1744 \times 336}} = \frac{728}{765.496} = \mathbf{+0.951}.$$

Problem 11. Find the coefficient of correlation between the sales and expenses of the following 10 firms;

Firms	:	1	2	3	4	5	6	7	8	9	10
Sales ('000)	:	50	50	55	60	65	65	65	60	60	50
Expenses ('000)	:	11	13	14	16	16	15	15	14	13	13

(B.Com., Osmania, Mysore)

Solution :

Calculation of Coefficient of Correlation

X	$x = X - \overline{X}$ $= X-58$	x^2	Y	$y = Y - \overline{Y}$ $= Y-14$	y^2	xy
50	−8	64	11	−3	9	24
50	−8	64	13	−1	1	8
55	−3	9	14	0	0	0
60	+2	4	16	+2	4	4
65	+7	49	16	+2	4	14
65	+7	49	15	+1	1	7
65	+7	49	15	+1	1	7
60	+2	4	14	0	0	0
60	+2	4	13	−1	1	−2
50	−8	64	13	−1	1	8
$\Sigma X = 580$	$\Sigma x = 0$	$\Sigma x^2 = 360$	$\Sigma Y = 140$	$\Sigma y = 0$	$\Sigma y^2 = 22$	$\Sigma xy = 70$

$$\overline{X} = \frac{\Sigma X}{N} = \frac{580}{10} = \mathbf{58} \qquad \overline{Y} = \frac{\Sigma Y}{N} = \frac{140}{10} = \mathbf{14}$$

$$r = \frac{\Sigma xy}{\sqrt{\Sigma x^2 \times \Sigma y^2}} \qquad \Sigma xy = 70\,; \Sigma x^2 = 360\,; \Sigma y^2 = 22$$

$$= \frac{70}{\sqrt{360 \times 22}} = \frac{70}{88.99}$$

$$r = \mathbf{+0.786}$$

Alternate Method :

Mean :

$$\overline{X} = \frac{\Sigma X}{N} = \frac{580}{10} = \mathbf{58} \qquad \overline{Y} = \frac{\Sigma Y}{N} = \frac{140}{10} = \mathbf{14}$$

Standard Deviation:

$$\sigma_x = \sqrt{\frac{\Sigma dx^2}{N}} = \sqrt{\frac{360}{10}} = \sqrt{36} = \mathbf{6} \qquad \sigma_y = \sqrt{\frac{\Sigma dy^2}{N}} = \sqrt{\frac{22}{10}} = \sqrt{2.2} = \mathbf{1.483}.$$

Coefficient of Correlation :

$$r = \frac{\Sigma dxdy}{N\sigma x.\sigma y}$$

$$\Sigma dxdy = 70\,; N = 10\,; \sigma x = 6\,; \sigma y = 1.483$$

$$r = \frac{70}{10 \times 6 \times 1.483} = \frac{70}{88.98} = \mathbf{+0.7866}.$$

Problem 12. Find the coefficient correlation from the following data

X	78	36	98	25	75	82	90	62	65	39
Y	84	51	91	60	68	62	86	58	53	47

(B.Com. Madurai)

Solution :

Computation of Coefficient of Correlation

X	$dx = X - 65$	dx^2	Y	$dy = Y - 66$	dy^2	$dxdy$
78	13	169	84	18	324	234
36	−29	841	51	−15	225	435
98	33	1089	91	25	625	825
25	−40	1600	60	−6	36	240
75	10	100	68	2	4	20
82	17	289	62	−4	16	−68
90	25	625	86	20	400	500
62	−3	9	58	−8	64	24
65	0	0	53	−13	169	0
39	−26	676	47	−19	361	494
$\Sigma X = 650$	$\Sigma dx = 0$	$\Sigma dx^2 = 5,398$	$\Sigma y = 660$	$\Sigma dy = 0 = 2224$	$\Sigma dy^2 = 2704$	$\Sigma dxdy$

Coefficient of Correlation :

$$r = \frac{\Sigma dxdy}{\sqrt{\Sigma dx^2 \times \Sigma dy^2}}$$

$$\Sigma dxdy = 2704; \Sigma dx^2 = 5398; \Sigma dy^2 = 2224$$

$$r = \frac{2704}{\sqrt{5398 \times 2224}}$$

$$= \frac{2704}{3464.85}$$

$$r = \mathbf{0.780}$$

Problem 13. Compute the coefficient of correlation of the following score of A and B :

A :	5	10	5	11	12	4	4	2	7	1
B :	1	6	2	8	5	1	4	6	5	2

(B.Com., Madurai)

Solution :

We can calculate coefficient of correlation without taking deviation of the items. We can use direct method. The formula gives the same answer as one gets when deviations of items are taken from mean or assumed mean. The point is illustrated by solving the above problem under direct method.

Computation of Coefficient of Correlation

X	X^2	Y	Y^2	XY
5	25	1	1	5
10	100	6	36	60
5	25	2	4	10
11	121	8	64	88
12	144	5	25	60
4	16	1	1	4
3	9	4	16	12
2	4	6	36	12
7	49	5	25	35
1	1	2	4	2
$\Sigma X = 60$	$\Sigma X^2 = 494$	$\Sigma Y = 40$	$\Sigma Y^2 = 212$	$\Sigma XY = 288$

$$r = \frac{N\Sigma XY - (\Sigma X)(\Sigma Y)}{\sqrt{N\Sigma X^2 - (\Sigma X)^2}\sqrt{N\Sigma Y^2 - (\Sigma Y^2)}}$$

$$= \frac{10 \times 288 - 60 \times 40}{\sqrt{10 \times 494 - (60)^2}\sqrt{10 \times 212 - (40)^2}}$$

$$= \frac{2880 - 2400}{\sqrt{4940 - 3600}\sqrt{2120 - 1600}}$$

$$= \frac{480}{\sqrt{1340 \times 520}}$$

$$= \frac{480}{834.75}$$

$$= \mathbf{+0.575}$$

$$= \mathbf{+0.58.}$$

Problem 14. The above problem (No. 13) is solved by taking deviations from arithmetic mean. We get similar answer, as above.

Solution :

Computation of Coefficient of Correlation

X	$dx = X - \overline{X}$ $= \overline{X} - 6$	dx^2	Y	$dy = Y - \overline{Y}$ $= Y - 4$	dy^2	$dxdy$
5	−1	1	1	−3	9	+3
10	+4	16	6	+2	4	+8
5	−1	1	2	−2	4	+2
11	+5	25	8	+4	16	+20
12	+6	36	5	+1	1	+6
4	−2	4	1	−3	9	+6
3	−3	9	4	0	0	0
2	−4	16	6	+2	4	−8
7	+1	1	5	+1	1	+1
1	−5	25	2	−2	4	+10
$\Sigma X = 60$	$\Sigma dx = 0$	$\Sigma dx^2 = 134$	$\Sigma y = 40$	$\Sigma dy = 0$	$\Sigma dy^2 = 52$	$\Sigma dxdy = 48$

$$\overline{X} = \frac{60}{10} = \mathbf{6} \qquad \overline{Y} = \frac{40}{10} = \mathbf{4}$$

$$r = \frac{\Sigma dxdy}{\sqrt{\Sigma dx^2 \times \Sigma dy^2}}$$

$$\Sigma dxdy = 48\,;\ \Sigma dx^2 = 134\,;\ \Sigma dy^2 = 52$$

$$r = \frac{48}{\sqrt{134 \times 52}} = \frac{48}{\sqrt{6968}} = \frac{48}{83.475} = +0.575 = \mathbf{+0.58.}$$

Problem 15. Calculate the Pearson's coefficient of correlation from the following taking 100 and 50 as the assumed averages of X and Y respectively :

X	104	111	104	114	118	117	105	108	106	100	104	105
Y	57	55	47	45	45	50	64	63	66	62	69	61

C.A.

Solution :

Computation of Coefficient of Correlation

X	dx = X−100	dx^2	Y	dy = Y−50	dy^2	$dxdy$
104	4	16	57	7	49	28
111	11	121	55	5	25	55
104	4	16	47	−3	9	−12
114	14	196	45	−5	25	−70
118	18	324	45	−5	25	−90
117	17	289	50	0	0	0
105	5	25	64	14	196	70
108	8	64	63	13	169	104
106	6	36	66	16	256	96
100	0	0	62	12	144	0
104	4	16	69	19	361	76
105	5	25	61	11	121	55
	$\Sigma d\,x = 96$	$\Sigma\ dx^2 = 1128$		$\Sigma dy\ = 84$	$\Sigma dy^2 = 1380$	$\Sigma\ dx\ dy = 312$

Coefficient of Correlation:

$$r = \frac{\Sigma dxdy \times N - (\Sigma dx)(\Sigma dy)}{\sqrt{\Sigma dx^2 \times X - (\Sigma dx)^2}\sqrt{(\Sigma dy^2 \times N - (\Sigma dy)^2}}$$

$$\Sigma dxdy = 312 : N = 12; \quad \Sigma dx = 96; \Sigma dy = 84;$$

$$\Sigma dx^2 = 1128; \Sigma dy^2 = 1380$$

$$r = \frac{312 \times 12 - (96)(84)}{\sqrt{1128 \times 12 - (96)^2}\sqrt{1380 \times 12 - (84)^2}}$$

$$= \frac{3744 - 8064}{\sqrt{13536 - 9216}\sqrt{16560 - 7056}}$$

$$= \frac{-4320}{\sqrt{4320 \times 9504}}$$

$$= \frac{-4320}{6407.6}$$

$$r = -0.6742$$

$$= \mathbf{-0.674}$$

Problem 16. Calculate the coefficient of correlation between infant mortality and overcrowding from the following data :

Infant mortality	109	122	96	142	151	124	125	102	109
% of population								156	122
overcrowded	14.9	6.3	5.8	12.2	33.2	13.3	14.6	8.8	4.9
								39.8	6.3

(*B.Com.*)

Solution :

Computation of Coefficient of Correlation

Infant mortality Rate X	$dx = X - 122$	dx^2	*% of population overcrowded (Y)*	$dy = Y - 10$	dy^2	$dxdy$
109	−13	169	14.9	+4.9	24.01	−63.7
122	0	0	6.3	−3.7	13.69	0
96	−26	676	5.8	−4.2	17.64	+109.2
142	+20	400	12.2	+2.2	4.84	+44.0
151	+29	841	33.2	+23.2	538.24	+ 672.8
124	+2	4	13.3	+3.3	10.89	+6.6
125	+3	9	14.6	+4.6	21.16	+13.8
102	−20	400	8.8	−1.2	1.44	+24.0
109	−13	169	4.9	−5.1	26.01	+66.3
156	+34	1156	39.8	+29.8	888.04	+1013.2
122	0	0	6.3	−3.7	13.69	0
$N = 11$	$\Sigma dx = +16$	$\Sigma dx^2 = 3824$		$\Sigma dy = +50.1$	$\Sigma dy^2 = 1559.65$	$\Sigma dxdy = 1886.2$

$$r = \frac{\Sigma dx\, dy \times N - (\Sigma dx \times \Sigma dy)}{\sqrt{\Sigma dx^2 \times N - (\Sigma dx)^2}\sqrt{\Sigma dy^2 \times N - (\Sigma dy)^2}}$$

$$\Sigma dxdy = 1886.2\,; \Sigma dx = +16\,; \Sigma dy = +\,50.1.$$

$$\Sigma dx^2 = 3824\,; \Sigma dy^2 = 1559.65\,; N = 11.$$

$$r = \frac{1886.2 \times 11) - (16 \times 50.1)}{\sqrt{3824 \times 11 - (16)^2}\sqrt{1559.65 \times 11 - (50.1)^2}}$$

$$= \frac{20748.2 - 801.6}{\sqrt{42064 - 256}\sqrt{17156.15 - 2510.01}}$$

$$= \frac{19946.6}{\sqrt{41808 \times 14646.14}}$$

$$= \frac{19,946.6}{24745.22}$$

$$r = \mathbf{+0.806}$$

Problem 17. Making use of the data summarised below calculate the coefficient of correlation.

Case	1	2	3	4	5	6	7	8
X	10	6	9	10	12	13	11	9
Y	9	4	6	9	11	13	8	4

(*B.Com. Delhi*)

Solution :

Computaion of Coefficient of Correlation

	X			Y			
Case	*X*	$dx = X-10$	dx^2	*Y*	$dy = Y-8$	dy^2	$dxdy$
1	10	0	0	9	+1	1	0
2	6	−4	16	4	−4	16	+16
3	9	−1	1	6	−2	4	+2
4	10	0	0	9	+1	1	0
5	12	+2	4	11	+3	9	+6
6	13	+3	9	13	+5	25	+15
7	11	+1	1	8	0	0	0
8	9	−1	1	4	−4	16	4
	$\Sigma X = 80$	$\Sigma dx = 0$	$\Sigma dx^2 = 32$	$\Sigma y = 64$	$\Sigma dy = 0$	$\Sigma dy^2 = 72$	$\Sigma dxdy = 43$

$$\overline{X} = \frac{\Sigma X}{N} = \frac{80}{8} = \mathbf{10}; \overline{Y} = \frac{\Sigma Y}{N} = \frac{64}{8} = \mathbf{8}$$

$$r = \frac{\Sigma dxdy}{\sqrt{\Sigma dx^2 \times \Sigma dy^2}}$$

$$\Sigma dxdy = 43; \Sigma dx^2 = 32; \Sigma dy^2 = 72$$

$$r = \frac{43}{\sqrt{32 \times 72}}$$

$$= \frac{43}{48}$$

$$r = \mathbf{+0.896}$$

Problem 18. The following table gives the marks obtained by a group of 12 students in two examinations *A* and *B*. Calculate the correlation coefficient between the marks obtained in the two examinations and interpret the result :

Students	*Marks in Examination* A	B	*Students*	*Marks in Examination* A	B
1	15	18	7	20	18
2	13	16	8	16	15
3	17	18	9	18	21
4	14	15	10	17	17
5	18	19	11	19	18
6	12	16	12	21	20

(*B.A., Econ., Hons., Delhi*)

Solution :

Computation of Coefficient of Correlation

Students	*Marks in A*			*Marks in B*			$dxdy$
	X	$dx = X - 18$	dx^2	Y	$dy = Y - 18$	dy^2	
1	15	−3	9	18	0	0	0
2	13	−5	25	16	−2	4	+10
3	17	−1	1	18	0	0	0
4	14	−4	16	15	−3	9	+12
5	18	0	0	19	+1	1	0
6	12	−6	36	16	−2	4	+12
7	20	+2	4	18	0	0	0
8	16	−2	4	15	−3	9	+ 6
9	18	0	0	21	+3	9	0
10	17	−1	1	17	−1	1	+ 1
11	19	+1	1	18	0	0	0
12	21	+3	9	20	+2	4	+ 6
		$\Sigma dx = -16$	$\Sigma dx^2 = 106$		$\Sigma dy = -5$	$\Sigma dy^2 = 41$	$\Sigma dxdy = 47$

$$r = \frac{(\Sigma dxdy \times N) - (\Sigma dx \times \Sigma dy)}{\sqrt{\Sigma dx^2 \times N - (\Sigma dx)^2}\sqrt{(\Sigma dy^2 \times N - (\Sigma dy)^2}}$$

$$\Sigma dxdy = +47; \Sigma dx = -16; \Sigma dy = -5; \Sigma dx^2 = 106;$$

$$\Sigma dy^2 = 41; N = 12$$

$$= \frac{(47 \times 12) - (-16 \times -5)}{\sqrt{106 \times 12 - (-16)^2}\sqrt{41 \times 12 - (-5)^2}}$$

$$= \frac{564 - 80}{\sqrt{1272 - 256}\sqrt{492 - 25}}$$

$$= \frac{484}{\sqrt{1016 \times 467}}$$

$$= \frac{484}{688 \cdot 82} = \mathbf{0.7026.}$$

$$r = \mathbf{+0.703.}$$

Problem 19. The index numbers of prices of all commodities in Bombay and in Calcutta were as under :

Month	*Index No. of Commodity Prices in Calcutta*	*Index No. of Commodity Prices in Bombay*
Jan.	169	204
Feb.	182	222
March	182	225
April	192	228
May	198	229
June	209	233
July	227	249
Aug.	238	266
Sept.	250	255
Oct.	253	255

(*B. Com.*)

Solution :

Computation of Coefficient of Correlation

Month	*Index No. of Commodity (Calcutta)*			*Index No. of Commodity (Bombay)*			$dxdy$
	X	$dx = X - 209$	dx^2	Y	$dy = Y - 229$	dy^2	
Jan.	169	−40	1600	204	−25	625	+ 1000
Feb.	182	−27	729	222	−7	49	+ 189
March	182	−27	729	225	−4	16	+ 108
April	192	−17	289	228	−1	1	+ 17
May	198	−11	121	229	0	0	0
June	209	0	0	233	+4	16	0
July	227	+18	324	249	+20	400	+ 360
Aug.	238	+29	841	266	+37	1369	+1073
Sept.	250	+41	1681	255	+26	676	+1066
Oct.	253	+44	1936	255	+26	676	+1144
$N = 10$		$\Sigma dx = +10$	$\Sigma dx^2 = 8250$		$\Sigma dy = +76$	$\Sigma dy^2 = 3828$	$\Sigma dxdy = 4957$

$$r = \frac{(\Sigma dxdy \times N) - (\Sigma dx \times \Sigma dy)}{\sqrt{\Sigma dx^2 \times N - (\Sigma dx)^2}\sqrt{\Sigma dy^2 \times N - (\Sigma dy)^2}}$$

$$\Sigma dxdy = 4957; \Sigma dx = 10; \Sigma dy = 76; \Sigma dx^2 = 8250; \Sigma dy^2 = 3828; N = 10$$

$$r = \frac{(4957 \times 10) - (10 \times 76)}{\sqrt{8250 \times 10 - (10)^2}\sqrt{3828 \times 10 - (76)^2}}$$

$$= \frac{49570 - 760}{\sqrt{82500 - 100}\sqrt{38280 - 5776}}$$

$$= \frac{48,810}{\sqrt{82400 \times 32504}}$$

$$= \frac{48,810}{51,752 \cdot 58}$$

$$r = \mathbf{+0.943}$$

Problem 20. Find Karl Pearson's coefficient of correlation between the values of X and Y given below and calculate the probable error.

X :	78	89	96	69	59	79	68	61
Y :	125	137	156	112	107	136	123	108

Assume 69 and 112 as the mean values for X and Y respectively

(*B.Com. Bangalore*)

Solution :

Computation of Coefficient of Correlation

X	$dx = X - 69$	dx^2	Y	$dy = Y - 112$	dy^2	$dxdy$
78	+9	81	125	+13	169	117
89	+20	400	137	+25	625	500
96	+27	729	156	+44	1936	1188
69	0	0	112	0	0	0
59	−10	100	107	− 5	25	50
79	+10	100	136	+24	576	240
68	− 1	1	123	+11	121	− 11
61	− 8	64	108	− 4	16	32
	$\Sigma dx = 47$	$\Sigma dx^2 = 1475$		$\Sigma dy = 108$	$\Sigma dy^2 = 3468$	$\Sigma dxdy = 2116$

Coefficient of correlation :

$$r = \frac{\Sigma dxdy \times N - (\Sigma dx)(\Sigma dy)}{\sqrt{\Sigma dx^2 \times N - (\Sigma dx)^2}\sqrt{\Sigma dy^2 \times N - (\Sigma dy)^2}}$$

$$\Sigma dxdy = 2116; N = 8; \Sigma dx = 47; \Sigma dy = 108; \Sigma dx^2 = 1475; \Sigma dy^2 = 3468$$

$$r = \frac{2116 \times 8 - (47)(108)}{\sqrt{1475 \times 8 - (47)^2}\sqrt{3468 \times 8 - (108)^2}}$$

$$= \frac{16928 - 5076}{\sqrt{11800 - 2209}\sqrt{27744 - 11664}}$$

$$= \frac{11852}{\sqrt{9591 \times 16080}} = \frac{11852}{12418 \cdot 67} = \mathbf{+0.9543}.$$

$$\text{Probable Error} = 0.6745\frac{1 - r^2}{\sqrt{N}} = \frac{0.6745(1 - 0.6745(1 - 0.954^2)}{\sqrt{8}}$$

$$= \frac{0.6745 \times 0.09}{2.828}$$

$$= \mathbf{+0.021}.$$

Problem 21. A department store gives in-service training to its salesmen which is followed by a test. It is considering whether it should terminate the service any salesman who does not do well in the test. The following data give the test scores and sales made by nine salesmen during a certain period:

Test scores :	14	19	24	21	26	22	15	20	19
(Sales ('00) Rs. :	31	36	48	37	50	45	33	41	39

Calcualte the correlation coefficient between the test scores and sales. Does it indicate that the termination of services of low test scores is justified ?

(*C.A.*)

Solution :

Computation of Coefficient of Correlation

Test Scores			*Sales('00)*			
X	$dx = X - \overline{X}$ $X - 20$	dx^2	Y	$dY = Y - \overline{Y}$ $Y - 40$	dy^2	$dxdy$
14	−6	36	31	−9	81	+54
19	−1	1	36	−4	16	+4
24	+4	16	48	+8	64	+32
21	+1	1	37	−3	9	−3
26	+6	36	50	+10	100	+60
22	+2	4	45	+5	25	+10
15	−5	25	33	−7	49	+35
20	0	0	41	+1	1	0
19	−1	1	39	−1	1	+1
$\Sigma X = 180$	$\Sigma dx = 0$	$\Sigma dx^2 = 120$	$\Sigma y = 360$	$\Sigma dy = 0$	$\Sigma dy^2 = 346$	$\Sigma dxdy = 193$

$$\overline{X} = \frac{\Sigma X}{N} = \frac{180}{9} = \mathbf{20}$$

$$\overline{Y} = \frac{\Sigma Y}{N} = \frac{360}{9} = \mathbf{40}.$$

$$r = \frac{\Sigma dxdy}{\sqrt{\Sigma dx^2 \times \Sigma dy^2}} \quad \Sigma dxdy = 193; \quad \Sigma dx^2 = 120; \quad \Sigma dy^2 = 346$$

$$= \frac{193}{\sqrt{120 \times 346}} = \frac{193}{203 \cdot 76}$$

$$\therefore \; r = \mathbf{+0.947}.$$

Thus, there is a high degree of positive correlation between test scores and sales. Therefore, the termination of services of low test scores is justified.

Problem 22. From the following table compute the coefficient of correlation between savings bank deposits and strikes and lockouts over a period of seven years.

Saving deposits (' 00,000) :	51	54	56	59	65	60	70
Strikes and lockouts :	58	44	33	36	23	33	13

(*B.Com. Madurai*)

Solution :

Computation of Coefficient of Correlation

Saving deposits ('00,000) X	dx $= X - 60$	dx^2	*Strikes and lockouts* Y	dy $= X - 36$	dy^2	$dxdy$
51	−9	81	58	+22	484	−198
54	−6	36	44	+8	64	−48
56	−4	16	33	−3	9	+12
59	−1	1	36	0	0	0
65	5	25	23	−13	169	−65
60	0	0	33	−3	9	0
70	10	100	13	−23	529	−230
	$\Sigma dx = -5$	$\Sigma dx^2 = 259$		$\Sigma dy = -12$	$\Sigma dy^2 = 1264$	$\Sigma dxdy = -529$

Coefficient of Correlation :

$$r = \frac{\Sigma dxdy \times N - (\Sigma dx)(\Sigma dy)}{\sqrt{\Sigma dx^2 \times N - (\Sigma dx)^2}\sqrt{\Sigma dy^2 \times N - (\Sigma dy)^2}}$$

$$\Sigma dxdy = -529; \quad N = 7; \quad \Sigma dx = -5; \quad \Sigma dy = -12;$$

$$\Sigma dx^2 = 259; \Sigma dy^2 = 1264$$

$$r = \frac{-529 \times 7 - (-5)(-12)}{\sqrt{259 \times 7 - (-5)^2}\sqrt{1264 \times 7 - (-12)^2}}$$

$$= \frac{(-3703) - (60)}{\sqrt{1813 - 25}\sqrt{8848 - 144}}$$

$$= \frac{-3763}{\sqrt{1788 \times 8704}}$$

$$= \frac{-3763}{3944 \cdot 97}$$

$$r = \mathbf{-0.95}$$

Problem 23. From the following information relating to the Stock Exchange Quotations for two shares A and B, ascertain, by using Pearson's coefficient of correlation, whether shares A and B are correlated, in their prices :

Price share (A) Rs. :	160	164	172	182	166	170	178
Price share (B) Rs. :	292	280	260	234	266	254	230

(*B.Com. Madurai*)

Solution :

Computation of Coefficient of Correlation

Price Share A			*Price Share B*			
X	$dx = X - 170$	dx^2	Y	$dy = Y - 260$	dy^2	$dxdy$
160	−10	100	292	+32	1024	−320
164	−6	36	280	+20	400	−120
172	+2	4	260	0	0	0
182	+12	144	234	−26	676	−312
166	− 4	16	266	+ 6	36	− 24
170	0	0	254	− 6	36	0
178	+8	64	230	−30	900	−240
	$\Sigma dx = 2$	$\Sigma dx^2 = 364$		$\Sigma dy = -4$	$\Sigma dy^2 = 3072$	$\Sigma dxdy = -1016$

Coefficient of Correlation :

$$r = \frac{\Sigma dxdy \times N - (\Sigma dx)(\Sigma dy)}{\sqrt{\Sigma dx^2 \times N - (\Sigma dx)^2}\sqrt{(\Sigma dx^2 \times N - (\Sigma dy)^2}}$$

$$\Sigma dxdy = -1016; N = 7; \Sigma dx = 2; \Sigma dy = -4;$$

$$\Sigma dx^2 = 364; \Sigma dy^2 = 3072$$

$$r = \frac{-1016 \times 7 - (2)(-4)}{\sqrt{364 \times 7 - (2)^2}\sqrt{3072 \times 7 - (-4)^2}}$$

$$= \frac{-7112 - (-8)}{\sqrt{2548 - 4}\sqrt{21504 - 16}}$$

$$= \frac{-7104}{\sqrt{2544 \times 21488}} = \frac{-7104}{7393.6} = \mathbf{-0.96}.$$

Problem 24. Find out Karl Pearson's co-efficient of correlation in the following series relating to prices and supply of a commodity.

Price : (Rs.)	11	12	13	14	15	16	17	18	19	20
Supply : (Kgs.)	30	29	29	25	24	24	24	21	18	15

(*B.Com., Andhra*)

Solution :

Computation of Coefficient of Correlation

X Series			*Y Series*			
Price $(Rs)(X)$	$dx =$ $X-15$	dx^2	*Supply* $Kgs.(Y)$	$dy = Y$ -24	dy^2	$dxdy$
11	−4	16	30	6	36	−24
12	−3	9	29	5	25	−15
13	−2	4	29	5	25	−10
14	−1	1	25	1	1	− 1
15	0	0	24	0	0	0
16	1	1	24	0	0	0
17	2	4	24	0	0	0
18	3	9	21	−3	9	− 9
19	4	16	18	−6	36	−24
20	5	25	15	−9	81	−45
	$\Sigma dx = 5$	$\Sigma dx^2 = 85$		$\Sigma dy = -1$	$\Sigma dy^2 = 213$	$\Sigma dxdy = -128$

Coefficient of Correlation :

$$r = \frac{\Sigma dxdy \times N - (\Sigma dx)(\Sigma dy)}{\sqrt{\Sigma dx^2 \times N - (\Sigma dx)^2 \Sigma dy^2 \times N - (\Sigma dy)^2}}$$

$$\Sigma dxdy = -128; \quad N = 10; \quad \Sigma dx = 5; \quad \Sigma dy = -1; \Sigma dx^2 = 85;$$

$$\Sigma dy^2 = 213$$

$$r = \frac{(-128 \times 10) - (5 \times -1)}{\sqrt{85 \times 10 - (5)^2 \times 213 \times 10 - (-1)^2}}$$

$$= \frac{-1280 - (-5)}{\sqrt{850 - 25 \times 2130 - 1}} = \frac{-1280 + 5}{\sqrt{825 \times 2129}}$$

$$= \frac{-1275}{\sqrt{825 \times 2129}} = \frac{-1275}{1325.30} = \mathbf{-0.96}.$$

Problem 25. Find out the co-efficient of correlation in the following case :

Height of fathers in inches	Height of sons in inches
65	67
66	68
67	64
67	68
68	72
69	70
71	69
73	70

(*B.Com., Andhra, M.A., Allahabad*)

Solution :

Computation of Coefficient of Correlation

X Series			*Y Series*			
Height of father in inches (X)	*Deviation from assumed mean dx* (67)	dx^2	*Height of Son in inches* (Y)	*Deviation from assumed mean 68* dy	dy^2	*deviation of x and y series* $dxdy$
65	−2	4	67	−1	1	2
66	−1	1	68	0	0	0
67	0	0	64	−4	16	0
67	0	0	68	0	0	0
68	1	1	72	4	16	4
69	2	4	70	2	4	4
71	4	16	69	1	1	4
73	6	36	70	2	4	12
$\Sigma X = 546$	$\Sigma dx = 10$	$\Sigma dx^2 = 62$	$\Sigma y = 548$	$\Sigma dy = 4$	$\Sigma dy^2 = 42$	$\Sigma dxdy = 26$

Coefficient of Correlation :

$$r = \frac{\Sigma dxdy \times N - (\Sigma dx)(\Sigma dy)}{\sqrt{\Sigma dx^2 \times N - (\Sigma dx)^2 \times \Sigma dy^2 \times N - (\Sigma dy)^2}}$$

$$\Sigma dxdy = 26 ; \Sigma dx = 10 ; \Sigma dy = 4 ; \Sigma dx^2 = 62; \Sigma dy^2 = 42;$$

$$N = 8$$

$$r = \frac{26 \times 8 - 10 \times 4}{\sqrt{(62 \times 8 - (10^2) \times (42 \times 8 - 4^2)}}$$

$$= \frac{208 - 40}{\sqrt{(496 - 100)(336 - 16)}} = \frac{168}{\sqrt{396 \times 320}} = \frac{168}{355.98}$$

$$r = \mathbf{+0.47}$$

Problem 26. Compute Karl Pearson's coefficient of correlation in the following series relating to cost of living and wages :

Wages :	100	101	103	102	100	99	97	98	96	95
Cost of living :	98	99	99	97	95	92	95	94	90	91

(*B.Com.,Bangalore,Karnataka, Gujarat*)

Solution :

Computation of Coefficient of Correlation

Wages (X)	$dx = X - 100$	dx^2	*Cost of living Y*	$dy = Y - 95$	dy^2	$dxdy$
100	0	0	98	+3	9	0
101	+1	1	99	+4	16	+ 4
103	+3	9	99	+4	16	+12
102	+2	4	97	+2	4	+ 4
100	0	0	95	0	0	0
99	−1	1	92	−3	9	+ 3
97	−3	9	95	0	0	0
98	−2	4	94	−1	1	+ 2
96	−4	16	90	−5	25	+20
95	−5	25	91	−4	16	+20
	$\Sigma dx = -9$	$\Sigma dx^2 = 69$		$\Sigma dy = 0$	$\Sigma dy^2 = 96$	$\Sigma dxdy = 65$

$$r = \frac{\Sigma dxdy - \frac{\Sigma dx \times \Sigma dy}{N}}{\sqrt{\Sigma dx^2 - \frac{(\Sigma dx)^2}{N}}\sqrt{\Sigma dy^2 - \frac{(\Sigma dy)^2}{N}}}$$

$\Sigma dxdy = 65; \quad \Sigma dx = -9; \quad \Sigma dy = 0; \quad \Sigma dx^2 = 69; \quad \Sigma dy^2 = 96; \quad N = 10$

$$r = \frac{65 \times 10 - (-9 \times 0)}{\sqrt{(69 \times 10 - (-9)^2 \; 96 \times 10 - (0)^2}}$$

$$= \frac{650}{\sqrt{609 \times 960}} = \frac{650}{764.62}$$

$$r = \mathbf{+0.85}.$$

Problem 27. Find the correlation coefficient between the income and expenditure of a wage earner and comment on the result.

Month :	*Jan.*	*Feb.*	*March*	*April*	*May*	*June*	*July*
Income :	46	54	56	56	58	60	62
Expenditure :	36	40	44	54	42	58	54

(*B.Com. Banaras*)

Solution :

Computation of Correlation Coefficient

Month	*Income*			*Expenditure*			
	X	$dx = X - 55$	dx^2	Y	$dy = Y - 45$	dy^2	$dxdy$
Jan.	46	−9	81	36	−9	81	+81
Feb.	54	−1	1	40	−5	25	+5
March	56	+1	1	44	−1	1	−1
April	56	+1	1	54	+9	81	+9
May	58	+3	9	42	−3	9	−9
June	60	+5	25	58	+13	169	+65
July	62	+7	49	54	+9	81	+63
		$\Sigma dx = +7$	$\Sigma dx^2 = 167$		$\Sigma dy = +13$	$\Sigma dy^2 = 447$	$\Sigma dxdy = 213$

$$r = \frac{(\Sigma dxdy \times N) - (\Sigma dx \times \Sigma dy)}{\sqrt{\Sigma dx^2 \times N - (\Sigma dx)^2}\sqrt{\Sigma dy^2 \times N - (\Sigma dy)^2}}$$

$\Sigma dxdy = 213; \quad \Sigma dx = +7; \quad \Sigma dy = +13; \quad \Sigma dx^2 = 167; \quad \Sigma dy^2 = 447; \quad N = 7$

$$r = \frac{(213 \times 7) - (7 \times 13)}{\sqrt{(167 \times 7 - (7)^2}\sqrt{447 \times 7 - (13)^2}}$$

$$= \frac{1491 - 91}{\sqrt{(1169 - 49)}\sqrt{3129 - 169}}$$

$$= \frac{1400}{\sqrt{1120 \times 2960}}$$

$$= \frac{1400}{1820.77}$$

$$= 0.7689$$

$$r = \mathbf{+0.769}.$$

Thus, there is a positive correlation between income and expenditure.

Problem 28. Calculate the Pearson's coefficient of correlation from the following data using 44 and 26 respectively as the origin of X and Y:

X:	43	44	46	40	44	42	45	42	38	40	42	57
Y:	29	31	19	18	19	27	27	29	41	30	26	10

(*C.A.*)

Solution :

Computation of Correlation Coefficient

X	$dx = X - 44$	dx^2	Y	$dy = Y - 26$	dy^2	$dxdy$
43	−1	1	29	+3	9	− 3
44	0	0	31	+5	25	0
46	+2	4	19	−7	49	−14
40	−4	16	18	−8	64	+32
44	0	0	19	−7	49	0
42	−2	4	27	+1	1	− 2
45	+1	1	27	+1	1	+ 1
42	−2	4	29	+3	9	− 6
38	−6	36	41	+15	225	−90
40	−4	16	30	+4	16	−16
42	−2	4	26	0	0	0
57	+13	169	10	−16	256	−208
$\Sigma X = 523$	$\Sigma dx = -5$	$\Sigma dx^2 = 255$	$\Sigma Y = 306$	$\Sigma dy = -6$	$\Sigma dy^2 = 704$	$\Sigma dxdy = -306$

$$r = \frac{\Sigma dxdy - \dfrac{\Sigma dx \times \Sigma dy}{N}}{\sqrt{\Sigma dx^2 - \dfrac{(\Sigma dx)^2}{N}}\sqrt{\Sigma dy^2 - \dfrac{(\Sigma dy)^2}{N}}}$$

$\Sigma dxdy = -306;\quad \Sigma dx = -5;\quad \Sigma dy = -6;\quad \Sigma dx^2 = 255;\quad \Sigma dy^2 = 704;\quad N = 12$

$$r = \frac{(-306) - \dfrac{(-5) \times (-6)}{12}}{\sqrt{255 - \dfrac{(-5)^2}{12}}\sqrt{704 - \dfrac{(-6)^2}{12}}}$$

$$= \frac{(-306 \times 12) - (-5 \times -6)}{\sqrt{255 \times 12 - (-5)^2}\sqrt{704 \times 12 - (-6)^2}}$$

$$= \frac{-3672 - (+30)}{\sqrt{3060 - (25)}\sqrt{8448 - 36}}$$

$$= \frac{-3702}{\sqrt{3035 \times 8412}}$$

$$= \frac{-3702}{5052.76}$$

$$= \mathbf{-0.733}.$$

Problem 29. Calculate the coefficient of correlation between age of cars and annual maintenance cost and comment :

Age of cars (years) (X) :	2	4	6	7	8	10	12
Annual maintenance cost ('00) (Y) :	16	15	18	19	17	21	20

(*B.Com. Andhra*)

Solution :

Computation of Coefficient of Correlation

X	$dx = X - \overline{X}(X-7)$	dx^2	Y	$dy = Y - \overline{Y}(Y-18)$	dy^2	$dxdy$
2	−5	25	16	−2	4	+10
4	−3	9	15	−3	9	+ 9
6	−1	1	18	0	0	0
7	0	0	19	+1	1	0
8	+1	1	17	−1	1	− 1
10	+3	9	21	+3	9	+ 9
12	+5	25	20	+2	4	+10
$\Sigma X = 49$	$\Sigma dx = 0$	$\Sigma dx^2 = 70$	$\Sigma Y = 126$	$\Sigma dy = 0$	$\Sigma dy^2 = 28$	$\Sigma dxdy = +37$

$$\overline{X} = \frac{\Sigma X}{N} = \frac{49}{7} = 7$$

$$\overline{Y} = \frac{\Sigma Y}{N} = \frac{126}{7} = \mathbf{18}$$

$$\Sigma dxdy = +37$$

$$\Sigma dx^2 = 70$$

$$\Sigma dy^2 = 28$$

$$N = 7$$

$$r = \frac{\Sigma dxdy}{\sqrt{\Sigma dx^2 \sqrt{\Sigma dy^2}}}$$

$$= \frac{37}{\sqrt{70 \times 28}}$$

$$= \frac{37}{44.27}$$

$$= 0.8357$$

$$r = \mathbf{+0.8357.}$$

Problem 30. The following table gives the marks obtained by a student in ten tests during the year. Calculate the correlation coefficient.

Test No. :	1	2	3	4	5	6	7	8	9	10
Marks in Accounts :	77	54	27	52	14	35	90	25	56	60
Marks in English :	35	58	60	40	50	40	35	56	34	42

(*B.Com. Agra*)

Solution :

Computation of Coefficient of Correlation

Test No.	*Marks in Accounts* X	$x = (X - \overline{X})$ $\overline{X} = 49$	x^2	*Marks in English*	$y = (Y - \overline{Y})$ $\overline{Y} = 45$	y^2	xy
1	77	+28	784	35	−10	100	−280
2	54	+ 5	25	58	+13	169	+ 65
3	27	−22	484	60	+15	225	−330
4	52	+ 3	9	40	−5	25	− 15
5	14	−35	1225	50	+5	25	−175
6	35	−14	196	40	−5	25	+ 70
7	90	+41	1681	35	−10	100	−410
8	25	−24	576	56	+11	121	−264
9	56	+ 7	49	34	−11	121	− 77
10	60	+11	121	42	−3	9	− 33
	$\Sigma X = 490$	$\Sigma x = 0$	$\Sigma x^2 = 5150$	$\Sigma Y = 450$	$\Sigma y = 0$	$\Sigma y^2 = 920$	$\Sigma xy = -1449$

Coefficient of Correlation :

$$r = \frac{\Sigma xy}{\sqrt{\Sigma x^2 \times \Sigma y^2}}$$

$$\Sigma xy = -1449; \quad \Sigma x^2 = 5150; \quad \Sigma y^2 = 920$$

$$r = \frac{-1449}{\sqrt{5150 \times 920}}$$

$$= \frac{-1449}{2176.69}$$

$$= \mathbf{-0.666}.$$

Problem 31. Calculate the value of coefficient of correlation between price and supply. What is its probable error? Interpret the value of coefficient of correlation.

Price :	8	10	15	17	20	22	24	25
Supply :	25	30	32	35	37	40	42	45

(*B.Com. Andhra*)

Solution :

Calculation of Coefficient of Correlation

X	$dx = X - 20$	dx^2	Y	$dy = Y - 35$	dy^2	$d_{(x)}d_{(y)}$
8	−12	144	25	−10	100	120
10	−10	100	30	−5	25	50
15	−5	25	32	−3	9	15
17	−3	9	35	0	0	0
20	0	0	37	+2	4	0
22	+2	4	40	+5	25	10
24	+4	16	42	+7	49	28
25	+5	25	45	+10	100	50
	$\Sigma dx = -19$	$\Sigma dx^2 = 323$		$\Sigma dy = +6$	$\Sigma dy^2 = 312$	$\Sigma dxdy = +273$

$$r = \frac{(\Sigma dxdy \times N) - (\Sigma dx \times \Sigma dy)}{\sqrt{\Sigma dx^2 \times N - (\Sigma dx)^2}\sqrt{\Sigma dy^2 \times N - (\Sigma dy)^2}}$$

$$\Sigma dxdy = 273; \quad \Sigma dx = -19; \quad \Sigma dy = +6; \quad \Sigma dx^2 = 323; \quad \Sigma dy^2 = 312;$$

$$r = \frac{(273 \times 8) - (-19 \times 6)}{\sqrt{323 \times 8 - (-19)^2}\sqrt{312 \times 8 - (+6)^2}}$$

$$= \frac{(2184) - (-114)}{\sqrt{2584 - 361}\sqrt{2496 - 36}}$$

$$= \frac{2184 + 114}{\sqrt{2223} \times \sqrt{2460}}$$

$$= \frac{2298}{\sqrt{2223} \times \sqrt{2460}}$$

$$= \frac{2298}{2338.49}$$

$$= \mathbf{+0.98}.$$

Probable Error of the Coefficient :

$$\text{P.E.} = 0.6745 \frac{1 - (0.98)^2}{\sqrt{8}}$$

$$= 0.6745 \frac{1 - 0.9604}{2.83}$$

$$= 0.6745 \frac{0.0396}{2.83} = 0.6745 \times 0.013 = \mathbf{0.009}.$$

$r = +0.98$. There is a very high degree of positive correlation between the price and supply. In other words, if price rises, supply rises; and price falls, supply falls.

Problem 32. Relationship between height and weight of a batch of students is given in the following series.

Height (*ins*)	*Weight* (*lbs*)	*Height* (*ins*)	*Weight* (*lbs*)
48	100	53	115
49	105	54	125
50	104	55	130
51	107	56	132
52	111	57	135

Find coefficient of correlation and coefficient of variation.

(*B.Com., Andhra*)

Solution :

Computation of Coefficient of Correlation and Coefficient of Variation

X Series			*Y Series*			
Heights in inches X	$dx = X - 52$	dx^2	*Weights in lbs Y*	$dy = Y - 115$	dy^2	$dxdy$
48	−4	16	100	−15	225	60
49	−3	9	105	−10	100	30
50	−2	4	104	−11	121	22
51	−1	1	107	− 8	64	8
52	0	0	111	− 4	16	0
53	1	1	115	0	0	0
54	2	4	125	10	100	20
55	3	9	130	15	225	45
56	4	16	132	17	289	68
57	5	25	135	20	400	100
	$\Sigma dx = 5$	$\Sigma dx^2 = 85$		$\Sigma dy = 14$	$\Sigma dy^2 = 1540$	$\Sigma dxdy = 353$

Height (*X series*)

$$\text{Mean} : \overline{X} = A + \frac{\Sigma dx}{N}$$
$$= 52 + \frac{5}{10} = 52.5$$
$$= \mathbf{52.5.}$$

Standard Deviation :

$$\sigma = \sqrt{\frac{\Sigma dx^2}{N} - \left(\frac{\Sigma dx}{N}\right)^2}$$
$$\Sigma dx^2 = 85; \quad N = 10; \quad \Sigma dx = 5$$
$$\sigma = \sqrt{\frac{85}{10} - \left(\frac{5}{10}\right)^2}$$
$$= \sqrt{8.5 - (0.5)^2}$$
$$= \sqrt{8.5 - .25}$$
$$= \sqrt{8.25}$$
$$= \mathbf{2.872.}$$

Weight (*Y Series*)

$$\overline{Y} = 115 + \frac{14}{10} = 115 + 1.4$$
$$= \mathbf{116.4}$$

Standard Deviation :

$$\Sigma dy^2 = 1540; \quad N = 10; \quad \Sigma dy = 14$$
$$\sigma = \sqrt{\frac{1540}{10} - \left(\frac{14}{10}\right)^2}$$
$$= \sqrt{154 - (1.4)^2}$$
$$= \sqrt{154 - 1.96}$$
$$= \sqrt{152.04}$$
$$\mathbf{12.33.}$$

Coefficient of Correlation :

$$r = \frac{\Sigma dxdy \times N - (\Sigma dx)(\Sigma dy)}{\sqrt{\Sigma dx^2 \times N - (\Sigma dx)^2}\sqrt{\Sigma dy^2 \times N - (\Sigma dy)^2}}$$

$$\Sigma dxdy = 353 : N = 10; \quad \Sigma dx = 5; \quad \Sigma dy = 14; \quad \Sigma dx^2 = 85; \quad \Sigma dy^2 = 1540$$

$$r = \frac{353 \times 10 - (5 \times 14)}{\sqrt{85 \times 10 - (5)^2 (1540 \times 10 - (14)^2}}$$

$$= \frac{3530 - 70}{\sqrt{(850 - 25)(15400 - 196)}} = \frac{3460}{\sqrt{825 \times 15204}} = \frac{3460}{3541.65}$$

$$r = \mathbf{+0.977}.$$

Coefficient of Variation of Height :

$$\text{C.V.} = \frac{\sigma}{\overline{X}} \times 100 \quad \sigma = 2.872; \quad \overline{X} = 52.5$$

$$= \frac{2.872}{52.6} \times 100$$

$$= \mathbf{5.47\%}.$$

Coefficient of Variation of Weight :

$$\sigma = 12.33; \quad \overline{X} = 116.4$$

$$\text{C.V.} = \frac{12.33}{116.4} \times 100$$

$$= \mathbf{10.59\%}.$$

The coefficient of variation of weight (10.59 %) is higher than the coefficient of variation of height (5.47%). Hence weight is more variable than height.

Problem 33. Calculate Pearson's coefficient of correlation between advertisement cost and sales as per the data given below:

Advertisement Cost ('000) :	39	65	62	90	82	75	25	98	36	78
Sales ('00,000) :	47	53	58	86	62	68	60	91	51	84

(*C.A. Inter*)

Solution :

Calculation of Coefficient of Correlation

X	$dx = X - 65$ dx	dx^2	Y	$dy = Y - 66$ dy	dy^2	$dxdy$
39	−26	676	47	−19	361	+494
65	0	0	53	−13	169	0
62	−3	9	58	− 8	64	+ 24
90	+25	625	86	+20	400	+500
82	+17	289	62	− 4	16	−68
75	+10	100	68	+ 2	4	+20
25	−40	1600	60	− 6	36	+240
98	+33	1089	91	+25	625	+825
36	−29	841	51	−15	225	+435
78	+13	169	84	+18	324	+234
$\Sigma x = 650$	$\Sigma dx = 0$	Σdx^2 $= 5398$	$\Sigma y = 660$	$\Sigma dy = 0$	Σdy^2 $= 2224$	$\Sigma dxdy$ $= 2704$

$$\overline{X} = \frac{650}{10} = \mathbf{65} \qquad \overline{Y} = \frac{\Sigma Y}{N} = \frac{660}{10} = \mathbf{66}$$

$$r = \frac{\Sigma dxdy}{\sqrt{\Sigma dx^2 \times \Sigma dy^2}} \qquad \Sigma dxdy = 2704; \quad \Sigma dx^2 = 5398; \quad \Sigma dy^2 = 2224$$

$$= \frac{2704}{\sqrt{5398 \times 2224}}$$

$$= \frac{2704}{3464.85}$$

$$r = \mathbf{+0.78}.$$

Problem 34. Calculate Karl Pearson's coefficient of correlation between the following pairs of values.

X ·	100	110	115	116	120	125	130	135
Y :	18	18	17	16	16	15	13	10

(*B. Com. Andhra*)

Solution :

Computation of Coefficient of Correlation

X	$dx = X - 120$	dx^2	Y	$dy = Y - 16$	dy^2	$dxdy$
100	−20	400	18	2	4	−40
110	−10	100	18	2	4	−20
115	−5	25	17	1	1	−5
116	−4	16	16	0	0	0
120	0	0	16	0	0	0
125	5	25	15	−1	1	−5
130	10	100	13	−3	9	−30
135	15	225	10	−6	36	−90
$\Sigma X = 951$	$\Sigma dx = -9$	$\Sigma dx^2 = 891$	$\Sigma Y = 123$	$\Sigma dy = -5$	$\Sigma dy^2 = 55$	$\Sigma dxdy = -190$

Coefficient of Correlation :

$$r = \frac{\Sigma\, dxdy \times N - (\Sigma dx)(\Sigma dy)}{\sqrt{\Sigma dx^2 \times N - (\Sigma dx)^2}\sqrt{\Sigma dy^2 \times N - (\Sigma dy)^2}}$$

$$\Sigma dxdy = -190; \quad N = 10; \quad \Sigma dx = -9; \quad \Sigma dy = -5; \quad \Sigma dx^2 = 891;$$

$$\Sigma dy^2 = 55$$

$$r = \frac{-190 \times 8 - (-9)(-5)}{\sqrt{891 \times 8 - (-9)^2}\sqrt{55 \times 8 - (-5)^2}}$$

$$= \frac{-1520 - 45}{\sqrt{7128 - 81}\sqrt{440 - 25}}$$

$$= \frac{-1565}{\sqrt{7047 \times 415}} = \frac{-1565}{1710.12}$$

$$r = \mathbf{-.0.915}.$$

Problem 35. Calculate the coefficient of correlation for the ages of husband and wife :

Age of husband :	23	27	28	29	30	31	33	35	36	39
Age of wife :	18	22	23	24	25	26	28	29	30	32

(*ICWA*)

Solution :

Computation of Coefficient of Correlation

Age of husband X	$dx = X - 31$	dx^2	*Age of wife Y*	$dy = Y - 25$	dy^2	$dxdy$
23	−8	64	18	−7	49	56
27	−4	16	22	−3	9	12
28	−3	9	23	−2	4	6
29	−2	4	24	−1	1	2
30	−1	1	25	0	0	0
31	0	0	26	1	1	0
33	+2	4	28	3	9	6
35	+4	16	29	4	16	16
36	+5	25	30	5	25	25
39	+8	64	32	7	49	56
$\Sigma x = 311$	$\Sigma dx = +1$	$\Sigma dx^2 = 203$	$\Sigma y = 257$	$\Sigma dy = 7$	$\Sigma dy^2 = 163$	$\Sigma dxdy = 179$

Coefficient of correlation :

$$r = \frac{\Sigma dxdy \times N - (\Sigma dx)(\Sigma dy)}{\sqrt{\Sigma dx^2 \times N - (\Sigma dx)^2}\sqrt{\Sigma dy^2 \times N - (\Sigma dy)^2}}$$

$$\Sigma dxdy = 179; \quad N = 10; \quad \Sigma dx = 1; \quad \Sigma dy = 7; \quad \Sigma dx^2 = 203; \quad \Sigma dy^2 = 163$$

$$r = \frac{179 \times 10 - (1)(7)}{\sqrt{203 \times 10 - (1)^2}\sqrt{163 \times 10 - (7)^2}}$$

$$= \frac{1790 - 7}{\sqrt{2030 - 1}\sqrt{1630 - 49}} = \frac{1783}{\sqrt{2029 \times 1581}} = \frac{1783}{1791.05}$$

$$r = +\mathbf{0.995}.$$

Problem 36. Find Karl Pearson's coefficient of correlation from the following data :

Wages	*Cost of living*	*Wages*	*Cost of living*
104	98	99	92
101	99	97	95
102	99	98	94
102	97	96	90
100	95	95	91

(*B. Com. Aligarh*)

Solution :

Computation of Coefficient of Correlation

Wages X	$x = (X - \overline{X})\overline{X} = 99$	x^2	*Cost of living* Y	$y = (Y - \overline{Y})\overline{Y} = 95$	y^2	xy
100	+1	1	98	3	9	+3
101	+2	4	99	4	16	+8
102	+3	9	99	4	16	+12
102	+3	9	97	2	4	+6
100	+1	1	95	0	0	0
99	0	0	92	−3	9	0
97	−2	4	95	0	0	0
98	−1	1	94	−1	1	+1
96	−3	9	90	−5	25	+15
95	−4	16	91	−4	16	+16
$\Sigma X = 990$	$\Sigma X = 0$	$\Sigma x^2 = 54$	$\Sigma y = 950$	$\Sigma Y = 0$	$\Sigma y^2 = 96$	$\Sigma xy = 61$

Coefficient of Correlation :

$$r = \frac{\Sigma XY}{\sqrt{\Sigma X^2 \times \Sigma Y^2}} \quad \Sigma XY = 61\,;\ \Sigma x^2 = 54\,;\ \Sigma y^2 = 96$$

$$= \frac{61}{\sqrt{54 \times 96}} = \frac{61}{72} = \mathbf{+0.85}$$

Problem 37. Calculate Karl Pearson's coefficient of correlation between price and supply of a commodity from the following data :

Price (Rs.) :	17	18	19	20	21	22	23	24	25	26
Supply (Kg.) :	38	37	38	33	32	33	34	29	26	23

(B.Com. Shivaji)

Solution :

Computation of Coefficient of Correlation

Price (X)	$dx = X - A = X - 20$	dx^2	*Supply* Y	$dy = Y - A = Y - 30$	dy^2	$dxdy$
17	−3	9	38	+8	64	−24
18	−2	4	37	+7	49	−14
19	−1	1	38	+8	64	−8
20	0	0	33	+3	9	0
21	+1	1	32	+2	4	+2
22	+2	4	33	+3	9	+6
23	+3	9	34	+4	16	+12
24	+4	16	29	−1	1	−4
25	+5	25	26	−4	16	−20
26	+6	36	23	−7	49	−42
	$\Sigma dx = +15$	$\Sigma dx^2 = 105$		$\Sigma dy = +23$	$\Sigma dy^2 = 281$	$\Sigma dxdy = -92$

$$r = \frac{(\Sigma\, dxdy \times N) - (\Sigma\, dx \times \Sigma\, dy)}{\sqrt{\Sigma dx^2 \times N - (\Sigma dx)^2}\sqrt{\Sigma dy^2 \times N - (\Sigma\, dy)^2}}$$

$$\Sigma\, dxdy = -92\,; \Sigma dx = +15\,; \Sigma dy = +23\,; \Sigma dx^2 = 105\,;$$
$$\Sigma dy^2 = 281\,; N = 10$$
$$r = \frac{-92 \times 10 - (15 \times 23)}{\sqrt{105 \times 10 - (15)^2}\sqrt{281 \times 10 - (23)^2}}$$
$$r = \frac{-920 - (+345)}{\sqrt{1050 - 225}\sqrt{2810 - 529}}$$
$$= \frac{-1265}{\sqrt{825 \times 2281}}$$
$$= \frac{-1265}{1371.8}$$
$$= \mathbf{-0.922}.$$

Thus, there is negative correlation.

Problem 38. Find if there is any significant correlation between the heights and weight given below :

Height in inches :	57	59	62	63	64	65	55	58	57
Weight in lbs :	113	117	126	126	130	129	111	116	112

(*B.Com. Aligarh*)

Solution:

Computation of Coefficient of Correlation

Height in inches X	*Deviation from* $\overline{X}$ (60)=dx	dx^2	*Weight in lbs Y*	*Deviation from* $\overline{Y}$ (120)=dy	dy^2	$dxdy$
57	−3	9	113	−7	49	21
59	−1	1	117	−3	9	3
62	+2	4	126	+6	36	12
63	+3	9	126	+6	36	18
64	+4	16	130	+10	100	40
65	+5	25	129	+9	81	45
55	−5	25	111	−9	81	45
58	−2	4	116	−4	16	8
57	−3	9	112	−8	64	24
$\Sigma X = 540$		$\Sigma dx^2 = 102$	$\Sigma x = 1080$		$\Sigma dy^2 = 472$	$\Sigma\, dxdy = 216$

Mean :

$$\overline{X} = \frac{\Sigma X}{N} = \frac{540}{9} = \mathbf{60.} \qquad \overline{Y} = \frac{\Sigma Y}{N} = \frac{1080}{9} = \mathbf{120\ lbs.}$$

Coefficient of Correlation :

$$r = \frac{\Sigma\, dxdy}{\sqrt{\Sigma\, dx^2 \times \Sigma\, dy^2}}$$
$$\Sigma\, dxdy = 216\,; \Sigma dx^2 = 102;\ \Sigma dy^2 = 472$$
$$r = \frac{216}{\sqrt{102 \times 472}} = \frac{216}{219.42} = 0.984$$
$$r = \mathbf{+0.98}.$$

Problem 39. Calculate Pearson's coefficient of correlation from the following data. Take 65 and 70 as the assumed average of the variate X and Y respectively.

X :	45	55	56	58	60	65	68	70	75	80	85
Y :	56	50	48	60	62	64	65	70	74	82	90

(*ICWA*)

Solution :

Computation of Coefficient of Correlation

X	$dx = X-65$	dx^2	Y	$dy = Y-70$	dy^2	$dxdy$
45	−20	400	56	−14	196	280
55	−10	100	50	−20	400	200
56	−9	81	48	−22	484	198
58	−7	49	60	−10	100	70
60	−5	25	62	−8	64	40
65	0	0	64	−6	36	0
68	3	9	65	−5	25	−15
70	5	25	70	0	0	0
75	10	100	74	4	16	40
80	15	225	82	12	144	180
85	20	400	90	20	400	400
	$\Sigma\, dx = 2$	$\Sigma\, dx^2 = 1414$		$\Sigma\, dy = -49$	$\Sigma\, dy^2 = 1865$	$\Sigma\, dxdy = 1393$

Coefficient of Correlation :

$$r = \frac{\Sigma\, dxdy \times N - (\Sigma\, dx)(\Sigma\, dy)}{\sqrt{\Sigma dx^2 \times N - (\Sigma dx)^2}\sqrt{\Sigma dy^2 \times N - (\Sigma\, dy)^2}}$$

$$\Sigma\, dxdy = 1393\,;\ N = 11\,;\ \Sigma dx = 2\,;\ \Sigma dy = -49\,;\ \Sigma dx^2 = 1414\,;\ \Sigma dy^2 = 1865$$

$$r = \frac{1393 \times 11 - (2)(-49)}{\sqrt{1414 \times 11 - (2)^2}\sqrt{1865 \times 11 - (-49)^2}}$$

$$= \frac{15323 + 98}{\sqrt{15554 - 4}\sqrt{20515 - 2401}}$$

$$= \frac{15421}{\sqrt{15550 \times 18114}}$$

$$= \frac{15421}{16783}$$

$$= +0.9189$$

$$(\text{or}) = \mathbf{+0.92}$$

Problem 40. From the following data, examine whether input of oil and output of electricity can be said to be correlated.

Input of oil :	6.9	8.2	7.8	4.8	9.6	8.0	7.7
Output of electricity :	1.9	3.5	6.5	1.3	5.5	3.5	2.2

(*B. Com. Madras*)

Solution:

Computation of Coefficient of Correlation

Input of oil			*Output of Electricity*			
X	$dx{=}X{-}8$	dx^2	Y	$dy = Y{-}3.5$	dy^2	$dxdy$
6.9	−1.1	1.21	1.9	−1.6	2.56	+1.76
8.2	+0.2	0.04	3.5	0	0	0
7.8	−0.2	0.04	6.5	−3.0	9.00	−0.60
4.8	−3.2	10.24	1.3	−2.2	4.84	+7.04
9.6	+1.6	2.56	5.5	+2.0	4.00	+3.20
8.0	0	0	3.5	0	0	0
7.7	−0.3	0.09	2.2	−1.3	1.69	+0.39
	$\Sigma dx = -3$	$\Sigma dx^2 = 14.18$		$\Sigma dy = -0.1$	$\Sigma dy^2 = 22.09$	$\Sigma dxdy = 11.79$

Coefficient of Correlation :

$$r = \frac{\Sigma\, dxdy \times N - (\Sigma\, dx)(\Sigma\, dy)}{\sqrt{\Sigma dx^2 \times N - (\Sigma dx)^2}\sqrt{\Sigma dy^2 \times N - (\Sigma\, dy)^2}}$$

$$\Sigma\, dxdy = 11.79;\ N = 7;\ \Sigma dx = -0.3;\ \Sigma dy = -0.1;\ \Sigma dx^2 = 14.18;\ \Sigma dy^2 = 22.09$$

$$r = \frac{11.79 \times 7 - (-3)(-0.1)}{\sqrt{14.18 \times 7 - (-3)^2}\sqrt{22.09 \times 7 - (-0.1)^2}}$$

$$= \frac{82.53 - 0.3}{\sqrt{99.26 - 9}\sqrt{154.63 - 0.01}}$$

$$= \frac{82.23}{\sqrt{90.26 \times 154.62}}$$

$$= \frac{82.23}{118.14}$$

$$= \mathbf{+0.696}.$$

Problem 41. Find out the coefficient of correlation between output and cost of the automobile factory from the following data :

Output of cars ('000) :	3.5	4.2	5.6	6.5	7.0	8.2	8.8	9	9.7	10
Cost per car (Rs.'000) :	9.8	9.4	8.8	8.4	8.3	8.2	8.2	8	8.0	8.1

(*B.Com. Saurashtra*)

Solution :

Computation of Coefficient of Correlation

Output of cars ('000) X	$dx = X-7$	dx^2	*Cost per car* ($Rs.$'000) Y	$dy = Y-8.4$	dy^2	$dxdy$
3.5	−3.5	12.25	9.8	1.4	1.96	−4.9
4.2	−2.8	7.84	9.4	1.0	1.00	−2.8
5.6	−1.4	1.96	8.8	0.4	0.16	−0.56
6.5	−0.5	0.25	8.4	0	0	0
7.0	0	0	8.3	−0.1	0.01	0
8.2	1.2	1.44	8.2	−0.2	0.04	−0.24
8.8	1.8	3.24	8.2	−0.2	0.04	−0.36
9.0	2.0	4.0	8.0	−0.4	0.16	−0.8
9.7	2.7	7.29	8.0	−0.4	0.16	−1.08
10.0	3.0	9.0	8.1	−0.3	0.09	−0.9
	$\Sigma dx = 2.5$	$\Sigma dx^2 =$ 47.27		$\Sigma dy = 1.2$	Σdy^2 = 3.62	$\Sigma\, dxdy =$ −11.64

Coefficient of Correlation :

$$r = \frac{\Sigma\, dxdy \times N - (\Sigma\, dx)(\Sigma\, dy)}{\sqrt{\Sigma dx^2 \times N - (\Sigma dx)^2}\sqrt{\Sigma dy^2 \times N - (\Sigma\, dy)^2}}$$

$$\Sigma\, dxdy = -11.64;\ N = 10;\ \Sigma dx = 2.5;\ \Sigma dy = 1.2;\ \Sigma dx^2 = 47.27;\ \Sigma dy^2 = 3.62$$

$$r = \frac{-11.64 \times 10 - (2.5)(1.2)}{\sqrt{47.27 \times 10 - (2.5)^2}\sqrt{3.62 \times 10 - (1.2)^2}}$$

$$= \frac{-116.40 - (3)}{\sqrt{472.7 - 6.25}\sqrt{36.2 - 1.44}} = \frac{-119.40}{\sqrt{466.45 \times 34.76}} = \frac{-119.40}{127.33}$$

$$= \mathbf{-0.938}.$$

Problem 42. Find a suitable coefficient of correlation for the following data.

Fertilizer used (metric tons):	15	18	20	24	30	35	40	50
Productivity (metric tons) :	85	93	95	105	120	130	150	160

(*B.Com., Madras*)

Solution:

Computation of Correlation Coefficient

X	$dx = x{-}30$	dx^2	Y	$dy = Y{-}120$	dy^2	$dxdy$
15	−15	225	85	−35	1225	+525
18	−12	144	93	−27	729	+324
20	−10	100	95	−25	625	+250
24	−6	36	105	−5	25	+30
30	0	0	120	0	0	0
35	5	25	130	+10	100	+50
40	10	100	150	+30	900	+300
50	20	440	160	+40	1600	+800
	$\Sigma dx = -8$	$\Sigma dx^2 = 1030$		$\Sigma dy = -12$	$\Sigma dy^2 = 5204$	$\Sigma dxdy = 2279$

$$r = \frac{\Sigma dxdy - \dfrac{\Sigma dx \times \Sigma dy}{N}}{\sqrt{\Sigma dx^2 - \dfrac{(\Sigma dx)^2}{N} \; \Sigma dy^2 - \dfrac{(\Sigma dy)^2}{N}}}$$

$$\Sigma dxdy = 2279; \Sigma dx = -8; \Sigma dy = -12; \Sigma dx^2 = 1030; \Sigma dy^2 = 5204; N = 8$$

$$r = \frac{(2279 \times 8) - (-8 \times -12)}{\sqrt{1030 \times 8 - (-8)^2 5204 \times 8 - (-12)^2}}$$

$$= \frac{18232 - 96}{\sqrt{(8240 - 64)(41632 - 144)}}$$

$$= \frac{18136}{\sqrt{8176 \times 41488}}$$

$$= \frac{18136}{18449}$$

$$= \mathbf{+0.98}$$

Problem 43. Calculate coefficient of correlation of the following figures relating to the consumption of fertilizer and the output of foodgrain in district X:

Chemical fertilizer used (in metric ton)	*Output of food (in metric ton)*	*Chemical fertilizer used (in metric ton)*	*Output of food (in metric ton)*
100	1000	170	1360
110	1050	180	1420
120	1080	190	1500
130	1150	200	1600
140	1200	210	1650
150	1220	220	1650
160	1300	230	1650

(*B.Com., Delhi*)

Solution:

Computation of Coefficient of Correlation

X	$dx = \frac{X-170}{10}$	dx^2	Y	$dy = \frac{Y-1500}{10}$	dy^2	$dxdy$
100	−7	49	1000	−50	2500	+350
110	−6	36	1050	−45	2025	+270
120	−5	25	1080	−42	1764	+210
130	−4	16	1150	−35	1225	+140
140	−3	9	1200	−30	900	+90
150	−2	4	1220	−28	784	+56
160	−1	1	1300	−20	400	+20
170	0	0	1360	−14	196	0
180	+1	1	1420	−8	64	−8
190	+2	4	1500	0	0	0
200	+3	9	1600	+10	100	+30
210	+4	16	1650	+15	225	+60
220	+5	25	1650	+15	225	+75
230	+6	36	1650	+15	225	+90
	$\Sigma dx - 7$	$\Sigma dx^2 = 231$		$\Sigma dy = -217$	$\Sigma dy^2 = 10633$	$\Sigma dxdy = 1383$

$$r = \frac{(\Sigma dxdy \times N) - (\Sigma dx \times \Sigma dy)}{\sqrt{\Sigma dx^2 \times N - (\Sigma dx)^2}\sqrt{\Sigma dy^2 \times N - (\Sigma dy)^2}}$$

$$\Sigma dxdy = 1383\,;\ \Sigma dx = -7\,;\ \Sigma dy = -217\,;\ \Sigma dx^2 = 231\,;\ \Sigma dy^2 = 10633\,;\ N = 14$$

$$r = \frac{(1383 \times 14) - (-7 \times -217)}{\sqrt{231 \times 14 - (-7)^2}\sqrt{10633 \times 14 - (-217)^2}}$$

$$= \frac{(19362) - (1519)}{\sqrt{(3234 - 49)}\sqrt{148862 - 47089}}$$

$$= \frac{17843}{\sqrt{3185 \times 101773}}$$

$$= \frac{17843}{18004}$$

$$= \mathbf{+0.99}$$

Problem 44. Marks secured by eleven students in two subjects are given below :

Subject I :	71	68	66	67	70	71	70	73	72	65	66
Subject II :	69	64	65	63	65	62	65	64	66	59	62

(B.A. Madurai)

Solution :

Computation of Coefficient of Correlation

Subject I			*Subject II*			
subject I X	$dx = (X - \overline{X})$ $\overline{X} = 69$	dx^2	*Subject II* Y	$dy = (Y - \overline{Y})$ $\overline{Y} = 64$	dy^2	$dxdy$
71	+2	4	69	+5	25	10
68	−1	1	64	0	0	0
66	−3	9	65	+1	1	−3
67	−2	4	63	−1	1	2
70	+1	1	65	+1	1	1
71	+2	4	62	−2	4	−4.
70	+1	1	65	+1	1	1
73	+4	16	64	0	0	0
72	+3	9	66	+2	4	6
65	−4	16	59	−5	25	20
66	−3	9	62	−2	4	6
$\Sigma X = 759$		$\Sigma dx^2 = 74$	$\Sigma Y = 704$		$\Sigma dy^2 = 66$	$\Sigma dxdy = 39$

Mean : $\overline{X} = \frac{\Sigma X}{N} = \frac{759}{11} = \mathbf{69}$ $\quad\quad \overline{Y} = \frac{\Sigma Y}{N} = \frac{704}{11} = \mathbf{64.}$

Coefficient of correlation :

$$r = \frac{\Sigma dxdy}{\sqrt{\Sigma dx^2 \times \Sigma dy^2}}$$

$$\Sigma dxdy = 39; \Sigma dx^2 = 74; \Sigma dy^2 = 66$$

$$r = \frac{39}{\sqrt{74 \times 66}}$$

$$= \frac{39}{\sqrt{4884}}$$

$$= \frac{39}{69.84}$$

$$r = \mathbf{+0.56.}$$

Problem 45. The following data were collected in an experiment on jute in a village of West Bengal, in which the length X (in cm.) of green plants and the weight Y (in gm.) of dry fibre were recorded for 8 plants :

Plant No. :	1	2	3	4	5	6	7	8
X (in cm.) :	172	148	162	183	160	141	150	190
Y (in gm.) :	6.4	2.3	3.5	4.7	4.1	2.9	2.8	6.6

Calculate the correlation coefficient between X and Y.

(B.Com. Burdwan)

Solution :

Computation of Coefficient of Correlation

Y	$dx = X - 172$	dx^2	Y	$dy = \frac{Y-4}{0.1}$	dy^2	$dxdy$
172	0	0	6.4	+24	576	0
148	−24	576	2.3	−17	289	+408
162	−10	100	3.5	−5	25	+50
183	+11	121	4.7	+7	49	+77
160	−12	144	4.1	+1	1	−12
141	−31	961	2.9	−11	121	+341
150	−21	484	2.8	−12	144	+264
190	+18	324	6.6	+26	676	+468
	$\Sigma dx = -70$	$\Sigma dx^2 = 2710$		$\Sigma dy = 13$	$\Sigma dy^2 = 1881$	$\Sigma dxdy = 1596$

Coefficient of Correlation :

$$r = \frac{\Sigma dxdy \times N - (\Sigma dx)(\Sigma dy)}{\sqrt{\Sigma dx^2 \times N - (\Sigma dx)^2}\sqrt{\Sigma dy^2 \times N - (\Sigma dy)^2}}$$

$$\Sigma dxdy = 1596; \quad N = 8; \quad \Sigma dx = -70; \quad \Sigma dy = 13; \quad \Sigma dx^2 = 2710; \quad \Sigma dy = 1881$$

$$r = \frac{1596 \times 8 - (-70)(13)}{\sqrt{2710 \times 8 - (-70)}\sqrt{1881 \times 8 - (13)^2}}$$

$$= \frac{12768 + 910}{\sqrt{21680 - 4900}\sqrt{15048 - 169}}$$

$$= \frac{13678}{\sqrt{16780 \times 14879}} = \frac{13678}{15800} = +0.866$$

$(or) \quad = \mathbf{+0.87}$

Problem 46. Calculate Karl Pearson's coefficient of correlation and its probable error from the following data of imports and exports :

Year	*Value of imports*	*Value of exports*
1994	903	620
1995	1036	625
1996	904	573
1997	961	640
1998	1122	642
1999	1092	661
2000	1131	685
2001	1190	793
2002	1314	816
2003	1350	805

(*B.Com. Lucknow*)

Solution :

Computation of Coefficient of Correlation

Year	*X*	*dx* $= X - 1100$	dx^2	*Y*	*dy* $= Y - 680$	dy^2	*dxdy*
1994	903	−197	38809	620	−60	3600	11,820
1995	1036	−64	4096	625	−55	3025	3520
1996	904	−196	38416	573	−107	11449	20,972
1997	961	−139	19321	640	−40	1600	5560
1998	1122	+22	484	642	−38	1444	−836
1999	1092	−8	64	661	−19	361	152
2000	1131	+31	961	685	+5	25	155
2001	1190	+90	8100	793	+113	12769	10,170
2002	1314	+214	45796	816	+136	18496	29,104
2003	1350	250	62500	805	+125	15625	31,250
		$\Sigma dx = +3$	$\Sigma dx^2 = 2,18,547$		$\Sigma dy = +60$	$\Sigma dy^2 = 68,394$	$\Sigma dxdy = 1,11,867$

Coefficient of Correlation :

$$r = \frac{\Sigma dxdy \times N - (\Sigma dx)(\Sigma dy)}{\sqrt{\Sigma dx^2 \times N - (\Sigma dx)^2}\sqrt{\Sigma dy^2 \times N - (\Sigma dy)^2}}$$

$$\Sigma dxdy = 1,11,867; \quad N = 10; \quad \Sigma dx = 3; \quad \Sigma dy = 60;$$

$$\Sigma dx^2 = 2,18,547; \quad \Sigma dy^2 = 68394$$

$$r = \frac{1,11,867 \times 10 - (3)(60)}{\sqrt{2,18,547 \times 10 - (3)^2}\sqrt{68,394 \times 10 - (60)^2}}$$

$$= \frac{1,118,670 - 180}{\sqrt{2,185470 - 9}\sqrt{683940 - 3600}}$$

$$= \frac{11,18,490}{\sqrt{2185461 \times 680340}}$$

$$= \frac{11,18,490}{1478.33 \times 824.83}$$

$$= \frac{11,18490}{1219370.93}$$

$$= \mathbf{+0.9173}.$$

$$\text{Probable Error of } r = 0.6745\frac{1 - r^2}{\sqrt{N}}$$

$$= 0.6745\frac{1 - (0.9173)^2}{\sqrt{10}}$$

$$= 0.6745\frac{1 - 0.8414}{3.1623}$$

$$= 0.6745 \times \frac{0.1586}{3.1623}$$

$$= 0.6745 \times 0.05015$$

$$= \mathbf{0.0338}.$$

Problem 47. Ten recruits were subjected to selection test to ascertain their suitability or a certain course of training. At the end of the training they were given proficiency test. The marks secured by the recruits are recorded below :

S. No.	:	1	2	3	4	5	6	7	8	9	10
Section test Score (X)	:	44	49	52	52	47	76	65	60	63	58
Proficiency test Score (Y)	:	48	55	45	60	43	80	58	50	77	46

(*B. Com., Bombay*)

Solution :

Computation of Coefficient of Correlation

Serial No.	*Selection test score X*	$dx = X - 56$	dx^2	*Proficiency test score Y*	$dy = Y - 57$	dy^2	$dxdy$
1	44	−12	144	48	−9	81	108
2	49	−7	49	55	−2	4	14
3	52	−4	16	45	−12	144	48
4	52	−4	16	60	+3	9	−12
5	47	−9	81	43	−14	196	126
6	76	+20	400	80	+23	529	460
7	65	+9	81	58	+1	1	9
8	60	+4	16	50	−7	49	−28
9	63	+7	49	77	+20	400	140
10	58	+2	4	46	−11	121	−22
N=10		$\Sigma dx = 6$	$\Sigma dx^2 = 856$		$\Sigma dy = -8$	$\Sigma dy^2 = 1534$	$\Sigma dxdy = 843$

Coefficient of Correlation :

$$r = \frac{\Sigma dxdy \times N - (\Sigma dx)(\Sigma dy)}{\sqrt{\Sigma dx^2 \times N - (\Sigma dx)^2}\sqrt{\Sigma dy^2 \times N - (\Sigma dy)^2}}$$

$$\Sigma dxdy = 843; \quad \Sigma dx = 6; \quad \Sigma dy = -8; \quad N = 10; \quad dx^2 = 856; \quad dy^2 = 1534$$

$$r = \frac{843 \times 10 - (6 - 8)}{\sqrt{856 \times 10 - (6)^2}\sqrt{1534 \times 10 - (-8)^2}}$$

$$= \frac{8430 + 48}{\sqrt{8560 - 36 \times 15340 - 64}}$$

$$= \frac{8478}{\sqrt{8524 \times 15276}} = \frac{8478}{11411}$$

$$= \mathbf{+0.743}$$

(or) $= \mathbf{+0.74}$.

Thus there is a high degree of positive correlation between selection test scores and proficiency test scores.

Problem 48. The following are the results of an Examination

Age of candidates	*Candidates appeared*	*Successful candidates*	*Age of candidates*	*Candidates appeared*	*Successful candidates*
13–14	200	124	18–19	400	252
14–15	300	180	19–20	250	145
15–16	100	65	20–21	150	81
16–17	50	34	21–22	25	12
17–18	150	99	22–23	75	33

Calculate coefficient of correlation between age and successful candidates in the examination.

(*B.Com. Rajasthan*)

Solution :

Computation of Coefficient of Correlation

Age	*m*	$dx = m - 17.5$	dx^2	*Success in %* Y	$dy = Y - 59$	dy^2	$dxdy$
13–14	13.5	−4	16	$\frac{124}{200} \times 100 = 62$	3	9	−12
14–15	14.5	−3	9	$\frac{180}{300} \times 100 = 60$	1	1	−3
15–16	15.5	−2	4	$\frac{65}{100} \times 100 = 65$	6	36	−12
16–17	16.5	−1	1	$\frac{34}{50} \times 100 = 68$	9	81	−9
17–18	17.5	0	0	$\frac{99}{150} \times 100 = 66$	7	49	0
18–19	18.5	1	1	$\frac{252}{400} \times 100 = 63$	4	16	4
19–20	19.5	2	4	$\frac{145}{250} \times 100 = 58$	−1	1	−2
20–21	20.5	3	9	$\frac{81}{150} \times 100 = 54$	−5	25	−15
21–22	21.5	4	16	$\frac{12}{25} \times 100 = 48$	−11	121	−44
22–23	22.5	5	25	$\frac{33}{75} \times 100 = 44$	−15	225	−75
		$\Sigma dx = 5$	$\Sigma dx^2 = 85$		$\Sigma dy = -2$	$\Sigma dy^2 = 564$	$\Sigma dxdy = -168$

Coefficient of Correlation :

$$r = \frac{\Sigma dxdy \times N - (\Sigma dx)(\Sigma dy)}{\sqrt{\Sigma dx^2 \times N - (\Sigma dx)^2}\sqrt{\Sigma dy^2 \times N - (\Sigma dy)^2}}$$

$$\Sigma dxdy = -168; \quad N = 10;$$

$$\Sigma dx = 5; \quad dy = -2 \quad \Sigma dx^2 = 85;$$

$$\Sigma dy^2 = 564$$

$$r = \frac{-168 \times 10 - (5)(-2)}{\sqrt{85 \times 10 - (5)^2}\sqrt{564 \times 10 - (-2)^2}}$$

$$= \frac{-1680 + 10}{\sqrt{850 - 25}\sqrt{5640 - 4}}$$

$$= \frac{-1670}{\sqrt{825 \times 5636}}$$

$$= \frac{-1670}{2156}$$

$$= \mathbf{-0.77}$$

Problem 49. Calculate coefficient of correlation between age and playing habit from the following data.

Age in years	*Population*	*No. of players*
15–20	1500	1200
20–25	2000	1560
25–30	4000	2280
30–35	3000	1500
35–40	2500	1000
40–45	1000	300
45–50	800	200
50–55	500	50
55–60	200	6

(B.Com)

Solution :

To Calculate the coefficient of correlation between age and playing habit, first we have to find out the playing habit in percentage. The workings are shown below :

Population	*No. of Players*	*% of Players*
1500	1200	$\frac{1200}{1500} \times 100 = 80$
2000	1560	$\frac{1560}{2000} \times 100 = 78$
4000	2280	$\frac{2280}{4000} \times 100 = 57$
3000	1500	$\frac{1500}{3000} \times 100 = 50$
2500	1000	$\frac{1000}{2500} \times 100 = 40$
1000	300	$\frac{300}{1000} \times 100 = 30$
800	200	$\frac{200}{800} \times 100 = 25$
500	50	$\frac{50}{500} \times 100 = 10$
200	6	$\frac{6}{200} \times 100 = 3$

Computation of Coefficient of Correlation

Age in year	*M.P.* X	$dx = \left(\frac{X - 37.5}{5}\right)$	dx^2	*Players per* 100 Y	$dy = (Y - 40)$	dy^2	$dxdy$
15–20	17.5	−4	16	80	+40	1600	−160
20–25	22.5	−3	9	78	+38	1444	−114
25–30	27.5	−2	2	57	+17	289	−34
30–35	32.5	−1	1	50	+10	100	−10
35–40	37.5	0	0	40	0	0	0
40–45	42.5	1	1	30	−10	100	−10
45–50	47.5	2	4	25	−15	225	−30
50–55	52.5	3	9	10	−30	900	−90
55–60	57.5	4	16	3	−37	1369	−148
		$\Sigma dx = 0$	$\Sigma dx^2 = 60$		$\Sigma dy = 13$	$\Sigma dy^2 = 6027$	$\Sigma dxdy = -596$

Coefficient of Correlation :

$$r = \frac{\Sigma dxdy \times N - (\Sigma dx)(\Sigma dy)}{\sqrt{\Sigma dx^2 \times N - (\Sigma dx)^2}\sqrt{\Sigma dy^2 \times N - (\Sigma dy)^2}}$$

$$\Sigma dxdy = -596; \quad N = 9; \quad \Sigma dx = 0; \quad \Sigma dy = 13$$

$$\Sigma dx^2 = 60; \quad \Sigma dy^2 = 6027$$

$$r = \frac{-596 \times 9 - (0)(13)}{\sqrt{60 \times 9 - (0)^2}\sqrt{6027 \times 9 - (13)^2}}$$

$$= \frac{-5364}{\sqrt{540 \times 54243 - 169}}$$

$$= \frac{-5364}{\sqrt{540 \times 54074}}$$

$$= \frac{-5364}{5403.69}$$

$$= \mathbf{-0.993}$$

Problem 50. The following table gives the distribution of the total population and those who are totally and partially blind among them. Find out if there is any relation between age and blindness :

Age	:	0–10	10–20	20–30	30–40	40–50	50–60	60–70	70–80
No. of persons ('000)	:	100	60	40	36	24	11	6	3
Blind	:	55	40	40	40	36	22	18	15

(*B.Com. Madurai, Punjab, Kanpur, Osmania, Rajasthan, Bhagalpur*)

Solution :

Computation of Coefficient of Correlation

Age				*Blindness*			
Age group	*m*	$dx = \frac{m-45}{10}$	dx^2	*Blind per lakh*	$dy = Y - 180$	dy^2	$dxdy$
0–10	5	−4	16	55	−125	15,625	500
10–20	15	−3	9	$\frac{40}{60,000} \times 1,00,000 = 67$	−113	12,769	339
20–30	25	−2	4	$\frac{40}{40,000} \times 1,00,000 = 100$	−80	6,400	160
30–40	35	−1	1	$\frac{40}{36,000} \times 1,00,000 = 111$	−69	4,761	69
40–50	45	0	0	$\frac{36}{24,000} \times 1,00,000 = 150$	−30	900	0
50–60	55	1	1	$\frac{22}{11,000} \times 1,00,000 = 200$	20	400	20
60–70	65	2	4	$\frac{18}{6000} \times 1,00,000 = 300$	120	14,400	240
70–80	75	3	9	$\frac{15}{3000} \times 1,00,000 = 500$	320	1,02,400	960
		$\Sigma dx = -4$	$\Sigma dx^2 = 44$		$\Sigma dy = 43$	$\Sigma dy^2 =$ 1,57,655	$\Sigma dxdy =$ 2,288

Coefficient of correlation :

$$r = \frac{\Sigma dxdy \times N - (\Sigma dx))(\Sigma dy)}{\sqrt{\Sigma dx^2 \times N - (dx)^2}\sqrt{\Sigma dy^2 \times N - (dy)^2}}$$

$$\Sigma dxdy = 2288; \quad N = 8; \quad \Sigma dx = -4; \Sigma dy = 43; \quad \Sigma dx^2 = 44; \quad \Sigma dy^2 = 1,57,655$$

$$r = \frac{2288 \times 8 - (-4)(43)}{\sqrt{44 \times 8 - (-4)^2}\sqrt{1,57,655 \times 8 - (43)^2}}$$

$$= \frac{18304 + 172}{\sqrt{336 \times 1259391}} = \frac{18476}{20570.74}$$

$$r = \mathbf{+0.898}$$

Problem 51. The following table gives the frequency according to age groups of marks obtained by 67 students in an intelligence test:

Test marks	*Age in years*				
	18	19	20	21	Total
200–250	4	4	2	1	11
250–300	3	5	4	2	14
300–350	2	6	8	5	21
350–400	1	4	6	10	21

Is there any relationship between age and intelligence? (*B. Com.*)

Solution :

Computation of Coefficient of Correlation

Total Marks			Age in years → X	18	19	20	21				
	Y	m	dy \ dx	-2	-1	0	1	f	fdy	fdy²	fdxdy
	200–250	225	-2	4 [16]	4 [8]	2 [0]	1 [-2]	11	-22	44	22
	250–300	275	-1	3 [6]	5 [5]	4 [0]	2 [-2]	14	-14	14	9
	300–350	325	0	2 [0]	6 [0]	8 [0]	5 [0]	21	0	0	0
	350–400	375	1	1 [-2]	4 [-4]	6 [0]	10 [10]	21	21	21	4
			f	10	19	20	18	N = 67	Σfdy = -15	Σfdy2 = 79	Σfdxdy = 35
			fdx	-20	-19	0	18	Σfdx = -21			
			fdx²	40	19	0	18	Σfdx² = 77			
			fdxdy	20	9	0	6	Σfdxdy = 35			

Coefficient of Correlation:

$$r = \frac{\Sigma f dx dy \times N - (\Sigma f dx)(\Sigma f dy)}{\sqrt{\Sigma f dx^2 \times N - (\Sigma f dx)^2}\sqrt{\Sigma f dy^2 \times N - (\Sigma f dy)^2}}$$

$$\Sigma f dx dy = 35; \quad N = 67; \quad \Sigma f dx = -21; \quad \Sigma f dy = -15; \quad \Sigma f dx^2 = 77; \quad \Sigma f dy^2 = 79$$

$$r = \frac{35 \times 67 - (21)(-15)}{\sqrt{77 \times 67 - (-21)^2}\sqrt{79 \times 67 - (-15)^2}}$$

$$= \frac{2345 - 315}{\sqrt{5159 - 441}\sqrt{5293 - 225}}$$

$$= \frac{2030}{\sqrt{4718 \times 5068}}$$

$$= \frac{2030}{4889.87}$$

$$r = \mathbf{+0.4151.}$$

Problem 52. The following table gives the distribution of the ages in years of husbands and wives in 100 couples :

Age of wives	*Age of husbands* 20–25	25–30	30–35	35–40
15–20	20	10	3	2
20–25	4	28	6	4
25–30	–	5	11	–
30–35	–	–	2	–
35–40	–	–	–	5

Calculate the coefficient of correlation between the age of the husband and the age of the wife.

(B.Com., Bombay)

Solution:

Computation of Coefficient of Correlation

			Age of husbands							
		X	20–25	25–30	30–35	35–40				
		m	22.5	27.5	32.5	37.5				
Y (Age of Wives)	m	dy \ dx	-1	0	1	2	f	fdy	Σfdy^2	$\Sigma fdxdy$
15–20	17.5	-2	20 [40]	10 [0]	3 [-6]	2 [-8]	35	-70	140	26
20–25	22.5	-1	4 [4]	28 [0]	6 [-6]	4 [-8]	42	-42	42	-10
25–30	27.5	0		5 [0]	11 [0]		16	0	0	0
30–35	32.5	1			2 [2]		2	2	2	2
35–40	37.5	2				5 [20]	5	10	20	20
		f	24	43	22	11	N = 100	Σfdy = -100	Σfdy^2 = 204	$\Sigma fdxdy$ = 38
		fdx	-24	0	22	22	Σfdx = 20			
		fdx^2	24	0	22	44	Σfdx^2 = 90			
		fdxdy	44	0	- 10	4	$\Sigma fdxdy$ = 38			

Coefficient of Correlation :

$$r = \frac{\Sigma fdxdy \times N - (\Sigma fdx)(\Sigma fdy)}{\sqrt{\Sigma fdx^2 \times N(\Sigma fdx^2)}\sqrt{\Sigma fdy^2 \times N - (\Sigma fdy)^2}}$$

$$\Sigma fdxdy = 38; \quad N = 100; \quad \Sigma fdx = 20; \Sigma fdy = -100; \quad \Sigma fdx^2 = 90; \quad \Sigma fdy^2 = 204$$

$$r = \frac{38 \times 100 - (20)(-100)}{\sqrt{90 \times 100 - (20)^2}\sqrt{204 \times 100} - (-100)^2}$$

$$= \frac{3800 - (-2000)}{\sqrt{9000 - 400}\sqrt{20400 - 10000}}$$

$$= \frac{5800}{\sqrt{8600 \times 10400}} = \frac{5800}{9457.27} = 0.6133$$

$$r = \mathbf{+0.61}.$$

Problem 53. Compute the correlation coefficient and the probable error for the following data :

Sales revenue (*Rs. '000*)	*Advertising expenditure* (*'000*) 5–15	15–25	25–35	35–45	Total
75–125	4	1	–	–	5
125–175	7	6	2	1	16
175–225	1	3	4	2	10
225–275	1	1	3	4	9
Total :	13	11	9	7	40

(*M.B.A. Delhi*)

Solution :

Computation of Coefficient of Correlation

X \ Y			5-15	15-25	25-35	35-45				
		m	10	20	30	40				
X	m	dx \ dy	-2	-1	0	1	f	fdx	fdx^2	fdxdy
75-125	100	-2	4 [16]	1 [2]			5	-10	20	18
125-175	150	-1	7 [14]	6 [6]	2 [0]	1 [-1]	16	-16	16	19
175-225	200	0	1 [0]	3 [-0]	4 [0]	2 [0]	10	0	0	0
225-275	250	+1	1 [-2]	1 [-1]	3 [0]	4 [4]	9	9	9	1
		f	13	11	9	7	N = 40	Σfdx = -17	Σfdx^2 =45	Σfdxdy = 38
		fdy	-26	-11	0	7	Σfdy = -30			
		fdy^2	52	11	0	7	Σfdy^2 = 70			
		fdxdy	28	7	0	3	Σfdxdy = 38			

$$r = \frac{\Sigma fdxdy - \dfrac{\Sigma fdx \times \Sigma fdy}{N}}{\sqrt{\Sigma fdx^2 - \dfrac{(\Sigma fdx^2)}{N}}\sqrt{\Sigma fdy^2 - \dfrac{(\Sigma fdy^2)}{N}}}$$

$$\Sigma fdxdy = 38; \quad \Sigma fdx = -17; \quad \Sigma fdy = -30; \quad \Sigma fdx^2 = 45; \quad \Sigma fdy^2 = 70; \quad N = 40.$$

$$r = \frac{38 - \dfrac{(17 \times -30)}{40}}{\sqrt{45 - \dfrac{(-17)^2}{40}}\sqrt{70 - \dfrac{(-30)}{40}}}$$

$$= \frac{(38 \times 40) - (-17 \times -30)}{\sqrt{45 \times 40 - (-17)^2}\sqrt{70 \times 40 - (-30)^2}}$$

$$= \frac{1520 - 510}{\sqrt{1800 - 289}\sqrt{2800 - 900}} = \frac{1010}{\sqrt{1511 \times 1900}} = \frac{1010}{1694.37}$$

$$r = \mathbf{+0.596.}$$

Problem 54. Calculate the coefficient of correlation between the age of mothers and daughters from the following data :

Ages of Mothers	*Age of daughters in years* 5–10	10–15	15–20	20–25	25–30	Total
15–25	6	3	–	–	–	9
25–35	3	16	10	–	–	29
35–45	–	10	15	7	–	32
45–55	–	–	7	10	4	21
55–65	–	–	–	4	5	9
Total :	9	29	32	21	9	100

(*B.Com., Mysore, M.A. Punjab*)

Solution :

Computation of Coefficient of Correlation

Age of mothers in years (rows) / Age of daughters in years (columns); cell entries: frequency [product $f \cdot dx \cdot dy$ in box]

y	m	dy \ X	5–10	10–15	15–20	20–25	25–30	f	fdy	fdy^2	fdxdy
		m	7.5	12.5	17.5	22.5	27.5				
		dx	-2	-1	0	1	2				
15–25	20	-2	6 [24]	3 [6]				9	-18	36	30
25–35	30	-1	3 [6]	16 [16]	10 [0]			29	-29	29	22
35–45	40	0		10 [0]	15 [0]	7 [0]		32	0	0	0
45–55	50	1			7 [0]	10 [10]	4 [8]	21	21	21	18
55–65	60	2				4 [8]	5 [20]	9	18	36	28
		f	9	29	32	21	9	N = 100	Σfdy = -8	Σfdy^2 = 122	Σfdxdy = 98
		fdx	-18	-29	0	21	18	Σfdx = -8			
		fdx^2	36	29	0	21	36	Σfdx^2 = 122			
		fdxdy	30	22	0	18	28	Σfdxdy = 98			

Coefficient of Correlation :

$$r = \frac{\Sigma fdxdy \times N - (\Sigma fdx)(\Sigma fdy)}{\sqrt{\Sigma fdx^2 \times N - (\Sigma fdx)^2}\sqrt{\Sigma fdy^2 \times N(\Sigma fdy)^2}}$$

$$\Sigma fdxdy = 98; \quad N = 100; \quad \Sigma fdx = -8; \quad \Sigma fdy = -8; \quad \Sigma fdx^2 = 122; \quad \Sigma fdy^2 = 122.$$

$$r = \frac{98 \times 100 - (-8)(-8)}{\sqrt{122 \times 100 - (-8)^2}\sqrt{122 \times 100 - (-8)^2}}$$

$$= \frac{9800 - 64}{\sqrt{12,200 - 64}\sqrt{12,200 - 64}}$$

$$= \frac{9736}{\sqrt{12136}\sqrt{12136}}$$

$$= \frac{9736}{12136}$$

$$= 0.8022$$

$$r = \mathbf{+0.8}.$$

Problem 55. Calculate the coefficient of correlation between the ages of husbands and wives from the following table :

Ages of wives (years)	*Ages of Husbands (years)* 20–30	30–40	40–50	50–60	60–70	Total
15–25	5	9	3	–	–	17
25–35	–	10	25	2	–	37
35–45	–	1	12	2	–	15
45–55	–	–	4	16	5	25
55–65	–	–	–	4	2	6
Total :	5	20	44	24	7	100

(*B.Com. Delhi*)

Solution :

Computation of Coefficient of Correlation

Age of wives			X → Age of Husbands	20–30	30–40	40–50	50–60	60–70				
			m	25	35	45	55	65				
y	m	dy	dx	-2	-1	0	1	2	f	fdy	fdy^2	fdxdy
15–25	20	-2		5 [20]	9 [18]	3 [0]			17	-34	68	38
25–35	30	-1			10 [10]	25 [0]	2 [-2]		37	-37	37	8
35–45	40	0			1 [0]	12 [0]	2 [0]		15	0	0	0
45–55	50	1				4 [0]	16 [16]	5 [10]	25	25	25	26
55–65	60	2					4 [8]	2 [8]	6	12	24	16
		f		5	20	44	24	7	N =100	Σfdy = -34	Σfdy^2 = 154	Σfdxdy = 88
		fdx		-10	-20	0	24	14	Σfdx = 8			
		fdx^2		20	20	0	24	28	Σfdx^2 = 92			
		fdxdy		20	28	0	22	18	Σfdxdy = 88			

Coefficient of Correlation :

$$r = \frac{\Sigma f dxdy \times N - (\Sigma f dx)(\Sigma f dy)}{\sqrt{\Sigma f dx^2 \times N - (\Sigma f dx)^2}\sqrt{\Sigma f dy^2 \times N - (\Sigma f dy)^2}}$$

$$\Sigma f dxdy = 88; \quad N = 100; \quad \Sigma f dx = 8; \quad \Sigma f dy = -34;$$

$$\Sigma f dx^2 = 92; \quad \Sigma f dy^2 = 154$$

$$r = \frac{88 \times 100 - (8)(-34)}{\sqrt{92 \times 100 - (8)^2}\sqrt{154 \times 100 - (-34)^2}}$$

$$= \frac{8,800 + 272}{\sqrt{9200 - 64}\sqrt{15,400 - 1156}}$$

$$= \frac{9072}{\sqrt{9,136 \times 14,244}}$$

$$= \frac{9072}{11407}$$

$$= \mathbf{+0.795}$$

Problem 56. Determine Karl Pearson's correlation coefficient from the following bi-variate frequency distribution and also calculate probable error :

	Age of wives (years)				
Age of husbands	16–23	23–30	30–37	37–44	44–51
18–25	9	3	–	–	–
25–32	–	20	10	4	–
32–39	–	–	12	5	3
39–46	–	–	8	7	5
46–53	–	–	–	10	4

(*M.A. Ecos., Kurukshetra*)

Solution :

Computation of Coefficient of Correlation

			Age of wives								
		Y	16–23	23–30	30–37	37–44	44–51				
		m	19.5	26.5	33.5	40.5	47.5				
X (Age of husbands)	m	dx \ dy	-2	-1	0	1	2	f	fdx	fdx²	fdxdy
18–25	21.5	-2	9 [36]	3 [6]				12	-24	48	42
25–32	28.5	-1		20 [20]	10 [0]	4 [-4]		34	-34	34	16
32–39	35.5	0			12 [0]	5 [0]	3 [0]	20	0	0	0
39–46	42.5	1			8 [0]	7 [7]	5 [10]	20	20	20	17
46–53	49.5	2				10 [20]	4 [16]	14	28	56	36
		f	9	23	30	26	12	N= 100	Σfdy = -10	Σfdy² = 158	Σfdxdy = 111
		fdy	-18	-23	0	26	24	Σfdx = 9			
		fdy²	36	23	0	26	48	Σfdx² = 133			
		fdxdy	36	26	0	23	26	Σfdxdy = 111			

$$r = \frac{\Sigma f dx dy - \dfrac{\Sigma f dx \times \Sigma f dy}{N}}{\sqrt{\Sigma f dx^2 - \dfrac{(\Sigma f dx)^2}{N}}\sqrt{\Sigma f dy^2 - \dfrac{(\Sigma f dy)^2}{N}}}$$

$$\Sigma f dx dy = 111; \quad \Sigma f dx = -10; \quad \Sigma f dy = 9; \quad \Sigma f dx^2 = 158; \quad \Sigma f dy^2 = 133; \quad N = 100;$$

$$r = \frac{111 - \dfrac{(-10)(9)}{100}}{\sqrt{158 - \dfrac{(-10)^2}{100}}\sqrt{133 - \dfrac{(9)^2}{100}}}$$

$$= \frac{111 + 0.9}{\sqrt{158 - 1}\sqrt{133 - 0.81}}$$

$$= \frac{111.9}{\sqrt{157 \times 132.19}}$$

$$= \frac{111.9}{144.06}$$

$$r = \mathbf{+0.7768.}$$

$$\text{P.E.} = 0.6745 \frac{1 - r^2}{\sqrt{N}}$$

$$= 0.6745 \frac{1 - (.7768)^2}{\sqrt{100}}$$

$$= \frac{0.6745 \times 0.397}{10}$$

$$= \frac{0.2678}{10}$$

$$= 0.02678 \quad = \mathbf{+0.027}.$$

Problem 57. Find the coefficient of correlation between the marks obtained by sixty candidates at an examination in two subjects—Economics and Statistics—from the data given below :

Marks in Statistics	*Marks in Economics*			
	5–15	15–25	25–35	35–45
0–10	1	1	–	–
10–20	3	6	5	1
20–30	1	8	9	2
30–40	–	3	9	3
40–50	–	–	4	4

(*B.Com., Nagpur*)

Solution :

Computation of Coefficient of Correlation

Marks in Statistics			Marks in Economics							
		x	5–15	15–25	25–35	35–45				
		m	10	20	30	40				
y	m	dy \ dx	-1	0	1	2	f	fdy	fdy²	fdxdy
0–10	5	-2	1 [2]	1 [0]			2	-4	8	2
10–20	15	-1	3 [3]	6 [0]	5 [-5]	1 [-2]	15	-15	15	-4
20–30	25	0	1 [0]	8 [0]	9 [0]	2	20	0	0	0
30–40	35	1		3 [0]	9 [9]	3 [6]	15	15	15	15
40–50	45	2			4 [8]	4 [16]	8	16	32	24
		Total	5	18	27	10	N = 60	Σfdy = 12	Σfdy² = 70	Σfdxdy = 37
		fdx	-5	0	27	20	Σfdx = 42			
		fdx²	5	0	27	40	Σfdx² = 72			
		fdxdy	5	0	12	20	Σfdxdy = 37			

Coefficient of Correlation :

$$r = \frac{\Sigma f dx dy \frac{(\Sigma f dx \times \Sigma f dy)}{N}}{\sqrt{\Sigma f dx^2 - \left(\frac{\Sigma f dx}{N}\right)^2}\sqrt{\Sigma f dy^2 - \left(\frac{\Sigma f dy}{N}\right)^2}}$$

$$= \frac{\Sigma f dx dy \times N - \Sigma f dx \times \Sigma f dy}{\sqrt{\Sigma f dx^2 \times N - (\Sigma f dx^2)}\sqrt{\Sigma f dy^2 \times N - (\Sigma f dy)^2}}$$

$$\Sigma f dx dy = 37; \quad N = 60; \quad \Sigma f dx = 42; \quad \Sigma f dy = 12$$

$$\Sigma f dx^2 = 72; \quad \Sigma f dy^2 = 70$$

$$r = \frac{37 \times 60 - (42)(12)}{\sqrt{72 \times 60 - (42)^2}\sqrt{70 \times 60 - (12)^2}}$$

$$= \frac{2220 - 504}{\sqrt{4320 - 1764}\sqrt{4200 - 144}} = \frac{1716}{\sqrt{2556 \times 4056}} = \frac{1716}{3219} = +\mathbf{0.533}$$

Alternatively:

$$r = \frac{1716}{\sqrt{2556 \times 4056}} = \frac{1716}{\sqrt{1,03,67,136}} = \frac{1716}{3219.80}$$

$$r = +\mathbf{0.5329} = \mathbf{0.533}$$

Problem 58. The following table gives the ages of husbands and wives at the time of their marriages. Calculate the correlation coefficient between the ages of husbands and wives.

Ages of husbands	*Ages of wives*			
	10–20	20–30	30–40	40–50
10–20	20	26	–	–
20–30	8	14	37	–
30–40	–	4	18	3
40–50	–	–	4	6

(*B.Com., Delhi*)

Solution :

Computation of Coefficient of Correlation

Age of Husbands				Age of wives							
			x	10–20	20–30	30–40	40–50				
			m	15	25	35	45				
			dx	-10	0	+10	+20				
y	m	dy		-1	0	+1	+2	f	fdy	fdy^2	fdxdy
10–20	15	-10	-1	[20] 20	[0] 26			46	-46	46	20
20–30	25	0	0	[0] 8	[0] 14	[0] 37		59	0	0	0
30–40	35	+10	+1		[0] 4	[18] 18	[6] 3	25	25	25	24
40–50	45	+20	+2			[8] 4	[24] 6	10	20	40	32
			f	28	44	59	9	N=140	Σfdy = -1	Σfdy^2 = 111	Σfdxdy = 76
			fdx	-28	0	59	18	Σfdx = 49			
			$fdxd^2$	28	0	59	36	Σfdx^2 = 123			
			fdxdy	20	0	26	30	Σfdxdy = 76			

$$r = \frac{\Sigma fdxdy \times N - (\Sigma fdx \times \Sigma fdy)}{\sqrt{\Sigma fdx^2 \times N - (\Sigma fdx)^2}\sqrt{\Sigma fdy^2 \times N - (\Sigma fdy)^2}}$$

$\Sigma fdxdy = 76$; $\Sigma fdx = 49$; $\Sigma fdy = -1$; $\Sigma fdx^2 = 123$; $\Sigma fdy^2 = 111$; $N = 140$

$$r = \frac{76 \times 140 - (49 \times -1)}{\sqrt{123 \times 140 - (49)^2}\sqrt{111 \times 140 - (-1)^2}}$$

$$= \frac{10640 + 49}{\sqrt{17220 - 2401}\ \sqrt{15540 - 1}}$$

$$= \frac{10689}{\sqrt{14819 \times 15539}} = \frac{10689}{15174.7}$$

$$r = \mathbf{+0.7044}$$

Problem 59. Calculate Karl Pearson's coefficient of correlation from the data given below :

Marks	*Ages in years*				
	18	19	20	21	22
20–25	3	2	–	–	–
15–20	–	5	4	–	–
10–15	–	–	7	10	–
5–10	–	–	–	3	2
0–5	–	–	–	3	1

(*B.Com. Delhi*)

Solution :

Computation of Coefficient of Correlation

Marks (y)	m	dy	x (Age in years) m: 18, dx: -2	19, dx: -1	20, dx: 0	21, dx: 1	22, dx: 2	Total	fdy	fdy^2	fdxdy
20–25	22.5	2	3 [-12]	2 [-4]				5	10	20	-16
15–20	17.5	1		5 [-5]	4 [0]			9	9	9	5
10–15	12.5	0			7 [0]	10 [0]		17	0	0	0
5–10	7.5	-1				3 [-3]	2 [-4]	5	-5	5	-7
0–5	2.5	-2				3 [-6]	1 [-4]	4	-8	16	-10
		Total	3	7	11	16	3	N = 40	Σfdy = 6	Σfdy^2 = 50	Σfdxdy = -38
		fdx	-6	-7	0	16	6	ΣFdx = 9			
		fdx^2	12	7	0	16	12	Σfdx^2 = 47			
		fdxdy	-12	-9	0	-9	-8	Σfdxdy = -38			

$$r = \frac{\Sigma fdxdy \times N - (\Sigma fdx)(\Sigma fdy)}{\sqrt{\Sigma fdx^2 \times N - (\Sigma fdx)^2}\sqrt{\Sigma fdy^2 \times N - (\Sigma fdy)^2}}$$

$$\Sigma fdxdy = -38; \quad N = 40; \quad \Sigma fdx = 9; \quad \Sigma fdy = 6; \Sigma fdx^2 = 47; \quad \Sigma fdy^2 = 50$$

$$r = \frac{-38 \times 40 - (9)(6)}{\sqrt{47 \times 40 - (9)^2}\sqrt{50 \times 40 \times (6)^2}}$$

$$= \frac{-1520 - 54}{\sqrt{1880 - 81}\sqrt{2000 - 36}} = \frac{-1574}{\sqrt{1799 \times 1964}} = \frac{-1574}{1880}$$

$$= \mathbf{-0.837}$$

Problem 60. The following are the marks obtained by the students in class of Statistics and Law :

R.No.	Marks in Statistics	Marks in Law	R.No.	Marks in Statistics	Marks in Law
1	15	13	13	14	11
2	0	1	14	9	3
3	1–	2	15	8	5
4	3	7	16	13	4
5	16	8	17	10	10
6	2	9	18	13	11
7	18	12	19	11	14
8	5	9	20	11	7
9	4	17	21	12	18
10	17	16	22	18	15
11	6	6	23	9	15
12	19	18	24	7	3

Prepare a correlation table taking the magnitude of each class interval as four marks and first class interval as equal to 0 and less than 4. Calculate Karl Pearson's coefficient of correlation between the marks in Statistics and marks in Law from the correlation table.

(B.Com. Bombay)

Solution :

Bivariate Frequency Table

Marks in Law	Marks in Statistics: 0–4	4–8	8–12	12–16	16–20	
0–4	// 2	/ 1	/ 1			4
4–8	/ 1	/ 1	// 2	/ 1		5
8–12	/ 1	/ 1	/ 1	// 2	/ 1	6
12–16			// 2	/ 1	// 2	5
16–20		/ 1		/ 1	// 2	4
	4	4	6	5	5	24

Computation of Coefficient of Correlation

Marks in Law				Marks in Statistics								
			x	0–4	4–8	8–12	12–16	16–20				
			m	2	6	10	14	18				
	Y	m	dy \ dx	-2	-1	0	1	2	f	fdy	fdy²	fdxdy
	0–4	2	-2	2 [8]	1 [2]	1 [0]			4	-8	16	10
	4–8	6	-1	1 [2]	1 [1]	2 [0]	1 [-1]		5	-5	5	2
	8–12	10	0	1 [0]	1 [0]	1 [0]	2 [0]	1 [0]	6	0	0	0
	12–16	14	1			2 [0]	1 [1]	2 [4]	5	5	5	5
	16–20	18	2		1 [-2]		1 [2]	2 [8]	4	8	16	8
			f	4	4	6	5	5	N=24	Σfdy = 0	Σfdy2 = 42	Σfdxdy = 25
			fdx	-8	-4	0	5	10	Σfdx = 3			
			fdx²	16	4	0	5	20	Σfdx2 = 45			
			fdxdy	10	1	0	2	12	Σfdxdy = 25			

$$r = \frac{\Sigma f dxdy - \dfrac{(\Sigma f dx \times \Sigma f dy)}{N}}{\sqrt{\Sigma f dx^2 - \dfrac{(\Sigma f dx)^2}{N}}\sqrt{\Sigma f dy^2 - \dfrac{(\Sigma f dy)^2}{N}}}$$

$$\Sigma f dxdy = 25; \quad \Sigma f dx = 3; \quad \Sigma f dy = 0;$$

$$\Sigma f dx^2 = 45; \quad \Sigma f dy^2 = 42; \quad N = 24$$

$$r = \frac{25 - \dfrac{3 \times 0}{24}}{\sqrt{45 - \dfrac{(3)^2}{24}}\sqrt{42 - \dfrac{(0)}{24}}}$$

$$= \frac{25}{\sqrt{44.625 \times 42}}$$

$$= \frac{25}{43.29}$$

$$= 0.5775$$

$$= \mathbf{0.578}.$$

Problem 61. Find out the coefficient of correlation from the following data :

Marks in Economics	*Marks in Statistics* 0–10	10–20	20–30	30–40	40–50	Total
0–10	4	6	–	–	–	10
10–20	–	5	9	1	–	15
20–30	–	–	4	3	3	10
30–40	–	–	–	6	3	9
40–50	–	–	–	4	2	6
Total:	4	11	13	14	8	50

(*B.Com., Kanpur*)

Solution :

Computation of Coefficient of Correlation

Marks in Economics Y	m	dy \ Marks in Statistics x	0–10	10–20	20–30	30–40	40–50	f	fdy	fdy^2	fdxdy
		m	5	15	25	35	45				
		dx	-2	-1	0	1	2				
0–10	5	-2	4 [16]	6 [12]				10	-20	40	28
10–20	15	-1		5 [5]	9 [0]	1 [-1]		15	-15	15	+4
20–30	25	0			4 [0]	3 [0]	3 [0]	10	0	0	0
30–40	35	1				6 [6]	3 [6]	9	9	9	12
40–50	45	2				4 [8]	2 [8]	6	12	24	16
		f	4	11	13	14	8	N =50	Σfdy = -14	Σfdy2 = 88	Σfdxdy = 60
		fdx	-8	-11	0	14	16	Σfdx = 11			
		fdx^2	16	11	0	14	32	Σfdx2 = 73			
		fdxdy	16	17	0	13	14	Σfdxdy = 60			

Coefficient of Correlation:

$$r = \frac{\Sigma fdxdy \times N - (\Sigma fdx)(\Sigma fdy)}{\sqrt{\Sigma fdx^2 \times N - (\Sigma fdx)^2}\sqrt{\Sigma fdy^2 \times N - (\Sigma fdy)^2}}$$

$$\Sigma fdxdy = 60; \quad N = 50; \quad \Sigma fdx = 11; \quad \Sigma fdy = -14; \quad \Sigma fdx^2 = 73;$$

$$\Sigma fdy^2 = 88$$

$$r = \frac{60 \times 50 - (11)(-14)}{\sqrt{73 \times 50 - (11)^2}\sqrt{88 \times 50 - (-14)^2}}$$

$$= \frac{3,000 + 154}{\sqrt{3,650 - 121}\sqrt{4400 - 196}}$$

$$= \frac{3154}{\sqrt{3529 \times 4204}}$$

$$= \frac{3154}{3851.74}$$

$$= 0.8189$$

$$r = \mathbf{+0.819}.$$

Problem 62. Find the coefficient of correlation from the following table ;

Y	*X*	5	10	15	20	25	30	Total
10		–	1	1	2	8	12	24
15		1	2	5	9	80	11	108
20		2	15	42	98	36	8	201
25		5	20	51	37	10	2	125
30		8	16	8	5	4	1	42
Total :		16	54	107	151	138	34	500

Solution :

Computation of Coefficient of Correlation

y	x →	5	10	15	20	25	30				
	dy \ dx	-3	-2	-1	0	1	2	f	fdy	fdy^2	fdxdy
10	-2		1 [4]	1 [2]	2 [0]	8 [-16]	12 [-48]	24	-48	96	-58
15	-1	1 [3]	2 [4]	5 [5]	9 [0]	80 [-80]	11 [-22]	108	-108	108	-90
20	0	2 [0]	15 [0]	42 [0]	98 [0]	36	8 [0]	201	0	0	0
25	1	5 [-15]	20 [-40]	51 [-51]	37 [0]	10 [10]	2 [4]	125	125	125	-92
30	2	8 [-48]	16 [-64]	8 [-16]	5 [0]	4 [8]	1 [4]	42	84	168	-116
	f	16	54	107	151	138	34	N= 500	Σfdy = 53	Σfdy^2 = 497	Σfdxdy = -356
	fdx	-48	-108	-107	0	138	68	Σfdx = -57			
	fdx^2	144	216	107	0	138	136	Σfdx^2 = 741			
	fdxdy	-60	-96	-60	0	-78	-62	Σfdxdy = -356			

Coefficient of Correlation :

$$r = \frac{\Sigma fdxdy \times N - (\Sigma fdx)(\Sigma fdy)}{\sqrt{\Sigma fdx^2 \times N - (\Sigma fdx)^2}\sqrt{\Sigma fdy^2 \times N - (\Sigma fdy)^2}}$$

$$\Sigma fdxdy = -356; \quad N = 500; \quad \Sigma fdx = -57; \quad \Sigma fdy = 53; \quad \Sigma fdx^2 = 741;$$

$$\Sigma fdy^2 = 497$$

$$r = \frac{-356 \times 500 - (-57)(53)}{\sqrt{741 \times 500 - (-57)^2}\sqrt{497 \times 500 - (53)^2}}$$

$$= \frac{-1,78,000 - (-3021)}{\sqrt{3,70,500 - 3249}\sqrt{2,48,500 - 2809}}$$

$$= \frac{-174979}{\sqrt{367251 \times 2,45,691}}$$

$$= \frac{-174979}{299970}$$

$$= \mathbf{-0.58}$$

Problem 63. Family income and its percentage spent on food in the case of hundred families gave the following bivariate frequency distribution. Calculate the coefficient of correlation and interpret its value :

Food expenditure (in %)	*Family income (Rs.)*				
	200–300	300–400	400–500	500–600	600–700
10–15	–	–	–	3	7
15–20	–	4	9	4	3
20–25	7	6	12	5	–
25–30	3	10	19	8	–

(*MBA, Delhi*)

Solution :

Calculation of Coefficient of Correlation

Food expenditure in % y	m	dy	x: 200–300	300–400	400–500	500–600	600–700	f	fdy	fdy^2	fdxdy
		m	250	350	450	550	650				
		dx	-2	-1	0	1	2				
10–15	12.5	-1				3 [-3]	7 [-14]	10	-10	10	-17
15–20	17.5	0		4 [0]	9 [0]	4 [0]	3 [0]	20	0	0	0
20–25	22.5	1	7 [-14]	6 [-6]	12 [0]	5 [5]		30	30	30	-15
25–30	27.5	2	3 [-12]	10 [-20]	19 [0]	8 [16]		40	80	160	-16
		f	10	20	40	20	10	N = 100	Σfdy = 100	Σfdy^2 = 200	Σfdxdy = -48
		fdx	-20	-20	0	20	20	Σfdx = 0			
		fdx^2	40	20	0	20	40	Σfdx^2 = 120			
		fdxdy	-26	-26	0	18	-14	Σfdxdy = -48			

Coefficient of Correlation :

$$r = \frac{\Sigma fdxdy \times N - (\Sigma fdx)(\Sigma fdy)}{\sqrt{\Sigma fdx^2 \times N - (\Sigma fdx)^2}\sqrt{\Sigma fdy^2 \times N - (\Sigma fdy)^2}}$$

$$\Sigma fdxdy = -48; \quad N = 100; \quad \Sigma fdx = 0; \quad \Sigma fdy = 100; \quad \Sigma fdx^2 = 120;$$

$$\Sigma fdy^2 = 200$$

$$r = \frac{-48 \times 100 - (0)(100)}{\sqrt{120 \times 100 - (0)^2}\sqrt{200 \times 100 - (100)^2}}$$

$$= \frac{-4800}{\sqrt{12,000 \times 20,000 - 10,000}} = \frac{-4800}{\sqrt{12,000 \times 10,000}} = \frac{-4800}{10,954.45}$$

$$r = \mathbf{-0.4381.}$$

Problem 64. Calculate from the data reproduced below pertaining to 66 selected villages in Meerut District, the value of r between total cultivable area and the area under wheat.

Area under wheat (in acres)	*Total cultivable area (in acres)* 0–500	500–1000	1000–1500	1500–2000	2000–2500	*Total*
0–200	12	6	–	–	–	18
200–400	2	18	4	2	1	27
400–600	–	4	7	3	–	14
600–800	–	1	–	2	1	4
800–1000	–	–	–	1	2	3
Total	14	29	11	8	4	66

(*B.Com.*)

Solution :

Computation of Coefficient of Correlation

Total cultivable area in acres (x); Area under wheat in Acres (y)

y	m	dy	x: 0-500	500-1000	1000-1500	1500-2000	2000-2500	f	fdy	fdy²	fdxdy
		m	250	750	1250	1750	2250				
		dx	-2	-1	0	1	2				
0-200	100	-2	12 [48]	6 [12]				18	-36	72	60
200-400	300	-1	2 [4]	18 [18]	4 [0]	2 [-2]	1 [-2]	27	-27	27	18
400-600	500	0		4 [0]	7 [0]	3 [0]		14	0	0	0
600-800	700	1		1 [-1]		2 [2]	1 [2]	4	4	4	3
800-1000	900	2				1 [2]	2 [8]	3	6	12	10
		f	14	29	11	8	4	N=66	Sfdy =-53	Σfdy² =115	Σfdxdy =91
		fdx	28	-29	0	8	8	Σfdx= -41			
		fdx²	56	29	0	8	16	Σfdx² =109			
		fdxdy	52	29	0	2	8	Σfdxdy =91			

Coefficient of correlation :

$$r = \frac{\Sigma f dx dy \times N - (\Sigma f dx)(\Sigma f dy)}{\sqrt{\Sigma f dx^2 \times N - (\Sigma f dx)^2}\sqrt{\Sigma f dy^2 \times N - (\Sigma f dy)^2}}$$

$$\Sigma f dx dy = 91; \quad N = 66; \quad \Sigma f dx = -41; \quad \Sigma f dy = -53; \quad \Sigma f dx^2 = 109; \quad \Sigma f dy^2 = 115$$

$$r = \frac{91 \times 66 - (-41)(-53)}{\sqrt{109 \times 66 - (41)^2}\sqrt{115 \times 66 - (-53)^2}}$$

$$= \frac{6006 - 2173}{\sqrt{7194 - 1681}\sqrt{(7590 - 2809)}}$$

$$= \frac{3833}{\sqrt{5513 \times 4781}}$$

$$= \frac{3833}{5133.9} = \mathbf{+0.746}$$

Problem 65. The following table gives the number of students having different heights and weights :

Height in Centimetres	*Weight in Kilograms* 55–60	60–65	65–70	70–75	75–80	*Total*
150–155	1	3	7	5	2	18
155–160	2	4	10	7	4	27
160–165	1	5	12	10	7	35
165–170	–	3	8	6	3	20
Total:	4	15	37	28	16	100

Do you find any relation between height and weight. *(B. Com.)*

Solution:

			Weight in kilograms								
		x	55–60	60–65	65–70	70–75	75–80				
		m	57.5	62.5	67.5	72.5	77.5				
Height in cm y	m	dy \ dx	-2	-1	0	1	2	f	fdy	fdy²	fdxdy
150–155	152.5	-1	1 [2]	3 [3]	7 [0]	5 [5]	2 [-4]	18	-18	18	-4
155–160	157.5	0	2 [0]	4 [0]	10 [0]	7 [0]	4 [0]	27	0	0	0
160–165	162.5	1	1 [-2]	5 [-5]	12 [0]	10 [10]	7 [14]	35	35	35	17
165–170	167.5	2		3 [-6]	8 [0]	6 [12]	3 [12]	20	40	80	18
		f	4	15	37	28	16	N =100	Σfdy = 57	Σfdy2 = 133	Σfdxdy = 31
		fdx	-8	-15	0	28	32	Σfdx = 37			
		fdx²	16	15	0	28	64	Σfdx² = 123			
		fdxdy	0	-8	0	17	22	Σfdxdy = 31			

Coefficient of Correlation:

$$r = \frac{\Sigma f dxdy \times N - (\Sigma f dx)(\Sigma f dy)}{\sqrt{\Sigma f dx^2 \times N - (\Sigma f dx)^2}\sqrt{\Sigma f dy^2 \times N - (\Sigma f dy)^2}}$$

$$\Sigma f dxdy = 31; \quad N = 100; \quad \Sigma f dx = 37; \quad \Sigma f dy = 57; \quad \Sigma f dx^2 = 123; \quad \Sigma f dy^2 = 133$$

$$r = \frac{31 \times 100 - (37)(57)}{\sqrt{123 \times 100 - (37)^2}\sqrt{133 \times 100 - (57)^2}}$$

$$= \frac{3100 - 2109}{\sqrt{12300 - 1369}\sqrt{13300 - 3249}}$$

$$= \frac{991}{\sqrt{10931 \times 10051}}$$

$$= \frac{991}{10481.77}$$

$$r = \mathbf{+0.0945.}$$

Problem 66. The correlation table given below shows the ages of husband and wife for 53 married couples, calculate the coefficient of correlation between the age of husband and that of his wife.

Age of husband	*Age of wife* 15–25	25–35	35–45	45–55	55–65	65–75	*Total*
15–25	1	1	–	–	–	–	2
25–35	2	12	1	–	–	–	15
35–45	–	4	10	1	–	–	15
45–55	–	–	3	6	1	–	10
55–65	–	–	–	2	4	2	8
65–75	–	–	–	–	1	2	3
Total	3	17	14	9	6	4	53

(*B.Com.*)

Solution :

Computation of Coefficient of Correlation

			Age of Wife									
		x	15–25	25–35	35–45	45–55	55–65	65–75				
		m	20	30	40	50	60	70				
y	m	dy \ dx	-2	-1	0	1	2	3	f	fdy	fdy^2	fdxdy
Age of Husband 15–25	20	-2	1 [4]	1 [2]					2	-4	8	6
25–35	30	-1	2 [4]	12 [12]	1 [0]				15	-15	15	16
35–45	40	0		4 [0]	10 [0]	1 [0]			15	0	0	0
45–55	50	1			3 [0]	6 [6]	1 [2]		10	10	10	8
55–65	60	2				2 [4]	4 [16]	2 [12]	8	16	32	32
65–75	70	3					1 [6]	2 [18]	3	9	27	24
		f	3	17	14	9	6	4	N=53	$\Sigma fdy = 16$	$\Sigma fdy^2 = 92$	$\Sigma fdxdy = 86$
		fdx	-6	-17	0	9	12	12	$\Sigma fdx = 10$			
		fdx^2	12	17	0	9	24	36	$\Sigma fdx^2 = 98$			
		fdxdy	8	14	0	10	24	30	$\Sigma fdxdy = 86$			

Coefficient of Correlation :

$$r = \frac{\Sigma fdxdy \times N - (\Sigma fdx)(\Sigma fdy)}{\sqrt{\Sigma fdx^2 \times N - (\Sigma fdx)^2}\sqrt{\Sigma fdy^2 \times N - (\Sigma fdy)^2}}$$

$$\Sigma fdxdy = 86; \quad N = 53; \quad \Sigma fdx = 10; \quad \Sigma fdy = 16; \quad \Sigma fdx^2 = 98; \quad \Sigma fdy^2 = 92$$

$$r = \frac{86 \times 53 - (10)(16)}{\sqrt{98 \times 53 - (10)^2}\sqrt{92 \times 53 - (16)^2}}$$

$$= \frac{4558 - 160}{\sqrt{5194 - 100}\sqrt{4876 - 256}}$$

$$= \frac{4398}{\sqrt{5094 \times 4620}} = \frac{4398}{4851.21} = 0.9065$$

$$r = \mathbf{+0.907}.$$

Problem 67. From the following table calculate the coefficient of correlation between the ages of fathers and sons and estimate the probable error of the result obtained :

Ages of father Years	*Age of sons* 2	6	10	14	18	22	26	30	*Total*
55–60	–	–	–	–	–	6	5	3	14
50–55	–	–	–	–	8	10	6	2	26
45–50	–	–	–	2	13	8	4	–	27
40–45	–	–	–	14	18	3	–	–	35
35–40	–	–	15	20	8	–	–	–	43
30–35	6	15	25	16	–	–	–	–	59
25–30	15	26	20	1	–	–	–	–	62
20–25	22	10	2	–	–	–	–	–	34
Total :	43	48	62	53	47	27	15	5	300

(*M.Com.*)

Solution :

Computation of Coefficient of Correlation

Ages of Fathers (rows) / Age of Sons (columns)

		x	2	6	10	14	18	22	26	30				
y	m	dy \ dx	-4	-3	-2	-1	0	1	2	3	f	fdy	fdy^2	fdxdy
55–60	57.5	4						6 (24)	5 (40)	3 (36)	14	56	224	100
50–55	52.5	3					8 (0)	10 (30)	6 (36)	2 (18)	26	78	234	84
45–50	47.5	2				2 (-4)	13 (0)	8 (16)	4 (16)		27	54	108	28
40–45	42.5	1				14 (-14)	18 (0)	3 (3)			35	35	35	-11
35–40	37.5	0			15 (0)	20 (0)	8 (0)				43	0	0	0
30–35	32.5	-1	6 (+24)	12 (+36)	25 (+50)	16 (+16)					59	-59	59	+126
25–30	27.5	-2	15 (+120)	26 (156)	20 (80)	1 (2)					62	-124	248	358
20–25	22.5	-3	22 (264)	10 (90)	2 (12)						34	-102	306	366
		f	43	48	62	53	47	27	15	5	N = 300	Σfdy = -62	Σfdy^2 = 1214	Σfdxdy = 1051
		fdx	-172	-144	-124	-53	0	27	30	15	Σfdx = -421			
		fdx^2	688	432	248	53	0	27	60	45	Σfdx^2 = 1553			
		fdxdy	408	282	142	0	0	73	92	54	Σfdxdy = 1051			

Coefficient of Correlation:

$$r = \frac{\Sigma fdxdy \times N - (\Sigma fdx)(\Sigma fdy)}{\sqrt{\Sigma fdx^2 \times N - (\Sigma fdx)^2}\sqrt{\Sigma fdy^2 \times N - (\Sigma fdy)^2}}$$

$$\Sigma fdxdy = 1051; \quad N = 300; \quad \Sigma fdx = -421; \quad \Sigma fdy = -62;$$

$$\Sigma fdx^2 = 1553; \quad \Sigma fdy^2 = 1214$$

$$r = \frac{1051 \times 300 - (-421)(-62)}{\sqrt{1553 \times 300 - (421)^2}\sqrt{1214 \times 300 - (62)^2}}$$

$$= \frac{3,15,300 - 26,102}{\sqrt{4,65,900 - 177241}\sqrt{364200 - 3844}}$$

$$= \frac{2,89,198}{\sqrt{2,88,659 \times 360356}}$$

$$= \frac{289198}{322200}$$

$$= +0.89$$

$$\text{Probable Error} = 0.6745\frac{1-r^2}{\sqrt{N}} = 0.6745\frac{1-(0.896)^2}{\sqrt{300}}$$

$$= 0.6745\frac{1-0.80}{17.32} = \frac{0.6745 \times 0.2}{17.32}$$

$$= \mathbf{0.0078}$$

Problem 68. A survey regarding the incomes and savings of 100 school teachers in a certain city provided in the following data :

Income (Rs.)	*Savings (Rs)*				
	50	100	150	200	*Total*
400	8	4	–	–	12
600	–	12	24	6	42
800	–	9	7	2	18
1000	–	–	10	5	15
1200	–	–	9	4	13
	8	25	50	17	100

Calculate the coefficient of correlation between incomes and savings.

(*B.Com. Rajasthan*)

Solution :

Let the savings be denoted by X and income be denoted by Y

Computation of Coefficient of Correlation

Income y	dy \ dx (Savings x)	50 (-1)	100 (0)	150 (1)	200 (2)	f	fdy	fdy²	fdxdy
400	-2		8 (16)	4 (0)		12	-24	48	16
600	-1		12 (0)	24 (-24)	6 (-12)	42	-42	42	-36
800	0		9 (0)	7 (0)	2 (0)	18	0	0	0
1000	1			10 (10)	5 (10)	15	15	15	20
1200	2			9 (18)	4 (16)	13	26	52	34
	f	8	25	50	17	N=100	Σfdy = -25	Σfdy² = 157	Σfdxdy = 34
	fdx	-8	0	50	34	Σfdx = 76			
	fdx²	8	0	50	68	Σfdx² = 126			
	fdxdy	16	0	4	14	Σfdxdy = 34			

Coefficient of Correlation

$$r = \frac{\Sigma fdxdy \times N - (\Sigma fdx)(\Sigma fdy)}{\sqrt{\Sigma fdx^2 \times N - (\Sigma fdx)^2}\sqrt{\Sigma fdy^2 \times N - (\Sigma fdy)^2}}$$

$$\Sigma f dx dy = 34; \quad N = 100; \quad \Sigma f dx = 76; \quad \Sigma f dy = -25$$

$$\Sigma f dx^2 = 126; \quad \Sigma f d^2 = 157$$

$$r = \frac{34 \times 100 - (76)(-25)}{\sqrt{126 \times 100 - (76)^2}\sqrt{157 \times 100 - (-25)^2}}$$

$$= \frac{3400 + 1900}{\sqrt{12600 - 5776}\sqrt{15,700 - 625}}$$

$$= \frac{5300}{\sqrt{6824 \times 15075}}$$

$$= \frac{5300}{10142}$$

$$= \mathbf{+0.523}$$

Problem 69. A computer while calculating correlation coefficient between two variables X and Y from 25 pairs of observations obtained the following results :

$N = 25; \quad \Sigma X = 125; \quad \Sigma X^2 = 650; \quad \Sigma Y = 100; \quad \Sigma Y^2 = 460; \quad \Sigma XY = 508$

It was, however, discovered at the time of checking that two pairs of observations were not correctly copied. They were taken as (6,14) and (8,6) while the correct values were (8,12) and (6,8). Prove that the correct value of the correlation coefficient should be 2/3.

(ICWA Final)

Solution :

Corrected $\Sigma x = 125 - 6 - 8 + 8 + 6 = 125$

Corrected $\Sigma y = 100 - 14 - 6 + 12 + 8 = 100$

Corrected $\Sigma x^2 = 650 - 6^2 - 8^2 + 8^2 + 6^2 = 650$

Corrected $\Sigma y^2 = 460 - 14^2 - 6^2 + 12^2 + 8^2 = 436$

Corrected $\Sigma xy = 508 - (6 \times 14) - (18 \times 6) + (8 \times 12) + (6 \times 8) = 520$

$$\text{Corrected } r = \frac{\Sigma xy - \dfrac{\Sigma x \times \Sigma y}{N}}{\sqrt{\Sigma x^2 - \dfrac{(\Sigma x)^2}{N}}\sqrt{\Sigma y^2 - \dfrac{(\Sigma y)^2}{N}}}$$

$$= \frac{520 - \dfrac{125 \times 100}{25}}{\sqrt{650 - \dfrac{(125)^2}{25}}\sqrt{436 - \dfrac{(100)^2}{25}}}$$

$$= \frac{(520 \times 25) - (125 \times 100)}{\sqrt{(650 \times 25) - (125)^2}\sqrt{(436 \times 25) - (100)^2}}$$

$$= \frac{13,000 - 12500}{\sqrt{16250 - 15625}\sqrt{10900 - 10,000}}$$

$$= \frac{500}{\sqrt{625}\sqrt{900}}$$

$$= \frac{500}{25 \times 30}$$

$$= \frac{500}{750}$$

$$r = +\frac{2}{3} \text{ or } \mathbf{+0.67}$$

Problem 70. The total of the multiplication of deviation of x and $y = 3044$.

Number of pairs of the observations is 10. Total of the deviations of $x = -170$. Total of the deviations of $y = -20$. Total of the squares of deviations of $x = 8288$. Total of the squares of deviations of $y = 2264$.

Find out the coefficient of correlation when the arbitrary means of x and y are 82 and 68 respectively.

(*B.Com., Rajasthan*)

Solution :

$$r = \frac{\Sigma dxdy - \dfrac{\Sigma dx \times \Sigma dy}{N}}{\sqrt{\Sigma dx^2 - \dfrac{(\Sigma dx)^2}{N}}\sqrt{\Sigma dy^2 - \dfrac{(\Sigma dy)^2}{N}}}$$

$$\Sigma dxdy = 3044, \quad \Sigma dx = -170, \quad \Sigma dy = -20$$

$$\Sigma dx^2 = 8288, \quad \Sigma dy^2 = 2264, \quad N = 10$$

$$r = \frac{3044 - \dfrac{(-170)(-20)}{10}}{\sqrt{8288 - \dfrac{(-170)^2}{10}}\sqrt{2264 - \dfrac{(-20)^2}{10}}}$$

$$= \frac{(3044 \times 10) - (-170 \times -20)}{\sqrt{8288 \times 10 - (-170)^2}\sqrt{2264 \times 10 - (-20)^2}}$$

$$= \frac{30440 - 3400}{\sqrt{82880 - 28900}\sqrt{22640 - 400}}$$

$$= \frac{27040}{\sqrt{53980}\sqrt{22240}}$$

$$= \frac{27040}{34648}$$

$$= \mathbf{+0.78}$$

Problem 71. Calculate the coefficient of correlation between X and Y series from the following data :

	X series	*Y series*
No. of pairs of observations	15	15
Arithmetic mean	25	18
Standard Deviation	3.01	3.03
Sum of squares of deviation from mean	136	138

Summation of product deviations of X and Y series from their respective arithmetic means = 122.

(*B.Com. Delhi*)

Solution :

$$r = \frac{\Sigma xy}{\sqrt{\Sigma x^2 \times \Sigma y^2}}$$

$$\Sigma xy = 122; \quad \Sigma x^2 = 136; \quad \Sigma y^2 = 138$$

$$r = \frac{122}{\sqrt{136 \times 138}}$$

$$= \frac{122}{137}$$

$$= \mathbf{+0.89}$$

Problem 72. A computer while calculating the correlation coefficient between the variables X and Y obtained the following constants :

$N = 30; \quad \Sigma X = 120; \quad \Sigma X^2 = 600; \quad \Sigma Y = 90; \quad \Sigma Y^2 = 250; \quad \Sigma XY = 356$

It was, however, later discovered at the time of checking that it had copied down two pairs of observations as :

X	Y
8	10
12	7

while the corrected values were:

X	Y
8	12
10	8

Obtain the correct value of the correlation coefficient between X and Y.

(*B.Com. Madurai*)

Solution :

Corrected $\Sigma x = 120 - 8 - 12 + 8 + 10 = 118$

Corrected $\Sigma x^2 = 600 - 8^2 - 12^2 + 8^2 + 10^2 = 556$

Corrected $\Sigma y = 90 - 10 - 7 + 12 + 8 = 93$

Corrected $\Sigma y^2 = 250 - 10^2 - 7^2 + 12^2 + 8^2 = 309$

Corrected $\Sigma xy = 356 - (8 \times 10) - (12 \times 7) + (8 \times 12) + (10 \times 8) = 368$

$$\text{Corrected } r = \frac{\Sigma xy - \dfrac{\Sigma x \times \Sigma y}{N}}{\sqrt{\Sigma x^2 - \dfrac{(\Sigma x)^2}{N}}\sqrt{\Sigma y^2 - \dfrac{(\Sigma y)^2}{N}}}$$

$$= \frac{368 - \dfrac{118 \times 93}{30}}{\sqrt{556 - \dfrac{(118)^2}{30}}\sqrt{309 - \dfrac{(93)^2}{30}}}$$

$$= \frac{(368 \times 30) - (118 \times 93)}{\sqrt{556 \times 30 - (118)^2}\sqrt{309 \times 30 - (93)^2}}$$

$$= \frac{11040 - 10974}{\sqrt{16680 - 13924}\sqrt{9270 - 8649}}$$

$$= \frac{66}{\sqrt{2756 \times 621}}$$

$$= \frac{66}{1308}$$

$$= \mathbf{+0.05}$$

Problem 73. Number of pairs of observations of X and $Y = 8$

X series Arithmetic Mean = 74.5

X series Assumed Mean = 69.0

X series Standard Deviation = 13.07

Y series Arithmetic Mean = 125.5

Y series Assumed Mean = 112.0

Y series Standard Deviation = 15.85

Sum of products of corresponding deviations of X and Y series = +2176.

Calculate the coefficient of correlation between X and Y series.

(*B.Com., Rajasthan*)

Solution :

$$r = \frac{\Sigma XY - N(\overline{X}_1 - A_1)(\overline{X}_2 - A_2)}{N\sigma_x\sigma_y}$$

$$\Sigma Xy = 2176; \quad N = 8; \quad \overline{X}_1 = 74.5; \quad \overline{X}^2 = 125.5; \quad A_1 = 69;$$

$$A_2 = 112; \sigma_x = 13.07; \quad \sigma_y = 15.85$$

$\overline{X}_1$ = Mean of X Series A_1 = Assumed mean of X Series

$\overline{X}_2$ = Mean of Y Series A_2 = Assumed mean of Y Series

N = Number (pairs) Observation:

$$r = \frac{2176 - 8(74.5 - 69)(125.5 - 112)}{8 \times 13.07 \times 15.85}$$

$$= \frac{2176 - 8 \times 5.5 \times 13.5}{8 \times 13.07 \times 15.85}$$

$$= \frac{2176 - 594}{1657.276}$$

$$= \frac{1582}{1657.276}$$

$$= +\mathbf{0.955}.$$

Thus, there is a high degree of Positive Correlation between X and Y.

Problem 74. A correlation coefficient of -0.5 does not mean that 50% of the data are explained. Comment.

(*B.A. Ecos., Delhi*)

Solution:

$$r = -0.5$$

$$r^2 = 0.25$$

(or) **25%.**

In this problem only 25% of the variation has been explained and remaining 75% of the variation is due to other factors. Therefore, when $r = -0.5$, it is wrong to mean that 50% of the data are explained.

RANK CORRELATION

Problem 75. Two judges in a beauty competition rank the 12 entries as follows:

X:	1	2	3	4	5	6	7	8	9	10	11	12
Y:	12	9	6	10	3	5	4	7	8	2	11	1

(*M.A. Delhi*)

Solution:

Computation of Rank Correlation

X	Y	$(X-Y)_D$	D^2
1	12	−11	121
2	9	−7	49
3	6	−3	9
4	10	−6	36
5	3	2	4
6	5	1	1
7	4	3	9
8	7	1	1
9	8	1	1
10	2	8	64
11	11	0	0
12	1	11	121
			$\Sigma D^2 = 416$

$$\begin{aligned} r_s &= 1 - \frac{6\Sigma D^2}{N_3 - N} \\ &= 1 - \frac{6 \times 416}{12^3 - 12} \\ &= 1 - \frac{2496}{1728 - 12} \\ &= 1 - \frac{2496}{1716} \\ &= 1 - 1.4545 \\ &= \mathbf{-0.4545}. \end{aligned}$$

Problem 76. The following table gives the score obtained by 11 students in English and Tamil Translation. Find the rank correlation coefficient.

Scores in English :	40	46	54	60	70	80	82	85	85	90	95
Scores in Tamil :	45	45	50	43	40	75	55	72	65	42	70

(*B.Sc., Annamalai*)

Solution:

Computation of Rank Correlation Coefficient

Scores in English X	*Rank* (x)	*Scores in Tamil Y*	*Rank* (y)	$D = R(X) - R(Y)$	D^2
40	11	45	7.5	+3.5	12.25
46	10	45	7.5	+2.5	6.25
54	9	50	6	+3.0	9.00
60	8	43	9	−1.0	1.00
70	7	40	11	−4.0	16.00
80	6	75	1	+5.0	25.00
82	5	55	5	0	0
85	3.5	72	2	+1.5	2.25
85	3.5	65	4	−0.5	0.25
90	2	42	10	−8	64.00
95	1	70	3	−2	4.00
					$\Sigma D^2 = 140$

Rank Correlation Coefficient:

$$
\begin{aligned}
r_s &= 1 - \frac{6\left[\Sigma D^2 + \frac{1}{12}(m^3 - m) + \frac{1}{12}(m^3 - m) + \frac{1}{12}(m^3 - m)\right]}{N^3 - N} \\
&= 1 - \frac{6\left[140 + \frac{1}{12}(2^3 - 2) + \frac{1}{12}(2^3 - 2)\right]}{11^3 - 11} \\
&= 1 - \frac{6[140 + 0.5 + 0.5]}{1320} \\
&= 1 - \frac{846}{1320} \\
&= \frac{474}{1320} \\
&= \mathbf{+0.359}.
\end{aligned}
$$

Problem 77. The ranks of the same 15 students in two subjects A and B are given below ; the two numbers within the brackets denoting the ranks of the same student in A and B respectively. (1,10), (2,7) (3,2), (4,6) (5,4), (6,8), (7,3) (8,1), (9,11), (10, 15), (11,9), (12,5), (13,14), (14,12), (15,13).

Use Spearman's formula to find the rank correlation coefficient.

(*ICWA*)

Solution :

Calculation of Rank Correlation

Subject A. Rank X	*Subject B. Rank* Y	$D = x - y$	D^2
1	10	−9	81
2	7	−5	25
3	2	1	1
4	6	−2	4
5	4	1	1
6	8	−2	4
7	3	4	16
8	1	7	49
9	11	−2	4
10	15	−5	25
11	9	+2	4
12	5	7	49
13	14	−1	1
14	12	2	4
15	13	2	4
			$\Sigma d^2 = 272$

Spearman's rank correlation coefficient :

$$
\begin{aligned}
r_s &= 1 - \frac{6\Sigma D^2}{N(N^2 - 1)} \qquad \Sigma D^2 = 272; \quad N = 15 \\
&= 1 - \frac{6 \times 272}{15^3 - 15} \\
&= 1 - \frac{1632}{3375 - 15} \quad = 1 - \frac{1632}{3360} \quad = 1 - 0.486 \quad = \mathbf{+0.514}.
\end{aligned}
$$

Problem 78. Calculate Spearman's rank correlation coefficient between advertisement cost and sales from the following data :

Advertisement Cost (Rs.'1000) :	39	65	62	90	82	75	25	98	36	78
Sales (Rs. '00,000) :	47	53	58	86	62	68	60	91	51	84

(*B.Com.*)

Solution :

Computation of Rank Correlation Coefficient

Advertisement Cost X	*Rank* x	*Sales* Y	*Rank* y	$D = x - y$	D^2
39	8	47	10	−2	4
65	6	53	8	−2	4
62	7	58	7	0	0
90	2	86	2	0	0
82	3	62	5	−2	4
75	5	68	4	1	1
25	10	60	6	4	16
98	1	91	1	0	0
36	9	51	9	0	0
78	4	84	3	1	1
					$\Sigma D^2 = 30$

Rank Correlation Coefficient :

$$r_s = 1 - \frac{6\Sigma D^2}{N^3 - N} \qquad \Sigma D^2 = 30; \quad N = 10$$

$$= 1 - \frac{6 \times 30}{10^3 - 10}$$

$$= 1 - \frac{180}{990}$$

$$= 1 - 0.1818$$

$$= 0.8182$$

$$= \mathbf{+0.82}.$$

Problem 79. Calculate the Rank Correlation coefficient for the following table of marks of students in two subjects :

First Subject	*Second subject*
80	36
64	38
54	39
49	41
48	27
35	43
32	45
29	52
20	51
18	42
15	40
10	50

(*M.A. Econ., Madurai*)

Solution :

Computation of Rank Correlation

Ist subject Marks X	*Rank* x	*Second subject Marks* Y	*Rank* Y	*Rank difference* $D = x - y$	D^2
80	1	36	11	−10	100
64	2	38	10	−8	64
54	3	39	9	−6	36
49	4	41	7	−2	4
48	5	27	12	−8	64
35	6	43	5	+1	1
32	7	45	4	+3	9
29	8	52	1	+7	49
20	9	51	2	+7	49
18	10	42	6	+4	16
15	11	40	8	+3	9
10	12	50	3	+9	81
					$\Sigma D^2 = 482$

Rank Correlation :

$$r_s = 1 - \frac{6\Sigma D^2}{N(N^2-1)} \qquad \Sigma D^2 = 482; \quad N = 12$$

$$= 1 - \frac{6 \times 482}{12(12^2-1)}$$

$$= 1 - \frac{2892}{1716}$$

$$= 1 - 1.685$$

$$= \mathbf{-0.685}.$$

Problem 80. From the following data calculate the coefficient of rank correlation between X and Y :

X :	36	56	20	65	42	33	44	50	15	60
Y :	50	35	70	25	58	75	60	45	80	38

(*B.Com. Bombay*)

Solution :

Calculation of Rank Correlation Coefficient

X	R_1	Y	R_2	$R_1 - R_2$ D	D^2
36	7	50	6	1	1
56	3	35	9	−6	36
20	9	70	3	6	36
65	1	25	10	−9	81
42	6	58	5	1	1
33	8	75	2	6	36
44	5	60	4	1	1
50	4	45	7	−3	9
15	10	80	1	9	81
60	2	38	8	−6	36
					$\Sigma D^2 = 318$

$$r_s = 1 - \frac{6\Sigma D^2}{N(N^2-1)} = 1 - \frac{6 \times 318}{10(10^2-1)} = 1 - \frac{1908}{990} = 1 - 1.927 = \mathbf{-0.927}.$$

Problem 81. Following are the ranks obtained by 10 students in two subjects, Statistics and Mathematics. To what extent the knowledge of the students in the two subjects is related?

Statistics :	1	2	3	4	5	6	7	8	9	10
Mathematics :	2	4	1	5	3	9	7	10	6	8

(*B.Com., Bombay*)

Solution :

Computation of Rank Correlation

Rank of Statistics X	*Rank of Mathematics* Y	$D = (X - Y)$	D^2
1	2	−1	1
2	4	−2	4
3	1	+2	4
4	5	−1	1
5	3	+2	4
6	9	−3	9
7	7	0	0
8	10	−2	4
9	6	+3	9
10	8	+2	4
			$\Sigma D^2 = 40$

Rank Correlation :

$$r_s = 1 - \frac{6\Sigma D^2}{N^3 - N} \qquad \Sigma D^2 = 40; \quad N = 10$$

$$= 1 - \frac{6 \times 40}{10^3 - 10} = 1 - \frac{240}{990} = 1 - 0.24$$

$$r_s = \mathbf{+0.76}.$$

Problem 82. From the following data calculate the rank correlation coefficient after making adjustment for tied ranks.

X	48	33	40	9	16	16	65	24	16	57
Y	13	13	24	6	15	4	20	9	6	19

(*M.Com. Meerut*)

Solution :

Computation of Rank Correlation

X	*Rank* (x)	Y	*Rank* (y)	$D = (R(x) - R(y))$	D^2
48	8	13	5.5	2.5	6.25
33	6	13	5.5	0.5	0.25
40	7	24	10	−3	9.0
9	1	6	2.5	−1.5	2.25
16	3	15	7	−4	16.00
16	3	4	1	2	4.0
65	10	20	9	1	1.0
24	5	9	4	1	1.0
16	3	6	2.5	0.5	0.25
57	9	19	8	1	1.0
					$\Sigma D^2 = 41$

16 is repeated 3 times in *X* items ; Hence $m = 3$, 13 and 6 are repeated twice in *Y* items Hence $m = 2$. Therefore the formula is :

$$r_s = 1 - \frac{6[\Sigma D^2 + 1/12(m^3 - m) + 1/12(m^3 - m)]}{N^3 - N}$$

$$= 1 - \frac{6[41 + 1/12(3^3 - 3) + 1/12(2^3 - 2) + 1/12(2^3 - 2)]}{10^3 - 10}$$

$$= 1 - \frac{6(41 + 2 + 0.5 + 0.5)}{990}$$

$$= 1 - \frac{264}{990}$$

$$= 1 - 0.267$$

$$r_s = \mathbf{+0.733}$$

Problem 83. Following are the scores of ten students in a class and their I.Q.

Student	*Scores*	*I.Q.*
1	35	100
2	40	100
3	25	110
4	55	140
5	85	150
6	90	130
7	65	100
8	55	120
9	45	140
10	50	110

(*B.Com. Delhi*

Solution :

Computation of Rank Correlation Coefficient

Student	*Scores*	R_1	*I.Q.*	R_2	$R_1 - R_2$	$(R_1 - R_2)^2$ D^2
1	35	9	100	9	0	0.00
2	40	8	100	9	−1.0	1.00
3	25	10	110	6.5	−3.5	12.25
4	55	4.5	140	2.5	2.0	4.00
5	85	2	150	1	1.0	1.00
6	90	1	130	4	−3	9.00
7	65	3	100	9	−6	36.00
8	55	4.5	120	5	−0.5	0.25
9	45	7	140	2.5	4.5	20.25
10	50	6	110	6.5	−0.5	0.25
						$\Sigma D^2 = 84$

$$r_s = 1 - \frac{6[\Sigma D^2 + \frac{1}{12}(m^3 - m) + \frac{1}{12}(m^3 - m)]}{N^3 - N}$$

$$= 1 - \frac{6\left[84 + \frac{1}{12}(2^3 - 2) + \frac{1}{12}(2^3 - 2) + \frac{1}{12}(2^3 - 2) + \frac{1}{12}(3^3 - 3)\right]}{10^3 - 10}$$

$$= 1 - \frac{6(84 + 0.5 + 0.5 + 0.5 + 2.0)}{990} = 1 - \frac{6 \times 87.5}{990}$$
$$= 1 - \frac{525}{990}$$
$$= 1 - 0.53$$
$$= \mathbf{+0.47}$$

Problem 84. Quotation of index number of security prices of a certain joint stock company and of prices of preference shares and debentures are given below :

Preference share Price (X)	73.2	85.8	78.9	75.8	77.2	81.2	83.8
Debenture price (Y)	97.8	99.2	98.8	98.3	98.3	96.7	97.1

Use the method of rank correlation to determine the relationship between preference share prices and debenture prices.

(*B.Com. Madras*)

Solution :

Computation of Rank Correlation

Preference share Price X	*Rank X* (x)	*Debentures Price Y*	*Rank Y* y	$D = x - y$	D^2
73.2	7	97.8	5	2	4
85.2	1	99.2	1	0	0
78.0	4	98.8	2	2	4
75.8	6	98.3	3.5	2.5	6.25
77.2	5	98.3	3.5	1.5	2.25
81.2	3	96.7	7	−4.0	16.0
83.8	2	97.1	6	−4.0	16.0
					$\Sigma D^2 = 48.50$

Rank Correlation :

$$r_{(s)} = 1 - \frac{6[\Sigma D^2 + \frac{1}{12}(m^3 - m) + \frac{1}{12}(m^3 - m)]}{N^3 - N}$$

Debentures Price (Y) 98.3 is repeated 2 times. $\Sigma D^2 = 48.50$, $N = 7$

$$r_s = 1 - \frac{6\left[48.50 + \frac{1}{12}(2^3 - 2)\right]}{7^3 - 7}$$
$$= 1 - \frac{6(48.50 + 0.5)}{336}$$
$$= 1 - \frac{6(49)}{336} = 1 - \frac{294}{336}$$
$$= 1 - 0.875$$
$$r_s = \mathbf{+0.125}$$

Problem 85. The coefficient of rank correlation of marks obtained by 10 students in English and Economics was found to be 0.5. It was later discovered that the difference in ranks in the two subjects obtained by one of the students was wrongly taken as 3 instead of 7. Find the correct coefficient of rank correlation.

(*B.Com. Bombay*)

Solution :

$$r_s = 1 - \frac{6\Sigma D^2}{N(N^2-1)} \qquad r_s = 0.5; \quad N = 10$$

Substituting the above values in the formula, we get

$$0.5 = 1 - \frac{6\Sigma D^2}{10(10^2-1)} \qquad 0.5 = 1 - \frac{6\Sigma D^2}{990}$$

$$\frac{6\Sigma D^2}{990} = 1 - 0.5 \qquad \frac{6\Sigma D^2}{990} = 0.5$$

$$6\Sigma D^2 = 0.5 \times 990 \quad \Sigma D^2 = \frac{0.5 \times 990}{6} \qquad \Sigma D^2 = 82.5$$

Correct Value of $\Sigma D^2 = 82.5 - 3^2 + 7^2 \quad = 122.5$

Corrected $r_s = 1 - \frac{6 \times 122.5}{990} = 1 - \frac{735}{990} = 1 - 0.7424 = 0.2576$

$r_s = \mathbf{+0.26}$

Problem 86. The ranks of the same 16 students in tests in Mathematics and Statistics were as follows, the two numbers within brackets denoting the ranks of the same students in Mathematics and Statistics respectively.

(1,1) (2,10) (3,3) (4,4) (5,5) (6,7) (7,2) (8,6) (9,8) (10,11) (11,15) (12,9) (13,14) (14,12) (15,16) (16,13)

(*i*) Calculate the rank correlation coefficient for proficiencies of this group in Mathematics and Statistics.

(*ii*) What does the value of the coefficient obtained indicate ?

(*iii*) If you had found out Karl Pearson's simple coefficient of correlation between the ranks of these 16 students, would your result have been the same as in (*i*) or any different.

(*B.Com. Banaras*)

Solution :

Calculation of Rank Correlation Coefficient

R_1	R_2	$R_1 - R_2(D)$	D_2
1	1	0	0
2	10	−8	64
3	3	0	0
4	4	0	0
5	5	0	0
6	7	−1	1
7	2	5	25
8	6	2	4
9	8	1	1
10	11	−1	1
11	15	−4	16
12	9	3	9
13	14	−1	1
14	12	2	4
15	16	1	1
16	13	3	9
			$\Sigma D^2 = 136$

$$r_s = 1 - \frac{6\Sigma D^2}{N^3 - N}$$

$$r_s = 1 - \frac{6 \times 136}{16^3 - 16} = 1 - \frac{816}{4080} = 1 - 0.2 = +\mathbf{0.8}$$

Computation of Correlation Coefficient

X	$dx = x - 10$	dx^2	Y	$dy = Y - 10$	dy^2	$dxdy$
1	−9	81	1	−9	81	81
2	−8	64	10	0	0	0
3	−7	49	3	−7	49	49
4	−6	36	4	−6	36	36
5	−5	25	5	−5	25	25
6	−4	16	7	−3	9	12
7	−3	9	2	−8	64	24
8	−2	4	6	−4	16	8
9	−1	1	8	−2	4	2
10	0	0	11	1	1	0
11	1	1	15	5	25	5
12	2	4	9	−1	1	−2
13	3	9	14	4	16	12
14	4	16	12	2	4	8
15	5	25	16	6	36	30
16	6	36	13	3	9	18
	$\Sigma dx = -24$	$\Sigma dx^2 = 376$		$\Sigma dy = -24$	$\Sigma dy^2 = 376$	$\Sigma dxdy = +308$

$$r = \frac{(\Sigma dxdy \times N) - (\Sigma dx \times \Sigma dy)}{\sqrt{\Sigma dx^2 \times N - (\Sigma dx)^2}\sqrt{\Sigma dy^2 \times N - (\Sigma dy)^2}}$$

$$\Sigma dxdy = 308; \quad \Sigma dx = -24; \quad \Sigma dy = -24$$

$$\Sigma dx^2 = 376; \quad \Sigma dy^2 = 376; \quad N = 16$$

$$r = \frac{(308 \times 16) - (-24 \times -24)}{\sqrt{376 \times 16 - (-24)^2}\sqrt{376 \times 16 - (-24)^2}}$$

$$= \frac{4928 - 576}{\sqrt{6016 - 576}\sqrt{6016 - 576}}$$

$$= \frac{4352}{5440}$$

$$r = +\mathbf{0.8}$$

Thus, when the ranks are not repeated the answer obtained by the Karl Pearson's method and Spearman's method comes out to be the same.

Problem 87. Ten competitors in a beauty contest are ranked by three judges in the following order :

1st Judge	1	5	4	8	9	6	10	7	3	2
2nd Judge	4	8	7	6	5	9	10	3	2	1
3rd Judge	6	7	8	1	5	10	9	2	3	4

Use the Rank correlation coefficient to discuss which pair of judges have nearest approach to common tastes in beauty.

(B.Com. Guru Nanak)

Solution:

Calculation for Rank Correlation Coefficient

I Judge (R_1)	*Ranks. II Judge* (R_2)	*III Judge* (R_3)	$D_1 = R_1 - R_2$	D_1^2	D_2 $R_1 - R_3$	D_2^2	D_3 $R_2 - R_3$	D_3^2
1	4	6	−3	9	−5	25	−2	4
5	8	7	−3	9	−2	4	1	1
4	7	8	−3	9	−4	16	−1	1
8	6	1	2	4	7	49	5	25
9	5	5	4	16	4	16	0	0
6	9	10	−3	9	−4	16	−1	1
10	10	9	0	0	1	1	1	1
7	3	2	4	16	5	25	1	1
3	2	3	1	1	0	0	−1	1
2	1	4	1	1	−2	4	−3	9
				$\Sigma D_1^2 = 74$		$\Sigma D_2^2 = 156$		$\Sigma D_3^2 = 44$

$$\text{(I \& II Judge)} = 1 - \frac{6\Sigma D_1^2}{N^3 - N} = 1 - \frac{6 \times 74}{990} = 1 - 0.45 = \mathbf{0.55}$$

$$\text{(I \& III Judges)} = 1 - \frac{6\Sigma D_2^2}{N^3 - N} = 1 - \frac{6 \times 156}{990} = 1 - 0.945 = \mathbf{0.055}$$

$$\text{(II \& III Judges)} = 1 - \frac{6\Sigma D_3^2}{N^3 - N} = 1 - \frac{6 \times 44}{990} = 1 - 0.27 = \mathbf{0.73}$$

Since rank correlation is the maximum between second and third judges, we can say that II and III judges have nearest approach in common tastes of beauty.

Problem 88. Ten competitors in a voice contest are ranked by three judges in the following orders :

First Judge :	1	6	5	10	3	2	4	9	7	8
Second Judge :	3	5	8	4	7	10	2	1	6	9
3rd judge :	6	4	9	8	1	2	3	10	5	7

Use the rank correlation to gauge which pair of judges have the nearest approach to common likings in voice. *(M.A. Econ., Delhi)*

Solution :

Computation of Rank Correlation

First Judge R_1	*Second Judge* R_2	*Third Judge* R_3	$D_1^2 = (R_1 - R_2)^2$	$D_2^2 = (R_2 - R_3)^2$	$D_3^2 = (R_1 - R_3)^2$
1	3	6	4	9	25
6	5	4	1	1	4
5	8	9	9	1	16
10	4	8	36	16	4
3	7	1	16	36	4
2	10	2	64	64	0
4	2	3	4	1	1
9	1	10	64	81	1
7	6	5	1	1	4
8	9	7	1	4	1
			$\Sigma D_1^2 = 200$	$\Sigma D_2^2 = 214$	$\Sigma D_3^2 = 60$

Rank Correlation :

1st and 2nd Judge :

$$r_s = 1 - \frac{6\Sigma D_1{}^2}{N^3 - N} = 1 - \frac{6 \times 200}{10^3 - 10} = 1 - \frac{1200}{990} = 1 - \mathbf{1.212}$$
$$= \mathbf{-0.212.}$$

2nd and 3rd Judge:

$$r_s = 1 - \frac{6 \times 214}{10^3 - 10} = 1 - \frac{1284}{990} = 1 - 1.2969 = \mathbf{0.297}.$$

1st and 3rd Judge:

$$r_s = 1 - \frac{6 \times 60}{10^3 - 10} = 1 - \frac{360}{990} = 1 - 0.364 = \mathbf{+0.636}$$

The first and the third judges have the nearest approach to common likings in voice as the rank correlation is positive and the highest :

CONCURRENT DEVIATION

Problem 89. Find the coefficient of concurrent deviation for the following data :

Year :	1	2	3	4	5	6	7
Supply :	150	154	160	172	160	165	180
Price :	200	180	170	160	190	180	172

(B.Com., Meerut)

Solution :

Computation of Coefficient of Concurrent Deviation[1pt]

Year	*Supply X*	*Direction change dx*	*Price Y*	*Direction change of dy*	*dxdy*
1	150		200		
2	154	+	180	–	–
3	160	+	170	–	–
4	172	+	160	–	–
5	160	–	190	+	–
6	165	+	180	–	–
7	180	+	172	–	–
					$\Sigma dxdy = 0$

Coefficient of Concurrent Deviation :

$$r_{(c)} = \pm\sqrt{\pm\frac{2C - N}{N}} \qquad C = 0; N = 6$$
$$= \pm\sqrt{\pm\frac{2 \times 0 - 6}{6}}$$
$$= \pm\sqrt{-(-1)}$$
$$= \pm\sqrt{(+1)}$$
$$= \mathbf{-1.}$$

Problem 90. Calculate coefficient of concurrent deviation from the following data :

Price	*Imports*	*Price*	*Imports*
368	22	384	26
384	21	395	24
385	24	403	29
361	20	400	28
347	22	385	27

(*M.Com. Madras*)

Solution :

Computation of Coefficient of Concurrent Deviation

Price X	*Direction of change of* $X = dx$	*Imports* y	*Direction of change of* $Y = dy$	*Concurrent deviation* $dxdy$
368		22		
384	+	21	−	−
385	+	24	+	+
361	−	20	−	+
347	−	22	+	−
384	+	26	+	+
395	+	24	−	−
403	+	29	+	+
400	−	28	−	+
385	−	27	−	+
				$C = 6$

$$r_c = \pm\sqrt{\pm\left(\frac{2C - N}{N}\right)}$$

$$C = 6 \quad N = 9$$

$$r_c = \pm\sqrt{\pm\left(\frac{2 \times 6 - 9}{9}\right)} = \pm\sqrt{\pm\left(\frac{12 - 9}{9}\right)} = \pm\sqrt{0.333} = \mathbf{+0.577}$$

Problem 91. Define 'Coefficient of Concurrent Deviations' and comment on its usefulness.

Calculate the coefficient of concurrent deviations from the data given below :

Computation of Coefficient of Concurrent Deviation

Months	*Supply*	*Price*
Jan.	160	292
Feb.	164	280
March	172	260
April	182	234
May	166	266
June	170	254
July	178	230
Aug.	192	190
Sep.	186	200

(*B.Com. Madras*)

Solution :

Calculation of Coefficient of Concurrent Deviation

Month	*Supply X*	*Direction of change compared to previous year = dx*	*Price Y*	*Direction of change compared to previous year = dy*	*dxdy*
Jan.	160		292		
Feb.	164	+	280	−	−
March	172	+	260	−	−
April	182	+	234	−	−
May	166	−	266	+	−
June	170	+	254	−	−
July	178	+	230	−	−
August	192	+	190	−	−
Sep.	186	−	200	+	−
					$\Sigma dxdy = 0$

Coefficient of Concurrent Deviation

$$r_{(c)} = \pm\sqrt{\pm\left(\frac{2C-N}{N}\right)} \qquad C = 0; \quad N = 8$$

$$= \pm\sqrt{\pm\left(\frac{2\times 0-8}{8}\right)}$$

$$= \pm\sqrt{\pm\left(\frac{-8}{8}\right)}$$

$$= \pm\sqrt{-(-1)} \quad = \pm\sqrt{(+1)} \quad = \pm -\mathbf{1}.$$

Problem 92. Calculate coefficient of correlation by concurrent deviation method from the following data :

X	30	40	50	50	20	10	60	70	40
Y	90	70	80	100	100	60	75	85	95

(B.Com. Madurai)

Solution :

Computation of Coefficient of Concurrent Deviation

X	*Direction of change of X = dx*	*Y*	*Direction of change of Y = dy*	*Concurrent deviation dxdy*
30		90		
40	+	70	−	−
50	+	80	+	+
50	=	100	+	0
20	−	100	=	0
10	−	60	−	+
60	+	75	+	+
70	+	85	+	+
40	−	95	+	−
				$C = 4$

$$r_c = \pm\sqrt{\pm\left(\frac{2C - N}{N}\right)}$$

$$C = 4; \quad N = 8$$

$$= \pm\sqrt{\pm\left(\frac{2 \times 4 - 8}{8}\right)}$$

$$= \pm\sqrt{\pm\left(\frac{8 - 8}{8}\right)}$$

$$= \pm\sqrt{\frac{0}{8}}$$

$$= \mathbf{0}$$

Problem 93. Calculate the coefficient of correlation by the method of current deviation from the following data :

Year :	1	2	3	4	5	6	7	8	9
Supply :	80	82	86	91	83	85	89	96	93
Price :	146	140	130	117	133	127	115	94	100

(*B.Com., Punjab*)

Solution :

Computation of Coefficient of Concurrent Deviation

Year	*Supply* *X*	*Direction of change compared to previous year* $= dx$	*Price*	*Direction of change* $= dy$	*Concurrent Deviation*
1	80		146		
2	82	+	140	–	–
3	86	+	130	–	–
4	91	+	117	–	–
5	83	–	133	+	–
6	85	+	127	–	–
7	89	+	115	–	–
8	96	+	94	–	–
9	93	–	100	+	–
					$\Sigma dxdy = 0$

Coefficient of Concurrent Deviation :

$$r_{(c)} = \pm\sqrt{\pm\left(\frac{2C - N}{N}\right)}$$

$$C = 0; \quad N = 8$$

$$r_c = \pm\sqrt{\pm\left(\frac{2 \times 0 - 8}{8}\right)}$$

$$= \pm\sqrt{\pm\left(\frac{-8}{8}\right)} = \pm\sqrt{(+1)} = \mathbf{-1.}$$

Problem 94. Compute the coefficient of the concurrent deviations for the following data in X and Y:

Months	X	Y
Jan.	8.5	60
Feb.	9.2	65
Mar.	9.3	61
Apr.	8.5	74
May	7.2	92
June	5.9	157
July	5.1	130
Aug.	6.6	106
Sep.	7.7	58
Oct.	7.6	80
Nov.	8.2	52
Dec.	9.2	45

(*B.Com., Gurunanak*)

Solution :

Computation of Coefficient of Concurrent Deviation

Months	X	*Direction of change* dx	Y	*Direction of change* dy	*Concurrent Deviation* $dxdy$
Jan.	8.5		60		
Feb.	9.2	+	65	+	+
March	9.3	+	61	−	−
April	8.5	−	74	+	−
May	7.2	−	92	+	−
June	5.9	−	157	+	−
July	5.1	−	130	−	+
Aug.	6.6	+	106	−	−
Sep.	7.7	+	58	−	−
Oct.	7.6	−	80	+	−
Nov.	8.2	+	52	−	−
Dec.	9.2	+	45	−	−
					$\Sigma dxdy = 2$

Coefficient of Concurrent Deviation :

$$r_{(c)} = \pm\sqrt{\pm\left(\frac{2C-N}{N}\right)} \qquad C = 2; \quad N = 11$$

$$= \pm\sqrt{\pm\left(\frac{2\times 2-11}{11}\right)}$$

$$= \pm\sqrt{\pm\left(\frac{4-11}{11}\right)}$$

$$= \pm\sqrt{\pm\left(\frac{-7}{11}\right)}$$

$$= \pm\sqrt{-(-0.6364)} \quad = \pm\sqrt{(+0.6364)} \quad = \mathbf{-0.798}.$$

7
REGRESSION

FORMULAE

	X on Y	Y on X
Regression Equations	$X = a + by$ $X - \overline{X} = bxy(Y - \overline{Y})$	$Y = a + bx$ $Y - \overline{Y} = byx(X - \overline{X})$
Normal Equations	$\Sigma X = Na + b\Sigma Y$ $\Sigma XY = a\Sigma Y + b\Sigma Y^2$	$\Sigma Y = Na + b\Sigma X$ $\Sigma XY = a\Sigma X + b\Sigma X^2$
Regression Coefficients	$bxy = r\frac{\sigma_x}{\sigma_y}$	$byx = r\frac{\sigma_y}{\sigma_x}$
When Deviations are taken from Mean	$r\frac{\sigma_x}{\sigma_y} = \frac{\Sigma xy}{\Sigma y_2}$ $x = (X - \overline{X});\ y(Y - \overline{Y})$	$r\frac{\sigma_y}{\sigma x} = \frac{\Sigma xy}{\Sigma x_2}$
When Deviations are taken from Assumed Mean	$r\frac{\sigma_x}{\sigma_y} = \frac{\Sigma dxdy - \frac{(\Sigma dx)(\Sigma dy)}{N}}{\Sigma dy^2 - \frac{(\Sigma dy)^2}{N}}$ $dx = (X - A)dy = (Y - Y)$	$r\frac{\sigma_y}{\sigma_x} = \frac{\Sigma dxdy - \frac{(\Sigma dx)(\Sigma dy)}{N}}{\Sigma dx^2 - \frac{(\Sigma dx)^2}{N}}$
When the original Values of X and Y Series are taken	$r\frac{\sigma_x}{\sigma_y} = \frac{\Sigma XY - N\overline{X}\,\overline{Y}}{\Sigma Y^2 - N(\overline{Y})^2}$	$r\frac{\sigma_y}{\sigma_x} = \frac{\Sigma XY - \overline{X}\,\overline{Y}}{\Sigma X^2 - N(\overline{X})^2}$

Coefficient of Correlation $r = \sqrt{bxy \times byx}$

REGRESSION

Problem 1. From the following data find the coefficient of correlation and obtain the two regression equations:

X:	1	2	3	4	5	6	7	8	9
Y:	9	8	10	12	11	13	14	16	15

(*M. Com. Kurukshetra*)

Solution:

Computation of Regression Equations

X	$dx = (X - \overline{X})$ $\overline{X} = 5$	dx^2	Y	$dy = (Y - \overline{Y})$ $\overline{Y} = 12$	dy^2	$dxdy$
1	−4	16	9	−3	9	12
2	−3	9	8	−4	16	12
3	−2	4	10	−2	4	4
4	−1	1	12	0	0	0
5	0	0	11	−1	1	0
6	1	1	13	1	1	1
7	2	4	14	2	4	4
8	3	9	16	4	16	12
9	4	16	15	3	9	12
$\Sigma X = 45$		$\Sigma dx^2 = 60$	$\Sigma Y = 108$		$\Sigma dy^2 = 60$	$\Sigma dxdy = 57$

$$\text{Mean: } \overline{X} = \frac{\Sigma X}{N} = \frac{43}{9} \quad \overline{Y} = \frac{\Sigma Y}{N} = \frac{108}{9}$$
$$= \mathbf{5}. \qquad = \mathbf{12}.$$

Regression Coefficient:

$$bxy = \frac{\Sigma dxdy}{\Sigma dy^2} = \frac{57}{60}$$
$$= 0.95.$$

the value of Σdx^2 and Σdy^2 are the same.So bxy and byx are also having the same value. Regression Equation of X on Y:

$$(X - \overline{X}) = bxy\,(Y - \overline{Y}) = X - 5 = 0.95(Y - 12)$$
$$(X - 5) = 0.95\,Y - 11.4$$
$$X = 0.95\,Y - 11.4 + 5$$
$$= 0.95\,Y - 6.4.$$

Regressioin Eqation of Y on X:

$$Y - \overline{Y} = byx(X - \overline{X}) = Y - 12 = 0.95(X - 5)$$
$$Y - 12 = 0.95 \quad X - 4.75$$
$$Y = 0.95\,X - 4.75 + 12$$
$$= 0.95 \quad X + 7.25$$

Coefficient of Correlation:

$$= \sqrt{bxy \times byx}$$
$$= \sqrt{0.95 \times 0.95}$$
$$= +0.95.$$

Problem 2. Calculate correlation and regression coefficients from the following data:

X:	2	4	6	8	10	12	14
Y:	4	2	5	10	4	11	12

(*M.A. Madurai*)

Find the estimate of Y when X = 13.

Solution:

Computation of Regression Coefficient

X	$dx = X - 8$	dx^2	Y	$dy = Y - 7$	dy^2	$dxdy$
2	−6	36	4	−3	9	+18
4	−4	16	2	−5	25	+20
6	−2	4	5	−2	4	+4
8	0	0	10	+3	9	0
10	2	4	4	−3	9	−6
12	4	16	11	+4	16	+16
14	6	36	12	+5	25	+30
$\Sigma X = 56$		$\Sigma dx^2 = 112$	$\Sigma Y = 48$	$\Sigma dy = -1$	$\Sigma dy^2 = 97$	$\Sigma dxdy = 82$

Regression Coefficient of X on Y:

$$bxy = \frac{\Sigma dxdy - \dfrac{\Sigma dx \times \Sigma dy}{N}}{\Sigma dy^2 - \dfrac{(\Sigma dy)^2}{N}} = \frac{82 - \dfrac{(0)-(-1)}{7}}{97 - \dfrac{(-1)^2}{7}} = \frac{82}{96.86}$$

$$= 0.85$$

$$byx = \frac{\Sigma dxdy - \dfrac{\Sigma dx \times \Sigma dy}{N}}{\Sigma dx^2 - \dfrac{(\Sigma dx)^2}{N}} = \frac{82 - \dfrac{(0)-(-1)}{7}}{112 - \dfrac{(0)^2}{7}} = \frac{82}{112}$$

$$= \mathbf{0.73}$$

Coefficient of Correlation:

$$r = \sqrt{bxy \times byx} = \sqrt{0.85 \times 0.73} = \sqrt{0.6205} = +0.79$$

Regression Equation of Y on X

$$Y - \overline{Y} = byx(X - \overline{X}) \qquad \text{Mean: } \overline{X} = \frac{\Sigma X}{N} = \frac{56}{7} = \mathbf{8}$$

$$Y - 6.86 = 0.73\,(X - 8)$$

$$Y - 6.86 = 0.73\,X - 5.84$$

$$Y = 0.73\,X - 5.84 + 6.86$$

$$= \mathbf{0.73\,X + 1.02} \qquad \overline{Y} = \frac{\Sigma Y}{N} = \frac{48}{7} = \mathbf{6.86}$$

When $X = 13$

$$Y = 0.73\,(13) + 1.02$$

$$= 9.49 + 1.02$$

$$Y = \mathbf{10.51}$$

Problem 3. Find the coefficient of correlation (r) between X and Y from the following data:

X:	3	6	5	4	4	6	7	5
Y:	3	2	3	5	3	6	6	4

Also find the line of regression of Y or X and predict the average values of Y when X is given to be 9. (*M. Com., Meerut*)

Solution :

Computation of Coefficient of Correlation and Regression Equation

X.	$x = X - \overline{X}$ $\overline{X} = 5$	x^2	Y	$y = Y - \overline{Y}$ $\overline{Y} = 4$	y^2	xy
3	−2	4	3	−1	1	+2
6	+1	1	2	−2	4	−2
5	0	0	3	−1	1	0
4	−1	1	5	+1	1	−1
4	−1	1	3	−1	1	+1
6	+1	1	6	+2	4	+2
7	+2	4	6	+2	4	+4
5	0	0	4	0	0	0
$\Sigma X = 40$		$\Sigma dx^2 = 12$	$\Sigma Y = 32$		$\Sigma y^2 = 16$	$\Sigma xy = 6$

Coefficient of correlation: $r = \dfrac{\Sigma xy}{\sqrt{\Sigma x^2 \times \Sigma y^2}} = \dfrac{6}{\sqrt{12 \times 16}} = \dfrac{6}{13.86}$

Coefficeint of Correlation = 0.433

$$\text{Mean: } \overline{X} = \frac{\Sigma X}{N} = \frac{40}{8} = 5 \quad \overline{Y} = \frac{\Sigma Y}{N} = \frac{32}{8} = 4$$

$$r\frac{\sigma y}{\sigma x} \text{ or } byx = \frac{\Sigma xy}{\Sigma x^2} = \frac{6}{12}$$

$$= \mathbf{+0.5}$$

Regression of Y on X:

$$Y - \overline{Y} = byx(X - \overline{X})$$
$$Y - 4 = 0.5(X - 5)$$
$$Y - 4 = 0.5X - 2.5$$
$$Y = 0.5X - 2.5 + 4$$
$$Y = \mathbf{0.5X + 1.5}$$

When $X = 9$,

$$Y = 0.5 \times 9 + 1.5 = 4.5 + 1.5$$
$$Y = \mathbf{6}$$

Problem: 4 The following table gives aptitute test scores and productivity indices of 8 randomly selected workers.Find the equation to the line which can be used to predict the productivity index from the aptitude score.Estimate the productivity index of a worker whose test score is 66.

Aptitude score (X)	: 57	58	59	59	60	61	62	64
Productivity index (Y)	: 67	68	65	68	72	72	69	71

(*M. Com., Meerut*)

Solution :

To find the productivity index from the aptitude score we have to find the Regression Equation of Y on X

X	$x = (X - 60)$ $\overline{X} = 60$	x^2	Y	$y = Y - \overline{Y}$ $\overline{Y} = 69$	y^2	xy
57	−3	9	67	−2	4	6
58	−2	4	68	−1	1	2
59	−1	1	65	−4	16	4
59	−1	1	68	−1	1	1
60	0	0	72	+3	9	0
61	1	1	72	+3	9	3
62	2	4	69	0	0	0
64	4	16	71	+2	4	8
$\Sigma X = 480$		$\Sigma x^2 = 36$	$\Sigma Y = 552$		$\Sigma y^2 = 44$	$\Sigma xy = 24$

$$\text{Mean : } \frac{\Sigma X}{N} = \frac{480}{8} \; \overline{Y} = \frac{\Sigma Y}{N} = \frac{552}{8}$$

$$\overline{X} = \mathbf{60} \; \overline{Y} = \mathbf{69}$$

$$byx = \frac{\Sigma xy}{\Sigma x^2} = \frac{24}{36}$$

$$= \mathbf{+0.67}$$

Regressiion Equation of Y on X

$$Y - \overline{Y} = byx\,(X - \overline{X})$$

$$Y - 69 = 0.67\,(X - 60)$$

$$Y - 69 = 0.67X - 40.2$$

$$Y = 0.67X - 40.2 + 69$$

$$= \mathbf{0.67\,X + 28.8}$$

When $X = 66$,

$$Y = 0.67 \times 66 + 28.8$$

$$= 44.22 + 28.8$$

$$Y = \mathbf{73.02}$$

Problem: 5 Estimate the values of X corresponding to $Y = 200$ from the following data:

X	200	248	297	338	463	493
Y	137	147	184	196	276	260

(*B. Com., Madras*)

Solution :

Computation of Regression Equation

X	$dx = X - 338$	dx^2	Y	$dy = Y - 196$	dy^2	$dxdy$
200	−138	19044	137	−59	3481	8142
248	−90	8100	147	−49	2401	4410
297	−41	1681	184	−12	144	492
338	0	0	196	0	0	0
463	125	15625	276	80	6400	10,000
493	155	24025	260	64	4096	9,920
ΣX = 2039	Σdx = 11	Σdx^2 = 68,475	ΣY = 1200	$\Sigma dy = 24$	Σdy^2 = 16,522	$\Sigma dxdy$ = 32964

$$\text{Mean: } \overline{X} = \frac{\Sigma X}{N} = \frac{2039}{6} = \mathbf{339.8}$$

$$\overline{Y} = \frac{\Sigma Y}{N} = \frac{1200}{6} = \mathbf{200}$$

$$bxy \text{ or } r\frac{\sigma x}{\sigma y} = \frac{\Sigma dxdy - \dfrac{\Sigma dx \times \Sigma dy}{N}}{\Sigma dy^2 - \dfrac{(\Sigma dy)^2}{N}}$$

$$= \frac{32964 - \left(\dfrac{11 \times 24}{6}\right)}{16522 - \dfrac{(24)^2}{6}} = \frac{32964 - 44}{16522 - 96}$$

$$= \frac{32,920}{16,426} = \mathbf{2.004}$$

Regression Equation of X on Y:

$$X - \overline{X} = bxy \quad (Y - \overline{Y})$$

$$X - 341.5 = 2.004 \quad (Y - 200)$$

$$X - 341.5 = 2.004 \quad Y - 400.8$$

$$X = 2.004 \quad Y - 400.8 + 339.8$$

$$X = 2.004Y - 61$$

When $Y = 200$,

$$X = 2.004(200) - 61$$

$$= 400.8 - 61$$

$$= \mathbf{339.8}$$

Problem 6. The following figures relate to years of service and income in hundreds of rupees of the employees of an organisation.Find the initial start for a person applying for a job after having served in another factory for a period of 12 years in a similar capacity.

Length of Srvice (years)	: 11	7	9	5	8	6	10
Income (hundreds of rupees)	: 7	5	3	2	6	4	8

(*B. Com., Bombay*)

Solution : Let length of Service be denoted by X and income by Y

Computation for the Regression Equation

X	$X = X - \overline{X}$ $\overline{X} = 8$	x^2	$\overline{Y}$	$y = Y - \overline{Y}$ $\overline{Y} = 5$	y^2	xy
11	+3	9	7	+2	4	6
7	−1	1	5	0	0	0
9	+1	1	3	−2	4	−2
5	−3	9	2	−3	9	+9
8	0	0	6	+1	1	0
6	−2	4	4	−1	1	+2
10	+2	4	8	+3	9	+6
$\Sigma X = 56$		$\Sigma x^2 = 28$	$\Sigma Y = 35$		$\Sigma y^2 = 28$	$\Sigma xy = 21$

$$\text{Mean : } \overline{X} = \frac{\Sigma X}{N} = \frac{56}{7} = 8$$

$$\overline{Y} = \frac{\Sigma Y}{N} = \frac{35}{7} = \mathbf{5}$$

$$r\frac{\sigma y}{\sigma x} = \frac{\Sigma xy}{\Sigma x^2} = \frac{21}{28} = 0.75$$

Regression equation of Y on X:

$$Y - \overline{Y} = r\frac{\sigma y}{\sigma x}(X - \overline{X})$$

$$Y - 5 = 0.75\,(X - 8)$$

$$Y - 5 = 0.75\,X - 6$$

$$Y = 0.75\,X - 6 + 5$$

$$= 0.75\,X - 1$$

When $X = 12$,

$$Y = 0.75 \times 12 - 1$$

$$= 9 - 1$$

$$= \mathbf{8} \text{ or Rs. } 800$$

Problem 7. Given the bivariate data:

X:	1	5	3	2	1	1	7	3
Y:	6	1	0	0	1	2	1	5

(*a*) Fit a regression line of Y on X and hence predict X if $Y = 2$.
(*b*) Fit a regression line of X on Y and hence predict Y if $X = 5$.
(*c*) Calculate Karl Pearson's correlation coefficient.

(*M. Com., Rajasthan*)

Solution:

Computation for Regression Equation

X	$dx = X - 3$	dx^2	Y	$dy = Y - 2$	dy^2	$dxdy$
1	−2	4	6	+4	16	−8
5	+2	4	1	−1	1	−2
3	0	0	0	−2	4	0
2	−1	1	0	−2	4	2
1	−2	4	1	−1	1	2
1	−2	4	2	0	0	0
7	+4	16	1	−1	1	−4
3	0	0	5	+3	9	0
$\Sigma X =$ 23	$\Sigma dx = -1$	$\Sigma dx^2 =$ 33	$\Sigma Y =$ 16	$\Sigma dy = 0$	$\Sigma dy^2 = 36$	$\Sigma dxdy =$ −10

Regression Equation of X on Y:

$$(X - \overline{X}) = bxy(Y - \overline{Y})$$

$$\text{Mean : } \overline{X} = \frac{\Sigma X}{N} = \frac{23}{8} \quad \overline{Y} = \frac{\Sigma Y}{N} = \frac{16}{8} = 2$$

$$= 2.875$$

$$bxy = \frac{\Sigma dxdy - \dfrac{\Sigma dx \times \Sigma dy}{N}}{\Sigma dy^2 - \dfrac{(\Sigma dy)^2}{N}} \quad \frac{-10 - \dfrac{(-1)(0)}{8}}{36 - \dfrac{(0)^2}{8}}$$

$$= \frac{-10}{36} = -0.278$$

Substituting the Values in the equation:

$$(X - 2.875) = -0.278(Y - 2)$$

$$X - 2.875 = -0.278Y + 0.556$$

$$X = -0.278Y + 0.556 + 2.875$$

$$= \mathbf{-0.278Y + 3.431}$$

When $Y = 2.5$,

$$X = -0.278 \times 2.5 + 3.431$$

$$= -0.695 + 3.431$$

$$X = \mathbf{2.736}$$

Regression Equation of Y on X:

$$Y - \overline{Y} = byx(X - \overline{X})$$

$$byx = \frac{\Sigma dxdy - \dfrac{(\Sigma dx) \times (\Sigma dy)}{N}}{\Sigma dx^2 - \dfrac{(\Sigma dx)^2}{N}}$$

$$= \frac{-10}{33 - 0.125} = \frac{-10}{32.875}$$

$$= -0.304$$

Substituting the value in the formula

$$
\begin{aligned}
Y-2 &= -0.304\,(X-2.875)\\
Y-2 &= -0.304\,X+0.874\\
Y &= -0.304\,X+0.874+2\\
&= -0.304\,X+2.874
\end{aligned}
$$

When X is 5,

$$
\begin{aligned}
Y &= -0.304\times 5+2.874\\
&= -1.52+2.874\\
Y &= \mathbf{1.354}
\end{aligned}
$$

Coefficient of Correlation:

$$
\begin{aligned}
r &= \sqrt{bxy\times byx}=\sqrt{-0.278\times -0.304}\\
&= \mathbf{+0.291}
\end{aligned}
$$

Problem 8. You are given the following observation on X and Y:

X:	0	1	3	6	8
Y:	1	3	2	5	4

Using linear regression of Y on X, estimate the proportion variance of Y due to X.Also give the proportion of variance of Y which remains unexplained. *(M. Com., Delhi)*

Solution: The proportion of variance of Y due to X will be given by r^2 and the proportion of variance of Y which remains unexplained will be given by $1-r^2$.

Computation of Coefficient of Correlation

X	$dx=(X-4)$	dx^2	Y	$dy=(Y-3)$	dy^2	$dxdy$
0	−4	16	1	−2	4	8
1	−3	9	3	0	0	0
3	−1	1	2	−1	1	1
6	2	4	5	2	4	4
8	4	16	4	1	1	4
$\Sigma X = 18$	$\Sigma dx=-2$	$\Sigma dx^2 = 46$	$\Sigma Y = 15$	$\Sigma dy = 0$	$\Sigma dy^2 = 10$	$\Sigma dxdy = 17$

Coefficient of Correlation:

$$
\begin{aligned}
&= \frac{\Sigma dxdy - \dfrac{\Sigma dx\times\Sigma dy}{N}}{\sqrt{\Sigma dx^2-\dfrac{(\Sigma dx)^2}{N}}\sqrt{\Sigma dy^2-\dfrac{(\Sigma dy)^2}{N}}}\\
&= \frac{17-\dfrac{(-2)(0)}{5}}{\sqrt{46-\dfrac{(-2)^2}{5}}\sqrt{10-\dfrac{(0)^2}{5}}}\\
&= \frac{17}{\sqrt{452}}=\frac{17}{21.26}\\
r &= \mathbf{+0.8}.
\end{aligned}
$$

Therefore,

$$r^2 = \mathbf{0.64.}$$

The proportion of variance of Y due to X is 0.64 or 64%.The proportion of variance of Y which remains unexplained $= 1 - r^2 = 1 - 0.64 = 0.36$ or 36%.

Problem 9. Fit a straight line regression of Y on X from the following table:

X:	0	1	2	3	4	5	6
Y:	2	1	3	2	4	3	5

(*B.A.* (*Eco.Hons.*), *Delhi*)

Solution:

Computation of Regression Equations

X	X^2	Y	XY
0	0	2	0
1	1	1	1
2	4	3	6
3	9	2	6
4	16	4	16
5	25	3	15
6	36	5	30
$\Sigma X = 21$	$\Sigma x^2 = 91$	$\Sigma Y = 20$	$\Sigma XY = 74$

Regression of Y on X:

$$Y = a + bX$$

The two normal equations are:

$$\Sigma Y = b\Sigma X + Na$$
$$\Sigma XY = a\Sigma X + b\Sigma X^2$$

Substituting the values we get,

$$\Sigma Y = 20;\ \Sigma X = 21;\ N = 7;\ \Sigma X^2 = 91;\ \Sigma XY = 74$$
$$20 = 7a + 21b \quad (1)$$
$$74 = 21a + 91b \quad (2)$$

Multiplying (1) by 3 we get

$$60 = 21a + 63b$$

Subtracting (3) from (2) we get

$$14 = 28b$$
$$28b = 14$$
$$b = \frac{14}{28} = 0.5$$
$$\text{When} \quad b = 0.5$$
$$7a + 21b = 20 = 7a + 21 \times 0.5 = 20$$
$$7a + 10.5 = 20 \qquad 7a = 20 - 10.5$$
$$7a = 9.5 \qquad \therefore \quad a = 1.357$$
$$\therefore \quad Y = 1.357 + 0.5X.$$

Problem 10. The following are the marks in Statistics (X) and Mathematics (Y) of ten students:

X:	56	55	58	58	57	56	60	64	69	57
Y:	68	67	67	70	65	68	70	66	68	66

Calculate the coefficient of correlation and estimate the marks in mathematics of a student who secures 62 marks in Statistics. (*B. Com. Bombay*)

Solution :

Computation of Coefficient of Correlation and Regression

Marks in Statistics X	$dx = X - 59$	dx^2	*Marks in Maths Y*	$dx = Y - 67$	dy^2	$dxdy$
56	−3	9	68	+1	1	−3
55	−4	16	67	0	0	0
58	−1	1	67	0	0	0
58	−1	1	70	+3	9	−3
57	−2	4	65	−2	4	+4
56	−3	9	68	+1	1	−3
60	+1	1	70	+3	9	+3
64	+5	25	66	−1	1	−5
69	+10	100	68	+1	1	+10
57	−2	4	66	−1	1	+2
$\Sigma X = 590$	$\Sigma dx = 0$	$\Sigma dx^2 = 170$	$\Sigma Y = 675$	$\Sigma dy = 5$	$\Sigma dy^2 = 27$	$\Sigma dxdy = +5$

Coefficient of Correlation:

$$r = \frac{\Sigma dxdy - \dfrac{\Sigma dx \times \Sigma dy}{N}}{\sqrt{\Sigma dx^2 - \dfrac{(\Sigma dx)^2}{N}}\sqrt{\Sigma dy^2 - \dfrac{(\Sigma dy)^2}{N}}}$$

$$= \frac{5 - \dfrac{(0) \times (5)}{10}}{\sqrt{170 - \dfrac{(0)^2}{10}}\sqrt{27 - \dfrac{(5)^2}{10}}}$$

$$= \frac{5}{\sqrt{170 \times 24.5}}$$

$$= \frac{5}{64.5}$$

$$r = +0.078$$

$$\text{Mean : } \overline{X} = \frac{\Sigma X}{N} = \frac{590}{10} = \mathbf{59.}$$

$$\overline{Y} = \frac{\Sigma Y}{N} = \frac{675}{10} = 67.5.$$

$$byx \text{ or } r\frac{\sigma_y}{\sigma_x} = \frac{\Sigma dxdy - \frac{\Sigma dx \times \Sigma dy}{N}}{\Sigma dx^2 - \frac{(\Sigma dx)^2}{N}}$$

$$= \frac{5 - \frac{(0)(5)}{10}}{170 - \frac{0^2}{10}} = \frac{5}{170}$$

$$byx = 0.0294 = \mathbf{0.03}.$$

Regression Equation of Y on X:

$$Y - \overline{Y} = byx \quad (X - \overline{X})$$
$$Y - 67.5 = 0.03 \quad (X - 59)$$
$$Y - 67.5 = 0.03 \quad X - 1.77$$
$$Y = 0.03 \quad X - 1.77 + 67.5$$
$$= 0.03 \quad X + 65.73.$$

When $X = 62,$

$$Y = 0.03(62) + 65.73$$
$$= 1.86 + 65.73$$
$$= \mathbf{67.59}.$$

Problem 11. From the following table showing age of cars of a certain make and annual maintenance costs, obtain the regression equation for costs related to age:

Age of cars (years) :	2	4	6	7	8	10	12
Annual maintenance Cost (Rs.) :	1600	1500	1800	1900	1700	2100	2000

(*B. Com., Bombay*)

Solution : Let the age of cars be denoted by X and the annual maintenance cost by Y.

Computation for the Regression of Y on X

X	$x = (X - \overline{X})$ $\overline{X} = 7$	x^2	Y	$y = Y - \overline{Y}$ $\overline{Y} = 1800$	y^2	xy
2	−5	25	1600	−200	40,000	1000
4	−3	9	1500	−300	90,000	900
6	−1	1	1800	0	0	0
7	0	0	1900	+100	10,000	0
8	1	1	1700	−100	10,000	−100
10	3	9	2100	+300	90,000	900
12	5	25	2000	+200	40,000	1000
ΣX = 49		$\Sigma x^2 =$ 70	$\Sigma Y =$ 12,600		$\Sigma y^2 =$ 2,80,000	$\Sigma xy =$ 3700

$$\text{Mean}: \quad \overline{X} = \frac{\Sigma X}{N} = \frac{49}{7} = 7$$

$$\overline{Y} = \frac{\Sigma Y}{N} = \frac{12,600}{7} = 1,800$$

$$r\frac{\sigma y}{\sigma x} \text{ or } byx = \frac{\Sigma xy}{\Sigma x^2} = \frac{3700}{70} = 52.86$$

Regression Equation of Y on X:

$$Y - \overline{Y} = byx\,(X - \overline{X})$$

$$Y - 1800 = 52.86\,(X - 7)$$

$$X - 1800 = 52.86\,X - 370.02$$

$$\overline{Y} = 52.86\,X - 370.02 + 1800$$

$$= 52.86\,X + \mathbf{1429.98}$$

Problem 12. The following data give the hardness (X) and tensile strength (Y) of 7 samples of a metal in certain units.Find the linear regression equation Y on X.

X:	146	152	158	164	170	176	182
Y:	75	78	77	79	82	85	86

(*I.C.W.A.*)

Solution :

Computation for the Linear Regression Equation of Y on X

X	$dx = X - 164$	dx^2	Y	$dy = Y - 80$	dy^2	$dxdy$
146	−18	324	75	−5	25	90
152	−12	144	78	−2	4	24
158	− 6	36	77	−3	9	18
164	0	0	79	−1	1	0
170	+ 6	36	82	2	4	12
176	+12	144	85	5	25	60
182	+18	324	86	6	36	108
$\Sigma X = 1148$	$\Sigma dx = 0$	$\Sigma dx^2 = 1008$	$\Sigma Y = 562$	$\Sigma dy = 2$	$\Sigma dy^2 = 104$	$\Sigma dxdy = 312$

$$\text{Mean}: \quad \overline{X} = \frac{\Sigma X}{N} = \frac{1148}{7} \qquad \overline{Y} = \frac{\Sigma Y}{N} = \frac{562}{7}$$

$$= 164 \qquad = 80.29$$

$$r\frac{\sigma_y}{\sigma_x} = \frac{\Sigma dxdy - \dfrac{\Sigma dx \times \Sigma dy}{N}}{\Sigma dx^2 - \dfrac{(\Sigma dx)^2}{N}}$$

$$= \frac{312 - \dfrac{(0)(2)}{7}}{1008 - \dfrac{(0)^2}{8}}$$

$$= \frac{312}{1008} = +0.3095 \text{ or } + 0.31$$

Regression Equation of Y on X:

$$Y - \overline{Y} = r\frac{\sigma_y}{\sigma_x} \quad (X - \overline{X})$$

$$Y - 80.29 = 0.31\,(X - 164)$$

$$Y - 80.29 = 0.31\,X - 50.84$$

$$Y = 0.31 \quad X - 50.84 + 80.29$$

$$Y = \mathbf{0.31 \quad X + 29.45.}$$

Problem 13. From the following data obtain the two regression equations:

Sales	: 91	97	108	121	67	124	51	73	111	57
Purchases	: 71	75	69	97	70	91	39	61	80	47

Hence or otherwise find correlation coefficient between sales and purchases.

(*C.A.Intermediate*)

Solution :

Computation of Regression Equatioins

Salses X	$(X - \overline{X})\overline{X} = 90$ dx	dx^2	*Purchases* Y	$dy = (Y - \overline{Y}$ $\overline{Y} = 70$	dy^2	$dxdy$
91	1	1	71	1	1	1
97	7	49	75	5	25	35
108	18	324	69	− 1	1	−18
121	31	961	97	27	729	837
67	−23	529	70	0	0	0
124	34	1156	91	21	441	714
51	−39	1521	39	−31	961	1209
73	−17	289	61	− 9	81	153
111	21	441	80	10	100	210
57	−33	1089	47	−23	529	759
ΣX $= 900$		Σdx^2 $= 6360$	$\Sigma y = 700$		Σdy^2 $= 2868$	$\Sigma dxdy$ $= 3,900$

Mean : $\overline{X} = \frac{\Sigma X}{N} = \frac{900}{10} = \mathbf{90.}$

$\overline{Y} = \frac{\Sigma Y}{N} = \frac{700}{10} = \mathbf{70.}$

Regression Coefficient:

$bxy = \frac{\Sigma dxdy}{\Sigma dy^2} = \frac{3900}{2868} = \mathbf{1.36.}$

$byx = \frac{\Sigma dxdy}{\Sigma dx^2} = \frac{3900}{6360} = \mathbf{0.61.}$

Regression of X on Y:

$$(X - \overline{X}) = b_x y(Y - \overline{Y})$$
$$(X - 90) = 1.36(Y - 70)$$
$$(X - 90) = 1.36 \quad Y - 95.2$$
$$X = 1.36 \quad Y - 95.2 + 90$$
$$X = \mathbf{1.36} \quad Y - \mathbf{5.2}.$$

Regression of Y on X:

$$(Y - \overline{Y}) = b_y x(X - \overline{X})$$
$$(Y - 70) = 0.61(X - 90)$$
$$(Y - 70) = 0.61\,X - 54.9$$
$$Y = 0.61\,X - 54.9 + 70$$
$$Y = \mathbf{0.61}\,X + \mathbf{15.1}.$$

Coefficient of Correlation:

$$\begin{aligned} r &= \sqrt{bxy \times byx} \\ &= \sqrt{1.36 \times 0.61} \\ &= \sqrt{0.8296} \\ &= \mathbf{+0.91}. \end{aligned}$$

Problem 14. Fit a regression line of Y on X for the following:

X:	40	70	50	60	80	50	90	40	60	60
Y:	2.5	6	4.5	5	4.5	2	5	3	4.5	3

(*B.A. Madurai*)

Solution :

Computation of Regression Equation

X	$dx = (X - \overline{X})$ $\overline{X} = 60$	dx^2	Y	$dy = (Y - \overline{Y}$ $\overline{Y} = 4$	dy^2	$dxdy$
40	−20	400	2.5	−1.5	2.25	30
70	+10	100	6.0	+2.0	4.0	20
50	−10	100	4.5	+0.5	0.25	− 5
60	− 0	0	5.0	+1.0	1.0	0
80	+20	400	4.5	+0.5	0.25	10
50	−10	100	2.0	−2.0	4.0	20
90	+30	900	5.0	+1.0	1.0	30
40	−20	400	3.0	−1.0	1.0	20
60	0	0	4.5	+0.5	0.25	0
60	0	0	3.0	−1.0	1.0	0
ΣX = 600		Σdx^2 = 2400	ΣY = 40		$\Sigma y^2 = 15.00$	$\Sigma dxdy$ = 125

$$\text{Mean : } \overline{X} = \frac{\Sigma X}{N} = \frac{600}{10} = \mathbf{60.} \qquad \overline{Y} = \frac{\Sigma Y}{N} = \frac{40}{10} = \mathbf{4.}$$

$$byx = \frac{\Sigma dxdy}{\Sigma dx^2} = \frac{125}{2400} = 0.052.$$

Regression Equation of Y on X:

$$\begin{aligned} Y - \overline{Y} &= byx(X - \overline{X}) \\ Y - 4 &= 0.052(X - 60) \\ Y - 4 &= 0.052\,X - 3.12 \\ Y &= 0.052\,X - 3.12 + 4 \\ Y &= \mathbf{0.052\,X + 0.88.} \end{aligned}$$

Problem 15. Find the regression line of Y on X for the following data and estimate Y when $X = 9$.

X:	18	26	28	31	25	19	35
Y:	11	16	19	17	14	11	24

(*B. Com., Bombay*)

Solution :

Computation of Regression Equation

X	$x = (X - \overline{X})$ $\overline{X} = 26$	x^2	Y	$y = (Y - \overline{Y}$ $\overline{Y} = 16$	y^2	xy
18	−8	64	11	−5	25	40
26	0	0	16	0	0	0
28	+2	4	19	+3	9	6
31	+5	25	17	+1	1	5
25	−1	1	14	−2	4	2
19	−7	49	11	−5	25	35
35	+9	81	24	+8	64	72
ΣY = 182		Σx^2 = 224	ΣY = 112		$\Sigma y^2 =$ = 128	$\Sigma xy = 160$

$$\text{Mean : } \quad \overline{X} = \frac{\Sigma X}{N} = \frac{182}{7} \quad \overline{Y} = \frac{\Sigma Y}{N} = \frac{112}{7}$$

$$= \mathbf{26.} \qquad\qquad = \mathbf{16.}$$

$$b_{yx} \text{ or } r \quad \frac{\Sigma xy}{\Sigma x^2}$$

$$= \frac{160}{224} = 0.71$$

Regression equation of Y on X:

$$\begin{aligned} Y - \overline{Y} &= b_{yx}(X - \overline{X}) \\ Y - 16 &= 0.71\,(X - 26) \\ Y - 16 &= 0.71\,X - 18.46 \\ Y &= 0.71\,X - 18.46 + 16 \\ &= 0.71\,X - 2.46. \end{aligned}$$

When $X = 9,$

$$Y = 0.71(9) - 2.46$$
$$= 6.39 - 2.46$$
$$= +3.93.$$

Problem 16. From the following data of the age of husband and the age of wife, form two regression lines and calculate the husband's age when the wife's age is 16.

Husband's age	:	36	23	27	28	28	29	30	31	33	35
Wife's age	:	29	18	20	22	27	21	29	27	29	28

(*B. Com., Bangolore*)

Solution : Let the husband's age be denoted by X and wife's age be denoted by Y.

Computation of Regression Equation

Husband's age X	$dx = (X - \overline{X})$ $\overline{X} = 30$	dx^2	*Wife's age* Y	$dy = (Y - \overline{Y})$ $\overline{Y} = 25$	dy^2	$dxdy$
36	6	36	29	4	16	24
23	−7	49	18	−7	49	49
27	−3	9	20	−5	25	15
28	−2	4	22	−3	9	6
28	−2	4	27	2	4	− 4
29	−1	1	21	−4	16	4
30	0	0	29	4	16	0
31	1	1	27	2	4	2
33	3	9	29	4	16	12
35	5	25	28	3	9	15
$\Sigma X = 300$		$\Sigma dx^2 = 138$	$\Sigma Y = 250$		$\Sigma y^2 = 164$	$\Sigma dxdy = 123$

Mean : $\overline{X} = \dfrac{\Sigma X}{N} \dfrac{300}{10} = \mathbf{30.}$ $\qquad \overline{Y} = \dfrac{\Sigma Y}{N} \dfrac{250}{10} = \mathbf{25.}$

Regression Coefficient:

$$bxy = \frac{\Sigma dxdy}{\Sigma dy^2} = \frac{123}{164} = \mathbf{0.75.}$$

Regression Coefficient:

$$byx = \frac{\Sigma dxdy}{\Sigma dx^2} = \frac{123}{138} = \mathbf{0.89.}$$

Regression Equation of X on Y:

$$(X - \overline{X}) = b_{xy}(Y - \overline{Y})$$
$$X - 30 = 0.75(Y - 25)$$
$$X - 30 = 0.75 \quad Y - 18.75$$
$$X = 0.75 \quad Y - 18.75 + 30$$
$$= \mathbf{0.75 \quad Y + 11.25.}$$

Regression Equation of Y on X:

$$Y - \overline{Y} = b_{yx}(X - \overline{X})$$
$$Y - 25 = 0.89(X - 30)$$
$$Y - 25 = 0.89 \quad (X - 26.7.$$
$$Y = 0.89 \quad X - 26.7 + 25$$
$$= 0.89 \quad X - \mathbf{1.7}$$

When the wife's age $(Y) = 16$, the husband's age (X)=

$$X = 0.75 \times 16 + 11.25$$
$$= 12 + 11.25$$
$$= \mathbf{23.25}.$$

Problem 17. The following table shows the number of motor registrations in a certain territory for a term of 5 years and the sale of motor tyres by a firm in that territory for the same period.

Year	*Motor Registration*	*No.of Tyres sold*
1	600	1,250
2	630	1,100
3	720	1,300
4	750	1,350
5	800	1,500

Find the regression equation to estimate the sale of tyres when motor registration is known.Estimate sale of tyres when registration is 850.

(B. Com., Bombay)

Solution : Let the number of motor registration be denoted by X and the No.of tyres sold be denoted by Y.

Computation of Regression Equation

X	$dx = (X - \overline{X})$ $\overline{X} = 700$	dx^2	Y	$dy = (Y - \overline{Y})$ $Y = 1300$	dy^2	$dxdy$
600	−100	10,000	1250	−50	2500	5,000
630	− 70	4,900	1100	−200	40,000	14,000
720	20	400	1300	0	0	0
750	50	2,500	1350	50	2,500	2,500
800	100	10,000	1500	200	40,000	20,000
ΣX =3500		$\Sigma dx^2 =$ 27,800	ΣY = 6500		85,000	$\Sigma dxdy$ $= 41,500$

$$\text{Mean : } \overline{X} = \frac{\Sigma X}{N} = \frac{3500}{5} = \mathbf{700}. \qquad \overline{Y} = \frac{\Sigma Y}{N} = \frac{6500}{5} = \mathbf{1300}.$$

Regression Coefficient:

$$byx = \frac{\Sigma dxdy}{\Sigma dx^2} = \frac{41,500}{27,800}$$
$$= \mathbf{1.493}.$$

Regression equation of Y on X:

$$Y - \overline{Y} = b_{yx}(X - \overline{X})$$
$$Y - 1300 = 1.493(X - 700)$$

$$Y - 1300 = 1.493 \quad X - 1045.1$$
$$Y = 1.493 \quad X - 1045.1 + 1300$$
$$Y = 1.493 \quad X + 254.9.$$

When Motor Registration $(X) = 850$, the sale of tyres is

$$Y = 1.493 \times 850 + 254.9$$
$$= 1269.05 + 254.9$$
$$= 1523.95$$
$$Y = \mathbf{1524}.$$

Problem 18. For a group of children, mean age is 10 years with S.D. 2.5 years.The average height of the group is 125 cms with S.D.of 13 cms.The coefficient of correlation between age and height is 0.6. Write the equation of two regression lines and explain their use.

(B. Com., Bombay)

Solution : Let the age be denoted by X and height by Y Regression Equation of X on Y.

$$X - \overline{X} = r\frac{\sigma x}{\sigma y}(Y - \overline{Y})$$
$$X - 10 = 0.6 \times \frac{2.5}{13}(Y - 125)$$
$$X - 10 = 0.6 \times 0.19(Y - 125)$$
$$X - 10 = 0.114 \quad Y - 14.25$$
$$X = 0.114Y - 14.25 + 10$$
$$X = \mathbf{0.114Y - 4.25}$$

Regression Equation of Y on X:

$$Y - \overline{Y} = r\frac{\sigma y}{\sigma x}(X - \overline{X})$$
$$Y - 125 = 0.6 \times \frac{13}{2.5}(X - 10)$$
$$Y - 125 = 0.6 \times \frac{13}{2.5}(X - 10)$$
$$Y - 125 = 3.12X - 31.2$$
$$Y = 3.12X - 31.2 + 125$$
$$Y = \mathbf{3.12X + 93.8}$$

Problem 19. The heights (in cm.) of a group of fathers and sons are given below:

Height of father	:	158	160	163	165	167	170	172	175	177	181
Height of son	:	163	158	167	170	160	180	170	175	172	175

Find the lines of regression and estimate the height of the son when the height of father is 164 cm.

(B. Com., Madras)

Solution : Let the height of fathers be denoted by X and height of sons by Y.

Computation of Regression Equatioin

Height of father in Cms.X	$dx = (X) -170$	dx^2	*Height of sons in Cms Y*	$dy = Y -170$	dy^2	$dxdy$
158	−12	144	163	− 7	49	84
160	−10	100	158	−12	144	120
163	− 7	49	167	− 3	9	21
165	− 5	25	170	0	0	0
167	− 3	9	160	−10	100	30
170	0	0	180	+10	100	0
172	2	4	170	0	0	0
175	5	25	175	5	25	25
177	7	49	172	2	4	14
181	11	121	175	5	25	55
$\Sigma X = 1688$	$\Sigma dx = -12$	$\Sigma dx^2 = 526$	$\Sigma Y = 1690$	$\Sigma dy = -10$	$\Sigma dy^2 = 456$	$\Sigma dxdy = 349$

$$\text{Mean}: \quad \overline{X} = \frac{\Sigma X}{N} = \frac{1688}{10} = \mathbf{168.8} \qquad \overline{Y} = \frac{\Sigma Y}{N} = \frac{1690}{10} = \mathbf{169}$$

$$bxy \quad or \quad r\frac{\sigma x}{\sigma y} = \frac{\Sigma dxdy - \left(\frac{\Sigma dx \times \Sigma dy}{N}\right)}{\Sigma dy^2 - \frac{(\Sigma dy)^2}{N}}$$

$$= \frac{349 - \left(\frac{-12 \times -10}{10}\right)}{456 - \frac{(-10)^2}{10}}$$

$$= \frac{349 - 12}{456 - 10} = \frac{337}{446}$$

$$= \mathbf{0.76}$$

$$byx \quad or \quad r\frac{\sigma y}{\sigma x} = \frac{\Sigma dxdy - \left(\frac{\Sigma dx \times \Sigma dy}{N}\right)}{\Sigma dx^2 - \frac{(\Sigma dx)^2}{N}}$$

$$= \frac{349 - \left(\frac{12 \times -10}{10}\right)}{526 - \frac{(-12)^2}{10}}$$

$$= \frac{349 + 12}{526 - 14.4} = \frac{361}{511.6}$$

$$= \mathbf{+0.71}$$

Regression Equation of X on Y:

$$\begin{aligned}
(X - \overline{X}) &= bxy\,(Y - \overline{Y}) \\
X - 168.8 &= 0.76\,(Y - 169) \\
X - 168.8 &= 0.76\,Y - 128.44 \\
X &= 0.76Y - 128.44 + 168.8 \\
X &= \mathbf{0.76Y - 40.36}
\end{aligned}$$

Regression Equation of Y on X:

$$\begin{aligned}
(Y - \overline{Y}) &= byx\,(X - \overline{X}) \\
(Y - 169) &= 0.71\,(X - 168.8) \\
Y - 169 &= 0.71X - 119.85 \\
Y &= 0.71X - 119.85 + 169 \\
Y &= \mathbf{0.71X + 49.15}
\end{aligned}$$

When the height of the father $(X) = 164$, the height of the son (Y) is:

$$\begin{aligned}
Y &= 0.71(164) + 49.15 \\
&= 116.44 + 49.15 \\
&= \mathbf{165.59}
\end{aligned}$$

Problem 20. Find out the regression equation showing the regression of capacity utilization on production from the following data:

	Average	*Standard Deviation*
Production (in lakh units)	35.6	10.5
Capacity utilization (in percentage)	84.8	8.5

$r = 0.62$

Estimate the production when the capacity utilization is 70%.

(*M.B.A., Himachal Pradesh*)

Solution :

Production be denoted by X

Capacity utilization be denoted by Y

Regression equation of X on Y:

$$(X - \overline{X}) = r\frac{\sigma_x}{\sigma_y}(Y - \overline{Y})$$

$$\overline{X} = 35.6; \quad r = 0.62; \quad \sigma_x = 10.5; \sigma_y = 8.5; \quad \overline{Y} = 84.8$$

$$\begin{aligned}
(X - 35.6) &= 0.62 \times \frac{10.5}{8.5}(Y - 84.8) \\
(X - 35.6) &= 0.77 \quad Y - 65.3 \\
X &= 0.77 \quad Y - 65.3 + 35.6 \\
&= \mathbf{0.77 \quad Y - 29.7.}
\end{aligned}$$

When

$$\begin{aligned}
Y &= 70 \\
X &= 0.77 \times 70 - 29.7 \\
&= 53.9 - 29.7 \\
&= \mathbf{24.2.}
\end{aligned}$$

The estimated production is 2,42,000 units when the capacity utilization is 70%.

Problem 21. Find the regression equations from the following data:

Age of husband	:	18	19	20	21	22	23	24	25	26	27
Age of wife	:	17	17	18	18	19	19	19	20	21	22

(*M. Com. Kurukshetra*)

Solution : Let age of husband be denoted by X and age of wife by Y.

Computation of Regression Equatioin

X	$dx = (X - 22)$	dx^2	Y	$dy = Y - 19$	dy^2	$dxdy$
18	−4	16	17	−2	4	8
19	−3	9	17	−2	4	6
20	−2	4	18	−1	1	2
21	−1	1	18	−1	1	1
22	0	0	19	0	0	0
23	1	1	19	0	0	0
24	2	4	19	0	0	0
25	3	9	20	+1	1	3
26	4	16	21	+2	4	8
27	5	25	22	+3	9	15
$\Sigma X = 225$	$\Sigma dx = 5$	$\Sigma dx^2 = 85$	$\Sigma Y = 190$	$\Sigma dy = 0$	$\Sigma dy^2 = 24$	$\Sigma dxdy = 43$

Mean : $\overline{X} = \frac{\Sigma X}{N} = \frac{225}{10} = \mathbf{22.5}$

$$bxy = \frac{\Sigma dxdy - \frac{\Sigma dx \times \Sigma dy}{N}}{\Sigma dy^2 - \frac{(\Sigma dy)^2}{N}} = \frac{43 - \frac{5 \times 0}{10}}{24 - \frac{(0)^2}{10}} = \frac{43}{24} = \mathbf{1.79.}$$

$Y = \frac{\Sigma Y}{N} = \frac{190}{10} = \mathbf{19}.$

$$byx = \frac{\Sigma dxdy - \frac{\Sigma dx \times \Sigma dy}{N}}{\Sigma dx^2 - \frac{(\Sigma dx)^2}{N}} = \frac{43 - \frac{5 \times 0}{10}}{85 - \frac{(5)^2}{10}} = \frac{43}{82.5} = \mathbf{0.52.}$$

Regression of X on Y:

$$(X - \overline{X}) = bxy(Y - \overline{Y})$$
$$X - 22.79 = 1.79(Y - 19)$$
$$X - 22.5 = 1.79 \quad Y - 34.01$$
$$X = 1.79 \quad Y - 34.01 + 22.5$$
$$X = 1.79 \quad Y - 11.51.$$

Regression of Y on X:

$$Y - \overline{Y} = byx(X - \overline{X})$$
$$Y - 19 = 0.52(X - 22.5)$$
$$Y - 19 = 0.52 \quad X - 11.7$$
$$Y = 0.52 \quad X - 11.7 + 19$$
$$Y = 0.52 \quad X + 7.3$$

Problem 22. Calculate the two regression equations of X on Y and Y on X from the data given below taking deviations from actual means of X and Y:

Price (Rs.)	:	10	12	13	12	16	15
Amount demanded	:	40	38	43	45	37	43

Estimate the likely demand when the price is Rs.20. (*M.A. Econ. Kurukshetra*)

Solution : Let price be denoted by X and demand denoted by Y.

Computation of Regression Equation

X	$x = (X - \overline{X})$ $\overline{X} = 13$	x^2	Y	$y = Y - \overline{Y}$ $\overline{Y} = 41$	y^2	xy
10	−3	9	40	−1	1	+3
12	−1	1	38	−3	9	+3
13	−0	0	43	+2	4	0
12	−1	1	45	+4	16	−4
16	+3	9	37	−4	16	−12
15	+2	4	43	+2	4	+4
$\Sigma X = 78$		$\Sigma x^2 = 24$	$\Sigma Y = 246$		$\Sigma y^2 = 50$	$\Sigma xy = -6$

$$\text{Mean : } \overline{X} = \frac{\Sigma X}{N} = \frac{78}{6} = \mathbf{13.} \qquad \overline{Y} = \frac{\Sigma Y}{N} = \frac{246}{6} = \mathbf{41.}$$

$$bxy = \frac{\Sigma xy}{\Sigma y^2} = \frac{-6}{50} = \mathbf{-0.12.}$$

$$byx = \frac{\Sigma xy}{\Sigma x^2} = \frac{-6}{24} = \mathbf{-0.25.}$$

Regression Equation of X on Y:

$$\begin{aligned} (Y - \overline{X}) &= bxy(Y - \overline{Y}) \\ X - 13 &= -0.12(Y - 41) \\ X - 13 &= -0.12 \quad Y + 4.92 \\ X &= -0.12 \quad Y + 4.92 + 13 \\ X &= \mathbf{-0.12 \quad Y + 17.92} \end{aligned}$$

Regression Equation of Y on X:

$$\begin{aligned} Y - \overline{Y} &= byx(X - \overline{X}) \\ Y - 41 &= -0.25(X - 13) \\ Y - 41 &= -0.25\,X + 3.25 \\ Y &= -0.25\,X + 3.25 + 41 \\ Y &= \mathbf{-0.25\,X + 44.25.} \end{aligned}$$

$$\begin{aligned} \text{When} \quad X &= 20 \\ Y &= -0.25(20) + 44.25 \\ &= 5 + 44.25. \\ Y &= \mathbf{49.25.} \end{aligned}$$

Problem 23. Price indices of cotton and wool are given below for the 12 months of a year. Obtain the equations of lines of regression between the indices:

Price index of cotton (X)	:	78	77	85	88	87	82
Price index of wool (Y)	:	84	82	82	85	89	90
Price index of cotton (X)	:	81	77	76	83	97	93
Price index of wool (Y)	:	88	92	83	89	98	99

(*B. Com. Madras*)

Solution : Let price index of cotton be denoted by X and wool by Y.

Computation of Regression Equation

X	$dx = X - 84$	dx^2	Y	$dy = Y - 88$	dy^2	$dxdy$
78	−6	36	84	−4	16	24
77	−7	49	82	−6	36	42
85	1	1	82	−6	36	−6
88	4	16	85	−3	9	−12
87	3	9	89	1	1	3
82	−2	4	90	2	4	−4
81	−3	9	88	0	0	0
77	−7	49	92	4	16	−28
76	−8	64	83	−5	25	40
83	−1	1	89	1	1	−1
97	13	169	98	10	100	130
93	9	81	99	11	121	99
$\Sigma X = 1004$	$\Sigma dx = -4$	$\Sigma dx^2 = 488$	$\Sigma y = 1061$	$\Sigma dy = 5$	$\Sigma dy^2 = 365$	$\Sigma dxdy = 287$

Mean : $\overline{X} = A + \frac{\Sigma dx}{N} = 84 - \frac{4}{12} = \mathbf{83.67}$

$Y = A + \frac{\Sigma dy}{N} = 88 + \frac{5}{12} = 88.42$

$bxy = \frac{\Sigma dxdy}{\Sigma dy^2} = \frac{287}{365} = \mathbf{0.79}$

$byx = \frac{\Sigma dxdy}{\Sigma dx^2} = \frac{287}{488} = \mathbf{0.59}$

Regression Equation of X on $\overline{Y}$:

$$Y - \overline{X} = bxy(Y - Y)$$
$$X - 83.67 = 0.79(Y - 88.42)$$
$$X - 83.67 = 0.79Y - 69.85$$
$$X = 0.79Y - 69.85 + 83.67$$
$$X = \mathbf{0.79Y + 13.82}.$$

Regression of Y on X:

$$Y - \overline{Y} = byx(X - \overline{X})$$
$$Y - 88.42 = 0.59(X - 83.67)$$
$$Y - 88.42 = 0.59X - 49.37$$
$$Y = 0.59X - 49.37 + 88.42$$
$$Y = \mathbf{0.59X + 39.05}.$$

Problem 24. From the data given below:

(*a*) Fit a regression line of Y on X and therefore, predict Y, When $X = 10$.

(*b*) Fit a regression line of X on Y, when $Y = 3$.

(*c*) Calculate Karl Pearson's coefficient correlation.

X:	1	5	3	2	1	1	7	3
Y:	6	1	0	0	1	2	1	5

(*B. Com.*)

Solution :

Computation of Regression Equatioin

X	$dx = X - 3$	dx^2	Y	$dy = Y - 2$	dy^2	$dxdy$
1	−2	4	6	+4	16	−8
5	+2	4	1	−1	1	−2
3	0	0	0	−2	4	0
2	−1	1	0	−2	4	2
1	−2	4	1	−1	1	2
1	−2	4	2	0	0	0
7	+4	16	1	−1	1	−4
3	0	0	5	+3	9	0
$\Sigma X = 23$	$\Sigma dx = -1$	$\Sigma dx^2 = 33$	$\Sigma Y = 16$	$\Sigma dy = 0$	$\Sigma dy^2 = 36$	$\Sigma dxdy = -10$

$$\text{Mean : } \overline{X} = \frac{\Sigma X}{N} = \frac{23}{8} = \mathbf{2.9} \qquad \overline{Y} = \frac{\Sigma Y}{N} = \frac{16}{8} = 2$$

$$bxy = \frac{\Sigma dxdy - \frac{\Sigma dx\, \Sigma dy}{N}}{\Sigma dy^2 - \frac{(\Sigma dy)^2}{N}} = \frac{-10 - \frac{(-1)(0)}{8}}{36 - \frac{(0)^2}{8}} = \frac{-10}{36} = \mathbf{-0.28}.$$

$$byx = \frac{\Sigma dxdy - \frac{\Sigma dx\, \Sigma dy}{N}}{\Sigma dx^2 - \frac{(\Sigma dx)^2}{N}} = \frac{-10 - \frac{(-1)(0)}{8}}{33 - \frac{(-1)^2}{8}} = \frac{-10}{33 - 0.13} = \frac{-10}{32.87} = \mathbf{-0.3}.$$

(a) Regression Equation of Y on X:

$$\begin{aligned} Y - \overline{Y} &= byx(X - \overline{X}) \\ Y - 2 &= -0.3(X - 2.9) \\ Y - 2 &= -0.3\,X + 0.87 \\ Y &= -0.3\,X + 0.87 + 2 \\ Y &= -0.3\,X + 2.87. \end{aligned}$$

When

$$\begin{aligned} X &= 10, \\ Y &= -0.3(10) + 2.87 \\ &= -3 + 2.87 \\ &= \mathbf{0.13}. \end{aligned}$$

(b) Regression Equation of X on Y:

$$\begin{aligned} X - \overline{X} &= bxy(Y - \overline{Y}) \\ X - 2.9 &= 0.28 \quad (Y - 2) \\ X - 2.9 &= -0.28 \quad Y + 0.56 \\ X &= -0.28 \quad Y + 0.56 + 2.9 \end{aligned}$$

$$X = -\mathbf{0.28} \quad Y + \mathbf{3.46}.$$

When
$$Y = 3,$$
$$X = -0.28(3) + 3.46$$
$$= -0.84 + 3.46$$
$$X = \mathbf{2.62}.$$

(*c*) Karl Pearson's Coefficient of Correlation:

$$r = \sqrt{bxy \times byx}$$
$$= \sqrt{-0.28 \times -0.3}$$
$$= \sqrt{0.84}$$
$$r = \mathbf{+0.29}.$$

Problem 25. A panel of two judges 'p' and 'Q' graded seven dramatic performances by independently awarding marks as follows:

Performance	:	1	2	3	4	5	6	7
Marks by P	:	46	42	44	40	43	41	45
Marks by Q	:	40	38	36	35	39	37	41

The eighth performance, which judge *Q* could not attend, was awarded 37 marks by judge *P*.If judge *Q* had also been present, how many marks would be expected to have been awarded by him to the eighth performance.

(*B.Com. Hons. Delhi*)

Solution : Let Marks *P* be denoted by *X* and *Q* by *Y*.

Computation of Regression Equation

Performance	X	$dx = x - 40$	dx^2	Y	$dy = Y - 35$	dy^2	$dxdy$
1	46	6	36	40	5	25	30
2	42	2	4	38	3	9	6
3	44	4	16	36	1	1	4
4	40	0	0	35	0	0	0
5	43	3	9	39	4	16	12
6	41	1	1	37	2	4	2
7	45	5	25	41	6	36	30
	$\Sigma X = 301$	$\Sigma dx = 21$	$\Sigma dx^2 = 91$	$\Sigma Y = 266$	$\Sigma dy = 21$	$\Sigma dy^2 = 91$	$\Sigma dxdy = 84$

Mean : $\overline{X} = \dfrac{\Sigma X}{N} = \dfrac{301}{7} = \mathbf{43.}$ $\qquad \overline{Y} = \dfrac{\Sigma Y}{N} = \dfrac{266}{7} = \mathbf{38.}$

$$byx = \frac{\Sigma dxdy - \dfrac{\Sigma dx \times \Sigma dy}{N}}{\Sigma dx^2 - \dfrac{(\Sigma dx)^2}{N}} = \frac{84 - \dfrac{21 \times 21}{7}}{91 - \dfrac{(21)^2}{7}}$$

$$= \frac{84 - 63}{91 - 63} = \frac{21}{28} = \mathbf{0.75}.$$

Regression Equation of Y on X:

$$\begin{aligned} Y - \overline{Y} &= byx(X - \overline{X}) \\ Y - 38 &= 0.75(X - 43) \\ Y - 38 &= 0.75\,X - 32.25 \\ Y &= 0.75\,X - 32.25 + 38 \\ &= 0.75\,X + 5.75 \end{aligned}$$

When $X = 37$,

$$\begin{aligned} Y &= 0.75(37) + 5.75 \\ &= 27.75 + 5.75 \\ &= \mathbf{33.50}. \end{aligned}$$

If judge Q had been present, he would have awarded 33.50 marks.

Problem 26. You are given the data relating to purchases and sales. Obtain the two regression equations by least squares and estimate the likely sales when the purchases equal to 100.

Purchases (X) :	62	72	98	76	81	56	76	92	88	49
Sales (Y) :	112	124	131	117	132	96	120	136	97	85

(*CA Inter*

Solution :

X	$x = X - \overline{X}$ $\overline{X} = 75$	x^2	Y	$y = Y - \overline{Y}$ $\overline{Y} = 115$	y^2	xy
62	−13	169	112	−3	9	39
72	−3	9	124	9	81	−27
98	23	529	131	16	256	368
76	1	1	117	2	4	2
81	6	36	132	17	289	102
56	−19	361	96	−19	361	361
76	1	1	120	5	25	5
92	17	289	136	21	441	357
88	13	169	97	−18	324	−234
49	−26	676	85	−30	900	780
$\Sigma X = 750$		$\Sigma x^2 = 2240$	$\Sigma Y = 1150$		$\Sigma y^2 = 2690$	$\Sigma xy = 1753$

Mean : $\overline{X} = \dfrac{\Sigma X}{N} = \dfrac{750}{10} = 75$ $\qquad \overline{Y} = \dfrac{\Sigma Y}{N} = \dfrac{1150}{10} = 115$

$bxy = \dfrac{\Sigma xy}{\Sigma y^2} = \dfrac{1753}{2690}$ $\qquad byx = \dfrac{\Sigma xy}{\Sigma x^2} = \dfrac{1753}{2240}$

$= \mathbf{0.6515}$ *or* $\mathbf{0.65}$ $\qquad = \mathbf{0.7825}$ *or* $\mathbf{0.78}$

Regression Equation of X on Y:

$X - \overline{X} = bxy(Y - \overline{Y})$

Regression Equation of Y on X:

$Y - \overline{Y} = byx = (X - \overline{X})$

$$X - 75 = 0.65(Y - 115) \qquad Y - 115 = 0.78\,(X - 75)$$
$$X - 75 = 0.65 \quad Y - 74.75 \qquad Y - 115 = 0.78\,X - 58.5$$
$$X = 0.65 \quad Y - 74.75 + 75 \qquad Y = 0.78\,X - 58.5 + 115$$
$$X = 0.65 \quad Y + 0.25 \qquad Y = 0.78\,X + 56.5$$

When X or purchase = 100, expected sales i.e.

$$Y = 0.78(100) + 56.5$$
$$= 78 + 56.5$$
$$Y = \mathbf{134.5}$$

Problem 27. The following data give the monthly income and expenditure (in rupees) on food of 10 families.

Income :	120	90	80	150	130	140	110	95	70	105
Expenditure :	40	36	40	45	40	44	45	38	50	35

Calculate the linear regression of expenditure of food (Y) on income (X)

(*M.A., Econ., Punjab*)

Solution :

Computation for Regression Equation

Income X	$dx = X - 110/5$	dx^2	*Expenditure* Y	$dy = Y - 40$	dy^2	$dxdy$
120	+2	4	40	0	0	0
90	−4	16	36	−4	16	16
80	−6	36	40	0	0	0
150	+8	64	45	5	25	40
130	+4	16	40	0	0	0
140	+6	36	44	4	16	24
110	0	0	45	5	25	0
95	−3	9	38	−2	4	6
70	−8	64	50	10	100	--80
105	−1	1	35	−5	25	5
$\Sigma X =$ 1090	$\Sigma dx = -2$	$\Sigma dx^2 = 246$	$\Sigma Y = 413$	$\Sigma dy = 13$	$\Sigma dy^2 = 211$	$\Sigma dxdy = 11$

$$\text{Mean : } \bar{X} = \frac{\Sigma X}{N} = \frac{1090}{10} = \mathbf{109} \qquad \bar{Y} = \frac{\Sigma Y}{N} = \frac{413}{10} = \mathbf{41.3}$$

$$byx \text{ or } r\frac{\sigma y}{\sigma x} = \frac{\Sigma dxdy - \dfrac{\Sigma dx \times \Sigma dy}{N}}{\left(\Sigma dx^2 - \dfrac{(\Sigma dx)^2}{N}\right) cx}$$

$$= \frac{11 - \dfrac{(-2)(13)}{10}}{\left(246 - \dfrac{(-2)^2}{10}\right) 5} = \frac{11 + 2.6}{(246 - 0.4)5} = \frac{13.6}{245.6 \times 5}$$

$$= \frac{13.6}{1228} = \mathbf{0.011}$$

Regression Equation of Y on X:

$$\begin{aligned} Y - \overline{Y} &= byx\,(X - \overline{X}) \\ Y - 41.3 &= 0.011\,(X - 109) \\ Y - 41.3 &= 0.011\,X - 1.199 \\ Y &= 0.011 \quad X - 1.199 + 41.3 \\ &= \mathbf{0.011X + 40.101} \end{aligned}$$

Problem 28. Obtain the regression of Y on X and X on Y from the following table and estimate the blood pressure when the age is 50.

Age (X)	*Blood pressure* (Y)	*Age* (X)	*Blood pressure* (Y)
56	147	55	150
42	125	49	145
72	160	38	115
36	118	42	140
63	149	63	152
47	128	60	155

(*M.A. Econ., Punjab*)

Solution :

Computation of Regression Equations

Age (X)	$dx = X - 62$	dx^2	*Blood pressure* Y	$dy = Y - 140$	dy^2	$dxdy$
56	−6	36	147	+ 7	49	− 42
42	−20	400	125	−15	225	+300
72	+10	100	160	+20	400	+200
36	−26	676	118	−22	484	+572
63	+1	1	149	+ 9	81	+ 9
47	−15	225	128	−12	144	+180
55	−7	49	150	+10	100	− 70
49	−13	169	145	+ 5	25	− 65
38	−24	576	115	−25	625	+600
42	−20	400	140	0	0	0
68	+6	36	152	+12	144	+ 72
60	−2	4	155	+15	225	− 30
$\Sigma X = 628$	$\Sigma dx = -116$	$\Sigma dx^2 = 2672$	$\Sigma Y = 1684$	$\Sigma dy = 4$	$\Sigma dy^2 = 2502$	$\Sigma dxdy = 1726$

Regression Equation of Y on X:

$$\begin{aligned}
(Y-\overline{Y}) &= byx(X-\overline{X}) \\
Y-140.33 &= 1.14(X-52.33) \\
Y-140.33 &= 1.14 \quad X-59.66 \\
Y &= 1.14 \quad X-59.66+140.33 \\
Y &= \mathbf{1.14}\,X+\mathbf{80.67}.
\end{aligned}$$

When

$$\begin{aligned}
X &= 50, \\
Y &= 1.14\,X+80.67 \\
Y &= 1.14(50)+80.67 \\
&= 57+80.67 \\
&= \mathbf{137.67}.
\end{aligned}$$

$$\text{Mean}: \overline{X} = \frac{\Sigma X}{N} = \frac{628}{12} = \mathbf{52.33} \qquad \overline{Y} = \frac{\Sigma Y}{N} = \frac{1684}{12} = \mathbf{140.33}$$

$$\begin{aligned}
bxy \quad or \quad r\frac{\sigma_x}{\sigma_y} &= \frac{\Sigma dxdy - \dfrac{\Sigma dx \times \Sigma dy}{N}}{\Sigma dy^2 - \dfrac{(\Sigma dy)^2}{N}} \\
&= \frac{1726 - \dfrac{(-116 \times 4)}{12}}{2502 - \dfrac{(4)^2}{12}} \\
&= \frac{1726 - \dfrac{(-464)}{12}}{2502 - \dfrac{16}{12}} \\
&= \frac{1726+38.67}{2502-1.33} \\
&= \frac{1764.67}{2500.67} \\
byx &= \mathbf{0.71}.
\end{aligned}$$

$$\begin{aligned}
bxy \quad or \quad r\frac{\sigma_y}{\sigma_x} &= \frac{\Sigma dxdy - \dfrac{(\Sigma dy)\,(\Sigma dx)}{N}}{\Sigma dx^2 - \dfrac{(\Sigma dx)^2}{N}} \\
&= \frac{1726 - \dfrac{(4)(-116)}{12}}{2672 - \dfrac{(-116)^2}{12}} \\
&= \frac{17.26+38.67}{2672-1121.33} \\
&= \frac{1764.67}{1550.67} \\
&= \mathbf{1.14}.
\end{aligned}$$

Regression Equation of X on Y:

$$X - \overline{X} = bxy(Y - \overline{Y})$$
$$X - 52.33 = 0.71(Y - 140.33)$$
$$X - 52.33 = 0.71 \quad Y - 99.63$$
$$X = 0.71 \quad Y - 99.63 + 52.33$$
$$X = \mathbf{0.71} \quad Y - \mathbf{47.30}.$$

Problem 29. By using simultaneous equation method, find out:
(*a*) Regression equation of Y on X
(*b*) Regression equation of X on Y
(*c*) The most probable value of Y, when $X = 10$.

X:	1	2	3	4	5
Y:	2	5	3	8	7.

(*B. Com.*)

Solution :

Regression Equation of Y on X

$Y = a + bX$

The simultaneous equations are

$$\Sigma Y = Na + b\Sigma X$$
$$\Sigma XY = a\,\Sigma X + b\Sigma X^2$$

Regression Equation of X on Y:

$$X = a + bY.$$

The simultaneous equations are

$$\Sigma X = Na + b\Sigma Y$$
$$\Sigma XY = a\,\Sigma Y + b\Sigma Y^2$$

X	X^2	Y	Y^2	XY
1	1	2	4	2
2	4	5	25	10
3	9	3	9	9
4	16	8	64	32
5	25	7	49	35
$\Sigma X = 15$	$\Sigma X^2 = 55$	$\Sigma Y = 25$	$\Sigma Y^2 = 151$	$\Sigma XY = 88$

(*a*) By substituting the values

$$25 = 5\,a + 15\,b \quad \ldots(1)$$
$$88 = 15\,a + 55\,b \quad \ldots(2)$$

Multiplying equation 1 by 3 and subtract it from equation (2)

$$88 = 15\,a + 55\,b \quad \ldots(2)$$
$$75 = 15\,a + 45\,b \quad \ldots(3)$$
$$13 = 10\,b$$
$$b = 1.3$$

(*b*) By substituting the values

$$15 = 5\,a + 25\,b \quad \ldots(1)$$
$$88 = 25\,a + 151\,b \quad \ldots(2)$$

Multiplying equation (*a*) by 5 and subtract it from equation 2.

$$88 = 25\,a + 151\,b \quad \ldots(2)$$
$$75 = 25\,a + 125\,b \quad \ldots(3)$$
$$13 = 26\,b$$
$$b = 0.5$$

But substituting the value of b in equation (1)

$$25 = 5a + 15(1.3)$$
$$25 = 5a + 19.5$$
$$5a = 25 - 19.5$$
$$a = \frac{5.5}{5} = \mathbf{1.1}$$
$$Y = \mathbf{1.1 + 1.3\,X}$$

By substituting the values in the equation (1) we get:

$$15 = 5a + 25(.5)$$
$$15 = 5a + 12.5$$
$$5a = 15 - 12.5$$
$$a = \frac{2.5}{5} = \mathbf{0.5}$$
$$X = \mathbf{0.5 + 0.5\,Y}$$

(c) When $X = 10$

$$Y = a + bX$$
$$= 1.1 + 1.3(10)$$
$$= 1.1 + 13$$
$$= \mathbf{14.1}$$

Problem 30. Given the following data, calculate the expected value of Y when $X = 12$:

	X	Y	
Average	7.6	14.8	
Standard Deviation	3.6	2.5	$r = 0.99$

(*B. Com., Mysore*)

Solution :

We have to find out regression equation of Y on X in order to calculate the expected value of Y when X is 12.

Regression Equation of Y on X:

$$(Y - \overline{Y}) = r\frac{\sigma_y}{\sigma_x}(X - \overline{X})$$
$$\overline{Y} = 14.8;\quad r = 0.99;\quad \sigma_y = 2.5;\quad \sigma_x = 3.6;\quad \overline{X} = 7.6$$
$$(Y - 14.8) = 0.99 \times \frac{2.5}{3.6}(X - 7.6)$$
$$(Y - 14.8) = 0.99 \times 0.69(X - 7.6)$$
$$Y - 14.8 = 0.68\,X - 5.17$$
$$Y = 0.68\,X - 5.17 + 14.8$$
$$= \mathbf{0.68\,X + 9.63}.$$

When X is 12,

$$Y = 0.68 \times 12 + 9.63$$
$$= 8.16 + 9.63$$
$$= \mathbf{17.79}.$$

Problem 31. Given the following data, estimate the marks in Mathematics obtained by a student who has scored 60 marks in English.

Mean of marks in Mathematics	80
Mean of marks in English	50
S.D.of marks in Mathematics	15
S.D.of marks in English	10
Coefficient of correlation	0.4

(*B. Com.*)

Solution :

Let marks in Mathematics be denoted by X and marks in English by Y.

Regression Equation of X on Y:

$$\begin{aligned} X-\overline{X} &= r\frac{\sigma x}{\sigma y}\left(Y-\overline{Y}\right) \\ X-80 &= 0.4\times\frac{15}{10}(Y-50) \\ X-80 &= 0.4\times 1.5(Y-50) \\ X-80 &= 0.6Y-30 \\ X &= 0.6Y-30+80 \\ X &= \mathbf{0.6Y+50} \end{aligned}$$

When $Y=60$,

$$\begin{aligned} X &= 0.6(60)+50 \\ &= 36+50 \\ X &= \mathbf{86} \end{aligned}$$

Hence for a student who has obtained 60 marks in English, the likely marks in Mathematics are 86.

Problem 32. From the following data of rainfall and production of rice, find the most likely production corresponding to the rainfall 40 cms.

	Rainfall	Production (quintals)
Mean	35	50
Standard Deviation	5	8
Correlation coefficient	+0.8	

(*M. Com., Kurukshetra*)

Solution : Production depends upon rainfall.Hence production be denoted by Y and ranifall by X.

Regression Equation of Y on Y:

$$\begin{aligned} Y-\overline{Y} &= r\frac{\sigma y}{\sigma x}X-\overline{X} \\ Y-50 &= 0.8\times\frac{8}{5}(X-35) \\ Y-50 &= 0.8\times 1.6(X-35) \\ Y-50 &= 1.28X-44.8 \\ Y &= 1.28X-44.8+50 \\ Y &= 1.28X+5.2 \end{aligned}$$

When $X=40$

$$\begin{aligned} Y &= 1.28(40)+5.2 \\ &= 51.2+5.2 \\ &= \mathbf{56.4}\text{ quintals.} \end{aligned}$$

Problem 33. You are given the following information:

	Price (Rs.)	Amount demanded (thousand units)
Arithmetic Mean	10	35
Standard Deviation	2	5
Correlation coefficient	+0.8	

Obtain the regression equation of amount demanded on price and estimate likely demand when price is Rs. 12.5.

(M.A. Econ., Punjab)

Solution :

Let the pricebe denoted by X and the amount demanded by Y.

Regression Equation of Y on X:

$$
\begin{aligned}
(Y - \overline{Y}) &= r\frac{\sigma y}{\sigma x}(X - \overline{X}) \\
(Y - 35) &= 0.8 \times \frac{5}{2}(X - 10) \\
Y - 35 &= 0.8 \times 2.5(X - 10) \\
Y - 35 &= 2X - 20 \\
Y &= 2\ \ X - 20 + 35 \\
&= \mathbf{2\,X + 15} \\
\text{When}\quad X &= 12.5, \quad Y\ is \\
Y &= 2 \times 12.5 + 15 \\
&= 25 + 15 \\
&= \mathbf{40}
\end{aligned}
$$

When the price is Rs. 12.5, the likely demand would be 40.

Problem 34. In a correlation analysis, between production and price of a commodity, the following constants were obtained:

	Production Index	Price Index
Arithmetic mean	110	98
Standard Deviation	12	5

Correlation between production and price −0.4

Write down the regression equation of price on production and calculate the price index when the prouction index is 116.

(Business Management, Madras)

Solution : Let production index be denoted by X and price index be denoted by Y.

Regression Equation of Y on X:

$$
\begin{aligned}
Y - \overline{Y} &= r\frac{\sigma_y}{\sigma_x}(X - \overline{X}) \\
Y - 98 &= -0.4 \times \frac{5}{12}(X - 110) \\
Y - 98 &= -0.167\,X + 18.37 \\
Y &= -0.167\,X + 18.37 + 98 \\
&= -0.167\,X + 116.37
\end{aligned}
$$

When the production index $(X) = 116$, the price index

$$\begin{aligned} Y &= -0.167 \times 116 + 116.37 \\ &= -19.37 + 116.37 \\ &= \mathbf{97}. \end{aligned}$$

Problem 35. You are given the following results for the heights (*X*) and weights (*Y*) of 1000 workers of a factory.

Mean $(\overline{X}) = 68"$ | *Mean* $(\overline{Y}) = 150$ lbs.
S.D.(X) = 2.5" | S.D.(Y) = 20 lbs.

$r = 0.6.$

Estimate from above data:

(*a*) The weight of a particular factory worker who is 5' tall.
(*b*) The height of a particular factory worker whose weight is 200 lbs.

(*B. Com. Mysore*)

Solution :

(*i*) Regression equation of *Y* on *X*:

$$\begin{aligned} Y - \overline{Y} &= r\frac{\sigma_y}{\sigma_x}(X - \overline{X}) \\ Y - 150 &= 0.6\frac{20}{2.5}(X - 68) \\ Y - 150 &= 4.8(X - 68) \\ Y - 150 &= 4.8X - 326.4 \\ Y &= 4.8X + 150 - 326.4 \\ &= 4.8X - 176.4 \end{aligned}$$

When $X = 60$, Y will be

$$\begin{aligned} Y &= 4.80 \times 60 - 176.4 \\ &= 288 - 176.4 \\ &= \mathbf{111.6}. \end{aligned}$$

The weight of a factory worker, who is 5 feet tall, is **111.6** lbs.

(*ii*) Regression equation of $\overline{X}$ on *Y*:

$$\begin{aligned} X - \overline{X} &= r\frac{\sigma_x}{\sigma_y}(Y - \overline{Y}) \\ X - 68 &= 0.6\frac{2.5}{20}(Y - 150) \\ X - 68 &= 0.075(Y - 150) \\ X - 68 &= 0.075Y - 11.25 \\ X &= 0.075y + 68 - 11.25 \\ X &= 0.075y + 56.75 \end{aligned}$$

When $Y = 200$ X will be

$$\begin{aligned} X &= 0.075 \times 200 + 56.75 \\ X &= 15 + 56.75 \\ X &= \mathbf{71.75}. \end{aligned}$$

Thus the height of a particular factory worker whose weight is 200 lbs= **71.75** inches.

Problem 36. The correlation coefficient between the variables X and Y is $r = 0.60$.If $\sigma_x = 1.50$, $\sigma_y = 2.00$, $\overline{X} = 10$ and $\overline{Y} = 20$, find the equations of the regression lines.

(*I.C.W.A., Final*)

(*i*) Y on X; (2) X on Y.

Solution :

Regression Equation of X on Y:

$$\begin{aligned}(X-\overline{X}) &= r\frac{\sigma_x}{\sigma_y}(Y-\overline{Y})\\ (X-10) &= 0.6\times\frac{1.50}{2}(Y-20)\\ (X-10) &= 0.6\times 0.75\,(Y-20)\\ X-10 &= 0.45\,Y-9\\ X &= 0.45\,Y-9+10\\ &= \mathbf{0.45\,Y+1}.\end{aligned}$$

Regression Equation of Y on X:

$$\begin{aligned}(Y-\overline{Y}) &= r\frac{\sigma_y}{\sigma_x}(X-\overline{X})\\ (Y-20) &= 0.6\times\frac{2}{1.50}(X-10)\\ Y-20 &= 0.6\times 1.33\quad(X-10)\\ Y-20 &= 0.8\,X-8\\ Y &= 0.8\,X-8+20\\ &= \mathbf{0.8\,X+12}.\end{aligned}$$

Problem 37. The following data based on 450 students, are given for marks in Statistics and Economics at a certain examination.

	Statistics	*Economics*
Mean marks	40	48
Standard deviation	12	16

Sum of the products of deviation of marks from their respective means is 42075. Give the equations to the two lines of regressions.

Estimate the average marks in Economics of the candidate who obtained 50 marks in Statistics.

(*B. Com. Madurai*)

Solution : Let marks in statistics be denoted by X and marks in Economics by Y.

Coefficient of Correlation:

$$\begin{aligned}r &= \frac{\Sigma dxdy}{N\sigma_x\sigma_y} = \frac{42075}{450\times 12\times 16} = \frac{42075}{86400}\\ &= \mathbf{+0.49}.\end{aligned}$$

Regression Equation of X on Y:

$$X-\overline{X} = r\frac{\sigma_x}{\sigma_y}(Y-\overline{Y})$$

$$
\begin{aligned}
X - 40 &= 0.49 \times \frac{12}{16}(Y - 48) \\
X - 40 &= 0.49 \times 0.75 \quad (Y - 48) \\
X - 40 &= 0.37 \quad Y - 17.76 \\
X &= 3.37Y - 17.76 + 40 \\
X &= \mathbf{3.37\,Y + 22.24}.
\end{aligned}
$$

Regression Equation of Y on X:

$$
\begin{aligned}
Y - \overline{Y} &= r\frac{\sigma_y}{\sigma_x}\left(X - \overline{X}\right) \\
Y - 48 &= 0.49 \times \frac{16}{12}(X - 40) \\
Y - 40 &= 0.49 \times 1.33 \quad (X - 40) \\
Y - 48 &= 0.65 \quad X - 26 \\
Y &= 0.65 \quad X - 26 + 48 \\
Y &= 0.65 \quad X + 22.
\end{aligned}
$$

When $X = 50,$

$$
\begin{aligned}
Y &= 0.65(50) + 22 \\
&= 32.5 + 22 \\
Y &= \mathbf{54.5}.
\end{aligned}
$$

Problem 38. The following data relate to marks obtained by 250 students in Accountancy and Statistics in M. Com. Examination of a University:

Subject	*Arithmetic Mean*	*Standard Deviation*
Accountancy	48	4
Statistics	55	5

Coefficient of correlation between marks in Accountancy and Statistics is +0.8 Draw the two lines of regression and estimate the marks obtained by a student in Statistics who securred 50 marks in Accountancy. (*M. Com. Delhi*)

Solution :

Regression Equation of Y on X

$$
\begin{aligned}
\left(Y - \overline{Y}\right) &= r\frac{\sigma_y}{\sigma_x}\left(X - \overline{X}\right) \\
(Y - 55) &= 0.8\frac{5}{4}(X - 48) \\
(Y - 55) &= 0.8 \times 1.25(X - 48) \\
Y - 55 &= 1\,(X - 48) \\
Y &= X - 48 + 55 \\
Y &= X + 7
\end{aligned}
$$

Regression Equation of X on Y

$$
(X - \overline{X}) = r\frac{\sigma_x}{\sigma_y}\left(Y - \overline{Y}\right)
$$

$$
\begin{aligned}
(X-48) &= 0.8\frac{4}{5}(Y-55)\\
X-48 &= 0.8\times 0.8(Y-55)\\
X-48 &= 0.64(Y-55)\\
X-48 &= 0.64\quad Y-35.2\\
X &= 0.64Y-35.2+48\\
X &= 0.64Y+12.8\\
\text{When}\qquad X &= 50,\\
Y &= 7+50\\
Y &= \mathbf{57}
\end{aligned}
$$

When a student obtained 50 marks in Accountancy, he secures 57 marks in Statistics.

Problem 39. The following results were worked out from scores in Statistics and Mathematics in a certain examination:

	Score in Statistics (X)	*Score in Mathematics* (Y)
Mean	39.5	47.5
Standard Deviation	10.8	17.8

Karl Pearson's correlation coefficient between X and $Y = +0.42$

Find both regression lines. Use these regression lines to estimate the value of Y for $X = 50$ and also estimate the value of X for $Y = 30$.

(*B. Com. Delhi*)

Solution :

Regression Equation of X on Y

$$
\begin{aligned}
(X-\overline{X}) &= r\frac{\sigma_x}{\sigma_y}(Y-\overline{Y})\\
(X-39.5) &= 0.42\frac{10.8}{17.8}(Y-47.5)\\
X-39.5 &= 0.42\times 0.61\quad (Y-47.5)\\
X-39.5 &= 0.26Y-12.35\\
X &= 0.26Y-12.35+39.5\\
X &= 0.26Y+27.15
\end{aligned}
$$

Regression Equation of Y on X

$$
\begin{aligned}
(Y-\overline{Y}) &= r\frac{\sigma_y}{\sigma_x}(X-\overline{X})\\
(Y-47.5) &= 0.42\frac{17.8}{10.8}(X-39.5)\\
Y-47.5 &= 0.42\times 1.65(X-39.5)\\
Y-47.5 &= 0.69X-27.26\\
Y &= 0.69X-27.26+47.5\\
Y &= 0.69X+20.24
\end{aligned}
$$

$$\begin{aligned}
\text{When} \quad X &= 50 \\
Y &= 0.69 \times 50 + 20.24 \\
&= 34.5 + 20.24 \\
&= \mathbf{54.74} \\
\text{When} \quad Y &= 30 \\
X &= 0.26 \times 30 + 27.15 \\
&= 7.8 + 27.15 \\
&= \mathbf{34.95}
\end{aligned}$$

Problem 40 You are given the following data:

	X	Y
Arithmetic Mean	36	85
Standard Deviation	11	8

Correlation coefficient between X and $Y = 0.66$.

(*i*) Find two regression equations.

(*ii*) Estimate value of X when $Y = 75$.

(*C.A.Inter*)

Solution :

(*i*) Regression Equation of X on Y:

$$\begin{aligned}
(X - \overline{X}) &= r\frac{\sigma_x}{\sigma_y}(Y - \overline{Y}) \\
X - 36 &= 0.66 \times \frac{11}{8}(Y - 85) \\
X - 36 &= 0.66 \times 1.38\,(Y - 85) \\
X - 36 &= 0.91\,Y - 77.35 \\
X &= 0.91\,Y - 77.35 + 36 \\
&= \mathbf{0.91\,Y - 41.35}
\end{aligned}$$

Regression Equation of Y on X:

$$\begin{aligned}
(Y - \overline{Y}) &= r\frac{\sigma_y}{\sigma_x}(X - \overline{X}) \\
(Y - 85) &= 0.66 \times \frac{8}{11}(X - 36) \\
Y - 85 &= 0.66 \times 0.73\,(X - 36) \\
Y - 85 &= 0.48\,X - 17.28 \\
Y &= 0.48\,X - 17.28 + 85 \\
&= \mathbf{0.48\,X + 67.72}.
\end{aligned}$$

$$\begin{aligned}
(ii) \quad \text{When} \quad Y &= 75, \text{the value of } X \text{ is} \\
X &= 0.91 \times 75 - 41.35 \\
&= 68.25 - 41.35 \\
&= \mathbf{26.9}.
\end{aligned}$$

Problem 41. From the following data, write down the equation of the regression line.

	Average	*S.D.*
Marks in Maths	48.4	8.4
Marks in English	35.6	10.5

$r = 0.62$

Estimate the marks in Mathematics corresponding to 70 marks in English.

(B. Com., Madras)

Solution : Let Marks in maths be denoted by X and English by Y. Regression Equation of X on Y:

$$X - \overline{X} = r\frac{\sigma x}{\sigma y}(Y - \overline{Y})$$

$$X - 48.4 = 0.62\frac{8.4}{10.5}(Y - 35.6)$$

$$X - 48.4 = 0.62 \times 0.8 \quad (Y - 35.6)$$

$$X - 48.4 = 0.496Y - 17.66$$

$$X = 0.496Y - 17.66 + 48.4$$

$$X = \mathbf{0.496\,Y + 30.74}$$

Regression Equation of Y on X:

$$Y - \overline{Y} = r\frac{\sigma y}{\sigma x} \quad (X - \overline{X})$$

$$Y - 35.6 = 0.62 \times \frac{10.5}{8.4}(X - 48.4)$$

$$Y - 35.6 = 0.62 \times 1.25(X - 48.4)$$

$$Y - 35.6 = 0.775X - 37.51$$

$$Y = 0.775X - 37.51 + 35.6$$

$$Y = \mathbf{0.775\,X - 1.91}$$

When Marks in English $(Y) = 70$ marks in Mathematics or

$$X = 0.496(70) + 30.74$$

$$= 34.72 + 30.74$$

$$= \mathbf{65.46} \text{ or } \mathbf{65.5}$$

Problem 42. The following data give the correlation coefficient, means and standard deviation of rainfall and yield of paddy in a certain tract.

	Yield per Acre in lbs.	*Annual Rainfall in* Inches
Mean	937.5	18.3
S.D.	38.4	2.0

$r = 0.58$

Estimate the most likely yield of paddy when the annual rainfall is 22 inches, other factors being assumed to remain the same.

(M. Com., Delhi, Agra, M.A. Eco., Delhi,)

Solution : Let yield per acre be denoted by X and annual rainfall by Y.

Regression Equation of X on Y:

$$X - \overline{X} = r\frac{\sigma x}{\sigma y}(Y - \overline{Y})$$

$$X - 937.5 = 0.58 \times \frac{38.4}{2}(Y - 18.3)$$

$$X - 937.5 = 0.58 \times 19.2(Y - 18.3)$$

$$X - 937.5 = 11.14Y - 203.86$$

$$X = 11.14Y - 203.86 + 937.5$$

$$X = \mathbf{11.14Y + 733.64}$$

When annual rainfall $(Y) = 22$, the yield of paddy

$$X = 11.14(22) + 733.64$$

$$= 245.08 + 733.64$$

$$= \mathbf{978.72}$$

Problem 43. You are supplied with the following data only:

$$\text{Variance of } X = 36$$

$$12X - 15Y + 99 = 0$$

$$60X - 27Y = 321$$

Calculate:

(*a*) the average value of X and Y
(*b*) Coefficient of Correlation between X and Y. (*M. Com., Agra*)

Solution :

We have

(*a*) $12\ X - 15\ Y + 99 = 0$ (1)

$60\ X - 27\ Y = 321$ (2)

Multiply (1) by 5,

$60\ X - 75 = -495$ (3)

Deducting (2)from (3),

$$-48\ Y = -816$$

$$\therefore\ Y = \frac{816}{48} = \mathbf{17}$$

Substituting the Values in (1)

$12\ X - 15 \times 17 = -99$

(*or*) $12\ X - 255 = -99$

(*or*) $12\ X = -99 + 255$

(*or*) $12\ X = 156$

$X = \frac{156}{12} = 13$

Thus $\overline{X} = 13; \overline{Y} = 17$

$$(b) \qquad 12X - 15Y = -99$$
$$-15Y = -12X - 99$$
$$-Y = \frac{12}{15}$$

$$(or) \qquad -Y = 0.8X - 6.6 (\text{ regression of } Y \text{ on } X)$$
$$byx\left(r\frac{\sigma y}{\sigma x}\right) = \mathbf{0.8}$$
$$60 \quad X = 27Y + 321$$
$$(or) X = \frac{27y}{60} + \frac{321}{60}$$
$$(or) \qquad X = 0.45Y + 5.35 (\text{regression of } X \text{ on } Y)$$
$$bxy\left(r\frac{\sigma x}{\sigma y}\right) = 0.45$$

$$r = \sqrt{r\frac{\sigma x}{\sigma y} \times r\frac{\sigma y}{\sigma x}}$$
$$= \sqrt{0.45 \times 0.8}$$
$$= \sqrt{0.360}$$
$$= \mathbf{+0.6}$$

Problem: 44. In a correlation study, the following values are obtained:

	X		T
Mean	65		67
Standard Deviation	2.5		3.5
Coefficient of correlation		0.8	

Find the two regression equations that are associated with the above values.

(M. Com., Calicut
B. Com., Hons.Delhi
B. Com., Gauhati
Shivaji.)

Solution :

Regression Equation of X on Y:

$$(X - \overline{X}) = r\frac{\sigma x}{\sigma y}(Y - \overline{Y})$$
$$\overline{X} = 65; r = 0.8; \sigma x = 2.5; \sigma y = 3.5; \overline{Y} = 67$$
$$(X - 65) = 0.8 \times \frac{2.5}{3.5}(Y - 67)$$
$$(X - 65) = 0.8 \times 0.71 \quad (Y - 67)$$
$$X - 65 = 0.57Y - 38.19$$
$$X = 0.57Y - 38.19 + 65$$
$$= \mathbf{0.57\,Y + 26.81}$$

Regression Equation of Y on X:

$$(Y - \overline{Y}) = r\frac{\sigma y}{\sigma x}(X - \overline{X})$$

$$
\begin{aligned}
Y - 67 &= 0.8 \times \frac{3.5}{2.5}(X - 65) \\
Y - 67 &= 0.8 \times 1.4(X - 65) \\
Y - 67 &= 1.12\,X - 72.8 \\
Y &= 1.12\,X - 72.8 + 67 \\
&= \mathbf{1.12\,X - 5.8}
\end{aligned}
$$

Problem 45. Assuming that there is a linear relationship between height (X) and weight (Y) of residents of a certain locality; estimate the height of an individual whose weight is 150 lbs, from the following data:

Mean height	= 65 inches
Mean weight	= 160 lbs.
Standard deviation of height	= 3 inches
Standard deviation of weight	= 20 lbs.

Coefficient of correlation between height and weight = 0.60.

Also, find the most likely weight of a person whose height is 68 inches.

(M. Com., Delhi)

Solution :

Regression Equation of X on Y:

$$
\begin{aligned}
X - \overline{X} &= r\frac{\sigma x}{\sigma y}(Y - \overline{Y}) \\
X - 65 &= 0.6 \times \frac{3}{20}(Y - 160) \\
X - 65 &= 0.09\,(Y - 160) \\
X - 65 &= 0.09\,Y - 14.4 \\
X &= 0.09\,Y - 14.4 + 65 \\
&= \mathbf{0.09\,Y + 50.6}
\end{aligned}
$$

When $Y = 150$ lbs,

$$
\begin{aligned}
X &= 0.09 \times 150 + 50.6 \\
&= 13.5 + 50.6 \\
&= \mathbf{64.1\ inches}
\end{aligned}
$$

Regression Equation of Y on X:

$$
\begin{aligned}
Y - \overline{Y} &= r\frac{\sigma y}{\sigma x}(X - \overline{X}) \\
Y - 160 &= 0.6 \times \frac{20}{3}(X - 65) \\
Y - 160 &= 4\ \ (X - 65) \\
Y - 160 &= 4\ \ X - 260 \\
Y &= 4\ \ X - 260 + 160 \\
&= \mathbf{4X - 100}
\end{aligned}
$$

When $X = 68$ inches,

$$\overline{Y} = 4 \times 68 - 100$$
$$= 272 - 100$$
$$= \mathbf{172\,lbs}$$

Problem 46. From the following data, write down the equation of the regression line.

	X		Y
Arithmetic mean	60		120
Standard deviation	3.36		7.24
Correlation coefficient		+0.98	

(*B. Com*).

Solution :

Regression Equation of X on Y:

$$X - \overline{X} = r\frac{\sigma x}{\sigma y}(Y - \overline{Y})$$
$$X - 60 = 0.98\frac{3.36}{7.24}(Y - 120)$$
$$X - 60 = 0.98 \times 0.47\,(Y - 120)$$
$$X - 60 = 0.46\,Y - 55.2$$
$$X = 0.46\,Y - 55.2 + 60$$
$$X = \mathbf{0.46\,Y + 4.8}$$

Regression Equation of Y on X:

$$Y - \overline{Y} = r\frac{\sigma y}{\sigma x}(X - \overline{X})$$
$$Y - 120 = 0.98\frac{7.24}{3.36}(X - 60)$$
$$Y - 120 = 0.98 \times 2.15\,(X - 60)$$
$$Y - 120 = 2.11\,X - 126.6$$
$$Y = 2.11\,X - 126.6 + 120.$$
$$Y = \mathbf{2.11\,X - 6.6}$$

Problem 47. Following are the marks in Malayalam and English in annual examination:

	Malayalam (X)		*English* (Y)
Mean	40		50
S.D.	10		16
r		+0.5	

Estimate the score of English when score in Malayalam is 50 and score in Malayam when score in English is 30.

(*B. Com., Calicut*)

Solution :

Regression Equation of X on Y:

$$X - \overline{X} = r\frac{\sigma x}{\sigma y}(Y - \overline{Y})$$

$$
\begin{aligned}
X - 40 &= 0.5 \times \frac{10}{16}(Y - 50) \\
X - 40 &= 0.5 \times 0.63\,(Y - 50) \\
X - 40 &= 0.32\,Y - 16 \\
X &= 0.32\,Y - 16 + 40 \\
X &= \mathbf{0.32\,Y + 24}
\end{aligned}
$$

When $Y = 30$,

$$
\begin{aligned}
X &= 0.32(30) + 24 \\
&= 9.6 + 24 \\
X &= \mathbf{33.6}
\end{aligned}
$$

Regression Equation of Y on X:

$$
\begin{aligned}
Y - \overline{Y} &= r\frac{\sigma y}{\sigma x}\,(X - \overline{X}) \\
Y - 50 &= 0.5 \times \frac{16}{10}(X - 40) \\
Y - 50 &= 0.5 \times 1.6\,(X - 40) \\
Y - 50 &= 0.8\,X - 32 \\
Y &= 0.8\,X - 32 + 50 \\
Y &= \mathbf{0.8\,X + 18}
\end{aligned}
$$

When $X = 50$,

$$
\begin{aligned}
Y &= 0.8(50) + 18 \\
&= 40 + 18 \\
Y &= \mathbf{58}
\end{aligned}
$$

Problem 48. Given:

	X series	*Y series*
Mean	18	100
S.D.	14	20

Coefficient of Correlation between X and Y series is $+0.8$

Find out the most probable value of Y if X is 70, and most probable value of X if Y is 90.

(*b*) If two regression coefficients are 0.8 and 0.6, what would be the value of the coefficient of correlation.

(*M. Com., Allahabad*)

Solution :

Regression of X on Y

$$
\begin{aligned}
(X - \overline{X}) &= r\frac{\sigma x}{\sigma y}\,(Y - \overline{Y}) \\
\overline{X} = 18; r &= 0.8; \sigma x = 14; \sigma y = 20; \overline{Y} = 100 \\
(X - 18) &= 0.8 \times \frac{14}{20}(Y - 100)
\end{aligned}
$$

$$
\begin{aligned}
(X - 18) &= 0.8 \times 0.7\,(Y - 100) \\
X - 18 &= 0.56\,Y - 56 \\
X &= 0.56\,Y - 56 + 18 \\
&= \mathbf{0.56\,Y - 38}
\end{aligned}
$$

When Y is 90

$$
\begin{aligned}
X &= (0.56 \times 90) - 38 \\
&= 50.4 - 38 \\
&= \mathbf{12.4}
\end{aligned}
$$

The most probable value of X when Y is 90 = 12.4

Regression of Y on X:

$$
\begin{aligned}
(Y - \overline{Y}) &= r\frac{\sigma y}{\sigma x}(X - \overline{X}) \\
Y - 100 &= 0.8 \times \frac{20}{14}(X - 18) \\
Y - 100 &= 0.8 \times 1.43\,(X - 18) \\
Y - 100 &= 1.14\,X - 20.52 \\
Y &= 1.14\,X - 20.52 + 100 \\
Y &= 1.14\,X + 79.48
\end{aligned}
$$

When X is 70

$$
\begin{aligned}
Y &= (1.14 \times 70) + 79.48 \\
&= 79.8 + 79.48 \\
&= \mathbf{159.28}
\end{aligned}
$$

Coefficient of correlation $= \sqrt{bxy \times byx}$

$$
\begin{aligned}
bxy = 0.8;\ byx &= 0.6 \\
r = \sqrt{0.8 \times 0.6} &= \sqrt{0.48} \\
&= \mathbf{+0.69}
\end{aligned}
$$

Problem 49. The following data are given for marks of 100 students in paper I and II in certain subjects:

A.M.of marks (Out of 100) in paper I = 39.5

A.M.of marks (Out of 100) in paper II = 47.5

S.D.of marks (Out of 100) " I = 10

S.D.of marks (Out of 100) " II = 16.8

Coefficient of correlation between the marks in Paper I and Paper II = 0.42. Find the A.M.of marks of (out of 200) if Paper I and Paper II are combined.Also give the expectation marks in Paper II for a candidate who secured 50 marks in Paper I.

(B. Com., Bombay, Poona)

Solution :

Combined Mean = 39.5 + 47.5 = 87

$\overline{X}_{12} = 87$ marks (out of 200)

Let Marks in paper I be denoted by X and paper II by Y.

Regression equation of $\overline{Y}$ on X:

$$\begin{aligned} Y - \overline{Y} &= r\frac{\sigma y}{\sigma x}(X - \overline{X}) \\ Y - 47.5 &= 0.42 \times \frac{16.8}{10}(X - 39.5) \\ Y - 47.5 &= 0.42 \times 1.68\,(X - 39.5) \\ Y - 47.5 &= 0.71\,X - 28.05 \\ Y &= 0.71\,X - 28.05 + 47.5 \\ &= 0.71\,X + 19.45 \end{aligned}$$

When Marks in Paper I = 50 marks in Paper II i.e.

$$\begin{aligned} Y &= 0.71\,(50) + 19.45 \\ &= 35.5 + 19.45 \\ &= \mathbf{54.95} \\ &= \mathbf{55} \end{aligned}$$

Problem 50. Explain the concept of Regression:

From the following data, write down the equations to the regression lines:

	Average	*S.D.*
Marks in Mathematics	48.4	8.4
Marks in English	35.6	10.5

$r = 0.62$

Estimate the marks in Mathematics corresponding to 70 marks in English.

(*B. Com Madras*)

Solution :

Regression of X on Y:

$$\begin{aligned} (X - \overline{X}) &= r\frac{\sigma x}{\sigma y}(Y - \overline{Y}) \\ \overline{X} = 48.4; r &= 0.62; \sigma x = 8.4; \sigma y = 10.5; \overline{Y} = 35.6 \\ (X - 48.4) &= 0.62 \times \frac{8.4}{10.5}(Y - 35.6) \\ X - 48.4 &= 0.496\,(Y - 35.6) \\ X &= 0.496\,Y - 17.66 + 48.4 \\ &= \mathbf{0.496\,Y + 30.74} \end{aligned}$$

Regression of Y on X:

$$(Y - \overline{Y}) = r\frac{\sigma y}{\sigma x}(X - \overline{X})$$

$$Y - 35.6 = 0.62 \times \frac{10.5}{8.4}(X - 48.4)$$
$$Y - 35.6 = 0.62 \times 1.25\,(X - 48.4)$$
$$Y - 35.6 = 0.775\,(X - 48.4)$$
$$Y = 0.775\,X - 37.51 + 35.6$$
$$Y = \mathbf{0.775\,X - 1.91}$$

When Y is 70,

$$X = (0.496 \times 70) + 30.74$$
$$= 34.72 + 30.74$$
$$= \mathbf{65.46}$$

Marks in Mathematics corresponding to 70 marks in English are 65.5.

Problem 51. You are given below the following information about advertisement and sales:

	Adv. Exp.(X) ('00,000)		*Sales (Y)* ('00,000)
Mean	10		90
S.D.	3		12
r		0.8	

(*a*) Calculate the two regression lines.

(*b*) Find the likely sales when advertisement expenditure is Rs.15 lakhs.

(*c*) What shoul be advertisement expenditure if the company wants to attain sales target of Rs.120 lakhs?

(*M.A. Econ. Punjab*)

Solution :

(*a*.) Regression Equation of X on Y =

$$X - \overline{X} = r\frac{\sigma x}{\sigma y}(Y - \overline{Y}) \quad X - 10 = 0.8 \times \frac{3}{12}(Y - 90)$$
$$X - 10 = 0.8 \times 0.25\,(Y - 90)$$
$$X - 10 = 0.2\,Y - 18$$
$$X = 0.2Y - 18 + 10$$
$$X = \mathbf{0.2\,Y - 8}$$

Regression Equation of Y on X:

$$Y - \overline{Y} = r\frac{\sigma y}{\sigma x}(X - \overline{X})$$
$$Y - 90 = 0.8 \times \frac{12}{3}(X - 10)$$
$$Y - 90 = 0.8 \times 4\,(X - 10)$$
$$Y - 90 = 3.2X - 32$$
$$Y = 3.2\,X - 32 + 90$$
$$Y = \mathbf{3.2\,X + 58}$$

(*b.*) When advertisement expenditure $(X) = 15$ lakhs,

$$\begin{aligned} \text{Sales}(Y) &= 3.2(15) + 58 \\ &= 48 + 58 \\ Y &= \mathbf{106\,lakhs.} \end{aligned}$$

(*c.*) When sales target $(Y) =$ Rs. 120 lakhs,

$$\begin{aligned} \text{Advertisement Expenditure}(X) &= 0.2(120) - 8 \\ &= 24 - 8 \\ X &= \mathbf{16\,lakhs} \end{aligned}$$

Problem 52. The following data, based on 450 students, are given for marks in Statistics and Economics at a certain examination.

Mean marks in Statistics	40
Mean marks in Economics	48
S.D. of marks (Statistics)	12
Variance of marks (Economics)	256

Sum of the products of deviations of marks from their respective mean 42075.

Give the equations of the two lines of regression and estimate the average marks in Economics of candidates who obtained 50 marks in Statistics. (*M. Com. Nagpur*)

Solution :

Variance of marks (Economics) $= \sqrt{256}$

Standard Deviation of marks (Economics) = 16

Coefficient of Correlation $= \dfrac{\Sigma xy}{N\sigma x\sigma y} = \dfrac{42075}{450 \times 12 \times 16} = \mathbf{0.49}$

Let marks in Statistics be denoted by X and marks in Economics be denoted by Y.

Regression Equation of X on Y:

$$\begin{aligned} X - \overline{X} &= r\frac{\sigma x}{\sigma y}(Y - \overline{Y}) \\ X - 40 &= 0.49 \times \frac{12}{16}(Y - 48) \\ X - 40 &= 0.49 \times 0.75\,(Y - 48) \\ X - 40 &= 0.37Y - 17.76 \\ X &= 0.37Y - 17.76 + 40 \\ X &= \mathbf{0.37\,Y + 22.24} \end{aligned}$$

Regression Equation of Y on X:

$$\begin{aligned} Y - \overline{Y} &= r\frac{\sigma y}{\sigma x}(X - \overline{X}) \\ Y - 48 &= 0.49 \times \frac{16}{12}(X - 40) \\ Y - 48 &= 0.49 \times \frac{1.33}{(X - 40)} \\ Y - 48 &= 0.65X - 26 \end{aligned}$$

$$
\begin{aligned}
Y &= 0.65X - 26 + 48 \\
&= \mathbf{0.65X + 22} \\
\text{When} \quad X &= 50, \\
Y &= 0.65(50) + 22 \\
&= 32.5 + 22 \\
&= \mathbf{54.5}
\end{aligned}
$$

Problem 53. Given that the means of X and Y are 65 and 67, their standard deviations are 2.5 and 3.5 respectively and the coefficient of correlation between them is 0.8.

(1) Write down the two regression lines

(2) Obtain the best estimate of X when $Y = 70$

(3) Using the estimated value of X as the given value of X, estimate corresponding value of Y.

(B.A. Madurai)

Soluton :

(i) Regression line of Y on X is.

$$
\begin{aligned}
Y &- \overline{Y} = r\frac{\sigma y}{\sigma x}(X - \overline{X}) \\
Y &- 67 = 0.8\,\frac{3.5}{2.5}(X - 65) \\
Y &- 67 = 1.12(X - 65) \\
Y &- 67 = 1.12\,X - 72.8 \\
\text{or} \quad Y &- 1.12\,X = -72.8 + 67 \\
\text{(or)} \quad Y &- 1.12X = -5.8 \\
\text{(or)} \quad Y &- 1.12\,X + 5.8 = 0
\end{aligned}
$$

Regression line of X on Y is:

$$
\begin{aligned}
X &- \overline{X} = r\frac{\sigma x}{\sigma y}(Y - \overline{Y}) \\
X &- 65 = 0.8\frac{2.5}{3.5}(Y - 67) \\
X &- 65 = 0.57\,(Y - 67) \\
X &- 65 = 0.57\,Y - 38.19 \\
X &- 0.57\,Y = -38.19 + 65 \\
X &- 0.57\,Y = -26.81 \\
\text{(or)}\, X &- 0.57\,Y - 26.81 = 0
\end{aligned}
$$

(2) When $Y = 70$

$$
\begin{aligned}
X &- 0.57\,Y - 26.81 = 0 \\
\text{(or)} \quad X &= 0.57 \times 70 + 26.81 \\
X &= 39.9 + 26.81 \\
X &= \mathbf{66.71}
\end{aligned}
$$

(3) When $X = 66.71$

$$\begin{aligned} Y &- 1.12X + 5.8 = 0 \\ \text{i.e. } Y &= 1.12 + 66.71 - 5.8 \\ &= 74.71 - 5.8 \\ Y &= \mathbf{68.91} \end{aligned}$$

Problem 54. Given the following data, calculate:

(*i*) The probable value of Y when $X = 12$

(*ii*) The probable value of X when $Y = 30$
$\overline{X} = 27.6$, $\overline{Y} = 14.8$, $\sigma x = 40$, $\sigma y = 20$ $r = 0.8$

(*B. Com., Mysore*)

Soluton :

Regression of X on Y:

$$\begin{aligned} (X - \overline{X}) &= r\frac{\sigma x}{\sigma y}(Y - \overline{Y}) \\ X = 27.6; r &= 0.8; \sigma x = 40; \sigma y = 20; \overline{Y} = 14.8 \\ (X - 27.6) &= 0.8\frac{40}{20}(Y - 14.8) \\ X - 27.6 &= 1.6Y - 23.68 \\ X &= 1.6Y - 23.68 + 27.6 \\ X &= 1.6Y + 3.92 \end{aligned}$$

Regression Equation of Y on X:

$$\begin{aligned} (Y - \overline{Y}) &= r\frac{\sigma y}{\sigma x}(X - \overline{X}) \\ Y - 14.8 &= 0.8 \times \frac{20}{40}(X - 27.6) \\ Y - 14.8 &= 0.8 \times 0.5\,(X - 27.6) \\ Y - 14.8 &= 0.4X - 11.04 \\ Y &= 0.4X - 11.04 + 14.8 \\ Y &= 0.4X + 3.76 \end{aligned}$$

(*i*) The proboble value of Y when $X = 12$

$$\begin{aligned} Y &= (0.4 \times 12 + 3.76 = 4.8 + 3.76 \\ &= \mathbf{8.56} \end{aligned}$$

(*ii*) The probable value of X when $Y = 30$,

$$\begin{aligned} X &= (1.6 \times 30) + 3.92 \\ &= 48 + 3.92 \\ &= \mathbf{51.92} \end{aligned}$$

Problem 55. Given that the means of X and Y are 14.6 and 12.7, their S.D.are 10.77 and 7.68 respectively and the coefficient of correlation between them is +0.654.

(*a*) Write down the two equations.

(*b*) Obtain the best estimate of X when $Y = 16$.

(*B. Com.*)

Solution:

Regression Equation of X on Y =

$$
\begin{aligned}
(X - \overline{X}) &= r\frac{\sigma x}{\sigma y}(Y - \overline{Y}) \\
X - 14.6 &= 0.654\frac{10.77}{7.68}(Y - 12.7) \\
X - 14.6 &= 0.654 \times 1.4\,(Y - 12.7) \\
X - 14.6 &= 0.92\,Y - 11.68 \\
X &= 0.92\,Y - 11.68 + 14.6 \\
&= \mathbf{0.92\,Y + 2.92}
\end{aligned}
$$

Regression Equation of Y on X:

$$
\begin{aligned}
Y - \overline{Y} &= r\frac{\sigma y}{\sigma x}(X - \overline{X}) \\
Y - 12.7 &= 0.654\frac{7.68}{10.77}(X - 14.6) \\
Y - 12.7 &= 0.654 \times 0.71\,(X - 14.6) \\
Y - 12.7 &= 0.46\,X - 6.72 \\
Y &= 0.46\,X - 6.72 + 12.7 \\
Y &= \mathbf{0.46\,X + 5.98}
\end{aligned}
$$

(*b*) When $Y = 16$,

$$
\begin{aligned}
X &= 0.92(16) + 2.92 \\
&= 14.72 + 2.92 \\
X &= \mathbf{17.64}
\end{aligned}
$$

Problem 56. From 10 observations on price (X) and supply (Y) the following data were obtained:

$\Sigma X = 130,\ \Sigma Y = 220,\ \Sigma X^2 = 2288,\ \Sigma Y^2 = 5506,\ \Sigma XY = 3467$

Obtain the lines of regression and estimate the supply when the price is 16 untis.

(*B.A. Delhi*)

Solution :

Regression of Y on X is $Y = a + bx$.

To find out the value of a and b, we can use the following equations

$$
\begin{aligned}
\Sigma Y &= Na + b\Sigma X \\
\Sigma XY &= a\Sigma X + b\Sigma X^2
\end{aligned}
$$

$\Sigma Y = 220; N = 10; \Sigma X = 130; \Sigma XY = 3467; \Sigma X^2 = 2288$

Substituting the values in the formula

$$220 = 10\,a + 130\,b \quad (1)$$

$$3467 = 130\,a + 2288\,b \quad (2)$$

Multiply the equation (1) by 13

$$2860 = 130\,a + 1690\,b \qquad (3)$$

Subtract (3) from (2)

$$\begin{aligned} 607 &= 598\,b \\ \therefore \quad b &= \frac{607}{598} = 1.02 \end{aligned}$$

Substituting the value in (1)

$$\begin{aligned} 220 &= 10\,a + 130(1.02) \\ 220 &= 10\,a + 132.6 \\ 10a &= 87.4 \\ a &= \mathbf{8.74.} \end{aligned}$$

Putting the values in the equation

$$\begin{aligned} i.e. \quad Y &= a + bX \\ Y &= 8.74 + 1.02X \\ X &= 16, \\ \therefore \quad Y &= 8.74 + 1.02(16) \\ &= 8.74 + 16.32 \\ &= \mathbf{25.06.} \end{aligned}$$

Problem 57. Find the means of variable X and Y and the correlation coefficient, given the following regression equations:

$$2Y - X = 50$$
$$3Y - 2X = 10$$

(B. Com.)

Solution :

$$\begin{aligned} 2Y - X &= 50 & \ldots(1) \\ 3Y - 2X &= 10 & \ldots(2) \end{aligned}$$

Multiply Equation (1) by 2 and subtract equation (2) from it

$$\begin{aligned} 4Y - 2X &= 100 & \ldots(3) \\ 3Y - 2X &= 10 & \ldots(2) \\ \hline Y &= \mathbf{90} \end{aligned}$$

By substituting the value of Y in the first equation

$$\begin{aligned} 2(90) - X &= 50 \\ 180 - X &= 50 \\ -X &= 50 - 180 \\ -X &= -130 \\ X &= 130 \\ \text{Therefore,} \quad \overline{X} &= 130; \overline{Y} = 90 \end{aligned}$$

We assume that

$$2Y - X = 50 \text{ is the regression equation of } Y \text{ on } X.$$
$$3Y - 2X = 10 \text{ is the regression equation of } X \text{ on } Y.$$

Regression of Equation X on Y:

$$3Y - 2X = 10 \quad or$$
$$2X = 3Y - 10$$
$$X = \frac{3}{2}Y - \frac{10}{2}$$
$$X = 1.5Y - 5$$

Regression Equation of Y on X:

$$2Y - X = 50 \quad or$$
$$2Y = X + 50$$
$$Y = \frac{X}{2} + \frac{50}{2}$$
$$= 0.5X + 25$$

Regression Coefficient of X on Y:

$$bxy = \mathbf{1.5}$$

Regression coefficient of Y on X:

$$byx = \mathbf{0.5}.$$

Coefficient of Correlation: $\sqrt{bxy \times byx}$

$$= \sqrt{1.5 \times 0.5}$$
$$= \sqrt{0.75}$$
$$r = \mathbf{0.87}.$$

Problem 58. For a bivariate data,

the mean value of X	$= 53.2$
the mean value of Y	$= 27.9$
the regression coefficient of Y on X	$= -1.5$
the regression coefficient of X on Y	$= -0.2$

Find (*i*) the most probable value of Y when $X = 60$ and
(*ii*) r, the coefficient of correlation

(*B. Com., Bombay*)

Solution : In order to find out the most probable value of Y when $X = 60$, we must know the regression equation of Y on X

(*i*) Regression of Y on X:

$Y - \overline{Y} = r\dfrac{\sigma y}{\sigma x}(X - \overline{X})$; $\overline{Y} = 27.9$; $\overline{X} = 53.2$

Regression coefficient of Y on $X = r\dfrac{\sigma y}{\sigma x} = -1.5$

Substituting the values we get

$$Y - 27.9 = -1.5(X - 53.2)$$
$$Y - 27.9 = -1.5X + 79.8$$
$$Y = -1.5X + 79.8 + 27.9$$
$$Y = -1.5X + 107.7$$

When X is 60,

$$Y = -1.5 \times 60 + 107.7$$
$$= -90 + 107.7$$
$$= \mathbf{17.7}$$

The most probable value of Y when $X = 60$ is 17.7

(*ii*) The coefficient of correlation is the square root of the two regression coefficients.

$$\begin{aligned} r &= \sqrt{bxy \times byx} \\ bxy &= \text{Regression coefficient of } X \text{ on } Y = -1.5 \\ byx &= \text{Regression coefficient of } Y \text{ on } X = -0.2 \\ r &= \sqrt{-1.5 \times -0.2} \\ &= \sqrt{0.3} \\ &= \mathbf{0.548} \end{aligned}$$

Problem 59. The lines of regression of a bivariate population are:

$$\begin{aligned} 8X - 10Y + 66 &= 0 \qquad \ldots(*) \\ 40X - 18Y &= 214 \qquad \ldots(**) \end{aligned}$$

The variance of X is 9. Find

(*i*) The mean values of X and Y.

(*ii*) Correlation coefficient between X and Y.

(*iii*) Standard deviation of Y.

(*I.C.W.A. Final, C.A. Inter., B.A. Punjab*)

Solution :

$$\begin{aligned} (i) \text{ We have } 40X - 18Y &= 214 \qquad \ldots(1) \\ 8X - 10Y + 66 &= 0 \qquad \ldots(2) \end{aligned}$$

Multiplying equation (2) by 5,

$$40X - 50Y = -330 \qquad \ldots(3)$$

Subtracting (3) from (1)

$$\begin{aligned} -32Y &= -544 \\ \therefore \quad Y &= \frac{-544}{-32} = 17. \end{aligned}$$

Putting this value in (1)

$$\begin{aligned} 40X - 18 \times 17 &= 214 \\ (or) \quad 40X &= 214 + 306 \\ (or) \quad 40X &= 520 \\ \therefore \quad X &= \frac{520}{40} = 13. \end{aligned}$$

Mean of $\overline{X} = 13$; Mean of $\overline{Y} = \mathbf{17}$.

(*ii*) Rewriting the equation (2)

$$\begin{aligned} 10y &= 8X + 66 \\ i.e., \quad Y &= \frac{8}{10}X + \frac{66}{10} \\ \text{(or)} \quad Y &= 0.8X + 6.6 \text{(regression line of } Y \text{ on } X) \\ \therefore \quad r &= \frac{\sigma_y}{\sigma_x} = \mathbf{0.8}(byx) \end{aligned}$$

(*ii*) Rewriting equation (1)

$$40X = 18Y + 214$$

$$\text{(or)} \quad X = \frac{18}{40}Y + \frac{214}{40}$$

$$\text{(or)} \quad X = 0.45Y + 5.35 \text{(regression line of } X \text{ on } Y)$$

$$\therefore \quad r\frac{\sigma_y}{\sigma_x} = 0.45(b_{xy})$$

$$r = \sqrt{r\frac{\sigma_y}{\sigma_x} \times r\frac{\sigma_x}{\sigma_y}} \quad \text{(or)} \sqrt{b_{yx} \times b_{xy}}$$

Substituting the values in the formula

$$r = \sqrt{0.8 \times 0.45}$$
$$= \sqrt{0.360}$$
$$= +0.6.$$

(*iii*)

$$\sigma_x{}^2 = 9 \text{ or } \sigma_x = 3$$

$$r\frac{\sigma_y}{\sigma_x} = 0.8$$

$$\text{i.e.} \quad 0.6\frac{\sigma_y}{3} = 0.8$$

$$\text{i.e.} \quad 0.6\,\sigma_y = 2.4$$

$$\therefore \quad \sigma_y = \frac{2.4}{0.6} = \mathbf{4.}$$

Alternatively:

$$r\frac{\sigma_x}{\sigma_y} = 0.45$$

$$\text{i.e.} \quad 0.6 \times \frac{3}{\sigma_y} = 0.45$$

$$\text{Hence} \quad \sigma_y = \frac{0.6 \times 3}{0.45} = \mathbf{4.}$$

Problem 60. From the following data calculate

(*i*) Correlation coefficient

(*ii*) Standard Deviation of Y (σ_y)

$$X = 0.85\,Y$$
$$Y = 0.89\,X$$
$$\sigma_x = 3$$

(*M. Com. Raj.*)

Solution :

(*i*) Coefficient of Correlation:

$$r = \sqrt{b_{xy} \times b_{yx}}$$
$$= \sqrt{0.85 \times 0.89}$$
$$= \sqrt{0.7565}$$
$$= \mathbf{0.869.}$$

(*ii*) Standard Deviation of *Y*:

$$r \times \frac{\sigma_x}{\sigma_y} = 0.85$$

$$0.869 \times \frac{3}{\sigma_y} = 0.85$$

$$0.85\sigma_y = 3 \times 0.869$$

$$0.85\sigma_y = 2.607$$

$$\sigma_y = \frac{2.607}{0.85}$$

$$\sigma_y = \mathbf{3.067}.$$

Problem 61. The following calculations have been made for prices of 12 stocks (*X*) on the Calcutta Stock Exchange on a certain day along with the volume of sales in thousands of shares (*Y*).From these calculations find the regression equation of prices of stocks, on the volume of sales of shares.

$\Sigma X = 580$, $\Sigma Y = 370$, $\Sigma XY = 11494$, $\Sigma X^2 = 41658$, $\Sigma Y^2 = 17206$

(*M. Com. Rajasthan*)

Solution :

$$\overline{X} = \frac{\Sigma X}{N} = \frac{580}{12} = \mathbf{48.33}. \qquad \overline{Y} = \frac{\Sigma Y}{N} = \frac{370}{12} = \mathbf{30.83}.$$

When figures are given in original values:

$$r\frac{\sigma_x}{\sigma_y} or b_{xy} = \frac{\Sigma XY - N\overline{XY}}{\Sigma Y^2 - N\left(\overline{Y}\right)^2}$$

$$= \frac{11494 - 12(48.33 \times 30.83)}{17206 - 12(30.83)^2}$$

$$= \frac{11494 - 12(1490.01)}{17206 - 12(950.49)}$$

$$= \frac{11,494 - 17880.12}{17,206 - 11405.88}$$

$$= \frac{-6386.12}{5800.12}$$

$$= \mathbf{-1.101}.$$

Regression Equation of *X* on *Y*:

$$X - \overline{X} = r\frac{\sigma_x}{\sigma_y}\left(Y - \overline{Y}\right)$$

$$X - 48.33 = -1.101\,(Y - 30.83)$$

$$X - 48.33 = -1.101\,Y + 33.94$$

$$X = -1.101\,Y + 33.94 + 48.33$$

$$X = \mathbf{-1.101\,Y + 82.27}.$$

Problem 62. The regression line of *Y* on *X* and *X* on *Y* are given by:

$Y = 11.64 - 0.5$ X and $X = 19.13 - 0.87$ Y

Find, Mean of *X* and *Y* and *r*.

(*B.A. Annamalai*)

Solution :

$$\overline{Y} = 11.64 - 0.5 \quad X \qquad \ldots(1)$$
$$\overline{X} = 19.13 - 0.87 \quad Y \qquad \ldots(2)$$

Multiply(1)by2.

$$2Y = 23.28 - X \qquad \ldots(3)$$

Rearranging the equations and subtracting

$$\begin{aligned} 2\overline{Y} + X &= 23.28 \\ 0.87\overline{Y} + X &= 19.13 \\ \hline 1.13\overline{Y} &= 4.15 \\ \therefore \quad \overline{Y} &= \frac{4.15}{1.13} = \mathbf{3.67} \end{aligned}$$

Substituting in (2), we get

$$\begin{aligned} \overline{X} &= 19.13 - 0.87 \times 3.67 \\ \overline{X} &= 19.13 - 3.19 \\ &= \mathbf{15.94} \\ b_{xy} &= -0.87 \quad b_{yx} = -0.5 \\ r &= \sqrt{b_{xy} \times -0.5} \\ &= \sqrt{-0.87 \times -0.5} \\ &= +0.659 \\ r &= \mathbf{0.66}. \end{aligned}$$

Problem 63. Obtain the regression equation of Y on X and X on Y and the value of r from the following table giving the marks in Accountancy and Statistics.

Marks in Statistics		*Marks in Accountancy*				
		5–15	15–25	25–35	35–45	Total
	0–10	1	1	–	–	2
	10–20	3	6	5	1	15
	20–30	1	8	9	2	20
	30–40	–	3	9	3	15
	40–50	–	–	4	4	8
	Total	5	18	27	10	60

Solution :

$$\text{Mean: } \overline{X} = A + \frac{\Sigma f dx}{N} \times C \qquad A = 20;\ \Sigma f dx = 42;\ N = 60;\ C = 10$$
$$= 20 + \frac{42}{60} \times 10 = \mathbf{27}.$$
$$\overline{Y} = A + \frac{\Sigma f dy}{N} \times C \qquad A = 25;\ \Sigma f dy = 12;\ N = 60;\ C = 10$$
$$= 25 + \frac{12}{60} \times 10 = 27.$$

Computation for Regression equation

Y	m	dx	X: 5-15	15-25	25-35	35-45	f	fdy	fdy²	fdxdy
		m	10	20	30	40				
		dx	-1	0	1	2				
0-10	5	-2	1 [2]	1 [0]			2	-4	8	2
10-20	15	-1	3 [3]	6 [0]	5 [-5]	1 [-2]	15	-15	15	-4
20-30	25	0	1 [0]	8 [0]	9 [0]	2 [0]	20	0	0	0
30-40	35	1		3 [0]	9 [9]	3 [6]	15	15	15	15
40-50	45	2			4 [8]	4 [16]	8	16	32	24
		f	5	18	27	10	N=60	fxy =12	fdy² =70	fdxdy =37
		fdx	-5	0	27	20	fdx =42			
		fdx²	5	0	27	40	fdx² =72			
		fdxdy	5	0	12	20	fdxdy =37			

$$bxy = \frac{\Sigma faxdy - \frac{(\Sigma fdx \times \Sigma fdy)}{N}}{\Sigma fdy^2 - \frac{(\Sigma fdy)^2}{N}} \times \frac{i_x}{i_y}$$

$$= \frac{37 - 42 \times \frac{12}{60}}{70 - \frac{(12)^2}{60}} \times \frac{10}{10}$$

$$= \frac{37 - 8.4}{70 - 2.4} = \frac{28.6}{67.6}$$

$$= \mathbf{0.423}.$$

$$byx = \frac{\Sigma fdxdy - \frac{\Sigma fdy \times \Sigma fdx}{N}}{\Sigma fdx^2 - \frac{(\Sigma fdx)^2}{N}} \times \frac{i_y}{i_x}$$

$$= \frac{37 - \frac{12 \times 42}{60}}{72 - \frac{(42)^2}{60}} \times \frac{10}{10}$$

$$= \frac{37 - 8.4}{72 - 29.4} \times \frac{10}{10} = \frac{286}{426}$$

$$= \mathbf{0.67}.$$

Regression Equation of Y on X:

$$Y - \overline{Y} = byx\left(X - \overline{X}\right)$$
$$Y - 27 = 0.67(X - 27)$$

Regression Equation of X on Y:

$$X - \overline{X} = bxy\left(Y - \overline{Y}\right)$$
$$X - 27 = 0.423(Y - 27)$$

$$Y - 27 = 0.67X - 18.09 \qquad X - 27 = 0.423Y - 11.42$$
$$Y = 0.67X - 18.09 + 27 \qquad X = 0.423Y - 11.42 + 27$$
$$Y = \mathbf{0.67X + 8.91}. \qquad X = \mathbf{0.423\,Y + 15.58}.$$

Coefficient of Correlation:

$$\begin{aligned} r &= \sqrt{bxy \times byx} \\ &= \sqrt{0.423 \times 0.67} \\ &= \sqrt{0.283} \\ &= \mathbf{+0.532}. \end{aligned}$$

Problem 64. Following is the distribution of students according to their height and weight.

	Weight in lbs.			
Height in inches	90–100	100–110	110–120	120–130
50–55	4	7	5	2
55–60	6	10	7	4
60–65	6	12	10	7
65–70	3	8	6	3

Calculate: (*i*) the two coefficients of regression, and (*ii*) obtain the two rgression equations. (*M. Com., Delhi*)

Solution : Let weight be denoted by X and height by Y.

Computation for Regression Equation

			Weight in ibs							
		x	90-100	100-110	110-120	120-130				
		m	95	105	115	125				
Y	m	dy \ dx	-1	0	1	2	f	fdy	fdy²	fdxdy
50-55	52.5	-1	4 [4]	7 [0]	5 [-5]	2 [-4]	18	-18	18	-5
55-60	57.5	0	6 [0]	10 [0]	7 [0]	4 [0]	27	0	0	0
60-65	62.5	1	6 [-6]	12 [0]	10 [10]	7 [14]	35	35	35	18
65-70	67.5	2	3 [-6]	8 [0]	6 [12]	3 [12]	20	40	80	18
		f	19	37	28	16	N=100	Σfdy =57	Σfdy² =133	Σfdxdy =31
		fdx	-19	0	28	32	Σfdx =41			
		fdx²	19	0	28	64	Σfdx² =111			
		fdxdy	-8	0	17	22	Σfdxdy =31			

(Height in Inches)

$$\text{Mean: } \overline{X} = A + \frac{\Sigma f dx}{N} \times C = 105 + \frac{41}{100} \times 10$$
$$= 105 + 4.1 = \mathbf{109.1}.$$
$$\overline{Y} = A + \frac{\Sigma f dy}{N} \times C = 57.5 + \frac{57}{100} \times 10$$
$$= 57.5 + 5.7 = \mathbf{63.2}.$$

(*i*) Regression Coefficient

$$bxy = \frac{\Sigma f dxdy - \dfrac{\Sigma f dx \times \Sigma f dy}{N}}{\Sigma f dy^2 - \dfrac{(\Sigma f dy)^2}{N}} \times \frac{i_x}{i_y}$$
$$= \frac{31 - \dfrac{(41 \times 57)}{100}}{133 - \dfrac{(57)^2}{100}} \times \frac{10}{5} = \frac{31 - 23.37}{133 - 32.49} \times 2$$
$$= \frac{7.63 \times 2}{100.51} = \frac{15.26}{100.51} = 0.1518$$
$$bxy = \mathbf{0.15}.$$
$$byx = \frac{\Sigma f dxdy - \dfrac{\Sigma f dy \times \Sigma f dx}{N}}{\Sigma f dx^2 - \dfrac{(\Sigma f dx)^2}{N}} \times \frac{i_y}{i_x}$$
$$= \frac{31 - \dfrac{57 \times 41}{100}}{111 - \dfrac{(41)^2}{100}} \times \frac{5}{10} = \frac{31 - 23.37}{111 - 16.81} \times \frac{1}{2}$$
$$= \frac{7.63}{94.19 \times 2} = \frac{7.63}{188.38} = \mathbf{0.04}.$$

Regression Equation of X on Y:

$$X - \overline{X} = bxy\,(Y - \overline{Y})$$
$$X - 109.1 = 0.15\,(Y - 63.2)$$
$$X - 109.1 = 0.15\,Y - 9.48$$
$$X = 0.15\,Y - 9.48 + 109.1.$$
$$= \mathbf{0.15\,Y + 99.62}.$$

Regression Equation of Y on X:

$$(Y - \overline{Y}) = byx\,(X - \overline{X})$$
$$Y - 63.2 = 0.04\,(X - 109.1)$$
$$Y - 63.2 = 0.04\,X - 4.36$$
$$Y = 0.04\,X - 4.36 + 63.2$$
$$Y = \mathbf{0.04\,X + 58.84}.$$

Problem 65. The following are the marks obtained by 132 students in test X and test Y:

X	30–40	40–50	50–60	60–70	70–80	Total
Y						
20–30	2	5	3	–	–	10
30–40	1	8	12	6	–	27
40–50	–	5	22	14	1	42
50–60	–	2	16	9	2	29
60–70	–	1	8	6	1	16
70–80	–	–	2	4	2	8
Total	3	21	63	39	6	132

Calculate:

(*a*) The correlation coefficient.

(*b*) The regression equations. (*B. Com.*)

Solution :

Y	m	dy \ x	30-40	40-50	50-60	60-70	70-80	f	fdy	fdy²	fdxdy
		m	35	45	55	65	75				
		dx	-2	-1	0	1	2				
20-30	25	-2	2 [8]	5 [10]	3 [0]			10	-20	40	18
30-40	35	-1	1 [2]	8 [8]	12 [0]	6 [-6]		27	-27	27	4
40-50	45	0		5 [0]	22 [0]	14 [0]	1 [0]	42	0	0	0
50-60	55			2 [-2]	16 [0]	9 [9]	2 [4]	29	29	29	11
60-70	65	2		1 [-2]	8 [0]	6 [12]	1 [4]	16	32	64	14
70-80	75	3			2 [0]	4 [12]	2 [12]	8	24	72	24
		f	3	21	63	39	6	N-132	Σfxy =38	Σfdy² =232	Σfdxdy =71
		fdx	-6	--21	0	39	12	Σfdx =24			
		fdx²	12	21	0	39	24	Σfdx² =96			
		fdxdy	10	14	0	27	20	Σfdxdy = 71			

(*a*) Cceefficient of Correlation:

$$bxy = \frac{\Sigma f dxdy - \dfrac{\Sigma f dx \times \Sigma f dy}{N}}{\Sigma f dy^2 - \dfrac{(\Sigma f dy)^2}{N}}$$

$$= \frac{71 - \dfrac{24 \times 38}{132}}{232 - \dfrac{(38)^2}{132}} = \frac{64.09}{232 - 10.94}$$

$$= \frac{64.09}{221.06} = \mathbf{0.29}.$$

$$byx = \frac{\Sigma fdxy - \dfrac{\Sigma fdy \times \Sigma fdx}{N}}{\Sigma fdx^2 - \dfrac{(\Sigma fdx)^2}{N}}$$

$$= \frac{71 - \dfrac{38 \times 24}{132}}{96 - \dfrac{(24)^2}{132}} = \frac{64.09}{96 - 4.36}$$

$$= \frac{64.09}{91.64} = 0.70.$$

$$r = \sqrt{bxy \times byx}$$

$$= \sqrt{0.29 \times 0.70}$$

$$= \sqrt{0.203}$$

$$= \mathbf{0.45}.$$

Mean:

$$\overline{X} = A + \frac{\Sigma fdx}{N} \times C$$

$$= 55 + \frac{24}{132} \times 10 = \mathbf{56.82}$$

$$\overline{Y} = 45 + \frac{38}{132} \times 10 = \mathbf{47.88}$$

(*b*) Regression Equation of X on Y:

$$X - \overline{X} = bxy\left(Y - \overline{Y}\right)$$

$$X - 56.82 = 0.29\,(Y - 47.88)$$

$$X - 56.82 = 0.29\,Y - 13.89$$

$$X = 0.29\,Y - 13.89 + 56.82$$

$$X = \mathbf{0.29\,Y + 42.93}.$$

(*c*) Regression Equation of Y on X:

$$Y - \overline{Y} = byx\left(X - \overline{X}\right)$$

$$Y - 47.88 = 0.70\,(X - 56.82)$$

$$Y - 47.88 = 0.70\,X - 39.77$$

$$Y = 0.70\,X - 39.77 + 47.88$$

$$Y = \mathbf{0.70\,X + 8.11}.$$

8

INDEX NUMBER

Unweighted Indices, Weighted Indices, Cost of Living Indices Base Shifting, Splicing and Chain Indices

FORMULAE

A. Unweighted Index. (*a*) Simple Aggregative Index $P_{01} = \frac{\Sigma P_1}{P_0} \times 100$ (*b*)(*i*) Simple Average of price Relative Index. $P_{01} = \frac{\frac{\Sigma P_1}{P_0} \times 100}{N}$ (*ii*) When the Geometric mean is used $P_{01} = anti \log \frac{\Sigma \log P}{N}$	P_1 = Price of the current year P_0 = Price of the base year N = Number of items $P = \frac{P_1}{P_0} \times 100$
B. Weighted Index Number (*a*) Weighted Aggregative Index (*i*) Laspeyre's Index $P_{01(La)} = \frac{\Sigma P_1 q_1}{\Sigma P_0 q_0} \times 100$ (*ii*) Paasche's Index $P_{01(Pa)} = \frac{\Sigma P_1 q_1}{\Sigma P_0 q_0} \times 100$ (*iii*) Bowley's Index $P_{01}\,(B) = \frac{\frac{\Sigma P_1 q_0}{\Sigma P_0 q_0} + \frac{\Sigma P_1 q_1}{\Sigma P_0 q_1} \times 100}{2}$ $or = \frac{L+P}{2}$ (*iv*) Fisher's Ideal Index $P_{01}(F) = \sqrt{\frac{\Sigma P_1 q_0}{\Sigma P_0 q_0} \times \frac{\Sigma P_1 q_1}{\Sigma P_0 q_1} \times 100}$ $or\, P_{01} = \sqrt{L \times P} \times 100$ (*v*) Marshall Edgeworth's Index $P_{01}(Ma) = \frac{\Sigma P_1(q_0 + q_1)}{\Sigma P_0(q_0 + q_1)} \times 100$ or $= \frac{\Sigma P_1 q_0}{\Sigma P_0 q_0} + \frac{\Sigma P_1 q_1}{\Sigma P_0 q_1} \times 100$	q_0 = Base year quantities q_1 = Current quantities L = Laspeyre's Index P = Paasche's Index

(*vi*) Kelly's Index $P_{01}(K) = \frac{\Sigma P_1 q}{\Sigma P_0 q} \times 100$	$q = \frac{q_0 + q_1}{2}$
C. Weighted Average of Price Relative Method $P_{01} = \frac{\Sigma PV}{V}$	$P = \frac{P_1}{P_0} \times 100$ for each item $V = P_0 q_0$ i.e. Value weights
D. Consumer Price Index (*i*) Aggregative Expenditure Method Consumer Price Index $= \frac{\Sigma P_1 q_0}{\Sigma P_0 q_0} \times 100$ (*ii*) Family Budget Method Consumer Price Index $= \frac{\Sigma PW}{\Sigma W}$ (*iii*) Consumer Price Index $= \frac{\Sigma IW}{\Sigma W}$	$P = \frac{P_1}{P_0} \times 100$ W = Weight I = Index Number
E. Time Reversal test (*i*) Time Reversal Test is satisfied when $P_{01} \times P_{10} = 1$ (*ii*) Factor Reversal Test is satisfied $P_{01} \times Q_{01} = \frac{\Sigma P_1 q_1}{\Sigma P_0 q_0}$	$P_{01} = \sqrt{\frac{\Sigma P_1 q_0}{\Sigma P_0 q_1} \times \frac{\Sigma P_1 q_1}{\Sigma P_0 q_1}}$ $P_{10} = \sqrt{\frac{\Sigma P_0 q_1}{\Sigma P_1 q_1} \times \frac{\Sigma P_0 q_0}{\Sigma P_1 q_0}}$ $Q_{01} = \sqrt{\frac{\Sigma q_1 P_0}{\Sigma q_0 P_0} \times \frac{\Sigma q_1 P_1}{\Sigma q_0 P_1}}$

Problem 1.

Commodity	*Price in* 2002	*Price in* 2003
A	90	95
B	40	50
C	90	110
D	30	35

Construct an index number for 2003, taking 2002 as base. (*B.Com.*)

Solution :

Computation of Price Index

Commodity	*Price in* 2002 P_0	*Price in* 2003 P_1
A	90	95
B	40	50
C	90	110
D	30	35
	$\Sigma P_0 = 250$	$\Sigma P_1 = 290$

Index Number $(P_{01}) = \frac{\Sigma P_1}{\Sigma P_0} \times 100 = \frac{290}{250} \times 100 = \mathbf{116}$

This means that the prices have increased in the year 2003 to the extent of 16%, when compared with the prices of 2002.

Problem 2. Prepare Index numbers (1991 = 100) of prices of a commodity from the following data :

Year	: 1991	1992	1993	1994	1995	1996	1997	1998	1999	2000
Prices	: 40	42	35	33	39	40	42	48	55	70

(*B.Com. Andhra*)

Solution : **Computation of Price Index**

Year	*Price*	*Index number* $= \frac{\text{Current Year Price}}{\text{Base Year Price}} \times 100$
1991	40	100
1992	42	$\frac{42}{40} \times 100 = 105$
1993	35	$\frac{35}{40} \times 100 = 87.5$
1994	33	$\frac{33}{40} \times 100 = 82.5$
1995	39	$\frac{39}{40} \times 100 = 97.5$
1996	40	$\frac{40}{40} \times 100 = 100$
1997	42	$\frac{42}{40} \times 100 = 105$
1998	48	$\frac{48}{40} \times 100 = 120$
1999	55	$\frac{55}{40} \times 100 = 137.5$
2000	70	$\frac{70}{40} \times 100 = 175.$

Problem 3. Compute a price index for the following by a (*a*) Simple aggregate and (*b*) average of price relative method by using both arithmetic mean and geometric mean.

Commodity	*A*	*B*	*C*	*D*	*E*	*F*
Price in 1998 (Rs.)	20	30	10	25	40	50
Price in 2003 (Rs.)	25	30	15	35	45	55

(*B.Com. Kerala*)

Solution : **Computation for Price Index**

Commodity	*Price in* 1998 P_0	*price in* 2003 P_1	*Price Relative* $P_{01} = (P_1 \div P_0 \times 100)$	*logP*
A	20	25	125	2.0969
B	30	30	100	2.0000

Cont...

C	10	15	150	2.1761
D	25	35	140	2.1461
E	40	45	112.5	2.0510
F	50	55	110	2.0414
	$\Sigma P_0 = 175$	$\Sigma P_1 = 205$	$\Sigma P = 737.5$	$\Sigma \log P = 12.5115$

(*a*) Simple Aggregate Index $= \dfrac{\Sigma P_1}{\Sigma P_0} \times 100$

$$= \frac{205}{175} \times 100$$

$$= \mathbf{117.143.}$$

(*b*) (*i*) Arithmetic Mean of Price Relatives,

$$= \frac{\Sigma P_{01}}{N}$$

$$= \frac{737.5}{6}$$

$$= \mathbf{122.92.}$$

(*ii*) Geometric Mean of Price Relative Index :

$$= \text{Antilog}\left[\frac{\Sigma \log P}{N}\right]$$

$$= \text{Antilog}\left[\frac{12.5115}{6}\right]$$

$$= \text{Antilog } 2.0853$$

$$= \mathbf{121.7.}$$

WEIGHTED INDICES

Problem 4. Calculate the weighted price index from the following data :

Materials Required	*Unit*	*Quantity Required*	*Price during* 1999 *Rs.*	2003 *Rs.*
Cement	100 Ibs	500 Ibs	5.0	8.0
Timber	c.ft.	2,000 c.ft.	9.5	14.2
Steel sheet	cwt.	50 cwt.	34.0	42.0
Bricks	per '000	20,000	12.00	24.00

(*B.A. Hons. Delhi,*)

Solution :

The quantity consumed (weights) neither relates to current year nor to base year. Here the weights are fixed. The appropriate index can be found out by applying Kelly's method.

Materials Required	*Unit*	*Quantity* q	*Price during* 1999(P_0)	2003(P_1)	P_0q	P_1q
Cement	100 Ibs	500 Ibs	5.0	8.0	25	40
Timber	c.ft.	2,000 c.ft.	9.5	14.2	19,000	28,400
Steel sheet	cwt.	50 cwt.	34.0	42.0	1,700	2,100
Bricks	per '000	20,000	12.0	24.0	240	480
					$\Sigma P_0q = 20,965$	$\Sigma P_1q = 31,020$

$$P_{01} = \frac{\Sigma p_1 q}{\Sigma p_0 q}$$
$$= \frac{31,020}{20,965} \times 100$$
$$= \mathbf{148.}$$

Problem 5. From the following data prepare the weighted index number for the food group for 2003 with 1997 as the base period.

Items in the food groups	*Weights*	*Price per Unit* 1997 *Rs.*	*Price per Unit* 2003 *Rs.*
Rice	35	1.50	1.60
Wheat	10	1.00	1.20
Gram	15	1.20	1.80
Milk	16	1.20	1.80
Ghee	4	10.00	14.00
Oil	8	6.00	6.50
Sugar	6	1.60	2.00
Salt	1	0.10	0.20
Vegetables	5	1.20	1.40

(*B.Com., Mysore*)

Solution :

Computation of weighted Index Number

Items	*Weights* W	P_0	P_1	I *or* $P = \frac{P_1}{P_0} \times 100$	PW
Rice	35	1.50	1.60	106.66	3733.45
Wheat	10	1.00	1.20	120.00	1200.00
Gram	15	1.20	1.80	150.00	2250.00
Milk	16	1.20	1.80	150.00	2400.00
Ghee	4	10.00	14.00	140.00	560.00
Oil	8	6.00	6.50	108.33	866.64
Sugar	6	1.60	2.00	125.00	750.00
Salt	1	0.10	0.20	200.00	200.00
Vegetables	5	1.20	1.40	116.67	538.35
	$\Sigma W = 100$				$\Sigma PW = 12543.44$

$$\text{Weighted Index} = \frac{\Sigma PW}{\Sigma W} = \frac{12543.44}{100} = \mathbf{125.43}.$$

Problem 6. Calculate the Index number, using the aggregate expenditure method for the year 2003 with 2000 as base year, from the following data :

Commodity	*Quantity in units*	*Price per unit* 2000 (*Rs.*)	*Price per unit in* 2003 (*Rs.*)
A	100	8	12.0
B	25	6	7.50
C	10	5	5.25
D	20	48	52.00
E	65	15	16.50
F	30	19	27.00

(*B.Com. Bombay*)

Solution :

Computation of Index Number by using Aggregate Expenditure Method

Commodity	q_0	P_0	P_1	P_1q_0	P_0q_0
A	100	8	12.00	1200.00	800
B	25	6	7.50	187.50	150
C	10	5	5.25	52.50	50
D	20	48	52.00	1040.00	960
E	65	15	16.50	1072.50	975
F	30	19	27.00	810.00	570
				$\Sigma P_1q_0 = 4362.50$	$\Sigma P_0q_0 = 3505$

$$P_{01} = \frac{\Sigma P_1q_0}{\Sigma P_0q_0} \times 100 = \frac{4362.50}{3505} \times 100 = \mathbf{124.47}.$$

Problem 7. From the following data, prepare "quantity index numbers" for the year 2003 taking 2000 as the base year :

Year	*Commodity I*		*Commodity II*		*Commodity III*	
	Price	*Quantity*	*Price*	*Quantity*	*Price*	*Quantity*
2000	5	10	8	6	6	3
2003	4	12	7	7	5	4

(*ICWA*)

Solution :

Computation of Quantity Index Number

Commodity	2000		2003		q_1P_0	q_0P_0	q_1P_1	q_0P_1
	P_0	q_0	P_1	q_1				
I	5	10	4	12	60	50	48	40
II	8	6	7	7	56	48	49	42
III	6	3	5	4	24	18	20	15
					$\Sigma q_1P_0 = 140$	$\Sigma q_0P_0 = 116$	$\Sigma q_1P_1 = 117$	$\Sigma q_0P_1 = 97$

$$Q_{01}(L) = \frac{\Sigma q_1P_0}{\Sigma q_0P_0} \times 100$$

$$= \frac{140}{116} \times 100$$

$$= \mathbf{120.69}$$

$$Q_{01}(P_a) = \frac{\Sigma q_1P_1}{\Sigma q_0P_1} \times 100$$

$$= \frac{117}{97} \times 100$$

$$= \mathbf{120.62}.$$

$$Q_{01}(F) = \sqrt{Q_{01}(L_a)Q_{01}(P_a)}$$

$$= \sqrt{120.69 \times 120.62}$$

$$= \mathbf{120.65}.$$

Problem 8. Compute a quantity index for the following data :

Commodity	*Quantity* 2000	2003	*Price in* 2000 *in Rs.*
A	40	50	40
B	30	40	30
C	10	20	10
D	5	10	5

Solution :

Computation of Quantity Index

Commodity	*Quantity*		*Price in Rs. 2000*		
	2000(q_0)	2003(q_1)	P_0	q_1P_0	q_0P_0
A	40	50	40	2000	1600
B	30	40	30	1200	900
C	10	20	10	200	100
D	5	10	5	50	25
			Total	3450	2625

Laspeyre's formula :

$$Q_{01} = \frac{\Sigma q_1 p_0}{\Sigma q_0 P_0} \times 100 = \frac{3450}{2625} \times 100 = \mathbf{131.4}.$$

There has been a net increase of 31.4 % in the quantities of commodities included in the index number compared to 2000.

Problem 9. From the following data calculate Fisher's ideal index :

Item	*Price per unit in Rs.*		*Quantities used*	
	1998	2003	1998	2003
A	9.25	15	5	5
B	8	12	10	11
C	4	5	6	6
D	1	1.25	4	8

(*B.Com. Madras*)

Solution :

Computation of Fisher's Ideal Index

Commodity	*Base year* 1998		*Current Year* 2003		P_0q_0	P_1q_0	P_0q_1	P_1q_1
	price P_0	*Quantity* q_0	*Price* P_1	*Quantity* q_1				
A	9.25	5	15	5	46.25	75	46.25	75
B	8	10	12	11	80	120	88	132
C	4	6	5	6	24	30	24	30
D	1	4	1.25	8	4	5	8	10
					$\Sigma P_0q_0 =$ 154.25	ΣP_1q_0 = 230	$\Sigma P_0q_1 =$ 166.25	ΣP_1q_1 = 247

$$\text{Fisher's Ideal Index} = \sqrt{\text{Laspeyre's} \times \text{Paache's Index}}$$

$$= \sqrt{\frac{\Sigma P_1 q_0}{\Sigma P_0 q_0} \times \frac{\Sigma P_1 q_1}{\Sigma P_0 q_1}} \times 100$$

$$= \sqrt{\frac{230}{154.25} \times \frac{247}{166.25}} \times 100$$

$$= \sqrt{1.491 \times 1.486} \times 100$$

$$= \sqrt{2.216} \times 100$$

$$= 1.489 \times 100$$

$$= \mathbf{148.9}.$$

Problem 10. Calculate Fisher's Ideal Index from the data given below and show that it satisfies time reversal test and factor reversal test.

	2000		2001	
Commodity	*Price*	*Quantity*	*Price*	*Quantity*
A	10	49	12	50
B	12	25	15	20
C	18	10	20	12
D	20	5	40	2

(*B.Com. Hons. Delhi*)

Solution :

Computation of Fisher's Ideal Index

Commodites	2000		2001		P_1q_0	P_0q_0	P_1q_1	P_0q_1
	P_0	q_0	P_1	q_1				
A	10	49	12	50	588	490	600	500
B	12	25	15	20	375	300	300	240
C	18	10	20	12	200	180	240	216
D	20	5	40	2	200	100	80	40
					$\Sigma P_1q_0 =$ 1363	$\Sigma P_0q_0 =$ 1070	$\Sigma P_1q_1 =$ 1220	$\Sigma P_0q_1 =$ 996

Fisher's Ideal Index :

$$
\begin{aligned}
P_{01} &= \sqrt{\frac{\Sigma P_1q_0}{\Sigma P_0q_0} \times \frac{\Sigma P_1q_1}{\Sigma P_0q_1}} \times 100 \\
&= \sqrt{\frac{1363}{1070} \times \frac{1220}{996}} \times 100 \\
&= \sqrt{1.274 \times 1.225} \times 100 \\
&= \sqrt{1.5607} \times 100 \\
&= 1.2493 \times 100 \\
&= \mathbf{124.93}
\end{aligned}
$$

Time Reversal Test :

Time Reversal is satisfied when

$$
\begin{aligned}
P_{01} \times P_{10} &= 1 \\
P_{01} \times P_{10} &= \sqrt{\frac{\Sigma P_1q_0}{\Sigma P_0q_0} \times \frac{\Sigma P_1q_1}{\Sigma P_0q_1}} \sqrt{\frac{\Sigma P_0q_1}{\Sigma P_1q_1} \times \frac{\Sigma P_0q_0}{\Sigma P_1q_0}} \\
&= \sqrt{\frac{1363}{1070} \times \frac{1220}{996} \times \frac{996}{1220} \times \frac{1070}{1363}} \\
&= \sqrt{1} \\
&= \mathbf{1}
\end{aligned}
$$

Factor Reversal Test :

Factor Reversal Test is satisfied when

$$P_{01} \times Q_{01} = \frac{\Sigma P_1 q_1}{\Sigma P_0 q_0}$$

$$P_{01} \times Q_{01} = \sqrt{\frac{\Sigma P_1 q_0}{\Sigma P_0 q_0} \times \frac{\Sigma P_1 q_1}{\Sigma P_0 q_1}}\sqrt{\frac{\Sigma q_1 P_0}{\Sigma q_0 P_0} \times \frac{\Sigma q_1 P_1}{\Sigma q_0 P_1}}$$

$$= \sqrt{\frac{1363}{1070} \times \frac{1220}{996} \times \frac{996}{1070} \times \frac{1220}{1363}}$$

$$= \sqrt{\frac{1220 \times 1220}{1070 \times 1070}}$$

$$= \frac{1220}{1070} i.e. = \frac{\Sigma P_1 q_1}{\Sigma P_0 q_0}$$

Hence both Time Reversal Test and Factor Reversal Tests are satisfied by Fisher's Ideal Index.

Problem 11. Calculate quantity index by (*i*) Laspeyre's method, (*ii*) Paasche's method and (*iii*) Fisher's method.

Commodity	2000		2002	
	Price	*Total value*	*Price*	*Total value*
A	10	100	12	144
B	12	144	14	196
C	14	196	16	256
D	16	256	18	324
E	18	324	20	400

(*B.Com. Madurai*)

Solution :

Commodity	2000		2002					
	P_0	q_0	P_1	q_1	$P_1 q_0$	$P_0 q_0$	$P_1 q_1$	$P_0 q_1$
A	10	10	12	12	120	100	144	120
B	12	12	14	14	168	144	196	168
C	14	14	16	16	224	196	256	224
D	16	16	18	18	288	256	324	288
E	18	18	20	20	360	324	400	360
					$\Sigma P_1 q_0 =$ 1160	$\Sigma P_0 q_0 =$ 1020	$\Sigma P_1 q_1$ = 1320	$\Sigma P_0 q_1 =$ 1160

$$P_{01}(L_a) = \frac{\Sigma P_1 q_0}{\Sigma P_0 q_0} \times 100$$

$$= \frac{1160}{1020} \times 100$$

$$= \mathbf{113.73}$$

$$P_{01}(P_a) = \frac{\Sigma P_1 q_1}{\Sigma P_0 q_1} \times 100$$

$$= \frac{1320}{1160} \times 100$$
$$= \mathbf{113.8}$$
$$P_{01}(F) = \sqrt{L \times P}$$
$$= \sqrt{113.73 \times 113.8}$$
$$= \mathbf{113.76}$$

Problem 12. Calculate index number from the following data :

	Base year		*Current year*	
	Kilo	*Rate (Rs)*	*Kilo*	*(Rate Rs)*
Bread	10	3	8	3.25
Meat	20	15	15	20
Tea	2	25	3	23

(*B.Com. Madurai*)

Solution :

Computation of Index Numbers

	Base Year		*Current Year*					
	Rate (Rs)	*Kilo*	*Rate (Rs)*	*Kilo*	P_1q_0	P_0q_0	P_1q_1	P_0q_1
Bread	3	10	3.25	8	32.50	30	26	24
Meat	15	20	20.00	15	400.00	300	300	225
Tea	25	2	23.00	3	46.00	50	69	75
					$\Sigma P_1q_0 =$ 478.50	ΣP_0q_0 = 380	ΣP_1q_1 = 395	$\Sigma P_0q_1 =$ 324

(*a.*) Laspeyre's Index :

$$P_{01}(L_a) = \frac{\Sigma P_1q_0}{\Sigma P_0q_0} \times 100 = \frac{478.50}{380} \times 100 = \mathbf{125.9}$$

(*b.*) Paasche's Index :

$$P_{01}(P_a) = \frac{\Sigma P_1q_1}{\Sigma P_0q_1} \times 100 = \frac{395}{324} \times 100 = \mathbf{121.9}$$

(*c.*) Bowley's Index :

$$P_{01}(B) = \frac{\frac{\Sigma P_1q_0}{\Sigma P_0q_0} + \frac{\Sigma P_1q_1}{\Sigma P_0q_1} \times 100}{2}$$

$$= \frac{\frac{478.5}{380} \times \frac{395}{324}}{2} \times 100 = \mathbf{123.9}$$

$$\text{or} = \frac{L+P}{2} = \frac{125.9 + 121.9}{2} = \mathbf{123.9}$$

(*d.*) Fisher's Index :

$$P_{01}(F) = \sqrt{L \times P} \times 100 \text{ or } \sqrt{\frac{\Sigma P_1 q_0}{\Sigma P_0 q_0} \times \frac{\Sigma P_1 q_1}{\Sigma P_0 q_1}} \times 100$$

$$= \sqrt{\frac{478.50}{380} \times \frac{395}{324}} \times 100$$

$$= \sqrt{1.259 \times 1.219} \times 100$$

$$= 1.2388 \times 100$$

$$= \mathbf{123.88}$$

(*e.*) Marshall Edgeworth Index :

$$P_{01}(Ma) = \frac{\Sigma P_1 q_0 + \Sigma P_1 q_1}{\Sigma P_0 q_0 + \Sigma P_0 q_1} \times 100$$

$$= \frac{478.5}{380} + \frac{395}{324} \times 100$$

$$= \frac{873.5}{704} \times 100$$

$$= 1.2408 \times 100$$

$$= \mathbf{124.08}$$

Problem 13. It is stated that the Marshall Edgeworth index number is a good approximation to the ideal index number, verify using the following data.

	2000		2003	
Commodity	*Price*	*Quantity*	*Price*	*Quantity*
A	2	74	3	82
B	5	125	4	140
C	7	40	6	33

(*B.Com. Bombay*)

Solution :

Computation of Index Number

Commodity	P_0	q_0	P_1	q_1	$P_1 q_0$	$P_0 q_0$	$P_1 q_1$	$P_0 q_1$
A	2	74	3	82	222	148	246	164
B	5	125	4	140	500	625	560	700
C	7	40	6	33	240	280	198	231
					$\Sigma P_1 q_0 =$ 962	$\Sigma P_0 q_0$ = 1053	$\Sigma P_1 q_1 =$ 1004	$\Sigma P_0 q_1 =$ 1095

Marshall Edgeworth Index :

$$P_{01}(Ma) = \frac{\Sigma P_1 (q_0 + q_1)}{\Sigma P_0 (q_0 + q_1)} \times 100 \frac{\Sigma P_1 q_0 + \Sigma P_1 q_1}{\Sigma P_0 q_0 + \Sigma P_0 q_1}$$

$$= \frac{962 + 1004}{1053 + 1095} \times 100 = \frac{1966}{2148} \times 100$$

$$= \mathbf{91.53}$$

Fisher's Price Index :

$$
\begin{aligned}
P_{01}(F) &= \sqrt{\frac{\Sigma P_1 q_0}{\Sigma P_0 q_0} \times \frac{\Sigma P_1 q_1}{\Sigma P_0 q_1}} \times 100 \\
&= \sqrt{\frac{962}{1053} \times \frac{1004}{1095}} \times 100 \\
&= \sqrt{0.914 \times 0.917} \times 100 \\
&= \sqrt{0.8381} \times 100 = 0.9155 \times 100 \\
&= \mathbf{91.55}
\end{aligned}
$$

Marshall Edgeworth index number is a good approximation to the ideal index number.

Problem 14. Given the data :

	Commodities	
	A	*B*
P_0	1	1
q_0	10	5
P_1	2	X
q_1	5	2

where p and q respectively stand for price and quantity. Find X, if the ratio between Laspeyre's and Paasche's index number is

L : P = 28 : 27 [*M.A. (Ecos.) Delhi*]

Solution :

Computation of Ideal Index Number

Commodities	P_0	q_0	P_1	q_1	$P_1 q_0$	$P_0 q_0$	$P_1 q_1$	$P_0 q_1$
A	1	10	2	5	20	10	10	5
B	1	5	X	2	$5X$	5	$2X$	2
					$\Sigma P_1 q_0 =$ $20 + 5X$	$\Sigma P_0 q_0$ $= 15$	$\Sigma P_1 q_1 =$ $10 + 2X$	$\Sigma P_0 q_1 = 7$

$$
\begin{aligned}
\text{Laspeyre's Index } P_{01(L)} &= \frac{P_1 q_0}{\Sigma P_0 q_0} \\
&= \frac{20 + 5X}{15} \\
\text{Paasche's Index } P_{01(pa)} &= \frac{\Sigma P_1 q_1}{\Sigma P_0 q_1} \\
&= \frac{10 + 2X}{7}
\end{aligned}
$$

$$
\begin{aligned}
\frac{20 + 5X/15}{10 + 2X/7} &= \frac{28}{27} = \frac{20 + 5X}{15} \times \frac{7}{10 + 2x} = \frac{28}{27} \\
\frac{140 + 35X}{150 + 30X} &= \frac{28}{27} \\
3780 + 945X &= 4200 + 840X \\
945X - 840X &= 4200 - 3780
\end{aligned}
$$

$$105X = 420$$
$$X = \frac{420}{105}$$
$$= \mathbf{4}$$

Problem 15. With the help of the following data prove that Fisher's Ideal Index satisfies both the time reversal test and factor reversal test.

Commidity	2000		2001	
	Price	*Value*	*Price*	*Value*
A	15	60	16	82
B	16	75	20	90
C	23	80	24	98
D	9	40	12	50
E	14	58	18	74

(*M. Com. Jodhpur*)

Solution :

Computation of Ideal Index Number

Commodity	2000		2001					
	Price P_0	*Quantity* q_0	*Price* P_1	*Quantity* q_1	P_1q_0	P_0q_0	P_1q_1	P_0q_1
A	15	60	16	82	960	900	1312	1230
B	16	75	20	90	1500	1200	1800	1440
C	23	80	24	98	1920	1840	2352	2254
D	9	40	12	50	480	360	600	450
E	14	58	18	74	1044	812	1332	1036
					$\Sigma P_1q_0 =$ 5904	$\Sigma P_0q_0 =$ 5112	$\Sigma P_1q_1 =$ 7396	$\Sigma P_0q_1 =$ 6410

Time Reversal Test :

Time Reversal Test is satisfied when

$$P_{01} \times P_{10} = 1$$

$$P_{01} \times P_{10} = \sqrt{\frac{\Sigma P_1q_0}{\Sigma P_0q_0} \times \frac{\Sigma P_1q_1}{\Sigma P_0q_1}}\sqrt{\frac{\Sigma P_0q_1}{\Sigma P_1q_1} \times \frac{\Sigma P_0q_0}{\Sigma P_1q_0}}$$
$$= \sqrt{\frac{5904}{5112} \times \frac{7396}{6410} \times \frac{6410}{7396} \times \frac{5112}{5904}}$$
$$= \sqrt{1}$$
$$= \mathbf{1}$$

Factor Reversal Test :

Factor Reversal Test is satisfied when

$$P_{01} \times Q_{01} = \frac{\Sigma P_1q_1}{\Sigma P_0q_0}$$

$$P_{01} \times Q_{01} = \sqrt{\frac{\Sigma P_1 q_0}{\Sigma P_0 q_0} \times \frac{\Sigma P_1 q_1}{\Sigma P_0 q_1}} \sqrt{\frac{\Sigma q_1 p_0}{\Sigma q_0 p_0} \times \frac{\Sigma q_1 p_1}{\Sigma q_0 p_1}}$$

$$= \sqrt{\frac{5904}{5112} \times \frac{7396}{6410} \times \frac{6410}{5112} \times \frac{7396}{5904}}$$

$$= \sqrt{\frac{7396}{5112} \times \frac{7396}{5112}}$$

$$= \frac{7396}{5112} \; i.e. = \frac{\Sigma P_1 q_1}{\Sigma P_0 q_0}$$

Hence the given data satisfies both the time reversal test and factor reversal test.

Problem 16. Calculate the Laspeyre's and the Paasche's Index numbers from the following data and comment on the relative merits of the two.

	Base year		*Current year*	
Commodity	*Quantity*	*price per lb. Rs.*	*Quantity*	*Price per lb Rs.*
A	10.0	0.80	11.0	0.70
B	8.0	0.85	9.0	0.80
C	5.0	1.30	5.5	0.80

(*B.Com. Madras*)

Solution :

Computation of Laspeyre's and Paasche's Indices

	Base	*Year*	*Current*	*Year*				
Commodity	*price* P_0	*Quantity* q_0	*price* P_1	*Quantity* q_1	$P_0 q_0$	$P_0 q_1$	$P_1 q_0$	$P_1 q_1$
A	0.80	10.0	0.70	11.0	8.0	8.8	7.0	7.7
B	0.85	8.0	0.90	9.0	6.8	7.65	7.2	8.1
C	1.30	5.0	0.80	5.5	6.5	7.15	4.0	4.4
					$\Sigma P_0 q_0 = 21.3$	$\Sigma P_0 q_1 = 23.6$	$\Sigma P_1 q_0 = 18.2$	$\Sigma P_1 q_1 = 20.2$

$$\text{Laspeyre's Index} = \frac{\Sigma P_1 q_0}{\Sigma P_0 q_0} \times 100$$

$$= \frac{18.2}{21.3} \times 100$$

$$= \mathbf{85.44}$$

$$\text{Paasche's Index} = \frac{\Sigma P_1 q_1}{\Sigma P_0 q_1} \times 100$$

$$= \frac{20.2}{23.6} \times 100$$

$$= \mathbf{85.59}$$

Problem 17. Calculate the Laspeyre's, Paasche's and Fisher's Ideal Index number for the following data, treating 2000 as the base year.

Commodity	2000 Quantity	2000 Price	2001 Quantity	2001 Price
Wheat	562	170	632	72
Rice	535	192	756	70
Sugar	639	195	926	95
Ghee	128	187	255	92
Fuel	542	185	632	92
Gold	217	150	314	180

(*Sri Venkateswara*)

Solution :

Computation of Fisher's Ideal Index

Commodity	2000 P_0	q_0	2001 P_1	q_1	P_1q_0	P_0q_0	P_1q_1	P_0q_1
Wheat	170	562	72	632	40,464	95,540	45,504	1,07,440
Rice	192	535	70	756	37,450	1,02,720	52,920	1,45,152
Sugar	195	639	95	926	60,705	1,24,605	87,970	1,80,570
Ghee	187	128	92	255	11,776	23,936	23,460	47,685
Fuel	185	542	92	632	49,864	1,00,270	58,144	1,16,920
Gold	150	217	180	314	39,060	32,550	56,520	47,100
					$\Sigma P_1q_0 = 2,39,319$	$\Sigma P_0q_0 =$ 4,79,621	$\Sigma P_1q_1 =$ 3,24,518	$\Sigma P_0q_1 =$ 6,44,867

$$\text{Laspeyre's Index} = \frac{\Sigma P_1q_0}{\Sigma P_0q_0} \times 100 = \frac{2,39,319}{4,79,621} \times 100 = \mathbf{49.90}$$

$$\text{Paasche's Index} = \frac{\Sigma P_1q_1}{\Sigma P_0q_1} \times 100 = \frac{3,24,518}{6,44,867} \times 100 = \mathbf{50.32}$$

$$\text{Fisher's Ideal Index} = \sqrt{\frac{\Sigma P_1q_0}{\Sigma P_0q_0} \times \frac{\Sigma P_1q_1}{\Sigma P_0q_1}} \times 100$$

$$= \sqrt{\frac{2,39,319}{4,79,621} \times \frac{3,24,518}{6,44,867}} \times 100$$

$$= \sqrt{0.499 \times 0.503} = \sqrt{0.2509} \times 100$$

$$= 0.5009 \times 100$$

$$= \mathbf{50.09}$$

Problem 18. Using the data given below calculate price index number for the year 2003 by (*i*) Laspeyre's formula, (*ii*) Paasche's formula and (*iii*) Fisher's formula with the year 2002 as base.

Commodity	Price (Rs.) 2002	Price (Rs.) 2003	Quantity ('000 kg.) 2002	Quantity ('000 kg.) 2003
Rice	9.3	4.5	100	90
Wheat	6.4	3.7	11	10
Pulses	5.1	2.7	5	3

(*I.C.W.A., Final*)

Solution :

Computation of Laspeyre's Index, paasche's Index and Fisher's Index

Commodity	2002 P_0	2002 q_0	2003 P_1	2003 q_1	P_1q_0	P_0q_0	P_1q_1	P_0q_1
Rice	9.3	100	4.5	90	450.0	930.0	405.0	837.0
Wheat	6.4	11	3.7	10	40.7	70.4	37.0	64.0
Pulses	5.1	5	2.7	3	13.5	25.5	8.1	15.3
					$\Sigma P_1q_0 = 504.2$	$\Sigma P_0q_0 = 1025.9$	$\Sigma P_1q_1 = 450.1$	$\Sigma P_0q_1 = 916.3$

$$\text{Laspeyre's Index} = \frac{\Sigma P_1q_0}{\Sigma P_0q_0} \times 100 = \frac{504.2}{1025.9} \times 100 = \mathbf{49.15}$$

$$\text{Passche's Index} = \frac{\Sigma P_1q_1}{\Sigma P_0q_1} \times 100 = \frac{450.1}{916.3} \times 100 = \mathbf{49.12}$$

$$\text{Fisher's Ideal Index} = \sqrt{\text{Laspeyre's Index} \times \text{Paasche's Index}} = \sqrt{49.15 \times 49.12} = \sqrt{2414.248} = \mathbf{49.13}$$

Problem 19. Calculate the index number by the application of Laspeyre's formula and Paasche's formula from the following data.

Commodity	Units consumed 1998	Units consumed 2003	Price per unit 1998	Price per unit 2003
A	20	16	1.2	2.0
B	35	38	2.1	2.4
C	10	9	3.0	4.1
D	45	50	0.8	1.2

(*B.A. Bombay*)

Solution :

Computation of Laspeyre's and Paasche's Index

Commodity	1998		2003					
	P_0	q_0	P_1	q_1	P_1q_0	P_0q_0	P_1q_1	P_0q_1
A	1.2	20	2.0	16	40.0	24.00	32.00	19.20
B	2.1	35	2.4	38	84.0	73.50	91.20	79.80
C	3.0	10	4.1	9	41.0	30.00	36.90	27.00
D	0.8	45	1.2	50	54.0	30.00	60.00	40.00
					$\Sigma P_1q_0 =$ 219	$\Sigma P_0q_0 =$ 163.50	$\Sigma P_1q_1 =$ 220.10	$\Sigma P_0q_1 =$ 166

$$\text{Laspeyre's Index } P_{01(L)} = \frac{\Sigma P_1q_0}{\Sigma P_0q_0} \times 100 = \frac{219}{163.50} \times 100 = \mathbf{133.94}$$

$$\text{Paasche's Index } P_{01(P)} = \frac{\Sigma P_1q_1}{\Sigma P_0q_1} \times 100 = \frac{220.10}{166} \times 100 = \mathbf{132.59}$$

Problem 20. Calculate from the following data the Fisher's Ideal Index and show that it satisfies Time Reversal and Factor Reversal Tests:

	Item	*A*	*B*	*C*	*D*	*E*
Price	1995	8	2	1	2	1
	2003	20	6	2	5	5
Quantity	1995	50	15	20	10	40
	2003	60	10	25	8	30

(*B.Com., Mysore*)

Solution :

Calculation of Ideal Index Number

Item	1995		2003					
	P_0	q_0	P_1	q_1	P_1q_0	P_0q_0	P_1q_1	P_0q_1
A	8	50	20	60	1000	400	1200	480
B	2	15	6	10	90	30	60	20
C	1	20	2	25	40	20	50	25
D	2	10	5	8	50	20	40	16
E	1	40	5	30	200	40	150	30
					$\Sigma P_1q_0 =$ 1380	$\Sigma P_0q_0 =$ 510	$\Sigma P_1q_1 =$ 1500	$\Sigma P_0q_1 =$ 571

Fisher's Ideal Index :

$$P_{01} = \sqrt{\frac{\Sigma P_1 q_0}{\Sigma P_0 q_0} \times \frac{\Sigma P_1 q_1}{\Sigma P_0 q_1}} \times 100$$

$$= \sqrt{\frac{1380}{510} \times \frac{1500}{571}} \times 100$$

$$= \sqrt{2.706 \times 2.627} \times 100$$

$$= 2.666 \times 100$$

$$= \mathbf{266.6}$$

Time Reversal Test :

Time Reversal Test is satisfied when

$$P_{01} \times P_{10} = 1.$$

$$P_{01} \times P_{10} = \sqrt{\frac{\Sigma P_1 q_0}{\Sigma P_0 q_0} \times \frac{\Sigma P_1 q_1}{\Sigma P_0 q_1}} \sqrt{\frac{\Sigma P_0 q_1}{\Sigma P_1 q_1} \times \frac{\Sigma P_0 q_0}{\Sigma P_1 q_0}}$$

$$= \sqrt{\frac{1380}{510} \times \frac{1500}{571} \times \frac{571}{1500} \times \frac{510}{1310}}$$

$$= \sqrt{1}$$

$$= \mathbf{1}$$

Factor Reversal Test :

Factor Reversal Test is satisfied when :

$$P_{01} \times Q_{10} = \frac{\Sigma P_1 q_1}{\Sigma P_0 q_0}$$

$$P_{01} \times Q_{01} = \sqrt{\frac{\Sigma P_1 q_0}{\Sigma P_0 q_0} \times \frac{\Sigma P_1 q_1}{\Sigma P_0 q_1}} \sqrt{\frac{\Sigma q_1 P_0}{\Sigma q_0 P_0} \times \frac{\Sigma q_1 P_1}{\Sigma q_0 P_1}}$$

$$= \sqrt{\frac{1380}{510} \times \frac{1500}{571} \times \frac{571}{510} \times \frac{1500}{1380}}$$

$$= \sqrt{\frac{1500}{510} \times \frac{1500}{510}}$$

$$= \frac{1500}{510} \text{ that is } = \frac{\Sigma P_1 q_1}{\Sigma P_0 q_0}$$

Hence Time Reversal Test and Factor Reversal Test are satisfied by Fisher's Ideal Index.

Problem 21. With the help of the following data construct Fisher's Index Number :

	Wheat		*Rice*		*Gram*	
Year	*Quantity*	*Price*	*Quantity*	*Price*	*Quantity*	*Price*
1997	15	15.3	5	20.2	10	4
2003	12	22.3	4	27.4	8	7

(*B.Com., Agra*)

Solution : Since we are given both current year and base year prices and quantities, the appropriate index would be the Fisher's ideal Index.

Computation of Fisher's Ideal Index

Commodity	1997		2003		P_1q_0	P_0q_0	P_1q_1	P_0q_1
	P_0	q_0	P_1	q_1				
Wheat	15.3	15	22.3	12	334.5	229.5	267.6	183.6
Rice	20.2	5	27.4	4	137.0	101.0	109.6	80.8
Gram	4.0	10	7.0	8	70.0	40.0	56.0	32.0
					$\Sigma P_1q_0 =$ 541.5	$\Sigma P_0q_0 =$ 370.5	$\Sigma P_1q_1 =$ 433.2	$\Sigma P_0q_1 =$ 296.4

$$P_{01} = \sqrt{\frac{\Sigma P_1q_0}{\Sigma P_0q_0} \times \frac{\Sigma P_1q_1}{\Sigma P_0q_1}} \times 100$$

$$= \sqrt{\frac{541.5}{370.5} \times \frac{433.2}{296.4}} \times 100$$

$$= \sqrt{1.462 \times 1.462} \times 100$$

$$= 1.462 \times 100$$

$$= \mathbf{146.2}$$

Problem 22. With the help of the following data prove that Fisher's Ideal satisfies both the time reversal test and factor reversal test.

Quantity	1993		2003	
	price	*Value*	*Price*	*Value*
A	5	50	6	72
B	7	84	10	80
C	10	80	12	96
D	4	20	5	30
E	8	56	8	64

(*M. Com., Jodhpur*)

Solution :

Computation of Fisher's Ideal Index

Commodity	1993		2003		P_1q_0	P_0q_0	P_1q_1	P_0q_1
	P_0	q_0	P_1	q_1				
A	5	10	6	12	60	50	72	60
B	7	12	10	8	120	84	80	56
C	10	8	12	8	96	80	96	80
D	4	5	5	6	25	20	30	24
E	8	7	8	8	56	56	64	64
					$\Sigma P_1q_0 =$ 357	$\Sigma P_0q_0 =$ 290	$\Sigma P_1q_1 =$ 342	$\Sigma P_0q_1 =$ 284

Time Reversal Test :

Time Reversal test is satisfied when $P_{01} \times P_{10} = 1$

$$P_{01} \times P_{10} = \sqrt{\frac{\Sigma P_1 q_0}{\Sigma P_0 q_0} \times \frac{\Sigma P_1 q_1}{\Sigma P_0 q_1}} \sqrt{\frac{\Sigma P_0 q_1}{\Sigma P_1 q_1} \times \frac{\Sigma P_0 q_0}{\Sigma P_1 q_0}}$$

$$= \sqrt{\frac{357}{290} \times \frac{342}{284}} \sqrt{\frac{284}{342} \times \frac{290}{357}}$$

$$= \sqrt{1} = \mathbf{1}$$

Factor Reversal Test :

Factor Reversal Test is satisfied when $P_{01} \times Q_{01} = \frac{\Sigma P_1 q_1}{\Sigma P_0 q_0}$

$$P_{01} \times Q_{01} = \sqrt{\frac{\Sigma P_1 q_0}{\Sigma P_0 q_0} \times \frac{\Sigma P_1 q_1}{\Sigma P_0 q_1}} \sqrt{\frac{\Sigma q_1 P_1}{\Sigma q_0 P_0} \times \frac{\Sigma q_1 P_1}{\Sigma q_0 P_1}}$$

$$= \sqrt{\frac{357}{290} \times \frac{342}{284} \times \frac{284}{290} \times \frac{342}{357}} = \sqrt{\frac{342}{290} \times \frac{342}{290}}$$

$$= \frac{342}{290} \text{ that is } \frac{\Sigma P_1 q_1}{\Sigma P_0 q_0}$$

Therefore the given data prove that Fisher's ideal index satisfies both the time reversal test and factor reversal test.

Problem 23. The following figures relate to the prices and quantities of certain commodities. Construct an index number from the following data for the year 2003, taking 1998 as the base year.

Commodity	*Quantity consumed*	*price (in Rs.) in* 1998	*Price (in Rs.) in* 2003
A	50	32	40
B	35	30	30
C	55	16	24
D	45	40	52
E	15	35	42

(*B.Com., Shivaji*)

Solution : Since the weights are fixed, the appropriate method for computing the index is Kelley's method.

Computation of Weighted Price Index

Commodity	*Quantity consumed*	*Price (in Rs.)*		$P_0 q$	$P_1 q$
		1998	2003		
	q	P_0	P_1		
A	50	32	40	1600	2000
B	35	30	30	1050	1050
C	55	16	24	880	1320
D	45	40	52	1800	2340
E	15	35	42	525	630
				$\Sigma P_0 q = 5855$	$\Sigma P_1 q = 7340$

$$P_{01(K)} = \frac{\Sigma P_1 q}{\Sigma P_0 q} \times 100$$
$$= \frac{7340}{5855} \times 100$$
$$= \mathbf{125.36}$$

Problem 24. From the data given construct an index number of the group of four commodities by using Fisher's Ideal Formula :

	Base year		*Current year*	
Commodities	*Price per unit*	*Expenditure (Rs.)*	*Price per unit*	*Expenditure (Rs.)*
1	2	40	5	75
2	4	16	8	40
3	1	10	2	24
4	5	25	10	60

(*B.Com., Bombay, Jammu, Madurai*)

Solution : From the given price and expenditure we can obtain the quantities consumed by dividing expenditure for each commodity by the respective price.

Computation of Fisher's Ideal Index

	Base Year		*Current Year*					
Commodity	*Per unit* P_0	*Quantity* q_0	*Price per unit* P_1	*Quantity* q_1	P_1q_0	P_0q_0	P_1q_1	P_0q_1
1	2	20	5	15	100	40	75	30
2	4	4	8	5	32	16	40	20
3	1	10	2	12	20	10	24	12
4	5	5	10	6	50	25	60	30
					$\Sigma P_1q_0 = 202$	$\Sigma P_0q_0 = 91$	$\Sigma P_1q_1 = 199$	$\Sigma P_0q_1 = 92$

$$\text{Fisher's Ideal Index} = \sqrt{\frac{\Sigma P_1q_0}{\Sigma P_0q_0} \times \frac{\Sigma P_1q_1}{\Sigma P_0q_1}} \times 100$$
$$= \sqrt{\frac{202}{91} \times \frac{199}{92}} \times 100$$
$$= \sqrt{2.22 \times 2.16} \times 100$$
$$= \sqrt{4.7952} \times 100$$
$$= 2.1898 \times 100$$
$$= \mathbf{218.98}$$

Problem 25. Construct Fisher's Ideal index from the following data and show that it satisfies the Time Reversal Test :

	P_0	P_1	Q_0	Q_1
Wheat	30	35	5	4
Rice	32	37	7	5
Gram	20	18	3	4

(*B.Com. Andhra*)

Solution :

Computation of Fisher's Ideal Index

Commodity	P_0	q_0	P_1	q_1	P_1q_0	P_0q_0	P_1q_1	P_0q_1
Wheat	30	5	35	4	175	150	140	120
Rice	32	7	37	5	259	224	185	160
Gram	20	3	18	4	54	60	72	80
					ΣP_1q_0 = 488	ΣP_0q_0 = 434	ΣP_1q_1 = 397	ΣP_0q_1 = 360

Fisher's Ideal Index

$$(P_{01}) = \sqrt{\frac{\Sigma P_1q_0}{\Sigma P_0q_0} \times \frac{\Sigma P_1q_1}{\Sigma P_0q_1}} \times 100$$

$$= \sqrt{\frac{488}{434} \times \frac{397}{360}} \times 100$$

$$= \sqrt{1.124 \times 1.103} \times 100$$

$$= \sqrt{1.2397} \times 100$$

$$= 1.1134 \times 100$$

$$= \mathbf{111.34}$$

Problem 26. Calculate Fisher's Ideal Index from the data given below :

Commodity	*Price*		*Quantity*	
	2002	2003	2002	2003
A	8	10	20	30
B	12	15	10	10
C	6	8	16	20
D	4	6	8	10

(*M.B.A. Rohtak*)

Solution :

Computation of Ideal Index

Commodity	*Price* P_0	P_1	*Quantity* q_0	q_1	P_1q_0	P_0q_0	P_1q_1	P_0q_1
A	8	10	20	30	200	160	300	240
B	12	15	10	10	150	120	150	120
C	6	8	16	20	128	96	160	120
D	4	6	8	10	48	32	60	40
					ΣP_1q_0 = 526	ΣP_0q_0 = 408	ΣP_1q_1 = 670	ΣP_0q_1 = 520

$$\text{Fisher's Ideal Index} = \sqrt{\frac{\Sigma P_1 q_0}{\Sigma P_0 q_0} \times \frac{\Sigma P_1 q_1}{\Sigma P_0 q_1}} \times 100$$

$$= \sqrt{\frac{526}{408} \times \frac{670}{520}} \times 100$$

$$= \sqrt{1.289 \times 1.288} \times 100$$

$$= \sqrt{1.660} \times 100$$

$$= 1.2885 \times 100$$

$$= \mathbf{128.85}$$

Problem 27. Construct an appropriate index number for purposes of comparison from the following data :

Year	*Rice*		*Wheat*		*Jowar*	
	Price	*Quantity*	*Price*	*Quantity*	*Price*	*Quantity*
1995	7	40	6	10	4	5
2002	14	30	11	7	6	6

(*B.Com., Madras*)

Solution :

Computation of Fisher's Index Number

Group	*Base year* 1995		*Current year* 2002		$P_1 q_0$	$P_0 q_0$	$P_1 q_1$	$P_0 q_1$
	Price P_0	*Qty.* q_0	*Price* P_1	*Qty.* q_1				
Rice	7	4	14	30	560	280	420	210
Wheat	6	10	11	7	110	60	77	42
Jowar	4	5	6	6	30	20	36	24
					$\Sigma P_1 q_0 = 700$	$\Sigma P_0 q_0 = 360$	$\Sigma P_1 q_1 = 533$	$\Sigma P_0 q_1 = 276$

$$\text{Fisher's Index } (P_{01}) = \sqrt{\frac{\Sigma P_1 q_0}{\Sigma P_0 q_0} \times \frac{\Sigma P_1 q_1}{\Sigma P_0 q_1}} \times 100$$

$$= \sqrt{\frac{700}{360} \times \frac{533}{276}} \times 100$$

$$= \sqrt{1.944 \times 1.931} \times 100$$

$$= \sqrt{3.753864} \times 100$$

$$= 1.938 \times 100$$

$$= \mathbf{193.8}.$$

Problem 28. From the following prove that the Fisher's Ideal Index satisfies both the Time Reversal Test and the Factor Reversal Test.

Commodity	Base year Price	Base year Quantity	Current year Price	Current year Quantity
A	6	50	10	56
B	2	100	2	120
C	4	60	6	60
D	10	30	12	24

(B.Com., Madras., Mysore, Jabalpur)

Solution :

Computation of Fisher's Ideal Index

Commodity	Base Year		Current Year					
	P_0	q_0	P_1	q_1	P_1q_0	P_0q_0	P_1q_1	P_0q_1
A	6	50	10	56	500	300	560	336
B	2	100	2	120	200	200	240	240
C	4	60	6	60	360	240	360	240
D	10	30	12	24	360	300	288	240
					$\Sigma P_1q_0 = 1420$	$\Sigma P_0q_0 = 1040$	$\Sigma P_1q_1 = 1448$	$\Sigma P_0q_1 = 1056$

Time Reversal Test.

Time Reversal Test is satisfied when

$$\begin{aligned} P_{01} \times P_{10} &= \sqrt{\frac{\Sigma P_1q_0}{\Sigma P_0q_1} \times \frac{\Sigma P_1q_1}{\Sigma P_0q_1}}\sqrt{\frac{\Sigma P_0q_1}{\Sigma P_1q_1} \times \frac{\Sigma P_1q_0}{\Sigma P_1q_1}} = 1 \\ &= \sqrt{\frac{1420 \times 1448}{1040 \times 1056} \times \frac{1056}{1448} \times \frac{1040}{1420}} = \sqrt{1} \\ &= \mathbf{1} \end{aligned}$$

Factor Reversal Test :

Factor Reversal Test is satisfied when

$$\begin{aligned} P_{01} \times Q_{01} &= \sqrt{\frac{\Sigma P_1q_0}{\Sigma P_0q_0} \times \frac{\Sigma P_1q_1}{\Sigma P_0q_1}} \times \sqrt{\frac{\Sigma q_1P_0}{\Sigma q_0P_0} \times \frac{\Sigma q_1P_1}{\Sigma q_0P_1}} \\ &= \frac{\Sigma P_1q_1}{\Sigma P_0q_0} \\ &= \sqrt{\frac{1420 \times 1448}{1040 \times 1056} \times \frac{1056}{1040} \times \frac{1448}{1420}} = \sqrt{\frac{1448}{1056} \times \frac{1448}{1056}} \\ &= \frac{1448}{1056}\ i.e = \frac{\Sigma P_1q_1}{\Sigma P_0q_1} \end{aligned}$$

Therefore Fisher's ideal index satisfies both the Time Reversal Test and Factor Reversal Test.

Problem 29. From the data given below show that Fisher's Ideal Index satisfied both Time Reversal and Factor Reversal Tests.

	2002		2003	
Commodities	P_0	q_0	P_1	q_1
A	6	10	8	12
B	10	5	10	8
C	5	8	7	10
D	15	12	20	15
E	20	15	25	10

(*B.Com., Banaras*)

Solution :

Computation of Fisher's Index

	2002		2003					
Commodity	P_0	q_0	P_1	q_1	P_1q_0	P_0q_0	P_1q_1	P_0q_1
A	6	10	8	12	80	60	96	72
B	10	5	10	8	50	50	80	80
C	5	8	7	10	56	40	70	50
D	15	12	20	15	240	180	300	225
E	20	15	25	10	375	300	250	200
					$\Sigma P_1q_0 = 801$	$\Sigma P_0q_0 = 630$	$\Sigma P_1q_1 = 796$	$\Sigma P_0q_1 = 627$

Time Reversal Test :

Time Reversal Test is satisfied when $P_01 \times P_10 = 1$.

$$\begin{aligned} P_{01} \times P_{10} &= \sqrt{\frac{\Sigma P_1q_0}{\Sigma P_0q_0} \times \frac{\Sigma P_1q_1}{\Sigma P_0q_1}}\sqrt{\frac{\Sigma P_0q_1}{\Sigma P_1q_1} \times \frac{\Sigma P_0q_0}{\Sigma P_1q_0}} \\ &= \sqrt{\frac{801}{630} \times \frac{796}{627} \times \frac{627}{796} \times \frac{630}{801}} \\ &= \sqrt{1} \\ &= \mathbf{1} \end{aligned}$$

Factor Reversal Test :

Factor Reversal Test is satisfied when $P_{01} \times Q_{01} = \frac{\Sigma P_1q_1}{\Sigma P_0q_0}$

$$\begin{aligned} P_{01} \times Q_{01} &= \sqrt{\frac{\Sigma P_1q_0}{\Sigma P_0q_0} \times \frac{\Sigma P_1q_1}{\Sigma P_0q_1}}\sqrt{\frac{\Sigma q_1P_0}{\Sigma q_0P_0} \times \frac{\Sigma q_1P_1}{\Sigma q_0P_1}} \\ &= \sqrt{\frac{801}{630} \times \frac{796}{627} \times \frac{627}{630} \times \frac{796}{801}} \\ &= \sqrt{\frac{796}{630} \times \frac{796}{630}} \\ &= \frac{796}{630} \quad \text{that is} = \frac{\Sigma P_1q_1}{\Sigma P_0q_0} \end{aligned}$$

Therefore the given data satisfied both Time Reversal and Factor Reversal Test.

Problem 30. The following table gives the data of production in million tons and price per ton of four principal crops in India during the years 1996 and 2002 Construct Fisher's ideal index number of prices for theyear 2002.

Commodity	*Production in million tons*		*Price (Rupees per ton)*	
	1996	2002	1996	2002
A	25	30	150	300
B	10	12	120	200
C	2	3	600	1,000
D	1	2	200	300

(*B.A., Kerala*)

Solution :

Computation of Fisher's Ideal Index

Commodity	1996		2002					
	P_0	q_0	P_1	q_1	P_1q_0	P_0q_0	P_1q_1	P_0q_1
A	150	25	300	30	7500	3750	9000	4500
B	120	10	200	12	2000	1200	2400	1440
C	600	2	1000	3	2000	1200	3000	1800
D	200	1	300	2	300	200	600	400
					$\Sigma P_1q_0 =$ 11,800	ΣP_0q_0 = 6350	$\Sigma P_1q_1 =$ 15000	$\Sigma P_0q_1 =$ 8140

Fisher's Ideal Index :

$$P_{01}(F) = \sqrt{\frac{\Sigma P_1q_0}{\Sigma P_0q_0} \times \frac{\Sigma P_1q_1}{\Sigma P_0q_1}} \times 100$$

$$= \sqrt{\frac{11800}{6350} \times \frac{15000}{8140}} \times 100$$

$$= \sqrt{1.858 \times 1.843} \times 100$$

$$= \sqrt{3.424} \times 100$$

$$= 1.850 \times 100$$

$$= \mathbf{185}$$

Problem 31. Construct with the help of the data given below Fisher's Ideal Index, and show how it satisfies the Time Reversal Test.

Commodity	*Base year price (Rs.)*	*Base year Quantity*	*Current year price*	*Current year Quantity*
Wheat	8	50	20	60
Ghee	2	15	6	10
Firewood	1	20	2	25
Sugar	2	10	5	8
Cloth	1	40	3	30

Solution :

Commodity	Base year		Current year		P_1q_0	P_0q_0	P_1q_1	P_0q_1
	Price P_0	Quantity q_0	Price P_1	Quantity q_1				
Wheat	8	50	20	60	1000	400	1200	480
Ghee	2	15	6	10	90	30	60	20
Firewood	1	20	2	25	40	20	50	25
Sugar	2	10	5	8	50	20	40	16
Cloth	1	40	3	30	120	40	90	30
					$\Sigma P_1q_0 = 1300$	$\Sigma P_0q_0 = 510$	$\Sigma P_1q_1 = 1440$	$\Sigma P_0q_1 = 571$

$$\text{Fisher's Ideal Index :} = \sqrt{\frac{\Sigma P_1q_0}{\Sigma P_0q_0} \times \frac{\Sigma P_1q_1}{\Sigma P_0q_1}} \times 100$$

$$= \sqrt{\frac{1300}{510} \times \frac{1440}{571}} \times 100$$

$$= \sqrt{2.549 \times 2.522} \times 100$$

$$= 2.5354 \times 100$$

$$= \mathbf{253.54}$$

Time Reversal Test :

Time Reversal Test is satisfied when

$$P_{01} \times P_{10} = \sqrt{\frac{\Sigma P_1q_0}{\Sigma P_0q_0} \times \frac{\Sigma P_1q_1}{\Sigma P_0q_1}} \sqrt{\frac{\Sigma P_0q_0}{\Sigma P_1q_0} \times \frac{\Sigma P_0q_1}{\Sigma P_1q_1}} = 1$$

$$P_{01} \times P_{10} = \sqrt{\frac{1300}{510} \times \frac{1440}{571} \times \frac{510}{1300} \times \frac{571}{1440}}$$

$$= \sqrt{1}$$

$$= \mathbf{1}$$

Thus Fisher's Ideal Index satisfies Time Reversal Test.

Problem 32. Using the following data, construct Fisher's Ideal Index number and show how it satisfies Factor Reversal test and Time Reversal test.

Commodity	*Price (Rs.) per unit*		*Number of units*	
	Base year	*Current year*	*Base year*	*Current year*
A	6	10	50	56
B	2	2	100	120
C	4	6	60	60
D	10	12	30	24
E	8	12	40	36

(*B.Com., Mysore*)

Solution :

Commodities	Base year		Current year		P_0q_0	P_1q_0	P_1q_1	P_0q_1
	Price per Unit(P_0)	No. of Units(q_0)	Price per per unit P_1	No. of units q_1				
A	6	50	10	56	300	500	560	336
B	2	100	2	120	200	200	240	240
C	4	60	6	60	240	360	360	240
D	10	30	12	24	300	360	288	240
E	8	40	12	36	320	480	432	288
					$\Sigma P_0q_0 = 1360$	$\Sigma P_1q_0 = 1900$	$\Sigma P_1q_1 = 1880$	$\Sigma P_0q_1 = 1344$

Fisher's Ideal Index

$$P_{01} = \sqrt{\frac{\Sigma P_1q_0}{\Sigma P_0q_0} \times \frac{\Sigma P_1q_1}{\Sigma P_0q_1}} \times 100$$
$$= \sqrt{\frac{1900}{1360} \times \frac{1880}{1344}} \times 100$$
$$= \sqrt{1.954} \times 100$$
$$= 1.398 \times 100$$
$$= \mathbf{139.8}$$

Factor Reversal Test is satisfied if

$$P_{01} \times Q_{01} = \frac{\Sigma P_1q_1}{\Sigma P_0q_0}$$

$$P_{01} \times Q_{01} = \sqrt{\frac{\Sigma P_1q_0}{\Sigma P_0q_0} \times \frac{\Sigma P_1q_1}{\Sigma P_0q_1} \times \frac{\Sigma q_1P_0}{\Sigma q_0P_0} \times \frac{\Sigma q_1P_1}{\Sigma q_0P_1}}$$
$$= \sqrt{\frac{1900}{1360} \times \frac{1880}{1334} \times \frac{1334}{1360} \times \frac{1880}{1900}}$$
$$= \sqrt{\frac{1880}{1360} \times \frac{1880}{1360}} = \frac{1880}{1360} \text{ i.e.}$$
$$= \frac{\Sigma P_1q_1}{\Sigma P_0q_0}$$

Fisher's Ideal Index satisfies factor reversal test.

Time Reversal test is satisfied if

$$P_{01} \times P_{10} = 1$$
$$= \sqrt{\frac{\Sigma P_1q_0}{\Sigma P_0q_0} \times \frac{\Sigma P_1q_1}{\Sigma P_0q_1} \times \frac{\Sigma P_0q_1}{\Sigma P_1q_1} \times \frac{\Sigma P_0q_0}{\Sigma P_1q_0}}$$

Substituting the values from the table

$$= \sqrt{\frac{1900}{1360} \times \frac{1880}{1344} \times \frac{1344}{1880} \times \frac{1360}{1900}}$$

$$= \sqrt{1}$$
$$= \mathbf{1}$$

Time Reversal test is satisfied by Fisher's formula.

Problem 33. The following figures relate to the prices and quantities of certain commodities. Construct an appropriate index number and show if it satisfies the Time Reversal test.

Commodity	2002 *Price*	2002 *Quantities*	2003 *Price*	2003 *Quantities*
Wheat	30	50	32	50
Gram	25	40	30	35
Barley	18	50	16	55

(*B.Com. Osmania*)

Solution :

Calculation of the Time Reversal Test

Commodity	2002 *Price* P_0	2002 *Qty.* q_0	2003 *Price* P_1	2003 *Qty.* q_1	P_1q_0	P_0q_0	P_1q_1	P_0q_1
Wheat	30	50	32	50	1600	1500	1600	1500
Gram	25	40	30	35	1200	1000	1050	875
Barley	18	50	16	55	800	900	880	990
					$\Sigma P_1q_0 = 3600$	$\Sigma P_0q_0 = 3400$	$\Sigma P_1q_1 = 3530$	$\Sigma P_0q_1 = 3365$

Time Reversal Test

$$P_{01} = \sqrt{\frac{\Sigma P_1q_0}{\Sigma P_0q_0} \times \frac{\Sigma P_1q_1}{\Sigma P_0q_1}}$$
$$= P_1q_0 = 3600$$
$$= P_0q_0 = 3400$$
$$= P_1q_1 = 3530$$
$$= P_0q_1 = 3365$$
$$P_{10} = \sqrt{\frac{\Sigma P_0q_1}{\Sigma P_1q_1} \times \frac{\Sigma P_0q_0}{\Sigma P_1q_0}}$$
$$P_{01} \times P_{10} = \sqrt{\frac{\Sigma P_1q_0}{\Sigma P_0q_0} \times \frac{\Sigma P_1q_1}{\Sigma P_0q_1} \times \frac{\Sigma P_0q_1}{\Sigma P_1q_1} \times \frac{\Sigma P_0q_0}{\Sigma P_1q_0}}$$
$$= \sqrt{\frac{3600}{3400} \times \frac{3530}{3365} \times \frac{3365}{3530} \times \frac{3400}{3600}}$$
$$= \sqrt{1}$$
$$= \mathbf{1}$$

COST OF LIVING INDEX

Problem 34. Calculate the index number of crime for 2001 with 1990 as base :

	1990('000)	2001('000)	*Weight*
Robberies	13	8	6
Car thefts	15	22	5
Cycle thefts	249	185	4
Pocket picking	328	259	1
Thefts by servants	497	448	2

(*B.Com. Kurukshetra*)

Solution :

Index Number of Crime for 2001

	1990	2001	*Weight* W	*Crime Relative* $P = \frac{P_1}{P_0} \times 100$	PW
Robberies	13	8	6	$\frac{8}{13} \times 100 = 61.54$	369.24
Car Thefts	15	22	5	$\frac{22}{15} \times 100 = 146.67$	733.35
Cycle Thefts	249	185	4	$\frac{185}{249} \times 100 = 74.30$	297.20
Pocket Picking	328	259	1	$\frac{259}{328} \times 100 = 78.96$	78.96
Thefts by Servants	497	448	2	$\frac{448}{497} \times 100 = 90.14$	180.28
			$\Sigma W = 18$		$\Sigma PW = 1659.03$

$$\text{Index Number of Crime} = \frac{\Sigma PW}{\Sigma W} = \frac{1659.03}{18} = \mathbf{92.17}.$$

Problem 35. In the construction of a certain Cost of Living Index Number the following group index numbers were found. Calculate the cost of Living Index Number by using (*i*) the weighted arithmetic mean, (*ii*) the weighted geometric mean.

Group	*Index Number*	*Weights*
1. Food	350	5
2. Fuel and lighting	200	1
3. Clothing	240	1
4. House Rent	160	1
5. Miscellaneous	250	2

(*B.Com., Bombay, Madhurai Andhra*)

Solution :

Computation of Price Index by A.M. and G.M

Group	*Index Number* I	*Weights* W	IW	*log I*	$\log I \times W$
Food	350	5	1750	2.5441	12.7205
Fuel+lighting	200	1	200	2.3010	2.3010
Clothing	240	1	240	2.3802	2.3802
House Rent	160	1	160	2.2041	2.2041
Miscellaneous	250	2	500	2.3979	4.7958
		$\Sigma W = 10$	$\Sigma IW = 2850$		$\Sigma \log I \times W = 24.4016$

The Consumer Price Index using by A.M. :

$$P_{01} = \frac{\Sigma IW}{\Sigma W} = \frac{2850}{10}$$
$$= \mathbf{285}.$$

Consumer Price Index using G.M. :

$$P_{01} = \frac{\Sigma \, log \, IW}{\Sigma W}$$
$$= \text{Antilog} \frac{24.4016}{10}$$
$$= \text{Antilog}(2.4401)$$
$$= \mathbf{275.5}.$$

Problem 36. Compute price index for the following data by applying weighted average of price relative, using (*i*) arithmetic mean and (*ii*) geometric mean :

Item	*Price in* 2001 *Rs.*	*Price in* 2002 *Rs.*	*Quantity in* 2001
Wheat	2.00	2.50	40 kg
Sugar	3.00	3.25	20 kg
Milk	1.50	1.75	10 lit

(*B.Com.*)

Solution:

Computation of Price Index

Item	*Price* P_0	*Price* P_1	*Quantity* q_0	$V = P_0 q_0$	$P = \frac{P_1}{P_0} \times 100$	PV	*Log P*	$\Sigma(logP)V$
Wheat	2.00	2.50	40	80	125	10,000	2.0969	167.7520
Sugar	3.00	3.25	20	60	108.33	6499.8	2.0346	122.0760
Milk	1.50	1.75	10	15	116.67	1750.05	2.0668	31.002
				$\Sigma V = 155$		$\Sigma PV = 18249.85$		$\Sigma(logP)V = 320.83$

(*a*) Arithmetic Mean :

$$P_{01} = \frac{\Sigma PV}{\Sigma V} = \frac{18249.85}{155} = \mathbf{117.74.}$$

(*b*) Geometric Mean :

$$P_{01} = \text{Antilog}\frac{\Sigma(\log P)V}{\Sigma V} = \text{Antilog}\frac{320.83}{155} = \text{Antilog } 2.0699 = \mathbf{117.4.}$$

Problem 37. Following information relating to workers in an industrial town is given :

Items of consumption	*Consumer price index in* 2000 (1990 = 100)	*Proportion of expenditure on item*
1. Food, drinks and tobacco	225	52%
2. Clothing	175	8%
3. Fuel and lighting	115	10%
4. Housing	250	14%
5. Miscellaneous	150	16%

Average wages per month in 1990 is Rs. 200. What should be the average wage per worker per month in 2000 in that town so that the standard of living of the workers does not fall below the 1990 level. (*B.A. Hons. Econ. Delhi*)

Solution :

Computation of Aggregate Index

Item of Computation	*Index in* 2000	*Weight W*	*IW*
Food, drinks and tobacco	225	52	11700
Clothing	175	8	1400
Fuel and lighting	155	10	1550
Housing	250	14	3500
Miscellaneous	150	16	2400
		$\Sigma W = 100$	$\Sigma IW = 20,550$

$$Index = \frac{\Sigma IW}{\Sigma W} = \frac{20550}{100} = 205.50$$

In order to keep the standard of living, the Average Wage per worker should be Rs. 205.50 *i.e.* there should be an increase of Rs. 105.50. Here, when the worker gets Rs. 200 in

1990, he must get Rs. 205.50 ×2 = Rs. 411. Thus, if the worker gets 411, his standard does not fall below 1990 level.

Problem 38. The following data show the consumer price index number (base : November 2000 = 100) for December 2003 for a certain class of families in West Bengal, separately for the five broad groups of items. Compute the overall consumer price index from the given data :

Item group	*Weight of group*	*Group index*
Food	58.55	91.4
Clothing	5.37	106.5
Fuel and Light	6.15	102.2
Housing	9.61	100.2
Miscellaneous	20.32	100.3

(*B.A. Econ. Hons., Calcutta*)

Solution :

Computation of Consumer Price Index

Item group	*Weight* W	*Group Index* I	IW
Food	58.55	91.4	5351.47
Clothing	5.37	106.5	571.91
Fuel and Light	6.15	102.2	628.53
Housing	9.61	100.2	961.0
Miscellaneous	20.32	100.3	2038.09
	$\Sigma W = 100$		$\Sigma IW = 9551.00$

$$\text{Consumer Price Index} = \frac{\Sigma IW}{\Sigma W} = \frac{9551}{100} = \mathbf{95.51}.$$

Problem 39. Explain the significance of the Family Budget Enquiry in the construction of cost of living index number.

The weights attached to certain items and the price relatives of these items are given below :

Item	*Weights*	*Price relative*
Food	55	150
Clothing	25	120
House rent	8	175
Miscellaneous	12	168

Calculate the cost of living index number based on these data. (*B.Com., Andhra*)

Solution :

Computation of Cost of Living Index

Item	*Price Relatives* P	*Weight* V	*Weighted Relatives* P.V.
Food	150	55	8,250
Clothing	120	25	3,000
House Rent	175	8	1,400
Miscellaneous	168	12	2,016
		$\Sigma V = 100$	$\Sigma IV = 14666$

P = Price Relative; V = Weight

$$\text{Cost of Living Index Numbers} = \frac{\Sigma PV}{\Sigma V} = \frac{14,666}{100} = \mathbf{146.66}.$$

Problem 40. The following are the group index numbers and the group weights of an average working class family's budget. Construct the cost of living index number :

Group	*Food*	*Fuel and lighting*	*Clothing*	*Rent*	*Miscellaneous*
Index Number	352	220	230	160	190
Weight	48	10	8	12	15

(*I.C.W.A.*)

Solution :

Cost of Living Index

Groups	*Index Number* I	*Weight* W	*IW*
Food	352	48	16,896
Fuel and lighting	220	10	2,200
Clothing	230	8	1,840
Rent	160	12	1,920
Miscellaneous	190	15	2,850
		$\Sigma W = 93$	$\Sigma IW = 25,706$

$$\text{Cost of Living} = \frac{\Sigma IW}{\Sigma W} = \frac{25,706}{93} = \mathbf{276.4}.$$

Problem 41. The following table gives the group price index number and percentage of expenditure on various groups, obtained from inquiries into the budget of the middle class families of Bombay.

Group	*Percentage of Expenditure*	*Group price* 2000	*Index Number* 2002
Food	35	350	440
Fuel and lighting	10	220	330
Clothing	20	230	400
Rent	15	160	105
Miscellaneous	20	190	340

What changes are seen in the level of cost of living of 2002 as compared to that of 2000?

(*B.A., Econ., Bombay*)

Solution :

Computation of Cost of Living index

Group	*Price in Rupees* 2000 P_0	2002 P_1	*Taking* 2000 *as base* $P = \frac{P_1}{P_0} \times 100$	*Percentage of Expenditure V*	$P \times V$
Food	350	440	$\frac{440}{350} \times 100 = 125.71$	35	4399.85
Fuel and lighting	220	330	$\frac{330}{220} \times 100 = 150.00$	10	1500.00
Clothing	230	400	$\frac{400}{230} \times 100 = 173.91$	20	3478.20
Rent	160	105	$\frac{105}{160} \times 100 = 65.62$	15	984.30
Miscellaneous	190	340	$\frac{340}{190} \times 100 = 178.94$	20	3578.80
				$\Sigma V = 100$	$\Sigma PV =$ 13941.15

$$\text{Cost of Living Index} = \frac{\Sigma PV}{\Sigma V} = \frac{13941.15}{100} = 139.4115 = \mathbf{139.41}$$

Problem 42. In calculating a certain cost of living index number, the following weights were used. Food 15, clothing 3, rent 4, fuel and light 2, miscellaneous 1. Calculate the index for a date when the average percentage increases in prices of items in the various groups over the base period were 32, 54, 47, 78 and 58 respectively.

Suppose a business executive was earning Rs. 2050 in the base period, what should be his salary in the current period if his standard of living is to remain the same.

(*B.Com. Punjab, Bombay*)

Solution :

Computation of Cost of Living Index

Group	*Average % increase in price*	*Group Index I*	*Weight W*	*IW*
Food	32	132	15	1980
Clothing	54	154	3	462
Rent	47	147	4	588
Fuel and Light	78	178	2	356
Miscellaneous	58	158	1	158
			$\Sigma W = 25$	$\Sigma IW = 3544$

$$\text{Cost of Living Index} = \frac{\Sigma IW}{\Sigma W} = \frac{3544}{25} = \mathbf{141.76.}$$

The business executive should get Rs. 2906.08 $\left(\frac{2050 \times 141.76}{100}\right)$, to maintain the same standard of living.

Problem 43. An enquiry into the budgets of middle class families in a city gave the following information :

	A	*B*	*C*	*D*	*E*
Expenses (Percent)	30	15	20	10	25
Prices (1994)	100	20	70	20	40
Prices (2003)	90	20	60	15	55

What are the changes in the cost of living figures of 2003 as compared to those 1994?

(*B.Com. Kerala*)

Solution :

Computation of Cost of Living Index

Items	*Weight V*	P_0	P_1	$P = \frac{P_1}{P_0} \times 100$	*PV*
A	30	100	90	90	2,700
B	15	20	20	100	1,500
C	20	70	60	85.7	1,714
D	10	20	15	75.0	750
E	25	40	55	137.5	3437.5
	$\Sigma V = 100$				$\Sigma PV = 10,101.5$

$$\text{Cost of Living Index} = \frac{\Sigma PV}{\Sigma V} \times 100 = \frac{10,101.5}{100} = \mathbf{101.02}$$

There is 1.02% change in the cost of living index of 2003 as compared to 1994.

Problem 44. In the construction of a certain cost of Living Index Number, the following group index numbers were found. Calculate the cost of Living Index Number by using :

(*i*) The weighted arithmetic mean, and
(*ii*) The weighted geometric mean.

Group	*Index Number*	*Number*
Food	352	48
Fuel and Lighting	200	10
Clothing	230	8
House Rent	160	12
Miscellaneous	190	15

(*B.Com., Gujarat., Rajasthan I.C.W.A.,*)

Solution :

Computation of Cost of Living Index

Group	*Index No. I*	*Weight W*	*IW*	*log I*	*W log I*
Food	352	48	16,896	2.5465	122.232
Fuel and Lighting	200	10	2000	2.3010	23.010
Clothing	230	8	1840	2.3617	18.894
House Rent	160	12	1920	2.2041	26.449
Miscellaneous	190	15	2850	2.2788	34.182
		$\Sigma W = 93$	$\Sigma IW =$ 25,506		$\Sigma W log I = 224.77$

(*i*) Cost of Living index (using the weighted A. M.)

$$= \frac{\Sigma IW}{\Sigma W} = \frac{25506}{93} = \mathbf{274.26}$$

$$= \mathbf{274.26}$$

(*ii*) Cost of Living Index (using weighted G.M.)

$$= \text{Antilog}\left(\frac{\Sigma W \log I}{\Sigma W}\right)$$

$$= \text{Antilog}\left(\frac{224.77}{93}\right)$$

$$= \text{Antilog}\ (2.419)$$

$$= \mathbf{261.1}$$

Problem 45. An enquiry into the budgets of the middle class families in a certain city in India gave the following information :

Expenses on	*Food* 35%	*Fuel* 10%	*Clothing* 20%	*Rent* 15%	*Misc.* 20%
Price 2000 (Rs.)	150	25	75	30	40
Price 2002 (Rs.)	145	23	65	30	45

What is the cost of living index number of 2002 as compared with that of 2000 ?
(B.Com., Kerala, karnatak I.C.W.A., Final)

Solution : **Computation of Cost of Living Index**

Items	*Price in* 2000 (*Rs*)	*Price in* 2002 (*Rs*)	*Price Relatives* *P*	*Weight* *W*	*Weighted Relatives PW*
Food	150	145	$\frac{145}{150} \times 100 = 96.7$	35	3384.5
Fuels	25	23	$\frac{23}{25} \times 100 = 92.0$.	10	920.0
Clothing	75	65	$\frac{65}{75} \times 100 = 86.7$	20	1734.0
Rent	30	30	$\frac{30}{30} \times 100 = 100.0$	15	1500.0
Misc.	40	45	$\frac{45}{40} \times 100 = 112.5$	20	2250.0
				$\Sigma W =$ $= 100$	$\Sigma PW =$ 9788.5

$$\text{Cost of Living Index for 2002} = \frac{\Sigma PW}{\Sigma W} = \frac{9788.5}{100} = \mathbf{97.89}$$

Problem 46. Calculate the index number of prices for 2003 on the basis of 1993 from the data given below.

Commodities	*Weights*	*Price per unit*	*Price per unit*
		1993	2003
A	40	16.00	20.00
B	25	40.00	60.00
C	5	0.50	0.50
D	20	5.12	6.25
E	10	2.00	1.50

(M.S.W., Lucknow)

Solution : **Computation of Price Index**

Commodities	*Weights V*	*Price per unit* 1993 (P_0)	*Price per unit* 2003 (P_1)	*Price Relatives* $P = \frac{P_1}{P_0} \times 100$	*Weighted Relatives IV*
A	40	16.00	20.00	125	5,000
B	25	40.00	60.00	150	3,750
C	5	0.50	0.50	100	500
D	20	5.12	6.25	122.1	2442
E	10	2.00	1.50	75	750
	$\Sigma V = 100$				$\Sigma IV =$ 12442

$$\text{Index Number of prices for 2003} = \frac{\Sigma PV}{\Sigma V} = \frac{12442}{100} = \mathbf{124.42}$$

Problem 47. The price quotations of four different commodities for 2002 and 2003 are given below. Calculate the index number for 2003 with 2002 as base by using (*i*) the simple average of price relatives, and (*ii*) the weighted average of price relatives,

Commodities	*Unit*	*Weight*	*Price in (Rs.)* 2002	2003
A	Kg.	5	2.00	4.50
B	Quintal	7	2.50	3.20
C	Dozen	6	3.00	4.50
D	Kg.	2	1.00	1.80

(*I.C.W.A.*)

Solution :

Computation of Index Number

Commodity	*Unit*	*Weight V*	P_0	P_1	$P = \frac{P_1}{P_0} \times 100$	*PV*
A	kg	5	2.00	4.50	225	1,125
B	Quintal	7	2.50	3.20	128	896
C	Dozen	6	3.00	4.50	150	900
D	Kg.	2	1.00	1.80	180	360
		$\Sigma V = 20$			$\Sigma P = 683$	$\Sigma PV =$ 3,281

$$\text{Simple Average of Price Relatives } (P_{01}) = \frac{\Sigma P}{N} = \frac{683}{4} = \mathbf{170.75}$$

Weighted Average of Price Relatives

$$P_{01} = \frac{\Sigma PV}{\Sigma V} = \frac{3281}{20} = \mathbf{164.05}$$

Problem 48. Calculate the Index Number using both the Aggregate Expenditure method and Family Budget method for the year 2003 with 2000 as base year from the following data.

Commodity	*Quantity in units in* 2000	*Price per unit in* 2000 (*Rs.*)	*Price per unit in* 2003 (*Rs.*)
A	100	8.00	12.00
B	25	6.00	7.50
C	10	5.00	5.25
D	20	48.00	52.00
E	25	15.00	16.50
F	30	9.00	27.00

(*B.Com., Bangalore*)

Solution :

(A) Computation of Index by Aggregate Expenditure Method

Commodity	Q_0	*Price in Rs.* 2000	2003	*Aggregate Expenditure*	
		P_0	P_1	P_0q_0	$P1q_0$
A	100	8.00	12.00	800.00	1200.00
B	25	6.00	7.50	150.00	187.50
C	10	5.00	5.25	50.00	52.50
D	20	48.00	52.00	960.00	1040.00
E	25	15.00	16.50	375.00	412.50
F	30	9.00	27.00	270.00	810.00
				$\Sigma P_0q_0 = 2605$	$\Sigma P_1q_0 =$ 3702.50

Aggregate Expenditure Method :

$$\text{Cost of Living Index} = \frac{\Sigma P_1q_0}{\Sigma P_0q_0} \times 100 = \frac{3702.5}{2605} \times 100 = \mathbf{142.13}$$

(B) Computation of Family Budget Index

Commodity	q_0	*Price in Rs.* 2000	2003	*Price Relative*	*Weight*	
		P_0	P_1	$P = \frac{P_1}{P_0} \times 100$	$V = P_0q_0$	PV
A	100	8.00	12.00	150.00	800	120000.00
B	25	6.00	7.50	125.00	150	18750.00
C	10	5.00	5.25	105.00	50	5250.00
D	20	48.00	52.00	108.33	960	103996.80
E	25	15.00	16.50	110.00	375	41250.00
F	30	9.00	27.00	300.00	270	81000.00
					$\Sigma V = 2605$	$\Sigma PV =$ 3, 70, 246.8

Family Budget Method.

$$\text{Cost of Living Index} = \frac{\Sigma PV}{\Sigma V} = \frac{3,70,246.8}{2605} = \mathbf{142.13}$$

Problem 49. Calculate the Cost of Living Index from the following data.

Item	*Quantity Consumed per year in the given year*	*price per unit in rupees* Base Year	given year
Rice	2 1/2 qtl×12	12	25
Pulses	3 kg × 12	4	0.6
Oil	2kg × 12	1.5	2.2
Clothing	6 metres × 12	0.75	1.0
Housing		20 per month	30 per month
Miscellaneous		10 per month	15 per month

(*M. Com. Rohtak*)

Solution :

Computation of Cost of Living Index

Items	*Quantity consumed per year* q_1	P_0	P_1	P_1q_1	P_0q_1
Rice	30 qtl.	12.0	25.0	750.0	360.0
Pulses	36 Kg.	0.40	0.6	21.6	14.4
Oil	24 Kg.	1.50	2.2	52.8	36.0
Clothing	72 Mts.	0.75	1.0	72.0	54.0
Housing		20 per month	30 per month	360.0	240.0
Miscellaneous		10 per month	15 per month	180.0	120.0
				$\Sigma P_1q_1 = 1436.4$	$\Sigma P_0q_1 = 824.4$

Here current year's quantities are given. Hence we apply paache's method.

$$\text{Cost of Living Index} = \frac{\Sigma P_1q_1}{\Sigma P_0q_1} \times 100 = \frac{1436.4}{824.4} \times 100 = 1.7424 \times 100 = \mathbf{174.24}$$

Problem 50. The table below shows the average wages in rupees per day of a group of industrial workers during the years 1990–2001. The consumer price indices for these years with 1990 as base year are also shown.

Determine the real wages of the workers during the years 1990–2001 as compared with their wages in 1990.

Year	*Average wage of workers*	*Consumer price index*
1990	1.19	100 (1990=100)
1991	1.33	107.6
1992	1.44	106.6
1993	1.57	107.6
1994	1.75	116.2
1995	1.84	118.8
1996	1.89	119.8
1997	1.94	120.2
1998	1.97	119.9
1999	2.13	121.7
2000	2.28	125.9
2001	2.45	129.3

(*ICWA*)

Solution :

Computation of Real Wages

Year	*Average wage of workers* (1)	*Consumer Price Index* (1990 = 100)(2)	*Real wages of worker* (3) $= \frac{(1)}{(2)} \times 100$
1990	1.19	100	$\frac{1.19}{100} \times 100 = 1.19$
1991	1.33	107.6	$\frac{1.33}{107.6} \times 100 = 1.24$
1992	1.44	106.6	$\frac{1.44}{106.6} \times 100 = 1.35$
1993	1.57	107.6	$\frac{1.57}{107.6} \times 100 = 1.46$
1994	1.75	116.2	$\frac{1.75}{116.2} \times 100 = 1.51$
1995	1.84	118.8	$\frac{1.84}{118.8} \times 100 = 1.55$
1996	1.89	119.8	$\frac{1.89}{119.8} \times 100 = 1.58$
1997	1.94	120.2	$\frac{1.94}{120.2} \times 100 = 1.61$
1998	1.97	119.9	$\frac{1.97}{119.9} \times 100 = 1.64$
1999	2.13	121.7	$\frac{2.13}{121.7} \times 100 = 1.75$
2000	2.28	125.9	$\frac{2.28}{125.9} \times 100 = 1.81$
2001	2.45	129.3	$\frac{2.45}{129.3} \times 100 = 1.89$

The purchasing power of the rupee in any year as compared to year 1990, is given by the reciprocal of the corresponding consumer price index.

Hence the purchasing power of rupee in 2001, as compared to the year 1990 is $\frac{100}{129.3} = 0.77$

This implies that in 2001 we have to spend Re. 1 for buying a commodity which cost 77 paise in 1990. This means that although the average wage of the worker in 2001 is more than double his wages in 1990, in fact he is not better off than in 1990, since the purchasing power of the rupee has in reality, sloped to Rs. 0.77 *i.e.* seventy-seven paise only.

Problem 51. The employees of a Coal Mines Ltd. have presented the following data in support of their contention that they are entitled to a wage adjustment. Dollar amounts shown represent the average weekly take-home pay of the group :

Year	*Pay (in \$)*	*Index*
1998	280	125
1999	300	130
2000	350	138.5
2001	420	150.4

(*a*) Compute the real wages based on the take-home pay and the price indices given.

(*b*) Compute the amount of pay needed in 2001 to provide buying power equal to that enjoyed in 1998. (*B. Com. Bombay*)

Solution:

$$\text{Real Wages} = \frac{\text{Money Wages}}{\text{Price Index}} \times 100$$

Year	*Pay in \$*	*Price Index*	*Real Wages*
1998	280	125	$\frac{280}{125} \times 100 = 224$
1999	300	130	$\frac{300}{130} \times 100 = 230.77$
2000	350	138.5	$\frac{350}{138.5} \times 100 = 252.70$
2001	420	150.4	$\frac{420}{150.4} \times 100 = 279.25$

$$\frac{420 \times 224}{279.25} = \mathbf{336.90}$$

Problem 52. From the figures given below calculate the index numbers of real wages taking 1998 as base :

Year	*Average Monthly wage*	*Consumer Price Index No.* (1998=100)
1998	220	100
1999	232	120
2000	243	130
2001	150	150
2002	171	180

(*M. Com. Delhi*)

Solution :

$$\text{Real Wage} = \frac{\text{Monthly Wage}}{\text{Price Index}} \times 100$$

Computation of Index Numbers

Year	*Average Monthly Wages*	*Consumer Price Index No.* 1998 = 100	*Real per capita income*	*Index NO. of Real Wages*
1998	220	100	220	$\frac{220}{100} \times 100 = 220$
1999	232	120	$\frac{232}{120} \times 100 = 193.33$	$\frac{193.33}{100} \times 100 = 193.33$
2000	243	130	$\frac{243}{130} \times 100 = 186.92$	$\frac{186.92}{100} \times 100 = 186.92$
2001	250	150	$\frac{250}{150} \times 100 = 166.66$	$\frac{166.66}{100} \times 100 = 166.66$
2002	271	180	$\frac{271}{180} \times 100 = 150.56$	$\frac{150.56}{100} \times 100 = 150.56$

CHAIN INDICES, SPLICING AND BASE SHIFTING

Problem 53. Construct chain index numbers from the link relatives given below :

Year	:	1998	1999	2000	2001	2002
Link index	:	100	105	95	115	102

(B.Com., Hons., Delhi)

Solution :

Computation of Chain Base Index

Year	*Link Relative*	*Chain Index Number*
1998	100	100
1999	105	$\frac{105}{100} \times 100 = 105$
2000	95	$\frac{95 \times 105}{100} = 99.75$
2001	115	$\frac{115 \times 99.75}{100} = 114.71$
2002	102	$\frac{102 \times 114.71}{100} = 117$

Problem 54. Convert the following fixed base index number into chain base index numbers :

Year	1998	1999	2000	2001	2002	2003
F.B.I	376	392	408	380	392	400

(B. Com. Punjab)

Solution :

Computation of Chain Base Index Numbers

Year	*F.B.I*	*Link Relatives*	*Chain Index*
1998	376	...	376
1999	392	$\frac{392}{376} \times 100 = 104.26$	$\frac{376 \times 104.26}{100} = 392$
2000	408	$\frac{408}{392} \times 100 = 104.08$	$\frac{392 \times 104.08}{100} = 408$
2001	380	$\frac{380}{408} \times 100 = 93.14$	$\frac{408 \times 93.14}{100} = 380$
2002	392	$\frac{392}{380} \times 100 = 103.16$	$\frac{380 \times 103.16}{100} = 392$
2003	400	$\frac{400}{392} \times 100 = 102.04$	$\frac{392 \times 102.4}{100} = 400$

Problem 55. From the chain index numbers given below, find fixed base index numbers :

Year	:	1998	1999	2000	2001	2002
Chain base index	:	80	110	120	90	140

(*B.Com., Madras*)

Solution :

Current Year Fixed Base Index =

$$\frac{\text{Current Year Chain base Index} \times \text{Previous Year F.B.I}}{100}$$

Computation of Fixed Base Index

Year	*Chain Base Index*	*Fixed base Index*
1998	80	80
1999	110	$\frac{80}{100} \times 110 = 88$
2000	120	$\frac{88}{100} \times 120 = 105.60$
2001	90	$\frac{105.6 \times 90}{100} = 95.04$
2002	140	$\frac{95.04 \times 140}{100} = 133.06$

Problem 56. Reconstruct the following index numbers by shifting base to : (*i*) 2000 and (*ii*) 2002.

Year	1995	1996	1997	1998	1999	2000	2001	2002
Index No.	120	150	160	180	200	200	210	240

Solution :

Computation of Index Numbers

Year	*Index Number*	2000	2002
1995	120	$\frac{120}{200} \times 100 = 60$	$\frac{120}{240} \times 100 = 50$
1996	150	$\frac{150}{200} \times 100 = 75$	$\frac{150}{240} \times 100 = 62.5$
1997	160	$\frac{160}{200} \times 100 = 80$	$\frac{160}{240} \times 100 = 66.66$
1998	180	$\frac{180}{200} \times 100 = 90$	$\frac{180}{240} \times 100 = 75$
1999	200	$\frac{200}{200} \times 100 = 100$	$\frac{200}{240} \times 100 = 83.33$
2000	200	$\frac{200}{200} \times 100 = 100$	$\frac{200}{240} \times 100 = 83.33$
2001	210	$\frac{210}{200} \times 100 = 105$	$\frac{210}{240} \times 100 = 87.5$
2002	240	$\frac{240}{200} \times 100 = 120$	$\frac{240}{240} \times 100 = 100$

Problem 57. Two sets of indices, one with 1989 as base and the other with 1997 as base are given below :

(*a*) Year	*Index No.*	(*b*) Year	*Index No.*
1989	100	1997	100
1990	110	1998	105
1991	120	1999	90
1992	190	2000	95
1993	300	2001	102
1994	330	2002	110
1995	360	2003	96
1996	390		
1997	400		

The index (*a*) with 1989 was discontiued in 1997. You are required to splice the second index number (*b*) with 1997 base to the first index number.

(*B.Com.*)

Solution :

$$\frac{\text{Index Number of Current Year} \times \text{Old Index of New Base Year}}{100}$$

Computation of I.Nos.

Year	*Index Number* (*a*) *with* 1989 *as base*	*Index Number* (*b*) *with* 1997 *as base*	
1989	100		
1990	110		
1991	120		
1992	190		
1993	300		
1994	330		
1995	360		
1996	390		
1997	400	100	$100 \times \frac{400}{100} = 400$
1998		105	$105 \times \frac{400}{100} = 420$
1999		90	$90 \times \frac{400}{100} = 360$
2000		95	$95 \times \frac{400}{100} = 380$
2001		102	$102 \times \frac{400}{100} = 408$
2002		110	$110 \times \frac{400}{100} = 440$
2003		96	$96 \times \frac{400}{100} = 384$

Problem 58. From the chain base index numbers given below, prepare fixed base index numbers and verify the answers.

Year	1999	2000	2001	2002	2003
Index	110	160	140	200	150

(*B.Com., Delhi*)

Solution : The formula to find out fixed base index :
Fixed base index of current year,

$$\frac{\text{Chain base index of the current year} \times \text{Fixed base index of the previous year}}{100}$$

Computation of Index Numbers

Year	*Chain base index*	*Conversion*	*Fixed base index*	*Verification Chain base Index*
1999	110		110.0	110
2000	160	$\frac{160}{100} \times 110$	176.0	$\frac{176}{110} \times 100 = 160$
2001	140	$\frac{140}{100} \times 176$	246.4	$\frac{246.4}{176} \times 100 = 140$
2002	200	$\frac{200}{100} \times 246.4$	492.8	$\frac{492.8}{246.4} \times 100 = 200$
2003	150	$\frac{150}{100} \times 492.8$	739.2	$\frac{739.2}{492.8} \times 100 = 150$

Problem 59. Calculate the Chain Base Index Numbers chained to 1999 from the average price of following three commodities :

Commodities	1999	2000	2001	2002.	2003
Wheat	4	6	8	10	12
Rice	16	20	24	30	36
Sugar	8	10	16	20	24

(*B.Com., Kurukshetra*)

Solution :

Computation of Chain Base Index

	Percentage based on preceding year				
Commodities	1999	2000	2001	2002	2003
Wheat	100	150	133.33	125	120
Rice	100	125	120.000	125	120
Sugar	100	125	160.00	125	120
Total of Link Relatives	300	400	413.33	375	360
Average Link Relatives	100	133.33	137.78	125	120
Chain Index (1999 = 100)	100	$\frac{100 \times 133.33}{100}$ = 133.33	$\frac{137.78 \times 133.33}{100}$ = 183.70	$\frac{125 \times 183.70}{100}$ 229.62	$\frac{120 \times 229.62}{100}$ = 275.54

Problem 60. From the following data of wholesale prices of cotton, construct Index Numbers by chain base method.

Year :	1994	1995	1996	1997	1998	1999	2000	2001	2002	2003
Price :	75	50	65	60	72	70	69	75	84	80

(*B. Com., Mysore*)

Solution : **Computation of Chain Base Index**

Year	*Price*	*Link Relatives*	*Chain Base Index*
1994	75	100	100
1995	50	$\frac{50}{75} \times 100 = 66.67$	$\frac{66.67 \times 100}{100} = 66.67$
1996	65	$\frac{65}{50} \times 100 = 130$	$\frac{130 \times 66.67}{100} = 86.67$
1997	60	$\frac{60}{65} \times 100 = 92.31$	$\frac{92.31 \times 86.67}{100} = 80$
1998	72	$\frac{72}{60} \times 100 = 120$	$\frac{120 \times 80}{100} = 96$
1999	70	$\frac{70}{72} \times 100 = 97.22$	$\frac{97.22 \times 96}{100} = 93.33$
2000	69	$\frac{69}{70} \times 100 = 98.57$	$\frac{98.57 \times 93.33}{100} = 92$
2001	75	$\frac{75}{69} \times 100 = 108.69$	$\frac{108.69 \times 92}{100} = 100$
2002	84	$\frac{84}{75} \times 100 = 112$	$\frac{112 \times 100}{100} = 112$
2003	80	$\frac{80}{84} \times 100 = 95.24$	$\frac{95.24 \times 112}{100} = 106.67$

Problem 61. The following table gives the money wages and cost of living index number based on 1997:

Year	:	1997	1998	1999	2000	2001	2002	2003
Wages	:	65	70	75	80	90	100	120
Cost of Living Index number	:	100	110	120	130	150	200	250

Calculate real wages (*M. Com. Rajasthan*)

Solution : **Computation of cost of living Index**

Year (1)	*Wages (in Rs.)* (2)	*Cost of Living Index Number* (3)	*Deflated money wages or Real Wages* $\frac{Col.(2)}{Col.(3)} \times 100$ (4)
1997	65	100	65
1998	70	110	$\frac{70}{110} \times 100 = 63.64$
1999	75	120	$\frac{75}{120} \times 100 = 62.5$
2000	80	130	$\frac{80}{130} \times 100 = 61.54$
2001	90	150	$\frac{90}{150} \times 100 = 60$
2002	100	200	$\frac{100}{120} \times 100 = 50$
2003	120	250	$\frac{120}{250} \times 100 = 48$

9

ANALYSIS OF TIME SERIES

(Methods of Measuring Trend)

1. **Graphic Method**
2. **Semi-Average Method**
3. **Moving Average Method**
4. **Method of Least Squares**
5. **Seasonal Variation**

FORMULAE

Method of Least Squares : The equation of the straight line trend or linear trend in the first degree Parabola is : $Yc = a + bX$	Yc = required trend value X = unit of time, a and b = Constants or unknowns.
The values of the constants a and b can be calculated by the following two normal equations $\Sigma Y = Na + b\Sigma X$ $\Sigma XY = a\Sigma X + b\Sigma X^2$	N = Number of years or months for which data are given
When $X = 0$ (when middle year is taken as origin) the equation to know the value of a and b is : $a = \frac{\Sigma Y}{N}, \quad b = \frac{\Sigma XY}{\Sigma X^2}$	
The Equation of the second degree Parabola is : $Y = a + bX + cX^2$	

Seasonal Variation

a. Method of Simple Averages (Weekly, Monthly or Quarterly)

b. Ratio to Trend Method

c. Ratio to Moving Average Method

d. Link Relative Method

Graphic Method and Semi-Average Method

Problem 1. With the help of the graph paper obtain the Trend values.

Year	1996	1997	1998	1999	2000	2001	2002
Value	65	85	95	75	100	80	130

(*B. Com.*)

Solution :

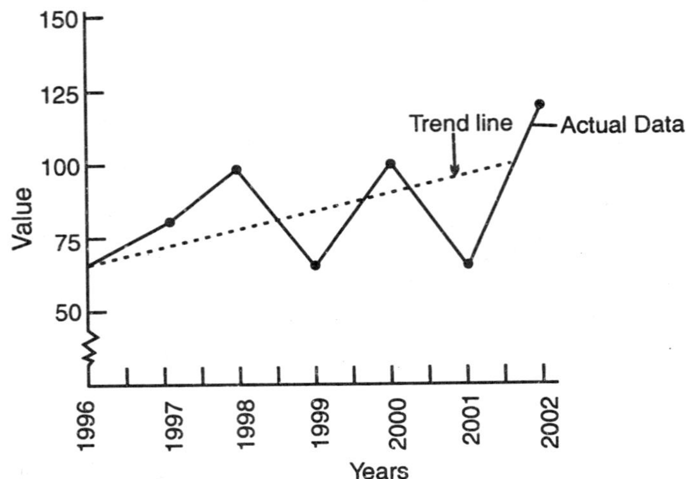

Problem 2. Draw a trend line by the method of semi-averages.

Year	1993	1994	1995	1996	1997	1998	1999	2000	2001	2002
Sales (' 000)	210	200	215	205	220	235	210	235	225	245

Solution :

Trend by the Method of Semi-averages

Year	*Sales ('000)*
1993	210
1994	200
1995	$215 = \frac{1050}{5} = 210$
1996	205
1997	220
1998	235
1999	210
2000	$235 = \frac{1150}{5} = 230$
2001	225
2002	245

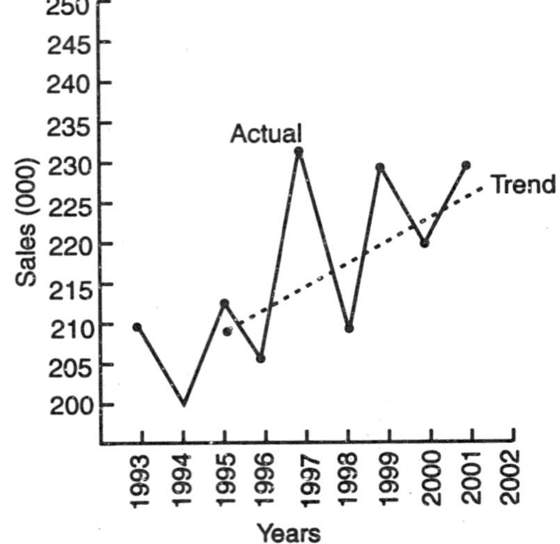

Problem 3. The following figures are given relating to the output in a factory. Draw a trend line with the help of method of semi-averages.

Years	*Output (Units)*
1996	600
1997	800
1998	1000
1999	800
2000	1200
2001	1000
2002	1400

(*B., Com.*)

Solution :

Trend by Method of Semi-averages

Year	*Output (in units)*
1996	600
1997	$800 = \frac{2400}{3} = 800$
1998	1000
1999	800 Middle item left out
2000	1200
2001	$1000 = \frac{3600}{3} = 1200$
2002	1400

Production in Units

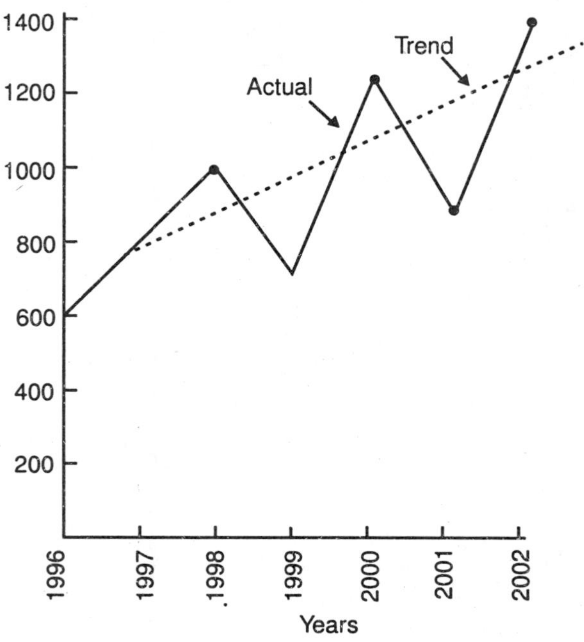

Moving Average Method

Problem 4. The following figures relate to the profits of a commercial concern for 8 years. Find the 3 yearly moving average.

Years	*Profits (Rs.)*	*Years*	*Profits (Rs.)*
1995	15,420	1999	26,120
1996	14,470	2000	31,950
1997	15,520	2001	35,370
1998	21,020	2002	35,670

(*B. Com., Osmania*)

Solution :

Computation of Trend Method of 3 Yearly Moving Average

Years	*Profits (Rs)*	*3 Yearly Moving Total*	*3 Yearly Moving Average*
1995	15,420	—	—
1996	14,470	45,410	15136.66 or 15,137
1997	15,520	51,010	17003.33 or 17,003
1998	21,020	62,660	20886.66 or 20,887
1999	26,120	79,090	26363.33 or 26,363
2000	31,950	93,440	31146.66 or 31,147
2001	35,370	1,02,990	34330
2002	35,670	—	—

Problem 5. Find the centred 4-year moving averages from the following time series data :

Years	:	1995	1996	1997	1998	1999	2000	2001	2002
Output	:	30.1	45.4	39.3	41.4	42.2	46.4	46.6	49.2

(*I.C.W.A*)

Solution :

Computation of Trend Method of 4 Yearly Moving Average

Years	*Productions (mn. Ibs)*	*4 Yearly Total*	*4 Yearly Moving average*	*4 Yearly moving average centred*
1995	30.1			
1996	45.4			
		156.2	39.05	
				40.57
1997	39.3			
		168.3	42.08	
				42.21
1998	41.4			
		169.03	42.33	
				43.24

Continued.

1999	42.2			
		176.6	44.15	
				45.13
2000	46.4			
		184.4	46.1	
2001	46.6			
2002	49.2			

Problem 6. Calculate the long-term trend and short-term oscillations with a three-year period from the following data :

Year	*Output of tea (tones)*	*Year*	*Output of tea (tonnes)*
1995	1632	1999	2620
1996	1557	2000	3120
1997	1652	2001	3236
1998	2100	2002	3562

(*B. Com., Kerala*)

Solution :

Computation of 3 Yearly Moving Average

Year (1)	*Output of tea (tonnes)* y (2)	3 *Yearly Moving Totals* (3)	3 *Yearly Moving Average (Trend Value)* (4)	*Short-term Oscillations* $5 = \frac{2}{4} \times 100$ (5)
1995	1632	—	—	—
1996	1557	4841	1613.67	96.49
1997	1652	5309	1769.67	93.35
1998	2100	6372	2124.00	98.87
1999	2620	7840	2613.33	100.26
2000	3120	8976	2992.00	104.28
2001	3236	9918	3306.00	97.88
2002	3562	—	—	—

Problem 7. Production of rice in a district during the last 10 years is given below :

Year	*Production (in tons)*	*Year*	*Production (in tons)*
1993	11,200	1998	14,500
1994	12,300	1999	11,600
1995	10,600	2000	14,300
1996	13,400	2001	13,600
1997	13,800	2002	15,400

Using a 3-yearly moving average, indicate the trend in the production of rice in the district.

(*B. Com., Andhra*)

Solution :

Computation of 3 Yearly Moving Average

Year	*Production (in tons)*	*3 Yearly Moving Total*	*3 Yearly Moving Average*
1993	11,200	–	–
1994	12,300	34,100	11,366.7
1995	10,600	36,300	12,100.0
1996	13,400	37,800	12,600.0
1997	13,800	41,700	13,900.0
1998	14,500	39,900	13,300.0
1999	11,600	40,400	13,466.7
2000	14,300	39,500	13,166.7
2001	13,600	43,300	14,433.3
2002	15,400	–	–

Problem 8. Construct a four-yearly centered moving average from the following data :

Year	:	1940	1950	1960	1970	1980	1990	2000
Imported cotton consumption in India (in '000 bales)	:	129	131	106	91	95	84	93

(*I.C.W.A.*)

Solution :

Computation of 4 Yearly Moving Average

Year	*Imported Cotton consumption (in '000 bales)*	*4 Yearly moving totals*	*4 Yearly Moving average*	*4 Yearly Moving average centered*
1940	129	–		
1950	131	–		
		457	114.25	
				110.00
1960	106			
		423	105.75	
				99.88
1970	91			
		376	94.00	
				92.38
1980	95			
		363	90.75	
1990	84	–		
2000	93	–		

Problem 9. Calculate trend values by taking 5 yearly period of moving average from the data given below :

Year	*Production (in tonnes)*
1987	4
1988	5
1989	6
1990	7
1991	9
1992	6
1993	5
1994	7
1995	8
1996	7
1997	6
1998	8
1999	9
2000	10
2001	7
2002	9

(*M.B.A, Rohtak; B.Com., Madras*)

Solution :

Computation of 5 Yearly Moving Average

Year	*Production (m. tones)*	*5 Yearly Moving Total*	*5 Yearly Moving Average*
1987	4	—	—
1988	5	—	—
1989	6	31	6.2
1990	7	33	6.6
1991	9	33	6.6
1992	6	34	6.8
1993	5	35	7.0
1994	7	33	6.6
1995	8	33	6.6
1996	7	36	7.2
1997	6	38	7.6
1998	8	40	8.0
1999	9	40	8.0
2000	10	43	8.6
2001	7	—	—
2002	9	—	—

Problem 10. Work out the centered 4 yearly moving average for the following data :

Year	Tonnage of goods carried	Year	Tonnage of goods carried
1991	2204	1997	2904
1992	2500	1998	3098
1993	2360	1999	3172
1994	2680	2000	2952
1995	2424	2001	3248
1996	2634	2002	3172

(*Osmania B. Com*

Solution :

Computation of 4 yearly Moving Average

Year	Tonnage of goods carried	4 Yearly Moving Total	4 Yearly Moving average	4 Yearly moving average centred
1991	2,204	—		
1992	2,500	—		
		9,744	2436	
1993	2,360			2463.5
		9,964	2491	
1994	2,680			2507.75
		10,098	2524.5	
1995	2,424			2592.5
		10,642	2660.5	
1996	2,634			2712.75
		11,060	2765	
1997	2,904			2858.5
		11,808	2952	
1998	3,098			2991.75
		12,126	3031.5	
1999	3,172			3074.5
		12,470	3117.5	
2000	2,952			3126.75
		12,544	3136	
2001	3,248	—	—	—
2002	3,172	—	—	—

Problem 11. From the following data calculate the 4-yearly moving average and determine the trend values. Find the short term fluctuations. Plot the original data and the trend on a graph.

Year	Value	Year	Value
1993	50.0	1998	38.1
1994	36.5	1999	32.6
1995	43.0	2000	41.7
1996	44.5	2001	41.1
1997	38.9	2002	33.8

(*C.A. Inter.*

Solution :

Computation of 4 Yearly Moving Average

Year (1)	*Value* (2)	*4 Yearly moving Total* (3)	*4 Yearly moving average* (4)	*4 Yearly moving average centred* (5)	*Short term oscillation* $= \frac{2}{5} \times 100$ (6)
1993	50.0	—			
1994	36.5	—			
		174.0	43.50		
1995	43.0			42.1	102.14
		162.9	40.73		
1996	44.5			40.9	108.80
		164.5	41.13		
1997	38.9			39.8	97.74
		154.1	38.53		
1998	38.1			38.2	99.74
		151.3	37.83		
1999	32.6			38.1	85.56
		153.5	38.38		
2000	41.7			37.8	110.32
		149.2	37.30		
2001	41.1	—			
2002	33.8	—			

Problem 12. Compute the trend by four week moving average for the following data :

Where, x = *Week;* y = *Production*

x	y	x	y
1	82	11	75
2	73	12	73
3	74	13	75
4	75	14	76
5	73	15	75
6	72	16	75
7	76	17	78
8	76	18	76
9	74	19	78
10	75	20	79

(*B. Com., Bombay*)

Solution :

Computation of 4 Week Moving Average

Week	*Production*	*4-Week Moving Total*	*4-Week Moving Average*	*4-Week Moving Average Centred*
1	82			
2	73			
		304	76.0	
3	74			74.9
		295	73.8	
4	75			73.65
		294	73.5	
5	73			73.75
		296	74.0	
6	72			74.15
		297	74.3	
7	76			74.4
		298	74.5	
8	76			74.9
		301	75.3	
9	74			75.15
		300	75.0	
10	75			74.65
		297	74.3	
11	75			74.40
		298	74.5	
12	73			74.65
		299	74.8	
13	75			74.8
		299	74.8	
14	76			75.05
		301	75.3	
15	75			75.65
		304	76.0	
16	75			76.0
		304	76.0	
17	78			76.4
		307	76.8	
18	76			77.3
		311	77.8	
19	78			
20	79			

Problem 13. Calculate a 7 year moving average for the following data on the numbe of commercial and industrial failures in a country during 1987–2002.

Year	No. of failures	Year	No. of failures
1987	23	1995	9
1988	26	1996	13
1989	28	1997	11
1990	32	1998	14
1991	20	1999	12
1992	12	2000	9
1993	12	2001	3
1994	10	2002	1

(*C.A. Nv.*)

Solution :

Computation of 7 Yearly Moving Average

Year	No. of Failures	7 Yearly Moving Total	7 Yearly Moving Average
1987	23	—	—
1988	26	—	—
1989	28	—	—
1990	32	153	21.86 or 22
1991	20	140	20.00 or 20
1992	12	123	17.57 or 18
1993	12	108	15.43 or 15
1994	10	87	12.43 or 12
1995	9	81	11.57 or 12
1996	13	81	11.57 or 12
1997	11	78	11.14 or 11
1998	14	71	10.14 or 10
1999	12	63	9.0 or 9
2000	9	—	—
2001	3	—	—
2002	1	—	—

Problem 14. Assuming a four yearly cycle, calculate the trend by the method of moving average from the following data relating to the production of tea in India.

Year	Production (lbs.)	Year	Production (lbs.)
1993	464	1998	540
1994	515	1999	557
1995	518	2000	571
1996	467	2001	586
1997	502	2002	612

(*I.C.W.A*)

Solution :

Computation of 4-Yearly Moving Average

Year	*Production of tea (lbs)*	*4-Yearly Moving Total*	*4-Yearly Moving Average*	*4-Yearly Moving Average Centred*
1993	464			—
1994	515			—
		1964	491.00	
1995	518			495.8
		2002	500.50	
1996	467			503.6
		2027	506.75	
1997	502			511.6
		2066	516.50	
1998	540			529.5
		2170	542.50	
1999	557			553.0
		2254	563.50	
2000	571			572.5
		2326	581.50	
2001	586			
2002	612			

Problem 15. The following table shows the United States average monthly production of bituminous coal, in millions of tons, for years 1992 to 2002.

Year	*Average monthly production of coal in million tonnes*
1992	45
1993	38
1994	52
1995	43
1996	50
1997	54
1998	40
1999	48
2000	53
2001	60
2002	65

Calculate (i) 4 year moving average and (ii) 4 year centred moving average.

(*B.Com. Bombay*)

Solution :

Computation of Four-Yearly Moving Average

Year	*Average monthly production of cool in million tons*	*4-Yearly Moving Total*	*4-Yearly Moving Average Average*	*4-Yearly Moving average Centred*
1992	45	—	—	
1993	38	—	—	
		178	44.5	
1994	52			45.13
		183	45.75	
1995	43			47.75
		199	49.75	
1996	50			48.25
		187	46.75	
1997	54			47.38
		192	48	
1998	40			48.38
		195	48.75	
1999	48			49.5
		201	50.25	
2000	53			53.38
		226	56.5	
2001	60	—		
2002	65	—		

Problem 16. Estimate the trend values using the data given below by taking a four-yearly moving average :

Year	*Value*
1991	12
1992	25
1993	39
1994	54
1995	70
1996	87
1997	105
1998	100
1999	82
2000	65
2001	49
2002	34

Solution :

Computation of 4 Yearly Moving Average

Year	*Value*	*4-Yearly moving totals*	*4-Yearly Moving Average*	*4-Yearly Moving average centred*
1991	12	—	—	—
1992	25	—	—	—
		130	32.5	
1993	39			39.75
		188	47.0	
1994	54			54.75
		250	62.5	
1995	70			70.75
		316	79.0	
1996	87			84.75
		362	90.5	
1997	105			92.00
		374	93.5	
1998	100			90.75
		352	88.0	
1999	82			81.00
		296	74.0	
2000	65			65.75
		230	57.5	
2001	49	—	—	—
2002	34	—	—	—

Problem 17. The following data give daily sales of a shop observing a five-day week over four successive weeks. Determine the period of the moving averages and calculate the moving averages accordingly.

Day	:	1	2	3	4	5	6	7	8	9	10
Sales	:	26	29	35	47	51	26	32	37	46	53
Day	:	11	12	13	14	15	16	17	18	19	20
Sales	:	28	30	36	46	54	28	31	36	46	54

(*C.A. Intermediate*)

Solution :

Computation of 5-Day Moving Average

Day	*Sales*	*5-Day Moving Total*	*5-Day Moving Average*
1	26	—	—
2	29	—	—
3	35	188	37.6
4	47	188	37.6
5	51	191	38.2
6	26	193	38.6
7	32	192	38.4

Continued.

8	37	194	38.8
9	46	196	39.2
10	53	194	38.8
11	28	193	38.6
12	30	193	38.6
13	36	194	38.8
14	46	194	38.8
15	54	195	39.0
16	28	195	39.0
17	31	195	39.0
18	36	195	39.0
19	46	—	—
20	54	—	—

Problem 18. Take a five-yearly period of moving average and determine short-term oscillations from the following data :

Year	*Production*
1991	14
1992	17
1993	22
1994	28
1995	26
1996	18
1997	20
1998	24
1999	25
2000	29
2001	30
2002	23

(*B. Com. Bombay*)

Solution :

5-Yearly Moving Average

Year	*Production* ('000) (*Y*)	*5-Yearly Moving Total*	*5-Yearly Moving Average* (*Yc*)	*Short-term Oscillation* (*Y* − *Yc*)
1991	14	—	—	—
1992	17	—	—	—
1993	22	107	21.4	0.6
1994	28	111	22.2	5.8
1995	26	114	22.8	3.2
1996	18	116	23.2	−5.2
1997	20	113	22.6	−2.6
1998	24	116	23.2	0.8
1999	25	128	25.6	−0.6
2000	29	131	26.2	2.8
2001	30	—	—	—
2002	23	—	—	—

METHOD OF LEAST SQUARE

Problem 19.

Year	:	1993	1994	1995	1996	1997	1998	1999	2000	2001	2002
No. of Students	:	332	317	357	392	402	405	410	427	405	438

Draw a graph to represent the moving averages.

Solution :

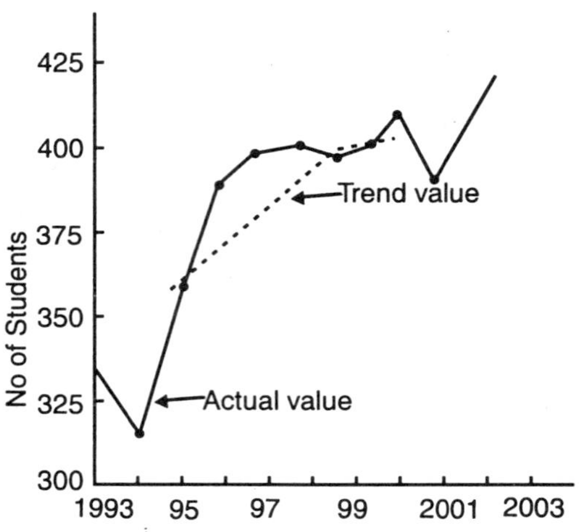

(*B. Com., Bombay*)

Computation of 5-Year Moving Average

Year	*5-Years Moving No. of Students*	*5-Years Moving Total*	*Average*
1993	332	—	—
1994	317	—	—
1995	357	1800	360.0
1996	392	1873	374.6 or 375
1997	402	1966	393.2 or 393
1998	405	2036	407.2 or 407
1999	410	2049	409.8 or 410
2000	427	2085	417.0
2001	405	—	—
2002	438	—	—

Problem 20. Fit a straight line trend by the method of least squares to the following data and calculate trend values :

Year	:	1996	1997	1998	1999	2000
Sales of T.V. Sets (in thousands)	:	4	6	7	8	10

Estimate the sales for the year 2005.

(*M. Com., HPU*)

Solution :

Computation of Trend Value

Year	*Sales of T.V.* ('000) Y	*Deviation from* 1998 X	X^2	*Trend value* XY	Yc
1996	4	−2	4	−8	4.2
1997	6	−1	1	−6	5.6
1998	7	0	0	0	7
1999	8	1	1	8	8.4
2000	10	2	4	20	9.8
$N = 5$	$\Sigma Y = 35$	$\Sigma X = 0$	$\Sigma X^2 = 10$	$\Sigma XY = 14$	

$$Yc = a + bX$$

Since = $X = 0$,

$$a = \frac{\Sigma Y}{N} = \frac{35}{5} = 7$$

$$b = \frac{\Sigma XY}{\Sigma X^2} = \frac{14}{10} = \mathbf{1.4}$$

$$Yc = 7 + 1.4X$$

$$Y_{1996} = 7 + (1.4 \times -2) = 7 - 2.8 = 4.2$$

$$Y_{1997} = 7 + (1.4 \times X - 1) = 7 - 1.4 = 5.6$$

$$Y_{1998} = 7 + (1.4 \times 0) = 7 + 0 = 7$$

$$Y_{1999} = 7 + (1.4 \times 1) = 7 + 1.4 = 8.4$$

$$Y_{2000} = 7 + (1.4 \times 2) = 7 + 2.8 = 9.8$$

For2005, $X = 7$

$$Y_{2005} = 7 + (1.4 \times 7) = 7 + 9.8 = \mathbf{16.8}$$

Thus the estimated sales of T.V. sets for the year 2005 will be 16.8 thousands.

Problem 21. Below are given the figures of production in '000 quintals of a sugar factory :

Year	*Production* ('000) *quintals*	*Year*	*Production* ('000) *quintals*
1994	80	1998	94
1995	90	1999	99
1996	92	2000	92
1997	83		

(*i*) Fit a straight line trend to these figures.

(*ii*) Plot these figures on graph and show the trend line.

(*B.Com Madurai, Calicut*)

Solution :

Fitting the Straight Line Trend

Year	*Production* ('000) (*Y*)	*Deviation from 1997 X*	X^2	XY	*Trend Value Yc*	*Short-term oscillations Y– Yc*
1994	80	−3	9	−240	84	−4
1995	90	−2	4	−180	86	+4
1996	92	−1	1	−92	88	+4
1997	83	0	0	−0	90	−7
1998	94	1	1	94	92	+2
1999	99	2	4	198	94	+5
2000	92	3	9	276	96	−4
$N = 7$	$\Sigma Y = 630$	$\Sigma X = 0$	$\Sigma X^2 = 28$	$\Sigma XY = 56$		

$$\text{Straight line trend is } Yc = a + bx$$
$$\Sigma Y = Na + b\Sigma x$$
$$\Sigma XY = a\Sigma x + b\,\Sigma x^2$$

Putting the values in the equation,

$$630 = 7a + 0 \qquad \therefore \qquad a = \frac{630}{7} = \mathbf{90}$$

$$56 = 0 + 28b \qquad \therefore \qquad b = \frac{56}{28} = \mathbf{2}$$

Thus, $Yc = 90 + 2x$

1994 $: x = -3;$ $Yc = 90 + 2(-3) = 84$

1995 $: x = -2;$ $Yc = 90 + 2(-2) = 86$

1996 $: x = -1;$ $Yc = 90 + 2(-1) = 88$

1997 $: x = 0;$ $Yc = 90 + 2(0) = 90$

1998 $: x = 1;$ $Yc = 90 + 2(1) = 92$

1999 $: x = 2;$ $Yc = 90 + 2(2) + 94$

2000 $: x = 3;$ $Yc = 90 + 2(3) = 96$

Alternatively

Deviation is taken from first year

Year	*Production* ('000) (*Y*)	*Deviation from* 1994	X^2	XY	*Trend Value Yc*	*Short term oscillation* $Y - Yc$
1994	80	0	0	0	84	−4
1995	90	1	1	90	86	+4
1996	92	2	4	184	88	+4
1997	83	3	9	249	90	−7
1998	94	4	16	376	92	+2
1999	99	5	25	495	94	+5
2000	92	6	36	552	96	−4
$N = 7$	$\Sigma Y = 630$	$\Sigma X = 21$	$\Sigma X^2 = 91$	$\Sigma XY = 1946$		

$$Yc = a + bx$$
$$\Sigma Y = Na + b\Sigma x$$
$$\Sigma XY = a\Sigma x + b\Sigma x^2$$

Substituting the values in the equations,

$$630 = 7a + 21b \quad (1)$$
$$1946 = 21a + 91b \quad (2)$$

Multiplying the equation (1) by (3)

$$1890 = 21a + 63b \quad (3)$$

Subtract (3) from (2)

$$1946 = 21a + 91b$$
$$1890 = 21a + 63b$$
$$56 = +28b$$
$$\therefore \quad b = \frac{56}{28} = 2$$

Substituting in equation (1)

$$630 = 7a + 21 \times 2$$
$$630 = 7a + 42$$
(or) $$7a = 630 - 42 = 588$$
$$\therefore \quad a = \frac{588}{7} = \mathbf{84}$$

Thus, $Yc = a + bx$

$1994; x$	$= 0;$	$Yc = 84 + 2(0) = 84$
$1995; x$	$= 1;$	$Yc = 84 + 2(1) = 86$
$1996; x$	$= 2;$	$Yc = 84 + 2(2) = 88$
$1997; x$	$= 3;$	$Yc = 84 + 2(3) = 90$
$1998; x$	$= 4;$	$Yc = 84 + 2(4) = 92$
$1999; x$	$= 5;$	$Yc = 84 + 2(5) = 94$
$2000; x$	$= 6;$	$Yc = 84 + 2(6) = 96$

Problem 22. Fit a straight line trend by the method of least square to the following data, relating to the net profits of a public sector concern.

Year	:	1996	1997	1998	1999	2000	2001	2002
Profits (Rs.)	:	300	700	600	800	900	700	1,000

(B. Com., Osmania)

Solution :

Computation of Trend Value

Year	*Profits (Rs) Y*	*Deviation from* 1999	*XY*	X^2	*Trend Value Yc*
1996	300	−3	−900	9	457.2
1997	700	−2	−1400	4	542.9
1998	600	−1	−600	1	628.6
1999	800	0	0	0	714.3
2000	900	1	900	1	800.0
2001	700	2	1400	4	885.7
2002	1000	3	3000	9	971.4
$N = 7$	$\Sigma Y = 5000$	$\Sigma X = 0$	$\Sigma XY = 2400$	$\Sigma X^2 = 28$	

$$Yc = a + bx$$

Since, $X = 0$

$$a = \frac{\Sigma Y}{N} = \frac{5000}{7} = \mathbf{714.3}$$

$$b = \frac{\Sigma XY}{\Sigma X^2} = \frac{2400}{28} = \mathbf{85.7}$$

Trend Value $Yc = 714.3 + 85.7x$

$$Y_{1996} = 714.3 + (85.7 \times -3) = 714.3 - 257.1 = 457.2$$
$$Y_{1997} = 714.3 + (85.7 \times -2) = 714.3 - 171.4 = 542.9$$
$$Y_{1998} = 714.3 + (85.7 \times -1) = 714.3 - 85.7 = 628.6$$
$$Y_{1999} = 714.3 + (85.7 \times 0) = 714.3 - 0 = 714.3$$
$$Y_{2000} = 714.3 + (85.7 \times 1) = 714.3 + 85.7 = 800.0$$
$$Y_{2001} = 714.3 + (85.7 \times 2) = 714.3 + 171.4 = 885.5$$
$$Y_{2002} = 714.3 + (85.7 \times 3) = 714.3 + 257.1 = 971.4$$

Problem 23. Calculate trend values by the method of least square from the data given below and estimate the sales for 2003.

Year	:	1996	1997	1998	1999	2000
Sales of Co. ('000,000)	:	70	74	80	86	90

(*B. Com. Banaras*)

Solution :

Calculation of Trend Values by the Method of Least Square

Year	*Sales Y*	*Deviation from 1998*		X^2	*Yc*
		X	*XY*		
1996	70	−2	−140	4	69.6
1997	74	−1	−74	1	74.8
1998	80	0	0	0	80.0
1999	86	1	86	1	85.2
2000	90	2	180	4	90.4
$N = 5$	$\Sigma Y = 400$	$\Sigma X = 0$	$\Sigma XY = 52$	$\Sigma X^2 = 10$	$\Sigma Yc = 400$

$$Yc = a + bx$$

Since, $\Sigma X = 0$

$$a = \frac{\Sigma Y}{N} = \frac{400}{5} = \mathbf{80}$$

$$b = \frac{\Sigma XY}{\Sigma X^2} = \frac{52}{10} = \mathbf{5.2}$$

Hence $Yc = 80 + 5.2x$

$$\therefore \quad Y_{1996} = 80 + 5.2\,(-2)$$
$$= 80 - 10.4 = 69.6$$
$$Y_{1997} = 80 - 5.2 = 74.8$$
$$Y_{1998} = 80 - 0 = 80.0$$
$$Y_{1999} = 80 + 5.2 = 85.2$$
$$Y_{2000} = 80 + 10.4 = 90.4$$

For 2003, X will be 5. Putting $X = 5$ in the equation

$$Y_{2003} = 80 + 5.2\,(5) = 80 + 26$$
$$= \mathbf{106}.$$

Thus the estimated sales for the year 2003 are Rs. 106 ('000,000)

Problem 24. The following are the annual profits, in thousands of rupees, in a certain business :

Year	:	1996	1997	1998	1999	2000	2001	2002
Profits (in Rs.'000)	:	60	72	75	65	80	85	95

(*a*) Use the method of Least Squares to fit a straight line to the above data.

(*b*) Also make an estimate of the profits for the year 2004.

(*B. Com. Bombay*)

Solution :

Computation of Trend Value

Year	*Profits* (*in '000 Rs.*) *Y*	*Deviation from* 1999 (X)	*XY*	X^2	*Yc*
1996	60	−3	−180	9	61.42
1997	72	−2	−144	4	66.28
1998	75	−1	−75	1	71.14
1999	65	0	0	0	76.00
2000	80	1	80	1	80.86
2001	85	2	170	4	85.72
2002	95	3	285	9	90.58
$N = 7$	$\Sigma Y = 532$	$\Sigma X = 0$	$\Sigma XY = 136$	$\Sigma X^2 = 28$	

$$Yc = a + bx$$

Since, $\Sigma X = 0$

$$a = \frac{\Sigma Y}{N} = \frac{532}{7} = \mathbf{76}$$

$$b = \frac{\Sigma XY}{\Sigma X^2} = \frac{136}{28} = \mathbf{4.86}$$

Hence $Yc = 76 + 4.86x$

$Y_{1996} = 76 + 4.86\,(-3) = 76 - 14.58 = 61.42$

$Y_{1997} = 76 + 4.86\,(-2) = 76 - 9.72 = 66.28$

$Y_{1998} = 76 + 4.86\,(-1) = 76 - 4.86 = 71.14$

$Y_{1999} = 76 + 4.86(0) = 76.00$

$Y_{2000} = 76 + 4.86\,(1) = 76 + 4.86 = 80.86$

$Y_{2001} = 76 + 4.86\,(2) = 76 + 9.72 = 85.72$

$Y_{2002} = 76 + 4.86\,(3) = 76 + 14.58 = 90.58$

For 2004, X will be 5. Putting $X = 5$ in the equation

$$Y_{2004} = 76 + 4.86\,(5) = 76 + 24.3 = \mathbf{100.3}$$

Thus, the expected profit for 2004 is **Rs. 1,00,300.**

Problem 25. Fit a straight line trend to the following data on the domestic demand for motor fuel.

Year	*Average monthly demand (million barrels)*	*Year*	*Average monthly demand (million barrels)*
1992	61	1998	96
1993	66	1999	100
1994	72	2000	103
1995	76	2001	110
1996	82	2002	114
1997	90		

(*B. A., Econ., Madurai*)

Solution :

Computation of Trend Value

Year	*Y*	*Time Deviation from mid year 1997(X)*	*XY*	X^2	*Trend value Yc*
1992	61	−5	25	−305	61.13
1993	66	−4	16	−264	66.54
1994	72	−3	9	−216	71.95
1995	76	−2	4	−152	77.36
1996	82	−1	1	−82	82.77
1997	90	0	0	0	88.18
1998	96	1	1	96	93.59
1999	100	2	4	200	99.0
2000	103	3	9	309	104.41
2001	110	4	16	440	109.82
2002	114	5	25	570	115.23
$N = 11$	$\Sigma Y = 970$	$\Sigma X = 0$	$\Sigma XY = 110$	$\Sigma X^2 = 596$	

$$Yc = a + bx$$

Since $\Sigma X = 0$ $\qquad a = \frac{\Sigma Y}{N} = \frac{970}{11} = \mathbf{88.18}$

$$b = \frac{\Sigma XY}{\Sigma X^2} = \frac{596}{110} = \mathbf{5.41}$$

Trend value $\qquad Yc = 88.18 + 5.41\ X$

$$Y_{1992} = 88.18 + (5.41 \times -5) = 88.18 - 27.05 = 61.13$$
$$Y_{1993} = 88.18 + (5.41 \times -4) = 88.18 - 21.64 = 66.54$$
$$Y_{1994} = 88.18 + (5.41 \times -3) = 88.18 - 16.23 = 71.95$$
$$Y_{1995} = 88.18 + (5.41 \times -2) = 88.18 - 10.82 = 77.36$$
$$Y_{1996} = 88.18 + (5.41 \times -1) = 88.18 - 5.41 = 82.77$$
$$Y_{1997} = 88.18 + (5.41 \times 0) = 88.18 - 0 = 88.18$$
$$Y_{1998} = 88.18 + (5.41 \times 1) = 88.18 + 5.41 = 93.59$$
$$Y_{1999} = 88.18 + (5.41 \times 2) = 88.18 + 10.82 = 99.0$$
$$Y_{2000} = 88.18 + (5.41 \times 3) = 88.18 + 16.23 = 104.41$$
$$Y_{2001} = 88.18 + (5.41 \times 4) = 88.18 + 21.64 = 109.82$$
$$Y_{2002} = 88.18 + (5.41 \times 5) = 88.18 + 27.05 = 115.23$$

Problem 26. The following table shows the number of salesmen working in a certain concern.

Year	:	1998	1999	2000	2001	2002
No. of Salesman	:	28	38	46	40	56

Use the method of least squares to fit a straight line trend and estimate the number of salesmen in 2003.

(*B. Com., Bombay*)

Solution :

Computation of Trend Value

Year	*No. of Salesmen Y*	*Deviation from 2000 (X)*	X^2	XY	*Trend Value Yc*
1998	28	−2	4	−56	30.0
1999	38	−1	1	−38	35.8
2000	46	0	0	0	41.6
2001	40	1	1	40	47.4
2002	56	2	4	112	53.2
$N = 5$	$\Sigma Y = 208$	$\Sigma X = 0$	$\Sigma X^2 = 10$	$\Sigma XY = 58$	

Trend Value $\qquad Yc = a + bx$

Since, $\Sigma X = 0$, $\qquad a = \frac{\Sigma Y}{N} = \frac{208}{5} = \mathbf{41.6}$

$$b = \frac{\Sigma XY}{\Sigma X^2} = \frac{58}{10} = \mathbf{5.8}$$

$$Yc = 41.6 + 5.8X$$

$$Y_{1998} = 41.6 + (5.8 \times -2) = 41.6 - 11.6 = 30.0$$

Similarly the other trend values can be obtained by putting

$$X = -1, 0, 1 \text{ and } 2.$$

For2003, $X = 3$

$$Y_{2003} = 41.6 + (5.8 \times 3) = 41.6 + 17.4 = \mathbf{59}$$

Hence the estimated number of salesmen in 2003 = 59

Problem 27. The following data give the total expenditure incurred by a certain college. Find the trend value.

Year	:	1996	1997	1998	1999	2000	2001	2002
Expenditure (*Rs. In Lakhs*)	:	1.5	1.8	2.0	2.3	2.4	2.6	3.0

Estimate the expenditure likely to be incurred by the college during 2003.

(*B. Com. Delhi*)

Solution :

Year	*Expenditure Y*	*Deviation from 1999* (*X*)	X^2	XY	*Trend Value Yc*
1996	1.5	−3	9	−4.5	1.54
1997	1.8	−2	4	−3.6	1.77
1998	2.0	−1	1	−2.0	2.00
1999	2.3	0	0	0	2.23
2000	2.4	1	1	2.4	2.46
2001	2.6	2	4	5.2	2.69
2002	3.0	3	9	9.0	2.92
$N = 7$	$\Sigma Y = 15.6$	$\Sigma X = 0$	$\Sigma X^2 = 28$	$\Sigma XY = 6.5$	

$$Yc = a + bX$$

Since, $\Sigma X = 0$,

$$a = \frac{\Sigma Y}{N} = \frac{15.6}{7} = \mathbf{2.23}$$

$$b = \frac{\Sigma XY}{\Sigma X^2} = \frac{6.5}{28} = \mathbf{0.23}$$

Trend Value $Yc = 2.23 + 0.23X$

$$Y_{1996} = 2.23 + (0.23X - 3) = 2.23 - 0.69 = 1.54$$

Similarly the other values can be obtained by putting

$$X = -2, -1, 0, 1, 2 \text{ and } 3.$$

$$Y_{2003} = 2.23 + (0.23 \times 4) = 2.23 + 0.92 = \mathbf{3.15}$$

The expenditure likely to be incurred by the college during 2003 is Rs. 3.15 lakhs.

Problem 28. Fit the straight line trend to the following figures by the method of least squares :

Year	:	1995	1996	1997	1998	1999	2000	2001
Sales in ('000 *tonnes*)	:	50	60	65	63	68	70	72

(*B. Com. Mysore*)

Solution :

Computation of Straight Line Trend

Year	*Sales in '000 tons Y*	*Deviation from mid-year 1998 (X)*	X^2	XY	*Trend Value Yc*
1995	50	−3	9	−150	54.46
1996	60	−2	4	−120	57.64
1997	65	−1	1	−65	60.82
1998	63	0	0	0	64.00
1999	68	1	1	68	67.18
2000	70	2	4	140	70.36
2001	72	3	9	216	73.54
$N = 7$	$\Sigma Y = 448$	$\Sigma X = 0$	$\Sigma X^2 = 28$	$\Sigma XY = 89$	

The equation of the straight line trend :

$$Yc = a + bX$$

Since, $\Sigma X = 0, a = \frac{\Sigma Y}{N} = \frac{448}{7} = \mathbf{64}$

$$b = \frac{\Sigma XY}{\Sigma X^2} = \frac{89}{28} = \mathbf{3.18}$$

Trend Value $Yc = 64 + (3.18X)$

$$Y_{1995} = 64 + (3.18 \times -3) = 64 - 9.54 = 54.46$$

Similarly the other value can be obtained by putting

$$X = -2, -1, 0, 1 \textit{ etc.}$$

Problem 29. Fit a straight line trend to the data given below by the method of least square :

Year	:	1996	1997	1998	1999	2000	2001	2002
Gross ex-factory value of output (Rs. crores)	:	672	824	968	1205	1464	1758	2058

(B. Com. Delhi,)

Solution :

Computation of Trend Value

Year	*Output Y*	*Deviation from 1999 (X)*	X^2	XY	*Trend value Yc*
1996	672	−3	9	−2016	579.64
1997	824	−2	4	−1648	812.57
1998	968	−1	1	−968	1045.50
1999	1205	0	0	0	1278.43
2000	1464	1	1	1464	1511.36
2001	1758	2	4	3516	1744.29
2002	2058	3	9	6174	1977.22
$N = 7$	$\Sigma Y = 8949$	$\Sigma X = 0$	$\Sigma X^2 = 28$	$\Sigma XY = 6522$	

$$Yc = a + bX$$

Since, $\Sigma X = 0$,

$$a = \frac{\Sigma Y}{N} = \frac{8949}{7} = \mathbf{1278.43}$$

$$= \frac{\Sigma XY}{\Sigma X^2} = \frac{6522}{28} = \mathbf{232.93}$$

Trend Value $Yc = 1278.43 + 232.93X$

$$Y_{1996} = 1278.43 + (232.93 \times -3) = 1278.43 - 698.79 = 579.64$$

Similarly the other trend value can be obtained by putting $X = -2, -1, 0, 1$, etc.

Problem 30. Below are given the figures of production (in thousand maunds) of sugar factory. Obtain the secular trend by fitting straight line.

Year	:	1994	1995	1996	1997	1998	1999	2000
Production	:	12	10	14	11	13	15	16

Also, plot the trend values to indicate the trend line. (*B. Com., Bombay*)

Solution :

Computation of Trend Value

Year	*Production*	*Deviation from 1997 (X)*	X^2	XY	*Trend Value Yc*
1994	12	−3	9	−36	10.75
1995	10	−2	4	−20	11.50
1996	14	−1	1	−14	12.25
1997	11	0	0	0	13.0
1998	13	1	1	13	13.75
1999	15	2	4	30	14.50
2000	16	3	9	48	15.25
$N = 7$	$\Sigma Y = 91$	$\Sigma X = 0$	$\Sigma X^2 = 28$	$\Sigma XY = 21$	

$$Y = a + bx$$

Since, $\Sigma X = 0$,

$$a = \frac{\Sigma Y}{N} = \frac{91}{7} = \mathbf{13}$$

$$b = \frac{\Sigma XY}{\Sigma X^2} = \frac{21}{28} = \mathbf{0.75}$$

Trend Value $Yc = 13 + 0.75X$

$$Y_{1994} = 13 + (0.75 \times -3) = 13 - 2.25 = 10.75$$

Similarly other trend value can be obtained by putting $X = -2, -1, 0, 1$, etc.

(See graph on page 595)

Problem 31. Calculate trend values from the data given below by applying the method of Least Squares :

Years	:	1996	1997	1998	1999	2000	2001	2002
Sales (Rs. Crores)	:	20	23	22	25	26	29	30

Estimate the likely Sales for the year 2005.

(*M.A., Econ., Kurukshetra*)

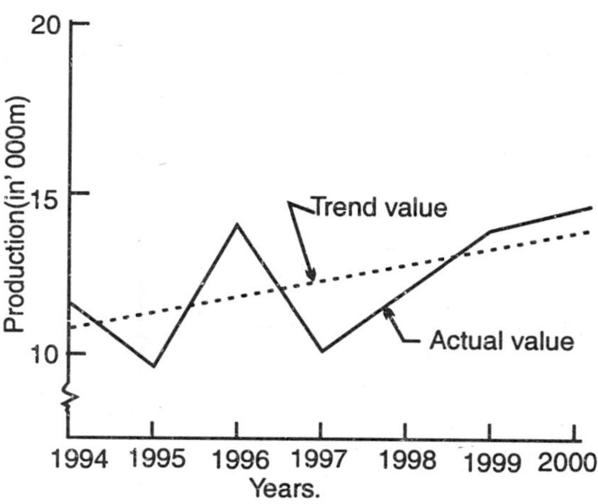

Solution :

Computation of Trend Value

Year	*Sales (Rs. crores) Y*	*Deviation from 1999 (X)*	X^2	XY	*Trend value Yc*
1996	20	−3	9	−60	20.08
1997	23	−2	4	−46	21.72
1998	22	−1	1	−22	23.36
1999	25	0	0	0	25.00
2000	26	1	1	26	26.64
2001	29	2	4	58	28.28
2002	30	3	9	90	29.92
$N = 7$	$\Sigma Y = 175$	$\Sigma X = 0$	$\Sigma X^2 = 28$	$\Sigma XY = 46$	

$$Yc = a + bX$$

Since, $\Sigma X = 0$,

$$a = \frac{\Sigma Y}{N} = \frac{175}{7} = \mathbf{25}$$

$$b = \frac{\Sigma XY}{\Sigma X^2} = \frac{46}{28} = \mathbf{1.64}.$$

Trend Value :

$$Yc = 25 + 1.64\,X$$

$$Y_{1996} = 25 + (1.64 \times -3) = 25 - 4.92 = 20.8$$

Similarly the trend values can be obtained by putting

$$X = -2, -1, 0, \text{ etc.}$$

For 2005,

$$X = 6$$

$$Y_{2005} = 25 + (1.64 \times 6) = 25 + 9.84 = \mathbf{34.84}$$

Hence the estimated sales for the year 2005 is Rs.**34.84 crores.**

Problem 32. Following are the profits of a concern from 1995 to 2001. Compute trend ordinates for the data :

Years	:	1995	1996	1997	1998	1999	2000	2001
Profits (*in thousand Rs.*)	:	75	70	72	65	50	54	41

(*B. Com., Hons., Utkal*)

Solution :

Computation of Trend Value

Year	*Profits* (*in Rs. '000*) Y	*Deviation from 1998* (X)	X^2	XY	*Trend Value Yc*
1995	75	−3	9	−225	77.71
1996	70	−2	4	−140	72.14
1997	72	−1	1	−72	66.57
1998	65	0	0	0	61.00
1999	50	1	1	50	55.43
2000	54	2	4	108	49.86
2001	41	3	9	123	44.29
$N = 7$	$\Sigma Y = 427$	$\Sigma X = 0$	$\Sigma X^2 = 28$	$\Sigma XY = -156$	

$$Yc = a + bX$$

Since, $\Sigma X = 0$,

$$a = \frac{\Sigma Y}{N} = \frac{427}{7} = \mathbf{61.}$$

$$b = \frac{\Sigma XY}{\Sigma X^2} = \frac{-156}{28} = \mathbf{-5.57.}$$

$$Yc = 61 - 5.57X$$

$$Y_{1995} = 61 - 5.57 \times -3 = 61 + 16.71 = 77.71$$

Similarly the other trend values can be obtained by putting $X = -2, -1, 0, 1$ etc.

Problem 33. Use the method of least squares to fit a straight line trend to the following data :

Year	*Sales* (*in '000 Rs.*)	*Year*	*Sales* (*in '000 Rs.*)
1992	25	1998	42
1993	29	1999	48
1994	28	2000	45
1995	36	2001	49
1996	37	2002	52
1997	42		

Obtain the trend values and estimate the sales in 2004.

(*B. A., Madurai*)

Solution :

Computation of Trend Value

Year	*Sales (in '000 Rs.) Y*	*Deviation from 1997 X*	X^2	XY	*Trend Value Yc*
1992	25	−5	25	−125	25.96
1993	29	−4	16	−116	28.64
1994	28	−3	9	−84	31.32
1995	36	−2	4	−72	34.00
1996	37	−1	1	−37	36.68
1997	42	0	0	0	39.36
1998	42	1	1	42	42.04
1999	48	2	4	96	44.72
2000	45	3	9	135	47.40
2001	49	4	16	196	50.08
2002	52	5	25	260	52.76
$N = 11$	$\Sigma Y = 433$	$\Sigma X = 0$	$\Sigma X^2 = 110$	$\Sigma XY = 295$	

$$Yc = a + bX$$

Since, $\Sigma X = 0$,

$$a = \frac{\Sigma Y}{N} = \frac{433}{11} = \mathbf{39.36}$$

$$b = \frac{\Sigma XY}{\Sigma X^2} = \frac{295}{110} = \mathbf{2.68}.$$

$$Yc = 39.36 + 2.68\ X$$

$$Y_{1992} = 39.36 + (2.68 \times -5) = 39.36 - 13.4 = 25.96$$

Similarly the other trend values can be obtained by putting

$$X = -4, -3, -2, \text{ etc.}$$

For 2004, $X = 7$

$$Y_{2004} = 39.36 + (2.68 \times 7) = 39.36 + 18.76 = \mathbf{58.12}.$$

Hence the estimated sales for 2004 = **Rs. 58.12 Thousands.**

Problem 34. The following table gives the sterling assets of R.B.I. in crores of rupees.
(*a*) Represent the data graphically.
(*b*) Fit a straight line trend.
(*c*) Show the trend on the graph

Year	1996–97	1997–98	1998–99	1999–2000	2000–2001	2001–2002
Assets	83	92	71	90	169	191

Also estimate the figures for 2006–2007.

(*B. Com., Mysore*)

Solution :

Computation of Trend Value

Year	*Y*	*Time deviation from the mid-year (X)*	X^2	XY	*Trend Value Yc*
1996–97	83	−2.5	6.25	−207.5	59.5
1997–98	92	−1.5	2.25	−138.0	82.1
1998–99	71	−0.5	0.25	−35.5	104.7
1999–00	90	0.5	0.25	45.0	127.3
2000–01	169	1.5	2.25	253.5	149.9
2001–02	191	2.5	6.25	477.5	172.5
$N = 6$	$\Sigma Y = 696$	$\Sigma X = 0$	$\Sigma X^2 = 17.50$	$\Sigma XY = 395$	

Since, $\Sigma X = 0; Y = a + bX$

Trend Value for the Year = Average + (Rate of Growth × Time deviation)

$$\text{Average} = \frac{\text{Total Sterling Assets}}{\text{No. of Years}} = \frac{696}{6} = \mathbf{116}$$

116 is the trend value for the middle year

$$\text{Rate of growth} = \frac{\Sigma XY}{\Sigma X^2} = \frac{395}{17.50} = \mathbf{22.6}$$

∴ Trend value for

$$\begin{aligned}
1996-97 &= 116 + (22.6 \times -2.5) = 116 - 56.5 = 59.5 \\
1997-98 &= 116 + (22.6 \times -1.5) = 116 - 33.9 = 82.1 \\
1998-99 &= 116 + (22.6 \times -0.5) = 116 - 11.3 = 104.7 \\
1999-00 &= 116 + (22.6 \times 0.5) = 116 + 11.3 = 127.3 \\
2000-01 &= 116 + (22.6 \times 1.5) = 116 + 33.9 = 149.9 \\
2001-02 &= 116 + (22.6 \times 2.5) = 116 + 56.5 = 172.5
\end{aligned}$$

Estimation of the Sterling assets for 2006–2007

Time Deviation from the middle year = 7.5

$$\begin{aligned}
\text{Trend Value for 2006–2007} &= 116 + (22.6 \times 7.5) \\
&= 116 + 169.50 \\
&= \textbf{Rs. 285.50} \text{ crores}
\end{aligned}$$

(See graph on page 573)

Problem 35. Fit a straight line trend equation by the method of least squares and estimate the trend values.

Year	:	1995	1996	1997	1998	1999	2000	2001	2002
Value	:	80	90	92	83	94	99	92	104

(*C.A. Intermediate*)

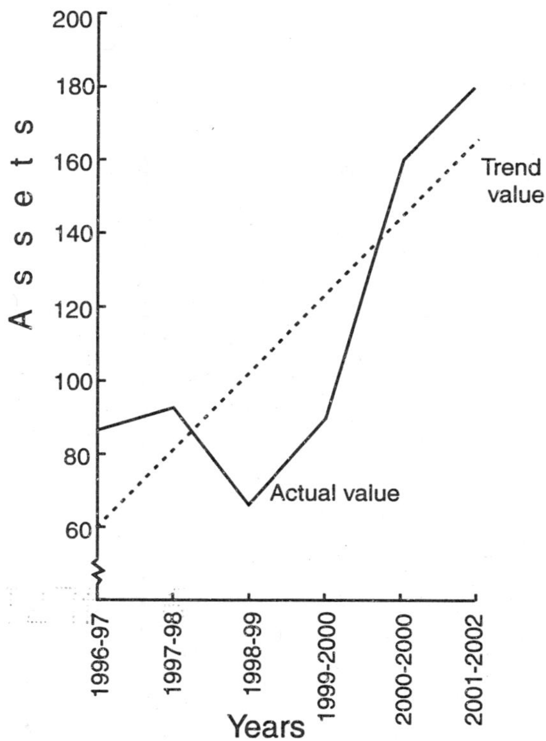

Solution :

Computation of Trend Value

Year	*Value Y*	*Deviation trend from 1998.5*	*Multiplying deviation by 2 (X)*	X^2	XY	*Trend Value Yc*
1995	80	−3.5	−7	49	−560	83.0
1996	90	−2.5	−5	25	−450	85.5
1997	92	−1.5	−3	9	−276	88.0
1998	83	−0.5	−1	1	−83	90.5
1999	94	0.5	1	1	94	93.0
2000	99	1.5	3	9	297	95.5
2001	92	2.5	5	25	460	98.0
2002	104	3.5	7	49	728	100.5
$N = 8$	$\Sigma Y = 734$			$\Sigma X^2 = 168$	$\Sigma XY = 210$	

$$Yc = a + bx$$

Since, $X = 0$,

$$a = \frac{\Sigma Y}{N} = \frac{734}{8} = \mathbf{91.75}$$

$$b = \frac{\Sigma XY}{\Sigma X^2} = \frac{210}{168} = \mathbf{1.25}$$

Trend Value : $Yc = 91.75 + 1.25\,X$

$$Y_{1995} = 91.75 + (1.25 \times -7) = 91.75 - 8.75 = 83$$

Similarly the other trend values can be obtained by putting

$X = -5, -3$ etc.

Problem 36. Find the trend of industrial employment in a city from the following data for 1993–2002.

Year	1993	1994	1995	1996	1997	1998	1999	2000	2001	2002
No. of Workers Employed (lakhs)	3.2	3.3	3.7	3.9	3.6	4.3	4.8	4.8	5.4	6.3

(*B. Com., Madurai*)

Solution :

Computation of Trend Value

Year	*No. of Workers employed y*	*Deviation from 1997.5*	*Multiplying Deviation by 2 (X)*	X^2	XY	*Trend Value Yc*
1993	3.2	−4.5	−9	81	−28.8	2.926
1994	3.3	−3.5	−7	49	−23.1	3.238
1995	3.7	−2.5	−5	25	−18.5	3.550
1996	3.9	−1.5	−3	9	−11.7	3.862
1997	3.6	−0.5	−1	1	−3.6	4.174
1998	4.3	0.5	1	1	4.3	4.486
1999	4.8	1.5	3	9	14.4	4.798
2000	4.8	2.5	5	25	24.0	5.110
2001	5.4	3.5	7	49	37.8	5.442
2002	6.3	4.5	9	81	56.7	5.734
$N = 10$	$\Sigma Y = 43.3$		$\Sigma X = 0$	$\Sigma X^2 = 330$	$\Sigma XY = 51.5$	

$$Yc = a + bx$$

Since, $X = 0$,
$$a = \frac{\Sigma Y}{N} = \frac{43.3}{10} = \mathbf{4.33}$$

$$b = \frac{\Sigma XY}{N} = \frac{51.5}{330} = \mathbf{0.156}$$

Trend Value
$$Yc = 4.33 + (0.156X)$$

$$Y_{1993} = 4.33 = (0.156 \times -9) = 4.33 - 1.404 = 2.926$$

Similarly the other values can be obtained by putting

$$X = -7, -5, -3 \text{ etc.}$$

Problem 37. The weights of a calf taken at weekly intervals are given below. Fit a straight line using the method of least squares and calculate the average rate of growth per week.

Weekly Age (X)	*Weight (Y)*	*Weekly Age (X)*	*Weight (Y)*
1	52.5	6	81.1
2	58.7	7	87.2
3	65.0	8	95.5
4	70.2	9	102.2
5	75.4	10	108.4

Also estimate the weight of the calf when age is (*i*) 12 weeks (*ii*) 15 weeks.

(*B. Com. Bombay*)

Solution :

Computation of Trend Value

Age (X)	*Weight Y*	*Deviation from 5.5*	*Multiplication of deviation by 2*	X^2	XY	*Trend value Yc*
1	52.5	−4.5	−9	81	−472.5	51.90
2	58.7	−3.5	−7	49	−410.9	58.06
3	65.0	−2.5	−5	25	−325.0	64.22
4	70.2	−1.5	−3	9	−210.6	70.38
5	75.4	−0.5	−1	1	−75.4	76.54
6	81.1	0.5	1	1	81.1	82.70
7	87.2	1.5	3	9	261.6	88.86
8	95.5	2.5	5	25	477.5	95.02
9	102.2	3.5	7	49	715.4	101.18
10	108.4	4.5	9	81	975.6	107.34
$N = 10$	$\Sigma Y = 796.2$			$\Sigma X^2 = 330$	$\Sigma XY = 1016.8$	

$$Yc = a + bX$$

Since, $X = 0$,

$$a = \frac{\Sigma Y}{N} = \frac{796.2}{10} = \mathbf{79.62}$$

$$b = \frac{\Sigma XY}{\Sigma X^2} = \frac{1016.8}{330} = \mathbf{3.08}$$

$$Yc = 79.62 + 3.08\, X$$

$$Y_1 = 79.62 + (3.08 \times -9) = 79.62 - 27.72 = 51.90$$

Similarly the other trend values can be obtained by putting

$$X = -7, -5 \text{ etc.}$$

For 12 weeks calf, the weight $(X) = 13$

$$Y_{12} = 79.62 + 3.08 \times 13 = 79.62 + 40.04 = \mathbf{119.66}$$

For 15 weeks calf, the weight $(X) = 19$

$$Y_{15} = 79.62 + (3.08 \times 19) = 79.62 + 58.52 = \mathbf{138.14}.$$

Problem 38. Fit a straight line trend by the method of least squares to the following data and estimate the value for 2004 from the same :

Year :	1995	1996	1997	1998	1999	2000	2001	2002
Value:	380	400	650	720	690	695	600	850

(*B. Com. Himachal*)

Solution :

Computation of Trend Values

Year	*Value Y*	*Devaition from 1998.5*	*Multiplication of deviation by 2 (X)*	X^2	*XY*	*Trend value Yc*
1995	380	−3.5	−7	49	−2660	440.01
1996	400	−2.5	−5	25	−2000	492.33
1997	650	−1.5	−3	9	−1950	544.65
1998	720	−0.5	−1	1	−720	596.97
1999	690	0.5	1	1	690	649.29
2000	695	1.5	3	9	2085	701.61
2001	600	2.5	5	25	3000	753.93
2002	850	3.5	7	49	5950	806.25
$N = 8$	$\Sigma Y = 4985$		$\Sigma X = 0$	$\Sigma X^2 = 168$	$\Sigma XY = 4395$	

$$Yc = a + bX$$

Since, $\Sigma X = 0$,

$$a = \frac{\Sigma Y}{N} = \frac{4985}{8} = 623.125 = \mathbf{623.13}.$$

$$b = \frac{\Sigma XY}{\Sigma X^2} = \frac{4395}{168} = \mathbf{26.16}$$

Trend Value $Yc = 623.13 + 26.16\,X$

$$Y_{1995} = 623.13 + (26.26 \times -7) = 623.13 - 183.12 = 440.01$$

Similarly the other values can be obtained by putting $X = -5, -3, -1$ etc.

For 2004 X = 11

$$Y_{2004} = 623.13 + (26.16 \times 11) = 623.13 + 287.76 = \mathbf{910.89}$$

Hence the estimated value for 2004 = **910.89**.

Problem 39. From the data given below determine the line of trend and hence find the expected value for 2003.

Year :	1993	1994	1995	1996	1997	1998	1999	2000	2001	2002
Production (in tons) :	110.2	143.3	143.3	134.5	138	55	74	129	150	140

(*B. Com. Madras*)

Solution :

Computation of Trend Values

Year	*Production in tons Y*	*Deviation from X 1997.5*	*Multiplying deviation by 2 (X)*	X^2	*XY*	*Yc*
1993	110.2	−4.5	−9	81	−991.8	122.27
1994	143.3	−3.5	−7	49	−1003.1	122.15
1995	143.3	−2.5	−5	25	−716.5	122.03
1996	134.5	−1.5	−3	9	−403.5	121.91
1997	138.0	−0.5	−1	1	−138.0	121.79
1998	55.0	0.5	1	1	55	121.67
1999	74.0	1.5	3	9	222	121.55
2000	129.0	2.5	5	25	645	121.43
2001	150.0	3.5	7	49	1050	121.31
2002	140.0	4.5	9	81	1260	121.19
$N = 10$	$\Sigma Y = 1217.3$			$\Sigma X^2 = 330$	$\Sigma XY = -20.9$	

$$Yc = a + bx$$

Since, $\Sigma X = 0$, $$a = \frac{\Sigma Y}{N} = \frac{1217.3}{10} = \mathbf{121.73}$$

$$b = \frac{\Sigma XY}{\Sigma X^2} = \frac{-20.9}{330} = \mathbf{-0.06}.$$

Trend Value $$Yc = 121.73 + (-0.06\ X)$$

$$Y_{1993} = 121.73 + (-0.06 \times -9) = 121.73 + 0.54 = 122.27$$

$$Y_{1994} = 121.73 + (-0.06 \times -7) = 121.73 + 0.42 = 122.15$$

Similarly the other values can be obtained by putting $X = -7, -5, -3, -1$ etc.
For 2003, X will be $= 11$

$$\therefore \quad Y_{2003} = 121.73 + (-0.06 \times 11) = 121.73 - 0.66 = \mathbf{121.07}$$

Hence the expected value for 2003 is 121.07 tons.

Problem 40. Fit a straight line trend by the method of least squares to the following data. Assuming that the same rate of change continues, what would be the earnings for the year 2002.

Year	:	1993	1994	1995	1996	1997	1998	1999	2000
Earnings (Rs. Lakhs)	:	38	40	65	72	69	60	87	95

(*B. Com. Delhi*)

Solution :

Computation of Trend Value

Year	*Earnings (Rs. Lakh) Y*	*Deviation taken from 1996.5*	*Multiplying deviation by 2 (X)*	X^2	XY	*Trend value Yc*
1993	38	−3.5	−7	49	−266	40.06
1994	40	−2.5	−5	25	−200	47.40
1995	65	−1.5	−3	9	−195	54.74
1996	72	−0.5	−1	1	−72	62.08
1997	69	0.5	1	1	69	69.42
1998	60	1.5	3	9	180	76.76
1999	87	2.5	5	25	435	84.10
2000	95	3.5	7	49	665	91.44
$N = 8$	$\Sigma Y = 526$			$\Sigma X^2 = 168$	$\Sigma XY = 616$	

$$Yc = a + bx$$

Since, $X = 0$, $$a = \frac{\Sigma Y}{N} = \frac{526}{8} = \mathbf{65.75}$$

$$b = \frac{\Sigma XY}{\Sigma X^2} = \frac{616}{168} = \mathbf{3.67}$$

The trend value $$Yc = 65.75 + 3.67\ X$$

$$Y_{1993} = 65.75 + (3.67 \times -7) = 65.75 - 25.69 = 40.06$$

Similarly the other trend value can be obtained by putting $X = -5, -3, -1, 1, 3, 5, 7$.
For 2002, $X = 11$

$$Y_{2002} = 65.75 + (3.67 \times 11) = 65.75 + 40.37 = \mathbf{106.12}$$

Problem 41. Obtain the straight line trend equation and tabulate against each year after estimation of the trend and short term fluctuations:

Year	:	1994	1995	1996	1997	1998	1999	2000	2001	2002
Value	:	380	400	650	720	690	620	670	950	1040

(*Inter C.A.*)

Solution :

Computation of Straight Line Trend

Year	*Value Y*	*Deviation from* 1998 (*X*)	X^2	XY	*Trend value Yc*	*Short-term fluctuations* (*Y– Yc*)
1994	380	−4	16	−1520	398.0	−18.0
1995	400	−3	9	−1200	468.5	−68.5
1996	650	−2	4	−1300	539.0	111.0
1997	720	−1	1	−720	609.5	110.5
1998	690	0	0	0	680.0	10.0
1999	620	1	1	620	750.5	−130.5
2000	670	2	4	1340	821.0	−151.0
2001	950	3	9	2850	891.5	58.5
2002	1040	4	16	4160	962.0	78.0
$N = 9$	$\Sigma Y = 6120$	$\Sigma X = 0$	$\Sigma X^2 = 60$	$\Sigma XY = 4230$		

$$Yc = a + bX$$

Since, $X = 0$,

$$a = \frac{\Sigma Y}{N} = \frac{6120}{9} = \mathbf{680}$$

$$b = \frac{\Sigma XY}{\Sigma X^2} = \frac{4230}{60} = \mathbf{70.5}$$

Trend value $\quad Yc = 680 + 70.5\,X$

$$Y_{1994} = 680 + (70.5 \times -4) = 680 - 282 = 398$$

Similarly the other trend values can be obtained by putting $X = -3, -2, -1, 0, 1$ etc.

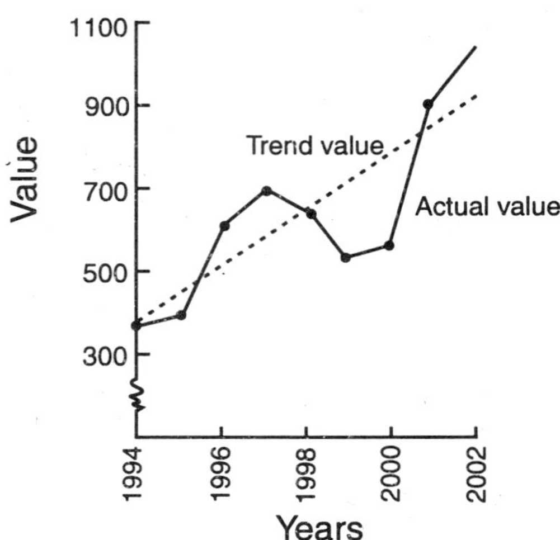

Problem 42. Fit a parabolic curve of second degree to the data given below and estimate the value for 2002 and comment on it :

Year	:	1996	1997	1998	1999	2000
Sales (in '000 Rs.)	:	10	12	13	10	8

(*M. Com. Delhi*)

Solution :

Computation of Second Degree Parabola

Year	*Sales (in '000 Rs.) Y*	*Deviation from 1998 X*	XY	X^2	X^2Y	X^4	*Trend values Yc*
1996	10	−2	−20	4	40	16	10.086
1997	12	−1	−12	1	12	1	12.057
1998	13	0	0	0	0	0	12.314
1999	10	1	10	1	10	1	10.857
2000	8	2	16	4	32	16	7.686
$N = 5$	$\Sigma Y = 53$	$\Sigma X = 0$	$\Sigma XY = -6$	$\Sigma X^2 = 10$	$\Sigma X^2Y = 94$	$\Sigma X^4 = 34$	

Since

$$\begin{aligned} \Sigma X &= 0 \text{ the equations are:} \\ \Sigma Y &= Na \times C\Sigma X^2 \\ \Sigma XY &= b\Sigma X^2 \\ \Sigma X^2Y &= a\Sigma X^2 + C\Sigma X^4 \end{aligned}$$

Substituting the values

$$53 = 5a + 10c \quad (1)$$
$$-6 = 10b \quad (2)$$
$$94 = 10a + 34c \quad (3)$$

From Equation (2) $b = \frac{-6}{10} = \mathbf{-0.6}$

Multiplying equation (1) by 2 and subtract equation (3) from (4)

$$106 = 10a + 20c \quad (4)$$
$$94 = 10a + 34c$$
$$12 = -14c \quad (5)$$
$$c = \frac{-12}{14} = -0.857$$

Putting the value of c in equation (3)

$$\begin{aligned} 94 &= 10a + 34(0.0857) \\ 10a - 29.138 &= 94 \\ 10a &= 94 + 26.138 \\ a &= \frac{123.138}{10} = 12.3138 = 12.314 \end{aligned}$$

Hence the second degree parabolic equation :

$$\begin{aligned}
Yc &= 12.314 - 0.6\,X - 0.857 \quad X^2 \\
Y_{1996} &= 12.314 + (-0.6 \times -2) + (-0.857)\,(4) \\
&= 12.314 + 1.2 - 3.428 \\
&= 13.514 - 3.428 = \mathbf{10.086} \\
Y_{1997} &= 12.314 + (-0.6 \times -1) + (-0.857 \times 1) \\
&= 12.314 + 0.6 - 0.857 \\
&= 12.914 - 0.857 \\
&= \mathbf{12.057}. \\
Y_{1998} &= 12.314 + (-0.6 \times 0) + (-0.857 \times 0) \\
&= \mathbf{12.314}. \\
Y_{1999} &= 12.314 + (-0.6 \times 1) + (-0.857 \times 1) \\
&= 12.314 - 0.6 - 0.857 \\
&= \mathbf{10.857}. \\
Y_{2000} &= 12.314 + (-0.6 \times 2) + (-0.857 \times 4) \\
&= 12.314 - 1.2 - 3.428 \\
&= 12.314 - 4.628 \\
&= \mathbf{7.686}. \\
\text{For2002,} \quad X &= 4, \; X^2 = 16 \\
Y_{2002} &= 12.314 + (-0.6 \times 4) + (-0.857 \times 16) \\
&= 12.314 - 2.4 - 13.712 \\
&= 12.314 - 16.112 \\
&= \mathbf{-3.798}.
\end{aligned}$$

Problem 43. Fit a second degree parabola to the following data and also estimate the value for 2005 with your comment :

Year	:	1970	1975	1980	1985	1990	1995	2000
Production (*in* '000 *Units*)	:	6	8	9	10	12	11	8

(*M. Com. Delhi*)

Solution :

$$Yc = a + bX + cX^2$$

The values of a, b, and c can be calculated by the following eqations.

$$\begin{aligned}
\Sigma Y &= Na + b\Sigma X + c\Sigma X^2 \\
\Sigma XY &= a\Sigma X + b\Sigma X^2 + c\Sigma X^3 \\
\Sigma X^2 Y &= a\Sigma X^2 + b\Sigma X^2 + c\Sigma X^4
\end{aligned}$$

Computation of Trend Value

Year	Production (in '000 units) Y	X	X^2	X^4	XY	X^2Y	Trend value Yc
1970	6	−3	9	81	−18	54	5.57
1975	8	−2	4	16	−16	32	8.071
1980	9	−1	1	1	−9	9	9.786
1985	10	0	0	0	0	0	10.715
1990	12	1	1	1	12	12	10.858
1995	11	2	4	16	22	44	10.215
2000	8	3	9	81	24	72	8.786
$N = 7$	$\Sigma Y = 64$	$\Sigma X = 0$	$\Sigma X^2 = 28$	$\Sigma X^4 = 196$	$\Sigma XY = 15$	$\Sigma X^2Y = 223$	

Since $\Sigma X = 0$ the equations are:

$$\Sigma Y = Na + c\Sigma X^2 \quad (1)$$

$$\Sigma XY = b\Sigma X^2 \quad (2)$$

$$\Sigma X^2Y = a\Sigma X^2 + c\Sigma X^4 \quad (3)$$

Substituting the values we get

$$64 = 7a + 28c \quad (1)$$

$$15 = 28b \quad (2)$$

$$223 = 28a + 196c \quad (3)$$

From equation (2) $b = \frac{15}{28} = \mathbf{0.536}$.

Multiplying equation (1) by 4 and subtract equation (3) from (4)

$$256 = 28a + 112c \quad (4)$$

$$223 = 28a + 196c$$

$$+33 = -84c$$

$$c = \frac{33}{-84} = \mathbf{-0.393}$$

Substituting the value of c in equation (1)

$$64 = 7a + 28 \times -0.393$$

$$64 = 7a - 11.004$$

$$7a - 11.004 = 64$$

$$7a = 64 + 11.004$$

$$a = \frac{75.004}{7}$$

$$= \mathbf{10.715}.$$

$$\begin{aligned} \text{Hence} \quad Yc &= 10.715 + 0.536X - 0.393\,X^2 \\ Y_{1970} &= 10.715 + (0.536 \times -3) + (-0.393 \times 9) \\ &= 10.715 - 1.608 - 3.537 \\ &= 10.715 - 5.145 \\ &= \mathbf{5.57} \end{aligned}$$

Similarly the other trend values can be obtained by putting X = −2, −1, 0 etc.

$$\begin{aligned} \text{For 2005,} \quad X &= 4, X^2 = 16 \\ Y_{2005} &= 10.715 + (0.536 \times 4) + (-0.393 \times 16) \\ &= 10.715 + 2.144 - 6.288 \\ &= \mathbf{6.571}. \end{aligned}$$

Hence the estimated value for 2005 = 6.571. ('000)

Problem 44. The sales of a company for last eight years are.

Year	:	1993	1994	1995	1996	1997	1998	1999	2000
Sales ('000)	:	52	45	98	92	110	185	175	220

Estimate sales figure for 2001 using an equation of the form $Y = ab^x$ where X = years and Y = sales.

(M. Com. Delhi)

Solution :

Fitting the equation of the form $Y = ab^x$

Year	*Sales Y*	*Deviation from* 1996 (*X*)	*Log Y*	X^2	*X Log Y*
1993	52	−3	1.7160	9	−5.1480
1994	45	−2	1.6532	4	−3.3064
1995	98	−1	1.9912	1	−1.9912
1996	92	0	1.9638	0	0
1997	110	1	2.0414	1	2.0414
1998	185	2	2.2672	4	4.5344
1999	175	3	2.2430	9	6.7290
2000	220	4	2.3424	16	9.3969
$N = 8$	$\Sigma Y = 977$	$\Sigma X = 4$	$\Sigma Log\,Y = 16.2182$	$\Sigma X^2 = 44$	$\Sigma X\,LogY = 12.2288$

$Y = ab^x$ in the logarithmic form we get

Log Y = log a× log b

The value of *a* and *b* can be obtained by solving the two normal equations.

$$\begin{aligned} \Sigma \log Y &= N \log a + \log b \Sigma X \\ \Sigma X \log Y &= \log a \Sigma X + \log b \Sigma X^2 \\ 16.2182 &= 8 \log a + 4 \log b \quad (1) \\ 12.2288 &= 4 \log a + 44 \log b \quad (2) \end{aligned}$$

Multiplying equation (2) by 2 and substract equation (1) from it

$$24.4576 = 8\log + 88\log b$$
$$16.2182 = 8\log a + 4\log b$$
$$8.2394 = 84\log b$$
$$84\log b = 8.2394$$
$$\log b = \frac{8.2394}{84} = \mathbf{0.0981}$$

Putting the value of log b in equation (1)

$$16.2182 = 8\log a + 4\,(0.0981)$$
$$16.2182 = 8\log a + 0.3924$$
$$8\log a = 16.2182 - 0.3924$$
$$\log a = \frac{15.8258}{8} = \mathbf{1.978}$$
$$\log Y = 1.978 + 0.0981\,X$$
$$\text{For2001, } X = 5$$
$$\log Y = 1.978 + (0.0981 \times 5) = 1.978 + 0.4905 = 2.4685$$
$$Y = \text{Antilog}\,(\log Y)$$
$$Y = \text{Antilog}\,(2.4685) = \mathbf{294.1}$$

Hence the estimated sales for 2001 = **294100**

Problem 45. Below are given the figures of production (in thousand quintals) of a sugar actory.

Year	*Production (thousand quintals)*	*Year*	*Production (thousand quintals)*
1991	77	1996	91
1993	88	1997	98
1994	94	2000	90
1995	85		

(*I*) Fit a straight line by the 'least squares' method, and tabulate the trend values.
(*II*) Eliminate the trend. What components of the time series are thus left over ?
(*III*) What is the monthly increase in the production of sugar? (*M. Com. Delhi, Andhra*)

Solution :

Computation of Trend Value

Year	*Production*	*Deviation from 1995 X*	X^2	XY	*Trend Value Yc*	$Y - Yc$
1991	77	−4	16	−308	83.283	−6.283
1993	88	−2	4	−176	86.043	+1.957
1994	94	−1	1	−94	87.423	+6.577
1995	85	0	0	0	88.803	−3.803
1996	91	1	1	91	90.183	+0.817
1997	98	2	4	196	91.563	+6.437
2000	90	5	25	450	95.703	−5.733
$N = 7$	$\Sigma Y = 623$	$\Sigma X = 1$	$\Sigma X^2 = 51$	$\Sigma XY = 159$		

$$Yc = a + bx$$

Since ΣX is not 0, the values of a and b can be obtained by using the normal equation.

$$\Sigma Y = Na + b\Sigma X \quad (1)$$

$$\Sigma XY = a\Sigma X + b\Sigma X^2 \quad (2)$$

$$623 = 7a + b \quad (1)$$

$$159 = a + 51b \quad (2)$$

Multiplying equation (2) by 7 we get

$$1113 = 7a + 357 \quad (3)$$

. Subtracting equation (1) from (3) we get

$$490 = 356\,b$$

$$b = \frac{490}{356} = \mathbf{1.38}$$

Substituting the value of b in the equation (1)

$$623 = 7a + 1.38$$

$$7a \quad +1.38 = 623$$

$$7a = 623 - 1.38$$

$$a = \frac{621.62}{7} = \mathbf{88.803}$$

$$Yc = a + bx$$

(*ii*) $Y_{1991} = 88.803 + (1.38)(-4) = 88.803 - 5.52$

$= \mathbf{83.283}$

$$Y_{1993} = 88.803 + (1.38 - 2) = 88.803 - 2.76 = 86.043$$

$$Y_{1994} = 88.803 + (1.38 \times -1) = 88.803 - 1.38 = 87.423$$

$$Y_{1995} = 88.803$$

$$Y_{1996} = 88.803 + (1.38 \times 1) = 88.803 + 1.38 = 90.183$$

$$Y_{1997} = 88.803 + (1.38 \times 2) = 88.803 + 2.76 = 91.563$$

$$Y_{2000} = 88.803 + (1.38 \times 5) = 88.803 + 6.9 = 95.703$$

(*ii*) If we eliminate the trend, the components of time series left over are cyclical and irregular variation.

(*iii*) The monthly increase in the production of sugar is

$$\frac{b}{12} = \frac{1.38}{12}$$

$= \mathbf{0.115\ thousand\ quintals}$

Problem 46. Population figures for a city are as given below. Fit a Curve of the type $Y = ab^x$ and estimate the population for 2005.

Year	1999	2000	2001	2002	2003
Population ('000)	132	142	157	170	191

(*M. Com. Delhi*)

Solution :

Fitting the Equation of the form $Y = ab^x$

Year	*Pop. In ('000s) Y*	*Deviation from 2001 (X)*	*Log Y*	*X Log Y*	X^2
1999	132	−2	2.1206	−4.2412	4
2000	142	−1	2.1523	−2.1523	1
2001	157	0	2.1959	0	0
2002	170	1	2.2304	2.2304	1
2003	191	2	2.2810	4.5620	4
$N = 5$	$\Sigma Y = 792$	$\Sigma X = 0$	$\Sigma LogY = 10.9802$	$\Sigma LogY = 0.3989$	$\Sigma X^2 = 10$

$$Log\ a = \frac{\Sigma \log Y}{N} = \frac{10.9802}{5} = \mathbf{2.19604}$$

$$Log\ b = \frac{\Sigma X\, LogY}{\Sigma X^2} = \frac{0.3989}{10} = \mathbf{0.03989}$$

$$Log\ Y = 2.19604 + 0.03989X$$

$$\text{For2005, } X = 4$$

$$\text{Log } Y_{2005} = 2.19604 + 0.03989 \times 4$$

$$= 2.19604 + 0.15956$$

$$= 2.3556$$

$$Y_{2005} = \text{Antilog}(\log Y)$$

$$= \text{Antilog}(2.3556)$$

$$= \mathbf{226.8}$$

Hence the estimated population for 2005 = **226800**

SEASONAL VARIATION

Problem 47. The following table shows the sales recorded in a particular area during a typical period of 4 weeks. Assuming that the trend value during the period remains the same, calculate seasonal indices (here daily indices) as percentage of grand average.

Weeks	*Sun*	*Mon*	*Tuesday*	*Wednesday*	*Thursday*	*Fri*	*Sat.*
1	1800	1610	1700	1640	1530	1810	760
2	1900	1650	1690	1470	1580	1900	800
3	2100	1620	1690	1530	1450	1900	820
4	2000	1650	1700	1550	1500	1800	850
Total	7700	6530	6780	6190	6060	7410	3230

(*B. Com.*)

Solution :

Computation of Seasonal Indices

Days	*Ist Week*	*IInd Week*	*IIIrd Week*	*IVth Week*	*Total*	*Seasonal Indices (% of daily total to average daily total)*
Sun.	1800	1900	2100	2000	7800	124.09
Mon.	1610	1650	1620	1650	6530	103.89
Tue.	1700	1690	1690	1700	6780	107.86
Wed.	1640	1470	1530	1550	6190	98.48
Thur.	1530	1580	1450	1500	6060	96.41
Fri.	1810	1900	1900	1800	7410	117.89
Sat.	760	800	820	850	3230	51.38
				Total	44000	700.00
				Average daily Total	6285.7	100

$$\text{Daily Index} = \frac{\text{Daily Total}}{\text{Average of daily total}} \times 100$$

$$\text{Daily Index}\,(Sun.) = \frac{7800}{6285.7} \times 100 = \mathbf{124.09}$$

This process will be continued for other days.

Problem 48. The following gives the price per article on the first of each month.

Year	*Jan.*	*Feb.*	*Mar.*	*April*	*May*	*June*	*July*	*Aug.*	*Sept.*	*Oct.*	*Nov.*	*Dec.*
2001	18	19	20	21	23	24	26	26	28	25	23	20
2002	18	21	21	21	22	24	25	26	27	24	23	21
2003	19	17	20	22	23	25	25	26	26	24	22	20

Calculate the seasonal variation for each of the months January to December.

(M.A. (Eco) Madurai

Solution :

Computation of Seasonal Variation

Months	*Price per article in Rs.*			*Monthly total 3 years (4)*	*3–Yearly average col. (4) ÷ (3) (5)*	*Monthly average expressed as average of monthly % of the average*
	(1) 2001	(2) 2002	(3) 2003			
Jan.	18	18	19	55	18.33	$\frac{18.33}{22.64} \times 100 = 80.9$
Feb.	19	21	17	57	19.00	$\frac{19.00}{22.64} \times 100 = 83.9$
Mar.	20	21	20	61	20.33	$\frac{20.33}{22.64} \times 100 = 89.8$
April	21	21	22	64	21.33	$\frac{21.33}{22.64} \times 100 = 94.2$
May	23	22	23	68	22.66	$\frac{22.66}{22.64} \times 100 = 100.08$

Months	Price per article in Rs.			Monthly total 3 years (4)	3–Yearly average col. (4) ÷ (3) (5)	Monthly average expressed as average of monthly % of the average
	(1) 2001	(2) 2002	(3) 2003			
June	24	24	25	73	24.33	$\frac{24.33}{22.64} \times 100 = 107.5$
July	26	25	25	76	25.33	$\frac{25.33}{22.64} \times 100 = 111.9$
Aug.	26	26	26	98	26.00	$\frac{26.00}{22.64} \times 100 = 114.9$
Sep.	28	27	26	81	27.00	$\frac{27.00}{22.64} \times 100 = 119.3$
Oct.	25	24	24	73	24.33	$\frac{24.33}{22.64} \times 100 = 107.5$
Nov.	23	23	22	68	22.66	$\frac{22.66}{22.64} \times 100 = 100.09$
Dec.	20	21	20	61	20.33	$\frac{20.33}{22.64} \times 100 = 89.8$
Total				815	271.63	1199.26
Average = $\frac{815}{2}$ and $\frac{271.63}{12}$				67.91	22.64	100

Problem 49. Assuming the trend is absent, determine if there is any seasonality in the lata given below.

Year	*1st Quarter*	*2nd Quarter*	*3rd Quarter*	*4th Quarter*
2000	3.7	4.1	3.3	3.5
2001	3.7	3.9	3.6	3.6
2002	4.0	4.1	3.3	3.1
2003	3.3	4.4	4.0	4.0

(*B. Com., Delhi*)

Solution :

Computation of Seasonal Indices

Year	*Ist Quarter*	*IInd Quarter*	*IIIrd Quarter*	*IVth Quarter*
2000	3.7	4.1	3.3	3.5
2001	3.7	3.9	3.6	3.6
2002	4.0	4.1	3.3	3.1
2003	3.3	4.4	4.0	4.0
Total	14.7	16.5	14.2	14.2
Seasonal Average	3.675	4.125	3.55	3.55
Seasonal Index	98.7	110.7	95.3	95.3

Calculation of Seasonal Index

$$\text{General Average} = \frac{3.675 + 4.125 + 3.55 + 3.55}{4}$$

$$= \frac{14.90}{4} = \mathbf{3.725}$$

$$\text{Seasonal Index} = \frac{\text{Quarterly Average}}{\text{Genral Average}} \times 100$$

$$\text{Seasonal Index for Ist Quarter} = \frac{3.675}{3.725} \times 100 = 98.7$$

$$\text{Seasonal Index for IInd Quarter} = \frac{4.125}{3.725} \times 100 = 110.7$$

$$\text{Seasonal Index for IIIrd Quarter} = \frac{3.55}{3.725} \times 100 = 95.3$$

$$\text{Seasonal Index for IVth Quarter} = \frac{3.55}{3.725} \times 100 = 95.3$$

Problem 50. From the data given below calculate seasonal indices for I, II, III and IV quarters assuming the trend is absent.

Quarters	1999	2000	2001	2002	2003
I	40	42	41	45	44
II	35	37	35	36	38
III	38	39	38	36	38
IV	40	38	40	41	42

(*M. Com. Jodhpur*)

Solution :

Computation of Seasonal Indices

Year	*Ist Quarter*	*IInd Quarter*	*IIIrd Quarter*	*IVth Quarter*
1999	40	35	38	40
2000	42	37	39	38
2001	41	35	38	40
2002	45	36	36	41
2003	44	38	38	42
Total	212	181	189	201
Average	42.4	36.2	37.8	40.2
Seasonal Index	108.16	92.35	96.43	102.55

Calculation of Seasonal Index :

$$\text{The average of averages} : \frac{42.4 + 36.2 + 37.8 + 40.2}{4}$$

$$\text{(General Average)} = \frac{156.6}{4} = \mathbf{39.2}$$

$$\text{Seasonal Index} = \frac{\text{Quarterly Average}}{\text{General Average}} \times 100$$

$$\text{S.I. for Ist Quarter} = \frac{42.4}{39.2} \times 100 = 108.16$$

$$\text{S. I. for IInd Quarter} = \frac{36.2}{39.2} \times 100 = 92.35$$

$$\text{S.I. for IIIrd Quarter} = \frac{37.8}{39.4} \times 100 = 96.43$$

$$\text{S.I. for IVth Quarter} = \frac{40.2}{39.2} \times 100 = 102.55$$

Problem 51. Compute the average seasonal movement for the following series.

Year	*Quarterly Production*			
	I	*II*	*III*	*IV*
1999	3.5	3.9	3.4	3.6
2000	3.5	4.1	3.7	4.0
2001	3.5	3.9	3.7	4.2
2002	4.0	4.6	3.8	4.5
2003	4.1	4.4	4.2	4.5

(*B. Com., Annamalai*)

Solution :

Computation of Seasonal Indices

Year	*Ist Quarter*	*IInd Quarter*	*III Quarter*	*IVth Quarter*
1999	3.5	3.9	3.4	3.6
2000	3.5	4.1	3.7	4.0
2001	3.5	3.9	3.7	4.2
2002	4.0	4.6	3.8	4.5
2003	4.1	4.4	4.2	4.5
Total	18.6	20.9	18.8	20.8
Average	3.72	4.18	3.76	4.16
Seasonal Index	94.18	105.82	95.19	105.32

Seasonal Indices :

$$\text{Seasonal Average} = \frac{3.72 + 4.18 + 3.76 + 4.16}{4} = \frac{15.82}{4}$$

$$= \mathbf{3.96}$$

$$\text{Index} = \frac{\text{Quarterly Average}}{\text{General Average}} \times 100$$

$$\text{Seasonal Index for Ist Quarter} = \frac{3.72}{3.96} \times 100 = 93.94$$

$$\text{Seasonal Index for IInd Quarter} = \frac{4.18}{3.96} \times 100 = 105.56$$

$$\text{Seasonal Index for IIIrd Quarter} = \frac{3.76}{3.96} \times 100 = 94.95$$

$$\text{Seasonal Index for IVth Quarter} = \frac{4.16}{3.96} \times 100 = 105.05$$

Problem 52. Find the Seasonal Index from the following table by ratio to moving average method.

Seasons	1999	2000	2001	2002	2003
I Quarter	40	42	41	45	44
II Quarter	35	37	35	36	38
III Quarter	38	39	38	36	38
IV Quarter	40	38	42	41	42

(*B. Com. Andhra*)

Solution :

Computation of Seasonal Index

Year 1	*Quarter* 2	*Given values* 3	*4–Quarterly moving total* 4	*4–Quarterly moving average* 5	*4–Quarterly moving average centred* 6	*Given figures as % of moving average* = (3/6 × 100) 7
1999	I	40				
	II	35				
			→ 153	38.25		
	III	38			→ 38.50	98.70
			→ 155	38.75		
	IV	40			→ 39.00	102.56
			→ 157	39.25		
2000	I	42			→ 39.38	106.65
			→ 158	39.50		
	II	37			→ 39.25	94.27
			→ 156	39.00		
	III	39			→ 38.88	100.31
			→ 155	38.75		
	IV	38			→ 38.50	98.70
			→ 153	38.25		
2001	I	41			→ 38.13	107.53
			→ 152	38.00		
	II	35			→ 38.50	90.90
			→ 156	39.00		
	III	38			→ 39.50	96.20
			→ 160	40.00		
	IV	42			→ 40.13	104.66
			→ 161	40.25		

Year 1	*Quarter* 2	*Given values* 3	*4–Quarterly moving total* 4	*4–Quarterly moving average* 5	*4–Quarterly moving average centred* 6	*Given figures as % of moving average* = (3/6 × 100) 7
2002	I	45			→ 40.00	112.50
			→ 159	39.75		
	II	36			→ 39.63	90.84
			→ 158	39.50		
	III	36			→ 39.38	91.42
			→ 157	39.25		
	IV	41			→ 39.50	103.80
			→ 159	39.75		
2003	I	44			→ 40.00	110.00
			→ 161	40.25		
	II	38			→ 40.38	94.11
			→ 162	40.50		
	III	38				
	IV	42				

Problem 53. Obtain seasonal fluctuations from the following time series : Quarterly output of coal for four years :

Year	*Quarters* *I*	*II*	*III*	*IV*
2000	65	58	56	61
2001	58	63	63	67
2002	70	59	56	52
2003	60	55	51	58

(*ICWA*)

Solution :

Computation of Seasonal Fluctuations

Year	*Quarter*	*Quarterly output of coal* (1)	4 *Quarterly moving Total* (2)	4 *Quarterly moving average* (3)	4 *Quarterly moving average centered* (4)	*Short term fluctuation* (1)–(4) = (5)	*Seasonal fluctuation* (*Refer Table*)
2000	I	65	–	–	–	–	–
	II	58	–	–	–	–	–
			→ 240	60			
	III	56			→ 60.38	–4.38	–2.96
			→ 243	60.75			
	IV	61			→ 61.38	–0.38	–0.96
			→ 248	62.00			
2001	I	68			→ 62.88	+5.12	+5.37
			→ 255	63.75			
	II	63			→ 64.50	–1.50	–1.29
			→ 261	65.25			

	III	63			→ 65.50	−2.50	−2.96
			→ 263	65.75			
	IV	67			→ 65.25	+1.75	−0.96
			→ 259	64.75			
2002	I	70			→ 63.88	+6.12	+5.37
			→ 252	63.00			
	II	59			→ 61.13	−2.13	−1.29
			→ 237	59.25			
	III	56			→ 58.00	−2.00	−2.96
			→ 227	56.75			
	IV	52			→ 56.25	−4.25	−0.96
			→ 223	55.75			
2003	I	60			→ 55.13	+4.87	+5.37
			→ 218	54.50			
	II	55			→ 55.25	−0.25	−1.29
			→ 224	56.00			
	III	51	–	–	–	–	–
	IV	58	–	–	–	–	–

Average Seasonal Fluctuations

Year	*Qr. I*	*Qr. II*	*Qr. III*	*Qr. IV*
2000	–	–	−4.38	−0.38
2001	+5.12	−1.50	−2.50	+1.75
2002	+6.12	−2.13	−2.00	−4.25
2003	+4.87	−0.25	–	–
	16.11	−3.88	−8.88	−2.88
	5.37	−1.29	−2.96	−0.96

Problem 54. Calculate the Seasonal Indices by the Link Relative method from the data given below :

Output of Wheat in Million Tonnes

Year	*I Quarter*	*II Quarter*	*III Quarter*	*IV Quarter*
1999	60	65	62	69
2000	62	68	65	68
2001	65	70	64	62
2002	70	75	68	67
2003	72	80	70	78

(*B. Com.*)

Solution :

Computation of Seasonal Indices

		Link Relatives		
Year	*Ist Quarter*	*IInd Quarter*	*IIIrd Quarter*	*IVth Quarter*
1999		108.3	95.4	111.3
2000	89.9	109.7	95.6	104.6
2001	95.6	107.7	91.4	96.9

2002	112.9	107.1	90.7	98.5
2003	107.5	111.1	87.5	111.4
Total of L.R.	405.9	543.9	460.6	522.7
Arithmetic mean	101.475	108.78	92.12	104.54
Chain Relatives	100	108.78	100.208	104.757
Adjusted C.R.	100	108.78 – 1.575 = 107.205	100.208 – 3.15 = 97.058	104.757 – 4.725 = 100.032
Seasonal Index	98.94	$\frac{107.205}{101.073} \times 100$ = 106.07	$\frac{97.058}{101.073} \times 100$ = 96.03	$\frac{100.032}{101.073} \times 100$ = 98.97

$$\text{Link Relative for any Quarter} = \frac{\text{Current Quarter's Value}}{\text{Previous Quarter's Value}} \times 100$$

$$\text{Link Relative for IInd Qr. of 1999} = \frac{65}{60} \times 100 = 108.3$$

$$\text{Link Relative for IIIrd Qr. of 1999} = \frac{62}{65} \times 100 = 95.4$$

$$\text{Link Relative for IVth Qr. of 1999} = \frac{69}{62} \times 100 = 111.3$$

Similarly the other Quarter's Link Relatives can be calculated.

Chain Relatives :

Chain Relatives for Ist Qr. = 100 (by assuming).

$$\text{C.R. for IInd Qr.} = \frac{\text{Link Relative for IIQr.} \times \text{C.R.Ist Qr.}}{100}$$

$$= \frac{108.78}{100} \times 100 = \mathbf{108.78}$$

$$\text{C.R. for IIIrd Qr.} = \frac{92.12 \times 108.78}{100} = \mathbf{100.208}$$

$$\text{C.R. for IVth Qr.} = \frac{104.54 \times 100.208}{100} = \mathbf{104.757}$$

The New (second) C.R. for Ist Quarter :

$$= \frac{\text{L.R. of Ist Qr.} \times \text{C.R. of last (IVth) Qr.}}{100}$$

$$= \frac{101.475 \times 104.757}{100}$$

$$= 106.30$$

Correction factor Qr.= $\frac{1}{4}$ (New C.R of Ist Qr. − 100)

$$= \frac{106.30 - 100}{4} = \frac{6.30}{4} = 1.575$$

Quarter I = 106.30 − 6.30 = 100

Quarter II = 108.78 − 1.575 = 107.205

Quarter III = 100.208 − 3.15 = 97.058

Quarter IV = 104.757 − 4.725 = 100.032

Average of Corrected C.R.

$$= \frac{100 + 107.205 + 97.058 + 100.032}{4}$$

$$= \frac{404.295}{4} = \mathbf{101.073}$$

Seasonal Indices : Quarter II = $\frac{107.205}{101.073} \times 100 = 106.07$

Quarter III = $\frac{97.058}{101.073} \times 100 = 96.03$

Quarter IV = $\frac{100.032}{101.073} \times 100 = 98.97$

Problem 55. Calculate the seasonal variation indices by the method of link relatives for the following figures :

Quarterly Figures for Five Years

	Year				
Quarter	1999	2000	2001	2002	2003
I	45	48	49	52	63
II	54	56	63	65	70
III	72	63	70	75	84
IV	60	56	65	72	66

(*M. Com., Rajasthan*)

Solution :

Computation of Seasonal Indices by Link Relative Method

	Link Relatives			
Year	*Ist Quarter*	*IInd Quarter*	*IIIrd Quarter*	*IVth Quarter*
1999	–	120.00	133.33	83.33
2000	80.00	116.67	112.50	88.89
2001	87.50	128.57	111.11	92.86
2002	80.00	125.00	115.38	96.00
2003	87.50	111.11	120.00	78.57
Total of L.R.	335.00	601.35	592.32	439.65
Arithmetic Mean	83.75	120.27	118.46	87.93

Chain Relative	100	120.27	142.47	125.27
Adjusted C.R.	100	119.04	141.01	121.58
Seasonal Indices	83.05	98.86	117.11	100.97

$$\text{Link Relative for a Quarter} = \frac{\text{current Quarter's Value}}{\text{Previous Quarter's Value}} \times 100$$

$$\text{Link Relative for IInd Qr.} = \frac{54}{45} \times 100 = \mathbf{120}$$

$$\text{Link Relative for IIIrd Qr.} = \frac{72}{54} \times 100 = \mathbf{133.33}$$

$$\text{Link Relative for IVth Qr.} = \frac{60}{72} \times 100 = \mathbf{83.33}$$

Similarly the other Quarter's L. R. can be calculated.

Chain Relatives :

Chain Relatives for Ist Qr. = 100 (by assuming).

$$\text{C.R. for IInd Qr.} = \frac{\text{L.R. for IInd Qr.} \times \text{C.R. Ist Qr.}}{100}$$

$$= \frac{120.27}{100} \times 100 = \mathbf{120.27}$$

$$\text{C.R. for IIIrd Qr.} = \frac{\text{L.R. for IIIrd Qr.} \times \text{C.R. IInd Qr.}}{100}$$

$$= \frac{118.46 \times 120.27}{100} = \mathbf{142.47}$$

$$\text{C.R. for IVth Qr.} = \frac{87.93 \times 142.47}{100} = \mathbf{125.27}$$

The New (second) C.R. for Ist Quarter :

$$= \frac{\text{L.R. of Ist Qr.} \times \text{ C.R. of last (IVth) Qr.}}{100} = \frac{83.75 \times 125.27}{100}$$

$$= \mathbf{104.91}$$

$$\text{Correction factor} = \frac{1}{4}\left(\frac{\text{New C.R. of Ist Qr.} - 100}{4}\right)$$

$$= \frac{104.91 - 100}{4} = \frac{4.91}{4} = \mathbf{1.23}$$

Adjusted Chain Relative :

Quarter I = 104.91 – 4.91 = **100**

Quarter II = 120.27 – 1.23 = **119.04**

Quarter III = 142.47 – 2.46 = **141.01**

Quarter IV = 125.27 – 3.69 = **121.58**

Average of Adjusted C.R. :

$$= \frac{100 + 119.04 + 141.01 + 121.58}{4}$$

$$= \frac{481.63}{4} = 120.41$$

Seasonal Indices :

Quarter I $= \frac{100}{120.41} \times 100 = \mathbf{83.05}$

Quarter II $= \frac{119.04}{120.41} \times 100 = \mathbf{98.96}$

Quarter III $= \frac{141.01}{120.41} \times 100 = \mathbf{117.11}$

Quarter IV $= \frac{121.58}{120.41} \times 100 = \mathbf{100.97}$

Problem 56. Calculate the Seasonal Index from the following data using the average method :

Year	I Qr.	II Qr.	III Qr.	IV Qr.
1999	72	68	80	70
2000	76	70	82	74
2001	74	66	84	80
2002	76	74	84	78
2003	78	74	86	82

(*C A Inter*)

Solution :

Computation of Seasonal Indices

Year	*I Qr.*	*II Qr.*	*III Qr.*	*IV Qr.*
1999	72	68	80	70
2000	76	70	82	74
2001	74	66	84	80
2002	76	74	84	78
2003	78	74	86	82
Total	376	352	416	384
Average	75.2	70.4	83.2	76.8
Seasonal Index	98.43	92.15	108.9	100.52

$$\text{Average of Averages} = \frac{75.2 + 70.4 + 83.2 + 76.8}{4}$$

$$= \frac{305.6}{4} = 76.4$$

Seasonal Index = (Arithmetic Mean ÷ Average of Averages) × 100

$$\frac{75.2}{76.4} \times 100 = 98.43 \qquad \frac{70.4}{76.4} \times 100 = 92.15$$

$$\frac{83.2}{76.4} \times 100 = 108.9 \qquad \frac{76.8}{76.4} \times 100 = 100.52$$

Problem 57. Using a quarterly moving average in respect of the following data, find
(*a*) trend,
(*b*) short–term fluctuations,

Year	*Ist Quarter*	*2nd Quarter*	*3rd Quarter*	*4th Quarter*
1999	35	86	67	124
2000	38	109	91	176
2001	47	158	104	226
2002	61	177	134	240
2003	72	206	141	307

(*C.A., Inter*)

Solution :

Computation of Seasonal Fluctuations

Year	*Quarter* (1)	*Y* (2)	*4 Yearly moving total* (3)	*4 Yearly moving average* (4)	*4 Yearly moving average centred* (5)	*Short term fluctuation* 6 = (2–5)	*Seasonal fluctuations* (*Refer Table*)
1999	Ist	35	–				
	2nd	86	–				
			→ 312	78.0			
	3rd	67			→ 78.38	−11.38	−19.22
			→ 315	78.75			
	4th	124			→ 81.63	+42.37	+68.38
			→ 338	84.5			
2000	Ist	38			→ 87.50	−49.50	−74.69
			→ 362	90.5			
	2nd	109			→ 97.00	+12.0	+25.28
			→ 414	103.5			
	3rd	91			→ 104.63	−13.63	−19.22
			→ 423	105.75			
	4th	176			→ 111.88	+64.12	+68.38
			→ 472	118.0			
2001	Ist	47			→ 119.63	−72.63	−74.69
			→ 485	121.25			
	2nd	158			→ 127.50	+30.50	+25.28
			→ 535	133.75			
	3rd	104			→ 135.50	−31.50	−19.22
			→ 549	137.25			
	4th	226			→ 139.63	+86.37	+68.38
			→ 568	142.0			
2002	Ist	61			→ 145.75	−84.75	−74.69
			→ 598	149.5			
	2nd	177			→ 151.25	+25.75	+25.28
			→ 612	153.0			
	3rd	134			→ 154.38	−20.38	−19.22
			→ 623	155.75			

	4th	240			→ 159.38	+80.62	+68.38
			→ 652	163.0			
2003	Ist	72			→ 163.88	−91.88	−74.68
			→ 659	164.75			
	2nd	206			→ 173.13	+32.87	+25.28
			→ 726	181.5			
	3rd	141	–				
	4th	307	–				

Quarter		*Deviation from Trend*		
Year	*Ist Quarter*	*IInd Quarter*	*IIIrd Quarter*	*IVth Quarter*
1999	–	–	−11.38	+ 42.37
2000	−49.50	+12.00	−13.63	+ 64.12
2001	−72.63	+30.50	−31.50	+ 86.37
2002	−84.75	+25.75	−20.38	+ 80.62
2003	−91.88	+32.87	–	–
Total	−298.76	+101.12	−76.89	+273.48
Average	−74.69	+25.28	−19.22	+68.37

Problem 58. Calculate seasonal indices from the following data with the help of the method of link relatives :

Quarter	1998	1999	2000	2001	2002
I	31	42	49	47	51
II	39	44	53	51	54
III	45	57	65	62	66
IV	36	45	55	50	58

(*B. Com.*)

Solution :

Computation of Seasonal Indices

		Link Relatives		
Year	*Ist Quarter*	*IInd Quarter*	*IIIrd Quarter*	*IVth Quarter*
1998	–	125.8	115.4	80.0
1999	116.7	104.8	129.5	78.9
2000	108.9	108.2	122.6	84.6
2001	85.5	108.5	121.6	80.6
2002	102.0	105.9	122.2	87.9
Total of L.R.	413.1	553.2	611.3	412.0
Arithmetic Mean	103.3	110.6	122.3	82.4
Chain Relative	100	110.6	135.3	111.5
Adjusted C.R.	100	106.8	127.7	101.1
Seasonal Indices	91.8	98.1	117.3	92.8

$$\text{Link Relative for any Quarter} = \frac{\text{current Quarter's Value}}{\text{Previous Quarter's Value}} \times 100$$

$$\text{L.R. for IInd Quarter} = \frac{39}{31} \times 100 = \mathbf{125.8}$$

$$\text{L.R. for IIIrd Quarter} = \frac{45}{39} \times 100 = \mathbf{115.4}$$

$$\text{L.R. for IVth Quarter} = \frac{36}{45} \times 100 = \mathbf{80.0}$$

Similarly the other Quarter's Link Relatives can be calculated.

Chain Relatives :

Chain Relatives for Ist Quarter = 100 (by assumption).

$$\text{C.R. for IInd Quarter} = \frac{\text{L.R. for II Qr.} \times \text{C.R. Ist Qr.}}{100}$$

$$= \frac{110.6 \times 100}{100} = \mathbf{110.6}$$

$$\text{C.R. for IIIrd Quarter} = \frac{122.3 \times 110.6}{100} = \mathbf{135.3}$$

$$\text{C.R for IVth Qr.} = \frac{82.4 \times 135.3}{100} = \mathbf{111.5}$$

The New C.R. (second) for Ist Quarter :

$$= \frac{\text{L.R. of Ist Qr.} \times \text{C.R. of last (IVth) Qr.}}{100} = \frac{103.3 \times 111.5}{100} = \mathbf{115.2}$$

$$\text{Correction factor} = \frac{1}{4}\,(\text{New C.R of Ist Qr.} - 100)$$

$$= \frac{1}{4}(115.2 - 100)$$

$$= \frac{15.2}{4} = \mathbf{3.8}$$

Adjusted C.R. are obtained by subtracting 1 × 3.8, 2 × 3.8, 3 × 3.8 from the chain relatives of the IInd, IIIrd and IVth Qrs. respectively. i.e

Qr. II = 110.6 – 3.8 = **106.8**

Qr. III = 135.3 – 7.6 = **127.7**

Qr. IV = 111.5 – 11.4 = **101.1**

$$\text{Average of Corrected C.R.} = \frac{100 + 106.8 + 127.7 + 101.1}{4}$$

$$= \frac{435.6}{4} = \mathbf{108.9}$$

Seasonal Indices :

$$\text{Qr. I} = \frac{100}{108.9} \times 100 = \mathbf{91.8}$$

$$\text{Qr. II} = \frac{106.8}{108.9} \times 100 = \mathbf{98.1}$$

$$\text{Qr. III} = \frac{127.7}{108.9} \times 100 = \mathbf{117.3}$$

$$\text{Qr. IV} = \frac{101.1}{108.9} \times 100 = \mathbf{92.8}$$

10

INTERPOLATION AND EXTRAPOLATION

A. Graphic method
B. Algebraic Method
   1. Binomial Expansion Method
   2. Newton's Method
   3. Lagrange Method
   4. Parabolic Method

FORMULAE

1. Binomial Expansion Method Condition :
   1. The X variable advanced by equal intervals. i.e. 5, 10, 15 etc.

2. The value of X for which Y is to be interpolated is one of the class limits of X Series. When the method is applied, the terminal $(Y-1)^n$ must be expanded and Y is made equal to zero.

$$(Y-1)^n = y^n - n\,y^{n-1} + \frac{n(n-1)}{2!}\,y^{n-2} - \frac{n(n-1)\,(n-2)}{3!}\,y^{n-3} + \ldots\ldots = 0$$

$n =$ the number of known values

In other words, we have the following result:

No. of known values	Equation for determining the unknown values
2 or $\Delta_0{}^2$	$Y_2 - 2Y_1 + Y_0 = 0$
3 or $\Delta_0{}^3$	$Y_3 - 3Y_2 + 3Y_1 - Y_0 = 0$
4 or $\Delta_0{}^4$	$Y_4 - 4Y_3 + 6Y_2 - 4Y_1 + Y_0 = 0$
5 or $\Delta_0{}^5$	$Y_5 - 5Y_4 + 10Y_3 - 10Y_2 + 5Y_1 - Y_0 = 0$
6 or $\Delta_0{}^6$	$Y_6 - 6Y_5 + 15Y_4 - 20Y_3 + 15Y_2 - 6Y_1 + Y_0 = 0$
7 or $\Delta_0{}^7$	$Y_7 - 7Y_6 + 21Y_5 - 35Y_4 + 35Y_3 - 21Y_2 + 7Y_1 - Y_0 = 0$

2.Newton's Method Condition :
The X variable advanced by equal intervals :That is 5, 10, 15 etc.

$$Y_x = Y_0 + x\Delta_0' + \frac{x(x-1)}{2!}\Delta_0^2 + \frac{x(x-1)\,(x-2)}{3!}\Delta_0^3 + \frac{x(x-1)\,(x-2)(x-3)}{4!}\Delta_0^4 \;\ldots\ldots$$

Y_x = the figure to be interpolated
Y_0 = the value of Y at origin

$$x = \frac{\text{Year of interpolation} - \text{the value at origin}}{\text{Differences between two adjoining years}}$$

	Δ = are the difference between various values
3. Lagrange's method Conditions : When X series advanced by unequal intervals $Y_x = \frac{(x-x_1)(x-x_2)(x-x_3)......(x-x_n)}{(x_0-x_1)(x_0x_2)(x_0-x_3)......(x_0-x_n)}$ $+ Y_1 \frac{(x-x_0)(x-x_2)(x-x_3)(x-x_n)}{(x_1-x_0)(x_1-x_2)(x_1-x_3)(x_1-x_n)}$ $+ Y_2 \frac{(x-x_0)(x-x_1)(x-x_3)(x-x_n)}{(x_2-x_0)(x_2-x_1)(x_2-x_3)(x_2-x_n)}$ $+ Y_3 .....$ $+ Y_n \frac{(x-x_0)(x-x_1)(x-x_2)....(x-x_{n-1})}{(x_n-x_0)(x_n-x_1)(x_n-x_2)....(x-x_{n-1})}$	Y, x = the figure to be interpolated x_0, x_1, x_2 = The given values Y_0, Y_1, Y_2 = Corresponding values of Y variable Y_n = The figure to be interpolated
4. Parabolic Method $Y = a + bx + cx^2 + dx^3 + ... nx^n$	a, b, c, d are constants

GRAPHIC METHOD

Problem 1. From the following data interpolate graphically the expectation of life at the age of 22 :

Age	:	10	15	20	25	30	35
Expectation of life	:	35.4	32.2	29.1	26.0	23.1	20.4

What are the underlying assumptions when you interpolate a value ?

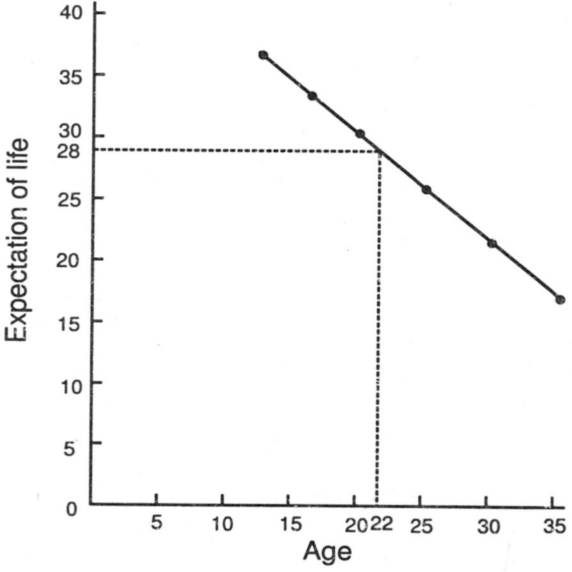

Expectation of life at the age of 22 is 28.

Problem 2. The following table gives the profits of a firm for the period 1997 to 2002. The figure for 2001 is missing. Interpolate the same by graphic method.

Year	:	1997	1998	1999	2000	2001	2002
Profits in Lakhs	:	108	113	110	110	?	114

(*B.Com., Osmania*)

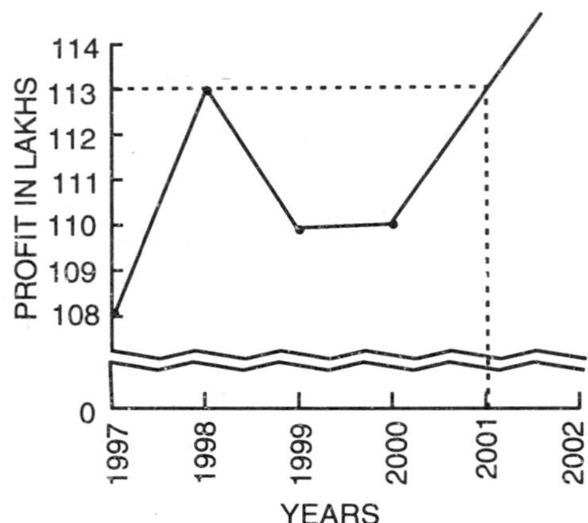

Binomial Expansion Method

Problem 3. Estimate the missing term in the following table :

X	:	1	2	3	4	5
Y	:	2	4	8	?	32

(*B. Com., Poona*)

Solution :

X	Y	X	Y
1	$2(Y_0)$	4	$?\ (Y_3)$
2	$4(Y_1)$	5	$32\ (Y_4)$
3	$8(Y_2)$		

In this problem, 4 values are known :

$$Y_4 - 4Y_3 + 6Y_2 - 4Y_1 + Y_0 = 0$$

(or) $$32 - (4Y_3) + (6 \times 8) - (4 \times 4) + 2 = 0$$

(or) $$32 - 4Y_3 + 48 - 16 + 2 = 0$$

(or) $$82 - 16 - 4Y_3 = 0$$

(or) $$66 - 4Y_3 = 0$$

(or) $$4Y_3 = 66$$

$$Y_3 = \frac{66}{4}$$

$$\doteqdot \mathbf{16.5}.$$

Problem 4. Estimate Y_1 from the following incomplete table :

X	:	1	2	3	4	5
Y	:	7	?	13	21	37

State the necessary assumptions made.

(*I.C.W.A., Inter*)

Solution :

X	Y	X	Y
1	$7(Y_0)$	4	$21(Y_3)$
2	? (Y_1)	5	$37(Y_4)$
3	$13(Y_2)$		

Known values are four. The missing value can be interpolated by Binomial Expansion Method. The equation is

$$Y_4 - 4Y_3 + 6Y_2 - 4Y_1 + Y_0 = 0$$

Substituting the values :

$$37 - (4 \times 21) + (6 \times 13) - 4Y_1 + 7 = 0$$

(or) $37 - 84 + 78 - 4Y_1 + 7 = 0$

(or) $122 - 84 - 4Y_1 = 0$

(or) $38 - 4Y_1 = 0$

(or) $4Y_1 = 38$

$$Y_1 = \frac{38}{4} = \mathbf{9.5}$$

Problem 5. Using an appropriate formula for interpolation estimate the average number of children born per month aged 30–34 :

Age of mother (in years)	*Average No. of children born*	*Age of mother (in years)*	*Average No. of children born*
15–19	0.7	30–34	?
20–24	2.1	35–39	5.7
25–29	3.1	40–44	5.8

(*B. Com., Bangalore*)

Solution :

Age of mother	*No. of children born*
15–19	0.7 (Y_0)
20–24	2.1 (Y_1)
25–29	3.1 (Y_2)
30–34	? (Y_3)
35–39	5.7 (Y_4)
40–44	5.8 (Y_5)

$$\Delta_0^5 = Y_5 - 5Y_4 + 10Y_3 - 10Y_2 + 5Y_1 - Y_0 = 0$$

Substituting the given values, we get

$$\Delta_0^5 = 5.8 - (5 \times 5.7) + 10Y_3 - (10 \times 3.1) + (5 \times 2.1) - 0.7 = 0$$

$$= 5.8 - 28.5 + 10Y_3 - 31 + 10.5 - 0.7 = 0$$
$$= 16.3 - 60.2 + 10Y_3 = 0$$
$$= -43.9 + 10Y_3 = 0$$
$$10Y_3 = 43.9$$
$$Y_3 = \frac{43.9}{10}$$
$$= \mathbf{4.39}$$

Hence the expected average number of children born per mother, in the age group 30–40 is 4.39.

Problem 6. The values of a function $f(x)$ are given for equidistant values of x:

x	:	4	5	6	7	8
$f(x)$	:	3.11	2.96	2.85	...	2.70

Obtain as best an approximation of f (7) as possible.

(I.C.W.A)

Solution :

x	y	x	y
4	$3.11(y_0)$	7	$?(y_3)$
5	$2.96(y_1)$	8	$2.70(y_4)$
6	$2.85(y_2)$		

Since known values are four, the equation is

$$y_4 - 4y_3 + 6y_2 - 4y_1 + y_0 = 0$$

Substituting :

$$2.70 - (4y_3) + (6 \times 2.85) - (4 \times 2.96) + 3.11 = 0$$
(or) $$2.70 - 4y_3 + 17.10 - 11.84 + 3.11 = 0$$
(or) $$22.91 - 11.84 - 4y_3 = 0$$
(or) $$11.07 - 4y_3 = 0$$
(or) $$4y_3 = 11.07$$
$$y_3 = \frac{11.07}{4}$$
$$= \mathbf{2.77.}$$

Problem : 7. The following table gives the amount of cement (Y) in thousands of tonnes manufactured in India. Find the missing figure.

Years	*Output*
1997	39
1998	85
1999	?
2000	151
2001	264
2002	388

(ICWA)

Solution :

Years	*Output*
1997	39(y_0)
1998	85 (y_1)
1999	? (y_2)
2000	151 (y_3)
2001	264 (y_4)
2002	388 (y_5)

The missing value can be interpolated by the Binomial Expansion Method. Known values are 5. Therefore, fifth leading differences will be zero. Here we have to find the value of y_2 and the equation :

$$y_5 - 5y_4 + 10y_3 - 10y_2 + 5y_1 - y_0 = 0$$
$$388 - (5 \times 264) + (10 \times 151) - (10y_2) + (5 \times 85) - 39 = 0$$
$$388 - 1320 + 1510 - 10y_2 + 425 - 39 = 0$$

(or) $$2323 - 1359 - 10y_2 = 0$$

(or) $$10y_2 = (2323 - 1359) = 964$$

(or) $$10y_2 = 964$$

$$\therefore \quad y_2 = \frac{964}{10} = \mathbf{96.4}.$$

Therefore, the estimated amount of cement manufactured in 1999 is 96.4 thousand tonnes.

Problem 8. Below are given weighted index numbers of cost of living of labourers in an industrial center in India. Interpolate to find out the missing index number for 2000 to the nearest integer using all the figures :

Year	:	1997	1998	1999	2001	2002
Index	:	173	149	145	131	141

(*B.Com.*)

Solution:

Year	*Index*
1997	173 (y_0)
1998	149 (y_1)
1999	145 (y_2)
2000	? (y_3)
2001	131 (y_4)
2002	141 (y_5)

We have to find out the value of y_3 or $\Delta_0^5 = 0$

$$y_5 - 5y_4 + 10y_3 - 10y_2 + 5y_1 - y_0 = 0$$
$$= 141 - (5 \times 131) + 10y_3 - (10 \times 145) + (5 \times 149) - 173 = 0$$

(or) $$= 141 - 655 + 10y_3 - 1450 + 745 - 173 = 0$$

(or) $$= 886 - 2278 + 10y_3 = 0$$

$$
\begin{aligned}
\text{(or)} \quad &= -1392 + 10y_3 = 0 \\
\text{(or)} \quad &= 10y_3 = 1392 \\
y_3 &= \frac{1392}{10} \\
&= \mathbf{139.2}.
\end{aligned}
$$

Problem 9. Using any method of interpolation find the population for 1981

Age (year)	*Population in (lakhs)*
1961	2522
1971	2514
1991	3168
2001	3613

(*B.Com., Mysore*)

Solution :

Known values are four. Binomial Expansion method is suitable.

$$Y_4 - 4y_3 + 6y_2 - 4y_1 + y_0 = 0$$

x	y	x	y
1961	2522 (y_0)	1991	3168 (y_3)
1971	2514 (y_1)	2001	3613 (y_4)
1981	? (y_2)		

Putting the values in the equation :

$$
\begin{aligned}
3613 - (4 \times 3168) + (6y_2) - (4 \times 2514) + 2522 &= 0 \\
\text{(or)} \quad 3,613 - 12,672 + 6y_2 - 10,056 + 2522 &= 0 \\
\text{(or)} \quad 6135 - 22728 + 6y_2 &= 0 \\
\text{(or)} \quad - 16593 + 6y_2 &= 0 \\
\text{(or)} \quad 6y_2 &= 16593 \\
y_2 &= \frac{16593}{6} \\
&= \mathbf{2765.5}
\end{aligned}
$$

Therefore, the population for 1981 is 2765.5 lakhs.

Problem 10. Use any suitable algebraic method of interpolation to find the value of y for $x = 3$ from the table below :

X	1	2	3	4	5
Y	2,16,000	2,26,981	...	2,50,047	2,62,144

(*I.A.S., B.Com., Madras*)

Solution :

X	Y	Z
1	2,16,000	y_0
2	2,26,981	y_1
3	?	y_2
4	2,50,047	y_3
5	2,62,144	y_4

Known values are 4.

$$Y_4 - 4y_3 + 6y_2 - 4y_1 + y_0 = 0$$
$$= 2,62,144 - (4 \times 2,50,047) + (6 \times y_2) - (4 \times 2,26,981) + 2,16,000 = 0$$
$$= 2,62,144 - 10,00,188. + 6y_2 - 9,07,924 + 2,16,000 = 0$$
$$4,78,144 + 6y_2 - 19,08,112$$
$$6y_2 = 14,29,968$$
$$y_2 = \frac{14,29,968}{6} = 2,38,328$$
$$y_2 = 2,38,328.$$

Problem 11. Interpolate the missing figure in the following table with the help of a suitable formula.

Year	:	1996	1997	1998	1999	2000	2001
No. of Factories	:	200	225	250	255	?	265

(*B.Com., Mysore*)

Solution:

x	y	x	y
1996	200 (y_0)	1999	255 (y_3)
1997	225 (y_1)	2000	? (y_4)
1998	250 (y_2)	2001	265 (y_5)

We have to find the Value of y_4

$$y_5 - 5y_4 + 10y_3 - 10y_2 + 5y_1 - y_0 = 0$$
$$265 - 5y_4 + (10 \times 255) - (10 \times 250) + (5 \times 225) - 200 = 0$$
(or) $$265 - 5y_4 + 2550 - 2500 + 1125 - 200 = 0$$
(or) $$3940 - 2700 - 5y_4 = 0$$
(or) $$1240 - 5y_4 = 0$$
(or) $$5y_4 = 1240$$
$$y_4 = \frac{1240}{5}$$
$$= \mathbf{248}.$$

Problem 12. Describe any algebraic method of interpolation you know of, stating the assumptions involved. Find by algebraic method of interpolation the number for 2000 from the following table of index numbers of production of a certain article in India :

Year :	1998	1999	2001	2002
Index No. :	100	107	157	212

(*B.Com., Madras*)

Solution :

x	y	x	y
1998	100 (y_0)	2001	157 (y_3)
1999	107 (y_1)	2002	212 (y_4)
2000	? (y_2)		

$$
\begin{aligned}
\Delta_0^4 &= y_4 - 4y_3 + 6y_2 - 4y_1 + y_0 = 0 \\
\text{(or)} \quad &= 212 - (4 \times 157) + 6y_2 - (4 \times 107) + 100 = 0 \\
\text{(or)} \quad &= 212 - 628 + 6y_2 - 428 + 100 = 0 \\
\text{(or)} \quad &= 312 - 1056 + 6y_2 = 0 \\
\text{(or)} \quad &- 744 + 6y_2 = 0 \\
\text{(or)} \quad 6y_2 &= 744 \\
y_2 &= \frac{744}{6} \\
&= \mathbf{124}
\end{aligned}
$$

Problem 13. Describe any two methods of interpolation and state the assumptions underlying them. Use one of these methods to estimate the business done in 2000 from the following data :

Year :	1997	1998	1999	2001	2002
Business (in lakhs Rs.):	150	235	368	525	780

(*B.Com., Madras*)

Solution :

$$
\begin{aligned}
(y-1)^n &= y_5 - 5y_4 + 10y_3 - 10y_2 + 5y_1 - y_0 = 0 \\
&= 780 - (5 \times 525) + (10y_3) - (10 \times 368) + (5 \times 235) - (150) = 0 \\
&= 780 - 2625 + 10y_3 - 3680 + 1175 - 150 = 0 \\
&= 1955 + 10y_3 - 6455 = 0 \\
&= 10y_3 - 4500 = 0 \\
\therefore \quad y_3 &= \frac{4500}{10} = 450
\end{aligned}
$$

The probable value of business for the year 2000 is 450 lakhs.

Problem 14. Find by interpolation the number of policies in force in 1999 from the following data :

Year	:	1996	1997	1998	2000	2001	2002
Number in force (lakhs)	:	66	73	81	99	106	112

(*B. Com., Madras*)

Solution :

x	y	x	y
1996	66 (y_0)	2000	99 (y_4)
1997	73 (y_1)	2001	106 (y_5)
1998	81 (y_2)	2002	112 (y_6)
1999	? (y_3)		

$$y_6 - 6y_5 + 15y_4 - 20y_3 + 15y_2 - 6y_1 + y_0 = 0$$

$$112 - (6 \times 106) + (15 \times 99) - 20y_3 + (15 \times 81) - (6 \times 73) + 66 = 0$$

(or) $$112 - 636 + 1485 - 20y_3 + 1215 - 438 + 66 = 0$$

(or) $$2878 - 1074 - 20y_3 = 0$$

(or) $$1804 - 20y_3 = 0$$

(or) $20y_3 = 1804$

$$y_3 = \frac{1804}{20}$$

$$= \mathbf{90.2}\ \textbf{lakhs.}$$

Problem 15. The working class cost of living index numbers for a certain place are given below for certain years. Interpolate the missing number :

Year	:	1997	1998	1999	2000	2001	2002
Index No.	:	320	300	?	280	278	250

(*B. Com. Mysore*)

Solution :

x	y	x	y
1997	320 (y_0)	2000	280 (y_3)
1998	300 (y_1)	2001	278 (y_4)
1999	? (y_2)	2002	250 (y_5)

Known values are 5. The formula is

$$Y_5(y-1)^5 = 0 \quad \text{or} \quad \Delta_0^5 = 0$$

$$Y_5 - 5y_4 + 10y_3 - 10y_2 + 5y_1 - y_0 = 0$$

$$250 - (5 \times 278) + (10 \times 280) - 10y_2 + (5 \times 300) - 320 = 0$$

(or) $$250 - 1390 + 2800 - 10y_2 + 1500 - 320 = 0$$

(or) $$4550 - 1710 - 10y_2 = 0$$

(or) $$2840 - 10y_2 = 0$$

(or) $$10y_2 = 2840$$

$$y_2 = \frac{2840}{10}$$

$$= \mathbf{284.}$$

Problem 16. Estimate the production for the year 1999 and 2001 with the help of the following table.

Year :	1996	1997	1998	1999	2000	2001	2002
Production (in '000 tonnes) :	200	220	260	?	350	?	430

(*M. Com. Agra, B. Com. Punjab*)

Solution :

x	y	x	y
1996	200 (y_0)	2000	350 (y_4)
1997	220 (y_1)	2001	? (y_5)
1998	260 y_2)	2002	430 (y_6)
1999	? (y_3)		

We need two equations to estimate two unknowns, y_3 and y_5

$$y_5 - 5y_4 + 10y_3 - 10y_2 + 5y_1 - y_0 = 0$$

(or) $$y_5 - 5 \times 350 + 10y_3 - 10 \times 260 + 5 \times 200 = 0$$

$$
\begin{aligned}
\text{(or)}\quad & y_5 - 1750 + 10y_3 - 2600 + 1100 - 200 = 0 \\
\text{(or)}\quad & y_5 + 10y_3 + 1100 - 4550 = 0 \\
\text{(or)}\quad & y_5 + 10y_3 - 3450 = 0 \\
\text{(or)}\quad & y_5 + 10y_3 = 3450 \qquad (1)
\end{aligned}
$$

Similarly

$$
\begin{aligned}
& Y_6 - 5y_5 + 10y_4 - 10y_3 + 5y_2 - y_1 = 0 \\
\text{(or)}\quad & 430 - 5y_5 + 10 \times 350 - 10y_3 + 5 \times 260 - 220 = 0 \\
\text{(or)}\quad & 430 - 5y_5 + 3500 - 10y_3 + 1300 - 200 = 0 \\
\text{(or)}\quad & 5230 - 220 - 5y_5 - 10y_3 = 0 \\
\text{(or)}\quad & -5y_5 - 10y_3 + 5010 = 0 \\
\text{(or)}\quad & 5y_5 + 10y_3 = 5010 \qquad (2)
\end{aligned}
$$

Subtracting equation (1) from (2)

i.e

$$
\begin{aligned}
5y_5 + 10y_3 &= 5010 \\
y_5 + 10y_3 &= 3450 \\
\hline
4y_5 &= 1560
\end{aligned}
$$

$$y_5 = 1560 \div 4 = \mathbf{390} \quad \therefore \quad (Eq.1) \quad 390 + 10y_3 = 3450$$

$$10y_3 = 3450 - 390 = 3060 \qquad \therefore \quad y_3 = \frac{3060}{10} = 306$$

Thus, the estimated production for 1999 is 306 ('000) tons and for 2001 is 390 ('000) tons

Problem 17. The number of members of international statistical society are :

X	1990	1991	1992	1993	1994	1995	1996	1997	1998	1999
Y	845	867	?	846	821	772	?	757	761	796

Make the best estimate you can of the members in 1992 and 1996.

(*B.Com., Punjab*)

Solution : Two equations are needed, since two values are unknown.

x	y	x	y
1990	845 (y_0)	1995	772 (y_5)
1991	867 (y_1)	1996	? (y_6)
1992	? (y_2)	1997	757 (y_7)
1993	846 (y_3)	1998	761 (y_8)
1994	821(y_4)	1999	796 (y_9)

$$\Delta^8 y_0 = 0 \qquad\qquad \Delta^8 y_1 = 0$$

$$\Delta^8 y_0 = y_8 - 8y_7 + 28y_6 - 56y_5 + 70y_4 - 56y_3 + 28y_2 - 8y_1 + y_0 = 0$$
$$\Delta^8 y_1 = y_9 - 8y_8 + 28y_7 - 56y_6 + 70y_5 - 56y_4 + 28y_3 - 8y_2 + y_1 = 0$$

Substituting the values in the formula

$$761 - (8 \times 757) + 28y_6 - (56 \times 772) + (70 \times 821) - (56 \times 846) + 28y_2 - 8 \times 867 + 845 = 0$$

$$\text{or } 761 - 6056 + 28y_6 - 43232 + 57470 - 47376 + 28y_2 - 6936 + 845 = 0$$

(or) $$28y_6 + 28y_2 + 59076 - 1,03,600 = 0$$

(or) $$28y_6 + 28y_2 = 44524 \quad (1)$$

$$796 - (8 \times 761) + (28 \times 757) - 56y_6 + (70 \times 772) - (56 \times 821) + (28 \times 846) - 8y_2 + 867 = 0$$

$$796 - 6088 + 21196 - 56y_6 + 54040 - 45976 + 23688 - 8y_2 + 867 = 0$$

(or) $$-56y_6 - 8y_2 + 100587 - 52064 = 0$$

(or) $$56y_6 - 8y_2 + 48523 = 0$$

(or) $$56y_6 - 8y_2 = 48,523 \quad (2)$$

Multiply equation(1) by 2, thus,

$$56y_6 + 56y_2 = 89048 \quad (3)$$

Subtract equation (2) from (3), we get

$$48y_2 = 40,525$$

$$y_2 = \frac{40525}{48}$$

$$\therefore \quad y_2 = \mathbf{844.27}$$

Putting the value in equation (1)

$$28y_6 + (28 \times 844.27) = 44524$$

$$28y_6 = 44,524 - 23639.56$$

$$28y_6 = 20884.44$$

$$y_6 = \frac{20884.44}{28}$$

$$= \mathbf{745.87}$$

Therefore missing values for 1992 is 844.27 and for 1996 is 745.87.

NEWTON'S METHOD

Problem 18. Given the following table construct a difference table and from it estimate y when $x = 0.35$ by using Newton's backward interpolation formula

x :	0	0.1	0.2	0.3	0.4
y :	1	1.095	1.179	1.251	1.310

(Answer to be given correct to 6 decimal places)

(I.C.W.A., Intermediate)

Solution :

x	y	*Differences*			
		Δ^1	Δ^2	Δ^3	Δ^4
0	1 (y_0)				
		+.095 $\Delta^1{}_0$			
0.1	1.095		−0.011 $\Delta^2{}_0$		
		+.084 $\Delta^1{}_1$		−0.011 $\Delta^3{}_0$	
0.2	1.179		−0.012		0 $\Delta^4{}_0$
		+.072 $\Delta^1{}_2$		−0.001	
0.3	1.251		−0.013		
		+.059 $\Delta^1{}_3$			
0.4	1.31				

$$x = \frac{0.35 - 0}{0.1} = 3.5$$

$$\begin{aligned}
yx &= y_0 + x\Delta_0{}^1 + \frac{x(x-1)}{2!}\Delta^2{}_0 + \frac{x(x-1)(x-2)}{3!}\Delta^3{}_0 \\
&\qquad + \frac{x(x-1)(x-2)(x-3)}{4!}\Delta^4{}_0 \\
&= 1 + 3.5 \times 0.095 + \frac{3.5 \times 2.5}{2}(-0.011) + \frac{3.5 \times 2.5 \times 1.5}{2 \times 3}(-0.011) \\
&\qquad + \frac{3.5 \times 2.5 \times 1.5 \times 0.5}{2 \times 3 \times 4} \times 0 \\
&= 1 + 0.3325 - 0.048125 - 0.002188 + 0 \\
&= 1.3325 - 0.050313 \\
&= \mathbf{1.282187}
\end{aligned}$$

When $x = 0.35$, $y =$ **1.282187**

Problem 19. From the following table estimate by interpolation the number of units of a commodity supplied when the price is Rs. 4.

Price in rupees :	1	3	5	7	9
No. of units supplied :	256	625	935	1201	1333

(*B. Com., Calcutta*)

Solution :

Price (x)	*No. of units* (y)	Δ^1	Δ^2	Δ^3	Δ^4
1	256 (y_0)				
		369$\Delta^1{}_0$			
3	625 (y_1)		−59 $\Delta^2{}_0$		
		310		15 $\Delta^3{}_0$	
5	935 (y_2)		−44		−105 $\Delta^4{}_0$
		266		−90	
7	1201 (y_3)		−134		
		132			
9	1333 (y_4)				

$$x = \frac{4-1}{2} = 1.5$$

$$\begin{aligned}
y_x &= y_0 + x\Delta_0^1 + \frac{x(x-1)}{2!}\Delta_0^2 + \frac{x(x-1)(x-2)}{3!}\Delta_0^3 \\
&\quad + \frac{x(x-1)(x-2)(x-3)}{4!}\Delta_0^4 \\
&= 256 + 1.5 \times 369 + \frac{1.5(1.5-1)}{2}(-59) + \frac{1.5(1.5-1)(1.5-2)}{2 \times 3}(15) \\
&\quad + \frac{1.5(1.5-1)(1.5-2)(1.5-3)}{2 \times 3 \times 4}(-105) \\
&= 256 + 1.5 \times 369 + \frac{1.5 \times 0.5}{2}(-59) + \frac{(1.5 \times 0.5 \times -0.5)}{2 \times 3}(15) \\
&\quad + \frac{1.5 \times 0.5 \times -0.5 \times -1.5}{2 \times 3 \times 4}(-105) \\
&= 256 + 553.5 - 22.125 - 0.9375 - 2.4609 \\
&= 809.5 - 25.5234 \text{ or } 25.5 \\
&= \mathbf{784.}
\end{aligned}$$

Problem 20. The following are the annual premiums charged by the Life Insurance Corporation of India for a policy of Rs. 1,000. Calculate the premium payable at the age of 26.

Age in years :	20	25	30	35	40
Premium (Rs.) :	23	26	30	35	42

(*M. Com., Agra*)

Solution :

Age year x	*Premium (y)*		*First* Δ^1		*Second* Δ^2		*Third* Δ^3		*Fourth* Δ^4	
20	23	y_0								
			+3	$\Delta^1{}_0$						
25	26	y_1			+1	$\Delta^2{}_0$				
			+4	$\Delta^1{}_1$			0	$\Delta^3{}_0$		
30	30	y_2			+1	$\Delta^2{}_1$			+1	$\Delta^4{}_0$
			+5	$\Delta^1{}_2$			+1	$\Delta^3{}_1$		
35	35	y_3			+2	$\Delta^2{}_2$				
			+7	$\Delta^1{}_3$						
40	42	y_4								

$$\begin{aligned}
y_x &= y_0 + x\Delta^1{}_0 + \frac{x(x-1)}{2!}\Delta^2{}_0 + \frac{x(x-1)\,(x-2)}{3!}\Delta^3{}_0 \ldots. \\
&\quad + \frac{x(x-1),(x-2)\,(x-3)}{4!} \times \Delta^4{}_0
\end{aligned}$$

$$x = \frac{26-20}{5} = \frac{6}{5} = 1.2$$

$$\begin{aligned}
y_x &= 23 + 1.2(3) + \frac{1.2(1.2-1)}{1 \times 2} \times 1 + \frac{1.2(1.2-1)(1.2-2)}{1 \times 2 \times 3} \times 0 \\
&\quad + \frac{1.2(1.2-1)(1.2-2)(1.2-3)}{1 \times 2 \times 3 \times 4} \times 1 = 23 + 3.6 + 0.12 + 0 + 0.014
\end{aligned}$$

$= \mathbf{26.734}$

(or) $= \mathbf{Rs.26.73}$.

Problem 21. The expectation of life at different ages for males (all India) is shown below :

Age (years)	:	20	25	30	35	40
Expectation of life (years)	:	33	29.8	26.6	23.5	20.5

Use Newton's formula and estimate the expectation of life at the age of 32 years.

(*B. Com., Bangalore*)

Solution:

Age	*Expectation of life*	*Differences* Δ^1		Δ^2		Δ^3		Δ^4	
$20(x_0)$	$33\ (y_0)$								
		-3.2	$\Delta^1{}_0$						
$25\ (x_1)$	$29.8\ (y_1)$			0	$\Delta^2{}_0$				
		-3.2	$\Delta^1{}_1$			$+0.1$	$\Delta^3{}_0$		
$30\ (x_2)$	$26.6\ (y_2)$			$+0.1$	$\Delta^2{}_1$			-0.1	$\Delta^4{}_0$
		-3.1	$\Delta^1{}_2$			0			
$35(x_3)$	$23.5(y_3)$			$+0.1$	$\Delta^2{}_2$				
		-3	$\Delta^1{}_3$						
$40\ (x_4)$	$20.5\ (y_4)$								

$$x = \frac{32-20}{5} = \frac{12}{5} = 2.4$$

$$y_x = y_0 + x\Delta^1{}_0 + \frac{x(x-1)}{2!}\Delta^2{}_0 + \frac{x(x-1)(x-2)}{3!}\Delta^3{}_0 + \frac{x(x-1)(x-2)(x-3)}{4!}\Delta^4{}_0$$

$$= 33 + (2.4 \times -3.2) + \frac{2.4(2.4-1)}{2} \times 0 + \frac{2.4(2.4-1)(2.4-2)}{2 \times 3}(0.1) + \frac{2.4(2.4-1)(2.4-2)(2.4-3)}{2 \times 3 \times 4}(-0.1)$$

$$= 33 - 7.68 + \frac{2.4 \times 1.4}{2} \times 0 + \frac{2.4 \times 1.4 \times 0.4}{6} \times 0.1 + \frac{2.4 \times 1.4 \times 0.4 \times -0.6}{24} \times (-0.1)$$

$$= 33 - 7.68 + 0 + 0.0224 + 0.0034$$

$$= 33.0258 - 7.68$$

$$= 25.3458$$

or $= \mathbf{25.4}$.

Problem 22. Estimate the expectation of life at the age of 16 years from the following data, by using Newton's formula :

Age in years	:	10	15	20	25	30	35
Expectation of life	:	35.4	32.3	29.2	26	23.2	20.4

(*B. Com., Kurukshetra*)

Solution :

Age Years (x)	Expectation of life	Δ^1		Δ^2		Δ^3		Δ^4		Δ^5	
10 (x_0)	35.4 (y_0)										
		−3.1	$\Delta^1{}_0$								
15 (x_1)	32.3 (y_1)			0	$\Delta^2{}_0$						
		−3.1	$\Delta^1{}_2$			−0.1	$\Delta^3{}_0$				
20 (x_2)	29.2(y_2)			−0.1	$\Delta^2{}_1$			0.6	$\Delta^4{}_0$		
		−3.2	$\Delta^1{}_3$			0.5	$\Delta^3{}_1$			−1.5	$\Delta^0{}_5$
25 (x_3)	26.0 (y_3)			0.4	$\Delta^2{}_2$			−0.9	$\Delta^4{}_1$		
		−2.8	$\Delta^1{}_4$			−0.4	$\Delta^3{}_2$				
30 (x_4)	23.2 (y_4)			0	$\Delta^2{}_3$						
		−2.8	$\Delta^1{}_5$								
35 (x_5)	20.4 (y_5)										

(The Δ^1 through Δ^5 columns sit under the heading *Differences*.)

$$x = \frac{16-10}{5} = \frac{6}{5} = 1.2$$

$$y_x = y_0 + x\Delta^1{}_0 + \frac{x(x-1)}{2!}\Delta^2{}_0 + \frac{x(x-1)(x-2)}{3!}\Delta^3{}_0 + \frac{x(x-1)(x-2)(x-3)}{4!}\Delta^4{}_0 + \frac{x(x-1)(x-2)(x-3)(x-4)}{5!}\Delta^5{}_0$$

$$y_x = 35.4 + 1.2(-3.1) + \frac{1.2(1.2-1)}{2}\times 0 + \frac{1.2(1.2-1)(1.2-2)}{2\times 3}\times(-0.1) + \frac{1.2(1.2-1)(1.2-2)(1.2-3)}{2\times 3\times 4}\times(0.6) + \frac{1.2(1.2-1)(1.2-2)(1.2-3)(1.2-4)}{2\times 3\times 4\times 5}(-1.5)$$

$$= 35.4 - 3.72 + \frac{1.2\times 0.2}{2}\times 0 + \frac{1.2\times 0.2(-0.8)}{6}(-0.1) + \frac{1.2\times 0.2(-0.8)(-1.8)\times(0.6)}{24} + \frac{1.2\times 0.2\times(-0.8)(-1.8)(-2.8)}{120}(-1.5)$$

$$= 35.4 - 3.72 + 0 + 0.0032 + 0.0086 + 0.0121$$

$$= 35.4239 - 3.72$$

$$= 31.7039 \text{ or } \mathbf{31.7}$$

Expectation of life at the age of 16 = **31.7**

Problem 23. Given the following pairs of corresponding values of X and Y :

X :	20	25	30	35	40
Y :	73	198	573	1198	1450

Estimate the Value of Y for $X = 22$

(*M. Com., Jammu*)

Solution :

X	Y	*Differences*							
		Δ^1		Δ^2		Δ^3		Δ^4	
20	73 (y_0)								
		125	${\Delta^1}_0$						
25	198 (y_1)			250	${\Delta^2}_0$				
		375	${\Delta^1}_1$			0	${\Delta^3}_0$		
30	573 (y_2)			250	${\Delta^2}_1$			−623	${\Delta^4}_0$
		625	${\Delta^1}_2$			−623	${\Delta^3}_1$		
35	1198 (y_3)			−373	${\Delta^2}_2$				
		252	${\Delta^1}_3$						
40	1450 (y_4)								

$$x = \frac{22-20}{5} = 0.4$$

$$y_x = y_0 + x{\Delta^1}_0 + \frac{x(x-1)}{2!}{\Delta^2}_0 + \frac{x(x-1)(x-2)}{3!}{\Delta^3}_0 + \frac{x(x-1)(x-2)(x-3)}{4!}{\Delta^4}_0$$

$$= 73 + 0.4 \times 125 + \frac{0.4(0.4-1)}{2} \times 250 + \frac{0.4(0.4-1)(0.4-2)}{2 \times 3} \times 0 + \frac{0.4(0.4-1)(0.4-2)(0.4-3)}{2 \times 3 \times 4}(-623)$$

$$= 73 + 0.4 \times 125 + \frac{0.4 \times -0.6}{2} \times 250 + \frac{0.4 \times -0.6 \times -1.6}{6} \times 0 + \frac{0.4 \times -0.6 \times -1.6 \times -2.6}{24} \times (-623)$$

$$= 73 + 50 - 30 + 0 + 25.9168$$

$$= 148.9168 - 30$$

$$= 118.9168 \text{ or } \mathbf{118.92}$$

Problem 24. Below are given the wages earned by workers per month in a certain factory. Calculate the number of workers earning more than Rs. 75 per month.

Weekly wages	*No. of workers*	*Weekly wages*	*No. of workers*
Upto Rs. 50	50	Upto Rs. 80	500
Upto Rs. 60	150	Upto Rs. 90	700
Upto Rs. 70	300	Upto Rs. 100	800

(*B. Com., Lucknow*)

Solution :

Weekly wages (X)	*No. of workers Y*	*Differences*									
		Δ^1		Δ^2		Δ^3		Δ^4		Δ^5	
Upto Rs.											
,, 50	50 y_0										
		100	$\Delta^1{}_0$								
,, 60	150 y_1			50	$\Delta^2{}_0$						
		150	$\Delta^1{}_1$			0	$\Delta^3{}_0$				
,, 70	300 y_2			50	$\Delta^2{}_1$			−50	$\Delta^4{}_0$		
		200	$\Delta^1{}_2$			−50	$\Delta^3{}_1$			0	$\Delta^5{}_0$
,, 80	500 y_3			0	$\Delta^2{}_2$			−50	$\Delta^4{}_1$		
		200	$\Delta^1{}_3$			−100	$\Delta^3{}_2$				
,, 90	700 y_4			−100	$\Delta^2{}_3$						
		100	$\Delta^1{}_4$								
,, 100	800 y_5										

$$x = \frac{75-50}{10} = \frac{25}{10} = 2.5$$

$$y_x = y_0 + x\Delta^1{}_0 + \frac{x(x-1)}{2!}\Delta^2{}_0 + \frac{x(x-1)(x-2)}{3!}\Delta^3{}_0$$

$$+\frac{x(x-1)(x-2)(x-3)}{4!}\Delta^4{}_0 + \frac{x(x-1)(x-2)(x-3)(x-4)}{5!}\Delta^5{}_0$$

$$= 50 + 2.5 \times 100 + \frac{2.5(2.5-1)}{2} \times 50 + \frac{2.5(2.5-1)(2.5-2)}{2 \times 3} \times 0$$

$$+\frac{2.5(2.5-1)(2.5-2)(2.5-3)}{2 \times 3 \times 4}(-50)$$

$$+\frac{2.5(2.5-1)(2.5-2)(2.5-3)(2.5-4)}{2 \times 3 \times 4 \times 5} \times 0$$

$$= 50 + 250 + 93.75 + 0 + 1.95 + 0$$

$$= \mathbf{395.7 \quad or \quad 396}$$

Hence workers earning wages upto Rs. 75 are 396. There are 800 workers. Therefore, number of workers earning more than Rs. 75 per month is 800−396 = 404 workers.

Problem 25. Using Newton's method of interpolation, estimate from the following data, the number of workers earning Rs. 24 or more but less than Rs. 25 :

Earning less than	:	20	25	30	35	40
No. of workers	:	296	599	804	918	966

(*M. Com., Meerut*)

Solution :

Earning (Rs)	*No. of Workers*		*Differences*							
			Δ^1		Δ^2		Δ^3		Δ^4	
Less than 20	296	(y_0)								
			+ 303	$\Delta^1{}_0$						
,, 25	599	(y_1)			−98	$\Delta^2{}_0$				
			+205	$\Delta^1{}_1$			+7	$\Delta^3{}_0$		
,, 30	804	(y_2)			−91	$\Delta^2{}_1$			+18	$\Delta^4{}_0$
			+114	$\Delta^1{}_2$			+25	$\Delta^3{}_1$		
,, 35	918	(y_3)			−66	$\Delta^2{}_2$				
			+48	$\Delta^1{}_3$						
,, 40	966	(y_4)								

$$y_x = y_0 + x\Delta^1{}_0 + \frac{x(x-1)}{1 \times 2}\Delta^2{}_0 + \frac{x(x-1)(x-2)}{1 \times 2 \times 3}\Delta^3{}_0 + \frac{x(x-1)(x-2)(x-3)}{1 \times 2 \times 3 \times 4}\Delta^4{}_0$$

$$x = \frac{24-20}{25-20} = \frac{4}{5} = 0.8$$

$$y_{24} = 296 + 0.8 \times 303 + \frac{0.8(0.8-1)}{2} \times -98 + \frac{0.8(0.8-1)(0.8-2)}{2 \times 3} \times 7 + \frac{0.8(0.8-1)(0.8-2)(0.8-3)}{2 \times 3 \times 4} \times 18$$

$$= 296 + 242.4 + \frac{0.8 \times -0.2}{2} \times -98 + \frac{0.8 \times -0.2 \times -1.2}{6} \times 7 + \frac{0.8 \times -0.2 \times -1.2 \times -2.2}{24} \times 18$$

$$= 296 + 242.4 + \frac{(-0.16 \times -98)}{2} + \frac{0.192}{2} \times 7 - \frac{0.422}{24} \times 18$$

$$= 296 + 242.4 + 7.84 + 0.224 - 0.317$$

$$= 546.46 - 0.317 = 546.147 \quad \text{or} \quad = \mathbf{546}$$

No. of workers earning less than Rs. 25 = 599.
No. of workers earning less than Rs. 24 = 546.
Therefore No. of workers earning between Rs. 24 and 25 = (599-546) = **53**

Problem 26. Estimate the number of students who get more than 48 but not more than 50 marks from the following data :

Marks upto	:	45	50	55	60	65
No. of students	:	447	484	505	511	514

(*M.A. Econ., Jabalpur*)

Solution :

Marks	No. of Students		Differences							
			Δ^1		Δ^2		Δ^3		Δ^4	
Upto 45	447	y_0								
			+ 37	$\Delta^1{}_0$						
,, 50	484	y_1			−16					
			+21	$\Delta^1{}_1$		$\Delta^2{}_0$				
,, 55	505	y_2			−15		+1			
			+6	$\Delta^1{}_2$		$\Delta^2{}_1$		$\Delta^3{}_0$		
,, 60	511	y_3			−3		+12		+11	$\Delta^4{}_0$
			+3	$\Delta^1{}_3$		$\Delta^2{}_2$		$\Delta^3{}_1$		
,, 65	514	y_4								

$$yx = y_0 + x\Delta^1{}_0 + \frac{x(x-1)}{1\times 2}\Delta^2{}_0 + \frac{x(x-1)(x-2)}{1\times 2\times 3}\Delta^3{}_0 + \frac{x(x-1)(x-2)(x-3)}{1\times 2\times 3\times 4}\Delta^4{}_0$$

$$x = \frac{48-45}{5} = 0.6$$

$$y_{48} = 447 + 0.6\times 37 + \frac{0.6(0.6-1)}{2}\times -16 + \frac{0.6(0.6-1)(0.6-2)}{6}\times 1 + \frac{0.6(0.6-1)(0.6-2)(0.6-3)}{24}\times 11$$

$$= 447 + 22.2 + \frac{0.6\times -0.4}{2}\times -16 + \frac{0.6\times -0.4\times -1.4}{6}\times 1 + \frac{0.6\times -0.4\times -1.4\times -2.4}{24}\times 11$$

$$= 447 + 22.2 + 1.92 + 0.056 - 0.37$$

$$= 471.176 - 0.37 = 470.806 \quad \text{or} \quad \mathbf{471} \text{ approximately}$$

The No. of students getting marks upto 50 = 484 ; But No. of students getting marks upto 48 = 471. Therefore the No. of students getting more than 48 marks but not more than 50 = 484−471 = 13.

Problem 27. From the following table of yearly premium for policies maturing at different ages, estimate the premium for policies maturing at the age of 47 years :

Age (years)	:	45	50	55	60	65
Premium (in Rs)	:	287	240	208	186	171

(*B. Com., Gujarat*)

Solution :

Age	Premium		Differences Δ^1		Δ^2		Δ^3		Δ^4	
45	287	y_0								
			−47	$\Delta^1{}_0$						
50	240	y_1			+15	$\Delta^2{}_0$				
			−32	$\Delta^1{}_1$			−5	$\Delta^3{}_0$		
55	208	y_2			+10	$\Delta^2{}_1$			+2	$\Delta^4{}_0$
			−22	$\Delta^1{}_2$			−3	$\Delta^3{}_1$		
60	186	y_3			+7	$\Delta^2{}_2$				
			−15	$\Delta^1{}_3$						
65	171	y_4								

$$y_x = y_0 + x\Delta^1{}_0 + \frac{x(x-1)}{2}\Delta^2{}_0 + \frac{x(x-1)(x-2)}{2 \times 3}\Delta^3{}_0 + \frac{x(x-1)(x-2)(x-3)}{2 \times 3 \times 4}\Delta^4{}_0$$

$$x = \frac{47-45}{5} = 0.4$$

$$y_{47} = 287 + 0.4 \times (-47) + \frac{0.4(0.4-1)}{2} \times 15 + \frac{0.4(0.4-1)(0.4-2)}{6} \times -5 + \frac{0.4(0.4-1)(0.4-2)(0.4-3)}{24} \times 2$$

$$= 287 - 18.8 + \frac{0.4 \times -0.6}{2} \times 15 + \frac{0.4 \times -0.6 \times -1.6}{6} \times -5 + \frac{0.4 \times -0.6 \times -1.6 \times -2.6}{24} \times 2$$

$$= 287 - 18.8 - 1.8 - 0.32 - 0.0832$$

$$= 287 - 21 = \mathbf{266}$$

The premium for policies maturing at the age of 47 years = **Rs. 266**

Problem 28. Find out the number of students securing second division in the University Examination from the following figures :

Marks obtained (out of 100)	:	0–20	20–40	40–60	60–80	80–100
No. of students	:	5	26	85	54	30

(48% and above but less than 60% marks makes second division)

(*M. Com., Rajasthan*)

Solution :

Marks less than (X)	No. of Students (Y)		Differences							
			Δ^1		Δ^2		Δ^3		Δ^4	
20 (x_0)	5	(y_0)								
			26	$\Delta^1{}_0$						
40 (x_1)	31	(y_1)			59	$\Delta^2{}_0$				
			85	$\Delta^1{}_1$			−90	$\Delta^3{}_0$		
60 (x_2)	116	(y_2)			−31	$\Delta^2{}_1$			97	$\Delta^4{}_0$
			54	$\Delta^1{}_2$			7	$\Delta^3{}_1$		
80 (x_3)	170	(y_3)			−24	$\Delta^2{}_2$				
			30	$\Delta^1{}_3$						
100 (x_4)	200	(y_4)								

$$x = \frac{48-20}{20} = \frac{28}{20} = 1.4$$

$$\begin{aligned}
y_{48} &= y_0 + x\Delta^1{}_0 + \frac{x(x-1)}{2!}\Delta^2{}_0 + \frac{x(x-1)(x-2)}{3!}\Delta^3{}_0 \\
&\quad + \frac{x(x-1)(x-2)(x-3)}{4!}\Delta^4{}_0 \\
&= 5 + 1.4 \times 26 + \frac{1.4(1.4-1)}{2}(59) + \frac{1.4(1.4-1)(1.4-2)}{2 \times 3}(-90) \\
&\quad + \frac{1.4(1.4-1)(1.4-2)(1.4-3)}{2 \times 3 \times 4}(97) \\
&= 5 + 36.4 + \frac{1.4 \times 0.4}{2} \times 59 + \frac{1.4 \times 0.4 \times -0.6}{6}(-90) \\
&\quad + \frac{1.4 \times 0.4 \times -0.6 \times -1.6}{24} \times 97 \\
&= 5 + 36.4 + 16.52 + 5.04 + 2.17 \\
&= 65.13 \quad \text{or} \quad 65
\end{aligned}$$

No. of students getting less than 60% marks = 116 (given)

No. of students getting less than 48% marks = 65

Therefore, the number of students getting second division above 48% but less than 60% = 116−65 = **51**

Problem 29. From the data given below estimate the number of persons living between the age of 35 and 42 :

Age (in years)	:	20	30	40	50
No. of persons	:	513	439	346	243

(*M. Com., Nagpur*)

Solution :

Age (years) (X)	*No. of Persons* (Y)	*Differences*					
		Δ^1		Δ^2		Δ^3	
20	513 (y_0)	−74	$\Delta^1{}_0$				
30	439 (y_1)			−19	$\Delta^2{}_0$		
		−93	$\Delta^1{}_1$			+9	$\Delta^3{}_0$
40	346 (y_2)			−10	$\Delta^2{}_1$		
		−103	$\Delta^1{}_2$				
50	243 (y_3)						

No. of persons living at 35 years.

$$x = \frac{35-20}{10} = \frac{15}{10} = 1.5$$

$$y_x = y_0 + x\Delta^1{}_0 + \frac{x(x-1)}{2!}\Delta^2{}_0 + \frac{x(x-1)(x-2)}{3!}\Delta^3{}_0$$

$$= 513 + (1.5 \times -74) + \frac{1.5(1.5-1)}{2}(-19) + \frac{1.5(1.5-1)(1.5-2)}{2 \times 3} \times 9$$

$$= 513 - 111 + \frac{1.5 \times 0.5}{2}(-19) + \frac{1.5 \times 0.5 \times 0.5}{6}(9)$$

$$= 513 - 111 - 7.125 - 0.5625 = 513 - 118.6875$$

$$= 394.3125 \quad \text{(or)} \quad \mathbf{394}$$

No. of persons living at 42 :

$$x = \frac{42-20}{10} = 2.2$$

$$y_{42} = 513 + 2.2(-74) + \frac{2.2(2.2-1)}{2} \times -19 + \frac{(2.2-1)(2.2-2)}{2 \times 3} \times 9$$

$$= 513 - 162.8 - 25.08 + 0.36 = 325.48 \quad \text{(or)} \quad 325$$

Persons living at 42 = 325
Persons living at 35 = 394
No. of persons living between 35 and 42 is 69 i.e. 394−325

Problem 30: Using an appropriate formula for interpolation, estimate the number of students who obtained less than 45 marks from the following :

Marks	:	0–40	40–50	50–60	60–70	70–80
No. of students	:	31	42	51	35	31

(*B. Com., Bangalore, Alahabad, Nagpur, Rajasthan, Jodhpur*)

Solution :

X (*Less than*)	f	cf.	*Differences*							
			Δ^1		Δ^2		Δ^3		Δ^4	
40	31	$31(y_0)$								
			42	$\Delta^1{}_0$						
50	42	$73(y_1)$			9	$\Delta^2{}_0$	−25	$\Delta^3{}_0$		
			51	$\Delta^1{}_1$						
60	51	$124(y_2)$			−16	$\Delta^2{}_1$			37	$\Delta^4{}_0$
			35	$\Delta^1{}_2$						
70	35	$159\ (y_3)$			−4	$\Delta^2{}_2$	12	$\Delta^3{}_1$		
			31	$\Delta^1{}_3$						
80	31	$190\ (y_4)$								

$$x = \frac{45-40}{10} = \frac{5}{10} = 0.5$$

$$y_x = y_0 + x\Delta_0^1 + \frac{x(x-1)}{2}\Delta_0^2 + \frac{x(x-1)(x-2)}{3!}\Delta_0^3 + \frac{x(x-1)(x-2)(x-3)}{4!}\Delta_0^4$$

$$= 31 + 0.5 \times 42 + \frac{0.5(0.5-1)}{2}9 + \frac{0.5(0.5-1)(0.5-2)}{2\times 3}(-25) + \frac{0.5(0.5-1)(0.5-1)(0.5-3)}{2\times 3\times 4}37$$

$$= 31 + 0.5 \times 42 + \frac{0.5 \times -0.5}{2} \times 9 + \frac{0.5 \times -0.5 \times -1.5}{2 \times 3}(-25) + \frac{0.5 \times -0.5 \times -1.5 \times -2.5}{2 \times 3 \times 4} \times 37$$

$$= 31 + 21 - 1.125 - 1.5625 - 1.4453$$

$$= 52 - 4.1328$$

$$= 47.8672 \quad \text{or} \quad 48$$

Hence, the number of students who obtained less than 45 marks is 48.

Problem 31. The weekly wages to 492 employees of a soap factory are as under :

Rs.	*Employees*
Not more than 40	212
Not more than 45	296
Not more than 50	368
Not more than 55	429
Not more than 60	460
Not more than 65	481
Not more than 70	490
Not more than 75	492

Using Newton's method, interpolate the number of employees who get more than Rs. 42 but not more than Rs. 45.

(*M. Com., Agra, M.A., Rajasthan, I.C.W.A*)

Solution :

Wages	y	Δ^1	Δ^2	Δ^3	Δ^4	Δ^5	Δ^6	Δ^7
40	212 y_0							
		84 $\Delta^1{}_0$						
45	296 y_1		-12 $\Delta^2{}_0$					
		72 $\Delta^1{}_1$		1 $\Delta^3{}_0$				
50	368 y_2		-11 $\Delta^2{}_1$		-20 $\Delta^4{}_0$			
		61 $\Delta^1{}_2$		-19 $\Delta^3{}_1$		59 $\Delta^5{}_0$		
55	429 y_3		-30 $\Delta^2{}_2$		39 $\Delta^4{}_1$		-120 $\Delta^6{}_0$	
		31 $\Delta^1{}_3$		20 $\Delta^3{}_2$		-61 $\Delta^5{}_1$		210 $\Delta^7{}_0$
60	460 y_4		-10 $\Delta^2{}_3$		-22 $\Delta^4{}_2$		90 $\Delta^6{}_1$	
		21 $\Delta^1{}_4$		-2 $\Delta^3{}_3$		29 $\Delta^5{}_2$		
65	481 y_5		-12 $\Delta^2{}_4$		7 $\Delta^4{}_3$			
		9 $\Delta^1{}_5$		5 $\Delta^3{}_4$				
70	490 y_6		-7 $\Delta^2{}_5$					
		2 $\Delta^1{}_6$						
75	492 y_7							

$$x = \frac{42-40}{5} = 0.4$$

$$\begin{aligned}
y_x &= y_0 + x\Delta_0^1 + \frac{x(x-1)}{1\times 2}\Delta_0^2 + \frac{x(x-1)(x-2)}{1\times 2\times 3}\Delta_0^3 \\
&\quad + \frac{x(x-1)(x-2)(x-3)}{1\times 2\times 3\times 4}\Delta_0^4 + \frac{x(x-1)(x-2)(x-3)(x-4)}{1\times 2\times 3\times 4\times 5}\Delta^5 \\
&\quad + \frac{x(x-1)(x-2)(x-3)(x-4)(x-5)}{1\times 2\times 3\times 4\times 5\times 6}\Delta_0^6 \\
&\quad + \frac{x(x-1)(x-2)(x-3)(x-4)(x-5)(x-6)}{1\times 2\times 3\times 4\times 5\times 6\times 7}\Delta_0^7 \\
&= 212 + 0.4\times 84 + \frac{0.4(0.4-1)}{2}\times -12 + \frac{0.4(0.4-1)(0.4-2)}{2\times 3}\times 1 \\
&\quad + \frac{0.4(0.4-1)(0.4-2)(0.4-3)}{2\times 3\times 4}\times -20 \\
&\quad + \frac{0.4(0.4-1)(0.4-2)(0.4-3)(0.4-4)}{2\times 3\times 4\times 5}\times 59 \\
&\quad + \frac{0.4(0.4-1)(0.4-2)(0.4-3)(0.4-4)(0.4-5)}{2\times 3\times 4\times 5\times 6}\times -120 \\
&\quad + \frac{0.4(0.4-1)(0.4-2)(0.4-3)(0.4-4)(0.4-5)(0.4-6)}{2\times 3\times 4\times 5\times 6\times 7}\times 210 \\
&= 212 + 33.6 + 1.44 + 0.06 + 0.83 + 1.77 + 2.75 + 3.85 \\
&= 256.30 \quad \text{or} \quad 256
\end{aligned}$$

Thus, the number of employees who get not more than Rs. 42 = 256.

The number of employees who get not more than Rs 45 = 296.

Therefore, number of employees who get between Rs. 42 and Rs. 45 = 296−256 = **40.**

Problem 32. Interpolate the figure of population for the year 1986 from the following data :—

Year	:	1970	1980	1990	2000
Population of a *town*	:	25,494	29,003	32,528	36,070

(*I.C.W.A.*)

Solution :

Year (x)	*Population* (y)	*Differences*		
		Δ^1	Δ^2	Δ^3
1970	25494 (y_0)			
		$+3509\ \Delta^1_0$		
1980	29003 (y_1)		$+16\ \Delta^2_0$	
		$+3525\ \Delta^1_1$		$+1\ \Delta^3_0$
1990	32528 (y_2)		$+17\ \Delta^2_1$	
		$+3542\ \Delta^1_2$		
2000	36070 (y_3)			

$$x = \frac{1986 - 1970}{10} = \frac{16}{10} = \mathbf{1.6}$$

$$y_{(1986)} = y_0 + x\Delta^1_0 + \frac{x(x-1)}{2!}\Delta^2_0 + \frac{x(x-1)(x-2)}{3!}\Delta^3_0$$

$$= 25494 + 1.6 \times 3509 + \frac{1.6(1.6-1)}{2} \times 16 + \frac{1.6(1.6-1)(1.6-2)}{2 \times 3} \times 1$$

$$= 25494 + 5614.4 + 7.68 - 0.064$$

$$= 31,116.08 - 0.064 = \mathbf{31,116.016}$$

The population for the year 1986 is 31, 116.

Problem 33. From the following data estimate the number of students getting marks between 20 and 25.

Marks		*No. of persons*	Marks		*No. of persons*
Below	10	20	Below	40	210
,,	20	45	,,	50	325
,,	30	115			

(*B. Com., Nagpur*)

Solution :

Marks Below	No. of students	*Differences*							
		Δ^1		Δ^2		Δ^3		Δ^4	
10	20 (y_0)								
		+25	Δ^1_0						
20	45 (y_1)			+45	Δ^2_0				
		+70	Δ^1_1			−20	Δ^3_0		
30	115 (y_2)			+25	Δ^2_1			+15	Δ^4_0
		+95	Δ^1_2			−5	Δ^3_1		
40	210 (y_3)			+20	Δ^2_2				
		+115	Δ^1_3						
50	325 (y_4)								

$$x = \frac{25-10}{10} = 1.5$$

$$y_x = y_0 + x\Delta^1{}_0 + \frac{x(x-1)}{2!}\Delta^2{}_0 + \frac{x(x-1)(x-2)}{3!}\Delta^3{}_0 + \frac{x(x-1)(x-2)(x-3)}{4!}\Delta^4{}_0$$

$$= 20 + 1.5 \times 25 + \frac{1.5(1.5-1)}{2} \times 45 + \frac{1.5(1.5-1)(1.5-2)}{2 \times 3} \times -20 + \frac{1.5(1.5-1)(1.5-2)(1.5-3)}{2 \times 3 \times 4} \times 15$$

$$= 20 + 37.5 + \frac{1.5 \times 0.5}{2} \times 45 + \frac{1.5 \times 0.5 \times -0.5}{2 \times 3} \times -20 + \frac{1.5 \times -0.5 \times -0.5 \times -1.5}{2 \times 3 \times 4} \times 15$$

$$= 20 + 37.5 + 16.875 + 1.25 + 0.3516 = 75.9766$$

$$= \mathbf{76.}$$

Thus the number of students getting less than 25 marks = 76

The number of students getting less than 20 marks = 45

Therefore the number of students who are getting marks between 20 and 25 = 76−45 = **31**.

Problem 34. The following are the marks obtained by 492 candidates in certain examination :

Not	*more*	*than*	40	*marks*	210	*candidates*
,,	,,	,,	45	,,	253	,,
,,	,,	,,	50	,,	307	,,
,,	,,	,,	55	,,	381	,,
,,	,,	,,	60	,,	413	,,
,,	,,	,,	65	,,	492	,,

Find out the candidates (*a*) who secured more than 48 but not more than 50 marks, (*b* less than 48 but not less than 45 marks. (*B. Com., Nagpur I.C.W.A.*

Solution :

Marks not more than	*No. of Candidates*	*Differences*									
		Δ^1		Δ^2		Δ^3		Δ^4		Δ^5	
40	210 (y_0)										
		43	Δ^1_0								
45	253 (y_1)			11	$\Delta^2{}_0$						
		54	$\Delta^1{}_1$			9	$\Delta^3{}_0$				
50	307 (y_2)			20	$\Delta^2{}_1$			−71	$\Delta^4{}_0$		
		74	$\Delta^1{}_2$			−62	$\Delta^3{}_1$			222	$\Delta^5{}_0$
55	381 (y_3)			−42	$\Delta^2{}_2$			151	$\Delta^4{}_1$		
		32	$\Delta^1{}_3$			89	$\Delta^3{}_2$				
60	413 (y_4)			47	$\Delta^2{}_3$						
		79	$\Delta^1{}_4$								
65	492 (y_5)										

$$x = \frac{48-40}{5} = 1.6$$

$$y_x = 210 + 1.6 \times 43 + \frac{1.6(1.6-1)}{1 \times 2} \times 11 + \frac{1.6(1.6-1)(1.6-2)}{1 \times 2 \times 3} \times 9$$
$$+ \frac{1.6(1.6-1)(1.6-2)(1.6-3)}{1 \times 2 \times 3 \times 4} \times (-71)$$
$$+ \frac{1.6(1.6-1)(1.6-2)(1.6-3)(1.6-4)}{1 \times 2 \times 3 \times 4 \times 5} \times 222$$
$$= 210 + 68.8 + 5.28 - 0.576 - 1.5904 - 2.3869$$
$$= 284.08 - 4.55 = 279.53 \quad \text{or} \quad 280.$$

(a) No. of candidates obtained marks more than 48 = 280
No. of candidates obtained marks more than 50 = 307 (given)

∴ No. of candidates who secured more than 48 but not more than 50 } = 307 – 280 = 27.

(b) No. of candidates obtained marks more than 45 = 253
No. of candidates obtained marks less than 48 = 280

∴ No. of candidates obtained marks, less than 48 but not less than 45 } = 280 – 253 = 27.

Problem 35. From the following table, find the number of workers falling in the earning group of Rs. 25 to Rs. 35 :

Earnings (Rs.) (Up to)	:	10	20	30	40	50	60
No. of workers	:	50	150	300	500	700	800

(*M.A., Rajasthan*)

Solution :

x	y		Δ^1		*Differences* Δ^2		Δ^3		Δ^4		Δ^5	
10	50	y_0										
			100	Δ^1_0								
20	150	y_1			50	Δ^2_0						
			150	Δ^1_1			0	Δ^3_0				
30	300	y_2			50	Δ^2_1			–50	Δ^4_0		
			200	Δ^1_2			–50	Δ^3_1			0	Δ^5_0
40	500	y_3			0	Δ^2_2			–50	Δ^4_1		
			200	Δ^1_3			–100	Δ^3_2				
50	700	y_4			–100	Δ^2_3						
			100	Δ^1_4								
60	800	y_5										

We have to find the number of workers earning upto Rs. 25.
By Newton's formula

$$x = \frac{25-10}{10} = 1.5$$

$$\begin{aligned} y_{25} &= 50 + 1.5(100) + \frac{1.5(1.5-1)}{2} \times 50 \\ &\quad + \frac{1.5(1.5-1)(1.5-2)}{6} \times 0 \\ &\quad + \frac{1.5(1.5-1)(1.5-2)(1.5-3)}{24} \times (-50) \\ &\quad + \frac{1.5(1.5-1)(1.5-2)(1.5-3)(1.5-4)}{120} \times 0 \\ &= 50 + 150 + 18.75 + 0 - 1.172 + 0 \\ &= 217.578 \\ &= \mathbf{218}. \end{aligned}$$

Hence the number of workers earning up to Rs. 25 is 218.

To find the number of workers earning upto Rs. 35

$$\begin{aligned} x &= \frac{35-10}{10} = 2.5 \\ y_{35} &= 50 + (2.5)100 + \frac{2.5(2.5-1)}{2} \times 50 \\ &\quad + \frac{2.5(2.5-1)(2.5-2)}{6} \times 0 \\ &\quad + \frac{2.5(2.5-1)(2.5-2)(2.5-3)}{24} \times (-50) \\ &\quad + \frac{2.5(2.5-1)(2.5-2)(2.5-3)(2.5-4)}{120} \times 0 \\ &= 50 + 250 + 93.75 + 0 + 1.95 + 0 \\ &= 395.7 \\ &= \mathbf{396}. \end{aligned}$$

Hence the number of workers falling in the group of Rs. 25 to Rs. 35 is

$$\begin{aligned} & y_{35} - y_{25} \\ =\ & 396 - 218 \\ =\ & \mathbf{178}. \end{aligned}$$

LAGRANGE'S METHOD

Problem 36. The following table gives the normal weight of a baby during the first six months of life.

Age in months	*Weight in Lbs.*
0	5
2	7
3	8
5	10
6	12

Estimate the weight of a baby at the age of 4 months.

(*I.C.W.A., B. Com., Kerala, Punjab*)

Solution :

Age	*Weight*	*Age*	*Weight*
0 (x_0)	5 (y_0)	5 (x_3)	10 (y_3)
2 (x_1)	7 (y_1)	6 (x_4)	12 (y_4)
3 (x_2)	8 (y_2)		

$$\textbf{Formula : } yx = y_0\frac{(x-x_1)(x-x_2)(x-x_3)(x-x_4)}{(x_0-x_1)(x_0-x_2)(x_0-x_3)(x_0-x_4)} + y_1\frac{(x-x_0)(x-x_2)(x-x_3)(x-x_4)}{(x_1-x_0)(x_1-x_2)(x_1-x_3)(x_1-x_4)} + y_2\frac{(x-x_0)(x-x_1)(x-x_3)(x-x_4)}{(x_2-x_0)(x_2-x_1)(x_2-x_3)(x_2-x_4)} + y_3\frac{(x-x_0)(x-x_1)(x-x_2)(x-x_4)}{(x_3-x_0)(x_3-x_1)(x_3-x_2)(x_3-x_4)} + y_4\frac{(x-x_0)(x-x_1)(x-x_2)(x-x_3)}{(x_4-x_0)(x_4-x_1)(x_4-x_2)(x_4-x_3)}.$$

Step 1

$$y_x = 5\frac{(4-2)(4-3)(4-5)(4-6)}{(0-2)(0-3)(0-5)(0-6)} + 7\frac{(4-0)(4-3)(4-5)(4-6)}{(2-0)(2-3)(2-5)(2-6)} + 8\frac{(4-0)(4-2)(4-5)(4-6)}{(3-0)(3-2)(3-5)(3-6)} + 10\frac{(4-0)(4-2)(4-3)(4-6)}{(5-0)(5-2)(5-3)(5-6)} + 12\frac{(4-0)(4-2)(4-3)(4-5)}{(6-0)(6-2)(6-3)(6-5)} +$$

Step 2

$$y_x = 5\frac{(2)(1)(-1)(-2)}{(-2)(-3)(-5)(-6)} + 7\frac{(4)(1)(-1)(-2)}{(2)(-1)(-3)(-4)} + 8\frac{(4)(2)(-1)(-2)}{(3)(1)(-2)(-3)} + 10\frac{(4)(2)(1)(-2)}{(5)(3)(2)(-1)} + 12\frac{(4)(2)(1)(-1)}{(6)(4)(3)(1)}.$$

$$= 5\left(\frac{4}{180}\right) + 7\left(\frac{8}{-24}\right) + 8\left(\frac{16}{18}\right) + 10\left(\frac{-16}{-30}\right) + 12\left(\frac{-18}{72}\right)$$

or $= 0.11 - 2.33 + 7.11 + 5.33 - 1.33$

or $= 12.55 - 3.66$

$= 8.89$ lbs.

Thus, the weight of a baby at the age of 4 months is 8.89 or **8.9** lbs.

Problem 37. The following table gives the normal weight of babies during the first twelve months of life :

Age (in months)	:	0	2	5	8	10	12
Weights (lbs.)	:	7.5	10.25	15	16	18	21

Find the weight of a 7 month old baby. (*M.A., Delhi*)

Solution :

AGE *In months*	*WEIGHT* *(lb)*
0 x_0	7.5 y_0
2 x_1	10.25 y_1
5 x_2	15 y_2
8 x_3	16 y_3
10 x_4	18 y_4
12 x_5	21 y_5

Formulae : Lagrange method :

$$\begin{aligned} y_x &= Y_0 \frac{(x-x_1)(x-x_2)(x-x_3)(x-x_4)(x-x_5)}{(x_0-x_1)(x_0-x_2)(x_0-x_3)(x_0-x_4)(x_0-x_5)} \\ &\quad + Y_1 \frac{(x-x_0)(x-x_2)(x-x_3)(x-x_4)(x-x_5)}{(x_1-x_0)(x_1-x_2)(x_1-x_3)(x_1-x_4)(x_1-x_5)} \\ &\quad + Y_2 \frac{(x-x_0)(x-x_1)(x-x_3)(x-x_4)(x-x_5)}{(x_2-x_0)(x_2-x_1)(x_2-x_3)(x_2-x_4)(x_2-x_5)} \\ &\quad + Y_3 \frac{(x-x_0)(x-x_1)(x-x_2)(x-x_4)(x-x_5)}{(x_3-x_0)(x_3-x_1)(x_3-x_2)(x_3-x_4)(x_3-x_5)} \\ &\quad + Y_4 \frac{(x-x_0)(x-x_1)(x-x_2)(x-x_3)(x-x_5)}{(x_4-x_0)(x_4-x_1)(x_4-x_2)(x_4-x_3)(x_4-x_5)} \\ &\quad + Y_5 \frac{(x-x_0)(x-x_1)(x-x_2)(x-x_3)(x-x_4)}{(x_5-x_0)(x_5-x_1)(x_5-x_2)(x_5-x_3)(x_5-x_4)} \end{aligned}$$

$$\begin{aligned} Y_x &= 7.5 \frac{(7-2)(7-5)(7-8)(7-10)(7-12)}{(0-2)(0-5)(0-8)(0-10)(0-12)} \\ &\quad +10.25 \frac{(7-0)(7-5)(7-8)(7-10)(7-12)}{(2-0)(2-5)(2-8)(2-10)(2-12)} \\ &\quad +15 \frac{(7-0)(7-2)(7-8)(7-10)(7-12)}{(5-0)(5-2)(5-8)(5-10)(5-12)} \\ &\quad +16 \frac{(7-0)(7-2)(7-5)(7-10)(7-12)}{(8-0)(8-2)(8-5)(8-10)(8-12)} \\ &\quad +18 \frac{(7-0)(7-2)(7-5)(7-8)(7-12)}{(10-0)(10-2)(10-5)(10-8)(10-12)} \\ &\quad +21 \frac{(7-0)(7-2)(7-5)(7-8)(7-10)}{(12-0)(12-2)(12-5)(12-8)(12-10)} \\ &= 7.5 \frac{(5)(2)(-1)(-3)(-5)}{(-2)(-5)(-8)(-10)(-12)} \end{aligned}$$

$$+10.25\,\frac{(7)\,(2)\,(-1)\,(-3)(-5)}{(2)\,(-3)\,(-6)\,(-8)(-10)}$$
$$+15\frac{(7)\,(5)\,(-1)\,(-3)(-5)}{(5)\,(3)\,(-3)\,(-5)(-7)}$$
$$+16\frac{(7)\,(5)\,(2)\,(-3)(-5)}{(8)\,(6)\,(3)\,(-2)(-4)}$$
$$+18\frac{(7)\,(5)\,(2)\,(-1)(-5)}{(10)\,(8)\,(5)\,(2)(-2)}$$
$$+21\frac{(7)\,(5)\,(2)\,(-1)(-3)}{(12)\,(10)\,(7)\,(4)(2)}$$

$$Y_x = 7.5\times\left(\frac{-150}{-9,600}\right)+10.25\left(\frac{-210}{2880}\right)+15\left(\frac{-525}{-1575}\right)$$
$$+16\left(\frac{+1050}{1152}\right)+18\left(\frac{350}{-1,600}\right)+21\left(\frac{210}{6720}\right)$$
$$y_x = 0.12-0.75+5+14.58-3.94+0.65$$
$$= 20.35-4.69$$
$$= 15.66.$$

Thus the weight of a seven month old baby is 15.66 lbs.

Problem : 38. The values of x and y are given below :

x	:	5	6	9	11
y	:	12	10	14	16

Find the value of y when x=10 by using Lagrange's method. (*M.A.Econ., Punjab*)

Solution :

x	5 (x_0)	6 (x_1)	9 (x_2)	11 (x_3)
y	12	10	14	16
	(y_0)	(y_1)	(y_2)	(y_3)

$$y_x = y_0\frac{(x-x_1)(x-x_2)(x-x_3)}{(x_0-x_1)(x_0-x_2)(x_0-x_3)}$$
$$+y_1\frac{(x-x_0)(x-x_2)(x-x_3)}{(x_1-x_0)(x_1-x_2)(x_1-x_3)}$$
$$+y_2\frac{(x-x_0)(x-x_1)(x-x_3)}{(x_2-x_0)(x_2-x_1)(x_2+x_3)}$$
$$+y_3\frac{(x-x_0)(x-x_1)(x-x_2)}{(x_3-x_0)(x_3-x_1)(x_3-x_2)}$$
$$= 12\frac{(10-6)\,(10-9)\,(10-11)}{(5-6)\,(5-9)\,(5-11)}+10\frac{(10-5)\,(10-9)\,(10-11)}{(6-5)\,(6-9)\,(6-11)}$$
$$+14\frac{(10-5)\,(10-6)\,(10-11)}{(9-5)\,(9-6)\,(9-11)}+16\frac{(10-5)\,(10-6)\,(10-9)}{(11-5)\,(11-6)\,(11-9)}$$
$$= 12\frac{4\times1\times-1}{-1\times-4\times-6}+10\frac{5\times1\times-1}{1\times-3\times-5}$$
$$+14\frac{5\times4\times-1}{4\times3\times-2}+16\frac{5\times4\times1}{6\times5\times2}$$

$$
\begin{aligned}
&= 12\frac{-4}{-24}+10\frac{-5}{15}+14\frac{-20}{-24}+16\frac{20}{60}\\
&= 2-3.33+11.67+5.33\\
&= 19.00-3.33\\
&= \mathbf{15.67}
\end{aligned}
$$

Therefore, when $x = 10$, $y = 15.67$

Problem 39. Find by Lagrange's formula the value of y when x = 8 from the following data :

x	:	5	9	11	12
y	:	121	73	25	16

(*B. Sc., Madras*)

Solution :

X	y	x	y
5 $(_{x0})$	121 $(_{y0})$	11 $(_{x2})$	25$(_{y2})$
9 $(_{x1})$	73 $(_{y1})$	12 $(_{x3})$	16 $(_{y3})$

$$
\begin{aligned}
y_x = \; & y_0\frac{(x-x_1)(x-x_2)(x-x_3)}{(x_0-x_1)(x_0-x_2)(x_0-x_3)}+\\
& y_1\frac{(x-x_0)(x-x_2)(x-x_3)}{(x_1-x_0)(x_1-x_2)(x_1-x_3)}+\\
& y_2\frac{(x-x_0)(x-x_1)(x-x_3)}{(x_2-x_0)(x_2-x_1)(x_2-x_3)}+\\
& y_3\frac{(x-x_0)(x-x_1)(x-x_2)}{(x_3-x_0)(x_3-x_1)(x_3-x_2)}
\end{aligned}
$$

Substituting the corresponding value, we get

$$
\begin{aligned}
y_x &= 121\frac{(8-9)\,(8-11)\,(8-12)}{(5-9)\,(5-11)\,(5-12)}+73\frac{(8-5)\,(8-11)\,(8-12)}{(9-5)\,(9-11)\,(9-12)}+\\
&\quad 25\frac{(8-5)\,(8-9)\,(8-12)}{(11-5)\,(11-9)\,(11-12)}+16\frac{(8-5)\,(8-9)\,(8-11)}{(12-5)\,(12-9)\,(12-11)}\\
&= 121\frac{(-1)\,(-3)\,(-4)}{(-4)\,(-6)\,(-7)}+73\frac{(3)\,(-3)\,(-4)}{(4)\,(-2)\,(-3)}\\
&\quad +25\frac{(3)\,(-1)\,(-4)}{(6)\,(2)\,(-1)}+16\frac{(3)\,(-1)\,(-3)}{(7)\,(3)\,(1)}\\
&= 121\times\frac{-1}{-14}+73\times\frac{3}{2}-25+16\times\frac{3}{7}\\
&= 8.64+109.5-25+6.86\\
&= 125-25\\
&= 100
\end{aligned}
$$

Therefore, when x = 8, the value of y = **100**

Problem 40. From the following temperature readings taken on a particular day, estimate temperature at 3 a.m. and 5 a.m.

Time	:	2 a.m.	6 a.m.	10 a.m.	2 p.m.
Temp ($^\circ$C)	:	40.2	42.4	51.0	72.4

(*B.Com., Madurai, Madras*)

Solution :

To Calculate the temperature at 3 a.m.

Time	*Temperature* ($^\circ$ *C*)
2 a.m. (x_0)	40.2 (y_0)
6 a.m. (x_1)	42.4 (y_1)
10 a.m.(x_2)	51.0 (y_2)
2 p.m. (x_3)	72.4 (4_2)

$$\begin{aligned} Y &= Y_0 \frac{(x-x_1)(x-x_2)(x-x_3)}{(x_0-x_1)(x_0-x_2)(x_0-x_3)} + \\ & Y_1 \frac{(x-x_0)(x-x_2)(x-x_3)}{(x_1-x_0)(x_1-x_2)(x_1-x_3)} + \\ & Y_2 \frac{(x-x_0)(x-x_1)(x-x_3)}{(x_2-x_0)(x_2-x_1)(x_2-x_3)} + \\ & Y_3 \frac{(x-x_0)(x-x_1)(x-x_2)}{(x_3-x_0)(x_3-x_1)(x_3-x_2)} \end{aligned}$$

Substituting the corresponding values, we get

$$\begin{aligned} Y &= 40.2 \frac{(3-6)(3-10)(3-14)}{(2-6)(2-10)(2-14)} + \\ & 42.4 \frac{(3-2)(3-10)(3-14)}{(6-2)(6-10)(6-14)} + \\ & 51.0 \frac{(3-2)(3-6)(3-14)}{(10-2)(10-6)(10-14)} + \\ & 72.4 \frac{(3-2)(3-6)(3-10)}{(14-2)(14-6)(14-10)} + \\ \therefore \quad Y &= 40.2 \frac{-3 \times -7 \times -11}{-4 \times -8 \times -12} + \\ & 42.4 \frac{1 \times -7 \times -11}{4 \times -4 \times -8} + \\ & 51.0 \frac{1 \times -3 \times -11}{8 \times 4 \times -4} + \\ & 72.4 \frac{1 \times -3 \times -7}{12 \times 8 \times 4} \\ Y &= \left(40.2 \times \frac{77}{128}\right) + \left(42.4 \times \frac{77}{128}\right) \\ & - \left(51.0 \times \frac{33}{128}\right) + \left(72.4 \times \frac{7}{128}\right) \\ &= 24.2 + 25.5 - 13.1 + 3.9 \\ &= 53.6 - 13.1 \\ &= 40.5 \end{aligned}$$

$\therefore$ Temperature at 3 a.m. is 40.5 $^\circ$ C.

(*b*) To Calculate the temperature at 5 a.m.

Time	*Temperature* ($^\circ$ C)
2 (x_0)	40.2 (y_0)
5 (x)	Y =?
6 (x_1)	42.4 (y_1)
10 (x_2)	51.0 (y_2)
14 (x_3)	72.4 (y_3)

The formula is

$$\begin{aligned} Y &= Y_0 \frac{(x-x_1)(x-x_2)(x-x_3)}{(x_0-x_1)(x_0-x_2)(x_0-x_3)} + \\ &\quad Y_1 \frac{(x-x_0)(x-x_2)(x-x_3)}{(x_1-x_0)(x_1-x_2)(x_1-x_3)} + \\ &\quad Y_2 \frac{(x-x_0)(x-x_1)(x-x_3)}{(x_2-x_0)(x_2-x_1)(x_2-x_3)} + \\ &\quad Y_3 \frac{(x-x_0)(x-x_1)(x-x_2)}{(x_3-x_0)(x_3-x_1)(x_3-x_2)} \end{aligned}$$

Substituting the corresponding values, we get

$$\begin{aligned} Y &= 40.2 \frac{(5-6)(5-10)(5-14)}{(2-6)(2-10)(2-14)} + \\ &\quad 42.4 \frac{(5-2)(5-10)(5-14)}{(6-2)(6-10)(6-14)} + \\ &\quad 51.0 \frac{(5-2)(5-6)(5-14)}{(10-2)(10-6)(10-14)} + \\ &\quad 72.4 \frac{(5-2)(5-6)(5-10)}{(14-2)(14-6)(14-10)} + \\ \text{i.e., } Y &= 40.2 \frac{-1 \times -5 \times -9}{-4 \times -8 \times -12} + \\ &\quad 42.4 \frac{3 \times -5 \times -9}{4 \times -4 \times -8} + \\ &\quad 51.0 \frac{3 \times -1 \times -9}{8 \times 4 \times -4} + \\ &\quad 72.4 \frac{3 \times -1 \times -5}{12 \times 8 \times 4} \\ Y &= 40.2 \times \frac{15}{128} + 42.4 \times \frac{135}{128} \\ &\quad -51.0 \times \frac{27}{128} + 72.4 \times \frac{5}{128} \\ &= 4.7 + 44.7 - 10.8 + 2.8 \\ &= 52.2 - 10.8 \\ &= 41.4 \end{aligned}$$

$\therefore$ The temperature at 5 a.m. is **41.4 $^\circ$ C**

Problem 41. Given the values:

x	:	14	17	31	35
$f(x)$	:	68.7	64.0	44.0	39.1

Calculate the value of $f(x)$ corresponding to $x = 27$.

(*B.Sc., Madras*)

Solution :

14 x_0	68.7 y_0	31x_2	44.0 y_2
17 x_1	64.0 y_1	35 x_3	39.1 y_3

The formula is

$$\begin{aligned} Y_x &= Y_0 \frac{(x - x_1)(x - x_2)(x - x_3)}{(x_0 - x_1)(x_0 - x_2)(x_0 - x_3)} + \\ &\quad Y_1 \frac{(x - x_0)(x - x_2)(x - x_3)}{(x_1 - x_0)(x_1 - x_2)(x_1 - x_3)} + \\ &\quad Y_2 \frac{(x - x_0)(x - x_1)(x - x_3)}{(x_2 - x_0)(x_2 - x_1)(x_2 - x_3)} + \\ &\quad Y_3 \frac{(x - x_0)(x - x_1)(x - x_2)}{(x_3 - x_0)(x_3 - x_1)(x_3 - x_2)} \end{aligned}$$

Substituting the corresponding values, we get

$$\begin{aligned} Y &= 68.7 \frac{(27 - 17)(27 - 31)(27 - 35)}{(14 - 17)(14 - 31)(14 - 35)} + \\ &\quad 64.0 \frac{(27 - 14)(27 - 31)(27 - 35)}{(17 - 14)(17 - 31)(17 - 35)} + \\ &\quad 44.0 \frac{(27 - 14)(27 - 17)(27 - 35)}{(31 - 14)(31 - 17)(31 - 35)} + \\ &\quad 39.1 \frac{(27 - 14)(27 - 17)(27 - 31)}{(35 - 14)(35 - 17)(35 - 31)} \\ Y &= 68.7 \frac{10 \times -4 \times -8}{-3 \times -17 \times -21} \\ &\quad 64.0 \frac{13 \times -4 \times -8}{3 \times -14 \times -18} \\ &\quad 44.0 \frac{13 \times 10 \times -8}{17 \times 14 \times -4} \\ &\quad 39.1 \frac{13 \times 10 \times -4}{21 \times 18 \times 4} \\ &= \left(68.7 \times \frac{320}{-1071}\right) + \left(64 \times \frac{416}{756}\right) + \left(44 \times \frac{-1040}{-952}\right) \\ &\quad + \left(39.1 \times \frac{-520}{1512}\right) \\ &= -20.53 + 35.22 + 48.07 - 13.45 \\ &= -33.98 + 83.29 \\ &= 49.31 \end{aligned}$$

Thus, when $x = 27$, $f(x)$=**49.31**

Problem 42. Estimate by a suitable method of interpolation the number of persons whose daily income is Rs. 19 but does not exceed Rs. 25 from the following data :

Income in Rs.	*No. of persons*
1 *but not exceeding* 9	50
10 -do- 19	70
19 -do- 28	203
28 -do- 37	406
37 -do- 46	304

(*M.A. Econ., Rajasthan*)

Solution :

Income		*No. of persons*
Income not exceeding Rs.	9 (x_0)	50 (y_0)
,,	19 (x_1)	120 (y_1)
,,	28(x_2)	323 (y_2)
,,	37 (x_3)	729 (y_3)
,,	46 (x_4)	1033 (y_4)

$x = 25$

$$y_x = y_0 \frac{(x-x_1)(x-x_2)(x-x_3)(x-x_4)}{(x_0-x_1)(x_0-x_2)(x_0-x_3)(x_0-x_4)} +$$

$$y_1 \frac{(x-x_0)(x-x_2)(x-x_3)(x-x_4)}{(x_1-x_0)(x_1-x_2)(x_1-x_3)(x_1-x_4)} +$$

$$y_2 \frac{(x-x_0)(x-x_1)(x-x_3)(x-x_4)}{(x_2-x_0)(x_2-x_1)(x_2-x_3)(x_2-x_4)} +$$

$$y_3 \frac{(x-x_0)(x-x_1)(x-x_2)(x-x_4)}{(x_3-x_0)(x_3-x_1)(x_3-x_2)(x_3-x_4)} +$$

$$y_4 \frac{(x-x_0)(x-x_1)(x_3-x_2)(x-x_3)}{(x_4-x_0)(x_4-x_1)(x_4-x_2)(x_4-x_3)}$$

$$= 50 \frac{(25-19)(25-28)(25-37)(25-46)}{(9-19)(9-28)(9-37)(9-46)} +$$

$$120 \frac{(25-9)(25-28)(25-37)(25-46)}{(19-9)(19-28)(19-37)(19-46)} +$$

$$323 \frac{(25-9)(25-19)(25-37)(25-46)}{(28-9)(28-19)(28-37)(28-46)} +$$

$$729 \frac{(25-9)(25-19)(25-28)(25-46)}{(37-9)(37-19)(37-28)(37-46)} +$$

$$1033 \frac{(25-9)(25-19)(25-28)(25-37)}{(46-9)(46-19)(46-28)(46-37)}$$

$$= 50 \frac{(6) \times (-3) \times (-12) \times (-21)}{(-10) \times (-19)(-28)(-37)} +$$

$$120 \frac{(16)(-3)(-12)(-21)}{(10)(-9)(-18)(-27)} +$$

$$323 \frac{(16)(6)(-12)(-21)}{(19)(9)(-9)(-18)} +$$

$$729\frac{(16)(6)(-3)(-21)}{(28)(18)(9)(-9)}+$$

$$1033\frac{(16)(6)(-3)(-12)}{(37)(27)(18)(9)}$$

$$= 50\left(\frac{-567}{24605}\right)+120\left(\frac{-112}{-405}\right)+323\left(\frac{448}{513}\right)$$

$$+729\left(\frac{28}{-189}\right)+1033\left(\frac{64}{+2997}\right)$$

$$= -1.15+33.19+282.07-108+22.06$$

$$= +337.32-109.15$$

$$= 228.17.$$

Hence No. of persons whose income does not exceed Rs. 25 = 228.

No. of persons whose income does not exceed Rs. 19 = 120.

Therefore, the number of persons whose income is Rs. 19 but not exceeding Rs. 25 is 228–120 = **108.**

Problem 43. Determine the percentage of criminals under 35 years.

Age	*Percentage of criminals*
Under 25 years	52.0
,, 30 ,,	67.3
,, 40 ,,	84.1
,, 50 ,,	94.4

(*B.Com., Nagpur*)

Solution :

Age under	*Percentage of criminals*
$25(x_0)$	$52.0\ (y_0)$
$30(x_1)$	$67.3\ (y_1)$
$40(x_2)$	$84.1\ (y_2)$
$50(x_3)$	$94.4\ (y_3)$

$$y_x = y_0\frac{(x-x_1)(x-x_2)(x-x_3)}{(x_0-x_1)(x_0-x_2)(x_0-x_3)}+y_1\frac{(x-x_0)(x-x_2)(x-x_3)}{(x_1-x_0)(x_1-x_2)(x_1-x_3)}$$

$$+y_2\frac{(x-x_0)(x-x_1)(x-x_3)}{(x_2-x_0)(x_2-x_1)(x_2-x_3)}+y_3\frac{(x-x_0)(x-x_1)(x-x_2)}{(x_3-x_0)(x_3-x_1)(x_3-x_2)}$$

$$= 52\frac{(35-30)(35-40)(35-50)}{(25-30)(25-40)(25-50)}$$

$$+67.3\frac{(35-25)(35-40)(35-50)}{(30-25)(30-40)(30-50)}$$

$$+84.1\frac{(35-25)(35-30)(35-50)}{(40-25)(40-30)(40-50)}$$

$$+94.4\frac{(35-25)(35-30)(35-40)}{(50-25)(50-30)(50-40)}$$

$$= 52\times\frac{(5)(-5)(-15)}{(-5)(-15)(-25)}+67.3\frac{(10)(-5)(-15)}{(5)(-10)(-20)}$$

$$+84.1\frac{(10)(5)(-15)}{(15)(10)(-10)}+94.4\frac{(10)(5)(-5)}{(25)(20)(10)}$$

$$= 52 \times \left(\frac{1}{-5}\right) + 67.3\left(\frac{15}{20}\right) + 84.1\left(\frac{+5}{+10}\right) + 94.4\left(\frac{-1}{20}\right)$$

$$= -10.4 + 50.48 + 42.05 - 4.72$$

$$= 92.53 - 15.12$$

$$= \mathbf{77.41.}$$

Thus, the percentage of criminals under 35 years of age is 77.4 %.

Problem 44. From the following data estimate the number of persons earning wage between Rs. 60 and 70.

Wages in Rs. : Below	:	40	40-60	60-80	80-100	100-120
No. of persons (in thousands)	:	250	120	100	70	50

(*B. Com., Banaras, M.A., Agra*)

Solution :

Wages below Rs.	*No. of persons* (000)
40 (x_0)	250 (y_0)
60 (x_1)	370 (y_1)
80 (x_2)	470 (y_2)
100(x_3)	540 (y_3)
120(x_4)	590 (y_4)

$$y_x = y_0\frac{(x-x_1)(x-x_2)(x-x_3)(x-x_4)}{(x_0-x_1)(x_0-x_2)(x_0-x_3)(x_0-x_4)} + y_1\frac{(x-x_0)(x-x_2)(x-x_3)(x-x_4)}{(x_1-x_0)(x_1-x_2)(x_1-x_3)(x_1-x_4)} + y_2\frac{(x-x_0)(x-x_1)(x-x_3)(x-x_4)}{(x_2-x_0)(x_2-x_1)(x_2-x_3)(x_2-x_4)} + y_3\frac{(x-x_0)(x-x_1)(x-x_2)(x-x_4)}{(x_3-x_0)(x_3-x_1)(x_3-x_2)(x_3-x_4)} + y_4\frac{(x-x_0)(x-x_1)(x-x_2)(x-x_3)}{(x_4-x_0)(x_4-x_1)(x_4-x_2)(x_4-x_3)}$$

Substituting the values in the formula :

$$y_x = 250\frac{(70-60)(70-80)(70-100)(70-120)}{(40-60)(40-80)(40-100)(40-120)} + 370\frac{(70-40)(70-80)(70-100)(70-120)}{(60-40)(60-80)(60-100)(60-120)} + 470\frac{(70-40)(70-60)(70-100)(70-120)}{(80-40)(80-60)(80-100)(80-120)} + 540\frac{(70-40)(70-60)(70-80)(70-120)}{(100-40)(100-60)(100-80)(100-120)} + 590\frac{(70-40)(70-60)(70-80)(70-100)}{(120-40)(120-60)(120-80)(120-100)}$$

$$
\begin{aligned}
y_x &= 250\frac{(-10)\times(-10)(-30)(-50)}{(-20)(-40)(-60)(-80)} + \\
&370\frac{(30)(-10)(-30)(-50)}{(20)(-20)(-40)(-60)} + \\
&470\frac{(30)(10)(-30)(-50)}{(40)(20)(-20)(-40)} + \\
&540\frac{(30)(10)(-10)(-50)}{(60)(40)(20)(-20)} + \\
&590\frac{(30)(10)(-10)(-30)}{(80)(60)(40)(20)} \\
&= 250\times\frac{-5}{128} + 370\times\frac{-15}{-32} + 470\times\frac{45}{64} \\
&+540\times\frac{5}{-32} + 590\frac{3}{128} \\
&= -9.77 + 173.44 + 330.47 - 84.38 + 13.83 \\
&= 517.74 - 94.15 \\
&= 423.59.
\end{aligned}
$$

The number of persons earning wages below Rs. 70 is 423.59 (thousand).
The number of persons earning wages below Rs. 60 is 370.
Therefore the number of persons earning wages between Rs. 60 and Rs. 70 is

53.59 (thousand) i.e. 423.59−370 = 53.59.

Problem 45. Given the following table, find log 656 :

No	:	654	658	659	661
Log	:	2.8156	2.8182	2.8189	2.8202

(*I.C.W.A.*)

Solution :

No.	*Log*	*No.*	*Log*
654	2.8156 (y_0)	659	2.8189 (y_2)
658	2.8182 (y_1)	661	2.8202 (y_3)

By using Lagrange's formula :

$$
\begin{aligned}
&2.8156\frac{(656-658)(656-659)(656-661)}{(654-658)(654-659)(654-661)} + \\
&2.8182\frac{(656-654)(656-659)(656-661)}{(658-654)(658-659)(658-661)} + \\
&2.8189\frac{(656-654)(656-658)(656-661)}{(659-654)(659-658)(659-661)} + \\
&2.8202\frac{(656-654)(656-658)(656-659)}{(661-654)(661-658)(661-659)} \\
&= 2.8156\frac{(-2)(-3)(-5)}{(-4)(-5)(-7)} + 2.8182\frac{2\times(-3)(-5)}{4\times(-1)\times(-3)} \\
&+2.8189\frac{2\times(-2)(-5)}{5\times1\times(-2)} + 2.8202\frac{2\times(-2)(-3)}{7\times3\times2}
\end{aligned}
$$

$$= 0.6033 + 7.0455 - 5.6378 + 0.8058$$
$$= 8.4546 - 5.6378$$
$$= 2.8168.$$

Thus the log of 656 is **2.8168.**

Problem 46. From the table given below, interpolate by the Lagrange's formula th number of persons under 30 years of age :

Age	:	10–15	15–20	20–25	25–35	35–45	45–55
No. of persons (thousands)	:	193.5	880	933	1,636	1,221	830

(*M.A., Allahabad, B. Com., Madras*)

Solution :

Age	*No. of persons* ('000)
Below 15	193.5 (y_0)
,, 20	1073.5 (y_1)
,, 25	2006.5 (y_2)
,, 35	3642.5 (y_3)
,, 45	4863.5 (y_4)
,, 55	5693.5 (y_5)

Formula :

$$y_x = y_0 = \frac{(x-x_1)(x-x_2)(x-x_3)(x-x_4)(x-x_5)}{(x_0-x_1)(x_0-x_2)(x_0-x_3)(x_0-x_4)(x_0-x_5)} +$$

$$y_1 = \frac{(x-x_0)(x-x_2)(x-x_3)(x-x_4)(x-x_5)}{(x_1-x_0)(x_1-x_2)(x_1-x_3)(x_1-x_4)(x_1-x_5)} +$$

$$y_2 = \frac{(x-x_0)(x-x_1)(x-x_3)(x-x_4)(x-x_5)}{(x_2-x_0)(x_2-x_1)(x_2-x_3)(x_2-x_4)(x_2-x_5)} +$$

$$y_3 = \frac{(x-x_0)(x-x_1)(x-x_2)(x-x_4)(x-x_5)}{(x_3-x_0)(x_3-x_1)(x_3-x_2)(x_3-x_4)(x_3-x_5)} +$$

$$y_4 = \frac{(x-x_0)(x-x_1)(x-x_2)(x-x_3)(x-x_5)}{(x_4-x_0)(x_4-x_1)(x_4-x_2)(x_4-x_3)(x_4-x_5)} +$$

$$y_5 = \frac{(x-x_0)(x-x_1)(x-x_2)(x-x_3)(x-x_4)}{(x_5-x_0)(x_5-x_1)(x_5-x_2)(x_5-x_3)(x_5-x_4)} +$$

$$y_x = 193.5\,\frac{(30-20)(30-25)(30-35)(30-45)(30-55)}{(15-20)(15-25)(15-35)(15-45)(15-55)} +$$

$$1073.5\,\frac{(30-15)(30-25)(30-35)(30-45)(30-55)}{(20-15)(20-25)(20-35)(20-45)(20-55)} +$$

$$2006.5\,\frac{(30-15)(30-20)(30-35)(30-45)(30-55)}{(25-15)(25-20)(25-35)(25-45)(25-55)} +$$

$$3642.5\,\frac{(30-15)(30-20)(30-25)(30-45)(30-55)}{(35-15)(35-20)(35-25)(35-45)(35-55)} +$$

$$4863.5\,\frac{(30-15)(30-20)(30-25)(30-35)(30-55)}{(45-15)(45-20)(45-25)(45-35)(45-55)} +$$

$$
\begin{aligned}
& 5693.5\frac{(30-15)(30-20)(30-25)(30-35)(30-45)}{(55-15)(55-20)(55-25)(55-35)(55-45)}+\\
= \;& 193.5\frac{(10)(5)(-5)(-15)(-25)}{(-5)(-10)(-20)(-30)(-40)}+\\
& 1073.5\frac{(15)(5)(-5)(-15)(-25)}{(5)(-5)(-15)(-25)(-35)}+\\
& 2006.5\frac{(15)(10)(-5)(-15)(-25)}{(10)(5)(-10)(-20)(-30)}+\\
& 3642.5\frac{(15)(10)(5)(-15)(-25)}{(20)(15)(10)(-10)(-20)}+\\
& 4863.5\frac{(15)(10)(5)(-5)(-25)}{(30)(25)(20)(10)(-10)}+\\
& 5693.5\frac{(15)(10)(5)(-5)(-15)}{(40)(35)(30)(20)(10)}.\\
= \;& 193.5\left(\frac{-5}{-64}\right)+1073.5\left(\frac{-3}{7}\right)+2006.5\left(\frac{-15}{-16}\right)\\
& +3642.5\left(\frac{15}{32}\right)+4863.5\left(\frac{1}{-16}\right)+5693.5\left(\frac{3}{448}\right)\\
= \;& 15.12-460.07+1881.09+1707.42-303.97+38.13\\
= \;& 3641.76-764.04\\
= \;& 2877.72 \quad \text{or} \quad \mathbf{2878}.
\end{aligned}
$$

Thus the number of persons under 30 years of age = 2878 thousand.

Problem 47. Use Lagrange' interpolation formula to find y when x = 0, given the following table :

x	:	-1	-2	2	4
y	:	-1	-9	11	69

(*I.C.W.A*)

Solution :

x		y	
-1	x_0	-1	y_0
-2	x_1	-9	y_1
2	x_2	11	y_2
4	x_3	69	y_3

$$
\begin{aligned}
y_0 = \;& (-1)\frac{(x+2)(x-2)(x-4)}{(-1+2)(-1-2)(-1-4)}\\
& +(-9)\frac{(x+1)(x-2)(x-4)}{(-2+1)(-2-2)(-2-4)}\\
& +11\frac{(x+1)(x+2)(x-4)}{(2+1)(2+2)(2-4)}+69\frac{(x+1)(x+2)(x-2)}{(4+1)(4+2)(4-2)}.
\end{aligned}
$$

The estimated value of y_0, when $x = 0$ is obtained by putting $x = 0$ in brackets.

$$y_0 = (-1)\frac{2(-2)(-4)}{1(-3)(-5)}+(-9)\frac{1(-2)(-4)}{(-1)(-4)(-6)}$$

$$+(11)\frac{1(2)(-4)}{3(4)(-2)} + (69)\frac{1(2)(-2)}{(5)(6)(2)}$$

$$= -\frac{16}{15} + 3 + \frac{11}{3} - \frac{23}{5}$$

$$= -1.07 + 3.00 + 3.67 - 4.60$$

$$= -5.67 + 6.67$$

$$= 1.$$

PARABOLIC METHOD

Problem 48. The pressure of wind in pounds per square foot, corresponding to the velocity in miles per hour has been determined by experiment to be approximately as follows :

Velocity	:	20	30	40	50
Pressure	:	2	4.4	7.9	13.2

Estimate the pressure for a velocity of 35 miles per hour.

Solution :

Velocity	20	30	35	40	50
Deviation from 35 (x)	-3	-1	0	1	3
Pressure (y)	2	4.4	?	7.9	13.2

Four values are known. Parabola of 3rd order,

$$y = a + bx + cx^2dx^3$$

Substituting :

$$2 = a - 3b + 9c - 27d \quad (1)$$

$$4.4 = a - b + c - d \quad (2)$$

$$y_0 = a \quad (3)$$

$$7.9 = a + b + c + d \quad (4)$$

$$13.2 = a + 3b + 9c + 27d \quad (5)$$

Add equations (1) and (5)

$$15.2 = 2a + 18c \quad (6)$$

Add equations (2) and (4)

$$12.3 = 2a + 2c \quad (7)$$

Multiply equations (7) by (9)

$$110.7 = 18a + 18c \quad (8)$$

Subtracting equation (6) from (8)

$$95.5 = 16a$$

$$a = \frac{95.5}{16}$$

$$\therefore \quad a = 5.96875$$

$$= \mathbf{5.97}.$$

Therefore, the estimated pressure for a velocity of 35 miles = **5.97.**

Problem 49. What is interpolation? The following table gives the death rate per one lakh population on account of a cetain ailment :

Year	:	1998	2000	2002
Death Rate	:	160	175	180

Estimate by the algebraic method, the death for 2001. (*B.Com., Madras*)

Solution :

Taking deviation from 2001

x	1998	2000	2001	2002
y	160	175	?	180
x	-3	-1	0	1

$$y = a + bx + cx^2$$

$$160 = a - 3b + 9c \quad (1)$$
$$175 = a - b + c \quad (2)$$
$$y_0 = a \quad (3)$$
$$180 = a + b + c \quad (4)$$

Multiply (2) by (3)

$$525 = 3a - 3b - 3c \quad (5)$$

Deduct equation (1) from (5)

$$365 = 2a - 6c \quad (6)$$

Multiply equation (4) by (3)

$$540 = 3a + 3b + 3c \quad (7)$$

Add equation (1) and (7)

$$700 = 4a + 12c$$

(or) $$350 = 2a + 6c \quad (8)$$

Add equation (8) and (6)

$$715 = 4a$$
$$a = \frac{715}{4}$$
$$= \mathbf{178.75.}$$

Problem 50. Interpolate the population of Jabalpur for the year 1986 in the following data obtained from census record :

Year	:	1971	1981	1991	2001
Population	:	453	470	484	504

(*Nagpur B. Com.,*)

Solution :

Taking deviation of years from 1986

x	:	1971	1981	1986	1991	2001
y	:	453	470	y_0	484	504
x		-3	-1	0	$+1$	$+3$

Four values are known, a parabola of the third order will be taken :

$$y = a + bx + cx^2 + dx^3$$

Substituting the values in the formula :

$$453 = a - 3b + 9c - 27d \quad (1)$$

$$470 = a - b + c - d \quad (2)$$

$$y_0 = a \quad (3)$$

$$484 = a + b + c + d \quad (4)$$

$$504 = a + 3b + 9c + 27d \quad (5)$$

Adding Equation (1) and (5)

$$957 = 2a + 18c \quad (6)$$

Adding Equation (2) and (4)

$$954 = 2a + 2c \quad (7)$$

Multiply Equation (7) by 9

$$8586 = 18a + 18c \quad (8)$$

Subtract Equation (6) from Equation (8), we get

$$7629 = 16a$$

$$\therefore \quad a = \frac{7629}{16}$$

$$= \mathbf{476.81}. \quad \text{or} \quad 477$$

Thus, the population for the year 1986 = 477

11

ASSOCIATION OF ATTRIBUTES

Symbols used :

(A), (B), (C), denote positive attributes

(α), (β), (Υ) denote negative attributes

(α) = Not (A) (β) = Not (B) (Υ) = Not (C)

Missing frequencies can be found out with the help of 2 × 2 contingency table or Nine square table.

	A	α	Total
B	(AB)	(αB)	(B)
β	(Aβ)	(αβ)	(β)
Total	A	(α)	N

Vertical total

$(AB) + (A\beta) = (A)$

$(\alpha B) + (\alpha\beta) = (\alpha)$

$(A) + (\alpha) = (N)$

$(AB) = (A) - (A\beta)$

$(A\beta) = (A) - (AB)$

$N - (\alpha) = (A)$

$(AB) + (A\beta) = (A)$

Horizontal total

$(AB) + (\alpha B) = (B)$

$(A\beta) + (\alpha\beta) = (\beta)$

$(B) + (\beta) = N.$

$(\alpha B) = (B) - (AB)$

$N - (\beta) = B$

$(AB) + (\alpha B) = (B)$

Types of Association

Positive association if $(AB) > \dfrac{(A)\,(B)}{N}$

Negative association if $(AB) < \dfrac{(A)\,(B)}{N}$

Independent if $(AB) = \dfrac{(A)\,(B)}{N}$

Yule's Coefficient of Association $Q = \dfrac{(AB)\,(\alpha\beta) - (A\beta)\,(\alpha B)}{(AB)\,(\alpha\beta) + (A\beta)\,(\alpha B)}$

Problem 1. Given N=2500 ; (A)=420 ; (AB)=85 ;(B)=670 Prepare 2×2 contingency table and compute Yule's coefficient of association and interpret the result.

(B.Com.)

Solution :

Given

	(A)	(α)	Total
(B)	85		670
(β)			
Total	420		2500 N

Remaining Values

	(A)	(α)	Total
(B)		585 $(\alpha\beta)$	
(β)	335 $(A\beta)$	1495$(\alpha\beta)$	1830(β)
Total		2080 (α)	

$$
\begin{aligned}
Q &= \frac{(AB)\,(\alpha\beta) - (A\beta)\,(\alpha B)}{(AB)\,(\alpha B) + (A\beta)\,(\alpha B)} \\
&= \frac{(85 \times 1495) - (335 \times 585)}{(85 \times 1495) + (335 \times 585)} \\
&= \frac{127075 - 195975}{127075 + 195975} \\
&= \frac{-68900}{323050} \\
&= \mathbf{-0.21}
\end{aligned}
$$

There is negative association

Problem 2. For two attributes A and B, we have (AB)=8; (A)=18, $(\alpha\beta)$=5 ; N= 35. Calculate the coefficient of association. *(B.A. Bombay)*

Solution :

Given

	(A)	(α)	
(B)	8		
(β)		5	
	18		35
			N

Missing Values are

	(A)	(α)	
(B)	8	12	20
(β)	10	5	15
	18	17	35
			N

$$
\begin{aligned}
Q &= \frac{(AB)(\alpha\beta) - (\alpha B)(A\beta)}{(AB)(\alpha\beta) + (\alpha\beta)(A\beta)} \\
&= \frac{8 \times 5 - 12 \times 10}{8 \times 5 + 12 \times 10} \\
&= \frac{40 - 120}{40 + 120} \\
&= \frac{-80}{160} \\
&= \mathbf{-0.5}
\end{aligned}
$$

Problem 3. Find whether A and B are independent in the following case :
$(AB) = 256\,;\ (\alpha B) = 768\,;\ (A\beta) = 48\,;\ (\alpha\beta) = 144$ *(B. Sc. Madurai Kamaraj)*

$$
\begin{aligned}
(A) &= (AB) + (A\beta) = 256 + 48 = \mathbf{304} \\
(B) &= (AB) + (\alpha B) = 256 + 768 = \mathbf{1024}
\end{aligned}
$$

$$(\alpha) = (\alpha B) + (\alpha\beta) = 768 + 144 = \mathbf{912}$$
$$N = (A) + (\alpha) = 304 + 912 = \mathbf{1216}$$
$$(AB) = \frac{(A) \times (B)}{N} = \frac{304 \times 1024}{1216} = \mathbf{256}$$

Since $(AB) = \frac{(A) \times (B)}{N}$, the attributes are independent

Problem 4. Given the following information. (A)=490, (AB) =294, (α)=570, (αB)=380. Show whether attributes A and B are positively associated, negatively associated, or independent.

(M.Com., Ujjain)

Solution :

294 (AB)	380 (αB)	674 (B)
196 $(A\beta)$	190 $(\alpha\beta)$	386 (β)
490 (A)	570 (α)	1060 N

$$\text{Expectation of } (AB) = \frac{(A) \times (B)}{N}$$
$$= \frac{490 \times 674}{1060} = 311.5$$

Since actual observation (AB) =294 is less than expectation (311.5). The attributes are negatively associated.

Problem : 5 For two attributes A and B, we have (AB)= 35; (A)=55 ; N=100; $(\alpha\beta)$=20. Calculate the coefficient of association.

(B.A. Bombay, Madurai)

Solution :

	(A)	(α)	
(B)	35	25(60-35)	60(35+25)
(β)	20(55-35)	20	40(100-60)
	55	45(100-55)	100

(or)

$$(\alpha) = N - (A) = 100 - 55 = 45$$
$$(A\beta) = (A) - (AB) = 55 - 35 = 20$$
$$(B) = N - (\beta) = 100 - 40 = 60$$
$$(\alpha B) = (B) - (AB) = 60 - 35 = 25$$

Yule's Coefficient of Association :

$$Q = \frac{(AB)(\alpha\beta) - (A\beta)(\alpha B)}{(AB)(\alpha\beta) + (AB)(\alpha B)}$$

$$= \frac{35 \times 20 - 20 \times 25}{35 \times 20 + 20 \times 25}$$

$$= \frac{700 - 500}{700 + 500}$$

$$= \frac{200}{1200}$$

$$= \mathbf{+0.167}$$

Problem 6. Show whether A and B are independent, positively associated or negatively associated.

$(AB)= 128$, $(\alpha B) = 384$, $(A\beta) = 24$, $(\alpha\beta) = 72$ *(B. A. Madurai)*

Solution :

$$(A) = (AB) + (A\beta) = 128 + 24 = 152$$

$$(B) = (AB) + (\alpha B) = 128 + 384 = 512$$

$$(\alpha) = (\alpha B) + (\alpha\beta) = 384 + 72 = 456$$

$$(N) = (A) + (\alpha) = 152 + 456 = 608$$

$$\frac{(A) \times (B)}{N} = \frac{152 \times 512}{608} = 128$$

$$(AB) = 128$$

Hence (A) and (B) are independent.

Problem 7. Following data relate to literacy and unemployment in a group of 500 persons. You are required to calculate Yule's Coefficient of Association between literacy and unemployment. Interpret it.

Literate unemployed	220
Literate Employed	20
Illiterate Employed	180

(M. Com., Agra, Vikram, C.A.)

220 (AB)	80 (αB)	300 (B)
20 $(A\beta)$	180 $(\alpha\beta)$	200 (β)
240 (A)	260 (α)	500 (N)

(A) = literacy

(α) = illiteracy

(B) = Unemployment

(β) = Employment

$$(\beta) = (A\beta) + (\alpha\beta) = 20 + 180 = \mathbf{200}$$

$$(B) = N - (\beta) = 500 - 200 = \mathbf{300}$$

$$(\alpha B) = (B) - (AB) = 300 - 220 = \mathbf{80}$$

$$(A) = (AB) + (A\beta) = 220 + 20 = \mathbf{240}$$

$$(\alpha) = (\alpha B) + (\alpha\beta) = 80 + 180 = \mathbf{260}$$

$$Q = \frac{(AB)(\alpha\beta) - (A\beta)(\alpha B)}{(AB)(\alpha B) + (A\beta)(\alpha\beta)}$$

$$= \frac{(220 \times 180) - (20 \times 80)}{(220 \times 180) + (20 \times 80)} = \frac{39,600 - 1600}{39,600 + 1600} = \frac{38,000}{41,200}$$

$$= +0.92$$

There is a positive association between literacy and unemployment.

Problem 8. In a report on consumers' preference it was given that out of 500 persons surveyed 410 preferred variety A, 380 preferred variety B and 270 persons liked both. Are the data consistent?

(*M. Com., Delhi*)

Solution :

(A) denote consumers who like variety A

(B) denote consumers who like variety B.

270 (AB)	110 (380–270) (αB)	380 (B)
140 (410–270) $(A\beta)$	–20 (90–110) $(\alpha\beta)$	120 (500–380) (β)
410 (A)	90 (500–410) (α)	500 N

No. There is no consistency in the given data as $(\alpha\beta) = -20$

Problem 9 : $N = 1{,}500$; $(A) = 383$; $(B) = 360$; $(AB) = 35$ Prepare 2×2 contingency table and compute Yule's coefficient of association and interpret the result.

(*M. Com. Allahabad*)

Solution :

	(A)	(α)	Total
(B)	35 (AB)	325 (αB)	360 (B)
(β)	348 $(A\beta)$	792 $(\alpha\beta)$	1140 (β)
Total	383 (A)	1117 (α)	1500 N

Yule's Coefficient of association

$$Q = \frac{(AB)(\alpha\beta) - (A\beta)(\alpha B)}{(AB)(\alpha\beta) + (A\beta)(\alpha B)}$$

$$= \frac{(35 \times 792) - (348 \times 325)}{(35 \times 792) + (348 \times 325)}$$

$$= \frac{27720 - 113100}{27720 + 113100}$$

$$= \frac{-85380}{140820}$$

$$= -0.606$$

There is a negative association.

Problem 10 : Investigate the association between darkness of eye colour in father and son from the following data:

Father with dark eyes and sons with dark eyes = 500

Father with dark eyes and sons with not dark eyes = 790

Father with not dark eyes and sons with dark eyes = 890

Father with not dark eyes and sons with not dark eyes = 7820

(*B. Com. Madurai, Agra*)

Solution :

(A) =Fathers with dark eyes

(α) =Fathers with not darks eyes

(B) = Sons with dark eyes

(β) =Sons with not dark eyes

Given data are :

$$\begin{aligned} (AB) &= 500 \\ (A\beta) &= 790 \\ (\alpha B) &= 890 \\ (\alpha\beta) &= 7820 \\ (A) &= (AB) + (A\beta) \\ &= 500 + 790 = 1290 \\ (\alpha) &= (\alpha B) + (\alpha\beta) \\ &= 890 + 7820 = 8710 \end{aligned}$$

Percentage of dark eyed amongst the sons of dark eyed fathers,

$$\frac{(AB) \times 100}{(A)} = \frac{500 \times 100}{1290} = \mathbf{38.76\%}$$

Percentage of dark eyed amongst the sons of not dark eyed fathers,

$$\frac{(\alpha B) \times 100}{(\alpha)} = \frac{890 \times 100}{8710} = \mathbf{10.22\%}$$

Thus there is a positive association between darkness of eye colour in fathers and sons.

Problem 11. Test for association between extravagance in fathers and extravagance in sons from the following data :

Extravagant fathers with extravagant sons = 327

Miserly fathers with extravagant sons = 741

Extravagant fathers with miserly sons = 545

Miserly fathers with miserly sons = 234

(*B. Sc., Madras*)

Solution :

Let (*A*) denote extravagant fathers,
(*α*) denote miserly fathers,
(*B*) denote extravagant sons
(*β*) denote miserly sons

We are given

$$(AB) = 327$$
$$(A\beta) = 545$$
$$(\alpha B) = 741$$
$$(\alpha\beta) = 234$$

$$\begin{aligned} Q &= \frac{(AB)(\alpha\beta) - (A\beta)(\alpha B)}{(AB)(\alpha\beta) + (A\beta)(\alpha B)} \\ &= \frac{(327 \times 234) - (545 \times 741)}{(327 \times 234) + (545 \times 741)} \\ &= \frac{76518 - 403845}{76518 + 403845} \\ &= -\frac{-327327}{480363} \\ &= \mathbf{-0.681} \quad \text{There is negative association} \end{aligned}$$

Problem 12. Do you find any association between the tempers of brothers and sisters from the following data :

Good-natured brothers and good-natured sisters	1230
Good-natured brothers and sullen sisters	850
Sullen brothers and good-natured sisters	530
Sullen brothers and sullen sisters	980

Solution :

(*A*) denote good natured brothers

(*α*) denote sullen natured brothers

(*B*) denote good natured sisters

(*β*) denote sullen natured sisters

The given data are :

$$\begin{aligned} (AB) &= 1230 & (A) &= (AB) + (A\beta) \\ (A\beta) &= 850\,; & &= 1230 + 850 = \mathbf{2080} \\ (\alpha B) &= 530\,; & (\alpha) &= (\alpha B) + (\alpha\beta) \\ (\alpha\beta) &= 980\,; & &= 530 + 980 = \mathbf{1510} \end{aligned}$$

Percentage of good natured sisters amongst the sisters of good natured brothers, *i.e.*,

$$\frac{(AB) \times 100}{(A)} = \frac{1230 \times 100}{2080} = 59.13\%$$

Percentage of good natured sisters amongst the sisters of sullen brothers, i.e.,
Brothers, i.e.,

$$\frac{(\alpha B) \times 100}{(\alpha)} = \frac{530 \times 100}{1510} = 35\%.$$

These two percentages bring out the fact that the tempers of the brothers and sisters are positively associated.

Problem 13. Eighty-eight residents of an Indian city, who were interviewed during a sample survey, and classified below according to their smoking and tea drinking habits. Calculate Yule's coefficient of Association and comment on its value.

	Smokers	*Non-smokers*
Drinking Tea	40	33
Non-drinking	3	12

(*M. Com., Delhi*)

Solution : Let A and B denote smokers and those drinking tea respectively.

α and β non-smokers and those not drinking tea respectively.

$$AB = 40\,;\ (A\beta) = 3\,;\ (\alpha B) = 33\,;\ (\alpha\beta) = 12$$

$$\begin{aligned} Q &= \frac{(AB)(\alpha\beta) - (A\beta)(\alpha B)}{(AB)(\alpha\beta) + (A\beta)(\alpha B)} \\ &= \frac{40 \times 12 - 3 \times 33}{40 \times 12 + 3 \times 33} \\ &= \frac{480 - 99}{480 + 99} \\ &= \frac{381}{579} \\ &= \mathbf{+0.658} \end{aligned}$$

There is positive association between drinking tea and smoking.

Problem 14. In an experiment on immunization of cattle from tuberculosis the following results were obtained :

	Affected	*Unaffected*
Inoculated	12	26
Not Inoculated	16	6

By calculating Yule's Coefficient of Association, examine the effect of vaccine in controlling the disease

(*M.A., Econ., Gorakhpur*)

Solution :

(A) : denote affected

(α) : denote unaffected

(B) : denote inoculated

(β) : denote not inoculated.

The given data are :

$$(AB)=12\ ;\ (A\beta)=16\ ;\ (\alpha B)=26\ ;\ (\alpha\beta)=6$$

$$\begin{aligned} Q &= \frac{(12 \times 6) - (16 \times 26)}{(12 \times 6) + (16 \times 26)} \\ &= \frac{72 - 416}{72 + 416} \\ &= \frac{-344}{488} \\ &= \mathbf{-0.705} \end{aligned}$$

There is a negative association between tuberculosis and inoculation. Hence, vaccine is effective in controlling the disease.

Problem 15 : In an investigation relating to health and nutrition of children between the age of one and five years two groups of children were compared, one belonging to the well-to-do class 125 in number, and the other belonging to the poor class, 124 in number. The following results were obtained :

	Poor children (percent)	*Well-to-do children (percent)*
Below Normal weight	75	23
Above ,, ,,	5	42

Find the coefficient of association between the weight of children and their parents financial condition.

(*M.Com., Gorakhpur*)

Solution

(A) = Poor children

(α) = well-to-do-children

(B) = Below normal weight

(β) = Above normal weight.

The given data :

$(AB) = 75$; $(A\beta) = 5$; $(\alpha B) = 23$; $(\alpha\beta) = 42$

Yule's coefficient of Association (or)

$$
\begin{aligned}
Q &= \frac{(AB)(\alpha\beta) - (A\beta)(\alpha B)}{(AB)(\alpha\beta) + (A\beta)(\alpha B)} \\
&= \frac{(75 \times 42) - (5 \times 23)}{(75 \times 42) + (5 \times 23)} \\
&= \frac{3150 - 115}{3150 + 115} \\
&= \frac{3035}{3265} \\
&= \mathbf{+0.93}
\end{aligned}
$$

Therefore, there is a positive association between the weight of the children and their economic status.

Problem 16. Calculate the coefficient of association between the intelligence of fathers and sons from the following data :

Intelligent fathers with intelligent sons	=	300
Intelligent fathers with dull sons	=	100
Dull fathers with intelligent sons	=	50
Dull fathers with dull sons	=	500

Solution :

(A) denotes intelligent fathers ; (α) dull fathers

(B) denotes intelligent sons ; (β) dull sons.

Given data are :

$$(AB) = 300$$
$$(A\beta) = 100$$
$$(\alpha B) = 50$$
$$(\alpha\beta) = 500$$

$$Q = \frac{(AB)(\alpha\beta) - (A\beta)(\alpha B)}{(AB)(\alpha\beta) + (A\beta)(\alpha B)}$$
$$= \frac{(300 \times 500) - (100 \times 50)}{(300 \times 500) + (100 \times 50)}$$
$$= \frac{150000 - 5000}{150000 + 5000}$$
$$= \frac{145000}{155000}$$
$$= \frac{145}{155}$$
$$Q = \mathbf{+0.935}$$

There is positive association.

Problem 17 : Investigate the association between eye colour in father and son from the following data :

Fathers with dark eyes and sons with dark eyes	= 100
Fathers with not dark eyes and sons with dark eyes	= 180
Fathers with dark eyes and sons with not dark eyes	= 160
Fathers with not dark eyes and sons with not dark eyes	= 1,560

(*M.A., Econ, Agra*)

Solution :

Let A denote fathers with dark eyes,
α denote fathers with not dark eyes,

B denote sons with dark eyes
β denote sons with not dark eyes.

Thus : $(AB) = 100$ (given in the question)
$(\alpha B) = 180$ (,,)
$(A\beta) = 160$ (,,)
$(\alpha\beta) = 1560$ (,,)

$$Q = \frac{(AB)(\alpha\beta) - (A\beta)(\alpha\beta)}{(AB)(\alpha\beta) + (A\beta)(\alpha\beta)}$$
$$= \frac{(100 \times 1560) - (160 \times 180)}{(100 \times 1560) + (160 \times 180)}$$
$$= \frac{156000 - 28800}{156000 + 28800}$$
$$= \frac{127200}{184800}$$
$$= \mathbf{+0.69}$$

There is positive association.

Problem 18. Calculate the Coefficient of association between intelligence in father and son from the following data :

Intelligent fathers with intelligent sons	248
Intelligent fathers with dull sons	81
Dull fathers with intelligent sons	92
Dull fathers with dull sons	579

(*M.A., Agra, M. Com., Rajasthan,* it B. com., *Madurai*)

Solution :

(A) : Intelligent fathers (α) : dul fathers

(B) : Intelligent sons (β) : dull sons.

Given data are :

$(AB) = 248\,; (A\beta) = 81$

$(\alpha B) = 92\,; (\alpha\beta)\, 579$

$$Q = \frac{(AB)(\alpha\beta) - (A\beta)(\alpha B)}{(AB)(\alpha\beta) + (A\beta)(\alpha B)}$$

$$= \frac{(248 \times 579) - (81 \times 92)}{(248 \times 579) + (81 \times 92)}$$

$$= \frac{143592 - 7452}{143592 + 7452}$$

$$= \frac{136140}{151044}$$

$Q = +\mathbf{0.9}$ There is positive association

Problem 19. In a co-educational institution, out of 200 students 150 were boys. They took an examination and it was found that 120 passed, 10 girls had failed. Is there any association between sex and success in the examination ?

(*MBA, M. Com., Himachal*)

Solution :

(A) denote boys and (α) denote girls

(B) denote those who passed the examination and (β) denote those who failed.

120	40	160
30	10	40
150	50	200

$$Q = \frac{(AB)(\alpha\beta) - (A\beta)(\alpha B)}{(AB)(\alpha\beta) + (A\beta)(\alpha B)}$$

$$= \frac{(120 \times 10) - (30 \times 40)}{(120 \times 10) + (30 \times 40)}$$

$$= \frac{1200 - 1200}{1200 + 1200} = \frac{0}{2400} = 0$$

Therefore, there is no association between sex and success in the examination.

Problem 20. The following table gives the number of blind and insane in two cities :

	City A	City B
Total population	2,70,000	1,60,200
Number of blind	1,000	2,000
Number of insane	6,000	1,000
Number of insane Among the blind	19	9

(*a*) Obtain the measure of association between blindness and insanity in each of the two age-groups.

(*b*) Do you consider that blindness and insanity are associated with each other in the two age-groups or is more in one age-group than the other ?

(*M.Com., Rajasthan*)

City A

	(*A*)	(α)	
(*B*)	19	5981	6000
(β)	981	263019	264000
	1000	269000	270000

City B

	(*A*)	α	
(*B*)	9	991	1000
(β)	1991	157209	159200
	2000	158200	160200

(*A*) denotes blindness (α) denotes Non-blindness

(*B*) denotes insanity (β) Sanity

$$Q = \frac{(AB)(\alpha\beta) - (A\beta)(\alpha B)}{(AB)(\alpha\beta) - (AB)(\alpha B)}$$

$$Q = \frac{(19 \times 263019) - (981 \times 5981)}{(19 \times 263019) + (981 \times 5981)}$$

$$= \frac{49,97,361 - 58,67,361}{49,97,361 + 58,67,361}$$

$$= \frac{-8,70,000}{1,08,64,722}$$

$$= \mathbf{-0.08}$$

$$Q = \frac{(9 \times 157209) - (1991 \times 991)}{(9 \times 157209) + (1991 \times 991)}$$

$$= \frac{1414881 - 1973081}{1414881 + 1973081}$$

$$= \frac{-558200}{3387962}$$

$$= \mathbf{-0.165}$$

Problem 21. 1660 candidates appeared for a competitive examination. 422 were successful. 256 had attended a coaching class ; and of these 150 came out successful. Estimate the utility of the coaching classes.

(*B. Com. Mysore*)

We have to find out Yule's Coefficient of Association.

Let (*A*) = successful candidates

(α) = failures

(*B*) = Attended coaching classes.

(β) = Not attended coaching classes.

Given

	(*A*)	(α)	
(B)	150		256
(β)			
	422		1660

N

Missing Values are:

	106 (αB)	
272 ($A\beta$)	1132 ($\alpha\beta$)	1404 (β)
	1238 (α)	

$$Q = \frac{150 \times 1132 - 272 \times 106}{150 \times 1132 + 272 \times 106}$$

$$= \frac{169,800 - 28,832}{169,800 + 28,832}$$

$$= \frac{1,40,968}{1,98,632}$$

$$= +\mathbf{0.71} \quad \text{Coaching classes are useful.}$$

Problem 22. Investigate the association between eye colour of husbands and eye colour of wives from the data given below :

Husbands with light eyes and wives with not light eyes = 214
Husbands with light eyes and wives with light eyes = 309
Husbands with not light eyes and wives with light eyes = 132
Husbands with not light eyes and wives with not light eyes = 112

(*M. Com. Delhi, Madurai, Punjab*)

Solution :

Let (A) denote husbands with light eyes
(α) denote husbands with not light eyes
(B) denote wives with light eyes
(β) denote wives with not light eyes

The given data in terms of symbols are
$(AB) = 309$; $(A\beta) = 214$; $(\alpha B) = 132$ $(\alpha\beta) = 112$

$$Q = \frac{(AB)(\alpha\beta) - (A\beta)(\alpha B)}{(AB)(\alpha\beta) + (A\beta)(\alpha B)}$$

$$= \frac{(309 \times 112) - (214 \times 132)}{(309 \times 112) + (214 \times 132)}$$

$$= \frac{34608 - 28248}{34608 + 28248}$$

$$= \frac{6360}{62856}$$

$$= +\mathbf{0.1}$$

Problem 23. 1,500 candidates appeared for a competitive examinations. 425 were successful, 250 had attended a coaching class and of these 150 came out successful. Estimate the utility of the coaching class.

(*M. Com., Rajasthan Univ.*)

Solution :

	(A) Coaching	(α) No Coaching	Total
(B) Success	150	275	425
(β) No Success	100	975	1075
Total	250	1250	1500

$$Q = \frac{(AB)(\alpha\beta) - (A\beta)(\alpha B)}{(AB)(\alpha\beta) + (A\beta)(\alpha B)}$$

$$(AB) = 150;\ (A\beta) = 100;\ (\alpha B) = 275;\ (\alpha\beta) = 975$$

$$Q = \frac{(150 \times 975) - (100 \times 275)}{(150 \times 975) + (100 \times 275)}$$

$$= \frac{146250 - 27500}{146250 + 27500}$$

$$= \frac{118750}{173750}$$

$$= +\mathbf{0.68} \text{ Coaching classes are useful.}$$

Problem 24. The following summary data relate to the adult population of a small village :

Adult population	600
No. of employed	240
Literate adult population employed	80
No. of literates	200

Determine whether literacy and employment are associated variables or not.

(*B. Com., Madurai*)

Solution :

Let (A) = literate

(α) = illiterate

(B) = employed

(α) = unemployed

	(A)	(α)	Total
(B)	80	160	240
(β)	120	240	360
Total	200	400	600

$$Q = \frac{(AB)(\alpha\beta) - (A\beta)(\alpha B)}{(AB)(\alpha\beta) + (A\beta)(\alpha B)}$$

$$= \frac{(80 \times 240) - (120 \times 160)}{(80 \times 240) + (120 \times 160)}$$

$$= \frac{19200 - 19200}{19200 + 19200}$$

$$= \frac{0}{38,400}$$

$$= \mathbf{0}$$

Therefore, there is no association between literacy and employment.

Problem 25. In a group of 400 students, the number of married is 160. Out of 120 students who failed, 48 belonged to the married group. Find out whether the attributes of marriage and failure are independent.

(*M. Com. Jodhpur*)

Solution :

Let (A) denote married students

(α) denote unmarried students

(B) denote failure

(β) denote passed students

	(A)	(α)	
(B)	48 (AB)	72 $(\alpha\beta)$	120 (B)
(β)	112 $(A\beta)$	168 $(\alpha\beta)$	280 (β)
Total	160 (A)	240 (α)	400 (N)

$$\begin{aligned} Q &= \frac{(AB)(\alpha\beta) - (A\beta)(\alpha B)}{(AB)(\alpha\beta) + (A\beta)(\alpha B)} \\ &= \frac{(48 \times 168) - (112 \times 72)}{(48 \times 168) + (112 \times 72)} \\ &= \frac{8064 - 8064}{8064 + 8064} \\ &= \frac{0}{16,128} \\ &= \mathbf{0} \end{aligned}$$

Since $Q = 0$, marriage and failure are independent.

Problem 26. In an examination at which 600 candidates appeared, boys outnumbered girls by 16% of all candidates. Number of passed candidates exceeded the number of failed candidates by 310. Boys failing in the examination numbered 88. Find coefficient association between male sex and success in examination.

(*M. Com., Agra M. A. (Econ.) Rajasthan*)

Solution :

(A) = Boys (α) = girls

(B) = Successful (β) = failure

Boys are outnumbered by 16% $= \dfrac{600 \times 16}{100} = \mathbf{96.}$

No. of girls $= 600 - 96 = \dfrac{504}{2} = \mathbf{252.}$

No. of boys $= \dfrac{504}{2} + 96 = 252 + 96 = \mathbf{348}$

(β) = No. of failed candidates $= \dfrac{600 - 310}{2} = \mathbf{145.}$

	(A)	(α)	
(B)	260 (AB)	195 (αB)	455 (B)
(β)	88 $(A\beta)$	57 $(\alpha\beta)$	145 (β)
	384 (A)	252 (α)	600 N

$$\begin{aligned} Q &= \frac{(AB)(\alpha\beta)-(A\beta)(\alpha B)}{(AB)(\alpha\beta)+(A\beta)(\alpha B)} \\ &= \frac{(260\times 57)-(88\times 195)}{(260\times 57)+(88\times 195)} \\ &= \frac{14820-17160}{14820+17160} \\ &= \frac{-2340}{31980} \\ &= \mathbf{-0.07}. \end{aligned}$$

Problem 27. Out of 3,000 unskilled workers of a factory, 2,000 come from rural areas and out of 1200 skilled workers, 300 come from rural areas. Determine the association between skill and residence by the method of proportions.

(B.A. Madurai Kamraj)

Solution :

Let (A) denote skilled workers.

(α) denote unskilled workers.

(B) denote workers from rural areas.

(β) denote workers from urban areas.

$(A) = 1200$; $(\alpha) = 3000$; $(B) = 2000$; $(\alpha B) = 2000$; $(AB) = 300$

$$\frac{(AB)}{(A)} = \frac{300}{1200} = 0.25$$

$$\frac{(\alpha B)}{(\alpha)} = \frac{300}{1200} = 0.67$$

$$\frac{(\alpha B)}{(\alpha)} > \frac{(AB)}{(A)} \; i.e. \, 0.67 > 0.25,$$

there is negative association between skill and residence.

Problem 28. In an assortive matching study to find whether tall husbands tend to marry tall wives, the following information about the wives of 125 tall and 125 short husbands was published :

	Tall Husbands	*Short Husbands*
Tall wives	56%	13%
Short wives	11%	48%

Find the coefficient of association between the stature of wives and husbands ignoring medium sized wives.

(I.A.S.)

Solution :

Let A and B denote tall husbands and tall wives respectively.

α and β denote short husbands and short wives respectively.

$AB = 56$; $(A\beta)$=11 ; (αB)=13 ; $(\alpha\beta)$=48

$$\begin{aligned} Q &= \frac{(AB)(\alpha\beta)-(A\beta)(\alpha B)}{(AB)(\alpha\beta)+(A\beta)(\alpha B)} \\ &= \frac{56\times 48-11\times 13}{56\times 48+11\times 13} \end{aligned}$$

$$= \frac{2688 - 143}{2688 + 143}$$
$$= \frac{2545}{2851}$$
$$= \mathbf{+0.9}.$$

Problem 29. In an anti-malarial campaign in a certain area, quinine was administered to 812 persons out of a total population of 3248. The numnber of fever cases is shown below:

Treatment	*Fever*	*No. Fever*
Quinine	20	792
No quinine	220	2216

$(\alpha)$and (β)denote no treatment of quinine and no attack of fever respectively.

(AB)=20 ; $(A\beta)$=792 ; (αB)=220 ; $(\alpha\beta)$=2216

$$= \frac{(AB)(\alpha\beta) - (A\beta)(\alpha B)}{(AB)(\alpha\beta) + (A\beta)(\alpha B)}$$
$$= \frac{20 \times 2216 - 792 \times 220}{20 \times 2216 + 792 \times 220}$$
$$= \frac{44320 - 174240}{44320 + 174240}$$
$$= -\frac{1,29,920}{2,18,560}$$
$$= \mathbf{-0.59}.$$

There is negative association between treatment of quinine and attack of fever.

Hence quinine is useful in checking malaria.

Problem 30. Can vaccination be regarded as a preventive measure for small-pox from the data given below ?

Of 1,482 persons in a locality exposed to small-pox, 368 in all were attacked.

Of **1,482** Persons, 343 had been vaccinated and of these only 35 were attacked.

Solution :

Let A be the attribute of vaccination,

a, the attribute of non-vaccination

B, the attribute of exemption from attack of small-pox.

β, the attribute of attack of small-pox.

N=1482 ; (A)=343 ; (β)=368 ; $(A\beta)$=35

$$(AB) = (A) - (A\beta) = 343 - 35 = 308$$
$$a = N - (A) = 1482 - 343 = 1139$$
$$(aB) = (B) - (AB) = N - (\beta) - (AB)$$
$$= 1482 - 368 - 308 = 806$$

Percentage of vaccinated who were not attacked

$$= \frac{(AB)}{(A)} \times 100 = \frac{308}{343} = 100$$
$$= \mathbf{90\%}.$$

Percentage of not vaccinated who were not attacked

$$= \frac{aB}{A} \times 100 = \frac{806}{1139} \times 100$$
$$= \mathbf{71\%}.$$

The comparison of the two percentages shows that vaccination and exemption from attack are positively associated. Therefore vaccination may be regarded as preventive measure for small-pox.

Problem 31. From the data given below test whether there is association between economic status and economic achievement :

	Rich	*Poor*
Educated	508	1559
Uneducated	905	1114

(*B.A. Annamalai*)

Solution :

Let (A) = Rich ; (α) = Poor ; (B) = Educated (β) = Uneducated.

The given data are :

$$(AB) = 508$$
$$(A\beta) = 905$$
$$(\alpha B) = 1559$$
$$(\alpha\beta) = 1114$$

$$Q = \frac{(AB)(\alpha\beta) - (A\beta)(\alpha B)}{(AB)(\alpha\beta) + (A\beta)(\alpha B)}$$
$$= \frac{(508 \times 1114) - (905 \times 1559)}{(508 \times 1114) + (905 \times 1559)}$$
$$= \frac{5,65,912 - 14,10,895}{5,65,912 + 14,10,895}$$
$$= -\frac{-8,44,983}{19,76,807}$$
$$= \mathbf{-0.43}.$$

The coefficient of association between richness and education is negative.

Problem 32. Calculate Yule's Coefficient of Association between marriage and failure of students from the following data pertaining to 500 students :

	Passed	*failed*	*Total*
Married	90	65	155
Unmarried	260	110	370

(*M.Com., Gorakhpur*)

Solution :

Let (A) denote married students.

(α) denote unmarried students

(B) denote failed students

(β) denote passed students

The given values are :

$(AB) = 65$; $(A\beta) = 90$; $(\alpha B) = 110$; $(\alpha\beta) = 260$

$$\begin{aligned} Q &= \frac{(AB)(\alpha\beta) - (A\beta)(\alpha B)}{(AB)(\alpha\beta) + (A\beta)(\alpha B)} \\ &= \frac{(65 \times 260) - (90 \times 110)}{(65 \times 260) + (90 \times 110)} \\ &= \frac{16900 - 9900}{16900 + 9900} \\ &= -\frac{7,000}{26,800} \\ &= \mathbf{+0.26}. \end{aligned}$$

Problem 33. From the data given below, compare the association between literacy and unemployment in the rural and urban areas and give reasons for the difference, if any

	Rural	*Urban*
Total Number of Adult Males	25 lakhs	200 lakhs
Literate Males	10 ,,	40 ,,
Unemployed Males	5 ,,	12 ,,
Literate and unemployed Males	3 ,,	4 ,,

(*M.Com., Agra*)

Solution :

Let A represent literate males.

B represent unemployed males.

Rural ('00,000)

	A	α	Total
B	3 (AB)	(5−3) 2 (αB)	5 (β)
β	(10−3) 7 $(A\beta)$	(20−7) 13 $(\alpha\beta)$	(25−5) 20 (β)
Total	10 (A)	(25−10) 15 (α)	25 N

Urban

B	4 (AB)	(12−4) 8 (αB)	12 (β)
β	(40−4) 36 $(A\beta)$	(188−36) 152 $(\alpha\beta)$	(200−12) 188 (β)
Total	40 (A)	(200−40) 160 (α)	200 N

$$\begin{aligned} Q &= \frac{(AB)(\alpha\beta) - (A\beta)(\alpha B)}{(AB)(\alpha\beta) + (A\beta)(\alpha B)} \\ &= \frac{(3 \times 13) - (7 \times 2)}{(3 \times 13) + (7 \times 2)} \\ &= \frac{39 - 14}{39 + 14} \end{aligned}$$

$$= \frac{25}{53}$$
$$= \mathbf{+0.47}.$$

$$Q = \frac{(4 \times 152) - (36 \times 8)}{(4 \times 152) + (36 \times 8)}$$
$$= \frac{608 - 288}{608 + 288}$$
$$= \frac{320}{896}$$
$$= \mathbf{+0.357}.$$

Problem 34. Calculate the coefficient of association between illiteracy and criminality from the data given below and interpret it.

The total population of a city is 2,44,000 out of which 40,000 are literates. The number of criminals in the group of literates is 300 and in the group of illiterates is 4,000

(*M.Com. Agra*)

Solution :

Let (A) denote literate (α) denote illiterate

(B) denote criminals (β) denote non-criminals.

The missing frequencies can be found out with the help of nine square table ;

	(A)	(α)	Total
(B)	300	4000	4300
(β)	39700	200000	239700
Total	40000	204000	244000

$$Q = \frac{(AB)(\alpha\beta) - (A\beta)(\alpha B)}{(AB)(\alpha\beta) + (A\beta)(\alpha B)}$$
$$= \frac{(300 \times 200000) - (39700 \times 4000)}{(300 \times 200000) + (39700 \times 4000)}$$
$$= \frac{60000000 - 158800000}{60000000 + 158800000} \ (or) \frac{600 - 1588}{600 + 1588}$$
$$= \frac{-988}{2188}$$
$$= \mathbf{-0.45}.$$

There is disassociation between literates and criminals. That is, there is an association between illiteracy and criminality.

Problem 35. The following table gives the number of literates and criminals in three cities of U.P.

	Kanpur	*Allahabad*	*Agra*
Total number (in '000)	244	184	230
Literates (in '000)	40	47	33
Literate criminals (in '00)	3	2	33
Illiterate criminals (in '00)	40	20	24

Compare the degree of association between criminality and illiteracy in each of the three towns.

(*M.A., Allahabad, M. Com., Agra, M. Com., Vikram*)

Solution :

(A) = Illiterate (α) = literate (values in '00)
(B) = criminals (β) = Non-criminals

Kanput

	(A)	(α)	
(B)	40	3	43
(β)	2000	397	2397
	2040	400	2440

Allahbad

	(A)	(α)	
(B)	20	2	22
(β)	1350	468	1818
	1370	470	1840

Agra

	(A)	(α)	
(B)	24	2	26
(β)	1946	328	2274
	1970	330	2300

$$Q = \frac{(AB)(\alpha\beta) - (A\beta)(\alpha B)}{(AB)(\alpha\beta) + (A\beta)(\alpha B)}$$

$$\text{Kanpur} \quad Q = \frac{(40 \times 397) - (2000 \times 3)}{(40 \times 397) + (2000 \times 3)} = \frac{15880 - 6000}{15880 + 6000} = \frac{9880}{21880} = +0.45$$

$$\text{Allahabad} \quad Q = \frac{(20 \times 468) - (1350 \times 2)}{(20 \times 468) + (1350 \times 2)} = \frac{9360 - 2700}{9360 + 2700} = \frac{6660}{12060} = +0.55$$

$$\text{Agra} \quad Q = \frac{(24 \times 328) - (1946 \times 2)}{(24 \times 328) + (1946 \times 2)} = \frac{7872 - 3892}{7872 - 3892} = \frac{3980}{11764} = +0.34$$

In all the cases, we get positive associations. Thus, we can say that there is association between illiteracy and criminality. It is highest in Allahabad and lowest in Agra.

Alternatively : Let (A) denote literate, (α) denote illiterate, (B) denote criminals, (β) denote non-criminality.

Thus Q (Kanpur) $= -0.45$
Q (Allahabad) $= -0.55$
Q (Agra) $= -0.34$

Problem 36. From the table below compare the intensity of association between literacy and unemployment among males in urban areas with that in rural areas :

	Total	*Literate*	*Unemployed*	*Literate unemployed*
Urban ('00000)	25	10	5	3
Rural ('00000)	200	40	12	4

(*M.A. Agra*)

Solution :

Let (A) denote literate ; (B) denote unemployment.

Given values are :

	(A)	(α)	Total
(B)	3		5
(β)			
Total	10		25
			N

	(A)	(α)	Total
(B)	4		12
(β)			
Total	40		200
			N

Complete Values are:

	(A)	(α)	Total
(B)	3	2	5
(β)	7	13	20
Total	10	15	25 N

	(A)	(α)	Total
(B)	4	8	12
(β)	36	152	188
Total	40	160	200 N

$$Q = \frac{(AB)(\alpha\beta) - (A\beta)(\alpha B)}{(AB)(\alpha\beta) + (A\beta)(\alpha B)}$$

Urban

$$Q = \frac{(3 \times 13) - (7 \times 2)}{(3 \times 13) + (7 \times 2)} = \frac{39 - 14}{39 + 14} = \frac{25}{53} = \mathbf{+0.47}$$

Rural

$$Q = \frac{(4 \times 152) - (36 \times 8)}{(4 \times 152) + (36 \times 8)} = \frac{608 - 288}{608 + 288} = \frac{320}{896} = \mathbf{+0.36}$$

Therefore, the intensity of association between literate and unemployment is more in urban areas than in rural areas.

Problem 37. According to a survey the following results were obtained :

	Boys	*Girls*
No. of candidates appeared at An examination	800	200
Married	150	50
Married and successful	70	20
Unmarried and successful	550	110

Find the association between marital status and the success at the examination both for boys and girls.

(*MBA, U.P.*)

Solution:

Let (A) denote married

(α) denote unmarried

(B) denote success

(β) denote non success

Boys

	(A)	(α)	Total
(B)	70 (AB)	550 (αB)	
(β)			
Total	150 (A)		800 N

Girls

	(A)	(α)	Total
(B)	20 (AB)	110 (αB)	
(β)			
Total	50 (A)		200 N

Missing values are:

	(A)	(α)	Total
(B)			620 (B)
(β)	80 (AB)	100 (αβ)	180 (β)
Total		650 (α)	N

	(A)	(α)	Total
(B)			130 (B)
(β)	30 (Aβ)	40 (αβ)	70 B
Total		150 (x)	N

$$Q = \frac{(AB)(\alpha\beta) - (A\beta)(\alpha B)}{(AB)(\alpha\beta) + (A\beta)(\alpha B)}$$

$$Q = \frac{(70 \times 100) - (80 \times 550)}{(70 \times 100) + (80 \times 550)}$$

$$= \frac{7,000 - 44,000}{7,000 + 44,000}$$

$$= \frac{-37,000}{51,000}$$

$$= \mathbf{-0.73}$$

$$Q = \frac{(20 \times 40) - (30 \times 110)}{(20 \times 40) + (30 \times 110)}$$

$$= \frac{800 - 3300}{800 + 3300}$$

$$= \frac{-2,500}{41,00}$$

$$= \mathbf{-0.61}$$

In both cases there are negative associations between marital status and success.

Problem 38. The following summary appears in a report on a survey covering 1000 fields. Scrutinize the numbers, and point out if there be any mistake or misprint in them.

Manured fields	= 510
Irrigated fields	= 490
Fields growing improved varieties	= 427
Fields both irrigated and manured	= 189
Fields both manured and growing improved varieties	= 140
Fields both irrigated and growing improved varieties	= 85

(*Delhi, M.A., Econ., M. Com., Allahabad; I.A.S*)

Solution :

Let A denote manured fields,

B denote irrigated fields,

C denote fields growing improved varieties

$N = 1000$, $(A) = 510$; $(B) = 490$; $(C) = 427$: $(AB) = 189$; $(AC) = 140$; $(BC) = 85$.

Here we are having three attributes. The condition for consistency is

$$(AB)+(BC)+(AC) > (A)+(B)+(C)- N$$

$$189+85+140 > 510+490+427-1000$$

$$414 > 427$$

414 is less than 427. Hence this is not correct. Therefore there is a misprint or mistake in the given data.

Problem 39. From the following, find whether blindness and baldness are associated :

Total population	= 16264000
Number of bald headed	= 24441
Number of blind	= 7623
Number of bald headed blind	= 221

(*M. Sc., Agra*)

Solution : Let A denote for bald headed and B for blindness.

$$\begin{aligned} N &= 1,62,64,000 \\ (A) &= 24,441 \\ (B) &= 7,623 \\ (AB) &= 921 \\ (AB) &= \frac{(A)\times(B)}{N} \\ &= \frac{24,441\times 7693}{1,62,64,000} \\ &= 11.56 \\ (AB) &= 221. \end{aligned}$$

$$\text{Therefore } (AB) > \frac{(A)\,(B)}{N}$$

Hence there is positive association between bald headed and blind persons.

Problem 40. The following table gives the distribution of students according to age in completed years and regular players among them :

Age in years	:	15	16	17	18	19	20
No. of Students	:	250	200	150	120	100	80
Regular Players	:	200	150	90	48	30	12

Calculate the co-efficient of association between maturity and playing habit, on the assumption that maturity is attained in 18th year of age.

(*M.A., Rajasthan Univ.*)

Solution :

No. of minor players = 250 + 200 + 150 = 600

No. of mature players = 120 +100 +80 = 300

No. of minor regular players = 200 + 150 + 90 = 440

No. of mature regular players = 48 + 30 +12 = 90

Let (A) denote maturity and (B) denote regular playing. (α) denote minority and (β) denote not regular playing.

$$(AB) = 90$$

$$(\alpha B) = 440$$

$$(A\beta) = (A) - (AB) = 300 - 90 = 210$$

$$(\alpha\beta) = (\alpha) - (\alpha\beta) = 600 - 440 = 160$$

Yule's Coefficient of Association :

(or)

$$
\begin{aligned}
Q &= \frac{(AB)(\alpha\beta) - (A\beta)(\alpha B)}{(AB)(\alpha\beta) + (A\beta)(\alpha B)} \\
&= \frac{90 \times 160 - 210 \times 440}{90 \times 160 + 210 \times 440} \\
&= \frac{14400 - 92400}{14400 + 92400} \\
&= \frac{-78,000}{1,06,800} \\
&= -0.73
\end{aligned}
$$

Thus there is a negative association between maturity and playing habits.

12
PROBABILITY

p = probability of success

q = probability of failure

Probability of an event happening $= \dfrac{P}{(P+q)}$

(or) $\dfrac{\text{No. of favourable cases}}{\text{Total No. of equally likely cases}}$

$$
\begin{aligned}
{}^{n}p_{n} &= \frac{n!}{(n-n)!} = n! \\
{}^{n}p_{r} &= \frac{n!}{(n-r)!} \\
{}^{n}C_{n} &= 1\left(\frac{(n!)}{(n-n)!n!}\right) \\
n_{cr} &= \frac{n!}{(n-r)!r!}
\end{aligned}
$$

$P(A \text{ or } B) = P(A) + P(B)$

$P(A \text{ and } B) = P(A) \times P(B)$

Problem 1. What is the probability of getting 3 white balls in a draw of 3 balls from a box containing 6 white and 5 red balls ?

Solution :

The number of favourable cases of drawing 3 white balls $= {}^{6}C_{3}$

The number of all possible $= {}^{11}C_{3}$

Hence the required probability $= \dfrac{{}^{6}C_{3}}{{}^{11}C_{3}} = \mathbf{\dfrac{4}{33}}$

Problem 2. A bag contains 5 green and 10 white balls. If one ball is drawn from it, find the chance that the ball drawn is green.

Solution :

The total number of ways in which one green ball can be drawn out of 15 is ${}^{15}C_{1}$

Favourable number of ways in which one green ball can be drawn is ${}^{5}C_{1}$

Hence the required probability $= \dfrac{{}^{5}C_{1}}{{}^{15}C_{1}} = \dfrac{1}{3}$

Problem 3. From a pack of 52 cards, 4 cards are drawn at random. What is the probability that (*a*) all of them are spades, (*b*) one is of each unit ?

Solution :

Total number of ways in which 4 cards are drawn $= {}^{52}C_{4}$

The ways of drawing 4 spades $= {}^{13}C_{4}$

(*a*) The probability that all of them are spades $= \dfrac{{}^{13}C_{4}}{{}^{52}C_{4}}$

(*b*) The probability that one is of each unit

$$= {}^{13}C_1 \times {}^{13}C_1 \times {}^{13}C_1 \times {}^{13}C_1$$
$$= 13 \times 13 \times 13 \times 13$$
$$= 13^4$$

The required Probability $= \dfrac{13^4}{^{52}C_4} = \mathbf{\dfrac{2197}{20285}}$

Problem 4. Five cards are drawn from a pack. What is the probability of its being 4 kings and the remaining card be other.

Solution :

Number of ways of drawing four kings $= {}^4C_4$

Number of ways of drawing a card out of 48 (remaining) $= {}^{48}C_1$

Exhaustive cases $= {}^{52}C_5$

The required probability $= \dfrac{{}^4C_4 \times {}^{48}C_1}{^{52}C_5}$

$$= \frac{1 \times 48 \times 5 \times 4 \times 3 \times 2}{52 \times 51 \times 50 \times 49 \times 48} = \mathbf{\frac{1}{54145}}$$

Problem 5. What is the chance of drawing without bias four aces successively from a pack of 52 cards ?

Solution :

Chance of drawing an ace in the first draw $= \dfrac{4}{52}$

Chance of drawing an ace in the second draw $= \dfrac{3}{51}$

Chance of drawing an ace in the third draw $= \dfrac{2}{50}$

Chance of drawing an ace in the fourth draw $= \dfrac{1}{49}$

The required problability $= \dfrac{4}{52} \times \dfrac{3}{51} \times \dfrac{2}{50} \times \dfrac{1}{49} = \mathbf{\dfrac{1}{270725}}$

Problem 6. In a bag there are 4 white and 10 yellow balls. Two balls are drawn at random. What is the probability that of these two balls, one is white and the other yellow.

Solution :

Total number of selecting 2 balls out of 14 $= {}^{14}C_2$

One white ball can be drawn $= {}^4C_1$

One yellow ball can be drawn $= {}^{10}C_1$

The probability of drawing two balls of different colour $= \dfrac{{}^4C_1 \times {}^{10}C_1}{^{14}C_2}$

$$= \mathbf{\frac{40}{91}}$$

Problem 7. An urn contains 10 balls, three of which are white, 4 blue and 3 black. Three balls are drawn at random from the urn, *i.e.* every ball has an equal chance of being included in the three. What is the chance that the three balls are of different colours ?

Solution :

$$\begin{aligned} &\text{Total number of exhaustive cases} &&= {}^{10}C_3 \\ (a)\quad &\text{Probability of drawing a white ball} &&= {}^{3}C_1 \\ &\text{Probability of drawing a blue ball} &&= {}^{4}C_1 \\ &\text{Probability of drawing a black ball} &&= {}^{3}C_1 \\ &\text{The required probability} &&= \frac{{}^{3}C_1 \times {}^{4}C_1 \times {}^{3}C_1}{{}^{10}C_3} \\ & &&= \frac{3 \times 4 \times 3}{120} = \mathbf{\frac{3}{10}} \end{aligned}$$

Problem 8. In an urn there are 4 white and 4 black balls. What is the probability of drawing the first ball white, the second black, the third white, and fourth black, and so on.

Solution :

Four white balls are to occupy four odd places, *viz.* 1,3,5 and 7, and can be arranged in 4!. The black balls are to occupy four even places, *viz.*, 2, 4, 6 and 8 can be arranged in 4 !

$$\left.\begin{array}{l}\text{Therefore, the required}\\ \text{probability}\end{array}\right\} = \frac{4! \times 4!}{8!} = \mathbf{\frac{1}{70}}$$

Problem 9. Two drawings each of 4 balls are made from a box containing 10 white and 6 green balls. What is the chance that the first drawing will give 4 white and the second 4 green balls.

(*a*) The balls drawn are replaced before the second draw.

(*b*) The balls drawn are not being replaced before the draw.

Solution :

(*a*) The balls are replaced :

Four white balls are drawn in ${}^{10}C_4$

Probability of drawing 4 white balls $= \dfrac{{}^{10}C_4}{{}^{16}C_4}$

Four green balls are drawn in ${}^{6}C_4$

Probability of drawing 4 green balls $\dfrac{{}^{6}C_4}{{}^{16}C_4}$

The required probability $= \dfrac{{}^{10}C_4}{{}^{16}C_4} \times \dfrac{{}^{6}C_4}{{}^{16}C_4} = \mathbf{\dfrac{9}{2366}}$

(*b*) The ball not replaced:

Four balls (white) in first draw can be drawn ${}^{10}C_4$

Four green balls in second draw can be drawn ${}^{6}C_4$

In the second draw the total number of balls in the box $16 - 4 = 12$

∴ The required probability :

$$\frac{{}^{10}C_4}{{}^{16}C_4} \times \frac{{}^{6}C_4}{{}^{12}C_4} = \mathbf{\frac{6}{715}}$$

Problem 10. From a pack of 52 cards, one card is drawn at random. Find the chance of drawing or drawing not a diamond, drawing or drawing not an ace.

Solution :

Probability of drawing a diamond $= \frac{13}{52}$

Probability of not drawing a diamond $= \frac{39}{52}$

Probability of drawing an ace $= \frac{4}{52}$

Probability of not drawing an ace $= \frac{48}{52}$

Probability of drawing a diamand ace $= \frac{1}{52}$

Probability of not drawing a diamand ace $= \frac{51}{52}$

Problem 11. A bag contains 25 balls marked 1 to 25. One ball is drawn at randam. What is the probability that it is marked with a number multiple 5 or 7.

Solution :

Sample space consists of 25 points.

The favourable events to draw a multiple of 5 are 5 (5, 10, 15, 20 and 25) : Therefore the probability that it is marked with a number of multiple of 5 $= \frac{5}{25}$ or $\frac{1}{5}$

In the same way, the events favourable to draw a multiple of 7 are 3 (7, 14 and 21). Therefore, the probability that it is marked with a number of multiple of 7 $= \frac{3}{25}$

Hence, the required probability of drawing with a multiple of 5 or 7 is $\frac{5}{25} + \frac{3}{25} = \frac{8}{25}$

Problem 12. What is the chance of getting two sixes in two rolling of a single die ?

Solution :

$$\left.\begin{array}{l}\text{The probability of getting a}\\ \text{Six in first roll}\end{array}\right\} = \frac{1}{6}$$

$$\left.\begin{array}{l}\text{The probability of getting a}\\ \text{Six in second roll}\end{array}\right\} = \frac{1}{6}$$

$$\left.\begin{array}{l}\text{The probability of getting}\\ \text{two sixes in two roll}\end{array}\right\} = \frac{1}{6} \times \frac{1}{6} = \mathbf{\frac{1}{36}}$$

(INDEPENDENT EVENT)

Problem 13. Find the chance of throwing head or tail alternatively in 3 successive tossings of a coin ?

Solution :

$$\left.\begin{array}{l}\text{The probability of getting a}\\ \text{head or tail in a toss}\end{array}\right\} = \frac{1}{2}$$

(a) First chance HTH

(b) (or) second chance THT

Probability of (a) $= \frac{1}{2} \times \frac{1}{2} \times \frac{1}{2} = \frac{1}{8}$

Probability of (b) $= \frac{1}{2} \times \frac{1}{2} \times \frac{1}{2} = 1/8$

Therefore, the required probability $= \frac{1}{8} + \frac{1}{8} = \frac{1}{4}$

Problem 14. What is the probability of getting all the heads in four throws of coin ?

(*M. Com. Aligarh*)

Solution :

Probability of getting a head in a throw $= \frac{1}{2}$

All the events are independent

The required probability $= \frac{1}{2} \times \frac{1}{2} \times \frac{1}{2} \times \frac{1}{2} = \mathbf{\frac{1}{16}}$

Problem 15. Urn A contains 3 white and 4 red balls. Urn B contains 4 white and 5 black. If an urn is chosen at random and a ball is drawn from it, what is the probability that the ball so drawn is a white one.

(*M. Com. Udaipur*)

Solution :

Probability of selecting any urn $= \frac{1}{2}$

Probability of drawing a white from urn A $= \frac{3}{7}$

Probability of drawing a white from urn B $= \frac{4}{9}$

The required probability $= \frac{1}{2} \times 3/7 + \frac{1}{2} \times 4/9$

$$= \frac{3}{14} + \frac{4}{18} = \frac{27+28}{126} = \mathbf{\frac{55}{126}}$$

Problem 16. Four cards are drawn from a pack of 52 cards without replacement. What is the probability that they are all of different suits ?

Solution :

The required probability would be :

$$1 \times \frac{39}{51} \times \frac{26}{50} \times \frac{13}{49} = \frac{2197}{20825}$$

Problem 17. A bag contains 4 white, 3 black and 5 red balls. What is the probability of getting a white or red ball at random in a single draw ?

Solution :

The probability of getting a white ball $= \frac{4}{12}$

The probability of getting a red ball $= \frac{5}{12}$

The probability of getting a white or a red $= \frac{4}{12} + \frac{5}{12} = \frac{9}{12}$

(or) 75%

Problem 18. There are two ways to enter a building and three ways to go out. In how many ways can you enter and leave the building

Solution :

A, B will denote the entrances

a, b, c will denote the exits.

$3 \times 2 = 6$ ways (Aa, Ab, Ac, Ba, Bb, Bc)

Problem 19. What is the chance of getting a king in a draw from a pack of 52 cards ?

Solution :

The total number of cases that can happen = 52 (52 cards are there.)

The total number of kings are 4 ; hence favourable cases = 4

The probability of drawing a king = $\frac{4}{52} = \frac{1}{13}$

Problem 20. Two coins are tossed simultaneously. What is the probability of getting a head and a tail ?

Solution :

The possible combinations of the two coins turning up with head (H) or tail (T) are HH, HT, TH, TT. The favourable ways are two out of these four possible ways and all these are equally likely to happen. Hence the probability of getting a head and a tail is

$$= \frac{2}{4} = \frac{1}{2}$$

Problem 21. One card is drawn at random from a well shuffled pack of 52 cards. What is the probability that it will be (a) a diamond (b) a queen ?

Solution :

There are 13 diamond cards in the pack of 52 cards. The number of ways in which a card can be drawn from that pack is 52. The number of favourable to the event happening is 13.

Hence probability of drawing a diamond = $\frac{13}{52} = \frac{1}{4}$

There are four queens in the pack and so the number of ways favourable to the event is 4.

The probability = $\frac{4}{52} = \frac{1}{13}$

Problem 22. Two cards are drawn from a pack of cards at random. What is the probability that it will be (a) a diamond and a heart (b) a king and a queen (c) two kings ?

Solution :

(a) The number of ways of drawing 2 cards from out of 52

$$= {}^{52}C_2 = \frac{52 \times 51}{1 \times 2} = 26 \times 51$$

The number of ways of drawing a diamond and heart = 13×13

The required probability = $\frac{13 \times 13}{26 \times 51} = \frac{13}{102}$

(b) The number of ways of drawing a king and a queen = 4×4

The required probability = $\frac{4 \times 4}{26 \times 51} = \frac{8}{663}$

(c) Two kings can be drawn out of 4 kings in

$$^{4}C_2 = 6 \text{ ways} = \frac{6}{26 \times 51} = \frac{1}{221}$$

Problem 23. A bag contains 7 red, 12 white and 4 green. Balls. What is the probability that :

(a) 3 balls drawn are all white and

(b) 3 balls drawn are one of each colour ?

(*B.Com. Andhra*)

Solution :

Total number of balls = 7 + 12 + 4 = 23

Number of possible ways of drawing 3 out of 12 white = $^{12}C_3$

Total number of possible ways of drawing 3 out of 23 balls = $^{23}C_3$

Therefore, probability of drawing 3 white balls = $\frac{^{12}C_3}{^{23}C_3} = \frac{220}{1771} = 0.1242$

(*b*) Number of possible ways of drawing 1 out of 7 red = $^{7}C_1$

Number of possible ways of drawing 1 out of 12 white = $^{12}C_1$

Number of possible ways of drawing 1 out of 4 green = $^{4}C_1$

Therefore, the probability of drawing balls of different colours

$$\frac{^{7}C_1 \times ^{12}C_1 \times ^{4}C_1}{^{23}C_3} = \frac{7 \times 12 \times 4}{1771} = 0.1897$$

Problem 24. Two dice are thrown. Find the probability that

(*a*) the total of the numbers on the dice is 8,
(*b*) the first die shows 6.
(*c*) the total of the numbers on the dice is greater than 8,
(*d*) the total of the numbers on the dice is 13,
(*e*) both the dice show the same number,
(*f*) the sum of the numbers shown by the dice is less than 5.
(*g*) the sum of the numbers shown by the dice is exactly 6.

Solution :

	FIRST DIE					
SECOND DIE	1	2	3	4	5	6
1	(1,1)	(1,2,)	(1,3)	(1,4)	(1,5)	(1,6)
2	(2,1)	(2,2)	(2,3)	(2,4)	(2,5)	(2,6)
3	(3,1)	(3,2)	(3,3)	(3,4)	(3,5)	(3,6)
4	(4,1)	(4,2)	(4,3)	(4,4)	(4,5)	(4,6)
5	(5,1)	(5,2)	(5,3)	(5,4)	(5,5)	(5,6)
6	(6,1)	(6,2)	(6,3)	(6,4)	(6,5)	(6,6)

(*a*) The cases which have a total of 8 are

(2,6), (3,5),(4,4), (5,3), (6,2) = 5

Therefore, the probability = $\frac{5}{36}$

(*b*) The first die shows 6 in the following cases

(6,1), (6,2), (6,3), (6,4), (6,5), (6,6) = 6

Therefore the probability = $\frac{6}{36} = \frac{1}{6}$

(*c*) The cases which give a total of more than 8 are (3,6), (4,5), (4,6), (5,4),(5,5), (5,6), (6,6), (6,4), (6,3), (6,5) = 10

Therefore the probability of getting more than 8 $= \frac{10}{36} = \frac{5}{18}$

(*d*) The probability of getting 13 or more than 13 is impossible therefore the probability = 0.

(*e*) The favourable cases are :

(1,1), (2,2), (3,3), (4,4), (5,5), (6,6) = 6

Therefore the probability $= \frac{6}{36} = \frac{1}{6}$

(*f*) The cases of which have less than 5 are 6 and they are

(1,1), (1,2), (1,2),(2,1),(2,2) and (3,1)

Therefore the probability $= \frac{6}{36} = \frac{1}{6}$

(*g*) The cases of which have exactly 6 are 5

(5,1), (4,2), (3,3), (2,4), (1,5)

Therefore the probability is $= \frac{5}{36}$

Problem 25. Mr. x is selected for interview for 3 posts. For the first post there are 5 candidates, for the second there are 4 and for the third there are 6. If the selection of each candidate is equally likely, find the chance that Mr. x will be selected for at least one post.

(*B.A. Econ. Calcutta*)

Solution :

Probability of no selection for the first post $= \frac{4}{5}$

Probability of no selection for the second post $= \frac{3}{4}$

Probability of no selection for the third post $= \frac{5}{6}$

All the events are independent. Therefore, the probability of selection at least for one post.

$$= 1 - \frac{4}{5} \times \frac{3}{4} \times \frac{5}{6}$$

$$= 1 - \frac{3}{6} = \frac{3}{6} = \frac{1}{2} \text{ or } \mathbf{50\%}$$

Problem 26. Two cards are drawn at random from a well shuffled pack of 52 cards. What is the probability that :

(*a*) both are aces,

(*b*) both are red,

(*c*) at least one is an ace ?

(*B.Com.*)

Solution :

Let A indicate the event of drawing 2 aces.

$$P(AA) = P(A) \times P\left(\frac{A}{A}\right)$$

$$P(A) = \text{drawing of an ace first.}$$

$P\left(\frac{A}{A}\right)$ = conditional probability of an ace at the second draw, given that the first was an acc.

Therefore,

$$P(A) = \frac{4}{52} \quad P\left(\frac{A}{A}\right) = \frac{3}{51}$$

$$P(AA) = \frac{4}{52} \times \frac{3}{51} = \frac{12}{2652} = \frac{1}{221}$$

(*b*) Let R indicate the events of drawing 2 red cards.

$$P(RR) = P(R) \times P\left(\frac{R}{R}\right) = \frac{26}{52} \times \frac{25}{51} = \frac{650}{2652} = \frac{25}{102}$$

(*c*) Let E indicate the event of drawing an ace. Then the probability that at least an ace is drawn is denoted by $P(E)$. Probability of not drawing an ace:

$$P(EE) = P(E) \times P\left(\frac{E}{E}\right) = \frac{48}{52} \times \frac{47}{51} = \frac{2256}{2652} = \left(\frac{188}{221}\right)$$

Therefore, probability of drawing at least an ace

$$= 1 - \frac{188}{221} = \frac{33}{221}$$

Problem 27. The odds in favour of a certain event are 2 to 5 and the odds against another event independent of the former are 5 to 6. Find the chance that one at least of the events will happen.

Solution :

The chance that the 1st event happens and the 2nd one does not happen

$$= 2/7 \times 5/11 = 10/77.$$

The chance that the 1st event does not happen and the 2nd happens

$$= 5/7 \times 6/11 = 30/77.$$

The chance that both the events happen

$$= 2/7 \times 6/11 = 12/77.$$

The chance that one at least of the event will happen

$$= 10/77 + 30/77 + 12/77 = 52/77$$

Alternatively :

The first event does not happen $= 1 - \frac{2}{7} = \frac{5}{7}$

The second event does not happen $= 1 - \frac{6}{11} = \frac{5}{11}$

$\therefore$ The chance that both do not happen $= \frac{5}{7} \times \frac{5}{11} = \frac{25}{77}$

The chance that one at least will happen $= 1 - \frac{25}{77} = \frac{52}{77}$.

Problem 28. Suppose it is 11 to 5 against a person who is now 38 years of age living till he is 73 and 5 to 3 against B now 43 living till he is 78, find the chance that at least one of these persons will be alive 35 years hence. *(B.Com. Bombay)*

Solution :

The probability that A will die within 35 years $= \frac{11}{16}$

The probability that B will die within 35 years $= \frac{5}{8}$

The probability that both will die within 35 years $= \frac{11}{16} \times \frac{5}{8} = \frac{55}{128}$

The probability that both of them will not die *i.e.* at least one of them will be alive $= 1 - \frac{55}{128} = \frac{73}{128}$

or $\frac{73}{128} \times 100 =$ **57%**

Problem 29. There are 3 economists, 4 engineers, 2 statisticians and 1 doctor. A committee of 4 from among them is to be formed. Find the probability that the committee :

(*i*) Consists of one of each kind ;
(*ii*) Has at least one economist ;
(*iii*) Has the doctor as a member and three others.

(B.Com Bombay)

Solution :

In all there are 10 members.

A committee of 4 can be formed in ${}^{10}C_4$

$${}^{10}C_4 = \frac{10 \times 9 \times 8 \times 7}{4!} = 210$$

(*i*) Number of cases for the committee to consist one of each kind is

$${}^{3}C_1 \times {}^{4}C_1 \times {}^{2}C_1 \times 1 = 4 \times 3 \times 2 \times 1 = 24$$

Hence required probability $= \frac{24}{210} = \frac{4}{35}$.

(*ii*) Committee has at least one economist and the probability is 1–P (no economist). Selecting no economist means, the selection is to be made out of remaining *i.e.* 7, which can be in

$${}^{7}C_4 \text{ } i.e. \text{ } \frac{7 \times 6 \times 5}{3 \times 2 \times 1} = \mathbf{35}$$

$$1-\text{P (no economist)}$$
$$= 1 - \frac{35}{210} = 1 - \frac{1}{6} = \mathbf{\frac{5}{6}}.$$

(*iii*) The committee must consist of a doctor and others are selected out of 9. That is

$$1 \times {}^9C_3 = \frac{1 \times 9 \times 8 \times 7}{3 \times 2 \times 1} = \mathbf{84}$$

$$\text{Therefore, the required probability} = \frac{84}{210} = \mathbf{\frac{2}{5}}$$

Problem 30. A can hit a target three times in five shots, B two times in five shots, and C three times in four shots. They fire a volley. What is the probability that two shots hit the target ? (*B. Com., Gujarat*)

Solution :

The probability of A hitting the target $= \frac{3}{5}$

The probability of B hitting the target $= \frac{2}{5}$

The probability of C hitting the target $= \frac{3}{4}$

The Probability that A and B hit and C misses it $= \frac{3}{5} \times \frac{2}{5} \times \frac{1}{4} = \frac{3}{50}$

The Probability that A and C hit and B misses it $= \frac{3}{5} \times \frac{3}{4} \times \frac{3}{5} = \frac{27}{100}$

The Probability that B and C hit and A misses it $= \frac{2}{5} \times \frac{3}{4} \times \frac{2}{5} = \frac{3}{25}$

$$\therefore \quad \text{The required probability} = \frac{3}{50} + \frac{27}{100} + \frac{3}{25} = \mathbf{\frac{45}{100}}.$$

Problem 31. The probability (*i*) that A can slove a problem in Statistics is 4/5, (*ii*) that B can solve it is 2/3, (*iii*) that C can solve it is 3/7. If all of them try independently, find the probability that the problem will be solved.

Solution :

Probability that A fails to solve the problem $= \frac{1}{5}$

Probability that B fails to solve the problem $= \frac{1}{3}$

Probability that C fails to solve the problem $= \frac{4}{7}$

The required probability,

$$= 1 - \frac{1}{5} \times \frac{1}{3} \times \frac{4}{7}$$
$$= 1 - \frac{4}{105}$$
$$= \mathbf{\frac{101}{105}}.$$

Problem 32. The probability that machine A will be performing a usual function in 5 years' time is **1/4** while the probability that machine B will still be operating usefully at the end of same period is 1/3.

Find the probability that in five years time :

(a) both machines will be performing a usual function,

(b) neither will be operating,

(c) only machine B will be operating, and

(d) at least one of the machines will be operating.

($ICMA$)

Solution :

Let A = Machine A function

Let B = Machine B function

Both machines will be performing :

(a)

$$P(A \text{ and } B) = P(A) \times P(B) = \frac{1}{4} \times \frac{1}{3} = \mathbf{\frac{1}{12}}$$

(b) Neither will be operating

$$= \frac{3}{4} \times \frac{2}{3} = \mathbf{\frac{1}{2}}$$

(c) Probability that only B will function

$$= \frac{3}{4} \times \frac{1}{3} = \mathbf{\frac{1}{4}}$$

(d) Probability that at least one of the machines will be operating

$$= \frac{1}{4} + \frac{1}{3} - \frac{1}{12} = \frac{6}{12} = \mathbf{\frac{1}{2}}$$

Problem 33. The odds against student X solving a Business Statistics problem are 8 to 6. and odds in favour of Y solving the same problem are 14 to 16. (i) What is the chance that the problem will be solved if both try ? (ii) What is the probability that they both, working independently of each other, solve the problem ? (iii) What is the probability that neither solves the problem ?

(CA)

Solution :

(i) The probability that X will solve the problem $= \dfrac{6}{8+6} = \dfrac{6}{14}$

The probability that Y will solve the problem $= \dfrac{14}{14+16} = \dfrac{14}{30}$

The probability that X fails to solve the problem $= \dfrac{8}{14}$

The probability that Y fails to solve the problem $= \dfrac{16}{30}$

Both of them fail to solve it $= \dfrac{8}{14} \times \dfrac{16}{30} = \dfrac{32}{105}$

The probability that the problems will be solved, if both try $= 1 - \dfrac{32}{105} = \dfrac{73}{105}$

(*ii*) Both of them solve independently and the probability $= \frac{6}{14} \times \frac{14}{30} = \frac{1}{5}$

(*iii*) None will solve the problem $= \frac{32}{105}$ (given above)

Problem 34. An urn contains 5 white and 7 black balls. A second urn contains 7 white and 8 black balls. One ball is drawn at random and put into the second urn without noticing its colour. A ball is then drawn at random from the second urn. What is the probability that it is white. (*B.Com., Bombay*)

Solution :

Probability of drawing a white ball from first urn $= \frac{5}{12}$

Probability of drawing a black ball from first urn $= \frac{7}{12}$

$$\left.\begin{array}{l}\text{The probability of drawing a}\\ \text{white ball from second urn}\\ \text{(The transferred ball may}\\ \text{be of any colour.)}\end{array}\right\} = \frac{8}{8+8}, \frac{7}{7+9} \quad \left(\frac{8}{16}\right)\left(\frac{7}{16}\right)$$

$$\left.\begin{array}{l}\text{Probability of drawing a white}\\ \text{ball from both urns}\end{array}\right\} = \frac{5}{12} \times \frac{8}{16} = \frac{5}{24}$$

$$\left.\begin{array}{l}\text{Probability of drawing a black}\\ \text{ball from first urns and a}\\ \text{white ball from second urn}\end{array}\right\} = \frac{7}{12} \times \frac{7}{16} = \frac{49}{192}$$

$$\text{The required probability} = \frac{5}{24} \times \frac{49}{192} = \frac{89}{192}$$

Problem 35. A sub-committee of 6 members is to be formed out of a group consisting of 7 men and 4 ladies. Calculate the probability that the sub-committee will consist of (*i*) exactly 2 ladies, and (*ii*) at least 2 ladies. (*B. A. Econ. Calcutta*)

Solution :

A sub-committee of 6 members can be formed out of 11 = $^{11}C_6$ ways.

Exhaustive No. of Cases $^{11}C_6$

$$\begin{aligned} ^{11}C_6 &= \frac{11!}{(11-5)!5!} \\ &= \frac{11!}{6!\,5!} = \frac{11 \times 10 \times 9 \times 8 \times 7}{5 \times 4 \times 3 \times 2} \\ &= \textbf{462 ways.} \end{aligned}$$

$$\text{(i)}\ \left.\begin{array}{l}\text{The probability that the sub-committee}\\ \text{consists of exactly 2 ladies, out of 4}\end{array}\right\} = {}^4C_2$$

Remaining 4 members out of 7 men = $^7C_4$

$$\therefore \left.\begin{array}{l}\text{The probability of forming the sub-}\\ \text{committee consists of exactly 2 ladies}\end{array}\right\} = \frac{^4C_2 \times {}^7C_4}{^{11}C_6}$$

$$= \frac{\dfrac{4 \times 3 \times 2}{2 \times 2} \times \dfrac{7!}{3! \times 4!}}{462}$$

$$= \frac{105}{231} = \mathbf{\frac{5}{11}}$$

(ii) The sub-committee consists of at least 2 ladies *i.e.* 2 or 3 or 4 ladies.

$$\text{The required probability } \} = \frac{{}^4C_2 \times {}^7C_4}{{}^{11}C_6} + \frac{{}^4C_3 \times {}^7C_3}{{}^{11}C_6} + \frac{{}^4C_4 \times {}^7C_2}{{}^{11}C_6}$$

$$= \frac{5}{11} + \frac{140}{462} + \frac{21}{462} = \frac{5}{11} + \frac{20}{66} + \frac{3}{66} = \mathbf{\frac{53}{66}}.$$

Problem 36. Two students X and Y work independently on a problem. The probability that X will solve it is $3/4$ and the probability that Y will solve it is $2/3$. What is the probability that the problem will be solved ?

Solution :

$$P(A \text{ or } B) = P(A) + P(B) - P(A \text{ and } B)$$

The probability that X will solve the problem is $= \dfrac{3}{4}$

The probability that Y will solve the problem is $= \dfrac{2}{3}$

The events are not mutually exclusive as both of them may solve the problem.

$$\text{Therefore the probability} = \frac{3}{4} + \frac{2}{3} - \left(\frac{3}{4} \times \frac{2}{3}\right)$$

$$= \frac{17}{12} - \frac{6}{12} = \frac{11}{12}$$

Alternatively :

The probability that X will solve it and Y fails to solve it

$$= \frac{3}{4} \times \frac{1}{3} = \frac{3}{12}$$

Probability that the problem will be solved

$$= \frac{2}{3} + \frac{3}{12} = \frac{11}{12}$$

Alternatively :

The probability that X will fail to solve and Y solves it

$$= \frac{1}{4} \times \frac{2}{3} = \frac{2}{12}$$

Probability that the problem will be solved

$$= \frac{3}{4} + \frac{2}{12} = \frac{11}{12}$$

Alternatively :

The probability that neither X nor Y will solve it

$$= \frac{1}{4} \times \frac{1}{3} = \frac{1}{12}$$

Hence the probability that the problem will be solved

$$= 1 - \frac{1}{12} = \frac{11}{12}.$$

Problem 37. A salesman has a 60 % chance of making a sale to each customer. The behaviour of successive customers is independent. If two customers A and B enter, what is probability that the salesman will make a sale to A or B ?

(*AIMA*)

Solution :

Probability of making a sale = 0.6

Probability of making no sale = 0.4

The required probability (makes a sales to A or B)

$$= 1 - (0.4 \times 0.4)$$
$$= 1 - 0.16$$
$$= 0.84 \text{ or } 84\%$$

Problem 38. An urn contains 8 white and 3 red balls. If two balls are drawn at random, find the probability that (*a*) both are white, (*b*) both are red and (*c*) one is of each colour.

(*B.A.* (*Hons.*) *Calcutta*)

Soloution :

Total number of balls in the urn = 8+3=11.

Two balls can be drawn out of 11 balls in $^{11}C_2$ ways.

Exhaustive number of cases = $^{11}C_2 = \frac{11 \times 10}{2} = 55.$

(*a*) Two white balls to be drawn

Out of 8 white, can be done in

$$^8C_2 = \frac{8 \times 7}{2} = 28 \text{ ways .}$$

The probability that both are white = $\frac{28}{55}$.

(*b*) Two red balls to be drawn

Out of 3 red balls can be done in $^3C_2$= 3 ways.

Hence, the probability that both are red = $\frac{3}{55}$.

(*c*) The number of favourable cases for drawing one white ball and one red ball is

$$^8C_1 \times ^3C_1 = 8 \times 3 = 24.$$

Therefore, the probability (one red and one white)

$$= \frac{24}{55}$$

Problem 39. Tickets are numbered from 1 to 100. They are well shuffled and a ticket is drawn at random. What is the probability that the drawn ticket has :

(*a*) an even number,

(*b*) a number 5 or a multiple of 5,

(*c*) a number which is greater than 75,

(*d*) a number which is a square ? (*M.B.A. Himachal*)

Solution :

(*a*) The total number of exhaustive, mutually exclusive and equal cases is 100. There are 50 even numbered tickets.

Therefore, favourable cases to the event is 50.

Therefore, the probability $= \frac{50}{100} = \frac{1}{2}$

(*b*) Suppose A denotes the number of happenings that the drawn ticket has a number 5 or a multiple of 5.

There are 20 cases i.e., 5, 10, 15, 20..........100.

Therefore, $P(A) = \frac{20}{100} = \frac{1}{5}$

(*c*) There are 25 cases, which have a number greater than 75. Say A will denote it.

Therefore, $P(A) = \frac{25}{100} = \frac{1}{4}$.

(*d*) There are 10 favourable cases which give squares between 1 and 100 *i.e.*, 1, 4, 9, 16, 25, 36, 49, 64, 81, 100.

Therefore, $P(A) = \frac{10}{100} = \frac{1}{10}$.

Problem 40. Find the chance of throwing more than 15 in one throw with 3 dice.

Solution :

Total number of cases = 6×6×6=216.

Throwing more than 15 means getting 16, 17 or 18.

Possible ways of throwing 16 are (6, 6, 4), (6, 5, 5), (6, 4, 6), (5, 5, 6), (5, 6, 5) and (4, 6, 6).

Number of favourable cases = 6.

The probability of getting 16 with three dice $= \frac{6}{216}$.

Possible ways of throwing 17 are (6, 6, 5), (6, 5, 6) and (5, 6, 6).

The probability of throwing 17 with the dice $= \frac{3}{216}$.

There is only one way of throwing 18 with three dice namely (6,6,6).

The probability of throwing 18 with three dice $= \frac{1}{216}$.

The three cases are mutually exclusive.

Therefore probability of throwing more than 15.

$$\frac{6}{216} + \frac{3}{216} + \frac{1}{216} = \frac{10}{216} = \frac{5}{108}.$$

Problem 41. A problem in statistics is given to three students A, B and C whose chances of solving it are 1/2, 1/3 and 1/4 respectively. What is the probability that the problem will be solved ?

Solution :

The probability that A fails to solve the problem $= 1 - \frac{1}{2} = \frac{1}{2}$

The probability that B a fails to solve the problem $= 1 - \frac{1}{3} = \frac{2}{3}$

The probability that C fails to solve the problem $= 1 - \frac{1}{4} = \frac{3}{4}$

The probability that the problem is not solved by A, B and $C = \frac{1}{2} \times \frac{2}{3} \times \frac{3}{4} = \frac{1}{4}$

Therefore, the probability that the problem is solved $= 1 - \frac{1}{4} = \mathbf{\frac{3}{4}}$ or **75%**.

Problem 42. From a pack of 52 cards, two cards are drawn at random. Find the chance that one is a knave and the other a queen.

Solution :

Sample space $= {}^{52}C_2$

Event space $= {}^4C_1 \times {}^4C_1$ (as there are 4 queens and 4 knaves)

$\therefore$ The required probability $= \frac{{}^4C_1 \times {}^4C_1}{{}^{52}C_2} = \frac{8}{663}$.

Problem 43. Five men in a company of 20 are graduates. If 3 men are picked out of the 20 at random, what is the probability that they are all graduates. What is the probability of at least one graduate ?

(*B. A. Econ. Calcutta*)

Solution :

3 men can be picked out of 20 and the exhaustive number of cases is ${}^{20}C_3 = 1140$ ways.

All three members are graduates, which can be in ${}^5C_3$ ways *i.e.*, 10.

Hence the probability that all the three men are graduates is :

$$\frac{10}{1140} = \mathbf{\frac{1}{114}}.$$

Probability of selecting at least one graduate = 1−P (selecting no graduate)

That is, selecting no graduates, means that all the three must be selected out of the 15 non-graduates, *i.e.* $\mathbf{{}^{15}C_3}$

$$\begin{aligned} {}^{15}C_3 &= \frac{15 \times 14 \times 13}{3 \times 2} = 455 \text{ ways} \\ & \quad 1 - P(\text{selecting no graduate}) \\ &= 1 - \frac{455}{1140} \\ &= \frac{685}{1140} = \mathbf{\frac{137}{228}}. \end{aligned}$$

Problem 44. The probability that a student passes a Physics test is 2/3 and the probability that he passes both Physics test and an English test is 14/45. The probability that he passes at least one test is 4/5. What is the probability that he passes the English test ?

(*M.A. Econ., Madras*)

Solution :

Let A denote that the student passes Physics test.

Let B denote that the student passes English test.

$$P(A) = \frac{2}{3}$$

$$P(A \text{ and } B) = \frac{14}{45}$$

$$P(A \text{ and } B) = \frac{4}{5}$$

$$\begin{aligned} P(B) &= P(A \text{ or } B) + P(A \text{ and } B) - \frac{1}{3} \\ &= \frac{4}{5} + \frac{14}{15} - \frac{1}{3} \\ &= \frac{36 + 14 - 30}{45} \\ &= \frac{50 - 30}{45} = \frac{20}{45} = \frac{4}{9} \end{aligned}$$

Problem 45. An electronic device is made up of three components A, B and C. The probability of the failure of component A is 0.01, that of B is 0.1 and that of C is 0.02 in some fixed period of time. Find the probability that the device will work satisfactorily during that period of time assuming that the three components work independently of one another

(*B. Com., Bombay*)

Solution :

Probability that component A fails = 0.01

Probability that component B fails = 0.1

Probability that component C fails = 0.02

The probability that the three components work independently

$$\begin{aligned} &= (1 - 0.01) \times (1 - 0.1)(1 - 0.02) \\ &= 0.99 \times 0.90 \times 0.98 \\ &= \mathbf{0.87318.} \end{aligned}$$

Problem 46. A piece of equipment will function only when all the three components A, B and C are working. The probability of A failing during one year is 0.15, that of B failing is 0.05 and that of C failing is 0.10. What is the probability that the equipment will fail before the end of the year.

(*M.Com., Delhi*)

Solution :

The probability that component A does not fail = 0.85

The probability that component B does not fail = 0.95

The probability that component C does not fail = 0.90

Therefore, all the components will work = 0.85 × 0.95 × 0.90 = 0.727

Hence the probability that the equipment will fail before the end of the year = 1−0.727 = 0.273.

Problem 47. The odds against A solving a problem are 10 to 7 and the odd in favour of B solving the problem are 15 to 12. What is the probability that if both of them try, the problem will be solved ?

(*B.Com.*)

Solution :

The probability that A will fail to solve the problem $= \frac{10}{17}$

The probability that B will fail to solve the problem $= \frac{12}{27}$

Therefore the compound probability of none of them solving the problem

$$= \frac{10}{17} \times \frac{12}{27}$$
$$= \mathbf{\frac{40}{123}}$$

Therefore the probability that the problem is solved either by A or B or both them

$$= 1 - \frac{40}{153} = \mathbf{\frac{113}{153}}$$

Problem 48. The odds against a certain event are 5 to 3 and the odds in favour of another event, independent of the former are 7 to 5. Find the chance that one at least of the events will happen.

(*M. Com. Rajasthan*)

Solution :

The probability of first event not taking place $\Big\} = \frac{5}{5+3} = \frac{5}{8}$

The probability of second event not taking place $\Big\} = \frac{5}{5+7} = \frac{5}{12}$

The probability of that neither of the two events takes place $\Big\} = \frac{5}{8} \times \frac{5}{12} = \frac{25}{96}$

Therefore, the probability of hapening at least one of the events $\Big\} = 1 - \frac{25}{96} = \mathbf{\frac{71}{96}}$

Problem 49. A problem in statistics is given to two students A and B. The odds in favour of A solving the problem are 6 to 9 and against B solving the problem are 12 to 10. If A and B attempt, find the probability of the problem being solved.

(*M. Com., Rajasthan*)

Solution :

Probability of A solving the problem : $\frac{6}{6+9} = \frac{6}{15}$

Probability of B solving the problem $= \frac{10}{12+10} = \frac{5}{11}$

Probability that A not solving it $= \frac{9}{15}$

Probability that B not solving it $= \frac{6}{11}$

Therefore, both of them fail to solve it $= \frac{9}{15} \times \frac{6}{11} = \frac{18}{55}$

Therefore, the probability that the problem will be solved : $= 1 - \frac{18}{55} = \frac{37}{55}$

Problem 50. An ordinary die is tossed twice and the difference between the number of spots turned is noted. Find the probability of a difference of 3.

(*B.A. Calcutta*)

Solution :

The event has the following six ways :

(1,4) (2,5) (3,6) (4,1) (5,2), (6,3) = 6 cases

The required Probability $= \dfrac{6}{10}$

Problem 51. In a factory there are 6 skilled workers and 4 unskilled workers. What is the probability that (*a*) a worker selected is skilled worker (*b*) two workers selected are skilled ?

Solution :

(*a*) Number of favourable cases $= {}^6C_1 = 6$

Total Number of equally likely case $= {}^{10}C_1 = 10$

Therefore, the required probability $= \dfrac{6}{10}$

(*b*) Number of favourable cases $= {}^6C_2 = \dfrac{6 \times 5}{1 \times 2}$

Total number of equally like cases $= {}^{10}C_2 = \dfrac{10 \times 9}{1 \times 2}$

The required probability $= \dfrac{{}^6C_2}{{}^{10}C_2} = \dfrac{6 \times 5}{1 \times 2} \times \dfrac{1 \times 2}{10 \times 9} = \dfrac{1}{3}$

Problem 52. A bag contains 10 white, 15 red and 8 green balls. A single draw of 3 balls is made. (*a*) What is the probability that a white, a red and a green balls are drawn ? (*b*) What would be the probability of getting all the three white balls ?

(*M. Com. Nagpur*)

Solution :

(*a*) Selection of a ball out of 10 white $= {}^{10}C_1$

Selection of a ball out of 15 red $= {}^{15}C_1$

Selection of a ball out of 8 green $= {}^8C_1$

No. of selections of 3 balls out of 33 $= {}^{33}C_3$

Therefore, the required probability $= \dfrac{{}^{10}C_1 \times {}^{15}C_1 \times {}^8C_1}{{}^{33}C_3}$

$$= \frac{10 \times 15 \times 8 \times 1 \times 2 \times 3}{33 \times 32 \times 31} = \frac{7200}{32736} = \frac{75}{\mathbf{341}}$$

(*b*) Favourable cases $= {}^{10}C_3$

Selection of 3 balls out of 33 $= {}^{33}C_3$

The required probability

$$= \frac{{}^{10}C_3}{{}^{33}C_3} = \frac{10 \times 9 \times 8}{3 \times 2 \times 1} \times \frac{3 \times 2 \times 1}{33 \times 32 \times 31}$$

$$= \frac{10 \times 9 \times 8}{33 \times 32 \times 31}$$

$$= \frac{\mathbf{15}}{\mathbf{682}}$$

Problem 53. Four cards are drawn from a full pack of cards. Find the probability that two are spades and two are hearts.

(*B. Com. Bombay*)

Solution :

Favourable cases are $^{52}C_4$

Number of ways for selecting two spades and two heart cards = $^{13}C_2 \times ^{13}C_2$

The required probability = $\dfrac{^{13}C_2 \times ^{13}C_2}{^{52}C_4}$

$$= \frac{13 \times 12}{1 \times 2} \times \frac{13 \times 12}{1 \times 2} \times \frac{1 \times 2 \times 3 \times 4}{52 \times 51 \times 50 \times 49} = \mathbf{\frac{468}{20825}}$$

Problem 54. There are 60 articles of which 20 are defective and 40 non-defective. If a sample of 10 is selected, find the probability of getting exactly 4 defectives and 6 non-defectives. *(B. Com.)*

Solution :

Sample space = $^{60}C_{10}$

The event space = $^{20}C_4 \quad \times ^{40}C_6$

The required probability = $\dfrac{^{20}C_4 \times ^{40}C_6}{^{60}C_{10}}$

Problem 55. If two cards are dawn from an ordinary pack, what is the probability that one will be a spade and other heart ?

Solution :

Favourable cases = $^{13}C_1 \times ^{13}C_1 = 13 \times 13$

Exhaustive cases = $^{52}C_2 = \left(\dfrac{52 \times 51}{2}\right) = 1326$

The required probability = $\dfrac{13 \times 13}{1326} = \dfrac{169}{1326} = \dfrac{13}{102}$

Problem 56. Four cards are drawn from a full pack of cards. What is the probability that out of 4 cards, two are spades ? *(B. Com.)*

Solution :

Exhaustive cases = $^{52}C_4$

Favourable cases = $^{13}C_2 \times ^{50}C_1 \times ^{49}C_1$

Required probability = $\dfrac{^{13}C_2 \times ^{50}C_1 \times ^{49}C_1}{^{52}C_4}$

Problem 57. A lot of 100 articles contains 10 defectives, 5 of these are selected at random from the lot. Find the probatility of having at least one defective.

Solution :

The probability of getting all defectives = $\dfrac{^{10}C_5 \times ^{90}C_0}{^{100}C_5}$

Problem 58. The probability that a boy will get a scholarship is 0.9 and that a girl will get is 0.8. What is the probability that at least one of them will get the scholarship ? *(M.A. (Eco.) Agra)*

Solution :

The boy will not get the scholarship = $1 - .9 = .1$

The girl will not get the scholarship = $1 - .8 = .2$

The probability that both of them will not get the scholarship

$$= 0.1 \times 0.2 = 0.02$$

Hence the probability that at least one of them will get the scholarship

$$= 1 - 0.02 = \mathbf{0.98}$$

Problem 59. An article manufactured by a company consists of two parts A and B, In the process of manufacture of part A 9 out of 10 are likely to be defective. Similarly 5 out 10 are likely to be defective in the manufacture of part B. Calculate the probability that the assembled parts will not be defective. (*CA*)

Solution :

Probability that the part A is defective $= 0.9$

Probability that the part B is defective $= 0.5$

Probability that the part A is not defective $= 0.1$

Probability that the part B is not defective $= 0.5$

The probability that the assembled parts will not be defective

$$= 0.1 \times 0.5 = \mathbf{0.05}$$

Problem 60. A problem in statistics is given to five students A, B, C, D and E. Their chances of solving, it are 1/2, 1/3, 1/4, 1/5 and 1/6. What is the probability that the problem will be solved. (*M. Com. Delhi*)

Solution : Events are independent.

Probability that A will fail to solve the problem $= 1 - \frac{1}{2} = \frac{1}{2}$

Probability that B will fail to solve the problem $= 1 - \frac{1}{3} = \frac{2}{3}$

Probability that C will fail to solve the problem $= 1 - \frac{1}{4} = \frac{3}{4}$

Probability that D will fail to solve the problem $= 1 - \frac{1}{5} = \frac{4}{5}$

Probability that E will fail to solve the problem $= 1 - \frac{1}{6} = \frac{5}{6}$

All of them will fail to solve the problem, then the probability

$$= \frac{1}{2} \times \frac{2}{3} \times \frac{3}{4} \times \frac{4}{5} \times \frac{5}{6} = \frac{1}{6}$$

Therefore, the probability that the problem will be solved

$$= 1 - \frac{1}{6} = \frac{5}{6}$$

Problem 61. In a single throw of two dice what is the probability of getting

(*a*) a total of 8,

(*b*) total different from 8 ?

Solution :

(*a*) Total of 8 can be had in the following ways :

2+6, 3+5, 4+4, 5+3, 6+2 = 5 ways

The number of equally likely ways that two dice can fall $= 6 \times 6 = 36$

Therefore, the required probability $= \frac{5}{36}$

(*b*) The required probability $= 1 - \frac{5}{36} = \frac{31}{36}$

Problem 62. What is the chance that a leap year, selected at random will contain 53 Sundays ?

(*B.A. Punjab, B. Com. Bombay*)

Solution : As a leap year consists of 366 days it contains 52 complete weeks and two more days.

The two consecutive days make the following combinations :

(*a*) Monday and Tuesday.

(*b*) Tuesday and Wednesday.

(*c*) Wednesday and Thursday.

(*d*) Thursday and Friday.

(*e*) Friday and Saturday.

(*f*) Saturday and Sunday, and

(*g*) Sunday and Monday.

If (*f*) or (*g*) occurs, then the year consists of 53 Sundays.

Therefore the number of favourable cases = 2

The total number of cases = 7

The probability $= \frac{2}{7}$.

Problem 63. Three ships A, B, and C sail from England to India. Odds in favour of their arriving safely are 2 : 5, 3 : 7 and 6 : 11 respectively. Find the chance that they all arrive safely.

Solution : Probability of ship A Arrives safely $= \frac{2}{7}$

Probability of ship B Arrives safely $= \frac{3}{10}$

Probability of ship C Arrives safely $= \frac{6}{17}$

Probability that all the ships

$$\text{Arrives safely} = \frac{2}{7} \times \frac{3}{10} \times \frac{6}{17} = \frac{36}{1190} = \frac{18}{538}$$

Problem 64. The odds against A solving a problem are 8 : 6 and the odds in favour of B solving it are 9 : 12. What is the probability that if both of them try it, it will be solved ?

Solution :

The probability of A not solving the problem $= \frac{8}{(8+6)} = \frac{8}{14}$

The probability of B not solving the problem $= \frac{12}{(9+12)} = \frac{12}{21}$

Hence the probability of both not solving the problem $\Big\} = \frac{8}{14} \times \frac{12}{21} = \frac{16}{49}$

Hence the probability of solving the problem $\Big\} = 1 - \frac{16}{49} = \frac{33}{49}$

Problem 65. A bag contains 7 red balls and 5 white balls, 4 balls are drawn at random. What is the probability that (*i*) all of them are red ; (*ii*) two of them are red and two white ?

(*M. Com. Calcutta*)

Solution :

(*i*) Favourable cases ${}^7C_4$ Exhaustive cases ${}^{12}C_4$

$$\text{Probability} = \frac{{}^7C_4}{{}^{12}C_4} = \frac{105}{495} = \frac{7}{33}$$

(*ii*) Favourable cases $= {}^7C_2 \times {}^5C_2$

Exhaustive cases $= {}^{12}C_4$

$$\text{Probability} = \frac{{}^7C_2 \times {}^5C_2}{{}^{12}C_4} = \frac{21 \times 10}{495} = \frac{14}{33}$$

Problem 66 : A university has to select an examiner from a list of 50 persons, 20 of them are women and 30 men, 10 of them knowing Hindi and 40 not, 15 of them being teachers and the remaining 35 not. What is the probability of the university selecting a Hindi-knowing women teacher ?

(*M. Com. Allahabad*)

Solution :

Probability of selecting a women $= \frac{20}{50}$

Probability of selecting a teacher $= \frac{15}{50}$

Probability of selecting Hindi-knowing teacher $= \frac{10}{50}$

The events are independent.

Therefore, the required probability $= \frac{20}{50} \times \frac{15}{50} \times \frac{10}{50} = \frac{3}{125}$

13

THEORETICAL DISTRIBUTION

Binomial Distribution, Poisson Distribution, Normal Distribution

Binomial

Constants of Binomial Distribution

No. of Successes (x)	*Probability*
0	$n_{co}p^o q^n = q^n$
1	$n_{c1}pq^{n-1}$
2	$n_{c2}p^2 q^{n-2}$
3	$n_{c3}p^3 q^{n-3}$
r	$n_{cr}p^r q^{(n-r)}$
n	$n_{cn}p^n q^o = p^n$

$(p+q)^n$ $=1$

Mean $= np$

Variance $= npq$

Standard Deviation $= \sqrt{npq}$

Skewness (β_1) $= \dfrac{(q-p)^2}{npq}$

Kurtosis (β_2) $=3 + \dfrac{1-6pq}{npq}$

Poisson

No. of Successes	*Probabilities*
0	$e - m$
1	$m.e^{-m}$
2	$\dfrac{m^2.e^{-m}}{2!}$
3	$\dfrac{m^3.e^{-m}}{3!}$
r	$\dfrac{m^r.e^{-m}}{r!}$
n	$\dfrac{m^n.e^{-m}}{n}$

Mean $= m=p$

Standard Deviation $= \sqrt{m}$

Skewness (β_1) $= \dfrac{1}{m}$

Kurtosis (β_2) $= 3 + \dfrac{1}{m}$

Variance $=$ m

Normal

$$Q_1 = \mu - 0.6745$$
$$Q_3 = \mu + 0.6745$$
$$Q_D = \frac{Q_3 - Q_1}{2} = 0.6745\sigma$$
$$Z = \frac{X - \mu}{\sigma}$$

Distance from the mean ordinates in terms of $\pm\sigma$	*Area under the curve*
Z = ±0.6745	50% = 0.50
Z = ±1.00	68.26% = 0.6826
Z = ±1.96	95% = 0.95
Z = ±2.00	95.44% = 0.9544
Z = ±2.58	99(%) = 0.99
Z = ±3.00	99.73% = 0.9973

BINOMIAL DISTRIBUTION

Problem 1. Bring out the fallacy, if any, in the following statement :

(a) The mean of a binomial distribution is 15 and its standard deviation is 5.

(B. Com.)

Solution :

$$\overline{X} = np = 15$$
$$\sigma = \sqrt{npq} = 5$$
$$\sigma^2 = npq = 25$$
$$q = \frac{npq}{np}$$
$$q = \frac{25}{15} = 1.67$$
$$p + q = 1.$$

However, the value of q cannot exceed one. Therefore, the statement is wrong.

Problem 2. Comment on the following :

For a binomial distribution, mean = 7 and variance = 11.

(I.C.W.A.)

Solution :

$$\text{Mean} = np = 7$$
$$\text{Variance} = npq = 11$$
$$q = \frac{npq}{np} = \frac{11}{7} = 1.57$$
$$q = 1.57 \text{ which is impossible.}$$

The value of q must be between 0 and 1. Therefore, the statement is wrong.

Problem 3. Eight coins are thrown simultaneously. Show that the probability of obtaining at least 6 heads is 37/56. (*ICWA*)

Solution :

Probability of at least 6 heads means, 6 or 7 or 8 heads

$$\begin{aligned}
\therefore \quad P(x \geq 6) &= P_{(6)} + P_{(7)} + P_{(8)} \\
&= {}^8C_6\left(\frac{1}{2}\right)^8 + {}^8C_7\left(\frac{1}{2}\right)^8 + {}^8C_8\left(\frac{1}{2}\right)^8 \\
&= \left(\frac{1}{2}\right)^8 [{}^8C_6 + {}^8C_7 + {}^8C_8] \\
&= \left(\frac{1}{2}\right)^8 [28 + 8 + 1] \\
&= \frac{1}{256} \times 37 \\
&= \frac{37}{256}
\end{aligned}$$

Problem 4. A box contains 100 transistors. 20 of which are defective, 10 are selected for inspection. Indicate what is the probability that:

(*i*) all 10 are defective, (*ii*) all 10 are good, (*iii*) at least one is defective and (*iv*) at the most 3 are defective. (*MBA, Himachal*)

Solution :

Probability of defective in the sample = 0.2

Probability of non-defective in the sample = 0.8

(i) All 10 are defective :

$$P_{(10)} = {}^{10}C_{10}(0.2)^{10}(0.8)^0 = \mathbf{(0.2)^{10}}.$$

(ii) All 10 are good

$$= \mathbf{1 - (0.2)^{10}}$$

(iii) At least one defective

The probability of at least one is defective is the sum of probability *viz.*

$$\begin{aligned}
P_{(1)} &+ P_{(2)} + P_{(3)} \ldots\ldots P_{(10)} \\
P_{(0)} &= {}^{10}C_0(0.2)^0(0.8)^{10} = (0.8)^{10} \\
&= \mathbf{P - (0.8)^{10}}
\end{aligned}$$

(iv) At the most 3 defective

$$\begin{aligned}
&P(x \leq 3) = P_{(0)} + P_{(1)} + P_{(2)} + P_{(3)} \\
= \; &{}^{10}C_0(0.8)^{10} + {}^{10}C_1(0.2)(0.8)^9 + {}^{10}C_2(0.2)^2(0.8)^8 + {}^{10}C_3(0.2)^3(0.8)^7
\end{aligned}$$

$$= 1 \times 0.1074 + 10 \times 0.027 + 45 \times 0.0067 + 120 \times 0.0017$$
$$= 0.1074 + 0.27 + 0.3 + 0.204$$
$$= \mathbf{0.8814}.$$

Problem 5. Three percent of a given lot of manufactured parts are defective. What is the probability that in a sample of four items none will be defective ?

(*B. Com. Bombay*)

Solution :

Probability of defective item = 0.03

$$q = 1 - P = 1 - 0.03 = 0.97$$
$$n = 4$$

Probability of getting 0 defective by binomial distribution

$$P_{(0)} = {}^4C_0(0.03)^0(0.97)^4$$
$$= (0.97)^4$$
$$= \mathbf{0.885}.$$

Problem 6. Four coins are tossed simultaneously. What is the probability of getting (*i*) 2 heads and 2 tails (*ii*) at least two heads, and (*iii*) at least one head.

(*CA*)

Solution :

Getting head = P

Getting tail = q.

The trials are independent.

(*i*)

$$P_{(x)} = {}^4C_x \left(\frac{1}{2}\right)^x \left(\frac{1}{2}\right)^{4-x}$$

Probability of getting 2 heads and 2 tails

$$P = {}^4C_2 \left(\frac{1}{2}\right)^2 \left(\frac{1}{2}\right)^2$$
$$= {}^4C_2 \left(\frac{1}{2}\right)^4$$
$$= \frac{4!}{2!2!} \times \left(\frac{1}{2}\right)^4$$
$$= \frac{4 \times 3}{2} \times \left(\frac{1}{2}\right)^4$$
$$= \mathbf{\frac{3}{8}}.$$

(*ii*) At least 2 heads mean 2 or 3 or 4 heads. Therefore, the probability of getting at least 2 heads is the sum of probabilities of $P_{(2)} + P_{(3)} + P_{(4)}$

$\therefore$ P (at least 2 heads) $= P_{(2)} + P_{(3)} + P_{(4)}$

$$= {}^4C_2 \left(\frac{1}{2}\right)^4 + {}^4C_3 \left(\frac{1}{2}\right)^4 + {}^4C_4 \left(\frac{1}{2}\right)^4$$
$$= \frac{3}{8} + \frac{1}{4} + \frac{1}{16} = \mathbf{\frac{11}{16}}.$$

(*iii*) P (at least 1 head)

$$= 1 - P \text{ (no head)}$$
$$= 1 - {}^4C_0 \left(\frac{1}{2}\right)^4$$
$$= 1 - \frac{1}{16}$$
$$= \mathbf{\frac{15}{16}}$$

Problem 7. Eight coins are tossed together and the occurrence of a head is termed a success. Write down the Binomial distribution of probabilities for the occurrence of 0, 1, ...8 heads. What is the arithmetic mean and variance of the distribution ?

(*B.A., Madurai*)

Solution :

Number of Successes	*Probability*
0	${}^8C_0 \left(\frac{1}{2}\right)^8$
1	${}^8C_1 \left(\frac{1}{2}\right) \left(\frac{1}{2}\right)^7$
2	${}^8C_2 \left(\frac{1}{2}\right)^2 \left(\frac{1}{2}\right)^6$
3	${}^8C_3 \left(\frac{1}{2}\right)^3 \left(\frac{1}{2}\right)^5$
4	${}^8C_4 \left(\frac{1}{2}\right)^4 \left(\frac{1}{2}\right)^4$
5	${}^8C_5 \left(\frac{1}{2}\right)^5 \left(\frac{1}{2}\right)^3$
6	${}^8C_6 \left(\frac{1}{2}\right)^6 \left(\frac{1}{2}\right)^2$
7	${}^8C_7 \left(\frac{1}{2}\right)^7 \left(\frac{1}{2}\right)$
8	${}^8C_8 \left(\frac{1}{2}\right)^8$

$$\text{Arithmetic Mean} = np$$
$$= 8 \times \frac{1}{2} = 4$$
$$\text{Variance} = npq$$
$$= 8 \times \frac{1}{2} \times \frac{1}{2} = \mathbf{2}$$

Problem 8. A coin is tossed six times. What is the probability of obtaining (*a*) 4 heads, (*b*) 5 heads, (*c*) 6 heads (*d*) getting 4 or more heads ? (*B.Com.*)

Solution :

(*a*) Probability of 4 heads

$$= {}^6C_4 P^4 q^2 = 15 \times \left(\frac{1}{2}\right)^4 \left(\frac{1}{2}\right)^2 = 0.234.$$

(*b*) Probability of 5 heads

$$= {}^6C_5 P^5 q = 6 \times \left(\frac{1}{2}\right)^5 \left(\frac{1}{2}\right) = 0.094.$$

(*c*) Probability of 6 heads

$$= {}^6C_6 P^6 q^0 = 1 \times \left(\frac{1}{2}\right)^6 \left(\frac{1}{2}\right)^0 = 0.016$$

(*d*) Probability of getting 4 or more heads

$$= 0.234 + 0.094 + 0.016 = 0.344.$$

Alternatively :

Probability of getting at least 4 heads (means we may get 4 heads or 5 heads or 6 heads)

$$P(x \leq 4) = P(4) + P(5) + P(6)$$

$$= {}^6C_4 \left(\frac{1}{2}\right)^4 \left(\frac{1}{2}\right)^2 +^6 C_5 \left(\frac{1}{2}\right)^5 \left(\frac{1}{2}\right) +^6 C_6 \left(\frac{1}{2}\right)^6 \left(\frac{1}{2}\right)^0$$

$$= {}^6C_4 \left(\frac{1}{2}\right)^6 +^6 C_5 \left(\frac{1}{2}\right)^6 +^6 C_6 \left(\frac{1}{2}\right)^6$$

$$= \left(\frac{1}{2}\right)^6 ({}^6C_4 +^6 C_5 +^6 C_6)$$

$$= \frac{1}{64} \times (15 + 6 + 1)$$

$$= \frac{1}{64} \times 22 = 0.344.$$

Problem 9. The average percentage of failure in a certain examination is 40. What is the probability that out of a group of 6 candidates, at least 4 passed in the examination.

(ICWA)

Solution :

All the trials are independent. The number of pass in the examination may be minimum 4 or 5 all of them may pass.

$$P = 1 - q$$

$$q = \frac{40}{100} = 0.4$$

$$P = 1 - 0.4 = 0.6$$

The probability of passing 4 or more candidates.

i.e.,

$$\begin{aligned} P(x \geq 4) &= P(x = 4) + P(x = 5) + P(x = 6) \\ &= P(4) + P(5) + P(6) \\ &= {}^6C_4(0.6)^4(0.4)^2 +^6 C_5(0.6)^5(0.4) +^6 C_6(0.6)^6 \\ &= (15 \times 0.1296 \times 0.16) + (6 \times 0.07776 \times 0.4) + (0.046656) \\ &= 0.311040 + 0.186624 + 0.046656 \\ &= 0.544320 \end{aligned}$$

Problem 10. Assuming that half the population is vegetarian so that the chance of an individual being a vegetarian is half and assuming that 100 investigators can take a sample of 10 individuals to see whether they are vegetarians, how many investigators would you expect to report that three people or less were vegetarians ?

(M.A.Delhi, ICWA, M.Com, Banaras, Nagpur)

Solution :

We have $P = \frac{1}{2}, q = 1 - \frac{1}{2} = \frac{1}{2}, n = 10, N = 100.$

Number of investigators getting 3 or less vegetarians *i.e.*, 0, 1, 2, 3 vegetarians *i.e.*, 0, 1, 2, 3 vegetarians

$$= 100 \times \left(\frac{1}{2}\right)^{10} + 100 \times {}^{10}C_1 \left(\frac{1}{2}\right)^1 \left(\frac{1}{2}\right)^9 + 100 \times {}^{10}C_2 \left(\frac{1}{2}\right)^2 \left(\frac{1}{2}\right)^8 + 100 \times {}^{10}C_3 \left(\frac{1}{2}\right)^3 \left(\frac{1}{2}\right)^7$$

$$= 100 \times \left(\frac{1}{2}\right)^{10} + 100 \times 10 \times \left(\frac{1}{2}\right)^{10} + 100 \times 45 \times \left(\frac{1}{2}\right)^{10} + 100 \times 120 \times \left(\frac{1}{2}\right)^{10}$$

$$= 100 \times \left(\frac{1}{2}\right)^{10} (1 + 10 + 45 + 120)$$

$$= 100 \times \frac{1}{1024} \times 176 = \mathbf{17} \text{ (approximately)}.$$

Problem 11. The probability of a defective bolt is 2. Find (*a*) the mean and S. D. for the distribution of defective bolts in a total of 1000 and (*b*) find the coefficient of skewness and kurtosis.

(*B. Com.*)

Solution :

(*a*)

$$P = 0.2\,;\ q = 0.8\,;\ n = 1000$$

$$\text{Mean} = np = 1000 \times 0.2 = 200$$

$$\text{S.D.} = \sqrt{npq} = \sqrt{1000 \times 0.2 \times 0.8} = 12.6$$

(*b*)

$$\beta_1 = \frac{(p-q)^2}{npq} = \frac{(0.8-0.2)^2}{1000 \times 0.2 \times 0.8} = \frac{0.36}{160} = 0.225$$

$$\beta_2 = 3 + \frac{1-6pq}{npq} = 3 + \frac{1 - 6 \times 0.2 \times 0.8}{1000 \times 0.2 \times 0.8} = 3.0025.$$

Problem 12. Five coins are tossed 3,200 times, find the frequencies of the distribution of heads and tails and tabulate the results. Calculate the mean number of successes and standard deviations.

(*C. A. Inter*)

Solution :

P=P (head with single coin) $= \frac{1}{2}\,;\ q = 1 - \frac{1}{2} = \frac{1}{2}\,;\ n = 5.$

Now using formula for binomial distribution probability of getting X head is given by

$$P(x) = {}^5C_x \left(\frac{1}{2}\right)^x \left(\frac{1}{2}\right)^{5-x} = {}^5C_1 \left(\frac{1}{2}\right)^5$$

$\therefore$ Frequency of x head is

$$f(x) = Np(x) = 3,200 \times {}^5C_x \left(\frac{1}{2}\right)^5$$

No. of heads (x)	$f(x) = 3,200 \times {}^5C_x \left(\frac{1}{2}\right)^5$
0	$f(0) = 3,200 \times {}^5C_0 \left(\frac{1}{2}\right)^5 = 100$
1	$f(1) = 3,200 \times {}^5C_1 \left(\frac{1}{2}\right)^5 = 500$
2	$f(2) = 3,200 \times {}^5C_2 \left(\frac{1}{2}\right)^5 = 1,000$
3	$f(3) = 3,200 \times {}^5C_3 \left(\frac{1}{2}\right)^5 = 1,000$
4	$f(4) = 3,200 \times {}^5C_4 \left(\frac{1}{2}\right)^5 = 500$
5	$f(5) = 3,200 \times {}^5C_5 \left(\frac{1}{2}\right)^5 = 100$
Total	3,200

Mean number of successes $= np = 5 \times \frac{1}{2} = 2.5$

Standard deviation $= \sqrt{npq} = \sqrt{5 \times \frac{1}{2} \times \frac{1}{2}} = 1.118.$

Problem 13. Twelve coins are tossed. What are the probabilities in a single tossing getting (*i*) 9 or more heads, (*ii*) less than 3 heads, (*iii*) at least 8 heads ? If the 12 coins are tossed 4096 times, or how many occasions would you expect these to be (*iv*) less than 3 heads, (*v*) at least 2 heads (*vi*) exactly 6 heads.

Solution :

(*i*) Probability of getting 9 or more heads is

$$P_{(9)} + P_{(10)} + P_{(11)} + P_{(12)}$$

$$P_{(9)} = {}^{12}C_9 \left(\frac{1}{2}\right)^9 \left(\frac{1}{2}\right)^3$$

$$P_{(10)} = {}^{12}C_{10} \left(\frac{1}{2}\right)^{10} \left(\frac{1}{2}\right)^2$$

$$P_{(11)} = {}^{12}C_{11} \left(\frac{1}{2}\right)^{11} \left(\frac{1}{2}\right)$$

$$P_{(12)} = {}^{12}C_{12} \left(\frac{1}{2}\right)^{12}$$

$$P \text{ (greater than 9)} = {}^{12}C_9 \left(\frac{1}{2}\right)^{12} + {}^{12}C_{10} \left(\frac{1}{2}\right)^{12} + {}^{12}C_{11} \left(\frac{1}{2}\right)^{12} + {}^{12}C_{12} \left(\frac{1}{2}\right)^{12}$$

$$= \left(\frac{1}{2}\right)^{12} [{}^{12}C_9 + {}^{12}C_{10} + {}^{12}c_{11} + {}^{12}C_{12}]$$

$$= \frac{1}{4096}(220 + 66 + 12 + 1)$$

$$= \frac{299}{4096}$$

(*ii*) Probability of getting less than 3 heads,

$$\begin{aligned} &= P_{(0)} + P_{(1)} + P_{(2)} \\ &= {}^{12}C_0 \left(\frac{1}{2}\right)^{12} + {}^{12}C_1 \left(\frac{1}{2}\right)^{12} + {}^{12}C_2 \left(\frac{1}{2}\right)^{12} \\ &= \left(\frac{1}{2}\right)^{12} [{}^{12}C_0 + {}^{12}C_1 + {}^{12}C_2] \\ &= \frac{1(1+12+66)}{4096} \\ &= \mathbf{\frac{79}{4096}} \end{aligned}$$

(*iii*) Probability of 8 heads $= {}^{12}C_8 \left(\frac{1}{2}\right)^{12} = \frac{495}{4096} = 0.1208$

Probability of 9 or more heads $= \frac{299}{4096} = 0.073$

$\therefore$ P (at least 8 heads) = 0.1208+0.073

= **0.1938**

(*iv*) Probability of less than 3 heads out of 4096 times

$$4096 \times \frac{79}{4096} = 79 \text{ times}$$

(*v*) Probability of at least 2 heads $= P(_0)$

$$1 - P_{(0)} + P_{(1)}$$

$$1 - {}^{12}C_0 \left(\frac{1}{2}\right)^{12} + {}^{12}C_1 \left(\frac{1}{2}\right)^{12}$$

$$1 - \frac{13}{4096} = \frac{4083}{4096}$$

$\therefore$ The number of occasions of getting at least 2 heads in 4096 tosses

$$4096 \times \frac{4083}{4096} = \mathbf{4083} \text{ times}$$

(*vi*) Probability of six heads.

$$\begin{aligned} P_{(6)} &= {}^{12}C_6 \left(\frac{1}{2}\right)^{12} \\ &= \frac{12.11.10.9.8.7}{6.5.4.3.2} \times \left(\frac{1}{2}\right)^{12} \\ &= \mathbf{\frac{924}{4096}} \end{aligned}$$

$\therefore$ The number of occasions of getting exactly 6 heads is.

$$4096 \times \frac{924}{4096} = \mathbf{924} \text{ times}$$

Problem 14. Is there any fallacy in the statement " the mean of a Binomial distribution is 20 and its standard deviation 7". (*M.A. Kurukshetra*)

Solution :

$$\begin{aligned} \text{Mean} &= np = 20 \\ \sigma &= \sqrt{npq} = 7 \\ \sigma^2 &= npq = 7^2 = 49 \\ q &= \frac{npq}{np} = \frac{49}{20} = 2.45 \end{aligned}$$

$p + q = 1$. The value of q lies between 0 and 1.

Therefore, the value of q should not exceed one.

Thus, the given statement is wrong.

Problem 15. Eight coins are thrown simultaneously. Find the chance of obtaining :

(*i*) at least 6 heads,

(*ii*) no heads,

(*iii*) all heads. (*M. Com. Meerut*)

Solution :

$$P = \frac{1}{2} \quad q = 1/2$$

(*i*) Probabilities of at least 6 heads implies that 6 or 7 or 8 heads.

(or) $P_{(6)}+)P_{(7)} + P_{(8)}$

$$\begin{aligned} P(r = 6, 7, 8) &= {}^8C_6 \left(\frac{1}{2}\right)^6 \left(\frac{1}{2}\right)^2 +^8 C_7 \left(\frac{1}{2}\right)^7 \left(\frac{1}{2}\right) +^8 C_8 \left(\frac{1}{2}\right)^8 \left(\frac{1}{2}\right)^0 \\ &= {}^8C_6 \left(\frac{1}{2}\right)^8 +^8 C_7 \left(\frac{1}{2}\right)^8 +^8 C_8 \left(\frac{1}{2}\right)^8 \\ &= \left(\frac{1}{2}\right)^8 [{}^8C_6 +^8 C_7 +^8 C_8] \\ &= \frac{1}{256} (28 + 8 + 1) \\ &= \mathbf{\frac{37}{256}} \end{aligned}$$

(*ii*) Probability of no head is

$$\begin{aligned} P(_0) &= {}^8C_0 = \left(\frac{1}{2}\right)^0 \left(\frac{1}{2}\right)^8 \\ &= 1 \times \frac{1}{256} \\ &= \mathbf{\frac{1}{256}} \end{aligned}$$

(*iii*) Probability of all heads is

$$\begin{aligned} P(_8) &= {}^8C_8 \left(\frac{1}{2}\right)^8 \\ &= 1 \times \frac{1}{256} \\ &= \mathbf{\frac{1}{256}} \end{aligned}$$

Problem 16. The probability that an evening college student will graduate is 0.4. Determine the probability that out of 5 students (*a*) none, (*b*), one, and (*c*) at least one will be graduate. (*B. Com. Bombay*)

Solution : By using binomial distribution

P (graduate) = 0.4

q (Non-graduate) = 0.6

$P^{(r)} = N_{cr}\ P^r\ q^{n-r}$

(*a*) Probability that none will graduate

$$P_{(0)} = {}^5C_0 (0.6)^5 = 0.0778 \text{ or } 0.08$$

(*b*) Probability that one will graduate

$$P_{(1)} = {}^5C_1 (0.4)(0.6)^4 = \mathbf{0.259}$$

(*c*) Probability that at least one will graduate

$$= 1 - P(\text{none will graduate}) = 1 - 0.08 = \mathbf{0.92}$$

Problem 17. The screws produced by a certain machine were checked by examining samples of 12. The following table shows the distribution of 128 samples according to the number of defective items they contained.

No. of defectives In a sample of 12	0	1	2	3	4	5	6	7	Total
No. of samples	7	6	19	35	30	23	7	1	128

Fit a binomial distribution and find the expected frequencies if the chance of screw being defective is $\frac{1}{2}$. Find the mean and variance of the fitted distribution. (*B. Com. Delhi*)

Solution :

Computation of frequencies

No. of defective	*Probabilities*	*Expected Frequency*	*Observed frequency*
0	$P_{(0)} = {}^7C_0 \left(\frac{1}{2}\right)^0 \left(\frac{1}{2}\right)^7 = \frac{1}{128}$	1	7
1	$P_{(1)} = {}^7C_1 \left(\frac{1}{2}\right)^1 \left(\frac{1}{2}\right)^6 = \frac{7}{128}$	7	6
2	$P_{(2)} = {}^7C_2 \left(\frac{1}{2}\right)^2 \left(\frac{1}{2}\right)^5 = \frac{21}{128}$	21	19
3	$P_{(3)} = {}^7C_3 \left(\frac{1}{2}\right)^3 \left(\frac{1}{2}\right)^4 = \frac{35}{128}$	35	35
4	$P_{(4)} = {}^7C_4 \left(\frac{1}{2}\right)^4 \left(\frac{1}{2}\right)^3 = \frac{35}{128}$	35	30
5	$P_{(5)} = {}^7C_5 \left(\frac{1}{2}\right)^5 \left(\frac{1}{2}\right)^2 = \frac{21}{128}$	21	23
6	$P_{(6)} = {}^7C_6 \left(\frac{1}{2}\right)^6 \left(\frac{1}{2}\right)^1 = \frac{7}{128}$	7	7
7	$P_{(7)} = {}^7C_7 \left(\frac{1}{2}\right)^7 \left(\frac{1}{2}\right)^0 = \frac{1}{128}$	1	1

Probabilities *i.e.* $p_{(x)} = {}^7C_x \left(\frac{1}{2}\right)^x \left(\frac{1}{2}\right)^{7-x}$

Expected frequencies $= 128\ p_{(x)}$

Arithmetic Mean $= np$

$$= 7 \times \frac{1}{2} = 3.5$$

Variance $= npq = 7 \times \frac{1}{2} \times \frac{1}{2} = 1.75$

POISSON

Problem 18. Between 2 and 4 P.M. the average number of phone calls per minute coming into the switchboard of a company is 2.5. Find the probability that during one particular minute there will be (*i*) no phone call at all, (*ii*) exactly 3 calls. (Given e^{-2}= 0.13534 and $e^{-0.5}$= 0.60650)

(*ICWA, C.A.*)

Solution :

(*i*)

$$m = 2.5$$

$$P_{(0)} = \frac{e^{-2.5}(2.5)^0}{0!}$$
$$= e^{-2.5}$$
$$= e^{-2.5} = e^{-2} \times e^{-.5}$$
$$= 0.13534 \times 0.60650$$
$$= \mathbf{0.0821}$$

(*ii*)

$$P_{(3)} = \frac{e^{-2.5}(2.5)^3}{3!}$$
$$= \frac{.0821 \times 15.625}{3 \times 2}$$
$$= \frac{1.2828}{6}$$
$$= \mathbf{0.214}$$

Problem 19. In a town 10 accidents took place in a span of 50 days. Assuming that the number of accidents per day follows the Poisson Distribution, find the probability that there will be three or more accidents in a day. (*MBA Madras*)

Solution :

$$m = \frac{10}{50} = 0.2$$

$$P(\text{3 or more accidents}) = 1 - [P_{(0)} + P_{(1)} + P_{(2)}]$$
$$= 1 - \left[e^{-.2} + e^{-.2} \times .2 + \frac{e^{-.2} \times (.2)^2}{2}\right]$$
$$= 1 - [e^{-.2}(1 + .2 + .02)]$$
$$= 1 - e^{-.2} \times 1.22$$
$$= 1 - 0.8187 \times 1.22$$
$$= 1 - 0.998$$
$$= \mathbf{0.002}$$

Problem 20. Assuming that on an average, 5% of the output of a factory making certain parts is defective and that 200 units are in a package, what is the probability that, at most 4 defective parts may be found in a package ? *(M. Com. Kerala)*

Solution :

$$m = 200 \times 0.05$$

$$P_{(x)} = \frac{e^{-10}(10)^x}{x!}$$

Probability of at most 4 defective parts in package

$$= P_{(0)} + P_{(1)} + P_{(2)} + P_{(3)} + P_{(4)}$$

$$= e^{-10}\left[1 + \frac{10}{1} + \frac{10^2}{2!} + \frac{10^3}{3!} + \frac{10^4}{4!}\right]$$

Problem 21. It is given that 3 % of electric bulbs manufactured by a company are defective. Using the Poisson approximation, find probability that a sample of 100 bulbs will contain (*i*) no defective, (*ii*) exactly one defective. *(B.A. Bombay)*

Solution :

$$n = 100 \quad P = 0.03$$

$$m = nP = 100 \times 0.03 = 3$$

$$P_{(0)} = e^{-m} = e^{-3} = 0.049 = 0.05$$

$$P_{(1)} = P_{(0)} \times m$$

$$= 0.05 \times 3$$

$$= \mathbf{0.15}$$

Problem 22. It is known from past experience that in a certain plant there are on the average 4 incidents per month. Find the probability that in a given year there will be less than 4 accidents. Assume Poisson distribution. *(M. Com. Delhi)*

Solution :

$$m = 4$$

$$P_{(x=r)} = \frac{e^{-m}m^r}{r!} = \frac{e^{-4}4^r}{r!}$$

The required probability that there will be less than 4 accidents is given as :

$$P(x < 4) = P(x = 0) + P(x = 1) + P(x = 2) + P(x = 3)$$

$$= e^{-4}\left(1 + 4 + \frac{4^2}{2!} + \frac{4^3}{3!}\right)$$

$$= e^{-4}(1 + 4 + 8 + 10.67)$$

$$= e^{-4} \times 23.67$$

$$= 0.01832 \times 23.67$$

$$= \mathbf{0.4336}$$

Problem 23. One fifth per cent of the blades produced by a blade manufacturing factory turn out to be defective. The blades are supplied in packets of 10. Use Poisson distribution to calculate the approximate number of packets containing no defective, one defective and two defective blades respectively in a consignment of 1,00,000 packets. *(MBA Madurai)*

(Given $e^{-.02} = .9802$)

Solution :

Here

$$P = \frac{1}{500}, n = 10$$

$$m = np = \frac{1}{500} \times 10 = 0.02.$$

Using the formula for Poisson distribution, the probability of x defective blades is

$$P^{(x)} = \frac{e^{-0.02}(0.02)^x}{x!}$$

The frequencies of 0, 1, 2, 3... defective blades given by

$$f^{(x)} = 1,00,000 \times \frac{e^{-0.02}(0.02)^x}{x!}$$

Number of packets with no defective blade

$$= 1,00,000 \times e^{-0.02} = 1,00,000 \times 0.9802 = 98,020$$

Number of packets with one defective blades

$$\begin{aligned} P_{(1)} &= \frac{e^{0.02}(0.02)}{1!} \\ &= 1,00,000 \times e^{-0.02} \times 0.02 \\ &= 98,020 \times 0.02 \\ &= 1960.4 \\ &= \mathbf{1960} \end{aligned}$$

Number of packets with two defective blades is

$$\begin{aligned} &= 1,00,000 \times e^{-0.02} \times \frac{(0.02)^2}{2!} \\ &= 98020 \times 0.0002 \\ &= 19.604 \\ &= \mathbf{20} \end{aligned}$$

Problem 24. A book contains 100 misprints distributed randomly throughout its 100 pages. What is the probability that a page observed at random contains at least two misprints. Assume Poisson Distribution.

(*B. Com. Delhi*)

Solution :

$$m = \frac{\text{Total Number of misprints}}{\text{Total Number of pages}} = \frac{100}{100} = 1$$

Probability that a page contains at least two misprints.

$$\begin{aligned} P(r > 2) &= 1 - [p(0) + p(1)] \\ P_{(r)} &= \frac{m^r e^{-m}}{r!} \\ P_{(0)} &= \frac{1^0 e^{-1}}{1!} = e^{-1} = \frac{1}{e} = \frac{1}{2.7183} \\ P_{(0)} + P_1 &= \frac{1}{2.7183} + \frac{1}{2.7183} = 0.736 \\ P(r > 2) &= 1 - [P^{(0)} + P_{(1)}] \\ &= 1 - 0.736 \\ &= \mathbf{0.264} \end{aligned}$$

Problem 25. If the mean of a Poisson distribution is 4, find, (1) Standard deviation, (2) β_1, (3) β_2,(4) μ_3 and (5) μ_4

Solution :

$$\begin{aligned} m &= 4 \\ S.D &= \sqrt{m} = \sqrt{4} = 2 \\ \beta_1 &= \frac{1}{m} = \frac{1}{4} = 0.25 \\ \beta_2 &= 3 + \frac{1}{m} = 3 + \frac{1}{4} = 3.25 \\ \mu_3 &= m = 4 \\ \mu_4 &= m + 3m^2 = 4 + 48 = 52 \end{aligned}$$

Problem 26. In a certain factory turning out optical lenses, there is a small chance 1/500 for any one lens to be defective. The lenses are supplied in packets of 10. Use Poisson distribution to calculate the approximate number of packets containing no defective, one defective, two defective, three defective lenses respectively in a consignment of 20, 000 packets. (Given $e^{-0.02} = 0.9802$). *(M. Com. Meerut, Delhi)*

Solution

$$N = 20,000\ n = 10$$

Probability of a defective lens $= \dfrac{1}{500}$

$$m = nP = 10 \times \frac{1}{500} = \frac{1}{50}(0.02)$$

Number of packets containing no defective lens

$$= 20,000 \times 0.9802 = \mathbf{19,604}.$$

Number of packets containing one defective lens

$$= 20,0000 \times 0.9802 \times 0.02 = \mathbf{392}.$$

Number of packets containing two defective lens

$$= \frac{20,000 \times 0.9802 \times (0.02)^2}{2} = 3.9208 = \mathbf{4}.$$

Number of packets containing three defective lenses

$$= \frac{20,000 \times 0.9802 \times (0.02)^3}{3 \times 2} = 0.026 = \mathbf{0}$$

Hence No. of packets containing four defective lenses is also zero.

Problem 27. Assuming that one in 80 births is a case of twins, calculate the probability of 2 or more sets of twins on a day when 30 births occur. Compare the results obtained by using (*i*) the Binomial distribution and (*ii*) Poisson approximation.

Solution :

(*i*) Using Binomial distribution :

$$\begin{aligned} P\text{ (twin birth)} &= \frac{1}{80} = 0.0125 \\ \therefore \quad q &= 1 - 0.0125 = 0.9875 \\ n &= 30 \end{aligned}$$

Probability of two or more sets on a day is

$$\begin{aligned} P(x \geq 20) &= 1 - P(x < 2) \\ &= 1 - P_{(0)} + P_{(1)} \\ P_{(0)} &= {}^{30}C_0(0.0125)^0(0.98750)^{30} \\ &= (0.98750)^{30} = \text{Antilog}(30 \log 0.9875) \\ &= \text{Antilog } (30 \times \bar{1}.9945) \\ &= \text{Antilog } (-30 + 29.835) \\ &= \text{Antilog } \bar{1}.8350 \\ &= 0.6839 \end{aligned}$$

$$\begin{aligned} P_{(1)} &= {}^{30}C_1(0.0125)(0.9875)^{29} \\ &= \text{Antilog}(\log 30 + \log 0.0125 + 29 \log 0.9875) \\ &= \text{Antilog}(1.4771 + \bar{2}.0969 + 29 \times \bar{1}.9945) \\ &= \text{Antilog}(1.4771 + \bar{2}.0969 + \bar{1}.8405) \\ &= \text{Antilog}\bar{1}.4145 \\ &= 0.2597. \end{aligned}$$

Therefore, the required probability

$$\begin{aligned} &= 1 - (0.6839 + 0.2597) \\ &= 1 - 0.9436 \\ &= \mathbf{0.0564}. \end{aligned}$$

(*ii*) By using Poisson approximation :

$$m = 0.375(np)$$

$$P_{(x)} = \frac{e^{-m} \times m^x}{x!} = \frac{e^{-0.375} \times 0.375^x}{x!}$$

Required Probability

$$\begin{aligned} &= 1 - [P_{(0)} + P_{(1)}] \\ &= 1 - e^{-0.375} + 0.375^{e-0.375} \\ &= 1 - e^{0.357}(1 + 0.357) \\ &= 1 - (0.6873 \times 1.375) \\ &= 1 - 0.945 \\ &= \mathbf{0.055}. \end{aligned}$$

Problem 28. Fit a Poisson distribution to the following data and calculate the theoretical frequencies :

x	:	0	1	2	3	4
f	:	123	59	14	3	1

(*B.Com. Gujarat*)

Solution :

x	0	1	2	3	4	
f	123	59	14	3	1	$\Sigma f = 200$
fx	0	59	28	9	4	$\Sigma fx = 100$

$$\text{Mean} = \frac{100}{200} = \mathbf{0.5.}$$

$$NP_{(0)} = Ne^{-m} = 200 \times e^{-0.5} = 200 \times 0.6065 = 121.3$$

Calculation of expected Frequencies

x	*Frequency* $(NP_{(x)})$	
0	$NP_{(0)} = 121.3$	121
1	$NP_{(0)} \times \frac{m}{1} = 121.3 \times 0.5 = 60.65$	61
2	$NP_{(1)} \times \frac{m}{2} = \frac{60.65 \times 0.5}{2} = 15.16$	15
3	$NP_{(2)} \times \frac{m}{3} = \frac{15.16 \times 0.5}{3} = 2.53$	3
4	$NP_{(3)} \times \frac{m}{4} = \frac{2.53 \times 0.5}{4} = 0.32$	0
	Total	200

Problem 29. The distribution of typing mistakes committed by a typist is given below. Assuming a poisson model, find out the expected frequencies :

Mistakes per page	:	0	1	2	3	4	5
Number of Pages	:	142	156	69	27	5	1

(*M. Com., Rajasthan, Delhi*)

Solution :

x	0	1	2	3	4	5	
f	142	156	69	27	5	1	$N = 400$
fx	0	156	138	81	20	5	$fx = 400$

$$\overline{X} = \frac{400}{400} = 1$$

$$e^{-1} = 0.3679$$

COMPUTATION OF EXPECTED FREQUENCIES

x	*Expected frequencies*		*observed frequencies*
0	$400 \times 0.3679 = 147.1$	147	142
1	$400 \times 0.3679 \times 1 = 147.1$	147	156
2	$\frac{400 \times 0.3679 \times (1)^2}{2!} = 73.9$	74	69
3	$\frac{400 \times 0.3679 \times (1)^3}{3!} = 24.5$	25	27
4	$\frac{400 \times 0.3679 \times (1)^4}{4!} = 6.1$	6	5
5	$\frac{400 \times 0.3679 \times (1)^5}{5!} = 1.2$	1	1
	Total :	400	400

Problem 30. Fit a poisson distribution to the following data :

No. of mistakes per page	0	1	2	3	4
No. of pages on Which mistakes occurred	109	65	22	3	1

(*B.Sc. Madurai, M. A. (Econ) Kurushetra*)

Solution :

x	0	1	2	3	4	
f	109	65	22	3	1	$N = 200$
fx	0	65	44	9	4	$\Sigma fx = 122$

$$\overline{X} = \frac{122}{200} = 0.61$$

$$e^{-0.61} = 0.5432$$

Compulation of Expected Frequencies

x	*Expected frequencies*	*Observed frequencies*
0	$NP_{(0)} = 200 \times 0.5432 = 108.64 = 109$	109
1	$NP_{(0)} \times \frac{m}{1} = 108.64 \times \frac{0.61}{1} = 66.28 = 66$	65
2	$NP_1 \times \frac{m}{2} = 66.28 \times \frac{0.61}{2} = 20.22 = 20$	22
3	$NP_{(2)} \times \frac{m}{3} = 20.22 \times \frac{0.61}{3} = 4.1 = 4$	3
4	$NP_{(3)} \times \frac{m}{4} = 4.1 \times \frac{0.61}{4} = 0.63 = 1$	1
	Total : 200	200

NORMAL

Problem 31. Find the probability that the standard normal variate lies between 0 to 1.5. (*B. Com.*)

Solution :

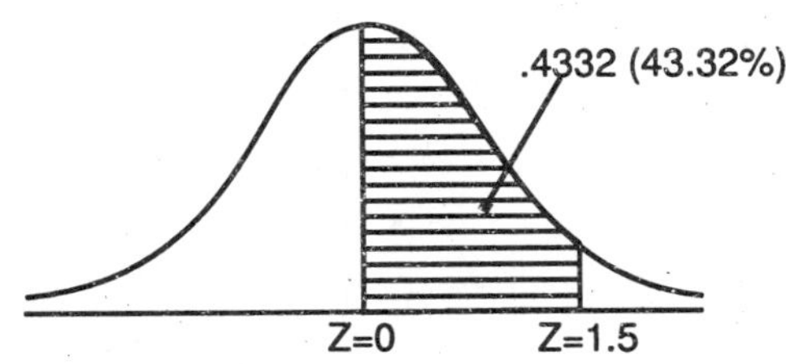

To find the area between $Z = 0$ and $Z = 1.5$, look the area between 0 to 1.5 from the table. It is 0.4332 or 43.32 % (shaded area).

Problem 32.

(*a*) Find the area to the left of $Z = 1.90$

(*b*) Find the area to the right of $Z = .25$

(*B.Com.*)

Solution :

(*a*) Area to the left of $Z = 0$ is 0.5

The area between $Z = 0$ And $Z = 1.9$ is $\frac{0.4713}{0.9713}$

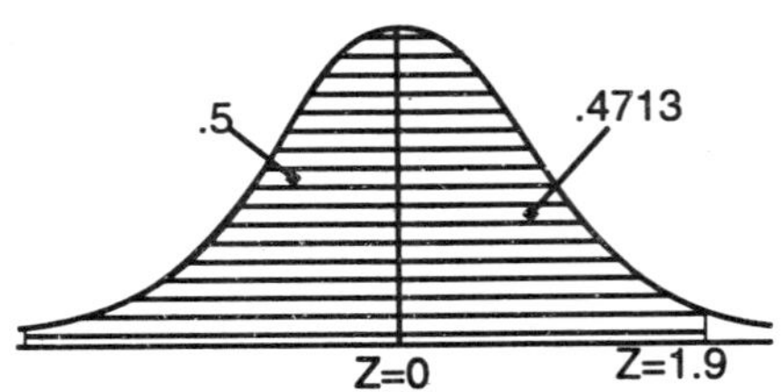

Therefore, the area to the left of $Z = 1.9$ is .9713 (shaded area).

(*b*)

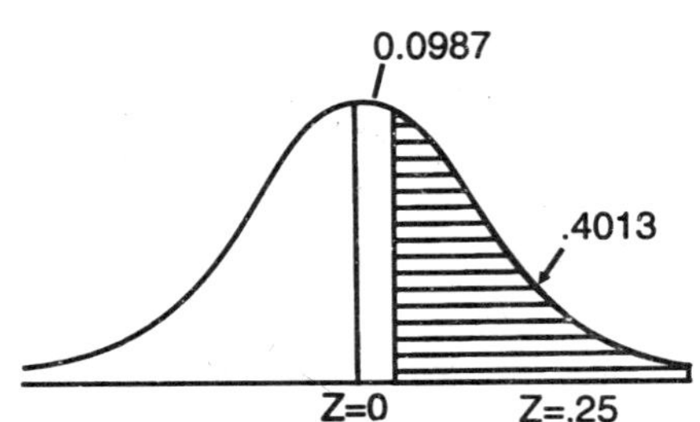

The value given in the table for $Z = .25$ is 0.0987.

Deduct this value from .5, we get .4013, which is required probability.

Problem 33. The life time of a certain kind of battery has a mean of 300 hours and a standard deviation of 35 hours. Assuming that the distribution of life times, which are measured to the nearest hour is normal, find the percentage of batteries which have life time of more than 370 hours.

(*B. Com.*)

Solution :

Corresponding $X = 370$ $Z = \frac{370 - 300}{35} = \frac{70}{35} = 2.$

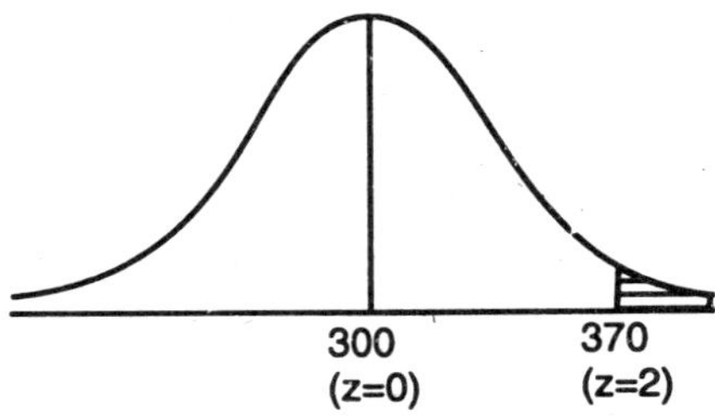

The area between $Z = 0$ and $Z = 2$ is .4772

The area of Z>2=.5−.4772 = .0228

Therefore the percentage of batteries having life time more than 370 hours = .0228×100 = **2.28%.**

Problem 34. A large number of measurements is normally distributed with a mean of 65.5" and a standard deviation of 6.2". Find the percentage of measurements that fall between 54.8" and 68.8".

(B. Com. Hons. Calcutta)

Solution :

Values of $Z = \dfrac{X - \overline{X}}{\sigma}$

When $Z = \dfrac{54.8 - 65.5}{6.2} = -1.73$

Area between $Z = 0$ and $Z = -1.73$ is .4582

When $X = 68.8$, $Z = \dfrac{68.8 - 65.5}{6.2} = .53$

Area between $Z = 0$ and $Z = .53$ is .2019

Total area between,

$$\begin{aligned} X &= 54.8 \text{ and } X = 68.8 \\ &= .2019 + .4582 = .6601 \end{aligned}$$

Percentage of measurement,

$$= .6601 \times 100 = 66.01\%$$

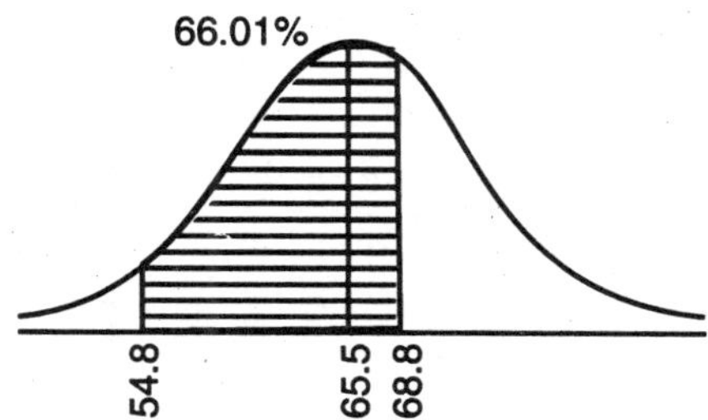

Problem 35. The scores made by candidate in a certain test are normally distributed with mean 500 and standard deviation 100. What per cent of candidates receive scores (*i*) less then 400 and 600?

(For a standard normal distribution $Z = \frac{X - \overline{X}}{\sigma}$ the area under the curve between $Z = 0$ and $Z = 1$ is 0.34134.)

(B. Com. Bombay)

Solution :

$$\overline{X} = 500$$
$$\sigma = 100$$

(*i*) For

$$\begin{aligned} X &= 400 \\ Z &= \frac{400 - 500}{100} = -1 \end{aligned}$$

Area between $Z = -1$ and $Z = 0$ is .34134

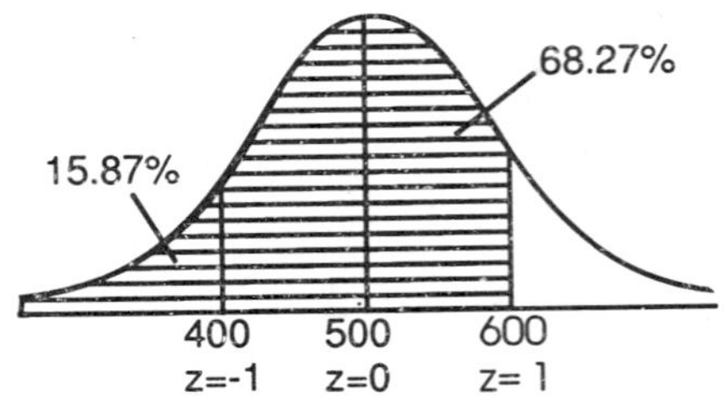

Area for $Z = -1 = .5 - .34134 = .15866$

Therefore, the percentage = $.15866 \times 100 = 15.87$ %.

(*ii*) When

$$X = 600, Z = \frac{600 - 500}{100} = 1$$

Area between $Z = 0$ and $Z = 1$ is .34134

Area between $X = 400$ to $X = 600$

i.e

$$\begin{aligned} Z &= -1 \text{ and } Z = 1 \text{ is } .34134 + .34134 \\ &= .68268 \\ &= 68.27\% \end{aligned}$$

Problem 36. The customer accounts of a certain departmental store have an average balance of Rs. 120 and a standard deviation of Rs. 40. Assuming that the account balances are normally distributed :

(1) What proportion of accounts is over Rs. 150?

(2) What proportion of accounts is between Rs. 100 and Rs. 150?

(3) What proportion of accounts is between Rs. 60 and Rs. 90?

(*B. Com.*)

Solution :

$$\text{Value of Z} = \frac{X - \overline{X}}{\sigma}$$

(1) When $X = 150$, $Z = \dfrac{150 - 120}{40} = .75$

To find the proportion of accounts greater than Rs. 150, we refer to right of $Z = .75$.

The area to the right of $Z = 0$ is .5

Area between $Z = 0$ and $Z = .75$ is .2734.

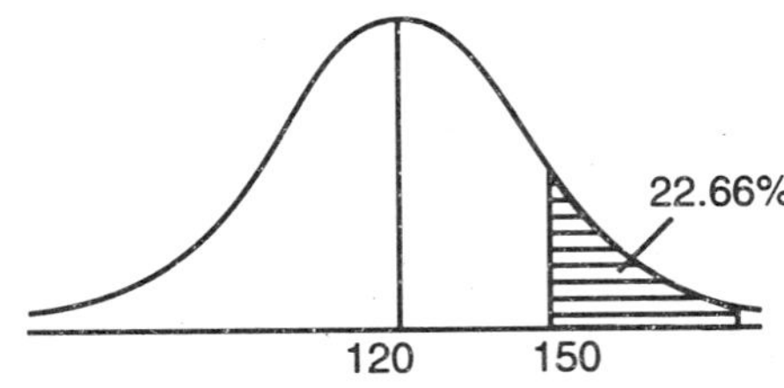

The area to the right of $Z = .75$ is $.5 - .2734 = .2266$

Hence 22.66 % of accounts have a balance in excess of Rs. 150 (shaded area)

(2) When $X = 100$, $Z = \dfrac{100 - 120}{40} = -.5$

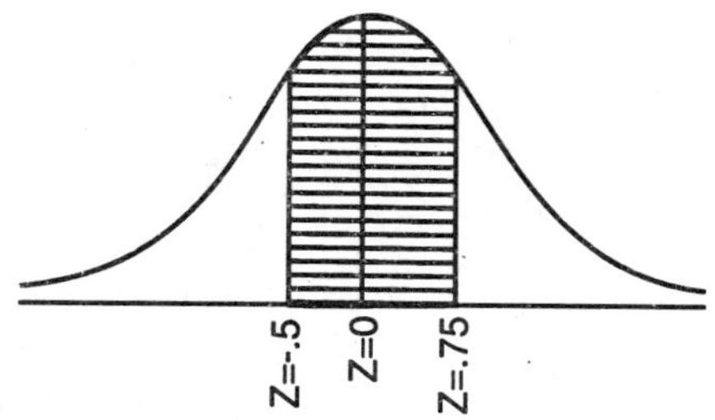

When $X = 150$, $Z = \dfrac{150 - 120}{40} = -.75$

The area between $Z = -.5$ and $Z = 0$ is .1915

The area between $Z = 0$ and $Z = .75$ is .2734

Therefore, the total area between

$Z = -.5$ and $Z = .75$ is $.1915 + .2734 = .4649$

Hence 46.5% of accounts have an average balance of accounts between Rs. 100 and Rs. 150.

(3) When $X = 60$, $Z = \dfrac{60 - 120}{40} = -1.5$

When $X = 90$, $Z = \dfrac{90 - 120}{40} = -.75$

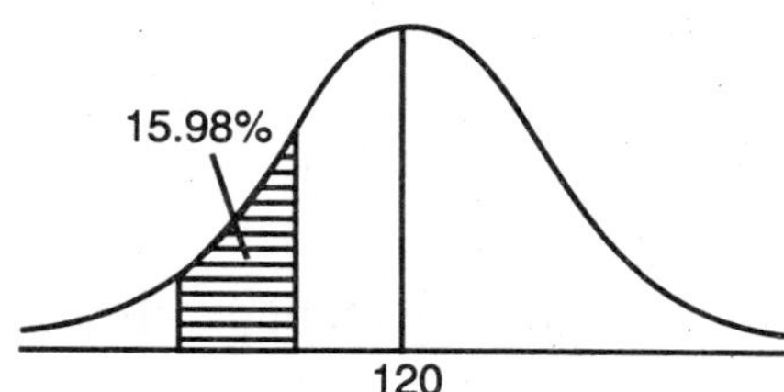

Area between $Z = 0$ to $Z = -1.5$ is .4332

Area between $Z = 0$ to $Z = -.75$ is .2734

Therefore, the area between $X = 90$ and $X = 60$

That is, $Z = -1.5$ to $Z = -.75$ is $.4332 - .2734 = .1598$.

Therefore, the account balances between Rs. 60 and Rs. 90 are 15.98%.

Problem 37. Assume the mean height of soldiers to be 68.22" with a variance of 10.8". How many soldiers in a regiment of 1,000 would you expect to be over six feet tall ?

(B. Com. Bombay)

Solution :

$$Z = \frac{X - \overline{X}}{\sigma}$$

$$X = 6' \text{ or } 72''$$

$$X = 68.22$$

$$\sigma = \sqrt{10.8} = 3.286$$

$$Z = \frac{72 - 68.22}{3.286} = 1.15$$

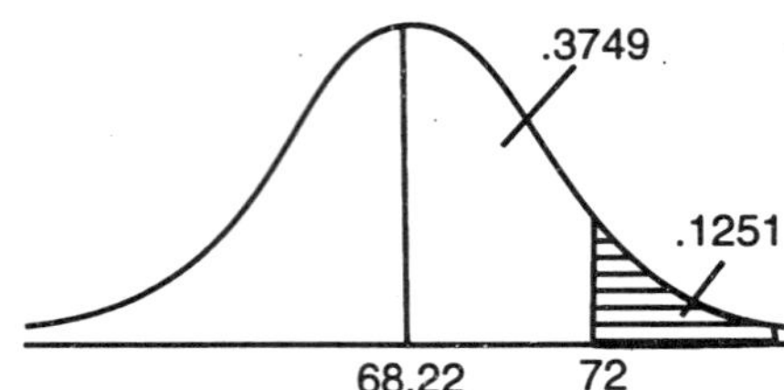

When $Z = 0$ and $Z = 1.15$, the area is .3749. The area to the right of the ordinate at 1.15 is $.5 - .3749 = .1251$. Therefore, the probability of soldiers, whose height is more than 6 feet, out of 1000 is $.1251 \times 1000 = 125.1$ or 125 soldiers.

Problem 38. 1,000 bulbs with a mean life 120 days are installed in a new factory ; their length of life is normally distributed with standard deviation 20 days. (*i*) How many bulbs will expire in less than 90 days ? (*ii*) If it is decided to replace all the bulbs together, what interval should be allowed between replacement if not more than 10 % should expire before replacement ?

(*MBA, Delhi*)

Solution :

$$\overline{X} = 120, \sigma = 20$$

(*i*) When $X = 90$, $Z = \frac{90-120}{20} = -1.5$

Area when $Z = 0$ and $Z = -1.5$ is 0.4332

$\therefore$ Area to the left of $Z = -1.5$ is $.5 - .4332 = .0668$.

Therefore, number of bulbs expected to expire in less than 90 days

$= .0668 \times 1000 =$ **66.8** or **67.**

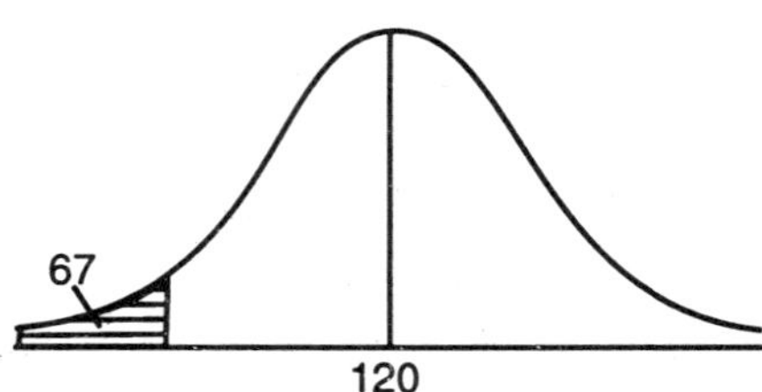

(*ii*) The value of standard normal variate to an area .4 *viz.* $.5 - .1$, is 1.28

$$\frac{X - 120}{20} = -1.28$$
$$X - 120 = 1.28 \times 20$$
$$X = 120 - 25.6$$
$$X = 94.4 \text{ or } \mathbf{94}.$$

Therefore the bulbs may be replaced after 94 days

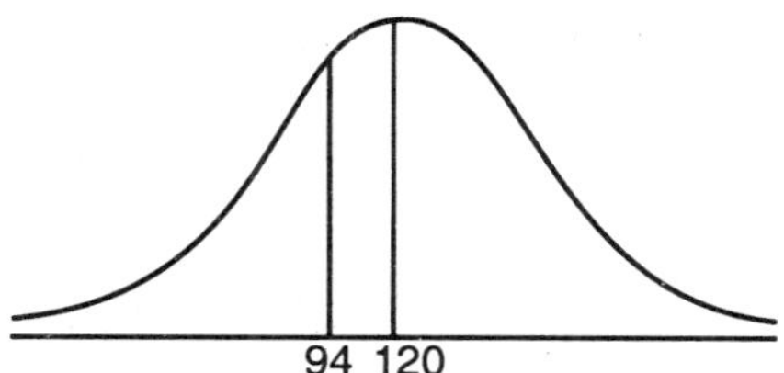

Problem 39. For a normal distribution in which $N = 1{,}000$, the mean is 40 and standard deviation is 8. Find (*i*) first quartile (*ii*) the third quartile and (*iii*) the inter-quartile range.

(*B. Com.*)

Solution :

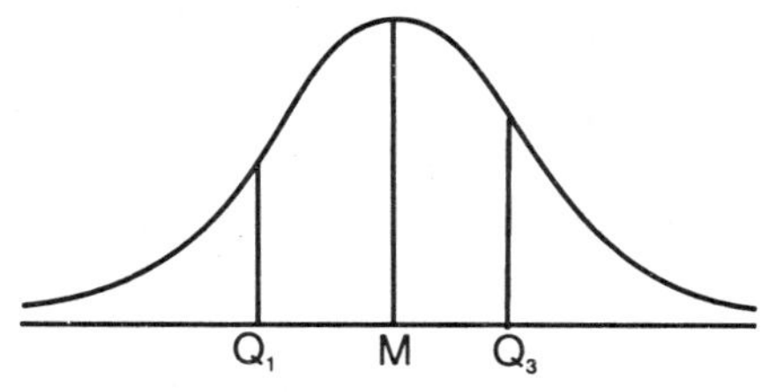

$$
\begin{aligned}
Q_1 &= \overline{X} - 0.6745\,\sigma \\
&= 40 - (0.6745 \times 8) \\
&= 40 - 5.396 \\
&= \mathbf{34.604}. \\
Q_3 &= \overline{X} + 0.6745\,\sigma \\
&= 40 + (0.6745 \times 8) \\
&= 40 + 5.396 \\
&= 45.396.
\end{aligned}
$$

Inter-quartile Range,

$$
\begin{aligned}
&= \frac{Q_3 - Q_1}{2} \\
&= \frac{45.396 - 34.604}{2} \\
&= \frac{10.792}{2} \\
&= \mathbf{5.396}.
\end{aligned}
$$

Problem 40. In a normal distribution 31 % of the items are under 45 and 8% are over 64. Find the mean and standard deviation of the distribution.

(*B. Com.*)

31% are under 45

8 % are over 64.

$$Z = \frac{45 - \overline{X}}{6} = -0.5 \text{ (from table)}$$

(Area to the left is 0.31, but right from this point, 0.31 to 0.5 is 0.19, the value corresponding to $Z = 0.5$)

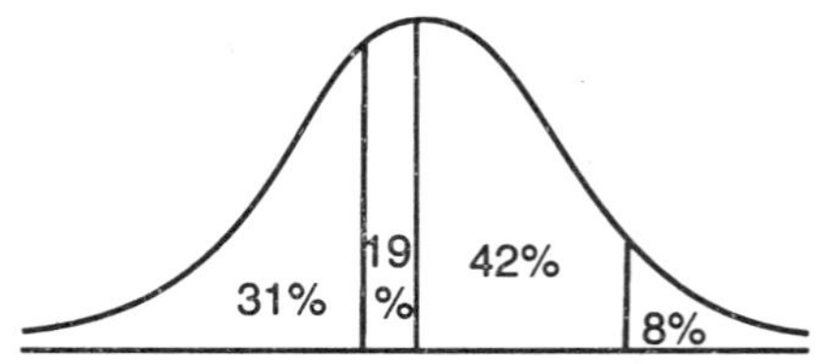

$$Z_1 = \frac{45 - \overline{X}}{\sigma} = -0.5$$

$$= \frac{45 - \overline{X}}{\sigma} = -0.5\,\sigma$$

$$= 45 - \overline{X} = -0.5\,\sigma$$

8 % of the items are above 64. The area to the right of ordinate at 64 = 0.8. The area to the left of the ordinate at $\overline{X}$ = 64 to the mean ordinate is 0.5–0.08 = 0.42. The value corresponding to this is 1.4 (from table)

$$Z_2 = \frac{64 - \overline{X}}{\sigma} = 1.4$$

$$= 64 - \overline{X} = 1.4\,\sigma$$

$$-\overline{X} = 0.5\,\sigma = -45(-)$$

$$-\overline{X} = \frac{-1.4\,\sigma = -64}{-1.96\,\sigma = 19}$$

$$\sigma = \frac{19}{1.9} = 10$$

Putting the value in equation :

$$45 - \overline{X} = -0.5\,(10)$$

$$45 - \overline{X} = -5$$

$$-\overline{X} = -5 - 45$$

$$-\overline{X} = -50$$

$$\overline{X} = 50$$

Problem 41. In a distribution exactly normal, 7% of the items are under 35 and 89% are under 63. What are the mean and standard deviation of the distribution ?

(*B. Com.*)

Solution :

When the percentage of items is 43 %, the Z = 1.4757.

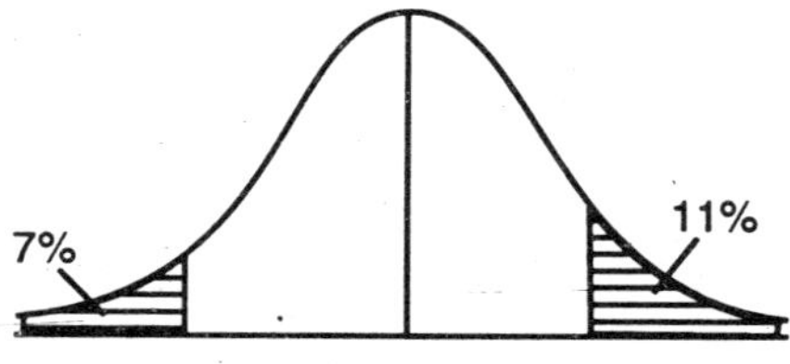

When the percentage of items is 39 % , the Z = 1.2263

Thus (1) $Z_1 = \frac{35 - \overline{X}}{\sigma} = -1.48$

(2) $Z_2 = \frac{63 - \overline{X}}{\sigma} = +1.23$

We have two equations :

$$35 - \overline{X} = -1.48\,\sigma$$
$$63 - \overline{X} = -1.23\,\sigma$$

Thus

$$35 - \overline{X} = -1.48\,\sigma \quad (1)$$
$$63 - \overline{X} = -1.23\,\sigma \quad (2)$$

By subtraction we get

$$-28 = -2.71\,\sigma$$
$$\sigma = \frac{-28}{-2.71} = 10.33$$

Putting the value in equation No. 1.

$$35 - \overline{X} = -1.48 \times (10.33)$$
$$- \overline{X} = -35 - 15.3$$
$$\overline{X} = 50.3$$

Problem 42. The average daily sale of 500 branch offices was Rs. 150 thousand and the standard deviation is Rs. 15 thousand. Assuming the distribution to be normal indicate how many branches have sales between :

Rs. 1,20,000 and Rs. 1,45, 000

Rs. 1,40,000 and Rs. 1,65, 000

(*M.B.A. Himachal*)

Solution :

(1) When

$$X = 1,20,000$$
$$Z = \frac{120 - 150}{15} = -2$$

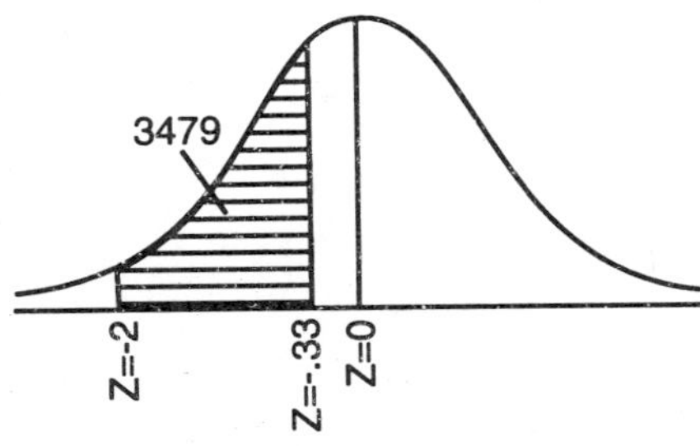

When

$$X = 1,45,000$$
$$Z_2 = \frac{145 - 150}{15} = -0.33$$

Area between $Z = 0$ and $Z = -2$ is 0.4772

Area between $Z = 0$ and $Z = -0.33$ is 0.1293

Therefore, the area between

$\overline{X} = 1,20,000$ and 1,45,000 is 0.4772–0.1293 = 0.3479

Therefore the number of branches having sales between

Rs. 1,20,000 and Rs. 1,45,000 = 5000×0.3479=174

(2) When $x = 1,40,000$

$$Z_1 = \frac{140 - 150}{15} = -0.67$$

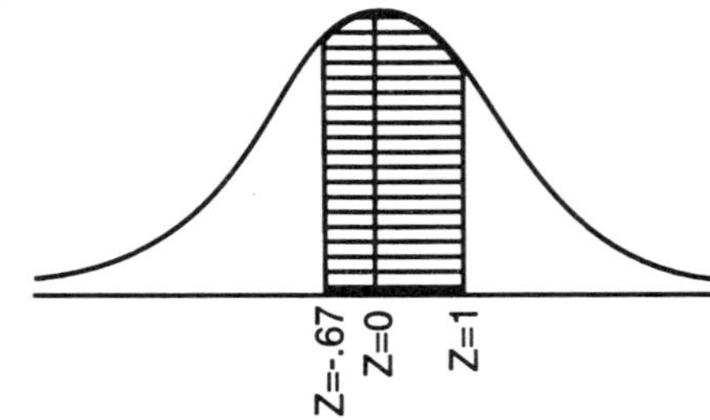

When $\overline{X} = 1,65,000$, $Z_2 = \dfrac{165 - 150}{15} = 1.$

Area between $Z = 0$ and $Z = -0.67 = 0.2486$

Area between $Z = 0$ and $Z = 1 = 0.3413$

Area between $Z = -0.67$ and $Z = 1$ is 0.5899

Therefore number of branches having sales between

$$\begin{aligned} \text{Rs.}1,40,000\text{and Rs, } 1,65,000 &= 500 \times 0.5899 \\ &= 294.95 \\ &= \mathbf{295}. \end{aligned}$$

Problem 43. The weekly wages of 1,000 workmen are normally distributed around a mean of Rs. 70 and with standard deviation of Rs. 5. Estimate the number of workers whose weekly wages will be

(*a*) between Rs. 70 and 72

(*b*) between Rs. 69 and Rs. 72

(*c*) more than Rs. 75

(*d*) less than Rs. 63

(*e*) more than Rs. 80

(*B.A., Delhi*)

Solution :

(*a*) When $\overline{X} = 70$, $Z_1 = 70 - 70 = 0$

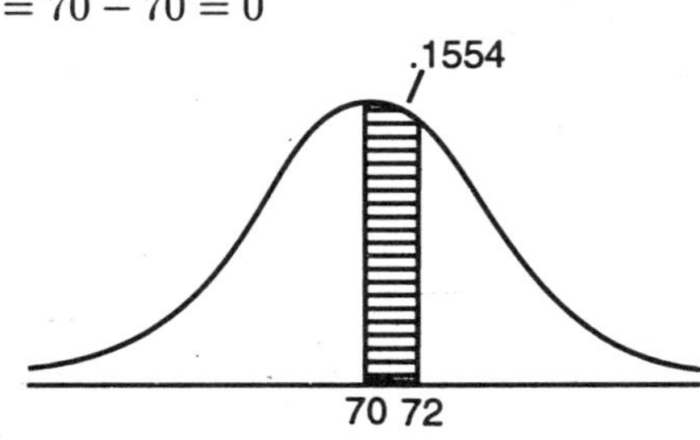

When $X = 72, Z_2 = \dfrac{72 - 70}{5} = 0.4$

Area between $Z = 0$ and $Z_2 = 0.4$ is 0.1554

Therefore, the number of workers with weekly wages between Rs. 70 and Rs. 72.

$$1000 \times 0.1554 = \mathbf{155}$$

(b) When $x = 69,\ Z_1 = \dfrac{69 - 70}{5} = \dfrac{-1}{5} = -0.2$

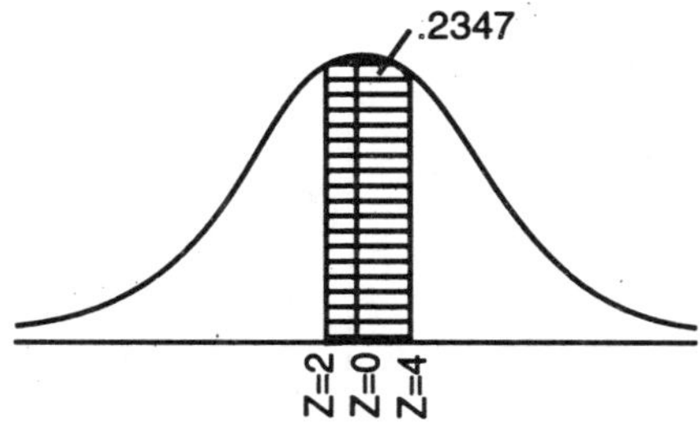

When $X = 72,\ Z_2 = \dfrac{72 - 70}{5} = \dfrac{2}{5} = 0.4$

Area between $Z_1 = 0$ and $Z_2 = -0.2 = 0.0793$

Area between $Z_1 = 0$ and $Z_2 = .04 = 0.1554$

Area between $Z_1 = -0.2$ and $Z_2 = 0.4 = 0.2347$

Therefore the number of workers with weekly wages between Rs. 69 and Rs. 72 = 1000×0.2347 = 234.7 = 235.

(c) When $X = 75,\ Z_2 = \dfrac{75 - 70}{5} = 1$

Are between $Z_1 = 0$ and $Z_2 = 1 = 0.3413$

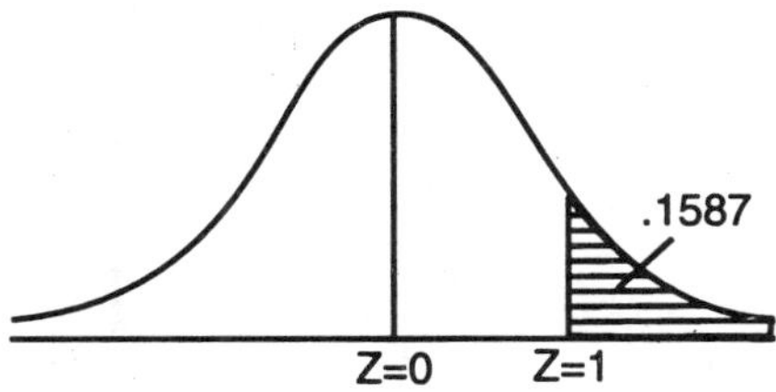

Area greater than Rs. 75 = 0.5−0.3413 = 0.1587

Therefore the number of workers with weekly wages more than Rs. 75 is 1,000×.1587 = 0.158.7 = **159.**

(d) When $X = 63,\ Z_1 = \dfrac{63 - 70}{5} = \dfrac{-7}{5} = -1.4$

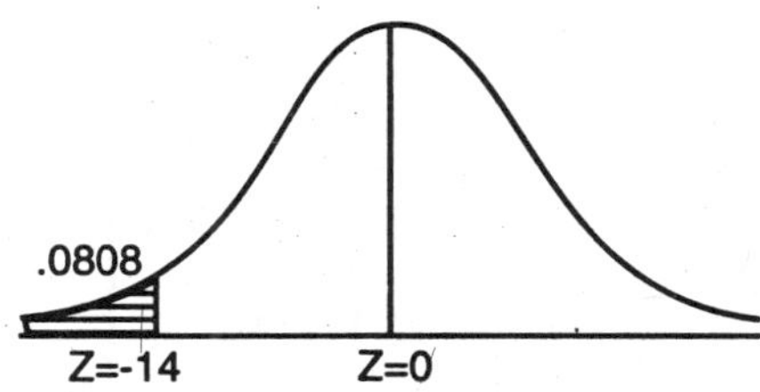

Area between $Z_1 = 0$ and $Z_2 = 1.4 = 0.4192$

Area less than Rs. 63 = 0.5−0.4192 = 0.0808

Therefore, the number of workers with weekly wages less than Rs. 63 is 1,000×0.0808 = 80.8 = **81**.

(*e*) When

$$x = 80, Z_2 = \frac{80 - 70}{5} = 2.$$

Area between

$$Z_1 = 0 \text{ and } Z_2 = \text{ is } 0.4772$$

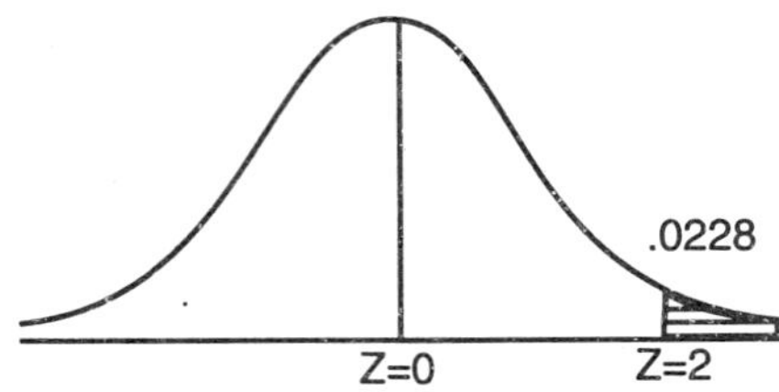

Area greater than Rs. 80 = 0.5−0.4772 = 0.0228

Therefore, the numbher of workers with weekly wages more than Rs. 80 is 1000 × 0.0228 =22.8=**23**

Problem 44. A sample of 100 dry battery cells tested to find the length of life produced the following results :

$$\overline{X} \quad = \quad 12 \text{ hours}, \sigma = 3 \text{ hours}$$

Assuming the data to be normally distributed, what percentage of battery cells are expected to have life:

(*a*) More than 15 hours

(*b*) Less then 6 hours and

(*c*) Between 10 and 14 hours

Given Z	:	2.5	2	1	0.67
Area	:	0.4938	0.4772	0.3413	0.2487

(*I.C.W.A.*)

Solution :

(*a*) When X = 15, $Z = \dfrac{15 - 12}{3} = 1$

Area to the right of Z = 1 is 0.5−.3413 = .1587

∴ The percentage of battery cells which have life more than 15 hours = .1587×100 = **15.87%**.

(*b*) When $X = 6$, $Z = \dfrac{6 - 12}{3} = -2$

Area to the left of $Z = -2$ is = .5−.4772 = .0228

∴ The percentage of battery cells which have life less than 6 hours = .0228×100 = 2.28%

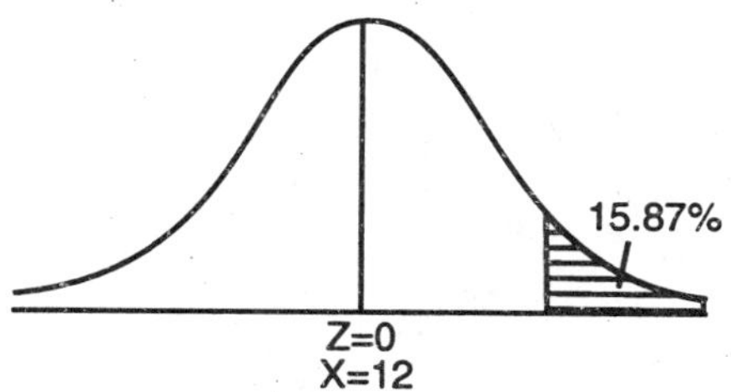

(c) When $X = 10$, $Z = \frac{10 - 12}{3} = -.67$

When $X = 14$, $Z = \frac{14 - 12}{3} = +.67$

Area to the right of $Z = -.67$ is 0.2487

Area to the left of $Z = +.67$ is $\frac{0.2487}{0.4974}$

Total area

$\therefore$ The percentage of cells which have life between 10 hours and 14 hours is $.4974 \times 100 = 49.74$ %.

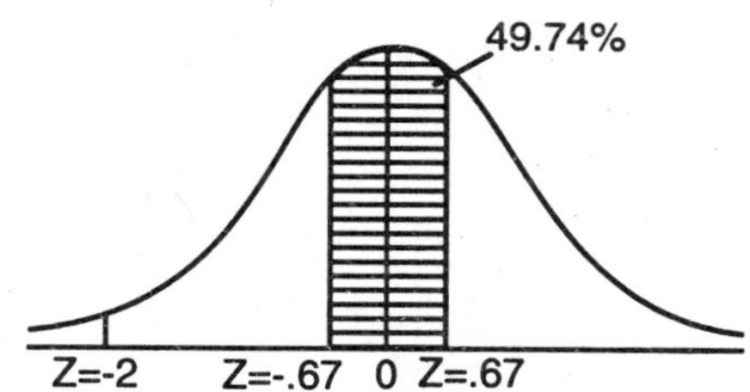

Problem 45. The life time of a certain type of battery has a mean life of 400 hours and standard deviation of 50 hours. Assuming normality for the distribution of life time, find :

(a) the percentage of batteries which have life-time of more than 350 hours.

(b) the life time value above which the best 25 % of the batteries will have their life, and

(c) the proportion of batteries that have a life-time between 300 hours to 500 hours.

(*B. Com. Shivaji*)

Solution :

Z=1 Z=0
X=400

(a) When $X = 350$, $Z = \frac{350 - 400}{50} = -1$

Area to the right of $Z = -1 = .3413+.5 = .8413$.

Therefore, 84.13% of the batteries have life time more than 350 hours.

(b)
$$Z = .675 = \frac{X - 400}{50}$$
$$.675 \times 50 = X - 400$$
$$33.75 + 400 = X$$
$$\therefore \quad X = 433.75 \text{ hours.}$$

Therefore, the best 25 % of the batteries will have life time more than 433.75 hours.

(c) When $X = 300$, $Z = \frac{300 - 400}{50} = -2$

When $X = 500$, $Z = \frac{500 - 400}{50} = 2$

When $Z = -2$, the area is .4772

When $Z = 2$, the area is $\frac{.4772}{.9544}$

$\therefore$ 95.44 %of batteries have life time between 300 to 500 hours.

Problem 46. Of a large group of men 5 % are under 60 inches in height and 40 % are between 60 and 65 inches. Assuming a normal distribution, find the mean height and standard deviation. (*M. Com. Andhra*)

Solution :

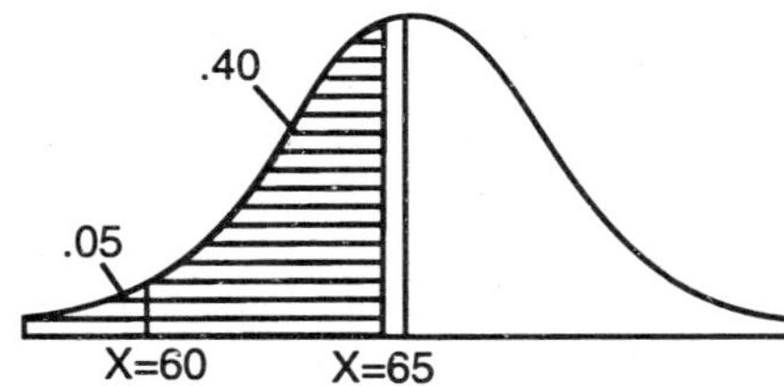

The area lying to the left of $X = 60$ is 0.05

The area between $Z = 0$ and $Z = \frac{60 - \overline{X}}{\sigma} = .5 - .05 = .45$

From table $Z = \frac{60 - \overline{X}}{\sigma} = -1.64$ (a)

Height of men between 60" and 65" = 40%

The area between the mean ordinate at 60" 65" is 0.4

The area between $Z = 0$ and $Z = \frac{65 - \overline{X}}{\sigma} = .05$

From table $Z = \frac{65 - \overline{X}}{6} = (.05) = -.13$ (b)

$$(a) \quad 60 - \overline{X} = -1.64\sigma$$

$$(b) \quad \frac{65 - \overline{X} = -.13\,\sigma}{-5 \;= -.1.51\,\sigma}$$

$$\sigma = \frac{5}{1.51} = 3.3.$$

Substituting the value in equation

$$\begin{aligned} 60 - \overline{X} &= -1.64\,(3.3) \\ 60 - \overline{X} &= -5.412 \\ 65.412 &= \overline{X} \\ \therefore \quad \overline{X} &= \mathbf{65.412} \end{aligned}$$

Problem 47. A student secures 72 marks in an examination in Sociology for which his class average is 54 and the standard deviation 20. He secures 76 marks in Statistics for which his class average is 52 and the standard deviation 12.

What can we say about the performance of this student with reference to these two examinations. (Convert Z scores or standard scores for both examinations and make your comments). *(B. A. Bombay)*

Solution :

Marks in Sociology $(X) = 72\ \overline{X}_{(x)} = 54\ \sigma_{(x)} = 20$

Marks in Statistics $(Y) = 76\ \overline{X}_{(y)} = 52\,\sigma_{(y)} = 12$

(Z) Score in Sociology $= \dfrac{72-54}{20} = \dfrac{18}{20} = 0.9$

(Z) Score in Statistics $= \dfrac{76-52}{12} = \dfrac{24}{12} = 2$

From the above, it is clear that the standard score in Statistics is greater than the standard score in Sociology. Therefore, the performance of the student is better in Statistics when comparing his performance in Sociology.

Problem 48. As a result of tests on 2,000 electric bulbs manufactured by a company it was found that the life time of the bulbs was normally distributed with and average life of 2040 hours and

Z	:	1.23	1.33	1.43	1.63	1.73	1.83
Area	:	0.3907	0.4082	0.4236	0.4484	0.4582	0.4667

(M. Com. Delhi)

Solution :

(*a*) When $X = 2150$, $Z = \dfrac{2150-2040}{60} = 1.83$

The area between $Z = 0$ and $Z = 1.83$ is .4667

Area to the right of $Z = .4667$ is $.5 - .4667 = .0333$

Required No. of bulbs $= .0333 \times 2000 =$ **67.**

(*b*) When $X = 1960$, $Z = \dfrac{1960-2040}{60} = -1.33$

Area between $Z = 0$ and $Z = 1.33$ is .4082

Area for less than $Z = -1.33$ is $.5 - .4082 = .0918$

Required No. of bulbs $= .0918 \times 2000 =$ **184.**

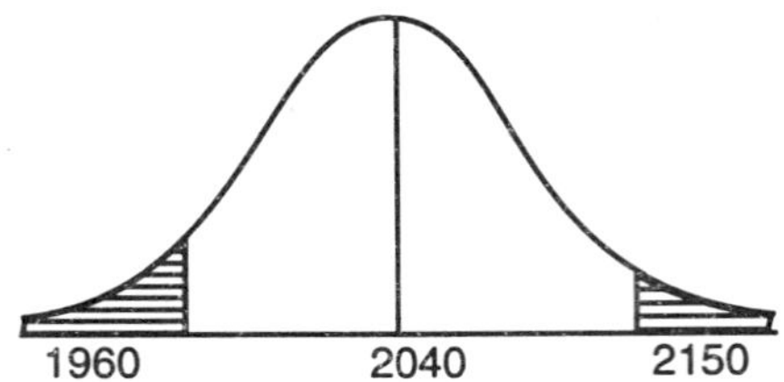

Problem 49. The mean weight of 500 male students in a certain college is 151 lbs. and the standard deviation is 15 lbs. Assuming the weights are normally distributed, find how many students weigh (A) between 120 and 155 lbs, and (B) more than 185 lbs.

(B. A. Bombay)

Solution :

(A) When $X = 120$, $Z = \dfrac{120 - 151}{15} = -2.07$

When $X = 155$, $Z = \dfrac{155 - 151}{15} = .27$

Area between

$$\begin{aligned} Z &= -2.07 \text{ and } Z = .27 \\ &= .4808 + .1064 \\ &= .5872. \end{aligned}$$

Therefore, the number of students weighing between 120 and 155 lbs.

$$= .5872 \times 500 = 293.6 \text{ or } \mathbf{294}$$

(B) When $X = 185$, $Z = \dfrac{185 - 151}{15} = 2.27$

Area to the right of Z = 2.27 is .5−**.4884** = .0116.

Therefore, the number of students weighing more than 185 lbs is 500×.0116 = 5.8 or 6.

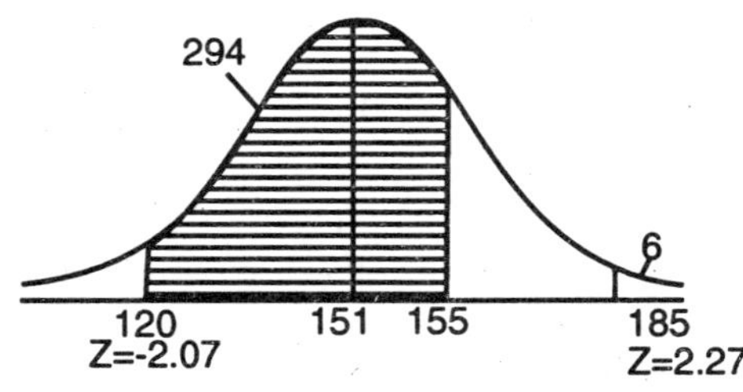

Problem 50. The results of a particular examination are given below in a summary form :

	Result	*% of candidates*
1.	Passed with distinction	10
2.	Passed	60
3.	Failed	30

It is known that a candidate gets plucked if he obtains less than 40 marks, out of 100 while he must obtain at least 75 marks in order to pass with distinction. Determine the mean and standard deviation of the distribution of marks assuming this to be normal.

(*M. Com. Delhi*)

Solution :

30 % students get marks less than 40.

$$Z = \frac{40 - \overline{X}}{\sigma} = -0.52 \text{ (from the table)}$$

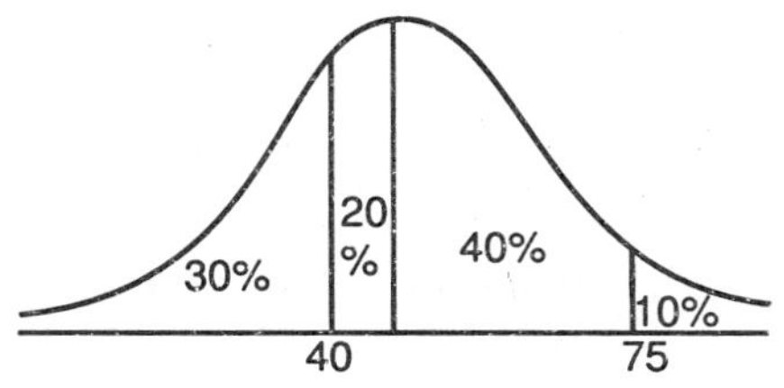

$$40 - \overline{X} = -0.52\,\sigma \qquad ...(i)$$

10% students get more than 75

$$40\% \text{ area } = 75 - \overline{X} = 1.28\,\sigma \qquad ...(ii)$$

Subtract (*i*) from (*ii*)

$$\begin{array}{r} 75 - \overline{X} = 1.28\,\sigma \\ 40 - \overline{X} = -0.52\,\sigma \\ \hline 35 = 1.8\,\sigma \end{array}$$

$$1.80\,\sigma = 35$$

$$\sigma = \frac{35}{1.8} = 19.4.$$

Mean :

$$\begin{aligned} 40 - \overline{X} &= -0.52 \times (19.4) \\ -\overline{X} &= -40 - 10.09 \\ -\overline{X} &= -50.09 \\ \overline{X} &= 50.09 \end{aligned}$$

Problem 51. The daily sales of a certain items are normally distributed with a mean of Rs. 8,000 and a variance of Rs. 10, 000.

(*a*) What is the probability that on a given day the sales will be less than Rs. 8,210 ?

(*b*) What percent of the days will the sales be between Rs. 8100 and Rs. 8210?

(*B. Com. Bombay*)

Solution :

(*a*) When $X = 8210$, $Z = \frac{8210 - 8000}{100} = 2.1$

Area between $Z = 0$ and $Z = 2.1$ is .4821

Area for $Z < 2.1$ is $.5 + .4821 = .9821$

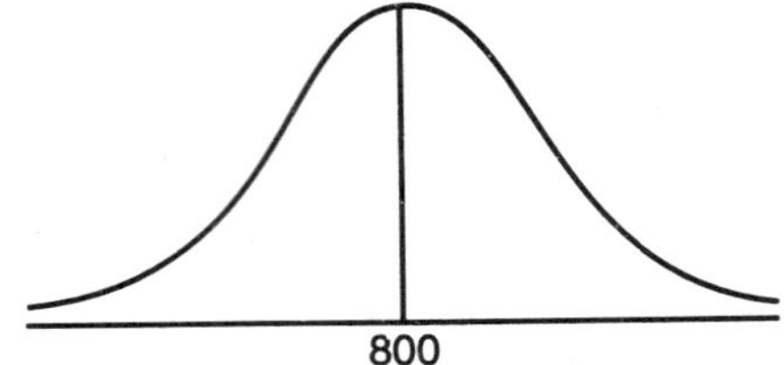

(b) When $X = 8100$, $Z = \dfrac{8100 - 8000}{100} = 1$

When $X = 8210$, $Z = 2.1$

Area between $Z = 0$ and $Z = 1$ is .3413

Required area (percentage) = .4821−.3413 = .1408 or 14.08 %

Problem 52. The mean and standard deviation of a normal distribution are 60 and 5 respectively. Find the inter-quartile range and the mean deviation of the distribution.

(*B. Com. Bombay*)

Solution :

Q_1 M Q_3

$$
\begin{aligned}
Q_1 &= \overline{X} - 0.6745\,\sigma \\
&= 60 - (0.6745 \times 5) \\
&= 60 - 3.3725 \\
&= 56.6275 \\
Q_3 &= \overline{X} + 0.6745\,\sigma \\
&= 60 + (0.6745 \times 5) \\
&= 60 + 3.3725 \\
&= 63.3725 \\
\text{Inter quartile range} &= \frac{Q_3 - Q_1}{2} \\
&= \frac{63.3725 - 56.6275}{2} \\
&= \mathbf{3.372.} \\
\text{Mean Deviation} &= \frac{4}{5}\sigma \\
&= \frac{4}{5} \times 5 \\
&= \mathbf{4.}
\end{aligned}
$$

Problem 53. The following table gives frequencies of occurrence of a variate X between certain limits :

Variate (X)	*Frequency* (f)
Less than 40	30
40 or more but less than 50	33
50 and more	37
	100

The distribution is exactly normal. Find the average and standard deviation of X.

(*M. Com. Delhi*)

Solution :

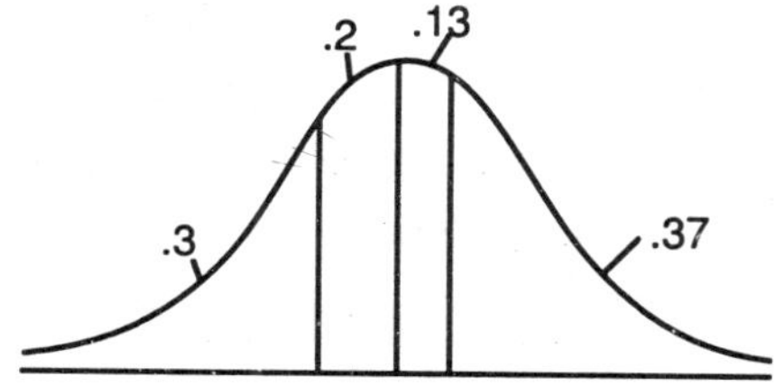

When $X = 40$, $Z_1 = \dfrac{40 - \overline{X}}{\sigma} = -0.53$ (from table)

When $X = 50$, $Z_2 = \dfrac{50 - \overline{X}}{\sigma} = 3.33$(from table)

$$\frac{40 - \overline{X}}{\sigma} = 0.53 \text{ or } 40 - \overline{X} = -0.53\,\sigma$$

$$\frac{50 - \overline{X}}{\sigma} = 0.33 \text{ or } 50 - \overline{X} = 0.33\,\sigma$$

By subtracting we get $10 = 0.86\,\sigma$

$$\sigma = \frac{10}{0.86} = \mathbf{11.62}$$

Substituting the value of σ in one equation, we get

$$50 - \overline{X} = 0.33\,(11.62)$$

$$\overline{X} = 50 - 3.84$$

$$\overline{X} = 46.16.$$

14

SAMPLING THEORY AND TEST OF SIGNIFICANCE

S.E. of No. of success $= \sqrt{npq}$

n : Size of sample;
p : probability of success in each trial;
$q = (1-p)$ *i.e.*, probability of failure.

S.E. of proportion of success $= \sqrt{\dfrac{pq}{n}}$

S.E. of difference in proportions :

or S.E.

$$(p_1 - p_2) = \sqrt{pq\left(\frac{1}{n_1} + \frac{1}{n_2}\right)}$$

where $\qquad p = \dfrac{n_1 p_1 + n_2 p_2}{n_1 + n_2}$

If S.E. $\dfrac{p_1 - p_2}{S.E.} > 1.96$ (5% level), not significant.

Large samples

S.E. $(\overline{X}) = \dfrac{\sigma p}{\sqrt{n}}$ $\qquad \sigma\, p = \sigma$ of population

$n =$ No. of observation.

S.E. of difference of means of two samples

$$\text{S.E. } (\overline{X_1} - \overline{X_2}) = \sqrt{\frac{\sigma_1^2}{n_1} + \frac{\sigma_2^2}{n_2}}$$

$$\text{S.E. } (\sigma_1 - \sigma_2) = \sqrt{\frac{\sigma_1^2}{2n_1} + \frac{\sigma_2^2}{2n_2}}$$

$$\text{S.E. } \qquad (r) = \frac{1 - r^2}{\sqrt{n}}$$

Problem 1. A coin is tossed 400 times and it turns up head 216 times. Discuss whether the coin may be an unbiased one, and explain briefly the theoretical principles you would use for this purpose. *(B. Com.)*

Solution :

An unbiased coin turn up head $= \frac{1}{2}$

$\therefore$ The expected number of heads in tosses 400 = 200

But the observed number of heads = 216

$$\text{S.E.} = \sqrt{npq}$$

$$= \sqrt{400 \times \frac{1}{2} \times \frac{1}{2}} = \sqrt{100} = 10$$

$$\text{Deviation from actual} = 216 - 200 = 16$$

$$Z = \frac{\text{Difference}}{S.E.} = \frac{16}{10} = \mathbf{1.6}$$

Since the observed deviation is 1.6 times the S.E, which is less than 1.96 SE (5% level), it can be concluded that the hypothesis is accepted. Therefore, the coin is an unbiased one.

Problem 2. In a sample of 400 parts manufactured by a factory, the number of defective parts was found to be 30. The company, however, claimed that only 5% of their product is defective. Is the claim tenable? (*ICWA*)

Solution :

P (Proportion of defectives in the sample) $= \frac{30}{400} = 0.075$

Null hypothesis $(H_0) : P = 0.05\ Q = .095$

$$\begin{aligned} Z &= \frac{p - P}{\sqrt{PQ/n}} \\ &= \frac{0.075 - 0.05}{\sqrt{0.05 \times 0.95/400}} \\ &= \frac{0.025}{\sqrt{0.00012}} \\ &= \frac{0.025}{0.011} \\ &= 2.27 \end{aligned}$$

The computed value of $Z = 2.27$, which is greater than 1.645% at 5% level of significance. Therefore, the null hypothesis is rejected. That is the Company's claim is not tenable.

Problem 3. A sample of size 400 was drawn and the sample mean was found to be 99. Test whether this sample could have come from a normal population with mean 100 and variance 64 at 5 % level of significance. (*M.A. Delhi*)

Solution :

$$\begin{aligned} Z &= \frac{\overline{x} - \mu}{\sigma\sqrt{n}} \quad \sigma^2 = 64 \quad \sigma = 8 \\ &= \frac{99 - 100}{8/\sqrt{400}} \\ &= \frac{-1 \times 20}{8} = -2.5 \end{aligned}$$

$2.5 > 1.96$, therefore, it is significant at 5% level of significance. The data are inconsistent. Hence, we conclude that the sample has not been drawn from the normal population with mean 100 and variance 64.

Problem 4. A machine puts out 16 imperfect articles in a sample of 500. After machine is overhauled, it puts out 3 imperfect articles in a batch of 100. Has the machine improved ? (*M. Com. Nagpur*)

Solution :

$$\begin{aligned} P_1 &= \frac{16}{500} = 0.032 \text{ (in the first sample)} \\ P_2 &= \frac{3}{500} = 0.03 \text{ (in the second sample)} \end{aligned}$$

Let us have the hypothesis that the machine has not improved after overhauling

$$\text{S.E } (p_1 - p_2) = \sqrt{pq\left(\frac{1}{n_1} + \frac{1}{n_2}\right)}$$

$$\text{Where } p = \frac{n_1 p_1 + n_2 p_2}{n_1 + n_2}$$

$$p = \frac{500 \times 0.032 + 100 \times 0.03}{500 + 100} = \frac{16 + 3}{600} = 0.03$$

$$q = 1 - 0.03 = 0.97$$

$$\text{SE } (p_1 - p_2) = \sqrt{pq\left(\frac{1}{n_1} + \frac{1}{n_2}\right)}$$

$$= \sqrt{(.03)(.97)\left(\frac{1}{500}\right) + \left(\frac{1}{100}\right)}$$

$$= \sqrt{(.03)(.97)[(.002) + (.01)]}$$

$$= 0.0187$$

$$Z = \frac{p_1 - p_2}{SE}$$

$$= \frac{0.032 - 0.03}{0.0187} = \frac{0.002}{0.0187} = 0.106$$

Since the difference is less than 2.58 *SE* (1% level), the result of the experiment supports the hypothesis. Therefore, we conclude that the machine has not improved after overhauling.

Problem 5. An operater claims that he produces 40 articles in an hour. A sample of 10 random hours shows the turns out as 43, 45, 38, 37, 41, 42, 44, 39, 43 and 38. Is the claim of the operative reasonable at 5 % significance level? Assume the distribution of hourly turnout of the operative to be normal and critical region at 5 % level employing one-tailed test for 9 df to be 1.833. *(B. Com.)*

Solution : Let the null hypothesis be that the average turnout of the operative is 40. This hypothesis is against the alternative hypothesis that turnout is less than 40.

$$\overline{X} = \frac{1}{10}(43 + 45 + 38 + 37 + 41 + 42 + 44 + 39 + 43 + 38) = \mathbf{41}.$$

$$S^2 = \frac{1}{9}(43 - 41)^2 + (45 - 41)^2 + (38 - 41)^2 + (37 - 41)^2 + (41 - 41)^2$$
$$+ (42 - 41)^2 + (44 - 41)^2 + (39 - 41)^2 + (43 - 41)^2 + (38 - 41)^2$$
$$= \frac{1}{9}(4) + (16) + (9) + (16) + (0) + (1) + (9) + (4) + (4) + (9)$$

$$\therefore \quad S = \frac{1}{9} \times 72 = 8$$
$$= \sqrt{8}$$
$$= \mathbf{2.8284}$$

$$\text{and} \quad t = \frac{\overline{X} - \mu}{S}\sqrt{n} = \frac{41 - 40}{2.8284} \times \sqrt{10}$$
$$= 1.118 < 1.833$$

Therefore the difference is not significant ; hence it could have arisen because of chance. The hypothesis cannot be rejected. The claim of the operative is tenable.

Problem 6. A sample size of 600 persons selected at random from a large city shows that the percentage of males in the sample is 53. It is believed that the ratio of males to total population in the city is $\frac{1}{2}$. Test whether this belief is confirmed by the observation.

(*B. Com., Calcutta*)

Solution : Let the null hypothesis be that the number of males to total population is ½ or 0.5

The observed value = 0.53

$$\text{S.E.} = \sqrt{\frac{pq}{n}} = \sqrt{\frac{1/2 \times 1/2}{600}} = \sqrt{\frac{1/4}{600}} = \sqrt{\frac{1}{2400}}$$

$$\text{S.E} = \frac{0.53 - 0.5}{S.E.} = \frac{0.53 - 0.5}{\sqrt{0.0004}}$$

$$= \frac{0.53 - 0.5}{0.02} = \frac{0.3}{0.02}$$

$$= \mathbf{1.5}$$

Since Z is less than 1.96, the difference is not significant at 5% level of confidence and could have arisen because of sampling fluctuations. Therefore the null hypothesis cannot be rejected. The belief is confirmed.

Problem 7. A random sample of 500 pineapples were taken from a large consignment and 65 were found to be bad. Show that the standard error of the population of bad ones in a sample of this size is 0.015, and deduce that the percentage of bad pineapples in the consignment almost certainly lies between 8.5 and 17.5. (*B. Com.*)

Solution :

Here

$$p = \frac{65}{300} = 0.13$$

$$q = 1 - 0.13 = 0.87$$

$$\text{S.E.} = \sqrt{\frac{pq}{n}} = \sqrt{\frac{0.13 \times 0.87}{500}}$$

$$= \sqrt{\frac{0.1131}{500}}$$

$$= \sqrt{.000226}$$

$$= 0.015$$

The limits of percentage of bad pineapples in the consignment are :

$$(0.13 \pm 3\,\text{S.E.}) \times 100 = (0.13 \pm 3 \times 0.015)100$$

$$= (0.13 \pm 0.045)\,100$$

$$= (0.13 \pm 4.5) = 17.5 \text{ and } 8.5$$

Note : (*i*) 3 *S.E.* limits are "almost certain".

Problem 8. Out of a consignment of 1,00,000 tennis balls, 400 were selected at random and examined. It was found that 20 of these were defective. How many defective balls you can reasonably expect to have in the whole consignment at 95% confidence level ?

(*Bombay*)

Solution :

Here

$$p = \frac{20}{400} = 0.05$$

$$q = 0.95$$

$$\overline{X} = np = 1,00,000 \times 0.05$$

$$= 5,000$$

$$\text{S.E.} = \sqrt{npq} = \sqrt{1,00,000 \times 0.05 \times 0.95}$$

$$= \sqrt{4750}$$

$$= 68.9$$

95 % confidence limits are

$5,000 \pm 1.96 \times 68.9 = 5,000 \pm 135.044$ or 5135 and 4,865

Problem 9. In a random sample of 1,000 persons from town A, 400 are found to be consumers of wheat. In a sample of 800 from town B, 400 are found to be consumers of wheat. Do these data reveal a significant difference between town A and town B, so far as the proportion of wheat consumers is concerned ? (*M.A., Punjab, Econ., B.Sc. Madurai*)

Solution : We take the hypothesis that the proportion of wheat consumers is concerned, the two towns do not differ.

$$S.E._{(p1-p2)} = \sqrt{pq\left(\frac{1}{n_1} + \frac{1}{n_2}\right)}$$

$$n_1 = 1000 \ p_1 = \frac{400}{1000} = 0.4$$

$$n_2 = 800 \ p_2 = \frac{400}{800} = 0.5$$

$$p = \frac{(1000 \times 0.4) + (800 \times 0.5)}{1000 + 800} = \frac{800}{1800} = \frac{4}{9}$$

$$q = 1 - \frac{4}{9} = \frac{5}{9}$$

$$S.E._{(p1-p2)} = \sqrt{\frac{4}{9} \times \frac{5}{9}\left(\frac{1}{1000} + \frac{1}{800}\right)}$$

$$= \sqrt{\frac{20}{81} \times \frac{9}{4000}} = 0.024$$

$$\frac{p_1 - p_2}{SE} = \frac{0.4 - 0.5}{0.024} = 4.17$$

4.17 is more than 2.58 SE (1% level). Therefore, we say that there is a significant difference between town A and town B, so far as the proportion of wheat consumers is concerned.

Problem 10. In a sample of 500 people from a village in Rajasthan, 280 are found to be rice eaters and the rest wheat eaters, Can we assume that both the food articles are equally popular ? (*M.A., Econ. Madras*)

Solution : We take the hypothesis that the food articles are equally popular.

Then, the expected frequency of wheat eaters and rice eaters are $= \left(\frac{500}{2}\right) = 250.250$

$$S.E. = \sqrt{npq} = \sqrt{500 \times \frac{1}{2} \times \frac{1}{2}} = \mathbf{11.18}$$

Difference between actual and observed = 280−250 = 30

$$\frac{\text{Difference}}{S.E} = \frac{30}{11.18} = \mathbf{2.68}$$

The difference is more than 2.58 S.E at 1% level. It is not because of sampling fluctuations. Therefore, we may assume that both the food articles are not equally popular.

Problem 11. A wholesaler in apples claims that only 4% of the apples supplied by him are defective. A random sample of 600 apples contained 36 defective apples. Test the claim of the wholesaler. *(B.A., Econ., Hons. Delhi)*

Solution :

$$S.E. = \sqrt{\frac{pq}{n}} = \sqrt{\frac{.96 \times .04}{600}} = 0.008$$

$$\begin{aligned} \text{95\% Confidence limit} &= \overline{X} \pm 1.96\,SE \\ &= .96 \pm 1.96\,(0.008) \\ &= .96 \pm 0.01568 \\ &= .94432 \text{ to } .97568 \end{aligned}$$

Out of 600 apples, good apples may be between .94432×600 = 566.59 to .97568×600 = 585.4 or 567 to 585.

Therefore the number of defective is expected between 15 to 33 apples. His claim is that 4% of apples are defective. But actual number is 36 defectives. Hence his claim cannot be accepted.

Problem 12. An examination was given to 50 students at college A and to 60 students at college B. At A, the mean grade was 75 with a standard deviation of 9. At B, the mean grade was 79 with a standard deviation of 7. Is there a significant difference between the performance of the students at A and those at B. given that $\alpha = 0.05$? $\alpha = 0.01$? *(M. Com., Delhi)*

Solution : Let us take the hypothesis that there is no difference in the grades obtained by students of college A and college B.

$$\begin{aligned} S.E. = (\overline{x_1} - \overline{x_2}) &= \sqrt{\frac{\sigma_1^2}{n_1} + \frac{\sigma_2^2}{n_2}} \\ n_1 = 50,\ n_2 &= 60,\ \sigma_1 = 9\,\sigma_2 = 7 \\ &= \sqrt{\frac{(9)^2 + (7)^2}{(50) + (60)}} \\ &= \sqrt{\frac{81}{50} + \frac{49}{60}} \\ &= \sqrt{1.62 + 0.817} = 1.56 \\ \frac{\text{Difference}}{SE} &= \frac{75 - 79}{1.56} = \frac{4}{1.56} = \mathbf{2.56} \end{aligned}$$

2.56 > 1.96 S.E. at 5% level of significance, therefore, we reject our hypothesis. But it is less than 2.58 SE at 1% level, it may be accepted.

Problem 13. in a random sample of 500 persons from Maharashtra, 200 are found to be consumers of vegetable oil. In another sampler of 400 persons from Gujarat, 200 are found to be consumers of vegetable oil. Discuss whether the data reveal a significant difference between Maharashtra and Gujarat so far as the proportion of vegetable oil consumers is concerned. *(B.A., Bombay; M. Com., Jodhpur, Meerut)*

Solution : Let the hypothesis be that there is no difference between Maharashtra and Gujarat so far as the proportion of vegetable oil consumers is concerned. *i.e.*, $p_1 = p_2$

$$S.E.(p_1 - p_2) = \sqrt{pq\left(\frac{1}{n_1} + \frac{1}{n_2}\right)}$$

$$p = \frac{n_1 p_1 + n_2 p_2}{n_1 + n_2}$$

$$p_1 = \frac{200}{500} = 0.4$$

$$p_2 = \frac{200}{400} = 0.5$$

$$p = \frac{(500 \times 0.4) + (400 \times 0.5)}{500 + 400} = \frac{4}{9}$$

$$q = 1 - \frac{4}{9} = \frac{5}{9}$$

$$S.E.(p_1 - p_2) = \sqrt{\frac{4}{9} \times \frac{5}{9}\left(\frac{1}{500} + \frac{1}{400}\right)}$$

$$= \sqrt{\frac{20}{81} \times \frac{9}{2000}} = \sqrt{\frac{1}{900}} = 0.033$$

$$p_1 - p_2 = 0.4 - 0.5 = 0.1$$

$$\frac{\text{Difference}}{S.E} = \frac{0.1}{.033} = 3.03$$

3.03 > 2.58 SE at 1% level of significance. Hence our hypothesis is rejected. Therefore, there is a significant difference between Maharashtra and Gujarat so far as the proportion of vegetable oil consumers is concerned.

Problem 14. A sample of 1000 students from Bombay University was taken and their average weight was found to be 112 pounds with a standard deviation of 20 pounds. Could the mean weight of students in the population be 120 pounds ?

(*M.A., Econ. Kurukshetra*)

Solution : The hypothesis is that there is no significant difference between the sample mean and population mean

$$S.E.(\overline{x}) = \frac{\sigma}{\sqrt{n}} = \frac{20}{\sqrt{1000}} = \frac{20}{31.623} = 0.632$$

$$\frac{\text{Difference}}{S.E} = \frac{120 - 112}{0.632} = 12.66$$

12.66 > 2.51 SE, 1% level of significance, therefore the mean weight of the students in the population could not be 120 lbs.

Problem 15. Out of 20,000 customers' ledger accounts, a sample of 600 was taken to test the accuracy of posting and balancing and 45 mistakes were found. Assign Limits within which the number of defective cases can be expected at 5% level. (*C.A.*,)

Solution :

$$p = \frac{45}{600} = 0.075$$

$$= 1 - 0.075 = 0.925$$

$$S.E. = \sqrt{\frac{pq}{n}}$$

$$= \sqrt{\frac{0.075 \times 0.925}{600}} = 0.0107\,(0.011)$$

95% confidence limits

$$p \pm 1.96 \text{ SE}$$
$$0.075 \pm 1.96\ (0.011)$$
$$0.075 \pm 0.022$$
$$0.053 \text{ and } 0.097 (5.3\% \text{ and } 9.7\%)$$

Therefore, at 5% level of significance, it is expected that the number of mistakes would vary between 5.3% and 9.7%.

Problem 16. Two groups consisting of 400 and 500 persons have mean height 68.5 inches and 66.1 inches and variances 6.4 and 6.0 respectively. Examine whether the difference in means is significant. *(B.A., Madras)*

Solution : Let the hypothesis be that there is no difference in the mean heights of the two groups

$$S.E.\ (\overline{x_1} - \overline{x_2}) = \sqrt{\frac{\sigma_1^2}{n_1} + \frac{\sigma_2^2}{n_2}}$$

$$\sigma_1^2 = 6.4 : n_1 = 400 : \sigma_2^2 = 6.0\,; n_2 = 500$$

$$S.E.\ (\overline{x_1} - \overline{x_2}) = \sqrt{\frac{6.4}{400} + \frac{6.0}{500}}$$
$$= \sqrt{0.016 + 0.012}$$
$$= \sqrt{0.028}$$
$$= 0.17$$
$$\overline{X_1} - \overline{X_2} = 68.5 - 66.1$$
$$= 2.4$$
$$\frac{\text{Difference}}{S.E} = \frac{2.4}{0.17}$$
$$= 14.12$$

14.12 > 2.58 *SE* at 1% level, we reject our hypothesis. Therefore, there is significant difference between the mean heights of the two groups.

Problem 17. A random sample of 1000 mill workers at Kanpur showed their mean wages to be Rs. 47 per month a standard deviation of Rs. 28. A sample of 1500 mill workers in Bombay showed their mean wages to be Rs. 49 per month with a standard deviation of Rs. 40. On the basis of these data would you say that the mean wages of mill workers in Bombay are higher than those at Kanpur ? *(M.A., Econ., Lucknow)*

Solution: Let us take the hypothesis that there is no difference in the mean wage of workers of two mills.

$$S.E.(\overline{X_1} - \overline{X_2}) = \sqrt{\frac{\sigma_1^2}{n_1} + \frac{\sigma_2^2}{n_2}}$$

$$\sigma_1 = 28\,; n_1 = 1000\,; \sigma_2 = 40\,; n_1 = 1500$$

$$S.E.(\overline{X_1} - \overline{X_2}) = \sqrt{\frac{(28)^2}{1000} + \frac{(40)^2}{1500}}$$
$$= \sqrt{\frac{784}{1000} + \frac{1600}{1500}}$$

$$= \sqrt{0.784 + 1.07}$$
$$= \sqrt{1.854}$$
$$= 1.36$$
$$\overline{X_1} - \overline{X_2} = 47 - 49 = 2$$
$$\frac{\text{Difference}}{S.E} = \frac{2}{1.36} = \mathbf{1.47}$$

1.47 < 1.96 SE at 5 % level, we accept the hypothesis.

Problem 18. A random sample of 1000 farms in a certain year gives an average yield of wheat 2000 lbs. per acre, with a S.D. of 192 lbs. A random sample of 1000 farms in the following year gives an average yield of 2100 lbs with a S.D. of 224 lbs. Can it be concluded that there is a significant difference in the mean yields.

Solution: Let us take the hypothesis that the mean yields do not differ significantly.

$$\text{S.E.}\,(\overline{X_1} - \overline{X_2}) = \sqrt{\frac{\sigma_1^2}{n_1} + \frac{\sigma_2^2}{n_2}}$$
$$\sigma_1 = 192\,;\ n_1 = 1000\,;\ \sigma_2 = 224\,;\ n_2 = 1000$$
$$\text{S.E.}\,(\overline{X_1} - \overline{X_2}) = \sqrt{\frac{(192)^2}{1000} + \frac{(224)^2}{1000}}$$
$$= \sqrt{\frac{36864}{1000} + \frac{50176}{1000}}$$
$$= \sqrt{36.864 + 50.176}$$
$$= \sqrt{87.04}$$
$$= 9.33$$
$$\overline{X_1} - \overline{X_2} = 2000 - 2100 = 100$$
$$\frac{\text{Difference}}{S.E} = \frac{100}{9.33} = \mathbf{10.72}.$$

10.72 > 2.58 S.E. at 1% level, there is significant difference in the mean yields.

Problem 19. From the data given below compute the standard error of the difference of the two sample means and find out if the two means significantly differ at a critical probability of 5 %

	Number of items	*Mean*	*Standard Deviation*
Sample B	36	181.5	3.0
Sample A	25	179.0	3.6

(*M.A. Econ., Gorakhpur*)

Solution: Hypothesis—no difference between the means.

$$\text{S.E.}\,(\overline{X}_1 - \overline{X}_2) = \sqrt{\frac{\sigma_1^2}{n_1} + \frac{\sigma_2^2}{n_2}}$$
$$\sigma_1 = 3\,;\ n_1 = 36\,;\ \sigma_2 = 3.6\,;\ n_2 = 25$$
$$\text{S.E.}\,(\overline{X}_1 - \overline{X}_2) = \sqrt{\frac{(3)^2}{36} + \frac{(3.6)^2}{25}}$$
$$= \sqrt{\frac{9}{36} + \frac{12.96}{25}}$$

$$= \sqrt{0.25 + 0.52}$$
$$= \sqrt{0.77}$$
$$= 0.88.$$
$$\overline{X}_1 - \overline{X}_2 = 181.5 - 179.0 = 2.5.$$
$$\frac{\text{Difference}}{S.E} = \frac{2.5}{0.88} = 2.84.$$

2.84 > 1.96 S.E. at 5 % level, the two groups differ significantly.

Problem 20. A large sample of 1089 members is found to have mean of 3.60 cm. Could it be regarded as a simple sample from a huge population whose mean is 3.90 cm. and standard deviation 2.60. cm. (*M.A. Econ., Gorakhpur*)

Solution : Let the hypothesis be that the sample came from population whose mean is 3.9 cm.

$$\text{S.E. } (\overline{X}) = \frac{\sigma}{\sqrt{n}}$$
$$\sigma = 2.6\,;\ n = 1,089$$
$$\text{S.E. } (\overline{X}) = \frac{2.6}{\sqrt{1,089}}$$
$$= \frac{2.6}{33}$$
$$= \mathbf{0.079}.$$
$$\text{Difference between } \overline{X} \text{ and } \mu = 3.60 - 3.90.$$
$$= \mathbf{0.3}.$$
$$\frac{\text{Difference}}{S.E} = \frac{0.3}{0.079}$$
$$= \mathbf{3.8}.$$

3.8 > 2.58 S.E. at 10 % level, we conclude that the sample does not come from a population with mean 3.9 and standard deviation 2.6 cm.

Problem 21. A random sample of 200 measurement from an infinite population gave a mean value of 50 and a standard deviation of 9. Determine the 95 percent confidence interval for the mean value of the population. (The limits given population ±1.96 standard deviation units include 75 percent of the measurements of a normally distributed variable). (*M. Com., Rajasthan*)

Solution :

$$S.E.(\overline{X}) = \frac{\sigma}{\sqrt{n}}$$
$$\sigma = 9\,;\ n = 200$$
$$S.E.(\overline{X}) = \frac{9}{\sqrt{200}}$$
$$= \frac{9}{14.24}$$
$$= 0.64.$$

95% Confidence interval

$$\overline{X} \pm 1.96\, S.E.$$
$$50 \pm 1.96\, S.E.$$
$$50 \pm 1.96\,(0.64)$$
$$50 \pm 1.25$$

48.75 and **51.25**

Problem 22. A company manufacturing electric light bulbs claims that the average life of its bulbs is 1600 hours. The average life and standard deviation of a random sample of 100 such bulbs were 1570 hours and 120 hours respectively. Should we accept the claim of the company ? *(B.A. Hons. Econ., Delhi)*

Solution: Let us take the hypothesis that there is no significant difference between sample mean and population mean.

$$\text{S.E. }(\overline{X}) = \frac{\sigma}{\sqrt{n}} = \frac{120}{\sqrt{100}} = 12$$

$$\frac{\text{Difference}}{S.E.(x)} = \frac{1600 - 1570}{12} = \frac{30}{12} = 2.5$$

2.5 > 1.96 S.E. at 5 % level of significance, the hypothesis can not be accepted. We can not accept the claim of the company.

Problem 23. It is claimed that a random sample of 100 tyres with a mean life of 15,269 km. is drawn from a population of tyres which has a mean life of 15,200 km. and standard deviation of 1,248 km. Test the validity of this claim. *(B.A., Hons. Econ., Delhi)*

Solution : A sample drawn from a population of tyres which has a mean life of 15,200 km. and σ=1248 km.

$$\overline{X} = 15,269\,;\ n = 100\,;\ \mu = 15,200\,;\ \sigma = 1,248$$

Substituting the values in the formula :

$$Z = \frac{\overline{X}-\mu}{\frac{\sigma}{\sqrt{n}}} = \frac{15,269 - 15200}{1248/\sqrt{100}} = \frac{69}{124.8} = \mathbf{0.55}.$$

Calculated value of $Z = 0.55 < 1.96$ (table value) at 5 % level of significance. Hence we accept the validity of claim.

Problem 24. Calculate standard error of mean from the following data, showing the amount paid by 100 firms in Calcutta on the occasion of Durga Puja :

Mid-value	:	39	49	59	69	79	89	99
No. of firms	:	2	3	11	20	32	25	7

(M.B.A., Rohtak)

Solution :

$$\text{S.E }\overline{X} = \frac{\sigma}{\sqrt{n}}$$

Computation of Standard Deviation

Mid value m	*f*	$d' \frac{m-69}{10}$	fd'	fd'^2
39	2	−3	−6	18
49	3	−2	−6	12
59	11	−1	−11	11
69	20	0	0	0
79	32	1	32	32
89	25	2	50	100
99	7	3	21	63
	$N = 100$		$\Sigma fd' = 80$	$\Sigma fd'^2 = 236$

$$\sigma = \sqrt{\frac{fd'^2}{N} - \left(\frac{\Sigma fd'}{N}\right)^2} \times C$$

$$= \sqrt{\frac{236}{100} - \left(\frac{80}{100}\right)^2} \times 10$$

$$= \sqrt{2.36 - 0.64} \times 10$$

$$= \sqrt{1.72} \times 10$$

$$= 1.131. \times 10$$

$$= \mathbf{13.11.}$$

$$\text{S.E. } \overline{X} = \frac{13.11}{\sqrt{100}}$$

$$= \frac{13.11}{10}$$

$$= \mathbf{1.311.}$$

Problem 25. Ten specimens of copper wires drawn from a large lot have the following breaking strength (in kg. Wt.)

578 572 570 568 572 578 570 572 596 584

Test whether the mean breaking strength of the lot may be taken to be 578 kg. wt.

(*B.A., Bombay*)

Solution : Hypothesis is that $\mu = 578$ kg. wt.

$$t = \frac{\overline{X} - \mu}{\sigma}\sqrt{n}$$

Computation of Mean and Standard Deviation

X	$(X - \overline{X})\overline{X} = 576$	$(X - \overline{X})^2$
578	+2	4
572	−4	16
570	−6	36
568	−8	64
572	−4	16
578	+2	4
570	−6	36
572	−4	16
596	+20	400
584	+8	64
$\Sigma X = 5760$		$\Sigma(X - \overline{X})^2 = 656$

$$\overline{X} = \frac{5760}{10} = 576$$

$$S. = \sqrt{\frac{\Sigma(X - \overline{X})^2}{n - 1}}$$

$$= \sqrt{\frac{656}{10 - 1}} = \sqrt{\frac{656}{9}} = \sqrt{72.89}$$

$$= 8.54$$

$$t = \frac{576 - 578}{8.54}\sqrt{10} = \frac{2}{8.54} \times 3.16$$

$$= \mathbf{0.74}.$$

$$df = 9 t_{0.05} = 2.26.$$

Table value is more than the calculated value. Therefore the hypothesis is accepted.

Problem 26. A random sample of size 16 has 53 as mean. The sum of the squares of the deviations taken from mean is 150. Can this sample be regarded as taken from the population having 56 as mean ? Obtain 95% and 99 % confidence limits of the mean of the population . (For v = 15, $t_{0.01}$= 2.95 and $t_{0.05}$= 2.13). (*B. Com., Gujarat*)

Solution :

$$t = \frac{\overline{X} - \mu}{\sigma}\sqrt{n}$$

$$\overline{X} = 53, \mu = 56, n = 16$$

$$S = \sqrt{\frac{\Sigma(X - \overline{X})^2}{n - 1}} = \sqrt{\frac{150}{15}} = \sqrt{10}$$

$$= \mathbf{3.16}$$

$$t = \frac{53 - 56}{3.16}\sqrt{16}$$

$$= \frac{3 \times 4}{3.16} = 3.79$$

$$df = 16 - 1 = 15$$

For $df = 15 t_{0.01} = 2.95.$

Calculated value i.e. 3.79 > 2.95, therefore the hypothesis is not supported. This sample cannot be regarded as taken from the population having 56 as mean.

95% confidence limit of the population mean

$$\overline{X} \pm \frac{S}{\sqrt{n}} t_{0.05}$$

$$= 53 \pm \frac{3.16}{4} \times 2.13$$

$$= 53 \pm 1.683$$

$$= 51.317 \text{ and } 54.683$$

99% confidence limit

$$\overline{X} \pm \frac{S}{\sqrt{n}} t_{0.01}$$

$$= 53 \pm \frac{3.16}{4} \times 2.95$$

$$= 53 \pm 2.33$$

$$= 50.67 \text{ and } 55.33.$$

Problem 27. The following results are obtained from a sample of 10 boxes of biscuits.

Mean weight of contents = 490 gms.

S.D. of the weight = 9 gm.

Could the sample come from a population having a mean of 500 gm.

(*M. Com., Rajasthan*)

Solution :

Let us take the hypothesis that μ=500 gm.

$$t = \frac{\overline{X} - \mu}{\sigma}\sqrt{n}$$

$$\overline{X} = 490;\ \mu = 500;\ \sigma = 9;\ n = 10$$

$$t = \frac{490 - 500}{9}\sqrt{10}$$

$$df = 10 - 1 = 9$$

$$= \frac{10}{9} \times 3.16$$

$$= \frac{31.6}{9}$$

$$= 3.51$$

$$df = 9, t_{0.01} = 3.25$$

3.51 > 3.25, our hypothesis is rejected.

Problem 28. A random sample of 27 pairs of observations from a bivariate normal population gave a coefficient of correlation 0.40. Is this value significant of correlation in the population ? *(B.A., Bombay)*

Solution : Let the hypothesis be that variables have $r = 0$

$$t = \frac{r - 0}{\sqrt{1 - r^2}} \times \sqrt{n - 2}$$

$$r = 0.40;\ n = 27$$

$$t = \frac{0.40}{\sqrt{1 - (0.4)^2}} \times \sqrt{27 - 2}$$

$$= \frac{0.4}{\sqrt{0.84}} \times \sqrt{25} = \frac{0.4 \times 5}{0.92}$$

$$= \mathbf{2.17}$$

Which is greater than 2.05 at $t_{0.05}$. Hence the hypothesis is rejected.

Problem 29. A random sample of 18 pairs of observations from a normal population gives a correlation coefficient of 0.52. Is it likely that the variables in the population are uncorrelated ? *(B.A., Poona)*

Solution : Let the hypothesis be that variables have $r = 0$

$$t = \frac{r - 0}{\sqrt{1 - r^2}} \times \sqrt{n - 2}$$

$$= \frac{r\sqrt{n - 2}}{\sqrt{1 - r^2}}$$

$$r = 0.52;\ n = 18$$

$$t = \frac{0.52\sqrt{18 - 2}}{\sqrt{1 - (0.52)^2}}$$

$$= \frac{0.52 \times \sqrt{16}}{\sqrt{1 - 0.2704}}$$

$$= \frac{0.52 \times 4}{\sqrt{0.7296}}$$

$$= \frac{2.08}{0.854}$$

$$= \mathbf{2.44.}$$

Which is less than the table value (2.58). Hence the hypothesis be accepted.

15

CHI SQUARE TEST

$$X^2 = \frac{\Sigma(0-E)^2}{E} \qquad O = \text{observed value}$$

E = Expected value

$V = n - k$ $\qquad V$ = (nu) degree of freedom

n = No. of frequency classes

k = No. of independent constraints.

V for a contingency table

$$V = (r-1)(c-1)$$

r = No. of rows

c = No. of columns.

Problem 1. Out of a sample of 120 persons in a village, 76 were administered a new drug for preventing influenza and out of them 24 persons were attacked by influenza. Out of those who were not administered the new drug, 12 persons were not affected by influenza, (a) Prepare 2×2 tables showing the actual and expected frequencies, (b) Use Chi-square test for finding out whether the new drug is effective or not.

(At 5 % level for one degree of freedom, the value of chi square is 3.84)

(CA)

Solution :

2×2 table

	A	α	
B	24	32	56(B)
β	52	12	64
	76 (A)	44	120 N

Let the influenza and new drug be independent. The expected frequencies are :

$\frac{76 \times 56}{120} = 35.5$	$\frac{56 \times 44}{120} = 20.5$	56
$\frac{76 \times 64}{120} = 40.5$	$\frac{64 \times 44}{120} = 23.5$	64
76	44	120

O	E	$O - E$	$(O - E)^2$	$\frac{(O - E)^2}{E}$
24	35.5	−11.5	132.25	3.725
52	40.5	11.5	132.25	3.265
32	20.5	11.5	132.25	6.451
12	23.5	−11.5	132.25	5.628
				$\Sigma\frac{(O - E)^2}{E} = 19.069$

$d.f=$ (2-1) (2-1) =1 ; $X^2 0.05$ for $5 d.f = 3.84$.

Calculated value of X^2 is 19.069 which is much higher than the table value. Therefore the hypothesis is rejected. Hence we conclude that the drug is undoubtedly effective in controlling the influenza.

Problem 2. The following data relate to the sales in a time of trade depression of a certain commodity demand :

Districts where Sales are	*District not hit by depression*	*Districts hit by depression*	*Total*
Satisfactory	250	80	330
Not satisfactory	140	30	170
Total	390	110	500

Do these data suggest that the sales are significantly affected by depression ?

(*B.Com. Karnataka*)

Solution : Let the hypothesis be that the sales are not significantly affected by depression.

Expectation of (AB) $\frac{A \times B}{N} = \frac{390 \times 330}{500} = 257.4$

The table of expected frequencies is

257.4	72.6	330
132.6	37.4	170
390	110	500

When applying X^2 test

O	E	$O - E$	$(O - E)^2$	$\frac{(O - E)^2}{E}$
250	257.4	−7.4	54.76	0.213
140	132.6	+7.4	54.76	0.413
80	72.6	+7.4	54.76	0.754
30	37.4	−7.4	54.76	1.464
				$\Sigma\frac{(O - E)^2}{E} = 2.844$

$$\begin{aligned} X^2 &= 2.844 \\ \nu &= (r-1)(C-1) \\ &= (2-1)(2-1) \\ &= 1 \end{aligned}$$

The calculated value 2.844 is less than the table value 3.841. Hence the hypothesis may be accepted. Thus we conclude that sales are not significantly affected by depression.

Problem 3. A tobacco company claims that there is no relationship between smoking and lung ailments. To investigate the claims random sample of 300 males in the age group of 40 to 50 is given medical test. The observed sample results are tabulated below :

	Lung ailment	*No lung ailment*	*Total*
Smokers	75	105	180
Non-smokers	25	95	120
Total	100	200	300

On the basis of this information, can it be concluded that smoking and lung ailments are independent ?

(At 5% level of significance the value of $X^2 = 3.841$ for 1 $d.f.$)

(*M. Com. Kurukshetra*)

Solution : Let us take the hypothesis that the smoking and lung ailment are not associated

Expectation of $(AB) = \frac{180}{300} \times 100 = 60$

The table of expected frequencies is :

60	120	180
40	80	120
100	200	300

When applying X^2 test :

O	E	$O - E$	$(O - E)^2$	$\frac{(O-E)^2}{E}$
75	60	15	225	3.750
25	40	−15	225	5.625
105	120	−15	225	1.875
95	80	15	225	2.813
				$\Sigma\frac{(O-E)^2}{E} = 14.063$

$$\begin{aligned} X^2 &= 14.063 \\ \nu &= (r-1)(c-1) = (2-1)(2-1) \\ &= 1 \end{aligned}$$

The table value of X^2 for 1 $d.\ f$ at 5 % level of significance is 3.841. The calculated value of X^2 is 14.063 which is more than the table value. Hence the hypothesis may be rejected. Thus we conclude that smoking and lung ailments are not independent *i.e.* they are associated attributes.

Problem 4. A dice is tossed 120 times with the following results :

No. turned up	1	2	3	4	5	6	Total
Frequency	30	25	18	10	22	15	120

Solution : Test the hypothesis that the dice is unbiased. (*M. Com. Delhi*)

The hypothesis is that the dice is an unbiased one. The expected frequency is $[120 \times 1/6] = 20$. Applying the X^2 test.

O	E	$O-E$	$(O-E)^2$	$\frac{(O-E)^2}{E}$
30	20	10	100	5.00
25	20	5	25	1.25
18	20	−2	4	0.20
10	20	−10	100	5.00
22	20	2	4	0.20
15	20	−5	25	1.25
			$\Sigma\frac{O-E)^2}{E} =$	12.90

$$d.f = n - 1 = 6 - 1 = 5$$

For 5 $d.f.$ at 5% level of significance, on the basis of table value is 11.07 which is less than the calculated value of $X^2 = 12.90$. Therefore the hypothesis which is an unbiased one, is rejected at 5% level of significance.

Problem 5. In a certain sample of 2,000 families, 1,400 families are consumers of tea. Out of 1,800 Hindu families, 1,236 families consume tea. Use Chi square test and state whether there is any significant difference between consumption of tea among Hindu and Non-Hindu families. (*CA*)

Solution : On tabulation of the information in a 2 × 2 contingency table we get :

	Hindu	*Non-Hindu*	*Total*
Consuming tea	1236	164	1400
Not consuming tea	564	36	600
Total	1800	200	2000

Hypothesis—The attributes are independent. On the basis of the independent, the expected frequencies are :

$\frac{1800 \times 1400}{2000}$ = 1260	1400—1260 = 140	1400
1,800—1260 =540	200—140 (600—540) = 60	600
1800	200	2,000

Calculation of X^2

O	E	$O-E$	$(O-E)^2$	$\frac{(O-E)^2}{E}$
1236	1260	−24	576	0.457
564	540	24	576	1.067
164	140	24	576	4.114
36	60	−24	576	9.600
				$\Sigma\frac{(O-E)^2}{E} = 15.238$

$d.f.$ is 1, Table value of X^2 0.05 for 1 $d.f = 3.841$.

The calculated value of X^2 15.238 is higher than the table value *i.e.* 3.841 ; therefore the null hypothesis is rejected.

Hence, the two communities differ significantly as far as consumption of tea is concerned.

Problem 6. 4 coins were tossed 160 times and the following results were obtained :

No. of heads	0	1	2	3	4
Observed frequencies	17	52	54	31	6

Under the assumption that coins are balanced, find the expected frequencies of getting 0, 1, 2, 3 or 4 heads and test the goodness of fit. (*M. Com. Delhi*)

Solution : Hypothesis is that the coins are unbiased.

X	*Expected frequency* $160^4\, C_z\, (.5)^4 = E$
0	$160 \times 4C_0(.5)^4 = 10$
1	$160 \times 4C_1(.5)^4 = 40$
2	$160 \times 4C_2(.5)^4 = 60$
3	$160 \times 4C_3(.5)^4 = 40$
4	$160 \times 4C_4(.5)^4 = 10$

When applying X^2

No. of heads	O	E	$O-E$	$(O-E)^2$	$(O-E)^2/E$
0	17	10	7	49	4.900
1	52	40	12	144	3.600
2	54	60	−6	36	0.600
3	31	40	−9	81	2.025
4	6	10	−4	16	1.600
					$\Sigma\frac{(O-E)^2}{E} = 12.725$

$d.f. = 5-1=4$; $X^2 0.05 = 9.488$

Calculated value of X^2 is 12.725 which is greater than the tabled value 9.488. Therefore, the fit is poor.

Problem 7. A survey of 200 families having three children selected at random gave the following results :

Male births	0	1	2	3
No. of families	40	58	62	40

Test the hypothesis that male and female births are equally likely at 5% level of significance. (*M. Com. Delhi*)

Solution :

Let the hypothesis be that the male and female births are equally likely.

Male births	O	E	$O—E$	$(O—E)^2$	$\frac{(O-E)^2}{E}$
0	40	50	−10	100	2.00
1	58	50	8	64	1.28
2	62	50	12	144	2.88
3	40	50	−10	100	2.00
					$\Sigma\frac{(O-E)^2}{E} = 8.16$

$$X^2 = 8.16, \quad \nu = 4 - 1 = 3$$

$$\nu = 3, X^2_{0.05} = 7.82$$

The calculated value of x^2 is 8.16. which is greater than the table value 7.82. Hence the hypothesis may be rejected. Thus we conclude that the male and female births are not equally likely at 5% level of significance.

Problem 8. From the adult male population of seven large cities random sample giving 2×7 contingency table of married and unmarried men, as given below were taken. Can it be said that there is a significant variation among the cities in the tendency of men to marry ?

City	*A*	*B*	*C*	*D*	*E*	*F*	*G*	*Total*
Married	133	164	155	106	153	123	146	980
Unmarried	36	57	40	37	55	33	36	294
Total	169	221	195	143	208	156	182	1274

(At (2-1) (7-1) d.f. take $X^2_{0.05}$= 12.6) (*B. Com., Gujarat, M. A. Punjab*)

Solution : Let us take the hypothesis that there is no significant variation among the cities in the tendency of men to marry.

$$\text{Expected number of married people in City } A = \frac{980}{1274} \times 169 = 130$$

$$\text{Expected number of married people in City } B = \frac{980}{1274} \times 221 = 170$$

$$\text{Expected number of married people in City } C = \frac{980}{1274} \times 195 = 150$$

$$\text{Expected number of married people in City } D = \frac{980}{1274} \times 143 = 110$$

$$\text{Expected number of married people in City } E = \frac{980}{1274} \times 208 = 160$$

$$\text{Expected number of married people in City } F = \frac{980}{1274} \times 156 = 120$$

$$\text{Expected number of married people in City } G = \frac{980}{1274} \times 182 = 140$$

The expected frequencies are :

130	170	150	110	160	120	140
39	51	45	33	48	36	42
169	221	195	143	208	156	182

When applying X^2test

0	E	$(O-E)$	$(O-E)^2$	$\Sigma\frac{(0-E)^2}{E}$
133	130	3	9	0.069
164	170	−6	36	0.212
155	150	5	25	0.167
106	110	−4	16	0.145
153	160	−7	49	0.306
123	120	3	9	0.075
146	140	6	36	0.257
36	39	−3	9	0.231
57	51	6	36	0.706
40	45	−5	25	0.556
37	33	4	16	0.485
55	48	7	49	1.021
33	36	−3	9	0.250
36	42	−6	36	0.857
				$\Sigma\frac{(0-E)^2}{E} = 5.337$

$$X^2 = \mathbf{5.337}$$
$$d.f = (2-1)(7-1)$$
$$= 6,\ x^2_{0.05}$$
$$= 12.6$$

The calculated value of $X^2 = 5.337$ which is less than the table value $= 12.6$. Hence the hypothesis may be accepted. Thus we conclude that there is no significant variation among the cities in the tendency of men to marry.

Problem 9. A survey of 320 families with 5 children each revealed the follwing distribution.

No. of boys	5	4	5	2	1	0
No. of girls	0	1	2	3	4	5
No. of families	14	56	110	88	40	12

Is the result consistent with the hypothesis that male and female births are equally probable ? You may use the following table giving the values of chi-square.

Solution: Let us take hypothesis that male and female births are equally probable. The expected number of families of are calculated below.

$$320\left(\frac{1}{2}+\frac{1}{2}\right)^5 = 320\left(\frac{1}{32}, \frac{5}{32}, \frac{10}{32}, \frac{10}{32}, \frac{5}{32}, \frac{1}{32}\right)$$
$$= 10,\ 50,\ 100,\ 100,\ 50,\ 10$$

When applying x^2 test

O	E	$O-E$	$(O-E)^3$	$\frac{(O-E)^2}{E}$
14	10	4	16	1.60
56	50	6	36	0.72
110	100	10	100	1.00
88	100	−12	144	1.44
40	50	−10	100	2.00
12	10	2	4	0.40
				$\Sigma\frac{(O-E)^2}{E} = 7.16$

$$x^2 = 7.16$$
$$d.f = 6 - 1 = 5$$
$$d.f \text{ or } \nu = 5,\ x^2_{0.05} = \mathbf{11.07}$$

The calculated value of $x^2 = 7.16$ which is less than the table value 11.07. Hence the hypothesis may be accepted. Thus we conclude that the results show that male and female births are equally probable.

Problem 10. From the data given below about the treatment of 500 patients suffering from a disease state whether the new treatment is superior to the conventional treatment.

	No. of patients		
	Favourable	*Not favourable*	*Total*
New	280	60	340
Conventional	120	40	160
Total	400	100	500

(Given for $V = 1$, $X^2_{0.05} = 3.84$) *(M. Com. Himachal)*

Solution : Hypothesis—No difference between new and the conventional treatment.

$$\text{Expectation of } (AB) = \frac{(A)\times(B)}{N} = \frac{340 \times 400}{500} = 272$$

The table of expected frequencies is :

272	68	340
128	32	160
400	100	500

When applying x^2 test

O	E	$(O-E)$	$(O-E)^2$	$\frac{(O-E)^2}{E}$
280	272	8	64	0.235
120	128	−8	64	0.500
60	68	−8	64	0.941
40	32	8	64	2.000
				$\Sigma\frac{(0-E)^2}{E} = 3.676$

$$\Sigma \frac{(0-E)^2}{E} = 3.676$$

$$\nu = (r—1)(c—1)$$
$$= (2—1)(2—1)$$
$$= 1$$
$$\nu = 1,\ X^2_{00.5} = 3.84.$$

The calculated value of X^2 is 3.676, which is less than the table value = 3.84. Hence the hypothesis may be accepted. Thus we conclude that there is no significant difference between the new and conventional treatment.

Problem 11. 200 digits were selected at random from a set of tables. The frequencies of the digits were :

Digit	:	0	1	2	3	4	5	6	7	8	9
f	:	18	19	23	21	16	25	22	20	21	15

Use the X^2 test to assess the correctness of the hypothesis that the digits were distributed in equal numbers in the tables from which these were chosen. *(B. Com., Bombay)*

Solution :

Hypothesis is that the digits were distributed in equal numbers in the tables. Then the expected frequency of each digit is 20 *i.e.* $\frac{200}{10}$.

Digits	*Frequency*		$O-E$	$(O-E)^2$	$\frac{(O-E)^2}{E}$
	O	*E*			
0	18	20	−2	4	0.2
1	19	20	−1	1	0.05
2	23	20	3	9	0.45
3	21	20	1	1	0.05
4	16	20	−4	16	0.8
5	25	20	5	25	1.25
6	22	20	2	4	0.2
7	20	20	0	0	0
8	21	20	1	1	0.05
9	15	20	−5	25	1.25
	200	200			$X^2 = 4.30$

$$\text{D.}f = 10–1 = 9$$

Decision : The computed value of x^2 = 4.3. At 0.05 level, the critical value of x^2 is 16.919. Since the computed value is less, our hypothesis may be accepted. Therefore, we conclude that the digits were distributed equally.

Problem 12. A certain drug was administered to 456 males, out of a total 720 in a certain locality, to test its efficacy against typhoid. The incidence of typhoid is shown below. Find out the effectiveness of the drug against the disease. (The table value of chi square for 1 d.f. at 5 % level of significance is 3.84).

	Infection	*No. Infection*	*Total*
Administering the drug	144	312	456
Without administering The drug	192	72	264
Total	336	384	720

(*M.B.A. Delhi*)

Solution :

2×2 Contingency Table

	Infection	*No infection*	*Total*
Administration of drug	144	312	456
No administration of drug	192	72	264
	336	384	720

Hypothesis. The drug is independent; not effective on the basis of the independent, the expected frequencies are :

$\frac{336 \times 456}{720} = 212.8$	243.2	456
123.2	140.8	264
336	384	720

O	E	$(O-E)^2$	$(O-E)^2$	$\frac{(O-E)^2}{E}$
144	212.8	−68.8	4733.44	22.24
192	123.2	+68.8	4733.44	38.42
312	243.2	+68.8	4733.44	19.46
72	140.8	−68.8	4733.44	33.62

$$\Sigma\frac{(0-E)^2}{E} = 113.74$$

Computed value of $x^2 = 113.74$ which is much greater than the table value of $x^2_{0.05}$ at 1 $d.f.$ = 3.841. Therefore, it is highly significant. The unit hypothesis is wrong. Therefore, the drug is definitely effective in controlling the typhoid.

Problem 13. From the following information, state whether the two attributes, *i.e.* condition of house and condition of child are independent.

Condition of child	*Condition of house*	
	Clean	Dirty
Clean	69	51
Fairly clean	81	20
Dirty	35	44

(*B. Com. Bombay*)

Solution : We take the hypothesis that the two attributes are independent. On this basis the expected frequencies are :

Condition of child	*Condition of House*		
	Clean	*Dirty*	*Total*
Clean	(*A*) 74	(α) 46	120
Fairly clean	(*B*) 62.28	(β) 38.72	101
Dirty	(*C*) 48.72	(Υ) 30.28	79
Total	185	115	300

$$E \text{ of } (A) = \frac{120 \times 185}{300} = 74$$

$$E \text{ of } (B) = \frac{101 \times 185}{300} = 62.28$$

$$E \text{ of } (C) = \frac{79 \times 185}{300} = 48.72$$

O	*E*	(*O-E*)	$(O\text{-}E)^2$	$\frac{(O-E)^2}{E}$
69	74	−5	25	0.34
81	62.28	18.72	350.44	5.63
35	48.72	13.72	188.24	3.86
51	46	15	25	0.54
20	38.72	18.72	350.44	9.05
44	30.28	13.71	188.24	6.22
				$E\frac{(O-E)^2}{E} = 25.64$

$$X^2 = 25.64$$

$$d.f = (\Upsilon - 1)(C - 1)$$

$$= (2 - 1)(3 - 1)$$

$$= 2.$$

For 2 d.f. x^2 at 5 % level of significance is 5.99.

The computed value of $x^2 = 25.54$ is greater than the table value of x^2 0.05 for $\nu = 2$ is 5.99. Therefore, the hypothesis is rejected. Thus, there is an association between the condition of child and condition and house.

Problem 14. From the following table test whether the colour of the sons' eye is associated with that of the fathers.

		Eye colour of sons		
		Not Light	*Light*	*Total*
Eye colour of fathers	Not light	230	148	378
	Light	151	471	622
	Total	381	619	1000

You may use the following value of X^2 0.05 = 3.84 for $V = 1$, 5.99 for $V = 2$, 7.82 for $V = 3$.

(*M. Com., Nagpur*)

Solution : The hypothesis is that the eye colour of fathers and sons is independent. On the basis of this, the expected frequencies are :

$\frac{378 \times 381}{1000} = 144$	234	378
237	385	622
381	619	1000

X^2test is calculated as follows :

O	E	$(O - E)$	$(O - E)^2$	$\frac{(O-E)^2}{E}$
230	144	86	7396	51.36
151	237	−86	7396	31.21
148	234	−86	7396	31.61
471	385	86	7396	19.21
				$\Sigma\frac{(0-E)^2}{E}$ 133.39

$$X^2 = 133.39$$

The table of X^2 at 5% level of significance for 1 *d.f.* is 3.84. The calculated value of X^2 is 133.39, which is much more than the table value = 3.84. Therefore, the hypothesis is wrong and we conclude that the eye colour of the sons depends on the eye colour of fathers.

Problem 15. In an experiment on the immunization of goats from anthrax the following results were obtained. Derive your inference on the vaccine.

	Died of Anthrax	*Survived*	*Total*
Inoculated with vaccine	2	10	12
Not inoculated	6	6	12
Total	8	16	24

(*M. Com., Calicut*)

Solution : Let us take the hypothesis the vaccine is not effective. Both the attributes are independent.

The expected frequencies are :

$\frac{8 \times 12}{24} = 4$	8	12
4	8	12
8	16	24

When applying X^2 test

O	E	$(O-E)$	$(O-E)^2$	$\frac{(O-E)^2}{E}$
2	4	−2	4	1.0
10	8	2	4	0.5
6	4	2	4	1.0
6	8	−2	4	0.5
24	24		16	3.0

$$X^2 = \Sigma\frac{(0-E)^2}{E} = 3.0$$

$$\nu = (r-1)(c-1) = (2-1)(2-1) = 1$$

The table value of X^2 for 1 *d.f.* at 5% level of significance is 3.841. The calculated value of X^2 is 3, which is less than the tabled value. Hence the null hypothesis may be accepted. Thus we conclude that the vaccine is ineffective in controlling the disease.

Problem 16. A certain drug was administered to 500 people out of a total of 800 included in the sample to test its efficacy against typhoid. The results are given below :

	Typhoid	*No typhoid*	*Total*
Drug	200	300	500
No Drug	280	20	300
Total	480	320	800

On the basis of these data, can it be concluded that the drug is effective in preventing typhoid (given for $V = 1$ X^2 $0.05 = 3.84$)

(*M A Kurukshetra*)

Solution : Let the hypothesis be "The drug is not effective in preventing typhoid."

The table of expected frequencies is :

$\frac{480 \times 500}{800} = 300$	$\frac{320 \times 500}{800} = 200$	500
$\frac{480 \times 300}{800} = 180$	$\frac{320 \times 300}{800} = 120$	300
480	320	800

N.B Alternatively, after finding out the first value, the remaining values can be obtained in the following manner.

$\frac{400 \times 500}{800} = 300$	500—300=200	500
480—300 = 180	320—200 = 120 (300—180) = 120	300
480	320	800

O	E	$(O-E)$	$(O-E)^2$	$\frac{(O-E)^2}{E}$
200	300	−100	10,000	33.33
280	180	+100	10,000	55.56
300	200	+100	10,000	50.00
20	120	−100	10,000	83.33
800	800			$\Sigma\frac{(O-E)^2}{E} = 222.22$

$$\begin{aligned} V &= (r-1)(c-1) \\ &= (2-1)(2-1) \\ &= 1 \times 1 \\ &= 1 \end{aligned}$$

$$d.f.\ 1.X^2 0.05 = 3.84$$

The computed value of X^2 is much greater than the table value. Therefore the hypothesis-the drug is not effective-rejected. Hence we conclude that the drug is effective preventing typhoid.

Problem 17. Out of 8,000 graduates in a town, 800 are females ; out of 1,600 graduate employees 120 are female. Use chi square test to determine if any distinction is made in appointment on the basis of sex. Value of chi square for 5% level for one degree of freedom is 3.84. (*CA*)

Solution : The information given in the question can be tabulated in a 2 × 2 table. Thus :

	Employed	*Unemployed*	*Total*
Male	1480	5720	7200
Female	120	680	800
Total	1600	6400	8000

We take the hypothesis that there is no distinction in appointment on the basis of sex.

The expected frequencies are :

$\frac{7200 \times 1600}{8000} = 1440$	5760	7200
160	640	800
1600	6400	8000

Applying X^2test

O	E	$(O-E)$	$(O-E)^2$	$\frac{(O-E)^2}{E}$
1480	1440	40	1600	1.111
120	160	−40	1600	10.000
5720	5760	−40	1600	0.278
680	640	40	1600	2.500
				$\Sigma\frac{(O-E)^2}{E} = 13.88$

$$X^2 = \Sigma\frac{(O-E)^2}{E} = 13.88$$

$$d.f = (r-1)(c-1)$$

$$= 1 \times 1$$

$$= 1$$

for $d.f.\ 1,\ X^2\ 0.05 = 3.84$

The calculated value of X^2 is 13.88 which is more than table value (3.84), therefore the hypothesis is rejected. It is confirmed that a distinction is made in appointment on the basis of sex.

16

PARTIAL AND MULTIPLE CORRELATION

PARTIAL CORRELATION, MULTIPLE CORRELATION, MULTIPLE REGRESSION ANALYSIS

FORMULAE

Partial Correlation

If there are three variables X_1, X_2 and X_3

$$r_{12.3} = \frac{r_{12} - r_{13}\,r_{23}}{\sqrt{1-r_{13}^2}\sqrt{1-r_{23}^2}}$$

$r_{12.3}$= Coefficient of correlation between X_1 and X_2 excluding X_3 (keeping X_3 constant)

$$r_{13.2} = \frac{r_{13} - r_{12}\,r_{23}}{\sqrt{1-r_{12}^2}\sqrt{1-r_{23}^2}}$$

$r_{13.2}$= Coefficient of correlation between X_1 and X_3 excluding X_2 (keeping X_2 constant)

$$r_{23.1} = \frac{r_{23} - r_{12}\,r_{13}}{\sqrt{1-r_{12}^2}\sqrt{1-r_{13}^2}}$$

$r_{23.1}$ = Coefficient of correlation between X_2 and X_3 excluding X_1 (keeping X_1 constant)

Multiple Correlation

$$r_{1.23} = \sqrt{\frac{r_{12}^2 + r_{13}^2 - 2r_{12}\,r_{13}\,r_{23}}{1-r_{23}^2}}$$

$R_{1.23}$ = Multiple coefficient correlation with X_1 as a dependent variable and X_2 and X_3 as two independent variables.

$$R_{2.13} = \sqrt{\frac{r_{12}^2 + r_{23}^2 - 2r_{12}\,r_{13}\,r_{23}}{1-r_{13}^2}}$$

$R_{2.13}$ = Multiple coefficient correlation with X_2 as a dependent variable and X_1 and X_3 as independent variable.

$$R_{3.12} = \sqrt{\frac{r_{31}^2 + r_{32}^2 - 2r_{12}\,r_{13}\,r_{23}}{1-r_{12}^2}}$$

$R_{3.12}$ = Multiple correlation coefficient with X_3 as a dependent variable and X_1 and X_2 as two independent variables.

Multiple Regression Equation

Regression Equation of X_1 on X_2 and X_3 is :

($X_{1.23}$= $a_{1.23}$ + $b_{12.3}$ X_2 + $b_{13.2}X_3$)

The values of $b_{12.3}$ and $b_{13.2}$ are determined by solving simultaneously the normal equations

$\Sigma X_1 = Na_{1.23} + b_{12.3}\,\Sigma X_2 + b_{13.2}\,\Sigma X_3$ $\Sigma X_1 X_2 = a_{1.23}\Sigma X_2 + b_{12.3}\,\Sigma X_2^2 + b_{13.2}\,\Sigma X_2 X_3$ $\Sigma X_1 X_3 = a_{1.23}\Sigma X_3 + b_{12.3}\,\Sigma X_2 X_3 + b_{13.2}\,\Sigma X_3$ Deviation taken from actual Mean $x_1 = b_{12..3}\,x_2 + b_{13..3}\,x_3$ The values of $b_{12.3}$ and $b_{13.2}$ can be obtained by solving simultaneously the following two normal equations $\Sigma x_1 x_2 = b_{12.3}\Sigma x_2^2 + b_{13.2}\,\Sigma x_2 x_3$ $\Sigma x_1 x_3 = b_{12.3}\Sigma x_2 x_3 + b_{13.2}\,\Sigma x_3^2$	$x_1 = X_1 - \overline{X}_1,$ $x_2 = X_2 - \overline{X}_2,$ $x_3 = x_2 - \overline{X}_3$
Partial Regression Coefficients $b_{12.3} = \frac{\sigma_1}{\sigma_2}\left(\frac{r_{12} - r_{13}\,r_{23}}{1 - r_{23}^2}\right)$ $b_{13.2} = \frac{\sigma_1}{\sigma_3}\left(\frac{r_{13} - r_{12}\,r_{23}}{1 - r_{23}^2}\right)$	σ_1, σ_2 and $\sigma_3$are the standard deviations of the variables X_1, X_2, X_3, r_{12}, r_{13} and r_{23} = the product movement correlation coefficient between X_1 and X_2 between X_1 and X_3 between X_2 and X_3 respectively.

PARTIAL CORRELATION

Problem 1. The following zero-order correlation coefficients are given :

$r_{12} = 0.98$, $r_{13} = 0.44$, and $r_{23} = 0.54$

Calculate the partial correlation coefficient between first and the third variables keeping the effect of second variable constant.

(*M. Com. Delhi*)

Solution: We have to find the value of $r_{13.2}$.

$$r_{13.2} = \frac{r_{13} - r_{12}\,r_{23}}{\sqrt{1 - r_{13}^2}\,\sqrt{1 - r_{23}^2}}$$

$$r_{13.2} = \frac{0.44 - (0.98)(0.54)}{\sqrt{1 - (0.98)^2}\,\sqrt{1 - (0.54)^2}}$$

$$= \frac{0.44 - 0.5292}{\sqrt{1 - 0.9604}\,\sqrt{1 - 0.2916}}$$

$$= \frac{-0.0892}{\sqrt{0.0396}\,\sqrt{0.7084}}$$

$$= \frac{-0.0892}{0.199 \times 0.842}$$

$$= \frac{-0.0892}{0.1676}$$

$$r_{13.2} = \mathbf{-0.532}$$

Problem 2. On the basis of observations made on 39 cotton plants, the total correlation of yield of cotton(x_1), number of bolls *i.e.*, seed vessels (x_2) and height (x_3) are found to be

$$r_{12} = 0.8,\ r_{13} = 0.65 \text{ and } r_{23} = 0.7$$

Compute the partial correlation between yiels of cotton and the number of bolls eliminating the effect of height.

(*M. Com. Kurukshetra*)

Solution : We have to find the partial correlation between yield of cotton and the number of bolls eliminating the effect of height, $r_{12.3}$

$$r_{12.3} = \frac{r_{12} - r_{13}\,r_{23}}{\sqrt{1-r_{13}^2}\,\sqrt{1-r_{23}^2}}$$

$$= \frac{0.8 - (0.65)(0.7)}{\sqrt{1-(0.65)^2}\,\sqrt{1-(0.7)^2}}$$

$$= \frac{0.8 - 0.455}{\sqrt{1-0.4225}\,\sqrt{1-0.49}}$$

$$= \frac{0.345}{\sqrt{0.5775}\,\sqrt{0.51}}$$

$$= \frac{0.345}{0.7599 \times 0.714}$$

$$= \frac{0.345}{0.543}$$

$$r_{12.3} = \mathbf{0.635}$$

Problem 3. Suppose a computer has found for a given set of values of x_1, x_2 and x_3

$$r_{12} = 0.91,\ r_{13} = 0.33 \text{ and } r_{23} = \mathbf{0.81}$$

Examine whether his computation may be said to be free from errors.

(*B. Com.*)

Solution :

$$r_{12.3} = \frac{r_{12} - r_{13}\,r_{23}}{\sqrt{1-r_{13}^2}\,\sqrt{1-r_{23}^2}}$$

$$= \frac{0.91 - (0.33)(0.81)}{\sqrt{1-(0.33)^2}\,\sqrt{1-(0.81)^2}}$$

$$= \frac{0.91 - 0.2673}{\sqrt{1-0.1089}\,\sqrt{1-0.6561}}$$

$$= \frac{0.6427}{\sqrt{0.8911}\,\sqrt{0.3439}}$$

$$= \frac{0.6427}{0.94 \times 0.59}$$

$$= \frac{0.6427}{0.5546} = 1.1589$$

It is greater than 1. Hence the computation is not free from errors.

Problem 4. If $r_{12} = 0.86$, $r_{13} = 0.65$ and $r_{23} = 0.72$, prove that $r_{12.3} = 0.748$.

(*B. Com. Gujarat*)

Solution :

$$r_{12.3} = \frac{r_{12} - r_{13}\, r_{23}}{\sqrt{1-r_{13}^2}\,\sqrt{1-r_{23}^2}}$$
$$= \frac{0.86 - (0.65)(0.72)}{\sqrt{1-(0.65)^2}\,\sqrt{1-(0.72)}}$$
$$= \frac{0.86 - 0.468}{\sqrt{1-0.4225}\,\sqrt{1-0.5184}}$$
$$= \frac{0.392}{\sqrt{0.5775}\,\sqrt{0.4816}}$$
$$= \frac{0.392}{0.76 \times 0.69}$$
$$= \frac{0.392}{0.524}$$
$$= \mathbf{0.748}$$

Problem 5. From the following data, calculate $r_{12.3}$:

X_1	4	0	2	1	1	3	4	1
X_2	2	0	2	4	2	3	3	0
X_3	1	4	2	2	3	0	4	0

(B. Sc., Gujarat)

Solution :

Computation of r_{12}, r_{13}, r_{23}

$(X_1 - \overline{X}_1)$			$(X_2 - \overline{X}_2)$			$(X_3 - \overline{X}_3)$					
X_1	x_1	x_1^2	X_2	x_2	x_2^2	X_3	x_3	x_3^2	$x_1\ x_2$	$x_1\ x_3$	$x_2\ x$
4	+2	4	2	0	0	1	−1	1	0	−2	
0	−2	4	0	−2	4	4	+2	4	4	−4	−
2	0	0	2	0	0	2	0	0	0	0	
1	−1	1	4	+2	4	2	0	0	−2	0	
1	−1	1	2	0	0	3	+1	1	0	−1	
3	+1	1	3	+1	1	0	−2	4	1	−2	−
4	+2	4	3	+1	1	4	+2	4	2	+4	+
1	−1	1	0	−2	4	0	−2	4	2	+2	+
$\Sigma X_1 = 16$	$\Sigma x_1 = 0$	$\Sigma x_1^2 = 16$	$\Sigma X_2 = 16$	$\Sigma x_2 = 0$	$\Sigma x_2^2 = 14$	$\Sigma X_3 = 16$	$\Sigma x_3^2 = 0$	$\Sigma x_3^2 = 18$	$\Sigma x_1x_2 = 7$	$\Sigma x_1x_3 = -3$	Σx_2x =

$$r_{12.3} = \frac{r_{12} - r_{13}\, r_{23}}{\sqrt{1-r_{13}^2}\,\sqrt{1-r_{23}^2}}$$
$$r_{12} = \frac{\Sigma x_1 x_2}{\sqrt{\Sigma x_1^2 \Sigma x_2^2}} = \frac{7}{\sqrt{16 \times 14}} = \frac{7}{14.97}$$
$$= \mathbf{0.468}$$
$$r_{13} = \frac{\Sigma x_2 x_3}{\sqrt{\Sigma x_1^2 \Sigma x_3^2}} = \frac{-3}{\sqrt{16 \times 18}} = \frac{-3}{16.97}$$
$$= \mathbf{0.177} \text{ or } \mathbf{0.18}$$
$$r_{23} = \frac{\Sigma x_2 x_3}{\sqrt{\Sigma x_2^2 \Sigma x_3^2}} = \frac{0}{\sqrt{14 \times 18}}$$
$$= \mathbf{0}$$
$$r_{12.3} = \frac{0.468 - (0.18)\,(0)}{\sqrt{1-(-0.18)^2}\,\sqrt{1-(0)^2}} = \frac{0.468}{\sqrt{1-6.0324}} = \frac{0.468}{\sqrt{0.9676}}$$
$$= \frac{0.468}{0.983} = \mathbf{0.476}$$

Problem 6. In a trivariate distribution it is found that

$$r_{12} = 0.7,\ r_{13} = 0.61,\ r_{23} = 0.4$$

Find the value of $r_{23.1}$,, $r_{13.2}$ and $r_{12.3}$

(*B. Sc., Kanpur*)

Solution:

$$r_{23.1} = \frac{r_{23} - r_{12}\, r_{13}}{\sqrt{1 - r_{12}^2}\,\sqrt{1 - r_{13}^2}}$$

$$= \frac{0.4 - 0.7 \times 0.61}{\sqrt{1 - (0.7)^2}\,\sqrt{1 - (0.61)^2}}$$

$$= \frac{0.4 - 0.427}{\sqrt{0.51}\,\sqrt{0.628}}$$

$$= \frac{-0.027}{0.714 \times 0.792} = \frac{-0.027}{0.565} = \mathbf{0.0477}$$

$$r_{23.1} = \mathbf{-0.048}$$

$$r_{13.2} = \frac{r_{13} - r_{12}\, r_{23}}{\sqrt{1 - r_{12}^2}\,\sqrt{1 - r_{23}^2}}$$

$$= \frac{0.61 - (0.7)(0.4)}{\sqrt{1 - (0.7)^2}\sqrt{1 - (0.4)^2}}$$

$$= \frac{0.61 - 0.28}{\sqrt{0.51}\,\sqrt{0.84}} = \frac{0.33}{0.714 \times 0.917} = \frac{0.33}{0.655}$$

$$r_{13.2} = \mathbf{0.504}$$

$$r_{12.3} = \frac{r_{12} - r_{12}\, r_{23}}{\sqrt{1 - r_{13}^2}\,\sqrt{1 - r_{23}^2}}$$

$$= \frac{0.7 - (0.61)(0.4)}{\sqrt{1 - (0.61)^2}\sqrt{1 - (0.4)^2}} = \frac{0.7 - 0.244}{\sqrt{0.628}\,\sqrt{0.84}}$$

$$= \frac{0.456}{0.792 \times 0.917} = \frac{0.456}{0.726}$$

$$r_{12.3} = \mathbf{0.628}$$

MULTIPLE CORRELATION

Problem 7. The following zero-order correlation coefficients are given :

$$r_{12} = 0.98,\ r_{13} = 0.44,\ r_{23} = 0.54$$

Calculate multiple correlation coefficient treating first variable as dependent and second and third variables as independent.

(*M. Com., Delhi*)

Solution : We have to find $R_{1.23}$, as we have to calculate multiple correlation coefficient, treating first variable as dependent and second and third as independent.

$$R_{1.23} = \sqrt{\frac{r_{12}^2 + r_{13}^2 - 2r_{12}\, r_{13}\, r_{23}}{1 - r_{23}^2}}$$

Substituting the given values

$$R_{1.23} = \sqrt{\frac{(0.98)^2 + (0.44)^2 - 2(0.98)(0.44)(0.54)}{1 - (0.54)^2}}$$

$$= \sqrt{\frac{0.9604 + 0.1936 - 0.4657}{1 - 0.2916}}$$

$$= \sqrt{\frac{1.154 - 0.4657}{0.7084}}$$

$$= \sqrt{\frac{0.6883}{0.7084}}$$

$$= \sqrt{0.9716}$$

$$R_{1.23} = \mathbf{0.986}$$

Problem 8. Given that $r_{12} = 0.6$, $r_{13} = 0.7$, $r_{23} = 65$, determine $R_{1.23}$. Calculate also the partial correlation coefficient $r_{23.1}$ (*B.A. Bombay*)

Solution :

$$R_{1.23} = \sqrt{\frac{r_{12}^2 + r_{13}^2 - 2r_{12}\,r_{13}\,r_{23}}{1 - r_{23}^2}}$$

Substituting the given values

$$R_{1.23} = \sqrt{\frac{(0.6)^2 + (0.7)^2 - 2(0.6)(0.7)(0.65)}{1 - (0.65)^2}}$$

$$= \sqrt{\frac{(0.36) + (0.49) - 0.546}{1 - 0.4225}}$$

$$= \sqrt{\frac{0.85 - 0.546}{0.5775}}$$

$$= \sqrt{\frac{0.304}{0.5775}}$$

$$= \sqrt{0.5264}$$

$$R_{1.23} = \mathbf{0.726}$$

$$r_{23.1} = \frac{r_{23} + r_{12}\,r_{13}}{\sqrt{1 - r_{12}^2}\,\sqrt{1 - r_{13}^2}}$$

$$= \frac{0.65 - (0.6)(0.7)}{\sqrt{1 - (0.6)^2}\,\sqrt{1 - (0.7)^2}} = \frac{0.65 - 0.42}{\sqrt{1 - 0.36}\,\sqrt{1 - 0.49}}$$

$$= \frac{0.23}{\sqrt{0.64}\,\sqrt{0.51}} = \frac{0.23}{\sqrt{0.3264}} = \frac{0.23}{0.57}$$

$$r_{23.1} = \mathbf{0.4}$$

Problem 9. A simple correlation coefficient between temperature x_1, corn yield x_2 and rainfall x_3 is

$$r_{12} = 0.59\ r_{13} = 0.46 \text{ and } r_{23}\ 0.77$$

Calculate partial correlation coefficients $r_{12.3}$, $r_{23.1}$, and $r_{13.2}$, Also calculate $R_{1.23}$ (*M.Com. Delhi*)

Solution:

$$r_{12.3} = \frac{r_{12} - r_{13}\, r_{23}}{\sqrt{1 - r_{13}^2}\,\sqrt{1 - r_{23}^2}}$$

$$= \frac{0.59 - (0.46)(0.77)}{\sqrt{1 - (0.46)^2}\sqrt{1 - (0.77)^2}} = \frac{0.59 - 0.3542}{\sqrt{1 - 2116}\sqrt{1 - 0.5929}}$$

$$= \frac{0.2358}{\sqrt{0.7884}\sqrt{0.4071}} = \frac{0.2358}{\sqrt{0.3209}} = \frac{0.2358}{0.5665}$$

$$= \mathbf{0.416}$$

$$r_{23.1} = \frac{r_{23} - r_{12}\, r_{13}}{\sqrt{1 - r_{12}^2}\,\sqrt{1 - r_{13}^2}} = \frac{0.77 - (0.59)(0.46)}{\sqrt{1 - (0.59)^2}\sqrt{1 - (0.46)^2}}$$

$$= \frac{0.77 - 2714}{\sqrt{1 - .3481}\sqrt{1 - .2116}} = \frac{0.4986}{\sqrt{0.6519}\sqrt{0.7884}} = \frac{0.4986}{\sqrt{0.5139}}$$

$$= \frac{0.4986}{0.7169} = \mathbf{0.695}$$

$$r_{13.2} = \frac{r_{13} - r_{12}\, r_{23}}{\sqrt{1 - r_{12}^2}\,\sqrt{1 - r_{23}^2}} = \frac{0.46 - (0.59)(0.77)}{\sqrt{1 - (0.59)^2}\sqrt{1 - (0.77)^2}}$$

$$= \frac{0.46 - 0.4543}{\sqrt{1 - 0.3481}\sqrt{1 - 0.5929}} = \frac{0.0057}{\sqrt{0.6519}\sqrt{0.4071}}$$

$$= \frac{0.0057}{0.2654} = \frac{0.0057}{\sqrt{0.5152}} = \mathbf{0.011}$$

$$R_{1.23} = \sqrt{\frac{r_{12}^2 + r_{13}^2 - 2r_{12}\, r_{13}\, r_{23}}{1 - r_{23}^2}}$$

$$= \sqrt{\frac{(0.59)^2 + (0.46)^2 - 2(0.59)(0.46)(0.77)}{1 - (0.77)^2}}$$

$$= \sqrt{\frac{0.3481 + 0.2116 - 0.4180}{1 - 0.5929}} = \sqrt{\frac{0.5597 - 0.4180}{0.4071}}$$

$$= \sqrt{\frac{0.1471}{0.4071}} = \sqrt{0.348}$$

$$= \mathbf{0.589}$$

Problem 10. Given that $r_{12} = 0.82$, $r_{13} = 0.77$, $r_{23} = 0.80$, determine $r_{23.1}$ and multiple correlation $R_{1.23}$ (*B. A. Bombay*)

Solution:

$$r_{23.1} = \frac{r_{23} - r_{12}\, r_{13}}{\sqrt{1 - r_{12}^2}\,\sqrt{1 - r_{13}^2}}$$

$$= \frac{0.80 - (0.82)(0.77)}{\sqrt{1 - (0.82)^2}\sqrt{1 - (0.77)^2}}$$

$$= \frac{0.80 - 0.6314}{\sqrt{1 - 0.6724}\sqrt{1 - 0.5929}}$$

$$= \frac{0.1686}{\sqrt{0.3276}\sqrt{0.4071}} = \frac{0.1686}{\sqrt{0.1334}}$$

$$= \frac{0.1686}{0.3652}$$

$$= \mathbf{0.4617}$$

$$R_{1.23} = \sqrt{\frac{r_{12}^2 + r_{13}^2 - 2r_{12}\,r_{13}\,r_{23}}{1 - r_{23}^2}}$$

$$= \sqrt{\frac{(0.82)^2 + (0.77)^2 - 2(0.82)(0.77)(0.80)}{1 - (0.80)^2}}$$

$$= \sqrt{\frac{(0.6724) + (0.5929) - (1.0102)}{1 - 0.64}}$$

$$= \sqrt{\frac{1.2653 - 1.0102}{0.36}}$$

$$= \sqrt{\frac{0.2551}{0.36}}$$

$$= \sqrt{0.7086} = 0.8418$$

$$= \mathbf{0.842}$$

REGRESSION EQUATION

Problem 11. In a trivariate distribution

$$\sigma_1 = 3, \quad \sigma_2 = 4, \quad \sigma_3 = 5$$

$$r_{23} = 0.4, \; r_{13} = 0.6, \; r_{12} = 0.7$$

Determine the regression equation of X_1 on X_2 and X_3 if the variates are measured from their means. *(B. Com., Gujarat,)*

Solution : When the variates are measured from mean, the regression equation of X_1 on X_2 and X_3 is given by :

$$b_{12.3} = \frac{\sigma_1}{\sigma_2} \times \frac{r_{12} - r_{13}\,r_{23}}{1 - r_{23}^2}$$

$$= \frac{3}{4} \times \frac{0.7 - (0.6)(0.4)}{1 - (0.4)^2}$$

$$= \frac{3}{4} \times \frac{0.7 - (0.24)}{1 - 0.16}$$

$$= \frac{3}{4} \times \frac{0.46}{0.84}$$

$$= \frac{3}{4} \times 0.5476$$

$$= \mathbf{0.41}$$

$$b_{13.2} = \frac{\sigma_1}{\sigma_3} \times \frac{r_{13} - r_{12}\,r_{23}}{1 - r_{23}^2}$$

$$= \frac{3}{5} \times \frac{0.6 - (0.7)(0.4)}{1 - (0.4)^2}$$

$$= \frac{3}{5} \times \frac{0.6 - 0.28}{1 - 0.16} = \frac{3}{5} \times \frac{0.32}{0.84}$$

$$= \frac{3}{5} \times 0.38$$

$$= \mathbf{0.228}$$

Therefore the required equation is

$X_1 = 0.41\ X_2 + 0.228\ X_3$ $\quad r_{12} = 0.28,\ r_{23} = 0.49,\ r_{31} = 0.51$

Problem 12. Given $\sigma_1 = 2.7 \quad \sigma_2 = 2.4 \quad \sigma_2 = 2.7$

Find the regression equation of X_3 on X_1 and X_2

(*B.A., Bombay*)

Solution : The regression equation of X_3 on X_1 and X_2 is

$$X_3 = b_{31.2}X_1 + b_{32..1}X_2$$

$$b_{31.2} = r_{31.2} \times \frac{\sigma_{3.12}}{\sigma_{1.23}}$$

$$b_{32.1} = r_{32.1} \times \frac{\sigma_{3.12}}{\sigma_{2.31}}$$

Hence we must find the values of $r_{31.2}, r_{32.1}, \sigma_{3.12}, \sigma_{1.23}, \sigma_{2.31}$

$$r_{31.2} = \frac{r_{31} - r_{23}\,r_{12}}{\sqrt{1-r_{23}^2}\,\sqrt{1-r_{12}^2}} = \frac{0.51-(0.49)(0.28)}{\sqrt{1-(0.49)^2}\,\sqrt{1-(0.28)^2}}$$

$$= \frac{0.51 -- 0.1372}{\sqrt{1-0.2401}\sqrt{1-0.0784}} = \frac{0.3728}{\sqrt{0.7599}\,\sqrt{0.9216}} = \frac{0.3728}{\sqrt{0.7003}}$$

$$= \frac{0.3728}{0.8368}$$

$$= \mathbf{0.446}$$

$$r_{32.1} = \frac{r_{32} - r_{12}\,r_{13}}{\sqrt{1-r_{12}^2}\,\sqrt{1-r_{13}^2}} = \frac{0.49-(0.28)(0.51)}{\sqrt{1-(0.28)^2}\sqrt{1-(0.51)^2}}$$

$$= \frac{0.49-0.1428}{\sqrt{1-0.0784}\sqrt{1-0.2601}} = \frac{0.3472}{\sqrt{0.9216}\,\sqrt{0.7399}} = \frac{0.3472}{\sqrt{0.6819}}$$

$$= \frac{0.3472}{\sqrt{0.6819}} = \frac{0.3472}{0.8258} = \mathbf{0.42}$$

$$\sigma_{3.12} = \sigma_3\sqrt{1-r_{31}^2}\sqrt{1-r_{32.1}^2} = 2.7\sqrt{1-(0.51)^2}\sqrt{1-(0.42)^2}$$

$$= 2.7 \times \sqrt{0.7399} \times \sqrt{0.8236}$$

$$= 2.70 \times 86 \times 0.91 = \mathbf{2.113}$$

$$\sigma_1.23 = \sigma\sqrt{1-r_1^2 2}\sqrt{1-r_{31.2}^2} = 2.7\sqrt{1-(0.28)^2}\sqrt{1-(0.446)^2}$$

$$= 2.7 \times \sqrt{0.9216}\,\sqrt{0.8011} = 2.7 \times 0.96 \times 0.895$$

$$= \mathbf{2.32}$$

$$r_{12.3} = \frac{r_{12} - r_{13}\,r_{23}}{\sqrt{1-r_{13}^2}\,\sqrt{1-r_{23}^2}} = \frac{0.28-(0.51)\,(0.49)}{\sqrt{1-(0.51)^2}\sqrt{1-(0.49)^2}}$$

$$\frac{0.28-0.2499}{\sqrt{1-0.2601}\,\sqrt{1-0.2401}} = \frac{0.0301}{\sqrt{0.7399}\,\sqrt{0.7599}}$$

$$= \frac{0.0301}{\sqrt{0.5623}}\,\frac{0.0301}{0.7499} = .\mathbf{04}$$

$$\sigma_{2.31} = \sigma_2\sqrt{1-r_{23}^2}\,\sqrt{1-r_{12.3}^2} = 2.4\sqrt{1-(0.49)^2}\sqrt{1-(0.04)^2}$$

$$= 2.4\sqrt{0.7599}\,\sqrt{0.9984} = 2.4 \times 0.87 \times 0.99$$

$$= \mathbf{2.07}$$

$$b_{31.2} = 0.446 \times \frac{2.113}{2.32} = \mathbf{0.406}$$

$$b_{32.1} = 0.42 \times \frac{2.113}{2.07} = \mathbf{0.429}$$

Substituting the values in the regression equation

$x_3 = \mathbf{0.406x_1 + 0.429x_2}$.

Problem 13. Find the multiple linear regression equation of X_1 on X_2 and X_3 from the data relating to three variables given below :

X_1	4	6	7	9	13	15
X_2	15	12	8	6	4	3
X_3	30	24	20	14	10	4

(B.A., Bombay)

Solution : The regression equation of X_1 on X_2 and X_3 is

$$X_1 = a_{1.23}, b_{12.3} + b_{13.2}X_3$$

By solving the following three normal equations, the value of the constants $a_{1.23}$, $b_{12.3}$ and , $b_{13.2}$ can be obtained

$$\Sigma X_1 = Na_{1.23} + b_{12.3}\Sigma X^2 + b_{13.2}\,\Sigma X_3$$
$$\Sigma X_1X_2 = a_{1.23}\Sigma X_2 + b_{12.3}\Sigma X_2^2 + b_{13.2}\Sigma X_2X_3$$
$$\Sigma X_1X_3 = a_{1.23}\Sigma X_3 + b_{12.3}\Sigma X_2X_3 + b_{13.2}\,\Sigma X_3^2$$

X_1	X_2	X_3	X_1X_2	X_1X_3	X_2X_3	X_1^2	X_2^2	ΣX_3^2
4	15	30	60	120	450	16	225	900
6	12	24	72	144	288	36	144	576
7	8	20	56	140	160	49	64	400
9	6	14	54	126	84	81	36	196
13	4	10	52	130	40	169	16	100
15	3	4	45	60	12	225	9	16
ΣX_1 =54	ΣX_2^2 =48	ΣX_3 =102	ΣX_1X_2 =339	ΣX_1X_3 =720	ΣX_2X_3 =1034	ΣX_1^2 =576	ΣX_2^2 =494	ΣX_3^2 =2188

Substituting the values in the normal equations :

$$6a_{1.23}, + 48b_{12.3} + 102b_{13.2} = 54 \quad (1)$$
$$48a_{1.23}, + 494b_{12.3} + 1034b_{13.2} = 339 \quad (2)$$
$$102a_{1.23}, + 1034b_{12.3} + 2188b_{13.2} = 720 \quad (3)$$

Multiplying equation (1) by 8 we get

$$48a_{1.23}, + 384b_{12.3} + 816b_{13.2} = 432 \quad (4)$$

Subtracting Eqn. (4) from (2), we get

$$110b_{12.3} + 218b_{13.2} = -93 \quad (5)$$

Multiplying Equation (1) by 17, we get

$$102a_{1.23}, + 816b_{12.3} + 1734b_{13.2} = 918 \quad (6)$$

Subtracting equation (3) from Equation (6), we get

$$218b_{12.3} + 454b_{13.2} = -198 \quad (7)$$

Multiplying equation (5) by 109, we get

$$11990b_{12.3} + 23762b_{13.2} = -10137 \quad (8)$$

Multiplying Eqn. (7) by 55, we get

$$11990b_{12.3} + 24970b_{13.2} = -10890 \qquad (9)$$

Subtracting Eqn. (8) from (9) we get

$$1208b_{12.3} = -753$$
$$b_{12.3} = \frac{-753}{1208} = \mathbf{-0.623}$$

Substituting the value in Eqn. 7, we get

$$218b_{12.3} + 454(-0.623) = -198$$
$$218b_{12.3} = -198 + 282.842$$
$$b_{12.3} = \frac{84.842}{218} = \mathbf{+0.389}$$

Substituting the values of $b_{12.3}$ and $b_{13.2}$ in Eqn. (1)

We get

$$6a_{1.23} + 48(0.389) + 102(-0.623) = 54$$
$$6a_{1.23} + 18.672 - 63.546 = 54$$
$$6a_{1.23} = 54 - 18.672 + 63.546$$
$$= 98.874$$
$$a_{1.23} = \frac{98.874}{6} = \mathbf{16.479}$$

Thus the multiple linear regression equation of X_1 on X_2 and X_3 is X_1= **16.479 + 0.389**$\mathbf{X_2}$-0.623 X_3.

17

MISCELLANEOUS

COEFFICIENT OF VARIATION

Problem 1. Given the following results relating to two groups containing 20 and 30 observations, calculate the coefficient of variation of all the 50 observations by combining both the groups.

	I	II
ΣX	45	55
ΣX^2	118	132

(*I.C.W.A.*)

Solution :

$$\overline{X}_1 = \frac{\Sigma X_1}{N} = \frac{45}{20} = \mathbf{2.45}$$

$$\overline{X}_2 = \frac{\Sigma X_2}{N} = \frac{55}{30} = \mathbf{1.83}$$

Combined Mean

$$\overline{X}_{12} = \frac{N_1\overline{X}_1 + N_2\overline{X}_2}{N_1 + N_2} = \frac{45+55}{20+30} = 2$$

$$d^1 = \overline{X}_1 - \overline{X}_{12} = 2.25 - 2 = 0.25 \quad \therefore \quad d_1^2 = 0.0625$$

$$d^2 = \overline{X}_2 - \overline{X}_{12} = 1.83 - 2 = -0.17 \quad \therefore \quad d_2^2 = 0.0289$$

$$\sigma_1 = \sqrt{\frac{1}{N_1}\Sigma X_1^2 - (\overline{X}_1)^2} = \sqrt{\frac{1}{20} \times 118 - (2.25)^2}$$

$$= \sqrt{5.9 - 5.0625} = \sqrt{0.8375}$$

$$= \mathbf{0.915}$$

$$\sigma_2 = \sqrt{\frac{1}{N_2}\Sigma X_2^2 - (\overline{X}_2)^2} = \sqrt{\frac{1}{30} \times 132 - (1.83)^2}$$

$$= \sqrt{4.4 - 3.3489} = \sqrt{1.0511}$$

$$= \mathbf{1.025}$$

Combined Standard Deviation :

$$\sigma_{12} = \sqrt{\frac{N_1\sigma_1^2 + N_1 d_1^2 + N_2\sigma_2^2 + N_2 d_2^2}{N_1 + N_2}}$$

$$= \sqrt{\frac{20 \times 0.915^2 + 20 \times 0.0625 + 30 \times 1.025^2 + 30 \times 0.0289}{20+30}}$$

$$= \sqrt{\frac{20 \times 0.8372 + 20 \times 0.0625 + 30 \times 1.0506 + 30 \times 0.0289}{50}}$$

$$= \sqrt{\frac{16.75 + 1.25 + 31.52 + 0.867}{50}}$$

$$= \sqrt{\frac{50.387}{50}}$$

$$= \sqrt{1.0079}$$

$$\sigma_{12} = \mathbf{1.003}$$

Coefficient of Variation :

$$= \frac{\sigma_{12}}{\overline{X}} \times 100$$

$$= \frac{1.003}{2} \times 100$$

$$C.V = \mathbf{50.15\%}$$

SKEWNESS

Problem 2. (*a*) In a moderately asymmetrical distribution, the mean and the median are respectively 25.6 and 26.1 inches. What is the mode of the distribution ?

(*b*) The measure of skewness for a certain distribution is −0.8. If the lower and upper quartiles are 44.1 and 56.6 respectively, find the median. (*I.C.W.A.*)

Solution : (*a*) In a moderately asymmetrical distribution, mode can be calculated by the formula :

$$\text{Mode} = 2 \text{ Median} - 2 \text{ Mean}$$

$$= 3(26.1) - 2(25.6)$$

$$= 78.3 - 51.2$$

$$\text{Mode} = \mathbf{27.1}$$

(*b*)

$$\text{Skewness} = \frac{Q_3 + Q_1 - 2 \text{ Median}}{Q_3 - Q_1}$$

$$-0.8 = \frac{56.6 + 44.1 - 2 \text{ Median}}{56.6 - 44.1}$$

$$-0.8 = \frac{100.7 - 2 \text{ Median}}{12.5}$$

$$-0.8 \times 12.5 = 100.7 - 2 \text{ Median}$$

$$-10 = 100.7 - 2 \text{ Median}$$

$$2 \text{ Median} = 100.7 + 10$$

$$\text{Median} = \frac{110.7}{2}$$

$$= \mathbf{55.35}$$

Problem 3. The median, mode and coefficient of skewness for a certain distribution are respectively 17.4, 15.3 and 0.35. Calculate the coefficient. (*I.C.W.A.*)

Solution :

$$\text{Median} = 17.4, \text{Mode} = 15.3$$

$$\text{Mode} = 3 \text{ Median} - 2 \text{ Mean}$$

$$15.3 = 3 \times 17.4 - 2 \text{ Mean}$$

$$15.3 = 52.2 - 2 \text{ Mean}$$

$$2 \text{ Mean} = 52.2 - 15.3$$

$$\text{Mean} = \frac{36.9}{2}$$

$$= 18.45$$

$$\text{Coefficient of skewness} = \frac{\text{Mean} - \text{Mode}}{\text{Standard Deviation}}$$

$$0.35 = \frac{18.45 - 15.3}{\sigma}$$

$$0.35\sigma = 18.45 - 15.3$$

$$\sigma = \frac{3.15}{0.35}$$

$$= \mathbf{9}$$

$$\text{Coefficient of Variation} = \frac{\sigma}{\overline{X}} \times 100$$

$$= \frac{9}{18.45} \times 100$$

$$= \mathbf{48.78\%}$$

Problem 4. The mean, median and the coefficient of variation of the weekly wages of a group of 100 workers are respectively Rs. 45, Rs. 42 and Rs. 40. Find the (*i*) mode, (*ii*) variance and (*iii*) coefficient of skewness for the distribution of wages. (*I.C.W.A.*)

Solution :

Mean = 45 ;

Median = 42;

and Coefficient of Variation = 40

(*i*)
$$\text{Mode} = 3\text{ Median} - 2\text{ Mean}$$

$$= 3(42) - 2(45)$$

$$= 126 - 90$$

$$= \mathbf{36}$$

(*ii*)
$$\text{Variance} = \sigma^2$$

$$\text{Coefficient of Variation} = \frac{\sigma \times 100}{\overline{X}}$$

$$40 = \frac{\sigma \times 100}{45}$$

$$\sigma = \frac{40 \times 45}{100}$$

$$= 18$$

$$\therefore \quad \text{Variance} = 18^2 = \mathbf{324}$$

(*iii*)
$$\text{Coefficient of Skewness} = \frac{\text{Mean} - \text{Mode}}{\sigma}$$

$$= \frac{45 - 36}{18}$$

$$= \mathbf{0.5}$$

REGRESSION

Problem 5. The profits y (Rs. lakhs) of a certain company in xth year of the life are given by :

x	1	2	3	4	5
y	2.18	2.44	2.78	3.25	3.83

Fit a second degree parabola $y = a + bX + cX^2$ to the data. *(I.C.W.A.)*

Solution :

$$Y = a + bX + cX^2$$

X	X^2	X^3	X^4	Y	XY	X^2Y
-2	4	-8	16	2.18	-4.36	8.72
-1	1	-1	1	2.44	-2.44	2.44
0	0	0	0	2.78	0	0
1	1	$+1$	1	3.25	3.25	3.25
2	4	$+8$	16	3.83	7.66	15.32
$\Sigma X = 0$	$\Sigma X^2 = 10$	$\Sigma X^3 = 0$	$\Sigma X^4 = 34$	$\Sigma Y = 14.48$	$\Sigma XY = 4.11$	$\Sigma X^2Y = 29.73$

$$\Sigma Y = Na + b\Sigma X + C\Sigma X^2$$
$$\Sigma XY = a\Sigma X + b\Sigma X^2 + C\Sigma X^3$$
$$\Sigma X^2Y = a\Sigma X^2 + b\Sigma X^2 + C\Sigma X^4$$

When $\Sigma X = 0$ the equations are reduced to

$$\Sigma Y = Na + CX^2$$
$$\Sigma XY = b\Sigma X^2$$
$$\Sigma X^2Y = a\Sigma X^2 + C\Sigma X^4$$

Substituting the values

$$14.48 = 5a + 10C \quad (1)$$
$$4.11 = 10b \quad (2)$$
$$29.73 = 10a + 34c \quad (3)$$

From Equation (2) we get

$$\text{b} = 0.411$$

Multiply Equation (1) by 2

$$28.96 = 10a + 20c \quad (4)$$

Subtracting equation (4) from (3) we get

$$0.77 = 14\text{ C}$$
$$\therefore \quad \text{C} = 0.055$$

Substitute the value in equation (1)

$$14.48 = 5a + 10 \times 0.055$$
$$-5a = 0.55 - 14.48$$
$$a = -\frac{-13.93}{-5}$$
$$= \mathbf{2.786}$$

INDEX NUMBER

Problem 6. An enquiry into the budgets of middle class families of a certain city revealed that on an average the percentage expenses on the different groups were :

Food	45
Rent	15
Clothing	12
Fuel & Light	8
Misc.	20

The group index numbers for the current year as compared with fixed base period were respectively 410, 150, 343, 248 and 285. Calculate the consumer price index number for the current year. Mr. X was getting Rs. 240 in the base period and Rs. 430 in the current year. State how much be ought to have received as extra allowance to maintain his former standard of living. (*I.C.W.A.*)

Solution :

Computation of Consumer Price Index

Groups	*Price Index* $P_1 (P_0 = 100)$	*Weight* q_0	$P_1 q_0$
Food	410	45	18,450
Rent	150	15	2,250
Clothing	343	12	4,116
Fuel and Light	248	8	1,984
Miscellaneous	285	20	5,700
		$\Sigma q_0 = 100$	$\Sigma P_1 q_0 = 32,500$

$$\text{Consumer Price Index} = \frac{\Sigma P_1 q_0}{\Sigma P_0 q^0} \times 100 = \frac{32500}{100 \times 100} \times 100$$
$$= 325\%$$

When $P_0 = 100$, Mr. X was getting Rs. 240 in the base period.

In the current year he ought to get $240 \times 325\%$ = Rs. 780

To maintain his former standard of living, he should receive an extra allowance of

Rs. 780 − Rs. 430 = **Rs. 350**

Problem 7. Construct Fisher's Ideal Index from the following data and show that it satisfies time reversal test and factor reversal test :

	2001		2003	
Article	*Price*	*Quantity*	*Price*	*Quantity*
A	10	6	15	5
B	12	10	15	10
C	18	5	27	3
D	8	5	12	4

(*B. Com., Delhi*)

Solution :

Computation of Fisher's Ideal Index

Article	2001		2003					
	P_0	q_0	P_1	q_1	P_1q_0	P_0q_0	P_1q_1	P_0q_1
A	10	6	15	5	90	60	75	50
B	12	10	15	10	150	120	150	120
C	18	5	27	3	135	90	81	54
D	8	5	12	4	60	40	48	32
					$\Sigma P_1q_0 = 435$	$\Sigma P_0q_0 = 310$	$\Sigma P_1q_1 = 354$	$\Sigma P_0q_1 = 256$

$$\text{Fisher's Ideal Index } P_{01} = \sqrt{\frac{\Sigma P_1q_0}{\Sigma P_0q_0} \times \frac{\Sigma P_1q_1}{\Sigma P_0q_1}} \times 100$$

$$= \sqrt{\frac{435}{310} \times \frac{354}{256}} \times 100$$

$$= \sqrt{1.403 \times 1.383} \times 100$$

$$= \sqrt{1.940} \times 100$$

$$= 1.3929 \times 100$$

$$= \mathbf{139.29}$$

Time Reversal Test is satisfied when

$$P_{01} \times P_{10} = 1$$

$$P_{01} \times P_{10} = \sqrt{\frac{\Sigma P_1q_0}{\Sigma P_0q_0} \times \frac{\Sigma P_1q_1}{\Sigma P_0q_1}} \sqrt{\frac{\Sigma P_0q_1}{\Sigma P_1q_1} \times \frac{\Sigma P_0q_0}{\Sigma P_1q_0}}$$

$$= \sqrt{\frac{435}{310} \times \frac{354}{256}} \sqrt{\frac{256}{354} \times \frac{310}{435}}$$

$$= \sqrt{1} = 1$$

Therefore Time Reversal Test is satisfied

Factor Reversal test is satisfied when

$$P_{01} \times Q_{01} = \frac{\Sigma P_1q_0}{\Sigma P_0q_0}$$

$$P_{01} \times Q_{01} = \sqrt{\frac{\Sigma P_1q_0}{\Sigma P_0q_0} \times \frac{\Sigma P_1q_1}{\Sigma P_0q_1}} \sqrt{\frac{\Sigma q_1P_0}{\Sigma q_0P_0} \times \frac{\Sigma q_1P_1}{\Sigma q_0P_1}}$$

$$= \sqrt{\frac{435}{310} \times \frac{354}{256} \times \frac{256}{310} \times \frac{354}{435}}$$

$$= \sqrt{\frac{354}{310} \times \frac{354}{310}}$$

$$= \frac{\mathbf{354}}{\mathbf{310}} \; i.e. = \frac{\mathbf{\Sigma P_1q_1}}{\mathbf{\Sigma P_0q_0}}$$

Therefore Factor Reversal Test is satisfied.

Problem 8. An index is at 100 in 1999. It rises 4% in 2000, falls 6% in 2001, falls 4% in 2002 and rises 3% in 2003. Calculate the index numbers for the five years with 2001 as base.

(M. Com., Delhi)

Solution :

Computation of Index Numbers

Year	*Index Number* (*Base year 1999 = 100*)	*Index Number* (*Base year 2001 = 100*)
1999	100	$\frac{100}{97.76} \times 100 = 102.29$
2000	100 + 4 =104	$\frac{104}{97.76} \times 100 = 106.38$
2001	$\frac{94}{100} \times 104 = 97.76$	100
2002	$\frac{96}{100} \times 97.76 = 93.85$	$\frac{93.85}{97.76} \times 100 = 96$
2003	$\frac{103}{100} \times 93.85 = 96.67$	$\frac{96.67}{97.76} \times 100 = 98.89$

Problem 9. From the following index numbers, prepare new ones by (a) considering the year 2001 as base and (b) using chain base method :

Year	:	1998	1999	2000	2001	2002	2003
Index Number	:	100	110	175	250	300	400

(B. Com., Poona)

Solution :

Computation of Index Numbers

		(*a*)	(*b*)
Year	*Index Number*	*Index Number* 2001 *as base*	*Chain Base Index Number*
1998	100	$\frac{100}{250} \times 100 = 40$	100
1999	110	$\frac{110}{250} \times 100 = 44$	$\frac{110}{100} \times 100 = 110$
2000	175	$\frac{175}{250} \times 100 = 70$	$\frac{175}{110} \times 100 = 159.09$
2001	250	$\frac{250}{250} \times 100 = 100$	$\frac{250}{175} \times 100 = 142.86$
2002	300	$\frac{300}{250} \times 100 = 120$	$\frac{300}{250} \times 100 = 120.00$
2003	400	$\frac{400}{250} \times 100 = 160$	$\frac{400}{300} \times 100 = 133.33$

Problem 10. Estimate the expectation of life at the age of 16 years by using the following data.

Age (in years)	:	10	15	20	25	30	35
Expectation of life (years)	:	35.4	32.3	29.2	26.0	23.2	20.4

(*I.C.W.A. Inter, B. Com., Kurukshetra*)

Solution :

x	y	*Differences*				
		Δ^1	Δ^2	Δ^3	Δ^4	Δ^5
10	35.4					
		$-3.1\ \Delta_0^1$				
15	32.3		$0\ \Delta_0^2$			
		-3.1		$-0.1\ \Delta_0^3$		
20	29.2		-0.1		$0.6\ \Delta_0 4$	
		-3.2		0.5		$-1.5\Delta_0 5$
25	26.0		$+0.4$		-0.9	
		-2.8		-0.4		
30	23.2		0			
		-2.8				
35	20.4					

$$x = \frac{16-10}{5} = 1.2$$

$$y_x = y_0 + x\Delta_0^{\ 1} + \frac{x(x-1)}{2!}\Delta_0^{\ 2} + \frac{x(x-1)(x-2)}{3!}\Delta_0^{\ 3}$$

$$+ \frac{x(x-1)(x-2)(x-3)}{4!}\Delta_0^{\ 4} + \frac{x(x-1)(x-2)(x-3)(x-4)}{5!}\Delta_0^{\ 5}$$

$$= 35.4 + 1.2 \times -3.1 + \frac{1.2(1.2-1)}{2} \times 0 + \frac{1.2(1.2-1)(1.2-2)}{2 \times 3}(-0.1)$$

$$+ \frac{1.2(1.2-1)(1.2-2)(1.2-3)}{2 \times 3 \times 4} \times 0.6$$

$$+ \frac{1.2(1.2-1)(1.2-2)(1.2-3)(1.2-4)}{2 \times 3 \times 4 \times 5} \times (-1.5)$$

$$= 35.4 - 3.72 + 0 + 0.0032 + 0.00864 + 0.012096$$

$$= 35.423936 - 3.72$$

$$= 31.703936.$$

Thus the estimated expectation of life at the age of 16 years = **31.7 years.**

PROBABILITY

Problem 11. The odds against a certain event are 5 to 2 and the odds in favour of another (independent) event are 6 to 5; find the chance that one at least of the events will happen.

Solution :

Probability against the event $= \frac{5}{7}$

Probability against the second event $= \frac{5}{11}$

Probability that no event will happen $= \frac{5}{7} \times \frac{5}{11} = \frac{25}{77}$

$\therefore$ The probability that at least one event will happen $\Big\} = 1 - \frac{25}{77} = \frac{52}{77}$

Problem 12. If in a bag there are 4 blue and 4 black balls and we draw 3 at random, what is the probability that the balls are black and not blue.

Solution :

Probability of drawing 3 black balls out of 4 $\Big\} = {}^4C_3$

Probability of drawing 3 balls out of 8 $\Big\} = {}^8C_3$

$\therefore$ The required probability $= \frac{{}^4C_3}{{}^8C_3} = \frac{4}{56} = \frac{1}{14}$

Problem 13. Find if a card taken out of well shuffled 52 cards is a (*a*) a spade, (*b*) an ace of spade, or (*c*) an ace of black colour.

Solution :

(*a*) There are 13 spade cards in 52 cards.
Probability of drawing a spade $= \frac{13}{52} = \mathbf{\frac{1}{4}}$

(*b*) There is one ace of spade in 52 cards.
Probability of drawing an ace of spade $= \mathbf{\frac{1}{52}}$

(*c*) There are 2 aces of black colour.
Probability of drawing aces of black colour $= \frac{2}{52}$ or $= \mathbf{\frac{1}{26}}$

Problem 14. A bag contains 15 white and 17 black balls. If one draw of 2 balls is made, what is the probability that one of them is white and the other black ?

Solution :

Total number of balls = 15 + 17 = 32

Probability of getting white ball $= \frac{15}{32}$

Probability of getting black ball $= \frac{17}{32}$

The probability of getting a white and black ball $= \frac{15}{32} \times \frac{17}{32} = \mathbf{\frac{255}{1024}}$

Problem 15. In a box there are 5 black pencils and 7 blue pencils. The other box contains 6 black pencils and 6 blue pencils. We drew one black pencil from any box of these two. What is the probability that the black pencil was drawn from the first box only ?

Solution :

Probability to draw a black from first box $\Big\} \frac{5}{12}$

Probability to draw a black from second box $\Big\} \frac{6}{12}$

Probability that pencil drawn from first box $\Big\} = \frac{5/12}{5/12 + 6/12}$

$$= \frac{5}{12} \times \frac{12}{11} = \mathbf{\frac{5}{11}}$$

Problem 16. There are 3 boxes. First has got 3 black pencils and 5 red ones, second has got 5 black pencils and 3 red ones, and the third has got 4 each. We drew one black pencil from one box. What is the probability that it was drawn from the first box ?

Solution : There are 3 boxes.

Every box has equal chance to be selected. Thus, in each case the probability $= \frac{1}{3}$

$$\text{The required probability} = \frac{\frac{1}{3} \times \frac{3}{8}}{\left(\frac{1}{3} \times \frac{3}{8}\right) + \left(\frac{1}{3} \times \frac{5}{8}\right) + \left(\frac{1}{3} \times \frac{4}{8}\right)}$$

$$= \frac{3/24}{3/24 + 5/24 + 4/24}$$

$$= \frac{3/24}{12/24}$$

$$= \frac{3}{24} \times \frac{24}{12} = \frac{3}{12} \text{ or } \mathbf{\frac{1}{4}}$$

Problem 17. Two cubical dice whose faces are marked with digits 1 to 6 are thrown simultaneously. Find the probability that the sum of the digits on the faces that turn up is 8.

Solution :

$$\left.\begin{array}{l}\text{Total number of ways}\\ \text{of turning up}\end{array}\right\} 6 \times 6 = 36$$

The favourable cases $= 5$

They are $6, 2; 5, 3; 4, 4; 3, 5; 2, 6$.

The required probability $= \mathbf{\frac{5}{36}}$

Problem 18. A tosses 2 coins. What is the probability that at least one tail would turn up ?

Solution :

Probability of head $= \frac{1}{2}$

Probability of tail $= \frac{1}{2}$

Probability of not turning up tail $= \frac{1}{2} \times \frac{1}{2} = \frac{1}{4}$ in two cases

Required Probability $= 1 - \frac{1}{4} = \mathbf{\frac{3}{4}}$

Problem 19. A cannot solve a problem selected at random in 25 % of cases and M in 36 % of cases. What is the probability that either of them can solve problem chosen at random.

Solution :

The probability that A cannot solve $= \frac{25}{100}$

The probability that M cannot solve $= \frac{36}{100}$

The probability that both of them fail to solve $= \frac{25}{100} \times \frac{36}{100} = \frac{9}{100}$

The required probability $= 1 - \frac{9}{100} = \frac{91}{100} = \mathbf{91\%}$

Problem 20. In a bag there are 6 blue and 8 white balls. What is the probability that 2 balls drawn in succession (without replacing any) are white ?

Solution :

Probability of drawing a white ball in first draw $\frac{8}{14}$

Probability of drawing a white ball in second draw $\frac{7}{13}$

Therefore, the required probability $= \frac{8}{14} \times \frac{7}{13} = \frac{56}{182} = \mathbf{\frac{4}{13}}$

SAMPLING

Problem 21. In a sample of 600 men from a certain city, 450 men are found to be smokers. In a sample of 900 from another city 450 are found to be smokers. Do the data indicate that the two cities are significantly different with respect to prevalence of smoking habit among men ?

(*M.A. Agra, M.B.A. Banaras, ICWA*)

Solution : Null hypothesis $P_1 = P_2$

$$P_1 = \frac{450}{650} = 0.75$$

$$P_2 = \frac{450}{900} = 0.5$$

(P_1 and P_2 = Proportion of smokers)

$$P = \frac{(600 \times 0.75) + 900 \times 0.50}{600 + 900} = \frac{900}{1500} = 0.6$$

$$\therefore \quad q = 1 - 0.6 = 0.4$$

$$SE_{(P_1 - P_2)} = \sqrt{\frac{0.6 \times 0.4}{600} + \frac{0.6 \times 0.4}{900}}$$

$$= \sqrt{0.0004 + 0.0003}$$

$$= 0.0265$$

$$Z = \frac{P_1 - P_2}{SE} = \frac{0.75 - 0.50}{0.0265} = \mathbf{9.43}$$

The computed value of Z = 9.43 lies in the rejection region. Therefore, there is a significant difference between the two cities with respect to prevalence of smoking habit among men.

Problem 22. A sample of 1000 days is taken from meteorological records of a certain district, and 120 of them are found to be foggy. What are the probable limits to the percentage of foggy days in the district ?

Solution :

Proportion of foggy days

$$= P = \frac{120}{1000} = \frac{3}{25}$$

$$q = \frac{22}{25}$$

Standard Error of the proportion of foggy days :

$$S.E = \sqrt{\frac{pq}{n}}$$

$$= \sqrt{\frac{3}{25} \times \frac{22}{25} \times \frac{1}{1000}}$$
$$= \sqrt{0.12 \times 0.88 \times 0.001}$$
$$= \sqrt{0.000106}$$
$$= 0.0103$$
$$= \mathbf{1.03\%}.$$

A simple sample should give a percentage within three times the standard error. Thus, the limits are 12% (3/25) ± 3.09, that is 8.91% and 15.9% (approximately).

Problem 23. In a newspaper article of 1600 works in Hindustani 64 percent of the words are found to be of Hindi origin, assuming the simple sampling conditions hold good, estimate the proportion of Hindi words in the writer's vocabulary and assign limits to that proportion :

Solution :

Assuming the conditions of simple sampling hold good, we have,

Proportion of words of Hindi origin or $P = \frac{64}{100}$

$$q = \frac{36}{100}$$

Standard error of proportion of words of Hindi origin

$$S.E = \sqrt{\frac{pq}{n}}$$
$$= \sqrt{\frac{64}{100} \times \frac{36}{100} \times \frac{1}{1600}}$$
$$= \sqrt{0.64 \times 0.36 \times 0.0006}$$
$$= \sqrt{0.00014}$$
$$= 0.012$$
$$= \mathbf{1.2\%}$$

A simple sample should give a percentage within three times the standard error. Thus the limits are 64 % ± 3.6, that is 60.4% and 67.6% (approximately).

Problem 24. 500 eggs are taken at random from a large consignment, and 50 are found to be bad. Estimate the percentage of bad eggs in the consignment and assign limits within which the percentage probably lies.

Solution :

Proportion of bad eggs in the sample :

$P = \frac{1}{10}$ and $q = \frac{9}{10}$

Standard Error of the proportion of bad eggs

$$S.E. = \sqrt{\frac{Pq}{n}}$$
$$= \sqrt{\frac{1}{10} \times \frac{9}{10} \times \frac{1}{500}}$$
$$= \sqrt{0.1 \times 0.9 \times 0.002}$$
$$= \sqrt{0.00018}$$

$$= 0.0134$$
$$= \mathbf{1.34\%}.$$

A simple sample should give a percentage within three times the standard error. Thus, the limits are 10% (1/10) ± 4.02, that is 5.98% and 14.02% (approximately).

Problem 25. The following table gives the proportion of dark coloured people in two cities.

City	*Total population observed*	*Percetage of dark coloured*
A	250	42
B	450	33

Can the difference observed in the percentage of dark coloured people be due to the fluctuations of sampling ?

Solution : The percentage of dark coloured people in two cities together is :

$$\begin{aligned}
A &= \frac{250 \times 42}{100} = \mathbf{105}\,;\ B = \frac{450 \times 33}{100} \\
&= 148.500 \text{ or } \mathbf{149} \\
P_0 &= \frac{(105 + 149) \times 100}{250 + 450} \\
&= \frac{254 \times 100}{700} \\
&= 36.29 \\
\therefore \quad q_0 &= 100 - 36.29 = 63.71 \\
\text{S.E.} &= \sqrt{P_0 q_0 \left(\frac{1}{n_1} + \frac{1}{n_2}\right)} \\
&= \sqrt{(36.29 \times 63.71)\left(\frac{1}{250} + \frac{1}{450}\right)} \\
&= \sqrt{2312.04 \times (0.004 + 0.002)} \\
&= \sqrt{13.872} \\
&= \mathbf{3.72\%}.
\end{aligned}$$

Problem 26. In certain sampling inspection, the number of defectives found in 10 samples of 100 each are given below :

16, 18, 11, 18, 21, 10, 20, 18, 17 and 21

Do these indicate that the quality characteristic under inspection is under statistical control ?

(B. Com)

Solution :

$$\begin{aligned}
\eta P &= \frac{16 + 18 + 11 + 18 + 21 + 10 + 20 + 18 + 17 + 21}{10} \\
&= \frac{170}{10} = 17 \\
P &= \frac{170}{100 \times 10} = 0.17 \qquad \therefore \qquad q = 1 - 0.17 = 0.83 \\
\eta P q &= \sqrt{100 \times 0.17 \times 0.83} \\
&= \sqrt{14.11} \\
&= 3.76
\end{aligned}$$

$$UCL = 17 + 3 \times 3.76 = 17 + 11.28 = 28.28$$
$$LCL = 17 - 3 \times 3.76 = 17 - 11.28 = \mathbf{5.72}$$

Sample points are within control limits, *i.e.* 5.72 to 28.28, and quality characteristic under inspection is under statistical control.

STANDARDISED RATES

Problem 27. Compute :

(1) General Fertility Rate,

(2) Total Fertility Rate, and

(3) The Gross Reproduction Rate from the following data :

Age group of child bearing females	15–19	20–24	25–29	30–34	35–39	40–44	45–49
No. of women ('000)	16	16.4	15.8	15.2	14.8	15	14.5
Total births	260	2244	1894	1320	916	280	145

Assume that the proportion of females birth is 46.2%. (*M. Com. Delhi*)

Solution :

Age	*No. of women* ('000)	*No. of births*	*Age specific fertility rate*
15–19	16	260	16
20–24	16.4	2244	137
25–29	15.8	1894	120
30–34	15.2	1320	87
35–39	14.8	916	62
40–44	15	280	19
45–49	14.5	145	10
Total:	107.7	7059	452

(1) $\text{GFR} = \dfrac{\text{No. of live births} \times 1000}{\text{No. of female population (15–49)}} = \dfrac{7059 \times 1000}{107700} = \mathbf{65.5}$

(2) TFR : $\Sigma(\text{SFR}) \times 5 = 452 \times 5 = \mathbf{2260}$

$$\text{TFR per woman} = \frac{2260}{1000} = \mathbf{2.26}$$

$$\text{G.R.R.} = \frac{\text{No. of female births}}{\text{Total births}} \times \mathbf{TFR}$$
$$= \frac{46.2 \times 2260}{100} = \mathbf{1044}$$

Problem 28. From the data given below calculate the gross reproduction rate and net reproduction rate :

Age group	*No. of children born to 100 women passing through the age group*	*Mortality Rate*
16–20	150	120
21–25	1500	180
26–30	2000	150
31–35	800	200
36–40	500	220
41–45	200	230
46–50	100	250

Sex ratio being males : females 52 : 48 (*B. Com. Delhi*)

Solution :

Age group	*No. of childern born to 1000 women passing through the age group*	*No. of female children*	*Survival rate* (1000) *Mortality Rate*	*No. of female children survived*
16–20	150	$150 \times \frac{48}{100} = 72$	880	$72 \times \frac{880}{1000} = 63.36$
21–25	1500	$1500 \times \frac{48}{100} = 720$	820	$720 \times \frac{820}{1000} = 590.40$
26–30	2000	$2000 \times \frac{48}{100} = 960$	850	$960 \times \frac{850}{1000} = 816.00$
31–35	800	$800 \times \frac{48}{100} = 384$	800	$384 \times \frac{800}{1000} = 307.20$
36–40	500	$500 \times \frac{48}{100} = 240$	780	$240 \times \frac{780}{1000} = 187.20$
41–45	200	$200 \times \frac{48}{100} = 96$	770	$96 \times \frac{770}{1000} = 73.92$
46–50	100	$100 \times \frac{48}{100} = 48$	750	$48 \times \frac{750}{1000} = 36.00$
		2,520		2074.08

$$\text{G.R.R} = \frac{\text{Total No. of female children born}}{1000}$$

$$= \frac{2520}{1000} = \mathbf{2.52} \text{ per woman}$$

$$\text{N.R.R.} = \frac{\text{No. of female children born and survived to 1000 women}}{1000}$$

$$= \frac{2074.08}{1000} = \mathbf{2.07} \text{ per woman}$$

Problem 29. Compute the crude and standardised death rates of the two populations A and B from following data ;

Age group	*A*		*B*	
	Population	*Deaths*	*Population*	*Deaths*
Below 5	15,000	360	40,000	1,000
5–30	20,000	400	52,000	1,040
Above 30	10,000	280	8,000	240

(*B. Com Andhra*)

Solution:

Age group	A			B		
	Population	*Deaths*	*Death rate*	*Population*	*Deaths*	*Death rate*
Below 5	15,000	360	24	40,000	1000	25
5–30	20,000	400	20	52,000	1,040	20
Above 30	10,000	280	28	8,000	240	30
Total :	45,000	1040		1,00,000	2,280	

Crude Death Rate :

$$\text{Town } (A) = \frac{\text{No. of deaths}}{\text{Population}} \times 1000 = \frac{1040 \times 1000}{45000} = \mathbf{23.1}$$

$$\text{Town } (B) = \frac{2280 \times 1000}{1,00,000} = \mathbf{22.8}$$

Standardised Death Rate :

$$\text{Town } (A) = \frac{(15,000 \times 24) + (20,000 \times 20) + (10,000 \times 28)}{15,000 + 20,000 + 10,000}$$

$$= \frac{3,60,000 + 4,00,000 + 2,80,000}{45,000}$$

$$= \frac{10,40,000}{44,000} = \mathbf{23.1}$$

Standardised Death Rate :

$$\text{Town } (B) = \frac{(15,000 \times 25) + (20,000 \times 20) + (10,000 \times 30)}{15,000 + 20,000 + 10,000}$$

$$= \frac{3,75,000 + 4,00,000 + 3,00,000}{45,000}$$

$$= \mathbf{23.89}$$

The death rate in town B is higher than town A.

Problem 30. The distribution of population according to different age groups and annual death rates specific to age groups of two towns A and B are as follows :

Age group	*Town A*		*Town B*	
	Population ('000)	*Death rate per* 1000	*Population* ('000)	*Death rate per* 1000
0–5	30	100	50	101
5–15	35	25	60	26
15–40	65	10	160	11
Above 40	20	30	30	31

Find :

(1) Crude death are for Town A and B

(2) The death rate of A as a standard population.

(*B. Com. Bombay*).

Solution :

Age group	*Town A*		*Town B*		*No. of Death*
	Population ('000)	*Specific death Rate*	*Population* ('000)	*Specific death Rate*	
0–5	30	100	50	101	3030
5–15	35	25	60	26	910
15–40	65	10	160	11	715
Above 40	20	30	30	31	620
Total:	150		300		5275

(1) CDR of Town A

$$= \frac{(30 \times 100) + (35 \times 25) + (65 \times 10) + (20 \times 30)}{150}$$

$$= \frac{3000 + 875 + 650 + 600}{150} = \frac{5125}{150} = \mathbf{34.17}$$

CDR of town B

$$= \frac{(50 \times 101) + (60 \times 26) + (160 \times 11) + (30 \times 31)}{300}$$

$$= \frac{5050 + 1560 + 1760 + 930}{300} = \frac{9300}{300} = \mathbf{31}.$$

(2) SDR of town B

$$\frac{5275}{150} = \mathbf{35.17}$$

Town A is more healthier.

Problem 31. Which of the two localities A and B is healthier ?

Age group	*Locality A*		*Locality B*	
	Population	*Death per 1000*	*Population*	*Death per1000*
0–10	600	30	400	40
10–20	1000	5	1500	4
20–60	3000	8	2400	10
Above 60	400	50	700	30

Take Locality A as standard.

(*B. Com. Bombay*)

Solution :

Standardised Death Rate of Locality A

$$= \frac{(600 \times 30) + (1000 \times 5) + (3000 \times 8) + (400 \times 50)}{600 + 1000 + 3000 + 400}$$

$$= \frac{18,000 + 5,000 + 24,000 + 20,000}{5,000}$$

$$= \frac{67000}{5000} = \mathbf{13.4}$$

Standardised Death Rate of Locality B

$$= \frac{(600 \times 40) + (1000 \times 4) + (3000 \times 10) + (400 \times 30)}{5,000}$$

$$= \frac{24,000 + 4,000 + 30,000 + 12000}{5,000}$$

$$= \frac{70,000}{5000}$$

$$= \mathbf{14}$$

Locality A is healthier than locality B, as SDR is lower.

Problem 32. From given data, make a comparative study of crude and standardized death rate for town A and town B.

Age group	*Town A*		*Town B*		*Standard population* ('000)
	Population (*'000*)	*Specific death rate*	*Population* (*'000*)	*Specific death rate*	
0–5	6	40	7	40	4
5–25	30	18	40	18	34
25–45	24	12	20	13	25
45–60	12	25	8	20	11
Above 60	8	34	5	44	6

(*B. Com. Bombay*)

Solution :

Age group	Town A			Town B		
	Population	Specific Death Rate	No. of Deaths	Population	Specific Death Rate	No. of Deaths
0–5	6,000	40	240	7,000	40	280
5–25	30,000	18	580	40,000	18	720
25–45	24,000	12	288	20,000	13	260
45–60	12,000	25	300	8,000	20	160
Above 60	8,000	34	272	5,000	44	220
Total :	80,000		1640	80,000		1640

$$\text{CDR for town } A = \frac{1640 \times 1000}{80,000} = 20.5$$

$$\text{CDR for town } B = \frac{1640 \times 1000}{80,000} = 20.5$$

The crude death rate for both the towns is the same. Since, different age groups have different specific death rates, in both towns, the crude death rate is not suitable for comparing the health conditions. Therefore, we have to use standardised death rate.

Standardised Population	Town A		Town B	
	Specific Death rate	No. of Deaths	Specific Death rate	No. of Deaths
4,000	40	160	40	160
34,000	18	612	18	612
25,000	12	300	13	325
11,000	25	275	20	220
6,000	34	204	44	264
80,000		1551		1581

$$\text{S.D.R. for town } A = \frac{1551 \times 1000}{80,000} = \mathbf{19.39}$$

$$\text{S.D.R. for town } B = \frac{1581 \times 1000}{80,000} = \mathbf{19.76}$$

Therefore, we conclude that town A is healthier than the town B, as SDR of town A is less than town B.

Problem 33. Which of the two places for which mortality data are given, is in your opinion more healthy ?

Age group	Locality A		Locality B	
	Population	Deaths	Population	Deaths
Under 5	4,500	135	4,000	144
5–15	10,000	40	10,500	63
15–65	12,000	75	13,500	81
Above 65	3,000	140	2,000	102
Total	30,000	390	30,000	390

Solution :

Age	Locality A			Locality B		
	Population	*Deaths*	*Death rate*	*Population*	*Deaths*	*Death rate*
Under 5	4,500	135	30	4,000	144	36
5–15	10,000	40	4	10,500	63	6
15–65	12,500	75	6	13,500	81	6
Above 65	3,000	140	47	2,000	102	51
Total :	30,000	390		30,000	390	

Crude Death Rate of locality A

$$= \frac{\text{No. of Deaths} \times 1000}{\text{Population}} = \frac{390 \times 1000}{30,000} = \mathbf{13}$$

Standard Death Rate = **13**

Standardised Death rate of locality B

$$= \frac{(4500 \times 36) + (10,000 \times 6) + (12500 \times 6) + (3000 \times 51)}{30,000}$$

$$= \frac{162,000 + 60,000 + 75000 + 153,000}{30,000}$$

$$= \frac{4,50,000}{30,000} = \mathbf{15}$$

Locality A is healthier than Locality B.

Problem 34. 200 candidates appeared for a competitive examination and 60 of them succeeded. 35 received special coaching and out of them 20 candidates succeeded. Prepare contingency 2×2 table and using Yule's Coefficient discuss whether special coaching is effective or not. (*CA*)

Solution :

(A) denote successful candidates

(B) denote those attended special coaching

	(A)		
B	20 (AB)	(15) (αB)	35 (B)
	40 ($A\beta$)	125 ($\alpha\beta$)	165 (β)
	60 (A)	140 (α)	N 200

$$Q = \frac{(AB)(\alpha\beta) - (A\beta)(\alpha B)}{(AB)(\alpha\beta) + (A\beta)(\alpha B)}$$

$$= \frac{(20 \times 125) - (40 \times 15)}{(20 \times 125) + (40 \times 15)}$$

$$= \frac{2500 - 600}{2500 + 600}$$

$$= \frac{1900}{3100}$$

$$= +\ \mathbf{0.613}$$

$Q = +\ 0.613$ and this shows that the special coaching is effective.

Problem 35. Out of 20,000 customer's ledger accounts, a sample of 600 accounts was taken to test the accuracy of posting and balancing wherein 45 mistakes were found. Assign limits within which the number of defective cases can be expected at 95% level. (*CA*)

Solution :

$$P = \frac{45}{600} = 0.075 \text{ or } 7.5\%$$

$$SE\,(p) = \sqrt{\frac{P(100 - P)}{n}}$$

$$= \sqrt{\frac{7.5 \times 92.5}{600}}$$

$$= \sqrt{\frac{693.75}{600}}$$

$$= \sqrt{1.156}$$

$$= 1.075$$

At 95% confidence limits, the percentage of defective cases are

$$P \pm 1.96\,SE$$

$$= 7.5 \pm 1.96 \times 1.075$$

$$= 7.5 \pm 2.107$$

$$= 5.393 \text{ and } 9.607$$

Hence the No. of defective cases may be :

$$20,000 \times \frac{5.393}{100} \text{ and } 20,000 \times \frac{9.607}{100}$$

That is between 1079 and 1921.

18

LOGARITHMS AND THEIR USES

In statistics, we may come across many mathematical operations to find out the result. Very often, tedious mathematical operations like divisions, powers, extracting root, etc. can be solved through logarithms. If logarithms are made use of in the process, much time and energy can be saved. The logarithm of a number is the power to which the base 10 should be raised to equal to that number. Thus, the log of 10 is 1 (10^1), of 100 is 2 $(10)^2$, of 1000 is 3 (10^3) and so on. But all the numbers are not so convenient ant their logs cannot be easily found out. For example, 56, 576, 846 etc. Here we have to consult with the logarithm table.

The logarithm of a number consists of two parts-characteristic and mantissa.

Characteristic :

It is the integral part of a logarithm and is ascertained by inspection. If the number is one or more than one, the characteristic is one less than the number of digits to the left of the decimal point. In other words, the characteristic of the log of a number is found by the formula, N-1, where N stands for the number of digits to the left of the decimal point. Thus the characteristic of 3 is 0 (number of digits-1), 45 is 1 (i.e., 2-1), 412 is 2 (i.e., 3-1).

Number	Characteristic
5	0 (1—1)
14	1 (2—1)
317	2(3—1)
2318	3 (4—1)
68437	4 (5—1)
236493	5 (6—1)

If the number is less than 1, the characteristic is one more than the number of zeros just to the right of the decimal point. In other words, the characteristic of a number less than 1 is found by the formula, N + 1, where N stands for the number of zeros to the right of decimal point. For example:

Number	Characteristic
.7841	—1 or $\bar{1}$
.0415	—2 or $\bar{2}$
.0056	—3 or $\bar{3}$
.00042	—4 or $\bar{4}$
.4868	—1 or $\bar{1}$
.89	—1 or $\bar{1}$

Mantissa

Mantissa of a number can be found out from the logarithm tables. It should be remembered that the mantissa of a number is always positive and is not changed by the position of the decimal point. But the characteristic can be positive as well as negative.

Mantissa is ascertained from logarithm tables and the characteristics by inspection. For example.

Number	Mantissa
1	.0000
11	.0414
42	.6232
442	.6454
44.2	.6454
4.42	.6454
.442	.6454

Explanation

To find out the mantissa, we have to look up the logarithm tables. Say, we have to find the mantissa of 5438. Refer logarithm table and note the figure opposite to 54 under 3 and add the mean difference under 8. If more than 4 figures are there, approximate the figures to the first 4 places. For example 14,578 can be approximated to 1458. The following example will illustrate the procedure.

Number	Characteristic	Mantissa	Logarithm
1	0	.0000	0.0000
10	1	.0000	1.0000
412	2	.6140	2.6140
5716	3	.7571	3.7571
87398	4	.9415	4.9415
4529.37	3	.6560	3.6560
13417	4	.1277	4.1277
1341.7	3	.1277	3.1277
134.417	2	.1284	2.1284
13.4417	1	.1284	1.1284
5617	3	.7495	3.7495
561.7	2	.7495	2.7495
56.17	1	.7495	1.74495
5.617	0	.7495	0.7495
.5617	$\bar{1}$	.7495	$\bar{1}.7495$
.05617	$\bar{2}$	.7495	$\bar{2}.7595$
.005617	$\bar{3}$	.7495	$\bar{3}.7495$
.0005617	$\bar{4}$	.7495	$\bar{4}.7495$
.00005617	$\bar{5}$	.7495	$\bar{5}.7495$

One can find out the logarithm of any number with the help of logarithm tables. Similarly, the number, the logarithm of which is given found out with the help of logarithm tables. To find out a number from the log of a number, first only the mantissa is taken into account. In antilog tables one can look up the number against the figures of mantissa. After finding out the number, the decimal point is considered by taking into account the characteristics. For example, how the number, the logarithm of which 2.4678 is to be obtained. The figure opposite to 46 under 7 is noted down. It is .2931. The mean difference opposite to 46 under 8 is 6, which is added to .2931, thus totaling to 2937. The characteristic is 2 ; then the decimal point is placed after the third (2+1) figure. So the number, the log of which is 2.4678 is 293.7

Uses of Logarithm :

1. *To multiply numbers*

If one wants to multiply with two or more figures, the work can easily and quickly be done with the help of log tables. The steps are :

1. Find out the logarithm of each value.
2. Add up all the logarithms.
3. Find out the antilogarithm of the total.

Example : Multiply $A \times B = \text{Log } A + \text{Log } B$

$AB = \text{Antilog of } (\log A + \log B)$

Example : Multiply 34 by 88

Log of	34	=	1.5315
Log of	88	=	1.9445
Total		=	3.4760

Then refer antilog to know the value of .4760 which is 2992. The characteristic is 3, therefore, put decimal point after (3+1) 4 digits, i.e., 2992 is the product.

Example : Multiply 3.4 with 8.8

Log of	3.4	=	0.5315
Log of	8.8	=	0.9445
Total		=	1.4760

Then refer antilog to know the value of 4760 which is 2992. The characteristic is 1, therefore put decimal point after 2 digits, i.e., 29.92 is the product.

2. *To divide the number :*

If one wants to divide one number by another, then find out the logarithm of the divisor and subtract it from the logarithm of the dividend and find out antilog of this difference. It will be the answer.

Example :

$A \div B$ =Anti log of (Log A-Log B)

Simplify :

Divide 468 by 16.2

Solution :

Log of	468	=	2.6702 (—)
Log of	16.2	=	1.2095
Total		=	1.4607

$461 \div 16.2 = \text{antilog of } 1.4607$

Look up the antilog table against 46 under 0, which is 2884 : and under 7 it is 5 which is added to 2884 = 2889. The characteristic is one ; so put decimal point after 2 figures. Thus the answer is 28.89. The procedure is similar to all types of figures of larger size.

3. *To raise a number to stated power :*

A number can be raised to any of its powers by multiplying the logarithm of the number by the exponent of power. The product is the log of the required power.

$\text{Log } x^n = \text{Anti log of } (n \log x)$

Example : Raise 3.5 to the 4th power

Log of 3.5 = 0.5441

Multiply 0.5441 by 4 ; We get 2.1764

Antilog of 2.1764 = 150.1

$$(3.5)^5 = 150.1$$

4. *To extract the root of a number :*

The logarithm of the number should be divided by the index of the root and the quotient is the log of the required root. Thus :

Steps :

1. Find the logarithm of the number.
2. Divide the logarithm by 2
3. Find out the antilog of the number, which is the answer.

Example : $\sqrt{x}$ =Antilog of $\left(\frac{\log x}{2}\right)$

Example :

Simplify : $\sqrt{256}$

Solution :

Log of 256 = 2.4082

To find root, divide 2.4082 by 2 ; we get 1.2041

Antilog of 1.2041 = 16

$$\sqrt{256} = 16$$

Example :

Simplify : $\sqrt{676}$

Solution : Log of 676 = 2.8299

2.8299 is divided by 2 = 1.41495 or 1.4150

Antilog of 1.4150 = 26.29

$$\sqrt{676} = 26$$

Example : Simplify : $\sqrt{0.0025}$

Solution : Log of 0.0025 = $\bar{3}.3979$ $\bar{3}.3979$ cannot be divided by 2 because the characteristic is negative. Hence

$$\frac{\bar{6} + 3.3979}{2} \; \bar{3} + 1.6990 = \bar{2}.6990$$

Antilog of .6990 = 0.5000

Since characteristic is $\bar{2}$, the root is .05

$$\sqrt{0.0025} = 0.05$$

Example .

Simplify : $\sqrt{\frac{248.3}{22}}$

Solution :

Log of	248.3	=	2.3950
Log of	22	=	1.3424
Total		=	1.0526

1.0526 divided by 2 = 0.5263

Antilog of 0.5263 = 3.359

$$\sqrt{\frac{248.3}{22}} = 3.359$$

Example :

Simplify :

$$\frac{3535}{\sqrt{3490 \times 4390}}$$

Solution :

Antilog of log $3535 - \frac{1}{2}(\log 3490 + \log 4390)$

$= \text{Antilog of } 3.5484 - \frac{1}{2}(3.5428 + 3.6425)$

$= \text{Antilog of } 3.5484 - \frac{1}{2}(7.1853)$

$= \text{Antilog of } 3.5484 - 3.5926$

$= \text{Antilog of } 1.9558$

$= \text{Antilog of } \bar{1}.9558$

$= 0.9033$

$$\therefore \quad \frac{3535}{\sqrt{3490 \times 4390}} = 0.9033$$

Example : Find $(0.0009725) \div (0.0681)$

Solution :

Log of	0.0009725	=	$\bar{4}.9879$
Log of	0.0681	=	2.8331
Total			−2.1548

Antilog of $\bar{2}.1548 = 0.01429$

$$\frac{0.0009725}{0.0681} = 0.01429$$

LOGARITHMS TABLES

	0	1	2	3	4	5	6	7	8	9	Mean Differences								
											1	2	3	4	5	6	7	8	9
10	0000	0043	0086	0128	0170	0212	0253	0294	0334	0374	4	8	12	17	21	25	29	33	37
11	0414	0453	0492	0531	0569	0607	0645	0682	0719	0755	4	8	11	15	19	23	26	30	34
12	0792	0828	0864	0899	0934	0969	1004	1038	1072	1106	3	7	10	14	17	21	24	28	31
13	1139	1173	1206	1239	1271	1303	1335	1367	1399	1430	3	6	10	13	16	19	23	26	29
14	1461	1492	1523	1553	1584	1614	1644	1673	1703	1732	3	6	9	12	15	18	21	24	27
15	1761	1790	1818	1847	1875	1903	1931	1959	1987	2014	3	6	8	11	14	17	20	22	25
16	2041	2068	2095	2122	2148	2175	2201	2227	2253	2279	3	5	8	11	13	16	18	21	24
17	2304	2330	2355	2380	2405	2430	2455	2480	2504	2529	2	5	7	10	12	15	17	20	22
18	2553	2577	2601	2625	2648	2672	2695	2718	2742	2765	2	5	7	9	12	14	16	19	21
19	2788	2810	2833	2856	2878	2900	2923	2945	2967	2989	2	4	7	9	11	13	16	18	20
20	3010	3032	3054	3075	3096	3118	3139	3160	3181	3201	2	4	6	8	11	13	15	17	19
21	3222	3243	3263	3284	3304	3324	3345	3365	3385	3404	2	4	6	8	10	12	14	16	18
22	3424	3444	3464	3483	3502	3522	3541	3560	3579	3598	2	4	6	8	10	12	14	15	17
23	3617	3636	3655	3674	3692	3711	3729	3747	3766	3784	2	4	6	7	9	11	13	15	17
24	3802	3820	3838	3856	3874	3892	3909	3927	3945	3962	2	4	5	7	9	11	12	14	16
25	3979	3997	4014	4031	4048	4065	4082	4099	4116	4133	2	3	5	7	9	10	12	14	15
26	4150	4166	4183	4200	4216	4232	4249	4265	4281	4298	2	3	5	7	8	10	11	13	15
27	4314	4330	4346	4362	4378	4393	4409	4425	4440	4456	2	3	5	6	8	9	11	13	14
28	4472	4487	4502	4518	4533	4548	4564	4579	4594	4609	2	3	5	6	8	9	11	12	14
29	4624	4639	4654	4669	4683	4698	4713	4728	4742	4757	1	3	4	6	7	9	10	12	13
30	4771	4786	4800	4814	4829	4843	4857	4871	4886	4900	1	3	4	6	7	9	10	11	13
31	4914	4928	4942	4955	4969	4983	4997	5011	5024	5038	1	3	4	6	7	8	10	11	12
32	5051	5065	5079	5092	5105	5119	5132	5145	5159	5172	1	3	4	5	7	8	9	11	12
33	5185	5198	5211	5224	5237	5250	5263	5276	5289	5302	1	3	4	5	6	8	9	10	12
34	5315	5328	5340	5353	5366	5378	5391	5403	5416	5428	1	3	4	5	6	8	9	10	11
35	5441	5453	5465	5478	5490	5502	5514	5527	5539	5551	1	2	4	5	6	7	9	10	11
36	5563	5575	5587	5599	5611	5623	5635	5647	5658	5670	1	2	4	5	6	7	8	10	11
37	5682	5694	5705	5717	5729	5740	5752	5763	5775	5786	1	2	3	5	6	7	8	9	10
38	5798	5809	5821	5832	5843	5855	5866	5877	5888	5899	1	2	3	5	6	7	8	9	10
39	5911	5922	5933	5944	5955	5966	5977	5988	5999	6010	1	2	3	4	5	7	8	9	10
40	6021	6031	6042	6053	6064	6075	6085	6096	6107	6117	1	2	3	4	5	6	8	9	10
41	6128	6138	6149	6160	6170	6180	6191	6201	6212	6222	1	2	3	4	5	6	7	8	9
42	6232	6243	6253	6263	6274	6284	6294	6304	6314	6325	1	2	3	4	5	6	7	8	9
43	6335	6345	6355	6365	6375	6385	6395	6405	6415	6425	1	2	3	4	5	6	7	8	9
44	6435	6444	6454	6464	6474	6484	6493	6503	6513	6522	1	2	3	4	5	6	7	8	9
45	6532	6542	6551	6561	6571	6580	6590	6599	6609	6618	1	2	3	4	5	6	7	8	9
46	6628	6637	6646	6656	6665	6675	6684	6693	6702	6712	1	2	3	4	5	6	7	7	8
47	6721	6730	6739	6749	6758	6767	6776	6785	6794	6803	1	2	3	4	5	5	6	7	8
48	6812	6821	6830	6839	6848	6857	6866	6875	6884	6893	1	2	3	4	4	5	6	7	8
49	6902	6911	6920	6928	6937	6946	6955	6964	6972	6981	1	2	3	4	4	5	6	7	8
50	6990	6998	7007	7016	7024	7033	7042	7050	7059	7067	1	2	3	3	4	5	6	7	8

(Contd.)

LOGARITHMS

	0	1	2	3	4	5	6	7	8	9	Mean Differences								
											1	2	3	4	5	6	7	8	9
51	7076	7084	7093	7101	7110	7118	7126	7135	7143	7152	1	2	3	3	4	5	6	7	8
52	7160	7168	7177	7185	7193	7202	7210	7218	7226	7235	1	2	2	3	4	5	6	7	7
53	7243	7251	7259	7267	7275	7284	7292	7300	7308	7316	1	2	2	3	4	5	6	6	7
54	7324	7332	7340	7348	7356	7364	7372	7380	7388	7396	1	2	2	3	4	5	6	6	7
55	7404	7412	7419	7427	7435	7443	7451	7459	7466	7474	1	2	2	3	4	5	5	6	7
56	7482	7490	7497	7505	7513	7520	7528	7536	7543	7551	1	2	2	3	4	5	5	6	7
57	7559	7566	7574	7582	7589	7597	7604	7612	7619	7627	1	2	2	3	4	5	5	6	7
58	7634	7642	7649	7657	7664	7672	7679	7686	7694	7701	1	1	2	3	4	4	5	6	7
59	7709	7716	7723	7731	7738	7745	7752	7760	7767	7774	1	1	2	3	4	4	5	6	7
60	7782	7789	7796	7803	7810	7818	7825	7832	7839	7846	1	1	2	3	4	4	5	6	6
61	7853	7860	7868	7875	7882	7889	7896	7903	7910	7917	1	1	2	3	4	4	5	6	6
62	7924	7931	7938	7945	7952	7959	7966	7973	7980	7987	1	1	2	3	3	4	5	6	6
63	7993	8000	8007	8014	8021	8028	8035	8041	8048	8055	1	1	2	3	3	4	5	5	6
64	8062	8069	8075	8082	8089	8096	8102	8109	8116	8122	1	1	2	3	3	4	5	5	6
65	8129	8136	8142	8149	8156	8162	8169	8176	8182	8189	1	1	2	3	3	4	5	5	6
66	8195	8202	8209	8215	8222	8228	8235	8241	8248	8254	1	1	2	3	3	4	5	5	6
67	8261	8267	8274	8280	8287	8293	8299	8306	8312	8319	1	1	2	3	3	4	5	5	6
68	8325	8331	8338	8344	8351	8357	8363	8370	8376	8382	1	1	2	3	3	4	4	5	6
69	8388	8395	8401	8407	8414	8420	8426	8432	8439	8445	1	1	2	2	3	4	4	5	6
70	8451	8457	8463	8470	8476	8482	8488	8494	8500	8506	1	1	2	2	3	4	4	5	6
71	8513	8519	8525	8531	8537	8543	8549	8555	8561	8567	1	1	2	2	3	4	4	5	5
72	8573	8579	8585	8591	8597	8603	8609	8615	8621	8627	1	1	2	2	3	4	4	5	5
73	8633	8639	8645	8651	8657	8663	8669	8675	8681	8686	1	1	2	2	3	4	4	5	5
74	8692	8698	8704	8710	8716	8722	8727	8733	8739	8745	1	1	2	2	3	4	4	5	5
75	8751	8756	8762	8768	8774	8779	8785	8791	8797	8802	1	1	2	2	3	3	4	5	5
76	8808	8814	8820	8825	8831	8837	8842	8848	8854	8859	1	1	2	2	3	3	4	5	5
77	8865	8871	8876	8882	8887	8893	8899	8904	8910	8915	1	1	2	2	3	3	4	4	5
78	8921	8927	8932	8938	8943	8949	8954	8960	8965	8971	1	1	2	2	3	3	4	4	5
79	8976	8982	8987	8993	8998	9004	9009	9015	9020	9025	1	1	2	2	3	3	4	4	5
80	9031	9036	9042	9047	9053	9058	9063	9069	9074	9079	1	1	2	2	3	3	4	4	5
81	9085	9090	9096	9101	9106	9112	9117	9122	9128	9133	1	1	2	2	3	3	4	4	5
82	9138	9143	9149	9154	9159	9165	9170	9175	9180	9186	1	1	2	2	3	3	4	4	5
83	9191	9196	9201	9206	9217	9217	9222	9227	9232	9238	1	1	2	2	3	3	4	4	5
84	9243	9248	9253	9258	9263	9269	9274	9279	9284	9289	1	1	2	2	3	3	4	4	5
85	9294	9299	9304	9360	9315	9320	9325	9330	9335	9340	1	1	2	2	3	3	4	4	5
86	9345	9350	9355	9360	9365	9370	9375	9380	9385	9390	1	1	2	2	3	3	4	4	5
87	9395	9400	9405	9410	9415	9420	9425	9430	9435	9440	0	1	1	2	2	3	3	4	4
88	9445	9450	9455	9460	9465	9469	9474	9479	9484	9489	0	1	1	2	2	3	3	4	4
89	9494	9499	9504	9509	9513	9518	9523	9528	9533	9538	0	1	1	2	2	3	3	4	4
90	9542	9547	9552	9557	9562	9566	9571	9576	9581	9586	0	1	1	2	2	3	3	4	4
91	9590	9595	9600	9605	9609	9614	9619	9624	9628	9633	0	1	1	2	2	3	3	4	4
92	9638	9643	9647	9652	9657	9661	9666	9671	9675	9680	0	1	1	2	2	3	3	4	4
93	9685	9689	9694	9699	9703	9708	9713	9717	9722	9727	0	1	1	2	2	3	3	4	4
94	9731	9736	9741	9745	9750	9754	9759	9763	9768	9773	0	1	1	2	2	3	3	4	4
95	9777	9782	9786	9791	9795	9800	9805	9809	9814	9818	0	1	1	2	2	3	3	4	4
96	9823	9827	9832	9836	9841	9845	9850	9854	9859	9863	0	1	1	2	2	3	3	4	4
97	9868	9872	9877	9881	9886	9890	9894	9899	9903	9908	0	1	1	2	2	3	3	4	4
98	9912	9916	9921	9926	9930	9934	9939	9943	9948	9952	0	1	1	2	2	3	3	4	4
99	9956	9961	9965	9969	9974	9978	9983	9987	9991	9996	0	1	1	2	2	3	3	3	4

ANTILOGARITHMS

	0	1	2	3	4	5	6	7	8	9	Mean Differences								
											1	2	3	4	5	6	7	8	9
.00	1000	1002	1005	1007	1009	1012	1014	1016	1019	1021	0	0	1	1	1	1	2	2	2
.01	1023	1026	1028	1030	1033	1035	1038	1040	1042	1045	0	0	1	1	1	1	2	2	2
.02	1047	1050	1052	1054	1057	1059	1062	1064	1067	1069	0	0	1	1	1	1	2	2	2
.03	1072	1074	1076	1079	1081	1084	1086	1089	1091	1094	0	0	1	1	1	1	2	2	2
.04	1096	1099	1102	1104	1107	1109	1112	1114	1117	1119	0	1	1	1	1	2	2	2	2
.05	1122	1125	1127	1130	1132	1135	1138	1140	1143	1146	0	1	1	1	1	2	2	2	2
.06	1148	1151	1153	1156	1159	1161	1164	1167	1169	1172	0	1	1	1	1	2	2	2	2
.07	1175	1178	1180	1183	1186	1189	1191	1194	1197	1199	0	1	1	1	1	2	2	2	2
.08	1202	1205	1208	1211	1213	1216	1219	1222	1225	1227	0	1	1	1	1	2	2	2	3
.09	1230	1233	1236	1239	1242	1245	1247	1250	1253	1256	0	1	1	1	1	2	2	2	3
.10	1259	1262	1265	1268	1271	1274	1276	1279	1282	1285	0	1	1	1	1	2	2	2	3
.11	1288	1291	1294	1297	1300	1303	1306	1309	1312	1315	0	1	1	1	2	2	2	2	3
.12	1318	1321	1324	1327	1330	1334	1337	1340	1343	1346	0	1	1	1	2	2	2	2	3
.13	1349	1352	1355	1358	1361	1365	1368	1371	1374	1377	0	1	1	1	2	2	2	3	3
.14	1380	1384	1387	1390	1393	1396	1400	1403	1406	1409	0	1	1	1	2	2	2	3	3
.15	1413	1416	1419	1422	1426	1429	1432	1435	1439	1442	0	1	1	1	2	2	2	3	3
.16	1445	1449	1452	1455	1459	1462	1466	1469	1472	1476	0	1	1	1	2	2	2	3	3
.17	1479	1483	1486	1489	1493	1496	1500	1503	1507	1510	0	1	1	1	2	2	2	3	3
.18	1514	1517	1521	1524	1528	1531	1535	1538	1542	1545	0	1	1	1	2	2	2	3	3
.19	1549	1552	1556	1560	1563	1567	1570	1574	1578	1581	0	1	1	1	2	2	3	3	3
.20	1585	1589	1592	1596	1600	1603	1607	1611	1614	1618	0	1	1	1	2	2	3	3	3
.21	1622	1626	1629	1633	1637	1641	1644	1648	1652	1656	0	1	1	2	2	2	3	3	3
.22	1660	1663	1667	1671	1675	1679	1683	1687	1690	1694	0	1	1	2	2	2	3	3	3
.23	1698	1702	1706	1710	1714	1718	1722	1726	1730	1734	0	1	1	2	2	2	3	3	4
.24	1738	1742	1746	1750	1754	1758	1762	1766	1770	1774	0	1	1	2	2	2	3	3	4
.25	1778	1782	1786	1791	1795	1798	1803	1807	1811	1816	0	1	1	2	2	2	3	3	4
.26	1820	1824	1828	1832	1837	1841	1845	1849	1854	1858	0	1	1	2	2	3	3	3	4
.27	1862	1866	1871	1875	1879	1884	1888	1892	1897	1901	0	1	1	2	2	3	3	3	4
.28	1905	1910	1914	1919	1923	1928	1932	1936	1941	1945	0	1	1	2	2	3	3	4	4
.29	1950	1954	1959	1963	1968	1972	1977	1982	1986	1991	0	1	1	2	2	3	3	4	4
.30	1995	2000	2004	2009	2014	2018	2023	2028	2032	2037	0	1	1	2	2	3	3	4	4
.31	2042	2046	2051	2056	2061	2065	2070	2075	2080	2084	0	1	1	2	2	3	3	4	4
.32	2089	2094	2099	2104	2109	2113	2118	2123	2128	2133	0	1	1	2	2	3	3	4	4
.33	2138	2143	2148	2153	2158	2163	2168	2173	2178	2183	0	1	1	2	2	3	3	4	4
.34	2188	2193	2198	2203	2208	2213	2218	2223	2228	2234	1	1	2	2	3	3	4	4	5
.35	2239	2244	2249	2254	2259	2265	2270	2275	2280	2286	1	1	2	2	3	3	4	4	5
.36	2291	2296	2301	2307	2312	2317	2323	2328	2333	2339	1	1	2	2	3	3	4	4	5
.37	2344	2350	2355	2360	2366	2371	2377	2382	2388	2393	1	1	2	2	3	3	4	4	5
.38	2399	2404	2410	2415	2421	2427	2432	2438	2443	2449	1	1	2	2	3	3	4	4	5
.39	2455	2460	2466	2472	2477	2483	2489	2495	2500	2506	1	1	2	2	3	3	4	5	5
.40	2512	2518	2523	2529	2535	2541	2547	2553	2559	2564	1	1	2	2	3	4	4	5	5
.41	2570	2576	2582	2588	2594	2600	2606	2612	2618	2624	1	1	2	2	3	4	4	5	5
.42	2630	2636	2642	2649	2655	2661	2667	2673	2679	2685	1	1	2	2	3	4	4	5	6
.43	2692	2698	2704	2710	2716	2723	2729	2735	2742	2748	1	1	2	3	3	4	4	5	6
.44	2754	2761	2767	2773	2780	2786	2793	2799	2805	2812	1	1	2	3	3	4	4	5	6
.45	2818	2825	2831	2838	2844	2851	2858	2864	2871	2877	1	1	2	3	3	4	5	5	6
.46	2884	2891	2897	2904	2911	2917	2924	2931	2938	2944	1	1	2	3	3	4	5	5	6
.47	2951	2958	2965	2972	2979	2985	2992	2999	3006	3013	1	1	2	3	3	4	5	5	6
.48	3020	3027	3034	3041	3048	3055	3062	3069	3076	3083	1	1	2	3	4	4	5	6	6
.49	3090	3097	3105	3112	3119	3126	3133	3141	3148	3155	1	1	2	3	4	4	5	6	6
.50	3162	3170	3177	3184	3192	3199	3206	3214	3221	3228	1	1	2	3	4	4	5	6	7

(Contd.)

ANTILOGARITHMS

	0	1	2	3	4	5	6	7	8	9	Mean Differences								
											1	2	3	4	5	6	7	8	9
.51	3236	3243	3251	3258	3266	3273	3281	3289	3296	3304	1	2	2	3	4	5	5	6	7
.52	3311	3319	3327	3334	3342	3350	3357	3365	3373	3381	1	2	2	3	4	5	5	6	7
.53	3388	3396	3404	3412	3420	3428	3436	3443	3451	3459	1	2	2	3	4	5	6	6	7
.54	3467	3475	3483	3491	3499	3508	3516	3524	3532	3540	1	2	2	3	4	5	6	6	7
.55	3548	3556	3565	3573	3581	3589	3597	3606	3614	3622	1	2	2	3	4	5	6	7	7
.56	3631	3639	3648	3656	3664	3673	3681	3690	3698	3707	1	2	3	3	4	5	6	7	8
.57	3715	3724	3733	3741	3750	3758	3767	3776	3784	3793	1	2	3	3	4	5	6	7	8
.58	3802	3811	3819	3828	3837	3846	3855	3864	3873	3882	1	2	3	4	4	5	6	7	8
.59	3890	3899	3908	3917	3926	3936	3945	3954	3963	3972	1	2	3	4	5	5	6	7	8
.60	3981	3990	3999	4009	4018	4027	4036	4046	4055	4064	1	2	3	4	5	6	6	7	8
.61	4074	4083	4093	4102	4111	4121	4130	4140	4150	4159	1	2	3	4	5	6	7	8	9
.62	4169	4178	4188	4198	4207	4217	4227	4236	4246	4256	1	2	3	4	5	6	7	8	9
.63	4266	4276	4285	4295	4305	4315	4325	4335	4345	4355	1	2	3	4	5	6	7	8	9
.64	4365	4375	4385	4395	4406	4416	4426	4436	4446	4457	1	2	3	4	5	6	7	8	9
.65	4467	4477	4487	4498	4508	4519	4529	4539	4550	4560	1	2	3	4	5	6	7	8	9
.66	4571	4581	4592	4603	4613	4624	4634	4645	4656	4667	1	2	3	4	5	6	7	9	10
.67	4677	4688	4699	4710	4721	4732	4742	4753	4764	4775	1	2	3	4	5	7	8	9	10
.68	4786	4797	4808	4819	4831	4842	4853	4864	4875	4887	1	2	3	4	6	7	8	9	10
.69	4898	4909	4920	4932	4943	4955	4966	4977	4989	5000	1	2	3	5	6	7	8	9	10
.70	5012	5023	5035	5047	5058	5070	5082	5093	5105	5117	1	2	4	5	6	7	8	9	11
.71	5129	5140	5152	5164	5176	5188	5200	5212	5224	5236	1	2	4	5	6	7	8	10	11
.72	5248	5260	5272	5284	5297	5309	5321	5333	5346	5358	1	2	4	5	6	7	9	10	11
.73	5370	5383	5395	5408	5420	5433	5445	5458	5470	5483	1	3	4	5	6	8	9	10	11
.74	5495	5508	5521	5534	5546	5559	5572	5585	5598	5610	1	3	4	5	6	8	9	10	12
.75	5623	5636	5649	5662	5675	5689	5702	5715	5728	5741	1	3	4	5	7	8	9	10	12
.76	5754	5768	5781	5794	5808	5821	5834	5848	5861	5875	1	3	4	5	7	8	9	11	12
.77	5888	5902	5916	5929	5943	5957	5970	5984	5998	6012	1	3	4	5	7	8	10	11	12
.78	6026	6039	6053	6067	6081	6095	6109	6124	6138	6152	1	3	4	6	7	8	10	11	13
.79	6166	6180	6194	6209	6223	6237	6252	6266	6281	6295	1	3	4	6	7	9	10	11	13
.80	6310	6324	6339	6353	6368	6383	6397	6412	6427	6442	1	3	4	6	7	9	10	12	13
.81	6457	6471	6486	6501	6516	6531	6546	6561	6577	6592	2	3	5	6	8	9	11	12	14
.82	6607	6622	6637	6653	6668	6683	6699	6714	6730	6745	2	3	5	6	8	9	11	12	14
.83	6761	6776	6792	6808	6823	6839	6855	6871	6887	6902	2	3	5	6	8	9	11	13	14
.84	6918	6934	6950	6966	6982	6998	7015	7031	7047	7063	2	3	5	6	8	10	11	13	15
.85	7079	7096	7112	7129	7145	7161	7178	7194	7211	7228	2	3	5	7	8	10	12	13	15
.86	7244	7261	7278	7295	7311	7328	7345	7362	7379	7396	2	3	5	7	8	10	12	13	15
.87	7413	7430	7447	7464	7482	7499	7516	7534	7551	7568	2	3	5	7	9	10	12	14	16
.88	7586	7603	7621	7638	7656	7674	7691	7709	7727	7745	2	4	5	7	9	11	12	14	16
.89	7762	7780	7798	7816	7834	7852	7870	7889	7907	7925	2	4	5	7	9	11	13	14	16
.90	7943	7962	7980	7998	8017	8035	8054	8072	8091	8110	2	4	6	7	9	11	13	15	17
.91	8128	8147	8166	8185	8204	8222	8241	8260	8279	8299	2	4	6	8	9	11	13	15	17
.92	8318	8337	8356	8375	8395	8414	8433	8453	8472	8492	2	4	6	8	10	12	14	15	17
.93	8511	8531	8551	8570	8590	8616	8630	8650	8670	8690	2	4	6	8	10	12	14	16	18
.94	8710	8730	8750	8770	8790	8810	8831	8851	8872	8892	2	4	6	8	10	12	14	16	18
.95	8913	8933	8954	8974	8995	9016	9036	9057	9078	9099	2	4	6	8	10	12	15	17	19
.96	9120	9141	9162	9183	9204	9226	9247	9268	9290	9311	2	4	6	8	11	13	15	17	19
.97	9333	9354	9376	9397	9419	9441	9462	9484	9506	9528	2	4	7	9	11	13	15	17	20
.98	9550	9572	9594	9616	9638	9661	9683	9705	9727	9750	2	4	7	9	11	13	16	18	20
.99	9772	9793	9817	9840	9863	9886	9908	9931	9954	9977	2	5	7	9	11	14	16	18	20

NATURAL SINES

	0' 0°.0	6' 0°.1	12' 0°.2	18' 0°.3	24' 0°.4	30' 0°.5	36' 0°.6	42' 0°.7	48' 0°.8	54' 0°.9	Mean Differences 1'	2'	3'	4'	5'
0	.0000	0017	0035	0052	0070	0087	0105	0122	0140	0157	3	6	9	12	15
1	.0175	0192	0209	0227	0244	0262	0279	0297	0314	0332	3	6	9	12	15
2	.0349	0366	0384	0401	0419	0436	0454	0471	0488	0506	3	6	9	12	15
3	.0523	0541	0558	0576	0593	0610	0628	0645	0663	0680	3	6	9	12	15
4	.0698	0715	0732	0750	0767	0785	0802	0819	0837	0854	3	6	9	12	15
5	.0872	0889	0906	0924	0941	0958	0976	0993	1011	1028	3	6	9	12	14
6	.1045	1063	1080	1097	1115	1132	1149	1167	1184	1201	3	6	9	12	14
7	.1219	1236	1253	1271	1288	1305	1323	1340	1357	1374	3	6	9	12	14
8	.1392	1409	1426	1444	1461	1478	1495	1513	1530	1547	3	6	9	12	14
9	.1564	1582	1599	1616	1633	1650	1668	1685	1702	1719	3	6	9	12	14
10	.1736	1754	1771	1788	1805	1822	1840	1857	1874	1891	3	6	9	12	14
11	.1908	1925	1942	1959	1977	1994	2011	2028	2045	2062	3	6	9	11	14
12	.2079	2096	2113	2130	2147	2164	2181	2198	2215	2232	3	6	9	11	14
13	.2250	2267	2284	2300	2317	2334	2351	2368	2385	2402	3	6	8	11	14
14	.2419	2436	2453	2470	2487	2504	2521	2538	2554	2571	3	6	8	11	14
15	.2588	2605	2622	2639	2656	2672	2689	2706	2723	2740	3	6	8	11	14
16	.2756	2773	2790	2807	2823	2840	2857	2874	2890	2907	3	6	8	11	14
17	.2924	2940	2957	2974	2990	3007	3024	3040	3057	3074	3	6	8	11	14
18	.3090	3107	3123	3140	3156	3173	3190	3206	3223	3239	3	6	8	11	14
19	.3256	3272	3289	3305	3322	3338	3355	3371	3387	3404	3	5	8	11	14
20	.3420	3437	3453	3469	3486	3502	3518	3535	3551	3567	3	5	8	11	14
21	.3584	3600	3616	3633	3649	3665	3681	3697	3714	3730	3	5	8	11	14
22	.3746	3762	3778	3795	3811	3827	3843	3859	3875	3891	3	5	8	11	14
23	.3907	3923	3939	3955	3971	3987	4003	4019	4035	4051	3	5	8	11	14
24	.4067	4083	4099	4115	4131	4147	4163	4179	4195	4210	3	5	8	11	13
25	.4226	4242	4258	4274	4289	4305	4321	4337	4352	4368	3	5	8	11	13
26	.4384	4399	4415	4431	4446	4462	4478	4493	4509	4524	3	5	8	10	13
27	.4540	4555	4571	4586	4602	4617	4633	4648	4664	4679	3	5	8	10	13
28	.4695	4710	4726	4741	4756	4772	4787	4802	4818	4833	3	5	8	10	13
29	.4848	4863	4879	4894	4909	4924	4939	4955	4970	4985	3	5	8	10	13
30	.5000	5015	5030	5045	5060	5075	5090	5105	5120	5135	3	5	8	10	13
31	.5150	5165	5180	5195	5210	5225	5240	5255	5270	5284	2	5	7	10	12
32	.5299	5314	5329	5344	5358	5373	5388	5402	5417	5432	2	5	7	10	12
33	.5446	5461	5476	5490	5505	5519	5534	5548	5563	5577	2	5	7	10	12
34	.5592	5606	5621	5635	5650	5664	5678	5693	5707	5721	2	5	7	10	12
35	.5736	5750	5764	5779	5793	5807	5821	5835	5850	5864	2	5	7	10	12
36	.5878	5892	5906	5920	5934	5948	5962	5976	5990	6004	2	5	7	9	12
37	.6018	6032	6046	6060	6074	6088	6101	6115	6129	6143	2	5	7	9	12
38	.6157	6170	6184	6198	6211	6225	6239	6252	6266	6280	2	5	7	9	11
39	.6293	6307	6320	6334	6347	6361	6374	6388	6401	6414	2	4	7	9	11
40	.6428	6441	6455	6468	6481	6494	6508	6521	6534	6547	2	4	7	9	11
41	.6561	6574	6587	6600	6613	6626	6639	6652	6665	6678	2	4	7	9	11
42	.6691	6704	6717	6730	6743	6756	6769	6782	6794	6807	2	4	6	9	11
43	.6820	6833	6845	6858	6871	6884	6896	6909	6921	6934	2	4	6	8	11
44	.6947	6959	6972	6984	6997	7009	7022	7034	7046	7059	2	4	6	8	10

NATURAL SINES

	0' 0°.0	6' 0°.1	12' 0°.2	18' 0°.3	24' 0°.4	30' 0°.5	36' 0°.6	42' 0°.7	48' 0°.8	54' 0°.9	Mean Differences				
											1'	2'	3'	4'	5'
45	.7071	7083	7096	7108	7120	7133	7145	7157	7169	7181	2	4	6	8	10
46	.7193	7206	7218	7230	7242	7254	7266	7278	7290	7302	2	4	6	8	10
47	.7314	7325	7337	7349	7361	7373	7385	7396	7408	7420	2	4	6	8	10
48	.7431	7443	7455	7466	7478	7490	7501	7513	7524	7536	2	4	6	8	10
49	.7547	7558	7570	7581	7593	7604	7615	7627	7638	7649	2	4	6	8	9
50	.7660	7672	7683	7694	7705	7716	7727	7738	7749	7760	2	4	6	7	9
51	.7771	7782	7793	7804	7815	7826	7837	7848	7859	7869	2	4	5	7	9
52	.7880	7891	7902	7912	7923	7934	7944	7955	7965	7976	2	4	5	7	9
53	.7986	7997	8007	8018	8028	8039	8049	8059	8070	8080	2	3	5	7	9
54	.8090	8100	8111	8121	8131	8141	8151	8161	8171	8181	2	3	5	7	8
55	.8192	8202	8211	8221	8231	8241	8251	8261	8271	8281	2	3	5	7	8
56	.8290	8300	8310	8320	8329	8339	8348	8358	8368	8377	2	3	5	6	8
57	.8387	8396	8406	8415	8425	8434	8443	8453	8462	8471	2	3	5	6	8
58	.8480	8490	8499	8508	8517	8526	8536	8545	8554	8563	2	3	5	6	8
59	.8572	8581	8590	8599	8607	8616	8625	8634	8643	8652	1	3	4	6	7
60	.8660	8669	8678	8686	8695	8704	8712	8721	8729	8738	1	3	4	6	7
61	.8746	8755	8763	8771	8780	8788	8796	8805	8813	8821	1	3	4	6	7
62	.8829	8838	8846	8854	8862	8870	8878	8886	8894	8902	1	3	4	5	7
63	.8910	8918	8926	8934	8942	8949	8957	8965	8973	8980	1	3	4	5	6
64	.8988	8996	9003	9011	9018	9026	9033	9041	9048	9056	1	3	4	5	6
65	.9063	9070	9078	9085	9092	9100	9107	9114	9121	9128	1	2	4	5	6
66	.9135	9143	9150	9157	9164	9171	9178	9184	9191	9198	1	2	3	5	6
67	.9205	9212	9219	9225	9232	9239	9245	9252	9259	9265	1	2	3	4	6
68	.9272	9278	9285	9291	9298	9304	9311	9317	9323	9330	1	2	3	4	5
69	.9336	9342	9348	9354	9361	9367	9373	9379	9385	9391	1	2	3	4	5
70	.9397	9403	9409	9415	9421	9426	9432	9438	9444	9449	1	2	3	4	5
71	.9455	9461	9466	9472	9478	9483	9489	9494	9500	9505	1	2	3	4	5
72	.9511	9516	9521	9527	9532	9537	9542	9548	9553	9558	1	2	3	3	4
73	.9563	9568	9573	9578	9583	9588	9593	9598	9603	9608	1	2	3	3	4
74	.9613	9617	9622	9627	9632	9636	9641	9646	9650	9655	1	2	2	3	4
75	.9659	9664	9668	9673	9677	9681	9686	9690	9694	9699	1	1	2	3	4
76	.9703	9707	9711	9715	9720	9724	9728	9732	9736	9740	1	1	2	3	3
77	.9744	9748	9751	9755	9759	9763	9767	9770	9774	9778	1	1	2	3	3
78	.9781	9785	9789	9792	9796	9799	9803	9806	9810	9813	1	1	2	2	3
79	.9816	9820	9823	9826	9829	9833	9836	9839	9842	9845	1	1	2	2	3
80	.9848	9851	9854	9857	9860	9863	9866	9869	9871	9874	0	1	1	2	2
81	.9877	9880	9882	9885	9888	9890	9893	9895	9898	9900	0	1	1	2	2
82	.9903	9905	9907	9910	9912	9914	9917	9919	9921	9923	0	1	1	2	2
83	.9925	9928	9930	9932	9934	9936	9938	9940	9942	9943	0	1	1	1	2
84	.9945	9947	9949	9951	9952	9954	9956	9957	9959	9960	0	1	1	1	2
85	.9962	9963	9965	9966	9968	9969	9971	9972	9973	9974	0	0	1	1	1
86	.9976	9977	9978	9979	9980	9981	9982	9983	9984	9985	0	0	1	1	1
87	.9986	9987	9988	9989	9990	9990	9991	9992	9993	9993	0	0	0	1	1
88	.9994	9995	9995	9996	9996	9997	9997	9997	9998	9998	0	0	0	0	0
89	.9998	9999	9999	9999	9999	1.000	1.000	1.000	1.000	1.000	0	0	0	0	0
90	1.000														

NATURAL COSINES

[Numbers in difference columns to be subtracted, not added.]

	0' 0°.0	6' 0°.1	12' 0°.2	18' 0°.3	24' 0°.4	30' 0°.5	36' 0°.6	42' 0°.7	48' 0°.8	54' 0°.9	Mean Differences 1	2	3	4	5
0	1.000	1.000	1.000	1.000	1.000	1.000	.9999	9999	9999	9999	0	0	0	0	0
1	.9998	9998	9998	9997	9997	9997	9996	9996	9995	9995	0	0	0	0	0
2	.9994	9993	9993	9992	9991	9990	9990	9989	9988	9987	0	0	0	1	1
3	.9986	9985	9984	9983	9982	9981	9980	9979	9978	9977	0	0	1	1	1
4	.9976	9974	9973	9972	9971	9969	9968	9966	9965	9963	0	0	1	1	1
5	.9962	9960	9959	9957	9956	9954	9952	9951	9949	9947	0	1	1	1	2
6	.9945	9943	9942	9940	9938	9936	9934	9932	9930	9928	0	1	1	1	2
7	.9925	9923	9921	9919	9917	9914	9912	9910	9907	9905	0	1	1	2	2
8	.9903	9900	9898	9895	9893	9890	9888	9885	9882	9880	0	1	1	2	2
9	.9877	9874	9871	9869	9866	9863	9860	9857	9854	9851	0	1	1	2	2
10	.9848	9845	9842	9839	9836	9833	9829	9826	9823	9820	1	1	2	2	3
11	.9816	9813	9810	9806	9803	9799	9796	9792	9789	9785	1	1	2	2	3
12	.9781	9778	9774	9770	9767	9763	9759	9755	9751	9748	1	1	2	3	3
13	.9744	9740	9736	9732	9728	9724	9720	9715	9711	9707	1	1	2	3	3
14	.9703	9699	9694	9690	9686	9681	9677	9673	9668	9664	1	1	2	3	4
15	.9659	9655	9650	9646	9641	9636	9632	9627	9622	9617	1	2	2	3	4
16	.9613	9608	9603	9598	9593	9588	9583	9578	9573	9568	1	2	2	3	4
17	.9563	9558	9553	9548	9542	9537	9532	9527	9521	9516	1	2	3	3	4
18	.9511	9505	9500	9494	9489	9483	9478	9472	9466	9461	1	2	3	4	5
19	.9455	9449	9444	9438	9432	9426	9421	9415	9409	9403	1	2	3	4	5
20	.9397	9391	9385	9379	9573	9367	9361	9354	9348	9342	1	2	3	4	5
21	.9336	9330	9323	9317	9311	9304	9298	9291	9285	9278	1	2	3	4	5
22	.9272	9265	9259	9252	9245	9239	9232	9225	9219	9212	1	2	3	4	6
23	.9205	9198	9191	9184	9178	9171	9164	9157	9150	9143	1	2	3	5	6
24	.9135	9128	9121	9114	9107	9100	9092	9085	9078	9070	1	2	4	5	6
25	.9063	9056	9048	9041	9033	9026	9018	9011	9003	8996	1	3	4	5	6
26	.8988	8980	8973	8965	8957	8949	8942	8934	8926	8918	1	3	4	5	6
27	.8910	8902	8894	8886	8878	8870	8862	8854	8846	8838	1	3	4	5	7
28	.8829	8821	8813	8805	8796	8788	8780	8771	8763	8755	1	3	4	6	7
29	.8746	8738	8729	8721	8712	8704	8695	8686	8678	8669	1	3	4	6	7
30	.8660	8652	8643	8634	8625	8616	8607	8599	8590	8581	1	3	4	6	7
31	.8572	8563	8554	8545	8536	8526	8517	8508	8499	8490	2	3	5	6	8
32	.8480	8471	8462	8453	8443	8434	8425	8415	8406	8396	2	3	5	6	8
33	.8387	8377	8368	8358	8348	8339	8329	8320	8310	8300	2	3	5	6	8
34	.8290	8281	8271	8261	8251	8241	8231	8221	8211	8202	2	3	5	7	8
35	.8192	8181	8171	8161	8151	8141	8131	8121	8111	8100	2	3	5	7	8
36	.8090	8080	8070	8059	8049	8039	8028	8018	8007	7997	2	3	5	7	8
37	.7986	7976	7965	7955	7944	7934	7923	7912	7902	7891	2	4	5	7	9
38	.7880	7869	7859	7848	7837	7826	7815	7804	7793	7782	2	4	5	7	9
39	.7771	7760	7749	7738	7727	7716	7705	7694	7683	7672	2	4	6	7	9
40	.7660	7649	7638	7627	7615	7604	7593	7581	7570	7559	2	4	6	8	9
41	.7547	7536	7524	7513	7501	7490	7478	7466	7455	7443	2	4	6	8	10
42	.7431	7420	7408	7396	7385	7373	7361	7349	7337	7325	2	4	6	8	10
43	.7314	7302	7290	7278	7266	7254	7242	7230	7218	7206	2	4	6	8	10
44	.7193	7181	7169	7157	7145	7133	7120	7108	7096	7083	2	4	6	8	10

NATURAL COSINES

[*Numbers in difference columns to be subtracted, not added.*]

	0' 0°.0	6' 0°.1	12' 0°.2	18' 0°.3	24' 0°.4	30' 0°.5	36' 0°.6	42' 0°.7	48' 0°.8	54' 0°.9	Mean Differences				
											1	2	3	4	5
45	.7071	7059	7046	7034	7022	7009	6997	6984	6972	6959	2	4	6	8	10
46	.6947	6934	6921	6909	6896	6884	6871	6858	6845	6833	2	4	6	8	11
47	.6820	6807	6794	6782	6769	6756	6743	6730	6717	6704	2	4	6	9	11
48	.6691	6678	6665	6652	6639	6626	6613	6600	6587	6574	2	4	7	9	11
49	.6561	6547	6534	6521	6508	6494	6481	6468	6455	6441	2	4	7	9	11
50	.6428	6414	6401	6388	6374	6361	6347	6334	6320	6307	2	4	7	9	11
51	.6293	6280	6266	6252	6239	6225	6211	6198	6184	6170	2	5	7	9	11
52	.6157	6143	6129	6115	6101	6088	6074	6060	6046	6032	2	5	7	9	11
53	.6018	6004	5990	5976	5962	5948	5934	5920	5906	5892	2	5	7	9	12
54	.5878	5864	5850	5835	5821	5807	5793	5779	5764	5750	2	5	7	9	12
55	.5736	5721	5707	5693	5678	5664	5650	5635	5621	5606	2	5	7	10	12
56	.5592	5577	5563	5548	5534	5519	5505	5490	5476	5461	2	5	7	10	12
57	.5446	5432	5417	5402	5388	5373	5358	5344	5329	5314	2	5	7	10	12
58	.5299	5284	5270	5255	5240	5225	5210	5195	5180	5165	2	5	7	10	12
59	.5150	5135	5120	5105	5090	5075	5060	5045	5030	5015	3	5	8	10	13
60	.5000	4985	4970	4955	4939	4924	4909	4894	4879	4863	3	5	8	10	13
61	.4848	4833	4818	4802	4787	4772	4756	4741	4726	4710	3	5	8	10	13
62	.4695	4679	4664	4648	4633	4617	4602	4586	4571	4555	3	5	8	10	13
63	.4540	4524	4509	4493	4478	4462	4446	4431	4415	4399	3	5	8	10	13
64	.4384	4368	4352	4337	4321	4305	4289	4274	4258	4242	3	5	8	11	13
65	.4226	4210	4195	4179	4163	4147	4131	4115	4099	4083	3	5	8	11	13
66	.4067	4051	4035	4019	4003	3987	3971	3955	3939	3923	3	5	8	11	14
67	.3907	3891	3875	3859	3843	3827	3811	3795	3778	3762	3	5	8	11	14
68	.3746	3730	3714	3697	3681	3665	3649	3633	3616	3600	3	5	8	11	14
69	.3584	3567	3551	3535	3518	3502	3486	3469	3453	3437	3	5	8	11	14
70	.3420	3404	3387	3371	3355	3338	3322	3305	3289	3272	3	5	8	11	14
71	.3256	3239	3223	3206	3190	3173	3156	3140	3123	3107	3	6	8	11	14
72	.3090	3074	3057	3040	3024	3007	2990	2974	2957	2940	3	6	8	11	14
73	.2924	2907	2890	2874	2857	2840	2823	2807	2790	2773	3	6	8	11	14
74	.2756	2740	2723	2706	2689	2672	2656	2639	2622	2605	3	6	8	11	14
75	.2588	2571	2554	2538	2521	2504	2487	2470	2453	2436	3	6	8	11	14
76	.2419	2402	2385	2368	2351	2334	2317	2300	2284	2267	3	6	8	11	14
77	.2250	2233	2215	2198	2181	2164	2147	2130	2113	2096	3	6	9	11	14
78	.2079	2062	2045	2028	2011	1994	1977	1959	1942	1925	3	6	9	11	14
79	.1908	1891	1874	1857	1840	1822	1805	1788	1771	1754	3	6	9	11	14
80	.1736	1719	1702	1685	1668	1650	1633	1616	1599	1582	3	6	9	12	14
81	.1564	1547	1530	1513	1495	1478	1461	1444	1426	1409	3	6	9	12	14
82	.1392	1374	1357	1340	1323	1305	1288	1271	1253	1236	3	6	9	12	14
83	.1219	1201	1184	1167	1149	1132	1115	1097	1080	1063	3	6	9	12	14
84	.1045	1028	1011	0993	0976	0958	0941	0924	0906	0889	3	6	9	12	14
85	.0872	0854	0837	0819	0802	0785	0767	0750	0732	0715	3	6	9	12	15
86	.0698	0680	0663	0645	0628	0610	0593	0576	0558	0541	3	6	9	12	15
87	.0523	0506	0488	0471	0454	0436	0419	0401	0384	0366	3	6	9	12	15
88	.0349	0332	0314	0297	0279	0262	0244	0227	0209	0192	3	6	9	12	15
89	.0175	0157	0140	0122	0105	0087	0070	0052	0035	0017	3	6	9	12	15
90	.0000														

NATURAL TANGENTS

	0' 0°.0	6' 0°.1	12' 0°.2	18' 0°.3	24' 0°.4	30' 0°.5	36' 0°.6	42' 0°.7	48' 0°.8	54' 0°.9	Mean Differences				
											1'	2'	3'	4'	5'
0	.0000	0017	0035	0052	0070	0087	0105	0122	0140	0157	3	6	9	12	15
1	.0175	0192	0209	0227	0244	0262	0279	0297	0314	0332	3	6	9	12	15
2	.0349	0367	0384	0402	0419	0437	0454	0472	0489	0507	3	6	9	12	15
3	.0524	0542	0559	0577	0594	0612	0629	0647	0664	0682	3	6	9	12	15
4	.0699	0717	0734	0752	0769	0787	0805	0822	0840	0857	3	6	9	12	15
5	.0875	0892	0910	0928	0945	0963	0981	0998	1016	1033	3	6	9	12	15
6	.1051	1069	1086	1104	1122	1139	1157	1175	1192	1210	3	6	9	12	15
7	.1228	1246	1263	1281	1299	1317	1334	1352	1370	1388	3	6	9	12	15
8	.1405	1423	1441	1459	1477	1495	1512	1530	1548	1566	3	6	9	12	15
9	.1584	1602	1620	1638	1655	1673	1691	1709	1727	1745	3	6	9	12	15
10	.1763	1781	1799	1817	1835	1853	1871	1890	1908	1926	3	6	9	12	15
11	.1944	1962	1980	1998	2016	2035	2053	2071	2089	2107	3	6	9	12	15
12	.2126	2144	2162	2180	2199	2217	2235	2254	2272	2290	3	6	9	12	15
13	.2309	2327	2345	2364	2382	2401	2419	2438	2456	2475	3	6	9	12	15
14	.2493	2512	2530	2549	2568	2586	2605	2623	2642	2661	3	6	9	12	16
15	.2679	2698	2717	2736	2754	2773	2792	2811	2830	2849	3	6	9	13	16
16	.2867	2886	2905	2924	2943	2962	2981	3000	3019	3038	3	6	9	13	16
17	.3057	3076	3096	3115	3134	3153	3172	3191	3211	3230	3	6	10	13	16
18	.3249	3269	3288	3307	3327	3346	3365	3385	3404	3424	3	6	10	13	16
19	.3443	3463	3482	3502	3522	3541	3561	3581	3600	3620	3	7	10	13	16
20	.3640	3659	3679	3699	3719	3739	3759	3779	3799	3819	3	7	10	13	17
21	.3839	3859	3879	3899	3919	3939	3959	3979	4000	4020	3	7	10	13	17
22	.4040	4061	4081	4101	4122	4142	4163	4183	4204	4224	3	7	10	14	17
23	.4245	4265	4286	4307	4327	4348	4369	4390	4411	4431	3	7	10	14	17
24	.4452	4473	4494	4515	4536	4557	4578	4599	4621	4642	4	7	11	14	18
25	.4663	4684	4706	4727	4748	4770	4791	4813	4834	4856	4	7	11	14	18
26	.4877	4899	4921	4942	4964	4986	5008	5029	5051	5073	4	7	11	15	18
27	.5095	5117	5139	5161	5184	5206	5228	5250	5272	5295	4	7	11	15	18
28	.5317	5340	5362	5384	5407	5430	5452	5475	5498	5520	4	8	11	15	19
29	.5543	5566	5589	5612	5635	5658	5681	5704	5727	5750	4	8	12	15	19
30	.5774	5797	5820	5844	5867	5890	5914	5938	5961	5985	4	8	12	16	20
31	.6009	6032	6056	6080	6104	6128	6152	6176	6200	6224	4	8	12	16	20
32	.6249	6273	6297	6322	6346	6371	6395	6420	6445	6469	4	8	12	16	20
33	.6494	6519	6544	6569	6594	6619	6644	6669	6694	6720	4	8	13	17	21
34	.6745	6771	6796	6822	6847	6873	6699	6924	6950	6976	4	9	13	17	21
35	.7002	7028	7054	7080	7107	7133	7159	7186	7212	7239	4	9	13	18	22
36	.7265	7292	7319	7346	7373	7400	7427	7454	7481	7508	5	9	14	18	23
37	.7536	7563	7590	7618	7646	7673	7701	7729	7757	7785	5	9	14	18	23
38	.7813	7841	7869	7898	7926	7954	7983	8012	8040	8069	5	9	14	19	24
39	.8008	8127	8156	8185	8214	8243	8273	8302	8332	8361	5	10	15	20	24
40	.8391	8421	8451	8481	8511	8541	8571	8601	8632	8662	5	10	15	20	25
41	.8693	8724	8754	8785	8816	8847	8878	8910	8941	8972	5	10	16	21	26
42	.9004	9036	9067	9099	9131	9163	9195	9228	9260	9293	5	11	16	21	27
43	.9325	9358	9391	9424	9457	9490	9523	9556	9590	9623	6	11	17	22	28
44	.9657	9691	9725	9759	9793	9827	9861	9896	9930	9965	6	11	17	23	29

NATURAL TANGENTS

	0' 0°.0	6' 0°.1	12' 0°.2	18' 0°.3	24' 0°.4	30' 0°.5	36' 0°.6	42' 0°.7	48' 0°.8	54' 0°.9	Mean Differences 1'	2'	3'	4'	5'
45	1.0000	0035	0070	0105	0141	0176	0212	0247	0283	0319	6	12	18	24	30
46	1.0355	0392	0428	0464	0501	0538	0575	0612	0649	0686	6	12	18	25	31
47	1.0724	0761	0799	0837	0875	0913	0951	0990	1028	1067	6	13	19	25	32
48	1.1106	1145	1184	1224	1263	1303	1343	1383	1423	1463	7	13	20	27	33
49	1.1504	1544	1585	1626	1667	1708	1750	1792	1833	1875	7	14	21	28	34
50	1.1918	1960	2002	2045	2088	2131	2174	2218	2261	2305	7	14	22	29	35
51	1.2349	2393	2437	2482	2527	2572	2617	2662	2708	2753	8	15	23	30	38
52	1.2799	2846	2892	2938	2985	3032	3079	3127	3175	3222	8	16	24	31	39
53	1.3270	3319	3367	3416	3465	3514	3564	3613	3663	3713	8	16	25	33	41
54	1.3764	3814	3865	3916	3968	4019	4071	4124	4176	4229	9	17	26	34	43
55	1.4281	4335	4388	4442	4496	4550	4605	4659	4715	4770	9	18	27	36	45
56	1.4826	4882	4938	4994	5051	5108	5166	5224	5282	5340	10	19	29	38	48
57	1.5399	5458	5517	5577	5637	5697	5757	5818	5880	5941	10	20	30	40	50
58	1.6003	6066	6128	6191	6255	6319	6383	6447	6512	6577	11	21	32	43	53
59	1.6643	6709	6775	6842	6909	6977	7045	7113	7182	7251	11	23	34	45	56
60	1.7321	7391	7461	7532	7603	7675	7747	7820	7893	7966	12	24	36	48	60
61	1.8040	8115	8190	8265	8341	8418	8495	8572	8650	8728	13	26	38	51	64
62	1.8807	8887	8967	9047	9128	9210	9292	9375	9458	9542	14	27	41	55	68
63	1.9626	9711	9797	9883	9970	2.0057	2.0145	2.0233	2.0323	2.0413	15	29	44	58	73
64	2.0503	0594	0686	0778	0872	0965	1060	1155	1251	1348	16	31	47	63	78
65	2.1445	1543	1642	1742	1842	1943	2045	2148	2251	2355	17	34	51	68	85
66	2.2460	2566	2673	2781	2889	2998	3109	3220	3332	3445	18	37	55	73	92
67	2.3559	3673	3789	3906	4023	4142	4262	4383	4504	4627	20	40	60	79	99
68	2.4751	4876	5002	5129	5257	5386	5517	5649	5782	5916	22	43	65	87	108
69	2.6051	6187	6325	6464	6605	6746	6889	7034	7179	7326	24	47	71	95	119
70	2.7475	7625	7776	7929	8083	8239	8397	8556	8716	8878	26	52	78	104	131
71	2.9042	9208	9375	9544	9714	9887	3.0061	3.0237	3.0415	3.0595	29	58	87	116	145
72	3.0777	0961	1146	1334	1524	1716	1910	2106	2305	2500	32	64	96	129	161
73	3.2709	2914	3122	3332	3544	3759	3977	4197	4420	4646	36	72	108	144	180
74	3.4874	5105	5339	5576	5816	6059	6305	6554	6806	7062	41	81	122	163	204
75	3.7321	7583	7848	8118	8391	8667	8947	9232	9520	9812	46	93	139	186	232
76	4.0108	0408	0713	1022	1335	1653	1976	2303	2635	2972	53	107	160	213	267
77	4.3315	3662	4015	4374	4737	5107	5483	5864	6252	6646					
78	4.7046	7453	7867	8288	8716	9152	9594	5.0045	5.0504	5.0970					
79	5.1446	1929	2422	2924	3435	3955	4486	5026	5578	6140					
80	5.6713	7297	7894	8502	9124	9758	6.0405	6.1066	6.1742	6.2432					
81	6.3138	3859	4596	5350	6122	6912	7720	8548	9395	7.0264					
82	7.1154	2066	3002	3962	4947	5958	6996	8062	9158	8.0285					
83	8.1443	2636	3863	5126	6427	7769	9152	9.0579	9.2052	9.3572					
84	9.5144	9.677	9.845	10.02	10.20	10.39	10.58	10.78	10.99	11.20					
85	11.43	11.66	11.91	12.16	12.43	12.71	13.00	13.30	13.62	13.95					
86	14.30	14.67	15.06	15.46	15.89	16.35	16.83	17.34	17.89	18.46					
87	19.08	19.74	20.45	21.20	22.02	22.90	23.86	24.90	26.03	27.27					
88	28.64	30.14	31.82	33.69	35.80	38.19	40.92	44.07	47.74	52.08					
89	57.29	63.66	71.62	81.85	95.49	114.6	143.2	191.0	286.5	573.0					
90	∞														

Mean Differences cease to be sufficiently accurate.